Are A Click Away

with McGraw-Hill's Homework Management system

COMING FALL 2009...

The updated and enhanced version of McGraw-Hill's Homework Manager and Homework Manager Plus

Introducing...

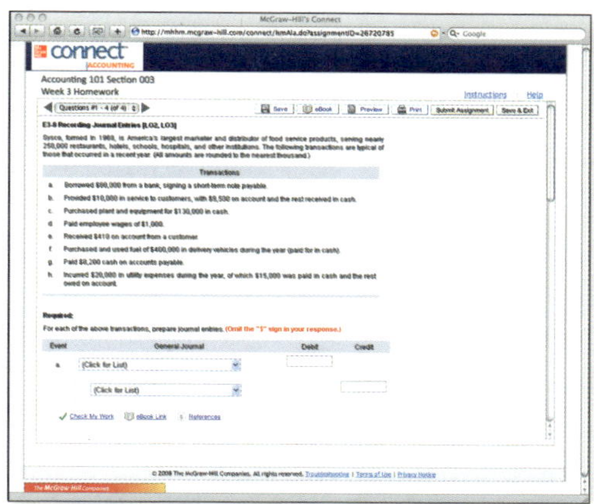

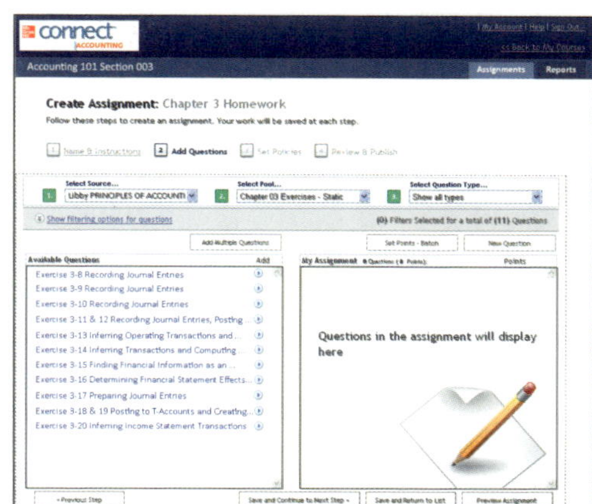

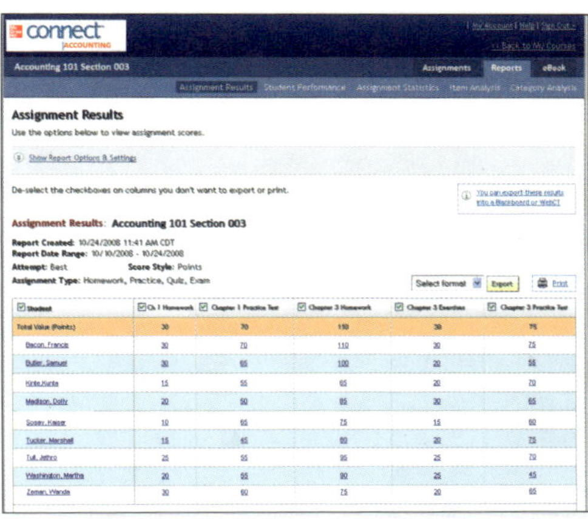

How did we improve our online homework and testing systems with Connect Accounting and Connect Accounting Plus*?

By listening to students and instructors who told us they wanted:

- Single entry point, registration and log on
- Better reports for instructors
- Enhanced ability to export reports and grades to Blackboard and WebCT
- Enhanced question selection including the ability to sort question by AACSB and learning objective tags
- Customizable assignment policies for instructors
- Student Assignment Preview for instructors
- Local time-zone support

*Connect Plus includes an interactive, integrated version of this textbook.

Better Grades

Q Need a tutor **at midnight**?

Struggling to understand the accounting cycle?

A 

Accounting Cycle Tutors

- Web-based Quantum Tutors for the Accounting Cycle are like having your own personal instructor
- Answers your questions
- Helps you think of better questions to ask
- Gives you unlimited chances to practice
- Has step-by-step feedback and instruction, including animated journal entries
- Is available when you need it, day or night
- Unlimited and convenient access to help you master the most important topic in this course, the accounting cycle

Q Always on the run? Juggling a **hectic schedule**?

Want to **study on the go**?

A

Text-specific iPod content

Download accounting videos, PowerPoints, and quizzes (see below) directly onto your iPod and take learning material with you wherever you go. Whether it's in the car, on the train, or waiting between classes – it's easy to get a quick refresher on key course information. Look for this iPod icon throughout the text. Icons connect your Media Integrated textbook with iPod study materials, making review and study time as easy as putting on headphones! Click on **www.mhhe.com/LLPW1e** to learn more about available iPod content.

iPod content includes:

- Lecture presentations – Audio and video, audio only, video only
- Interactive self quizzes *
- Accounting videos *

*Available for certain iPod models only

Don't have an iPod? Content can be viewed on any computer! Visit **www.mhhe.com/LLPW1e** for directions.

Visit **www.mhhe.com/ipod** to view a demonstration of our iPod content.

Are A Click Away

with McGraw-Hill's Web-Based Study Tools

Q Want an online, **searchable version** of your textbook?

Wish your textbook could be available online while you're doing your homework?

A

Connect Plus eBook

If your instructor has chosen Homework Manager Plus (or the updated version, *Connect Plus*, available fall 2009), you have an affordable and searchable online version of your book integrated with your other online homework tools.

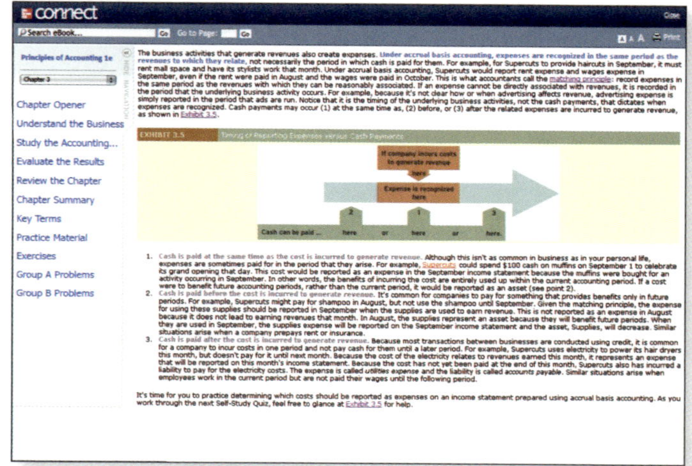

Connect Plus eBook offers features like:

- topic search
- adjustable text size
- jump to page number
- print by section

Q Want to get more **value** from your textbook purchase?

Think learning accounting should be a little bit more **interesting**?

A

Check out the companion website for this textbook www.mhhe.com/LLPW1e

We put it there for you. Go online for test tips and practice problems whenever you study. The companion website for this book includes **games, quizzes, and outlines** to help you study. Get more from your textbook – use the Online Learning Center.

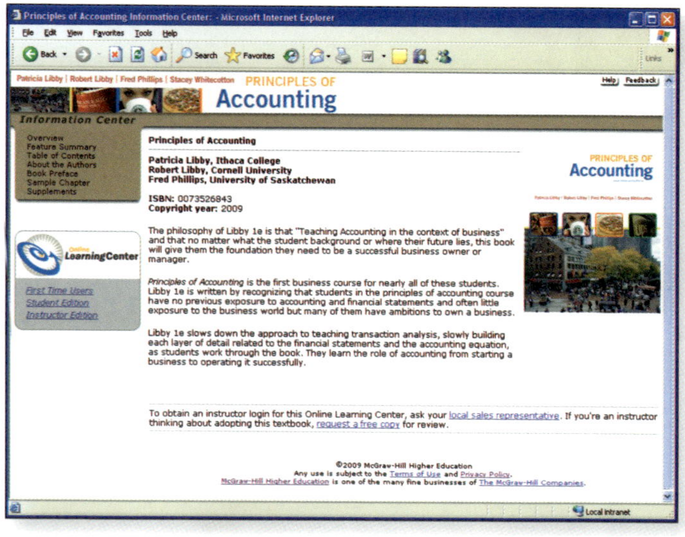

PRINCIPLES OF
Financial Accounting

PRINCIPLES OF
Financial Accounting

www.mhhe.com/LLPW1e

CHAPTERS 1–17

Patricia A. Libby
Ithaca College

Robert Libby
Cornell University

Fred Phillips
University of Saskatchewan

Stacey Whitecotton
Arizona State University

Boston Burr Ridge, IL Dubuque, IA New York San Francisco St. Louis
Bangkok Bogotá Caracas Kuala Lumpur Lisbon London Madrid Mexico City
Milan Montreal New Delhi Santiago Seoul Singapore Sydney Taipei Toronto

The McGraw·Hill Companies

PRINCIPLES OF ACCOUNTING
Published by McGraw-Hill/Irwin, a business unit of The McGraw-Hill Companies, Inc., 1221 Avenue of the Americas, New York, NY, 10020.

This book is printed on acid-free paper.

1 2 3 4 5 6 7 8 9 0 DOW/DOW 0 9 8

ISBN-13: 978-0-07-352684-3 (combined edition)
ISBN-10: 0-07-352684-3 (combined edition)
ISBN-13: 978-0-07-327395-2 (volume 1, chapters 1–12)
ISBN-10: 0-07-327395-3 (volume 1, chapters 1–12)
ISBN-13: 978-0-07-327396-9 (volume 2, chapters 12–25)
ISBN-10: 0-07-327396-1 (volume 2, chapters 12–25)
ISBN-13: 978-0-07-327408-9 (principles of financial accounting, chapters 1–17)
ISBN-10: 0-07-327408-9 (principles of financial accounting, chapters 1–17)

Vice president and editor-in-chief: *Brent Gordon*
Editorial director: *Stewart Mattson*
Publisher: *Tim Vertovec*
Senior sponsoring editor: *Alice Harra*
Senior developmental editor: *Kimberly D. Hooker*
Executive marketing manager: *Sankha Basu*
Manager of photo, design & publishing tools: *Mary Conzachi*
Full service project manager: *Elm Street Publishing Services*
Senior production supervisor: *Debra R. Sylvester*
Interior designer: *Pam Verros*
Senior photo research coordinator: *Jeremy Cheshareck*
Photo researcher: *Editorial Image, LLC*
Senior media project manager: *Susan Lombardi*
Cover design: *Cara Hawthorne*
Compositor: *Laserwords Private Limited*
Printer: *R. R. Donnelley*

The Library of Congress Cataloging-in-Publication Data

Principles of accounting / Patricia A. Libby . . . [et al.].
p. cm.
Includes index.
ISBN-13: 978-0-07-352684-3 (combined edition : alk. paper)
ISBN-10: 0-07-352684-3 (combined edition : alk. paper)
ISBN-13: 978-0-07-327395-2 (volume 1, ch. 1–12 : alk. paper)
ISBN-10: 0-07-327395-3 (volume 1, ch 1–12 : alk. paper)
[etc.]
1. Accounting. 2. Accounting—Textbooks. I. Libby, Patricia A.
HF5636.P75 2009
657—dc22

2008038810

www.mhhe.com

DEDICATION

*Herman and Doris Hargenrater,
Laura Libby, Oscar and Selma Libby.*

–Patricia and Robert Libby

*To the best teachers I've ever had:
my Mom and Dad, Barb, Harrison,
and Daniel.*

–Fred Phillips

*This book is dedicated to Mark, Riley,
and Carley Drayna. Thanks for all your
love and support.*

–Stacey Whitecotton

MEET THE AUTHORS

Patricia A. Libby

Patricia Libby is Associate Professor of Accounting at Ithaca College, where she teaches the undergraduate Principles of Accounting course. She previously taught graduate and undergraduate Principles of Accounting at Eastern Michigan University and the University of Texas. Before entering academe, she was an auditor with Price Waterhouse (now PricewaterhouseCoopers) and a financial administrator at the University of Chicago. She is also faculty adviser to Beta Alpha Psi, Ithaca College Accounting Association, and Ithaca College National Association of Black Accountants. She received her B.S. from Pennsylvania State University, her M.B.A. from DePaul University, and her Ph.D. from the University of Michigan; she is also a CPA.

Pat conducts research on using cases in the introductory course and other parts of the accounting curriculum. She has published articles in *The Accounting Review*, *Issues in Accounting Education*, and *The Michigan CPA*.

Robert Libby

Robert Libby is the David A. Thomas Professor of Accounting at Cornell University, where he teaches the introductory Principles of Accounting course. He previously taught at the University of Illinois, Pennsylvania State University, the University of Texas at Austin, the University of Chicago, and the University of Michigan. He received his B.S. from Pennsylvania State University and his M.A.S. and Ph.D. from the University of Illinois; he is also a CPA.

Bob is a widely published author and researcher specializing in behavioral accounting. He was selected as the American Accounting Association (AAA) Outstanding Educator in 2000, received the AAA Outstanding Service Award in 2006, and received the AAA Notable Contributions to the Literature Award in 1985 and 1996. He is the only person to have received all three of the Association's highest awards for teaching, service, and research. He has published numerous articles in *The Accounting Review; Journal of Accounting Research; Accounting, Organizations, and Society;* and other accounting journals. He has held a variety of offices including Vice President of the American Accounting Association and is a member of the American Institute of CPAs and the editorial boards of *The Accounting Review; Accounting, Organizations, and Society; Journal of Accounting Literature;* and *Journal of Behavioral Decision Making.*

Fred Phillips

Fred Phillips is Professor and the George C. Baxter Scholar at the University of Saskatchewan, where he teaches introductory Principles of Accounting. He also has taught introductory accounting at the University of Texas at Austin and the University of Manitoba. Fred has an undergraduate accounting degree, a professional accounting designation, and a Ph.D. from the University of Texas at Austin. He previously worked as an audit manager at KPMG.

Fred's main interest is accounting education. He has won 11 teaching awards, including three national case-writing competitions. Recently, Fred won the 2007 Alpha Kappa Psi Outstanding Professor award at The University of Texas at Austin, and in 2006 he was awarded the title Master Teacher at the University of Saskatchewan. He has published instructional cases and numerous articles in journals such as *Issues in Accounting Education*, *Journal of Accounting Research*, and *Organizational Behavior and Human Decision Processes*. He received the American Accounting Association Outstanding Research in Accounting Education Award in 2006 and 2007 for his articles. Fred is a past Associate Editor of *Issues in Accounting Education* and a current member of the Teaching, Learning & Curriculum and Two-Year College sections of the American Accounting Association. In his spare time, he likes to work out, play video games, and drink iced cappuccinos.

Stacey Whitecotton

Stacey Whitecotton is Associate Professor in the School of Accountancy at Arizona State University. She received her Ph.D. and Masters of Accounting from The University of Oklahoma and her B.B.A. from Texas Tech University.

Stacey teaches managerial accounting topics at the undergraduate level and in the MBA program. She was recognized as the Outstanding Undergraduate Teacher by the School of Accountancy and Information Management in 1999 and was awarded the John W. Teets Outstanding Graduate Teacher award in 2000–2001. She is currently serving as the faculty director for the W. P. Carey Online MBA program.

Stacey's research interests center around the use of decision aids to improve the decision-making behavior of financial analysts, managers, and auditors. Her research has been published in *The Accounting Review*, *Organizational Behavior and Human Decision Processes*, *Behavioral Research in Accounting*, *Auditing: A Journal of Practice and Theory*, and *The Journal of Behavioral Decision Making*.

Stacey and her husband Mark enjoy traveling and the many outdoor activities Arizona has to offer with their two kids, Riley and Carley.

What Does Pizza Have to Do with Accounting?

Teaching challenge: Motivating students to read the book

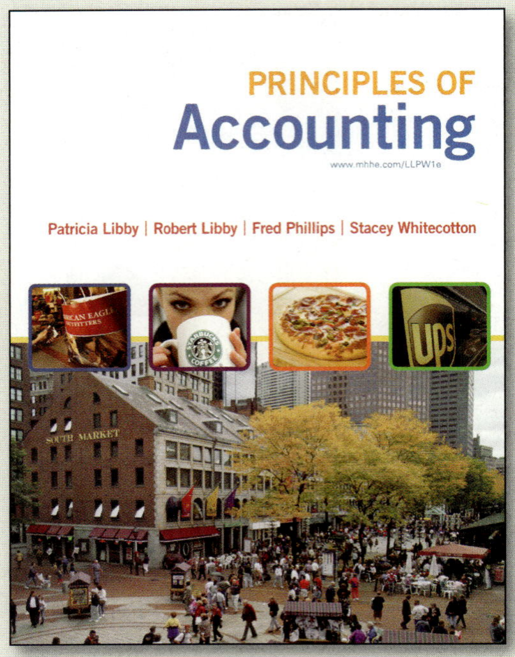

The number one challenge we hear from faculty is how to motivate students to read their textbook. Students taking Principles of Accounting don't yet know **why accounting matters** in their lives, so they aren't naturally drawn to reading their text.

However, most students do know about eating pizza, drinking Starbucks or their favorite coffee, shopping at retail stores like American Eagle, and shipping packages with UPS. Once they read about how these activities relate to accounting, they begin to see that **accounting is in their everyday lives.**

In addition, many of your students **imagine themselves starting and running a business** someday (or helping with a family business). So, our *Principles of Accounting* book opens with a novel idea: Chapters 1–4 are written around the true story of Mauricio Rosa, an immigrant from El Salvador who started Pizza Aroma, a small gourmet pizza restaurant in Ithaca, New York. Mauricio's actual experiences and decisions provide a consistent story line and create a framework for learning about accounting. In Chapter 1, Mauricio and his CPA discuss plans for starting his business, addressing topics such as choice of organizational form, accounting information needs, and financial statement reporting. In Chapter 2, Mauricio actually establishes Pizza Aroma by contributing capital, obtaining a bank loan, and investing in restaurant equipment. He learns how these activities affect Pizza Aroma's financial condition and how they are reported in the balance sheet. In Chapter 3, Pizza Aroma begins to earn revenue and incur expenses. He learns how these operating transactions affect the balance sheet and the income statement. Finally, in Chapter 4, Mauricio learns how the accounting records are adjusted prior to determining whether Pizza Aroma has been profitable.

The dialogue between Mauricio and Laurie in the first chapter invites students into a discussion like one they may have someday. Through this true story that

*The building cover has a busy marketplace that **depicts the essence of business, accounting, free enterprise, etc.,** and the crowd rushing off to wherever indicates that business is alive and well . . .*—Judy Daulton, Piedmont Technical College

*The examples follow through is an excellent case of how to close the books of accounts. The classifications of accounts make sense with easy understanding for the class. **The accounting cycle is clearly explained and easy to understand for the class.***—Shafi Ullah, Broward College

*The presentation of the **pizza case is awesome . . . it lends itself to a mystery and drives you to find out the ending** . . . excellent. . . .*—David Laurel, South Texas College

Libby/Libby/ Phillips/Whitecotton (LLPW) is the only book to use a true story to introduce students to accounting and the accounting cycle with a running case about a pizzeria.

"Others outside your business will also need financial information about your restaurant. For example, where will the money come from to start your business?"

"I'll contribute $30,000 from personal savings. But I'll still need to ask the bank for a $20,000 loan to buy equipment. What will the bank want to know?"

continues in the entire first 4 chapters (the accounting cycle), students see the relationship between accounting and business, and they get a mini-manual for how to start their own businesses. Students get captivated by the story and may not realize they are learning accounting principles in the process.

The choice of Pizza Aroma is purposeful: Students love pizza, they connect accounting to something in their everyday lives. More important, they learn to make the connection in the first few weeks that accounting can help them be successful. **When students understand why accounting matters to them, they want to read more.**

(Chapter One) is engaging with the interview approach. ***The business owner is at the same level of accounting knowledge as the students and asks the questions that are surely running through the students' minds. . . .*** —Patricia Walczak, Lansing Community College

Since ***many (of my students) have worked in fast-food establishments and certainly all have eaten pizza,*** *I think this should make it more interesting and understandable to them.*—Sandra Augustine, Hilbert College

Introducing balance sheet accounts in Chapter 2 and, exclusively, income accounts in Chapter 3 is a dynamic idea that makes sense! ***The focus on a proprietorship selling pizza through the first 4 chapters is a topic students can identify with.***—Marcia Sandvold, Des Moines Area Community College

Pizza Aroma: It's a true story

Pizza Aroma, Ithaca, NY

Author Patricia Libby and Owner Mauricio Rosa

Gourmet Pizza

How Can LLPW Ensure Students Will Master the Accounting Cycle?

Teaching challenge: Students struggle with the accounting cycle

Faculty understand that mastering the accounting cycle is essential to success in Principles of Accounting courses. The authors agree. They believe students struggle with the accounting cycle when transaction analysis is covered in one chapter. Students are often overwhelmed when they are exposed to the accounting equation, journal entries, and T-accounts for both balance sheet and income statement accounts in a single chapter.

*Slowing down the material by **breaking transaction analysis into two chapters is an excellent idea, which I think will help students greatly.** That is one of my biggest complaints about my current text; it goes too fast.*—Amy Haas, Kingsborough Community College

The Libby/Libby/Phillips/Whitecotton approach **covers transaction analysis over two chapters** so that students have the time to master the material. In Chapter 2 of *Principles of Accounting*, students are introduced to the accounting equation and transaction analysis for investing and financing transactions that affect only balance sheet accounts. This provides students the opportunity to learn the basic structure and tools used in accounting in a simpler setting than usual. Chapter 3 introduces operating transactions that affect income statement accounts. As a result of this slower building-block approach to transaction analysis, students are better prepared to learn adjustments, financial statement preparation, and more advanced topics.

*It is presented in a very organized manner. The students are **presented the journalizing/posting information (Chapters 2 and 3) at a slower pace,** giving them the opportunity to absorb and comprehend this difficult information. Chapter 4 then wraps up the entire cycle all at once, instead of presenting adjusting entries in one chapter and then ending the accounting cycle in another. In other words, in a **more efficient and easily understandable manner.**—Carol Pace, Grayson Community College*

*The concentration and reinforcement of the basic accounting equation allow the student to **master the equation before introducing the income statement concepts. Excellent idea.***
—Patricia Holmes, Des Moines Area Community College

LLPW is the only book offering a more patient, "building-block" approach to the accounting cycle, covering transaction analysis in 2 chapters instead of 1.

The following grid provides a detailed comparison of the Libby/Libby/Phillips/Whitecotton approach with the approach of other principles of accounting texts.

Accounting Cycle

Chapter	LLPW Approach	Other Approaches
1	Overview of Financial Statements and Users, Transaction Analysis with Accounting Equation	Overview of Financial Statements and Users, Transaction Analysis with Accounting Equation
2	Journal Entries and T-Accounts with Transactions affecting Balance Sheet Accounts only	Journal Entries and T-Accounts with Transactions affecting both Balance Sheet and Income Statement Accounts
3	Journal Entries and T-Accounts with Transactions affecting both Balance Sheet and Income Statement Accounts	Adjusting Entries, Financial Statement Preparation
4	Adjusting Entries, Financial Statement Preparation, Closing Process, (Worksheet)	Closing Process, Worksheet, (Reversing Entries), Financial Statement Preparation

First introducing income accounts in chapter 3 is great. I don't know any other text to do this.—Jeannie Harrington, Middle Tennessee State University

Learning accounting is like learning a foreign language where practice of new terms and concepts is essential. By taking a progressive building-block approach to Chapters 2 and 3, students have more time to master transaction analysis, which is the foundation for the rest of the course. Students have more time to practice and feel less overwhelmed.

It caught my attention from page 1 and I wanted to read on and find out how Pizza Aroma was going to do. *The first four chapters simplify the accounting process and explain accounting on an entry level for first time accounting students. Great Job!!!*—Susan Logorda, Lehigh Carbon Community College

How Can LLPW Help Students Learn Accounting in the Context of Business?

Teaching challenge: Many students don't have enough work experience to understand accounting in the context of business

Because many students don't have business experience, the authors teach accounting in the context of business by focusing each chapter on one well-known company and using that company as a consistent example throughout the chapter including the examples, financial statements, and data.

Great explanations; fantastic use of the real world examples. . . .—Shea Mears, Des Moines Area Community College

The authors focus every chapter of Principles of Accounting on a company that makes or provides something students use or see in their everyday lives. Chapters 1 through 4 focus on the true story of Pizza Aroma, a typical local small pizza restaurant. In Chapters 5–25, the authors profile well-known companies such as Starbucks (Chapter 21), American Eagle Outfitters (Chapter 7), Skechers (Chapter 9), Blockbuster (Chapter 25), General Mills (Chapter 14), Cedar Fair (Chapter 10), and Tombstone (Chapter 18).

The use of Cedar Fair for (chapter 10) is great. ***How fascinating this was to use roller coasters for depreciation examples.***—Jeannie Harrington, Middle Tennessee State University

Authors did a nice job of making it easy to read and understand. ***Supplemental information with real company*** *and use of extras like the coach's tips, self-study practice and exhibits, make this a better text than I currently use.*—Larry Dragosavac, Edison CC

LLPW is the only book that uses this unique "focus company approach" to teach accounting in the context of real business.

FOCUS COMPANIES

Ch 1: Introducing Accounting

Pizza Aroma

Ch 2: Balance Sheet

Pizza Aroma

Ch 3: Balance Sheet and Income Statement

Pizza Aroma

Ch 4: Adjusting and Closing the Books

Pizza Aroma

Ch 5: Accounting Systems

UPS

Ch 6: Merchandising

Wal-Mart

Ch 7: Inventories

American Eagle Outfitters

Ch 8: Internal Controls

The Home Depot

Ch 9: Receivables

Skechers

Ch 10: Long-lived Assets

Cedar Fair

Ch 11: Current Liabilities

General Mills

Ch 12: Partnerships

Bloom 'N Flowers

Ch 13: Corporations

Sonic Drive-In

Ch 14: Long-Term Liabilities

General Mills

Ch 15: Investments

Washington Post Companies

Ch 16: Statement of Cash Flows

Nautilus

Ch 17: Financial Statement Analysis

Lowe's

Ch 18: Managerial Accounting

Tombstone Pizza

Ch 19: Job Order Costing

Toll Brothers

Ch 20: Process Costing

CK Mondavi

Ch 21: Cost Behavior and Cost Volume Profit Analysis

Starbucks

Ch 22: Capital Budgeting

Mattel

Ch 23: Budgetary Planning

Cold Stone Creamery

Ch 24: Budgetary Control

Cold Stone Creamery

Ch 25: Standard Costing and Variance Analysis

Blockbuster

How Can LLPW Help Students Study and Practice?

***Principles of Accounting* offers a host of pedagogical tools that complement the different ways you like to teach and the ways your students like to learn. . . .**

Coach's Tips

Every student needs encouragement, and inclusion of Coach's Tips is just one way Libby/Libby/Phillips/Whitecotton fulfills that need. Coach's Tips appear throughout the text offering tips, advice, and suggestions about how to learn principles of accounting.

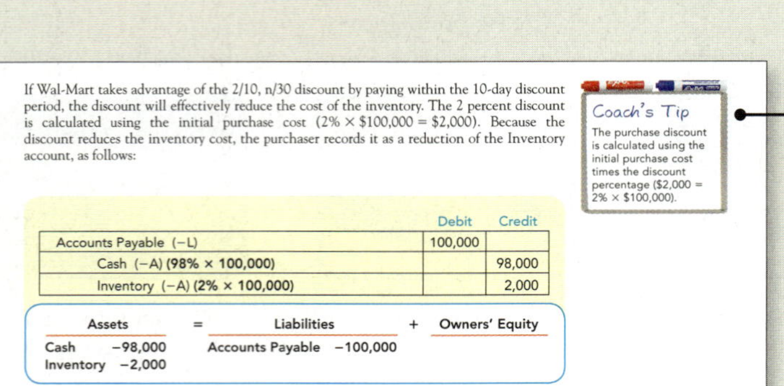

If Wal-Mart takes advantage of the 2/10, n/30 discount by paying within the 10-day discount period, the discount will effectively reduce the cost of the inventory. The 2 percent discount is calculated using the initial purchase cost (2% × $100,000 = $2,000). Because the discount reduces the inventory cost, the purchaser records it as a reduction of the Inventory account, as follows:

	Debit	Credit
Accounts Payable (−L)	100,000	
Cash (−A) **(98% × 100,000)**		98,000
Inventory (−A) **(2% × 100,000)**		2,000

Assets		=	Liabilities		+	Owners' Equity
Cash	−98,000		Accounts Payable	−100,000		
Inventory	−2,000					

Coach's Tip

The purchase discount is calculated using the initial purchase cost times the discount percentage ($2,000 = 2% × $100,000).

Self-Study Practice

Research shows that students learn best when they are actively engaged in the learning process. This active learning feature engages the student, provides interactivity, and promotes efficient learning. These practices ask students to pause at strategic points throughout each chapter to ensure they understand key points before moving ahead.

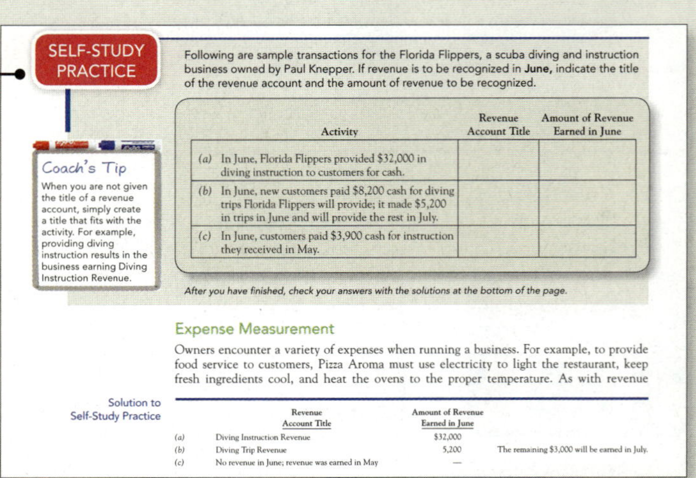

SELF-STUDY PRACTICE

Following are sample transactions for the Florida Flippers, a scuba diving and instruction business owned by Paul Knepper. If revenue is to be recognized in **June,** indicate the title of the revenue account and the amount of revenue to be recognized.

Activity	Revenue Account Title	Amount of Revenue Earned in June
(a) In June, Florida Flippers provided $32,000 in diving instruction to customers for cash.		
(b) In June, new customers paid $8,200 cash for diving trips Florida Flippers will provide; it made $5,200 in trips in June and will provide the rest in July.		
(c) In June, customers paid $3,900 cash for instruction they received in May.		

After you have finished, check your answers with the solutions at the bottom of the page.

Coach's Tip

When you are not given the title of a revenue account, simply create a title that fits with the activity. For example, providing diving instruction results in the business earning Diving Instruction Revenue.

Expense Measurement

Owners encounter a variety of expenses when running a business. For example, to provide food service to customers, Pizza Aroma must use electricity to light the restaurant, keep fresh ingredients cool, and heat the ovens to the proper temperature. As with revenue

Solution to Self-Study Practice

	Revenue Account Title	Amount of Revenue Earned in June	
(a)	Diving Instruction Revenue	$32,000	
(b)	Diving Trip Revenue	5,200	The remaining $3,000 will be earned in July.
(c)	No revenue in June; revenue was earned in May	—	

Spotlight On ETHICS

Accounting Scandals

Accounting scandals are driven by the fear of personal failure and greed. Initially, some people may appear to benefit from fraudulent reporting. In the long run, however, fraud harms most individuals and organizations. When it is uncovered, the corporation's stock price drops dramatically. In the case involving MicroStrategy, the stock price dropped 65 percent in a single day of trading, from $243 to $86 per share. Creditors are also harmed by fraud. WorldCom's creditors recovered only 42 percent of what they were owed. They lost $36 billion. Innocent employees also are harmed by fraud. At Enron, 5,600 employees lost their jobs and many lost all of their retirement savings.

Ethical conduct is just as important for small private businesses as it is for large public companies. Laurie's advice to Mauricio and to all managers is to strive to create an ethical environment and establish a strong system of checks and controls inside the company. Do not tolerate blatant acts of fraud, such as employees making up false expenses for reimbursement, punching in a time card belonging to a fellow employee who will be late for work, or copying

Spotlight On Ethics

This feature appears throughout the text stressing ethical issues that could be faced in relation to the chapter material and the importance of acting responsibly in business practice.

If Wal-Mart paid for the inventory after the 10-day discount period, it would not be eligible for the 2 percent discount. Instead, it would pay the full $100,000 owed. The payment would be recorded as a decrease in Accounts Payable (debit) and a decrease in Cash (credit) of $100,000.[2]

Spotlight On BUSINESS DECISIONS

To Take or Not to Take the Discount, That Is the Question

Purchasers usually pay within the discount period because the savings are much larger than they may appear to you. Although 2 percent might seem a small discount, if taken consistently on all purchases made during the year, it can add up to substantial savings. All the purchaser must do to earn the 2 percent discount is to pay the bill 20 days early (on the 10th day instead of the 30th). Over a year (365 days), this discount is equivalent to a 37 percent annual interest rate.* So even if purchasers must borrow from the bank at a high rate, such as 15 percent, they will still save a great deal by taking the discount.

Spotlight On Business Decisions

Good decision making is essential in business whether you are preparing, using, or analyzing accounting information. Spotlight On Business Decisions helps students develop good decision-making skills by illustrating the relevance of accounting in real-world decision making.

CHAPTER 4 Completing the Accounting Cycle 155

Spotlight On FINANCIAL REPORTING

Accrued Expenses in the Millions and Billions

Accrued expenses are significant liabilities for many companies. For example, Tootsie Roll Industries recently reported the following:

NOTE 2—ACCRUED LIABILITIES:
Accrued liabilities are comprised of the following:

	DECEMBER 31,	
(in thousands of dollars)	2006	2005
Compensation	$ 12,923	$ 15,756
Other employee benefits	5,631	5,213
Taxes, other than income	1,781	1,765
Advertising and promotions	17,854	14,701
Other	5,613	7,534
	$ 43,802	$ 44,969

The $43.8 million in total accrued liabilities represents 70 percent of Tootsie Roll's current liabilities and 27 percent of total liabilities.

Likewise, Wal-Mart Stores, Inc., reported approximately $14.7 billion in accrued liabilities, primarily from accrued wages and benefits owed to employees. This was 28 percent of current liabilities and 17 percent of total liabilities.

Spotlight On Financial Reporting

Concepts come to life when you see how well-known businesses apply them. Spotlight On Financial Reporting helps students to apply their knowledge to relevant, real-world financial reporting issues.

From Reading to Doing—Extensive End-of-Chapter Material to Help

Chapter Summary

End-of-chapter summaries complement the learning objectives outlined at the beginning of the chapter.

Chapter Summary

LO1 Define internal control and explain why it is needed. p. 344

- Internal control encompasses the methods an organization uses to protect against the theft of assets, to enhance the reliability of accounting information, to promote efficient and effective operations, and to ensure compliance with applicable laws and regulations.
- Internal controls are needed to ensure that people will behave in ways that benefit the organization. When internal controls operate effectively, they can improve an organization's efficiency and minimize waste, unintentional errors, and fraud.

LO2 Explain the common principles and limitations of internal control. p. 346

- The concept of internal control is broad. Most employees of a company will encounter five basic internal control principles: (1) establish responsibility for each task, (2) segregate duties so that one employee cannot initiate, approve, record, and handle a single transaction, (3) restrict access to assets and information to those employees who have been assigned responsibility for them, (4) document all procedures, and (5) independently verify work that has been done using information from others inside and outside the business.
- Internal controls are limited because they (1) are implemented only to the extent that their benefits exceed their costs and (2) may fail to operate effectively as a result of error and fraud.

LO3 Apply internal control principles to cash receipts and payments. p. 348

- When applied to cash receipts, internal control principles require that (1) cashiers be held individually responsible for the cash they receive, (2) different individuals be assigned to receive, maintain custody of, and record cash, (3) cash be stored in a locked safe until it has been securely deposited in a bank, (4) cash register receipts, cash count sheets, daily cash summary reports, and bank deposit slips be prepared to document the cash received and deposited, and (5) cash register receipts be matched to cash counts and deposits to independently verify that all cash was received and deposited.
- When applied to cash payments, internal control principles require that (1) only certain individuals or departments initiate purchase requests, (2) different individuals be assigned to order, receive, and pay for purchases, (3) access to checks and

Key Terms

Bank Reconciliation (p. 355)
Bonding (p. 347)
Cash (p. 360)
Cash Count Sheet (p. 350)
Cash Equivalents (p. 360)
Collude (p. 348)
Deposits in Transit (p. 357)
Electronic Funds Transfer (EFT) (p. 351)
Imprest System (p. 352)
Internal Control (p. 344)
NSF (Not Sufficient Funds) Checks (p. 357)
Outstanding Check (p. 357)
Override (p. 348)
Petty Cash Fund (p. 353)
Remittance Advice (p. 351)
Sarbanes-Oxley (SOX) Act of 2002 (p. 344)
Segregation of Duties (p. 346)
Voucher (p. 352)
Voucher System (p. 352)

See complete glossary in back of text.

Key Terms

Terms, definitions, and page references are given.

Questions

Each chapter includes 10–20 questions that ask students to explain and discuss terms and concepts discussed in the chapter.

Questions

1. What are internal controls and why are they needed?
2. What aspect(s) of the Sarbanes-Oxley Act of 2002 might counteract the incentive to commit fraud?
3. What aspect(s) of the Sarbanes-Oxley Act of 2002 might reduce opportunities for fraud?
4. What aspect(s) of the Sarbanes-Oxley Act of 2002 might allow the good character of employees to prevail?
5. From the perspective of a CEO or CFO, what does internal control mean?
6. What are five common internal control principles?
7. Why is it a good idea to assign each task to only one employee?
8. Why should responsibilities for certain duties, like cash handling and cash recording, be separated? What specific responsibilities should be separated?
9. What are some of the methods for restricting access?
10. In what ways does documentation act as a control?
11. In what ways can independent verification occur?
12. In what way does a mandatory vacation policy act as a control?
13. What are the three limitations of internal control?
14. What is the primary internal control goal for cash receipts?
15. What internal control functions are performed by a cash register? How are these functions performed when cash is received by mail?
16. How is cash received in person independently verified?
17. What is the primary internal control goal for cash payments?
18. In what ways is a petty cash system similar to and different from an imprest payroll system?
19. Describe three ways in which banking services help businesses control cash.
20. What are the purposes of a bank reconciliation? What balances are reconciled?
21. Define *cash* and indicate the types of items that should be reported as cash. Define *cash equivalents* and give two examples of a cash equivalent.

Multiple Choice

1. Which of the following accounts would not appear in a closing journal entry?
   a. Interest Revenue.
   b. Accumulated Depreciation.
   c. Owner's Capital.
   d. Salary Expense.

Quiz 4-1
www.mhhe.com/LLPW1e

2. Which account is least likely to appear in an adjusting journal entry?
   a. Cash.
   b. Interest Receivable.
   c. Accumulated Depreciation.
   d. Salaries Payable.

Multiple-Choice Questions

Each chapter includes 10 multiple-choice questions that let students practice basic concepts. Solutions are provided for all questions.

LLPW is written by best-selling authors whose books are well-known for the quality of their end-of-chapter problem material.

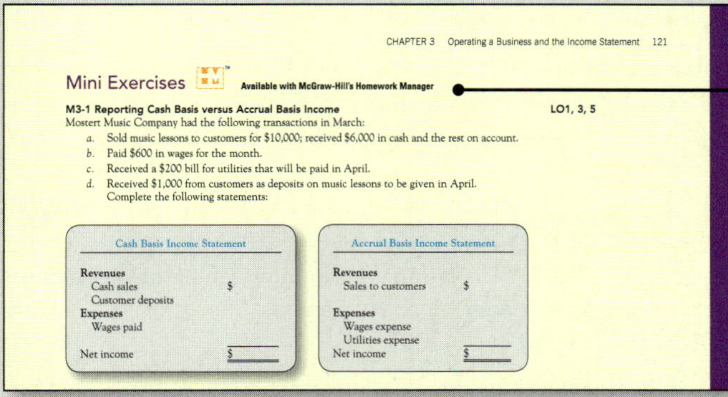

CHAPTER 3 Operating a Business and the Income Statement 121

Mini Exercises Available with McGraw-Hill's Homework Manager

M3-1 Reporting Cash Basis versus Accrual Basis Income LO1, 3, 5

Mostert Music Company had the following transactions in March:

a. Sold music lessons to customers for $10,000; received $6,000 in cash and the rest on account.
b. Paid $600 in wages for the month.
c. Received a $200 bill for utilities that will be paid in April.
d. Received $1,000 from customers as deposits on music lessons to be given in April.

Complete the following statements:

Cash Basis Income Statement	
Revenues	
Cash sales	$
Customer deposits	
Expenses	
Wages paid	
Net income	$

Accrual Basis Income Statement	
Revenues	
Sales to customers	$
Expenses	
Wages expense	
Utilities expense	
Net income	$

Mini Exercises

Assignments illustrate and apply single learning objectives from the chapter.

Exercises

Additional assignments illustrate and apply single and multiple learning objectives from the chapter.

____ 5. Internal auditing.
____ 6. Reviewing financial information for compliance with GAAP.

Exercises Available with McGraw-Hill's Homework Manager

E1-1 Categorizing Business Forms LO1

The following describes different businesses. Mark each with the appropriate letter to indicate whether it would be categorized as a sole proprietorship (S), partnership (P), or corporation (C).

____ 1. Alan Cohen and Carol Palmer own Cohen and Palmer, CPAs, an accounting firm. Both are personally liable for the firm's debts.

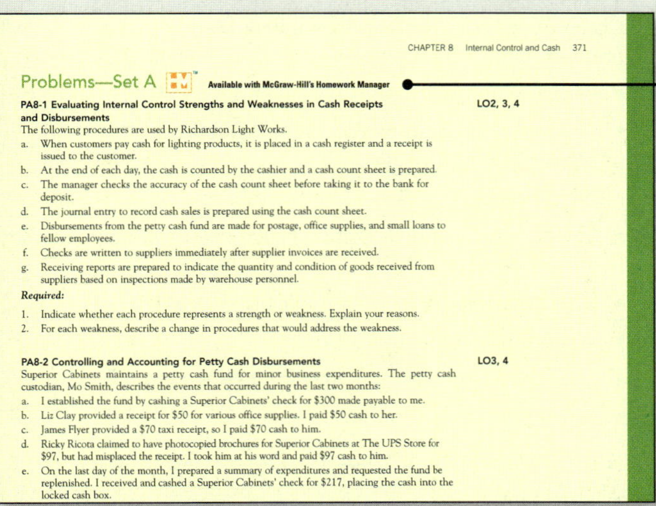

CHAPTER 8 Internal Control and Cash 371

Problems—Set A Available with McGraw-Hill's Homework Manager

PA8-1 Evaluating Internal Control Strengths and Weaknesses in Cash Receipts and Disbursements LO2, 3, 4

The following procedures are used by Richardson Light Works.

a. When customers pay cash for lighting products, it is placed in a cash register and a receipt is issued to the customer.
b. At the end of each day, the cash is counted by the cashier and a cash count sheet is prepared.
c. The manager checks the accuracy of the cash count sheet before taking it to the bank for deposit.
d. The journal entry to record cash sales is prepared using the cash count sheet.
e. Disbursements from the petty cash fund are made for postage, office supplies, and small loans to fellow employees.
f. Checks are written to suppliers immediately after supplier invoices are received.
g. Receiving reports are prepared to indicate the quantity and condition of goods received from suppliers based on inspections made by warehouse personnel.

Required:

1. Indicate whether each procedure represents a strength or weakness. Explain your reasons.
2. For each weakness, describe a change in procedures that would address the weakness.

PA8-2 Controlling and Accounting for Petty Cash Disbursements LO3, 4

Superior Cabinets maintains a petty cash fund for minor business expenditures. The petty cash custodian, Mo Smith, describes the events that occurred during the last two months:

a. I established the fund by cashing a Superior Cabinets' check for $300 made payable to me.
b. Liz Clay provided a receipt for $50 for various office supplies. I paid $50 cash to her.
c. James Flyer provided a $70 taxi receipt, so I paid $70 cash to him.
d. Ricky Ricota claimed to have photocopied brochures for Superior Cabinets at The UPS Store for $97, but had misplaced the receipt. I took him at his word and paid $97 cash to him.
e. On the last day of the month, I prepared a summary of expenditures and requested the fund be replenished. I received and cashed a Superior Cabinets' check for $217, placing the cash into the locked cash box.

Problems (Sets A and B)

Assignments illustrate and apply the chapter's learning objectives.

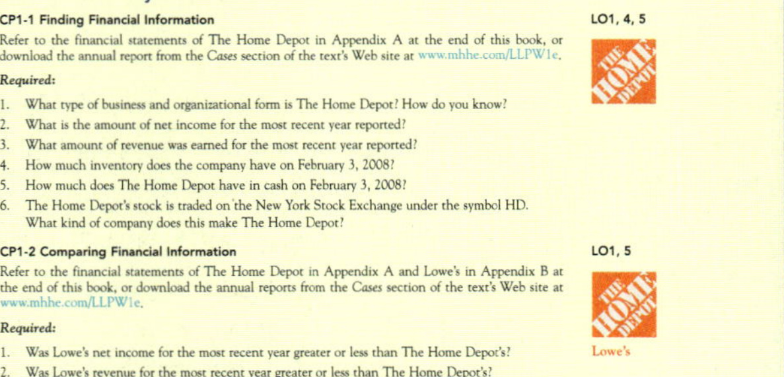

CHAPTER 1 The Role of Accounting in Starting a Business 45

Cases and Projects

CP1-1 Finding Financial Information LO1, 4, 5

Refer to the financial statements of The Home Depot in Appendix A at the end of this book, or download the annual report from the Cases section of the text's Web site at www.mhhe.com/LLPW1e.

Required:

1. What type of business and organizational form is The Home Depot? How do you know?
2. What is the amount of net income for the most recent year reported?
3. What amount of revenue was earned for the most recent year reported?
4. How much inventory does the company have on February 3, 2008?
5. How much does The Home Depot have in cash on February 3, 2008?
6. The Home Depot's stock is traded on the New York Stock Exchange under the symbol HD. What kind of company does this make The Home Depot?

CP1-2 Comparing Financial Information LO1, 5

Refer to the financial statements of The Home Depot in Appendix A and Lowe's in Appendix B at the end of this book, or download the annual reports from the Cases section of the text's Web site at www.mhhe.com/LLPW1e.

Required:

1. Was Lowe's net income for the most recent year greater or less than The Home Depot's?
2. Was Lowe's revenue for the most recent year greater or less than The Home Depot's?
3. Did Lowe's have more or less inventories than The Home Depot at the end of the year?

Cases and Projects

End-of-chapter cases and projects use data from The Home Depot's and Lowe's annual reports and show students how to draw information from an annual report, providing them with a valuable perspective on how information is used in decision making.

How Can McGraw-Hill Technology Help Students Study and Practice?

McGraw-Hill's Homework Manager System

Easy. Effective. Reliable.

McGraw-Hill's Homework Manager® and Homework Manager Plus.®

The #1 choice in web-based assessment, course management, and homework.

With Homework Manager and Homework Manager Plus system, instructors can create web-based assignments and assessments that can be customized to meet course needs. Assignments are based on content from the textbook, so terminology and problem styles are consistent, eliminating confusion for students.

Homework Manager and Homework Manager Plus include:

- Automatically graded homework
- Immediate student feedback
- Personalized gradebook
- Static and algorithmic exercises, problems, and select test bank questions
- Self-graded practice quizzes
- Online testbank
- Interactive, integrated eBook*

**eBook available only with McGraw-Hill's Homework Manager Plus*

EASY.

With a simple, four-step process and intuitive interface, Homework Manager and Homework Manager Plus system allows instructors to get their course online in less than an hour!

EFFECTIVE.

Instructors and students using McGraw-Hill's Homework Manager and Homework Manager Plus system report improved grades, greater retention, and increased student engagement.

RELIABLE.

Stability and support are as important to our customers as they are to us. Only Homework Manager and Homework Manager Plus offer a 24-hour support line to ensure you and your students stay connected.

To connect you with your students in even better ways, we're delighted to announce the new version of Homework Manager and Homework Manager Plus called CONNECT, coming in fall 2009. . . .

As with Homework Manager, Connect Accounting lets instructors easily deliver customized assignments, quizzes and tests online.

- Students can practice important skills on their own schedule and get instant feedback.
- Instructors get automatically graded homework, personalized student feedback and gradebook, static and algorithmic exercises, problems, and test questions.
- Access to an interactive eBook is available with Connect Accounting Plus.
- Continuous improvement: Homework Manager customers will find the following enhancements with CONNECT Accounting:
  - Single entry point, registration, and sign on
  - Enhanced gradebook reporting capabilities
  - The ability to export reports and grades to WebCT and Blackboard
  - Enhanced question selection including AACSB and learning objectives
  - Customizable assignment policies
  - Integrated, interactive eBook*
  - Student Assignment Preview for instructors
  - Local time-zone support

*eBook available only with McGraw-Hill CONNECT ACCOUNTING PLUS.

iPod Downloadable Content

Principles of Accounting gives students the option to download content for review and study to their Apple® iPods and most other MP3/MP4 devices. iPod icons appear throughout the text pointing students to chapter-specific audio lecture presentation slides and course-related videos.

McGraw-Hill has leading technology products for your classroom presentations, course management, labs, and self-study.

Carol Yacht's General Ledger and Peachtree

From one of the most trusted names in computer accounting education, Carol Yacht, comes a general ledger package that's a perfect fit for your course no matter how you like to teach it.

Students using Carol Yacht's General Ledger (CYGL) can move from financial statements to the specific journal entries with just a click of the mouse; changing an entry updates the financial statements on the fly, allowing students to see instantly how journal entries impact financial statements.

If you want your students to practice on the same software the professionals use, the CYGL CD includes Peachtree for use on numerous problems from the text.

Excel Templates

eXcel If they are going to work in accounting (or business in general), students have to know Microsoft Excel. *Principles of Accounting* offers Excel templates tied to specific end-of-chapter problems and annual report cases. This allows students to experience problem solving as it truly happens in real companies. The templates are available on the text Web site www.mhhe.com/LLPW1e.

Online Learning Center

www.mhhe.com/LLPW1e

For instructors, *Principles of Accounting*'s Online Learning Center (OLC) includes the Instructor's Resource Manual, PowerPoint slides, Solutions Manual, and Excel Template solutions tied to the end-of-chapter material. There are also links to professional resources.

For students and instructors, the OLC includes multiple-choice quizzes, Excel templates, The Home Depot and Lowe's Companies annual reports, check figures, Web links, and McGraw-Hill's Homework Manager (see below). Instructors can pull all of this material as part of another online course management system.

ALEKS®

www.business.aleks.com

ALEKS (Assessment and Learning in Knowledge Spaces) delivers precise, qualitative diagnostic assessments of students' knowledge, guides them in the selection of appropriate new study material, and records their progress toward mastery of curricular goals in a robust classroom management system.

ALEKS interacts with the student much as a skilled human tutor would, moving between explanation and practice as needed, correcting and analyzing errors, defining terms and chapter topics on request. By sophisticated modeling of a student's knowledge state for a given subject, ALEKS can focus clearly on what the student is most ready to learn next. When students focus on exactly what they are ready to learn, they build confidence and a learning momentum that fuels success.

ALEKS Math Prep for Accounting provides coverage of the basic math skills needed to succeed in introductory *Principles of Accounting*, while ALEKS for the Accounting Cycle provides a detailed, guided overview through every stage of the accounting cycle.

CourseSmart

http://www.coursesmart.com

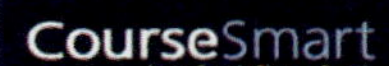

With the CourseSmart eTextbook, students can save up to 45 percent of the cost of a print book, reduce their impact on the environment, and access powerful Web tools for learning. CourseSmart is an online eTextbook, which means users access and view their textbook online when connected to the Internet. Students can also print sections of the book for maximum portability. CourseSmart eTextbooks are available in one standard online reader with full text search, notes and highlighting, and e-mail tools for sharing notes between classmates.

Quantum Tutors for the Accounting Cycle

Proven to Increase Test Scores by as Much as 50 percent

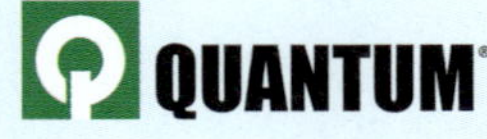

The Quantum Tutors for the Accounting Cycle help tutor students on the fundamental accounting concepts and problem-solving skills needed for principles and financial accounting courses. Just like working with an excellent instructor, students can enter their own work into the software, ask questions, and receive step-by-step feedback at a detailed level not available with any other software or homework management system. The Quantum Tutors are ideal when the student needs immediate help and the instructor is not available to answer questions. Accessed over the Internet, it offers students unlimited, convenient access day or night. It also allows them to study independently at their own pace.

We are happy to help you integrate technology into your course. Please call your local McGraw-Hill representative to learn more.

Instructor Resources

McGraw-Hill's Homework Manager

See page (xviii) for details.

Instructor CD-ROM

ISBN 0073274038

This integrated CD-ROM allows you to access most of the text's ancillary materials. You no longer need to worry about the various supplements that accompany your text. Instead, almost everything is available on one convenient CD-ROM: PowerPoint slides, Solutions Manual, Instructor's Resource Manual, Test Bank, and Computerized Test Bank.

Online Learning Center

www.mhhe.com/LLPW1e

See page (xix) for details.

Solutions Manual

Prepared by Patricia Libby, Robert Libby, Fred Phillips, and Stacey Whitecotton, the manual provides solutions for end-of-chapter questions, mini exercises, exercises, problems, and cases and projects. Available on the Instructor CD-ROM and text Web site.

Test Bank

Prepared by Laura Rickett, Kent State University, and Jay Holmen, University of Wisconsin–Eau Claire, this comprehensive Test Bank includes more than 2,000 true/false and multiple-choice questions, problems, essays, and matching questions. It is available on the Instructor CD-ROM.

Presentation Slides

Prepared by Jon Booker and Charles Caldwell at Tennessee Technological University and Susan Galbreath at David Lipscomb University, this option provides completely customized PowerPoint presentations for use in your classroom. Available on the Instructor CD-ROM and text Web site.

Instructor's Resource Manual

Prepared by J. Lowell Mooney, Georgia Southern University, supplements, including the Financial Accounting Videos, Study Guide, and PowerPoint slides, are topically cross-referenced in the Instructor's Manual to help instructors direct students to specific ancillaries to reinforce key concepts. Available on the Instructor CD-ROM and text Web site.

Algorithmic-Diploma Testbank

ISBN 0073274054

This feature allows you to add and edit questions; create up to 99 versions of each chapter test; attach graphic files to questions; import and export ASCII files; and select questions based on type, level of difficulty, or learning objective. This software provides password protection for saved tests and question databases and can run on a network.

EZ Test

McGraw-Hill's EZ Test is a flexible and easy-to-use electronic testing program that allows instructors to create tests from book-specific items. EZ Test accommodates a wide range of question types and allows instructors to add their own questions. Multiple versions of the test can be created, and any test can be exported for use with course management systems such as BlackBoard/WebCT. EZ Test Online is a new service that gives instructors a place to easily administer EZ Test–created exams and quizzes online. The program is available for Windows and Macintosh environments.

Excel Templates

Available on the text Web site www.mhhe.com/LLPW1e, these templates are tied to selected end-of-chapter material.

Instructor Excel Templates

This feature provides solutions to the student Excel Templates for selected end-of-chapter assignments. Available on the text Web site.

Check Figures

Prepared by Lu Ann Bean, Florida Institute of Technology, it provides key numbers in the solutions to the problems at the end of each chapter. Available on the text Web site.

Student Resources

Online Learning Center

www.mhhe.com/LLPW1e

Practice what you're learning. Lots of free practice problems are online whenever you're ready. Even at 1 A.M.

McGraw-Hill's Homework Manager

See page (xviii) for details.

Working Papers

Volume 1 (Chapters 1–12) 007327397X

Volume 2 (Chapters 12–25) 0073273988

Prepared by Jeannie Folk at College of DuPage, these items contain all of the forms necessary for completing end-of-chapter assignments.

Study Guide

Volume 1 (Chapters 1–12) 0073273929

Volume 2 (Chapters 12–25) 0073273937

Prepared by Jeannie Folk at College of DuPage, this outstanding learning tool gives students a deeper understanding of the course material and reinforces, step by step, what they are learning in the main text.

Check Figures

Available on the text Web site, www.mhhe.com/LLPW1e, check figures provide key numbers in solutions to end-of-chapter material.

iPod Downloadable Content

See below for details.

Excel Templates

Available on the text Web site www.mhhe.com/LLPW1e, these templates are tied to selected end-of-chapter material.

Carol Yacht's General Ledger and Peachtree

Carol Yacht's General Ledger Software is McGraw-Hill/Irwin's custom-built general ledger package. Carol Yacht's General Ledger can help you master every aspect of the general ledger, from inputting sales and cash receipts to calculating ratios for analysis or inventory valuations. Carol Yacht's General Ledger allows you to review an entire report and then double-click any single transaction to review or edit it. The report will then be updated on the fly to include the revised figures. When it comes to learning how an individual transaction affects the outcome of an entire report, no other approach matches that of Carol Yacht's General Ledger. Students can use Carol Yacht's General Ledger and Peachtree to solve numerous problems from the textbook.

iPod Downloadable Content

You are holding a media-integrated textbook that provides students portable educational content—just right for those students who want to study when and where it's most convenient for them. *Principles of Accounting* gives students the option to download content for review and study to their Apple® iPods and most other MP3/MP4 devices. iPod icons appear throughout the text pointing students to chapter-specific audio lecture presentation slides and course-related videos.

Photo Courtesy of Apple.®

Quick Reference to iPod Icons

Lectured slideshow–LP3-1
www.mhhe.com/LLPW1e

Lecture presentations available for download to your iPod, Zune, or MP3 device (audio and visual depending on your device)

Video 3-1
www.mhhe.com/LLPW1e

Topical videos available for download to your iPod, Zune, or MP3 (depending on your device)

Quiz 3-1
www.mhhe.com/LLPW1e

Multiple-choice quizzes available for download to your iPod, Zune, or MP3 (depending on your device)

Acknowledgments

Many dedicated instructors have devoted their time and effort to help us develop this text. We would like to acknowledge and thank all of our colleagues who helped guide our decisions. This text would not be what it is without the help of our dedicated contributors:

Reviewers

Alan Applebaum, Broward Community College
Leah Arrington, Northwest Mississippi Community College
Cynthia Ash, Davenport University
Sandy Augustine, Hilbert College
Collin Battle, Broward Community College
LuAnn Bean, Florida Institute of Technology
Sarah Beauchea, Berkeley College
Lisa Bernard, Pearl River Community College
Margaret Black, San Jacinto College
David Bland, Cape Fear Community College
Linda Bolduc, Mount Wachusett Community College
Patrick Borja, Citrus College
Thomas Branton, Alvin Community College
Gregory Brookins, Santa Monica College
Pennye Brown, Austin Peay State University
William P. Burke, Neumann College
Carla Cabarle, Minot State University
Michelle Cannon, Ivy Tech Community College of Indiana
Lloyd Carroll, Borough of Manhattan Community College
Lisa Cole, Johnson County Community College
Joan Cook, Milwaukee Area Technical College
Susan Cordes, Johnson County Community College
Christine Crosby, York Technical College
Judy Daulton, Piedmont Technical College
Passard Dean, Saint Leo University
Larry Dragosavac, Edison Community College
Karla Duckworth, Hinds Community College
Rebecca Evans, Blue Ridge Community College
Mary Falkey, Prince George Community College
John Gabeleman, Columbus State Community College
Patrick Geer, Hawkeye Community College
Gloria Grayless, Sam Houston State University
Joyce Griffin, Kansas City Kansas Community College
Amy Haas, Kingsborough Community College
Betty Harper, Middle Tennessee State University
Jeannie Harrington, Middle Tennessee State University
Paul Harris, Camden Community College
Patricia Holmes, Des Moines Area Community College
Robert Holtfreter, Central Washington University
Audrey Hunter, Broward Community College
Connie Hylton, George Mason University
Phillip Imel, Northern Virginia Community College
Thomas Kam, Hawaii Pacific University
Naomi Karolinski, Monroe Community College
Randy Kidd, Longview Community College
Thomas Knight, Borough of Manhattan Community College
Jerry Krueze, Western Michigan University
David Laurel, South Texas College
Susan Logorda, Lehigh Carbon Community College
Linda Mallory, Central Virginia Community College
Robert Mandau, Piedmont Technical College
Kenneth Mark, Kansas City Kansas Community College
Cynthia McCall, Des Moines Area Community College
Kevin McFarlane, Front Range Community College
Chris McNamara, Finger Lakes Community College
Shea Mears, Des Moines Area Community College
Terri Meta, Seminole Community College
Tammy Metzke, Milwaukee Area Technical College
Norma Montague, Central Carolina Community College
Karen Mozingo, Pitt Community College
Andrea Murowski, Brookdale Community College
Seved Noorian, Wentworth Institute of Technology
Shelly Ota, Leeward Community College
Carol Pace, Grayson Community College
Susan Pallas, Southeast Community College
Gregory L. Prescott, University of South Alabama
Timothy Prindle, Des Moines Area Community College
LaVonda Ramey, Schoolcraft College
Jenny Resnick, Santa Monica College
Carla Rich, Pensacola Junior College
Eric Rothenburg, Kingsborough Community College
Gary Rupp, SUNY–Farmingdale
Marcia Sandvold, Des Moines Area Community College
Richard Sarkisian, Camden Community College
Mona Seiler, Queensborough Community College
James Shimko, Sinclair Community College
Jay Siegel, Union County College
Alice Sineath, Forsyth Technical Community College
Lois Slutsky, Broward Community College–South Campus
Daniel Small, J. Sergeant Reynolds Community College
Robert Smolin, Citrus College
Laura Solano, Pueblo Community College
Laurel Stevenson, Seminole Community College
Janice Stoudemire, Midlands Technical College
Lynette Teal, Western Wisconsin Technical College
Lynda Thompson, Massasoit Community College
Judith Toland, Buck County Community College
Shafi Ullah, Broward Community College
Ski Vanderlaan, Delta College
Patricia Walczak, Lansing Community College
Scott Wallace, Blue Mountain Community College
Shane Warrick, Southern Arkansas University
Jack Wiehler, San Joaquin Delta College
Terrence Willyard, Baker College

TACTYC Focus Group Attendees (May 2006)

Patricia Walczak, Lansing Community College
Amy Haas, Kingsborough Community College
Mary Falkey, Prince George's Community College
Kenneth, Mark, Kansas City Kansas Community College
Allen Applebaum, Broward Community College
Audrey Hunter, Broward Community College
Scott Wallace, Blue Mountain Community College
Carla Rich, Pensacola Junior College
Marcia Sandvold, Des Moines Area Community College

TACTYC Focus Group Attendees (May 2007)

Amy Haas, Kingsborough Community College
Mary Falkey, Prince George Community College
Scott Wallace, Blue Mountain Community College
Patricia Holmes, Des Moines Area Community College
Ski Vanderlaan, Delta College
Lisa Cole, Johnson County Community College
Marcia Sandvold, Des Moines Area Community College

TACTYC Focus Group Attendees (May 2008)

Stanley Chapteru, Borough of Manhattan Community College
Paul Shinal, Cayuga Community College
Lois Slutsky, Broward Community College
Joan Cook, Milwaukee Area Technical College
John Gabelman, Columbus State Community College
Mary Halford, Prince George's Community College
Patty Holmes, Des Moines Area Community College
Marcia Sandvold, Des Moines Area Community College
Harvey Man, Manhattan Community College
Ron Dougherty, Tech Community College–Columbus
Natasha Librizzi, Milwaukee Area Technical College
Mary Falkey, Prince George's Community College
Melvin Williams, College of the Mainland
Carol Hutchinson, Asheville Buncombe Technical College

Principles of Accounting Symposium Attendees (March 2008)

Beverly Beatty, Anne Arundel Community College
George Bernard, Seminole Community College
Carla Cabarle, Minot State University
Chapterris Crosby, York Technical College
Steve Doster, Shawnee State University
Robert Dunlevy, Montgomery County Community College
Richard Fredericsk, Lasell College
John Gabelman, Columbus State Community College
Gloria Grayless, Sam Houston State University
Jeannie Harrington, Middle Tennessee State University
William Herd, Springfield Technical Community College
Susan Logorda, Lehigh Carbon Community College
Cathryn Nash, Dekalb Technical College
LaVonda Ramey, Schoolcraft College
Pamela Strysick, Broward Community College
Mario Tripaldi, Hudson County Community College
David Verduzco, University of Texas at Austin

Design Reviewers (WebEx, November 2007)

Paul Harris, Camden Community College
Audrey Hunter, Broward County Community College
Amy Haas, Kingsborough Community College
Kevin McFarlane, Front Range Community College
Patrick Geer, Hawkeye Community College
Patricia Holmes, Des Moines Area Community College
Sandra Augustine, Hilbert College
David Bland, Cape Fear Community College
David Laurel, South Texas College
Hoossein Noorian, Wentworth Institute of Technology
Margaret Black, San Jacinto College
Terri Meta, Seminole Community College
Lynda Thompson, Massasoit Community College
Jeannie Harrington, Middle Tennessee State University
John Gabelman, Columbus State Community College
Thomas Kam, Hawaii Pacific University
Tammy Metzke, Milwaukee Area Technical College
Chris McNamara, Finger Lakes Community College
Constance Hylton, George Mason University
Tom Branton, Alvin Community College
Lisa Cole, Johnson County Community College
Lois Slutksy, Broward Community College
Shane Warrick, South Arkansas University

We are grateful to the following individuals who helped develop, critique, and shape the text and ancillary package: Cheryl Bartlett, Central New Mexico Community College; Jeannie Folk, College of DuPage; Kimberly Temme, Maryville University of Saint Louis; Angela Sandberg, Jacksonville State University; Patricia Holmes, Des Moines Area Community College; LuAnn Bean, Florida Technical Institute; Beth Woods, Accuracy Counts; Laura Rickett, Kent State University; J. Lowell Mooney, Georgia Southern University; Rada Brooks, University of California–Berkeley; Jay Holmen, University of Wisconsin–Eau Claire; Susan Galbreath, David Lipscomb University; Jon Booker, Tennessee Technological University; Charles Caldwell, Tennessee Technological University; Matthew Muller, Adirondack Community College, Carol Yacht; Jack Terry, ComSource Associates, Inc.; and James Aitken, Central Michigan University.

Special thanks to Alan Cohen, Ithaca College, and John Gabelman, Columbus State Community College, and their Principles of Accounting Students, for class testing.

Last, we thank a talented group of individuals at McGraw-Hill/Irwin whose extraordinary efforts made all of this come together. We would especially like to thank our editorial director, Stewart Mattson; Tim Vertovec, our publisher; Alice Harra, our sponsoring editor; Kimberly Hooker, our developmental editor; Sankha Basu, our marketing manager; Mary Conzachi, our project manager; Martha Beyerlein, our freelance project manager; Pam Verros and Cara Hawthorne, our designers; Debra Sylvester, our production supervisor; Susan Lombardi, our media producer; Jeremy Cheshareck, our photo research coordinator; David Tietz, our photo researcher; and Marcy Lunetta, our permission researcher.

Patricia A. Libby
Robert Libby
Fred Philips
Stacey Whitecotton

Assurance of Accuracy

Dear Colleagues,

Accuracy has always been our top priority in producing a textbook. We test every word through your eyes and those of our many professional copy editors, line editors, accuracy checkers, and contributing supplement authors. We have taken every effort to ensure the accuracy of this first edition of *Principles of Accounting* including the following:

- ***Three drafts of manuscript***: We wrote and edited the entire manuscript three times, reading each other's chapters and making sure our voices, vocabulary, and pedagogy were consistent throughout.
- ***Three rounds of accuracy checking***: Three professional accuracy checkers individually tested every problem at different stages of the production so that you don't have any surprises.
- ***Two rounds of professional line editing***: A large investment was made to ensure consistency of voice and appropriate reading level.
- ***Two hundred and sixty reviews:*** Detailed reviews of every chapter from principles instructors around the country were compiled, synthesized, studied, and acted upon during each draft of our manuscript.
- ***Forty*** students participated in a class test of Chapters 1–4.
- ***Thirty-six*** members at three different conferences of Teachers of Accounting at Two-Year Colleges participated in focus groups held in 2006 (Atlanta), 2007 (Indianapolis), and 2008 (San Antonio) where we spent several hours listening to their advice that helped us shape the content and pedagogy.
- ***Twenty-six*** faculty attendees of McGraw-Hill's Principles of Accounting Symposium in 2008 (Las Vegas) spent several days discussing the challenges of teaching principles of accounting.
- ***Twenty-five*** professors served as design reviewers via WebEx to critique the design and overall visual appeal of the text and challenged us to help their students with a book that says "You can do it!" through its design.

All of our editorial advisers, reviewers, and attendees are listed on page xxii.

You and your students can be assured that our dedication and commitment to producing an error-free text has gone into every page of *Principles of Accounting*.

Pat Libby Bob Libby Fred Phillips Stacey M Whitecotton

Patricia Libby | Robert Libby | Fred Phillips | Stacey Whitecotton

To Our Students and Readers: Advice on How to Read Your Textbook

Dear Students,

The following advice is generated from an in-depth study of 172 undergraduate students of varying backgrounds, all of whom were enrolled in an introductory accounting course.

- **Read the chapters to learn rather than just to get through them.** Learning doesn't miraculously occur just because your eyes have skimmed all the assigned lines of the textbook. You have to think and focus while reading to ensure that you sink the material into your understanding and memory. Use the learning objectives in the text to focus on what's really important in each chapter.

- **Don't get discouraged if you initially find some material challenging to learn.** At various times, both the best and weakest students describe themselves as "confused" and "having a good grasp of the material," "anxious" and "confident," and "overwhelmed" and "comfortable." The simple fact is that learning new material can be challenging and initially confusing. Success doesn't appear to depend as much on whether you become confused as it does on what you do when you become confused.

- **Clear up confusion as it arises.** A key difference between the most and least successful students is how they respond to difficulty and confusion. When successful students are confused or anxious, they immediately try to enhance their understanding through rereading, self-testing, and seeking outside help if necessary. In contrast, unsuccessful students try to reduce anxiety by delaying further reading or by resorting to memorizing without understanding. Aim to clear up confusion when it arises because accounting in particular is a subject for which your understanding of later material depends on your understanding of earlier material.

- **Think of reading as the initial stage of studying.** Abandon the idea that "studying" occurs only during the final hours before an exam. By initially reading with the same intensity that occurs during later reviews for an exam, you can create extra time for practicing exercises and problems. This combination of concentrated reading and extensive practice is likely to contribute to better learning and superior exam scores.

To learn more about the study on which this advice is based, see B. J. Phillips and F. Phillips, "Sink or Skim: Textbook Reading Behaviors of Introductory Accounting Students," *Issues in Accounting Education* 22 (February 2007), pp. 21–44.

Brief Table of Contents

Chapter 1 **The Role of Accounting in Starting a Business 2**

Chapter 2 **Establishing a Business and the Balance Sheet 48**

Chapter 3 **Operating a Business and the Income Statement 96**

Chapter 4 **Completing the Accounting Cycle 144**

Chapter 5 **Accounting Systems 202**

Chapter 6 **Merchandising Operations 260**

Chapter 7 **Inventories 302**

Chapter 8 **Internal Control and Cash 342**

Chapter 9 **Receivables 380**

Chapter 10 **Long-Lived Tangible and Intangible Assets 416**

Chapter 11 **Current Liabilities and Payroll 466**

Chapter 12 **Partnerships 504**

Chapter 13 **Accounting for Corporations 558**

Chapter 14 **Long-Term Liabilities 598**

Chapter 15 **Accounting for Investments 640**

Chapter 16 **Reporting and Interpreting the Statement of Cash Flows 680**

Chapter 17 **Financial Statement Analysis 728**

Appendix A A-1

Appendix B B-1

Appendix C C-1

Appendix D D-1

Glossary G-1

Credits PC-1

Business Index I-1

Subject Index I-4

Table of Contents

Chapter 1

The Role of Accounting in Starting a Business 2

PIZZA AROMA 3

Business Types and Organizational Forms 4
Business Types 4
Organizational Forms 4
Accounting and Business Decisions 6
Accounting Defined 6
Accounting Professionals 6
Users of Financial Information 6
Basic Financial Reports 8
The Accounting Equation 9
Pizza Aroma Illustration 10
Financial Statements 13
Professional Standards and Ethical Conduct 22
Generally Accepted Accounting Principles 23
Ethical Conduct 24
Epilogue for Pizza Aroma 25
Demonstration Case 26
Supplement 1A: Overview of Career Choices for Accounting Professionals 27
Chapter Summary 28
Key Terms 30
Questions 30
Multiple Choice 31
Mini Exercises 31
Exercises 33
Problems—Set A 38
Problems—Set B 42
Cases and Projects 45

Chapter 2

Establishing a Business and the Balance Sheet 48

PIZZA AROMA 49

Determine the Effects of Business Activities 50
Nature of Business Transactions 50
Balance Sheet Accounts 51
Transaction Analysis 52
Analysis of Pizza Aroma's Transactions 53
Prepare Accounting Records 57
The Accounting Cycle 57
Analyzing Business Transactions 57
Recording Transaction Effects 58
Posting Transaction Effects 60
Pizza Aroma's Accounting Records 62
Preparing a Trial Balance 64
Prepare a Balance Sheet 67
Classified Balance Sheet 67
Limitations of the Balance Sheet 68
Summary of the Accounting Cycle 70
Demonstration Case 71
Chapter Summary 74
Key Terms 75
Questions 75
Multiple Choice 76
Mini Exercises 76
Exercises 80
Problems—Set A 85
Problems—Set B 88
Cases and Projects 92

Chapter 3

Operating a Business and the Income Statement 96

PIZZA AROMA 97

Recognizing Operating Activities 98
Income Statement Accounts 98
Operating Cycle 99
Measure Operating Activities 100
Cash-Based Measurements 100
Accrual Basis Accounting 101
Expanded Transaction Analysis Model 103
Analysis of Pizza Aroma's Transactions 106
Prepare an Income Statement 112
Unadjusted Trial Balance 112
Classified Income Statements 112
Limitations of the Income Statement 114

Demonstration Case 115
Chapter Summary 118
Key Terms 119
Questions 119
Multiple Choice 120
Mini Exercises 121
Exercises 125
Problems—Set A 133
Problems—Set B 136
Cases and Projects 139

Chapter 4

Completing the Accounting Cycle 144

PIZZA AROMA 145

Adjusting Revenues and Expenses 146
Reasons for Adjustments 146
Types of Adjustments 147
Analysis of Adjustments 147

Preparing Financial Statements 160
Adjusted Trial Balance 160
Relationships among Financial Statements 161
Classified Income Statement 162
Statement of Owner's Equity 162
Classified Balance Sheet 163

Completing the Accounting Cycle 164
Closing the Books 164
Preparing a Post-Closing Trial Balance 167

Analyzing Financial Information 169
Computing and Interpreting Key Ratios 169
Analyzing Net Profit Margin (NPM) 169
Making Comparisons to Benchmarks 170

Demonstration Case 171
Supplement 4: Using an Accounting Workshop 175
Chapter Summary 177
Key Terms 179
Questions 179
Multiple Choice 179
Mini Exercises 180
Exercises 183
Problems—Set A 191
Problems—Set B 195
Cases and Projects 199

Chapter 5

Accounting Systems 202

THE UPS STORE 203

Manual versus Computerized Accounting Information Systems 204

Components of an Accounting Information System 206
Accounts Receivable Subsidiary Ledger 206
Accounts Payable Subsidiary Ledger 208

Special Journals and Posting of Transactions 209
Revenue Journal 209
Cash Receipts Journal 212
Purchases Journal 216
Cash Payments Journal 217
Use of the General Journal 218
Summary of the Recording Process 219

Basic Theory of Accounting Information Systems 221
Underlying Assumptions 221
Developmental Phases 221

Computerized Accounting Information Systems 222
Advantages and Disadvantages 222
Peachtree Complete 2008—An Illustration 223

Demonstration Case 225
Chapter Summary 228
Key Terms 228
Questions 229
Multiple Choice 229
Mini Exercises 230
Exercises 233
Problems—Set A 243
Problems—Set B 250
Cases and Projects 257

Chapter 6

Merchandising Operations 260

WAL-MART 261

Operating Cycles and Inventory Systems 262
- Operating Cycles 262
- Inventory Systems 262

Recording Merchandise Purchases 265
- Purchases on Account 265
- Transportation Cost (Freight-In) 265
- Purchase Returns and Allowances 266
- Purchase Discounts 266
- Summary of Purchase-Related Transactions 268

Recording Merchandise Sales 270
- Cash Sales 270
- Sales Returns and Allowances 271
- Credit Card Sales 271
- Sales on Account and Sales Discounts 272
- Transportation Cost (Freight-Out) 273
- Summary of Sales-Related Transactions 273
- Comparison of Sales and Purchases Accounting 274

Preparing and Analyzing the Income Statement 276
- Multistep Income Statement for Merchandisers 276
- Gross Profit Percentage 277
- Comparison to Benchmarks 278

Demonstration Case A 279
Demonstration Case B 280
Supplement 6A: Periodic Inventory Records 281
Supplement 6B: Closing Entries for a Merchandiser 283
Chapter Summary 283
Key Terms 283
Questions 285
Multiple Choice 285
Mini Exercises 286
Exercises 288
Problems—Set A 293
Problems—Set B 295
Cases and Projects 298

Chapter 7

Inventories 302

AMERICAN EAGLE OUTFITTERS 303

Reporting Inventory and Cost of Goods Sold 304
- Balance Sheet and Income Statement Reporting 304
- Cost of Goods Sold Equation 305

Choosing Among Inventory Closing Methods 306
- Cost Flow Methods under a Perpetual Inventory System 308
- First-In, Last Out (FIFO) 308
- Last-In, First-Out (LIFO) 309
- Weighted Average Cost 310
- Financial Statement Effects of Inventory Costing Methods 310

Reporting Inventory at the Lower of Cost or Market 312

Identifying the Effects of Inventory Errors 314
- Income Statement Effects 314
- Balance Sheet Effects 315

Evaluating Inventory Management 316
- Inventory Turnover Analysis 316
- Comparison to Benchmarks 317

Demonstration Case 318
Supplement 7A: Cost Flow Methods under a Periodic Inventory System 320
Supplement 7B: Estimating Inventory Gross Profit Method 323
Chapter Summary 324
Key Terms 325
Questions 325
Multiple Choice 325
Mini Exercises 326
Exercises 328
Problems—Set A 333
Problems—Set B 336
Cases and Projects 339

Chapter 8

Internal Control and Cash 342

THE HOME DEPOT 343

Internal Control 344
- Definition and Purpose 344
- Sarbanes-Oxley Act of 2002 344
- Common Control Principles 346
- Control Limitations 348

Internal Control of Cash 348
- Cash Receipts 349
- Cash Payments 351
- Bank Procedures and Reconciliation 355

Financial Reporting of Cash 360
- Cash and Cash Equivalents 360

Demonstration Case A 361
Demonstration Case B 361
Chapter Summary 362
Key Terms 363
Questions 363
Multiple Choice 364
Mini Exercises 365
Exercises 368
Problems—Set A 371
Problems—Set B 374
Cases and Projects 378

Chapter 9

Receivables 380

SKECHERS 381

Types of Receivables 382

Accounts Receivable 383
- Accounting for Bad Debts: The Allowance Method 383
- Recording Estimated Bad Debt Expense 383
- Method for Estimating Bad Debts 385
- Other Issues 388

Notes Receivable and Interest Revenue 390
- Calculating Interest 390
- Recording Notes Receivable and Interest Revenue 390

Evaluating Receivables Management 393
- Receivables Turnover Analysis 393
- Comparison to Benchmarks 394

Demonstration Case A 395
Demonstration Case B 397
Supplement 9A: Direct Write-Off Method 398
Chapter Summary 398
Key Terms 399
Questions 400
Multiple Choice 400
Mini Exercises 401
Exercises 403
Problems—Set A 408
Problems—Set B 410
Cases and Projects 412

Chapter 10

Long-Lived Tangible and Intangible Assets 416

CEDAR FAIR 417

Definition and Classification 418
- Tangible Assets 418
- Intangible Assets 418

Tangible Assets: Acquisition, Use, Impairment, and Disposal 419
- Acquisition of Tangible Assets 419
- Use of Tangible Assets 423
- Impairment of Tangible Assets 430
- Disposal and Exchange of Tangible Assets 431

Intangible Assets: Types, Acquisition, Use, and Disposal 433
- Types of Intangible Assets 433
- Acquisition, Use, and Disposal of Intangible Assets 434

Evaluation of Long-Lived Asset Use 436
- Turnover Analysis 436
- Impact of Differences in Depreciation 437

Demonstration Case 439
Supplement 10A: Natural Resources 442
Supplement 10B: Changes in Depreciation 443

Supplement 10C: Exchanging Assets 443
Chapter Summary 444
Key Terms 445
Questions 446
Multiple Choice 446
Mini Exercises 447
Exercises 450
Problems—Set A 456
Problems—Set B 457
Cases and Projects 459

Chapter 11

Current Liabilities and Payroll 466

GENERAL MILLS, INC. 467

Reporting Liabilities 468
- Measuring Liabilities 468
- Classifying Liabilities 468
- Calculating and Interpreting the Current Ratio 469

Accounting for Current Liabilities 470
- Accounts Payable 470
- Notes Payable 470
- Current Portion of Long-Term Debt 472
- Other Current Liabilities 473

Payroll Accounting 473
- Calculating the Payroll 478
- Recording the Payroll 480
- Applying Internal Control Principles 484

Demonstration Case A 485
Demonstration Case B 486
Demonstration Case C 487
Supplement 11A: Employee Benefits 488
Chapter Summary 489
Key Terms 490
Questions 490
Multiple Choice 491
Mini Exercises 492
Exercises 494
Problems—Set A 497
Problems—Set B 499
Cases and Projects 501

Chapter 12

Partnerships 504

BLOOM'N FLOWERS 505

Partnerships Compared to Similar Organizations 506
- Characteristics of Partnerships 506
- Similar Forms of Business 507

Accounting for Partnerships 509
- Formation: Recording Cash and Noncash Contributions 509
- Division of Income (or Loss): Four Methods 511
- Preparation of Financial Statements 516

Changes of Ownerships in a Partnership 517
- Admission of a Partner 517
- Withdrawal of a Partner 521
- Death of Partner 525

Liquidation of a Partnership 526
- No Capital Deficiency 527
- Capital Deficiency 529

Ratio Analysis 533
- Partner Return on Equity 533

Demonstration Case A 534
Demonstration Case B 536
Demonstration Case C 538
Demonstration Case D 539
Chapter Summary 539
Key Terms 541
Questions 541
Multiple Choice 541
Mini Exercises 542
Exercises 545
Problems—Set A 549
Problems—Set B 552
Cases and Projects 555

Chapter 13

Accounting for Corporations 558

SONIC CORP. 559

Characteristics of the Corporate Form 560
- Ownership 560
- Laws and Taxes 560

Formation 561
Financing 562
Accounting for Stock Transactions 562
Common and Preferred Stock 563
Treasury Stock 565
Financial Statement Reporting 567
Accounting for Dividends and Splits 568
Cash Dividends on Common Stock 568
Cash Dividends on Preferred Stock 570
Stock Dividends 572
Stock Splits 573
Statement of Retained Earnings 574
Financial Ratio Analysis 575
Earnings per Share (EPS) 576
Price/Earnings (P/E) Ratio 577
Demonstration Case A 577
Demonstration Case B 579
Chapter Summary 580
Key Terms 580
Questions 581
Multiple Choice 581
Mini Exercises 582
Exercises 584
Problems—Set A 590
Problems—Set B 593
Cases and Projects 595

Chapter 14

Long-Term Liabilities 598
GENERAL MILLS, INC. 599

Long-Term Liabilities 600
Making Financing Decisions 600
Measuring Liabilities 600
Accounting for Long-Term Liabilities 601
Discounted Notes 601
Bonds Payable 604
Lease Liabilities 610
Analyzing Long-Term Liabilities 611
Debt-to-Assets Ratio 611
Times Interest Earned Ratio 612
Demonstration Case A 613
Demonstration Case B 614
Demonstration Case C 615
Supplement 14A: Discounting Future Payments 616
Supplement 14B: Effective-Interest Method of Amortization 619
Supplement 14C: Straight-Line Method of Amortization 622
Chapter Summary 623
Key Terms 624
Questions 625
Multiple Choice 625
Mini Exercises 626
Exercises 628
Problems—Set A 631
Problems—Set B 634
Cases and Projects 637

Chapter 15

Accounting for Investments 640
THE WASHINGTON POST COMPANY 641

An Overview 642
Reasons Companies Invest 642
Identifying Investment Types and Accounting Methods 643
Accounting for Passive Investments 644
Debt Investments Held to Maturity: Amortized Cost Method 644
Investments in Stock of Significant Influence 645
Investments in Stock for Control 645
Securities Available for Sale: Market Value Method 646
Comparison of Available-for-Sale and Trading Securities 650
Accounting for Influential Investments 654
Investments for Significant Influence: Equity Method 654
Investments with Controlling Interests: Consolidated Statements 658

Evaluating Total Invested Capital 660
Return on Assets (ROA) 660
Comparison to Benchmarks 660

Demonstration Case A 661
Demonstration Case B 662
Demonstration Case C 663
Chapter Summary 664
Key Terms 665
Questions 665
Multiple Choice 666
Mini Exercises 667
Exercises 668
Problems—Set A 671
Problems—Set B 674
Cases and Projects 677

Chapter 16

Reporting and Interpreting the Statement of Cash Flows 680

NAUTILUS INC. 681

Classifications of the Statement of Cash Flows 682
The Relationship between Business Activities and Cash Flows 682
Cash Flows from Operating Activities 683
Cash Flows from Investing Activities 684
Cash Flows from Financing Activities 684
Net Increase (Decrease) in Cash 684
Relationships to the Balance Sheet and Income Statement 685

Reporting Cash Flows from Operating Activities—Indirect Method 687
Depreciation and Gains and Losses on Sale of Long-Term Assets 689
Changes in Current Assets and Current Liabilities 689

Reporting Cash Flows from Investing Activities 693
Plant and Equipment 693
Land and Investments 694

Reporting Cash Flows from Financing Activities 694
Long-Term Debt 694
Contributed Capital 694
Retained Earnings 694

Preparing and Evaluating the Statement of Cash Flows 696
Format for the Statement of Cash Flows 696
Noncash Investing and Financing Activities 696
Supplemental Cash Flow Information 698
Free Cash Flow 698
Quality of Income Ratio 698

Demonstration Case A: Indirect Method 699
Supplement 16A: Reporting Cash Flows from Operating Activities—Direct Method 700
Demonstration Case B: Direct Method (Supplement A) 704
Supplement 16B: Spreadsheet Approach: Indirect Method 705
Chapter Summary 707
Key Terms 707
Questions 708
Multiple Choice 708
Mini Exercises 709
Exercises 712
Problems—Set A 719
Problems—Set B 721
Cases and Projects 723

Chapter 17

Financial Statement Analysis 728

LOWE'S 729

Release of Financial Information 730
Preliminary Press Release 730
Quarterly and Annual Reports 730
Securities and Exchange Commission (SEC) Filings 731
Investor Information Web Sites 731

Horizontal (Trend) Analysis 732
Preparing Comparative Balance Sheets and Comparative Income Statements 732
Revealing Changes through Trend Analyses 732

Vertical (Common Size) Analysis 734
Preparing a Common Size Balance Sheet and Income Statement 735
Interpreting Common Size Statements 735

Financial Ratios 736

Profitability Ratios 736

Liquidity Ratios 740

Solvency Ratios 742

Accounting Decisions and Ratio Analysis 744

Demonstration Case 745

Supplement 17A: Nonrecurring and Other Special Items 746

Chapter Summary 747

Key Terms 747

Questions 747

Multiple Choice 747

Mini Exercises 748

Exercises 749

Problems—Set A 755

Problems—Set B 758

Cases and Projects 761

Appendix A A-1

Appendix B B-1

Appendix C C-1

Appendix D D-1

Glossary G-1

Credits PC-1

Business Index I-1

Subject Index I-4

PRINCIPLES OF

Financial Accounting

1 The Role of Accounting in Starting a Business

At the beginning of each chapter, you'll see a list of learning objectives that identify the key topics you need to master. You can also use the list as an outline for taking notes as you read through the chapter.

LEARNING OBJECTIVES

After studying this chapter, you should be able to:

Lectured slideshow–LP1-1
www.mhhe.com/LLPW1e

LO1 Categorize business types and organizational forms.

LO2 Describe accounting and its role in business decisions.

LO3 Identify users of financial information.

LO4 Describe the fundamental accounting equation and elements of financial statements.

LO5 Explain the structure of basic financial statements.

LO6 Understand the importance of ethical decisions in financial reporting and business.

Focus Company: PIZZA AROMA, Ithaca, NY

"A Small Business Comes to Life"

Have you ever walked into a local store or restaurant and thought, I'm good at this, and I can do it better? But when you thought about it further, you realized that you did not have all the knowledge you needed to start the business and monitor its success. How would you know you really could do it better? Where would you get good advice? Who else would be interested in how well your business did? In the next four chapters, you will learn about the start of a real business—one person's dream turned into reality—and two of the authors of this text are now regular customers.

About two decades ago, Mauricio Rosa and his wife emigrated from El Salvador to the United States to build a better life. While working in pizza shops in Massachusetts and New York, Mauricio perfected a gourmet pizza concept that caught the attention of a business owner in Ithaca, New York. Thinking that great gourmet pizza would be a new and exciting addition to the restaurant scene in Ithaca, the man encouraged Mauricio to start his own pizza business there.

Although the idea interested Mauricio, he had many questions to ask and decisions to make before attempting such a venture. The business owner suggested that Mauricio contact Laurie Hensley, a local CPA (certified public accountant), to ask her advice. The two met at her Ithaca office at the beginning of April.

ORGANIZATION OF THE CHAPTER

BUSINESS TYPES AND ORGANIZATIONAL FORMS	ACCOUNTING AND BUSINESS DECISIONS	BASIC FINANCIAL REPORTS	PROFESSIONAL STANDARDS AND ETHICAL CONDUCT
• Business Types • Organizational Forms	• Accounting Defined • Accounting Professionals • Users of Financial Information	• The Accounting Equation • Pizza Aroma Illustration • Financial Statements	• Generally Accepted Accounting Principles • Ethical Conduct

Throughout this text, we will provide you with tips to highlight explanations of selected topics. Please read them carefully.

Coach's Tip

In this chapter, the conversation between Mauricio and Laurie is important to the flow of the material. Please do not skip the dialogue.

BUSINESS TYPES AND ORGANIZATIONAL FORMS

"Hi, Laurie. I'm opening a gourmet pizza restaurant named Pizza Aroma, and I have lots of questions."

"It's nice to meet you, Mauricio, and I'm glad to help. We should start by talking about what type of business you're establishing and how you want to organize it."

Learning Objective 1

Categorize business types and organizational forms.

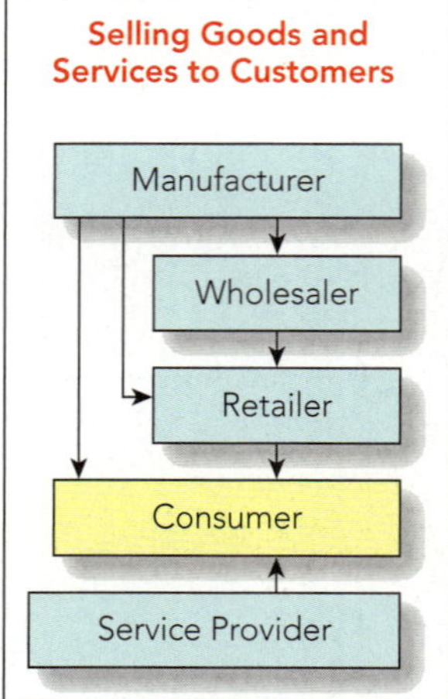

Business Types

Laurie explained the types of businesses. Most businesses, whether they are large like Wal-Mart or small like a pizza restaurant, exist so their owners can earn a profit. These businesses earn their profits by selling goods or services to customers for more than the cost of producing them.[1] Mauricio's pizza restaurant is a service business. **Service companies** do not make or sell goods; instead, they provide a service to customers or clients. Hilton Hotels provides lodging services, Southwest Airlines provides air transportation services, and Mauricio's restaurant will provide food service. Other companies earn profits in other ways. **Manufacturers** make products from raw inputs. For example, Dell uses various plastic, metal, and electronic components to build computers. **Merchandisers** sell the goods that manufacturers produced. Merchandisers that sell exclusively to other businesses are called wholesalers. Those that sell to customers are called retailers. Wal-Mart, Macy's, Linens 'n Things, and Best Buy are retailers.

Organizational Forms

One of the first decisions Mauricio must make is to determine how to organize his business. Laurie outlined for him the three major ways that businesses can be organized, each of which has unique strengths and weaknesses.[2]

Sole Proprietorship

A **sole proprietorship** is owned by one individual who often manages the business as well. Sole proprietorships are relatively inexpensive to form. Because they are not legally separate from their owners, all of their profits (or losses) become part of the proprietor's taxable income. The proprietor is also personally liable for all of the business's debts.

Key terms such as sole proprietorship are printed in blue type throughout the text. Each is listed at the end of the chapter and defined at the end of the book in the glossary.

[1] Some organizations (such as city governments, colleges, and the United Way) are considered nonprofit because the objective is to provide benefits to society rather than to earn a profit.

[2] For additional information on starting, financing, and managing a small business, go to the U.S. Small Business Association Web site at www.sba.gov.

Partnership

A **partnership** is similar to a proprietorship, but it has two or more owners rather than one. A partnership agreement outlines how the profits (or losses) are to be shared and how the ownership of the business can change (for example, by adding a new partner, buying out an existing partner, or dissolving the partnership). As sole proprietors attempt to expand their businesses, they often add partners to obtain the resources the business needs to grow.

Corporation

Unlike a proprietorship or partnership, a **corporation**[3] is a separate legal entity. This means that corporations are taxed separately from their owners, and their owners cannot be held liable for more than their investments in the corporation—a major advantage to an investor.

A corporation's ownership is divided into shares of stock. When a relatively small number of individuals own the stock, the corporation is a privately held company. Public companies, on the other hand, sell stock on the stock market to reach many more individuals.

In addition to the limited liability advantage, another major advantage of a corporation is that, at any time, stockholders can sell all or part of their shares to someone else. These advantages make it easier for a corporation to raise large amounts of money to finance its growth. A corporation's major disadvantage is the higher cost of its creation, primarily due to higher legal fees. Most of the big-name companies you are familiar with, such as Home Depot, The Gap, and Papa John's, are corporations. A share of stock is shown above.

Percentage of Organizational Forms in the United States

Partnerships 6%
Corporations 21%
Sole Proprietorships 73%

Source: 1997 U.S. Economic Census, Legal Forms of Organizations, www.census.org.

Coach's Tip

The best way to know whether you are reading the chapter carefully enough is to see how well you do on a short exercise. Therefore, at important points throughout each chapter, you will find an exercise that will help you to reinforce the concepts you have just learned and provide feedback on how well you learned them. We urge you not to skip these practices.

"Although I certainly think the corporate form has its advantages, I intend to start out as a **sole proprietor.** If I decide to grow my business beyond what I can personally afford, then I'll consider changing it by adding a partner or establishing a corporation."

Complete this short practice exercise to make sure you understand how to categorize businesses.

SELF-STUDY PRACTICE

Match the following terms to the most appropriate statements. Select only one statement to describe each term.

1. _____ Corporation
2. _____ Merchandiser
3. _____ Public company
4. _____ Sole proprietorship
5. _____ Manufacturer
6. _____ Partnership
7. _____ Service provider

A. Sells goods made by manufacturers to customers.
B. Has two or more individuals who have agreed on how to share the profits.
C. Is a separate legal and accounting entity that sells stock to owners.
D. Makes products from raw inputs.
E. Provides a service to customers or clients.
F. Sells stock on the stock market.
G. Is a business owned by one individual.

After you have finished, check your answers with the solutions at the bottom of the page.

[3] Another form of business is a **limited liability company** or **LLC** in which a partnership can be organized as a corporation to limit liability to the partners' individual investments. However, it is taxed as a partnership with each partner paying taxes on his or her percentage of the profits.

Solution to Self-Study Practice

1. C 2. A 3. F 4. G 5. D 6. B 7. E

"Laurie, I believe passionately that I can make the best pizza around using the highest quality ingredients. I brought a copy of my menu and some samples of my pizza for you to try. What do you think?"

"Wow, Mauricio! This is awesome. I think you're going to sell a lot of pizza, and it's going to be the best in town. But the question is, can you do it at a profit? Let me explain how accounting and accounting professionals can help."

ACCOUNTING AND BUSINESS DECISIONS

Learning Objective 2
Describe accounting and its role in business decisions.

Laurie defined accounting and the role it plays in business decisions.

Accounting Defined

To know just how successful his company will be, Mauricio will need to establish and maintain a system of financial recordkeeping—that is, an accounting system. **Accounting** is an information system designed by an organization to capture (analyze, record, and summarize) the activities affecting its financial condition and performance and then communicate the results to decision makers, both inside and outside the organization. When business owners, managers, investors, and creditors talk about business operations, they use accounting as their language, so accounting is often referred to as the **language of business.**

Video 1-1
www.mhhe.com/LLPW1e

Accounting Professionals

Every organization needs accountants to help its owner(s) understand the financial effects of business decisions and to assist in communicating financial information for making decisions. Accountants who are employed by a single business or nonprofit organization work in **private accounting**. Like Laurie, accountants who charge a fee for their services to businesses and nonprofit organizations work in **public accounting**. Laurie is a licensed **certified public accountant** (CPA) who has passed a rigorous exam and been in practice in public accounting. Supplement 1-A to this chapter illustrates the wide variety of career choices available to accounting professionals. Some accounting graduates start their careers in CPA firms and then decide to move into private accounting within businesses, government organizations such as the Internal Revenue Service (IRS) and the Federal Bureau of Investigation (FBI), or nonprofit organizations such as the American Red Cross. Many of them become top managers of large companies. After earning a graduate degree, some devote their careers to teaching and research.

Because today's cost of computers and accounting software such as Peachtree[4] is low, most small business owners do their own bookkeeping and hire public accountants to provide assistance and advice. Because Mauricio's business will be small, he decides to have Pizza Aroma contract with a CPA who will help him set up an accounting system for the business and advise him on key business decisions. As his business grows, Mauricio may then decide to hire a private accountant or to ask an independent CPA to review his financial records and accounting system.

"I feel confident now that there are professionals who can help me with my financial issues. How will an accounting system help me run my business?"

Learning Objective 3
Identify users of financial information.

Users of Financial Information

Whether focused on marketing, human resources, finance, or production and operations, all businesspeople need accounting information to understand the financial condition and performance of a business. As Exhibit 1.1 indicates, the accounting system produces two kinds of reports: managerial accounting reports and financial accounting reports.

[4] We illustrate the use of Peachtree in Chapter 5.

Exhibit 1.1 The Accounting System and Decision Makers

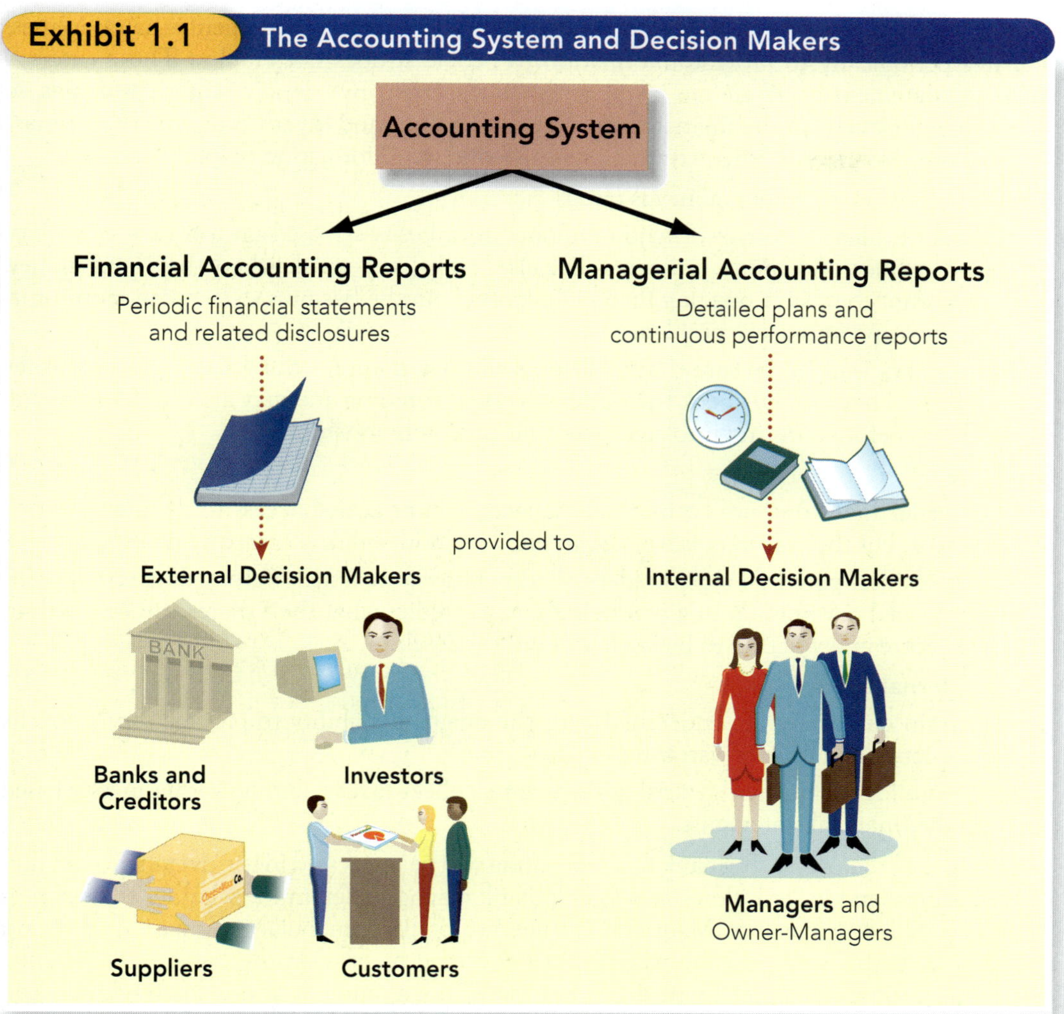

Managerial accounting reports include detailed financial plans and continually updated reports about the financial performance of the business. These reports are made available only to the company's managers (**internal users** of the information) so that they can make business decisions such as whether to build, buy, or rent a building; whether to continue or discontinue making particular products; how much to pay employees; and how much to borrow from creditors. **Sole proprietors** and **partners** who manage their own businesses and other **managers** who are hired by owners clearly have an interest in receiving the best, most up-to-date information for use in making these decisions.

As owner and manager of Pizza Aroma, Mauricio will regularly need managerial accounting reports to monitor the quantity of supplies on hand, evaluate the various costs associated with making and selling his gourmet pizza, and assess his employees' productivity. He will also use the information to forecast the possible effects of any changes he may consider, such as expanding his business to a second location or adding salads and desserts to the menu. Owners who do not manage their own businesses use accounting information to evaluate how effectively the managers are operating their companies.

"Others outside your business will also need financial information about your restaurant. For example, where will the money come from to start your business?"

"I'll contribute $30,000 from personal savings. But I'll still need to ask the bank for a $20,000 loan to buy equipment. What will the bank want to know?"

Laurie described financial accounting reports called **financial statements** that a business prepares periodically to provide information to people it does not employ. These **external financial statement users** are not given access to the company's detailed internal records, so they rely extensively on the financial statements. Creditors and investors are the two primary external user groups, but other external users also find the information helpful.

Creditors (anyone to whom money is owed)

- **Banks** evaluate the risk of lending money to a business based on a review of its past performance and future prospects. Because banks take a risk when they lend money, they want to receive ongoing financial reports from the business so they can monitor its progress and anticipate problems.
- **Suppliers** want to be sure that a business can pay them for the goods or services they deliver. They usually check the business's credit standing and may also ask for financial reports before entering into significant business relationships.

Investors

- **External investors,** unlike internal managers, do not have access to detailed internal records, but they are very interested in knowing how well the company is doing.
- Current and potential **stockholders** of corporations are a major group of external users. They need information that will help them to predict what their shares will be worth in the future and whether to buy, sell, or hold the stock.

Other external users

- Certain **customers** are concerned with the company's ability to provide service on its products and honor its warranties.
- Various local, state, and federal **governments** collect taxes and monitor businesses based on the financial statements.

In Pizza Aroma's case, the bank it borrows from will be interested in the overall profitability of the business and its cash flows, which help bank managers determine whether the business can make its loan payments. Mauricio will need to prepare financial information to obtain the loan from the bank, and he will need to continue to provide the bank with financial reports until the loan has been repaid. See Exhibit 1.1 for a summary of the difference between financial accounting reports such as these and the managerial accounting reports that are prepared for internal users.

SELF-STUDY PRACTICE

A. Define *accounting.*

B. For each of the following, indicate whether the person or entity is an internal user (I) or an external user (E) of accounting information.

1. _____ Banker	3. _____ Supplier	5. _____ Public company stockholder
2. _____ Manager	4. _____ Government	6. _____ Sole proprietor

After you have finished, check your answers with the solutions at the bottom of the page.

BASIC FINANCIAL REPORTS

Mauricio understood everything Laurie had told him, but he had another major concern.

"I want to be knowledgeable when I talk to my accountants and bankers, but I don't know much about accounting."

"This is a common concern for new business owners. Let's start with the most basic thing you need to know about accounting."

Solution to Self-Study Practice

A. Accounting is an information system designed to capture a business's financial condition and financial performance and communicate it to decision makers inside and outside the organization.

B. 1. E 2. I 3. E 4. E 5. E 6. I

The Accounting Equation

Learning Objective 4

Describe the fundamental accounting equation and elements of financial statements.

One of the keys to understanding financial reports is the concept that **what a business owns must equal what a business owes to its creditors and owners.** The business owns the **resources** it uses to generate profits, pay its creditors, and provide a return to the owners. It owes money to its creditors and owners who have **claims to the resources.** Accountants use special names for these: Resources a business owns are called **assets.** The claims it owes are called **liabilities** when they are held by creditors and **owners' equity** when they are held by investors. The result is the fundamental accounting equation that provides the structure for accounting and financial reporting.

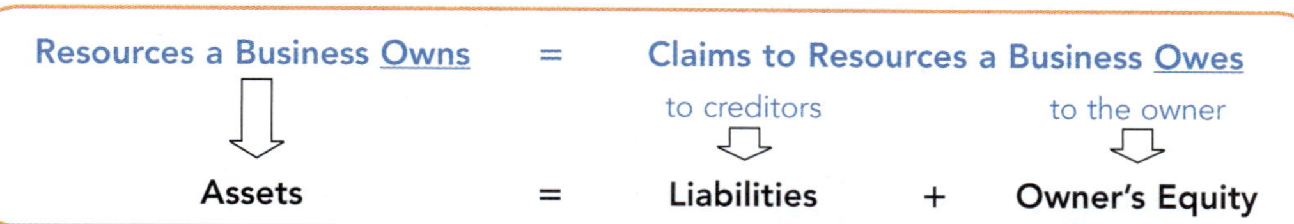

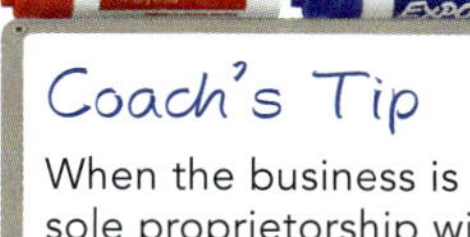

Coach's Tip

When the business is a sole proprietorship with one owner, like Pizza Aroma, *owner's equity* is singular. When the business has more than one owner, claims by the owners are called *owners' equity* (plural).

Because the elements of the accounting equation (Assets = Liabilities + Owner's Equity) are fundamental to reading and understanding financial statements, let's look at each in detail.

Assets

An asset is any resource controlled by the business that has measurable value and is expected to provide future benefits. Pizza Aroma's assets would include resources such as cash, supplies (including ingredients), and equipment such as tables, chairs, and pizza ovens. Initially, these assets would be reported in the business's financial statements at their purchase price, also called their historical cost.

However, not all valuable resources are reported as assets. For example, Mauricio's secret recipe for a specialty pizza may be a very valuable resource, but its value is difficult to measure. He created it himself rather than purchasing it from someone else (that is, the recipe has no measurable historical cost).

Liabilities

A liability is a measurable amount that a business owes to a creditor. What would be Pizza Aroma's liabilities? If it borrows from a bank, it would owe a liability called Notes Payable. This particular name is used because banks require borrowers to sign a legal document called a *note* that describes details about the business's promise to repay the bank.

The business would also owe payments to the suppliers who deliver ingredients and other supplies to the restaurant. When a company buys goods from suppliers, it usually does so on credit by promising to pay for them at a later date. The amount that is owed, as indicated on the supplier's bill or invoice, is called Accounts Payable because purchases made using credit are said to be "on account." Pizza Aroma could also owe wages to its employees (Wages Payable) and sales taxes to the government (Taxes Payable) among other liabilities. As you may have noticed, anything with the word **payable** in its name is considered a liability.

Owner's Equity

Owner's equity represents the owner's claim to the business. The claim arises for two reasons:

- First, the owner has a claim on amounts he or she invested in the business by making direct contributions to the company.
- Second, the owner has a claim on the amounts the company has earned through profitable business operations.

The goal of most business owners is to generate profits because this increases owners' equity and allows owners to receive more money back from the business than they put in (a return on their investment). Mauricio's goal should be to increase his stake (his equity) in the business by making more money than he invests (generating profits).

How will Mauricio know if the business is making profits that will increase his equity? You've heard that to reap a reward, you must expend effort—"no pain, no gain." This is the

Video 1-2
www.mhhe.com/LLPW1e

same concept behind measuring the profits in a business. Profits are generated when the total amount earned from selling goods and services is more than all of the costs incurred to generate those sales. This means Pizza Aroma will be profitable if it earns more from selling its gourmet pizzas (generating revenues) than its costs to make its pizzas and run the business (incurring expenses). The difference between total revenues and expenses is sometimes loosely called **profit** or **earnings,** but the preferred term in accounting is **net income.** Thus, the fundamental accounting equation can be expanded to show the effects of revenues, expenses, and owner investments and withdrawals:

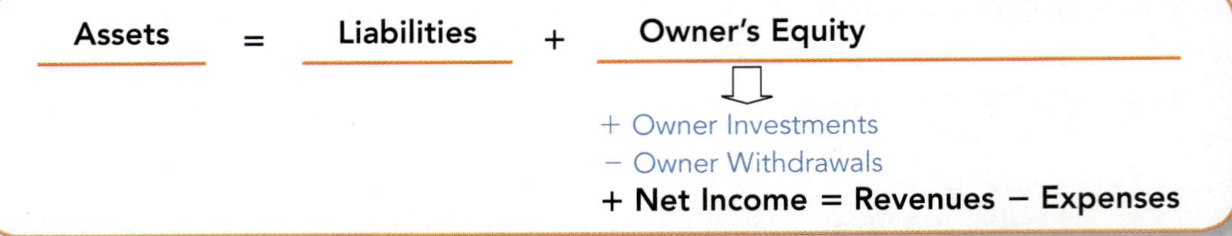

Revenues

Revenues are sales of goods or services to customers. They will be measured at the amount Pizza Aroma charges its customers for the pizza it delivers. Most restaurants receive cash and earn revenue at the time they provide the food service. If a business sells goods or services to customers "on account," then, instead of receiving cash on delivery, the company receives a different asset from the customer: a promise to pay, called Accounts Receivable.

Expenses

Expenses are all costs of doing business that are necessary to earn revenues. For Pizza Aroma, the expenses will include utilities, rent, wages to employees, advertising, insurance, repairs, and supplies used in making pizza. Some of these, such as supplies, insurance, and rent, are paid for before they are used to generate revenues. Other expenses, such as utilities and employees' wages, are paid for after they are used or owed to suppliers. Accountants say that expenses are **incurred** to generate revenues. This means that the activities giving rise to a cost (e.g., running an ad, using electricity) have occurred.

Pizza Aroma Illustration

"Mauricio, let me illustrate for you some common activities you can expect to undertake for Pizza Aroma to show how resources would balance with the claims to those resources made by creditors and owners.

Coach's Tip

Unless indicated otherwise in the text and assignments, analyze all activities from the standpoint of the **business.**

Laurie explained that activities of the business are reported separately from personal activities of its owners. This is called the **separate entity assumption**. The illustrated activities are shown from the standpoint of the effects on the business Pizza Aroma. It is important to learn in this section the types of activities businesses undertake and typical terms used by businesses. The process for analyzing these activities is the focus in Chapter 2.

(1) **Obtain Investments from Owners.** The first resource any new business needs is cash. Sole proprietors often begin by contributing their personal funds. They invest in the business because they expect a return on their investment. Let's assume Mauricio will contribute $30,000 of his personal funds to start the business.

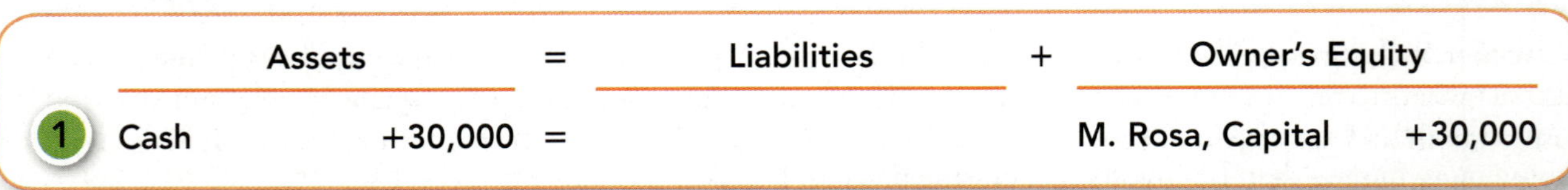

	Assets		=	Liabilities	+	Owner's Equity	
(1)	Cash	+30,000	=			M. Rosa, Capital	+30,000

2 **Borrow from Bank.** When Pizza Aroma needs more cash, it may borrow the money from a bank. The bank lends cash to the business and expects the loan to be repaid with interest. Assume Pizza Aroma obtains a $20,000 loan from a local bank.

	Assets		=	Liabilities		+	Owner's Equity	
2	Cash	+20,000	=	Notes Payable	+20,000			

3 **Purchase Equipment.** Once the financing is complete, the business can purchase the resources necessary to run the business, such as a building, equipment, and supplies. The business can either buy these resources with cash or borrow the money from suppliers and banks. Assume Pizza Aroma buys ovens, chairs, tables, counters, a refrigerator, a computer, a cash register, and pots, all for $40,000 in cash.

	Assets		=	Liabilities	+	Owner's Equity
3	Equipment	+40,000	=	No change		
	Cash	−40,000				

4 **Earn Revenues.** Now let's consider what happens if Pizza Aroma sells pizza in the first month of operations, earning revenues. Assume the business sells pizza to customers at the restaurant for $10,000 cash and delivers an additional $1,000 in pizza on account to local colleges. Selling goods and services "on account" means that Pizza Aroma will bill the colleges (customers) after delivering the pizza; it receives no cash on delivery. The customers' promise to pay the business is called Accounts Receivable.

	Assets		=	Liabilities	+	Owner's Equity	
4	Cash	+10,000	=			Pizza Revenue	+11,000
	Accounts Receivable	+ 1,000					

5 **Incur Expenses.** Businesses must incur many types of expenses to generate the revenues. Let's assume Pizza Aroma incurs the following expenses during the first month of operations, paying for everything in cash: Buying and using $4,000 in supplies and paying $2,000 for rent, $2,000 for wages to employees, $600 for utilities, $300 for insurance, and $100 for advertising.

	Assets		=	Liabilities	+	Owner's Equity	
5	Cash	− 9,000	=			Supplies Expense	− 4,000
						Rent Expense	− 2,000
						Wages Expense	− 2,000
						Utilities Expense	− 600
						Insurance Expense	− 300
						Advertising Expense	− 100

6 **Purchase Supplies on Account.** To be ready for business the following month, assume Pizza Aroma purchases "on account" $3,000 in pizza ingredients and supplies (flour, tomatoes, cheese, napkins, pizza boxes, utensils, and cups). Purchasing goods and services on account means that suppliers will bill Pizza Aroma for them after delivery rather than expecting cash on delivery. The company's promises to pay suppliers are called Accounts Payable.

	Assets		=	Liabilities		+	Owner's Equity	
6	Supplies	+3,000	=	Accounts Payable	+3,000			

7 Distribute Profits to Owners. The business can use any profits it earns to buy more assets, pay creditors, or distribute profits to the owners. Let's assume Pizza Aroma distributes $1,000 to Mauricio at the end of the first month of operations. Withdrawing a portion of profits is how Mauricio "pays" himself or "draws" from the business each month.

	Assets		=	Liabilities		+	Owner's Equity	
7	Cash	−1,000	=				M. Rosa, Drawing	−1,000

Exhibit 1.2 summarizes these activities.

When you first begin to study accounting, among the most difficult things to grasp are the various **account titles** for the many kinds of assets, liabilities, revenues, and expenses a business can have. Laurie showed Mauricio the list of common account titles (see Exhibit 1.3) that most businesses use and suggested that he refer to it often while learning accounting.

In Exhibit 1.3, notice that "receivables" are assets and "payables" are liabilities. Also note that a "prepaid" expense account is always an asset, and an "unearned" revenue account is always a liability. When you are trying to determine what to call an account that is not on the list (the "specific type of" accounts), keep it simple. For example, when supplies are used, call the expense account Supplies Expense.

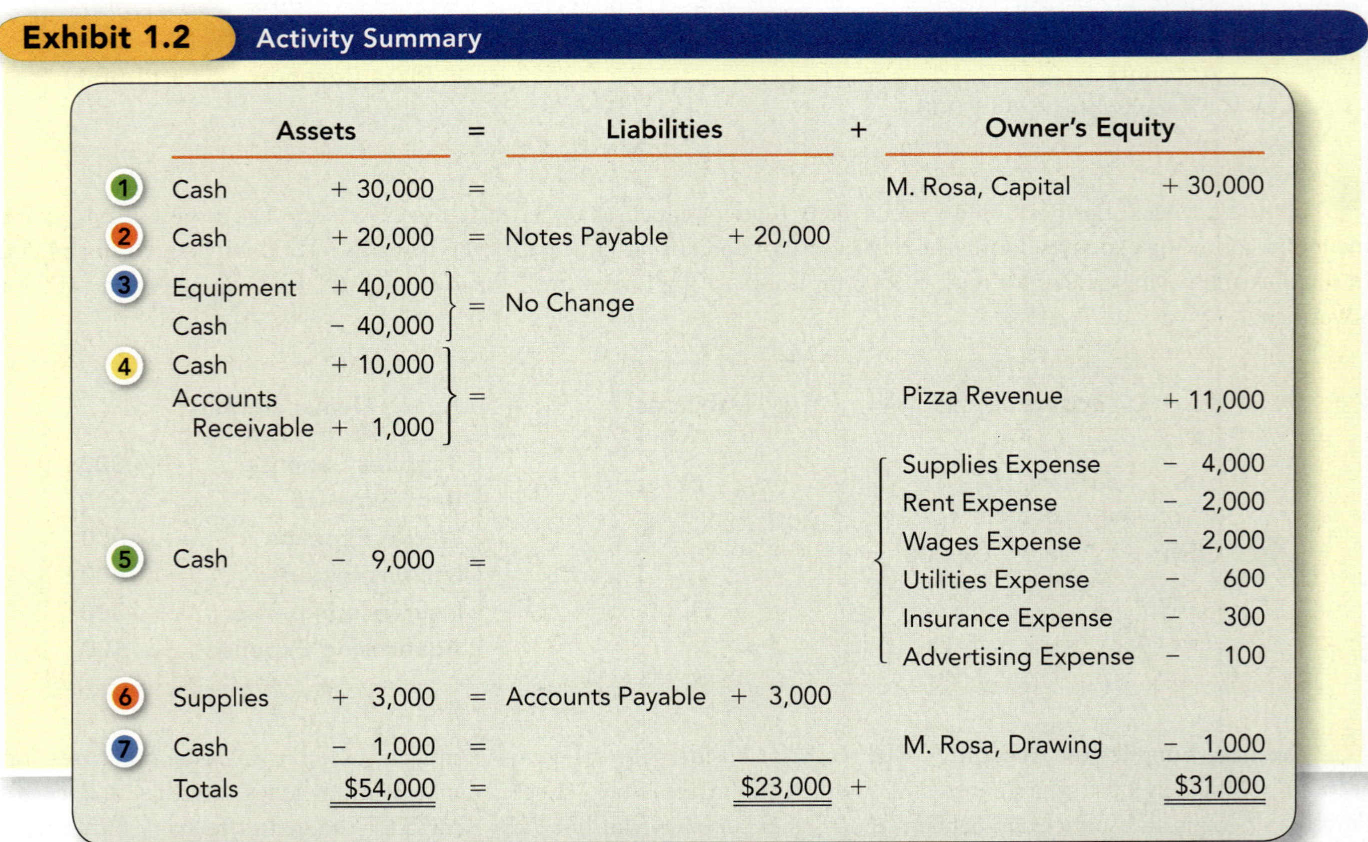

Exhibit 1.2 Activity Summary

	Assets		=	Liabilities		+	Owner's Equity	
1	Cash	+ 30,000	=				M. Rosa, Capital	+ 30,000
2	Cash	+ 20,000	=	Notes Payable	+ 20,000			
3	Equipment	+ 40,000	=	No Change				
	Cash	− 40,000						
4	Cash	+ 10,000	=				Pizza Revenue	+ 11,000
	Accounts Receivable	+ 1,000						
5	Cash	− 9,000	=				Supplies Expense	− 4,000
							Rent Expense	− 2,000
							Wages Expense	− 2,000
							Utilities Expense	− 600
							Insurance Expense	− 300
							Advertising Expense	− 100
6	Supplies	+ 3,000	=	Accounts Payable	+ 3,000			
7	Cash	− 1,000	=				M. Rosa, Drawing	− 1,000
	Totals	$54,000	=		$23,000	+		$31,000

Exhibit 1.3 Typical Account Titles

Assets	Liabilities	Owner's Equity
Cash Short-Term Investments Accounts Receivable Inventory (*to be sold to customers*) Supplies Prepaid Expenses (*rent, insurance, and advertising paid in advance*) Land Building Equipment Long-Term Investments Intangible Assets "Specific type of" asset	Accounts Payable (*to suppliers including utilities*) Short-Term Notes Payable Wages Payable Taxes Payable Interest Payable Unearned Revenues (*collections from customers before earning revenue*) Long-Term Notes Payable Bonds Payable "Specific type of" payable	"Proprietor's name," Capital "Proprietor's name," Drawing **Revenues** Sales Revenue; Investment Revenue; "Specific type of" revenue; Pizza Revenue; Fee Revenue; Service Revenue **Expenses** Cost of Goods Sold (*inventory sold to customers*); Advertising Expense; Insurance Expense; "Specific type of" expense; Rent Expense; Interest Expense; Wages Expense; Utilities Expense; Supplies Expense

Because the five financial statement elements and account titles are so important to understanding the rest of this chapter and other chapters, let's stop for a short practice exercise.

SELF-STUDY PRACTICE

For each of the following account titles, indicate what type of element it is. Use A for asset, L for liability, OE for owner's equity, R for revenue, and E for expense. Try to answer this quiz without referring to the exhibits just to see how well you have learned the terms.

1. _____ Supplies Expense
2. _____ Equipment
3. _____ M. Rosa, Capital
4. _____ Sales Revenue
5. _____ Wages Payable
6. _____ Accounts Receivable
7. _____ Fee Revenue
8. _____ Utilities Expense
9. _____ M. Rosa, Drawing
10. _____ Prepaid Rent

After you have finished, check your answers with the solutions at the bottom of the page.

Financial Statements

"Okay, I think I get it, but can you tell me how all those items relate to each other and how they are reported in the financial statements?"

Learning Objective 5

Explain the structure of basic financial statements.

This was a good question. Laurie explained that before statements can be prepared, it is necessary to determine balances in accounts. She created a new table in Exhibit 1.4 that included a separate coloumn for each asset and liability and a separate section for revenues and expenses. This table shows the effects of the same seven activities on each account along with each account's ending total. The various asset, liability, owner's equity, revenue, and expense accounts appear in different financial statements. The term *financial statements* refers to four accounting reports, typically prepared in the following order:

1. Income Statement.
2. Statement of Owner's Equity.
3. Balance Sheet.
4. Statement of Cash Flows.

Solution to Self-Study Practice

1. E 2. A 3. OE 4. R 5. L 6. A 7. R 8. E 9. OE 10. A

Exhibit 1.4 Account Balances

	Assets				=	Liabilities		+	Owner's Equity	
	Cash	Accounts Receivable	Supplies	Equipment	=	Accounts Payable	Note Payable		M. Rosa, Capital	
Beg.	$ 0	$ 0	$ 0	$ 0	=	$ 0	$ 0	+	$ 0	
1	+30,000				=				+30,000	Owner investment
2	+20,000				=		+20,000			
3	−40,000			+40,000	=	No change				
4	+10,000	+1,000			=				+11,000	Pizza Revenue
5	−9,000				=				−4,000	Supplies Expense
									−2,000	Rent Expense
									−2,000	Wages expense
									−600	Utilities Expense
									−300	Insurance Expense
									−100	Advertising Expense
6			+3,000		=	+3,000				
7	−1,000				=				−1,000	M. Rosa, Drawing
Totals	$10,000	$1,000	$3,000	$40,000	=	$3,000	$20,000		$31,000	
	$54,000					$23,000			$31,000	

"I think you'll understand these relationships better if I show you how Pizza Aroma's financial reports might look at the end of the first month of operation, based on the activities I discussed earlier."

> **Coach's Tip**
>
> To make good decisions, you need to know how financial statements are structured and where to find information in them. Therefore, it is most **important** that you learn the structure and content of each of the statements presented in this chapter. You will use them in future chapters.

Laurie wanted Mauricio to focus at this meeting on the structure of the financial statements and how, given the illustrated activities, Pizza Aroma's financial statements would be reported. She also emphasized that the structure of the financial statements she would present is typical for any size of business.

Financial statements can be prepared at any time during the year, although they are most commonly prepared monthly, every three months (quarterly), and at the end of the year (annual reports). Businesses are allowed to choose any date for the end of their accounting (or fiscal) year. For example, the toy maker Mattel uses a December 31 year-end because this is the start of its slow business period. It sells fewer toys in January through May than in the first three weeks of December. The only U.S. professional sports team operating as a public company—the Green Bay Packers, Inc.—has chosen a fiscal year-end of March 31, the month after the season wraps up with the Pro Bowl.

Income Statement

The income statement (also called the **statement of income** or **statement of operations**) reports a business's financial performance over a specific period. Although the term *profit* is used widely for this measure of performance, accountants prefer to use the technical term **net income** or **net earnings.** A company measures its success by selling goods and/or providing services for more than the costs to generate those revenues. Each revenue and expense account is an accumulation of activities over a period of time.

An initial look at the income statement in Exhibit 1.5 indicates a great deal about the statement's purpose and content. The heading identifies the name of the business, the title of the report, and the specified period (for the month ended May 31, 2009) covered by the statement. Larger businesses with thousands or millions of dollars in revenues and expenses add a fourth

Exhibit 1.5 Income Statement

Pizza Aroma
Income Statement
For the Month Ended May 31, 2009

		Heading
		Name of the entity
		Title of the statement
		Accounting period
Revenue		
Pizza revenue	$11,000	Revenue earned from the sale/delivery of pizza to customers
Total revenues	11,000	← **Total amount earned during May**
Expenses		
Supplies expense	4,000	Cost of supplies used in making and selling pizzas
Wages expense	2,000	Amount for employees' work in May
Rent expense	2,000	Rent for the month of May
Utilities expense	600	Utilities used in May
Insurance expense	300	Insurance coverage for May
Advertising expense	100	Advertising used in May
Total expenses	9,000	← **Total amount incurred in May to generate revenues**
Net income	**$ 2,000**	

line under the date to indicate that the numbers have been rounded to the nearest thousand "(in thousands)" or million "(in millions)."

Notice that an income statement for Pizza Aroma would have three major captions—revenues, expenses, and net income—corresponding to the income statement equation (Revenues − Expenses = **Net Income**). Individual types of revenues and expenses would be reported under the revenues and expenses headings. For Pizza Aroma, the revenue and expense accounts shaded in yellow in Exhibit 1.4 are reported on its income statement. These accounts are typical for most businesses, whether small or large. Notice that each major caption in Exhibit 1.5 has a subtotal, and the bottom line amount for net income has a double underline to highlight it.

A dollar sign is placed at the top and bottom of the column of numbers. In accounting, we assume we can report financial information in the standard monetary denomination of the country in which the business operates, such as reporting in dollars in the United States or euros in Germany. This is called the **monetary unit assumption**.

When listing the accounts on the income statement, revenues are on top, usually with the largest, most relevant revenue listed first. Then expenses are subtracted, again usually with the largest and most relevant expense listed first.

"So does the $2,000 of net income mean that I'll have that much more in cash?"

"No. Net income is a measure of how much better off your business is, not how much cash you made."

Laurie's point is one of the key understandings about the income statement. It is quite common for a business to provide goods or services to customers in one month but not collect cash from them until a later month. Similarly, expenses for the current month's activities may actually be paid in a different month. You will learn this in more detail later, but it is worth trying to understand from the beginning that revenues do not necessarily equal cash coming in during the month and expenses do not equal cash going out during the month.

Mauricio seemed disappointed with a projected net income of $2,000 for the first month. Laurie reassured him that it is typical for new businesses like Pizza Aroma to struggle initially to generate a profit because they have lots of expenses related to advertising and employee training but relatively little revenues due to a lack of a loyal customer base.[5] As you can probably expect, Pizza Aroma's net income would likely increase in the future after the business becomes established. By selling more pizza, revenues would increase without a major increase in expenses except for the cost of ingredients and supplies used in making the additional pizzas. Expenses such as employee wages and rent would likely not increase all that much.

"I guess that's not so bad. It does make me want to watch my expenses carefully and try to boost my pizza sales quickly. What about reporting what Pizza Aroma owes to the bank? Should we talk about the balance sheet?"

"Before we look at that, I want to show you the next statement that connects the income statement to the balance sheet, so you'll understand the relationships between the reports."

Statement of Owner's Equity

Pizza Aroma, a sole proprietorship, will report a **statement of owner's equity**. Corporations prepare a more comprehensive statement of stockholders' equity in a similar fashion. For Pizza Aroma, most changes in owner's equity will relate to generating and distributing earnings.

The heading in Exhibit 1.6 identifies the name of the entity, the title of the report, and the accounting period (for the period ended May 31, 2009). The green shaded accounts on Exhibit 1.4 along with net income are reported on the statement of owner's equity.

The statement starts with the owner's equity balance at the beginning of the period. Because Pizza Aroma is a new business, the beginning balance of owner's equity would be $0. Then it would add additional investments made by the owner during the period and the net income reported on the income statement ($2,000 in Exhibit 1.5). A **net loss** in which expenses exceed revenues would be subtracted. Finally, any withdrawals made by the owner for the period would be subtracted to determine the owner's equity balance at the end of the period. Investments by Mauricio and earning profits (net income) add to his ownership in the business, while distributing profits as withdrawals by Mauricio reduces his equity in the business. Again, notice the use of a dollar sign at the top and bottom of the column of numbers and the double underscore at the bottom.

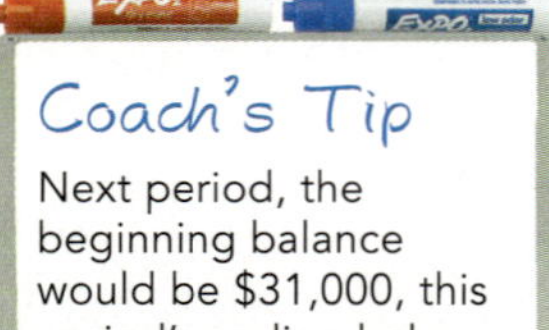

Coach's Tip

Next period, the beginning balance would be $31,000, this period's ending balance.

[5] In fact, 50 percent of all new businesses fail or close within the first six years of opening. Not many start out with a positive net income in the first month as projected of Pizza Aroma (Exhibit 1.5). Instead, most report a net loss in which their expenses exceed their revenues. For more information on small business failures, see Brian Headd, "Redefining Business Success: Distinguishing Between Closure and Failures," *Small Business Economics*, August 21, 2003, pp. 51–61.

Exhibit 1.6 Statement of Owner's Equity

PIZZA AROMA

Pizza Aroma
Statement of Owner's Equity
For the Month Ended May 31, 2009

Heading
Name of the entity
Title of the statement
Accounting period

M. Rosa, capital, May 1, 2009		$ 0	← **Last period's ending owner's equity balance**
Add:	Investments by owner	30,000	Initial and/or additional resources from owner
	Net income	2,000	Reported on the income statement (Exhibit 1.5)
Less:	Withdrawals by owner	(1,000)	Withdrawals made by owner
M. Rosa, capital, May 31, 2009		$31,000	← **This period's ending owner's equity balance**

Balance Sheet

The next financial report is the **balance sheet**, also known as the **statement of financial position.** The balance sheet's purpose is to report the amount of a business's assets, liabilities, and owner's equity at a specific point in time. Think of the balance sheet as a picture or snapshot of Pizza Aroma's resources and claims to its resources at the end of the day on May 31, 2009. Exhibit 1.7 shows a projected balance sheet for Pizza Aroma based on assumed activities for May, the first month of business.

Notice again that the heading specifically identifies the name of the entity and title of the statement. Unlike the other financial reports, the balance sheet is presented for a specific point in time (at May 31, 2009). The assets are listed in order of how soon they are to be used or turned into cash. Likewise, liabilities are listed in order of how soon each is to be paid or settled.

The blue shaded row at the bottom of Exhibit 1.4 provides the ending balances for the accounts on the balance sheet. It first lists the assets of the business that for Pizza Aroma total $54,000. The second section lists the business's liabilities and owner's equity balances, also totaling $54,000. The balance sheet balances because the resources equal the claims to the resources. The fundamental accounting equation reflects the business's financial position on May 31, 2009:

Assets	=	Liabilities	+	Owner's Equity
$54,000	=	$23,000	+	$31,000

In the assets section, Cash is the first asset reported. The $10,000 represents the total amount of cash expected to be on hand and in Pizza Aroma's bank account. The $1,000 reported as Accounts Receivable represents the amount that Pizza Aroma expects to collect from customers (local colleges) for prior pizza deliveries sold on credit. Pizza Aroma will allow area colleges to buy pizza for events on account by running a tab that Pizza Aroma sends as a bill after it makes the deliveries. The $3,000 reported for Supplies indicates the

Exhibit 1.7 Balance Sheet

PIZZA AROMA

Pizza Aroma Balance Sheet At May 31, 2009		**Heading** Name of the entity Title of the statement Point in time
Assets		
Cash	$ 10,000	Amount on hand and in the business's bank account
Accounts receivable	1,000	Amount owed by customers (colleges)
Supplies	3,000	Amount of food and paper supplies on hand
Equipment	40,000	Cost of ovens, tables, etc.
Total assets	**$54,000**	← **Total amount of the business's resources**
Liabilities and Owner's Equity		
Liabilities		
Accounts payable	$ 3,000	Amount owed to suppliers
Notes payable	20,000	Amount of loan owed to the bank
Total liabilities	23,000	
Owner's Equity		
M. Rosa, capital	31,000	Amount invested plus amount earned that is retained in the business (from Exhibit 1.6)
Total liabilities and owner's equity	**$54,000**	← **Total claims on the business's resources**

cost of pizza supplies that are expected to remain on hand at May 31, 2009. The same is true for the $40,000 of Equipment.

Under liabilities, the $3,000 of Accounts Payable is the amount Pizza Aroma is expected to owe to suppliers for food and paper supplies purchased on account. The Notes Payable is the written promise to repay the $20,000 loan from the bank.[6] As with all liabilities, these are financial obligations of the business arising from past business activities.

Finally, owner's equity of $31,000 reflects all contributions that Mauricio would have made during the month ($30,000) plus the restaurant's expected net income ($2,000) less Mauricio's withdrawals ($1,000). It matches the ending amount for owner's equity reported on the statement of owner's equity (see Exhibit 1.6).

"So, besides monitoring my revenues and expenses, it looks like I need to make sure I have enough assets to pay liabilities."

"Sharp observation! Your creditors are most interested in your ability to pay cash to them in the future. However, not all assets can easily be turned into cash, and not all revenues and expenses are received or paid in cash. So, there is one more financial statement."

Statement of Cash Flows

Pizza Aroma's projected income statement shows a positive net income of $2,000. However, net income does not necessarily equal cash because revenues are reported when earned and expenses are reported when incurred regardless of when cash is received or paid. The fourth financial report of interest to external users, then, is the statement of cash flows. It includes only those activities in the Cash column, reflecting changes much like a video camera with a telephoto lens focused on activities affecting only cash. See Exhibit 1.8 for Pizza Aroma's projected statement of cash flows for the month ended May 31, 2009, based on the illustrated activities. The statement of cash flows is divided into three types of business activities:

- Operating activities. These activities are directly related to running the business to earn profit. For Pizza Aroma, they include buying supplies, cleaning the facility, paying employees for their labor, buying advertising, renting a building, repairing ovens, and obtaining insurance.
- Investing activities. These activities involve buying and selling productive resources with long lives, such as buildings, land, equipment, and tools, as well as investing funds in other businesses and lending to others. Pizza Aroma is expected to purchase equipment for $40,000 cash.
- Financing activities. Any borrowing from banks, repaying bank loans, receiving investments from owners, or distributing business profits to owners are considered financing activities.

Many new businesses have **negative** cash flows from operations when they are just starting. In the long run, businesses need to generate positive cash flows from their operating activities to remain in business because of the limited amount of money banks and others will provide. Pizza Aroma's projected $1,000 cash flow from operating activities is lower than its net income of $2,000 but positive—better than expected of new companies.

Notes to the Financial Statements

The four basic financial statements are incomplete without notes that help those who study the statements to understand how the amounts were measured and what other information may affect their decisions. We will discuss the notes in other chapters.

[6] To simplify this discussion, interest on the Notes Payable is presented in future chapters. Interest Expense is the amount incurred during the period for using the borrowed funds; Interest Payable is the amount of interest not yet paid.

Exhibit 1.8 Statement of Cash Flows

Pizza Aroma Statement of Cash Flows For the Month ended May 31, 2009		
		Heading Name of the entity Title of the statement Accounting period
Cash Flows from Operating Activities		**Directly related to earning income**
Cash from customers	$ 10,000	Amount of cash received from customers
Cash to suppliers and employees	(9,000)	Amount of cash paid to suppliers and employees
Cash used in operating activities	**1,000**	
Cash Flows from Investing Activities		**Related to the sale/purchase of productive assets**
Purchase of equipment	(40,000)	
Cash used in investing activities	**(40,000)**	
Cash Flows from Financing Activities		**Activities with owners and banks**
Investment by owner	30,000	
Withdrawal by owner	(1,000)	
Borrowing from bank	20,000	
Cash provided by financing activities	**49,000**	
Change in Cash	10,000	**Sum of three flows ($1,000 + $[40,000] + $49,000)**
Beginning Cash balance, May 1, 2009	0	
Ending Cash balance, May 31, 2009	**$ 10,000**	**Amount reported on the balance sheet (Exhibit 1.7)**

"How does the whole picture fit together, and what will my external users look for?"

Relationships among the Financial Statements

Exhibit 1.9 shows how the four basic financial statements connect to one another. The arrow indicates that net income shown on the income statement is a component in determining the ending balance of owner's equity that is reported on the balance sheet. In addition, cash flows for the period added to the cash at the beginning of the period equal the cash reported on the balance sheet at the end of the period.

The financial statements are a key source of information when external users such as creditors and investors make decisions concerning a business. As you will see throughout this course, the amounts reported in the financial statements can be used to calculate percentages and ratios that reveal important insights about a company's performance. For now, however, let's consider how creditors and investors might gain valuable information simply by reading the dollar amounts reported in each financial statement.

Creditors are mainly interested in assessing two things:

1. **Is the company generating enough cash to make payments on its loan?** Answers to this question will come from the statement of cash flows. In particular, creditors would be interested in seeing whether operating activities are producing positive cash flows sufficient to make cash payments on loans. Pizza Aroma's net inflow of $1,000 cash from operating activities for the month is projected to be very good for a new business.
2. **Does the company have enough assets to cover its liabilities?** Answers to this question will come from comparing assets and liabilities reported on the balance sheet. At May 31, Pizza Aroma is expected to own slightly more than twice what it owes to creditors

Exhibit 1.9 Relationships among Pizza Aroma's Projected Financial Statements

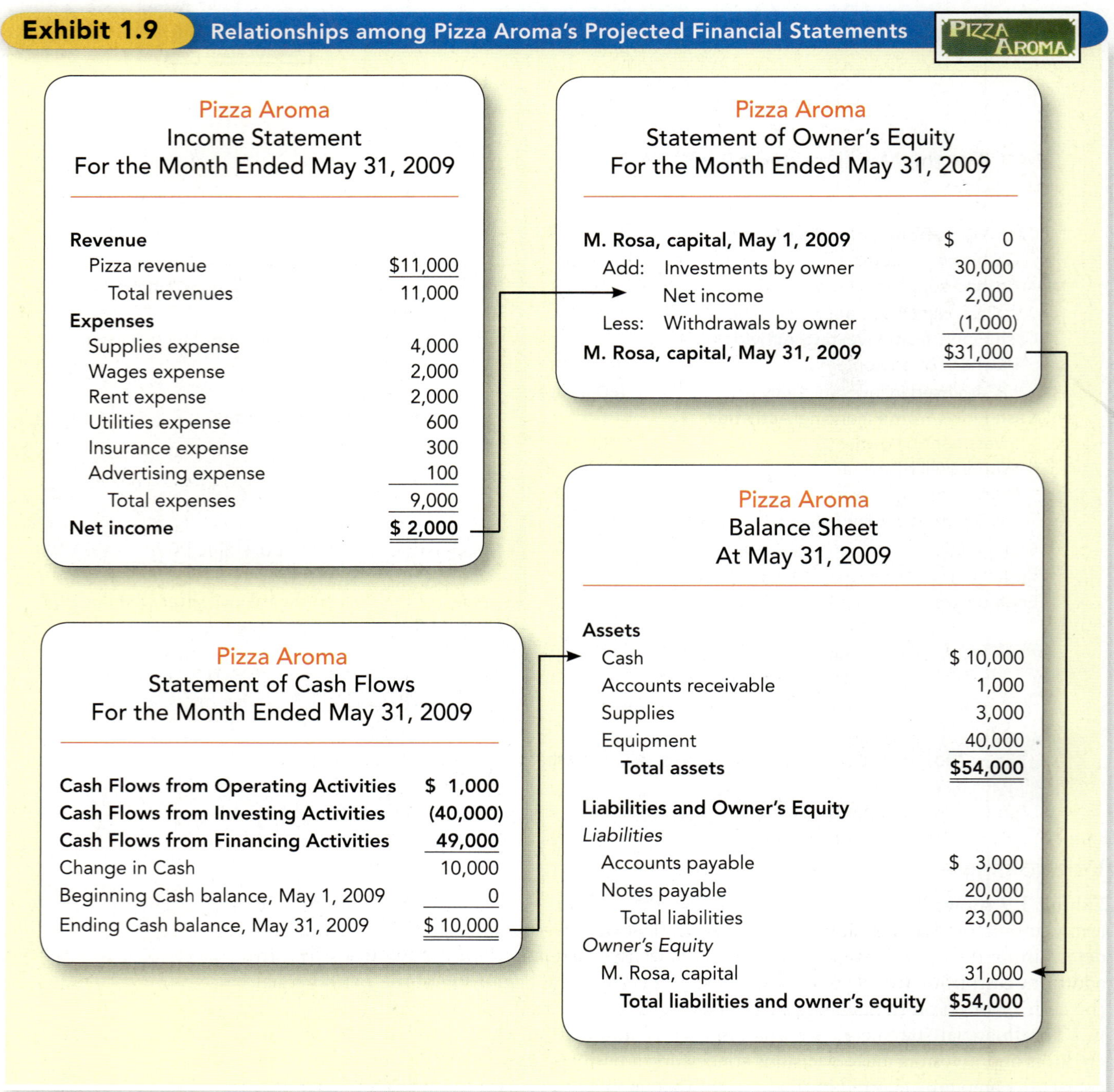

Pizza Aroma
Income Statement
For the Month Ended May 31, 2009

Revenue	
Pizza revenue	$11,000
Total revenues	11,000
Expenses	
Supplies expense	4,000
Wages expense	2,000
Rent expense	2,000
Utilities expense	600
Insurance expense	300
Advertising expense	100
Total expenses	9,000
Net income	**$ 2,000**

Pizza Aroma
Statement of Owner's Equity
For the Month Ended May 31, 2009

M. Rosa, capital, May 1, 2009	$ 0
Add: Investments by owner	30,000
Net income	2,000
Less: Withdrawals by owner	(1,000)
M. Rosa, capital, May 31, 2009	$31,000

Pizza Aroma
Statement of Cash Flows
For the Month Ended May 31, 2009

Cash Flows from Operating Activities	$ 1,000
Cash Flows from Investing Activities	(40,000)
Cash Flows from Financing Activities	49,000
Change in Cash	10,000
Beginning Cash balance, May 1, 2009	0
Ending Cash balance, May 31, 2009	$ 10,000

Pizza Aroma
Balance Sheet
At May 31, 2009

Assets	
Cash	$ 10,000
Accounts receivable	1,000
Supplies	3,000
Equipment	40,000
Total assets	**$54,000**
Liabilities and Owner's Equity	
Liabilities	
Accounts payable	$ 3,000
Notes payable	20,000
Total liabilities	23,000
Owner's Equity	
M. Rosa, capital	31,000
Total liabilities and owner's equity	**$54,000**

(total assets of $54,000 versus total liabilities of $23,000). With $10,000 in cash, Pizza Aroma could pay all of its accounts payable and part of its notes payable right now if needed.

Investors look for either an **immediate return** on their contributions to a company or a **long-term return** (increasing growth in owner's equity). Owner's equity is more likely to increase if a company is profitable. As a result, investors look closely at the income statement for information about the company's ability to generate profits. Pizza Aroma's expected net income of $2,000 for its first month of operations is a positive sign of future profitability, especially in light of the net losses reported by most start-up businesses.

A summary of the purposes, structures, and content of the four financial statements is provided in Exhibit 1.10.

Exhibit 1.10 Summary of Four Basic Financial Statements

Financial Statement	Purpose: To report	Structure	Examples of Content
Income Statement	The accountant's primary measure of economic performance *during the accounting period*.	Revenues − Expenses Net income	Sales Revenue Rent Expense Wages Expense Utilities Expense
Statement of Owner's Equity	The way that net income, owner investments, and owner withdrawals affected the company's financial position *during the accounting period*.	Beginning owner's equity + Additional investments + Net income (or − Net loss) − Withdrawals Ending owner's equity	Net income is from the income statement
Balance Sheet	The financial position (economic resources and sources of financing) of a business *at a specific point in time*.	Assets = Liabilities + Owner's Equity	Cash, Receivables, Supplies, Equipment, Accounts Payable, Notes Payable, Owner's Capital
Statement of Cash Flows	Inflows (receipts) and outflows (payments) of cash *during the accounting period* in the operating, investing, and financing categories.	± Cash flows from Operating Activities ± Cash flows from Investing Activities ± Cash flows from Financing Activities Change in cash + Beginning cash balance Ending cash balance	Cash collected from customers, Cash paid to suppliers, Cash paid to purchase equipment, Cash borrowed from banks

You have been introduced to new and important material. Before moving on, take a moment to complete two short exercises to make sure that you understand business activities and financial statements.

SELF-STUDY PRACTICE A

In the space provided, indicate the type of account (A = asset, L = liability, OE = owner's equity, R = revenue, E = expense) and whether the account is reported on the income statement (I/S) or balance sheet (B/S).

Account Title	Type	Statement
1. Land	________	________
2. Wages Expense	________	________
3. Prepaid Insurance	________	________
4. Rent Revenue	________	________
5. S. Mattson, Capital	________	________
6. Note Payable	________	________

After you have finished, check your answers with the solutions at the bottom of the page.

Solution to Self-Study Practice A

	Type	Statement		Type	Statement
1.	A	B/S	4.	R	I/S
2.	E	I/S	5.	OE	B/S
3.	A	B/S	6.	L	B/S

SELF-STUDY PRACTICE B

A year ago, you formed a Web design business (called WebTech) as a sole proprietorship by making a $100,000 investment in cash. For the year ended August 31, 2009, the business had revenues of $350,000 and expenses of $270,000, and you withdrew $10,000 from the business. The business had $210,000 in assets at year-end and owed suppliers and banks $40,000. Complete all of the white areas in the following financial statements with the appropriate terms or amounts.

WebTech
Income Statement
____

Revenues	$ 350,000
Expenses	______
______	$ ______

WebTech
____
For the Year Ended August 31, 2009

Beginning owner's equity	$ 0
Additional investments	100,000
Net income	______
Withdrawals	(10,000)
______	$ ______

WebTech
Balance Sheet
____

Assets	$ 210,000
Total assets	$ ______
Liabilities	$ ______
Owner's Equity	______
Total liabilities and owner's equity	$ ______

After you have finished, check your answers with the solutions at the bottom of the page.

Coach's Tip

Remember: Beginning balances for new companies are $0, and the balance sheet always balances.

Fill in the Blank: In the next period, beginning owner's equity would be ________.

PROFESSIONAL STANDARDS AND ETHICAL CONDUCT

"So, you've just seen how your financial statements should look in one month and how they relate to one another. Are you feeling okay with all this?"

"It actually makes me anxious to get started. But first, I've heard a lot about 'cooking the books.' How do users know the information they're getting is reliable and can be trusted?"

This is another important question. Laurie indicated that, to enhance the reliability of financial reporting, managers must apply accounting principles in an ethical business environment.

Solution to Self-Study Practice B

WebTech
Income Statement
For the Year Ended 8/31/09

Revenues	$ 350,000
Expenses	270,000
Net income	$ 80,000

WebTech
Statement of Owner's Equity
For the Year Ended 8/31/09

Beginning owner's equity	$ 0
Additional investments	100,000
Net income	80,000
Withdrawals	(10,000)
Ending owner's equity	$170,000

WebTech
Balance Sheet
At 8/31/09

Assets	$210,000
Total assets	$210,000
Liabilities	$ 40,000
Owner's equity	170,000
Total liabilities and owner's equity	$210,000

Solution to Coach's Tip
$170,000

Generally Accepted Accounting Principles

Learning Objective 6

Understand the importance of ethical decisions in financial reporting and business.

The system of financial statement reporting in use today has a long history going all the way back to a publication in 1494 by the Italian monk and mathematician Luca Pacioli. Now the primary responsibility for setting the rules of accounting rests with the Financial Accounting Standards Board (FASB) in the United States and the International Accounting Standards Board (IASB) in most other countries. As a group, these rules are called generally accepted accounting principles, or **GAAP** for short. ("GAAP" is pronounced like the name of the clothing store.)

For financial information to be useful, managers, creditors, owners, and others need to have confidence that the information is

- Relevant (it helps in making decisions).
- Reliable (it is unbiased and verifiable).
- Comparable (against other companies).
- Consistent (over time).

GAAP follow these guidelines to provide helpful information to users.

As a summary, Laurie showed Mauricio the information in Exhibit 1.11—the key concepts the FASB uses in developing new accounting principles. The concepts discussed in this chapter are highlighted in red; the rest will be introduced in later chapters. Mauricio was surprised at how many concepts he had already learned.

Many of the FASB's rules that result from following these key concepts are quite complex and apply mostly to large public companies. In future chapters, we will focus on accounting rules that have the greatest impact on financial statements at an appropriate introductory level.

"Who is responsible for ensuring that businesses follow GAAP?"

Laurie told Mauricio that a company's **managers have primary responsibility for following GAAP and preparing fair financial statements.** To provide additional assurance, some private companies and all public companies hire independent auditors to check their financial records. Following rules approved by the Public Company Accounting Oversight Board (PCAOB) and other accounting bodies, these auditors report whether, beyond a reasonable doubt, the financial statements represent what they claim to represent and whether they comply with GAAP. In a sense, GAAP are to auditors and accountants what the criminal code is to lawyers and the public. The Securities and Exchange Commission (SEC) is the government agency that supervises the work of the FASB and the PCAOB.

"Overall, users expect information that is truthful, and this assumes that the company is following strong ethical business and accounting practices."

Exhibit 1.11 Key Concepts for External Financial Reporting

Objective of External Financial Reporting

To provide useful economic information to external users for decision making

Useful information is

- Relevant, Reliable, Comparable, and Consistent

Elements to be Measured and Reported

- Assets, Liabilities, Owner's Equity, Revenues, and Expenses

Concepts for Measuring and Reporting Information

- **Assumptions:** Separate Entity, Monetary Unit, Continuity, Time Period
- **Principles:** Historical Cost, Revenue Recognition, Matching, Full Disclosure
- **Exceptions:** Cost Benefit, Materiality, Conservatism, Industry Practices

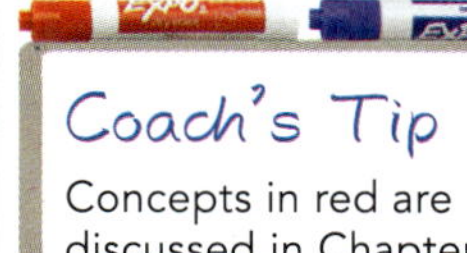

Coach's Tip

Concepts in red are discussed in Chapters 1 and 2. Those in black will be discussed in Chapters 3 and 4.

Ethical Conduct

Coach's Tip

Internal controls are designed to protect assets from loss and ensure the accuracy of the accounting records. Controls you have seen include the security tags on clothing and using a bank to keep cash safe. We will discuss many internal controls throughout the text.

Ethics refers to the standards of conduct for judging right from wrong, honest from dishonest, and fair from unfair. Intentional financial misreporting is both unethical and illegal. As you will see throughout this course, some accounting and business issues have clear answers that are either right or wrong. However, many situations require accountants, auditors, and managers to weigh the pros and cons of alternatives before making final decisions. To help ensure these decisions are made in a professional and ethical manner, the American Institute of Certified Public Accountants (AICPA) requires all its members to adhere to a **Code of Professional Conduct**.

Mauricio's concern about "cooking the books" likely stems from hearing about several high-profile accounting frauds that occurred a few years ago involving Enron, WorldCom (now owned by Verizon), Global Crossing, and Xerox. In response to these frauds, the U.S. Congress stepped into the crisis to create the **Sarbanes-Oxley Act of 2002.** The Act requires top managers of public companies to sign a report certifying their responsibilities for the financial statements, maintain an audited system of **internal controls** to ensure accuracy in the accounting reports, and maintain an independent committee to ensure that managers cooperate with auditors. As a result of the act, corporate executives now face severe consequences—20 years in prison and $5 million in fines—if they are found guilty of committing accounting fraud.

Spotlight On ETHICS

Accounting Scandals

Accounting scandals are driven by the fear of personal failure and greed. Initially, some people may appear to benefit from fraudulent reporting. In the long run, however, fraud harms most individuals and organizations. When it is uncovered, the corporation's stock price drops dramatically. In the case involving MicroStrategy, the stock price dropped 65 percent in a single day of trading, from $243 to $86 per share. Creditors are also harmed by fraud. WorldCom's creditors recovered only 42 percent of what they were owed. They lost $36 billion. Innocent employees also are harmed by fraud. At Enron, 5,600 employees lost their jobs and many lost all of their retirement savings.

Ethical conduct is just as important for small private businesses as it is for large public companies. Laurie's advice to Mauricio and to all managers is to strive to create an ethical environment and establish a strong system of checks and controls inside the company. Do not tolerate blatant acts of fraud, such as employees making up false expenses for reimbursement, punching in a time card belonging to a fellow employee who will be late for work, or copying someone's ideas and claiming them as his or her own. Also be aware that not all ethical dilemmas are clear-cut. Some situations will require you to weigh one moral principle (e.g., honesty) against another (e.g., loyalty). Advise your employees that, when faced with an ethical dilemma, they should follow a three-step process:

1. **Identify who will benefit from the situation** (often the manager or employee) and how others will be harmed (other employees, the company's reputation, owners, creditors, and the public in general).
2. **Identify the alternative courses of action.**
3. **Choose the alternative that is the most ethical**—and that you would be proud to have reported in the news.

Often, there is no one right answer to ethical dilemmas and hard choices will need to be made. In the end, however, following strong ethical practices is a key factor in business success and in ensuring good financial reporting.

As the meeting between Laurie and Mauricio concluded, Laurie made the following comments:

"I've enjoyed our meeting. For now, you don't need to worry about all the details; this is just an overview. But try to remember these points:

1. The elements of the financial reports.
2. The purpose and structure of the reports.
3. The account titles.
4. The key concepts.

If you do, the bookkeeping tasks we'll discuss later will be easier."

"Thanks, Laurie. I look forward to learning more."

Epilogue for Pizza Aroma

Not long after Mauricio's conversation with Laurie, *The Ithaca Journal* reported his restaurant's opening:

> Mauricio Rosa was ready to become a father twice on Monday — once to a newborn and once to a (new) business . . . Pizza Aroma. . . . He wasn't even sure he'd be there to see the first lunch-hour rush of his own: Dora was home . . . and he was waiting for a phone call telling him to head to the hospital. "I can't take any more excitement," Mauricio said. . . .
>
> Mauricio has 39 pizzas on the menu and 4 more he's concocted that he hasn't had time to tell the printer about yet. . . . "I just think what people would like better," Mauricio said of his creative impulses. . . .
>
> One thing he's learned about being successful is to use fresh ingredients, never frozen, never cheap, Mauricio said. He apparently has learned the businessman's art of diplomacy, too. What's his favorite? "Actually, everything is my favorite," he said.
>
> Kenneth Aaron, "Aroma," *The Ithaca Journal*, November 9, 1999, p. 6A.

Since then, Pizza Aroma has received the "Best Pizza" award several years in a row in the *Ithaca Times* readers' poll.

The next three chapters will take you step by step through the financing, investing, and operating decisions that occurred at Pizza Aroma during its first month of operations. We will look at the way accountants collect data about business activities and process it to construct the financial statements. The key to success in this course is to **practice** the skills that are presented in this text. It is very difficult to learn accounting without doing the assignments and keeping up with the reading.

Coach's Tip

At the end of most chapters, you will find one or more demonstration cases. These cases show you how to apply what you have learned to problems like the ones you will be asked to do as homework. It is worth your effort to treat these cases as if they are exam questions, and then check the suggested solutions.

Demonstration Case

This introductory case reviews the structure and content of the income statement, the statement of owner's equity, and the balance sheet.

In 2006, Rich Kolasa opened Rich's Repair Shop, a new bike repair business, as a sole proprietorship. Most of the repairs that Rich's shop does are paid for in cash. Rich receives an advance from a local bike rental store in return for an agreement to repair the store's bikes as needed. He also bills a regional bike club whenever his shop repairs a member's bicycle. Within one year, the repair shop grew so busy that Rich had to hire several employees. Following is an alphabetical list of the shop's accounts and their balances for 2009. The business's year ends on December 31.

Required:

1. For each account, indicate in the space provided:
   a. The type of account it is (A = asset, L = liability, OE = owner's equity, R = revenue, or E = expense).
   b. On which financial statement the account is found (I/S = income statement, SOE = statement of owner's equity, or B/S = balance sheet).

Element	Statement		
______	______	Accounts Payable	$ 7,000
______	______	Accounts Receivable	2,000
______	______	Cash (balance on December 31, 2009)	21,000
______	______	Equipment	83,000
______	______	Insurance Expense	5,000
______	______	Notes Payable (due in three years)	35,000
______	______	Rent Expense	24,000
______	______	Rich Kolasa, Drawing (during the year)	100,000
______	______	Service Revenues	311,000
______	______	Supplies Expense	12,000
______	______	Supplies	33,000
______	______	Utilities Expense	7,000
______	______	Wages Expense	120,000
______	______	Wages Payable	3,000

2. At the beginning of the year, the Rich Kolasa, Capital account held $41,000. During the year, he made an additional investment of $10,000 in cash in the business. Prepare an income statement, a statement of owner's equity, and a balance sheet for the year ended December 31, 2009, following the formats of Exhibits 1.5 to 1.7.
3. Describe the purpose of each of these statements.
4. Did financing for Rich's Repair Shop's assets come primarily from liabilities or from owner's equity?

Suggested Solution

1.

Element	Statement		
L	B/S	Accounts Payable	$ 7,000
A	B/S	Accounts Receivable	2,000
A	B/S	Cash (balance on December 31, 2009)	21,000
A	B/S	Equipment	83,000
E	I/S	Insurance Expense	5,000
L	B/S	Notes Payable (due in three years)	35,000
E	I/S	Rent Expense	24,000
OE	SOE	Rich Kolasa, Drawing (during the year)	100,000

R	I/S	Service Revenues	311,000
E	I/S	Supplies Expense	12,000
A	B/S	Supplies	33,000
E	I/S	Utilities Expense	7,000
E	I/S	Wages Expense	120,000
L	B/S	Wages Payable	3,000

2.

Rich's Repair Shop
Income Statement
For the Year Ended December 31, 2009

Revenues	
Service revenues	$ 311,000
Total revenues	311,000
Expenses	
Wages expense	120,000
Rent expense	24,000
Supplies expense	12,000
Utilities expense	7,000
Insurance expense	5,000
Total expenses	168,000
Net income	**$143,000**

Rich's Repair Shop
Statement of Owner's Equity
For the Year Ended December 31, 2009

Rich Kolasa, capital, Jan. 1, 2009	$ 41,000
Add: Additional investments	10,000
Net income	143,000
Less: Rich Kolasa, drawing	(100,000)
Rich Kolasa, capital, Dec. 31, 2009	**$ 94,000**

Rich's Repair Shop
Balance Sheet
At December 31, 2009

Assets	
Cash	$ 21,000
Accounts receivable	2,000
Supplies	33,000
Equipment	83,000
Total assets	**$139,000**
Liabilities and Owner's Equity	
Liabilities	
Accounts payable	$ 7,000
Wages payable	3,000
Notes payable	35,000
Total liabilities	45,000
Owner's Equity	
Rich Kolasa, capital	94,000
Total owner's equity	94,000
Total liabilities and owner's equity	**$139,000**

3. The income statement reports the economic performance (net income) of a business during the period. The statement of owner's equity reports the way net income, owner investments, and owner withdrawals affect the financial position of the business during the period. The balance sheet reports the business's financial position (its assets, liabilities, and owner's equity) at a specific point in time.
4. Financing for Rich's Repair Shop's assets is provided primarily from owner's equity ($94,000) rather than from liabilities ($45,000). Owner's equity includes a combination of owner investments, owner withdrawals, and net income over time.

Supplement 1A

Overview of Career Choices for Accounting Professionals

According to the government's labor department, accounting is one of the fastest growing fields with 49,000 new jobs a year expected to be added through 2014. The following summarizes the career opportunities available in private and public accounting.

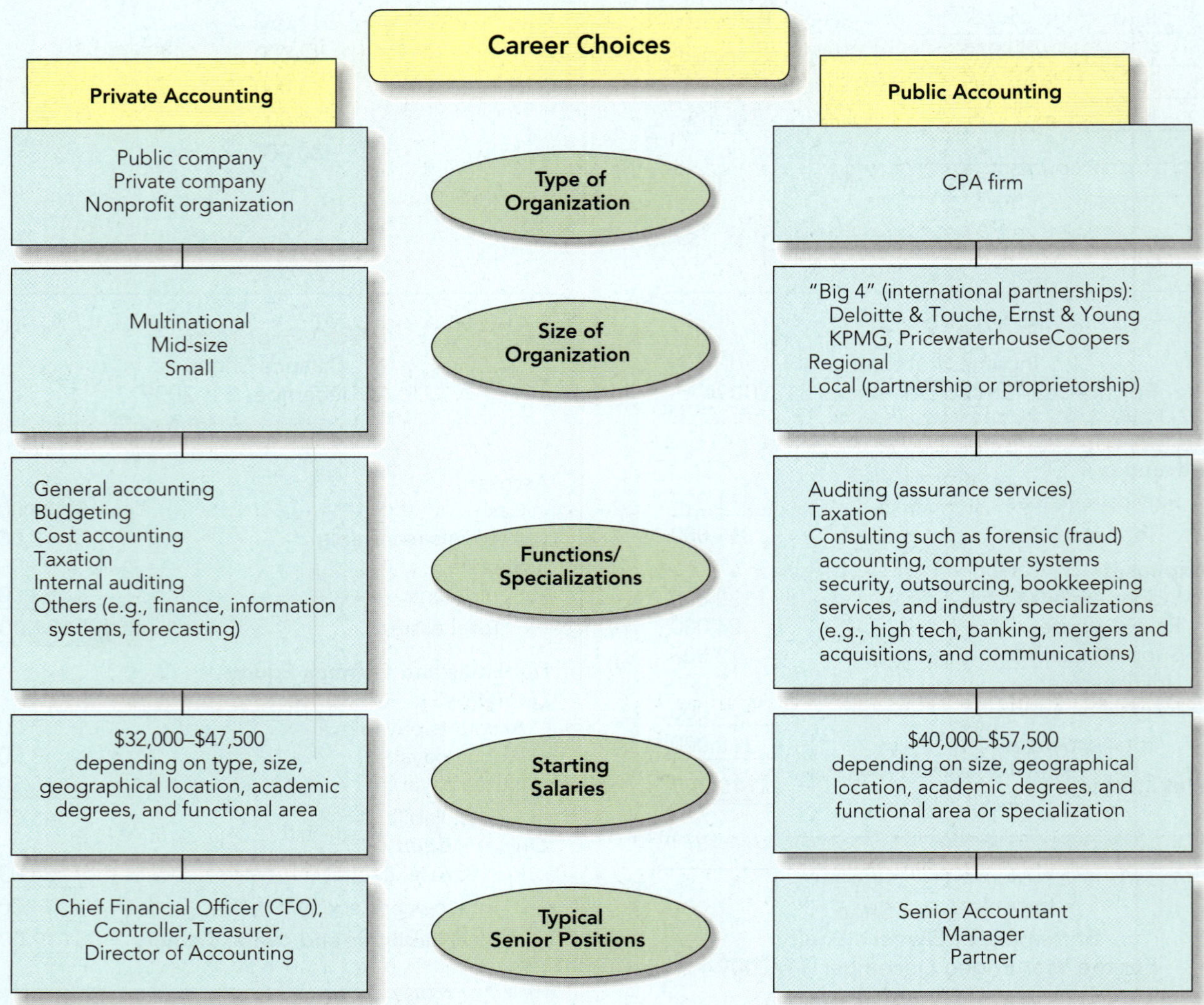

Source: 2008 Robert Half *Salary Guide*

Accountants may pursue a variety of certifications. In CPA firms, staff members become licensed certified public accountants (CPAs) when they have met the state's educational requirements, passed the certified public accounting examination, and practiced with supervision for a set period.[7] CPAs specializing in forensic accounting investigate fraud as Certified Fraud Examiners (CFE). In private accounting, accountants can earn alternative certifications, including Certified Management Accountant (CMA), Certified Internal Auditor (CIA), Certified Financial Manager (CFM), and Chartered Financial Analyst (CFA), among others. For additional information on accounting careers, certifications, salaries, and opportunities, visit www.aicpa.org, www.collegegrad.com, and www.imanet.org.

Chapter Summary

LO1 Categorize business types and organizational forms. p. 4

- Business Types
  Manufacturing businesses make products from raw inputs.
  Merchandising businesses sell manufactured goods to customers.
  Service businesses provide service to customers or clients; they do not make or sell products.
- Organizational Forms
  Sole proprietorships are owned by one individual, are relatively inexpensive to form, and are not legally separate from their owners. Thus, all profits or losses become part of the taxable income of the owner, who is also personally responsible for all of the business's debts.

[7] Each state sets its own requirements. At the time this text is being written, 44 states plus Puerto Rico, Guam, and Washington, D.C. require 150 credit hours of education to be eligible to take the CPA examination. For more information, visit the National Association of State Boards of Accountancy Web site (www.NASBA.org) and see an accounting faculty advisor.

Partnerships are legally similar to proprietorships, but they have two or more owners.

Corporations are separate legal entities (thus, they pay taxes) that sell shares of stock to investors (stockholders). Corporations are more costly to establish than sole proprietorships and partnerships. Stockholders in corporations cannot be held liable for more than their investment in the corporation. Private corporations sell stock to a few individuals; public corporations sell stock on the stock market.

LO2 Describe accounting and its role in business decisions. p. 6

- Accounting Defined

Accounting is an information system designed to capture and communicate a business's financial condition and performance to decision makers inside and outside the organization.

- Accounting Professionals

Private accountants are employed by a single business or nonprofit organization. Many pursue the Certified Management Accountant certification.

Public accountants charge fees for services to a variety of businesses and nonprofit organizations. Staff members of CPA firms become licensed certified public accountants.

LO3 Identify users of financial information. p. 6

- Users of Financial Information

Internal users (primarily managers, sole proprietors, and partners) are those inside the organization who make business decisions affecting the organization's operating, investing, and financing activities.

  - **Management accounting** is the area of accounting that produces financial information for internal users.

External users (primarily bankers, suppliers, governments, and stockholders in corporations) are not directly involved in running the business.

  - **Financial accounting** is the area of accounting that produces financial information for external users.

LO4 Describe the fundamental accounting equation and elements of financial statements. p. 9

- The Accounting Equation

The **fundamental accounting equation** is Assets = Liabilities + Owner's Equity.

The five financial statement elements are:

  - **Assets** are measurable economic resources that the business owns and are likely to provide future benefits.
  - According to the **historical cost principle,** assets are initially measured at the total cost to acquire them.
  - **Liabilities** are measurable and probable obligations that require the business to pay cash or deliver goods or services to others in the future.
  - **Owner's equity** is the difference between the assets the business owns and the liabilities it owes.
  - **Revenues** are the amounts that the business earned in delivering goods and services to customers.
  - **Expenses** are the amounts of resources an entity used to earn revenues during a period.

LO5 Explain the structure of basic financial statements. p. 13

- Financial Statements

Income statement

  - Its purpose is to report the performance of a business over a period of time.
  - The income statement equation is Revenues − Expenses = Net Income (or Net Loss).

Statement of owner's equity

  - Its purpose is to report the changes in owner's equity for a period of time and link the income statement to the balance sheet.
  - The owner's equity equation is Beginning Owner's Equity + Additional Investments + Net Income (or − Net Loss) − Withdrawals = Ending Owner's Equity.

Balance sheet

  - Its purpose is to report the amount of a business's assets, liabilities, and owner's equity at a particular point in time.
  - The balance sheet equation is Assets = Liabilities + Owner's Equity

Statement of cash flows

  - The purpose is to report the cash inflows and outflows for operating, investing, and financing activities during a period of time.
  - The cash flow equation is ± Cash from Operating Activities ± Cash from Investing Activities ± Cash from Financing Activities = Change in cash during the period.
    - **Operating activities**—those activities directly related to earning profits.
    - **Investing activities**—buying and selling productive resources primarily with long lives.
    - **Financing activities**—borrowing and repaying bank loans, receiving additional investments from owners, and withdrawing profits from the business by owners.
  - According to the **monetary unit assumption,** financial information is reported in the standard monetary unit of the country in which the business operates.

Notes to the financial statements explain how amounts were measured and provide additional information that may affect users' decisions.

LO6 Understand the importance of ethical decisions in financial reporting and business. p. 23

- Generally Accepted Accounting Principles
  The Financial Accounting Standards Board (FASB) sets the rules of accounting, which are the main source of **generally accepted accounting principles** (GAAP).
  Financially useful information should be **reliable, relevant, comparable,** and **consistent.**
  The Public Company Accounting Oversight Board (PCAOB) sets the rules for independent auditors.
- Ethical Conduct
  Ethics in business and accounting refers to the standards of conduct used to judge right from wrong, honest from dishonest, and fair from unfair. Ethical dilemmas harm employees, the business's reputation, the corporation's stock price, lenders, and the public in general.
  Companies need a strong system of **internal controls** to ensure the accuracy of their accounting records and to protect their assets from loss. An audit by independent auditors provides additional credibility regarding the strength of the companies' internal controls and the quality of their financial information.
  Independent auditors (CPAs) must adhere to an ethics code, the Code of Professional Conduct, when providing services to clients.

Key Terms

Accounting (p. 6)
Asset (p. 9)
Balance Sheet (p. 17)
Certified Public Accountant (p. 6)
Code of Professional Conduct (p. 24)
Comparable (p. 23)
Consistent (p. 23)
Corporation (p. 5)
Ethics (p. 24)
Expenses (p. 10)
Financial Accounting (p. 8)
Financial Accounting Standards Board (FASB) (p. 23)
Financing Activities (p. 18)
Fundamental Accounting Equation (p. 9)
Generally Accepted Accounting Principles (GAAP) (p. 23)
Historical Cost (p. 9)
Income Statement (p. 14)
Internal Controls (p. 24)
Investing Activities (p. 18)
Liability (p. 9)
Managerial Accounting (p. 7)
Monetary Unit Assumption (p. 15)
Net Income (p. 15)
Net Loss (p. 16)
Notes (p. 18)
Operating Activities (p. 18)
Owner's Equity (p. 9)
Partnership (p. 5)
Private Accounting (p. 6)
Public Accounting (p. 6)
Public Company Accounting Oversight Board (PCAOB) (p. 23)
Relevant (p. 23)
Reliable (p. 23)
Revenues (p. 10)
Securities and Exchange Commission (SEC) (p. 23)
Separate Entity Assumption (p. 10)
Sole Proprietorship (p. 4)
Statement of Cash Flows (p. 18)
Statement of Owner's Equity (p. 16)

See complete glossary in the back of text.

Questions

1. List the organizational forms for business and the primary strengths and weaknesses of each.
2. Define *accounting*.
3. Briefly distinguish
   a. financial accounting from managerial accounting and
   b. private accounting from public accounting.
4. The accounting process generates financial reports for both internal and external users. Describe some of the specific groups of internal and external users.
5. Write the fundamental accounting equation and define each of its elements.
6. Write the equation for the income statement and define each of its elements.
7. Briefly define *net income* and *net loss*.
8. Write the equation for the statement of owner's equity.
9. Write the equation for the statement of cash flows, and explain the three major types of activities reported on the statement.
10. Describe the purpose of the
    a. balance sheet,
    b. income statement,
    c. statement of owner's equity, and
    d. statement of cash flows.
11. What information should be included in the heading of each of the four primary financial statements?
12. What is the purpose of the notes to the financial statements?
13. Briefly describe the organizations responsible for developing accounting measurement rules (generally accepted accounting principles) in the United States.
14. What are *ethical dilemmas* in accounting, and who benefits and who is harmed by unethical behaviors?

Multiple Choice

Quiz 1-1
www.mhhe.com/LLPW1e

1. Which of the following is *not* a primary objective of external users who read a company's financial statements?
   a. Understanding the company's current financial state.
   b. Assessing the company's contribution to social and environmental policies.
   c. Predicting the company's future financial performance.
   d. Evaluating the company's ability to generate cash from sales.
2. Which of the following is *not* one of the four basic financial statements?
   a. Balance sheet
   b. Audit report
   c. Income statement
   d. Statement of cash flows
3. The income statement reports
   a. Net earnings or losses for a period of time.
   b. Revenues, expenses, and liabilities.
   c. Only revenue for which cash was received at the point of sale.
   d. Financial position of a business at a specific point in time.
4. Which of the following is *false* regarding the balance sheet?
   a. The accounts shown on a balance sheet represent the basic accounting equation for a particular business.
   b. The owner's equity balance shown on the balance sheet must agree to the ending owner's equity balance shown on the statement of owner's equity.
   c. The balance sheet summarizes the net changes in specific account balances over a period of time.
   d. The balance sheet reports the amount of assets, liabilities, and owner's equity of a business at a point in time.
5. Which of the following is *not* one of the items required to be shown in the heading of a financial statement?
   a. The financial statement preparer's name.
   b. The title of the financial statement.
   c. The financial reporting date or period.
   d. The name of the business entity.
6. A company reported assets of $130,000, liabilities of $20,000, expenses of $220,000, and net income of $40,000. Revenues and owner's equity would be reported as:

	Revenues	Owner's Equity
a.	$110,000	$180,000
b.	$180,000	$110,000
c.	$260,000	$110,000
d.	$260,000	$150,000

7. Which of the following is a liability?
   a. Prepaid expense
   b. Accounts receivable
   c. Wages payable
   d. Sales revenue
8. Which of the following regarding GAAP is *true?*
   a. GAAP is an abbreviation for goodie, another accounting problem.
   b. Changes in GAAP do not affect the amount of income reported by a company.
   c. GAAP is the abbreviation for generally accepted accounting principles.
   d. Changes to GAAP must be approved by the Senate Finance Committee.
9. Which of the following is *false?*
   a. Assets are the resources the business owns.
   b. Assets = Liabilities − Owner's Equity.
   c. Ethical decisions are an important component of sound financial reporting.
   d. The primary responsibility for the information in financial statements lies with management.
10. (Supplement 1-A) Public accountants provide which of the following services for clients?
   a. Internal auditing, cost accounting, and budgeting.
   b. Assurance, forensic, and consulting.
   c. Internal auditing, taxation, and consulting.
   d. Assurance, cost accounting, and bookkeeping.

Solutions to Multiple-Choice Questions

1. b 2. b 3. a 4. c 5. a 6. c 7. c
8. c 9. b 10. b

Mini Exercises  Available with McGraw-Hill's Homework Manager

M1-1 Matching Business Types to Definitions LO1

Match each term with its related definition by entering the appropriate letter on the blank provided.

Term	Definition
____ 1. Manufacturing business	A. Provides service to customers.
____ 2. Merchandising business	B. Produces goods from raw inputs.
____ 3. Service business	C. Sells goods produced by others to customers.

LO1

M1-2 Matching Business Forms to Definitions

Match each term with its related definition by entering the appropriate letter on the blank provided.

Term	Definition
____ 1. Sole proprietorship	A. Business owned by more than one individual who are liable for the debts of the business.
____ 2. Partnership	B. Business owned by one individual who pays taxes on the profits of the business.
____ 3. Corporation	C. Business that pays taxes and sells shares of stock to owners.

LO3

M1-3 Identifying Users of Financial Information

1. Who are the primary internal users of financial information, and what decisions do they make?
2. Who are the primary external users of financial information, and what decisions do they make?

LO4

P&G

M1-4 Identifying Elements of the Financial Statements

According to its annual report, "Procter & Gamble markets a broad range of laundry, cleaning, paper, beauty care, health care, food and beverage products in more than 140 countries around the world, with leading brands including Tide, Ariel, Crest, Crisco, Vicks and Max Factor." The following are items taken from its recent balance sheet and income statement. Mark each item in the following list with a letter(s) to indicate whether it would be reported as an asset (A), liability (L), or owners' equity (OE) account on the balance sheet or a revenue (R) or expense (E) account on the income statement.

____ 1. Accounts payable	____ 6. Interest expense
____ 2. Accounts receivable	____ 7. Inventories
____ 3. Cash	____ 8. Selling and administrative expenses
____ 4. Cost of goods sold	____ 9. Sales revenue
____ 5. Buildings	____ 10. Notes payable

LO4

Microsoft Corporation

M1-5 Identifying Elements of the Financial Statements

Microsoft Corporation manufactures home entertainment devices such as Xbox, creates software such as Word, and operates networks such as MSN Hotmail. The following items were presented in the company's financial statements. Mark each item from the balance sheet as an asset (A), liability (L), or owners' equity (OE) and each item from the income statement as a revenue (R) or expense (E).

____ 1. Inventories	____ 6. Owners' capital
____ 2. Accounts payable	____ 7. Accounts receivable
____ 3. Sales revenue	____ 8. Cash
____ 4. Property and equipment	____ 9. Promotion expense
____ 5. Notes payable	____ 10. Cost of goods sold

LO4

M1-6 Matching Financial Statement Items to the Four Basic Financial Statements

Match each element with its financial statement by entering the appropriate letter in the space provided.

Element	Financial Statement
____ 1. Expenses	A. Balance sheet
____ 2. Cash flows from investing activities	B. Income statement
____ 3. Assets	C. Statement of owner's equity
____ 4. Withdrawals	D. Statement of cash flows
____ 5. Revenues	
____ 6. Cash flows from operating activities	
____ 7. Liabilities	
____ 8. Cash flows from financing activities	

LO5

M1-7 Preparing an Income Statement

The Tea Room, a sole proprietorship owned by Gerry Stayman, earned revenues of $220,000 and incurred expenses of $150,000 during its first year of operations ended December 31, 2010. At the end of the year, The Tea Room owned assets of $180,000 and owed liabilities of $30,000. Gerry invested $100,000 cash to establish the new business and withdrew $20,000 during the year. Prepare the Tea Room's income statement for 2010.

LO5

M1-8 Preparing a Statement of Owner's Equity

Refer to the information in M1-7. Prepare a statement of owner's equity for 2010.

M1-9 Preparing a Balance Sheet LO5

Refer to the information in M1-7. Prepare a balance sheet at December 31, 2010.

M1-10 Determining the Effects of Business Activities LO5

For each of the following activities, indicate what the company owns (the account and effect) and what the company owes (the account and effect) using the fundamental accounting equation. An example is provided. Be sure to answer from the standpoint of the business.

a. Received $10,000 contribution from owner, Alecia Simpson.
b. Purchased a $4,000 computer for use in the business on account.
c. Provided $22,000 of service to customers for cash.
d. Paid employees $15,000 cash.
e. Withdrew $1,200 cash from the business profits.

	Assets		=	Liabilities		+	Owner's Equity
Example: Borrowed $30,000 from a bank.	Cash	+30,000		Notes Payable	+30,000		

M1-11 Identifying Definitions with Abbreviations LO6

The following is a list of important abbreviations used in the chapter and widely in business. Give the full designation of each abbreviation. The first one is an example.

Abbreviation	Full Designation
1. CPA	certified public accountant
2. GAAP	________________
3. FASB	________________
4. SEC	________________

M1-12 Identifying Ethical Dilemmas LO6

The following is a short list of scenarios. Write a brief statement about whether you believe the scenario is an ethical dilemma and, if so, who will be harmed by the unethical behavior.

1. You are a tax accounting professional and a client informs you that some of the receipts used in preparing the tax return are falsified.
2. A friend gives you his accounting homework assignment. You change his name to yours on the top of the paper and turn in the assignment as your work.
3. You are an employee at a local clothing store. Your manager asks you to sell her a few expensive items priced at $1,200 but charge her only $100.

M1-13 (Supplement 1-A) Identifying Areas of Accounting

For each of the following job responsibilities, identify the area of accounting (private accounting, public accounting, or both) that is most involved.

____ 1. Preparing financial statements for external users.
____ 2. Consulting.
____ 3. Cost accounting.
____ 4. Auditing by CPA.
____ 5. Internal auditing.
____ 6. Reviewing financial information for compliance with GAAP.

Exercises  Available with McGraw-Hill's Homework Manager

E1-1 Categorizing Business Forms LO1

The following describes different businesses. Mark each with the appropriate letter to indicate whether it would be categorized as a sole proprietorship (S), partnership (P), or corporation (C).

____ 1. Alan Cohen and Carol Palmer own Cohen and Palmer, CPAs, an accounting firm. Both are personally liable for the firm's debts.

____ 2. Crystal's Spa and Salon does not have separate legal existence apart from its one owner, Crystal Mullinex.

____ 3. Gimme Coffee is divided into 12,000 shares of stock.

____ 4. Johnson Boatyard does not pay taxes and has one owner.

LO4

E1-2 Inferring Values Using the Income Statement and Balance Sheet Equations

Review the chapter explanations of the income statement and the balance sheet equations. Apply these equations in each of the following independent cases to compute the two missing amounts for each case. Assume that it is the end of 2010, the first full year of operations for the company.

Independent Cases	Total Revenues	Total Expenses	Net Income (Loss)	Total Assets	Total Liabilities	Owner's Equity
A.	$100,000	$82,000	$_____	$150,000	$70,000	$_____
B.	_____	80,000	12,000	112,000	_____	60,000
C.	80,000	86,000	_____	104,000	26,000	_____
D.	50,000	_____	13,000	_____	22,000	77,000
E.	_____	81,000	(6,000)	_____	73,000	28,000

LO4, 5

OAKLEY

E1-3 Matching Financial Statement Items to the Four Basic Financial Statements

Oakley, Inc., manufactures sunglasses, goggles, shoes, watches, footwear, and clothing. Recently, the company reported the following items in its financial statements. Indicate whether these items appeared on the balance sheet (B/S), income statement (I/S), statement of owners' equity (SOE), or statement of cash flows (SCF).

____ 1. Total owners' equity

____ 2. Sales Revenue

____ 3. Total assets

____ 4. Cash flows from operating activities

____ 5. Total liabilities

____ 6. Net income

____ 7. Cash flows from financing activities

LO4

GENERAL MILLS

E1-4 Matching Financial Statement Items to Balance Sheet and Income Statement Categories

General Mills is a manufacturer of food products, such as Lucky Charms cereal, Pillsbury crescent rolls, and Jolly Green Giant vegetables. The following items were presented in the company's financial statements. Mark each item in the following list with letters to indicate whether it would be reported as an asset (A), liability (L), or owners' equity (OE) account on the balance sheet or a revenue (R) or expense (E) account on the income statement.

____ 1. Inventories

____ 2. Accounts Payable

____ 3. Income Tax Expense

____ 4. Equipment

____ 5. Accounts Receivable

____ 6. Notes Payable

____ 7. Owners' Capital

____ 8. Cost of Goods Sold

____ 9. Selling and Administrative Expenses

____ 10. Sales Revenue

LO4

Tootsie

Tootsie Roll Industries

E1-5 Matching Financial Statement Items to Balance Sheet and Income Statement Categories

Tootsie Roll Industries manufactures and sells candy. Major products include Tootsie Roll, Tootsie Roll Pops, Tootsie Pop Drops, Tootsie Flavor Rolls, Charms, and Blow-Pop lollipops. The following items were listed on Tootsie Roll's recent income statement and balance sheet. Mark each item in the following list with letters to indicate whether it would be reported as an asset (A), liability (L), or owners' equity (OE) account on the balance sheet or a revenue (R) or expense (E) account on the income statement.

____ 1. Accounts Payable

____ 2. Accounts Receivable

____ 3. Wages Payable

____ 4. Owners' Capital

____ 5. Income Tax Expense

____ 6. Inventories

____ 7. Cash

____ 8. Machinery

____ 9. Promotion and Advertising Expenses

____ 10. Sales Revenue

____ 11. Notes Payable to Banks

____ 12. Selling and Administrative Expenses

E1-6 Preparing Financial Statements LO5

John Clay organized Clay Company as a sole proprietorship on January 1, 2010. At the end of January 2010, the following monthly financial data are available:

Service Revenue	$130,000
Other Expenses	80,000
Wages Expense	15,000
Cash	30,000
Accounts Receivable from Customers	15,000
Supplies	42,000
Accounts Payable (to suppliers for merchandise purchased during the month)	26,000
J. Clay, Capital	26,000

John Clay made no withdrawals during January.

Required:

1. Using formats from the chapter, prepare an income statement, statement of owner's equity, and balance sheet for the month of January, including appropriate headings.
2. Discuss whether Clay Company will be able to pay its liabilities.

E1-7 Reporting Amounts on the Four Basic Financial Statements LO5

The following summary information was reported by Lucus Rock, the sole proprietor of Lucus Rock Company, for the year ending December 31, 2011. Amounts are in thousands (i.e., assets = $18,200,000).

Assets	$18,200	L. Rock, capital, December 31, 2010	$3,500
Liabilities	13,750	Cash flows from operating activities	1,600
Revenue	10,500	Cash flows from investing activities	(1,000)
Expenses	9,200	Cash flows from financing activities	(900)
L. Rock, drawings in 2011	500		
Additional investment by owner during 2011	150	Cash, December 31, 2010	1,000
		Cash, December 31, 2011	700

Required:

Prepare the four basic financial statements for 2011:

a. Income statement.
b. Statement of owner's equity.
c. Balance sheet.
d. Statement of cash flows.

E1-8 Preparing an Income Statement and Inferring Missing Values LO5 FedEx

FedEx is an industry leader in providing rapid delivery of packages and freight around the world. Its May 31, 2007, income statement contained the following items (in millions of dollars):

Salaries Expense	$ 8,051	Rent Expense	$1,598
Maintenance and Repairs Expense	1,440	Fuel Expense	2,946
Net income	?	Other Expenses	7,241
Delivery Revenues	22,527	Total Expenses	?

Required:

1. Solve for the missing amounts and prepare an income statement for the year ended May 31, 2007.
2. What is FedEx's largest expense?

E1-9 Preparing a Balance Sheet LO5

Dave & Buster's Inc. is a restaurant/entertainment company. Founded in 1982, Dave & Buster's provides high-quality food and beverage items and offers an extensive array of interactive entertainment attractions such as pocket billiards, shuffleboard, state-of-the-art simulators, and virtual reality and

traditional carnival-style amusements and games of skill. Its February 4, 2007, balance sheet contained the following items (in millions).

Cash	$ 10	Property and Equipment	$317
Owners' Capital	97	Other Assets	167
Accounts Payable	19	Wages Payable	46
Other Liabilities	91	Total Assets	507
Supplies	13	Total Liabilities and Owners' Equity	?
Notes Payable	254		

Required:

1. Prepare the balance sheet as of February 4, 2007, solving for the missing amount.
2. Which of Dave & Buster's assets has the highest total?
3. As of February 4, 2007, did most of the financing for assets come from creditors or owners?

LO5

E1-10 Completing a Balance Sheet and Inferring Net Income

Terry Lopez organized Read More Store as a sole proprietorship, contributing $100,000 cash to start the business. The store completed its first year of operations on December 31, 2010. On that date, the following financial items for the year were determined:

Cash on hand and in the bank	$ 48,900
Amounts due from customers from sales of books	26,000
Equipment	48,000
Amounts owed to publishers for books purchased	8,000
One-year note payable to a local bank	2,120
Terry Lopez, Capital account balance	112,780

The owner made no withdrawals during the year.

Required:

1. Using typical account titles, prepare a balance sheet as of the end of 2010.
2. Using the statement of owner's equity equation and an opening balance of $0, compute the amount of net income for the year.
3. As of December 31, 2010, did most of the financing for assets come from creditors or owners?

LO5

E1-11 Analyzing Revenues and Expenses and Computing Net Income

Assume that you are the sole proprietor of Collegiate Laundry Service that provides pick-up, cleaning, and delivery of laundry for students in local colleges. For the month of October 2010, you have the following information:

a. The business's records in October indicated $12,000 in laundry services for cash. They also showed 20 laundry services totaling $1,000 on account (due from college students in November).

b. You determined that the business used $800 in laundry supplies (the amount paid for the supplies) in October.

c. According to the business's checkbook in October, it paid $3,500 for employees' wages and $500 for other expenses. However, the business has not yet paid the $600 October advertising expense for newspaper advertisements run during October.

Required:

On the basis of the data given, what was net income for October? Show computations.

LO5

E1-12 Analyzing Revenues and Expenses and Completing an Income Statement

TNT Cleaning Service, owned by sole proprietor Kathy Terwilliger, has been operating for 20 years. The following financial items were determined for the fiscal year ended December 31, 2009:

Cleaning Service Revenue (cash received in 2009)	$150,000
Cleaning Service Revenue (services provided in 2009 with cash to be received in 2010)	16,000
Wages expense (2009 expense paid in 2009)	97,000
Wages expense (2009 expense to be paid in 2010)	5,775
Fuel expense	525
Advertising expense	9,025
Supplies expense	18,500

Required:

Prepare an income statement for TNT Cleaning Service for 2009.

E1-13 Matching Cash Flow Statement Items to Business Activity Categories

LO5

Tech Data

Tech Data Corporation is a leading distributor of computer peripherals and network solutions, and recently was ranked by *Fortune* as the second most admired company in its industry category. The following items were taken from its recent cash flow statement.

Required:

Indicate

1. Whether each item is a cash flow from operating (O), investing (I), or financing (F) activities.
2. The direction of the effect on cash (+ for cash increases and − for cash decreases).

O, I, or F	+ or −	
________	________	A. Cash paid to suppliers and employees.
________	________	B. Cash collected from customers.
________	________	C. Cash received from borrowing long-term debt.
________	________	D. Cash received from owners as additional investments.
________	________	E. Cash paid to purchase equipment.

E1-14 Matching Cash Flow Statement Items to Business Activity Categories

LO5

Coca-Cola Company

The Coca-Cola Company is one of the world's leading manufacturers, marketers, and distributors of nonalcoholic beverage concentrates and syrups producing more than 300 beverage brands. The following items were taken from a recent cash flow statement.

Required:

Indicate

1. Whether each item is a cash flow from operating (O), investing (I), or financing (F) activities.
2. The direction of the effect on cash (+ for cash increases and − for cash decreases).

O, I, or F	+ or −	
________	________	A. Cash paid for purchases of buildings and equipment.
________	________	B. Cash paid to owners as distributions of profits.
________	________	C. Cash received on sales of buildings and equipment.
________	________	D. Cash paid to suppliers and employees.
________	________	E. Cash received from owners as additional investments.
________	________	F. Cash received from borrowing long-term debt.
________	________	G. Cash received from customers.
________	________	H. Cash paid on long-term debt.

E1-15 Reporting Amounts on the Statement of Cash Flows

LO4

Microsoft Corporation

The following are independent cases.

a. During a recent year, General Mills delivered breakfast cereal to customers who paid or promised to pay amounts totaling $10,506 million. During the same period, General Mills collected $6,375 million in cash from its customers.
b. During a recent year, Microsoft delivered software to customers who paid or promised to pay amounts totaling $32.2 billion. During the same period, Microsoft collected $25.4 billion in cash from its customers.

Required:

1. Indicate which of the two amounts will be shown on General Mills' cash flow statement.
2. Indicate which of the two amounts will be shown on Microsoft's cash flow statement.

E1-16 Determining the Effects of Business Activities

LO5

For each of the following activities, indicate what the company owns (the account and effect) and what the company owes (the account and effect) using the fundamental accounting equation. Be sure to answer from the standpoint of the business. An example is provided.

1. Purchased a building for $40,000; paid $30,000 cash and signed a note payable for the rest.
2. Purchased $1,000 of supplies on account.
3. Provided $31,000 of consulting service to customers on account.
4. Paid employees $19,000 cash.
5. Received a $600 utility bill to be paid next month.
6. Provided $6,200 of consulting service to customers for cash.
7. Purchased a new copy machine for $3,000 cash.
8. Paid $5,000 cash as a withdrawal by owner.

	Assets		=	Liabilities	+	Owner's Equity	
Example: Received $100,000 contribution from owner, Carl Reyes.	Cash	+100,000				C. Reyes, Capital	+100,000

LO1, 2, 4, 5, 6

E1-17 Matching Definitions with Terms or Abbreviations

Match each definition with its related term or abbreviation by entering the appropriate letter on the blank provided.

____ 1. SEC
____ 2. Investing activities
____ 3. Private company
____ 4. Corporation
____ 5. Accounting
____ 6. Partnership
____ 7. FASB
____ 8. Financing activities
____ 9. Monetary unit
____ 10. GAAP
____ 11. Public company
____ 12. Operating activities

A. System that collects and processes financial information about an organization and reports that information to decision makers.
B. Measurement of information about a business in dollars or other national currency.
C. Unincorporated business owned by two or more persons.
D. Company that sells shares of its stock to a small number of individuals.
E. Incorporated business that issues shares of stock as evidence of ownership.
F. Purchases and disposals of long-term assets.
G. Transactions with lenders (borrowing and repaying cash) and owners (receiving additional investments from owners and providing withdrawals to owners).
H. Day-to-day activities related to a company's core business.
I. Securities and Exchange Commission.
J. Financial Accounting Standards Board.
K. Company that has its stock bought and sold by investors on established stock exchanges.
L. Generally accepted accounting principles.

Problems—Set A

HM™ **Available with McGraw-Hill's Homework Manager**

LO5

PA1-1 Preparing Financial Statements

Assume that Craig Reed is the sole proprietor of Nuclear Company. At the end of the first year of operations (December 31, 2010), the following financial data for the company are available:

Cash	$ 25,000	Notes Payable	$ 2,000
Accounts Receivable (from customers)	12,000	Service Revenue	140,000
Supplies	90,000	Wages Expense	60,000
Equipment	45,000	Advertising Expense	1,100
Accounts Payable (to suppliers)	57,370	Other Expenses	38,000

Mr. Reed invested $87,000 in cash to start up the business at the beginning of 2010. He withdrew $15,270 in cash from the business during 2010.

Required:

1. Prepare an income statement for the year ended December 31, 2010.
2. Prepare a statement of owner's equity for the year ended December 31, 2010.
3. Prepare a balance sheet at December 31, 2010.

PA1-2 Preparing Financial Statements

LO5

Assume that Dr. Aaron Jones is the sole owner of Family Medicine. At the end of the first year of operations (June 30, 2009), the following financial data for the company are available:

Cash	$13,500
Accounts Receivable (from patients)	9,500
Supplies	17,000
Equipment	76,000
Accounts Payable (to suppliers)	3,500
Notes Payable	21,000
Medical Service Revenue	90,000
Wages Expense	46,000
Utilities Expense	6,500
Other Expenses	2,000

Dr. Jones invested $62,000 in cash to start the practice at the beginning of the year and withdrew $6,000 in cash from the business during the year.

Required:

1. Prepare an income statement for the year ended June 30, 2009.
2. Prepare a statement of owner's equity for the year ended June 30, 2009.
3. Prepare a balance sheet at June 30, 2009.

PA1-3 Preparing Financial Statements

LO5

www.mhhe.com/LLPW1e

Electronic Arts

Electronic Arts is the world's leading developer and publisher of interactive entertainment software for personal computers and advanced entertainment systems made by Sony, Nintendo, and Microsoft. Assume that the company is revising its methods for displaying its financial statements, and the controller in the accounting department has asked you to create electronic worksheets that can be used as the standard format for financial statement reporting. The controller has provided you an alphabetical list of account names with corresponding balances as of September 30. All amounts are in thousands of dollars. She has asked you to use a spreadsheet program to create two worksheets that organize the accounts into a properly formatted balance sheet and income statement. Use formulas to compute the unknown amount.

Accounts Payable	$120,200	Other Liabilities	$333,600
Accounts Receivable	139,300	Owners' Capital	?
Cash	920,800	Promotion Expense	55,500
Cost of Goods Sold (expense)	198,900	Property and Equipment	307,100
Inventories	36,800	Research and Development Expense	22,500
Notes Payable	1,400	Sales Revenue	450,500
Other Assets	443,000	Selling Expense	98,100
Other Expenses	29,600		

Not knowing quite where to start, you e-mailed your friend Billy for advice on using a spreadsheet. Billy provided this very detailed reply:

From: BillyTheTutor@yahoo.com
To: HairZed@hotmail.com
Subject: Excel Help

Hey, pal. Long time, no chat. Here's the scoop on creating those worksheets with a screenshot that shows how to go. If you need more help, let me know and I'll submit an application for your position there. ☺

1. Start-up Excel to open a new spreadsheet file. You'll need only two worksheets for this assignment, so delete the third worksheet by clicking on the *Sheet3* tab at the bottom of the worksheet and selecting Edit/Delete Sheet in the pull-down menu. While you're at it, rename *Sheet1* and *Sheet2* to *Balance Sheet* and *Income Statement* by double-clicking on the worksheet tabs and typing in the new names.
2. Plan the layout for your reports. Use the first column as a blank margin, the second column for account names and their headings, and the third column for the numbers corresponding to each account name or total. If you want to apply the same format to all worksheets, begin by right-clicking on the tab at the bottom of a worksheet and choosing Select All Sheets. Next, resize the first column by clicking on the A at the top of that column, selecting Format/Column/Width. . . from the pull-down menu, and choosing a width of 2. Using this same procedure, resize columns B and C to 50 and 15, respectively.
3. Starting with cell B1, enter the company's name. Enter the report name and date in cells B2 and B3. To merge cells so these headings span more than one column, select the cells to be merged and click on [merge icon]. Continue with the body of the report in cell B5, entering any necessary amounts in column C.
4. To use formulas to compute subtotals and totals, the equals sign = is entered first into the cell and is followed immediately by the formula. So, to subtract cell C16 from C13, enter = C16-C13. To add a series of amounts, say C6 through C10, use a formula like =SUM(C6:C10), as shown in the screenshot.
5. After you get all the data entered and totals calculated, be sure to save the file. To do this, just click on File-Save As. . . and enter the file name.
6. If you need to print the worksheets, it might be best to highlight what you want printed, then click File/Print . . . and choose Selection in the dialog box that pops up.
7. Go to it, you accounting guru!

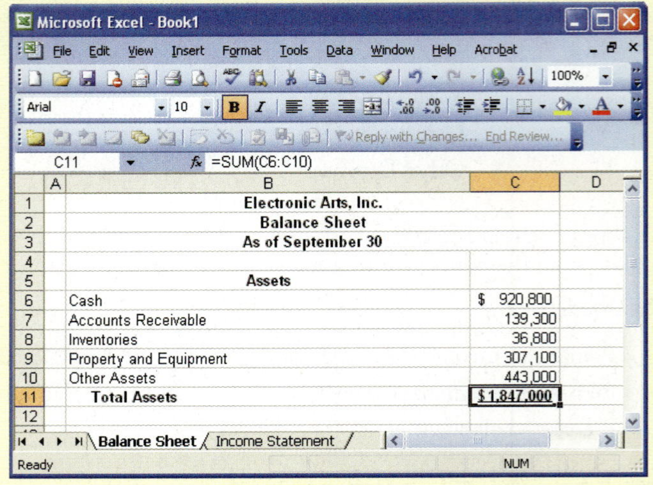

Required:
Follow Billy's advice to create a balance sheet and income statement with each statement saved on a separate worksheet in a file called *meEA.xls* where the *me* part of the file name uniquely identifies you.

LO5 PA1-4 Analyzing and Interpreting an Income Statement

Three individuals organized Pest Away Company on January 1, 2011, to provide insect extermination services. At the end of 2011, the following income statement was prepared:

PEST AWAY COMPANY
Income Statement
For the Year Ended December 31, 2011

Revenues	
Sales revenue ($192,000 in cash and $24,000 in credit)	$216,000
Expenses	
Wages expense	84,000
Supplies expense	33,000
Advertising expense	14,000
Utilities expense	13,000
Interest expense	8,000
Other expenses	25,000
Total expenses	177,000
Net income	$ 39,000

Required:

1. What was the average amount of monthly revenue?
2. What was the average amount of monthly wages expense?
3. Explain why Supplies Expense is reported as an expense.
4. Explain why Advertising Expense is reported as an expense.
5. Can you determine how much cash the company had on December 31, 2011? Answer yes or no, and explain your reasoning.

PA1-5 Reporting Amounts on the Four Basic Financial Statements

LO5

www.mhhe.com/LLPW1e

The following summary information was reported by Hannah Company, a sole proprietorship owned by Dan Hannah, for the quarter ending September 30, 2010.

Assets	$79,500	D. Hannah, Capital, June 30, 2010	$51,000
Liabilities	18,500		
D. Hannah, Capital, September 30, 2010	61,000	Cash flows from operating activities	15,700
Revenue	32,100	Cash flows from investing activities	(7,200)
Expenses	18,950	Cash flows from financing activities	(5,300)
D. Hannah, Drawings	4,900		
Additional investment by owner	1,750	Cash, June 30, 2010	3,200
		Cash, September 30, 2010	6,400

Required:

Prepare the four basic financial statements for the quarter:

a. Income statement.
b. Statement of owner's equity.
c. Balance sheet.
d. Statement of cash flows.

PA1-6 Reporting Amounts on the Four Basic Financial Statements (Challenging Problem)

LO5
OSI Restaurant Partners, Inc.

www.mhhe.com/LLPW1e

The following information for the year ended December 31, 2006, was reported by OSI Restaurant Partners, Inc., that owns and operates Outback Steakhouse and Carrabba's Italian Grill restaurants. Amounts are in millions of dollars.

Accounts Payable	$ 166	Other Liabilities	$ 330
Wages and Taxes Payable	120	Other Revenues	21
Cash (balance on January 1, 2006)	84	Owners' Capital (balance on January 1, 2006)	1,144
Cash (balance on December 31, 2006)	94	Property, Fixtures and Equipment	1,549
Food and Supplies Expense	1,415	Restaurant Sales Revenue	3,920
General and Administrative Expenses	235	Unearned Revenue (a liability)	187
Food and Supply Inventories	87	Utilities and Other Expenses	1,104
Notes Payable	235	Wages Expense	1,087
Other Assets	529		

Other information	
Cash paid to purchase equipment	$ 384
Cash paid to suppliers and employees	2,578
Cash received from customers	2,946
Cash received from bank borrowings	375
Repayments of bank borrowings	294
Cash received from sale of fixtures and equipment	32
Other cash outflows from financing activities	62
Other cash outflows from investing activities	2
Additional investment by owners	16
Withdrawals (distribution of profits to owners in cash)	39

Required:

Prepare the four basic financial statements for 2006:

a. Income statement.
b. Statement of owners' equity.
c. Balance sheet.
d. Statement of cash flows.

Problems—Set B  Available with McGraw-Hill's Homework Manager

LO5

PB1-1 Preparing Financial Statements

Assume that Marcia Waxman is the sole proprietor of the Write-r-Wrong Company. At the end of the first year of operations (April 30, 2011), the following financial data for the company are available:

Cash	$ 39,150	Notes Payable	$ 3,500
Accounts Receivable (from customers)	27,500	Service Revenue	270,000
Supplies	35,000	Supplies Expense	22,000
Equipment	208,000	Wages Expense	138,500
Accounts Payable (to suppliers)	47,800	Other Expenses	10,000

Ms. Waxman invested $186,000 in cash to start the business at the beginning of the year, May 1, 2010. She withdrew $27,150 in cash from the business during the year.

Required:

1. Prepare an income statement for the year ended April 30, 2011.
2. Prepare a statement of owner's equity for the year ended April 30, 2011.
3. Prepare a balance sheet at April 30, 2011.

LO5

PB1-2 Preparing Financial Statements

Assume that Elyse Rosati is the sole owner of Sweaters 'n Things Company. At the end of the first year of operations (December 31, 2012), the following financial data for the company are available:

Cash	$ 31,500	Notes Payable	$ 35,000
Accounts Receivable (from customers)	79,000	Sales Revenue	945,000
Inventories	152,000	Cost of Goods Sold (expense)	746,000
Fixtures and Equipment	140,000	Utilities Expense	42,500
Accounts Payable (to suppliers)	71,500	Other Expenses	2,000

Ms. Rosati invested $200,000 in cash to start the business at the beginning of the year and withdrew $58,500 in cash from the business during the year.

Required:

1. Prepare an income statement for the year ended December 31, 2012.
2. Prepare a statement of owner's equity for the year ended December 31, 2012.
3. Prepare a balance sheet at December 31, 2012.

LO5

PB1-3 Preparing Financial Statements

Best Buy Co. Inc. is a specialty retailer of consumer electronics, home-office products, entertainment software, appliances, and related services. Assume that the company is revising its methods for displaying its financial statements, and the controller in the accounting department has asked you to create electronic worksheets that can be used as the standard format for financial statement reporting. The controller has provided you an alphabetical list of account names with corresponding balances (in millions of dollars) as of December 31. He has asked you to use a spreadsheet program to create two worksheets that organize the accounts into a properly formatted balance sheet and income statement. Use formulas to compute the unknown amount.

Accounts Payable	$ 2,824	Other Liabilities	$ 2,063
Accounts Receivable	375	Owners' Capital	?
Cash	470	Promotion Expense	1,002
Cost of Goods Sold (expense)	27,165	Property and Equipment	2,464
Inventories	2,851	Research and Development Expense	2,051
Notes Payable	958	Sales Revenue	35,934
Other Assets	4,134	Selling Expense	3,717
Other Expenses	753	Other Revenue	131

Not knowing quite where to start, you e-mailed your friend Susan for advice on using a spreadsheet. Susan provided a very detailed reply.

From: SusanTutor@yahoo.com
To: PaloozaJoe@hotmail.com
Subject: Excel Help

Hey, friend. Long time, no chat. Here's the scoop on creating those worksheets with a screenshot that shows how to go. If you need more help, let me know and I'll submit an application for your position there. ☺

1. Start-up Excel to open a new spreadsheet file. You'll need only two worksheets for this assignment, so delete the third worksheet by clicking on the *Sheet3* tab at the bottom of the worksheet and selecting Edit/Delete Sheet in the pull-down menu. While you're at it, rename *Sheet1* and *Sheet2* to *Balance Sheet* and *Income Statement* by double-clicking on the worksheet tabs and typing in the new names.
2. Plan the layout for your reports. Use the first column as a blank margin, the second column for account names and their headings, and the third column for the numbers corresponding to each account name or total. If you want to apply the same format to all worksheets, begin by right-clicking on the tab at the bottom of a worksheet and choosing Select All Sheets. Next, resize the first column by clicking on the A at the top of that column, selecting Format/Column/Width. . . from the pull-down menu, and choosing a width of 2. Using this same procedure, resize columns B and C to 50 and 15, respectively.
3. Starting with cell B1, enter the company's name. Enter the report name and date in cells B2 and B3. To merge cells so these headings span more than one column, select the cells to be merged and click on [merge icon]. Continue with the body of the report in cell B5, entering any necessary amounts in column C.
4. To use formulas to compute subtotals and totals, the equals sign = is entered first into the cell and is followed immediately by the formula. So, to subtract cell C16 from C13, enter =C16-C13. To add a series of amounts, say C6 through C10, use a formula like =SUM(C6:C10), as shown in the screenshot.
5. After you get all the data entered and totals calculated, be sure to save the file. To do this, just click on File/Save As. . . and enter the file name.
6. If you need to print the worksheets, it might be best to highlight what you want printed, then click File/Print. . . and choose Selection in the dialog box that pops up.
7. Go to it, you accounting guru!

Microsoft Excel - PB1-3

C11 =SUM(C6:C10)

	A	B	C
1		Best Buy	
2		Balance Sheet	
3		As of December 31	
4		(in millions)	
5		ASSETS	
6		Cash	$ 470
7		Accounts Receivable	375
8		Inventories	2,851
9		Property and Equipment	2,464
10		Other Assets	4,134
11		Total Assets	$ 10,294
12			
13			

Balance Sheet / Income S

Required:

Follow Susan's advice to create a balance sheet and income statement with each statement saved on a separate worksheet in a file called *meBB.xls* where the *me* part of the file name uniquely identifies you.

PB1-4 Analyzing and Interpreting an Income Statement LO5

Lauren DiLorenzo organized Viva Lingerie Company on January 1, 2010, to manufacture undergarments with a French flair. At the end of 2010, the following income statement was prepared:

VIVA LINGERIE COMPANY
Income Statement
For the Year Ended December 31, 2010

Revenues	
Sales revenue (cash)	$276,000
Sales revenue (credit)	192,000
Total revenues	468,000
Expenses	
Cost of goods sold	236,000
Wages expense	148,000
Advertising expense	4,000
Interest expense	5,000
Utilities expense	12,000
Other expenses	15,000
Total expenses	420,000
Net income	$ 48,000

Required:

1. What was the average amount of monthly revenue?
2. What was the average amount of monthly selling expense?
3. Explain why cost of goods sold is reported as an expense.
4. Explain why utilities expense is reported as an expense.
5. Can you determine how much cash the company had on December 31, 2010? Answer yes or no, and explain your reasoning.

LO5

PB1-5 Reporting Amounts on the Four Basic Financial Statements

The following summary information was reported by Darryl Company, a sole proprietorship owned by Jane Darryl, for the year ending December 31, 2009.

Assets	$ 97,500	J. Darryl, Capital, January 1, 2009	$ 7,400
Liabilities	81,500		
J. Darryl, Capital, December 31, 2009	16,000	Cash flows from operating activities	20,200
Revenue	135,600	Cash flows from investing activities	(47,000)
Expenses	128,100	Cash flows from financing activities	40,100
Withdrawals	4,900	Cash, January 1, 2009	8,200
Additional investment by owner	6,000	Cash, December 31, 2009	21,500

Required:

Prepare the four basic financial statements for 2009:

a. Income statement.
b. Statement of owner's equity.
c. Balance sheet.
d. Statement of cash flows.

LO5

PB1-6 Reporting Amounts on the Four Basic Financial Statements (Challenging Problem)

The Cheesecake Factory Incorporated reported the following information for the 2006 fiscal year ended January 2, 2007. Amounts are in thousands of dollars.

Accounts Payable	$ 45,570	Other Assets	$ 186,453
Accounts Receivable	11,639	Other Liabilities	126,012
Wages and Other Expenses Payable	117,226	Other Revenues	8,171
Cash (balance on January 3, 2006)	31,052	Owners' Capital (balance on January 3, 2006)	646,699
Cash (balance on January 2, 2007)	44,790	Prepaid Rent	43,870
Food and Supplies Expense	333,528	Property and Equipment	732,204
General and Administrative Expenses	72,751	Restaurant Sales Revenue	1,315,325
Food and Supply Inventories	20,775	Utilities and Other Expenses	414,978
Notes Payable	39,381	Wages Expense	420,957

Other information

Additional investments by owners	$ 33,555
Cash paid to purchase equipment	243,211
Cash paid to suppliers and employees	1,123,353
Repayments of borrowings	170,242
Cash received from customers	1,276,008
Cash received from borrowings	175,000
Cash received from sale of long-term assets	115,975
Withdrawals (payments to owners)	49,994

Required:

Prepare the four basic financial statements for the 2006 fiscal year:

a. Income statement.
b. Statement of owners' equity.
c. Balance sheet.
d. Statement of cash flows.

Cases and Projects

CP1-1 Finding Financial Information

LO1, 4, 5

Refer to the financial statements of The Home Depot in Appendix A at the end of this book, or download the annual report from the *Cases* section of the text's Web site at www.mhhe.com/LLPW1e.

Required:

1. What type of business and organizational form is The Home Depot? How do you know?
2. What is the amount of net income for the most recent year reported?
3. What amount of revenue was earned for the most recent year reported?
4. How much inventory does the company have on February 3, 2008?
5. How much does The Home Depot have in cash on February 3, 2008?
6. The Home Depot's stock is traded on the New York Stock Exchange under the symbol HD. What kind of company does this make The Home Depot?

CP1-2 Comparing Financial Information

LO1, 5

Lowe's

Refer to the financial statements of The Home Depot in Appendix A and Lowe's in Appendix B at the end of this book, or download the annual reports from the *Cases* section of the text's Web site at www.mhhe.com/LLPW1e.

Required:

1. Was Lowe's net income for the most recent year greater or less than The Home Depot's?
2. Was Lowe's revenue for the most recent year greater or less than The Home Depot's?
3. Did Lowe's have more or less inventories than The Home Depot at the end of the year?
4. Did Lowe's have more or less cash than The Home Depot at the end of the year?
5. Is Lowe's the same type of business organization as The Home Depot?
6. On an overall basis, was Lowe's or The Home Depot more successful in the most recent fiscal year?

CP1-3 Examining an Annual Report: Internet-Based Team Research

LO1, 4, 5, 6

As a team, select an industry to analyze. Reuters provides lists of industries and their makeup at www.investor.reuters.com/Industries.aspx. Each group member should acquire the annual report (or Form 10-K filed with the SEC) for one publicly traded company in the industry with each member selecting a different company. (In addition to the company's own Web site, a great source is the SEC's Electronic Data Gathering, Analysis, and Retrieval (EDGAR) service. This free source is available by going to the Filings & Forms section of www.sec.gov and clicking on Search for Company Filings and then Companies & Other Filers.)

Required:

1. On an individual basis, each team member should write a short report that lists the following information for the business:
   a. What type of business organization is it?
   b. What types of products or services does it sell?
   c. On what day of the year does its fiscal year end?
   d. For how many years does it present complete (1) balance sheets, (2) income statements, and (3) cash flow statements?
   e. Are its financial statements audited by independent CPAs? If so, by whom?
   f. Did its total assets increase or decrease over the last year?
   g. Did its net income increase or decrease over the last year?
2. Then, as a team, write a short report comparing and contrasting your companies using these attributes. Discuss any patterns across the companies that you as a team observe. Provide potential explanations for any differences discovered.

CP1-4 Making Ethical Decisions: Real-Life Example

LO6

In September 2002, John Rigas, his three sons, and another executive from Adelphia Communications were charged with defrauding investors and lenders of more than a billion dollars. John Rigas went to prison in 2007. If others are convicted, each would face more than 30 years in prison. To understand the charges, you need to first understand a bit about Adelphia's history. Adelphia started as a one-town cable company in 1952 and, at the time the fraud accusations were made public, had grown into the sixth largest cable television provider in the country. With the company starting as a family-owned business, Adelphia's operations were always a central part of the personal lives of the Rigas family members. However, the extent to which their personal lives were mixed with the business activities was never clear to stockholders—at least not nearly as clear as when they were reported in an article in the August 12, 2002, issue of *Fortune*. After the following questions, we present a table from that article, which summarizes how the Rigas family allegedly used more than $1.2 billion dollars of Adelphia's money that ultimately belonged to Adelphia's stockholders.

Required:

1. What accounting concept is the Rigas family accused of violating?
2. Based on the information provided in the following table, can you determine which of the family's dealings are clearly inappropriate and which are clearly appropriate?
3. As a stockholder, how might you attempt to ensure that this type of behavior does not occur or, at least, does not occur without you knowing about it?
4. Aside from Adelphia's stockholders, who else might be harmed by the Rigas family's actions?

Family Assets, Sort of Some of the notable ways the Rigas family used Adelphia shareholder dollars.

On the Receiving End. . .	Who's Behind the Entity	How Much?
Dobaire Designs	Adelphia paid this company, owned by Doris Rigas (John's wife), for design services.	$371,000
Wending Creek Farms	Adelphia paid John Rigas's farm for lawn care and snowplowing.	$2 million
SongCatcher Films	Adelphia financed the production of a movie by Ellen Rigas (John's daughter).	$3 million
Eleni Interiors	The company made payments to a furniture store run by Doris Rigas and owned by John.	$12 million
The Golf Club at Wending Creek Farms	Adelphia began developing a ritzy golf club.	$13 million
Wending Creek 3656	The company bought timber rights that would eventually revert to a Rigas family partnership.	$26 million
Praxis Capital Ventures	Adelphia funded a venture capital firm run by Ellen Rigas's husband.	$65 million
Niagara Frontier Hockey LP	Adelphia underwrote the Rigas' purchase of the Buffalo Sabres hockey team.	$150 million
Highland 2000	Adelphia guaranteed loans to a Rigas family partnership, which used the funds to buy stock.	$1 billion
Total		**$1,271,371,000**

LO6 CP1-5 Making Ethical Decisions: A Mini-Case

You are one of three partners who own and operate Mary's Maid Service. The company has been operating for seven years. One of the other partners has always prepared the company's annual financial statements. Recently, you proposed that the statements be audited each year because it would benefit the partners and prevent possible disagreements about the division of profits. The partner who prepares the statements proposed that his Uncle Ray, who has a lot of financial experience, do the job and at little cost. Your other partner remained silent.

Required:

1. What position would you take on the proposal? Justify your response.
2. What would you strongly recommend? Give the basis for your recommendation.

LO5 CP1-6 Developing a Balance Sheet and Income Statement: Critical Thinking Exercise

On September 30, Jill and Jack started arguing about who is better off. Jack said he was better off because he had the latest PlayStation console that he bought last year for $350. Jill, on the other hand, argued that she was better off because she had $1,000 and a '75 Mustang that she bought two years ago for $800. Jack countered that Jill still owed $250 on her car and that Jack's dad promised to buy him a Porsche if he gets a great score in his accounting class. Jill pointed out that she inherited a collection of trading cards that she figured she could sell for about $250. Jack said he had $6,000 in his bank account then because he just received a $4,800 student loan. Jill knows that Jack still owes an $800 installment on this term's tuition.

Jill and Jack met again in early November. They asked how each other was doing. Jill claimed that she'd become much more successful than Jack. She had a part-time job and earned $500 per month. Jack laughed at Jill because he had won $950 on a lottery ticket he bought in October for which the "work" was standing in line for a minute. It was just what he needed because his apartment cost $450 each month. Jill, on the other hand, paid $120 for her share of the rent. Both Jill and Jack had other normal living costs that total $300 each month.

Required:

1. Prepare a report that compares what Jill and Jack each own and owe on September 30. Note any decisions you had to make when preparing your report. Which of the two is better off?
2. Prepare a report that compares what Jill and Jack each earned during October. Note any decisions you had to make when preparing your report. Which of the two is more successful?

2 Establishing a Business and the Balance Sheet

LEARNING OBJECTIVES

After studying this chapter, you should be able to:

Lectured slideshow–LP2-1
www.mhhe.com/LLPW1e

LO1 Identify what constitutes a business transaction and recognize common balance sheet account titles used in business.

LO2 Apply transaction analysis to simple business transactions in terms of the accounting model: Assets = Liabilities + Owner's Equity.

LO3 Determine the impact of business transactions on the balance sheet using two basic tools, journal entries and T-accounts.

LO4 Prepare a simple classified balance sheet.

Focus Company: PIZZA AROMA, Ithaca, NY

"Use of Accounting Tools"

As you learned in Chapter 1, Mauricio Rosa is the owner-manager of Pizza Aroma, a gourmet pizza restaurant in Ithaca, New York. In April, after an informative discussion about the role of accounting in starting a business, Mauricio hired Laurie Hensley to provide recordkeeping services for his new venture. Laurie told him that all businesses, large or small, need systems for gathering and organizing the detailed information that she and other accountants require. What would happen, for example, if FedEx did not have a system to monitor and evaluate the use of its $12.6 billion in airplanes, facilities, and package-handling and ground-support equipment (over half of all of its resources) or to track the 6.4 million packages and $96 million in revenues the company handles every day?[1] Clearly, big companies need well-organized systems for tracking their business activities and financial results. The same is true for small businesses like Pizza Aroma.

Laurie showed Mauricio how to create an accounting system for Pizza Aroma. In Chapters 2, 3, and 4, you will look at this business as if you were a manager. You will learn about the decisions that business managers make and see how Pizza Aroma's accounting system tracks its financial results from the revenues the restaurant earns from selling pizza to the costs of equipment, rent, employee wages, and those marvelous fresh ingredients that Mauricio uses. You will see how managers and others analyze and interpret these results before making new business decisions.

In particular, this chapter will focus on the activities that establish a business so it is ready to open its doors. In Chapter 3, we will focus on the operating activities that occur after a business is established, most importantly earning revenues and incurring expenses. We will conclude our discussion of the accounting system in Chapter 4.

[1] http://www.fedex.com/us/investorrelations/financialinfo/2007annualreport/.

ORGANIZATION OF THE CHAPTER

DETERMINE THE EFFECTS OF BUSINESS ACTIVITIES	PREPARE ACCOUNTING RECORDS	PREPARE A BALANCE SHEET
• Nature of Business Transactions • Balance Sheet Accounts • Transaction Analysis • Analysis of Pizza Aroma's Transactions	• The Accounting Cycle • Analyzing Business Transactions • Recording Transaction Effects • Posting Transaction Effects • Pizza Aroma's Accounting Records • Preparing a Trial Balance	• Classified Balance Sheet • Limitations of the Balance Sheet • Summary of the Accounting Cycle

DETERMINE THE EFFECTS OF BUSINESS ACTIVITIES

Nature of Business Transactions

Learning Objective 1

Identify what constitutes a business transaction and recognize common balance sheet account titles used in business.

As you saw in Chapter 1, Mauricio must make many decisions and undertake several activities to establish Pizza Aroma as a business. Those business activities that affect the accounting equation are called **transactions**. Which activities are accounting transactions? Transactions include two types of activities or events, external events and internal events.

- **External events** are measurable **exchanges between the business and others**—exchanges of assets and services from one entity for other assets or promises to pay from another entity. Businesses undertake these exchanges either to bring in profits or to acquire resources with the potential to bring in profits. In other words, businesses create value through exchanges. As Exhibit 2.1 shows, the external events at Pizza Aroma include:

  (1) Receiving a cash investment from Mauricio Rosa in exchange for an ownership stake in the business.

  (2) Borrowing cash from banks in exchange for Pizza Aroma's promise to repay the debt.

  (3) Acquiring equipment, ingredients, and paper supplies from suppliers in exchange for Pizza Aroma's cash payment or promise to pay.

  (4) Selling pizza to customers in exchange for their cash payments or promises to pay.

- **Internal events** include certain events that are not exchanges between the business and others but nevertheless have a direct and measurable effect on the entity. Examples

Exhibit 2.1 Business Exchanges

include the use of supplies and the use of a building over time. When Pizza Aroma uses its ovens and supplies to make and sell pizza, those activities are internal events.

Throughout this textbook, we will use the word *transaction* in a broad sense that includes both types of events.

You should note that some important activities are *not* reflected in the financial statements either because an exchange of assets has not yet occurred or because the assets are not measurable. If Pizza Aroma orders supplies, for example, no exchange of assets or services occurs. Only the supplier's promise to deliver and Pizza Aroma's promise to pay are exchanged—**an exchange of promises is not an accounting transaction.**

Balance Sheet Accounts

Once a transaction has been identified, names must be given to the items that have been exchanged. Companies use a standardized format called an account that is an individual record of both increases and decreases in a specific asset, liability, owner's equity, revenue, or expense. Each company establishes a **chart of accounts**—a list of all account titles and their numbers that are unique to each company. Exhibit 2.2 shows a partial chart of accounts that includes some common balance sheet account titles along with some simple account numbers. These accounts are usually organized by financial statement element with asset accounts listed first (the 100 series in the exhibit) followed by liabilities (the 200 series) and owner's equity (the 300 series). Pizza Aroma will use several of the accounts listed in Exhibit 2.2. (In Chapter 3, we will add revenue and expense accounts to the chart.) In doing assignments, if you are unsure of an account title, refer to this exhibit for help.

If you recognize some key words in an account title, you can tell what type of account it is. Recall the following points from Chapter 1:

- Accounts with **receivable** in the title are always assets; they represent amounts owed to the business by (receivable from) customers and others.
- Accounts with **payable** in the title are always liabilities; they represent amounts owed by the company to others to be paid in the future.

Coach's Tip

In homework problems, you will either be given the account names or expected to select appropriate names similar to the ones in Exhibit 2.2. After you have selected a name for an account, you must use that exact name in all transactions affecting that account.

Exhibit 2.2 Chart of Accounts (partial—balance sheet accounts only)

Account Number	Account Name	
101	Cash	— amount of coins, paper money, and funds in the bank
104	Investments	— amount of excess cash invested in stocks, bonds, certificates of deposit, etc.
106	Accounts Receivable	— amounts owed by customers buying goods or services on account
107	Notes Receivable	— signed promises to pay by customers, employees, and others
110	Inventory	— goods to be sold
115	Supplies	— pencils, boxes, paper, etc. to be used in future periods
120	Prepaid Rent	— amount paid to rent buildings and equipment in future periods
121	Prepaid Insurance	— amount paid to receive insurance coverage in future periods
122	Prepaid Advertising	— amount paid to advertise in future periods
140	Equipment	— trucks, machinery, computers, etc., to be used in future periods
145	Buildings	— structures acquired to use in future periods
160	Land	— real estate property acquired to use in future periods
180	Intangibles	— long-term rights such as patents and trademarks
201	Accounts Payable	— amounts owed to suppliers due to buying goods or services on account
205	Wages (or Salaries) Payable	— amounts owed to employees for work in past periods
210	Notes Payable	— signed promise by the company to repay borrowed money
217	Interest Payable	— amount due on notes payable as the cost of borrowing
230	Unearned Revenue	— amount received from customers in advance of delivering goods or services to them
300	"Owner's Name," Capital	— amount of equity owner has in the business
301	"Owner's Name," Drawing	— amount withdrawn by owner from the business

- Any account with **prepaid** in the title is an asset because it represents amounts paid to others for future benefits, such as insurance coverage and property rentals.
- Accounts with **unearned** in the title are always liabilities that represent amounts paid to the company in the past by others who expect to receive goods or services from the company in the future.

Although the account titles in Exhibit 2.2 are common ones, every company has a variation on the chart of accounts, depending on the nature of its business activities. Some companies may refer to Accounts Payable by another title, such as Trade Accounts Payable. Others may have no Unearned Revenue account. Still other companies may create account titles to fit their business activities. For example, FedEx has an account called Package Handling and Ground Support Equipment.[2]

Transaction Analysis

Learning Objective 2

Apply transaction analysis to simple business transactions in terms of the accounting model: Assets = Liabilities + Owner's Equity.

Now that Mauricio can identify accounting transactions and the accounts involved, what does he need to do to accumulate the effects of his transactions? For each transaction, Mauricio must perform what is called **transaction analysis.** Transaction analysis is the process of studying a transaction and its related documents to determine their effect on the business in terms of the accounting equation. Documents (also called source documents) are the sources of evidence that a business activity has occurred. Source documents include, for example, sales receipts, checks, invoices (bills) from suppliers, cash register tapes, and employee time cards.

Recall from Chapter 1 that the basic accounting equation for a business that is organized as a sole proprietorship is:

Video 2-1
www.mhhe.com/LLPW1e

Assets (A) = Liabilities (L) + Owner's Equity (OE)

There are two rules to follow in performing transaction analysis:

- **Dual effects:** Every transaction affects at least two accounts. It is critical that you correctly identify those accounts and the direction of the effect (whether an increase or a decrease). This is what accountants have developed into a system known as *double-entry bookkeeping*.
- **Balancing the accounting equation:** The accounting equation must remain in balance after each transaction is recorded.

To succeed in performing transaction analysis, you need a clear understanding of these principles. Slow down and think carefully as you read the following material.

Coach's Tip

In today's complex business environment, employers value people who understand how to analyze transactions. **Study this section well.**

Dual Effects

Every transaction has **at least two effects** on the basic accounting equation. Transactions with external parties involve an **exchange** through which the business entity both receives something and gives something else up. For example, suppose Pizza Aroma purchased some paper napkins for cash. In this exchange, Pizza Aroma would receive supplies (an increase in an asset) in return for giving up cash (a decrease in an asset).

Transaction	Pizza Aroma Received	Pizza Aroma Gave
Purchased paper napkins for cash	Supplies (increased)	Cash (decreased)
	NAPKINS +	−

[2] The accounts you see in the financial statements of most large businesses are actually summations (or aggregations) of several specific accounts. For example, Papa John's International keeps separate accounts for equipment, buildings, and land, but combines them under one title on the balance sheet, called Property and Equipment.

In this transaction, notice that Supplies and Cash were the two accounts that were affected. As you saw in Chapter 1, however, most supplies are purchased on credit and paid for later. In that case, Pizza Aroma would engage in *two* transactions: (1) the purchase of an asset on credit and (2) the eventual payment. In the first transaction, Pizza Aroma would receive supplies (an increase in an asset) and in return give a promise to the supplier to pay later, called an **Account Payable** (an increase in a liability). In the second transaction, Pizza Aroma would give up cash (a decrease in an asset) and eliminate or receive back its promise to pay (a decrease in the Accounts Payable liability).

Transactions	Pizza Aroma Received	Pizza Aroma Gave
(1) Purchased paper napkins on credit	Supplies (increased) +	Accounts Payable (increased) [a promise to pay] +
(2) Paid on its Accounts Payable	Accounts Payable (decreased) [a promise was eliminated] −	Cash (decreased) −

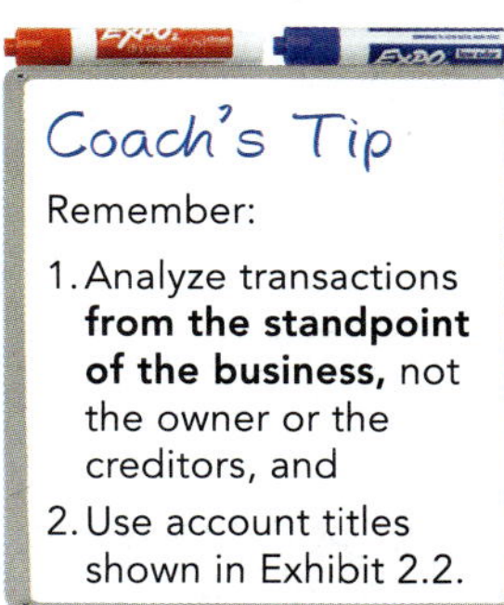

Balancing the Accounting Equation

The accounting equation must remain in balance after each transaction. That is, total assets (resources) must equal total liabilities and owner's equity (claims to resources). If all of the correct accounts have been identified and the appropriate direction of the effect on each account has been determined, the equation should remain in balance.

Based on these two rules, you can see that transaction analysis includes the following steps:

Transaction Analysis Steps

Step  : Ask yourself What did the company receive? and What did the company give in return?

- **Identify the accounts affected** (by name), making sure that at least two accounts change.
- **Classify them by the type of account** (A for asset, L for liability, and OE for owner's equity).
- **Determine the direction of the effect** (an increase [+] or a decrease [−]) on each account.

Step  : **Verify that the accounting equation (A = L + OE) remains in balance.**

Analysis of Pizza Aroma's Transactions

To illustrate the process of transaction analysis, let's analyze Pizza Aroma's transactions during the **first week** of May just before the restaurant began to sell pizza. Mauricio has found a store he can rent for a reasonable amount of money, but it will require some renovation as well as new equipment and furnishings. Thus, he needs to obtain cash to finance these activities. Mauricio has $30,000 of his own money to contribute, and he estimates Pizza Aroma will need to borrow $20,000 from a local bank to pay for everything Mauricio needs to do before he opens for business.

(*a*) RECEIVE INVESTMENT BY OWNER: To establish Pizza Aroma, a new gourmet pizza restaurant, the business receives $30,000 cash as an initial investment from owner-manager Mauricio Rosa.

1 *Identify and classify accounts and effects:*
Received: Cash (+A) $30,000 **Given:** Recognition of owner's investment, M. Rosa, Capital (+OE) $30,000

2 *Is the accounting equation in balance?*
Yes. The left side increased by $30,000 and the right side increased by $30,000.

	Assets	=	Liabilities	+	Owner's Equity
	Cash				M. Rosa, Capital
(*a*)	+30,000	=			+30,000

(*b*) BORROW FROM BANK: Mauricio negotiates with a local bank and signs a three-year, $20,000 note in Pizza Aroma's name (the loan is a liability of the business).

1 *Identify and classify accounts and effects:*
Received: Cash (+A) $20,000 **Given:** A written promise by the business to pay the bank, Notes Payable (+L) $20,000

2 *Is the accounting equation in balance?*
Yes. The left side increased by $20,000 and the right side increased by $20,000.

	Assets	=	Liabilities	+	Owner's Equity
	Cash		Notes Payable		M. Rosa, Capital
(*a*)	+30,000	=			+30,000
(*b*)	+20,000	=	+20,000		

Transactions (*a*) and (*b*) are **financing** transactions. Companies that need cash to buy or build additional facilities often seek funds from owners (investors), as in transaction (*a*), or from banks (creditors), as in transaction (*b*). Mauricio is excited; he has the cash he needs. Before he can renovate the store, however, he needs to pay rent to the building's owner.

(*c*) PREPAY RENT: Pizza Aroma pays $4,800 in advance to the building owner to cover rent for the store from May through October (six months).

1 *Identify and classify accounts and effects:*
Received: Prepaid Rent (+A) $4,800 **Given:** Cash (−A) $4,800

2 *Is the accounting equation in balance?*
Yes. The left side increased and decreased by the same amount, $4,800.

	Assets		=	Liabilities	+	Owner's Equity
	Cash	Prepaid Rent		Notes Payable		M. Rosa, Capital
(*a*)	+30,000		=			+30,000
(*b*)	+20,000		=	+20,000		
(*c*)	− 4,800	+4,800	=	No change		

Recall that any account with the word *prepaid* in the title is an asset. Prepaid rent represents Pizza Aroma's right to use the store in the future. Now it is time to renovate the space. Pizza Aroma hires a construction company to renovate the store including the installation of new ovens and refrigerators, work counters, tables, chairs, a computerized cash register, and a sign at a cost of $36,000. The business pays $33,000 cash to the construction company and owes the rest on account (due in 30 days).

(d) PURCHASE EQUIPMENT: A construction company renovates the store and installs equipment at a cost of $36,000; Pizza Aroma pays $33,000 in cash and promises to pay the balance next month.

1. *Identify and classify accounts and effects:*
   Received: Equipment (+A) $36,000 **Given:** Cash (−A) $33,000 and a promise to pay, Accounts Payable (+L) $3,000
2. *Is the accounting equation in balance?*
   Yes. The left side increased by $3,000 ($36,000 − $33,000) and the right side increased by $3,000.

	Assets			=	Liabilities		+	Owner's Equity
	Cash	Prepaid Rent	Equipment		Accounts Payable	Notes Payable		M. Rosa, Capital
(a)	+30,000			=				+30,000
(b)	+20,000			=		+20,000		
(c)	− 4,800	+4,800		=	No change			
(d)	**−33,000**		**+36,000**	**=**	**+3,000**			

Notice that more than two accounts were affected by this transaction.

Now Mauricio must acquire the ingredients he needs to make his dough and gourmet sauces. To serve the pizza to customers, he also needs paper and plastic supplies.

(e) PURCHASE SUPPLIES: Pizza Aroma orders and receives $2,000 in supplies on account from local fresh food suppliers.

1. *Identify and classify accounts and effects:*
   Received: Supplies (+A) $2,000 **Given:** A promise to pay, Accounts Payable (+L) $2,000
2. *Is the accounting equation in balance?*
   Yes. The left side increased by $2,000 and the right side increased by $2,000.

	Assets				=	Liabilities		+	Owner's Equity
	Cash	Supplies	Prepaid Rent	Equipment		Accounts Payable	Notes Payable		M. Rosa, Capital
(a)	+30,000				=				+30,000
(b)	+20,000				=		+20,000		
(c)	− 4,800		+4,800		=	No change			
(d)	−33,000			+36,000	=	+3,000			
(e)		**+2,000**			**=**	**+2,000**			

Mauricio gathers all of the documents that are related to the transactions that have taken place. One is a bill that he pays to one of Pizza Aroma's food suppliers.

(f) PAY ACCOUNT OWED TO SUPPLIER: Pizza Aroma pays $1,000 cash on account to a supplier.

1. *Identify and classify accounts and effects:*
   Received: A reduction in the amount owed to the supplier, Accounts Payable (−L) $1,000 **Given:** Cash (−A) $1,000
2. *Is the accounting equation in balance?*
   Yes. The left side decreased by $1,000 and the right side decreased by $1,000.

	Assets				=	Liabilities		+	Owner's Equity
	Cash	Supplies	Prepaid Rent	Equipment		Accounts Payable	Notes Payable		M. Rosa, Capital
(a)	+30,000				=				+30,000
(b)	+20,000				=		+20,000		
(c)	− 4,800		+4,800		=	No change			
(d)	−33,000			+36,000	=	+3,000			
(e)		+2,000			=	+2,000			
(f)	**− 1,000**				**=**	**−1,000**			

After paying the supplier, Mauricio realizes that he has not used all of Pizza Aroma's cash. Because he does not think the business will need another $6,000 for several months, he decides to invest the excess money in a savings account at a local bank. The investment, opened in Pizza Aroma's name, will earn interest while the cash is idle.

(g) INVEST EXCESS CASH: Pizza Aroma puts $6,000 cash in a savings account at a bank.

1. *Identify and classify accounts and effects:*
   Received: Investments (+A) $6,000 **Given:** Cash (−A) $6,000
2. Is the accounting equation in balance?
   Yes. The left side increased and decreased by $6,000.

	Assets					=	Liabilities		+ Owner's Equity
	Cash	Investments	Supplies	Prepaid Rent	Equipment		Accounts Payable	Notes Payable	M. Rosa, Capital
(a)	+30,000					=			+30,000
(b)	+20,000					=		+20,000	
(c)	− 4,800			+4,800		=	No change		
(d)	−33,000				+36,000	=	+3,000		
(e)			+2,000			=	+2,000		
(f)	− 1,000					=	−1,000		
(g)	− 6,000	+6,000				=	No change		
Totals	5,200	6,000	2,000	4,800	36,000	=	4,000	20,000	30,000
	$54,000						$54,000		

SELF-STUDY PRACTICE

Practice is the most effective way to develop your transaction analysis skills. Review the analysis of Pizza Aroma's transactions (pages 53–56); then complete the analysis of the following events. For each, identify and classify the accounts involved and the effects of the transaction on them. Then show the effects on the accounting equation at the bottom of the exercise. Repeat the steps until they become a natural part of your thought process.

1. Paul Knepper contributes $50,000 to establish a new scuba business, Florida Flippers, a sole proprietorship that offers scuba instruction and diving services.
   a. *Identify and classify accounts and effects:*
      Received: **Given:**
   b. *Is the accounting equation in balance?*
2. Florida Flippers buys a small building near the ocean for $250,000, paying $25,000 cash with Paul signing a 10-year note in Florida Flippers' name for the balance.
   a. *Identify and classify accounts and effects:*
      Received: **Given:**
   b. *Is the accounting equation in balance?*

	Assets		=	Liabilities	+	Owner's Equity
	Cash	Building		Notes Payable		P. Knepper, Capital
1.			=			
2.			=			

After you have finished, check your answers with the solutions at the bottom of the next page.

PREPARE ACCOUNTING RECORDS

The Accounting Cycle

Learning Objective 3

Determine the impact of business transactions on the balance sheet using two basic tools, journal entries and T-accounts.

As you have just learned, the first step in capturing financial information is to analyze each transaction. For most organizations, however, recording the transaction effects and keeping track of account balances in this way is impractical. To process the many transactions that businesses generate every day, most companies establish computerized accounting systems. These systems follow a cycle, called the accounting cycle. Exhibit 2.3 illustrates the three steps during the period:

1. **Analyze** transactions that result in exchanges between the company and external parties.
2. **Record** the effects in chronological order in the first accounting book, called the general journal.
3. **Post** (transfer) each effect in the general journal to a specific page in another accounting book, called the general ledger, in which each page represents a separate account.

In this chapter, you will learn how these activities affect the balance sheet accounts **during the period.** You will not learn about activities that affect the income statement accounts until Chapter 3, so you will have a chance to become comfortable with the accounting process first. In Chapter 4, you will learn about activities that occur at the **end of the period,** when accountants adjust the records, prepare financial statements, and set up the records for the next cycle.

Analyzing Business Transactions

As you saw earlier, transactions can increase or decrease assets, liabilities, and owner's equity. Now you will learn how to use the fundamental accounting equation to create a transaction analysis model that shows the **direction** of these effects—that is, whether they are increases or decreases. You can think of each individual account as looking like a T, with a left side and

Exhibit 2.3 The Accounting Cycle

DURING THE PERIOD

(Chapters 2 and 3)

- Analyze transactions
- Record journal entries in the general journal
- Post amounts to the general ledger

AT THE END OF THE PERIOD

(Chapter 4)

- Adjust revenues and expenses and related balance sheet accounts
- Prepare a complete set of financial statements and disseminate it to users
- Close revenues, gains, expenses, losses and owner's withdrawals to owner's equity

Solution to Self-Study Practice

1. a. Received: Cash (+A) $50,000. Given: Sole ownership, P. Knepper, Capital (+OE) $50,000.
   b. Yes. The left side increased by $50,000 and the right side increased by $50,000.
2. a. Received: Building (+A) $250,000. Given: Cash (−A) $25,000 and Notes Payable (+L) $225,000.
   b. Yes. The left side increased by $225,000 ($250,000 − $25,000) and the right side increased by $225,000.

	Assets		=	Liabilities	+	Owner's Equity
	Cash	Building		Notes Payable		P. Knepper, Capital
a.	+ 50,000		=			+ 50,000
b.	− 25,000	+ 250,000	=	+ 225,000		

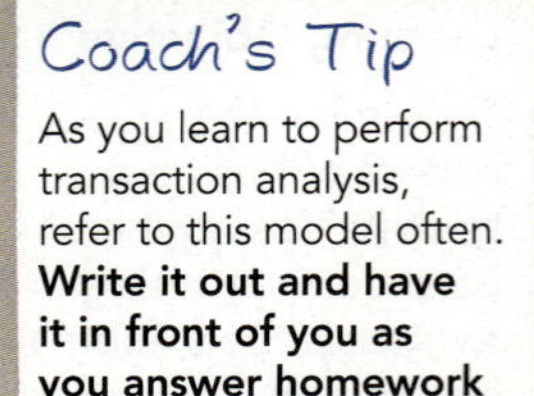

Coach's Tip

As you learn to perform transaction analysis, refer to this model often. **Write it out and have it in front of you as you answer homework assignments, especially in the next few chapters.**

Exhibit 2.4 Transaction Analysis Model

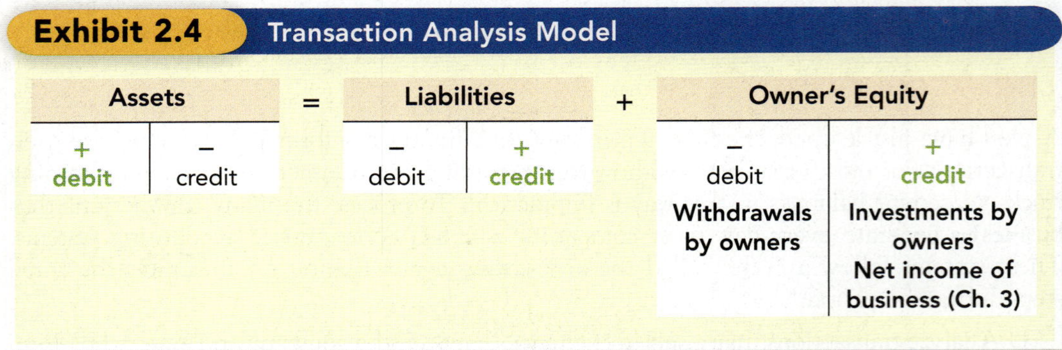

a right side (see Exhibit 2.4). Remember two important points about this model: **First and most important, the direction of the effect on a T-account depends on which side of the accounting equation's equal sign you are:**

- Because **assets** are shown on the **left** side of the equal sign in the accounting equation, an increase (+) is shown on the **left** side of the T-account.
- Because **liabilities and owner's equity** are shown on the **right** side of the equal sign in the accounting equation, an increase (+) is shown on the **right** side of the T-account.

The second important point to remember is that there are special accounting names for the left and right sides of the accounts:

- Debit is on the **left.** So, asset accounts that are on the left side of the equal sign in the accounting equation generally have debit balances. It is highly unusual for an asset account such as Inventory to have a negative (credit) balance.
- Credit is on the **right.** So liability and owner's equity accounts that are on the right side of the equal sign in the accounting equation generally have credit balances.

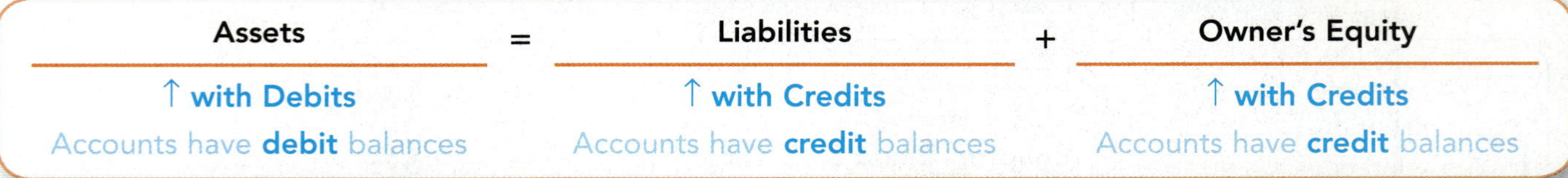

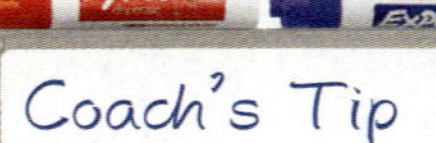

Coach's Tip

Why are they called "Debit" cards? From the bank's perspective, your bank account is a liability on the bank's books (the bank owes you money that you deposited at the bank) and liabilities are reduced with debits. When you use your debit card, the bank debits (reduces) your account.

Many students have trouble with accounting because they forget that debit means "left" and credit means "right." Perhaps someone once told you that you were a credit to your school or your family (a good thing). You also know that using your debit card to pay for purchases reduces the cash balance in your bank account (a bad thing). As a result, you may think that credits are good and debits are bad. Such is not the case. Just remember that **debit is the left side** of the T-account and **credit is the right side** of the T-account.

If you have identified the correct accounts and effects through transaction analysis, the accounting equation will remain in balance. Moreover, in any transaction, **the total dollar value of all debits must equal the total dollar value of all credits.** For an extra measure of assurance, add this equality check (Debits = Credits) to the transaction analysis process.

Recording Transaction Effects

You have learned that there are two types of records or books in a bookkeeping system: a general journal and a general ledger. After reviewing the business documents that support a transaction, the bookkeeper analyzes the effects of the transaction on the accounts and then enters them in the journal **in chronological order,** using a special form called the journal entry. The journal entry, then, is an accounting tool for expressing the effects of a transaction on the accounts. It is written in a debits-equal-credits format like the entries shown in the sample journal page in Exhibit 2.5.

Notice the following points about this formal handwritten way of recording journal entries:

- The first item in each entry is the date of the transaction.
- The *debited* account titles (listed in Exhibit 2.2 for Pizza Aroma) are written first (on top); the *credited* accounts are written below the debits and are indented to the right (both the words and the amounts) as a reminder to credit these accounts.

Exhibit 2.5 Formal Journal Page

General Journal				Page G1
Date	Account Titles and Explanation	Ref.	Debit	Credit
May 1	Cash		30,000	
	M. Rosa, Capital			30,000
	(Investment by owner.)			
May 2	Cash		20,000	
	Notes Payable			20,000
	(Borrowed from bank.)			
May 5	Equipment		36,000	
	Cash			33,000
	Accounts Payable			3,000
	(Purchased equipment paying part cash and the rest on credit.)			

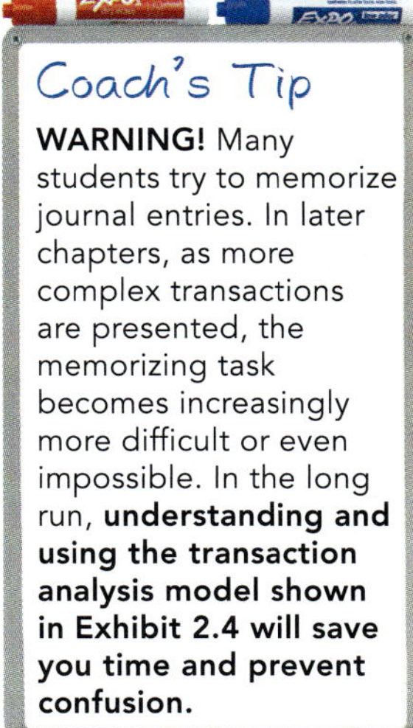

- Total debits (in the May 5 transaction, $36,000) equal total credits (in the May 5 transaction, $33,000 + $3,000).
- Because the journal is an internal record of the business, dollar signs are not necessary.
- The May 5 transaction affected three accounts. Any journal entry that affects more than two accounts is called a **compound entry.** Many transactions require a compound journal entry.
- When more than one account is debited, the order of the debited accounts does not matter. That means Buildings can be on the first line of a journal entry and Equipment can be on the second line when they are purchased, or vice versa. Likewise, the same is true for recording more than one credited account. Cash can be indented on the third line with Notes Payable indented on the fourth line when both are given to purchase buildings and equipment. Just make sure **debits are on top and the credits are on the bottom.**
- The reference column (Ref.) is used when the effects of the transactions are posted to the general ledger (the next step); it provides cross-references between the journal and the ledger. As you will soon see, the ledger page number will be the same as the account number from the chart of accounts in Exhibit 2.2.
- A description of the transaction with the necessary details is written below the debits and credits.
- A line is left blank after the description before the next journal entry begins.

In this text, we will present journal entries with slight changes to this formal way of recording entries to help you in your learning. For example, the May 5 entry in Exhibit 2.5 is the same as Transaction (*d*) in the Pizza Aroma illustration (page 55). The simplified journal entry we will use for Pizza Aroma is as follows:

Event	Account Titles	Debit	Credit
(*d*)	Equipment (+A)	36,000	
	Cash (−A)		33,000
	Accounts Payable (+L)		3,000

Here are the differences between the two ways of recording journal entries:

- Instead of a date, we will use a different form of reference to identify the event on which each transaction is based, such as the letter (*d*).
- To simplify the entry, we will omit the reference column and the description at the bottom of the entry.

- We will add the symbol A, L, or OE, along with the direction of the effect on the account (+ or −) next to each account title to clarify the effects of the transaction on the elements of the financial statements. This will help you to see that the accounting equation remains in balance.

Posting Transaction Effects

By themselves, journal entries show the effects of transactions, but they do not provide account balances. That is why the second book, the general **ledger,** is necessary. Each page in the ledger represents an account. After the journal entries have been recorded, the bookkeeper posts (transfers) the dollar amounts to each ledger page that the transaction affected so that the account balances can be computed. The ledger page number (that is, the account number) is then entered in the reference column in the journal, and the journal page number is entered in the reference column in the ledger. In most computerized accounting systems, these cross-references are entered automatically. In the manual accounting system that some small organizations still use, the ledger is often a three-ring binder with a separate page for each account. Exhibit 2.6 shows how the May 5 journal entry is posted to the appropriate ledger pages. Notice that the

Exhibit 2.6 Posting from the Journal to the Ledger

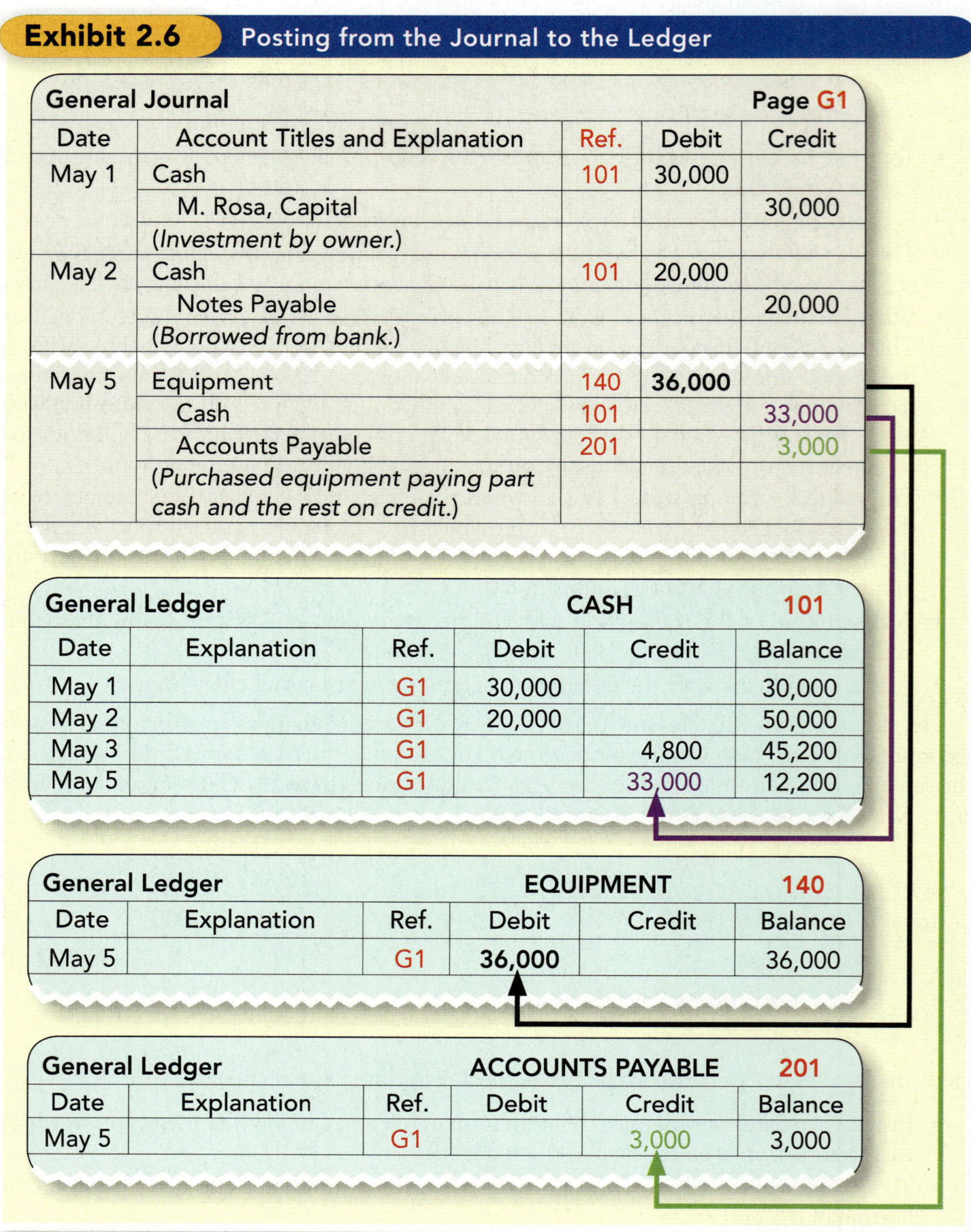

General Journal — Page G1

Date	Account Titles and Explanation	Ref.	Debit	Credit
May 1	Cash	101	30,000	
	M. Rosa, Capital			30,000
	(Investment by owner.)			
May 2	Cash	101	20,000	
	Notes Payable			20,000
	(Borrowed from bank.)			
May 5	Equipment	140	**36,000**	
	Cash	101		33,000
	Accounts Payable	201		3,000
	(Purchased equipment paying part cash and the rest on credit.)			

General Ledger — CASH — 101

Date	Explanation	Ref.	Debit	Credit	Balance
May 1		G1	30,000		30,000
May 2		G1	20,000		50,000
May 3		G1		4,800	45,200
May 5		G1		33,000	12,200

General Ledger — EQUIPMENT — 140

Date	Explanation	Ref.	Debit	Credit	Balance
May 5		G1	**36,000**		36,000

General Ledger — ACCOUNTS PAYABLE — 201

Date	Explanation	Ref.	Debit	Credit	Balance
May 5		G1		3,000	3,000

cash effects from each of the journal entries have been posted to the Cash ledger page. The right-hand column on the ledger page shows the running balance in the account.

Just as we simplified the journal entries, we will simplify the ledger pages in this text by using T-accounts. Each **T-account** represents the debit and credit columns of the ledger page. Exhibit 2.7 shows the T-accounts for Pizza Aroma's Cash, Equipment, and Accounts Payable accounts based on Transactions (*a*) through (*d*) on pages 54–55. Notice that in the T-account for the asset Cash, transactions that increase cash are shown on the left side and transactions that decrease cash are shown on the right side. For Accounts Payable, however, increases are shown on the right and decreases on the left, because Accounts Payable is a liability account.

In Exhibit 2.7, notice the following points:

- Every account starts with a beginning balance on the positive side. For balance sheet accounts, the ending balance from the prior period is the beginning balance for the current period. Because Pizza Aroma is a new business, the beginning balance in each account is zero.
- Because these are internal records, dollar signs are not necessary.
- Each line indicates the reference letter for the transaction. Thus, the effects can be traced back to the appropriate journal entry. These reference letters are very useful in finding errors that were made in posting the effects of transactions.
- To find the account balances, we can express the T-accounts as equations:

	Cash	Accounts Payable
Beginning balance	$ 0	$ 0
+ "+" side	+ 50,000	+ 3,000
− "−" side	− 37,800	− 0
Ending balance	$ 12,200	$ 3,000

  This method of balancing the accounts will be useful in answering analytical questions that ask you to determine a missing value in a particular account (that is, to solve for an unknown value).
- The ending balance is indicated on the positive side and is double underlined to highlight the amount.

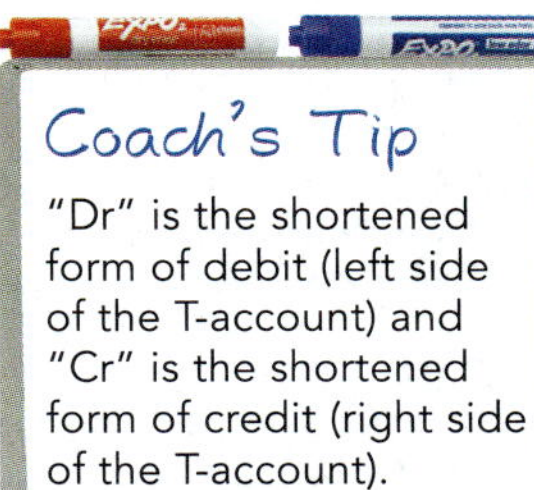

Exhibit 2.7 Posting from a Simplified Journal Entry to T-Accounts

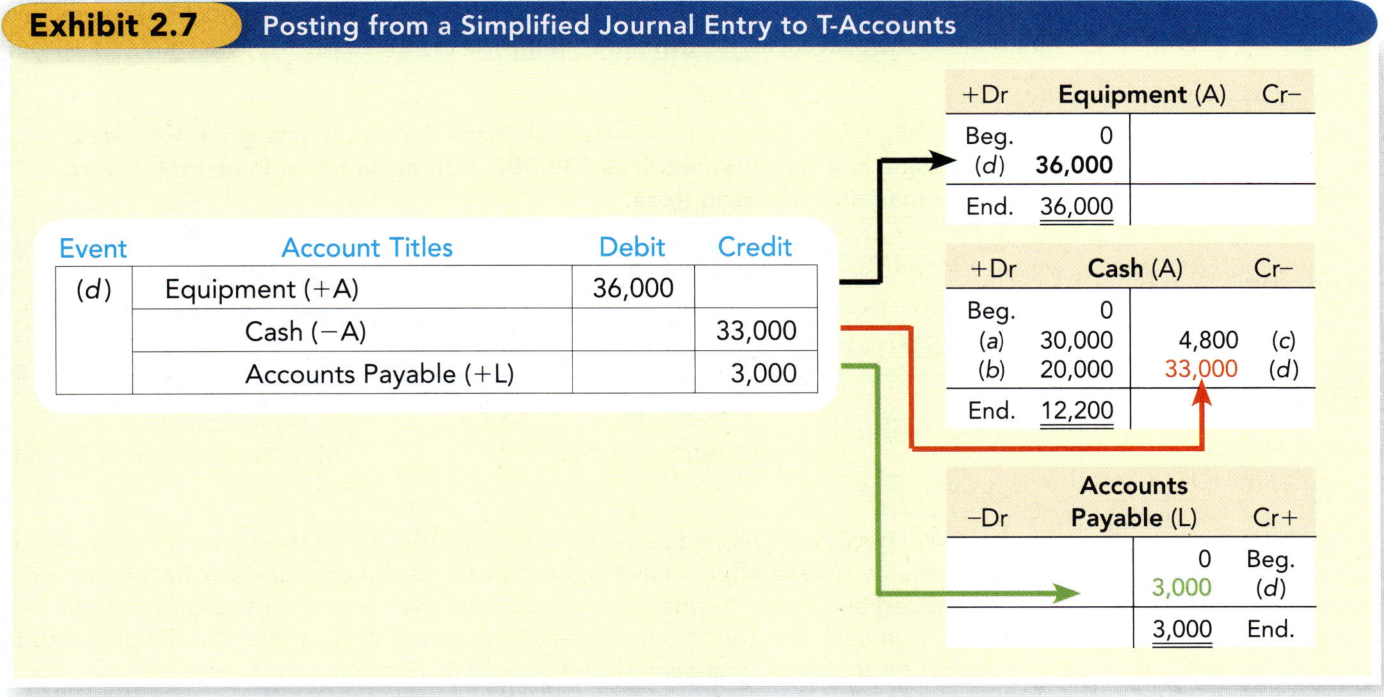

A final note on the terms *debit* and *credit:* Each word may be used as a verb, noun, and adjective. For example, you can say that Pizza Aroma's Cash account was debited (a verb) when the owner invested cash to start the business. That means that the amount was entered on the left side of the T-account. Or you can say that a credit (a noun) was entered on the right side of an account. Finally, Notes Payable may be described as a credit account (an adjective). We will use *debit* and *credit* instead of **left** and **right** throughout the rest of this textbook.

The next section illustrates the steps to follow in analyzing the effects of transactions using the transaction analysis model (Exhibit 2.4), recording those effects in journal entries (using our simplified version) and determining the account balances using T-accounts.

Pizza Aroma's Accounting Records

Mauricio hired Laurie to prepare Pizza Aroma's accounting records. She told Mauricio to keep the documents he received with each transaction. With these documents, she would be able to analyze each transaction, record the journal entries, and post the effects to the appropriate accounts. You are about to see how Laurie created the accounting records for Pizza Aroma based on the first week of activities—transactions (*a*) through (*g*) on pages 54–56—that established the new business. Laurie followed the accounting cycle process, using the simplified journal entry and T-account formats just introduced:

Coach's Tip

These critical concepts are basic to material throughout the rest of the text. The most effective way to learn it is to **practice, practice, practice—do your assigned homework!**

Step 1 **Analyze each transaction** by identifying and classifying accounts affected and the direction of the effects, checking to make sure that the accounting equation remains in balance and that debits equal credits in the double-entry recordkeeping system.

Step 2 **Record the journal entry,** reflecting the effects of the transaction on the accounting equation. Use the transaction letters (*a*) to (*g*) as references.

Step 3 **Post the effects** of each line of the journal entry to the appropriate T-account. Because Pizza Aroma is a new company, all beginning balances in the T-accounts (located in the margins of the following pages) will be $0.

Mauricio wanted to see what Laurie had prepared because he knew the information would help him in making future business decisions. On the morning before he opened the doors for his first day of business, Laurie explained everything to him. Just as she advised Mauricio, we urge you to **study this illustration carefully,** including the explanations of transaction analysis. Careful study is **essential** to understanding (1) the accounting model, (2) transaction analysis, (3) the dual effects of each transaction, and (4) the balancing concepts.

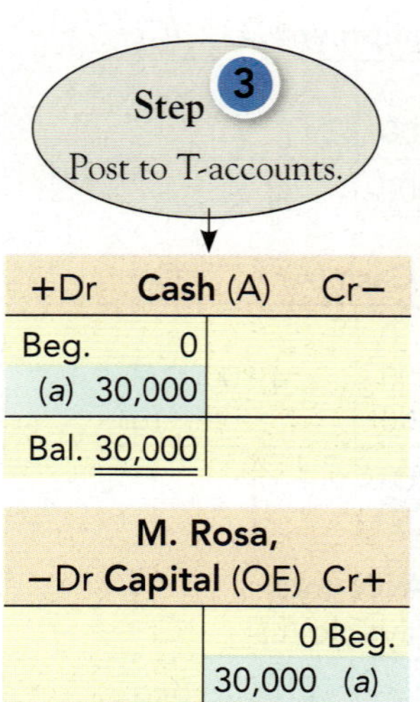

+Dr	Cash (A)	Cr−
Beg.	0	
(*a*)	30,000	
Bal.	30,000	

−Dr	M. Rosa, Capital (OE)	Cr+
	0	Beg.
	30,000	(*a*)
	30,000	Bal.

(*a*) INVESTMENT BY OWNER: To establish Pizza Aroma, a new gourmet pizza restaurant, the business receives $30,000 cash as an initial investment from owner-manager Mauricio Rosa.

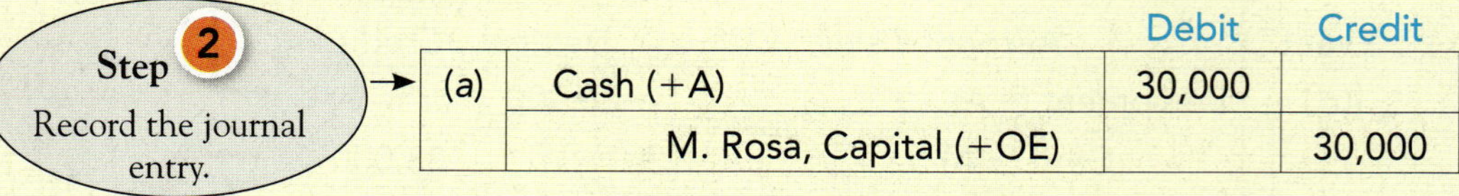

		Debit	Credit
(*a*)	Cash (+A)	30,000	
	M. Rosa, Capital (+OE)		30,000

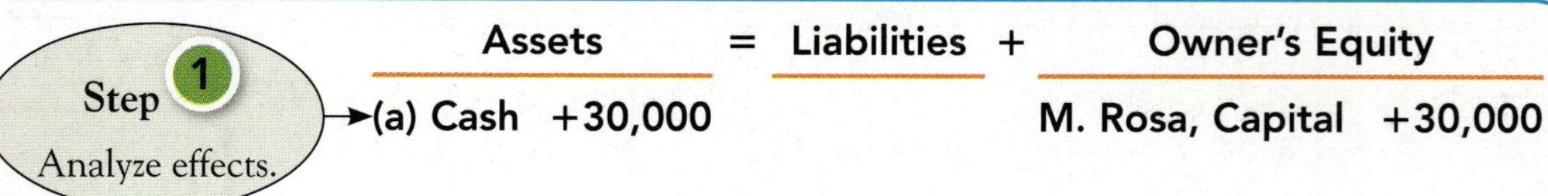

Equality checks: (1) Debits $30,000 = Credits $30,000; (2) the accounting equation is in balance. **These effects have been posted to the appropriate T-accounts** (see the shaded amounts). To post the amounts, transfer or copy the debit or credit amount on each line to the appropriate T-account. For example, the $30,000 debit is listed on the debit (increase) side of the Cash T-account.

(*b*) BORROW FROM BANK: Mauricio negotiates with a local bank and signs a three-year, $20,000 note in Pizza Aroma's name (a liability of the business).

		Debit	Credit
(*b*)	Cash (+A)	20,000	
	Notes Payable (+L)		20,000

Assets		=	Liabilities		+	Owner's Equity
(*b*) **Cash**	**+20,000**		**Notes Payable**	**+ 20,000**		

Equality checks: (1) Debits $20,000 = Credits $20,000; (2) the accounting equation is in balance.

+Dr Cash (A)	Cr−
Beg. 0	
(*a*) 30,000	
(*b*) 20,000	
Bal. 50,000	

−Dr Notes Payable (L)	Cr+
	0 Beg.
	20,000 (*b*)
	20,000 Bal.

(*c*) PREPAY RENT: Pizza Aroma pays $4,800 in advance to the building owner to cover rent for the store for May through October (six months).

		Debit	Credit
(*c*)	Prepaid Rent (+A)	4,800	
	Cash (−A)		4,800

Assets		=	Liabilities	+	Owner's Equity
(*c*) **Cash**	**− 4,800**				
Prepaid Rent	**+ 4,800**				

Equality checks: (1) Debits $4,800 = Credits $4,800; (2) the accounting equation is in balance.

+Dr Cash (A)	Cr−
Beg. 0	
(*a*) 30,000	4,800 (*c*)
(*b*) 20,000	
Bal. 45,200	

+Dr Prepaid Rent (A)	Cr−
Beg. 0	
(*c*) 4,800	
Bal. 4,800	

(*d*) PURCHASE EQUIPMENT: A construction company renovates the store and installs equipment at a cost of $36,000; Pizza Aroma pays $33,000 in cash and promises to pay the balance next month.

		Debit	Credit
(*d*)	Equipment (+A)	36,000	
	Cash (−A)		33,000
	Accounts Payable (+L)		3,000

Assets		=	Liabilities		+	Owner's Equity
(*d*) **Equipment**	**+ 36,000**		**Accounts Payable**	**+ 3,000**		
Cash	**− 33,000**					

Equality checks: (1) Debits $36,000 = Credits $36,000; (2) the accounting equation is in balance.

+Dr Cash (A)	Cr−
Beg. 0	
(*a*) 30,000	4,800 (*c*)
(*b*) 20,000	33,000 (*d*)
Bal. 12,200	

+Dr Equipment (A)	Cr−
Beg. 0	
(*d*) 36,000	
Bal. 36,000	

−Dr Accounts Payable (L)	Cr+
	0 Beg.
	3,000 (*d*)
	3,000 Bal.

(*e*) PURCHASE SUPPLIES: Pizza Aroma orders and receives $2,000 in supplies on account from local fresh food suppliers.

		Debit	Credit
(*e*)	Supplies (+A)	2,000	
	Accounts Payable (+L)		2,000

Assets		=	Liabilities		+	Owner's Equity
(*e*) **Supplies**	**+ 2,000**		**Accounts Payable**	**+ 2,000**		

Equality checks: (1) Debits $2,000 = Credits $2,000; (2) the accounting equation is in balance.

+Dr Supplies (A)	Cr−
Beg. 0	
(*e*) 2,000	
Bal. 2,000	

−Dr Accounts Payable (L)	Cr+
	0 Beg.
	3,000 (*d*)
	2,000 (*e*)
	5,000 Bal.

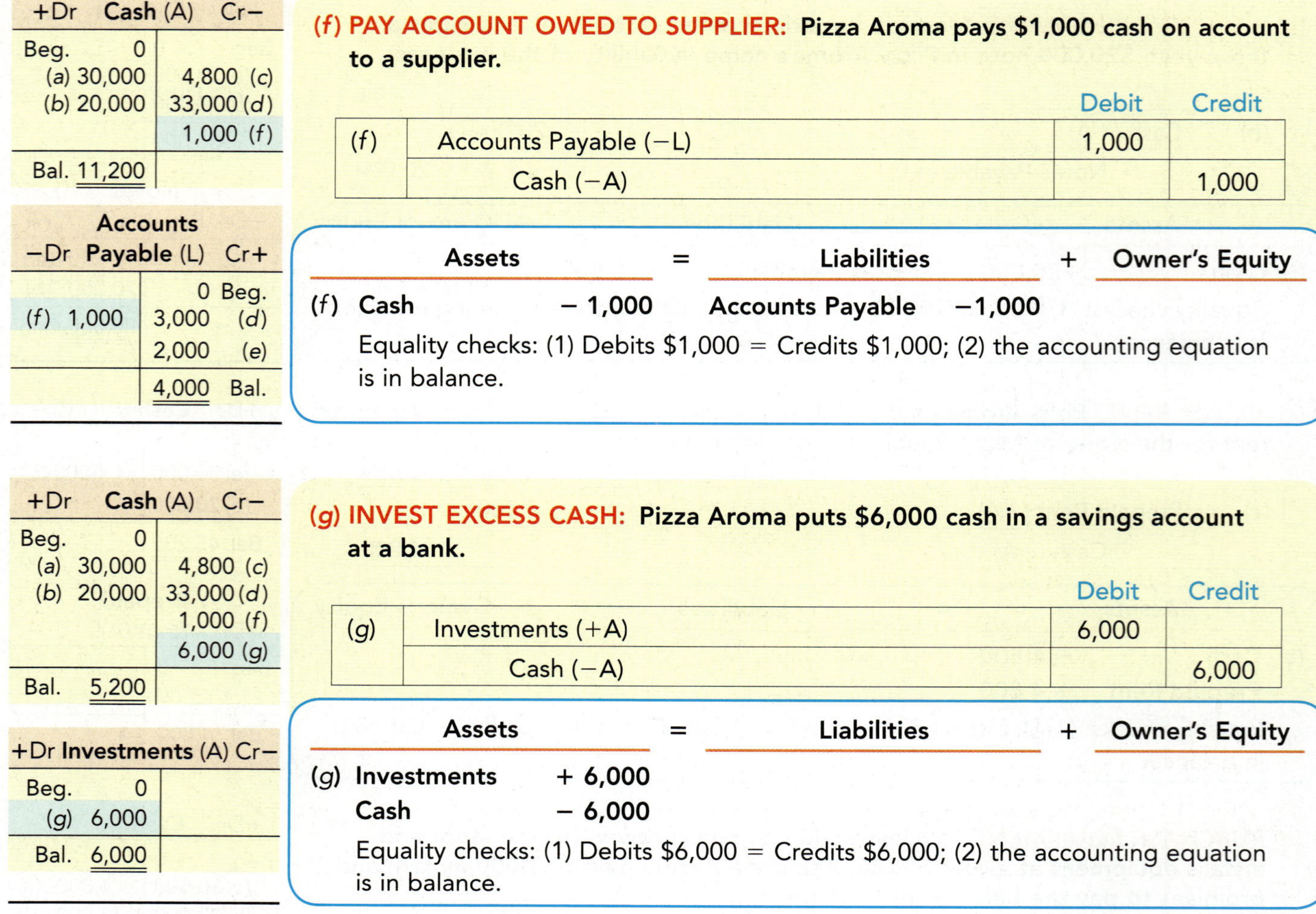

+Dr Cash (A) Cr−	
Beg. 0	
(a) 30,000	4,800 (c)
(b) 20,000	33,000 (d)
	1,000 (f)
Bal. 11,200	

−Dr Accounts Payable (L) Cr+	
	0 Beg.
(f) 1,000	3,000 (d)
	2,000 (e)
	4,000 Bal.

(f) PAY ACCOUNT OWED TO SUPPLIER: Pizza Aroma pays $1,000 cash on account to a supplier.

		Debit	Credit
(f)	Accounts Payable (−L)	1,000	
	Cash (−A)		1,000

Assets		=	Liabilities		+	Owner's Equity
(f) Cash	− 1,000		Accounts Payable	−1,000		

Equality checks: (1) Debits $1,000 = Credits $1,000; (2) the accounting equation is in balance.

+Dr Cash (A) Cr−	
Beg. 0	
(a) 30,000	4,800 (c)
(b) 20,000	33,000 (d)
	1,000 (f)
	6,000 (g)
Bal. 5,200	

+Dr Investments (A) Cr−	
Beg. 0	
(g) 6,000	
Bal. 6,000	

(g) INVEST EXCESS CASH: Pizza Aroma puts $6,000 cash in a savings account at a bank.

		Debit	Credit
(g)	Investments (+A)	6,000	
	Cash (−A)		6,000

Assets		=	Liabilities	+	Owner's Equity
(g) Investments	+ 6,000				
Cash	− 6,000				

Equality checks: (1) Debits $6,000 = Credits $6,000; (2) the accounting equation is in balance.

In addition to these transactions, two more activities took place during the first week of May:

- Mauricio hired two people to help him during the lunch and dinner hours beginning on May 8, the restaurant's opening. Because the employees have not yet worked for Pizza Aroma, the business does not yet owe them anything. The only thing that has occurred is an exchange of promises—Mauricio's promise to pay the employees and their promise to work. Hiring employees who have not yet provided any service to the business is not an accounting transaction, so nothing needs to be recorded.
- Mauricio used his personal funds to buy a larger car for his family. As you read in the epilogue of Chapter 1, he was about to expand his family, so he needed a bigger car. Under the separate entity assumption, each business must be accounted for as an individual organization, separate and apart from its owners. Therefore, this transaction does not affect Pizza Aroma.

Exhibit 2.8 summarizes the journal entries and T-accounts for transactions (*a*) through (*g*). Because this is a new company, the beginning balances in the T-accounts are $0.

Preparing a Trial Balance

We have just used the accounting system to capture the economic events that occurred during the first week of Pizza Aroma's existence. In that week, the business obtained financing from its owner and creditors and acquired the assets necessary to run the restaurant. So what was Pizza Aroma's financial position immediately before it opened its doors? To answer this question, we need to prepare a balance sheet for the end of the first week.

Exhibit 2.8 Summary of Pizza Aroma Transactions: Journal Entries and T-Accounts

Pizza Aroma
Journal Entries
May 1–7

		Debit	Credit
(a)	Cash (+A)	30,000	
	M. Rosa, Capital (+OE)		30,000
(b)	Cash (+A)	20,000	
	Notes Payable (+L)		20,000
(c)	Prepaid Rent (+A)	4,800	
	Cash (−A)		4,800
(d)	Equipment (+A)	36,000	
	Cash (−A)		33,000
	Accounts Payable (+L)		3,000
(e)	Supplies (+A)	2,000	
	Accounts Payable (+L)		2,000
(f)	Accounts Payable (−L)	1,000	
	Cash (−A)		1,000
(g)	Investments (+A)	6,000	
	Cash (−A)		6,000

Pizza Aroma T-Accounts as of May 7

+Dr	**Cash** (A) Cr−
Beg. 0	
(a) 30,000	4,800 (c)
(b) 20,000	33,000 (d)
	1,000 (f)
	6,000 (g)
Bal. 5,200	

+Dr	**Equipment** (A) Cr−
Beg. 0	
(d) 36,000	
Bal. 36,000	

+Dr	**Investments** (A) Cr−
Beg. 0	
(g) 6,000	
Bal. 6,000	

+Dr	**Prepaid Rent** (A) Cr−
Beg. 0	
(c) 4,800	
Bal. 4,800	

+Dr	**Supplies** (A) Cr−
Beg. 0	
(e) 2,000	
Bal. 2,000	

−Dr	**Accounts Payable** (L) Cr+
	0 Beg.
(f) 1,000	3,000 (d)
	2,000 (e)
	4,000 Bal.

−Dr	**Notes Payable** (L) Cr+
	0 Beg.
	20,000 (b)
	20,000 Bal.

−Dr	**M. Rosa, Capital** (OE) Cr+
	0 Beg.
	30,000 (a)
	30,000 Bal.

Before the financial statements are prepared, managers usually prepare a check on the accounting system, called a **trial balance.** As Exhibit 2.9 on page 67 shows, a trial balance is a list of individual accounts (shown in the left column), usually in financial statement order (assets, liabilities, owner's equity, revenues, and expenses). The ending debit or credit balances from the T-accounts are shown in the next two columns. Notice that debit balances are placed in the left of the two columns and credit balances are placed in the right column. The total of these two columns provides a check on the equality of the debits and credits. The trial balance summarizes account balances for preparation of financial statements and for review and analysis for any adjustments that may be needed (as discussed in Chapter 4). And, again, as an internal document, dollar signs are not required.

SELF-STUDY PRACTICE

For the following events to establish Florida Flippers, a new business, analyze each transaction, record the journal entries, and then post the entries to the T-accounts at the bottom of the exercise.

(*a*) Paul Knepper invests $50,000 to establish a new scuba business, Florida Flippers, a sole proprietorship offering scuba instruction and diving services.

		Debit	Credit
(*a*)			

Assets	=	Liabilities	+	Owner's Equity
(*a*)				

Equality checks: (1) Debits ______ = Credits ______; (2) is the accounting equation in balance? ______

(*b*) On behalf of Florida Flippers, Paul buys a small building near the ocean for $250,000, paying $25,000 cash and signing a note due in 10 years for the balance.

		Debit	Credit
(*b*)			

Assets	=	Liabilities	+	Owner's Equity
(*b*)				

Equality checks: (1) Debits ______ = Credits ______; (2) is the accounting equation in balance?

+Dr **Cash** (A) Cr−	
Beg. 0	
Bal.	

+Dr **Building** (A) Cr−	
Beg. 0	
Bal.	

−Dr **Notes Payable** (L) Cr+	
	0 Beg.
	Bal.

−Dr **P. Knepper, Capital** (OE) Cr+	
	0 Beg.
	Bal.

After you have finished, check your answers with the solutions at the bottom of the page.

Solution to Self-Study Practice

Journal Entries:

		Debit	Credit
(*a*)	Cash (+A)	50,000	
	P. Knepper, Capital (+OE)		50,000
(*b*)	Building (+A)	250,000	
	Cash (−A)		25,000
	Notes Payable (+L)		225,000

Equality Checks:

(a) Debits $50,000 = Credits $50,000; equation is in balance.
(b) Debits $250,000 = Credits $250,000; equation is in balance.

Transaction Analysis:

Assets		=	Liabilities		+	Owner's Equity	
(*a*) Cash	+ 50,000					(*a*) P. Knepper, Capital	+ 50,000
(*b*) Building	+ 250,000		(*b*) Notes Payable	+ 225,000			
Cash	− 25,000						

T-Accounts:

+Dr **Cash** (A) Cr−	
Beg. 0	
(*a*) 50,000	25,000 (*b*)
Bal. 25,000	

+Dr **Building** (A) Cr−	
Beg. 0	
(*b*) 250,000	
Bal. 250,000	

−Dr **Notes Payable** (L) Cr+	
	0 Beg.
	225,000 (*b*)
	225,000 Bal.

−Dr **P. Knepper, Capital** (OE) Cr+	
	0 Beg.
	50,000 (*a*)
	50,000 Bal.

Exhibit 2.9 Trial Balance for Pizza Aroma

PIZZA AROMA

Pizza Aroma
Trial Balance
On May 7

	Debit	Credit
Cash	5,200	
Investments	6,000	
Supplies	2,000	
Prepaid Rent	4,800	
Equipment	36,000	
Accounts Payable		4,000
Notes Payable		20,000
M. Rosa, Capital		30,000
Totals	54,000	54,000

Ending balances in T-accounts in Exhibit 2.8

Trial balance provides a check on debits = credits equality

Laurie showed Mauricio the trial balance she had created for Pizza Aroma. It showed a total of $54,000 in both the debit and credit columns. Thus, the debits equaled the credits. What happens, however, when the totals do not balance?

Locating and Correcting Errors

In a manual recordkeeping system, unequal totals may occur in a trial balance as a result of human error—that is, the type of error you might make when you are doing your homework. These errors can be traced and should be corrected before you proceed through the rest of the accounting cycle. Specifically, if the two columns are not equal, errors have occurred in one or more of the following activities:

- Totaling the debit and credit columns in the trial balance.
- Copying the ending balances (the amounts and whether a debit or credit balance) from the T-accounts (in the ledger) to the trial balance.
- Computing the ending balances in the T-accounts.
- Incorrectly posting the dollar effects of a transaction from a journal entry to the T-accounts. Examples would include (1) posting a $300 cash transaction as a debit instead of a credit to Cash and (2) posting a $330 credit as a $300 credit.
- Preparing journal entries in which the debits do not equal the credits.

To locate the error that is preventing the two columns in a trial balance from balancing, start with the first bulleted item in this list—that is, recompute the two columns. If the two columns remain unequal, proceed to the second bulleted item, and so on until you have found the error.

Certain other errors may occur in both manual and computerized recordkeeping systems, but they will not be identified by the trial balance. For example, posting $300 as a credit to Accounts Payable when it should have been a $300 credit to Cash will result in Cash being $300 too high on the debit side and Accounts Payable being $300 too high on the credit side. Because the debit and credit columns will be equal, however, this error will not show up in the trial balance.

PREPARE A BALANCE SHEET

Classified Balance Sheet

Learning Objective 4

Prepare a simple classified balance sheet.

Now for Mauricio's first look at Pizza Aroma's financial position before selling any pizza! Exhibit 2.10 illustrates the May 7 balance sheet based on the transactions in this chapter. Notice that assets and liabilities have been separated into classifications—current and

Exhibit 2.10 Classified Balance Sheet for Pizza Aroma

Pizza Aroma
Balance Sheet
At May 7, 2009

ASSETS		
Current Assets		
Cash	$ 5,200	Current assets
Investments	6,000	
Supplies	2,000	
Prepaid Rent	4,800	
Total current assets	18,000	
Equipment	36,000	← Noncurrent assets
Total Assets	$54,000	
LIABILITIES AND OWNER'S EQUITY		
Current Liabilities		
Accounts Payable	$ 4,000	← Current liabilities
Total current liabilities	4,000	
Notes Payable	20,000	← Noncurrent liabilities
Owner's Equity		
M. Rosa, Capital	30,000	
Total Liabilities and Owner's Equity	$54,000	

noncurrent. This creates a classified balance sheet. Most companies list assets **in order of liquidity,** or how soon an asset is expected to be turned into cash or used.

Current assets are those resources that Pizza Aroma will use or turn into cash within one year. Cash is the most liquid asset. Then investments can be turned in for cash at the business's discretion. Next Pizza Aroma will use supplies very quickly in making pizza, while Prepaid Rent will be used over six months. The only noncurrent asset for Pizza Aroma is equipment that is expected to last several years.

Just as assets are reported in order of liquidity, liabilities are listed on the balance sheet **in order of maturity,** or how soon an obligation is to be paid in cash such as Accounts Payable or settled by providing services such as Unearned Revenue. Those liabilities that Pizza Aroma will need to pay or settle within the coming year (in cash, services, or other current assets) are classified as current liabilities. At this point, only Accounts Payable is classified as current because most accounts payable are due within one to two months. Liabilities that are owed beyond a year are classified as noncurrent liabilities. Pizza Aroma owes notes payable to the bank in three years. Distinguishing current assets and current liabilities assists external users of the financial statements in assessing the amounts and timing of future cash flows.

Limitations of the Balance Sheet

Some people mistakenly believe that the balance sheet reports what a business is worth. Because the balance sheet lists the company's assets and liabilities, they reason that the net difference between the two must be the company's worth. In fact, "net worth" is the term many accountants and analysts use when referring to owner's equity. So why is it wrong to think of the balance sheet as reporting what a business is worth?

The answer comes from knowing that accounting is based on recording and reporting **transactions,** as you have seen over and over in this chapter. This reliance on transactions has two significant implications for the balance sheet: (1) it affects what is (and is not) recorded, and (2) it affects the amounts assigned to recorded items.

1. **What is (and is not) recorded?**
   - Only measurable exchanges, such as a purchase of ovens, are recorded. Because Pizza Aroma's name was not acquired in an exchange, you will not see it on the balance sheet. The same is true of Mauricio's gourmet pizza recipes.
2. **What amounts are assigned to recorded items?**
   - Following the historical cost principle, assets and liabilities are first recorded at the amounts that were measurable and accurate at the time the transaction occurred. The cost principle does not allow increases in asset values (and decreases in liability values) to be recorded unless external exchanges have caused the change in value.
   - Does that mean that if an asset's value falls over time, it will continue to be reported at its original cost? The answer is no. **Conservatism** requires that when doubt exists about the amount at which assets and liabilities (and revenues and expenses) should be reported, the least optimistic measurement should be used. Businesses should not overstate assets and revenues or understate liabilities and expenses.

Spotlight On FINANCIAL REPORTING

The Competition

PIZZA AROMA

As in most college towns, Pizza Aroma has many competitors from other local pizza restaurants to the big chains including Pizza Hut and Papa John's. The balance sheet of Papa John's, a corporation, follows. You will notice that the structure of the balance sheet and its account titles are quite similar to Pizza Aroma's, but the amounts are significantly larger. Also, instead of ownership by a sole proprietor, approximately 30 million shareholders own Papa John's.

Papa John's International, Inc.
Balance Sheet
At December 31, 2006
(In thousands)

Assets		
Current assets		
Cash	$ 12,979	For perspective, cash is nearly $13 million. Current assets
Accounts receivable, net	23,326	
Inventories	26,729	
Prepaid expenses	7,779	
Other current assets	13,730	
Total current assets	**84,543**	
Investments	1,254	Noncurrent assets
Property and equipment, net	197,722	
Notes receivable, net	12,104	
Intangibles	67,357	
Other assets	16,659	
Total assets	**$379,639**	
Liabilities and Stockholders' Equity		
Current liabilities		
Accounts payable	$ 29,202	Current liabilities
Income and other taxes payable	15,136	
Other current liabilities	57,758	
Total current liabilities	**102,096**	
Unearned fee revenue	7,562	Noncurrent liabilities
Long-term debt	96,511	
Other long-term liabilities	27,302	
Stockholders' equity	**146,168**	
Total liabilities and stockholders' equity	**$379,639**	

Spotlight On ETHICS

Motivation to Be Conservative

Why are accountants conservative? It is primarily because they know that outsiders such as bankers and owners who are not active in their businesses (or investors in the case of corporations) are going to use the financial statements to make decisions, and accountants do not want to mislead them. This is a very important ethical issue to accountants. If owners invest additional amounts into their businesses after relying on financial statements with inflated amounts for assets (and revenues) and amounts for liabilities (and expenses) that are too low, they may lose their money when things go wrong in the business. So, when faced with uncertainty about the numbers, accountants take a conservative approach.

Summary of the Accounting Cycle

Before Mauricio opens Pizza Aroma's newly painted doors for business, let's summarize the accounting cycle process in which the effects of business events move from the journal and the ledger to the company's balance sheet. Exhibit 2.11 illustrates the process for a fictitious construction company.

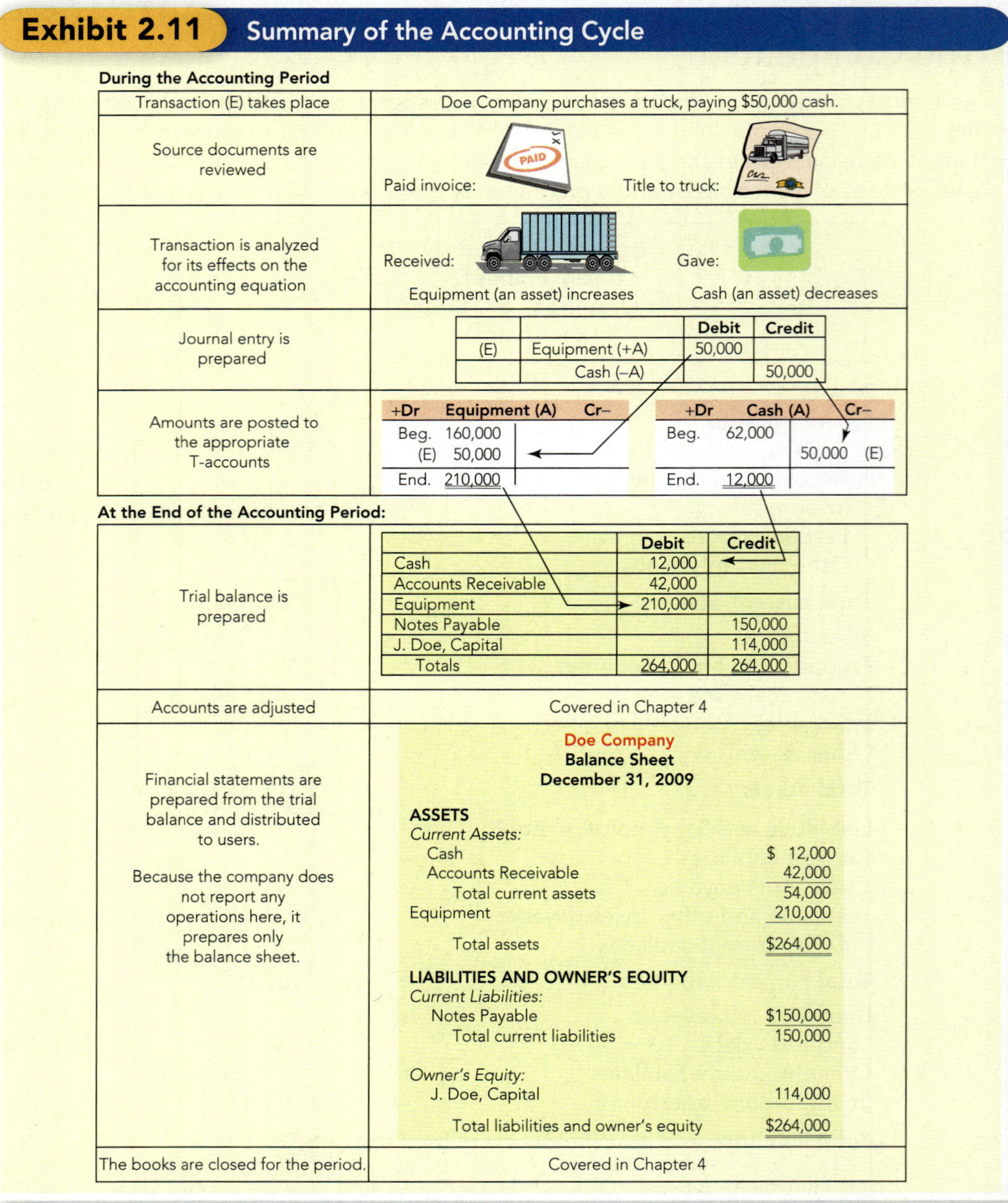

Exhibit 2.11 Summary of the Accounting Cycle

During the Accounting Period

Step	Illustration
Transaction (E) takes place	Doe Company purchases a truck, paying $50,000 cash.
Source documents are reviewed	Paid invoice: [PAID] Title to truck:
Transaction is analyzed for its effects on the accounting equation	Received: Equipment (an asset) increases. Gave: Cash (an asset) decreases
Journal entry is prepared	see journal entry below
Amounts are posted to the appropriate T-accounts	see T-accounts below

Journal entry:

		Debit	Credit
(E)	Equipment (+A)	50,000	
	Cash (–A)		50,000

T-accounts:

+Dr Equipment (A)	Cr–
Beg. 160,000	
(E) 50,000	
End. 210,000	

+Dr Cash (A)	Cr–
Beg. 62,000	
	50,000 (E)
End. 12,000	

At the End of the Accounting Period:

Trial balance is prepared

	Debit	Credit
Cash	12,000	
Accounts Receivable	42,000	
Equipment	210,000	
Notes Payable		150,000
J. Doe, Capital		114,000
Totals	264,000	264,000

Accounts are adjusted — Covered in Chapter 4

Financial statements are prepared from the trial balance and distributed to users.

Because the company does not report any operations here, it prepares only the balance sheet.

Doe Company
Balance Sheet
December 31, 2009

ASSETS	
Current Assets:	
Cash	$ 12,000
Accounts Receivable	42,000
Total current assets	54,000
Equipment	210,000
Total assets	$264,000
LIABILITIES AND OWNER'S EQUITY	
Current Liabilities:	
Notes Payable	$150,000
Total current liabilities	150,000
Owner's Equity:	
J. Doe, Capital	114,000
Total liabilities and owner's equity	$264,000

The books are closed for the period. — Covered in Chapter 4

As you can see, you need to know quite a bit about accounting to interpret and use financial statements intelligently. In this chapter, we focused on the transactions that establish a business. Next, you need to learn how the accounting system handles transactions related to operating activities, and how to report the effects of those transactions in the income statement. Those topics will be the focus of Chapters 3 and 4.

Demonstration Case

On April 1, 2010, Steve Delancey, a college student, started Goodbye Grass, a lawn care service business. Goodbye Grass's transactions to establish the business through April 30, 2010, follows:

(*a*) Received cash totaling $9,000 from Steve who will be the owner-manager of the business.

(*b*) Acquired rakes and other hand tools (equipment) for $600, paying the hardware store $200 cash and agreeing informally to pay the balance in three months.

(*c*) Ordered lawn mowers and edgers costing $4,000 from XYZ Lawn Supply, Inc.

(*d*) Purchased four acres of land for the future site of a storage garage; paid cash, $5,000.

(*e*) Received the mowers and edgers that had been ordered in (*c*), and signed a promissory note to pay XYZ Lawn Supply in full in 60 days.

(*f*) Sold one acre of land to the city for a park for $1,250, and accepted a note from the city indicating that Goodbye Grass will receive payment in six months.

(*g*) Steve borrowed $3,000 from a local bank for personal use.

Required:

1. Analyze each event to determine its effects on the accounting equation for Goodbye Grass.
2. Prepare journal entries to record the transactions (*a*)–(*g*).
3. Set up T-accounts for Cash, Note Receivable (from the city), Equipment (hand tools and mowing equipment), Land, Accounts Payable (to hardware store), Note Payable (to the equipment supply company), and S. Delancey, Capital. Indicate the beginning balances of $0 in each T-account, and then summarize the effects of each journal entry in the appropriate T-accounts.
4. Use the amounts in the T-accounts developed in requirement 3 to prepare a *classified* balance sheet for Goodbye Grass at April 30, 2010. Show the balances for all assets, liabilities, and owner's equity accounts.
5. As of April 30, 2010, has financing for Goodbye Grass's assets come primarily from liabilities or owner's equity?

Coach's Tip

For possible account names, see the chart of accounts in Exhibit 2.2.

Suggested Solution

1. Analyze transactions:

	Assets				=	Liabilities		+	Owner's Equity
	Cash	Note Receivable	Equipment	Land		Accounts Payable	Note Payable		S. Delancey, Capital
Beg.	$ 0	$ 0	$ 0	$ 0	=	$ 0	$ 0		$ 0
(*a*)	+9,000				=				+9,000
(*b*)	− 200		+ 600		=	+400			
(*c*)				No change*	=	No change			
(*d*)	−5,000			+5,000	=	No change			
(*e*)			+ 4,000		=		+4,000		
(*f*)		+1,250		−1,250	=	No change			
(*g*)				No change*	=	No change			
Totals	$3,800	$1,250	$ 4,600	$3,750	=	$400	$ 4,000		$9,000
	$13,400				=	$13,400			

*Event (*c*) is not a considered a transaction because it involves only the exchange of promises. Event (*g*) is not considered a transaction of the company because the separate entity assumption (from Chapter 1) states that personal transactions of the owners are separate from transactions of the business.

2. Record journal entries:

		Debit	Credit
(*a*)	Cash (+A)	9,000	
	S. Delancey, Capital (+OE)		9,000
(*b*)	Equipment (+A)	600	
	Cash (–A)		200
	Accounts Payable (+L)		400
(*c*)	This is not an accounting transaction, so a journal entry is not needed.		
(*d*)	Land (+A)	5,000	
	Cash (–A)		5,000
(*e*)	Equipment (+A)	4,000	
	Note Payable (+L)		4,000
(*f*)	Note Receivable (+A)	1,250	
	Land (–A)		1,250
(*g*)	This is not a transaction of the business, so a journal entry is not needed.		

3. Summarize journal entries in T-accounts:

Assets = **Liabilities** + **Owner's Equity**

+Dr **Cash** (A) Cr−

	Dr	Cr	
Beg. Bal.	0		
(*a*)	9,000	200	(*b*)
		5,000	(*d*)
End.	3,800		

+Dr **Equipment** (A) Cr−

	Dr	Cr
Beg. Bal.	0	
(*b*)	600	
(*e*)	4,000	
End.	4,600	

−Dr **Accounts Payable** (L) Cr+

Dr	Cr	
	0	Beg. Bal.
	400	(*b*)
	400	End.

Owner's Equity

−Dr **S. Delancey, Capital** (OE) Cr+

Dr	Cr	
	0	Beg. Bal.
	9,000	(*a*)
	9,000	End.

+Dr **Note Receivable** (A) Cr−

	Dr	Cr
Beg. Bal.	0	
(*f*)	1,250	
End.	1,250	

+Dr **Land** (A) Cr−

	Dr	Cr	
Beg. Bal.	0		
(*d*)	5,000	1,250	(*f*)
End.	3,750		

−Dr **Note Payable** (L) Cr+

Dr	Cr	
	0	Beg. Bal.
	4,000	(*e*)
	4,000	End.

4. Prepare a classified balance sheet from the T-accounts:

GOODBYE GRASS
Balance Sheet
At April 30, 2010

Assets		**Liabilities**	
Current Assets		*Current Liabilities*	
Cash	$ 3,800	Accounts Payable	$ 400
Note Receivable	1,250	Note Payable	4,000
Total Current Assets	5,050	Total Current Liabilities	4,400
Equipment	4,600		
Land	3,750	**Owner's Equity**	
		S. Delancey, Capital	9,000
Total Assets	$13,400	Total Liabilities and Owner's Equity	$13,400

5. The primary source of financing for Goodbye Grass's assets (totaling $13,400) has come from owner's equity ($9,000) rather than liabilities ($4,400).

Supplement 2A

Accounting Concepts Revisited

Recall from Chapter 1 that accounting is an information system designed to capture and communicate the results of business activities to decision makers. The word *capture* suggests the need for guidelines on how relevant business activities should be identified and measured. The word *communicate* suggests the need for guidelines on what to report and how to report it. Learning and understanding these key concepts will be helpful to you as you study because learning **how** the accounting process works will be easier if you know **why** the system works in a certain way. For a brief review of the key concepts that accountants follow in establishing **generally accepted accounting principles (GAAP),** see Exhibit 2.12.

Objective of Financial Reporting. The primary objective of financial reporting is to **provide useful economic information about a business in order to help external parties, primarily investors (in corporations) and creditors, to make sound financial decisions.** These external **decision makers** include, among others, current and potential owners, lenders, suppliers, customers, government agencies, and experts who provide financial advice. Certainly the bank that lends money to Pizza Aroma is a key external party that is most interested in the business's financial performance and condition. All decision makers are expected to have a reasonable understanding of accounting concepts and procedures—which may be one reason you are studying accounting.

Qualitative Characteristics of Financial Information. The information provided to external users of the financial statements must be **relevant.** Thus, it should be provided on a timely basis, and it should help users to assess both how well the company has met its past goals and how well it may be expected to do in the future. The information should also be **reliable.** Reliable information is not biased (that is, it does not favor any one party over another), and it can be verified (that is, others who review the evidence will arrive at the same result). Finally, information is of high quality when it is **comparable** to that of other companies and **consistent** in the use of measurement rules over time.

Elements of the Financial Statements. The elements of the financial statements are the categories of information to be measured and reported. On the balance sheet, the elements include assets, liabilities, and owner's equity.

Assets are resources with probable future benefits owned or controlled by the business as a result of past transactions. In other words, they are the resources the business can use to operate in the future.

Liabilities are probable debts or obligations (claims to a company's assets) that result from past transactions and will be paid for with assets or services in the future. Distinguishing between a company's current assets and current liabilities helps external users of the financial statements to assess the amount and timing of the company's future cash flows.

Owner's equity includes investments by the owner and the accumulated net income (or losses) from business operations (covered in Chapter 3), less any amounts withdrawn by the owner. The only investor in Pizza Aroma is Mauricio Rosa, the owner. His owner's equity account is called M. Rosa, Capital.

Accounting Assumptions. To measure and report the elements of the financial statements, accountants make four assumptions. Under the **separate entity assumption,** each business must be accounted for as an individual organization, separate and apart from its owners, all other persons, and other entities. Under the **monetary unit assumption,** each business accounts for and reports its financial results in terms of the national monetary unit (dollars in the United States, yen in Japan, euros in Germany).

Exhibit 2.12 Key Concepts for External Financial Reporting

Objective of External Financial Reporting

To provide useful economic information to external users for decision making

Useful information is:

- Relevant, Reliable, Comparable, and Consistent

Elements to be measured and reported

- Assets, Liabilities, Owner's Equity, Revenues, and Expenses

Concepts for Measuring and Reporting Information:

- **Assumptions:** Separate Entity, Monetary Unit, Continuity, Time Period
- **Principles:** Historical Cost, Revenue Recognition, Matching, Full Disclosure
- **Exceptions:** Cost benefit, Materiality, Conservatism, Industry Practices

Concepts in red are discussed in Chapters 1 and 2. Those in black will be discussed in Chapters 3 and 4.

A third basic assumption is important in understanding the information on the balance sheet. Under the continuity assumption (sometimes called the **going-concern assumption**), a business is assumed to continue operating long enough to meet its contractual commitments and plans. In future chapters (unless otherwise indicated), we will assume that the businesses we are discussing, including Pizza Aroma, meet the continuity assumption. The fourth assumption, time period, is discussed in Chapter 3.

Accounting Principles. Four principles guide the rules for measuring and reporting accounting transactions. For assets and liabilities, the **historical cost principle** states that on the date of the acquisition, cost is measured as the cash paid plus the dollar value at that time of any assets, privileges, or rights also given in the exchange. For example, if you trade your computer plus cash for a new car, the new car's cost equals the cash paid plus the computer's market value. Thus, in most cases, cost is relatively easy to determine and can be verified. The revenue, matching, and full disclosure principles are discussed in Chapter 3.

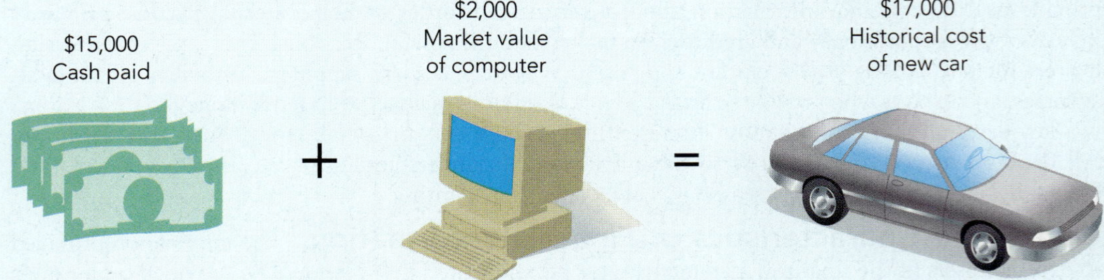

Constraints. In this chapter we introduced the constraint of **conservatism,** which requires that when doubt exists about the amount at which assets and liabilities should be reported, the least optimistic measurement should be used. If the value of an asset falls permanently below its historical cost, then the amount recorded for the asset should be reduced to that lower amount. Other constraints will be introduced in future chapters.

Chapter Summary

LO1 Identify what constitutes a business transaction and recognize common balance sheet account titles used in business. p. 50

- Nature of Business Transactions
  Transactions include:
  External exchanges—measurable exchanges of assets and services from one company for other assets or promises to pay from another company, and
  Internal events—those that are not exchanges between the business and others, but which have a direct and measurable effect on the entity, including use of supplies and use of a building over many years.
- Balance Sheet Accounts
  Typical balance sheet account titles include the following:
  Assets: Cash, Accounts Receivable, Inventories, Supplies, Buildings, and Equipment.
  Liabilities: Accounts Payable and Notes Payable.
  Owner's Equity: "Owner's Name," Capital.

LO2 Apply transaction analysis to simple business transactions in terms of the accounting model: Assets = Liabilities + Owner's Equity. p. 52

- Transaction Analysis
  Transaction analysis is based on dual effects and the basic accounting equation. *Dual effects* means that every transaction affects at least two accounts.
  - Transaction analysis follows a systematic approach: (1) determine whether a transaction exists; (2) examine the transaction for the accounts affected, classifying the accounts as assets, liabilities, or owner's equity and identifying the direction and amount of the effects; and (3) evaluate whether the accounting equation remains in balance.

LO3 Determine the impact of business transactions on the balance sheet using two basic tools, journal entries and T-accounts. p. 57

- The Accounting Cycle
  - During the accounting period, when a transaction occurs, it is analyzed, its effects are recorded in the general journal (using journal entries), and the amounts are posted to the general ledger (similar to T-accounts).
  - At the end of the accounting period, a trial balance is prepared; adjustments are analyzed, recorded, and posted; financial statements are prepared; and the records are closed.

- **Analyzing Business Transactions**
    - *Debit* is the left side of the T-account, and *credit* is the right side of the T-account.
    - Debits increase assets and decrease liabilities and owner's equity.
    - Credits decrease assets and increase liabilities and owner's equity.
- **Recording Transaction Effects**
  Journal entries express, in debit-equals-credit form, the effects of a transaction on various asset, liability, and owner's equity accounts. Journal entries are used to record financial information in the accounting system, which is later summarized by account in the ledger (T-accounts).
- **Posting Transaction Effects**
  T-accounts are a simplified version of the ledger, which summarizes transaction effects for each account. For assets, T-accounts show increases on the left (debit) side which are on the left side of the accounting equation, and decreases on the right (credit) side. For liabilities and owner's equity, T-accounts show increases on the right (credit) side which are on the right side of the accounting equation, and decreases on the left (debit) side.
- **Preparing a Trial Balance**
  A *trial balance* is prepared at the end of the accounting period prior to preparing the financial statements. Each account is listed along with its debit or credit balance (in separate columns). The purpose of the trial balance is to check that debits equal credits, summarize account balances, review and analyze necessary adjustments, and prepare financial statements.

LO4 Prepare a simple classified balance sheet. p. 67

- **Classified Balance Sheet**
  A *classified balance sheet* separately classifies assets as current if they will be used up or turned into cash within one year. Liabilities are classified as current if they will be paid, settled, or fulfilled within one year.
- **Limitations of the Balance Sheet**
    - Because accounting is transaction based, the balance sheet does not necessarily represent the current value of a business.
    - Some assets are not recorded because they do not arise from transactions.
    - The amounts recorded for assets and liabilities may not represent current values because, under the cost principle, they generally are recorded at cost, using the exchange amounts established at the time of the initial transaction.
    - The concept of conservatism states that when uncertainty exists about the value of an asset or liability, care should be taken to not overstate the reported value of assets or understate the reported value of liabilities.

Key Terms

Account (p. 51)
Accounting Cycle (p. 57)
Classified Balance Sheet (p. 68)
Conservatism (p. 69)
Continuity Assumption (p. 74)
Credit (p. 58)
Current Assets (p. 68)
Current Liabilities (p. 68)
Debit (p. 58)
Journal (p. 57)
Journal Entry (p. 58)
Ledger (p. 57)
T-account (p. 61)
Transactions (p. 50)
Trial Balance (p. 65)

See complete glossary in the back of text.

Questions

1. Define the following:
    a. Asset
    b. Current asset
    c. Liability
    d. Current liability
    e. Owner's capital
2. Define *transaction*, and give an example of each of the two types of events that are considered transactions.
3. For accounting purposes, what is an *account?* Explain why accounts are used in an accounting system.
4. What is the basic accounting equation?
5. Explain what *debit* and *credit* mean.
6. Briefly explain what *transaction analysis* means. What are the two principles underlying transaction analysis? What are the steps in performing transaction analysis?
7. What two different accounting equalities must be maintained in transaction analysis?
8. What is a *journal entry?* What is its typical format?
9. What is a *T-account?* What is its purpose?
10. What are the key features that all assets possess? What are the key features of all liabilities?
11. Explain what the following accounting terms mean:
    a. Separate entity assumption
    b. Conservatism

Multiple Choice

Quiz 2-1
www.mhhe.com/LLPW1e

1. Which of the following is not an asset?
   a. Cash
   b. Land
   c. Equipment
   d. Owner's Capital
2. Which of the following statements describe transactions that would be recorded in the accounting system?
   a. An exchange of an asset for a promise to pay.
   b. An exchange of a promise for another promise.
   c. Both of the above.
   d. None of the above.
3. Total assets on a balance sheet prepared on any date must agree with which of the following?
   a. The sum of total liabilities and net income as shown on the income statement.
   b. The sum of total liabilities and owner's equity.
   c. The sum of total liabilities and cash.
   d. The sum of total liabilities, owner's equity, and net income.
4. The dual effects concept can best be described as follows:
   a. When a transaction is recorded in the accounting system, at least two effects on the basic accounting equation will result.
   b. When an exchange takes place between two parties, both parties must record the transaction.
   c. When a transaction is recorded, both the balance sheet and the income statement must be impacted.
   d. When a transaction is recorded, one account will always increase and one account will always decrease.
5. The T-account is used to summarize which of the following?
   a. Increases and decreases to a single account in the accounting system.
   b. Debits and credits to a single account in the accounting system.
   c. Changes in specific account balances over a time period.
   d. All of the above describe how accountants use T-accounts.
6. Which of the following describes how assets are listed on the balance sheet?
   a. In alphabetical order.
   b. In order of magnitude, lowest value to highest value.
   c. From most current to least current.
   d. From least current to most current.
7. A company was recently formed with $50,000 cash invested by the owner. The company then borrowed $20,000 from a bank, and bought $10,000 of supplies on account. The company also purchased $50,000 of equipment by paying $20,000 in cash and signing a note for the remainder. What is the amount of total assets to be reported on the balance sheet?
   a. $110,000
   b. $100,000
   c. $90,000
   d. None of the above
8. Which of the following is/are true regarding *debits* and *credits?*
   a. In any given transaction, the total dollar amount of the debits and the total dollar amount of the credits must be equal.
   b. Debits decrease certain accounts and credits decrease certain accounts.
   c. Liabilities and owner's equity accounts usually end in credit balances; assets usually end in debit balances.
   d. All of the above.
9. What is/are the purpose(s) of the trial balance?
   a. To check that debits equal credits.
   b. To record the effects of transactions.
   c. To accumulate effects of transactions to determine account balances.
   d. All of the above.
10. Which of the following statements is/are true regarding the balance sheet?
   a. One cannot determine the true "current value" of a company by reviewing just its balance sheet.
   b. Certain assets that are not acquired through identifiable and measurable transactions are not reported on a company's balance sheet.
   c. A balance sheet shows only the ending balances, in a summarized format, of balance sheet accounts in the accounting system as of a particular date.
   d. All of the above.

Solutions to Multiple-Choice Questions

1. d 2. a 3. b 4. a 5. d 6. c 7. a
8. d 9. a 10. d

Mini Exercises 

Available with McGraw-Hill's Homework Manager

LO2 **M2-1 Identifying Increase and Decrease Effects on Balance Sheet Accounts**

Complete the following table by entering either the word *increases* or *decreases* in each column.

	Debit	Credit
Assets	______	______
Liabilities	______	______
Owner's equity	______	______

M2-2 Identifying Debit and Credit Effects on Balance Sheet Accounts

LO2

Complete the following table by entering either the word *debit* or *credit* in each column.

	Increase	Decrease
Assets	________	________
Liabilities	________	________
Owner's equity	________	________

M2-3 Matching Terms with Definitions

LO1, 2, 3

Match each term with its related definition by entering the appropriate letter in the space provided. There should be only one definition per term (that is, there are more definitions than terms).

Term	Definition
____ 1. Journal entry	A. Exchange of more than promises between a business and other parties.
____ 2. A = L + OE; Debits = Credits	B. Four periodic financial statements.
____ 3. Transaction	C. Two equalities in accounting that aid in providing accuracy.
____ 4. Liabilities	D. Recording results of transaction analysis in debit-equals-credit format.
____ 5. Assets	E. Account debited when money is borrowed from a bank.
____ 6. Income statement, balance sheet, statement of owner's equity, and statement of cash flows	F. Resources owned by the business with probable future economic benefits.
	G. Cumulative earnings of a company that have not been withdrawn by the owners.
	H. At least two effects for every transaction.
	I. Debts or obligations to be paid with assets or fulfilled with services.
	J. Assignment of dollar amounts to transactions.

M2-4 Classifying Accounts on a Balance Sheet

LO4

The following are a few of the accounts of Aim Delivery Service:

____ 1. Wages Payable	____ 9. Sales Taxes Payable
____ 2. Accounts Payable	____ 10. Equipment
____ 3. Accounts Receivable	____ 11. Notes Payable (due in six years)
____ 4. Buildings	____ 12. Notes Receivable (due in six months)
____ 5. Cash	____ 13. Prepaid Rent (for three months)
____ 6. "Owner's Name," Capital	____ 14. Investments (held for five months)
____ 7. Land	____ 15. Supplies
____ 8. Merchandise Inventory	____ 16. Utilities Payable

In the space provided, classify each as it would be reported on a balance sheet. Use the following code: (CA) current asset, (CL) current liability, (OE) owner's equity, (NCA) noncurrent asset, and (NCL) noncurrent liability.

M2-5 Identifying Accounts on a Classified Balance Sheet and Their Normal Debit or Credit Balances

LO1, 3
Hasbro, Inc.

According to a recent report of Hasbro, Inc., the company is "a worldwide leader in children's and family games and toys." Hasbro produces items under several brands including Tonka, Milton Bradley, Playskool, and Parker Brothers. The following are several accounts from a recent balance sheet:

a. Accounts Receivable	f. Property, Plant, and Equipment
b. Short-Term Loan (payable)	g. Accounts Payable
c. "Owners" Capital	h. Cash
d. Long-Term Debt (payable)	i. Accrued Liabilities Payable (e.g., Wages Payable)
e. Income Taxes Payable	j. Inventories

Required:

1. Indicate how each account normally should be categorized on a classified balance sheet. Use CA for current asset, NCA for noncurrent asset, CL for current liability, NCL for noncurrent liability, and OE for owner's equity
2. Indicate whether the account normally has a debit or credit balance.

LO3, 4
Blockbuster, Inc.

M2-6 Identifying Accounts on a Classified Balance Sheet and Their Normal Debit or Credit Balances

Blockbuster, Inc., is a leading global provider of rentable DVDs, videogames, and videocassettes. The following are several accounts included in a recent balance sheet:

a. Income Taxes Payable
b. Accounts Receivable
c. Movie Rental Supplies
d. "Owners'" Capital
e. Long-Term Debt
f. Property and Equipment
g. Prepaid Rent
h. Intangibles
i. Accounts Payable
j. Long-Term Liabilities
k. Cash
l. Accrued Liabilities Payable (e.g., Wages Payable)
m. Merchandise Inventories

Required:

1. Indicate how each account normally should be categorized on a classified balance sheet. Use CA for current asset, NCA for noncurrent asset, CL for current liability, NCL for noncurrent liability, and OE for owners' equity.
2. Indicate whether the account normally has a debit or credit balance.

LO1

M2-7 Identifying Events as Accounting Transactions

Do the following events result in a recordable transaction for The Toro Company? Answer yes or no for each.

____ 1. Toro purchased robotic manufacturing equipment that it paid for by signing a note payable.
____ 2. The Toro Company's president invested in another company.
____ 3. The company lent $550,000 to an employee.
____ 4. Toro ordered supplies from Office Max to be delivered next week.
____ 5. Toro received $250,000 in cash from its owners.
____ 6. The company borrowed $2,500,000 from a local bank.

LO1

M2-8 Identifying Events as Accounting Transactions

3M Company, headquartered in St. Paul, Minnesota, manufactures Post-It Notes and Scotch Tape, among many other products. With a strong commitment to sustainability, in 2006 alone, 3M expended about $18 million for capital projects related to protecting the environment. Do the following events result in a recordable transaction for 3M? Answer yes or no for each.

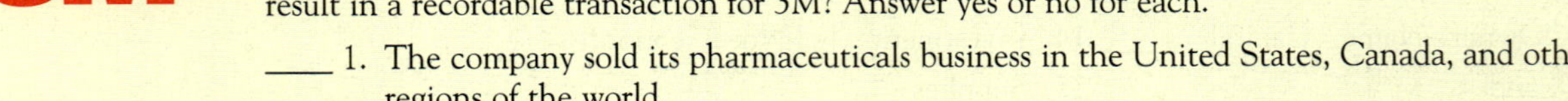

____ 1. The company sold its pharmaceuticals business in the United States, Canada, and other regions of the world.
____ 2. The company received additional investments from investors (its corporate owners).
____ 3. The company signed an agreement to rent a building in the United Kingdom; no cash was exchanged.
____ 4. The company paid for renovations to add pollution control devices to manufacturing facilities in California.
____ 5. The vice president of the company spoke at a sustainability luncheon in Indiana, which contributed to building the company's reputation as a responsible company.

LO2

M2-9 Determining Financial Statement Effects of Several Transactions

Spotlighter Company, a new sole proprietorship owned and managed by Ryan Terlecki, sells lighting fixtures. For each of the following transactions for the month of January 2009 (the first month of operations), indicate the accounts, amounts, and direction of the effects on the accounting equation. A sample is provided.

a. *(Sample)* Borrowed $3,940 from a local bank on a note due in six months.
b. Received $4,630 in cash from Ryan Terlecki.

c. Purchased $920 in equipment, paying $190 cash and promising the rest on a note due in one year.
d. Paid $372 cash for supplies.
e. Bought $700 of supplies on account.

Assets			=	Liabilities		+	Owner's Equity
a. Sample:	**Cash**	**+3,940**		**Notes Payable**	**+3,940**		

M2-10 Preparing Journal Entries LO3

For each of the transactions in M2–9 (including the sample), write the journal entry using the format shown in this chapter.

M2-11 Posting to T-Accounts LO3

For each of the transactions in M2–9 (including the sample), post the effects to the appropriate T-accounts and determine ending account balances. (*Note:* Remember to include beginning balances.)

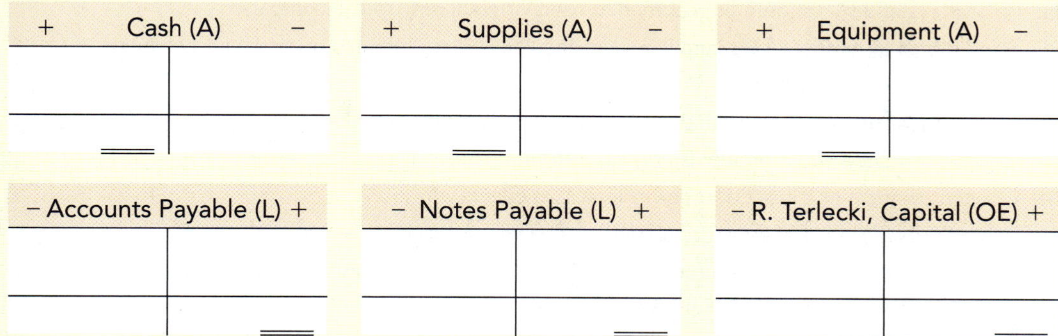

M2-12 Reporting a Classified Balance Sheet LO4

Given the transactions in M2–9 (including the sample), prepare a classified balance sheet for Spotlighter Company as of January 31, 2009.

M2-13 Preparing a Classified Balance Sheet LO4

The following accounts are taken from the financial statements of Trump Entertainments Resorts, Inc. at year-end December 31, 2006. Amounts have been rounded to the nearest thousand.

TRUMP ENTERTAINMENT RESORTS MARINA PLAZA TAJ MAHAL

General Expenses	$ 279,118	Cash	$ 127,382
Salaries Payable	28,099	Accounts Receivable	54,342
Interest Expense	130,144	Inventories	10,816
Other Assets	508,704	Other Current Assets	23,400
Accounts Payable	30,495	Property and Equipment	1,535,852
Other Current Liabilities	98,138	Long-Term Note Payable	1,690,996
Food and Beverage Revenue	123,091	"Owners'" Capital	412,768

Required:

1. Prepare a classified balance sheet at December 31, 2006. Note that some of the accounts in the list are not reported on the balance sheet.
2. Using the balance sheet, indicate whether the total assets of Trump Entertainments Resorts, Inc. at year-end were financed primarily by liabilities or owners' equity.

Exercises  Available with McGraw-Hill's Homework Manager

LO1, 2, 3

E2-1 Matching Terms with Definitions

Match each term with its related definition by entering the appropriate letter in the space provided. There should be only one definition per term (that is, there are more definitions than terms).

____ 1. Transaction	____ 6. Current assets
____ 2. Separate entity concept	____ 7. Notes payable
____ 3. Balance sheet	____ 8. Dual effects
____ 4. Liabilities	____ 9. Conservatism
____ 5. Assets = Liabilities + Owner's Equity	____ 10. Debit

A. Economic resources to be used or turned into cash within one year.
B. Reports assets, liabilities, and owner's equity.
C. Decreases assets; increases liabilities and owner's equity.
D. Increases assets; decreases liabilities and owner's equity.
E. Exchange of more than promises between a business and other parties.
F. Assumption that businesses will operate into the foreseeable future.
G. Accounts for a business separate from its owners.
H. Principle that assets should be recorded at their original cost to the company.
I. Standardized format used to accumulate data about each item reported on financial statements.
J. Basic accounting equation.
K. Two equalities in accounting that aid in providing accuracy.
L. Account credited when money is borrowed from a bank.
M. Concept that every transaction has at least two effects.
N. Debts or obligations to be paid or settled with assets or services.
O. Accounting concept that requires special care to be taken to avoid overstating assets and revenues or understating liabilities and expenses.

LO1

E2-2 Identifying Account Titles

The following are independent situations.

a. A company orders and receives 10 personal computers for office use for which it signs a note promising to pay $25,000 within three months.
b. A company purchases a new delivery truck for $21,000 cash. The truck has a $24,000 list ("sticker") price.
c. A women's clothing retailer orders 30 new display stands for $300 each for future delivery.
d. A new company is formed and the owner invests $12,000 cash.
e. A company purchases a piece of land for $50,000 cash. An appraiser for the buyer valued the land at $52,500.
f. A local company's owner buys a $10,000 car for personal use. Answer from the company's point of view.
g. A company borrows $1,000 from a local bank and signs a six-month note for the loan.
h. A company pays $1,500 owed on its note payable (ignore interest).

Required:

1. Indicate titles of the appropriate accounts, if any, affected in each of the preceding events. Consider what the business receives and gives in the exchange.
2. At what amount would you record the delivery truck in b? The piece of land in e? What measurement principle are you applying?
3. What reasoning did you apply in c? For f, what accounting concept did you apply?

LO1, 3

E2-3 Classifying Accounts and Their Usual Balances

As described in a recent annual report, Digital Diversions, Inc. (DDI) designs, develops, and distributes videogames for computers and advanced game systems such as Paystation, Y-Box, Tamecube, and Gamegirl. DDI has been operating for only one full year.

Required:

For each of the following accounts from DDI's recent balance sheet, complete the following table. Indicate whether the account is classified as a current asset (CA), noncurrent asset (NCA), current liability (CL), noncurrent liability (NCL), or owner's equity (OE), and whether the account usually has a debit (*dr*) or credit (*cr*) balance.

Account	Balance Sheet Classification	Debit or Credit Balance
1. Land	______	______
2. Wages Payable	______	______
3. Notes Payable (due in three years)	______	______
4. Accounts Receivable	______	______
5. Supplies	______	______
6. "Owners'" Capital	______	______
7. Machinery and Equipment	______	______
8. Accounts Payable	______	______
9. Cash	______	______
10. Taxes Payable	______	______

E2-4 Determining Financial Statement Effects of Several Transactions

LO1, 2

The following events occurred for Favata Company:

(*a*) Received $10,000 cash from owner, Jim Favata.

(*b*) Borrowed $7,000 cash from a bank.

(*c*) Purchased land for $12,000; paid $1,000 in cash and signed a note for the balance.

(*d*) Bought $800 of supplies on account.

(*e*) Purchased $3,000 of equipment, paying $1,000 in cash and signing a note due in six months for the rest.

Required:

For each of the events (*a*) through (*e*), perform transaction analysis and indicate the account, amount, and direction of the effect (+ for increase and − for decrease) on the accounting equation. Check that the accounting equation remains in balance after each transaction. Use the following headings:

Event	Assets	=	Liabilities	+	Owner's Equity

E2-5 Determining Financial Statement Effects of Several Transactions

LO1, 2
Nike, Inc.

Nike, Inc., with headquarters in Beaverton, Oregon, is one of the world's leading manufacturers of athletic shoes and sports apparel. The following activities occurred during a recent year. The amounts are presented in millions of dollars.

(a) Purchased $216.3 in property, plant, and equipment; paid by signing a $5.0 long-term note and fulfilling the rest with cash.

(b) Received $21.1 in cash from investors (corporate owners).

(c) One Nike owner personally borrowed $21.0 from a local bank.

Required:

1. For each of these events, perform transaction analysis and indicate the account, amount (in millions), and direction of the effect on the accounting equation. Check that the accounting equation remains in balance after each transaction. Use the following headings:

Event	Assets	=	Liabilities	+	Owner's Equity

2. Explain your response to transaction (*c*).

LO3

E2-6 Recording Activities

Refer to E2–4.

Required:

For each of the events in E2–4, prepare journal entries, checking that debits equal credits.

LO3

E2-7 Recording Activities

Refer to E2–5.

Required:

1. For each of the events in E2–5, prepare journal entries, checking that debits equal credits.
2. Explain your response to event (*c*).

LO3

E2-8 Analyzing the Effects of Transactions in T-Accounts

Julio Estella formed Estella Consulting to provide accounting and financial consulting services to clients. The following activities occurred during the year:

(*a*) Received $60,000 cash from Julio Estella to establish the sole proprietorship.

(*b*) Purchased equipment for use in the business at a cost of $12,000; one-fourth was paid in cash and the company signed a note for the balance (due in six months).

(*c*) Signed an agreement with a cleaning service to pay it $120 per week for cleaning the corporate offices, beginning next week.

(*d*) Julio Estella borrowed $10,000 for personal use from a local bank, signing a one-year note.

Required:

1. Create T-accounts for the following accounts: Cash, Equipment, Notes Payable, and Julio Estella, Capital. Beginning balances are zero. For each of the preceding transactions, record its effects in the appropriate T-accounts. Include good referencing and totals for each T-account.
2. Using the balances in the T-accounts, fill in the following amounts for the accounting equation:

Assets $ ______ = Liabilities $ ______ + Owner's Equity $ ______

3. Explain your response to events (*c*) and (*d*).

LO1

E2-9 Inferring Investing and Financing Transactions and Preparing a Balance Sheet

During its first week of operations, January 1–7, 2010, Home Comfort Furniture, a sole proprietorship owned by Sara Baine, completed six transactions with the dollar effects indicated in the following schedule:

	Assets			=	Liabilities	+	Owner's Equity
	Cash	Equipment	Land		Notes Payable		S. Baine, Capital
Beginning	$ 0	$ 0	$ 0	=	$ 0		$ 0
a.	+12,000			=			+12,000
b.	+50,000			=	+50,000		
c.	− 4,000		+12,000	=	+ 8,000		
d.	+ 4,000			=	+ 4,000		
e.	− 7,000	+7,000		=			
f.			+ 3,000	=	+ 3,000		
Ending							

Required:

1. Write a brief explanation of transactions (*a*) through (*f*). Explain any assumptions that you made.
2. Compute the ending balance in each account and prepare a classified balance sheet for Home Comfort Furniture on January 7, 2010.
3. As of January 7, 2010, has most of the financing for Home Comfort's assets come from liabilities or owner's equity?

E2-10 Explaining Investing and Financing Transactions and Preparing a Balance Sheet **LO1, 2, 3, 4**

During its first month of operations, March 2011, Faye's Fashions, a sole proprietorship owned and operated by Faye Miller, completed four transactions with the dollar effects indicated in the following schedule. Parentheses around a number are negative effects.

Accounts	DOLLAR EFFECT OF EACH OF THE FOUR TRANSACTIONS				Ending Balance
	(a)	*(b)*	*(c)*	*(d)*	
Cash	$50,000	$(4,000)	$5,000	$(4,000)	
Computer Equipment				4,000	
Delivery Truck		25,000			
Short-Term Notes Payable			5,000		
Long-Term Notes Payable		21,000			
F. Miller, Capital	50,000				

Required:

1. Write a brief explanation of transactions (*a*) through (*d*). Explain any assumptions that you made.
2. Compute the ending balance in each account and prepare a *classified* balance sheet for Faye's Fashions at the end of March 2011.
3. As of March 31, 2011, has most of the financing for Faye's Fashions' assets come from liabilities or owner's equity?

E2-11 Recording Journal Entries **LO3**

Assume that Hargett Company was organized on May 1, 2009, to compete with Stefanov Company—a company that sells office products. The following events occurred during the first month of Hargett Company's operations.

(*a*) Received $60,000 cash from Megan Hargett who organized Hargett Company.
(*b*) Borrowed $20,000 cash and signed a note due in two years.
(*c*) Ordered computer equipment costing $16,000.
(*d*) Purchased $10,000 in equipment, paying $1,000 in cash and signing a six-month note for the balance.
(*e*) Received and paid for the computer equipment ordered in (*c*).

Required:

Prepare journal entries for each transaction. Be sure to use good referencing and categorize each account as an asset (A), liability (L), or owner's equity (OE). If a transaction does not require a journal entry, explain the reason.

E2-12 Analyzing the Effects of Transactions Using T-Accounts; Preparing and Interpreting a Balance Sheet **LO1, 2, 3, 4**

Jonah Lee established Lee Delivery Company in 2010. The following transactions occurred during the year:

(*a*) Received $90,000 cash from Jonah Lee, the sole owner.
(*b*) Purchased land for $12,000, signing a two-year note (ignore interest).
(*c*) Bought two used delivery trucks at the start of the year at a cost of $10,000 each; paid $2,000 cash and signed a note due in three years for the rest (ignore interest).
(*d*) Sold one-fourth of the land for $3,000 to Birkins Moving, which signed a note agreeing to pay Lee Delivery Company in six months (ignore interest).
(*e*) Paid $52,000 cash to construct a garage for the trucks.
(*f*) Jonah Lee paid $122,000 cash for land for his personal use.

Required:

1. Analyze each item for its effects on the financial statements of Lee Delivery Company for the year ended December 31, 2010. Transaction (*a*) is presented as an example:

	Assets	=	Liabilities	+	Owner's Equity
	Cash				J. Lee, Capital
(*a*)	+90,000	=			+90,000

2. Record the effects of each item into a journal entry, using the simplified journal entry format shown in the chapter.
3. Summarize the effects of the journal entries by account, using the T-account format shown in the chapter.
4. Prepare a *classified* balance sheet for Lee Delivery Company on December 31, 2010.
5. Using the balance sheet, indicate whether Lee Delivery Company's assets at year-end were financed primarily by liabilities or owner's equity.

LO3 **E2-13 Explaining the Effects of Transactions on Balance Sheet Accounts Using T-Accounts**
Mashu Furniture Repair Service, a company owned by sole proprietor Doreen Mashu, began operations on June 1, 2009. The following T-accounts indicate the activities for the month of June.

Cash (A)	
Beg. 0	
(*a*) 17,000	10,000 (*b*)
	1,500 (*c*)

Supplies (A)	
Beg. 0	
(*c*) 1,500	

Building (A)	
Beg. 0	
(*b*) 50,000	

Notes Payable (L)	
	0 Beg.
	40,000 (*b*)

D. Mashu, Capital (OE)	
	0 Beg.
	17,000 (*a*)

Required:

Explain events (*a*) through (*c*) that resulted in the entries in the T-accounts. That is, for each account what transactions made it increase and/or decrease?

LO3 **E2-14 Analyzing the Effects of Transactions Using T-Accounts**
Ekar Company, formed by Catherine Ekar, has been operating for one year (2009). At the start of 2010, Ekar's T-account balances were as follows:

Assets:

Cash	
5,000	

Short-Term Investments	
2,000	

Equipment	
4,000	

Liabilities:

Short-Term Notes Payable	
	300

Long-Term Notes Payable	
	600

Owner's Equity:

C. Ekar, Capital	
	10,100

Required:

1. Using the data from these T-accounts, determine the amounts for the following on January 1, 2010:

Assets $ ______ = Liabilities $ ______ + Owner's Equity $ ______

2. Enter the following 2010 transactions in the T-accounts:
   (*a*) Sold $1,500 of the investments for $1,500 cash.
   (*b*) Sold one-fourth of the equipment for $1,000 in cash.
   (*c*) Borrowed $2,600 from a local bank, signing a note due in three years (ignore interest).
   (*d*) Paid $300 cash on a short-term note payable (ignore interest).
3. Compute ending balances in the T-accounts to determine amounts for the following on December 31, 2010:

Assets $ ______ = Liabilities $ ______ + Owner's Equity $ ______

Problems—Set A  Available with McGraw-Hill's Homework Manager

PA2-1 Determining Financial Statement Effects of Various Transactions LO1, 2

Lester's Home Healthcare Services was established on January 1, 2009, by Jennifer Lester, who invested $40,000 in the company. During the first month (January 2009), the company had the following five events:

(*a*) Collected a total of $40,000 from owner Jennifer Lester.

(*b*) Purchased a building for $65,000, equipment for $16,000, and three acres of land for $12,000; paid $13,000 in cash and signed a note for the balance that is due to be paid in 15 years. (*Note:* Five different accounts are affected.)

(*c*) Jennifer Lester personally lent $5,000 cash to another business.

(*d*) Purchased supplies for $3,000 cash.

(*e*) Sold one acre of land for $4,000 cash to another company.

Required:

1. Was Lester's Home Healthcare Services organized as a sole proprietorship, partnership, or corporation? Explain the basis for your answer.
2. During the first month, the records of the company were inadequate. You were asked to prepare the summary of the preceding transactions. To develop a quick assessment of their economic effects on Lester's Home Healthcare Services, you have decided to complete the spreadsheet that follows and to use plus (+) for increases and minus (−) for decreases for each account. Transaction (a) is presented as an example.

	Assets					=	Liabilities	+	Owner's Equity
	Cash	Supplies	Land	Building	Equipment		Notes Payable		J. Lester, Capital
(*a*)	+40,000					=			+40,000

3. How did you handle transaction (*c*) between Jennifer Lester and the other business? Why?
4. Based only on the completed spreadsheet, provide the following amounts (show computations):
   a. Total assets at the end of the month.
   b. Total liabilities at the end of the month.
   c. Total owner's equity at the end of the month.
   d. Cash balance at the end of the month.
   e. Total current assets at the end of the month.
5. As of January 31, 2009, has the financing for Lester's Home Healthcare Services investment in assets primarily come from liabilities or owner's equity?

PA2-2 Recording and Posting Transactions; Preparing and Interpreting the Balance Sheet LO2, 3, 4

eXcel www.mhhe.com/LLPW1e

Owner-manager Nicole Cade established Athletic Performance Company as a sole proprietorship on July 1, 2010. The company's chart of accounts included the following:

Accounts Payable	N. Cade, Capital
Building	Notes Payable
Cash	Supplies
Equipment	

During the month of July, the company had the following activities:

(*a*) Received $200,000 cash from Nicole Cade.

(*b*) Borrowed $30,000 cash from a local bank, payable June 30, 2012.

(*c*) Bought a factory building for $141,000; paid $41,000 in cash and signed a three-year note for the balance.

(*d*) Paid cash for equipment that cost $100,000.

(*e*) Purchased supplies for $10,000 on account.

Required:

1. Analyze transactions (*a*)–(*e*) to determine their effects on the accounting equation. Use the format shown in the demonstration case on page 71.

2. Record the transaction effects determined in requirement 1 using a journal entry format.
3. Summarize the journal entry effects from requirement 2 using T-accounts.
4. Prepare a *classified* balance sheet at July 31, 2010.
5. As of July 31, 2010, has the financing for Athletic Performance Company's assets primarily come from liabilities or owner's equity?

LO2, 3, 4

PA2-3 Recording and Posting Transactions; Preparing and Interpreting the Balance Sheet

Deliberate Speed Company was established as a sole proprietorship by Andrew Nguyen on July 1, 2009. The company's accounts at July 1, 2011, included the following:

Accounts Payable	$ 10,000	Equipment	$118,000
A. Nguyen, Capital	439,000	Land	200,000
Cash	26,000	Notes Payable	2,000
Factory Building	100,000	Supplies	7,000

During the month of July, the company had the following activities:

(*a*) Received $400,000 cash as an additional investment from Andrew Nguyen.

(*b*) Borrowed $90,000 cash from a local bank, payable June 30, 2013.

(*c*) Bought a factory building for $182,000; paid $82,000 in cash and signed a three-year note for the balance.

(*d*) Paid cash for equipment that cost $200,000.

(*e*) Purchased supplies for $30,000 on account.

Required:

1. Analyze transactions (*a*)–(*e*) to determine their effects on the accounting equation. Use the format shown in the demonstration case on page 71.
2. Record the transaction effects determined in requirement 1 using a journal entry format.
3. Summarize the journal entry effects from requirement 2 using T-accounts.
4. Prepare a *classified* balance sheet at July 31, 2011.
5. As of July 31, 2011, has the financing for Deliberate Speed Company's assets primarily come from liabilities or owner's equity?

LO1, 2

PA2-4 Determining Financial Statement Effects of Various Transactions

Russeck Company, formed by sole proprietor Kal Russeck, is a small manufacturing business that makes model trains to sell to toy stores. It has a small service department that repairs customers' trains for a fee. The company has been in business for five years. At the end of the most recent year, 2009, the accounting records reflected total assets of $500,000 and total liabilities of $200,000. During the current year, 2010, the following summarized events occurred:

(*a*) Received an additional investment of $100,000 cash from owner Kal Russeck.

(*b*) Borrowed $120,000 cash from the bank and signed a 10-year note.

(*c*) Built an addition on the factory for $200,000 and paid cash to the contractor.

(*d*) Purchased equipment for the new addition for $30,000, paying $3,000 in cash and signing a note due in six months for the balance.

(*e*) Returned a $3,000 piece of equipment from (*d*) because it proved to be defective; received a reduction of the note payable.

(*f*) Purchased a delivery truck (equipment) for $10,000; paid $5,000 cash and signed a nine-month note for the remainder.

(*g*) Kal Russeck lent $5,000 of his personal funds to Tom Mallard, his neighbor.

Required:

1. Complete the spreadsheet that follows, using plus (+) for increases and minus (−) for decreases for each account. The first transaction is used as an example.

	Assets			=	Liabilities	+	Owner's Equity
	Cash	Equipment	Building		Notes Payable		K. Russeck, Capital
(*a*)	+100,000			=			+100,000

2. Did you include event (*g*) in the spreadsheet? Why or why not?
3. Based on beginning balances plus the completed spreadsheet, provide the following amounts (show computations):
   a. Total assets at the end of the year.
   b. Total liabilities at the end of the year.
   c. Total owner's equity at the end of the year.
4. As of December 31, 2010, has the financing for Russeck Company's assets primarily come from liabilities or owner's equity?

PA2-5 Recording and Posting Transactions; Preparing and Interpreting the Balance Sheet

LO2, 3, 4

www.mhhe.com/LLPW1e

Peta Plastics Company has been operating for three years as a sole proprietorship owned and managed by James Peta. The December 31, 2009, account balances are:

Cash	$ 35,000	Land	$ 35,000
Accounts Receivable	5,000	Factory Building	120,000
Supplies	4,000	Accounts Payable	37,000
Notes Receivable (due 2011)	2,000	Notes Payable (due 2015)	80,000
Equipment	116,000	J. Peta, Capital	200,000

During the year 2010, the company had the following summarized activities:

(*a*) Purchased equipment that cost $20,000; paid $5,000 cash and signed a two-year note for the balance.
(*b*) Received an additional $20,000 cash investment from James Peta.
(*c*) Borrowed $30,000 cash from a local bank, payable June 30, 2015.
(*d*) Purchased $4,000 of additional supplies on account.
(*e*) Built an addition to the factory for $41,000; paid $12,000 in cash and signed a three-year note for the balance.
(*f*) Hired a new employee to start January 1, 2011, at an annual salary of $35,000.

Required:

1. Analyze transactions (*a*)–(*f*) to determine their effects on the accounting equation. Use the format shown in the demonstration case on page 71.
2. Record the transaction effects determined in requirement 1 using a journal entry format.
3. Summarize the journal entry effects from requirement 2 using T-accounts.
4. Explain your response to event (*f*).
5. Prepare a *classified* balance sheet at December 31, 2010.
6. As of December 31, 2010, has the financing for Peta Plastics Company's assets primarily come from liabilities or owner's equity?

PA2-6 Using Technology for Analyzing Transactions and Preparing a Balance Sheet

LO2, 3, 4
Elizabeth Arden

www.mhhe.com/LLPW1e

Assume that you recently obtained a part-time accounting position at the corporate headquarters of Elizabeth Arden in Miami Lakes, Florida. Elizabeth Arden is a leading marketer and manufacturer of prestige beauty products, prominently led by the Red Door line of fragrances. The following table summarizes accounts and their balances (in thousands) reported by Elizabeth Arden in a recent September 30 balance sheet.

Cash	$ 14,300	Short-Term Notes Payable	$ 125,000
Accounts Receivable	285,400	Accounts Payable	111,800
Inventories	199,700	Other Current Liabilities	75,700
Other Current Assets	31,600	Long-Term Debt	323,600
Property and Equipment	35,800	Other Long-Term Liabilities	10,100
Other Noncurrent Assets	224,100	"Owners" Capital	144,700

Determine how the balance sheet of Elizabeth Arden would change if the company were to enter into the following transactions (amounts in thousands) during October:

Oct. 2 Purchase an additional manufacturing facility at a cost of $17,000 by signing a note that becomes payable in three years.
Oct. 10 Use $4,000 cash to repay one of the short-term loans.

Oct. 21 Receive an additional $10,000 cash from investors (corporate owners).

Oct. 28 Use cash to buy land for $5,000.

Required:

Elizabeth Arden's controller has asked you to create a spreadsheet in which to display:

1. The account balances at September 30.
2. The effects of the four October transactions.
3. Totals that combine the September 30 balances with the October transactions. You think you might be ready to tackle this assignment, but just to be sure, you e-mail your friend Owen for advice. Here's his reply.

From: Owen@yahoo.com
To: Helpme@hotmail.com
Cc:
Subject: Excel Help

Wow, I can't believe you landed such a great job at EA. Congratulations!

- My thinking is that you'll really impress your boss if you set up the spreadsheet to look like a bunch of T-accounts, one beside another. Use two columns for each balance sheet account (with the account name spanning the two columns) to make it look just like a T-account. [To use the cell merge command to make a header span two columns, see PA1-3.] Here's a screen shot of how one part of the left-hand side of your worksheet might look just before you enter the October transactions.

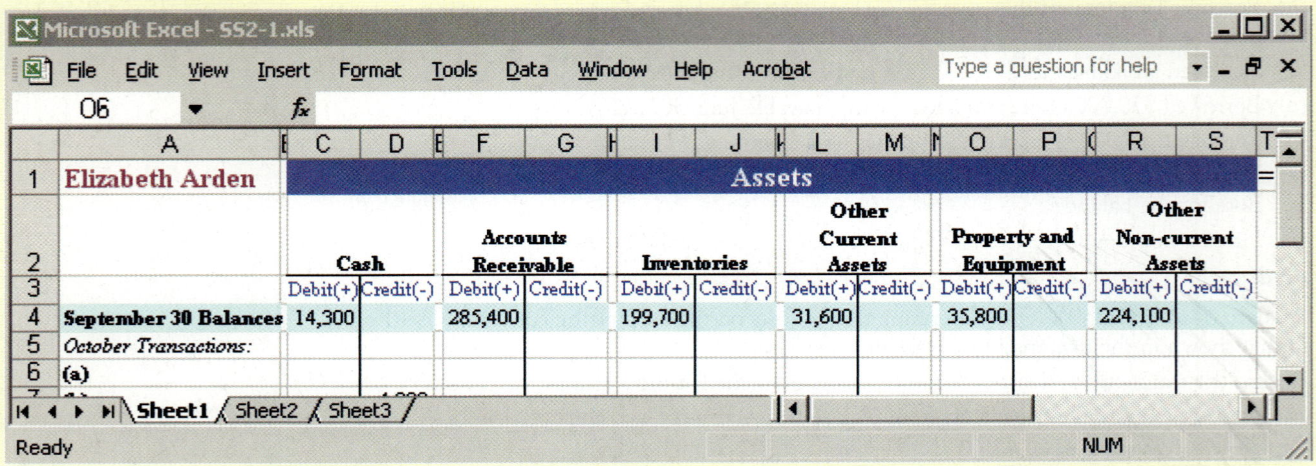

- For extra spreadsheet skills, you might also try creating a balance sheet with cells that are linked to the corresponding cells in the T-accounts. To do this, open a worksheet in the same file as the T-accounts. Then click on a cell in the balance sheet worksheet where you want to import a number from the T-accounts, then type =, then click on the tab for the T-account worksheet, click on the cell with the total to be transferred, and then press enter. This links the cells so that any changes to the T-accounts automatically update the balance sheet.
- I guess the only thing that's left is to remind you that to compute the ending balances in each T-account, you have to add the increases to the beginning balance and subtract the decreases. So, to compute the totals for a particular account, your formula might look like =(SUM(C4:C9)-SUM(D5:D9)).
- Oh yeah, when you've finished, don't forget to save the file using a name that uniquely identifies you.

Problems—Set B  Available with McGraw-Hill's Homework Manager

LO1, 2

PB2-1 Determining Financial Statement Effects of Various Transactions

Swish Watch Repair Company owned by Jacob Swish repairs expensive watches for customers. The company has been in business for three years. At the end of the most recent year, 2009, the accounting records reported total assets of $2,255,000 and total liabilities of $1,780,000. During the current year, 2010, the following summarized events occurred:

(*a*) Received an additional investment of $109,000 cash from Jacob Swish.

(*b*) Borrowed $186,000 cash from the bank and signed a 10-year note.

(*c*) Jacob Swish borrowed $85,000 from a local bank to acquire his summer cottage.

(*d*) Built an addition on the factory for $200,000 and paid cash to the construction company.

(*e*) Purchased equipment for the new addition for $44,000 and supplies for $18,000, paying $12,000 in cash and signing a six-month note for the balance.

(*f*) Returned a $4,000 piece of equipment, from (*e*) because it proved to be defective; received a cash refund.

Required:

1. Complete the spreadsheet that follows, using plus (+) for increases and minus (−) for decreases for each account. The first transaction is used as an example.

	Assets					=	Liabilities	+	Owner's Equity
	Cash	Supplies	Land	Equipment	Building		Notes Payable		J. Swish, Capital
(*a*)	+109,000					=			+109,000

2. Did you include event (*c*) in the spreadsheet? Why?
3. Based on beginning balances plus the completed spreadsheet, provide the following amounts (show computations):
   a. Total assets at the end of the year.
   b. Total liabilities at the end of the year.
   c. Total owner's equity at the end of the year.
4. As of December 31, 2010, has the financing for Swish Watch Repairs' assets primarily come from liabilities or owner's equity?

PB2-2 Recording and Posting Transactions; Preparing and Interpreting the Balance Sheet LO2, 3, 4

Susan Engel established Boston Bed & Breakfast as a sole proprietorship on July 1, 2009. The company's chart of accounts included the following:

Accounts Payable	Notes Payable
Building	S. Engel, Capital
Cash	Supplies
Equipment	

During the month of July, the company had the following activities:

(*a*) Received $160,000 cash from Susan Engel.

(*b*) Purchased a large existing bed and breakfast for $900,000; paid $90,000 as a down payment and signed a note payable from a local bank for the rest. The note is due on June 30, 2029.

(*c*) Purchased new kitchen appliances for $16,000 cash.

(*d*) Purchased supplies for $9,000 on account.

(*e*) Returned a defective appliance purchased in (c) for $3,000 and received a cash refund.

Required:

1. Analyze transactions (*a*)–(*e*) to determine their effects on the accounting equation. Use the format shown in the demonstration case on page 71.
2. Record the transaction effects determined in requirement 1 using a journal entry format.
3. Summarize the journal entry effects from requirement 2 using T-accounts.
4. Prepare a *classified* balance sheet at July 31, 2009.
5. As of July 31, 2009, has the financing for Boston Bed & Breakfast's assets primarily come from liabilities or owner's equity?

PB2-3 Recording and Posting Transactions; Preparing and Interpreting the Balance Sheet LO2, 3, 4

ETHAN ALLEN

Ethan Allen Interiors is a leading manufacturer and retailer of home furnishings with 315 retail stores in the United States and abroad. The following is adapted from Ethan Allen's June 30, 2007, balance sheet (year-end). Dollars are in thousands.

Cash	$147,879	Accounts Payable	$ 26,650
Other Current Assets	234,550	Wages and Other Expenses Payable	120,789
Property, Plant, and Equipment	322,185	Long-Term Liabilities	245,517
Intangibles and Other Assets	97,984	Owners' Capital	409,642

Assume that the following events occurred in the next quarter ended September 30, 2007:

(*a*) Paid $1,400 cash for new intangibles and other assets.

(*b*) Received $1,050 in cash as an additional investment from owners.

(*c*) Purchased property, plant, and equipment; paid $1,870 in cash and signed a note payable to repay the remaining $9,300 in two years.

(*d*) Sold, at cost, intangibles and other assets for $320 cash.

(*e*) Conducted negotiations to purchase a sawmill that is expected to cost $36,000.

Required:

1. Analyze transactions (*a*)–(*e*) to determine their effects on the accounting equation. Use the format shown in the demonstration case on page 71.
2. Record the transaction effects determined in requirement 1 using a journal entry format.
3. Summarize the journal entry effects from requirement 2 using T-accounts. Use the balances reported in the preceding list as the beginning balances for the quarter ended September 30, 2007.
4. Explain your response to event (*e*).
5. Prepare a *classified* balance sheet at September 30, 2007.
6. As of September 30, 2007, has the financing for Ethan Allen's assets primarily come from liabilities or owners' equity?

LO1, 2

PB2-4 Determining Financial Statement Effects of Various Transactions

Steve Limberg established The Swimmer's Cove, a sole proprietorship selling swimming apparel and equipment, in 2006. At December 31, 2011, the accounting records reflected total assets of $850,000 and total liabilities of $375,000. During the current year, 2012, the following summarized events occurred:

(*a*) Borrowed $10,000 cash from the local bank and signed a six-month note.

(*b*) Purchased a warehouse for $300,000 and a delivery van for $40,000; paid cash of $50,000 and signed a 20-year note for the rest.

(*c*) Ordered $150,000 in merchandise to be delivered in January 2013.

(*d*) Received an additional investment of $60,000 cash from owner Steve Limberg.

(*e*) Sold the delivery van to another business for $40,000; received $10,000 cash and the rest on a two-year note due from the other company.

(*f*) Purchased a short-term investment for $30,000 cash.

(*g*) Steve Limberg withdrew $25,000 cash from the business.

Required:

1. Complete the spreadsheet that follows, using plus (+) for increases and minus (−) for decreases for each account. The first transaction is used as an example.

	Assets					=	Liabilities	+	Owner's Equity	
	Cash	Short-term Investment	Notes Receivable	Equipment	Building		Notes Payable		S. Limberg, Capital	S. Limberg, Drawing
(*a*)	+10,000					=	+10,000			

2. Did you include event (*c*) in the spreadsheet? Why or why not?
3. Based on beginning balances plus the completed spreadsheet, provide the following amounts (show computations):
   a. Total assets at the end of the year.
   b. Total liabilities at the end of the year.
   c. Total owner's equity at the end of the year.
4. As of December 31, 2012, has the financing for The Swimmer's Cove's assets primarily come from liabilities or owner's equity?

LO2, 3, 4
Starbucks

PB2-5 Recording and Posting Transactions; Preparing and Interpreting the Balance Sheet

Starbucks is a coffee company—a big coffee company. During a 10-year period, the number of Starbucks locations increased from 165 to more than 5,800 stores—an average increase of 43 percent every year. The following is adapted from Starbucks' September 30, 2007, annual report, (Starbucks' year-end). Dollars are reported in thousands.

Cash	$ 281,300	Other Long-Term Assets	$ 757,000
Accounts Receivable	287,900	Accounts Payable and Other Current Liabilities	1,445,400
Inventories	691,700	Short-Term Notes Payable	710,200
Other Current Assets	435,600	Long-Term Debt	904,200
Property, Plant, and Equipment	2,890,400	Owners' Capital	2,284,100

Assume that the following events (dollars in thousands) occurred in the next quarter that ended December 31, 2007:

(*a*) Paid $10,000 cash for additional other long-term assets.

(*b*) Received $5,100 in cash as additional contributions (investments) from owners.

(*c*) Purchased property, plant, and equipment; paid $11,200 in cash and signed long-term loans for $9,500.

(*d*) Sold, at cost, other long-term assets for $6,000 cash.

(*e*) Conducted negotiations to purchase a coffee farm that is expected to cost $8,400.

Required:

1. Analyze transactions (*a*)–(*e*) to determine their effects on the accounting equation. Use the format shown in the demonstration case on page 71.
2. Record the transaction effects determined in requirement 1 using a journal entry format.
3. Summarize the journal entry effects from requirement 2 using T-accounts. Use the September 2007 ending balances (reported above) as the beginning balances for the October–December 2007 quarter.
4. Explain your response to event (*e*).
5. Prepare a *classified* balance sheet at December 31, 2007.
6. As of December 31, 2007, has the financing for Starbucks' assets primarily come from liabilities or owners' equity?

PB2-6 Using Technology for Analyzing Transactions and Preparing a Balance Sheet

LO2, 3, 4
The Estée Lauder Companies

Assume that you recently obtained a part-time accounting position at the corporate office of Estée Lauder headquartered in New York. Estée Lauder is one of the world's leading manufacturers and marketers of quality skin care, makeup, fragrance, and hair care products including brands such as Estée Lauder, Aramis, and Clinique. The following table summarizes accounts and their balances (in millions) reported by Estée Lauder in a recent June 30 balance sheet.

Cash	$ 369	Accounts Payable	$ 264
Accounts Receivable	771	Short-Term Notes Payable	90
Inventories	766	Other Current Liabilities	1,084
Other Current Assets	271	Long-Term Debt	432
Property and Equipment	758	Other Long-Term Liabilities	266
Other Noncurrent Assets	849	Owners' Capital	1,648

Determine how Estée Lauder's balance sheet would change if the company were to enter into the following transactions (amounts in millions) during July:

July 5 Purchase an additional research and development facility at a cost of $25 by signing a note that becomes payable in four years.

July 11 Use $10 cash to repay one of the short-term loans.

July 25 Receive an additional $30 cash from owners.

July 27 Use cash to buy land for $13.

Required:

Estée Lauder's controller has asked you to create a spreadsheet in which to display:

1. The account balances at June 30.
2. The effects of the four July transactions.
3. Totals that combine the June 30 balances with the July transactions. You think you might be ready to tackle this assignment, but just to be sure, you e-mail your friend Sally for advice. Here's her reply.

From: Sally@yahoo.com
To: Helpme@hotmail.com
Cc:
Subject: Excel Help

Wow, I can't believe you gave up that great job at EA. Good thing you landed another one so quickly!

- My thinking is that you'll really impress your boss if you set up the spreadsheet to look like a bunch of T-accounts, one beside another. Use two columns for each balance sheet account (with the account name spanning the two columns) to make it look just like a T-account. [To use the cell merge command to make a header span two columns, see PA1-3.] Here's a screen shot of how one part of the left-hand side of your worksheet might look just before you enter the July transactions.

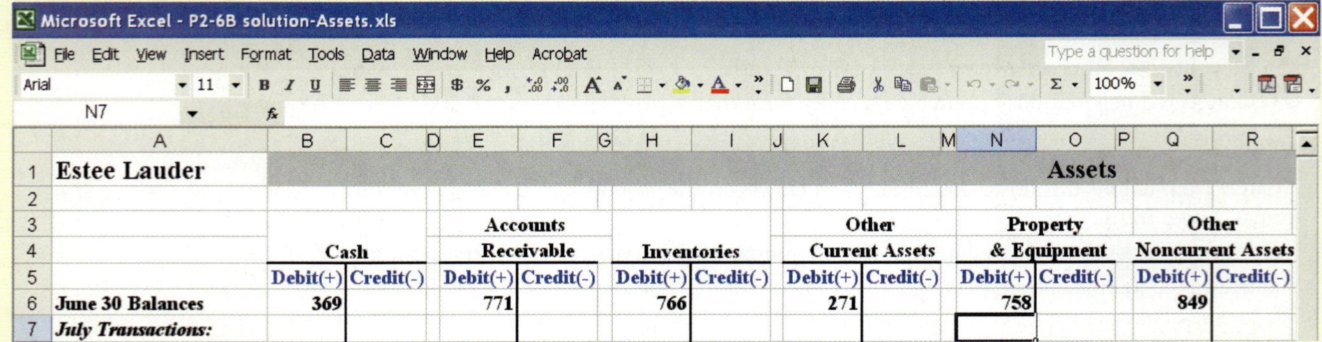

Microsoft Excel - P2-6B solution-Assets.xls

	A	B	C	E	F	H	I	K	L	N	O	Q	R
1	Estee Lauder	Assets											
2													
3				Accounts				Other		Property		Other	
4		Cash		Receivable		Inventories		Current Assets		& Equipment		Noncurrent Assets	
5		Debit(+)	Credit(-)	Debit(+)	Credit(-)	Debit(+)	Credit(-)	Debit(+)	Credit(-)	Debit(+)	Credit(-)	Debit(+)	Credit(-)
6	June 30 Balances	369		771		766		271		758		849	
7	*July Transactions:*												

- For extra spreadsheet skills, you might also try creating a balance sheet with cells that are linked to the corresponding cells in the T-accounts. To do this, open a worksheet in the same file as the T-accounts. Then click on a cell in the balance sheet worksheet where you want to import a number from the T-accounts, then type =, then click on the tab for the T-account worksheet, click on the cell with the total to be transferred, and then press enter. This links the cells so that any changes to the T-accounts automatically update the balance sheet.
- I guess the only thing that's left is to remind you that to compute the ending balances in each T-account, you have to add the increases to the beginning balance and subtract the decreases. So, to compute the totals for a particular account, your formula might look like =(SUM(B6:B11)-SUM(C6:C11)).
- Oh yeah, when you've finished, don't forget to save the file using a name that uniquely identifies you.

Cases and Projects

LO1, 2, 4

CP2-1 Finding and Analyzing Financial Information

Refer to the financial statements of The Home Depot in Appendix A at the end of this book, or download the annual report from the *Cases* section of the text's Web site at www.mhhe.com/LLPW1e.

Required:

1. What is the company's fiscal year-end? Where did you find the exact date?
2. Use the company's balance sheet from the most recent year to determine the amounts in the accounting equation (A = L + SE).
3. What is the amount of the company's current liabilities?
4. Has financing for the company's investment in assets primarily come from liabilities or stockholders' equity?

LO1, 2, 4

Lowe's

CP2-2 Comparing Financial Information

Refer to the financial statements of The Home Depot in Appendix A and Lowe's in Appendix B at the end of this book, or download the annual reports from the *Cases* section of the text's Web site at www.mhhe.com/LLPW1e.

Required:

1. Use the companies' balance sheets to determine the amounts in the accounting equation (A = L + OE) for the most recent year. Is Lowe's or The Home Depot larger in terms of total assets?

2. Does Lowe's have more or less current liabilities than The Home Depot?
3. On the balance sheet, Lowe's reports inventories of $7,611,000,000. Does this amount represent the expected selling price? Why or why not?
4. Has financing for Lowe's investment in assets primarily come from liabilities or stockholders' equity? Thinking back to Chapter 1, what does this imply about the risk assumed by Lowe's investors (corporate owners), relative to those investing in The Home Depot?

CP2-3 Examining the Balance Sheet: Internet-Based Team Research — LO2, 4

As a team, select an industry to analyze. Using your Web browser, each team member should acquire the annual report or 10-K for one publicly traded company in the industry, with each member selecting a different company. (See CP1-3 in Chapter 1 for a description of possible resources for these tasks.)

Required:

1. On an individual basis, each team member should write a short report that lists the following information.
   a. The date of the balance sheet.
   b. The major noncurrent asset accounts and any significant changes in them.
   c. The major noncurrent liability accounts and any significant changes in them.
   d. Any significant changes in total owners' equity (stockholders' equity for a corporation).
   e. Whether financing for the assets primarily comes from liabilities or stockholders' (owners') equity.
2. Then, as a team, write a short report comparing and contrasting your companies using the preceding information. Discuss any similarities across the companies that you as a team observe, and provide potential explanations for any differences discovered.

CP2-4 Examining Real-Life Fraud: Ethical Reasoning, Critical Thinking, and Communication — LO2

In the world of financial fraud, the "Ponzi scheme" is famous. Here is the story behind how the scam received its name. Charles Ponzi started the Security Exchange Company on December 26, 1919. He thought he had discovered a way to purchase American stamps in a foreign country at significantly lower amounts than they were worth in the United States. He claimed that his idea was so successful that anyone who gave money to his company would be repaid their original loan plus 50 percent interest within 90 days. Friends and family quickly offered their money to Ponzi, and they were handsomely rewarded, being repaid their original loan and the 50 percent interest within just 45 days.

Thanks to an article in *The New York Times*, word spread quickly about Ponzi's business, attracting thousands of people seeking a similar payback. He might have had a successful business had his idea actually worked. The problem, however, was that it did not. The 50 percent interest paid to early investors did not come from the profits of a successful underlying business idea (which did not even exist) but instead was obtained fraudulently from funds contributed by later lenders. Eventually, the Ponzi scheme collapsed on August 10, 1920, after an auditor examined his accounting records.

Required:

1. Assume that on December 27, 1919, each of Ponzi's first three lenders provided $5,000 to his company. Use the basic accounting equation to show the effects of these transactions on December 27, 1919.
2. If the first two lenders are repaid their original loan amounts plus the 50 percent interest promised to them, how much cash is left in Ponzi's business to repay the third lender? Given what you discovered, how was it possible for Ponzi's company to remain in "business" for over eight months?
3. Whom did Ponzi's scheme hurt?

Epilogue: After taking in nearly $15 million from 40,000 people, Ponzi's company failed with just $1.5 million in total assets. Ponzi spent four years in prison before jumping bail to become involved in fraudulently selling swampland in Florida. We're not kidding.

CP2-5 Analyzing a Mini Case: Ethical Reasoning, Critical Thinking, and Communication — LO1, 2, 4

You work as an accountant for a small land development company that desperately needs additional financing to continue in business. Your company's president is meeting with the manager of a local bank at the end of the month to try to obtain this financing. The president has approached you with two ideas to improve the company's reported financial position.

- First, he claims that because a big part of the company's value comes from its knowledgeable and dedicated employees, you should report their "intellectual abilities" as an asset on the balance sheet.
- Second, he claims that although the local economy is doing poorly and almost no one is buying land or new houses, he is optimistic that eventually things will turn around. For this reason, he asks you to continue reporting the company's land on the balance sheet at its cost rather than the much lower amount that real estate appraisers say it is really worth.

Required:

1. Thinking back to Chapter 1, why do you think the president is so concerned with the amount of assets reported on the balance sheet?
2. What accounting concept introduced in Chapter 2 relates to the president's first suggestion to report intellectual abilities as an asset?
3. What accounting concept introduced in Chapter 2 relates to the president's second suggestion to continue reporting land at its cost?
4. If you were to do as he asks, whom would the president's suggestions hurt? What should you do?

LO1, 4

CP2-6 Evaluating the Reliability of a Balance Sheet: Financial Analysis and Critical Thinking

Betsey Jordan asked a local bank for a $50,000 loan to expand her small company. The bank asked Betsey to submit a financial statement of the business to supplement the loan application. Betsey prepared the following balance sheet.

Balance Sheet
June 30, 2010

Assets	
Cash	$ 9,000
Inventory	30,000
Equipment	46,000
Personal residence (monthly payments, $2,800)	300,000
Remaining assets	20,000
Total assets	$405,000
Liabilities	
Short-Term debt to suppliers	$ 62,000
Long-Term debt on equipment	38,000
Total debt	100,000
Owner's equity	305,000
Total liabilities and owner's equity	$405,000

Required:

The balance sheet has several flaws. However, there is at least one major deficiency. Identify it and explain its significance.

LO1, 4

CP2-7 Preparing and Analyzing a Balance Sheet: Decision Making as a Financial Analyst

Your best friend from home writes you a letter about an investment opportunity that has come her way. Her neighbor Josh Dewey is establishing a new business and has asked her to lend the business $20,000 (her recent inheritance from her great-aunt's estate). Your friend has never loaned money to a company before and, knowing that you are a financial analyst, asks that you look over the balance sheet and send her some advice. An *unaudited* balance sheet, in only moderately good form, is enclosed with the letter:

Dewey, Cheetum, and Howe Services
Balance Sheet
For the Year Ending December 31, 2009

Accounts receivable	$ 8,000
Cash	1,000
Inventory	8,000
Furniture and fixtures	52,000
Delivery truck	12,000
Buildings (estimated market value)	98,000
Total assets	**$179,000**
Accounts payable	$ 16,000
Payroll taxes payable	13,000
Notes payable (due in three years)	15,000
Mortgage payable	50,000
Total liabilities	**$ 94,000**
J. Dewey, capital	$ 85,000
Total owners' equity	**$ 85,000**

The only footnote states that the building was recently purchased for $60,000 and carries a mortgage (shown in the liability section). The footnote further states that, in the company president's opinion, the building is "easily worth $98,000."

Required:

1. Draft a new balance sheet for your friend, correcting any errors you note. (If any of the account balances need to be corrected, you may need to adjust the owners' equity balance correspondingly.) If no errors or omissions exist, state so.
2. Write a letter to your friend explaining the changes you made to the balance sheet, if any, and offer your comments on the company's apparent financial condition based only on this information. Suggest other information your friend might want to review before coming to a final decision on whether to lend the money to the business.

3 Operating a Business and the Income Statement

LEARNING OBJECTIVES

After studying this chapter, you should be able to:

Lectured slideshow–LP3-1
www.mhhe.com/LLPW1e

LO1 Recognize common income statement accounts.

LO2 Describe a typical business operating cycle and explain the necessity for the time period assumption.

LO3 Explain the accrual basis of accounting and apply the revenue and matching principles to measure income.

LO4 Apply transaction analysis to examine and record the effects of operating activities on the financial statements.

LO5 Understand the purpose of a trial balance and prepare a simple income statement.

Focus Company: PIZZA AROMA, Ithaca, NY

"Opening the Doors"

In Chapter 2, Mauricio Rosa, owner-manager of Pizza Aroma, established his new gourmet pizza business. Using money he had contributed plus a loan from the bank, he purchased the ovens, counters, tables, chairs, and other equipment he needed to run the business. His next step was to make the critical decisions that would draw customers into the restaurant and provide them with the service that would keep them coming back—while making sure, of course, that he made a profit. What would Mauricio's operating strategy be?

Before launching into a discussion on strategy, we need to know something about the pizza business. Pizza is a global food, generating more than $32 billion[1] in sales each year. In this business, which depends heavily on human capital, companies compete through marketing and product quality. Mauricio insists on using only the highest quality, freshest ingredients, which requires an almost fanatical focus on testing ingredients and checking product quality—right down to the size of the black olives and the fat content of the meat and mozzarella.

Competition is stiff. The large pizza chains, mainly Pizza Hut, Papa John's, and Domino's, all tout the quality of their ingredients. In fact, Papa John's International, Inc., includes its motto, "Better Ingredients. Better Pizza" in its corporate logo. The big chains also use national radio and television advertising along with extensive local marketing efforts to draw in customers.

Pizza Aroma's uniqueness lies in its gourmet pizza, a niche the big chains do not emphasize. To succeed, then, Pizza Aroma needs an operating strategy that maintains quality while keeping costs low and operations simple. It also needs to advertise to the local community and colleges in novel and aggressive ways.

[1] http://www.pmq.com/mag/20061112/article.php?story=pizzapower2006.

For information about a business's recent financial performance—that is, the relative success of its operating activities—owners and other users of the financial statements turn to the income statement. In this chapter, we will focus on Pizza Aroma's operating activities as reflected on its income statement. To read and understand the income statement, you need to answer the following questions:

- How do business activities affect the income statement?
- How are business activities measured?
- How are business activities reported on the income statement?

ORGANIZATION OF THE CHAPTER

RECOGNIZE OPERATING ACTIVITIES	MEASURE OPERATING ACTIVITIES	PREPARE AN INCOME STATEMENT
• Income Statement Accounts • Operating Cycle	• Cash-Based Measurements • Accrual Basis Accounting • Expanded Transaction Analysis Model • Analysis of Pizza Aroma's Transactions	• Unadjusted Trial Balance • Classified Income Statements • Limitations of the Income Statement

RECOGNIZE OPERATING ACTIVITIES

Learning Objective 1

Recognize common income statement accounts.

Income Statement Accounts

Revenues

A business earns revenues when it exchanges its products or services for cash or a customer's promise to pay cash, called Accounts Receivable. When Pizza Aroma sells pizza to consumers, it has earned revenue. Pizza Aroma's primary revenue is **Pizza Revenue.**

Revenues earned

Expenses

Cash expenditures → Debt payments; Expenses; Asset purchases (will be expensed when used to generate revenues)

Some students confuse cash payments and **expenses.** Cash payments are outflows of money for any purpose, whether to buy equipment, pay off a bank loan, or pay a utility bill. An expense is defined more narrowly. If revenues are the positive benefits from the sale of a good or service, then expenses are the costs incurred to generate those revenues. Anything a business **uses** to generate revenues during a period is an expense, regardless of when it was or will be paid for.

What does this distinction mean for Pizza Aroma? It hires and pays employees to make and serve food. It uses electricity to operate equipment and light its facilities. It advertises its pizza and uses food ingredients and paper supplies during the course of business. All of these expenses are necessary to generate revenues. Some of them may result in cash payments at the time they are incurred; others may be incurred before or after cash is

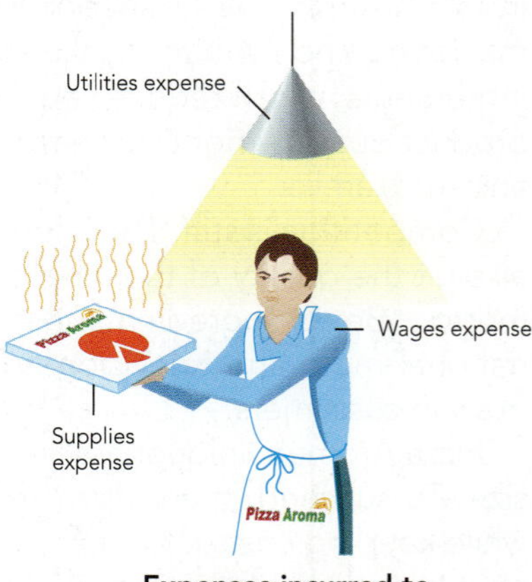

Expenses incurred to generate revenues

paid. In short, not all cash payments (such as buying equipment for cash) are expenses, and expenses are necessary to generate revenues.

Account titles may vary to fit a business's specific types of revenues and expenses. When you are trying to determine the account title to use for a particular revenue or expense, think about the nature of the business and the type of activity involved. For example, when a consulting firm provides services to clients, it earns Consulting Fee Revenue or Fee Revenue—not Sales Revenue because it did not sell a product to a customer. See Exhibit 3.1 for a partial chart of accounts for a pizza restaurant.

Operating Cycle

Learning Objective 2

Describe a typical business operating cycle and explain the necessity for the time period assumption.

The long-term objective of any business is to **turn cash into more cash.** If a company is to stay in business, this excess cash must be generated from operations—that is, from the activities for which the business was established—rather than from borrowing money or selling long-lived assets.

Companies buy inventory, supplies, and services such as electricity, as well as the work of their employees. Then they sell the inventory or services to customers. The period that begins when the company pays for its inventory and services and ends when customers pay cash to the company is known as the **operating (cash-to-cash) cycle**. The length of time for a company to complete its operating cycle depends on the nature of the business. The graphic in Exhibit 3.2 illustrates the operating cycle for Pizza Aroma that is typical of most businesses.

Pizza Aroma's operating cycle is relatively short, from the expenditure of cash to purchase ingredients from suppliers to the sale of pizzas to customers for cash. Some companies, however, pay for inventory well before they sell it. Toys R Us, for example, builds up its inventory months before the year-end holiday season. The company borrows funds from banks to pay for the inventory and then repays the loans with interest after receiving cash from customers. Many other companies receive cash from customers well after a sale takes place. For example, furniture stores such as Ethan Allen often sell furniture to customers who make regular monthly payments over several months or years.

The operating cycle is repeated continuously until a company goes out of business. However, decision makers need to receive information about a company's financial condition and performance periodically. To measure the income for a specific period, accountants follow the **time period assumption**,[2] which states that the long life of a company can be reported over shorter periods, such as months, quarters, and years.

[2] This is the fourth assumption accountants make as part of the key concepts for external financial reporting as shown in Exhibit 2.12 at the end of Chapter 2.

Exhibit 3.1 Chart of Accounts (partial—income statement accounts only)

Account Number	Account Name
401	Pizza Revenue
410	Investment Revenue
450	Gain on Sale of Assets
501	Wages Expense
503	Supplies Expense
506	Utilities Expense
507	Telephone Service Expense
510	Rent Expense
511	Insurance Expense
512	Advertising Expense
530	Interest Expense
550	Loss on Sale of Assets

Coach's Tip

Notice that the account numbers for income statement accounts start in the 400s. A full chart of accounts would start with assets (100s), liabilities (200s), and owner's equity accounts (300s) as shown in Exhibit 2.2.

Exhibit 3.2 Typical Business Operating Cycle

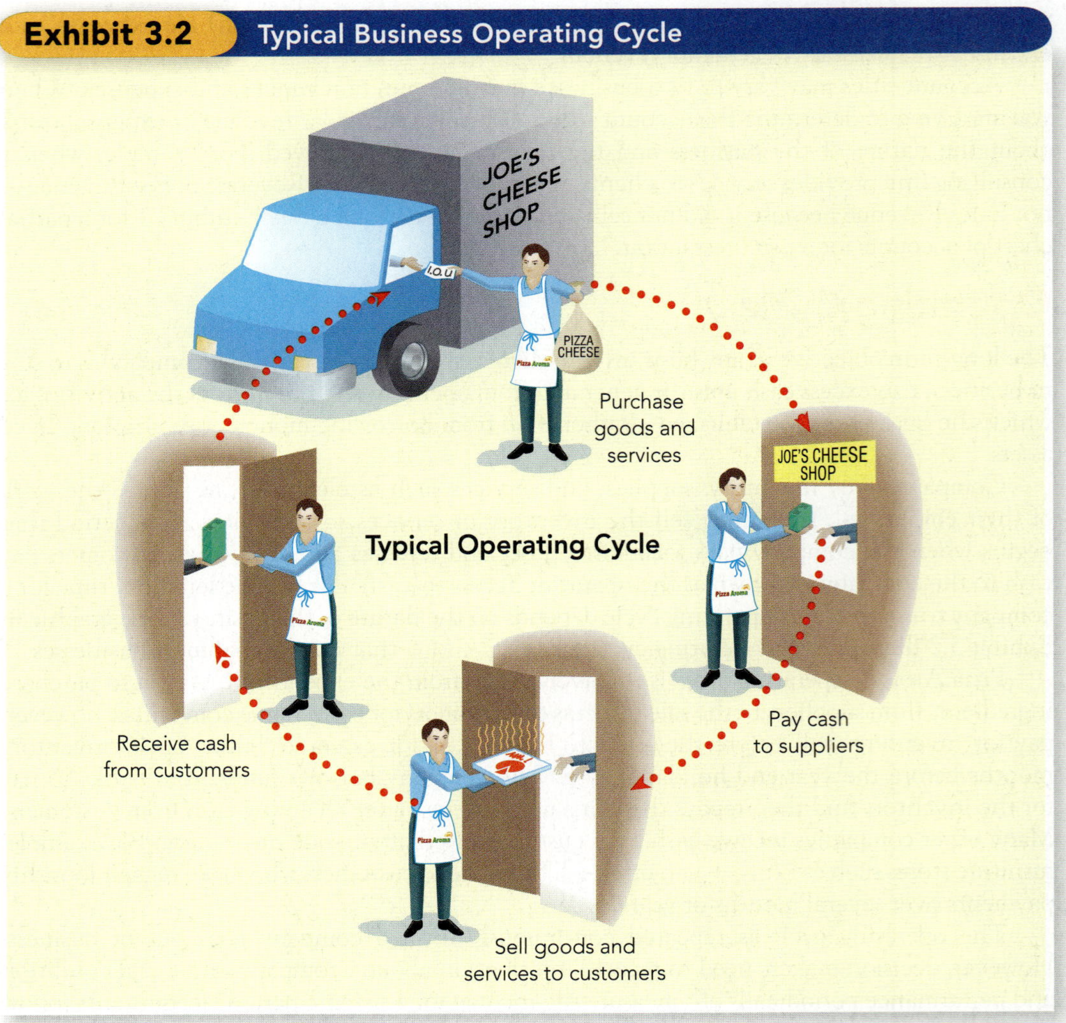

Learning Objective 3
Explain the accrual basis of accounting and apply the revenue and matching principles to measure income.

MEASURE OPERATING ACTIVITIES

Two issues arise in reporting periodic income to users:

1. **Recognition. When** should the effects of operating activities be recognized (recorded)?
2. **Measurement. What amounts** should be recognized (recorded)?

Cash-Based Measurements

CASH BASIS Income Measurement

	Revenues (= cash receipts)
–	Expenses (= cash payments)
	Net Income (cash basis)

How do you know if you are better off today than you were last month? You probably determine your personal financial position by looking at the cash balance in your bank account. That is, you measure your financial performance as the difference between your cash balance at the beginning of the period and your cash balance at the end of the period. If you have a higher cash balance at the end of the period than you did at the beginning, your cash receipts exceeded your cash disbursements. As long as you received and disbursed cash shortly before or after the activities that caused those cash flows, your increasing or decreasing cash balance will provide a timely measure of your financial performance. Reporting your income on this basis, called cash basis accounting, is usually good enough.

Cash basis accounting does not measure financial performance well when a company conducts transactions using credit rather than cash, however. Credit often introduces a significant delay between the time when an activity occurs and the time that it impacts a bank account balance. If you are paid for work once a month, for example, your hard work does not show up in your cash balance until the end of the month. Similarly, if you use a credit card to purchase groceries, those transactions will not affect your cash balance until you pay the bill the following month.

Because most businesses, including Pizza Aroma, use credit for their transactions, cash basis accounting is not likely to correspond to the business activities that actually occur during a given period. For this reason, generally accepted accounting principles do not allow cash basis accounting to be used for purposes of external reporting. Instead, generally accepted accounting principles require accrual basis accounting.

Accrual Basis Accounting

In accrual basis accounting (accrual accounting), a business recognizes revenues and expenses when the transaction that causes them occurs, not necessarily when the business receives or is paid cash. That is, **revenues are recognized when they are earned and expenses are recognized when they are incurred** (that is, when goods or services attained from others are used). The two basic accounting principles that determine when revenues and expenses are recorded under accrual basis accounting are the **revenue principle** and the **matching principle.**

ACCRUAL BASIS Income Measurement

	Revenues (= when earned)
–	Expenses (= when incurred)
	Net Income (accrual basis)

Revenue Measurement

Under accrual basis accounting, a business recognizes revenues (that is, measures and records them) when it delivers goods or services to the customer. The generally accepted accounting principle that businesses use to determine when to recognize revenue is the revenue principle. This rule requires recognizing (recording and reporting) revenue in the period in which it is **earned.**[3] Most businesses recognize revenue at the point of delivery of goods or services—when the business transfers title, risks, and rewards of ownership to the customer. As is typical in the fast-food industry, Pizza Aroma recognizes its revenues from pizza sales **at the time it delivers its gourmet pizza to customers,** as ordered.

Although businesses expect to receive cash in exchange for their goods and services, the timing of cash receipts from customers does not dictate when businesses report revenues. Instead, the key to determining when to report revenue is whether the business has done what it promised to do. Thus, cash can be received (1) in the **same** period as, (2) in a period **before,** or (3) in a period **after** the goods or services are delivered (see Exhibit 3.3). Let's see how to handle each of these cases.

1 **Cash is received in the same period as the goods or services are delivered.** This is the most common timing for Pizza Aroma because most customers pay cash within a few minutes of receiving their pizza. Pizza Aroma delivers the pizza to the customer as ordered, earning revenue in the process. In the exchange, Pizza Aroma receives cash from the customer.

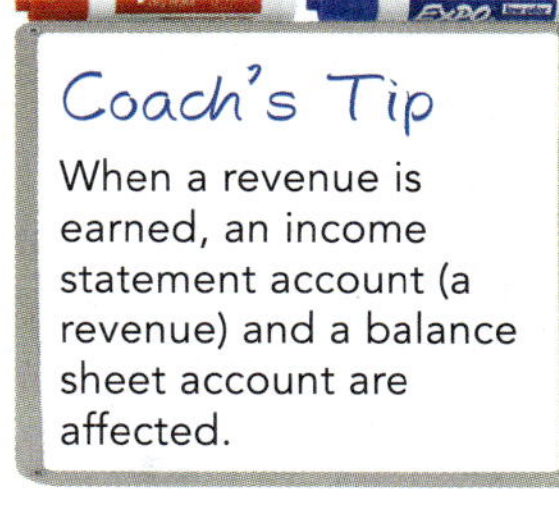

[3] Under the revenue principle, four criteria or conditions must normally be met for revenue to be recognized. If *any* of these criteria is *not* met, revenue normally is *not* recognized and cannot be recorded. The four criteria are (1) the company has delivered goods or performed services (that is, the company has performed), (2) the business has persuasive evidence of an arrangement with the customer, (3) the price is fixed or determinable, and (4) the collection of cash is reasonably assured.

Exhibit 3.3 Recording Revenues versus Cash Receipts

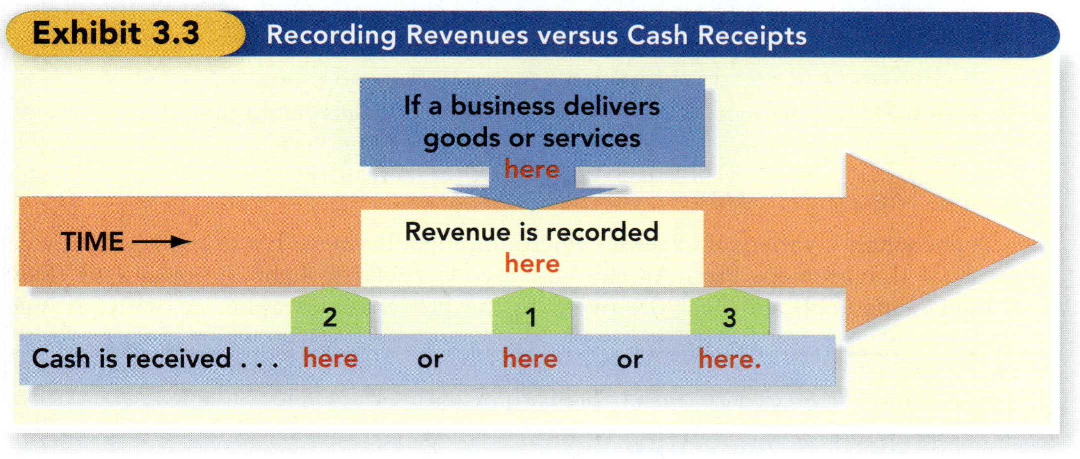

2 **Cash is received before the goods or services are delivered.** This situation occurs, for example, when Pizza Aroma accepts a large order for an event to be held next month. Pizza Aroma requires the customer to provide a deposit when the order is placed. Cash is recorded when it is received. However, because Pizza Aroma has not yet delivered the pizza, it records no revenue. So how does Pizza Aroma account for the other half of the transaction? The promise to deliver pizza in the future creates a liability called Unearned Revenue equal to the amount of the cash deposit received in advance. When Pizza Aroma delivers the pizza next month, it will record and report Pizza Revenue on the income statement and reduce the Unearned Revenue account because the liability has been satisfied. Following the revenue principle, a business records revenue when it delivers goods or services, not when it receives cash.

3 **Cash is received after the goods or services are delivered.** To boost business, Pizza Aroma also arranges to deliver pizza "on account" to some customers, such as college departments. That is, the restaurant delivers pizza when it is ordered and then bills the customer at the end of the month. When a business sells goods or services on account, it earns the revenue when it delivers the goods or services. Pizza Aroma earns revenue when it delivers the pizza, even though it has not yet received cash. At that time, Pizza Aroma records both the revenue and an asset called Accounts Receivable that represents the customer's promise to pay for the deliveries in the future. When the customer pays its monthly bill, Pizza Aroma will increase its Cash account and decrease Accounts Receivable.

As you can see, under the revenue principle, a business records revenue when it earns it **regardless of when it receives the cash.** It may receive cash before, during, or after the time it earned revenue. When the business receives cash before or after earning it, it makes one entry on the date it earns revenue and another on the date it receives cash. To cement this principle in your memory, practice applying it in the following exercise.

SELF-STUDY PRACTICE

Following are sample transactions for the Florida Flippers, a scuba diving and instruction business owned by Paul Knepper. If revenue is to be recognized in **June,** indicate the title of the revenue account and the amount of revenue to be recognized.

Activity	Revenue Account Title	Amount of Revenue Earned in June
(a) In June, Florida Flippers provided $32,000 in diving instruction to customers for cash.		
(b) In June, new customers paid $8,200 cash for diving trips Florida Flippers will provide; it made $5,200 in trips in June and will provide the rest in July.		
(c) In June, customers paid $3,900 cash for instruction they received in May.		

After you have finished, check your answers with the solutions at the bottom of the page.

Coach's Tip

When you are not given the title of a revenue account, simply create a title that fits with the activity. For example, providing diving instruction results in the business earning Diving Instruction Revenue.

Expense Measurement

Owners encounter a variety of expenses when running a business. For example, to provide food service to customers, Pizza Aroma must use electricity to light the restaurant, keep fresh ingredients cool, and heat the ovens to the proper temperature. As with revenue

Solution to Self-Study Practice

	Revenue Account Title	Amount of Revenue Earned in June	
(a)	Diving Instruction Revenue	$32,000	
(b)	Diving Trip Revenue	5,200	The remaining $3,000 will be earned in July.
(c)	No revenue in June; revenue was earned in May	—	

recognition, these expenses are recorded as incurred (that is, when goods or services obtained from others are used), **regardless of when Pizza Aroma pays cash.** Under accrual basis accounting, businesses apply the **matching principle**, which requires that the expenses incurred to generate revenues should be recognized (that is, recorded) in the same period **to match costs with the benefits.** And as with revenue recognition, expenses may be paid for (1) at the same time as, (2) before, or (3) after they are incurred to generate revenue (see Exhibit 3.4).

1 **Cash is paid in the same period as the expense is incurred to generate revenue.** Expenses are sometimes paid for in the period that they arise. For example, Pizza Aroma spends $50 cash now for balloons to celebrate its grand opening. It would report this cost on this month's income statement because the balloons were used for an activity occurring this month. In other words, the benefits of incurring the cost are entirely used up within the current accounting period.

2 **Cash is paid before the expense is incurred to generate revenue.** It is common for businesses to pay for something that provides benefits only in future periods. For example, Pizza Aroma buys paper plates now but does not use them until next month. The asset Supplies is increased and Cash is decreased. Given the matching principle, the expense from using these supplies is reported next month when the supplies are used to earn revenue, not now when purchased. This month, the supplies represent an asset because they will benefit a future period. When they are used later, Supplies Expense will be reported on next month's income statement and the asset Supplies will decrease. Similar situations arise when a company prepays rent or insurance.

3 **Cash is paid after the cost is incurred to generate revenue.** Although rent is paid and supplies are purchased before they are used, many costs are paid after receiving and using goods or services. For example, Pizza Aroma uses electricity to heat the ovens and light the restaurant this month but does not pay for its electricity usage until next month. Because the cost of the electricity relates to revenues earned now, it represents an expense that will be reported on this month's income statement. Because the cost has not yet been paid at the end of the month, a liability called Accounts Payable is created. Similar situations arise when employees work in the current period but are not paid their wages until the following period.

Now practice applying the matching principle by completing the exercise on the next page.

Expanded Transaction Analysis Model

Learning Objective 4

Apply transaction analysis to examine and record the effects of operating activities on the financial statements.

We have discussed the variety of business activities affecting the income statement and how to measure them. Now we will determine how to record those business activities in the accounting system and reflect them in the financial statements. To do so, we need to expand the transaction analysis model presented in Chapter 2 to include operating activities.

Exhibit 3.4 Recording Expenses versus Cash Payments

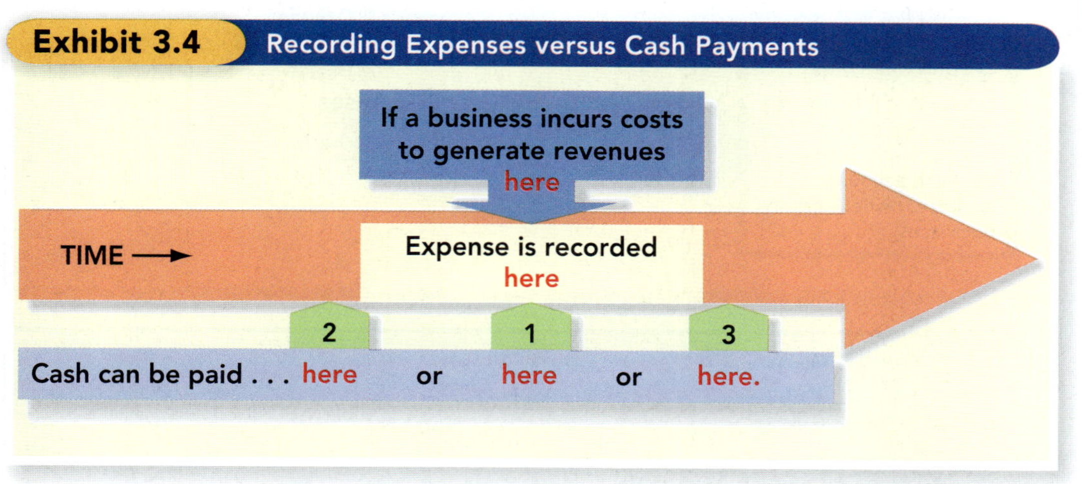

Video 3-1
www.mhhe.com/LLPW1e

SELF-STUDY PRACTICE

The following sample transactions are for Florida Flippers, a scuba diving and instruction business owned by Paul Knepper. Apply the matching principle. If an expense is incurred in **June,** indicate the title of the expense account and the amount of expense to be recognized.

Activity	Expense Account Title	Amount of Expense Incurred in June
(a) At the beginning of June, Florida Flippers paid a total of $6,000 cash for insurance for the months of June, July, and August.		
(b) In June, Florida Flippers paid $4,000 in wages to employees who worked in June.		
(c) In June, Florida Flippers paid $2,400 for electricity used in May.		

After you have finished, check your answers with the solutions at the bottom of the page.

Revenues

Increase net income and owner's equity

↑ with Credits

Accounts have credit balances

Expenses

Decrease net income and owner's equity

↑ with Debits

Accounts have debit balances

The complete transaction model includes all five accounting elements: Assets, Liabilities, Owner's Equity, Revenues, and Expenses (see Exhibit 3.5). Recall that revenues increase owner's equity, expenses decrease owner's equity, and revenue minus expenses equals net income. That means that when net income is positive, owner's equity increases; when net income is negative, owner's equity decreases.

Before illustrating the use of the expanded transaction analysis model, we should emphasize the following points:

- Revenues increase net income, which increases owner's equity. Because owner's equity increases on the credit side of the accounting equation, revenues have **credit** balances.
- Expenses decrease net income, thus decreasing owner's equity. Therefore, expenses have **debit** balances (they are the opposite of the credit balance of owner's equity). To increase an expense, then, you debit it, which decreases net income and owner's equity. When you debit an expense account, you are adding to the expenses.
- When revenues exceed expenses, the business reports net income, increasing owner's equity. However, when expenses exceed revenues, a net loss results, decreasing owner's equity.

Exhibit 3.5 Expanded Transaction Analysis Model

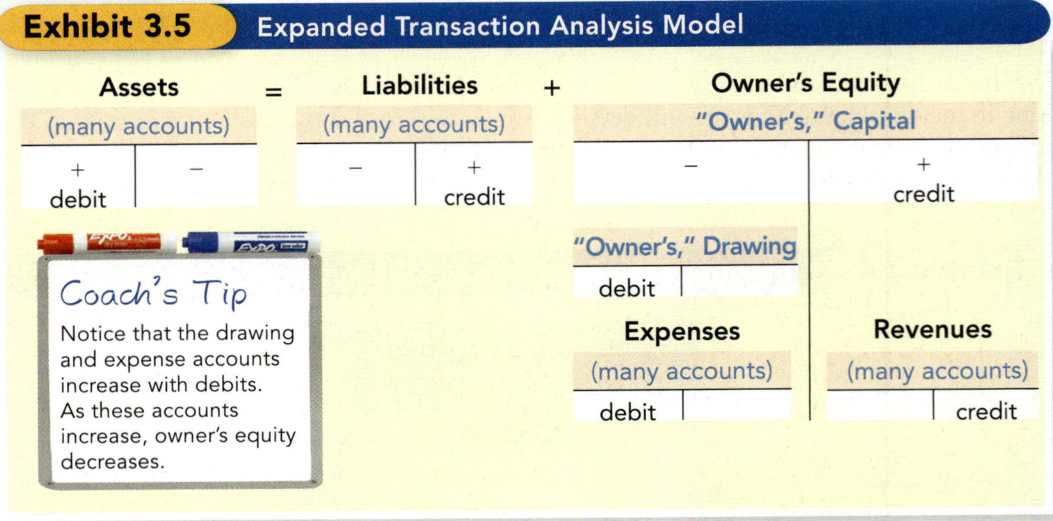

Solution to Self-Study Practice

	Expense Account Title	Amount of Expense Incurred in June	
(a)	Insurance Expense	$2,000	The remaining $4,000 will be used in July and August.
(b)	Wages Expense	4,000	
(c)	No expense in June; expense was incurred in May	—	

- Although the owner's drawing account is **not reported on the income statement,** it decreases owner's equity as expenses do. Therefore, the drawing account has a **debit** balance. As the owner withdraws more funds from the business, the drawing account balance increases with debits that, in turn, reduce the owner's overall stake in the business.

Owner's Drawing Account

Decreases owner's equity

↑ with Debits

Account has a debit balance

Furthermore, as you saw in Chapter 2, where we introduced the transaction analysis model:

1. All accounts can increase or decrease, although revenues and expenses tend to increase throughout the period. For balance sheet accounts on the left side of the accounting equation, the increase symbol + is written on the left side of the T-account. For balance sheet accounts on the right side of the accounting equation, the increase symbol + is written on the right side of the T-account.
2. Debits are written on the left side and credits on the right side of each T-account.
3. Every transaction affects at least two accounts.

To analyze transactions using the expanded transaction analysis model, follow these steps:

Step 

- **Identify the accounts affected** by name, making sure that at least two accounts change.
- **Classify them by type of account** (A for asset, L for liability, OE for owner's equity, R for revenue, or E for expense).
- **Determine the direction of the effect** (an increase [+] or decrease [−] in each account). Include also the direction of the effect of revenues and expenses on owner's equity (e.g., [+E, −OE]).

Step 

- **Verify** that the **accounting equation (A = L + OE) remains in balance.**
- **Verify** that the total dollar value of the **debits** in the transaction **equals** the total dollar value of the **credits.**

Refer to the expanded transaction analysis model shown in Exhibit 3.5 until you can construct it without assistance. **Study the exhibit carefully to make sure you understand the impact of revenues and expenses on both the balance sheet and the income statement.**

SELF-STUDY PRACTICE

For each of the following accounts, complete the table. Indicate whether:

1. The account will be reported on the balance sheet (B/S) or income statement (I/S).
2. The account is classified as a current asset (CA), noncurrent asset (NCA), current liability (CL), noncurrent liability (NCL), owner's equity (OE), revenue (R), or expense (E).
3. The account usually has a debit (Dr) or credit (Cr) balance.

Account	(1) Balance Sheet or Income Statement	(2) Classification on Financial Statement	(3) Debit or Credit Balance
a. Interest Expense	______	______	______
b. Cost of Goods Sold	______	______	______
c. Unearned Revenue	______	______	______
d. Equipment	______	______	______
e. Wages Payable	______	______	______
f. Sales Revenue	______	______	______
g. Prepaid Insurance	______	______	______
h. Accounts Receivable	______	______	______
i. Fee Revenue	______	______	______
j. Supplies Expense	______	______	______

After you have finished, check your answers with the solutions at the bottom of the next page.

Beginning balances in balance sheet accounts come from the May 7 trial balance in Exhibit 2.9.

Postings to T-Accounts

+ Cash (A)	−
Bal. 5,200	
(h) 12,000	
17,200	

− Pizza Revenue (R)	+
	0 Beg.
	12,000 (h)
	12,000

Analysis of Pizza Aroma's Transactions

The dough was ready; the sauce was simmering; the mushrooms, other veggies, and meats had been carefully sliced; the mozzarella had been perfectly grated; and several gourmet pizzas were in the oven when Mauricio opened the doors of Pizza Aroma on the first day of business. The restaurant had a good first month. Now let's analyze, record, and post the effects of the first month's operating activities to the T-accounts. Chapter 2 showed how to analyze transactions *(a)* to *(g)*; we will continue the analysis with transaction *(h)*.

(*h*) During May, Pizza Aroma sells pizza to restaurant customers for $12,000 cash.

		Debit	Credit
(*h*)	Cash (+A)	12,000	
	Pizza Revenue (+R, +OE)		12,000

Assets	=	Liabilities	+	Owner's Equity
(*h*) Cash +12,000				Pizza Revenue (+R) +12,000

Equality checks: (1) Debits $12,000 = Credits $12,000; (2) the accounting equation is in balance.

+ Accounts Receivable (A)	−
Bal. 0	
(*i*) 2,000	
2,000	

− Pizza Revenue (R)	+
	0 Beg
	12,000 (*h*)
	2,000 (*i*)
	14,000

(*i*) Pizza Aroma delivers $2,000 in pizza on account to various college departments.

		Debit	Credit
(*i*)	Accounts Receivable (+A)	2,000	
	Pizza Revenue (+R, +OE)		2,000

Assets	=	Liabilities	+	Owner's Equity
(*i*) Accounts Receivable +2,000				Pizza Revenue (+R) +2,000

Equality checks: (1) Debits $2,000 = Credits $2,000; (2) the accounting equation is in balance.

+ Cash (A)	−
Bal. 5,200	
(*h*) 12,000	
(*j*) 600	
17,800	

− Unearned Revenue (L)	+
	0 Beg.
	600 (*j*)
	600

(*j*) Fraternities place large orders for end-of-May graduation events and for mid-June reunion weekend, giving Pizza Aroma $600 cash on deposit in mid-May.

		Debit	Credit
(*j*)	Cash (+A)	600	
	Unearned Revenue (+L)		600

Assets	=	Liabilities	+	Owner's Equity
(*j*) Cash +600		Unearned Revenue +600		

Equality checks: (1) Debits $600 = Credits $600; (2) the accounting equation is in balance.

Solution to Self-Study Practice

	Account	Balance Sheet or Income Statement	Classification on Financial Statement	Debit or Credit Balance
a.	Interest Expense	I/S	E	Dr
b.	Cost of Goods Sold	I/S	E	Dr
c.	Unearned Revenue	B/S	CL	Cr
d.	Equipment	B/S	NCA	Dr
e.	Wages Payable	B/S	CL	Cr
f.	Sales Revenue	I/S	R	Cr
g.	Prepaid Insurance	B/S	CA	Dr
h.	Accounts Receivable	B/S	CA	Dr
i.	Fee Revenue	I/S	R	Cr
j.	Supplies Expense	I/S	E	Dr

(*k*) Pizza Aroma purchases $3,000 of additional supplies, paying $2,200 in cash and owing the rest on account.

		Debit	Credit
(*k*)	Supplies (+A)	3,000	
	Cash (−A)		2,200
	Accounts Payable (+L)		800

Assets		=	Liabilities		+	Owner's Equity
(*k*) Supplies	**+3,000**		**Accounts Payable**	**+800**		
Cash	**−2,200**					

Equality checks: (1) Debits $3,000 = Credits $3,000; (2) the accounting equation is in balance.

+ Supplies (A)	−
Bal. 2,000	
(*k*) 3,000	
5,000	

+ Cash (A)	−
Bal. 5,200	
(*h*) 12,000	2,200 (*k*)
(*j*) 600	
15,600	

− Accounts Payable (L)	+
	4,000 Bal.
	800 (*k*)
	4,800

(*l*) Pizza Aroma pays $800 cash for newspaper advertising during May.

		Debit	Credit
(*l*)	Advertising Expense (+E,−OE)	800	
	Cash (−A)		800

Assets		=	Liabilities	+	Owner's Equity	
(*l*) Cash	**−800**				**Advertising Expense (+E)**	**−800**

Equality checks: (1) Debits $800 = Credits $800; (2) the accounting equation is in balance.

+ Cash (A)	−
Bal. 5,200	
(*h*) 12,000	2,200 (*k*)
(*j*) 600	800 (*l*)
14,800	

+ Advertising Expense (E)	−
Beg. 0	
(*l*) 800	
800	

(*m*) Pizza Aroma pays $1,000 cash to employees for work during May.

		Debit	Credit
(*m*)	Wages Expense (+E, −OE)	1,000	
	Cash (−A)		1,000

Assets		=	Liabilities	+	Owner's Equity	
(*m*) Cash	**−1,000**				**Wages Expense (+E)**	**−1,000**

Equality checks: (1) Debits $1,000 = Credits $1,000; (2) the accounting equation is in balance.

+ Cash (A)	−
Bal. 5,200	
(*h*) 12,000	2,200 (*k*)
(*j*) 600	800 (*l*)
	1,000 (*m*)
13,800	

+ Wages Expense (E)	−
Beg 0	
(*m*) 1,000	
1,000	

(*n*) College departments pay Pizza Aroma $1,300 cash owed on their accounts (see event [i]).

		Debit	Credit
(*n*)	Cash (+A)	1,300	
	Accounts Receivable (−A)		1,300

Assets		=	Liabilities	+	Owner's Equity
(*n*) Cash	**+1,300**				
Accounts Receivable	**−1,300**				

Equality checks: (1) Debits $1,300 = Credits $1,300; (2) the accounting equation is in balance.

+ Cash (A)	−
Bal. 5,200	
(*h*) 12,000	2,200 (*k*)
(*j*) 600	800 (*l*)
(*n*) 1,300	1,000 (*m*)
15,100	

+ Accounts Receivable (A)	−
Bal. 0	
(*i*) 2,000	1,300 (*n*)
700	

+	Cash (A)	−
Bal.	5,200	
(*h*)	12,000	2,200 (*k*)
(*j*)	600	800 (*l*)
(*n*)	1,300	1,000 (*m*)
		600 (*o*)
	14,500	

+	Telephone Service Expense (E)	−
Beg.	0	
(*o*)	600	
	600	

(*o*) Pizza Aroma receives and pays a $600 bill for telephone service in May.

		Debit	Credit
(*o*)	Telephone Service Expense (+E, −OE)	600	
	Cash (−A)		600

Assets		=	Liabilities	+	Owner's Equity	
(*o*) Cash	−600				Telephone Service Expense (+E)	−600

Equality checks: (1) Debits $600 = Credits $600; (2) the accounting equation is in balance.

+	Cash (A)	−
Bal.	5,200	
(*h*)	12,000	2,200 (*k*)
(*j*)	600	800 (*l*)
(*n*)	1,300	1,000 (*m*)
		600 (*o*)
		2,400 (*p*)
	12,100	

+	Prepaid Insurance (A)	−
Bal.	0	
(*p*)	2,400	
	2,400	

(*p*) At the end of May, Pizza Aroma purchases insurance for its restaurant equipment, paying $2,400 cash to cover the months of June, July, and August.

		Debit	Credit
(*p*)	Prepaid Insurance (+A)	2,400	
	Cash (−A)		2,400

Assets		=	Liabilities	+	Owner's Equity
(*p*) Prepaid Insurance	+2,400				
Cash	−2,400				

Equality checks: (1) Debits $2,400 = Credits $2,400; (2) the accounting equation is in balance.

+	Cash (A)	−
Bal.	5,200	
(*h*)	12,000	2,200 (*k*)
(*j*)	600	800 (*l*)
(*n*)	1,300	1,000 (*m*)
		600 (*o*)
		2,400 (*p*)
		3,000 (*q*)
	9,100	

+	M. Rosa Drawing (OE)	−
Beg.	0	
(*q*)	3,000	
	3,000	

(*q*) Owner Mauricio Rosa withdraws $3,000 in cash at the end of May.

		Debit	Credit
(*q*)	M. Rosa, Drawing (−OE)	3,000	
	Cash (−A)		3,000

Assets		=	Liabilities	+	Owner's Equity	
(*q*) Cash	−3,000				M. Rosa, Drawing	−3,000

Equality checks: (1) Debits $3,000 = Credits $3,000; (2) the accounting equation is in balance.

Coach's Tip

NOTICE! The drawing account has a debit balance even though it is an owner's equity account because it reduces owner's equity. As the drawing account increases (is debited), owner's equity decreases.

See Exhibit 3.6 for a summary of the journal entries (*h*) through (*q*) and all T-accounts as of May 31.

Exhibit 3.6 Summary of Pizza Aroma's Journal Entries and T-Accounts

Pizza Aroma
Journal Entries
May 8–31

		Debit	Credit
(*h*)	Cash (+A)	12,000	
	Pizza Revenue (+R, +OE)		12,000
(*i*)	Accounts Receivable (+A)	2,000	
	Pizza Revenue (+R, +OE)		2,000
(*j*)	Cash (+A)	600	
	Unearned Revenue (+L)		600
(*k*)	Supplies (+A)	3,000	
	Cash (–A)		2,200
	Accounts Payable (+L)		800
(*l*)	Advertising Expense (+E, –OE)	800	
	Cash (–A)		800
(*m*)	Wages Expense (+E, –OE)	1,000	
	Cash (–A)		1,000
(*n*)	Cash (+A)	1,300	
	Accounts Receivable (–A)		1,300
(*o*)	Telephone Service Expense (+E, –OE)	600	
	Cash (–A)		600
(*p*)	Prepaid Insurance (+A)	2,400	
	Cash (–A)		2,400
(*q*)	M. Rosa, Drawing (–OE)	3,000	
	Cash (–A)		3,000

(*continued*)

Exhibit 3.6 Summary of Pizza Aroma's Journal Entries and T-Accounts *(continued)*

Pizza Aroma
T-Accounts
May 31

Assets

+	Cash (A)	–
Beg. 0		
(*a*) 30,000	4,800 (*c*)	
(*b*) 20,000	33,000 (*d*)	
(*h*) 12,000	1,000 (*f*)	
(*j*) 600	6,000 (*g*)	
(*n*) 1,300	2,200 (*k*)	
	800 (*l*)	
	1,000 (*m*)	
	600 (*o*)	
	2,400 (*p*)	
	3,000 (*q*)	
9,100		

+ Investments (A) –	
Beg. 0	
(*g*) 6,000	
6,000	

+ Accounts Receivable (A) –	
Beg. 0	
(*i*) 2,000	1,300 (*n*)
700	

+ Supplies (A) –	
Beg. 0	
(*e*) 2,000	
(*k*) 3,000	
5,000	

+ Prepaid Rent (A) –	
Beg. 0	
(*c*) 4,800	
4,800	

+ Prepaid Insurance (A) –	
Beg. 0	
(*p*) 2,400	
2,400	

+ Equipment (A) –	
Beg. 0	
(*d*) 36,000	
36,000	

Liabilities

– Accounts Payable (L) +	
	0 Beg.
(*f*) 1,000	3,000 (*d*)
	2,000 (*e*)
	800 (*k*)
	4,800

– Unearned Revenue (L) +	
	0 Beg.
	600 (*j*)
	600

– Notes Payable (L) +	
	0 Beg.
	20,000 (*b*)
	20,000

Owner's Equity

– M. Rosa, Capital (OE) +	
	0 Beg.
	30,000 (*a*)
	30,000

+ M. Rosa, Drawing (OE) –	
Beg. 0	
(*q*) 3,000	
3,000	

Expenses

+ Wages Expense (E) –	
Beg. 0	
(*m*) 1,000	
1,000	

+ Telephone Service Expense (E) –	
Beg. 0	
(*o*) 600	
600	

+ Advertising Expense (E) –	
Beg. 0	
(*l*) 800	
800	

Revenues

– Pizza Revenue (R) +	
	0 Beg.
	12,000 (*h*)
	2,000 (*i*)
	14,000

SELF-STUDY PRACTICE

Analyze each of Florida Flippers' selected transactions in **June;** then record the journal entries and post the effects to the T-accounts. Be sure to check to make sure that the accounting equation remains in balance and that debits equal credits in each journal entry.

(*a*) In June, new customers paid Florida Flippers $8,200 in cash for diving trips; $5,200 was for trips made in June, and the rest is for trips that will be provided in July.

(*b*) In June, customers paid $3,900 in cash for instruction they received in May.

(*c*) At the beginning of June, Florida Flippers paid a total of $6,000 cash for insurance to cover the months of June, July, and August.

(*d*) In June, Florida Flippers paid $4,000 in wages to employees who worked in June.

Coach's Tip

- For transaction (*b*), a journal entry had been recorded in May for what the customers owed to Florida Flippers.
- For transaction (*c*), record the entry at what it represents on the date of the exchange. Because the payment is for future insurance coverage, the entire amount is an asset.

Journal Entries

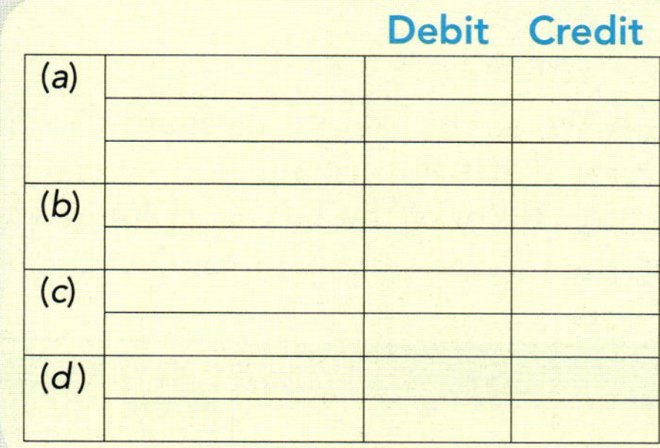

Effects

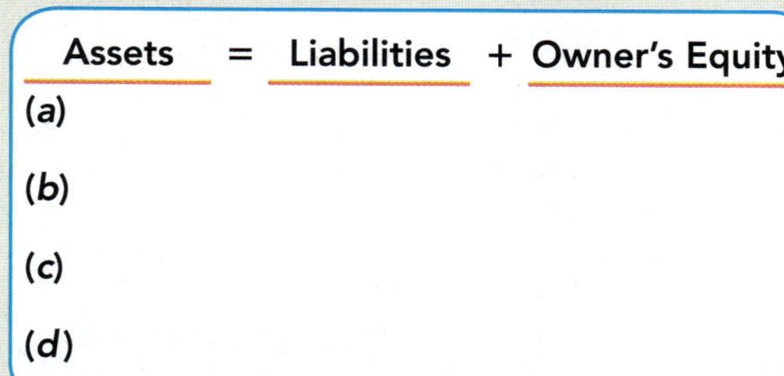

T-Accounts

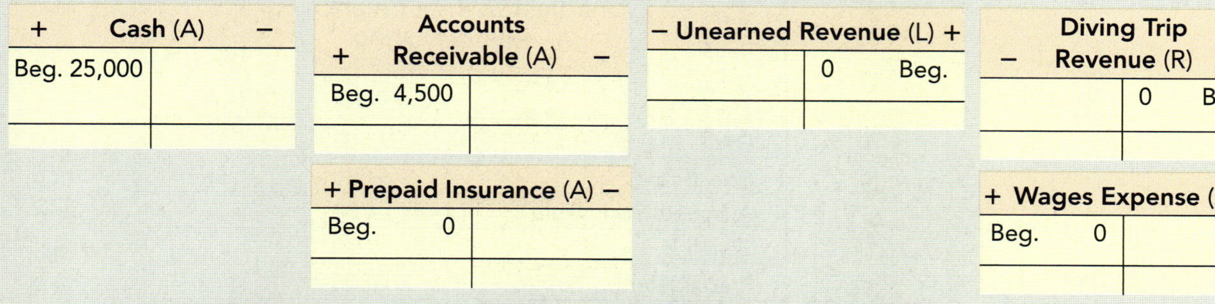

After you have finished, check your answers with the solutions at the bottom of the page.

Solution to Self-Study Practice

Journal Entries

		Debit	Credit
(*a*)	Cash (+A)	8,200	
	Diving Trip Revenue (+R, +OE)		5,200
	Unearned Revenue (+L)		3,000
(*b*)	Cash (+A)	3,900	
	Accounts Receivable (–A)		3,900
(*c*)	Prepaid Insurance (+A)	6,000	
	Cash (–A)		6,000
(*d*)	Wages Expense (+E, –OE)	4,000	
	Cash (–A)		4,000

Assets		=	Liabilities		+	Owner's Equity	
(*a*) Cash	+8,200		Unearned Revenue	+3,000		Diving Trip Revenue (+R)	+5,200
(*b*) Cash	+3,900						
Accts. Rec.	–3,900						
(*c*) Prepd. Ins.	+6,000						
Cash	–6,000						
(*d*) Cash	–4,000					Wages Expense (+E)	–4,000

+ Cash (A) –

	+	–	
Beg.	25,000		
(*a*)	8,200	6,000	(*c*)
(*b*)	3,900	4,000	(*d*)
	27,100		

+ Accounts Receivable (A) –

	+	–	
Beg.	4,500		
		3,900	(*b*)
Bal.	600		

– Unearned Revenue (L) +

–	+	
	0	Beg.
	3,000	(*a*)
	3,000	

– Diving Trip Revenue (R) +

–	+	
	0	Beg.
	5,200	(*a*)
	5,200	

+ Prepaid Insurance (A) –

	+	–
Beg.	0	
(*c*)	6,000	
	6,000	

+ Wages Expense (E) –

	+	–
Beg.	0	
(*d*)	4,000	
	4,000	

PREPARE AN INCOME STATEMENT

Unadjusted Trial Balance

Learning Objective 5

Understand the purpose of a trial balance and prepare a simple income statement.

Mauricio had a busy first month, and his gourmet pizzas became the rage. He was eager to find out how Pizza Aroma had performed financially. Did it make a profit, or even do better than expected? Laurie showed Mauricio the trial balance on May 31, 2009, but cautioned him that it was "unadjusted," meaning that some revenues and expenses had not yet been recorded. Mauricio needed to count the remaining supplies to determine how much the restaurant had used in May. Laurie needed to allocate the Prepaid Rent cost used in May, and she had to contact the bank to find out how much the investments had earned for the month. With that warning, Mauricio reviewed the **unadjusted trial balance** in Exhibit 3.7.

Based on the amounts in the trial balance, Laurie next showed Mauricio the preliminary income statement she had prepared, cautioning him again that it was unadjusted.

Classified Income Statements

As you learned in Chapter 2, the assets and liabilities shown on the balance sheet are classified as either current or noncurrent. This classification provides useful information to external decision makers who want to assess the timing and probability of the business's future cash flows. Similarly, the revenues and expenses shown on the income statement can be classified

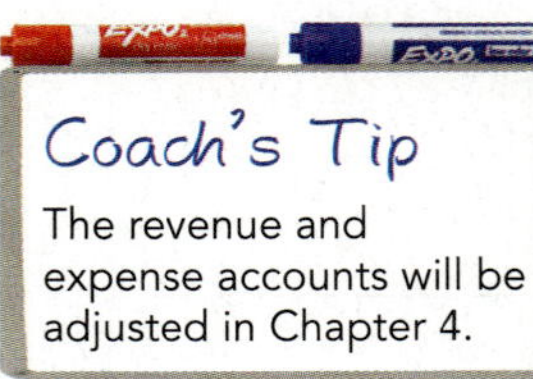

Coach's Tip

The revenue and expense accounts will be adjusted in Chapter 4.

Exhibit 3.7 Unadjusted Trial Balance

PIZZA AROMA

Pizza Aroma
Unadjusted Trial Balance
On May 31, 2009

		Debit	Credit
Balance sheet accounts	Cash	9,100	
	Investments	6,000	
	Accounts Receivable	700	
	Supplies	5,000	
	Prepaid Rent	4,800	
	Prepaid Insurance	2,400	
	Equipment	36,000	
	Accounts Payable		4,800
	Unearned Revenue		600
	Notes Payable		20,000
	M. Rosa, Capital		30,000
	M. Rosa, Drawing	3,000	
Income statement accounts	Pizza Revenue		14,000
	Investment Revenue		0
	Wages Expense	1,000	
	Supplies Expense	0	
	Utilities Expense	0	
	Telephone Service Expense	600	
	Rent Expense	0	
	Insurance Expense	0	
	Advertising Expense	800	
	Interest Expense	0	
	Totals	**69,400**	**69,400**

to create a more useful statement of financial performance. The three major classifications of amounts shown on the income statement are Operating Revenues, Operating Expenses, and Other Items.

Operating Revenues and Expenses

Operating revenues result from the sale of goods or services—that is, from the primary or central mission of the business. Mattel earns operating revenues by manufacturing toys and games. American Eagle Outfitters earns operating revenues by selling clothing. Pizza Aroma earns operating revenues by selling pizza.

Likewise, operating expenses are the costs directly related to the generation of operating revenues. Mattel's primary operating expense is Cost of Goods Sold, which represents the inventory that Mattel "uses up" to generate revenues. Pizza Aroma's largest operating expenses are Wages Expense and Supplies Expense, as is typical in the food service industry.

Other Items

Not all activities that affect the income statement are central to a business's operations. These **peripheral** (normal but not central) transactions are classified as Other Items on the income statement. For example, any interest or dividends that Pizza Aroma earns on its investments are stated as Investment Revenue. Because earning investment revenue is not the central focus of Pizza Aroma's business, its Investment Revenue account is classified under Other Items.

Similarly, the cost of borrowing money, called Interest Expense, is classified under Other Items. Incurring interest expense is not a central operating activity of most businesses except for financial institutions.

The separation of operating revenues and expenses from other items enables financial statement users to identify activities that should be ongoing as opposed to those that may not be. See Exhibit 3.8 for Pizza Aroma's classified income statement for May prepared using the amounts in the unadjusted trial balance.

Exhibit 3.8 Classified Income Statement: (from the unadjusted trial balance)

PIZZA AROMA

Pizza Aroma
Income Statement (unadjusted)
For the Month Ended May 31, 2009

Operating Revenues	
Pizza revenue	$14,000
Total operating revenues	14,000
Operating Expenses	
Wages expense	1,000
Supplies expense	0
Utilities expense	0
Telephone service expense	600
Rent expense	0
Insurance expense	0
Advertising expense	800
Total operating expenses	2,400
Operating Income	11,600
Other Items	
Investment revenue	0
Interest expense	(0)
Net Income	$11,600

Limitations of the Income Statement

There are many misconceptions about the meaning of net income. The most common one is that net income equals the amount of cash the business generated during the period. While that is the way that most of us think about our own income for a period, it is not the way to measure revenues and expenses on a company's income statement.

A second, related misconception is that a company's net income represents the change in the company's value during the period. While a company's net income is one source of value to the company, many other determinants of its value are not included in the income statement. A good example is the increase in the value of Pizza Aroma's name as its reputation for making great pizza grows.

A third common misconception is that the measurement of income involves only counting. Proper counting is critical to income measurement, but estimation also plays a role. For example, Pizza Aroma's equipment will not last forever. Instead, it will be "used up" over time to generate the company's revenue. It should therefore be expensed over the period in which it is used. Doing so requires an estimate of the period over which each category of equipment will be used. We will discuss this particular example in Chapter 4; many other examples of the role of estimates in income measurement will arise in later chapters.

Spotlight On ETHICS

Why All the Scandals?

You may have read about numerous accounting scandals, such as those at Enron and WorldCom (now owned by Verizon), in which managers have been accused of "cooking the books." Why did they do it? The simple answer is greed. Companies whose earnings have fallen often experience a decline in their stock prices, which usually leads to pay reductions or even job losses for senior executives. When a company is actually performing poorly, greed may lead some managers to falsify revenues and hide expenses to make it look like the company is still doing well.

While this sometimes fools people for a short time, it rarely works in the long run and often leads to very bad consequences. A few cases involving faulty revenue and expense accounting follow. As you look at these, imagine what it must have been like to be Bernie Ebbers—the person who received a 25-year prison sentence at the age of 65. It is probably just as bad as being Barry Minkow who was sentenced to 25 years in jail at the age of 21.

The CEO	The Fraud	Conviction/Plea	The Outcome
Bernie Ebbers, 65 WorldCom	Recorded operating expenses as if they were assets; resulted in the largest fraud in U.S. history	Convicted July 2005	Sentenced to 25 years
Sanjay Kumar, 44 Computer Associates	Recorded sales in the wrong accounting period	Pleaded guilty April 2006	Sentenced to 12 years
Martin Grass, 49 Rite Aid Corporation	Recorded rebates from drug companies before they were earned	Pleaded guilty June 2003	Sentenced to 8 years
Barry Minkow, 21 ZZZZ Best	Made up customers and sales to show profits when, in reality, the company was a sham	Convicted December 1988	Sentenced to 25 years

In this chapter, you learned how to measure and report revenues and expenses for the accounting period as a starting point for determining net income. The next step is to adjust the financial statements so that they will be complete and up to date at the end of the accounting period. The adjustment process is the main topic of Chapter 4, in which Laurie will help Mauricio to adjust Pizza Aroma's financial statements for May.

Demonstration Case

This is a continuation of the Goodbye Grass case, a lawn care service business, introduced in Chapter 2. Steve Delancey established the company in April 2010 as a sole proprietorship and purchased property and equipment. The following is the April 30, 2010, balance sheet based only on the activities for establishing the business (from Chapter 2):

GOODBYE GRASS
Balance Sheet
At April 30, 2010

Assets		**Liabilities**	
Current Assets		*Current Liabilities*	
Cash	$ 3,800	Accounts Payable	$ 400
Note Receivable	1,250	Notes Payable	4,000
Total Current Assets	5,050	Total Current Liabilities	4,400
Equipment	4,600		
Land	3,750	**Owner's Equity**	
		S. Delancey, Capital	9,000
Total Assets	$13,400	Total Liabilities and Owner's Equity	$13,400

The following activities occurred during May 2010 (the next month):

a. Purchased and used gasoline for mowers and edgers, paying $90 in cash at a local gas station.

b. Received $1,600 cash from the city in early May in advance for lawn maintenance service for May through August ($400 each month). The entire amount is to be recorded as Unearned Revenue (a liability).

c. Purchased in early May $300 of insurance covering six months, May through October. The entire payment is to be recorded as Prepaid Insurance (an asset).

d. Mowed lawns for residential customers who are billed every two weeks. Earned a total of $5,200 of service in May and billed customers.

e. Received payments of $3,500 from residential customers on their accounts.

f. Paid wages every two weeks. Total cash paid in May was $3,900.

g. Received a bill for $320 from the local gas station for additional gasoline purchased on account and used in May. The bill will be paid in June.

h. Paid $40 interest (one month's interest) in mid-May on notes owed to XYZ Lawn Supply.

i. Paid $100 on accounts payable.

j. Steve Delancey withdrew $2,000 from the business.

Required:

1. Analyze activities (*a*)–(*j*) to determine their effects on the basic accounting equation (Assets = Liabilities + Owner's Equity).
2. Prepare journal entries to record the transactions identified among activities (*a*)–(*j*).
3. Summarize the effects of each transaction in the appropriate T-accounts. Before entering these effects, set up T-accounts for Cash; Accounts Receivable; Note Receivable; Prepaid Insurance; Equipment; Land; Accounts Payable; Unearned Revenue; Notes Payable; S. Delancey, Capital; S. Delancey, Drawing; Mowing Revenue; Wages Expense; Fuel Expense; and Interest Expense. The beginning balance in each T-account should be the amount shown on the preceding April 30 balance sheet or $0 if the account does not appear on the balance sheet. After posting the journal entries to the T-accounts, compute ending balances for each T-account.
4. Use the amounts in the T-accounts to prepare an unadjusted trial balance for Goodbye Grass at May 31, 2010.
5. Prepare a *classified* (operating revenues and expenses separated from other revenues and expenses) income statement for May 2010 based on the unadjusted trial balance.

After completing the requirements, check your answers with the following suggested solution.

Suggested Solution

1. Analyze transactions

	Assets		=	Liabilities		+	Owner's Equity	
(*a*)	Cash	− 90					Fuel Expense (+E)	− 90
(*b*)	Cash	+ 1,600		Unearned Revenue	+ 1,600			
(*c*)	Cash	− 300						
	Prepaid Insurance	+ 300						
(*d*)	Accounts Receivable	+ 5,200					Mowing Revenue (+R)	+ 5,200
(*e*)	Cash	+ 3,500						
	Accounts Receivable	− 3,500						
(*f*)	Cash	− 3,900					Wages Expense (+E)	− 3,900
(*g*)				Accounts Payable	+ 320		Fuel Expense (+E)	− 320
(*h*)	Cash	− 40					Interest Expense (+E)	− 40
(*i*)	Cash	− 100		Accounts Payable	− 100			
(*j*)	Cash	− 2,000					S. Delancey, Drawing	− 2,000

2. Journal entries

		Debit	Credit
(*a*)	Fuel Expense (+E, −OE)	90	
	Cash (−A)		90
(*b*)	Cash (+A)	1,600	
	Unearned Revenue (+L)		1,600
(*c*)	Prepaid Insurance (+A)	300	
	Cash (−A)		300
(*d*)	Accounts Receivable (+A)	5,200	
	Mowing Revenue (+R, +OE)		5,200
(*e*)	Cash (+A)	3,500	
	Accounts Receivable (−A)		3,500
(*f*)	Wages Expense (+E, −OE)	3,900	
	Cash (−A)		3,900
(*g*)	Fuel Expense (+E, −OE)	320	
	Accounts Payable (+L)		320
(*h*)	Interest Expense (+E, −OE)	40	
	Cash (−A)		40
(*i*)	Accounts Payable (−L)	100	
	Cash (−A)		100
(*j*)	S. Delancey, Drawing (−OE)	2,000	
	Cash (−A)		2,000

3. T-accounts

Assets = Liabilities + Owner's Equity

Assets

+	Cash (A)		−
Bal.	3,800		
(b)	1,600	90	(a)
(e)	3,500	300	(c)
		3,900	(f)
		40	(h)
		100	(i)
		2,000	(j)
Bal.	2,470		

+	Accounts Receivable (A)		−
Beg.	0		
(d)	5,200	3,500	(e)
Bal.	1,700		

+	Note Receivable (A)		−
Bal.	1,250		
Bal.	1,250		

+	Prepaid Insurance (A)		−
Beg.	0		
(c)	300		
Bal.	300		

+	Equipment (A)		−
Bal.	4,600		
Bal.	4,600		

+	Land (A)		−
Bal.	3,750		
Bal.	3,750		

Liabilities

−	Accounts Payable (L)		+
		400	Bal.
(i)	100	320	(g)
		620	Bal.

−	Unearned Revenue (L)		+
		0	Beg.
		1,600	(b)
		1,600	Bal.

−	Notes Payable (L)		+
		4,000	Bal.
		4,000	Bal.

Owner's Equity

−	S. Delancey, Capital (OE)		+
		9,000	Bal.
		9,000	Bal.

+	S. Delancey, Drawing (OE)		−
Beg.	0		
(j)	2,000		
Bal.	2,000		

Expenses

+	Wages Expense (E)		−
Beg.	0		
(f)	3,900		
Bal.	3,900		

+	Fuel Expense (E)		−
Beg.	0		
(a)	90		
(g)	320		
Bal.	410		

+	Interest Expense (E)		−
Beg.	0		
(h)	40		
Bal.	40		

Revenues

−	Mowing Revenue (R)		+
		0	Beg.
		5,200	(d)
		5,200	Bal.

4. Unadjusted trial balance

GOODBYE GRASS
Unadjusted Trial Balance
As of May 31, 2010

Account Name	Debits	Credits
Cash	2,470	
Accounts Receivable	1,700	
Note Receivable	1,250	
Prepaid Insurance	300	
Equipment	4,600	
Land	3,750	
Accounts Payable		620
Unearned Revenue		1,600
Notes Payable		4,000
S. Delancey, Capital		9,000
S. Delancey, Drawing	2,000	
Mowing Revenue		5,200
Wages Expense	3,900	
Fuel Expense	410	
Interest Expense	40	
Totals	20,420	20,420

5. Unadjusted income statement

GOODBYE GRASS
Income Statement (unadjusted)
For the Month Ended May 31, 2010

Operating Revenues	
Mowing Revenue	$5,200
Total operating revenues	5,200
Operating Expenses	
Wages Expense	3,900
Fuel Expense	410
Total operating expenses	4,310
Operating Income	890
Other Items	
Interest Expense	(40)
Net Income	$ 850

Chapter Summary

LO1 Recognize common income statement accounts. p. 98

- Income Statement Accounts
  The income statement reports net income that is calculated by combining:
  Revenues. Amounts charged to customers for sales of goods or services provided.
  Expenses. Costs of business activities undertaken to earn revenues.
  See Exhibit 3.1 for an expanded list of account titles.

LO2 Describe a typical business operating cycle and explain the necessity for the time period assumption. p. 99

- Operating Cycle
  The process by which a company acquires and pays for goods and services and then sells goods and services to customers who pay cash to the company (the cash-to-cash cycle). The length of time to complete the cycle varies by company.
- Cash-Based Measurements
  Financial performance is measured as the difference between cash received and cash paid during a period. However, cash basis accounting does not measure financial performance well when transactions are conducted using credit rather than cash.

LO3 Explain the accrual basis of accounting and apply the revenue and matching principles to measure income. p. 100

- Accrual Basis Accounting
  The two key concepts underlying accrual basis accounting and the income statement are:
  Revenue principle. Recognize (record) revenues when they are earned.
  Matching principle. Recognize (record) expenses when they are incurred in generating revenue.

LO4 Apply transaction analysis to examine and record the effects of operating activities on the financial statements. p. 103

- Expanded Transaction Analysis Model
  The expanded transaction analysis model includes revenues, expenses, and the owner's drawing account as subcategories of owner's capital.
  - Revenues increase with credits, thus increasing owner's equity.
  - Expenses increase with debits, thus decreasing owner's equity.
  -

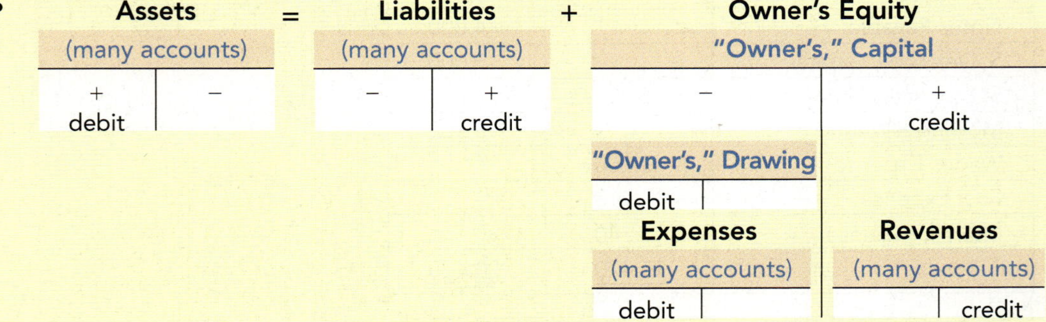

LO5 Understand the purpose of a trial balance and prepare a simple income statement. p. 112

- **Unadjusted Trial Balance**
  The unadjusted trial balance is a list of all accounts and their unadjusted balances and is used to check on the equality of recorded debits and credits.
- **Classified Income Statement**
  Revenues and expenses are classified into Operating Revenues, Operating Expenses, and Other Items on a classified income statement.
  - Operating revenues result from the sale of goods or services—the business's central mission.
  - Operating expenses are costs that are directly related to generating operating revenues in the same period.
  - Other items include revenues, expenses, gains, and losses that are not the business's primary mission. Examples include interest revenue, interest expense, and gains or losses on the sale of long-lived assets.
- **Limitations of the Income Statement**
  - Because of the application of accrual accounting concepts to measure revenues and expenses in a period, net income will **not** equal cash generated by a business during the same period. Under accrual accounting, revenues are recorded when earned and expenses are recorded when incurred regardless of the timing of the cash receipts and payments.
  - Net income is **not** the change in the value of a company during the period. Net income is one source of value, but the income statement does not include many other determinants of value change, such as the increase in value of a company's reputation for quality.
  - Estimation plays a key role in measuring income for a period.

Key Terms

Accrual Basis Accounting (accrual accounting) (p. 101)
Cash Basis Accounting (p. 100)
Matching Principle (p. 103)
Operating (Cash-to-Cash) Cycle (p. 99)
Revenue Principle (p. 101)
Time Period Assumption (p. 99)
Unadjusted Trial Balance (p. 112)

See complete glossary in the back of text.

Questions

1. Indicate the income statement equation and define each element.
2. When accounting was developed in the 14th and 15th centuries, businesses had very short lives. For instance, a business might have been created for a single shipment of goods from Europe to North America. After delivering the goods and distributing profits among those who financed the shipment, the business ceased to exist. In more recent centuries, businesses began to experience longer lives. Identify the accounting concept needed when accounting for businesses with long lives. Explain what this concept means and why it is necessary for modern-day accounting.
3. Define accrual basis accounting and contrast it with cash basis accounting.
4. Why is it appropriate to use a cash basis of accounting in your personal life but not in the business world?
5. What does it mean to "recognize" an accounting transaction?
6. When is revenue typically recognized under accrual basis accounting?
7. Explain the matching principle.
8. Explain why owner's equity increases by revenues and decreases by expenses.
9. Explain why revenues are recorded as credits and expenses as debits.
10. Complete the following table by entering either *debit* or *credit* in each cell:

Item	Increase	Decrease
Revenues		
Expenses		

11. Complete the following table by entering either *increase* or *decrease* in each cell:

Item	Debit	Credit
Revenues		
Expenses		

12. What is the difference between Accounts Receivable and Revenue?
13. What is the difference between Wages Payable and Wages Expense?
14. For each of the following situations, indicate whether it represents an accounting error and explain why it is or is

not an error. Also indicate whether a trial balance would indicate that an error exists for each situation.

a. Cash received from a customer who is paying on his or her account owed to the business was debited to Accounts Receivable and credited to Cash.

b. Revenue was recognized when a customer purchased a gift certificate for future use.

c. An expense was recorded as an asset.

d. The debit side of a journal entry was recorded in the accounts, but the credit side was not.

e. A business owner purchased a new car for personal use, but the business did not record this.

15. What are three limitations of the income statement that often lead to misconceptions?

Multiple Choice

1. Which of the following items is **not** a specific account in a company's chart of accounts?
   a. Accounts Receivable.
   b. Net Income.
   c. Revenue.
   d. Unearned Revenue.

Quiz 3-1
www.mhhe.com/LLPW1e

2. Which of the following accounts normally has a debit balance?
   a. Unearned Revenue.
   b. Rent Expense.
   c. Retained Earnings.
   d. Sales Revenue.

3. The matching principle controls
   a. Where on the income statement expenses should be presented.
   b. How costs are allocated between Cost of Goods Sold (sometimes called Cost of Sales) and general and administrative expenses.
   c. The ordering of current assets and current liabilities on the balance sheet.
   d. When costs are recognized as expenses on the income statement.

4. When should businesses that sell gift certificates to customers report revenue?
   a. When the gift certificate is sold and cash is received.
   b. When the gift certificate is used by the customer.
   c. At the end of the year in which the gift certificate is sold.
   d. None of the above.

5. How will a manager's decision to record a payment as an asset rather than as an expense affect net income for the business in the current period?
   a. Net income will be higher.
   b. Net income will be lower.
   c. Net income will not be affected by this decision.
   d. The effect cannot be determined.

6. When should a company report the cost of an insurance policy as an expense?
   a. When the company first signs the policy.
   b. When the company pays for the policy.
   c. When the company receives the benefits from the policy over its period of coverage.
   d. When the company receives payments from the insurance company for its insurance claims.

7. When expenses exceed revenues in a given period (and there are no gains or losses),
   a. Owner's equity will not be impacted.
   b. Owner's equity will be increased.
   c. Owner's equity will be decreased.
   d. One cannot determine the impact on owner's equity without additional information.

8. Which account is *least* likely to be debited when revenue is recorded?
   a. Accounts Payable
   b. Accounts Receivable
   c. Cash
   d. Unearned Revenue

9. Webby Company reported the following amounts on its income statement: Service Revenues, $31,600; Interest Expense, $300; and Net Income, $1,600. If the only other account reported on the income statement was for "selling expenses," what is its amount?
   a. $ 2,200
   b. $29,700
   c. $30,000
   d. $30,900

10. Which of the following is the entry a law firm would record when it receives a payment from a new client that will be earned when the firm provides services in the future?
    a. *Debit* to Accounts Receivable; *credit* to Legal Services Revenue.
    b. *Debit* to Unearned Revenue; *credit* to Legal Services Revenue.
    c. *Debit* to Cash; *credit* to Unearned Revenue.
    d. *Debit* to Unearned Revenue; *credit* to Cash.

Solutions to Multiple-Choice Questions

1. b	2. b	3. d	4. b	5. a	6. c	7. c
8. a	9. b	10. c				

Mini Exercises  Available with McGraw-Hill's Homework Manager

M3-1 Reporting Cash Basis versus Accrual Basis Income LO1, 3, 5

Mostert Music Company had the following transactions in March:

a. Sold music lessons to customers for $10,000; received $6,000 in cash and the rest on account.
b. Paid $600 in wages for the month.
c. Received a $200 bill for utilities that will be paid in April.
d. Received $1,000 from customers as deposits on music lessons to be given in April.

Complete the following statements:

Cash Basis Income Statement	
Revenues	
Cash sales	$
Customer deposits	
Expenses	
Wages paid	
Net income	$

Accrual Basis Income Statement	
Revenues	
Sales to customers	$
Expenses	
Wages expense	
Utilities expense	
Net income	$

M3-2 Identifying Revenues LO3

The following transactions are July 2011 activities of Ben's Extreme Bowling Center owned by Ben Baxter, who owns and operates several bowling centers. If revenue is to be recognized in **July,** indicate the amount. If revenue is not to be recognized in July, explain why.

Activity	Amount or Explanation
a. Collected $12,000 from customers for games played in July.	________
b. Billed a customer for $250 for a party held at the center on the last day of July. The bill is to be paid in August.	________
c. Received $1,000 in July from customers who purchased bowling equipment on account in June.	________
d. Received from the men's and women's bowling leagues advance payments totaling $1,500 for the fall season that starts in September.	________

M3-3 Identifying Expenses LO3

The following transactions are July 2011 activities of Ben's Extreme Bowling Center owned by Ben Baxter, who owns and operates several bowling centers. If an expense is to be recognized in **July,** indicate the amount. If an expense is not to be recognized in July, explain why.

Activity	Amount or Explanation
e. Paid $1,500 to plumbers for repairing a broken pipe in the restrooms in July.	________
f. Paid $2,000 for the June electricity bill (received and recorded as an expense at the end of June).	________
g. Paid $5,475 to employees for work in July.	________
h. Received the July electricity bill for $2,500 that will be paid in August.	________

LO1, 4

M3-4 Recording Revenues

For each transaction in M3-2, write the journal entry using the format shown in the chapter.

LO1, 4

M3-5 Recording Expenses

For each transaction in M3-3, write the journal entry using the format shown in the chapter.

LO4

M3-6 Determining the Financial Statement Effects of Operating Activities Involving Revenues

The following transactions are July 2011 activities of Ben's Extreme Bowling Center owned by Ben Baxter, who owns and operates several bowling centers. For each of the following transactions, complete the spreadsheet, indicating the amount and effect (+ for increase and − for decrease) of each transaction. Write NE if there is no effect. The first transaction is provided as an example.

	BALANCE SHEET			INCOME STATEMENT		
Transaction	Assets	Liabilities	Owner's Equity	Revenues	Expenses	Net Income
a. Collected $12,000 from customers for games played in July.	+12,000	NE	+12,000	+12,000	NE	+12,000
b. Billed a customer for $250 for a party held at the center on the last day of July. The bill is to be paid in August.						
c. Received $1,000 in July from customers who purchased bowling equipment on account in June.						
d. Received from the men's and women's bowling leagues advance payments totaling $1,500 for the fall season that starts in September.						

LO4

M3-7 Determining the Financial Statement Effects of Operating Activities Involving Expenses

The following transactions are July 2011 activities of Ben's Extreme Bowling Center owned by Ben Baxter, who owns and operates several bowling centers. For each of the following transactions, complete the spreadsheet, indicating the amount and effect (+ for increase and − for decrease) of each transaction. Write NE if there is no effect. The first transaction is provided as an example.

	BALANCE SHEET			INCOME STATEMENT		
Transaction	Assets	Liabilities	Owner's Equity	Revenues	Expenses	Net Income
e. Paid $1,500 to plumbers for repairing a broken pipe in the restrooms in July.	−1,500	NE	−1,500	NE	+1,500	−1,500
f. Paid $2,000 for the June electricity bill (received and recorded as an expense at the end of June).						
g. Paid $5,475 to employees for work in July.						
h. Received the July electricity bill for $2,500 that will be paid in August.						

LO5

M3-8 Preparing an Income Statement

Given the transactions in M3-6 and M3-7 (including the examples), prepare an income statement based on unadjusted account balances for Ben's Extreme Bowling Center for the month ended July 31, 2011.

LO3

M3-9 Identifying Revenues

The following transactions are February 2009 activities of Swing Hard, a sole proprietorship owned by Doris Heald. The business offers indoor golfing lessons. If revenue is to be recognized in February, indicate the amount. If revenue is not to be recognized in February, explain why.

Activity	Amount or Explanation
a. Collected $15,000 from customers for lessons given in February.	________
b. Sold a gift certificate for golf lessons for $150 cash in February.	________
c. Received $4,000 from customers for services provided to them on credit in January.	________
d. Collected $2,250 in advance payments for golf lessons to start in June.	________
e. Billed a customer $125 for golf lessons given at the end of February. The customer is to pay the bill in March.	________

M3-10 Identifying Expenses **LO3**

The following transactions are February 2009 activities of Swing Hard, a sole proprietorship owned by Doris Heald. The business offers indoor golfing lessons. If an expense is to be recognized in February, indicate the amount. If an expense is not to be recognized in February, explain why.

Activity	Amount or Explanation
f. Paid $1,750 for electricity used in the month of January; the bill was received and recorded at the end of January.	________
g. Received an $800 electricity bill for the month of February to be paid in March.	________
h. Paid $4,750 to its golf instructors for the month of February.	________

M3-11 Recording Revenues **LO1, 4**

For each transaction in M3-9, write the journal entry using the format shown in the chapter.

M3-12 Recording Expenses **LO1, 4**

For each transaction in M3-10, write the journal entry using the format shown in the chapter.

M3-13 Determining the Financial Statement Effects of Operating Activities Involving Revenues **LO4**

The following transactions are February 2009 activities of Swing Hard, a sole proprietorship owned by Doris Heald. The business offers indoor golfing lessons. For each of the following transactions, complete the spreadsheet, indicating the amount and effect (+ for increase and − for decrease) of each transaction. Write NE if there is no effect. The first transaction is provided as an example.

	BALANCE SHEET			INCOME STATEMENT		
Transaction	Assets	Liabilities	Owner's Equity	Revenues	Expenses	Net Income
a. Collected $15,000 from customers for lessons given in February.	+15,000	NE	+15,000	+15,000	NE	+15,000
b. Sold a gift certificate for golf lessons for $150 cash in February.						
c. Received $4,000 from customers for services provided to them on credit in January.						
d. Collected $2,250 in advance payments for golf lessons to start in June.						
e. Billed a customer $125 for golf lessons given at the end of February. The customer is to pay the bill in March.						

LO4

M3-14 Determining the Financial Statement Effects of Operating Activities Involving Expenses

The following transactions are February 2009 activities of Swing Hard, a sole proprietorship owned by Doris Heald. The business offers indoor golfing lessons. For each of the following transactions, complete the spreadsheet, indicating the amount and effect (+ for increase and − for decrease) of each transaction. Write NE if there is no effect. The first transaction is provided as an example.

	BALANCE SHEET			INCOME STATEMENT		
Transaction	Assets	Liabilities	Owner's Equity	Revenues	Expenses	Net Income
f. Paid $1,750 for electricity used in the month of January; the bill was received and recorded at the end of January.	−1,750	−1,750	NE	NE	NE	NE
g. Received an electricity bill for $800 for the month of February to be paid in March.						
h. Paid $4,750 to its golf instructors for the month of February.						

LO5

M3-15 Preparing an Income Statement

Given the transactions in M3-13 and M3-14 (including the examples), prepare an income statement based on unadjusted account balances for Swing Hard for the month ended February 28, 2009.

LO5

M3-16 Preparing an Income Statement from a Trial Balance

The following unadjusted trial balance as of December 31, 2010, is for Buckeroo U!, a sole proprietorship owned by Tim Carey. The company specializes in horse-breaking services and rodeo lessons.

Buckeroo U!
Unadjusted Trial Balance
As of December 31, 2010

Account Name	Debits	Credits
Cash	59,750	
Accounts Receivable	3,300	
Prepaid Insurance	1,200	
Equipment	64,600	
Land	23,000	
Accounts Payable		29,230
Unearned Revenues		1,500
Long-Term Notes Payable		74,000
T. Carey, Capital		16,000
Horse-Breaking Revenue		25,200
Rodeo Lesson Revenue		10,500
Wages Expense	4,130	
Maintenance Expense	410	
Interest Expense	40	
Totals	156,430	156,430

Required:

Using the unadjusted trial balance provided, create a *classified* income statement for Buckeroo U! for the year ended December 31, 2010.

M3-17 Preparing an Income Statement

LO5
Time Warner, Inc.

The following accounts are from a recent set of financial statements of Time Warner, Inc. Dollars are in millions.

Subscription Revenue	$22,222	Accounts Receivable	$6,411	Long-Term Debt	$20,238
Other Operating Revenues	13,818	Interest Expense	1,266	Other Operating Expenses	29,003
Salaries Expense	10,478	Accounts Payable	1,380	Unearned Revenue	1,473
Cash	4,220	Advertising Revenue	7,612	Equipment	13,676

Required:
Assume that the year ended on December 31, 2010. Prepare a *classified* income statement for the year. Note that some accounts listed are not reported on the income statement.

M3-18 Preparing an Income Statement

LO5
H&R Block

Henry and Richard Bloch founded H&R Block in 1955. Henry, who served as a navigator on a B-17 bomber in World War II, and Richard, who founded his first business in the 4th grade and attended Wharton at age 16, built H&R Block into the world's largest tax services company, serving more than 20 million people in 11 countries around the globe. The following accounts are from the financial statements of H&R Block at the end of a recent fiscal year. Dollars are in millions.

Cost of Services (an expense)	$2,383	Cash	$1,008	Other Operating Expenses	$ 837
Salaries Payable	331	Accounts Receivable	1,000	Long-Term Note Payable	418
Salaries Expense	1,113	Software Revenue	493	Owners' Capital	3,492
Accounts Payable	769	Other Operating Revenues	917		
Service Revenue	3,463	Interest Expense	49		

Required:
Assume that the year ended on April 30, 2009. Prepare a *classified* income statement for the year. Note that some accounts are not reported on the income statement.

Exercises

Available with McGraw-Hill's Homework Manager

E3-1 Matching Definitions with Terms

LO1, 3

Match each definition with its related term by entering the appropriate letter in the space provided.

Term	Definition
____ 1. Expenses	A. Record expenses when incurred in earning revenue.
____ 2. Matching principle	B. Liability account used to record the obligation to provide future services or return cash that has been received before revenues have been earned.
____ 3. Revenue principle	C. Costs that result when a company sacrifices resources to generate revenues.
____ 4. Cash basis accounting	D. Record revenues when earned, not necessarily when cash is received.
____ 5. Unearned Revenue	E. Record revenues when received and expenses when paid.
____ 6. Accrual basis accounting	F. Type of asset account used to record the benefits obtained when cash is paid before expenses are incurred.
____ 7. Prepaid Expenses	G. Record revenues when earned and expenses when incurred.

E3-2 Identifying Revenues

LO1, 3

According to the revenue principle, revenues should be recognized when they are earned, which happens when the company performs acts promised to the customer. For most businesses, this condition is met at the point of delivery of goods or services. The following transactions occurred in September 2009:

a. A customer purchases 10 MP3 song files from Apple's iTunes store. The customer promises to pay $10 within three months. Answer from Apple's standpoint.

b. The Home Depot provides a carpet installation service for $2,000 cash. A comparable installation from other companies costs $3,000.

c. AT&T is scheduled to install digital cable at 1,000 Austin-area homes next week. The installation charge is $100 per home. The terms require payment within 30 days of installation. Answer from AT&T's standpoint.

d. AT&T completes the installations described in (*c*). Answer from AT&T's standpoint.

e. AT&T receives payment from customers for the installations described in (*c*). Answer from AT&T's standpoint.

f. A customer purchases a ticket from AMR Corporation's American Airlines in September for $500 cash to travel in December. Answer from American Airlines' standpoint.

Required:
If revenue is to be recognized in September, indicate the revenue account affected and the amount for each transaction. If revenue is not to be recognized in September, explain why.

LO1, 3

E3-3 Identifying Revenues

According to the revenue principle, revenues should be recognized when they are earned, which happens when the company performs acts promised to the customer. For most businesses, this condition is met at the point of delivery of goods or services. The following transactions occurred in September 2010:

a. General Motors receives $26 million in contributions from new investors.

b. Cal State University receives $20,000,000 cash for 80,000 five-game season football tickets. None of the games has been played.

c. Cal State plays the first football game referred to in (*b*).

d. Hall Construction signs a contract with a customer to construct a new $500,000 warehouse. At the signing, Hall receives a check for $50,000 as a deposit to be applied against amounts earned during the first phase of construction. Answer from Hall's standpoint.

e. A popular snowboarding magazine company receives a total of $1,800 today from subscribers. The subscriptions begin in the next fiscal year. Answer from the magazine company's standpoint.

f. T-Mobile sells a $100 cell phone plan to a customer who charges the sale on his credit card. Answer from the standpoint of T-Mobile.

Required:
For each of the transactions, if revenue is to be recognized in September, indicate the revenue account affected and the amount. If revenue is not to be recognized in September, explain why.

LO1, 3

E3-4 Identifying Expenses

Under accrual basis accounting, expenses are recognized when incurred, which means the activity giving rise to the expense has occurred. Assume the following transactions occurred in January 2010:

a. Gateway pays its computer service technicians $90,000 in salary for the two weeks ended January 7. Answer from Gateway's standpoint.

b. At the beginning of January, Turner Construction pays $4,500 in worker's compensation insurance for the first three months of the year.

c. The McGraw-Hill Companies—publisher of this textbook and *BusinessWeek*—uses $1,000 worth of electricity and natural gas in January for which it has not yet been billed.

d. Pooler's Pools receives and pays a $1,500 invoice in January from a marketing firm for services received in January.

e. A consulting firm performs consulting services in January for a bookstore for $5,000. The terms indicate that payment is due from the bookstore within 30 days of the consultation. Answer from the bookstore's standpoint.

f. Tawanda Canoes has its delivery van repaired in January for $280 and charges the amount on account.

Required:
If an expense is to be recognized in January for each transaction, indicate the expense account affected and the amount. If an expense is not to be recognized in January, indicate why.

LO1, 3

E3-5 Identifying Expenses

Under accrual basis accounting, expenses are recognized when incurred, which means the activity giving rise to the expense has occurred. The following transactions occurred in January 2009:

a. American Express pays its salespersons $3,500 in commissions related to December financial advisory services sales. Answer from American Express's standpoint.

b. On January 31, American Express determines that it will pay its salespersons $4,200 in commissions related to January sales. The payment will be made in early February. Answer from American Express's standpoint.

c. The city of Omaha contracts with Waste Management, Inc. to provide trash collection services beginning in January. The city pays $7.2 million for the entire year. Answer from the city's standpoint.

d. The University of Florida orders 60,000 season football tickets from its printer and pays $6,000 in advance for the custom printing. The first game will be played in September. Answer from the university's standpoint.

e. A Houston Community College employee works eight hours at $15 per hour on January 31; payday is not until February 3. Answer from the college's point of view.

f. Wang Consulting paid $3,600 for a fire insurance policy on January 1. The policy covers 12 months beginning on January 1. Answer from Wang's point of view.

g. Ziegler Machines, a sole proprietorship selling farm equipment, receives a $230 phone bill at the end of January for calls made in January. The bill has not been paid to date.

Required:
For each transaction that is an expense to be recognized in January, indicate the expense account affected and the amount. If an expense is not to be recognized in January, indicate why.

E3-6 Determining Financial Statement Effects of Various Transactions LO4

The following transactions occurred during a recent year:

a. (*Example*) Received cash investment from owner.
b. Borrowed cash from local bank.
c. Purchased equipment on credit.
d. Earned revenue and collected cash.
e. Incurred expenses, on credit.
f. Earned revenue, on credit.
g. Paid cash on account.
h. Incurred expenses and paid cash.
i. Earned revenue, collected half in cash and the balance on credit.
j. Collected cash from customers on account.
k. Incurred expenses, paid half in cash and the balance on credit.
l. Paid insurance expense for the period.

Required:
For each transaction, complete the following table indicating its effect (+ for increase and − for decrease). Write NE if there is no effect. The first transaction is provided as an example.

	BALANCE SHEET			INCOME STATEMENT		
Transaction	Assets	Liabilities	Owner's Equity	Revenues	Expenses	Net Income
a. (*Example*)	+	NE	+	NE	NE	NE

E3-7 Determining Financial Statement Effects of Various Transactions LO4 Wolverine World Wide, Inc.

Wolverine World Wide, Inc., manufactures military, work, sport, and casual footwear and leather accessories under a variety of brand names, such as Caterpillar, Hush Puppies, Wolverine, and Steve Madden. The following transactions occurred during a recent year. Dollars are in thousands.

a. (*Example*) Received $49,000 cash from investors.
b. Purchased $300,000 of additional supplies on account.
c. Borrowed $58,000, signing a long-term note.
d. Purchased $18,600 in additional property, plant, and equipment for cash.
e. Incurred $87,000 in selling expenses, paying two-thirds in cash and owing the rest on account.
f. Incurred $4,700 in interest expense to be paid next year.

Required:
For each transaction, complete the following table, indicating the effect (+ for increase and − for decrease) and amount. Write NE if there is no effect. The first transaction is provided as an example.

	BALANCE SHEET			INCOME STATEMENT		
Transaction	Assets	Liabilities	Owner's Equity	Revenues	Expenses	Net Income
a. (*Example*)	+49,000	NE	+49,000	NE	NE	NE

LO4
Sysco

E3-8 Recording Journal Entries

Sysco, formed in 1969, is America's largest marketer and distributor of food service products, serving nearly 250,000 restaurants, hotels, schools, hospitals, and other institutions. The following transactions are typical of those that occurred in a recent year. (All amounts are rounded to the nearest thousand.)

a. Borrowed $80,000 from a bank, signing a short-term note payable.
b. Provided $10,000 in service to customers with $9,500 on account and the rest received in cash.
c. Purchased plant and equipment for $130,000 in cash.
d. Paid employee wages of $1,000.
e. Received $410 on account from customers.
f. Purchased and used fuel of $400,000 in delivery vehicles during the year (paid for in cash).
g. Paid $8,200 cash on accounts payable.
h. Incurred $20,000 in utility expenses during the year, of which $15,000 was paid in cash and the rest owed on account.

Required:
For each transaction, prepare journal entries. Determine whether the accounting equation remains in balance and debits equal credits after each entry.

LO4
Greek Peak

E3-9 Recording Journal Entries

Greek Peak is a ski resort in upstate New York. The company sells lift tickets, ski lessons, and ski equipment. It operates several restaurants and rents townhouses to vacationing skiers. The following hypothetical December 2011 transactions are typical of those that occur at the resort.

a. Borrowed $500,000 from the bank on December 1, signing a note payable due in six months.
b. Purchased a new snowplow for $20,000 cash on December 31.
c. Purchased ski merchandise for $10,000 on account to sell in the ski shop.
d. Incurred $22,000 in routine maintenance expenses for the chairlifts; paid cash.
e. Sold $72,000 of season passes for cash. The season begins in January.
f. Sold daily lift passes in December for a total of $76,000 cash.
g. Received a $320 deposit on a townhouse to be rented for five days in January.
h. Paid half the charges incurred on account in *(c)*.
i. Paid $18,000 in wages to employees for the month of December.

Required:
Prepare journal entries for each transaction. Be sure to categorize each account as an asset (A), liability (L), owners' equity (OE), revenue (R), or expense (E), and check that debits equal credits for each journal entry.

LO4

E3-10 Recording Journal Entries

Rowland & Sons Air Transport Service has been in operation for three years. The following transactions occurred in February 2009:

Feb. 1	Paid $200 for rent of hangar space in February.
Feb. 2	Purchased fuel costing $450 on account for the next flight to Dallas.
Feb. 4	Received customer payment of $800 to ship several items to Philadelphia next month.
Feb. 7	Flew cargo from Denver to Dallas; the customer paid $900 for the air transport.
Feb. 10	Paid pilot $1,200 in wages for flying in January.
Feb. 14	Paid $60 for an advertisement to run in the local paper on March 5.
Feb. 18	Flew cargo for two customers from Dallas to Albuquerque for $1,700; one customer paid $500 cash and the other asked to be billed.
Feb. 25	Purchased on account $1,350 in spare parts for the planes.
Feb. 27	Hugh Rowland, owner, withdrew $1,800 cash from the business.

Required:
Prepare journal entries for each transaction. Be sure to categorize each account as an asset (A), liability (L), owners' equity (OE), revenue (R), or expense (E).

LO4

E3-11 Recording Journal Entries and Posting to T-Accounts

Ricky's Piano Rebuilders, owned by Jon Ricky, has been operating for one year (2009). At the start of 2010, its income statement accounts had zero balances and its balance sheet account balances were as follows:

Cash	$ 6,000	Building	$ 22,000
Accounts Receivable	25,000	Accounts Payable	8,000
Supplies	1,200	Unearned Fee Revenue (deposits)	3,200
Equipment	8,000	Notes Payable	40,000
Land	6,000	J. Ricky, Capital	17,000

Required:

1. Create T-accounts for the balance sheet accounts and for these additional accounts: J. Ricky, Drawing; Piano Rebuilding Revenue; Rent Revenue; Wages Expense; and Utilities Expense. Enter the beginning balances.
2. Prepare journal entries for the following January 2010 transactions, using the letter of each transaction as a reference:
   a. Received a $500 deposit from a customer who wanted her piano rebuilt.
   b. Rented a part of the building to a bicycle repair shop for $300 received in January.
   c. Delivered five rebuilt pianos to customers who paid $14,500 in cash.
   d. Delivered two rebuilt pianos to customers for $7,000 charged on account.
   e. Received $6,000 from customers as payment on their accounts.
   f. Received an electric and gas utility bill for $350 for January services to be paid in February.
   g. Ordered $800 in supplies..
   h. Paid $1,700 on account in January.
   i. Paid $10,000 in wages to employees in January for work done this month.
   j. Received and paid cash for the supplies in *(g)*.
   k. Jon Ricky withdrew $10,000 cash from the business.
3. Post the journal entries to the T-accounts. Show the unadjusted ending balances in the T-accounts.

E3-12 Preparing an Unadjusted Trial Balance **LO5**

Refer to E3-11.

Required:

Use the balances in the completed T-accounts in E3-11 to prepare an unadjusted trial balance at the end of January 2010.

E3-13 Inferring Operating Transactions and Preparing an Unadjusted Trial Balance **LO4, 5**

Virtual Golf Center, owned by Mike McCall, operates indoor golf simulators that allow individual customers and golf club members to experience courses such as Pebble Beach and Augusta without leaving their own neighborhood. Its stores are located in rented space in malls and shopping centers. During its first month of business ended April 30, 2009, Virtual Golf Center completed eight transactions with the dollar effects indicated in the following schedule:

	Assets				=	Liabilities		+	Owner's Equity	
	Cash	Accounts Receivable	Supplies	Equipment		Accounts Payable	Unearned Revenue		M. McCall, Capital	
Beginning Balance	0	0	0	0		0	0		0	
(a)	+100,000								+100,000	
(b)	−30,000			+30,000						
(c)	−200		+1,000			+800				
(d)	+9,000	+1,000							+10,000	Sales Revenue
(e)	−1,000								−1,000	Wages Expense
(f)						+1,200			−1,200	Utilities Expense
(g)	+2,000						+2,000			
(h)	−5,000								−5,000	M. McCall, Drawing

Required:

1. Write a brief explanation of transactions *(a)* through *(h)*. Include any assumptions that you made.
2. Compute the ending balance in each account and prepare an unadjusted trial balance for Virtual Golf Center on April 30, 2009.

LO4
The Washington Post Company

E3-14 Inferring Transactions and Computing Effects Using T-Accounts

The Washington Post Company is best known for publishing *The Washington Post* but also publishes *Newsweek* magazine and owns Kaplan, Inc. (admissions test preparation services among other services) and various television stations and community newspapers. A recent annual report included the following accounts. Dollars are in millions.

+Dr Accounts Receivable (A) Cr−		
1/1	399	
	2,805	?
12/31	423	

+Dr Supplies (A) Cr−		
1/1	15	
	342	?
12/31	20	

−Dr Unearned Revenue (L) Cr+		
	439	1/1
?	2,643	
	509	12/31

Required:

1. For each T-account, describe the typical transactions that cause it to increase and decrease.
2. Solve for the missing amounts (in millions). (*Hint:* Express each T-account in equation format: Beginning + Increase Side − Decrease Side = Ending.)

LO1, 3, 5

E3-15 Finding Financial Information as an Investor

You are evaluating your current portfolio of investments to determine those that are not performing to your expectations. You have all of the companies' most recent annual reports.

Required:

For each of the following, indicate where you would locate the information in an annual report.

1. The total cost incurred for repairs and maintenance during the year.
2. Accounts receivable.
3. Description of a company's revenue recognition policy.
4. The cost of wages incurred during the year.

LO4

E3-16 Determining Financial Statement Effects of Several Transactions

Sifuentes Consulting, owned and managed by José Sifuentes, provides marketing consulting services. In January 2011, Sifuentes Consulting posted the following transactions.

a. *(Example)* Received \$9,500 cash for consulting services rendered in January.
b. Received an additional \$10,000 in cash as an investment from José Sifuentes.
c. Purchased \$12,000 of equipment, paying 25 percent in cash and owing the rest on a note due in two years.
d. Received \$7,500 cash for consulting services to be performed in February.
e. Bought \$1,000 of supplies on account.
f. Paid \$1,100 for December utility bill (recorded as expense in December 2010).
g. Received utility bill for January for \$1,250, due February 15.
h. Consulted for customers in January for fees totaling \$15,900, due in February.
i. Received \$12,000 cash for consulting services rendered in December.
j. Paid \$500 toward supplies purchased in (*e*).
k. J. Sifuentes withdrew \$3,000 cash from the business.

Required:

Indicate the accounts, amounts, and direction of the effects on the firm's accounting equation for each of the transactions. A sample is provided.

Assets		=	Liabilities	+	Owner's Equity	
(*a*) Cash	+9,500				Service Revenue (+R)	+9,500

E3-17 Preparing Journal Entries LO4

For each transaction in E3-16 (including the example), write the journal entry using the format shown in this chapter.

E3-18 Posting to T-Accounts LO4

For each transaction in E3-16 (including the example), post the effects to the appropriate T-accounts and determine ending account balances. Beginning account balances have been given. An example is provided.

+Dr	**Cash** (A)		Cr−
1/1/11	10,000		
(a)	*9,500*		

+Dr	**Accounts Receivable** (A)		Cr−
1/1/11	9,500		

+Dr	**Supplies** (A)		Cr−
1/1/11	800		

+Dr	**Equipment** (A)		Cr−
1/1/11	8,000		

−Dr	**Accounts Payable** (L)		Cr+
		5,000	1/1/11

−Dr	**Note Payable** (L)		Cr+
		0	1/1/11

−Dr	**Unearned Revenue** (L)		Cr+
		2,500	1/1/11

−Dr	**J. Sifuentes, Capital** (OE)		Cr+
		20,800	1/1/11

+Dr	**J. Sifuentes, Drawing** (OE)		Cr−
1/1/11	0		

−Dr	**Service Revenue** (R)		Cr+
		0	1/1/11
		9,500	*a.*

+Dr	**Utilities Expense** (E)		Cr−
1/1/11	0		

E3-19 Creating an Unadjusted Trial Balance LO5

Based on the transactions posted to T-accounts in E3-18, create an unadjusted trial balance for Sifuentes Consulting for the month ended January 31, 2011.

E3-20 Inferring Income Statement Transactions and Creating Financial Statements LO4, 5

An analysis of transactions made during July 2009 by Zelkind Tech Services, an Internet service provider owned by Josh Zelkind, during its first month of operations, follows. Increases and decreases in owner's equity are explained.

	Assets				= Liabilities	+ Owner's Equity	
	Cash	Accounts Receivable	Supplies	Equipment	Accounts Payable	J. Zelkind, Capital	
Beg.	0	0	0	0	0	0	
a.	+11,000					+11,000	Investment by owner
b.		+5,000				+5,000	Service Revenue
c.					+710	−710	Utilities Expense
d.	−6,000			+10,000	+4,000		
e.	+1,000					+1,000	Service Revenue
f.			+550		+550		
g.	−3,000				−3,000		
h.	−2,000					−2,000	Wage Expense
i.	−750					−750	Rent Expense
j.	+1,500	−1,500					
k.	−500					−500	J. Zelkind, Drawing

Required:

1. Describe the business activities that led to the accounting equation effects for each transaction (*a*)–(*k*).
2. Prepare a *classified* income statement for July and a *classified* balance sheet as of July 31, 2009. (*Hint:* You can determine the amount for owner's equity by completing the equation: Assets = Liabilities + Owner's Equity.)

LO1, 3, 4

E3-21 Determining Financial Statement Effects of Various Transactions

John "Bum" Andrews founded EZ Reader in January 2010 to provide a service in which an employee follows a student around reading assigned textbook chapters aloud so that the student will not have to. Selected transactions for EZ Readers' first month of business are as follows:

a. Received $50,000 cash from John Andrews to establish the business.
b. Billed customers $10,500 for services performed in January.
c. Purchased a car for $24,500 for use in the business. Paid in cash.
d. Purchased $2,400 of supplies on account.
e. Received $7,500 cash from customers billed in transaction (*b*).
f. Used $1,500 in utilities that will be paid in February.
g. Paid employees $3,500 cash for work done in January.
h. Paid $1,200 cash toward supplies purchased in transaction (*d*).

Required:

For each transaction, write (1) the name of the account being debited or credited, (2) the basic account type (A, L, OE, R, or E), (3) whether the account is increased (+) or decreased (−) due to the transaction, and (4) whether the account normally holds a debit or credit balance. Transaction (*a*) has been given as an example.

	DEBIT SIDE OF JOURNAL ENTRY				CREDIT SIDE OF JOURNAL ENTRY			
	Account Name	Account Type	Direction of Change	Normal Balance	Account Name	Account Type	Direction of Change	Normal Balance
a.	Cash	A	+	Debit	J. Andrews, Capital	OE	+	Credit

LO1, 3, 4, 5
Sigil Games Online

E3-22 Comprehensive Exercise

In 2002, Brad McQuaid and Jeff Butler founded Sigil Games Online, Inc. (now owned by Sony Online Entertainment) with the mission of creating massively multiplayer online (MMO) games. Its "vanguard" product has been the game *Vanguard: Saga of Heroes*, released in winter of 2007. The company intends to sell subscriptions to its game online. For the sake of this exercise, assume that Sigil has been selling subscriptions for *Vanguard* for one full year (2009) at $15 per month. At the start of 2010, its income statement accounts had zero balances, and its balance sheet account balances were as follows:

Cash	$ 1,500,000	Accounts Payable	$ 108,000
Accounts Receivable	150,000	Wages Payable	34,500
Supplies	14,700	Unearned Revenue	73,500
Equipment	874,500	Notes Payable	60,000
Land	1,200,000	McQuaid & Butler, Capital	3,885,200
Building	422,000		

In addition to these accounts, Sigil's chart of accounts includes the following: Subscription Revenue, Licensing Revenue, Wages Expense, Advertising Expense, and Utilities Expense.

Required:

1. Analyze these effect of the following January 2010 transactions on the accounting equation using the format shown in the demonstration case.
    a. Received $50,000 cash from customers for subscriptions earned in 2009.
    b. Received $25,000 cash from Electronic Arts, Inc., for licensing revenue earned in the month of January 2010.
    c. Purchased 10 new computer servers for $33,500; paid $10,000 cash and signed a note for the remainder owed.

d. Paid $10,000 for an Internet advertisement run on Yahoo! in January 2010.

e. Sold 15,000 monthly subscriptions at $15 each for services provided during the month of January 2010. Half was collected in cash and half was sold on account.

f. Received an electric and gas utility bill for $5,350 for January 2010 services. The bill will be paid in February.

g. Paid $10,000 in wages to employees in January 2010 for work done in 2009. The expense was recorded in 2009.

h. Purchased $3,000 of supplies on account.

i. Paid $378,000 in wages to employees for work done in January 2010.

j. Paid $3,000 cash to the supplier in (*h*).

2. Prepare journal entries for the January 2010 transactions listed in requirement 1 using the letter of each transaction as a reference.
3. Create T-accounts, enter the beginning balances shown, post the journal entries to the T-accounts, and show the unadjusted ending balances in the T-accounts.
4. Prepare an unadjusted trial balance as of January 31, 2010.

Problems—Set A

Available with McGraw-Hill's Homework Manager

PA3-1 Recording Nonquantitative Journal Entries

LO1, 3, 4

The following list includes a series of accounts for B-Ball Stores, a sole proprietorship owned by Ralph Ball. The business has been operating for three years. These accounts are listed alphabetically and numbered for identification. Following the accounts is a series of transactions. For each transaction, indicate the account(s) that should be debited and credited by entering the appropriate account number(s) to the right of each transaction. If no journal entry is needed, write *none* after the transaction. The first transaction is used as an example.

Account No.	Account Title	Account No.	Account Title
1	Accounts Payable	9	R. Ball, Capital
2	Accounts Receivable	10	R. Ball, Drawing
3	Cash	11	Rent Expense
4	Equipment	12	Service Revenue
5	Interest Expense	13	Supplies Expense
6	Interest Payable	14	Supplies
7	Note Payable	15	Wages Expense
8	Prepaid Insurance	16	Wages Payable

	Transactions	Debit	Credit
a.	(*Example:*) Purchased equipment for use in the business; paid one-third cash and signed a note payable for the balance.	4	3,7
b.	Received additional investment from R. Ball.		
c.	Paid cash for rent this period.		
d.	Collected cash for services performed this period.		
e.	Collected cash on accounts receivable for services performed last period.		
f.	Performed services this period on credit.		
g.	Paid cash on accounts payable for expenses incurred last period.		
h.	Employees worked this period but will not be paid until next period.		
i.	Purchased supplies to be used later; paid cash.		
j.	Paid three-fourths of the interest expense for the year; the balance will be paid next year.		
k.	Ralph Ball withdrew cash from the business.		
l.	On the last day of the current period, paid cash for an insurance policy covering the next two years.		

LO1, 3, 4

PA3-2 Recording Nonquantitative Journal Entries

The following is a series of accounts for Jay's Laundry Services owned and managed by Jay Lewis. The company has been operating for two years. The accounts are listed alphabetically and numbered for identification. Following the accounts is a series of transactions. For each transaction, indicate the account(s) that should be debited and credited by entering the appropriate account number(s) to the right of each transaction. If no journal entry is needed, write *none* after the transaction. The first transaction is given as an example.

Account No.	Account Title	Account No.	Account Title
1	Accounts Payable	9	Notes Payable
2	Accounts Receivable	10	Prepaid Insurance
3	Advertising Expense	11	Service Revenue
4	Buildings	12	Supplies Expense
5	Cash	13	Supplies
6	J. Lewis, Capital	14	Wages Expense
7	J. Lewis, Drawing	15	Wages Payable
8	Land		

	Transactions	Debit	Credit
a.	(*Example*) Received cash from owner Jay Lewis.	5	6
b.	Performed services for customers this period on credit.		
c.	Purchased on credit but did not use supplies this period.		
d.	Prepaid a fire insurance policy at the end of this period to cover the next 12 months.		
e.	Purchased a building this period by making a 20 percent cash down payment and signing a note payable for the balance.		
f.	Collected cash this year for services that had been provided and recorded in the prior year.		
g.	Paid cash this period for wages that had been earned and recorded last period.		
h.	Paid cash for supplies that had been purchased on accounts payable in the prior period		
i.	Paid cash for advertising expense incurred in the current period.		
j.	Ran advertising in local newspaper this period to be paid next period.		
k.	Collected cash for services rendered this period.		
l.	This period Jay Lewis sold his summer house on the lake to another person for an amount above the original purchase price.		
m.	Jay Lewis withdrew cash from the business.		

LO2, 3, 4

PA3-3 Recording Journal Entries

Ryan Olson organized MeToo, a company providing online networking management services on MySpace, Facebook, Friendster, and other electronic social networks. Ryan believes that college and high school students make up his target market. You have been hired to record the transactions occurring in the first two weeks of operations, beginning May 1, 2010.

a. May 1 Received $30,000 cash from Ryan Olson to establish the sole proprietorship.

b. May 1 Borrowed $50,000 from the bank to provide additional funding to begin operations; the note is due in two years.

c. May 1 Paid $2,400 for a one-year fire insurance policy (recorded as Prepaid Insurance).

d. May 3 Purchased furniture and fixtures for the store for $15,000 on account. The amount is due within 30 days.

e. May 5 Placed advertisements in local college newspapers for a total of $250 cash.

f. May 9 Sold services for $400 cash.

g. May 14 Made full payment for the furniture and fixtures purchased on account on May 3.

Required:

For each transaction, prepare a journal entry. If no entry is needed, explain why. Be sure to categorize each account as an asset (A), liability (L), owner's equity (OE), revenue (R), or expense (E).

PA3-4 Recording Journal Entries

LO1, 3, 4

www.mhhe.com/LLPW1e

Robin Harrington established Time Definite Delivery on January 1, 2011. The following transactions occurred during the company's most recent quarter.

a. Received $80,000 from Robin Harrington to establish the sole proprietorship.
b. Provided delivery service to customers, receiving $72,000 in accounts receivable and $16,000 in cash.
c. Purchased equipment costing $82,000 and signed a long-term note for the full amount.
d. Incurred repair costs of $3,000 on account.
e. Collected $56,000 from customers on account.
f. Borrowed $90,000 by signing a long-term note.
g. Prepaid $74,400 cash to rent equipment and aircraft next quarter.
h. Paid employees $38,000 for work done during the quarter.
i. Purchased (with cash) and used $49,000 in fuel for delivery equipment.
j. Paid $2,000 on accounts payable.
k. Ordered but have not yet received $700 in supplies.
l. Robin Harrington withdrew $8,000 cash from the business.

Required:

For each transaction, prepare a journal entry. If no entry is needed, explain why. Be sure to categorize each account as an asset (A), liability (L), owner's equity (OE), revenue (R), or expense (E).

PA3-5 Analyzing the Effects of Transactions Using T-Accounts and Preparing an Unadjusted Trial Balance

LO1, 3, 4, 5

www.mhhe.com/LLPW1e

Barbara Jones, a textbook editor, opened Barb's Book Fixing on February 1, 2010. The business specializes in editing accounting textbooks. You have been hired as manager. Your duties include maintaining the company's financial records. The following transactions occurred in February 2010, the first month of operations.

a. Received an investment of $16,000 cash from Barbara Jones to establish the sole proprietorship.
b. Paid three months' rent for the office at $800 per month (recorded as Prepaid Rent).
c. Purchased supplies for $300 cash.
d. Negotiated a two-year loan at the bank, depositing $10,000 in the company's bank account.
e. Used all of the money from (*d*) to purchase a computer for $2,500 and the balance for furniture and fixtures for the office.
f. Placed an advertisement that ran the same day in the local paper for $425 cash.
g. Made sales totaling $1,800; $1,525 was in cash and the rest on accounts receivable.
h. Incurred and paid employee wages of $420.
i. Collected accounts receivable of $50 from customers.
j. Had one of the computers repaired for $120 cash.
k. Barbara Jones withdrew $3,500 cash from the business.

Required:

1. Set up appropriate T-accounts for Cash; Accounts Receivable; Supplies; Prepaid Rent; Equipment; Furniture and Fixtures; Notes Payable; B. Jones, Capital; B. Jones, Drawing; Service Revenue; Advertising Expense; Wages Expense; and Repair Expense. All accounts begin with zero balances.
2. Record in the T-accounts the effects of each transaction for Barb's Book Fixing in February, referencing each transaction in the accounts with the transaction letter. Show the unadjusted ending balances in the T-accounts.
3. Prepare an unadjusted trial balance at the end of February.
4. Refer to the revenues and expenses shown on the unadjusted trial balance. Based on this information, write a short memo to Barbara offering your opinion on the results of operations during the first month of business.

PA3-6 Analyzing the Effects of Transactions Using T-Accounts and Preparing an Unadjusted Trial Balance

LO1, 3, 4, 5

www.mhhe.com/LLPW1e

Randy Ellis established Spicewood Stables in Dripping Springs, Texas, on April 1, 2010. The company provides stables, care for animals, and grounds for riding and showing horses. You have been hired as the new assistant controller. The following transactions for April 2010 are provided for your review.

a. Received from Randy Ellis $200,000 in cash to establish the business as a sole proprietorship.
b. Built a barn for $142,000. The company paid half the amount in cash on April 1 and signed a three-year note payable for the balance.

c. Provided $15,260 in animal care services for customers, all on credit.
d. Rented stables to customers who cared for their own animals; received cash of $13,200.
e. Received from a customer $1,500 to board her horse in May, June, and July.
f. Purchased hay and feed supplies on account for $3,210.
g. Paid $840 in cash for water utilities incurred in the month.
h. Paid $1,700 on accounts payable for previous purchases.
i. Received $1,000 from customers on accounts receivable.
j. Paid $4,000 in wages to employees who worked during the month.
k. At the end of the month, prepaid a two-year insurance policy for $3,600.
l. Received an electric utility bill for $1,200 for usage in April; the bill will be paid next month.

Required:

1. Set up appropriate T-accounts. All accounts begin with zero balances.
2. Record in the T-accounts the effects of each transaction for Spicewood Stables in April, referencing each transaction in the accounts with the transaction letter. Show the unadjusted ending balances in the T-accounts.
3. Prepare an unadjusted trial balance as of April 30, 2010.
4. Refer to the revenues and expenses shown on the unadjusted trial balance. Based on this information, write a short memo to Randy Ellis offering your opinion on the results of operations during the first month of business.

Problems—Set B

Available with McGraw-Hill's Homework Manager

LO1, 3, 4
Abercrombie & Fitch

PB3-1 Recording Nonquantitative Journal Entries

Abercrombie & Fitch Co. is a specialty retailer of casual apparel. The company's brand was established in 1892. It was first publicly traded in 1996 and was spun off from The Limited in 1998. The following is a series of accounts for Abercrombie. They are listed alphabetically and numbered for identification. Following the accounts is a series of transactions. For each transaction, indicate the account(s) that should be debited and credited by entering the appropriate account number(s) to the right of each transaction. If no journal entry is needed, write *none* after the transaction. The first transaction is given as an example.

Account No.	Account Title	Account No.	Account Title
1	Accounts Payable	8	Rent Expense
2	Accounts Receivable	9	Supplies Expense
3	Cash	10	Supplies
4	Equipment	11	Unearned Revenue
5	Interest Revenue	12	Wages Expense
6	Owners' Capital	13	Wages Payable
7	Prepaid Rent		

Transactions	Debit	Credit
a. (*Example*) Incurred wages expense; paid cash.	12	3
b. Collected cash on account.		
c. Sold gift certificates to customers; none redeemed this period.		
d. Purchased equipment, paying part in cash and charging the balance on account.		
e. Paid cash to suppliers on account.		
f. Received additional cash from owners.		
g. Paid rent to landlords for next month's use of mall space.		
h. Earned and received cash for interest on investments.		

PB3-2 Recording Nonquantitative Journal Entries

LO1, 3, 4

The following is a series of accounts for Cohen & Sons Consulting, owned and managed by Alan Cohen. The company has been operating for five years. The accounts are listed alphabetically and numbered for identification. Following the accounts is a series of transactions. For each transaction, indicate the account(s) that should be debited and credited by entering the appropriate account number(s) to the right of each transaction. If no journal entry is needed, write *none* after the transaction. The first transaction is given as an example.

Account No.	Account Title	Account No.	Account Title
1	Accounts Payable	10	Interest Revenue
2	Accounts Receivable	11	Land
3	Advertising Expense	12	Notes Payable
4	A. Cohen, Capital	13	Prepaid Rent
5	A. Cohen, Drawing	14	Supplies Expense
6	Buildings	15	Supplies
7	Cash	16	Wages Expense
8	Consulting Revenue	17	Wages Payable
9	Equipment		

	Transactions	Debit	Credit
a.	(*Example*) Received additional cash from owner Alan Cohen.	7	4
b.	Performed services for customers this period on credit.		
c.	Purchased on credit but did not use supplies this period.		
d.	Collected cash this year for services provided and recorded in the prior year.		
e.	Prepaid rent on the office this period for the next six months.		
f.	Purchased two cars this period, paying part cash and signing a note payable with the dealer for the balance.		
g.	Paid cash for advertising expense incurred in the current period.		
h.	Paid cash this period to employees for wages they had earned in the last period.		
i.	Paid cash for supplies that had been purchased on accounts payable in the prior period.		
j.	Ran advertising in local newspaper this period to be paid next period.		
k.	This period Alan Cohen purchased a condominium in Florida for personal use.		
l.	Collected cash for services rendered this period.		

PB3-3 Recording Journal Entries

LO1, 3, 4

Diana Mark is the president of ServicePro, a sole proprietorship that provides temporary employees for not-for-profit organizations. ServicePro has been operating for five years; its revenues are increasing with each passing year. You have been hired to help Diana in analyzing the following transactions for the first two weeks of April 2010:

a.	April 2	Purchased office supplies for $500 on account.
b.	April 5	Billed the local United Way office $1,950 for temporary services provided.
c.	April 8	Paid $250 for supplies purchased and recorded on account last period.
d.	April 8	Placed an advertisement in the local paper for $400 cash; the ad will run in May.
e.	April 9	Purchased a new computer for the office costing $2,300 cash.
f.	April 10	Paid employee wages of $1,200. Of this amount, $200 had been earned by employees in the prior period and already recorded in the Wages Payable account.
g.	April 11	Received $1,000 on account from the local United Way office (from [*b*] above).
h.	April 12	Purchased land as the site of a future office for $10,000. Paid $2,000 down and signed a note payable for the balance.

i. April 13 Received $80,000 cash as additional investment by owner Diana Mark.
j. April 14 Billed Family & Children's Service $2,000 for services rendered this month.
k. April 15 Received the April telephone bill for $245 to be paid next month.

Required:

For each transaction, prepare a journal entry. If no entry is needed, explain why. Be sure to categorize each account as an asset (A), liability (L), owner's equity (OE), revenue (R), or expense (E).

LO1, 3, 4

PB3-4 Recording Journal Entries

John Cirba established Cirba Moving & Storage on April 1, 2010. The following transactions occurred during the business's most recent quarter.

a. Received $100,000 from John Cirba to establish the sole proprietorship.
b. Purchased three moving vans costing $80,000 each, paying $50,000 as a down payment and signing a long-term note for the rest.
c. Provided moving services to customers, receiving $23,000 in cash and billing customers for $120,000 in services on account.
d. Incurred $3,000 of repair costs on one of the vans; the amount is payable next quarter on account.
e. Paid for and used $9,000 in fuel for the moving vans.
f. Collected $72,000 from customers on account.
g. Paid $1,000 cash to a marketing firm for advertising assistance.
h. Purchased $12,000 in insurance coverage for the next quarter.
i. Ordered, but have not yet received, $3,200 in new moving pads and dollies (equipment).
j. Paid $2,000 on accounts payable.
k. Paid employees $109,000 for work done during the quarter.
l. John Cirba withdrew $5,000 cash from the business.

Required:

For each transaction, prepare a journal entry. If no entry is needed, explain why. Be sure to categorize each account as an asset (A), liability (L), owner's equity (OE), revenue (R), or expense (E).

LO1, 3, 4, 5

PB3-5 Analyzing the Effects of Transactions Using T-Accounts and Preparing an Unadjusted Trial Balance

Jessica Pothier opened FunFlatables on June 1, 2011. The company rents out moon walks and inflatable slides for parties and corporate events. The business also has obtained the use of an abandoned ice rink located in a local shopping mall, where its rental products are displayed and available for casual hourly rental by mall patrons. The following transactions occurred during the first month of operations.

a. Received $50,000 cash contributions from Jessica to establish the sole proprietorship.
b. Purchased inflatable rides and inflation equipment, paying $20,000 cash.
c. Received $5,000 cash from casual hourly rentals at the mall.
d. Rented rides and equipment to customers for $10,000. Received cash of $2,000; the rest is due from customers.
e. Received $2,500 from a large corporate customer as a deposit on a party booking for July 4.
f. Began to prepare for the July 4 party by purchasing various party supplies on account for $600.
g. Paid $12,000 in cash for renting the mall space in June, July, and August.
h. Received $1,000 from customers on accounts receivable.
i. Paid $4,000 in wages to employees for work done during the month.
j. Paid $1,000 for running a television ad this month.
k. Jessica Pothier withdrew $6,000 cash from the business.

Required:

1. Set up appropriate T-accounts for Cash; Accounts Receivable; Supplies; Prepaid Rent; Equipment; Accounts Payable; Unearned Rent Revenue; J. Pothier, Capital; J. Pothier, Drawing; Rent Revenue; Wages Expense; and Advertising Expense. All accounts begin with zero balances.
2. Record in the T-accounts the effects of each transaction for FunFlatables in June, referencing each transaction in the accounts with the transaction letter. Show the unadjusted ending balances in the T-accounts.

3. Prepare an unadjusted trial balance for the end of June 2011.
4. Jessica has become alarmed at how quickly the business's cash balance has fallen. Refer to the revenues and expenses shown on the unadjusted trial balance and write a short memo to her offering your opinion on the results of operations during the first month of business.

PB3-6 Analyzing the Effects of Transactions Using T-Accounts and Preparing an Unadjusted Trial Balance LO1, 3, 4, 5

Margaret Foster established Body and Soul in Cortland, New York, on March 1, 2010. The company provides massage therapy and other spa services. You have been hired as the new business manager. The following transactions for March 2010 are provided for your review.

a. Received from Margaret Foster $50,000 in cash to establish the business as a sole proprietorship.
b. Paid $18,000 to rent store space for the business from March 1 to September 1 (six months).
c. Purchased massage tables, towels, and other necessary equipment; paid $8,000 in cash and owed $12,000 on account.
d. Provided spa services to customers for $20,000 cash.
e. Received $2,400 from customers as gift certificates for future spa services (recorded as unearned revenue).
f. Purchased spa supplies on account for $3,000.
g. Borrowed $10,000 from a local bank to renovate additional space in the store.
h. Paid $6,000 for a two-year insurance policy with coverage beginning on April 1, 2010.
i. Paid $1,200 on accounts payable for previous purchases.
j. Provided $600 in spa services to customers on account.
k. Ordered $2,500 in spa supplies for delivery in April.
l. Received an electric and gas utility bill for $1,500 for usage in March; the bill will be paid next month.
m. Paid $12,000 in wages to employees who worked during the month.
n. Margaret Foster withdrew $7,000 cash from the business.

Required:

1. Set up appropriate T-accounts. All accounts begin with zero balances.
2. Record in the T-accounts the effects of each transaction for Body and Soul in March, referencing each transaction in the accounts with the transaction letter. Show the unadjusted ending balances in the T-accounts.
3. Prepare an unadjusted trial balance as of March 31, 2010.
4. Refer to the revenues and expenses shown on the unadjusted trial balance. Based on this information, write a short memo to Margaret Foster offering your opinion on the results of operations during the first month of business.

Cases and Projects

CP3-1 Finding Financial Information LO1, 4

Refer to the financial statements of The Home Depot in Appendix A at the end of this book, or download the annual report from the *Cases* section of the text's Web site at www.mhhe.com/LLPW1e.

Required:

1. Did The Home Depot's total revenues increase or decrease in the most recent year? By how much? Calculate this change as a percentage of the previous year's total revenues by dividing the amount of the change by the previous year's revenues and multiplying by 100.
2. State the amount of the largest expense on the most recent income statement and describe the transaction represented by the expense. Did this expense increase or decrease from the previous year and by what percentage?

CP3-2 Comparing Financial Information LO1, 4

Lowe's

Refer to the financial statements of The Home Depot in Appendix A and Lowe's in Appendix B at the end of this book, or download the annual reports from the *Cases* section of the text's Web site at www.mhhe.com/LLPW1e.

Required:

1. Did Lowe's total revenues increase or decrease in the most recent year? By how much? Calculate this change as a percentage of the previous year's total revenues. Is the trend in Lowe's revenues more or less favorable than The Home Depot's?
2. State the amount of the largest expense on the most recent income statement of Lowe's and describe the transaction represented by the expense. Did this expense increase or decrease and by what percentage, as compared to the previous year? Is the trend in Lowe's largest expense more or less favorable than the trend for The Home Depot's largest expense?

LO1, 3, 5

CP3-3 Examining the Income Statement: Internet-Based Team Research

As a team, select an industry to analyze. Using your Web browser, each team member should acquire the annual report or 10-K for one publicly traded company in the industry, with each member selecting a different company. (See CP1-3 in Chapter 1 for a description of possible resources for these tasks.)

Required:

1. On an individual basis, each team member should write a short report that lists the following information:
   a. The major revenue and expense accounts on the most recent income statement.
   b. Description of how the company has followed the conditions of the revenue principle.
   c. The percentage of revenues that go to covering expenses and that are in excess of expenses (in other words, the percentage that remains as net income).
2. Then, as a team, write a short report comparing and contrasting your companies using these attributes. Discuss any patterns across the companies that you as a team observe. Provide potential explanations for any differences discovered.

LO1, 3, 4

CP3-4 Examining a Real-Life Example: Ethical Decision Making

Read the excerpt from a September 2, 2002, article in *Fortune* magazine and answer the questions that follow it.

> Forget about fraud. Companies don't need to lie, cheat, and steal to fool investors. Clever managers have always had, and continue to have, access to perfectly legal tricks to help make their balance sheets and income statements look better than they really are—tricks that *even today* won't jeopardize their ability to swear to the SEC that their books are on the up and up. . . . One of the most controversial of all number games—the one that got WorldCom in trouble—is to capitalize expenses. That can have a tremendous impact on the bottom line.

Required:

1. In this chapter, you learned that when a company incurs a cost, its accountants have to decide whether to record it as an asset or expense. When costs are recorded as an asset, they are said to be "capitalized." This builds on ideas first presented in Chapter 2, where you learned that it is appropriate to record costs as assets provided that they possess certain characteristics. What are those characteristics?
2. The author of the article argues that even with clear rules such as those referenced in requirement 1, accounting still allows managers to use "tricks" such as *capitalizing expenses*. What do you suppose the author means by the expression *capitalizing expenses?*
3. Suppose that, in the current year, a company inappropriately records a cost as an asset when it should be recorded as an expense. What is the effect of this accounting decision on the current year's net income? What is the effect of this accounting decision on the following year's net income?
4. Later in the article (not shown), the author says that the videogame industry is one in which companies frequently capitalize software development costs as assets. These costs include wages

paid to programmers, fees paid to graphic designers, and amounts paid to game testers. Evaluate whether software development costs are likely to possess the main characteristics possessed by all assets. Can you think of a situation in which software development costs might not possess these main characteristics?

5. Do you think it is always easy and straightforward to determine whether costs should be capitalized or expensed? Do you think it is always easy and straightforward to determine whether a manager is acting ethically or unethically? Give examples to illustrate your views.

CP3-5 Analyzing a Mini-Case: Ethical Decision Making

LO1, 3, 4

Mike Lynch is the manager of an upstate New York regional office for an insurance company. As the regional manager, his pay package includes a base salary, commissions, and a bonus when the region sells new policies in excess of its quota. Lately Mike has been under enormous pressure stemming largely from two factors. First, he is experiencing mounting personal debt due to a family member's illness. Second, compounding his worries, the region's sales of new insurance policies have dipped below the normal quota for the first time in years.

You have been working for Mike for two years, and like everyone else in the office, you consider yourself lucky to work for such a supportive boss. You also feel great sympathy for his personal problems over the last few months. In your position as accountant for the regional office, you are only too aware of the drop in new policy sales and the impact this will have on Mike's bonus. While you are working on the year-end financial statements, Mike stops by your office.

Mike asks you to change the manner in which you have accounted for a new property insurance policy for a large local business. A check for the premium, substantial in amount, came in the mail on December 31, the last day of the reporting year. The premium covers a period beginning on January 5. You deposited the check and correctly debited cash and credited an *unearned revenue* account. Mike says, "Hey, we have the money this year, so why not count the revenue this year? I never did understand why you accountants are so picky about these things anyway. I'd like you to change the way you've recorded the transaction. I want you to credit a *revenue* account. And anyway, I've done favors for you in the past, and I am asking for such a small thing in return." With that, he leaves your office.

Required:

Justify your answers to each of the following questions.

1. How should you handle this situation?
2. What are the ethical implications of Mike's request?
3. Who are the parties who would be helped or harmed if you went along with the request?
4. If you fail to comply with his request, how will you explain your position to him?

CP3-6 Analyzing Changes in Accounts and Preparing a Trial Balance: Critical Thinking

LO1, 4, 5

Stephen Hordichuk organized Hordichuk Painting Service Company as a sole proprietorship on January 20, 2010. The following is a schedule of the cumulative account balances immediately after each of the first ten transactions ending on January 31, 2010.

	CUMULATIVE BALANCES									
Accounts	*(a)*	*(b)*	*(c)*	*(d)*	*(e)*	*(f)*	*(g)*	*(h)*	*(i)*	*(j)*
Cash	$ 75,000	$ 70,000	$ 85,000	$ 71,000	$ 69,000	$ 61,000	$ 61,000	$ 46,000	$ 44,000	$ 60,000
Accounts Receivable			12,000	12,000	12,000	12,000	26,000	26,000	26,000	10,000
Supplies					5,000	5,000	5,000	5,000	5,000	5,000
Office Fixtures		20,000	20,000	20,000	20,000	20,000	20,000	20,000	20,000	20,000
Land				18,000	18,000	18,000	18,000	18,000	18,000	18,000
Accounts Payable					3,000	3,000	3,000	3,000	1,000	1,000
Notes Payable		15,000	15,000	19,000	19,000	19,000	19,000	19,000	19,000	19,000
S. Hordichuk, Capital	75,000	75,000	75,000	75,000	75,000	75,000	75,000	75,000	75,000	75,000
Paint Revenue			27,000	27,000	27,000	27,000	41,000	41,000	41,000	41,000
Wages Expense						8,000	8,000	23,000	23,000	23,000

Required:

1. Analyze the changes in this schedule for each transaction; then explain the transaction. Transactions *(a)* and *(b)* are examples.
   - *a.* Cash increased $75,000, and J. Hordichuk, Capital (owner's equity) increased $75,000. Therefore, transaction *(a)* was the receipt of $75,000 cash investment from the owner to establish the business.
   - *b.* Cash decreased $5,000, Office Fixtures (an asset) increased $20,000, and Notes Payable (a liability) increased $15,000. Therefore, transaction *(b)* was a purchase of office fixtures that cost $20,000. Payment was made as follows: cash, $5,000; notes payable, $15,000.
2. Based only on the preceding schedule, prepare an unadjusted trial balance.

LO1, 4, 5

CP3-7 Analyzing Transactions and Preparing an Unadjusted Trial Balance

Assume you recently started a new company that rents machines for making frozen drinks such as smoothies, frozen juices, tea slush, and iced cappuccinos. For $100, your business will deliver a machine, provide supplies (straws and paper cups), set up the machine, and pick up the machine the next morning. Other businesses in your city sell drink mix and other supplies. Being a one-person operation, you are responsible for everything from purchasing to marketing to operations to accounting.

You decide that you will just write notes about what happens during the month and then do the accounting at the end of the month. You figure this will be more efficient. Your notes said the following about your first month of operations:

- *a.* Oct. 2 Received $10,000 cash investment from the owner to establish Slusher Gusher.
- *b.* Oct. 12 Paid cash to buy three frozen drink machines on eBay at a total cost of $1,500.
- *c.* Oct. 13 Paid cash to buy $70 of supplies.
- *d.* Oct. 16 Received $500 cash for this past week's rentals.
- *e.* Oct. 20 Bought $100 of supplies on account.
- *f.* Oct. 23 Received $400 cash from customers who owe $200 more for services provided.
- *g.* Oct. 25 Received $100 cash from one of the customers who had not paid yet.
- *h.* Oct. 26 Ran an ad in the local paper today for $25 cash.
- *i.* Oct. 27 Received $150 cash for a two-machine All Saints Day party to be held on November 1.

Required:

Create a spreadsheet to record the effects of the October transactions and calculate end-of-month totals. Using the spreadsheet, prepare a trial balance that checks whether debits equal credits. Because you are dealing with your own business this time, you want to be extra sure that you do this just right, so you e-mail your friend Sally for advice. Her reply follows on the next page.

From: Sally@yahoo.com
To: Helpme@hotmail.com
Cc:
Subject: Excel Help

Wow, you're a CEO already? I always thought you were a mover and a shaker! So you want my advice on how to set up your spreadsheet? My advice is read the last e-mail I sent *[see PB2-6]*. The main thing that's new here is that you'll need to include some columns for revenue and expenses under the owner's equity heading. Here's a screen shot of how the right-hand side of your worksheet might look just before you enter the October transactions. Notice that because expenses decrease owner's equity , the debit side is used to record expenses.

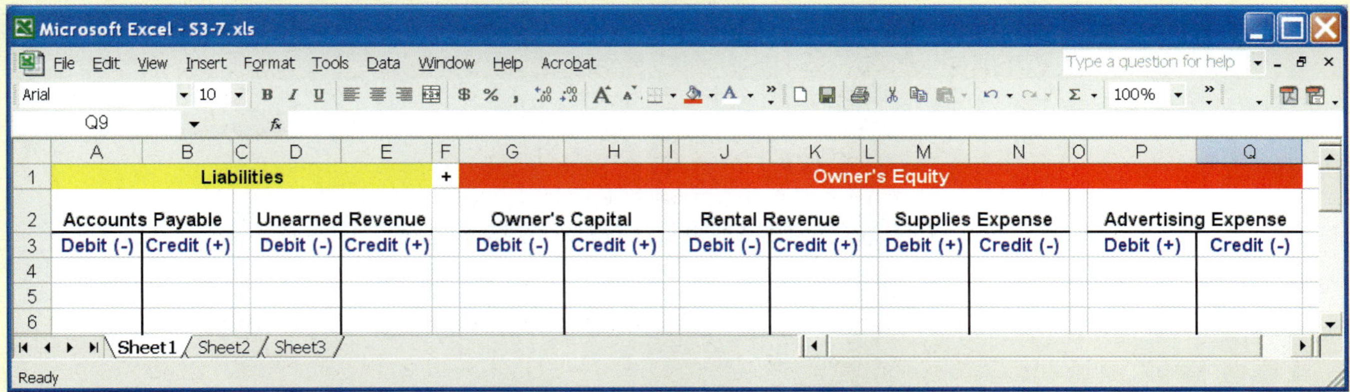

To prepare the trial balance, create three columns. In the first, copy and paste the account names (one per row). In the second column, link in each debit balance by entering = in a cell and then clicking on the debit total from the T-account. Repeat this with all accounts. Then do the same with the credit balances. At the bottom of the trial balance, use the SUM function to compute totals.

Don't forget to save the file using a name that uniquely identifies you (as my true hero).

4 Completing the Accounting Cycle

LEARNING OBJECTIVES

After studying this chapter, you should be able to:

Lectured slideshow–LP4-1
www.mhhe.com/LLPW1e

LO1 Explain the purpose of adjustments at the end of the accounting cycle.

LO2 Identify and analyze the adjustments necessary at the end of the period to update balance sheet and income statement accounts.

LO3 Present an income statement, statement of owner's equity, and balance sheet.

LO4 Explain the purpose and process of closing the books.

LO5 Compute and interpret the net profit margin ratio.

Focus Company: PIZZA AROMA, Ithaca, NY

Adjusting the Accounts, Closing the Books, and Analyzing Financial Information

In Chapter 3, you saw that Pizza Aroma sold a lot of pizza during its first month of operations—more than owner-manager Mauricio Rosa had expected. Mauricio was very curious to know how the business performed, so he made a simple computation:

- Using the preliminary income statement (in Exhibit 3.8), he found that net income was almost 83% of pizza revenue.[1] He knew that rival Papa John's usually reported a net income of only about 5% of its revenues.

Mauricio was very excited and eager to discuss these results with Laurie, his CPA.

At their meeting, Laurie congratulated Mauricio on having a good first month. However, she cautioned him that because he had been using **unadjusted amounts** in his computations, his results and comparisons were not meaningful. She emphasized that at the end of an accounting period, managers must make many evaluations and estimates (1) to update amounts already recorded in the accounting records and (2) to include events that had occurred but had not yet been recorded.

These adjustments ensure that the recognition of revenues and expenses will occur in the proper period, and that the measurement of assets and liabilities will represent their appropriate amounts. For example, this process would include updating the Supplies account to reflect the amounts used during the month, among many other adjustments. After the accounts have been adjusted, financial statements should be prepared for owners, creditors, and other users. Only then would Mauricio be able to compute and interpret useful ratios.

In this chapter, you will learn why adjustments are necessary in accrual basis accounting. Understanding the purpose of adjustments will help you to determine what adjustments

[1] Pizza Aroma: Net income \$11,600 ÷ Pizza revenue \$14,000 = 0.83, or 83%. Papa John's average from 2004 to 2006: Average net income \$44.2 million ÷ Average revenues \$965.2 million = 0.046, or about 5%.

are needed and how to record and summarize them. Then you will learn how to prepare Pizza Aroma's May 31 financial statements using the adjusted accounts and how to prepare its accounting records for the next period by "closing the books." Finally, you will learn a common ratio that is helpful in evaluating a business's financial performance.

ORGANIZATION OF THE CHAPTER

ADJUSTING REVENUES AND EXPENSES	PREPARING FINANCIAL STATEMENTS	COMPLETING THE ACCOUNTING CYCLE	ANALYZING FINANCIAL INFORMATION

• Reasons for Adjustments
• Types of Adjustments
• Analysis of Adjustments
  • Unearned Revenues
  • Accrued Revenues
  • Prepaid Expenses
  • Accrued Expenses
	• Adjusted Trial Balance
	• Relationships among Financial Statements
	• Classified Income Statement
	• Statement of Owner's Equity
	• Classified Balance Sheet
		• Closing the Books
		• Preparing a Post-Closing Trial Balance
			• Computing and Interpreting Key Ratios
			• Analyzing Net Profit Margin
			• Making Comparisons to Benchmarks

ADJUSTING REVENUES AND EXPENSES

Learning Objective 1

Explain the purpose of adjustments at the end of the accounting cycle.

See Exhibit 4.1 for the basic steps in the **accounting cycle.** As you saw in Chapters 2 and 3, the accounting cycle is the process in which businesses analyze, record, and post the effects of transactions; adjust the records at the end of the period; prepare the financial statements; and then prepare the accounting records for the next accounting cycle. In this chapter, you will study the *end-of-period* phase of this cycle, which focuses primarily on adjustments made to record revenues and expenses in the proper period and to update the balance sheet accounts.

Video 4-1
www.mhhe.com/LLPW1e

Reasons for Adjustments

Accounting systems are designed to record most recurring daily transactions, particularly those involving cash. As cash is received or paid, it is recorded in the accounting system. In general, this focus on cash works well, especially when cash receipts and payments occur in the same period as the activities that produce revenues and expenses. However, cash is not always received in the period in which the company earns the related revenue; likewise, cash is not always paid in the period in which the company incurs the related expense.

Exhibit 4.1 The Accounting Cycle

DURING THE PERIOD
(Chapters 2 and 3)
- Analyze transactions
- Record journal entries in the general journal
- Post amounts to the general ledger

AT THE END OF THE PERIOD
(Chapter 4)
- Adjust revenues and expenses and related balance sheet accounts
- Prepare a complete set of financial statements and disseminate the statements to users
- Close revenues, gains, expenses, losses, and withdrawals to owner's equity

How does the accounting system record revenues and expenses when one transaction is needed to record a cash receipt or payment and another transaction is needed to record revenue when it is earned or an expense when it is incurred? The solution to the problem created by such differences in timing is to record adjusting entries at the end of every accounting period so that:

- Revenues are recorded when they are earned (the **revenue principle**).
- Expenses are recorded when they are incurred to generate revenue (the **matching principle**).
- **Assets** are reported at amounts that represent the probable future benefits remaining at the end of the period.
- **Liabilities** are reported at amounts that represent the probable future sacrifices of assets or services owed at the end of the period.

Learning Objective 2

Identify and analyze the adjustments necessary at the end of the period to update balance sheet and income statements accounts.

Companies wait until the **end of the accounting period** to adjust their accounts in this way because adjusting the records daily would be very costly and time consuming. Adjusting entries are required every time a company wants to prepare financial statements for external users. In practice, almost every account could require an adjustment. Rather than trying to memorize an endless list of specific examples, you should focus instead on learning the general types of adjustments needed and the process used to determine how to adjust the accounts.

Types of Adjustments

There are four types of adjustments:

Revenues

- Unearned Revenues Previously recorded liabilities that were created when cash was received in advance and that must be adjusted for the amount of revenue actually earned during the period.
- Accrued Revenues Revenues that were earned but not yet recorded, with cash to be received in future periods.

Expenses

- Prepaid Expenses Previously recorded assets, such as Prepaid Rent, Supplies, and Equipment, that were created when cash was paid in advance and that must be adjusted for the amount of expense actually incurred during the period through use of the asset.
- Accrued Expenses are expenses that were incurred but not yet recorded, with cash to be paid in future periods.

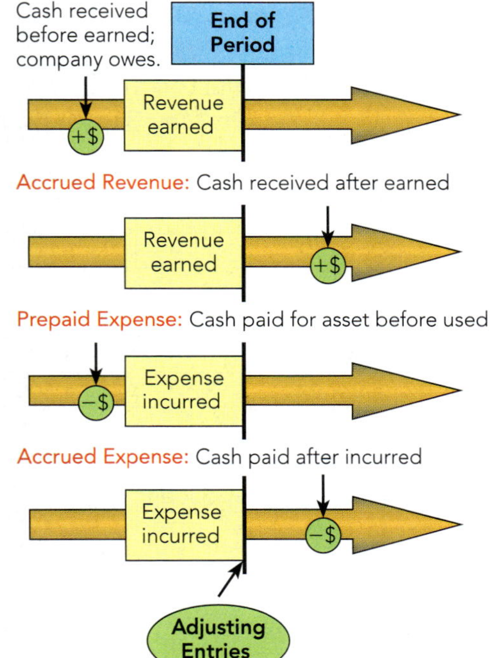

Each of these types of adjustments involves two entries:

- One for the cash receipt or payment.
- One for recording the revenue or expense in the proper period (through the adjusting entry).

We will illustrate the process involved in analyzing and adjusting the accounts by reviewing all adjustments Laurie made for Pizza Aroma before preparing the first month's statements.

Analysis of Adjustments

Analyzing adjustments at the end of the period involves three steps:

Step 1 ***Identify the type of adjustment.*** Unearned Revenue and Prepaid Expense accounts exist at the end of the period but are overstated, and the related revenue or expense is understated. Accrued Revenues and Accrued Expenses that have occured but have not been recorded are understated, as are the related receivable and payable accounts.

Step 2 ***Determine the amount*** of revenue earned or expense incurred during the period. Sometimes the amount is known, sometimes it is calculated, and sometimes it must be estimated. This will be the amount needed in the adjusting entry for the revenue or expense account.

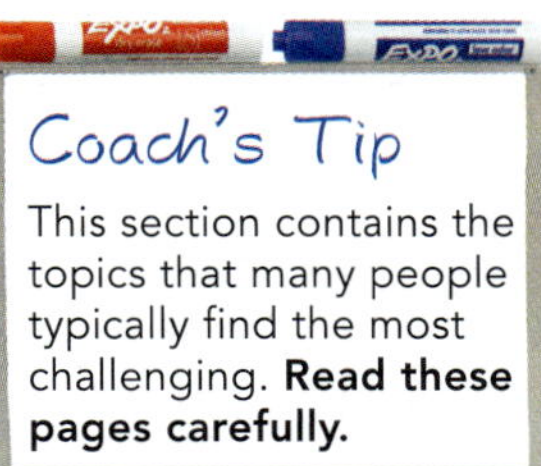

Step 3 ***Record the adjusting journal entry*** and post it to the appropriate accounts. Unearned Revenue or Prepaid Expense accounts, in which cash had previously been received

or paid, are reduced in adjusting entries to their remaining balance. For accrued revenues, the other half of the entry increases a receivable account; for accrued expenses, the other half of the entry increases a payable account.

Coach's Tip

Remember that all adjusting entries are made at the end of the period and then are posted to appropriate accounts affected.

So what are the adjustments needed for Pizza Aroma at the end of May?

Step 1 ***Identify type of adjustment*. Laurie showed Mauricio the unadjusted trial balance (see Exhibit 4.2) and pointed out the accounts that needed adjustment.**

As you can see, Pizza Aroma's adjustments included one unearned revenue account, one accrued revenue account, four prepaid expense accounts, and three accrued expense accounts. Let's begin with an analysis of the revenue adjustments. Note that the abbreviation *AJE* stands for adjusting journal entry.

Unearned Revenues

When a customer pays for goods or services before the company delivers them, the company records the amount of cash received in an Unearned Revenue account. This unearned revenue

Exhibit 4.2 Pizza Aroma's Unadjusted Trial Balance

PIZZA AROMA

Pizza Aroma
Unadjusted Trial Balance
On May 31, 2009

	Debit	Credit	To identify where adjustments are needed:
Cash	9,100		
Investments	6,000		Determine whether any interest has been earned. If so,
Interest Receivable	0		**Accrued Revenue** ⇒ Amount of interest earned and to be received
Accounts Receivable	700		
Supplies	5,000		**Prepaid Expense** ⇒ Determine amount of supplies used during period
Prepaid Rent	4,800		**Prepaid Expense** ⇒ Determine amount of rent used during period
Prepaid Insurance	2,400		**Prepaid Expense** ⇒ Determine amount of insurance used during period
Equipment	36,000		**Prepaid Expense** ⇒ Determine depreciation expense
Accumulated Depreciation		0	Represents the total amount of equipment used
Accounts Payable		4,800	
Wages Payable		0	**Accrued Expense** ⇒ Amount of wages incurred and owed to employees
Utilities Payable		0	**Accrued Expense** ⇒ Amount of utilities incurred and owed for period
Interest Payable		0	**Accrued Expense** ⇒ Amount of interest owed on debt for period
Unearned Revenue		600	**Unearned Revenue** ⇒ Determine amount earned for deliveries during period
Notes Payable		20,000	
M. Rosa, Capital		30,000	
M. Rosa, Drawing	3,000		
Pizza Revenue		14,000	Revenue from delivering pizza sold during period
Investment Revenue		0	Revenue on investments earned during period
Supplies Expense	0		Expense for supplies used during period
Wages Expense	1,000		Expense for wages incurred during period
Utilities Expense	0		Expense for utilities used during period
Telephone Service Expense	600		Expense for telephone service used during period
Rent Expense	0		Expense for rent used during period
Insurance Expense	0		Expense for insurance used during period
Advertising Expense	800		Expense for advertising used during period
Depreciation Expense	0		Expense for depreciation of equipment used during period
Interest Expense	0		Expense for interest incurred on debt during period
Totals	69,400	69,400	

is a liability representing the company's promise to perform or deliver the goods or services in the future. Recognition of (recording) the revenue is postponed (deferred) until the company meets its obligation.

AJE 1. During May, Pizza Aroma collected $600 in deposits from fraternities ordering pizza deliveries on upcoming graduation and reunion weekends. When received, the business recorded $600 cash as Unearned Revenue, a liability, to recognize its obligation to deliver pizzas in the future. Pizza Aroma earned no revenue when it received the cash because the company had not yet delivered the pizzas.

Step 2 ***Determine the amount.*** By the end of May, Pizza Aroma had delivered and earned $400 of the $600 in revenue associated with the graduation events. However, that $400 is still included in the Unearned Revenue account. Because only $200 in pizza remained to be delivered in June and was therefore unearned at the end of May, the $600 balance in the Unearned Revenue account is overstated by $400.

Step 3 ***Record the AJE.*** An adjusting entry is therefore necessary to reduce the Unearned Revenue account by $400 and increase the Pizza Revenue account by $400. After the entry is made, its effects are posted to the appropriate T-accounts.

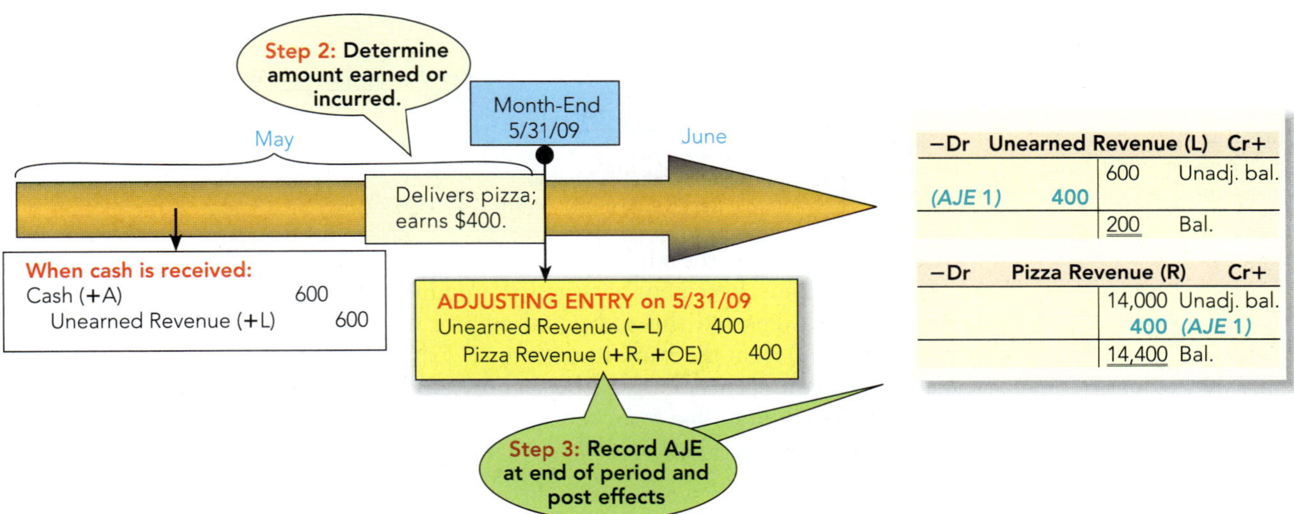

After the adjusting entry was made, the income statement reported the additional $400 of Pizza Revenue earned in May, and the balance sheet reported the remaining liability of $200 in the Unearned Revenue account.

Additional examples of unearned revenues for other companies include magazine subscriptions; season tickets to sporting events, plays, and concerts; airplane tickets sold in advance; and rent paid in advance by renters. Each of these requires an adjusting entry at the end of the accounting period to report the amount of revenue earned during the period.

Spotlight On FINANCIAL REPORTING

Millions, Even Billions in Unearned Revenue

In a recent year, Readers' Digest Association, producer of *Readers' Digest* magazine and 28 other magazines and numerous books, reported more than $390 million in current Unearned Revenues and $131 million in noncurrent Unearned Revenues for subscriptions sold in advance to customers. United Air Lines reported the following unearned revenues: (1) nearly $1.7 billion in Advance Ticket Sales and (2) more than $3.6 billion in unearned revenues in the account Mileage Plus Deferred Revenue representing the amount the company estimated it promised to customers for future flights under its frequent flyer program.

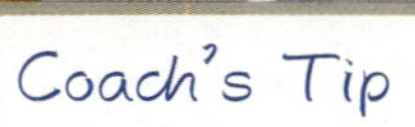

Coach's Tip

Accrued revenue is revenue that has been earned when the company performed a service or delivered goods, but nothing was recorded because cash was not yet received.

Accrued Revenues

Sometimes companies perform services or provide goods (that is, earn revenue) before customers pay. Because the cash that is owed for these goods and services has not yet been received, the revenue that was earned has not been recorded. Revenues that have been earned but have not yet been recorded at the end of the accounting period are called **accrued revenues.**

AJE 2. Near the beginning of May, Pizza Aroma deposited $6,000 cash in a savings account at a local bank. The savings account earns investment (or interest) revenue over time, but Pizza Aroma does not receive cash until a withdrawal is made when needed in the future.

Step 2 ***Amount.*** The bank statement has indicated that the savings account earned $30 during May.

Step 3 ***AJE.*** An adjusting entry is needed at the end of May to recognize the $30 in Investment Revenue earned but not yet received. The other half of the entry is to Interest Receivable.

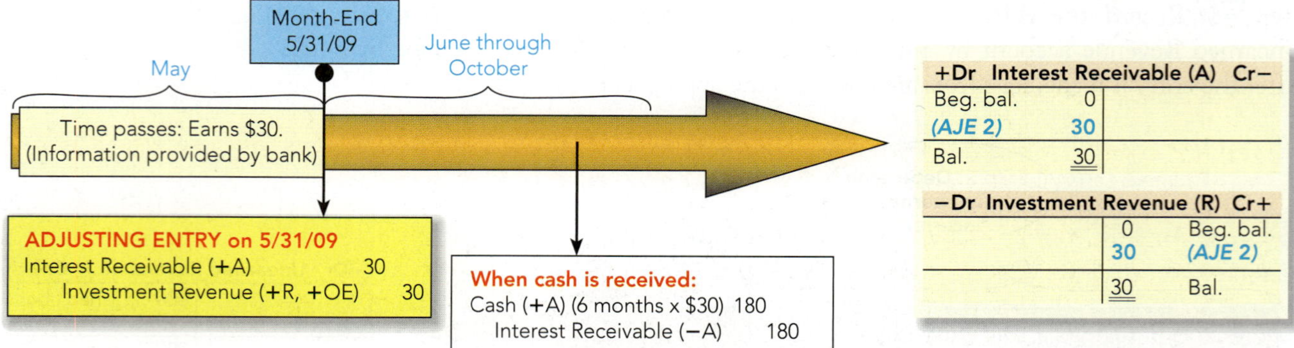

After Laurie recorded the adjusting entry and posted its effects to the appropriate accounts, Pizza Aroma's income statement reported the additional $30 revenue earned in May. The balance sheet also reported the additional current asset of $30, representing Pizza Aroma's right to receive $30 from the bank in the future. Pizza Aroma will make a similar adjustment at the end of each month as long as the savings account is open. Other examples of accrued revenue include amounts due from tenants who rent space from the company and interest earned on loans made to others.

Prepaid Expenses

Businesses use many assets over time to generate revenues. At the end of every period, they must make an adjustment to record the amount of the asset that was used during the period. Let's analyze Pizza Aroma's four prepaid expenses at the end of May.

Supplies. Supplies are prepaid expenses that must be adjusted for the dollar amount used during the period.

AJE 3. During May, Pizza Aroma purchased $5,000 in supplies. On May 31, Mauricio counted that $600 worth of supplies remained on hand.

Step 2 ***Amount.*** The easiest way to determine the dollar amount of supplies used is to add the dollar amount of supplies available at the beginning of the period plus any purchases made during the period and then subtract the dollar amount of supplies remaining on hand at the end of the period.

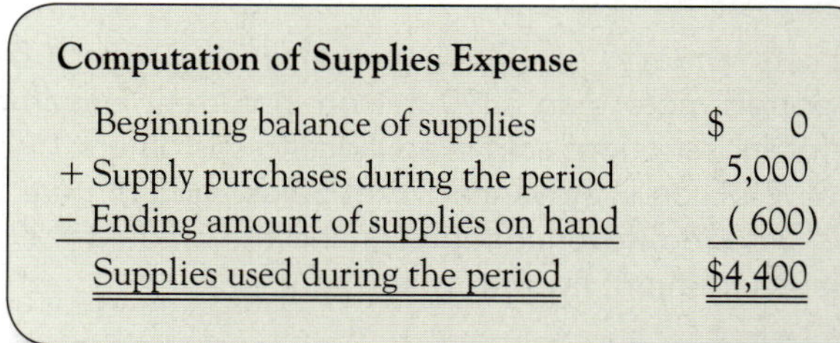

Computation of Supplies Expense

Beginning balance of supplies	$ 0
+ Supply purchases during the period	5,000
− Ending amount of supplies on hand	(600)
Supplies used during the period	$4,400

Step 3 *AJE.* An adjusting entry is needed to record the use of $4,400 of supplies during May.

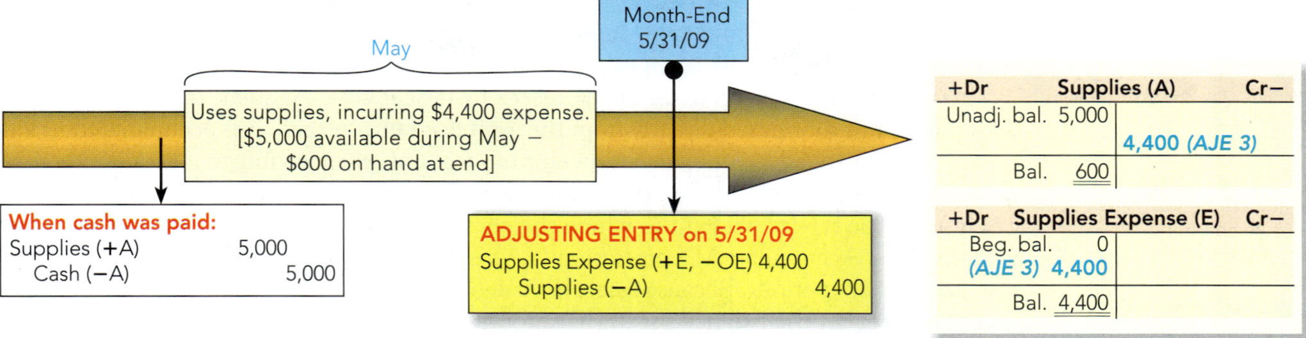

After the adjusting entry was recorded and its effects posted to the accounts, Pizza Aroma's income statement reported $4,400 of Supplies Expense, and the balance sheet reported the remaining $600 in Supplies.

Prepaid Rent. Like supplies, prepaid rent is a prepaid expense that must be adjusted for the amount used during the period.

AJE 4. At the beginning of May, Pizza Aroma paid $4,800 in advance to rent the store for six months (May through October).

Step 2 ***Amount.*** At the end of May, one month of the Prepaid Rent had been used to generate revenue: $4,800 × 1/6 = $800 of Rent Expense in May.

Step 3 *AJE.* An adjusting entry is needed to record the amount of rent used for the month.

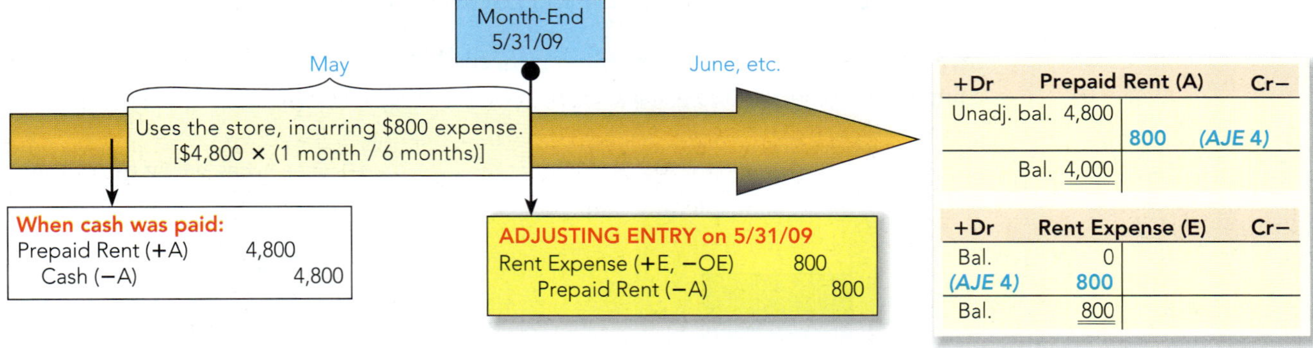

After the adjusting entry was recorded and its effects posted to the accounts, Pizza Aroma's income statement reported the additional $800 of Rent Expense incurred in May. The balance sheet also reported the remaining asset of $4,000, representing the unused portion of the Prepaid Rent. Pizza Aroma will make a similar adjustment at the end of each of the remaining five months.

Prepaid Insurance. Like rent, insurance is usually paid for before the coverage begins. At the end of May, Pizza Aroma purchased insurance for $2,400 covering June, July, and August. It recorded the asset Prepaid Insurance on that date. Because the insurance did not begin until June, none of the asset had been used by the end of May. Thus, **no adjusting entry was necessary at the end of May.** However, at the end of June, July, and August, an adjusting entry will be necessary to reduce the Prepaid Insurance account and record Insurance Expense of $800, representing one month of insurance coverage ($2,400 ÷ 3 months).

ADJUSTING ENTRY at the end of June, July, and August		
Insurance Expense (+E, −OE)	800	
Prepaid Insurance (−A)		800

Equipment. Unlike supplies that are purchased and then used over a relatively short period, buildings and equipment represent prepaid expenses that will be used over many years.

Building and equipment accounts increase when the assets are **acquired** and decrease when they are **sold.** However, these assets are also **used** over time to generate revenue. Thus, a part of their cost should be expensed in the same period (the matching principle). Accountants say that buildings and equipment **depreciate** over time as they are used. Depreciation **is an allocation of an asset's cost to an expense over its estimated useful life to the company.**

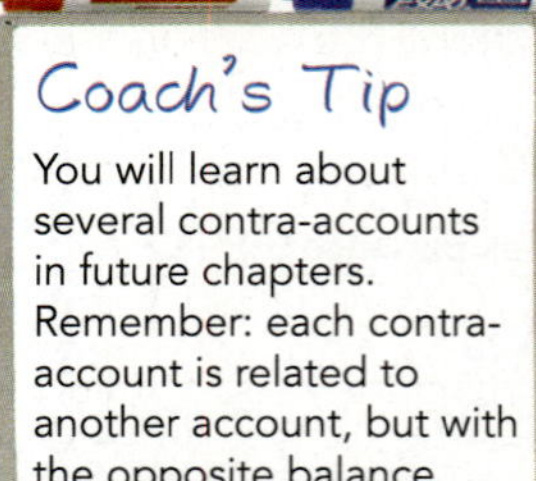

It is important to keep track of the asset's historical cost. As such, the amount that has been used is not subtracted directly from the asset account. Instead, it is accumulated in a new kind of account called a contra-account. Contra-accounts are accounts that are directly related to another account but with an opposite balance. To identify these accounts, we will place an x in front of the type of account to which the contra-account relates. For example, the contra-account titled Accumulated Depreciation (xA) is used to accumulate the amount of historical cost used in prior periods. Because assets have debit balances, Accumulated Depreciation has a credit balance. On the balance sheet, the amount that is reported for equipment is its net book value (also called the book value or carrying value), which equals the ending balance in the Equipment account minus the ending balance in the Accumulated Depreciation account.

+ Equipment (A)	−
Beginning bal. Buy	Sell
Ending bal.	

− Accumulated Depreciation (xA)	+
	Beginning bal. Used
	Ending bal.

Amount reported on the balance sheet = Net book value

AJE 5. At the beginning of May, Pizza Aroma purchased $36,000 in equipment that is expected to be used for many years. It was used for one month to generate revenue.

Step 2 ***Amount.*** Mauricio estimates that $300 is the cost allocation (depreciation) that must be adjusted to reflect the use of equipment in May. (The computations for estimating the amount of depreciation expense will be covered in detail in future chapters.)

Step 3 ***AJE.*** An adjusting entry is needed to record the allocation of the cost of equipment to reflect the estimate of the amount used to generate revenue in May.

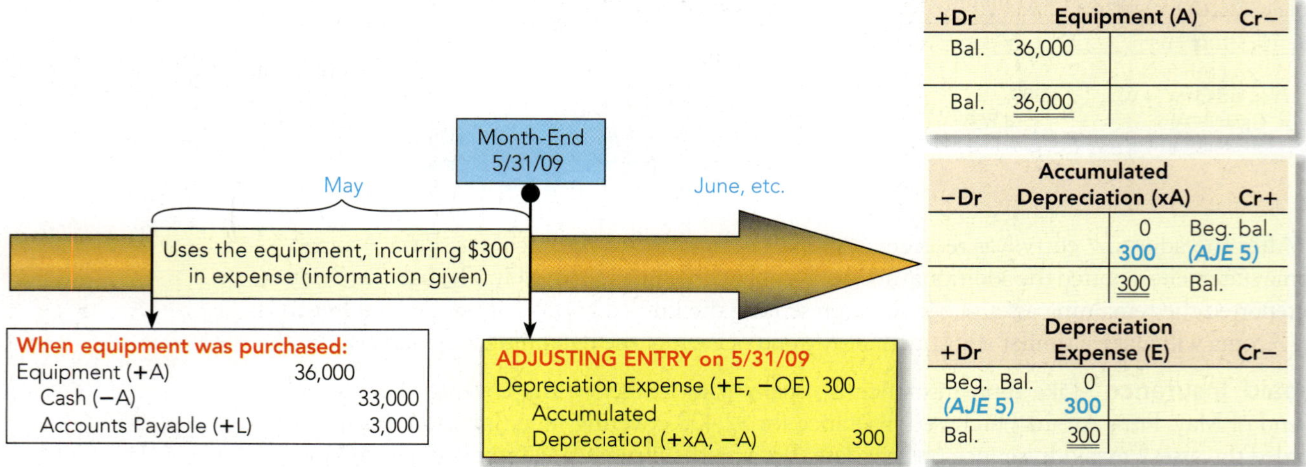

After the adjusting entry was recorded and its effects posted to the accounts, Pizza Aroma reported $300 of Depreciation Expense on the income statement and an increase in the contra-asset account Accumulated Depreciation. Notice that the Equipment account was not affected by the recording of depreciation for the month. However, the amount that was reported on the balance sheet at the end of May was $35,700, the equipment's net book value.

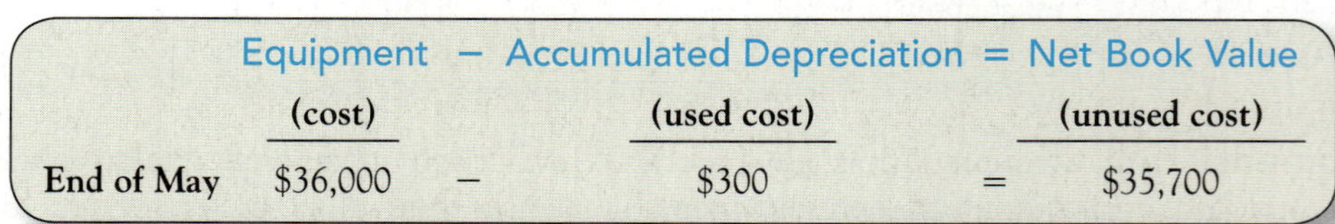

Each month, the amount of cost allocated to Depreciation Expense will increase the Accumulated Depreciation account. At the end of June, for example, Accumulated Depreciation will have a $600 balance, and the balance sheet will report a net book value of $35,400.

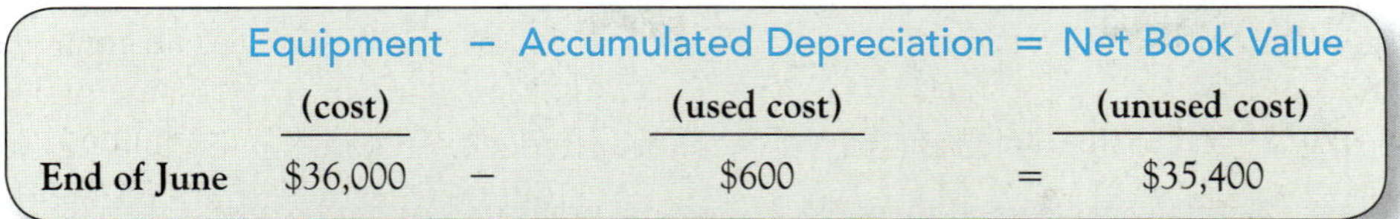

	Equipment (cost)	–	Accumulated Depreciation (used cost)	=	Net Book Value (unused cost)
End of June	$36,000	–	$600	=	$35,400

A common misconception held by students and others unfamiliar with accounting is that depreciation as used by accountants reflects a decline in an asset's *market value* (the amount the asset could be sold for). **In accounting, depreciation is simply a cost allocation concept, not a way to report a reduction in market value.** Depreciation Expense is reported each period on the income statement and describes the portion of the asset's historical cost that is estimated to have been used up during the period.

Accrued Expenses

Numerous expenses are incurred in the current period without being paid for until the next period. Common examples include Wages Expense for the wages owed to employees, Utilities Expense for the water, gas, and electricity used during the period, and Interest Expense incurred on debt. At the end of the period, an adjusting entry records these expenses in the proper period.

Wages. Businesses use the services of employees to generate revenue. Although a company may employ workers steadily, the business does not pay employees until after they work, usually at the end of the week, every two weeks, or the month. At the end of the accounting period, then, an adjusting entry records the expense for the wages owed to employees who have not yet been paid.

AJE 6. Pizza Aroma's employees worked the last week of May, but they will not be paid until June 1.

Step 2 ***Amount.*** Mauricio calculates the business incurred $100 of Wages Expense that was not recorded in May.

Step 3 ***AJE.*** An adjusting entry is needed to record the expense and the related liability, Wages Payable.

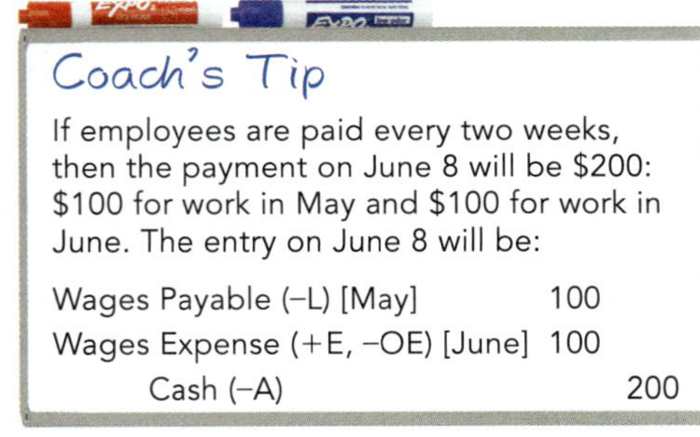

Coach's Tip

If employees are paid every two weeks, then the payment on June 8 will be $200: $100 for work in May and $100 for work in June. The entry on June 8 will be:

Wages Payable (–L) [May]	100	
Wages Expense (+E, –OE) [June]	100	
Cash (–A)		200

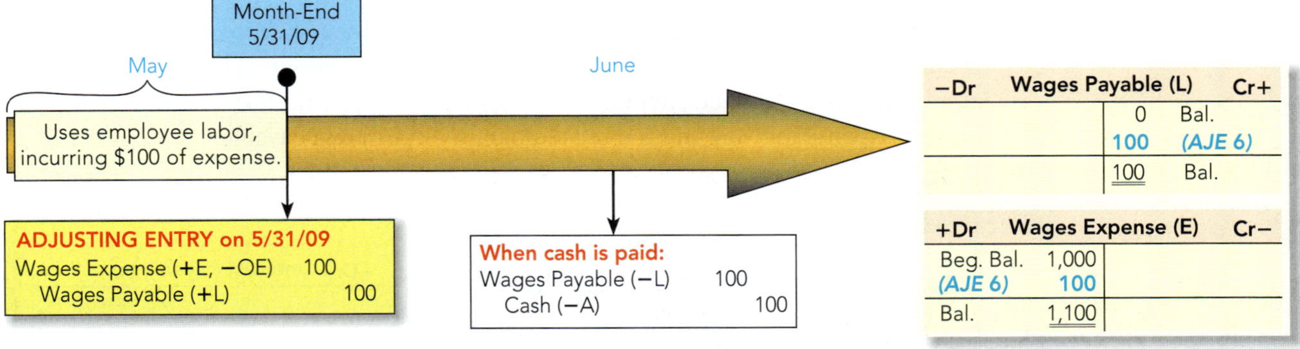

After the adjusting entry was recorded and its effects posted, Pizza Aroma's income statement reported $100 of Wages Expense. The balance sheet reported a current liability of $100 in Wages Payable.

Utilities. Businesses use electricity, gas, and telephone service over time but the utility companies bill them at the end of the period. To reflect usage of these utility services in the proper period, an adjusting entry must be made.

AJE 7. Pizza Aroma used utilities to generate revenue in May, but because no bill was received by the end of the month, no entry was made to recognize the expense incurred that month.

Step 2 ***Amount.*** Mauricio estimates that Pizza Aroma used $1,000 of electricity and gas in May.

Step 3 ***AJE.*** An adjusting entry is therefore needed to record the $1,000 of Utilities Expense incurred in May along with its related liability, Utilities Payable. The company will pay the bill in June when it is received.

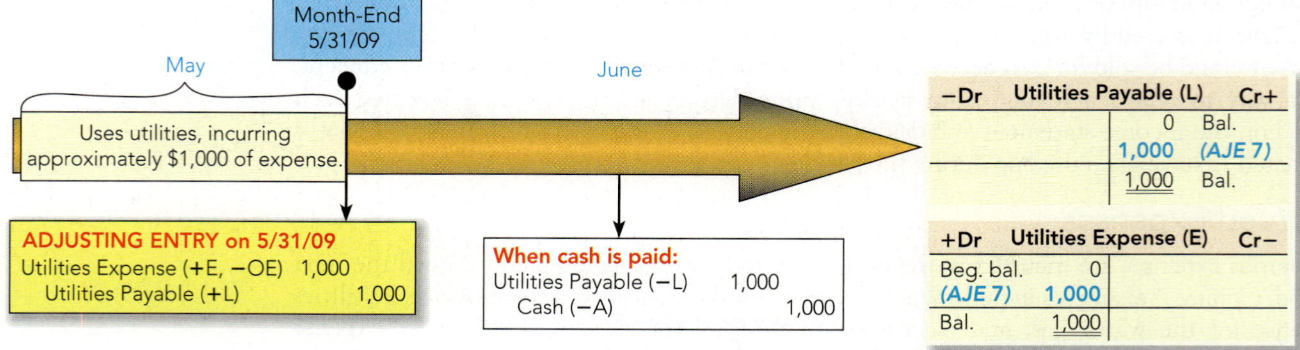

Similar to wages, Pizza Aroma's income statement reported $1,000 of Utilities Expense. In addition, the balance sheet reported another current liability Utilities Payable for $1,000.

Interest. When a company borrows funds, it must pay interest. Each day that passes, the company incurs interest expense (the cost of using borrowed funds). Most loans require payment of interest at the end of the month, quarter, or year. An adjusting entry is needed at the end of the period to record the accrual of any interest expense owed.

AJE 8. At the beginning of May, Pizza Aroma borrowed $20,000 from a local bank. This $20,000 is the **principal** of the loan that was recorded in Notes Payable in exchange for $20,000 cash from the bank. The loan requires Pizza Aroma to repay the principal in three years **plus interest** on May 1 each year. As each day in May passed, the company used the borrowed funds and incurred interest, but Pizza Aroma did not record any expense because no cash for the interest had yet been paid.

Step 2 ***Amount.*** With Laurie's assistance, Mauricio determined that $200 in interest expense was incurred during May. (The computations for determining the amount of interest expense will be covered in detail in future chapters.)

Step 3 ***AJE.*** At the end of May, the $20,000 principal recorded as Notes Payable remained due, so no adjustment to Notes Payable was necessary. However, one month of interest expense has been incurred. An adjusting entry is needed to record the $200 in Interest Expense for May and the related liability in Interest Payable.

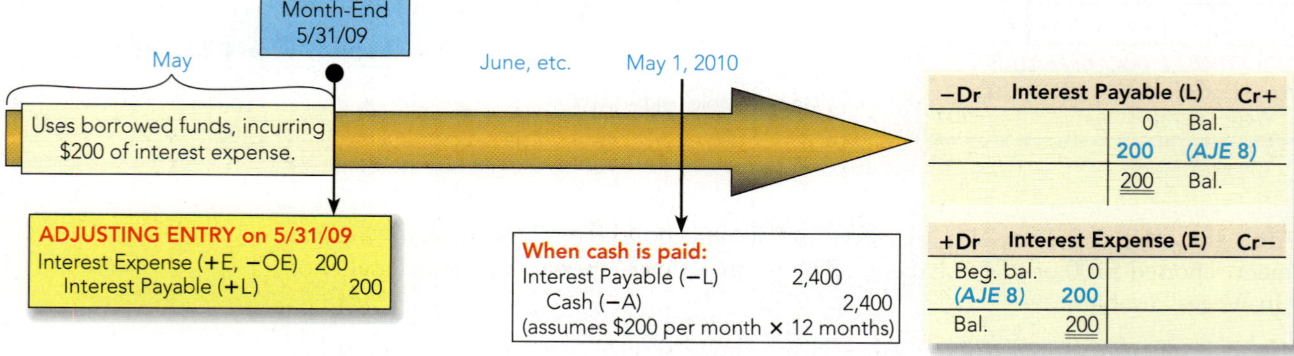

After recording and posting the adjusting entry, Pizza Aroma's income statement reported Interest Expense of $200. Another current liability, Interest Payable, for $200 is reported on the balance sheet.

Spotlight On FINANCIAL REPORTING

Accrued Expenses in the Millions and Billions

Accrued expenses are significant liabilities for many companies. For example, Tootsie Roll Industries recently reported the following:

NOTE 2—ACCRUED LIABILITIES:
Accrued liabilities are comprised of the following:

	DECEMBER 31,	
(in thousands of dollars)	**2006**	**2005**
Compensation	$ 12,923	$ 15,756
Other employee benefits	5,631	5,213
Taxes, other than income	1,781	1,765
Advertising and promotions	17,854	14,701
Other	5,613	7,534
	$ 43,802	$ 44,969

The $43.8 million in total accrued liabilities represents 70 percent of Tootsie Roll's current liabilities and 27 percent of total liabilities.

Likewise, Wal-Mart Stores, Inc., reported approximately $14.7 billion in accrued liabilities, primarily from accrued wages and benefits owed to employees. This was 28 percent of current liabilities and 17 percent of total liabilities.

Pizza Aroma's accounts have now been adjusted and all of the revenues and expenses for May properly recorded. See Exhibit 4.3 for a summary of the adjusting entries *AJE 1* through

Exhibit 4.3 Summary of Pizza Aroma's Adjusting Entries

PIZZA AROMA

Pizza Aroma
Adjusting Journal Entries
May 31, 2009

		Debit	Credit	
(AJE 1)	Unearned Revenue (−L)	400		Unearned revenue
	Pizza Revenue (+R, +OE)		400	
(AJE 2)	Interest Receivable (+A)	30		Accrued revenue
	Investment Revenue (+R, +OE)		30	
(AJE 3)	Supplies Expense (+E, −OE)	4,400		Prepaid expenses
	Supplies (−A)		4,400	
(AJE 4)	Rent Expense (+E, −OE)	800		
	Prepaid Rent (−A)		800	
(AJE 5)	Depreciation Expense (+E, −OE)	300		
	Accumulated Depreciation (+xA, −A)		300	
(AJE 6)	Wages Expense (+E, −OE)	100		Accrued expenses
	Wages Payable (+L)		100	
(AJE 7)	Utilities Expense (+E, −OE)	1,000		
	Utilities Payable (+L)		1,000	
(AJE 8)	Interest Expense (+E, −OE)	200		
	Interest Payable (+L)		200	

Exhibit 4.4 Summary of Pizza Aroma's T-Accounts after Adjustment

Pizza Aroma | T-Accounts | May 31, 2009

Assets

+	Cash (A) –
Bal. 9,100	
Bal. 9,100	

+	Investments (A) –
Bal. 6,000	
Bal. 6,000	

+	Interest Receivable (A) –
Unadj. bal. 0	
(AJE 2) 30	
Bal. 30	

+	Accounts Receivable (A) –
Bal. 700	
Bal. 700	

+	Supplies (A) –
Unadj. bal. 5,000	4,400 (AJE 3)
Bal. 600	

+	Prepaid Rent (A) –
Unadj. bal. 4,800	800 (AJE 4)
Bal. 4,000	

+	Prepaid Insurance (A) –
Unadj. bal. 2,400	
Bal. 2,400	

+	Equipment (A) –
Bal. 36,000	
Bal. 36,000	

–	Accumulated Depreciation (xA) +
	0 Unadj. bal.
	300 (AJE 5)
	300 Bal.

Liabilities

–	Accounts Payable (L) +
	4,800 Bal.
	4,800 Bal.

–	Wages Payable (L) +
	0 Unadj. bal.
	100 (AJE 6)
	100 Bal.

–	Utilities Payable (L) +
	0 Unadj. bal.
	1,000 (AJE 7)
	1,000 Bal.

–	Interest Payable (L) +
	0 Unadj. bal.
	200 (AJE 8)
	200 Bal.

–	Unearned Revenue (L) +
(AJE 1) 400	600 Unadj. bal.
	200 Bal.

–	Notes Payable (L) +
	20,000 Bal.
	20,000 Bal.

Owner's Equity

–	M. Rosa, Capital (OE) +
	30,000 Bal.
	30,000 Bal.

+	M. Rosa, Drawing (OE) –
Bal. 3,000	
Bal. 3,000	

Expenses

+	Supplies Expense (E) –
Unadj. bal. 0	
(AJE 3) 4,400	
Bal. 4,400	

+	Wages Expense (E) –
Unadj. bal. 1,000	
(AJE 6) 100	
Bal. 1,100	

+	Utilities Expense (E) –
Unadj. bal. 0	
(AJE 7) 1,000	
Bal. 1,000	

+	Telephone Service Expense (E) –
Bal. 600	
Bal. 600	

+	Rent Expense (E) –
Unadj. bal. 0	
(AJE 4) 800	
Bal. 800	

+	Advertising Expense (E) –
Bal. 800	
Bal. 800	

+	Interest Expense (E) –
Unadj. bal. 0	
(AJE 8) 200	
Bal. 200	

+	Depreciation Expense (E) –
Unadj. bal. 0	
(AJE 5) 300	
Bal. 300	

Revenues

–	Pizza Revenue (R) +
	14,000 Unadj. bal.
	400 (AJE 1)
	14,400 Bal.

–	Investment Revenue (R) +
	0 Unadj. bal.
	30 (AJE 2)
	30 Bal.

Coach's Tip

A T-account for Insurance Expense has not been listed here because it has a $0 balance.

AJE 8. Refer to Exhibit 4.4 for Pizza Aroma's T-accounts after the adjusting entries were made on May 31, 2009.

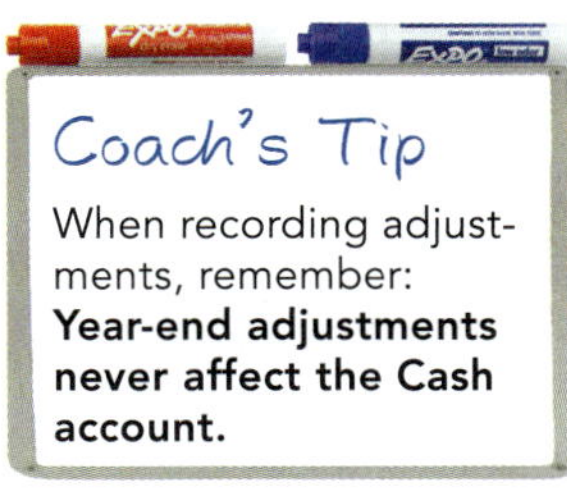

Coach's Tip

When recording adjustments, remember: **Year-end adjustments never affect the Cash account.**

Summary Exhibits

Using selected examples, Exhibit 4.5 summarizes the entries needed to adjust unearned and accrued revenues; Exhibit 4.6 summarizes those needed to adjust most prepaid and accrued expenses. Note that in both cases, the goal is to record revenues and expenses in the proper period. Note too that each adjusting entry involves one balance sheet and one income statement account and that **cash is never affected in the adjustment.**

Exhibit 4.5 Summary Illustration of Adjusting Unearned and Accrued Revenues

		Unearned Revenues (for deposits on future pizza deliveries)	Accrued Revenues (for interest earned on investments)
During the period	Entry when cash is received before company earns revenue	Cash (+A) 600 Unearned Revenue (+L) 600	None
End of period	**AJE** needed because company has earned revenue during period	Unearned Revenue (−L) 400 Pizza Revenue (+R, +OE) 400	Interest Receivable (+A) 30 Investment Revenue (+R, +OE) 30
Next period	Entry when cash is received after company earns revenue	None	Cash (+A) 30 Interest Receivable (−A) 30

Revenue recorded in proper period

Exhibit 4.6 Summary Illustration of Adjusting Prepaid and Accrued Expenses

		Prepaid Expenses (for renting a building)	Accrued Expenses (for amounts owed to workers)
During the period	Entry when cash is paid before company incurs expense	Prepaid Rent (+A) 4,800 Cash (−A) 4,800	None
End of period	**AJE** needed because company has incurred an expense during the period	Rent Expense (+E, −OE) 800 Prepaid Rent (−A) 800	Wages Expense (+E, −OE) 100 Wages Payable (+L) 100
Next period	Entry when cash is paid after company incurs expense	None	Wages Payable (−L) 100 Cash (−A) 100

Expense recorded in proper period

Now it's your turn to practice adjusting accounts at the end of the period. Review Pizza Aroma's adjustments and then complete the following Self-Study Practice.

SELF-STUDY PRACTICE

Florida Flippers, a scuba diving and instruction business, completed its operations on December 31, 2010. Follow the three-step process for each of the following adjustments.

Step 1: Identify the type of adjustment needed.

Step 2: Determine the amount of the adjustment affecting a revenue or expense account.

Step 3: Record the adjusting entries on December 31.

AJE 1: Florida Flippers received $6,000 from customers on November 15, 2010, for diving trips to the Bahamas in December and January. The $6,000 was recorded in Unearned Revenue on that date. By the end of December, one-third of the diving trips had been completed.

AJE 2: On December 30, 2010, Florida Flippers provided advanced diving instruction to 10 customers, who will pay the business $800 in January. No entry was made when the instruction was provided.

AJE 3: On September 1, 2010, Florida Flippers paid $24,000 for insurance for the 12 months beginning on September 1. The amount was recorded as Prepaid Insurance on September 1.

AJE 4: On March 1, 2010, Florida Flippers borrowed $300,000. Interest is payable each March 1 for three years. Interest incurred for the year was $20,000.

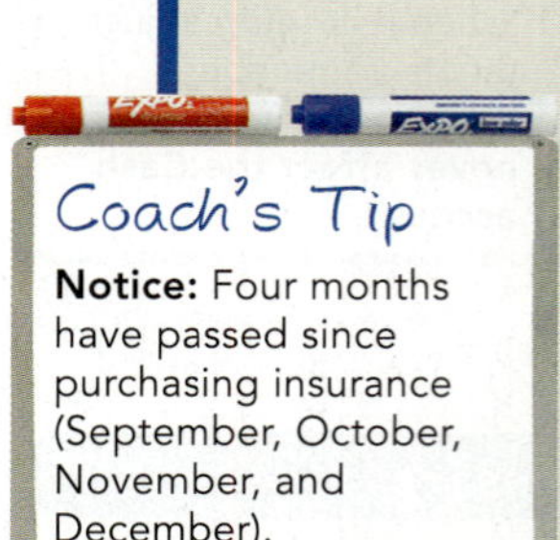

Coach's Tip

Notice: Four months have passed since purchasing insurance (September, October, November, and December).

	1 Type of Adjustment	2 Determination of Amount of Adjustment	3 Adjusting Journal Entry Accounts	Debit	Credit
AJE 1					
AJE 2					
AJE 3					
AJE 4					

After you have finished, check your answers with the solution at the bottom of the page.

Spotlight On ETHICS

Adjustments and a Question of Ethics

When a business's financial performance lags behind expectations, managers and owners may be tempted to manipulate accounting adjustments to improve the appearance of the financial statements. For example, managers may record cash received as a revenue even though the company did not earn the revenue in the current period. Or they may fail to accrue certain expenses at year-end. Because these unethical acts cause errors in the financial statements, any ratio analysis that is based on those statements will mislead users.

(continued)

Solution to Self-Study Practice

	Type	Amount	Adjusting Journal Entry Accounts	Debit	Credit
AJE 1	Unearned Revenue	$6,000 × 1/3 = $2,000 earned	Unearned Revenue (−L)	2,000	
			Diving Trip Revenue (+R, +OE)		2,000
AJE 2	Accrued Revenue	$800 earned (given)	Accounts Receivable (+A)	800	
			Diving Instruction Revenue (+R, +OE)		800
AJE 3	Prepaid Expense	$24,000 × 1/12 = $2,000 per month $2,000 × 4 months = $8,000 used	Insurance Expense (+E, −OE)	8,000	
			Prepaid Insurance (−A)		8,000
AJE 4	Accrued Expense	$20,000 incurred (given)	Interest Expense (+E, −OE)	20,000	
			Interest Payable (+L)		20,000

(continued)

Let's take a look at how Pizza Aroma's financial statements would be affected by failing to record one of the adjusting entries, *AJE 7* (see Exhibit 4.3). In analyzing the effects of this error on the financial statements, follow four steps:

1. Write down the adjusting entry that should have been made.

(AJE 7)	Utilities Expense (+E, −OE)	1,000	
	Utilities Payable (+L)		1,000

2. Post the effects of failing to record this entry on the following chart. Use U for understated and O for overstated. Because Utilities Expense was not recorded, expenses are understated.

BALANCE SHEET					INCOME STATEMENT				
Assets	=	Liabilities	+	Owner's Equity	Revenues	−	Expenses	=	Net Income
		U 1,000					U 1,000		

3. Beginning with the income statement (revenues, expenses, and net income), indicate the effects on the other elements. Use NE to indicate that there is no effect on an element.

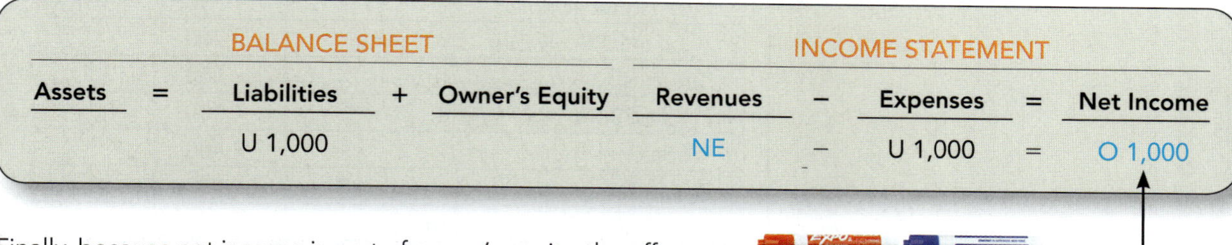

4. Finally, because net income is part of owner's equity, the effect on net income will also be the effect on owner's equity. Complete the rest of the balance sheet elements, checking that the accounting equation remains in balance (that is, assets = liabilities + owner's equity).

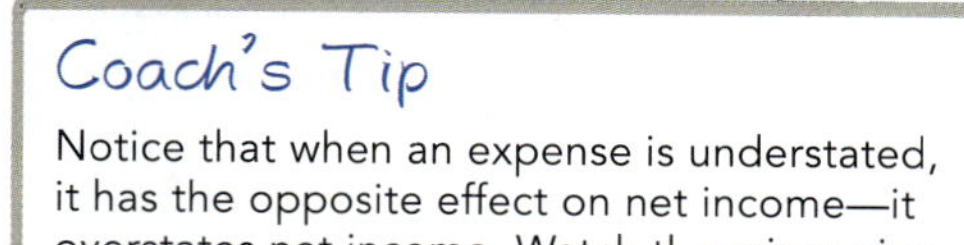

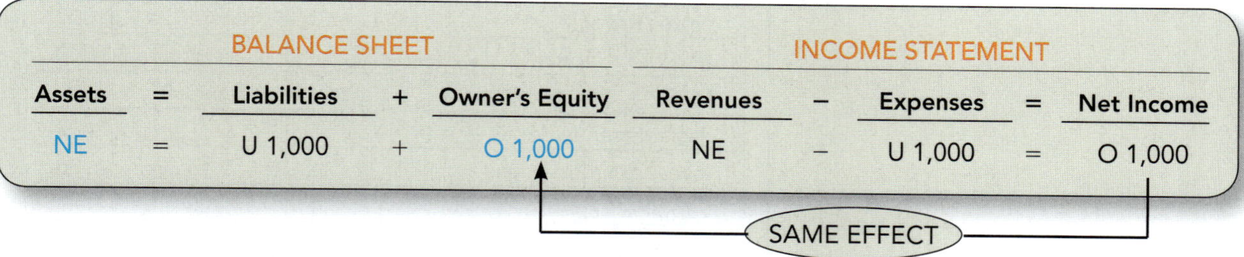

In sum, if *AJE 7* were not recorded, Pizza Aroma's expenses and liabilities would be understated, and its net income and owner's equity would be overstated. Any ratios that are based on these totals would also be in error.

Of course, errors sometimes occur without fraudulent intent. Still, research on many companies indicates that some managers do engage in fraudulent recording of adjusting entries. These studies are borne out by enforcement actions taken by the Securities and Exchange Commission (SEC). A recent SEC study reported 227 enforcement investigations in a five-year period. Of those, "126 involved improper revenue recognition and 101 involved improper expense recognition. . . 157 resulted in charges against at least one senior manager. . . . Furthermore, . . . 57 enforcement matters resulted in charges for auditing violations. . . ."[2] In many of these cases, the businesses involved, their managers, and their auditors were penalized for their actions.

[2] These statistics are reported in the Securities and Exchange Commission's study, "Report Pursuant to Section 704 of the Sarbanes-Oxley Act of 2002," January 27, 2003, p. 47.

Learning Objective 3

Present an income statement, statement of owner's equity, and balance sheet.

PREPARING FINANCIAL STATEMENTS

Adjusted Trial Balance

Pizza Aroma's accounts are now adjusted so that all revenues and expenses for May are properly recorded. Before Laurie prepares a complete set of financial statements, however, she checks to ensure that debit balances remained equal to credit balances after the adjustments were posted to all of the accounts in the ledger.[3] Exhibit 4.7 is the **adjusted trial balance** based on

[3] For a discussion and illustration of the use of a worksheet for end-of-period adjustments, refer to Supplement 4A of this chapter.

Exhibit 4.7 Pizza Aroma's Adjusted Trial Balance

PIZZA AROMA

Pizza Aroma
Adjusted Trial Balance
On May 31, 2009

		ADJUSTED	
		Debit	Credit
Balance sheet accounts	Cash	9,100	
	Investments	6,000	
	Interest Receivable	30	
	Accounts Receivable	700	
	Supplies	600	
	Prepaid Rent	4,000	
	Prepaid Insurance	2,400	
	Equipment	36,000	
	Accumulated Depreciation		300
	Accounts Payable		4,800
	Wages Payable		100
	Utilities Payable		1,000
	Interest Payable		200
	Unearned Revenue		200
	Notes Payable		20,000
	M. Rosa, Capital		30,000
	M. Rosa, Drawing	3,000	
Income statement accounts	Pizza Revenue		14,400
	Investment Revenue		30
	Supplies Expense	4,400	
	Wages Expense	1,100	
	Utilities Expense	1,000	
	Telephone Service Expense	600	
	Rent Expense	800	
	Insurance Expense	0	
	Advertising Expense	800	
	Interest Expense	200	
	Depreciation Expense	300	
	Totals	**71,030**	**71,030**

the updated balances in the T-accounts in Exhibit 4.4. Because the total debits of $71,030 equaled the total credits in the adjusted trial balance, Laurie prepared Pizza Aroma's financial statements for the month of May: an income statement, a statement of owner's equity, and a balance sheet.

Relationships among Financial Statements

As you learned in Chapter 1, the financial statements are interrelated—that is, the numbers from one statement flow into the next statement. Exhibit 4.8 illustrates the interconnections among the statements using the fundamental accounting equation. Starting on the bottom right, notice that

1. Revenue minus expenses yields net income on the **income statement.**
2. Net income, owner withdrawals, and any additional investments made by the owner during the period affect the balance in the owner's capital account on the **statement of owner's equity.**
3. The owner's capital account is a component of the **balance sheet.**

Thus, if a number on the income statement changes or is in error, it will impact the other statements.

Exhibit 4.8 also includes special labels for the accounts. Balance sheet accounts are considered **permanent,** indicating that they retain their balances from the end of one period to the beginning of the next. Revenue, expense, and the owner's drawing accounts are **temporary** accounts because their balances accumulate for a period but start with a zero balance at the beginning of the next period. These labels will be discussed in the section on *closing the books* following the presentation of Pizza Aroma's classified financial statements.

The structures of the classified financial statements as discussed in Chapters 1 through 3 are provided in summary formats in Exhibit 4.9. The connection between the income statement

Exhibit 4.8 Relationships of the Financial Statements

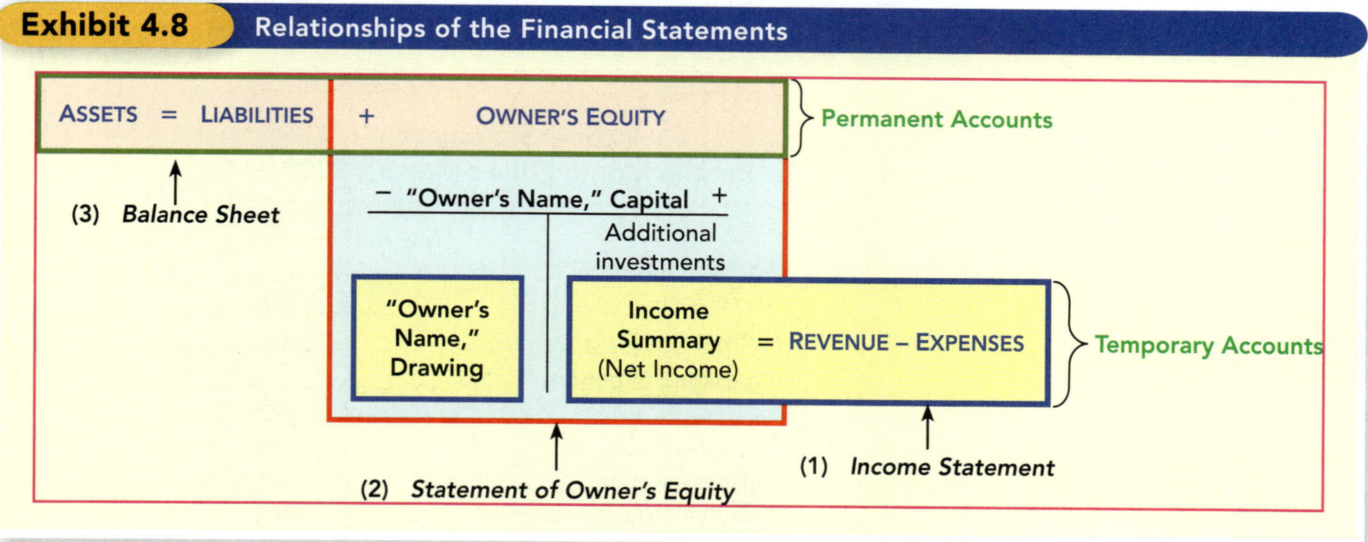

Exhibit 4.9 Formats of the Classified Financial Statements

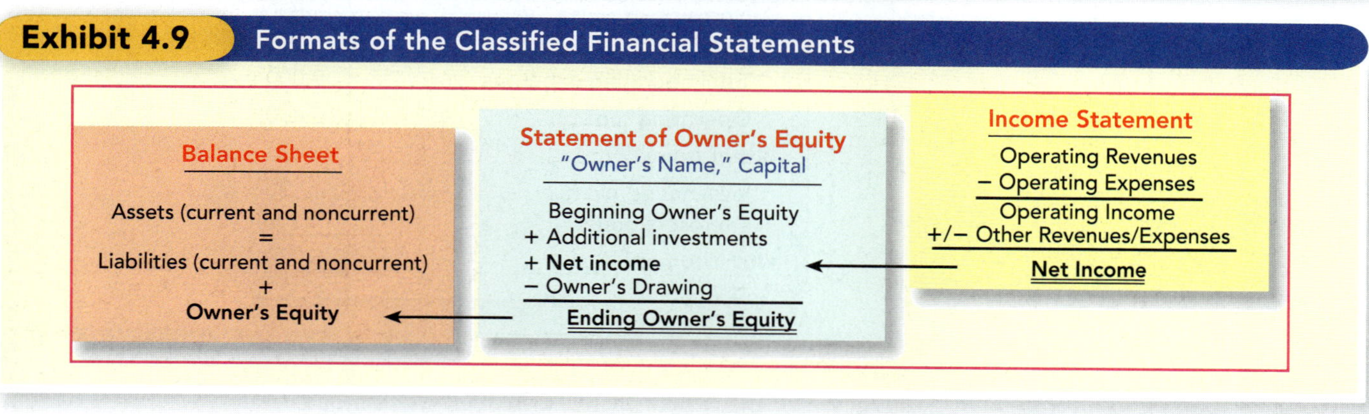

and statement of owner's equity is net income. The connection between the statement of owner's equity and the balance sheet is the ending balance in owner's equity.

Classified Income Statement

The income statement is prepared first because net income is a component of Owner's Equity. Laurie presented the following income statement for May (in Exhibit 4.10) to Mauricio for his review. Note that it is classified into operating revenue and expenses and other items (revenues and expenses not related to the central focus of the business).

Mauricio was very happy with Pizza Aroma's financial performance during its first month of operations. Before he established the business, Laurie had shown him a projected income statement for May (see Exhibit 1.5, page 15) that showed a projected revenue of $11,000. The actual revenue of $14,400 was about 31 percent higher than anticipated. Mauricio's strategy of aggressive advertising on college campuses together with word-of-mouth reports on the high quality of his gourmet pizza appears to have paid off in better-than-expected sales.

Pizza Aroma earned a net income of $5,230—more than double the $2,000 that Laurie had projected. Mauricio credits this success to his close attention to controlling costs while maintaining quality. He is greatly encouraged about the business's potential.

Statement of Owner's Equity

To connect net income to the balance sheet, the next statement to prepare is the statement of owner's equity. The beginning balance of the account called M. Rosa, Capital is affected by the amount of net income shown on the income statement, in addition to any investments or withdrawals the owner made during the period. The result is the ending balance in the M. Rosa, Capital account, which is a component of the balance sheet.

Exhibit 4.10 Pizza Aroma's Classified Income Statement

PIZZA AROMA

Pizza Aroma
Income Statement
For the Month Ended May 31, 2009

Operating Revenues	
Pizza revenue	$14,400
Total operating revenues	14,400
Operating Expenses	
Supplies expense	4,400
Wages expense	1,100
Utilities expense	1,000
Telephone service expense	600
Rent expense	800
Advertising expense	800
Depreciation expense	300
Total operating expenses	9,000
Operating Income	5,400
Other Items	
Investment revenue	30
Interest expense	(200)
Net Income	$ 5,230

Pizza Aroma
Statement of Owner's Equity
For the Month Ended May 31, 2009

M. Rosa, capital, May 1, 2009	$ 0
Additional investments	30,000
Net income	5,230
M. Rosa, drawing	(3,000)
M. Rosa, capital, May 31, 2009	$32,230

Classified Balance Sheet

The ending balance for M. Rosa, Capital, which is taken from the Statement of Owner's Equity, becomes the total Owner's Equity on the Balance Sheet. Note that the contra-asset account Accumulated Depreciation has been subtracted from the Equipment account to reflect the equipment's net book value (or carrying value) at month-end. Recall that assets are listed in order of their liquidity, and liabilities are listed in order of their due dates. Current assets are those that will be used or turned into cash within one year. Current liabilities are obligations that must be paid with current assets within one year.

Pizza Aroma
Balance Sheet
May 31, 2009

ASSETS	
Current Assets	
Cash	$ 9,100
Investments	6,000
Accounts receivable	700
Interest receivable	30
Supplies	600
Prepaid rent	4,000
Prepaid insurance	2,400
Total current assets	22,830
Equipment (cost, $36,000 less accumulated depreciation, $300)	35,700
Total assets	$58,530
LIABILITIES AND OWNER'S EQUITY	
Current Liabilities	
Accounts payable	$ 4,800
Wages payable	100
Utilities payable	1,000
Interest payable	200
Unearned revenue	200
Total current liabilities	6,300
Notes payable	20,000
Owner's Equity	
M. Rosa, Capital	32,230
Total liabilities and owner's equity	$58,530

Laurie explained to Mauricio that Pizza Aroma's balance sheet shows that it is in strong financial condition. The external user of Pizza Aroma's statements, the local bank, will be pleased to see that there are sufficient current assets ($22,830) to settle the current liabilities ($6,300) that will come due in the next 12 months. Mauricio noted that he would need to purchase more supplies for the coming month, especially given the restaurant's rapid growth in sales.

Preparing the financial statements and providing them to internal and external users is an important step in the accounting communication process. However, one additional step is necessary to complete the accounting cycle: closing the books.

COMPLETING THE ACCOUNTING CYCLE

Closing the Books

Learning Objective 4

Explain the purpose and process of closing the books.

Video 4-2
www.mhhe.com/LLPW1e

After adjusting entries have been recorded and posted, companies need to prepare the ledger accounts for the next period. This phase in the accounting cycle is called closing the books. However, only certain accounts are closed.

The ending balance in each of Pizza Aroma's asset, liability, and owner's equity accounts carries over as the beginning account balance for the next period. So the $9,100 cash balance on May 31, for example, becomes the cash balance at June 1, the beginning of the next accounting period. The balances in these permanent accounts are **not** reduced to zero (not closed) at the end of the accounting period.

In contrast, revenue, expense, and owner's drawing accounts accumulate data for the current accounting period only. As such, these accounts must begin each period with a zero balance. Therefore, the balances in these accounts, called temporary accounts, are closed (reduced to zero) at the end of each period.

The process of closing the books is simply a series of journal entries that are made for the following reasons:

1. To update the owner's capital account for (1) the net income or loss for the period and (2) any withdrawals during the period. Until the temporary accounts are closed, the owner's capital account in the ledger does not reflect the amount reported on the balance sheet.
2. To establish a zero balance in each of the temporary accounts in preparation for use in the next accounting period.

Closing entries are dated the last day of the accounting period, are entered in the journal in the usual debits-equal-credits format, and are immediately posted to the ledger (or T-accounts). **Temporary accounts with debit balances are credited and accounts with credit balances are debited.** The four closing entries (labeled CE) are:

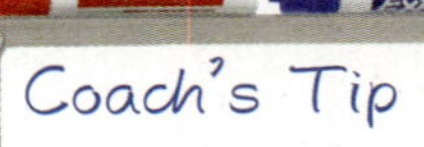

Coach's Tip

Note the following:

- Only income statement accounts (revenues and expenses) are closed to Income Summary.
- Make sure you close out the temporary accounts to a zero balance; record a debit for accounts with credit balances and a credit for accounts with debit balances.
- Owner's drawing is not an expense or reported on the income statement; as such, it is **not** closed to Income Summary.

CE 1 All revenue accounts are closed to a new temporary account called Income Summary used only for closing the books.[4] Because revenues have credit balances, each account is debited with a credit to Income Summary for the total of the revenues.

CE 2 All expense accounts are closed to the Income Summary account. Because expenses have debit balances, each account is credited with a debit to Income Summary for the total of the expenses.

CE 3 The Income Summary account, which should be equal to net income, is closed to the Owner's Capital account.

- If revenues exceed expenses (that is, the company had net income), Income Summary will have a credit balance. To close it, debit Income Summary and credit the owner's capital account.
- If expenses exceed revenues (that is, the company had a net loss), Income Summary will have a debit balance. To close it, credit Income Summary and debit the owner's capital account.

CE 4 The owner's drawing account is closed to the owner's capital account.

[4] Some companies do not use the Income Summary account. Instead, they close revenues and expenses directly to the Owner's Capital account.

Exhibit 4.11 is a simple illustration of how to record and post closing entries to the T-accounts. Notice that all of the temporary accounts have zero balances after closing the books and that the owner's capital account in the ledger is updated to match the amount reported on the balance sheet.

Companies usually close temporary accounts at the end of the fiscal year. Because Laurie wanted Mauricio to understand the necessity and effect of closing the books, she showed Mauricio the entries she would make to close Pizza Aroma's books at the end of May if this was the end of the fiscal year. Notice that the balances in the temporary accounts are the same as the ending amounts in the T-accounts shown in Exhibit 4.4.

Exhibit 4.11 Recording and Posting the Closing Entries (Simple Illustration)

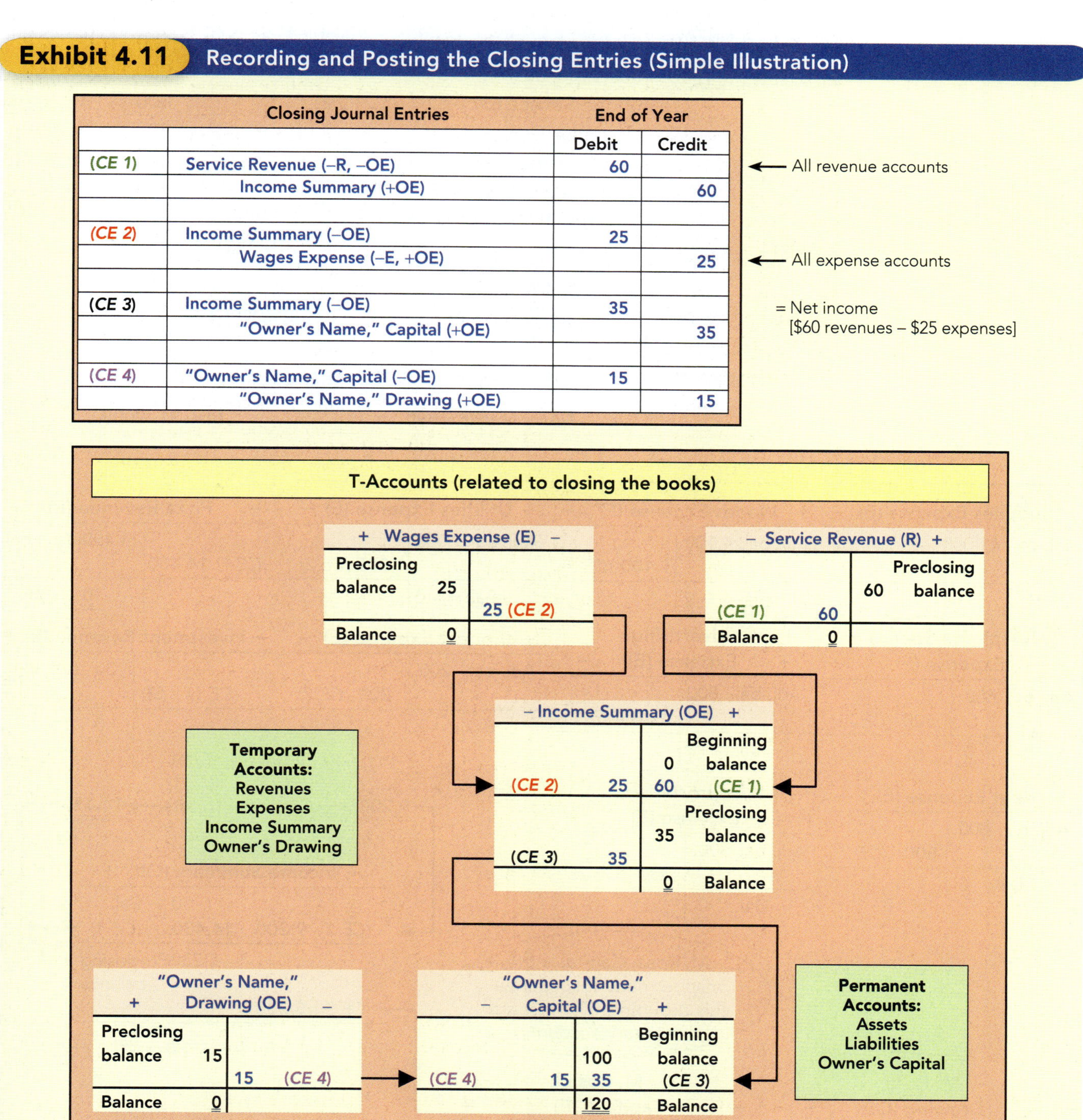

	Closing Journal Entries	End of Year Debit	End of Year Credit	
(CE 1)	Service Revenue (–R, –OE)	60		← All revenue accounts
	Income Summary (+OE)		60	
(CE 2)	Income Summary (–OE)	25		
	Wages Expense (–E, +OE)		25	← All expense accounts
(CE 3)	Income Summary (–OE)	35		= Net income [$60 revenues – $25 expenses]
	"Owner's Name," Capital (+OE)		35	
(CE 4)	"Owner's Name," Capital (–OE)	15		
	"Owner's Name," Drawing (+OE)		15	

Pizza Aroma
Closing Journal Entries
May 31, 2009

		Debit	Credit
(CE 1)	Pizza Revenue (−R, −OE)	14,400	
	Investment Revenue (−R, −OE)	30	
	Income Summary (+OE)		14,430
(CE 2)	Income Summary (−OE)	9,200	
	Supplies Expense (−E, +OE)		4,400
	Wages Expense (−E, +OE)		1,100
	Utilities Expense (−E, +OE)		1,000
	Telephone Service Expense (−E, +OE)		600
	Rent Expense (−E, +OE)		800
	Advertising Expense (−E, +OE)		800
	Interest Expense (−E, +OE)		200
	Depreciation Expense (−E, +OE)		300
(CE3)	Income Summary (−OE)	5,230	
	M. Rosa, Capital (+OE)		5,230
(CE 4)	M. Rosa, Capital (−OE)	3,000	
	M. Rosa, Drawing (+OE)		3,000

All revenue accounts

All expense accounts

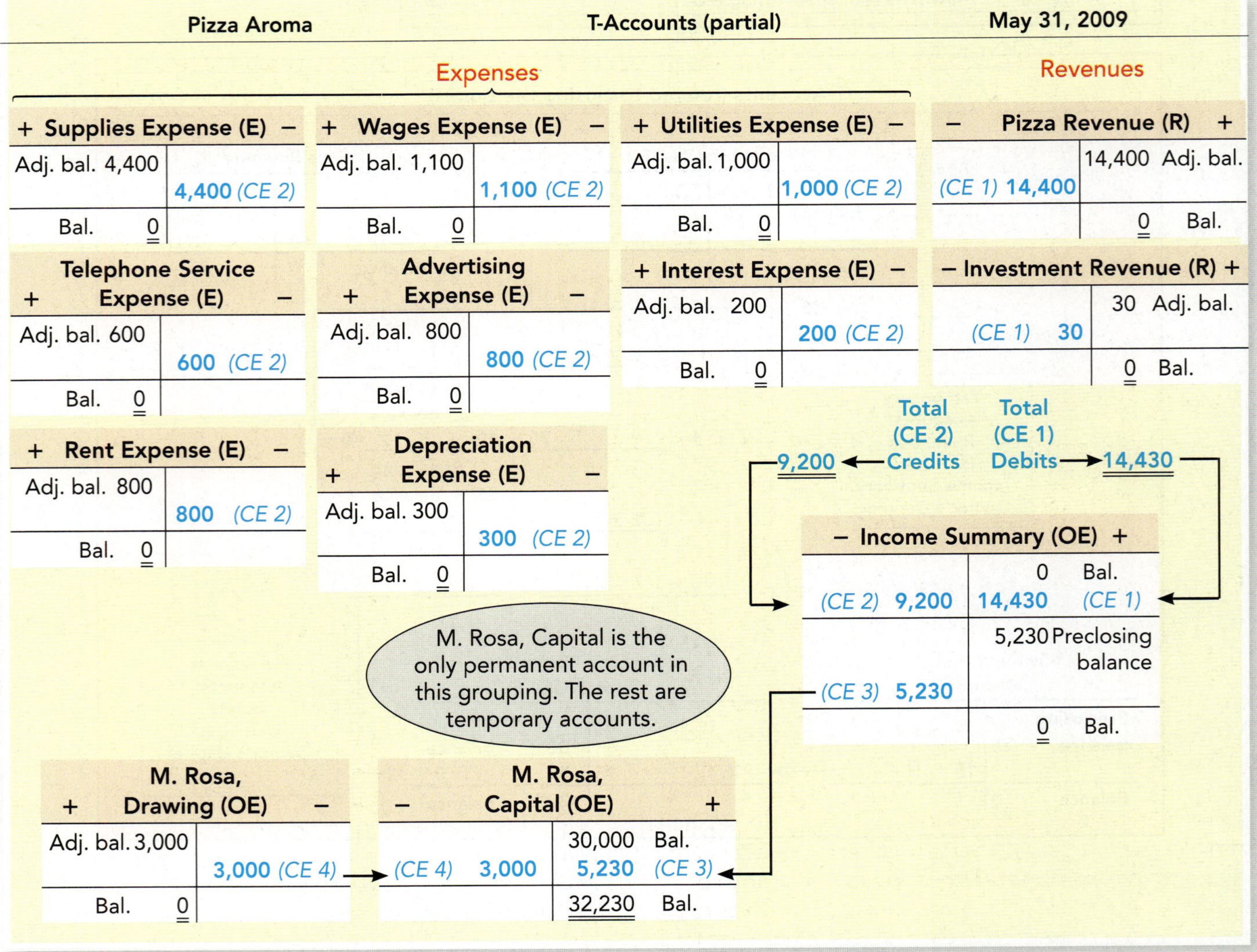

Now it's your turn to practice closing accounts at the end of the period. Review the closing entries just illustrated for Pizza Aroma and then complete the following Self-Study Practice.

SELF-STUDY PRACTICE

Florida Flippers, a scuba diving and instruction business owned by Paul Knepper, presented the following adjusted trial balance on December 31, 2010. Record all closing entries on December 31.

Florida Flippers
Trial Balance
On December 31, 2010

	Adjusted	
	Debit	**Credit**
Cash	14,000	
Accounts Receivable	800	
Supplies	11,700	
Prepaid Insurance	6,000	
Equipment	56,000	
Accumulated Depreciation		10,000
Building	250,000	
Accumulated Depreciation		12,500
Accounts Payable		6,000
Interest Payable		20,000
Unearned Revenue		4,000
Notes Payable		225,000
P. Knepper, Capital		50,000
P. Knepper, Drawing	12,000	
Diving Instruction Revenue		81,500
Diving Trip Revenue		30,000
Wages Expense	22,000	
Supplies Expense	3,000	
Fuel Expense	1,000	
Repairs Expense	3,000	
Utilities Expense	14,000	
Advertising Expense	3,000	
Depreciation Expense	22,500	
Interest Expense	20,000	
Totals	**439,000**	**439,000**

	Closing Journal Entries	Debit	Credit
CE 1			
CE 2			
CE 3			
CE 4			

After you have finished, check your answers with the solution at the bottom of the next page.

Preparing a Post-Closing Trial Balance

After Laurie completed the closing process for Pizza Aroma, all temporary accounts had a zero balance. The accounts were then ready for recording revenues and expenses in the new accounting period as well as any future withdrawals Mauricio might make. The ending balance in M. Rosa, Capital was updated and matched the balance sheet amount of $32,230. This balance was carried forward to become the beginning balance for the next period starting on June 1.

Just to make sure that all the temporary accounts have been closed and that the accounting records are still in balance, a **post-closing trial balance** should be prepared as the last step of the accounting cycle. Here is the one Laurie prepared for Pizza Aroma.

Pizza Aroma
Post-Closing Trial Balance
On May 31, 2009

	Debit	Credit
Cash	9,100	
Investments	6,000	
Interest Receivable	30	
Accounts Receivable	700	
Supplies	600	
Prepaid Rent	4,000	
Prepaid Insurance	2,400	
Equipment	36,000	
Accumulated Depreciation		300
Accounts Payable		4,800
Wages Payable		100
Utilities Payable		1,000
Interest Payable		200
Unearned Revenue		200
Notes Payable		20,000
M. Rosa, Capital		32,230
M. Rosa, Drawing	0	
Pizza Revenue		0
Investment Revenue		0
Supplies Expense	0	
Wages Expense	0	
Utilities Expense	0	
Telephone Service Expense	0	
Rent Expense	0	
Insurance Expense	0	
Advertising Expense	0	
Interest Expense	0	
Depreciation Expense	0	
Totals	**58,830**	**58,830**

Permanent accounts—balances carry forward to the next period (Cash through M. Rosa, Capital)

Temporary accounts—balances begin at $0 in the next period (M. Rosa, Drawing through Depreciation Expense)

Solution to Self-Study Practice

	Closing Journal Entries	Debit	Credit
CE 1	Diving Instruction Revenue (−R, −OE)	81,500	
	Diving Trip Revenue (−R, −OE)	30,000	
	Income Summary (+OE)		111,500
CE 2	Income Summary (−OE)	88,500	
	Wages Expense (−E, +OE)		22,000
	Supplies Expense (−E, +OE)		3,000
	Fuel Expense (−E, +OE)		1,000
	Repairs Expense (−E, +OE)		3,000
	Utilities Expense (−E, +OE)		14,000
	Advertising Expense (−E, +OE)		3,000
	Depreciation Expense (−E, +OE)		22,500
	Interest Expense (−E, +OE)		20,000
CE 3	Income Summary (−OE)	23,000	
	P. Knepper, Capital (+OE)		23,000
CE 4	P. Knepper, Capital (−OE)	12,000	
	P. Knepper, Drawing (+OE)		12,000

Notice that all temporary accounts have zero balances although some companies do not show accounts with zero balances. Also, note the trial balance still balances. The accounting cycle for the month of May is complete.

Managers find this last phase of the accounting cycle to be very busy. Adjusting the accounts, preparing statements, and closing the books may appear to happen on the last day of the period. However, this phase of the accounting cycle actually takes place after the end of the period, often extending over several weeks. Auditors usually conduct their audit tests and analyses at the same time. As an example of the time needed for the last phase, The Cheesecake Factory reported the date of the balance sheet as January 2, 2007, but the auditor PricewaterhouseCoopers dated the opinion February 22, 2007—a seven-week period before the accounting records were finally audited, adjusted, and closed.

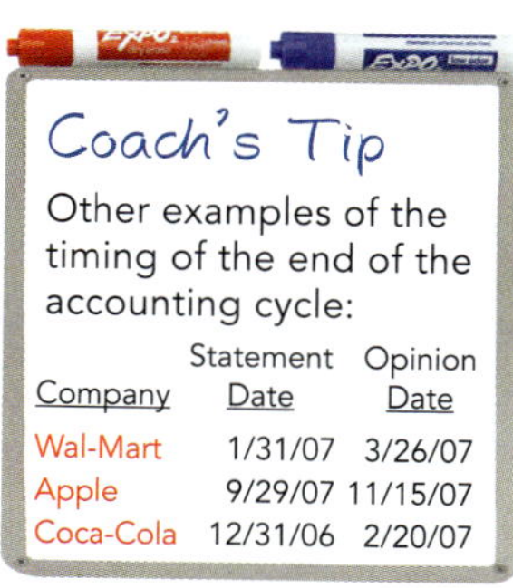

Coach's Tip

Other examples of the timing of the end of the accounting cycle:

Company	Statement Date	Opinion Date
Wal-Mart	1/31/07	3/26/07
Apple	9/29/07	11/15/07
Coca-Cola	12/31/06	2/20/07

ANALYZING FINANCIAL INFORMATION

Computing and Interpreting Key Ratios

Learning Objective 5

Compute and interpret the net profit margin ratio.

When Pizza Aroma's financial statements were complete and available for review, Laurie explained to Mauricio how to compute and interpret a key ratio that would provide information on his business's overall financial performance. Users of financial information rely on ratios in analyzing a company's past performance and financial condition as well as in predicting its future potential. Noting how ratios change over time in addition to how well they compare to competitors' ratios and to industry averages provides valuable information about a company's business decisions and strategies.

This chapter will introduce one financial ratio that was of particular interest to Mauricio in evaluating the results of Pizza Aroma's first month of business. Other ratios will be presented in later chapters of this textbook. In each instance, you will see a chart similar to the one presented below—**Accounting Decision Tools**—that summarizes the formula and its interpretation.

Analyzing Net Profit Margin (NPM)

The net profit margin provides information on managers' relative success at generating revenues and controlling costs.

Accounting Decision Tools

Name of Measure	Formula	What It Tells You
Net profit margin (NPM)	$\frac{\text{Net Income}}{\text{Total Sales (or Operating) Revenues}} \times 100$	• The percentage of every sales dollar generated during the period that was profit • A higher ratio means that managers are more effective at generating sales and/or controlling expenses

Using the information from Pizza Aroma's income statement presented in Exhibit 4.10, its net profit margin would be computed as follows:

$$\text{Net profit margin} \quad \frac{\text{Net Income}}{\text{Total Sales (or Operating) Revenues}} \times 100 = \frac{\$5{,}230}{\$14{,}400} \times 100 = 36.3\%$$

The net profit margin measures how effective management was in generating revenues and controlling costs and expenses during the period. For the first month of operation, Pizza Aroma realized 36.3 percent of net profit to revenue or \$0.363 for every dollar of pizza revenue. This is less than half the 83 percent that Mauricio originally computed based on the unadjusted accounts (see the beginning of the chapter), and another demonstration of the impact of year-end adjusting entries on results. Mauricio was concerned by this information because the business's performance was not as strong as he had originally thought. Laurie assured him that Pizza Aroma was doing very well for a new business.

Because managers' sales growth strategies and cost control measures impact this ratio, a rising net profit margin signals more effective management of sales and/or control of expenses. Financial analysts expect well-run businesses to maintain or improve their net profit margins over time.

Making Comparisons to Benchmarks

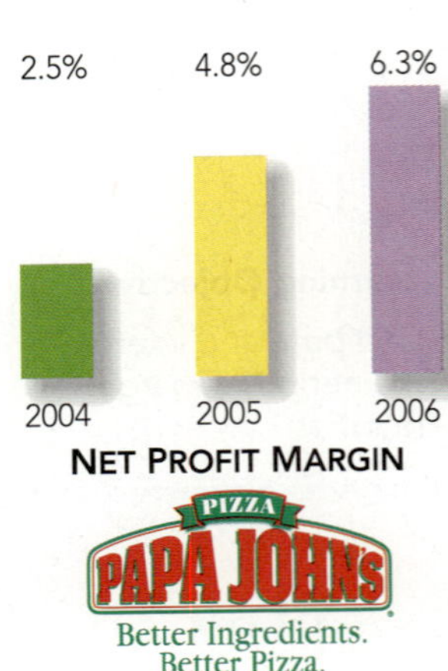

Comparing a company's ratio (1) over time and (2) to its competition provides additional useful information on the effectiveness of management.

Comparison over Time

We do not have historical data for Pizza Aroma for computing ratios over time, but we can analyze a competitor's NPM ratio over time to observe any trends. As you can see from the graphic in the margin, Papa John's has had an increasing NPM over time, more than doubling its NPM between 2004 and 2006. This suggests that its managers have become more effective at generating sales and/or controlling expenses. Pizza Aroma's ratio at 36.3 percent far surpasses the 6.3 percent net profit margin of Papa John's, a major international competitor.

Comparison to Competition

As Exhibit 4.12 shows, Papa John's, Domino's, and Yum! Brands (owner of Pizza Hut and several other restaurants) reported for 2006 a 6.3 percent, 7.4 percent, and 8.6 percent net profit margin ratio, respectively. All three companies fell short of the restaurant industry average of 13.3 percent, which includes large restaurant chains, not just pizza restaurants.

You should also be aware that the net profit margin can vary greatly between different types of industries. Exhibit 4.12 shows that auto and truck manufacturers recently reported an average net profit margin of 8.2 percent compared to the 14.3 percent reported by footwear companies and the 17.5 percent reported by pharmaceutical companies.

With Laurie's advice and support, Mauricio was energized by the strong results of his new business and the ratio information about Pizza Aroma's major competitors. He was ready to take on the challenges of expanding his customer base and building customer loyalty—while doing so at a profit.

In this chapter, you learned the importance of adjusting the accounts to measure revenue and expenses in the proper period. You also learned how to close the books at the end of the accounting period to update the owner's capital account and prepare the temporary accounts to accumulate the next period's financial information. In the following chapter, you will learn about the accounting information system.

Exhibit 4.12 Average Net Profit Margin Ratios by Industry

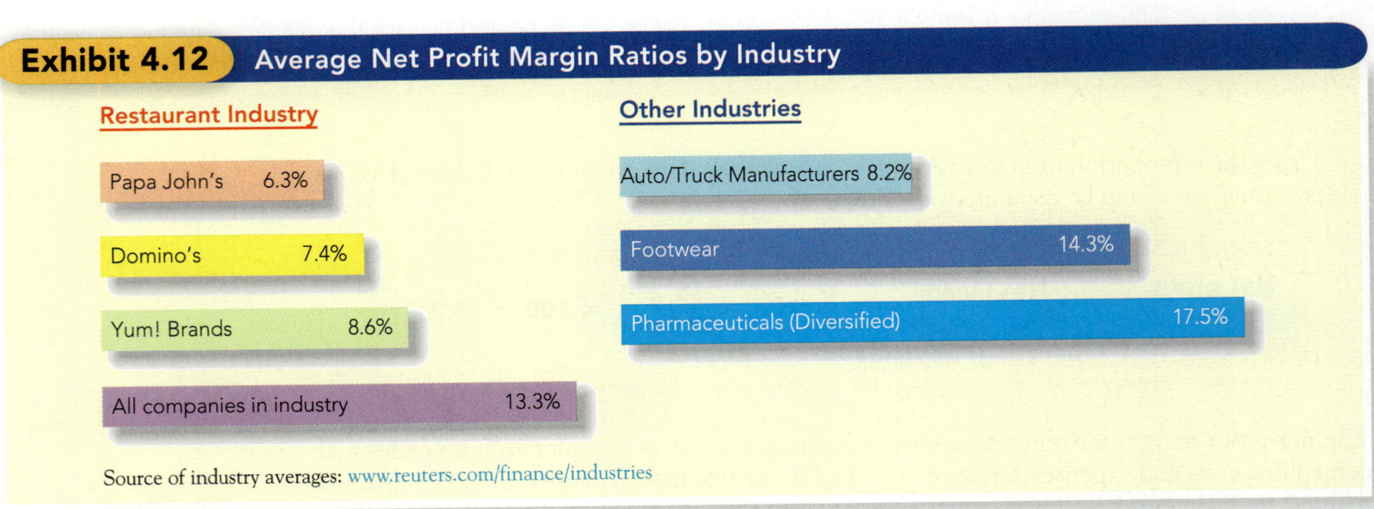

Source of industry averages: www.reuters.com/finance/industries

Demonstration Case

This final installment of the case of Goodbye Grass, the lawn care business started by Steve Delancey, covers three end-of-cycle activities: the adjustment process, financial statement preparation, and recording of closing entries. So far, no adjustments have been made to the accounts. The starting point for this process is the unadjusted trial balance as of May 31, 2010, which follows.

GOODBYE GRASS
Unadjusted Trial Balance
As of May 31, 2010

Account Name	Debits	Credits
Cash	2,470	
Accounts Receivable	1,700	
Note Receivable	1,250	
Prepaid Insurance	300	
Equipment	4,600	
Land	3,750	
Accounts Payable		620
Unearned Revenue		1,600
Notes Payable		4,000
S. Delancey, Capital		9,000
S. Delancey, Drawing	2,000	
Mowing Revenue		5,200
Wages Expense	3,900	
Fuel Expense	410	
Interest Expense	40	
Totals	20,420	20,420

In reviewing this unadjusted trial balance, you should be able to identify one unearned revenue account and two prepaid expense accounts that may need to be adjusted in addition to accruals that may be necessary regarding wages, interest expense on notes payable, and interest earned on the note receivable. The following information was determined at the end of the accounting cycle:

Revenues

- **Unearned Revenue**

  a. One-fourth of the $1,600 cash received from the city at the beginning of May for future mowing service was earned in May. The $1,600 in Unearned Revenue represents four months of service (May through August).

- **Accrued Revenue**

  b. Interest earned and receivable on Goodbye Grass's outstanding note receivable was $25 for the month of May.

Expenses

- **Prepaid Expenses**

  c. Insurance purchased at the beginning of May for $300 provided coverage for six months (May through October).

  d. Mowers, edgers, rakes, and hand tools (equipment) were used in May to generate revenues. The company estimates $25 in depreciation of this equipment in May.

- **Accrued Expenses**

  e. Wages were paid through the third week in May. Employees who worked the last week of May will be paid in June. Wages amount to $400.

  f. One month of interest on the $4,000 notes payable has been paid through mid-May. Another $20 of interest needs to be accrued and will be paid in June.

Required:

1. Analyze the effects of the required adjustments in items *a* through *f* on the basic accounting equation (Assets = Liabilities + Owner's Equity) and record the adjusting journal entries required at the end of May. Follow the steps outlined in the chapter: (1) Identify adjustments by type; (2) determine the amount of the revenue or expense to be recorded; and (3) record the adjusting entry and post the effects to the T-accounts.
2. Post the adjusting entry effects to the appropriate T-accounts. Obtain the beginning balances from the unadjusted trial balance and then calculate the adjusted May 31 balances.
3. Prepare an adjusted trial balance to ensure that debit and credit balances are equal, remembering to include all the accounts in the trial balance (not just the ones affected by the adjusting journal entries).
4. Prepare a *classified* income statement, a statement of owner's equity, and a *classified* balance sheet from the amounts in the adjusted trial balance.
5. Prepare the closing journal entries that would be required if Goodbye Grass's fiscal *year* ended May 31, 2010.

After completing requirements 1–5, check your answers with the following solution.

Suggested Solution

1. Analyze and record adjusting entries

All adjusting entries are written together at the end of this requirement.

a. **Unearned Revenue**

(1) ***Type:*** **Unearned Revenue**
(2) ***Amount:*** The unadjusted balance for Unearned Revenue is $1,600. One-fourth of that $1,600 ($400 = ¼ × $1,600) was earned in May.
(3) ***Entry:*** Therefore, an adjusting entry is needed to increase the Mowing Revenue account by the $400 earned in May and reduce the Unearned Revenue liability account by $400.

b. **Interest Revenue**

(1) ***Type:*** **Accrued Revenue**
(2) ***Amount:*** The business earned but has not yet recorded the $25 interest on its Note Receivable due from the city.
(3) ***Entry:*** Therefore, an adjusting entry is needed to increase the Interest Revenue account and create an Interest Receivable account for the amount earned and due from the city.

c. **Insurance**

(1) ***Type:*** **Prepaid Expense**
(2) ***Amount:*** The business received insurance coverage in May, so one month of the six-month prepaid insurance policy has been used ($300 × ⅙ = $50 used).
(3) ***Entry:*** Therefore, an adjusting entry is needed to increase the Insurance Expense account by the $50 incurred in May and reduce the Prepaid Insurance account by $50.

d. **Equipment**

(1) ***Type:*** **Prepaid Expense**
(2) ***Amount:*** The business estimates monthly depreciation on the equipment to be $25.
(3) ***Entry:*** Therefore, an adjusting entry is needed to increase the Depreciation Expense account by the $25 incurred and increase the contra-account Accumulated Depreciation by the amount of the equipment used in May.

e. **Wages**

(1) ***Type:*** **Accrued Expense**
(2) ***Amount:*** Employees who worked the last week in May will be paid in early June. The business used the employees' labor to generate revenues in May but has not yet recorded the $400 expense incurred.
(3) ***Entry:*** Therefore, an adjusting entry is needed to increase the Wages Expense account by $400 and create a Wages Payable account for the $400 owed to the employees.

f. **Interest Expense**

(1) ***Type:*** **Accrued Expense**
(2) ***Amount:*** The business owes two additional weeks of interest on the $4,000 note payable. The amount given is $20.
(3) ***Entry:*** Therefore, an adjusting entry is needed to increase the Interest Expense account by $20 and create an Interest Payable account for the $20 due the bank by the end of May.

Goodbye Grass
Adjusting Journal Entries
May 31, 2010

		Debit	Credit
(AJE a)	Unearned Revenue (−L)	400	
	Mowing Revenue (+R, +OE)		400
(AJE b)	Interest Receivable (+A)	25	
	Interest Revenue (+R, +OE)		25
(AJE c)	Insurance Expense (+E, −OE)	50	
	Prepaid Insurance (−A)		50
(AJE d)	Depreciation Expense (+E, −OE)	25	
	Accumulated Depreciation (+xA, −A)		25
(AJE e)	Wages Expense (+E, −OE)	400	
	Wages Payable (+L)		400
(AJE f)	Interest Expense (+E, −OE)	20	
	Interest Payable (+L)		20

2. Post adjusting entries to T-accounts

Assets = Liabilities + Owner's Equity

Assets

+ Cash (A)	−
Bal. 2,470	
Bal. 2,470	

+ Accounts Receivable (A)	−
Bal. 1,700	
Bal. 1,700	

+ Interest Receivable (A)	−
Unadj. bal. 0 AJE b 25	
Bal. 25	

+ Note Receivable (A)	−
Bal. 1,250	
Bal. 1,250	

+ Prepaid Insurance (A)	−
Unadj. bal. 300	50 AJE c
Bal. 250	

+ Equipment (A)	−
Bal. 4,600	
Bal. 4,600	

− Accumulated Depreciation (xA)	+
	0 Unadj. bal. 25 AJE d
	25 Bal.

+ Land (A)	−
Bal. 3,750	
Bal. 3,750	

Liabilities

− Accounts Payable (L)	+
	620 Bal.
	620 Bal.

− Unearned Revenue (L)	+
AJE a 400	Unadj. 1,600 bal.
	1,200 Bal.

− Wages Payable (L)	+
	Unadj. 0 bal. 400 AJE e
	400 Bal.

− Interest Payable (L)	+
	Unadj. 0 bal. 20 AJE f
	20 Bal.

− Notes Payable (L)	+
	4,000 Bal.
	4,000 Bal.

Owner's Equity

− S. Delancey, Capital (OE)	+
	9,000 Bal.
	9,000 Bal.

+ S. Delancey, Drawing (OE)	−
Bal. 2,000	
Bal. 2,000	

Expenses

+ Wages Expense (E)	−
Unadj. bal. 3,900 AJE e 400	
Bal. 4,300	

+ Fuel Expense (E)	−
Bal. 410	
Bal. 410	

+ Interest Expense (E)	−
Unadj. bal. 40 AJE f 20	
Bal. 60	

+ Insurance Expense (E)	−
Unadj. bal. 0 AJE c 50	
Bal. 50	

+ Depreciation Expense (E)	−
Unadj. bal. 0 AJE d 25	
Bal. 25	

Revenues

− Mowing Revenue (R)	+
	Unadj. 5,200 bal. 400 AJE a
	5,600 Bal.

− Interest Revenue (R)	+
	Unadj. 0 bal. 25 AJE b
	25 Bal.

3. Adjusted trial balance

GOODBYE GRASS
Adjusted Trial Balance
As of May 31, 2010

Account Name	Debits	Credits
Cash	2,470	
Accounts Receivable	1,700	
Interest Receivable	25	
Note Receivable	1,250	
Prepaid Insurance	250	
Equipment	4,600	
Accumulated Depreciation		25
Land	3,750	
Accounts Payable		620
Unearned Revenue		1,200
Wages Payable		400
Interest Payable		20
Notes Payable		4,000
S. Delancey, Capital		9,000
S. Delancey, Drawing	2,000	
Mowing Revenue		5,600
Interest Revenue		25
Wages Expense	4,300	
Fuel Expense	410	
Interest Expense	60	
Insurance Expense	50	
Depreciation Expense	25	
Totals	20,890	20,890

4. Income statement, statement of owner's equity, and balance sheet

GOODBYE GRASS
Income Statement
For the Month Ended May 31, 2010

Operating Revenues	
Mowing revenue	$5,600
Total operating revenue	5,600
Operating Expenses	
Wages expense	4,300
Fuel expense	410
Insurance expense	50
Depreciation expense	25
Total operating expenses	4,785
Operating Income	815
Other Items	
Interest revenue	25
Interest expense	(60)
Net Income	$ 780

GOODBYE GRASS
Statement of Owner's Equity
For the Month Ended May 31, 2010

S. Delancey, Capital, May 1, 2010	$ 9,000
Add: Additional investments	0
Net income	780
Less: S. Delancey, Drawing	(2,000)
S. Delancey, Capital, May 31, 2010	**$ 7,780**

GOODBYE GRASS
Balance Sheet
As of May 31, 2010

Assets		Liabilities	
Current Assets		*Current Liabilities*	
Cash	$ 2,470	Accounts Payable	$ 620
Accounts Receivable	1,700	Unearned Revenue	1,200
Interest Receivable	25	Wages Payable	400
Note Receivable	1,250	Interest Payable	20
Prepaid Insurance	250	Notes Payable	4,000
Total Current Assets	5,695	Total Current Liabilities	6,240
Equipment	4,600	**Owner's Equity**	
Less: Accumulated Depreciation	(25)	S. Delancey, Capital	7,780
Land	3,750		
Total Assets	**$14,020**	**Total Liabilities and Owner's Equity**	**$14,020**

5. Closing journal entries

Goodbye Grass
Closing Journal Entries
May 31, 2010

		Debit	Credit
(CE 1)	Mowing Revenue (−R, −OE)	5,600	
	Interest Revenue (−R, −OE)	25	
	Income Summary (+OE)		5,625
(CE 2)	Income Summary (−OE)	4,845	
	Wages Expense (−E, +OE)		4,300
	Fuel Expense (−E, +OE)		410
	Interest Expense (−E, +OE)		60
	Insurance Expense (−E, +OE)		50
	Depreciation Expense (−E, +OE)		25
(CE 3)	Income Summary (−OE)	780	
	S. Delancey, Capital (+OE)		780
(CE 4)	S. Delancey, Capital (−OE)	2,000	
	S. Delancey, Drawing (+OE)		2,000

Supplement 4A

Using an Accounting Worksheet

An accounting worksheet may be prepared to facilitate end-of-period accounting activities. If an accounting worksheet is used, it should be prepared before recording the adjusting and closing entries. The final worksheet provides all of the data needed to complete the remaining end-of-period steps, bringing together in one place the (1) unadjusted trial balance, (2) amounts for the adjusting entries, (3) income statement, (4) statement of owner's equity, and (5) balance sheet. Closing entries can also be prepared from the information provided on the worksheet.

The following simplified case for High-Rise Apartments shows how to prepare a worksheet at the end of the accounting period. High-Rise Apartments is a sole proprietorship for the management of rental properties in Collegetown. Brooks Lape owns and operates it.

Exhibit 4.13 includes a series of transparencies that correspond to the steps needed to complete the worksheet. You can turn over each transparency as directed. To help you, each step is color coded to match the columns on the worksheet. Follow these steps to develop the worksheet:

Step 1 ***Refer to Exhibit 4.13.*** Set up the worksheet format by entering the appropriate column headings. The left-hand column shows the account titles (taken directly from the ledger). There are six separate pairs of Debit–Credit columns. Notice that the last three pairs of Debit–Credit columns show the data for the financial statements. Enter the unadjusted trial balance as of the

(continued on page 177)

Exhibit 4.13 Accounting Worksheet

HIGH-RISE APARTMENTS
Worksheet for the Year Ended December 31, 2010

	Unadjusted Trial Balance		Adjusting Entries		Adjusted Trial Balance		Financial Statements: Income Statement		Owner's Equity		Balance Sheet	
Account Titles	Debit	Credit	Debit	Credit	Debit	Credit	Debit	Credit	Debit	Credit	Debit	Credit
Cash	12,297											
Rent Revenue Receivable												
Prepaid Insurance	2,400											
Maintenance Supplies	600											
Land	25,000											
Apartment Building	360,000											
Accumulated Depreciation-Building		10,000										
Unearned Rent Revenue		1,000										
Salaries Payable												
Interest Payable												
Notes Payable, Long-Term		30,000										
Mortgage Payable, Long-Term		238,037										
B. Lape, Capital (Jan. 1)		84,960										
B. Lape, Drawing	12,000											
Rent Revenue		127,463										
Advertising Expense	500											
Maintenance Supplies Expense	3,000											
Salary Expense	17,400											
Interest Expense	19,563											
Utilities Expense	34,500											
Miscellaneous Expenses	4,200											
Insurance Expense												
Depreciation Expense												
	491,460	491,460										

end of the accounting period directly from the ledger into the first pair of Debit–Credit columns. When all current entries for the period excluding the adjusting entries have been recorded in the journal and posted to the ledger, the amounts for the Unadjusted Trial Balance columns will equal the balances in the respective ledger accounts. Before going on to the next step, check the equality of the debits and credits by totaling each column ($491,460). Adding up the numbers in the columns in this way is called footing. When you use a worksheet, it is not necessary to develop a separate unadjusted trial balance because you can develop one on the worksheet.

Step 2 ***Refer to Exhibit 4.13a (turn over the first transparency).*** Complete the second pair of Debit–Credit columns, headed Adjusting Entries, by developing and then entering the amounts of the adjusting entries directly on the worksheet. The adjustments for High-Rise Apartments that are shown in Exhibit 4.13a were entered for illustration purposes. Review each entry to be sure you can explain why it was recorded. To facilitate examination for potential errors, the adjusting entries are usually referenced as illustrated in Exhibit 4.13a. Some of the adjusting entries may need one or more account titles in addition to those of the original trial balance (see the last five account titles in Exhibit 4.13a). After the adjusting entries on the worksheet are complete, check the equality of debits and credits for those amounts by totaling the two columns ($14,200 each).

Step 3 ***Refer to Exhibit 4.13b (turn over the second transparency).*** Complete the pair of Debit–Credit columns headed Adjusted Trial Balance. Although it is not essential, this pair of columns helps to ensure accuracy. The adjusted trial balance reflects the line-by-line combined amounts of the unadjusted trial balance, plus or minus the amounts entered as adjusting entries in the second pair of columns. For example, the Rent Revenue account shows a $128,463 credit balance under Unadjusted Trial Balance. Add to this amount the credit amount, $600, minus the debit amount, $500, for a combined amount of $128,563, and enter it as a credit under Adjusted Trial Balance. (Adding across rows in this way is called cross-footing.) For those accounts that were not affected by the adjusting entries, carry the unadjusted trial balance amount directly across to the Adjusted Trial Balance column. After you complete each line, check the equality of the debits and credits under Adjusted Trial Balance (column totals, $503,560).

Step 4 ***Refer to Exhibit 4.13c (turn over the third transparency).*** Extend the amount on each line under Adjusted Trial Balance horizontally across the worksheet and enter it under the heading for the financial statement on which it must be reported (income statement, owner's equity, or balance sheet). Carry debit amounts across as debits and credit amounts across as credits. Note that (1) each amount that you extended across the worksheet is entered under only one of the six remaining columns, and (2) debits remain debits and credits remain credits. Enter net income as a balancing debit amount in the Income Statement column and a credit amount in the Owner's Equity column. This amount represents the closing process entry that results in a debit to Income Summary (after revenues and expenses have been closed to the Income Summary) and a credit to B. Lape, Capital. (A net loss should be entered as a credit in the Income Statement column and a debit in the owner's equity column.)

Step 5 ***Refer to Exhibit 4.13d (turn over the fourth transparency).*** Sum the two Owner's Equity columns. The difference is the ending balance of B. Lape, Capital. Enter this amount ($109,260) as a balancing debit amount under Owner's Equity and a balancing credit under Balance Sheet (that is, an increase to owner's equity). At this point, the two Balance Sheet columns should sum to equal amounts. The continuous checking of the equality of debits and credits in each pair of Debit-Credit columns helps to ensure the correctness of the worksheet. You can prepare the financial statements for High-Rise Apartments directly from the completed worksheet in Exhibit 4.13d.

Chapter Summary

LO1 Explain the purpose of adjustments at the end of the accounting cycle. p. 146

- Reasons for Adjustments
  Adjustments are needed to ensure that:
  - Revenues are recorded when they are earned (the revenue principle).
  - Expenses are recorded when they are incurred to generate revenues (the matching principle).
  - Assets are reported at amounts representing the economic benefits remaining at the end of the current period.
  - Liabilities are reported at amounts owed at the end of the current period, which will require a future sacrifice of resources.

LO2 Identify and analyze the adjustments necessary at the end of the period to update balance sheet and income statement accounts. p. 147

- Types of Adjustments
  - Unearned revenues. Cash was received before it was earned. The adjusting entry (AJE) reduces the liability and increases the revenue account.

- Accrued revenues. Cash will be received after being earned in the current period. The AJE increases the revenue account and increases a receivable account.
- Prepaid expenses. Cash was paid for an asset before it was used to generate revenue. The AJE reduces the asset (or increases its contra-account) and increases a related expense.
- Accrued expenses. Cash will be paid after the expense was incurred. The AJE increases the expense account and increases a payable account.

- Analysis of Adjustments
  The process for preparing adjustments includes

  Step 1 Identify the type of adjustment. Review the trial balance.
  Step 2 Determine the amount of the revenue earned or expense incurred. Use of a timeline may help to determine the amount.
  Step 3 Record the adjusting journal entry and post it to the appropriate T-accounts (accounts in the ledger).

  Adjusting entries never affect the Cash account.

LO3 Present an income statement, statement of owner's equity, and balance sheet. p. 160

- Relationships among Financial Statements
  Net income is a component in determining ending owner's capital. Ending owner's capital is included on the balance sheet. Thus, an error on the income statement will cause the other statements to also be in error.
- Adjusted Trial Balance
  An adjusted trial balance is a list of all accounts with their adjusted debit or credit balances indicated in the appropriate columns to provide a check on the equality of debits and credits.
- Classified Income Statement
  Using the adjusted balances for revenues and expenses from the adjusted trial balance, a classified income statement lists operating revenues and then subtracts operating expenses to determine the operating income.
  - A revenue or expense is classified as "operating" if it is earned or incurred as part of the business's central operations (the primary focus of the business).
  - Other revenues and expenses that are not central to operations, such as interest revenue and interest expense, are added to or subtracted from operating income to determine net income.
- Statement of Owner's Equity
  A statement of owner's equity connects the income statement to the balance sheet.
- Classified Balance Sheet
  A classified balance sheet lists assets in order of liquidity and liabilities in order of their due dates. The ending balance of the owner's capital account on the statement of owner's equity is a component on the balance sheet.

LO4 Explain the purpose and process of closing the books. p. 164

- Closing the Books
  Closing entries are required
  (a) To transfer net income (or loss) and owner withdrawals during the period to the owner's capital account.
  (b) To prepare all temporary accounts (revenue, expense, and owner's drawing accounts) for the following year by establishing zero balances.

  The process includes four entries:
  CE1. Debit each revenue account and credit the total revenues to Income Summary, an account used only during the closing process. All revenues should now have zero balances.
  CE2. Credit each expense account and debit the total expenses to Income Summary. All expenses should now have zero balances.
  CE3. If net income is positive, then there should be a credit balance equal to the amount of net income in Income Summary. Debit Income Summary and credit the owner's capital account for the balance. Do just the opposite if there is a net loss. Income Summary should now have a zero balance.
  CE4. Debit the owner's capital account and credit the owner's drawing account for its balance. The drawing account should now have a zero balance, and there should be no additional temporary accounts to close.
- Preparing a Post-Closing Trial Balance
  A post-closing trial balance provides a final check on the equality of the accounting equation and ensures that all temporary accounts have been closed to a zero balance.

LO5 Compute and interpret the net profit margin ratio. p. 169

- **Computing and Interpreting Key Ratios**
  Users of financial information compute and interpret ratios in analyzing a company's past performance and financial condition and predicting future potential.
- **Analyzing Net Profit Margin (NPM)**
  A measure of how much profit management generated on every dollar of sales during the period:
  - Computation: NPM = (Net Income ÷ Sales (or operating) revenues) × 100
  - Assesses management's effectiveness at generating sales and/or controlling costs.
  - A higher ratio suggests management is more effective at generating sales and/or controlling costs.
- **Making Comparisons to Benchmarks**
  Ratios should be computed (1) for a company over time and (2) against competitors and industry averages to observe trends.

Key Terms

Accrued Expenses (p. 147)
Accrued Revenues (p. 147)
Adjusted Trial Balance (p. 160)
Adjusting Entries (p. 147)
Closing the Books (p. 164)
Contra-account (p. 152)
Depreciation (p. 152)
Income Summary (p. 164)
Net Book Value (also called *book value* or *carrying value*) (p. 152)
Net Profit Margin (p. 169)
Permanent Accounts (p. 164)
Prepaid Expenses (p. 147)
Temporary Accounts (p. 164)
Unearned Revenues (p. 147)

See complete glossary in the back of text.

Questions

1. Briefly explain the purposes of adjustments.
2. Explain the relationships between adjustments and (a) the time period assumption (from chapter 3), (b) the revenue principle, and (c) the matching principle.
3. List the four types of adjustments, and give an example of each type.
4. Explain the effect of adjusting journal entries on cash.
5. What is a contra-asset? Give an example of one.
6. Explain the differences between depreciation expense and accumulated depreciation.
7. What is an adjusted trial balance? What is its purpose?
8. On December 31, a company makes a $9,000 payment to rent a warehouse in January, February, and March of the following year. Show the accounting equation effects of the transaction on December 31, as well as the adjustments required on January 31, February 28, and March 31.
9. Using the information in question 8, determine the amounts and accounts that will be reported on the January 31 balance sheet and the income statement for the month ended January 31.
10. Using the information in question 8, prepare the journal entry and adjusting journal entries to be made on December 31, January 31, February 28, and March 31.
11. What is the equation for each of the following statements: (a) income statement, (b) statement of owner's equity, and (c) balance sheet?
12. Explain how the financial statements in question 11 relate to each other.
13. What is the purpose of closing journal entries?
14. How do permanent accounts differ from temporary accounts?
15. Why are the income statement accounts closed but the balance sheet accounts are not?
16. Is the owner's drawing account considered an asset, liability, or owner's equity account? Is it a permanent or temporary account? Does it normally have a debit or credit balance?
17. What is a post-closing trial balance? Is it a useful part of the accounting cycle? Explain.
18. How is a company's net profit margin computed and what does it measure?

Multiple Choice

1. Which of the following accounts would not appear in a closing journal entry?
   a. Interest Revenue.
   b. Accumulated Depreciation.
   c. Owner's Capital.
   d. Salary Expense.

Quiz 4-1
www.mhhe.com/LLPW1e

2. Which account is least likely to appear in an adjusting journal entry?
   a. Cash.
   b. Interest Receivable.
   c. Accumulated Depreciation.
   d. Salaries Payable.

3. When a concert promotions company collects cash for ticket sales two months in advance of the show date, which of the following accounts is affected?
   a. Accrued Liability.
   b. Accounts Receivable.
   c. Prepaid Expense.
   d. Unearned Revenue.

4. On December 31, an adjustment is made to reduce unearned revenue and report revenue earned during the period. How many accounts will be included in this adjusting journal entry?
   a. None.
   b. One.
   c. Two.
   d. Three.

5. An adjusting journal entry to recognize accrued salaries payable would cause which of the following?
   a. A decrease in assets and owner's equity.
   b. A decrease in assets and liabilities.
   c. An increase in expenses, liabilities, and owner's equity.
   d. An increase in expenses and liabilities and a decrease in owner's equity.

6. An adjusted trial balance
   a. Shows the ending balances in a "debit" and "credit" format before adjusting journal entries are posted.
   b. Is prepared after closing entries have been posted.
   c. Is a tool financial analysts use to review the performance of publicly traded companies.
   d. Shows the ending balances resulting from the adjusting journal entries in a "debit" and "credit" format.

7. Company A owns a building. Which of the following statements regarding depreciation is **false** from an accounting perspective?
   a. As the value of the building decreases over time, it "depreciates."
   b. Depreciation is an estimated expense to be recorded each period during the building's life.
   c. As depreciation is recorded, owner's equity is reduced.
   d. As depreciation is recorded, total assets are reduced.

8. Which of the following trial balances is used as a source for preparing the income statement?
   a. Unadjusted trial balance.
   b. Preadjusted trial balance.
   c. Adjusted trial balance.
   d. Post-closing trial balance.

9. Assume the balance in Prepaid Insurance is $2,500 but it should be $1,500. The adjusting journal entry should include which of the following?
   a. Debit to Prepaid Insurance for $1,000.
   b. Credit to Insurance Expense for $1,000.
   c. Debit to Insurance Expense for $1,000.
   d. Debit to Insurance Expense for $1,500.

10. Assume that a company receives a bill for $10,000 for advertising done during the current year. If this expense is not yet recorded by the end of the year, what will the adjusting journal entry include?
   a. Debit to Advertising Expense of $10,000.
   b. Credit to Advertising Expense of $10,000.
   c. Debit to Accrued Liabilities of $10,000.
   d. Need more information to determine.

Solutions to Multiple-Choice Questions

1. *b* 2. *a* 3. *d* 4. *c* 5. *d* 6. *d* 7. *a* 8. *c* 9. *c* 10. *a*

Mini Exercises  Available with McGraw-Hill's Homework Manager

LO2

M4-1 Understanding Concepts Related to Adjustments

Match each of the following situations to two applicable reasons that require an adjustment to be made.

____ & ____ 1. Northwest Airlines provided flights this month for customers who paid cash last month for tickets.

____ & ____ 2. Abercrombie & Fitch received a telephone bill for services this month, which must be paid next month.

____ & ____ 3. GSD + M (an advertising firm in Austin, Texas) completed work on an advertising campaign that will be billed and collected next month.

____ & ____ 4. The Tiger Woods Foundation used up some of the benefits of its 35,000-square-foot building when teaching students about forensic science, aerospace, and video production.

A. Revenue has been earned.
B. Expense has been incurred.
C. Liability has been incurred.
D. Liability has been fulfilled.
E. Asset has been created.
F. Asset has been used up.

M4-2 Preparing an Adjusted Trial Balance
LO3

Macro Company has the following adjusted accounts and balances at year-end (June 30, 2010):

Accounts Payable	$ 300	Depreciation Expense	$ 110	Prepaid Expenses	$ 40
Accounts Receivable	550	Insurance Expense	110	Salaries Expense	660
Accrued Liabilities	150	Interest Expense	180	Sales Revenue	3,600
Accumulated Depreciation	250	Interest Payable	30	Supplies	710
Buildings and Equipment	1,400	Interest Revenue	50	Supplies Expense	820
Cash	1,020	Land	200	Rent Expense	400
J. Macro, Capital	420	Long-Term debt	1,300	Unearned Revenue	100

Required:

Prepare an adjusted trial balance for Macro Company at June 30, 2010.

M4-3 Matching Transactions with Type of Adjustment
LO2

Match each transaction with the type of adjustment that will be required by entering the appropriate letter in the space provided.

Transaction	Type of Adjustment
____ 1. An expense has not yet been incurred but has been paid in advance.	A. Unearned revenue.
____ 2. Rent has not yet been collected but is already earned.	B. Accrued revenue.
____ 3. Office supplies on hand will be used next accounting period.	C. Prepaid expense.
____ 4. An expense has been incurred but not yet paid or recorded.	D. Accrued expense.
____ 5. Revenue has been collected in advance and will be earned later.	

M4-4 Matching Transactions with Type of Adjustment
LO2

Match each transaction with the type of adjustment that will be required by entering the appropriate letter in the space provided.

Transaction	Type of Adjustment
____ 1. Supplies for office use were purchased during the year for $500, and $100 of the office supplies remained on hand (unused) at year-end.	A. Unearned revenue. B. Accrued revenue. C. Prepaid expense.
____ 2. Interest of $250 on a note receivable was earned at year-end, although collection of the interest is not due until the following year.	D. Accrued expense.
____ 3. At year-end, wages payable of $3,600 had not been recorded or paid.	
____ 4. At year-end, service revenue of $2,000 was collected in cash but was only partly earned.	

M4-5 Determining Effects of Adjustments
LO2

For each of the following transactions for Sky Blue Company owned by sole proprietor Anna Cerveny, give the effects amounts and direction of effect (+ for increase or − for decrease) of the adjustments required at the end of the month on December 31, 2010. Use the following form. If an element is not affected, write NE for no effect.

a. Collected $1,200 rent for the period December 1, 2010, to February 28, 2011, that was credited to Unearned Rent Revenue on December 1, 2010.

b. Paid $2,400 for a two-year insurance premium on December 1, 2010; debited Prepaid Insurance for that amount.

c. Used a machine purchased on December 1, 2010, for $48,000. The company estimates *annual* depreciation of $4,800.

	BALANCE SHEET			INCOME STATEMENT		
Transaction	Assets	Liabilities	Owner's Equity	Revenues	Expenses	Net Income
a.						
b.						
c.						

LO2 **M4-6 Recording Adjusting Journal Entries**

Using the information in M4-5, for each transaction, (1) identify the type of adjustment and (2) prepare the adjusting journal entry required on December 31, 2010.

LO2 **M4-7 Determining Accounting Equation Effects of Adjustments**

For each of the following transactions for Sky Blue Company owned by sole proprietor Anna Cerveny, give the effects amounts and direction of effect (+ for increase or − for decrease) of the adjustments required at the end of the month on December 31, 2010. Use the following form. If an element is not affected, write NE for no effect.

a. Received a $600 utility bill for electricity usage in December to be paid in January 2011.

b. Owed wages to 10 employees who worked three days at $100 each per day at the end of December. The company will pay employees at the end of the first week of January 2011.

c. On December 1, 2010, loaned money to an employee who agreed to repay the loan in one year along with one full year of interest equal to $1,200.

	BALANCE SHEET			INCOME STATEMENT		
Transaction	Assets	Liabilities	Owner's Equity	Revenues	Expenses	Net Income
a.						
b.						
c.						

LO2 **M4-8 Recording Adjusting Journal Entries**

Using the information in M4-7, for each transaction, (1) identify the type of adjustment and (2) prepare the adjusting journal entry required on December 31, 2010.

LO3 **M4-9 Reporting an Income Statement**

Sky Blue Company, owned by sole proprietor Anna Cerveny, provides computer technology services to customers. The company has the following adjusted accounts at December 31, 2010.

Cash	$ 1,200	A. Cerveny, Capital	$ 3,400
Accounts Receivable	2,000	A. Cerveny, Drawing	300
Interest Receivable	30	Service Revenue	42,000
Prepaid Insurance	2,300	Interest Revenue	30
Notes Receivable	3,000	Rent Revenue	300
Equipment	12,000	Wages Expense	21,600
Accumulated Depreciation	300	Depreciation Expense	300
Accounts Payable	1,600	Utilities Expense	220
Wages Payable	3,820	Insurance Expense	100
Interest Payable	2,900	Rent Expense	9,000
Unearned Rent Revenue	600	Interest Expense	2,900

Prepare a *classified* income statement for 2010.

LO3 **M4-10 Reporting a Statement of Owner's Equity**

Refer to M4-9. Prepare a statement of owner's equity for 2010. Assume that the owner did not make any investments during the year.

LO3 **M4-11 Reporting a Balance Sheet**

Refer to M4-9. Prepare a *classified* balance sheet at December 31, 2010. Are Sky Blue Company's assets financed primarily by debt or equity?

LO4 **M4-12 Recording Closing Journal Entries**

Refer to the adjusted accounts in M4-9. Prepare closing journal entries on December 31, 2010.

LO5 **M4-13 Analyzing Financial Information**

Refer to M4-9. Compute the net profit margin ratio, and interpret what the result suggests for Sky Blue Company.

For M4-14 through M4-19, complete the following requirements:

1. What type of adjustment is this?
2. Prepare the adjusting journal entry on December 31.
3. In separate T-accounts for each account, enter the unadjusted balance, post the adjusting journal entry, and report the adjusted balance.

M4-14 Preparing and Posting Adjusting Journal Entries LO2

At December 31, the unadjusted trial balance of H&R Tacks reports Supplies Expense of $0 and Supplies of $9,000, representing the beginning cost of Supplies plus the amount purchased during the year. On December 31, supplies costing $1,300 are on hand. (See requirements on prior page.)

M4-15 Preparing and Posting Adjusting Journal Entries LO2

At December 31, the unadjusted trial balance of H&R Tacks reports Equipment of $38,000 and zero balances in Accumulated Depreciation and Depreciation Expense. Depreciation for the period is estimated to be $6,000. (See requirements on prior page.)

M4-16 Preparing and Posting Adjusting Journal Entries LO2

At December 31, the unadjusted trial balance of H&R Tacks reports Prepaid Insurance of $7,200 and Insurance Expense of $0. The insurance was purchased on July 1 and provides coverage for 12 months. (See requirements on prior page.)

M4-17 Preparing and Posting Adjusting Journal Entries LO2

At December 31, the unadjusted trial balance of H&R Tacks reports Unearned Revenue of $5,000 and Service Revenue of $33,800. One-half of the unearned revenue has been earned as of December 31. (See requirements on prior page.)

M4-18 Preparing and Posting Adjusting Journal Entries LO2

At December 31, the unadjusted trial balance of H&R Tacks reports Wages Payable of $0 and Wages Expense of $20,000. Employees have been paid for work done up to December 27, but the $1,200 they have earned for December 28–31 has not yet been paid or recorded. (See requirements on prior page.)

M4-19 Preparing and Posting Adjusting Journal Entries LO2

At December 31, the unadjusted trial balance of H&R Tacks reports Interest Payable of $0 and Interest Expense of $0. Interest incurred and owed in December totals $500. (See requirements on prior page.)

M4-20 Preparing an Adjusted Trial Balance LO3

The following alphabetical listing is the adjusted account balances for H&R Tacks, owned and managed by Jeremy Daily.

Accounts Payable	$ 400	Insurance Expense	$ 3,600	Prepaid Insurance	$ 3,600
Accounts Receivable	500	Interest Expense	500	Service Revenue	46,300
Accumulated Depreciation	6,000	Interest Payable	500	Supplies	1,300
Cash	5,000	J. Daily, Capital	27,700	Supplies Expense	7,700
Depreciation Expense	6,000	J. Daily, Drawing	200	Unearned Revenue	2,500
Equipment	38,000	Notes Payable	3,000	Wages Expense	21,200
				Wages Payable	1,200

Prepare an adjusted trial balance as of December 31.

M4-21 Closing the Books LO4

Refer to the adjusted account balances in M4-20. Prepare closing journal entries on December 31.

M4-22 Computing Net Profit Margin LO5

Refer to the adjusted account balances in M4-20.

Required:

1. Compute net income.
2. Compute net profit margin for H&R Tacks.
3. What does the result of your computation suggest about H&R Tacks?

Exercises

Available with McGraw-Hill's Homework Manager

E4-1 Preparing an Adjusted Trial Balance LO3

Gibson Consultants provides marketing research for clients in the retail industry. The company had the following adjusted balances at December 31, 2010:

Cash		Accumulated Depreciation		Accrued Liabilities	
173,000			18,100		25,650

Wages Expense		Advertising Expense		Supplies	
1,590,000		320,050		12,200	

Accounts Receivable		Prepaid Expenses		Interest Expense	
225,400		10,200		17,200	

Interest Payable	
	2,030

Consulting Fees Revenue	
	2,577,200

P. Gibson, Capital	
	?

Utilities Expense	
25,230	

Travel Expense	
23,990	

Building and Equipment	
323,040	

Investment Revenue	
	7,800

P. Gibson, Drawing	
5,000	

Unearned Consulting Fees	
	32,500

Training Expenses	
188,000	

Accounts Payable	
86,830	

Land	
60,000	

Notes Payable	
	160,000

Depreciation Expense	
18,600	

Investments	
145,000	

Rent Expense	
152,080	

Required:

1. Prepare an adjusted trial balance for Gibson Consultants at December 31, 2010. Solve for the '?' in the P. Gibson, Capital account (*Hint:* Remember: Assets = Liabilities + Owner's Equity.)
2. Assume that no investments were made by P. Gibson during the year. Does the P. Gibson, Capital balance determined in 1 represent the balance at December 31, 2010, or December 31, 2009? Explain.

LO2
Coach, Inc.

E4-2 Identifying Adjustments by Scanning a Trial Balance

Coach, Inc.—the maker of handbags and other women's and men's accessories—was owned by Sara Lee Corporation until April 2001, when Coach was spun off as a separate company. Assume the following adjusted balances were reported in Coach's trial balance and were used to prepare its July 2, 2009, year-end financial statements.

COACH INCORPORATED
Adjusted Trial Balance
At July 2, 2009
(millions of dollars)

	Debit	Credit
Cash	154,556	
Accounts Receivable	65,399	
Inventories	184,419	
Prepaid Expenses	25,671	
Property and Equipment	203,862	
Other Assets	713,215	
Accounts Payable		64,985
Wages Payable		185,502
Interest Payable		2,851
Notes Payable		3,270
Other Liabilities		57,748
Owners' Capital		644,114
Sales Revenue		1,710,423
Cost of Sales (used up inventory)	399,652	
Selling, General, and Administrative Expenses	688,961	
Interest Expense	13,641	
Interest Revenue		15,760
Other Expenses	235,277	
	2,684,653	2,684,653

Required:

1. Based on the information in the trial balance, identify any accounts that likely were unearned revenues or prepaid expenses requiring an adjusting entry as of July 2 (no computations are necessary).
2. Based on the information in the trial balance, identify any accounts that likely were accrued revenues or accrued expenses requiring an adjusting entry as of July 2 (no computations are necessary).

E4-3 Determining Adjustments and Accounting Equation Effects **LO1, 2**

MoBo, a wireless phone carrier owned by sole proprietor Morris Bonner, completed its first year of operations on December 31, 2011. All of the 2011 entries have been recorded except for the following:

a. At year-end, employees earned wages of $6,000 that will be paid on the next payroll date, January 6, 2012.

b. At year-end, the company had earned interest revenue of $3,000. It will be collected March 1, 2012.

Required:

1. What is the annual reporting period for this company?
2. Identify whether each required adjustment is an unearned revenue, accrued revenue, prepaid expense, or accrued expense.
3. Show the accounting equation effects (amounts and direction of effects) of each required adjustment. Use + for increase, − for decrease, or NE for no effect. Complete the following schedule:

	BALANCE SHEET			INCOME STATEMENT		
Transaction	Assets	Liabilities	Owner's Equity	Revenues	Expenses	Net Income
a.						
b.						

4. Why are these adjustments needed?

E4-4 Recording Adjusting Journal Entries **LO2**

Refer to E4-3.

Required:

Record the required adjusting journal entries for transactions *a* and *b*.

E4-5 Determining Adjustments and Accounting Equation Effects **LO1, 2**

Mary Fes, owner of Fes Company, has hired you to help with the accounting entries at the end of the year on December 31, 2009. In developing information for the adjusting journal entries, you learned the following:

a. A two-year insurance premium of $7,200 was paid on January 1, 2009, for coverage beginning on that date. As of December 31, 2009, the unadjusted balances were $7,200 for Prepaid Insurance and $0 for Insurance Expense.

b. At December 31, 2009, you obtained the following data relating to shipping supplies.

Balance in Shipping Supplies on December 31, 2008	$15,000
Shipping supplies purchased in 2009	72,000
Shipping supplies on hand, counted on December 31, 2009	10,000

Required:

1. Of the $7,200 paid for insurance, what amount should be reported on the 2009 income statement as Insurance Expense? What amount should be reported on the December 31, 2009, balance sheet as Prepaid Insurance?
2. What amount should be reported on the 2009 income statement as Shipping Supplies Expense? What amount should be reported on the December 31, 2009, balance sheet as Shipping Supplies?
3. Using the following format, indicate the accounting equation effects (amounts and direction of effects) of the adjustment required for (*a*) insurance and (*b*) shipping supplies. Use + for increase, − for decrease, or NE for no effect.

	BALANCE SHEET			INCOME STATEMENT		
Transaction	Assets	Liabilities	Owner's Equity	Revenues	Expenses	Net Income
a.						
b.						

LO2

E4-6 Recording Adjusting Journal Entries
Refer to E4-5.

Required:
Prepare adjusting journal entries at December 31, 2009, for (*a*) insurance and (*b*) shipping supplies.

LO2

E4-7 Recording Adjusting Journal Entries
Jaworski's Ski Store is completing the accounting process for its first year ended December 31, 2010. The transactions during 2010 have been journalized and posted. The following data are available to determine adjusting journal entries:

a. The balance in Office Supplies was $50 at December 31, 2009. Jaworski's purchased $800 of supplies during 2010. The unadjusted balance in Supplies Expense was $0 at December 31, 2010. A year-end count showed $100 of supplies on hand.

b. Wages earned by employees during December 2010, unpaid and unrecorded at December 31, 2010, amounted to $3,700. The last paychecks were issued December 28; the next payments will be made on January 6, 2011. The unadjusted balance in Wages Expense was $40,000 at December 31, 2010.

c. Jaworski's rents a portion of the store's basement for $1,100 per month to K. Frey. On November 1, 2010, the store collected six months' rent in the amount of $6,600 in advance from Frey. It was credited in full to Unearned Rent Revenue when collected. The unadjusted balance in Rent Revenue was $0 at December 31, 2010.

d. The store purchased delivery equipment at the beginning of the year 2010. The estimated depreciation for 2010 is $3,000, although none has been recorded yet.

e. On December 31, 2010, the unadjusted balance in Prepaid Insurance was $4,800. This was the amount paid in the middle of the year for a two-year insurance policy with coverage beginning on July 1, 2010. The unadjusted balance in Insurance Expense was $800, which was the cost of insurance from January 1 to June 30, 2010.

f. Jaworski's operates a repair shop doing some work for Frey. At the end of December 31, 2010, Frey had not paid for completed work amounting to $750. This amount has not yet been recorded as Repair Shop Revenue. Collection is expected during January 2011.

Required:
For each of the preceding items,

1. Identify the type of adjustment.
2. Prepare the adjusting journal entry that should be recorded at December 31, 2010.
3. Indicate the account names and adjusted balances that should be reported on Jaworski's year-end balance sheet and income statement.

LO2

E4-8 Determining Financial Statement Effects of Adjusting Journal Entries
Refer to E4-7.

Required:
For each transaction in E4-7, indicate the amount and direction of effects of the adjusting journal entry on the elements of the balance sheet and income statement. Use the following format: + for increase, – for decrease, and NE for no effect.

	BALANCE SHEET			INCOME STATEMENT		
Transaction	Assets	Liabilities	Owner's Equity	Revenues	Expenses	Net Income
a.						
b.						
etc.						

LO2, 4

E4-9 Recording Transactions Including Adjusting and Closing Journal Entries
Cooper Paving, owned by Chuck Cooper, uses the following accounts:

Codes	Accounts	Codes	Accounts
A	Accounts Receivable	J	Notes Payable
B	Accumulated Depreciation	K	Paving Equipment
C	Cash	L	Service Revenue
D	C. Cooper, Capital	M	Supplies
E	C. Cooper, Drawing	N	Supplies Expense
F	Depreciation Expense	O	Unearned Service Revenue
G	Income Summary	P	Wages Expense
H	Interest Expense	Q	Wages Payable
I	Interest Payable	R	None of the above

Required:
For each of the following independent situations, give the journal entry by entering the appropriate code(s) and amount(s). The first one is an example.

		DEBIT		CREDIT	
	Independent Situations	**Code**	**Amount**	**Code**	**Amount**
a.	(*Example*) Accrued wages, unrecorded and unpaid at year-end, $400.	P	400	Q	400
b.	Service revenue collected in advance, $600.				
c.	Amounts withdrawn by the owner during year, $900.				
d.	Depreciation expense for year, $1,000.				
e.	Service revenue earned but not yet collected at year-end, $1,000.				
f.	Balance in supplies account, $400; supplies on hand at year-end, $150.				
g.	At year-end, interest on notes payable not yet recorded or paid, $220.				
h.	Balance at year-end in Service Revenue account, $75,000. Give the journal entry to close this one account at year-end.				
i.	Balance at year-end in Interest Expense account, $420. Give the journal entry to close this one account at year-end.				

E4-10 Inferring Transactions from Accrual Accounts

LO2
Deere & Company

Deere & Company was incorporated in 1868 and today is the world's leading producer of agricultural equipment. The company also provides credit, managed health care plans, and insurance products for businesses and the general public. The following information is taken from a recent annual report (in millions of dollars):

Wages and Benefits Payable			
		Beg. bal.	981
	2,261	(a)	?
		End. bal.	1,060

Product Warranties Payable			
		Beg. bal.	507
(b)	?		565
		End. bal.	549

Interest Payable			
		Beg. bal.	129
	1,140	(c)	?
		End. bal.	140

Required:

1. For each accrued liability account, describe the typical transactions that cause it to increase and decrease.
2. Solve for the missing amounts for (*a*), (*b*), and (*c*) (in millions).

E4-11 Analyzing the Effects of Adjusting Journal Entries on the Income Statement and Balance Sheet

LO2, 3

On December 31, 2009, Laura's Pie Company, owned by Laura Anne, prepared an income statement and balance sheet, but the bookkeeper accidentally failed to take into account four adjusting journal entries. The income statement, prepared on this incorrect basis, reported income of $30,000. The balance sheet reflected total assets, $90,000; total liabilities, $40,000; and owner's equity, $50,000. The data for the four adjusting journal entries follow:

a. Depreciation of $8,000 for the year on equipment was not recorded.

b. Wages amounting to $17,000 for the last three days of December 2009 were not paid and not recorded (the next payroll will be on January 10, 2010).

c. Rent revenue of $4,800 was collected on December 1, 2009, for office space for the three-month period December 1, 2009, to February 28, 2010. The $4,800 was credited in full to Unearned Rent Revenue when collected.

d. The company borrowed $10,000 from a local bank on January 1, 2009. The note principal is due in three years but requires payment of $1,500 interest every January 1 with the next payment due on January 1, 2010. No interest has been paid or recorded for 2009.

Required:
Complete the following table to show the effects of the four adjusting journal entries (indicate deductions with parentheses):

Items	Net Income	Total Assets	Total Liabilities	Owner's Equity
Amounts reported	$30,000	$90,000	$40,000	$50,000
Effect of depreciation	______	______	______	______
Effect of wages	______	______	______	______
Effect of rent revenue	______	______	______	______
Effect of interest	______	______	______	______
Correct amounts	______	______	______	______

LO1, 2, 3

E4-12 Reporting an Adjusted Income Statement

Dyer Rental Store, a sole proprietorship owned by Jessica Dyer, completed its first year of operations on December 31, 2010. Because this is the end of the annual accounting period, the business's bookkeeper prepared the following tentative income statement:

Income Statement, 2010 (amounts are unadjusted)	
Rental Revenue	$114,000
Expenses	
Salaries and Wages Expense	28,500
Supplies Expense	12,000
Rent Expense	9,000
Utilities Expense	4,000
Gas and Oil Expense	3,000
Other Operating Expenses	1,000
Total expenses	57,500
Income	$ 56,500

You are an independent CPA hired by the business to audit its accounting systems and financial statements. In your audit, you developed additional data as follows:

a. Salaries and wages for the last three days of December amounting to $310 were not recorded or paid.

b. The $400 telephone bill for December 2010 has not been recorded or paid.

c. Depreciation on vans amounting to $23,000 for 2010 was not recorded.

d. Interest of $500 was not recorded on the note payable by Dyer Rental.

e. The Unearned Rental Revenue account includes $4,000 revenue earned in 2010.

f. Supplies costing $600 were used during 2010, but this has not yet been recorded.

Required:

1. Explain why adjusting entries are necessary.
2. For each item *a* through *f*, indicate the type of adjustment and then prepare the adjusting journal entry that should be recorded at December 31, 2010. If none is required, explain why.
3. Prepare a *classified* income statement for 2010 using adjusted amounts.

E4-13 Recording Adjusting Entries and Preparing an Adjusted Trial Balance LO2, 3

Ninja Sockeye Star, owned by Johnny Chen, had the following unadjusted accounts at the end of its second year of operations ending December 31, 2009. The accounts have normal debit or credit balances.

Cash	$12,000	Wages Payable	$ 0
Accounts Receivable	6,000	J. Chen, Capital	31,900
Prepaid Rent	2,400	Commissions Revenue	45,000
Equipment	21,000	Wages Expense	25,000
Accumulated Depreciation	1,000	Utilities Expense	12,500
Accounts Payable	1,000	Rent Expense	0
Utilities Payable	0	Depreciation Expense	0

Other data not yet recorded at December 31, 2009, follow:

a. Rent used during 2009, $1,200.
b. Depreciation expense for 2009, $1,000.
c. Utilities used in 2009 but not yet paid, $9,000.
d. Wages earned by employees in 2009 but not yet paid, $800.

Required:

1. Create T-accounts based on the accounts titles and balances at December 31, 2009.
2. Using the steps outlined in the chapter, (1) identify the type of adjustment of (*a*) through (*d*), (2) determine the amount, and (3) prepare the adjusting journal entries required at December 31, 2009.
3. Post the effects of the adjusting journal entries to the T-accounts and prepare an adjusted trial balance as of December 31, 2009.

E4-14 Recording Adjusting Entries and Preparing an Adjusted Trial Balance LO2, 3

Mint Cleaning, owned by Kat Slifer, had the following unadjusted accounts at the end of its second year of operations ending December 31, 2010. To simplify this exercise, the amounts given are in thousands of dollars and have normal debit or credit balances.

Cash	$38	Unearned Service Revenue	$ 27
Accounts Receivable	9	K. Slifer, Capital	80
Prepaid Insurance	16	K. Slifer, Drawing	16
Equipment	90	Service Revenue	179
Accumulated Depreciation	4	Supplies Expense	26
Accounts Payable	25	Wages Expense	120
Wages Payable	0		

Other data not yet recorded at December 31, 2010, follow:

a. One-fourth of the Prepaid Insurance expired during 2010.
b. Depreciation expense for 2010, $4.
c. Wages earned by employees but not yet paid in 2010, $7.
d. One-third of the Unearned Service Revenue was earned in 2010.

Required:

1. Create T-accounts based on the account titles and balances at December 31, 2010.
2. Using the steps outlined in the chapter, (1) identify the type of adjustment of *a* through *d*, (2) determine the amount, and (3) prepare the adjusting journal entries required at December 31, 2010.

3. Post the effects of the adjusting journal entries to the T-accounts and prepare an adjusted trial balance as of December 31, 2010.

LO3

E4-15 Reporting an Income Statement, Statement of Owner's Equity, and Balance Sheet

Refer to E4-14.

Required:

Using the adjusted balances in E4-14, prepare a *classified* income statement, statement of owner's equity, and *classified* balance sheet for 2010.

LO4

E4-16 Recording Closing Entries

Refer to E4-14.

Required:

1. Using the adjusted balances in E4-14, give the closing journal entries for 2010.
2. What is the purpose of closing the books at the end of the accounting period?

LO5

E4-17 Analyzing Financial Information Using Net Profit Margin

Refer to the financial statements created in E4-15.

Required:

Compute and interpret the net profit margin ratio for Mint Cleaning for 2010.

LO1, 2

E4-18 Recording Initial Transactions and Subsequent Adjustments

During the month of September, Texas Go-Kart Company had the following business activities:

a. Paid rent on September 1 on the track facility for six months at a total cost of $12,000.

b. Sold season tickets on September 1 for 12-month admission to the race track. Season ticket sales totaled $60,000.

c. Reserved the race track on September 1 for a private organization that will use the track one day per month beginning on September 15 for $2,000, to be paid in the following month.

d. Hired a new manager on September 1 at a monthly salary of $3,000 to be paid the first Monday following the end of the month. The manager started on September 2.

Required:

Using the following table, prepare

1. The journal entry, if any, required to record each of the initial business activities on September 1.
2. The adjusting journal entry, if any, required on September 30.

Ref / Date	Journal Entries and Adjusting Journal Entries	DEBIT	CREDIT
(*a*) Sept 1			
Sept 30			
(*b*) Sept 1			
Sept 30			
(*c*) Sept 1			
Sept 30			
(*d*) Sept 1			
Sept 30			

E4-19 Completing a Worksheet Starting with an Unadjusted Trial Balance (Chapter Supplement)

Fairbanks Company is completing its annual accounting information processing cycle at December 31, 2011. The following worksheet has been started.

Fairbanks Company
Unadjusted Trial Balance
December 31, 2011
(dollars in thousands)

Account No.	Account Titles	Debit	Credit
101	Cash	38	
102	Accounts Receivable	40	
103	Supplies	21	
104	Prepaid Insurance	4	
110	Equipment	80	
111	Accumulated Depreciation, Equipment		8
119	Accounts Payable		12
120	Wages Payable		
121	Interest Payable		
122	Unearned Revenue		10
123	Note Payable (due 2014)		25
130	K. Fairbanks, Capital		89
145	Service Revenue		108
146	Wages Expense	69	
147	Insurance Expense		
148	Depreciation Expense		
150	Interest Expense		
		252	252

Data not yet recorded for 2011:

a. Half of Prepaid Insurance was used in 2011.
b. Depreciation expense, $8
c. Wages earned by employees; not yet paid, $1.
d. Revenue collected by Fairbanks; not yet earned, $6.
e. Interest expense incurred; not yet paid, $3.

Required:
Complete the worksheet. Set up additional column headings for Adjusting Entries, Adjusted Trial Balance, Income Statement, Owner's Equity, and Balance Sheet.

Problems—Set A  Available with McGraw-Hill's Homework Manager

PA4-1 Recording Adjusting Journal Entries LO2

Jordan Company's annual accounting year ends on December 31. Jordan Broome owns and manages the company. It is now December 31, 2009, and all of the 2009 entries have been made except for the following:

a. The company owes interest of $400 on a bank loan taken out on October 1, 2009. The interest will be paid when the loan is repaid on September 30, 2010.
b. On September 1, 2009, Jordan collected six months' rent of $4,800 on storage space. At that date, Jordan debited Cash and credited Unearned Rent Revenue for $4,800.
c. The company earned service revenue of $3,000 on a special job completed December 29, 2009. Collection will be made during January 2010. No entry has been recorded.
d. On November 1, 2009, Jordan paid a $4,200, one-year premium for property insurance for coverage starting on that date. Prepaid Insurance was debited and Cash was credited for this amount.

e. At December 31, 2009, wages earned by employees totaled $1,100. The employees will be paid on the next payroll date, January 15, 2010.

f. Depreciation of $1,000 must be recognized on a service truck purchased this year.

g. On December 27, 2009, the company received a tax bill of $400 from the city for 2009 property taxes on land. The tax bill is payable during January 2010.

Required:
Following the steps outlined in the chapter, for each transaction:

1. Identify the type of adjustment (unearned revenue, accrued revenue, prepaid expense, or accrued expense).
2. Determine the amount of revenue or expense to be recorded.
3. Record the adjusting journal entry at December 31, 2009.

LO2

PA4-2 Determining Financial Statement Effects of Adjusting Journal Entries
Refer to PA4-1.

Required:
Using the following headings, indicate the effect of each adjusting journal entry and the amount of the effect. Use + for increase, − for decrease, and NE for no effect.

	BALANCE SHEET			INCOME STATEMENT		
Transaction	Assets	Liabilities	Owner's Equity	Revenues	Expenses	Net Income
a.						
b.						
etc.						

LO3, 4

www.mhhe.com/LLPW1e

PA4-3 Preparing an Adjusted Trial Balance, Closing Journal Entries, and Post-Closing Trial Balance
Dell is the world's largest computer systems company selling directly to customers. The following is a list of adjusted accounts and amounts reported for a recent fiscal year ended February 3. The accounts have normal debit or credit balances and the dollars are rounded to the nearest million.

Accounts Payable	$ 9,840	Long-Term Debt	$ 504
Accounts Receivable	5,452	Other Assets	14,635
Accrued Liabilities	6,087	Other Expenses	1,002
Accumulated Depreciation	749	Other Liabilities	2,549
Cash	9,807	Property, Plant, and Equipment	2,005
Cost of Goods Sold (inventory used)	45,958	Research and Development Expense	463
Dell Owners' Capital	9,174	Sales Revenue	55,908
Interest Revenue	227	Selling, General, and	
Inventories	576	Administrative Expenses	5,140

Required:

1. Prepare an adjusted trial balance at February 3, 2009. Is the Dell Owners' Capital balance of $9,174 the amount that would be reported on the balance sheet as of February 3, 2009?
2. Prepare the closing entries required at February 3, 2009.
3. Prepare a post-closing trial balance at February 3, 2009.

LO4, 5
Starbucks Corporation

www.mhhe.com/LLPW1e

PA4-4 Preparing Closing Entries and Computing and Analyzing Net Profit Margin
Starbucks Corporation purchases and roasts high-quality whole bean coffees and sells them along with fresh-brewed coffees, its exclusive line of Frappucino blended beverages, Italian-style espresso beverages, and premium teas. The following is a simplified list of accounts and amounts reported in its accounting records. The accounts have normal debit or credit balances, and the dollars are rounded to the nearest million. Assume that the year ended on September 30, 2010.

Accounts Payable	$ 221	Long-Term Debt	$ 196
Accounts Receivable	191	Other Current Assets	71
Accrued Liabilities	354	Other Long-Lived Assets	461
Accumulated Depreciation	300	Other Expenses	499
Cash	307	Prepaid Expenses	94
Cost of Sales (an expense for inventory sold)	2,605	Property, Plant, and Equipment	2,142
Depreciation Expense	340	Service Revenues	6,369
General and Administrative Expenses	357	Short-Term Bank Debt	476
Interest Revenue	92	Starbucks Owners' Capital	1,596
Inventories	546	Store Operating Expenses	2,166
		Unearned Revenue	175

Required:

1. Prepare the closing entries required at September 30, 2010.
2. Compute net profit margin for the year ended September 30, 2010.
3. In the year ended September 30, 2009, assume that Starbucks had an 8.6% net profit margin and that the industry ratio was 10.5%. What does this information suggest to you about Starbucks?

PA4-5 Recording Transactions (including adjusting journal entries), Preparing Financial Statements, Closing the Books, and Analyzing a Key Ratio: Comprehensive Review Problem (Chapters 2, 3, and 4)

LO1, 2, 3, 4, 5

www.mhhe.com/LLPW1e

Harry Hermann began operations of his machine shop (H-H Tool) on January 1, 2009. The annual reporting period ends December 31. The trial balance on January 1, 2011, follows (the amounts are rounded to thousands of dollars to simplify):

H-H Tool
Trial Balance
On January 1, 2011
(in thousands)

Account Titles	Debit	Credit	Account Titles	Debit	Credit
Cash	3		Utilities Payable		0
Accounts Receivable	5		H. Hermann, Capital		73
Supplies	12		H. Hermann, Drawing	0	
Land	0		Service Revenue		0
Equipment	60		Depreciation Expense	0	
Accumulated Depreciation		6	Wages Expense	0	
Other Assets	4		Interest Expense	0	
Accounts Payable		5	Supplies Expense	0	
Notes Payable		0	Utilities Expense	0	
Wages Payable		0	Other Operating Expenses	0	
Interest Payable		0		84	84

(continued)

Transactions during 2011 (summarized in thousands of dollars) follow:

a. Borrowed $12 cash on a short-term note payable dated March 1, 2011.
b. Purchased land for future building site, paid cash, $9.
c. Earned $160 in Service Revenue for 2011, including $40 on credit and $120 collected in cash.
d. Received an additional $3 investment by H. Hermann.
e. Recognized $70 in Wages Expense for 2011, paid in cash, and $15 of Other Operating Expenses on credit.
f. Collected accounts receivable from customers, $24.
g. Purchased other assets, $10 cash.

h. Paid accounts payable, $13.
i. Purchased supplies on account for future use, $18.
j. Signed a $25 service contract to start February 1, 2012.
k. Paid $17 cash to H. Hermann on his drawing account.

Data for adjusting journal entries follow:

l. Supplies counted on December 31, 2011, $10.
m. Depreciation for the year on the equipment, $6.
n. Accrued interest on notes payable, $1.
o. Wages earned by employees since the December 24 payroll not yet paid, $12.
p. Utility bill of $8 for December usage was received on December 31, 2011. It will be paid in 2012.

Required:

1. Set up T-accounts for the accounts on the trial balance and enter beginning balances.
2. Record journal entries for transactions (*a*) through (*k*) and post them to the T-accounts.
3. Prepare an unadjusted trial balance.
4. Record and post the adjusting journal entries (*l*) through (*p*).
5. Prepare an adjusted trial balance.
6. Prepare a classified income statement, statement of owner's equity, and classified balance sheet.
7. Prepare and post the closing journal entries.
8. Prepare a post-closing trial balance.
9. How much net income did H-H Tool generate during 2011? Is the company financed primarily by debt or equity?
10. Compute and interpret the net profit margin for H-H Tool for the year ended December 31, 2011.

PA4-6 Completing a Worksheet and Preparing Closing Entries (Chapter Supplement)
Anderson Plumbing Supply has partially completed the following worksheet for the year ended December 31, 2010:

	UNADJUSTED TRIAL BALANCE		ADJUSTING ENTRIES	
Account Titles	Debit	Credit	Debit	Credit
Cash	13,000			
Accounts Receivable	22,000			
Supplies	1,200			(*a*) 600
Interest Receivable			(*b*) 300	
Long-Term Note Receivable	9,000			
Equipment	80,000			
Accumulated Depreciation		35,000		(c) 10,000
Accounts Payable		10,000		
Short-Term Note Payable		12,000		
Interest Payable				(*d*) 720
Accrued Liabilities Payable				(*e*) 3,620
J. Anderson, Capital		55,000		
J. Anderson, Drawing	20,000			
Service Revenue		72,000		
Interest Revenue				(*b*) 300
Expenses (not detailed)	38,800		(*a*) 600	
Depreciation Expense			(c) 10,000	
Interest Expense			(*d*) 720	
Other Operating Expenses			(*e*) 3,620	
Totals	184,000	184,000	15,240	15,240

Required:

1. Use additional columns for Adjusted Trial Balance, Income Statement, Owner's Equity, and Balance Sheet to complete the worksheet.
2. Explain each of the adjustments.
3. Give the closing entries.
4. Why are the adjusting and closing entries journalized and posted?

Problems—Set B  Available with McGraw-Hill's Homework Manager

PB4-1 Recording Adjusting Journal Entries LO2

Greenly Company's annual accounting year ends on June 30. It is June 30, 2010, and all of the 2010 entries except the following adjusting journal entries have been made:

a. The company earned service revenue of $2,000 on a special job that was completed June 29, 2010. Collection will be made during July 2010; no entry has been recorded.

b. On March 30, 2010, Greenly paid a $3,200, six-month premium for property insurance for coverage starting on that date. Cash was credited and Prepaid Insurance was debited for this amount.

c. At June 30, 2010, wages of $900 earned by employees were not yet paid. The employees will be paid on the next payroll date, July 15, 2010.

d. On June 1, 2010, Greenly collected two months' maintenance revenue of $450. At that date, Greenly debited Cash and credited Unearned Maintenance Revenue for $450.

e. Depreciation of $1,500 must be recognized on a service truck purchased on July 1, 2007.

f. Cash of $4,200 was collected on May 1, 2010, for services to be rendered evenly over the next year beginning on May 1. Unearned Service Revenue was credited when the cash was received.

g. The company owes $600 interest on a bank loan taken out on February 1, 2010. The interest will be paid when the loan is repaid on January 31, 2011.

Required:

Following the steps outlined in the chapter, for each transaction:

1. Identify the type of adjustment (unearned revenue, accrued revenue, prepaid expense, or accrued expense).
2. Determine the amount of revenue or expense to be recorded.
3. Record the adjusting journal entry at June 30, 2010.

PB4-2 Determining Financial Statement Effects of Adjusting Journal Entries LO2

Refer to PB4-1.

Required:

Using the following headings, indicate the effect of each adjusting journal entry and the amount of the effect. Use + for increase, − for decrease, and NE for no effect.

	BALANCE SHEET			INCOME STATEMENT		
Transaction	Assets	Liabilities	Owner's Equity	Revenues	Expenses	Net Income
a.						
b.						
etc.						

LO3, 4
Pacific Sunwear of California

PB4-3 Preparing an Adjusted Trial Balance, Closing Journal Entries, and Post-Closing Trial Balance

Pacific Sunwear of California operates three chains of retail stores under the names Pacific Sunwear (also known as PacSun), Pacific Sunwear (PacSun) Outlet, and d.e.m.o. The following is a simplified list of adjusted accounts and amounts reported in the company's records for a recent year ended January 28. Dollars are in thousands.

Accounts Payable	$ 47,550	Inventories	$ 215,140
Accounts Receivable	12,679	Long-Term Liabilities	138,300
Accrued Liabilities	33,649	Sales Revenue	1,391,473
Accumulated Depreciation	247,140	Other Current Assets	81,357
Cash	95,185	Other Current Liabilities	14,896
Cost of Goods Sold (used inventory)	884,982	Other Long-Lived Assets	332,893
Depreciation Expense	74,617	Other Operating Expenses	76,734
Selling, General, and Administrative Expenses	309,218	PacSun Owners' Capital	534,513
		Prepaid Expenses	22,360
Interest Expense	7,269	Property, Plant, and Equipment	295,087

Required:

1. Prepare an adjusted trial balance at January 28, 2009. Is the PacSun Owners' Capital balance of $534,513 the amount that would be reported on the balance sheet as of January 28, 2009?
2. Prepare the closing entries required at January 28, 2009.
3. Prepare a post-closing trial balance at January 28, 2009.

LO4, 5
Federal Express Corporation

PB4-4 Preparing Closing Entries and Computing and Analyzing Net Profit Margin

Federal Express Corporation delivers packages and freight to over 220 countries via air and land routes. The company also owns FedEx Kinko's. The following is a simplified list of adjusted accounts and amounts reported in its accounting records. The accounts have normal debit or credit balances, and the dollars are rounded to the nearest million. Assume that the year ended on May 31, 2011.

Accounts Payable	$1,594	Long-Term Debt	$ 3,778
Accounts Receivable	1,429	Other Current Assets	836
Accrued Expenses Payable	1,755	Other Long-Lived Assets	5,199
Accumulated Depreciation	8,988	Other Expenses	8,009
Cash	257	Prepaid Expenses	125
Salary and Benefits Expense	8,051	Property and Equipment	16,905
Depreciation Expense	845	Service Revenues	22,527
Interest Expense	40	FedEx Owners' Capital	8,905
Interest Revenue	213	Landing Fees Expense	1,598
Spare Parts and Supplies	269	Fuel Expense	2,946

Required:

1. Prepare the closing entries required at May 31, 2011.
2. Compute net profit margin for the year ended May 31, 2011.
3. In the year ended May 31, 2010, assume that FedEx had a net profit margin of 5.1% and that the industry ratio was 11.7%. What does this information suggest to you about FedEx?

LO1, 2, 3, 4, 5

PB4-5 Recording Transactions (including adjusting entries), Preparing Financial Statements, Closing the Books, and Analyzing a Key Ratio Comprehensive Review Problem (Chapters 2, 3, and 4)

Alison Renny began operations of her furniture repair shop (Lazy Sofa Furniture) on January 1, 2010. The annual reporting period ends December 31. The trial balance on January 1, 2011, was as follows (the amounts are rounded to thousands of dollars to simplify):

Lazy Sofa Furniture
Trial Balance
On January 1, 2011
(in thousands)

Account Titles	Debit	Credit	Account Titles	Debit	Credit
Cash	5		Utilities Payable		0
Accounts Receivable	4		Unearned Revenue		0
Supplies	2		A. Renny, Capital		19
Small Tools	6		A. Renny, Drawing	0	
Equipment	0		Service Revenue		0
Accumulated Depreciation		0	Depreciation Expense		0
Other Assets	9		Wages Expense		0
Accounts Payable		7	Interest Expense		0
Notes Payable		0	Supplies Expense		0
Wages Payable		0	Utilities Expense		0
Interest Payable		0	Other Operating Expenses	0	0
				26	26

(continued)

Transactions during 2011 (summarized in thousands of dollars) follow:

a. Borrowed $21 cash on July 1, 2011, signing a short-term note payable.
b. Purchased equipment for $18 cash on July 1, 2011.
c. Received $5 cash as an additional investment from owner A. Renny.
d. Earned $65 in Service Revenue in 2011, including $9 on credit and $56 received in cash.
e. Recognized $28 in Wages Expense for 2011, paid in cash, and $7 of Other Operating Expenses on credit.
f. Purchased additional small tools, $3 cash.
g. Collected accounts receivable, $8.
h. Paid accounts payable, $11.
i. Purchased on account supplies for future use, $10.
j. Received a $3 deposit on work to start January 15, 2012.
k. Paid $10 cash to A. Renny on her drawing account.

Data for adjusting journal entries:

l. Supplies of $4 were counted on December 31, 2011.
m. Depreciation for 2011, $2.
n. Accrued interest on notes payable of $1.
o. Wages earned since the December 24 payroll not yet paid, $3.
p. Utility bill for $4 for December utility usage was received on December 31, 2011. It will be paid in 2012.

Required:

1. Set up T-accounts for the accounts on the trial balance and enter beginning balances.
2. Record journal entries for transactions (*a*) through (*k*) and post them to the T-accounts.
3. Prepare an unadjusted trial balance.
4. Record and post the adjusting journal entries (*l*) through (*p*).
5. Prepare an adjusted trial balance.
6. Prepare a classified income statement, statement of owner's equity, and classified balance sheet.
7. Prepare and post the closing journal entries.
8. Prepare a post-closing trial balance.

9. How much net income did Lazy Sofa Furniture generate during 2011? Is the company financed primarily by debt or equity?
10. Compute and interpret the net profit margin ratio for Lazy Sofa Furniture for the year ended December 31, 2011.

PB4-6 Completing a Worksheet and Preparing Closing Entries (Chapter Supplement)
Marine Pool Service & Repair, a sole proprietorship owned by Robert Horn, has been in operation for several years. Revenues have increased gradually from both the pool cleaning and repair services. The annual financial statements prepared in the past have not conformed to GAAP. The newly employed president decided that a balance sheet, income statement, and statement of owner's equity should be prepared in conformity with GAAP. The first step was to employ a full-time bookkeeper and engage a local CPA firm. It is now December 31, 2009, the end of the current accounting year. The bookkeeper has developed a trial balance from the ledger. A member of the staff of the CPA firm will advise and assist the bookkeeper in completing the accounting information processing cycle for the first time. The unadjusted trial balance at December 31, 2009, follows.

Marine Pool Service & Repair
Unadjusted Trial Balance
December 31, 2009

Debits		Credits	
Cash	27,500	Accumulated Depreciation	24,000
Accounts Receivable	2,080	Accounts Payable	8,000
Supplies	820	Wages Payable	0
Prepaid Insurance	800	Interest Payable	0
Land (for future building site-not in use)	5,000	Unearned Cleaning Revenue	4,000
Equipment	72,000	Note Payable	20,000
Remaining Assets (not detailed)	22,000	R. Horn, Capital	37,800
R. Horn, Drawing	3,000	Repair Revenue	72,000
Wages Expense	60,000	Cleaning Revenue	34,000
Advertising Expense	2,000		
Utilities Expense	1,400		
Maintenance Expense	3,200		
Supplies Expense	0		
Insurance Expense	0		
Depreciation Expense	0		
Interest Expense	0		
	199,800		199,800

Examination of the records and related documents provided the following additional information that should be considered for adjusting entries:

a. A physical count of office supplies inventory at December 31, 2009, reflected $70 on hand.
b. On July 1, 2009, a two-year insurance premium was paid amounting to $800; it was debited to Prepaid Insurance.
c. The equipment cost $72,000 when acquired. Annual depreciation expense is $12,000.
d. Unpaid and unrecorded wages earned by employees at December 31, 2009, amounted to $900.
e. The one-year, $20,000 note payable was signed on October 1, 2009. Interest of $600 is owed and will be paid in 2010. No entry has yet been made for the interest.
f. All but $1,000 of the Unearned Cleaning Revenue had been earned by December 31, 2009.
g. Gasoline, oil, and fuel purchased for the vehicles and used during the last two weeks of December 2009 amounting to $200 have not been paid for or recorded (this is considered maintenance expense).

Required:

1. Create and complete a worksheet.
2. Give the closing entries.

Additional problems are available at www.mhhe.com/LLPW1e. Click on Chapter 4 and select Additional Problems (PC4-1 through PC4-7).

Cases and Projects

CP4-1 Finding Financial Information

LO3

Refer to the financial statements of The Home Depot in Appendix A at the end of this book, or download the annual report from the *Cases* section of the text's Web site at www.mhhe.com/LLPW1e.

Required:

1. The company's Prepaid Advertising Expenses are included in the balance sheet under Other Current Assets. Refer to the notes to the financial statements to determine the amount of the Prepaid Advertising Expenses as of February 3, 2008.
2. How much did The Home Depot owe for salaries and related expenses at the end of the more recent year? Was this an increase or decrease from the previous year?
3. In which line of the balance sheet does The Home Depot include its intangible assets and what kinds of intangible assets does the company have?

CP4-2 Comparing Financial Information

LO2, 3

Lowe's

Refer to the financial statements of The Home Depot in Appendix A and Lowe's in Appendix B at the end of this book, or download the annual reports from the *Cases* section of the text's Web site at www.mhhe.com/LLPW1e.

Required:

1. Refer to the notes to the financial statements to determine how much The Home Depot and Lowe's each spent on advertising expenses in the most recent fiscal year.
2. How much did The Home Depot and Lowe's each owe for salaries and wages at the end of the most recent year? Provide one reason that would explain the difference between the two companies' accrued payroll liabilities.

CP4-3 Examining Adjustments: Internet-Based Team Research

LO2, 3, 5

As a team, select an industry to analyze. Using your Web browser, each team member should acquire the annual report or 10-K for one publicly traded company in the industry with each member selecting a different company. (See CP1-3 in Chapter 1 for a description of possible resources for these tasks.)

Required:

1. On an individual basis, each team member should write a short report listing the following:
   a. The company's total assets and total liabilities at the end of each year.
   b. The company's prepaid expenses and accrued liabilities at the end of each year.
   c. The percentage of prepaid expenses to total assets and the percentage of accrued liabilities to total liabilities.
   d. Describe and explain the types of accrued liabilities reported in the notes to the financial statements.
   e. Compute the company's net profit margin ratio for the most recent year and the prior year. What does this suggest to you about the company?
2. Discuss any patterns that you as a team observe. Then, as a team, write a short report comparing and contrasting your companies according to the preceding attributes. Provide potential explanations for any differences discovered.

CP4-4 Ethical Decision Making: A Real-Life Example

LO2

On December 12, 2002, the SEC filed a lawsuit against four executives of Safety-Kleen Corp., one of the country's leading providers of industrial waste collection and disposal services. The primary issue was that the executives had directed others in the company to record improper adjustments in 1999 and 2000, which had the effect of overstating net income during those periods. The following table was included in the SEC's court documents to demonstrate the (combined) effect of proper and improper adjustments on net income. (All amounts are in millions.)

	YEAR (QUARTER)				
	1999(Q1)	1999(Q2)	1999(Q3)	1999(Q4)	2000(Q1)
Net income before adjustments	$ 90.9	$ 76.7	$ 47.9	$ 57.3	$ 47.0
Effect of improper adjustments	36.6	30.9	75.5	53.1	69.8
Net income after adjustments	$127.5	$107.6	$123.4	$110.4	$116.8

The following excerpts from the SEC's complaint describe two of the allegedly improper adjustments:

Improper Capitalization of Operating Expenses

26. As part of the fraudulent accounting scheme, [three top executives] improperly recorded several adjusting entries to capitalize certain operating expenses. These adjustments caused the company to materially overstate both its assets and its earnings. For example, at the end of the third quarter of fiscal 1999, they improperly capitalized approximately $4.6 million of payroll expenses relating to certain marketing and start-up activities.

Improper Treatment of Accruals

33. During the fourth quarter of fiscal 1999, [the CFO] created additional fictitious income by directing [other accounting executives] to eliminate a $7.6 million accrual that had been established to provide for management bonuses that had been earned in fiscal 1999, but were to be paid the following quarter. Humphreys' action suggested that no bonuses were going to be paid for that year. In fact, the bonuses for 1999 were paid as scheduled.

Required:

1. Discuss whether large adjustments, such as those included by Safety-Kleen in 1999 and 2000, necessarily indicate improper accounting procedures.
2. What does the SEC's document mean in paragraph 26 when it says three top executives "improperly recorded several adjusting entries to *capitalize* certain operating expenses" (emphasis added). Drawing on concepts presented in Chapters 2 and 3, explain why it is improper to record payroll expenses for marketing personnel as assets.
3. Assume the $7.6 million in bonuses referred to in paragraph 33 were recorded in the third quarter of 1999. What journal entry would have been used to record this accrual? Assume this accrual was eliminated in the fourth quarter of 1999. What adjusting journal entry would have been recorded to eliminate (remove) the previous accrual? What journal entry would have been used to record the $7.6 million in bonuses paid in the first quarter of 2000 (assuming the accrual had been removed in the fourth quarter of 1999)? What accounting concept is violated by recording an expense for management bonuses when they are paid rather than when they are earned by managers?

Epilogue:

In April 2005, a federal judge found the company's former CEO and CFO liable for $200 million for their role in the fraud.

LO3
Escalade, Inc.

CP4-5 Aggregating Accounts on an Adjusted Trial Balance to Prepare an Income Statement, Statement of Owner's Equity, and Balance Sheet

Assume that you recently were hired for a job in Evansville, Indiana, at the head office of Escalade, Inc., which makes Goalrilla™ and Goaliath basketball systems and is the exclusive supplier of Ping Pong and Stiga equipment for table tennis. Your first assignment is to review the company's lengthy adjusted trial balance to determine the accounts that can be combined ("aggregated") into single line items that will be reported on the financial statements. By querying the accounting system, you were able to obtain the following alphabetical list of accounts and their adjusted balances (in thousands) as of December 31. Accounts have normal debit or credit balances.

Accounts Payable	$ 2,792	Interest Receivable	$ 415	Packaging Expenses	$ 1,010
Accounts Receivable	34,141	Inventory of Finished Goods	10,263	Prepaid Insurance	108
Accrued Interest Payable	42	Inventory of Goods Being Made	4,536	Prepaid Rent	434
Accrued Wages Payable	5,856	Inventory of Supplies and Materials	5,750	Rent Expense	7,350
Accrued Warranties Payable	1,324	Long-Term Bank Loan	14,000	Salaries Expense	3,582
Accumulated Depreciation	26,198	Long-Term Contract Payable	1,837	Sales Commissions Expense	3,349
Cash	3,370	Long-Term Note Payable	2,700	Sales of Basketball Systems	98,998
Cost of Goods Sold	111,164	Manufacturing Equipment	12,962	Sales of Other Products	28,710
Depreciation Expense	862	Notes Payable (current)	11,390	Sales of Ping Pong Tables	27,746
Escalade Owners' Capital	34,736	Notes Receivable	400	Shipping Expenses	1,448
Factory Buildings	7,070	Office Building	2,301	Transport Equipment	7,560
Income Tax Expense	5,804	Office Equipment	2,363	Unearned Revenue	8,144
Income Tax Payable	1,189	Office Supplies Expense	69	Utilities Expense	2,111
Insurance Expense	2,368	Other Accrued Liabilities	1,638	Wages Expense	3,024
Interest Expense	950	Other Long-Term Assets	28,310	Warehouse Buildings	3,000
				Warranties Expense	1,226

Required:

1. With the preceding account names and balances, prepare an adjusted trial balance using a spreadsheet.
2. Prepare an income statement, statement of owners' equity, and balance sheet that import their numbers from the adjusted trial balance or from the other statements where appropriate. If similar accounts can be aggregated into a single line item for each financial statement, use a formula to compute the aggregated amount. To be sure that you understand how to import numbers from other parts of a spreadsheet, you e-mail your friend Owen for advice. Here's his reply.

From: Owen@yahoo.com
To: Helpme@hotmail.com
Cc:
Subject: Excel Help

Hey, pal. You're bouncing from job to job like one of those ping-pong balls that your company sells. Okay, to import a number from another spreadsheet, you first click on the cell where you want the number to appear. For example, if you want to enter the Cash balance in the balance sheet, click on the cell in the balance sheet where the cash number is supposed to appear. Enter the equals sign (=) and then click on the tab that takes you to the worksheet containing the adjusted trial balance. In that worksheet, click on the cell that contains the amount you want to import into the balance sheet and then press enter. This will create a link from the adjusted trial balance cell to the balance sheet cell. At the end of this message, I've pasted a screen shot showing the formula I would enter on the balance sheet to import the total of three related inventory accounts from the adjusted trial balance. Don't forget to save the file using a name that indicates who you are.

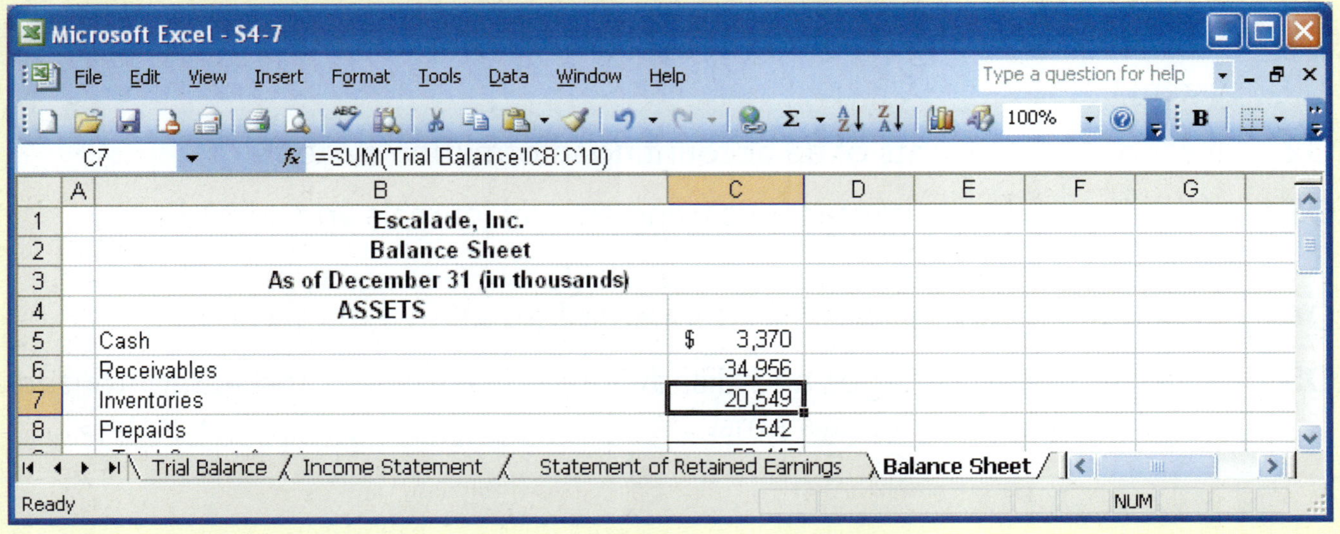

5 Accounting Systems

LEARNING OBJECTIVES

After completing this chapter, you should be able to:

Lectured slideshow–LP5-1
www.mhhe.com/LLPW1e

LO1 Describe processing methods of accounting information systems.

LO2 Describe components of an accounting information system.

LO3 Journalize and post transactions using special journals and subsidiary ledgers.

LO4 Explain the basic theory of accounting information systems.

LO5 Compare the advantages and disadvantages of manual and computerized accounting information systems.

Focus Company: THE UPS STORE®

Retail Packing, Shipping, Postal & Business Services

www.theupsstore.com/index.html

Just as universities and colleges have seen a huge demand for one-time photocopy services, United Parcel Service (UPS) has noticed considerable demand from individuals and small businesses for photocopy services as well as binding, laminating, collating, faxing, packaging, and shipping. In response to this demand, UPS created an opportunity for aspiring business managers to start their own full-service packaging and shipping stores under the familiar UPS Store name. Each UPS Store is independently owned and operated to provide packaging, copying, and shipping services to a variety of customers.

This chapter explains the methods that a UPS Store uses to track the amounts owed by customers. It also explains how the store tracks its own purchases of services and supplies and the payments it makes on account to creditors. We illustrate the tracking process first using a manual accounting system and then using a well-known computerized system.

ORGANIZATION OF THE CHAPTER

MANUAL VERSUS COMPUTERIZED ACCOUNTING INFORMATION SYSTEMS	COMPONENTS OF AN ACCOUNTING INFORMATION SYSTEM	SPECIAL JOURNALS AND POSTING OF TRANSACTIONS	BASIC THEORY OF ACCOUNTING INFORMATION SYSTEMS	COMPUTERIZED ACCOUNTING INFORMATION SYSTEMS
	• Accounts Receivable Subsidiary Ledger • Accounts Payable Subsidiary Ledger	• Revenue Journal • Cash Receipts Journal • Purchases Journal • Cash Payments Journal • Use of the General Journal • Summary of the Recording Process	• Underlying Assumptions • Developmental Phases	• Advantages and Disadvantages • Peachtree Complete 2008—An Illustration

Learning Objective 1

Describe processing methods of accounting information systems.

MANUAL VERSUS COMPUTERIZED ACCOUNTING INFORMATION SYSTEMS

The term **accounting information system (AIS)** refers to everything involved in collecting, processing, and distributing accounting information for managers to use internally or creditors and investors to use externally. Chapters 1–4 presented the basic elements of an accounting system. In reality, however, most businesses need a more detailed system than the one illustrated in those chapters. For example, The UPS Store needs to know more than the fact that together, customers owe $6,476. Rather, the store needs to know which specific customers owe which particular amounts. To provide this extra detail, an accounting information system must include some additional tools for tracking transactions as well as a certain degree of computerization.

Although a few small businesses still use a **manual accounting information system** that records and processes all financial information by hand on paper, today most accounting information systems are computerized. A **computerized accounting information system** uses a software program to perform basic bookkeeping functions. The program journalizes and posts transactions, prepares trial balances, and generates financial statements, all electronically. See Exhibit 5.1 for the features of computerized accounting systems, compared to manual systems.

Exhibit 5.1 Comparison of Features of Manual and Computerized Accounting Systems

	Manual System	Computerized System
Journalizing and posting	• Performed by hand • Extremely time consuming	• Performed by computer • Quick and easy
Handling of errors	• Error prone • Finding and correcting errors can be time consuming	• Virtually error free • Program identifies journal entries that are out of balance and will not record them until the error is corrected
Financial statement preparation	• Prepared by hand • Extremely time consuming	• Prepared by computer • Quick and easy
Accountant's responsibilities	• Mainly bookkeeping tasks	• Bookkeeping • Ensuring that all transactions and adjustments have been recorded

Although a computerized accounting system automates the basic bookkeeping functions, it does not eliminate the need for an accountant. Instead, it frees the accountant to focus on more important functions, such as:

- Ensuring that all transactions have been entered into the system.
- Making necessary adjustments at the end of each accounting period.

Because computerized accounting systems simplify the bookkeeping process, you might think they are easier to understand as well. As Exhibit 5.2 shows, however, that is not the case. The process of double-entry bookkeeping is easy to see and trace in a manual accounting system because every transaction results in recording both debits and credits in the same place and at the same time using the same journal entry. That is often not the case for a computerized system, which may use one computer module to record one part of a transaction and a different module to record other parts of the same transaction. In summarizing the results of the transaction, the program later combines information from the various modules.

Exhibit 5.2 Understanding Manual versus Computerized Accounting Systems

Manual Accounting System	Computerized Accounting System

Easier to Understand because transactions are: • Processed by hand • Easily traced back to specific journal entries • Easily traced to corresponding postings in the ledger accounts	**More Difficult to Understand** because some parts of a transaction are • Processed by different parts of the software • Often accessible only by specific program modules • Processed behind the scenes, making transactions difficult if not impossible to trace

The differences in Exhibit 5.2 explain why, in Chapters 1–4, you learned to process all steps in the accounting cycle by hand. As with any automated technology (such as spreadsheets and electronic calculators), you need to understand what the technology can do for you before you can use it properly. Because a manual system is easier to understand than a computerized system, we use it here to introduce the extra tools businesses need to track their accounting transactions. Later in this chapter, when we illustrate the computerized accounting program Peachtree Complete 2008, you will better appreciate what such programs can do for you.

SELF-STUDY PRACTICE

Indicate whether each of the following statements represents a characteristic of a manual (M) or computerized (C) accounting information system.

1. The accountant performs mainly bookkeeping tasks. _______
2. Journalizing, posting, and financial statement preparation are performed quickly and easily. _______
3. Debits and credits are recorded in the same place and at the same time using the same journal entry. _______
4. It frees the accountant to ensure that all transactions have been entered into the system and to make the necessary adjustments at the end of each accounting period. _______
5. Some transactions are difficult to trace because they are performed behind the scenes. _______

After you have finished, check your answers with the solution at the bottom of the page.

Solution to Self-Study Practice

1. M 2. C 3. M 4. C 5. C

Learning Objective 2

Describe components of an accounting information system.

COMPONENTS OF AN ACCOUNTING INFORMATION SYSTEM

The accounting steps illustrated in Chapters 1–4 involved recording transactions in the general journal, posting them to the general ledger accounts (sometimes represented by T-accounts), and summarizing the results in the financial statements. At the end of the accounting period, you could easily determine the total balance in any account by looking at either the financial statements or the general ledger accounts. But what if the following happens?

- A specific customer wants to know how much he owes The UPS Store on June 10 of the current year.
- The UPS Store needs to pay the accounts payable owed to a supplier on October 18.

General ledger account balances are not useful for supplying this type of detailed information because they report totals, not amounts pertaining to specific individuals or businesses.

To accomplish these tasks, businesses use subsidiary ledgers. A **subsidiary ledger** is used to group accounts that share a common feature. Two of the most frequently used subsidiary ledgers are:

1. The **accounts receivable subsidiary ledger** used to track accounts receivable transactions and balances for individual customers.
2. The **accounts payable subsidiary ledger** used to track accounts payable transactions and balances for individual creditors.

Accounts Receivable Subsidiary Ledger

Keeping detailed records for each individual customer is a massive undertaking, so The UPS Store uses an accounts receivable subsidiary ledger to manage the task. Assume that on September 30, The UPS Store has a total of $6,476 in Accounts Receivable as shown in the general ledger in the top portion of Exhibit 5.3. This balance consists of various amounts owed by individual customers. The accounts receivable subsidiary ledger contains the details of each customer's account, as shown in the bottom portion of Exhibit 5.3.

You can think of a general ledger account as a large file drawer and the accounts receivable subsidiary ledger as a collection of file folders for the various customers, arranged in alphabetical order. Each file folder contains the following information:

- The customer's name.
- A chronological record of the services charged to the customer's account.
- A chronological record of the payments the customer has made on the account.
- An up-to-date balance indicating the amount the customer currently owes.

If you examine the bottom portion of Exhibit 5.3 closely, you will see all four of these elements in the subsidiary ledger. Thus, The UPS Store has an up-to-date balance for each customer at all times.

The individual customer accounts in the accounts receivable subsidiary ledger and the Accounts Receivable general ledger account serve complementary purposes.

- The subsidiary ledger accounts capture and report a detailed transaction history for each customer.
- The general ledger account captures and reports the same information but in a highly summarized form.

Because the same information is captured in different places, accountants can use the Accounts Receivable general ledger account as a way to double-check the information recorded in the subsidiary ledger accounts. To use the general ledger account in this way, as a **control account**, the total of the subsidiary ledger accounts is computed at the end of each month. A list called a schedule of accounts receivable is prepared by listing each customer account name and balance as shown in Exhibit 5.4. Notice that the total of these balances in Exhibit 5.4 ($6,476) matches the ending balance in the Accounts Receivable control account (shown in the top of Exhibit 5.3), as it should if no errors are made.

Exhibit 5.3 Accounts Receivable Account and Accounts Receivable Subsidiary Ledger

General Ledger

Accounts Receivable				Acct. No. 110
Date	Item	Debit	Credit	Balance
Aug. 31	Bal.			5,416
Sep. 30		7,300		12,716
Sep. 30			6,240	6,476

Accounts Receivable Subsidiary Ledger

Downtown Dental Services				
Date	Item	Debit	Credit	Balance
Aug. 31	Bal.			2,410
Sep. 1		1,389		3,799
Sep. 18			2,410	1,389

Gallegos Gift Shop				
Date	Item	Debit	Credit	Balance
Aug. 31	Bal.			886
Sep. 12		1,825		2,711
Sep. 29			1,000	1,711

Keays Optical				
Date	Item	Debit	Credit	Balance
Aug. 31	Bal.			1,277
Sep. 20		2,298		3,575
Sep. 22			1,987	1,588

Matthews Custom Computers				
Date	Item	Debit	Credit	Balance
Aug. 31	Bal.			843
Sep. 21		1,788		2,631
Sep. 28			843	1,788

Coach's Tip

The total of the individual balances in the accounts receivable subsidiary ledger must equal the total for the Accounts Receivable account in the general ledger ($1,389 + $1,711 + $1,588 + $1,788 = $6,476).

Exhibit 5.4 Schedule of Accounts Receivable

Downtown Dental Services	$ 1,389
Gallegos Gift Shop	1,711
Keays Optical	1,588
Matthews Custom Computers	1,788
Total	$ 6,476

When using an accounts receivable subsidiary ledger, a company must record any transactions with customers on account in both the subsidiary ledger and the Accounts Receivable account. This requires that journal entries include the customers' names. For example, Exhibit 5.5 shows the journal entry to record services provided on account to Downtown Dental Services. Notice that the first line of the journal entry indicates the control account name (Accounts Receivable) as well as the subsidiary ledger account name (Downtown Dental Services). Both parts are needed because **transactions with customers on account are posted to both the**

Exhibit 5.5 General Journal Entry Involving a Subsidiary Ledger Account

Date	Account Titles	Ref.	Debit	Credit
Sep. 1	Accounts Receivable—Downtown Dental Services	110/✓	1,389	
	Fees Earned	410		1,389

control account and a subsidiary ledger account to ensure the control account balance equals the total of the subsidiary accounts.

When the debit to the Accounts Receivable control account and the related subsidiary account (Downtown Dental Services) is posted, the Ref. column (in Exhibit 5.5) indicates the account number (110) for the control account and a checkmark (✓) for the subsidiary account. A slash (/) separates the references to indicate that the debit has been posted in these two separate locations.

Accounts Payable Subsidiary Ledger

Much like the accounts receivable subsidiary ledger, the accounts payable subsidiary ledger provides detailed information on all purchases and payments that The UPS Store has made on account as well as the current balance owed to each individual creditor. Collectively, these balances add to the outstanding balance in the Accounts Payable account in the general ledger.

The accounts payable subsidiary ledger looks exactly like the accounts receivable subsidiary ledger. The only difference is that it tracks creditor transactions rather than customer transactions. At the end of the month, the accountant compiles a schedule of accounts payable to verify that the individual balances in the subsidiary ledger equal the balance in the Accounts Payable account in the general ledger. The procedures for recording transactions in the accounts payable subsidiary ledger are virtually identical to those for the accounts receivable subsidiary ledger.

Advantages of Subsidiary Ledgers

At this point, you may be thinking that subsidiary ledgers require a lot of extra work. In the long run, subsidiary ledgers actually save time and effort and simplify the accounting process. See Exhibit 5.6 for a summary of the many advantages of using subsidiary ledgers.

Exhibit 5.6 Advantages of Using Subsidiary Ledgers

- **Provides dedicated accounts for individual customers and creditors**
  Each customer or creditor has an individual account in which all transactions for that customer or creditor are recorded. Thus, the company can maintain accurate, up-to-date account balances for individual customers and creditors.
- **Reduces unnecessary detail in the general ledger accounts**
  Because the details of each transaction are entered into the subsidiary ledger accounts, only a summary entry must be made in the general ledger. This arrangement, which requires far fewer entries, reduces labor.
- **Makes locating errors in individual customer and creditor accounts easier**
  Because all details for individual customers or creditors are located only in the subsidiary ledgers, the potential for errors is reduced.
- **Allows for division of labor**
  If all accounts are located in one place, the work of maintaining them cannot be divided among several individuals. Because the accounts receivable and accounts payable subsidiary ledgers are updated separately from the general ledger, the three ledgers can be maintained by three different individuals, which reduces the risk of undetected errors.

To make sure you understand how subsidiary and control accounts work, take a moment to try the following Self-Study Practice.

SELF-STUDY PRACTICE

Indicate whether each of the following is a true (T) or false (F) statement regarding the components of an accounting information system.

1. Subsidiary ledgers can be used only for accounts receivable and accounts payable transactions. _______
2. A schedule of accounts receivable is a list of all transactions in the Accounts Receivable account in the general ledger. _______
3. One advantage of using subsidiary ledgers is that they make locating errors in individual customer and creditor accounts easier. _______
4. Another name for a subsidiary ledger account is a control account. _______
5. A checkmark in the Ref. column of the general journal indicates that the amount has been posted to the general ledger. _______

After you have finished, check your answers with the solution at the bottom of the page.

SPECIAL JOURNALS AND POSTING OF TRANSACTIONS

Learning Objective 3
Journalize and post transactions using special journals and subsidiary ledgers.

Imagine how many times a day companies such as The UPS Store collect money from customers and make payments to creditors. If accountants were to record a general journal entry each time Cash was debited or credited, they would be exhausted after only a few hours. Reading through earlier chapters, you yourself may have thought, "There must be an easier way to do this—I am writing Cash and Accounts Receivable over and over again!"

In this section, we introduce special journals, which provide an efficient way to account for repetitive, frequent transactions. By aggregating similar journal entries in one special journal, accountants can greatly reduce the amount of time and effort needed to journalize and post transactions. **Special journals do not eliminate the need for a general journal,** but they do allow the general journal to be used only for transactions that cannot be recorded efficiently in special journals.

Several types of special journals can be tailored to the needs of a particular business, but we limit our discussion to the four most common ones: the revenue journal, cash receipts journal, purchases journal, and cash payments journal.

Revenue Journal

Assume The UPS Store recorded the general journal entries shown in Exhibit 5.7.

Ordinarily, these four transactions would require you to perform the following tasks:

- Prepare the four journal entries shown.
- Post eight times to the general ledger accounts.
- Post four more times to the individual subsidiary ledger accounts.

Considering that the average UPS Store probably makes hundreds of such entries each day, it should be clear that no one has enough time to record them all in a general journal. Instead, accountants have created the revenue journal for recording these transactions efficiently. A revenue journal is used only for recording revenues earned on account, such as those in Exhibit 5.7. If a revenue journal were used instead of a general journal, those four transactions would be recorded as in Exhibit 5.8.

The five columns in the revenue journal in Exhibit 5.8 serve the following purposes:

1. ***Date.*** This column indicates the date on which a customer is billed for services provided on account. The bill is commonly called an invoice and may take the form of a sales slip or billing statement given to a customer at the time the services are provided.

Solution to Self-Study Practice

1. F—Subsidiary ledgers can be used for any group of accounts that share a common feature such as inventory or fixed assets.
2. F—It is a listing of individual customer account balances at the end of an accounting period.
3. T—This is one of many advantages of using subsidiary ledgers.
4. F—A control account is another name for a general ledger account that is supported by a subsidiary ledger.
5. F—A checkmark indicates that the amount has been posted to the subsidiary ledger.

Exhibit 5.7 General Journal

Date	Account Titles	Ref.	Debit	Credit
Sep. 1	Accounts Receivable—Downtown Dental Services	110/✓	1,389	
	Fees Earned	410		1,389
12	Accounts Receivable—Gallegos Gift Shop	110/✓	1,825	
	Fees Earned	410		1,825
20	Accounts Receivable—Keays Optical	110/✓	2,298	
	Fees Earned	410		2,298
29	Accounts Receivable—Matthews Custom Computers	110/✓	1,788	
	Fees Earned	410		1,788

2. ***Invoice No.*** All invoices are sequentially numbered, and the invoice number is shown in the Invoice No. column to ensure that all invoices have been accounted for at the end of the month. Thus, even if an invoice has been voided, it must be recorded as on the September 10 line of Exhibit 5.8.
3. ***Account Debited.*** The Account Debited column indicates the specific subsidiary account (customer) that is debited. Because all transactions in the revenue journal are debited to Accounts Receivable, indicating the name of the control account in this column is not needed.
4. ***Ref.*** This column is used to indicate whether an invoice has been recorded in a customer's account in the subsidiary ledger. For example, the checkmark in Exhibit 5.8 for Downtown Dental Services is placed in the Ref. column when the fees charged on account for Downtown Dental Services ($1,389) are debited to that customer's subsidiary ledger account. **Postings to the subsidiary ledger are done daily** to ensure that customer balances are always up to date.
5. ***Accounts Receivable Dr. Fees Earned Cr.*** This column lists the individual amounts charged to each customer, which have been recorded in the subsidiary ledger each day. These amounts have not been recorded in the general ledger, so they are totaled at the end of the month and recorded as a single entry in the Accounts Receivable control account and the Fees Earned revenue account in the general ledger. The total in this column of the revenue journal actually represents a journal entry, so it is posted to the ledger accounts just like any other journal entry. The debit is recorded first followed by the credit as indicated by the account numbers (110/410) in Exhibit 5.8. A benefit of using the revenue journal is that **postings to the general ledger are made at the end of the accounting period,** which saves time and makes the posting process more efficient.

Coach's Tip

Individual transactions are posted to customer accounts in the accounts receivable subsidiary ledger each day, but their total is posted only at the end of each month to the Accounts Receivable control account in the general ledger.

Exhibit 5.8 Revenue Journal

Revenue Journal — Page 2

Date	Invoice No.	Account Debited	Ref.	Accts Receivable Dr. Fees Earned Cr.
Sep. 1	820	Downtown Dental Services	✓	1,389
10	821	VOID	—	—
12	822	Gallegos Gift Shop	✓	1,825
20	823	Keays Optical	✓	2,298
29	824	Matthews Custom Computers	✓	1,788
		Total		7,300
				(110 / 410)

See Exhibit 5.9 for a summary of postings from the revenue journal to the subsidiary ledger and general ledger accounts.

Exhibit 5.9 Summary of Postings from the Revenue Journal

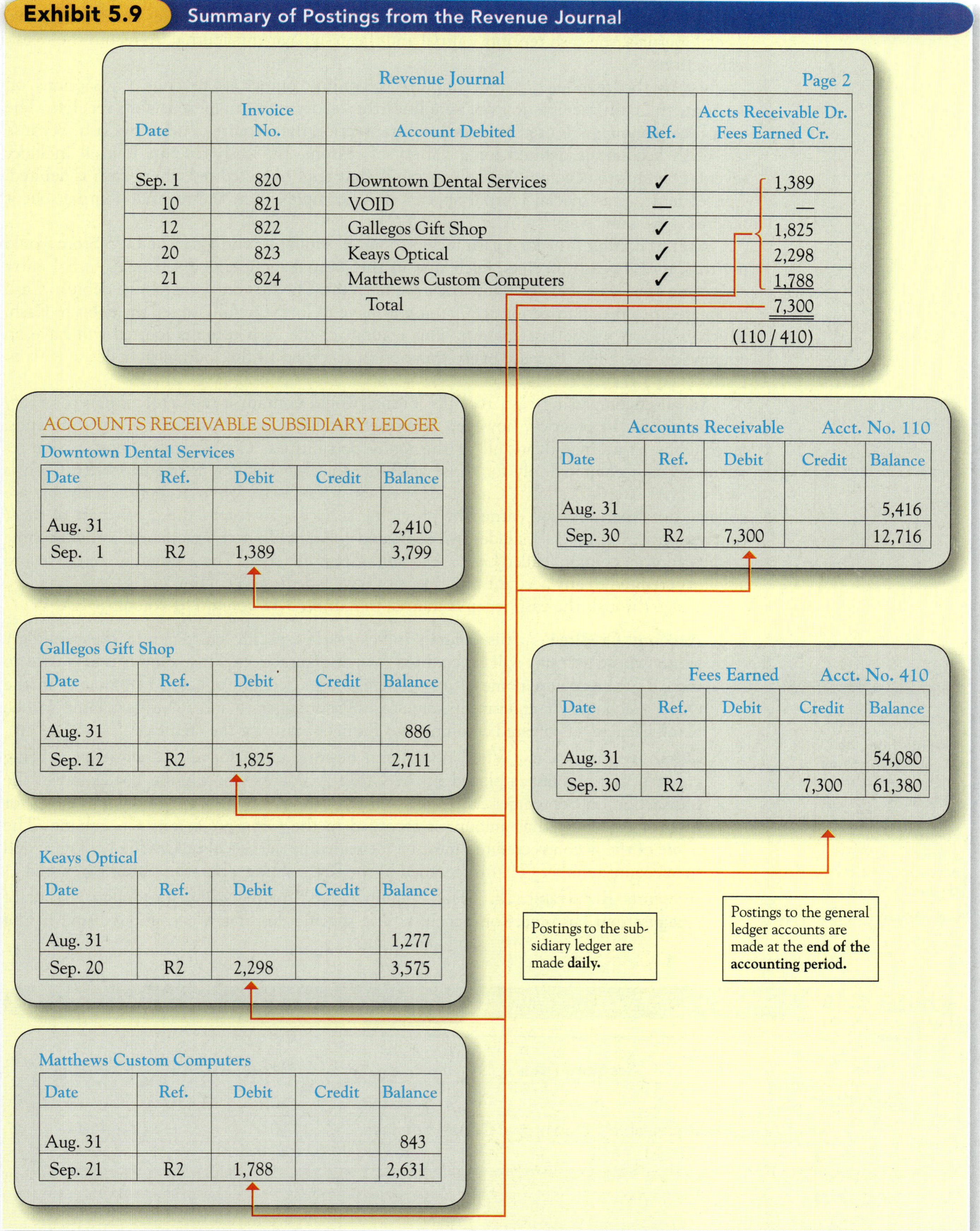

Revenue Journal — Page 2

Date	Invoice No.	Account Debited	Ref.	Accts Receivable Dr. Fees Earned Cr.
Sep. 1	820	Downtown Dental Services	✓	1,389
10	821	VOID	—	—
12	822	Gallegos Gift Shop	✓	1,825
20	823	Keays Optical	✓	2,298
21	824	Matthews Custom Computers	✓	1,788
		Total		7,300
				(110 / 410)

ACCOUNTS RECEIVABLE SUBSIDIARY LEDGER

Downtown Dental Services

Date	Ref.	Debit	Credit	Balance
Aug. 31				2,410
Sep. 1	R2	1,389		3,799

Gallegos Gift Shop

Date	Ref.	Debit	Credit	Balance
Aug. 31				886
Sep. 12	R2	1,825		2,711

Keays Optical

Date	Ref.	Debit	Credit	Balance
Aug. 31				1,277
Sep. 20	R2	2,298		3,575

Matthews Custom Computers

Date	Ref.	Debit	Credit	Balance
Aug. 31				843
Sep. 21	R2	1,788		2,631

Accounts Receivable — Acct. No. 110

Date	Ref.	Debit	Credit	Balance
Aug. 31				5,416
Sep. 30	R2	7,300		12,716

Fees Earned — Acct. No. 410

Date	Ref.	Debit	Credit	Balance
Aug. 31				54,080
Sep. 30	R2		7,300	61,380

Cash Receipts Journal

Until now, we have recorded individual cash receipts with a general journal entry such as the one in Exhibit 5.10. For a company such as The UPS Store, many transactions involve the Cash account. Given the heavy use of the Cash account, most companies prefer to use two special journals, the cash receipts journal and the cash payments journal, to record their cash transactions.

Just as the revenue journal simplifies recording numerous revenue transactions on account, the cash receipts journal simplifies the recording of numerous cash receipts. The **cash receipts journal** is used to record any transaction that requires a debit to Cash. Because the Cash account is debited for a variety of reasons, the cash receipts journal includes several columns to accommodate all accounts that might be credited when Cash is debited. Consequently, this special journal appears more complex than the revenue journal, but it functions the same way.

Refer to Exhibit 5.11 for a cash receipts journal similar to one that The UPS Store would use to record its cash receipts. Each line in the journal represents a separate journal entry consisting of at least one debit and at least one credit. The first entry includes a debit to Cash and a credit to Fees Earned for $820. You may have to look carefully to see the debit to Cash, which is shown in the last column. This column of the cash receipts journal will have an amount on every line because every transaction recorded in the journal includes a debit to Cash.

An all-encompassing cash receipts journal would contain a separate column for every possible credit. In practice, however, a business would require hundreds, if not thousands, of columns to accommodate all of the many possibilities. Consequently, most businesses set up specific columns only for those accounts that are credited frequently when Cash is received. At The UPS Store, Cash is debited most frequently when accounts receivable are collected or when fees are earned by providing services. To record the credit part of these transactions, Exhibit 5.11 includes two dedicated coloums. To accommodate all other possible credits, another column, called Other Accounts Cr., is included. This column is used to record amounts credited to any account that does not have a dedicated column.

Let's go through the cash receipts journal in Exhibit 5.11 column by column.

1. **Account Credited.** This column indicates the specific customer in the subsidiary ledger whose account will be credited for the transaction. This column is also used to indicate the account name of any general ledger account affected by amounts in the Other Accounts Cr. column. In some cases (September 15 and 30), this column will be blank because a dedicated column (Fees Earned) exists for the credits.
2. **Other Accounts Cr.** When no column heading exists for an account that is being credited, the amount is placed in the Other Accounts Cr. column. For example, the transaction on September 20 relates to interest revenue. Because no column exists for Interest Revenue, that amount is recorded in the Other Accounts Cr. column. The name of the account credited must be identified in the Account Credited column, and the account number (710) is recorded in the Ref. column when the amount is posted.
3. **Accounts Receivable Cr.** This column is used for recording the dollar amount of receipts from customers on account. The specific customer's account is listed in the

Coach's Tip

Postings from the Other Accounts Cr. column are typically made on a daily basis. Postings to the Accounts Receivable control account, Fees Earned, and Cash accounts must be done on a monthly basis.

Exhibit 5.10 General Journal

Date	Account Titles	Ref.	Debit	Credit
Sep. 18	Cash	105	2,410	
	Accounts Receivable—Downtown Dental Services	110/✓		2,410

Exhibit 5.11 Cash Receipts Journal

Cash Receipts Journal — Page 3

Date	Account Credited	Ref.	Other Accounts Cr.	Accounts Receivable Cr.	Fees Earned Cr.	Cash Dr.
Sep. 15					820	820
18	Downtown Dental Services	✓		2,410		2,410
20	Interest Revenue	710	80			80
22	Keays Optical	✓		1,987		1,987
28	Matthews Custom Computers	✓		843		843
29	Gallegos Gift Shop	✓		1,000		1,000
30			—	—	890	890
	Totals		80	6,240	1,710	8,030
			(✓)	(110)	(410)	(105)

Account Credited column. For example, the entry on September 18 illustrates a cash receipt of $2,410 on account from Downtown Dental Services. The ✓ indicates that the amount was posted to the accounts receivable subsidiary ledger. Subsidiary ledger postings are made on a daily basis.

4. **Fees Earned Cr.** This column is used for recording cash received from customers at the time services are provided.
5. **Cash Dr.** This column is used for recording the amount of each debit to Cash.

Posting to the General Ledger

The accounts receivable subsidiary ledger will be completely up to date on September 30 because all transactions involving individual customer accounts have been posted daily. However, in most cases, cash transactions involving the general ledger accounts are not posted from the cash receipts journal until the end of the month. So, at the end of the period, the columns in the cash receipts journal must be totaled and the totals posted to the general ledger accounts. Totaling the numbers in a column in this manner is to foot the column. These end-of-month totals are posted to the appropriate general ledger account as in the CR3 postings in Exhibit 5.12.

You must also crossfoot the columns in a multiple-column journal at the end of the accounting period. Doing so means verifying that debits equal credits for the footed totals in the journal. Look at the cash receipts journal in Exhibit 5.11. Notice that:

- The amounts in the credit columns ($80 + $6,240 + $1,710) add to a total of $8,030 and
- The total amount debited to Cash is $8,030.

Because the columns on this journal page crossfoot, we can be confident that the entry is in balance (that is, debits equal credits).

When footed column totals are posted to the general ledger accounts, the account number is shown beneath the total. The Other Accounts Cr. column is one exception to this procedure. The total in this column is not posted anywhere as a single total because postings from this column are made to the general ledger on a daily basis. The checkmark (✓) under the column total in Exhibit 5.11 indicates that the amounts in this column were posted individually. The totals in the remaining columns must be posted to the general ledger accounts as shown in Exhibit 5.12.

Exhibit 5.12 End-of-Month Posting to the General Ledger

Cash — Acct. No. 105

Date	Item	Ref.	Debit	Credit	Balance
Aug. 31	Bal.				4,220
Sep. 30		CR3	8,030		12,250

Accounts Receivable — Acct. No. 110

Date	Item	Ref.	Debit	Credit	Balance
Aug. 31	Bal.				5,416
Sep. 30		R2	7,300		12,716
Sep. 30		CR3		6,240	6,476

Fees Earned — Acct. No. 410

Date	Item	Ref.	Debit	Credit	Balance
Aug. 31	Bal.				54,080
Sep. 30		R2		7,300	61,380
Sep. 30		CR3		1,710	63,090

The Ref. columns of the Cash, Accounts Receivable, and Fees Earned accounts in the general ledger (Exhibit 5.12) indicate the journal page on which each entry originated. The abbreviation CR stands for cash receipts. Therefore, the abbreviation CR3 in the Ref. column of the Cash account indicates that the underlying details of this entry can be found on page 3 of the cash receipts journal.

Preparation of the Schedule of Accounts Receivable

Although the accounts receivable subsidiary ledger is updated daily, the Accounts Receivable control account is updated only at the end of the month. Throughout the month, the balances in the control account and the subsidiary accounts differ. To determine whether errors were made in updating these records, the Accounts Receivable general ledger control account is reconciled to the accounts receivable subsidiary ledger at the end of the month. Exhibit 5.13 shows that the September balances in the subsidiary ledger accounts equal the $6,476 general ledger balance in Exhibit 5.12, so no errors had been made.

Exhibit 5.14 (page 215) summarizes the postings from the cash receipts journal. Some of the detail in the general ledger accounts and subsidiary ledger accounts has been eliminated to save space.

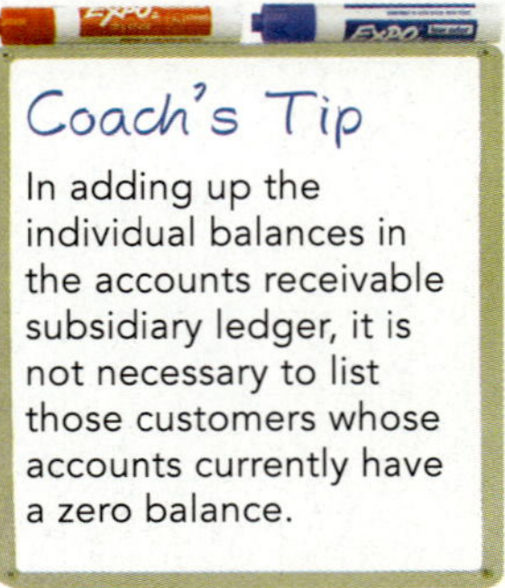

Coach's Tip

In adding up the individual balances in the accounts receivable subsidiary ledger, it is not necessary to list those customers whose accounts currently have a zero balance.

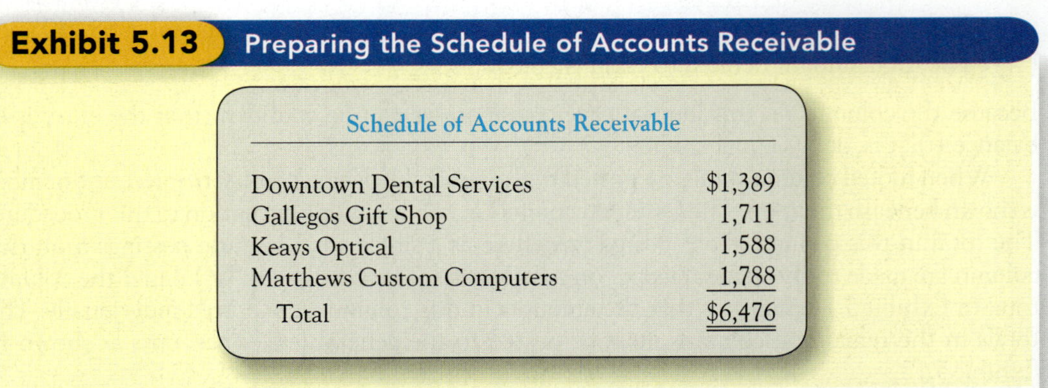

Exhibit 5.13 Preparing the Schedule of Accounts Receivable

Schedule of Accounts Receivable

Downtown Dental Services	$1,389
Gallegos Gift Shop	1,711
Keays Optical	1,588
Matthews Custom Computers	1,788
Total	$6,476

Exhibit 5.14 Summary of Postings from Cash Receipts Journal

Cash Receipts Journal Page 3

Date	Account Credited	Ref.	Other Accounts Cr.	Accounts Receivable Cr.	Fees Earned Cr.	Cash Dr.
Sep. 15					820	820
18	Downtown Dental Services	✓		2,410		2,410
20	Interest Revenue	710	80			80
22	Keays Optical	✓		1,987		1,987
28	Matthews Custom Computers	✓		843		843
29	Gallegos Gift Shop	✓		1,000		1,000
30					890	890
	Totals		80	6,240	1,710	8,030
			(✓)	(110)	(410)	(105)

ACCOUNTS RECEIVABLE SUBSIDIARY LEDGER

Downtown Dental Services

Date	Ref.	Debit	Credit	Balance
Aug. 31				2,410
Sep. 1	R2	1,389		3,799
Sep. 18	CR3		2,410	1,389

Gallegos Gift Shop

Date	Ref.	Debit	Credit	Balance
Aug. 31				886
Sep. 12	R2	1,825		2,711
Sep. 29	CR3		1,000	1,711

Keays Optical

Date	Ref.	Debit	Credit	Balance
Aug. 31				1,277
Sep. 20	R2	2,298		3,575
Sep. 22	CR3		1,987	1,588

Matthews Custom Computers

Date	Ref.	Debit	Credit	Balance
Aug. 31				843
Sep. 21	R2	1,788		2,631
Sep. 28	CR3		843	1,788

Cash Acct. No. 105

Date	Ref.	Debit	Credit	Balance
Aug. 31				4,220
Sep. 30	CR3	8,030		12,250

Accounts Receivable Acct. No. 110

Date	Ref.	Debit	Credit	Balance
Aug. 31				5,416
Sep. 30	R2	7,300		12,716
Sep. 30	CR3		6,240	6,476

Fees Earned Acct. No. 410

Date	Ref.	Debit	Credit	Balance
Aug. 31				54,080
Sep. 30	R2		7,300	61,380
Sep. 30	CR3		1,710	63,090

Interest Revenue Acct. No. 710

Date	Ref.	Debit	Credit	Balance
Aug. 31				0
Sep. 30	CR3		80	80

To make sure you understand how to use the revenue journal and the cash receipts journal, try the following Self-Study Practice.

SELF-STUDY PRACTICE

Indicate whether each of the following is a true (T) or false (F) statement regarding the use of special journals.

1. The revenue journal is used to record all transactions involving a credit to the Fees Earned account. _______
2. The Invoice No. column does not serve any useful purpose in the revenue journal. _______
3. Posting from the cash receipts journal and the revenue journal to the subsidiary ledger accounts is done at the end of the month. _______
4. Footing is the act of adding up a row of numbers to ensure that debits equal credits. _______
5. The notation (110/510) beneath a column of numbers in a journal indicates the date and time when a posting was made. _______

After you have finished, check your answers with the solution at the bottom of the page.

Coach's Tip

The purchases journal (below) has two different Ref. columns. The one on the left is used only to show the posting to the individual creditors for the Accounts Payable Cr. Column. The one on the right is used to identify the specific general ledger account that is debited when something is recorded in the Other Accounts Dr. column.

Purchases Journal

The **purchases journal** is used only to record purchases made and expenses incurred on account. Several columns are needed in this journal because the number of accounts that could be debited when Accounts Payable is credited is nearly limitless. The UPS Store, for example, might purchase any of the following items on account: store equipment, advertising, shipping supplies, and so on. The purchases journal must be able to accommodate each of them. Exhibit 5.15 is a page from a typical purchases journal.

Notice that some of the columns in the purchases journal are identical to those in the cash receipts journal (see Exhibit 5.11, page 213). Because of space considerations, we limit this analysis to those columns not discussed in connection with the cash receipts journal.

1. **Account Credited.** Because the purchases journal is used for recording all purchases made and expenses incurred on account, every transaction involves a creditor in the accounts payable subsidiary ledger. This column is used to identify the creditor whose subsidiary account is increased by each transaction.
2. **Accounts Payable Cr.** This column is used for recording the dollar amount of the credit to Accounts Payable.

Exhibit 5.15 Purchases Journal

Purchases Journal — Page 4

Date	Account Credited	Ref.	Accounts Payable Cr.	Shipping Supplies Dr.	Other Accounts Dr.		
					Accounts	Ref.	Amount
Sep. 11	XYZ Suppliers	✓	1,418	1,418			
18	Carlson Equipment	✓	2,000		Store Equipment	170	2,000
29	EmilRado Advertising Co.	✓	715		Advertising Expense	520	715
30	XYZ Suppliers	✓	500	500			
	Totals		4,633	1,918			2,715
			(210)	(115)			(✓)

Solution to Self-Study Practice

1. F—The revenue journal can be used only to record revenue transactions on account.
2. F—Keeping track of every invoice is important in the event an invoice is lost, misplaced, or otherwise unaccounted for.
3. F—Posting to the subsidiary ledger is performed on a daily basis.
4. F—Footing is adding up a column of numbers.
5. F—The 110 and 510 indicate that account 110 has been debited for the amount in the column and that a credit for the same amount has been placed into account 510.

3. **Shipping Supplies Dr.** When an account is used often (for example, the Shipping Supplies account at The UPS Store), a column should be created for it in the purchases journal. The number of Debit columns and the accounts they represent differs depending on the business. Commonly used debit columns in a purchases journal include Office Supplies, Equipment, and Inventory.
4. **Other Accounts Dr.** This column is used for identifying the name of any account being debited for which the purchases journal has no dedicated column.

Because the purchases journal has multiple columns, its columns must be footed and crossfooted like the ones in the cash receipts journal. Once the equality of debits and credits has been verified, the amounts can be posted. Remember that a checkmark (✓) below a column total indicates that the total should not be posted anywhere because the individual amounts were posted daily. After posting transactions from the purchases journal, selected general ledger accounts (illustrating an asset, liability, and expense) would appear as in Exhibit 5.16.

Coach's Tip

A separate column (Other Accounts Dr.) is required for any account that is debited but does not have a dedicated column. The additional column is required because the Account Credited column is used only to identify the specific subsidiary account being charged.

Cash Payments Journal

Just as the cash receipts journal is used to record all cash received by a business, a cash payments journal like the one in Exhibit 5.17 is used for recording all transactions involving cash payments.

1. **Check No.** All cash payments are made with sequentially numbered checks so that every check can be tracked. To ensure that every check has been accounted for, even voided checks are listed in the Cash Payments Journal as in Exhibit 5.17.
2. **Account Debited.** This column is for the name of the creditor whose account is being debited in the accounts payable subsidiary ledger or the specific general ledger account that is being debited in the Other Accounts Dr. column.
3. **Other Accounts Dr.** The dollar amounts recorded in this column are posted to general ledger accounts other than Cash and Accounts Payable. These accounts are identified by name in the Account Debited column.
4. **Accounts Payable Dr.** This is the dollar amount of those transactions that will be posted individually to the accounts payable subsidiary ledger and in total to the Accounts Payable general ledger account.

Because the cash payments journal is a multiple-column journal, its columns must be footed and cross-footed. If the column totals do not crossfoot, one or more errors have been made.

Exhibit 5.16 Posting to the General Ledger

Shipping Supplies — Acct. No. 115

Date	Item	Ref.	Debit	Credit	Balance
Aug. 31	Bal.				285
Sep. 30		P4	1,918		2,203

Accounts Payable — Acct. No. 210

Date	Item	Ref.	Debit	Credit	Balance
Aug. 31	Bal.				3,113
Sep. 30		P4		4,633	7,746

Advertising Expense — Acct. No. 520

Date	Item	Ref.	Debit	Credit	Balance
Aug. 31	Bal.				1,768
Sep. 29		P4	715		2,483

Exhibit 5.17 Cash Payments Journal

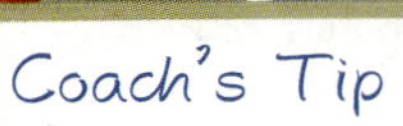

Coach's Tip

Amounts in the Other Accounts Dr. column must be posted daily. Amounts in the Accounts Payable Dr. column are posted daily to the subsidiary ledger and the total is posted at the end of the period to the Accounts Payable control account.

Cash Payments Journal — Page 8

Date	Check No.	Account Debited	Ref.	Other Accounts Dr.	Accounts Payable Dr.	Cash Cr.
Sep. 1	5601	Carlson Equipment	✓		1,228	1,228
2	5602	Advertising Expense	520	645		645
11	5603	VOID				
12	5604	EmilRado Advertising Co.	✓		365	365
26	5605	XYZ Suppliers	✓		1,538	1,538
29	5606	Shipping Supplies	115	325		325
30	5607	Salaries Expense	510	850		850
	Totals			1,820	3,131	4,951
				(✓)	(210)	(105)

As in earlier examples, the column totals in the cash payments journal must be posted to the appropriate general ledger accounts. See Exhibit 5.18 for selected general ledger accounts after the end-of-month postings have been made. The abbreviation used for all cash payment postings is CP8, indicating that the amounts recorded came from page 8 of the cash payments journal. **Notice that an entire month's worth of transactions has been recorded in the Cash account with nothing more than one debit and one credit.** This is the beauty (and ease) of using special journals.

A final step is required because the accounts payable subsidiary ledger has been updated continuously while the Accounts Payable control account was updated only at the end of the month. Thus, the Accounts Payable account in the general ledger must be reconciled with the related subsidiary ledger accounts through a schedule of accounts payable, as in Exhibit 5.19.

Use of the General Journal

Every business uses a general journal—even when it uses special journals—because certain transactions cannot be recorded in any of the special journals. Assume, for example, that The UPS Store purchased $4,000 of store equipment by issuing a note payable to Carlson

Exhibit 5.18 General Ledger after End-of-Month Postings

Cash — Acct. No. 105

Date	Item	Ref.	Debit	Credit	Balance
Aug. 31	Bal.				4,220
Sep. 30		CR3	8,030		12,250
Sep. 30		CP8		4,951	7,299

Accounts Payable — Acct. No. 210

Date	Item	Ref.	Debit	Credit	Balance
Aug. 31	Bal.				3,113
Sep. 30		P4		4,633	7,746
Sep. 30		CP8	3,131		4,615

Exhibit 5.19 Accounts Payable Control Account and Schedule of Accounts Payable

Accounts Payable — Acct. No. 210

Date	Item	Ref.	Debit	Credit	Balance
Aug. 31	Bal.				3,113
Sep. 30		P4		4,633	7,746
Sep. 30		CP8	3,131		4,615

Schedule of Accounts Payable

Carlson Equipment	$ 2,000
EmilRado Advertising Co.	715
XYZ Suppliers	1,900
Total	$ 4,615

Equipment. Initially, you might be tempted to record this entry in the purchases journal. However, the purchases journal can be used only for purchases made on account, and a note payable is not the same as an account payable. If this entry were recorded in the purchases journal, the note payable would never be recorded, and the balance in Accounts Payable would be $4,000 more than it should be. The proper treatment of this transaction is to record it in the general journal as in Exhibit 5.20.

In addition to this type of entry, the general journal is used to record all correcting entries, adjusting entries, and closing entries. So even though the general journal is used less often when special journals are used, it cannot be eliminated.

Coach's Tip

Transactions posted from a special journal should never be entered again into the general journal. To do so would be to journalize and post the transaction twice because special journals do in fact represent journal entries.

Summary of the Recording Process

See Exhibit 5.21 for an overview of the process for recording transactions when special journals and subsidiary ledgers are used.

Four points are worth emphasizing:

1. Transactions are entered into either the general journal or one of the four special journals, but not both.
2. Entries involving Accounts Receivable or Accounts Payable that are recorded in a special journal or in the general journal must be posted to **both** the subsidiary ledger account **and** the related general ledger control account.
3. Each month the subsidiary ledger accounts must be reconciled to the related control account in the general ledger (as indicated by the dotted line in Exhibit 5.21).
4. Information for preparing the financial statements must still be obtained from the general ledger.

See Exhibit 5.22 for a summary of the frequency of posting required for each of the journals.

Exhibit 5.20 Recording Unusual Transactions in the General Journal

Date	Account Titles and Explanation	Ref.	Debit	Credit
Sep. 1	Store Equipment	170	4,000	
	Notes Payable	250		4,000
	(Purchased equipment by issuing a note payable)			

Exhibit 5.21 Summary of the Recording Process for Special Journals and Subsidiary Ledgers

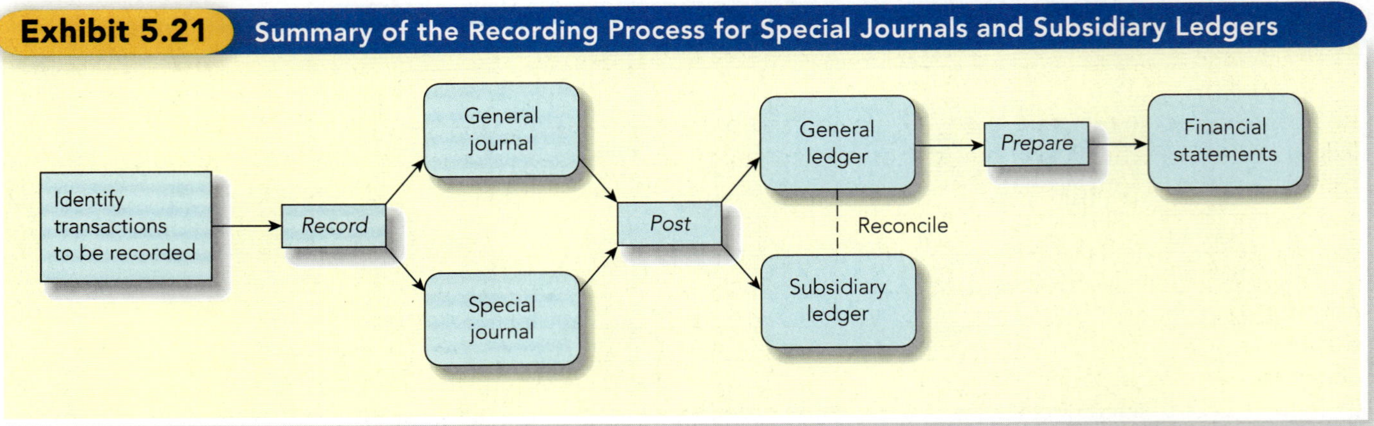

Exhibit 5.22 Frequency of Posting from Journals

Journal	Item	Posting Frequency
Revenue journal	Subsidiary Accounts Dr. (customers)	Daily
	Column totals to general ledger (GL)	Monthly
Cash receipts journal	Subsidiary Accounts Cr. (customers)	Daily
	Other Accounts Cr. items to GL	Daily
	Column totals (except Other) to GL	Monthly
Purchases journal	Subsidiary Accounts Cr. (creditors)	Daily
	Other Accounts Dr. items to GL	Daily
	Column totals (except Other) to GL	Monthly
Cash payments journal	Subsidiary Accounts Dr. (creditors)	Daily
	Other Accounts Dr. items to GL	Daily
	Column totals (except Other) to GL	Monthly
General journal	Subsidiary Accounts Dr./Cr. (all)	Daily
	General ledger accounts (all)	Daily

To make sure you understand how to use special journals, try the following Self-Study Practice.

SELF-STUDY PRACTICE

Indicate whether Legal Ease should use the revenue journal (R), cash receipts journal (CR), purchases journal (P), cash payments journal (CP), or general journal (G) to record each of the following events.

1. A check is written to Agro's Advertising for an advertisement in the local paper. ________
2. Cash is collected from a customer for a previous balance owed. ________
3. Legal Ease bought office supplies on account from Office Outlet, Inc. ________
4. Legal Ease prepared a legal brief on account for Superior Roofing. ________
5. End-of-period closing entries are made for Legal Ease. ________

After you have finished, check your answers with the solution at the bottom of the page.

Solution to Self-Study Practice

1. CP—All checks are essentially cash payments and, therefore, are recorded in the cash payments journal.
2. CR—Cash collections of any kind are recorded in the cash receipts journal.
3. P—Any purchases made on account are recorded in the purchases journal.
4. R—Services performed on account are recorded in the revenue journal.
5. G—Transactions that cannot be recorded in any of the special journals are recorded in the general journal.

BASIC THEORY OF ACCOUNTING INFORMATION SYSTEMS

Learning Objective 4

Explain the basic theory of accounting information systems.

In Chapters 2–4, you learned how to journalize and post daily transactions in the general ledger, prepare adjusting and closing entries, and generate end-of-period financial statements. During this process, you generated three different types of journal entries, three trial balances, and a set of general-purpose financial statements. This chapter has presented some additional tools for collecting and processing financial data efficiently and effectively.

The entire process described in Chapters 2–4 and in this chapter, along with the distribution of the resulting financial information to creditors and investors, is referred to as the accounting information system. An accounting information system includes the source documents used in preparing transactions (receipts, bills, checks) as well as the trial balances, journals, ledger accounts, schedules, and financial statements that are the end result of the process. In this section, we discuss some of the assumptions behind such systems and sketch the process of developing one from scratch.

Underlying Assumptions

The most effective accounting information systems have three basic features: usefulness, cost effectiveness, and flexibility.

1. **Usefulness.** An accounting information system must adequately meet the needs of a variety of different users whether they work in accounting, marketing, or production.
2. **Cost effectiveness.** As tempting as it might be to create the Rolls Royce of accounting systems, the benefits of an accounting system must be balanced against the costs of implementing and maintaining it.
3. **Flexibility.** An accounting information system must have the capacity to expand or shrink with a business's information needs.

How do you create an accounting information system that is useful, cost effective, and flexible? Achieving these goals requires a time-consuming development process.

Developmental Phases

The development of an accounting information system has four phases: analysis, design, implementation, and feedback.

1. **Analysis.** This first phase identifies the needs of both internal and external users. Internal users need to keep track of transactions with customers and creditors; investors need to assess the company's profitability; the bank needs to determine the likelihood that its loan will be repaid. A good accounting information system should adequately meet all these needs.
2. **Design.** In the second phase, design, planners create a cost-effective system that will meet the needs identified during the first phase. This step may require nothing more than selecting a suitable general ledger software program, or it may require creating a complex system that professional systems designers must implement. This phase of development must answer the critical question of whether the system will be manual or computerized.
3. **Implementation.** Proper implementation of the new system is critical to its success (or failure). A design that works "on paper" must be transformed into a workable, effective, and efficient system.
4. **Feedback.** A new accounting information system is likely to require occasional tweaking as certain aspects of its design prove unmanageable. In some cases, the business may even outgrow the system and require a more sophisticated design. Replacing an old design often involves switching from a manual to a computerized system.

Exhibit 5.23 summarizes the four phases in the development of an accounting information system.

In the next section, we examine a computerized accounting information system, the general ledger package Peachtree Complete 2008. But first, make sure you understand the

Exhibit 5.23 Development of an Accounting Information System

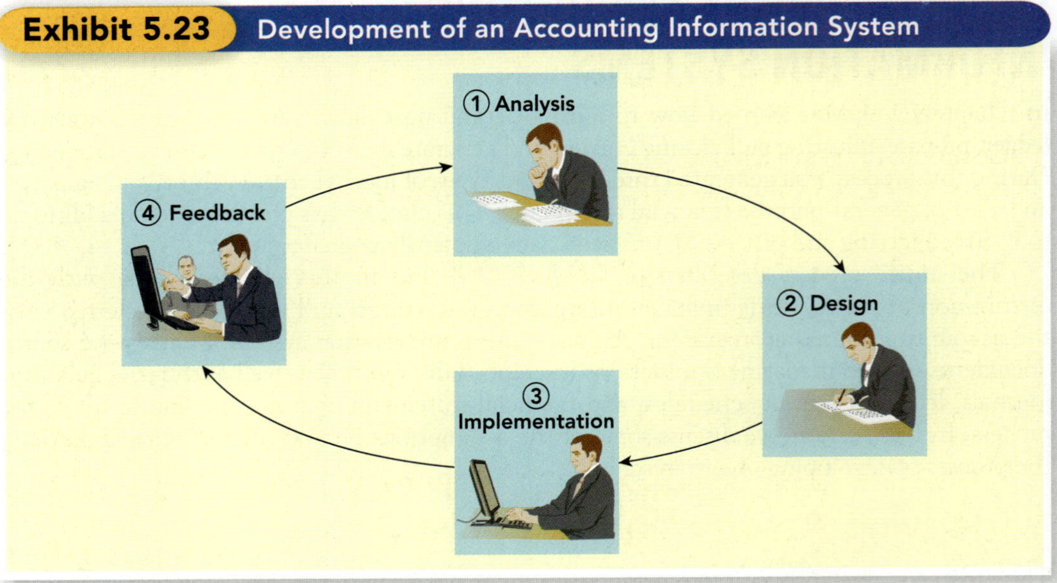

basic theory of accounting information systems by completing the following Self-Study Practice.

SELF-STUDY PRACTICE

Indicate whether each of the following statements regarding the basic theory of accounting information systems is true (T) or false (F).

1. Most accounting information systems are manual or computerized. ________
2. The underlying assumptions of accounting information systems are usefulness, flexibility, and design. ________
3. The correct order of the developmental phases of an accounting information system is design, analysis, implementation, and feedback. ________
4. A critical question that must be answered during the implementation phase of developing an accounting information system is whether the system will be manual or computerized. ________
5. A popular general ledger software package is Peachtree Complete 2008. ________

After you have finished, check your answers with the solution at the bottom of the page.

Learning Objective 5
Compare the advantages and disadvantages of manual and computerized accounting information systems.

COMPUTERIZED ACCOUNTING INFORMATION SYSTEMS

The use of computerized accounting information systems has become quite common, even by small businesses. Substantial declines in the cost of general ledger software packages and computer hardware are partly responsible for their increased use combined with an increase in user-friendly commercial general ledger software programs, such as Peachtree Complete 2008. What are the pros and cons of using such systems?

Advantages and Disadvantages

Computerized accounting information systems have three primary advantages:

1. **Fewer recording errors.** Computerized programs calculate invoice totals and account balances virtually without error.

Solution to Self-Study Practice

1. T.
2. F — The underlying assumptions of an accounting information system are usefulness, cost effectiveness, and flexibility.
3. F — The correct order of the development phases is analysis, design, implementation, and feedback.
4. F — This question is answered during the design phase of developing an accounting information system.
5. T.

2. **Simplified recordkeeping.** The information entered on a customer's invoice or creditor's bill is posted simultaneously to all subsidiary and general ledger accounts.
3. **Up-to-date balances.** Because account balances are always current, trial balances and/or financial statements can be generated at any time.

Compared to these advantages, computerized accounting systems have few disadvantages. These systems can create unexpected problems, however, such as:

1. **Information input errors.** That is, human errors can be made while inputting information into the system. Computers cannot distinguish between good information and bad information and will process both with dizzying speed.
2. **Lack of control over some accounting procedures.** Because much of the accounting process is performed internally in these programs, tracking down errors can be difficult.
3. **Ease of altering records.** Although changes and corrections are easier to make electronically than by hand, criminals also find it easier to commit fraud and/or engage in illegal activities electronically.

Peachtree Complete 2008—An Illustration

Assume managers at a local UPS Store recently analyzed their manual accounting information system. Based on projected growth of the business, managerial reporting requirements, and additional information requested by creditors, managers decided to convert to a computerized accounting information system. Because The UPS Store is a small service business with no complex reporting requirements, the managers agreed that the general ledger software package Peachtree Complete 2008 would easily accommodate both their managerial requirements and the information needs of any external users.

In this section, we examine various reports generated by Peachtree Complete 2008. This short example shows how the software generates and displays accounting reports similar to those shown earlier in this chapter using a manual system. The following reports are generated for The UPS Store:

1. **Sales Journal.** Peachtree Complete 2008 does not use a revenue journal. Instead, it prepares a sales journal. The major difference between the two is that a sales journal can be used by businesses that provide services as well as by those that sell goods (inventory). Unlike a manual accounting system, the sales journal contains both debit and credit columns. Compare the sales journal in Exhibit 5.24 to the Revenue Journal in Exhibit 5.8 (page 210).
2. **Cash receipts journal.** See Exhibit 5.25 for a cash receipts journal generated by Peachtree Complete 2008. Notice that it has only two columns containing the dollar amounts for debit and credit compared to the multiple columns in the manual version in Exhibit 5.11 (page 213).

Exhibit 5.24 Sales Journal

The UPS Store
Sales Journal
For the Period from Sep. 1, 2008 to Sep. 30, 2008

Filter criteria includes: Report order is by check date. Report is printed in detail format.

Date	Account ID	Invoice/CM #	Line Description	Debit Amnt	Credit Amnt
9/1/08	410	820	Shipping Fees Earned		1,389.00
	110		Downtown Dental Services	1,389.00	
9/10/08	110	821	Cash Customer		
9/10/08	110	821V	Cash Customer		
9/12/08	410	822	Shipping Fees Earned		1825.00
	110		Gallegos Gift Shop	1825.00	
9/20/08	410	823	Shipping Fees Earned		2,298.00
	110		Keays Optical	2,298.00	
9/21/08	410	824	Shipping Fees Earned		1,788.00
	110		Matthews Custom Computers	1,788.00	
		Total		7,300.00	7,300.00

Exhibit 5.25 Cash Receipts Journal

The UPS Store
Cash Receipts Journal
For the Period from Sep. 1, 2008 to Sep. 30, 2008

Filter criteria includes: Report order is by check date. Report is printed in detail format.

Date	Account ID	Transaction Ref	Line Description	Debit Amnt	Credit Amnt
9/15/08	410	101	Shipping Fees Earned		820.00
	105		Cash Customer	820.00	
9/18/08	110	2	Invoice: 757		2,410.00
	105		Downtown Dental Services	2,410.00	
9/20/08	710	Int	Interest Earned		80.00
	105		Albuquerque City Bank	80.00	
9/22/08	110	4	Invoice: 776		1,277.00
	110		Invoice: 823		710.00
	105		Keays Optical	1,987.00	
9/28/08	110	5	Invoice: 743		843.00
	105		Matthews Custom Computers	843.00	
9/29/08	110	6	Invoice: 755		886.00
	110		Invoice: 822		114.00
	105		Gallegos Gift Shop	1,000.00	
9/30/08	410	102	Shipping Fees Earned		890.00
	105		Cash Customer	890.00	
				8,030.00	**8,030.00**

3. **Customer ledgers.** Peachtree Complete 2008 refers to the accounts receivable subsidiary ledger simply as Customer Ledgers, as shown in Exhibit 5.26. Compare it to the accounts receivable subsidiary ledger in Exhibits 5.3 (page 207) and 5.14 (page 215).
4. **General ledger accounts.** See Exhibit 5.27 for the Accounts Receivable account in the general ledger as Peachtree Complete 2008 presented it. Note that the balance in the control account is the same as the balance in the customer ledgers. The transactions are not summarized as they are in a manual system. Instead they are very detailed because, unlike you and me, the computer does not get tired of posting. Note too that the references to the special journals (in the column labeled **Jrnl**) are SJ (sales journal) and CRJ (cash receipts journal).

Coach's Tip

Notice that the customer balances in the Balance column of Exhibit 5.26 are identical to those calculated manually in Exhibits 5.3 and 5.14. The only difference between manual and computerized accounting information systems is how the information is processed and displayed. The end result is the same using either process.

Exhibit 5.26 Customer Ledgers

The UPS Store
Customer Ledgers
For the Period from Aug. 31, 2008 to Sep. 30, 2008

Filter criteria includes: Report order is by ID. Report is printed in detail format.

Customer ID / Customer	Date	Trans No	Type	Debit Amt	Credit Amt	Balance
11	9/10/08	821	SJ			0.00
Cash Customer	9/10/08	821V	SJ			0.00
	9/15/08	101	CRJ	820.00	820.00	0.00
	9/30/08	102	CRJ	890.00	890.00	0.00
12	9/20/08	Int	CRJ	80.00	80.00	0.00
Albuquerque City Bank						
22	8/31/08	757	SJ	2,410.00		2,410.00
Downtown Dental Services	9/1/08	820	SJ	1,389.00		3,799.00
	9/18/08	2	CRJ		2,410.00	1,389.00
34	8/31/08	755	SJ	886.00		886.00
Gallegos Gift Shop	9/12/08	822	SJ	1,825.00		2,711.00
	9/29/08	6	CRJ		1,000.00	1,711.00
57	8/31/08	776	SJ	1,277.00		1,277.00
Keays Optical	9/20/08	823	SJ	2,298.00		3,575.00
	9/22/08	4	CRJ		1,987.00	1,588.00
66	8/31/08	743	SJ	843.00		843.00
Matthews Custom Computers	9/21/08	824	SJ	1,788.00		2,631.00
	9/28/08	5	CRJ		843.00	1,788.00
Report Total				**14,506.00**	**8,030.00**	**6,476.00**

Exhibit 5.27 General Ledger Accounts—Accounts Receivable

The UPS Store
General Ledger
For the Period from Sep. 1, 2008 to Sep. 30, 2008

Filter criteria includes: IDs: 110. Report order is by ID. Report is printed with shortened descriptions and with hide period subtotals.

Account ID Account Description	Date	Reference	Jrnl	Trans Description	Debit Amt	Credit Amt	Balance
110	9/1/08			Beginning Balance			5,416.00
Accounts Receivable	9/1/08	820	SJ	Downtown Dental	1,389.00		
	9/12/08	822	SJ	Gallegos Gift Shop	1,825.00		
	9/18/08	3	CRJ	Downtown Dental		2,410.00	
	9/20/08	823	SJ	Keays Optical	2,298.00		
	9/21/08	824	SJ	Matthews Custom	1,788.00		
	9/22/08	5	CRJ	Keays Optical - Inv		710.00	
	9/22/08	5	CRJ	Keays Optical - Inv		1,277.00	
	9/28/08	1	CRJ	Matthews Custom		843.00	
	9/29/08	6	CRJ	Gallegos Gift Shop		114.00	
	9/29/08	6	CRJ	Gallegos Gift Shop		886.00	
				Change	7,300.00	6,240.00	1,060.00
	9/30/08			**Ending Balance**			**6,476.00**

Clearly, the accumulation, presentation, and control of information is much easier, faster, and more accurate in a computerized accounting information system than in a manual system. However, users of a computerized system must take extra care to prevent both intentional misstatements and unintentional human errors.

Before you close this chapter, take a moment to complete the following Self-Study Practice.

SELF-STUDY PRACTICE

Indicate whether each of the following is an advantage of a computerized accounting system (C) or a manual accounting system (M).

1. Virtually all postings are error free. ________
2. Financial statement preparation takes relatively little time. ________
3. The process of double-entry accounting can be easily seen and traced. ________
4. The accountant has more time to spend on critical accounting issues. ________

After you have finished, check your answers with the solution at the bottom of the page.

Demonstration Case

Selected transactions of Miller Accounting, Inc., for the month of August, the first month of operations, are as follows:

Aug. 1 Issued Check 5280 for August office rent of $1,800.
3 Received $1,600 cash from Camel Enterprises for accounting services rendered today.
9 Issued Check 5281 for $850 of office supplies purchased today from Office Emporium.
12 Provided accounting services worth $2,500 on account to Willoby Warner (Invoice 201).
14 Purchased $6,000 of office equipment on account from Eli's Equipment.
16 Received $100 cash for office supplies sold to employees at cost.
21 Received $2,000 from Willoby Warner in payment of services provided on August 12.
23 Purchased $400 of office supplies on account from Rudy's Supplies.
27 Issued Check 5282 for $6,000 to Eli's Equipment as payment for August 14 purchase.
30 Purchased $20,000 office equipment from Rudy's Supplies by issuing a note payable.

Solution to Self-Study Practice

1. C—Because computers perform the postings, virtually no errors occur.
2. C—Computerized accounting systems are relatively efficient, whereas financial statements in a manual system must be prepared by hand and take a great deal of time.
3. M—Manual performance of all financial functions makes the double-entry process easier to see and trace.
4. C—Because performing tedious accounting functions takes less time, the accountant has more time to spend on important accounting issues.

Miller uses the following journals: a Revenue Journal, Cash Receipts Journal, Purchases Journal, Cash Payments Journal, and General Journal. Use the following account numbers where applicable: Office Supplies—115, Office Equipment—180, Notes Payable—250, and Rent Expense—615.

Required:

1. For each of the August transactions, indicate the journal in which to record the transaction.
2. Indicate whether the accounts receivable subsidiary ledger or the accounts payable subsidiary ledger would be affected by each transaction. If so, indicate the subsidiary ledger that would be affected. If not, write No effect.
3. Journalize all transactions for August in the appropriate journal. Post only to the subsidiary ledgers. However, record items in the Ref. column as if the daily postings to the general ledger accounts have been made.

Suggested Solution

1. Journal used to record transaction:

Aug. 1	Cash payments journal	Aug. 16	Cash receipts journal
3	Cash receipts journal	21	Cash receipts journal
9	Cash payments journal	23	Purchases journal
12	Revenue journal	27	Cash payments journal
14	Purchases journal	30	General journal

You may have placed the August 3 transaction in the revenue journal because it involved a customer. However, customers can charge services or simply pay for them at the time services are rendered. In this case, payment was made when the services were performed, requiring the use of the cash receipts journal. The same logic explains why the August 9 transaction is recorded in the cash payments journal rather than the purchases journal.

2. Subsidiary ledger affected:

Aug. 1	No effect	Aug. 16	No effect
3	No effect	21	Accounts receivable subsidiary ledger
9	No effect	23	Accounts payable subsidiary ledger
12	Accounts receivable subsidiary ledger	27	Accounts payable subsidiary ledger
14	Accounts payable subsidiary ledger	30	No effect

The transaction on August 3 has no impact on the accounts receivable subsidiary ledger because the customer paid cash for services rendered (this was not a collection on account). The same logic applies to the August 9 cash payment for office supplies.

3. Journalize transactions in the appropriate journal:

Revenue Journal — Page 1

Date	Invoice No.	Account Debited	Ref.	Accts Receivable Dr. Fees Earned Cr.
Aug. 12	201	Willoby Warner	✓	2,500

Cash Receipts Journal — Page 1

Date	Account Credited	Ref.	Other Accounts Cr.	Accounts Receivable Cr.	Fees Earned Cr.	Cash Dr.
Aug. 3					1,600	1,600
16	Office Supplies	115	100			100
21	Willoby Warner	✓		2,000		2,000

Purchases Journal — Page 1

Date	Account Credited	Ref.	Accounts Payable Cr.	Office Supplies Dr.	Other Accounts Dr.		
					Accounts	Ref.	Amount
Aug. 14	Eli's Equipment	✓	6,000		Office Equipment	180	6,000
23	Rudy's Supplies	✓	400	400			

The columns in this purchases journal differ somewhat from those used for The UPS Store. Special journals can be modified to meet the specific needs of each company, so be aware of the column headings the business uses.

Cash Payments Journal — Page 1

Date	Check No.	Account Debited	Ref.	Other Accounts Dr.	Accounts Payable Dr.	Cash Cr.
Aug. 1	5280	Rent Expense	615	1,800		1,800
9	5281	Office Supplies	115	850		850
27	5282	Eli's Equipment	✓		6,000	6,000

General Journal — Page 1

Date	Account Titles and Explanations	Ref.	Debit	Credit
Aug. 30	Office Equipment	180	20,000	
	Notes Payable	250		20,000
	(Equipment purchased on a Note Payable)			

This transaction involves a Note Payable rather than an Account Payable, so it is not entered in the purchases journal, which is reserved for purchases and charges made on account. If it were recorded in the purchases journal, the $20,000 would be credited erroneously to Accounts Payable rather than Notes Payable at the end of the accounting period.

ACCOUNTS RECEIVABLE SUBSIDIARY LEDGER

Willoby Warner

Date	Ref.	Debit	Credit	Balance
Aug. 12	R1	2,500		2,500
21	CR1		2,000	500

Note that the transaction with Camel Enterprises on August 3 has no impact on the accounts receivable subsidiary ledger.

ACCOUNTS PAYABLE SUBSIDIARY LEDGER

Eli's Equipment

Date	Ref.	Debit	Credit	Balance
Aug. 14	P1		6,000	6,000
27	CP1	6,000		0

Rudy's Supplies

Date	Ref.	Debit	Credit	Balance
Aug. 23	P1		400	400

Note that the transaction with Rudy's Supplies on August 30 has no impact on the accounts payable subsidiary ledger.

Chapter Summary

LO1 Describe processing methods of accounting information systems. p. 204

- Two different methods are used for processing accounting information.
    - Manual: all transactions are recorded and posted using paper and pen.
    - Computerized: all transactions are journalized and posted using proprietary software.
- Computerized accounting information systems can make the accounting function easier to perform, but the difficulty of following transactions through the system can make these systems more difficult to understand.

LO2 Describe components of an accounting information system. p. 206

- Accounts receivable subsidiary ledger: collects and maintains individual customer records for transactions made on account.
- Accounts payable subsidiary ledger: collects and maintains individual creditor records for transactions made on account.
- Advantages of using subsidiary ledgers:
    - Dedicated accounts for individual customers.
    - Omission of unnecessary detail from the general ledger accounts.
    - Ease of locating errors in individual customer and creditor accounts.
    - Division of labor.
- Control account—general ledger account that summarizes all transactions in the related subsidiary ledger.

LO3 Journalize and post transactions using special journals and subsidiary ledgers. p. 209

- Use the revenue journal to record all revenues earned from customers on account.
- Use the cash receipts journal to record all collections of cash (regardless of the purpose).
- Use the purchases journal to record all purchases or expenses recorded on account with creditors.
- Use the cash payments journal to record all payments of cash (regardless of the purpose).
- Use the general journal to record unusual, correcting, adjusting, and closing entries even if the business uses special journals.

LO4 Explain the basic theory of accounting information systems. p. 221

- The underlying assumptions of accounting information systems (AIS) are:
    - Usefulness: to adequately serve users, the AIS should be reliable, relevant, and accurate.
    - Cost effective: the usefulness of the AIS must be balanced against the cost of implementing it.
    - Flexibility: the AIS should meet the changing needs of a growing company.
- The developmental phases of an accounting system are:
    - Analysis: identify the needs of internal and external users.
    - Design: create a system that meets users' needs and determine whether it should be manual or computerized.
    - Implementation: transform a design on paper into a workable, effective, and efficient system.
    - Feedback: monitor the system periodically to ensure that needs are being met as planned.

LO5 Compare the advantages and disadvantages of manual and computerized accounting information systems. p. 222

- The advantages of using a computerized accounting information system include:
    - Fewer errors.
    - Simplified recordkeeping.
    - Up-to-date balances.
- The disadvantages of using a computerized accounting information system include:
    - Human errors made inputting information.
    - Loss of control over portions of the accounting process.
    - Ease of altering records and the potential for fraud.

Key Terms

Accounting Information System (AIS) (p. 204)
Accounts Payable Subsidiary Ledger (p. 206)
Accounts Receivable Subsidiary Ledger (p. 206)
Cash Payments Journal (p. 217)
Cash Receipts Journal (p. 212)
Computerized Accounting Information System (p. 204)
Control Account (p. 206)
Crossfoot the Columns (p. 213)
Foot (p. 213)
Manual Accounting Information System (p. 204)
Purchases Journal (p. 216)
Revenue Journal (p. 209)
Special Journal (p. 209)
Subsidiary Ledger (p. 206)

See complete glossary in back of text.

Questions

1. What is an accounting information system?
2. What is the key difference between manual and computerized accounting information systems?
3. Is it easier or more difficult to find errors in a computerized accounting information system? Why or why not?
4. Which is easier to understand: How a computerized accounting system functions or how a manual accounting system functions? Explain.
5. What is a subsidiary ledger? What type of information is contained in an accounts receivable subsidiary ledger?
6. What is a schedule of accounts receivable? Why is it necessary? When is it generated?
7. What are two advantages of using subsidiary ledgers?
8. Explain what a control account is. Describe each of the two control accounts illustrated in the chapter.
9. When subsidiary accounts are used without special journals, the Ref. column of the general journal will include a checkmark (✓) and an account number (210). What is the purpose of each?
10. What is a special journal? List the four special journals illustrated in the chapter.
11. What is the purpose of the revenue journal? How often are transactions posted to the general ledger Accounts Receivable account from this journal?
12. What is the purpose of the cash receipts journal? What types of transactions are recorded in this journal?
13. What types of transactions are recorded in the purchases journal?
14. What is the purpose of a cash payments journal? Are all cash payments recorded here? Why or why not?
15. Subsidiary ledger postings are made daily regardless of the special journal from which they are posted. Discuss the validity of this statement.
16. What does the following notation in the Ref. column of a special journal mean? CP4
17. Define the terms foot and crossfoot.
18. Is there a need for a general journal when special journals are used by a business? Why or why not?
19. What are the three underlying assumptions of accounting information systems?
20. Briefly describe the four developmental phases of an accounting information system.
21. List two advantages and two disadvantages of using a computerized accounting information system.

Multiple Choice

Quiz 5-1
www.mhhe.com/LLPW1e

1. All individual transactions with customers on account are tracked in the
   a. Accounts payable control account
   b. Accounts payable subsidiary ledger
   c. Accounts receivable control account
   d. Accounts receivable subsidiary ledger
2. A ✓ in the Ref. column of a special journal indicates that
   a. The transaction was posted to the applicable control account.
   b. The transaction was posted to the applicable general ledger account.
   c. The transaction was posted to the applicable subsidiary ledger.
   d. The transaction was not posted.
3. Which of the following is a true statement regarding special journals?
   a. The revenue journal is used for recording cash revenues.
   b. Posting to the subsidiary ledgers is done daily from all special journals and the general journal.
   c. The purchases journal is used for recording cash payments for purchases on account.
   d. In some cases the general journal will be used to record cash receipts.
4. Which of the following statements is false?
   a. The sum of the individual subsidiary accounts balances and the balance in the corresponding control account will not be equal until the end of the accounting period.
   b. Special journals are used to record repetitive, frequent transactions.
   c. Single column special journals must be crossfooted.
   d. The use of the general journal is not eliminated by the use of special journals.
5. In recording transactions to the subsidiary ledger and the control account, which of the following is a true statement?
   a. Transactions are posted daily to the subsidiary ledger and at the end of the accounting period to the control account.
   b. A transaction should be posted only to the subsidiary ledger or the control account; otherwise the transactions will be recorded twice.
   c. Both the control account and the subsidiary ledger should have identical balances at all times.
   d. All of these are true statements regarding the control account and subsidiary ledger.
6. Which of the following is a true statement regarding the use of subsidiary ledgers and special journals?
   a. The use of subsidiary ledgers reduces the number of transactions recorded in the control account.
   b. The use of subsidiary ledgers greatly increases individual efforts because everything is recorded twice.
   c. Special journals contain specific column headings that cannot be changed regardless of the type of business using them.
   d. A general journal is not required when special journals are used.

7. Which of the following is a true statement regarding the use of special journals?
   a. Crossfooting the revenue journal is a useful step that helps ensure errors are detected before amounts are posted to ledger accounts.
   b. Cash transactions can be recorded in any of the four special journals.
   c. All special journals contain at least two amount columns, one for the account debited and one for the account credited.
   d. A separate column is required when specific accounts are impacted that do not have a dedicated column in the special journal.
8. All of the following are true statements regarding posting from special journals except
   a. Postings to the subsidiary ledgers are made on a daily basis from the special journals.
   b. Postings to the control accounts are made at the end of the accounting period from the special journals.
   c. Postings to the subsidiary ledgers and control accounts are made on a daily basis from the general journal.
   d. Postings to the general ledger accounts are made at the end of the accounting period from the Other Accounts column of the special journals.
9. Which of the following is not a step in the development of an accounting information system?
   a. Implementation
   b. Flexibility
   c. Feedback
   d. Analysis
10. Which of the following is not an advantage of using a computerized accounting information system?
   a. Fewer transaction posting errors.
   b. Information input errors.
   c. Up-to-date balances in the subsidiary ledgers and general ledger at all times.
   d. Simplification of recordkeeping.

Solutions to Multiple-Choice Questions

1. d 2. c 3. b 4. c 5. a 6. a 7. d 8. d 9. b 10. b

Mini Exercises  Available with McGraw-Hill's Homework Manager

LO2 **M5-1 Identifying Appropriate Ledger for Specific Accounts**

Identify whether each of the following items would be found in the general ledger or a subsidiary ledger.

1. Accounts Payable—D & E Electric
2. Interest Earned
3. Office Supplies
4. Interest Receivable
5. Salaries Expense
6. Notes Payable
7. Accounts Receivable—Blaugrund
8. Notes Receivable

LO2 **M5-2 Determining Balance in Accounts Receivable Control Account**

Determine the balance in the Accounts Receivable control account (No. 110) as of August 31, 2009, by posting the following information about the revenues and receipts on account for Joy, Inc. during August 2009. Assume a balance of $2,000 in Accounts Receivable at July 31, 2009, all owed from Silky Somethings. You may omit any posting references.

	Revenues	Receipts
Lady-Like Apparel	$ 800	$ 200
Uptown Clothiers	147	147
Silky Somethings	675	375
Luxury Lingerie	950	950
Totals	$ 2,572	$ 1,672

LO2 **M5-3 Determining Balance in Accounts Payable Control Account**

Determine the balance in the Accounts Payable control account (No. 210) as of June 30, 2009, by posting the following purchases and payments made on account during June 2009. Assume a balance of $315 in Accounts Payable at May 31, 2009, all due to Midtown Suppliers. You may omit any posting references.

	Purchases	Payments
Classy Supplies, Inc.	$ 215	$ 112
Indigo Enterprises	52	52
Midtown Suppliers	410	515
Wholesale Suppliers Inc.	300	300
Totals	$ 977	$ 979

M5-4 Identifying Posting References in a Revenue Journal **LO3**

Using the revenue journal below, identify the appropriate posting reference for each of the letters (*a* – *f*) shown, as either:

1. An amount posted to the subsidiary ledger.
2. An amount posted to a general ledger account.
3. An amount not posted.

Revenue Journal Page 6

Date	Invoice No.	Account Debited	Ref.	Accts Receivable Dr. Fees Earned Cr.
Mar. 1	255	Koala Child Care	*a*	4,251
4	256	Blue Bird Day Care	*b*	2,795
15	257	Kindra Care	*c*	968
23	258	Leaning Tree Child Care	*d*	10,643
31	259	Creative Child Care	*e*	3,447
				22,104
				f

M5-5 Identifying Posting References in a Cash Receipts Journal **LO3**

Using the following cash receipts journal, identify the appropriate posting reference for each of the letters (*a* – *j*) shown, as either:

1. An amount posted to the subsidiary ledger.
2. An amount posted to a general ledger account.
3. An amount not posted.

Cash Receipts Journal Page 9

Date	Account Credited	Ref.	Other Accounts Cr.	Accounts Receivable Cr.	Fees Earned Cr.	Cash Dr.
Mar. 3	Koala Child Care	*a*		4,251		4,251
9	Blue Bird Day Care	*b*		1,000		1,000
15		*c*			2,741	2,741
18	Kindra Care	*d*		968		968
25	Interest Revenue	*e*	222			222
30	Leaning Tree Child Care	*f*	—	8,643	___	8,643
			222	14,862	2,741	17,825
			g	*h*	*i*	*j*

M5-6 Posting to the Accounts Receivable Control Account **LO2, 3**

Using the special journals presented in M5-4 and M5-5, determine the ending balance in the Accounts Receivable control account by posting the appropriate amounts into the following ledger account.

Accounts Receivable Acct. No. 110

Date	Item	Ref.	Debit	Credit	Balance
Feb 28	Balance				0

LO2, 3

M5-7 Posting to the Accounts Receivable Subsidiary Ledger and Preparing a Schedule of Accounts Receivable

Using the special journals from M5-4 and M5-5, perform the following tasks:

1. Assuming there are no balances in any of the customer accounts at February 28, post the necessary information to each of the customer accounts in the accounts receivable subsidiary ledger and determine the ending balance in each account.
2. Prepare a schedule of accounts receivable.

LO3

M5-8 Identifying the Appropriate Journal for Recording Transactions

Identify the appropriate journal that would be used to record each of the following transactions:

1. Cash paid for rent
2. Owner contribution of cash to business
3. Purchase of office supplies on account
4. Office supplies returned to supplier on account
5. Cash received for services rendered
6. Owner contribution of furniture to business
7. Cash payments to creditors on account
8. Revenue earned on account
9. Cash received from customers on account
10. Office supplies returned to supplier for cash

LO3

M5-9 Identifying the Appropriate Journal for Recording Transactions

Identify the appropriate journal that would be used to record each of the following transactions:

1. Revenue earned on account
2. Sales supplies returned to supplier for cash
3. Owner contribution of an automobile to the business
4. Cash payments to creditors on account
5. Purchase of sales supplies on account
6. Cash received for services rendered
7. Sales supplies returned to supplier on account
8. Cash received from customers on account
9. Owner contribution of cash to the business
10. Cash paid for annual fire insurance policy

LO3

M5-10 Identifying the Frequency of Posting from Various Journals

Freeburrow, Inc., uses a revenue journal, purchases journal, cash receipts journal, cash payments journal, and general journal for recording transactions. For each column of a special journal described below, indicate how often amounts in the column should be posted using the following: (The first one has been done for you.)

D—Daily only
T—In total only at the end of the accounting period
B—Both daily and in total at the end of the accounting period

Special Journal Column	Frequency of Posting
1. Cash column of a cash payments journal	T—In total only at the end of the accounting period
2. Other Accounts column of a cash receipts journal	
3. Column in a single column revenue journal	
4. Cash column of a cash receipts journal	
5. Fees Earned column of a cash receipts journal	
6. Accounts Payable column of a cash payments journal	
7. Other Accounts column of a cash payments journal	
8. All amounts recorded in a general journal	
9. Accounts Receivable column of a cash receipts journal	
10. Other Accounts column of a purchases journal	

M5-11 Identifying Columns in Special Journals LO3

Identify the special journal in which you would find the following column headings. (Note: Some column headings may be found in more than one special journal.)

1. Accounts Receivable Cr.
2. Accounts Payable Cr.
3. Ref.
4. Accts Receivable Dr./Fees Earned Cr.
5. Cash Cr.
6. Cash Dr.
7. Other Accounts Dr.
8. Accounts Payable Dr.
9. Other Accounts Cr.
10. Fees Earned Cr.

M5-12 Identifying the Underlying Assumptions of Accounting Information Systems LO4

Indicate whether each of the following statements regarding accounting information systems is true or false.

1. Flexibility in an accounting system is not realistic because accounting information systems are built to meet a specific need and any attempt to alter the system will render it unable to meet these needs.
2. An accounting information system must meet the needs of various users in a sufficient manner.
3. The underlying assumptions of accounting information systems require that an adequate system must be: Cost effective, flexible, and useful.
4. Accounting information systems can be manual or computerized.

M5-13 Matching Each Developmental Phase of an Accounting Information System with its Description LO4

Match each developmental phase with the related description by entering the appropriate letter in the space provided.

Phase	Description
1. Implementation	A. Determining whether the company will use a manual or computerized system.
2. Analysis	B. Identifying the needs of internal and external users of the system.
3. Feedback	C. Tweaking the system when portions of the system are unmanageable.
4. Design	D. Transforming the design into a workable, effective, and efficient system.

M5-14 Identifying Advantages and Disadvantages of Computerized Accounting Information Systems LO5

Indicate whether each of the following items is an advantage or disadvantage of using a computerized accounting information system:

Answer	Phase
______	1. Lack of control over portions of the accounting procedures
______	2. Simplification of recordkeeping
______	3. Up-to-date balances in the general ledger and subsidiary ledgers
______	4. Ease of altering records
______	5. Information input errors
______	6. Fewer posting errors

Exercises  Available with McGraw-Hill's Homework Manager

E5-1 Determining Account Balance in Accounts Receivable Control Account and Explaining How Items are Posted from Special Journals LO2, 3

Cluney Company uses the four special journals described in this chapter. On October 31, the balance in the Accounts Receivable control account was $50,000.

After footing and crossfooting the special journals for November, the following column totals were obtained from the special journals:

Revenue journal	$710,000
Cash receipts journal (Accounts Receivable Cr. column)	652,000

Required:

1. Determine the balance in the Accounts Receivable control account as of November 30 after all special journal postings have been made.
2. The total amount from the revenue journal of $710,000 is posted to which account(s) in the general ledger?

LO2, 3

E5-2 Determining Account Balance in Accounts Payable Control Account and Explaining How Items are Posted from Special Journals

Georgy Company uses the four special journals described in this chapter. On January 31, the balance in the Accounts Payable control account was $84,000.

After footing and crossfooting the special journals for February, the following column totals were obtained from the special journals:

Purchases journal (Accounts Payable column)	$ 278,000
Cash payments journal (Accounts Payable column)	283,000

Required:

1. Determine the balance in the Accounts Payable control account as of February 28 after all special journal postings have been made.
2. The total amount from the Accounts Payable column in the cash payments journal of $283,000 is posted to which account(s) in the general ledger?

LO2, 3

E5-3 Identifying Transactions in Accounts Receivable and Accounts Payable Ledgers

Various debit and credit transactions are presented in the following subsidiary ledger accounts:

Example 1:

Crystal Products, Inc.

Date	Account	Ref.	Debit	Credit	Balance
Jul. 31	Bal.				30,000
Aug. 31	*(a)*	CR5		30,000	0
Aug. 31	*(b)*	R2	27,000		27,000

Example 2:

Superior Supplies, Inc.

Date	Account	Ref.	Debit	Credit	Balance
Jul. 31	Bal.				16,000
Aug. 8	*(c)*	P4		21,500	37,500
Aug. 19	*(d)*	G1	1,500		36,000
Aug. 30	*(e)*	CP9	16,000		20,000

Required:

1. Identify the source of each transaction *(a)*–*(e)*.
2. Describe each transaction *(a)*–*(e)*.
3. Based on your responses for requirements 1 and 2, indicate whether Example 1 is taken from an accounts receivable subsidiary ledger or an accounts payable subsidiary ledger.

4. Based on your responses for requirements 1 and 2, indicate whether Example 2 is taken from an accounts receivable subsidiary ledger or an accounts payable subsidiary ledger.

E5-4 Identifying Proper Posting Treatment for Transactions in the Cash Payments Journal **LO2, 3**

The following cash payments journal was taken from the records of Lemski Corporation for the month of February:

Cash Payments Journal — Page 1

Date	Check No.	Account Debited	Ref.	Other Accounts Dr.	Accounts Payable Dr.	Cash Cr.
Feb. 8	361	Sales Supplies	*(a)*	900		900
14	362	Utilities Expense	*(b)*	1,450		1,450
21	363	Craig Company	*(c)*		12,000	12,000
25	364	Rent Expense	*(d)*	4,800		4,800
28	365	Wages Expense	*(e)*	2,400		2,400
		Totals		9,550	12,000	21,550
				(f)	*(g)*	*(h)*

Required:

For each of the posting references *(a)*–*(h)*, identify which of the following is the appropriate treatment of the item:

1. A posting to a general ledger account.
2. A posting to a subsidiary ledger account.
3. No posting is required.

E5-5 Matching Transactions to Revenue, Cash Receipts, and General Journals **LO3**

Indicate the journal in which each of the following transactions would be recorded by writing the letter of the appropriate journal in the space provided.

Transaction	Journal
___ 1. Provided services on account.	A. Revenue journal
___ 2. Investment of cash by the owner.	B. Cash receipts journal
___ 3. Received cash from customer on account.	C. General journal
___ 4. Provided services for cash.	
___ 5. Received cash from customer for services not yet rendered.	
___ 6. Recorded depreciation at the end of the accounting period.	

E5-6 Matching Transactions to Purchases, Cash Payments, and General Journals **LO3**

Indicate the journal in which each of the following transactions would be recorded by writing the letter of the appropriate journal in the space provided.

Transaction	Journal
___ 1. Recorded office supplies used at the end of the accounting period.	A. Purchases journal
___ 2. Purchased office furniture with a promissory note.	B. Cash payments journal
___ 3. Paid Rent for three months in advance.	C. General journal
___ 4. Paid for supplies purchased on account.	
___ 5. Purchased supplies on account.	
___ 6. Paid a one-year insurance policy in advance.	

LO3

E5-7 Matching Transactions to Appropriate Journal for Revenue- and Purchase-Related Transactions

Indicate the journal in which each of the following transactions would be recorded by writing the letter of the appropriate journal in the space provided.

Transaction	Journal
____ 1. Paid for office equipment purchased on account.	A. Revenue journal
____ 2. Provided services for customer for cash.	B. Cash receipts journal
____ 3. Returned office supplies purchased on account.	C. Purchases journal
____ 4. Accrued salaries for the month of December.	D. Cash payments journal
____ 5. Collected cash from customers on account.	E. General journal
____ 6. Provided services for customer on account.	
____ 7. Recorded depreciation on office equipment.	
____ 8. Purchased office supplies on account.	

LO3

E5-8 Recording Transactions in the Revenue Journal

Revenue-related transactions for King Enterprises are presented for the month of June, 2009.

Jun. 1 Issued invoice No. 101 to Rice Company; $1,600.
8 Issued invoice No. 102 to Barney's Bakes; $2,100.
11 Received cash from Rice Corporation on account; $1,444.
17 Issued invoice No. 103 to Lola, Inc.; $5,600.
20 Issued invoice No. 104 to Tony Company; $3,300.

Required:
Prepare a revenue journal with one column for dollar amounts. Assume no postings have been made to any subsidiary or general ledger accounts.

LO3

E5-9 Recording Transactions in the Revenue Journal

Revenue-related transactions for Prince Ltd. are presented for the month of August, 2009.

Aug. 5 Issued invoice No. 520 to Duke Company; $3,900.
9 Issued invoice No. 521 to Princess Rakes; $5,700.
12 Issued invoice No. 522 to Joker Corporation; $2,200.
20 Received cash from Duke Company on account; $3,900.
25 Issued invoice No. 523 to Knave Company; $4,100.

Required:
Prepare a revenue journal with one column for dollar amounts. Assume no postings have been made to any subsidiary or general ledger accounts.

LO2, 3

E5-10 Posting from the Revenue Journal to Control and Subsidiary Accounts

The revenue journal for Jungle Fever, Inc. is presented for the month of March 2009.

Revenue Journal — Page 12

Date	Invoice No.	Account Debited	Ref.	Accts Receivable Dr. Fees Earned Cr.
Mar. 5	1001	Macaw Incorporated		10,200
9	1002	Boa, Ltd.		9,400
18	1003	Macaw Incorporated		13,600
22	1004	Chimply Awesome, Inc.		1,500
31	1005	Boa, Ltd.		18,000
		Total		

Required:

1. Complete the revenue journal with a total.
2. Post the transactions in Jungle Fever's revenue journal to the Accounts Receivable control account (No. 110) and the related subsidiary ledger for the month of March. Use appropriate references, dates, and frequency of posting rules described in the chapter. Assume there was no previous balance in Accounts Receivable.

E5-11 Recording Transactions in the Cash Receipts Journal LO3

Transactions involving cash receipts for Percy Enterprises are presented for the month of July 2008.

Jul. 8 Received cash from Starrburst, Inc., for services rendered; $5,800.
11 Received cash from Haute Tamales Corporation on account; $1,950.
24 Received cash from Rollo Company on account; $200.
29 Received cash from Blow Popps Enterprises for services rendered; $350.
31 Received cash for supplies sold to employees at cost; $25.

Required:

Prepare a cash receipts journal for these transactions. The cash receipts journal should contain the following headings: Date; Account Credited; Ref.; Other Accounts Cr.; Accounts Receivable Cr.; Fees Earned Cr.; and Cash Dr. Assume no postings have been made to any subsidiary or general ledger accounts.

E5-12 Recording Transactions in the Cash Receipts Journal LO3

Transactions involving cash receipts for Prog Company are presented for the month of April 2008.

Apr. 2 Received cash from Gorm, Inc., on account; $2,800.
6 Received cash from Slock Corporation for services rendered; $400.
12 Received cash for supplies sold to employees at cost; $15.
22 Received cash from Tring Company on account; $3,600.
27 Received cash from Drong Enterprises for services rendered; $750.

Required:

Prepare a cash receipts journal for these transactions. The cash receipts journal should contain the following headings: Date; Account Credited; Ref.; Other Accounts Cr.; Accounts Receivable Cr.; Fees Earned Cr.; and Cash Dr. Assume no postings have been made to any subsidiary or general ledger accounts.

E5-13 Posting from the Cash Receipts Journal to Control Account and Subsidiary Ledger LO2, 3

The cash receipts journal for Jewel Company is presented for the month of November 2008.

Cash Receipts Journal — Page 9

Date	Account Credited	Ref.	Other Accounts Cr.	Accounts Receivable Cr.	Fees Earned Cr.	Cash Dr.
Nov. 3	Sapphire Enterprises			800		800
10	Diamond Corporation			1,300		1,300
17					15,800	15,800
21	Sapphire Enterprises			1,600		1,600
28	Interest Revenue		180			180
30	Diamond Corporation			7,700		7,700
	Totals					

Required:

1. Complete the cash receipts journal with totals.
2. Post the transactions shown in Jewel Company's cash receipts journal to the subsidiary ledger accounts, as well as the affected general ledger accounts for the month of November. Use appropriate references, dates, and frequency of posting rules described in the chapter. October 31

balances: Diamond Corporation—$12,200 and Sapphire Enterprises—$3,400. Use the following general ledger accounts and balances:

Account No.	Account Title	Oct. 31 Balance	Account No.	Account Title	Oct. 31 Balance
105	Cash	$12,000	410	Fees Earned	$2,400
110	Accounts Receivable	15,600	710	Interest Revenue	800

LO3

E5-14 Recording Transactions in the Revenue and Cash Receipts Journals

Revenue-related transactions for Foods Enterprises are presented for the month of January, 2008.

Jan. 1 Issued invoice No. 601 to Cheese Company; $1,600.
4 Received cash from Angus, Inc., for services rendered; $800.
12 Issued invoice No. 602 to Rogers Steaks; $2,100.
16 Received cash from Cheese Company on account; $1,444.
20 Issued invoice No. 603 to Bean, Inc.; $5,600.
23 Issued invoice No. 604 to Noodle Company; $3,300.
26 Received cash from Noodle Company on account; $600.
31 Received cash for supplies sold to employees at cost; $30.

Required:
Prepare a revenue journal and a cash receipts journal for these transactions. The cash receipts journal should contain the following headings: Date; Account Credited; Ref.; Other Accounts Cr.; Accounts Receivable Cr.; Fees Earned Cr.; and Cash Dr. Assume no postings have been made to any subsidiary or general ledger accounts.

LO3

E5-15 Recording Transactions in the Revenue and Cash Receipts Journals

Revenue-related transactions for Spot Enterprises are presented for the month of September 2009.

Sep. 2 Received cash from Angrila Corporation for services rendered; $60.
4 Issued invoice No. 421 to Rice Company; $2,500.
11 Issued invoice No. 422 to Barney's Bakes; $1,400.
16 Received cash from Holt, Inc., for services rendered; $1,100.
19 Issued invoice No. 423 to Lola, Inc.; $4,200.
22 Issued invoice No. 424 to Tony Company; $2,200.
24 Received cash for supplies sold to employees at cost; $40.
30 Received cash from Tony Company on account; $1,000.

Required:
Prepare a revenue journal and a cash receipts journal for these transactions. The cash receipts journal should contain the following headings: Date; Account Credited; Ref.; Other Accounts Cr.; Accounts Receivable Cr.; Fees Earned Cr.; and Cash Dr. Assume no postings have been made to any subsidiary or general ledger accounts.

LO3

E5-16 Recording Transactions in the Purchases Journal

Purchase-related transactions for Topo Company are presented for the month of February 2009.

Feb. 1 Received a bill from Rob's Rentals for February rent; $2,400.
2 Purchased office equipment on account from Eddie's Equipment; $6,000.
9 Received a bill from Irma's Insurance for a one-year flood insurance policy; $4,000.
10 Purchased office supplies on account from Otto's Supplies; $360.
16 Received a bill for cleaning services from Jane's Janitorial; $300.
22 Received a bill for office supplies from Office Mart; $225.

Required:
Prepare a purchases journal for these transactions. The purchases journal should contain the following headings: Date; Account Credited; Ref.; Accounts Payable Cr.; Office Supplies Dr.; Other Accounts Dr.; Ref.; and Amount. Assume no postings have been made to any subsidiary or general ledger accounts.

E5-17 Recording Transactions in the Purchases Journal

LO3

Purchase-related transactions for Gigio Company are presented for the month of May 2009.

May. 2 Received a bill from State Barn Insurance for a two-year fire insurance policy; $4,980.
7 Purchased store supplies on account from Supplies R Us; $250.
12 Received a bill from Mary Maids for cleaning services; $400.
25 Received a bill for advertising from The Daily Grind; $600.
30 Purchased store equipment on account from Equipment Wholesalers; $5,000.
31 Received a bill from Alice's Archives for advertising placed in their magazine; $1,200.

Required:

Prepare a purchases journal for these transactions. The purchases journal should contain the following headings: Date; Account Credited; Ref.; Accounts Payable Cr.; Advertising Expense Dr.; Other Accounts Dr.; Ref.; and Amount. Use appropriate references and dates, and assume no postings have been made to any subsidiary or general ledger accounts.

E5-18 Posting from the Purchases Journal to Control Account and Subsidiary Ledger

LO2, 3

The Purchases Journal for Crown Company is presented for the month of August 2009.

Purchases Journal

Page 3

Date	Account Credited	Ref.	Accounts Payable Cr.	Delivery Expense Dr.	Other Accounts Dr.		
					Accounts	Ref.	Amount
Aug. 1	Rent and Insurance, Inc.		3,500		Prepaid Insurance		3,500
8	Danny's Deliveries		145	145			
17	Super Supplies		200		Office Supplies		200
24	The Daily Herald		350		Advertising Expense		350
29	Danny's Deliveries		475	475			
30	Rent and Insurance, Inc.		2,500	___	Rent Expense		2,500
	Totals		7,170				

Required:

1. Complete the purchases journal with totals.
2. Post the transactions shown in Crown Company's purchases journal to the subsidiary ledger, as well as any affected general ledger accounts for the month of August. Assume no beginning balances in any accounts. Use appropriate references, dates, and frequency of posting rules described in the chapter. Use the following accounts: 115—Office Supplies; 140—Prepaid Insurance; 210—Accounts Payable; 520—Advertising Expense; 525—Delivery Expense; 615—Rent Expense.

E5-19 Recording Transactions in the Cash Payments Journal

LO3

Transactions involving cash payments for Klink Corporation are presented for the month of November 2009.

Nov. 5 Issued check No. 330 to Supply Outfitters on account; $450.
10 Issued check No. 331 to Southern Utilities for gas and electric; $725.
19 Issued check No. 332 to Phisher Company on account; $650.
26 Issued check No. 333 to Season's Deal on account; $1,400.
29 Issued check No. 334 to secretary for November wages; $1,200.
30 Issued check No. 335 to Allgreat Insurance for a one-year fire insurance policy; $2,400.

Required:

Prepare a cash payments journal for these transactions. The cash payments journal should contain the following headings: Date; Check No.; Account Debited; Ref.; Other Accounts Dr.; Accounts Payable Dr.; and Cash Cr. Assume no postings have been made to any subsidiary or general ledger accounts.

LO3

E5-20 Recording Transactions in the Cash Payments Journal
Transactions involving cash payments for Housin Company are presented for the month of January 2009.

Jan. 2 Issued check No. 801 to Mutual of Omaha for a one-year insurance policy; $1,600.
10 Issued check No. 802 to Sliver Enterprises on account; $950.
17 Issued check No. 803 to Digger Company on account; $1,100.
23 Issued check No. 804 to Northern Utilities for gas and electric; $820.
27 Issued check No. 805 to Wholesale Sellers on account; $5,000.
30 Issued check No. 806 to secretary for January wages; $1,800.

Required:
Prepare a cash payments journal for these transactions. The cash payments journal should contain the following headings: Date; Check No.; Account Debited; Ref.; Other Accounts Dr.; Accounts Payable Dr.; and Cash Cr. Assume no postings have been made to any subsidiary or general ledger accounts.

LO2, 3

E5-21 Posting from the Cash Payments Journal to Control Account and Subsidiary Ledger
The cash payments journal for Shrimp Enterprises is presented for the month of April 2009.

Cash Payments Journal — Page 6

Date	Check No.	Account Debited	Ref.	Other Accounts Dr.	Accounts Payable Dr.	Cash Cr.
Apr. 2	521	Store Supplies		500		500
8	522	Crayfish Corporation			750	750
13	523	Fishing Suppliers, Inc.			2,100	2,100
20	524	Advertising Expense		260		260
26	525	Lobsters, Ltd.			825	825
29	526	Wages Expense		910		910
		Totals				

Required:

1. Complete the cash payments journal with totals.
2. Post the transactions shown in Shrimp Enterprises cash payments journal to the subsidiary ledger accounts, as well as the affected general ledger accounts for the month of April. Use appropriate references, dates, and frequency of posting rules described in the chapter. March 31 balances: Crayfish Corporation—$1,750; Fishing Suppliers, Inc.—$2,100; and Lobsters, Ltd.—$1,000. Use the following general ledger accounts and balances:

Account No.	Account Title	Mar. 31 Balance	Account No.	Account Title	Mar. 31 Balance
105	Cash	$9,000	510	Wages Expense	$2,400
115	Store Supplies	250	520	Advertising Expense	800
210	Accounts Payable	4,850			

LO2, 3

E5-22 Recording Transactions in the Purchases and Cash Payments Journals
Transactions for Twilight Company are presented for the month of October 2009.

Oct. 3 Purchased postage meters on account from Potter's Postage Equipment; $1,000.
8 Issued check No. 1101 to Everything Postal for packaging supplies; $120.
12 Purchased bubble wrap on account from Everything Postal; $160.
18 Issued check No. 1102 to Southern Utilities for gas and electric; $155.
20 Received a bill for packaging supplies from Postal Suppliers; $80.
25 Received a bill for advertising charges from The Daily Post; $75.
31 Issued check No. 1103 to Everything Postal on account; $100.

Required:
Prepare a purchases journal and a cash payments journal for these transactions. The purchases journal should contain the following headings: Date; Account Credited; Ref.; Accounts Payable Cr.; Packaging Supplies Dr.; Other Accounts Dr.; Ref.; and Amount. The cash payments journal should contain the following headings: Date; Check No.; Account Debited; Ref.; Other Accounts Dr.; Accounts Payable Dr.; and Cash Cr. Assume no postings have been made to any subsidiary or general ledger accounts.

E5-23 Recording Transactions in the Purchases and Cash Payments Journals **LO3**

Purchase-related transactions for Tofflet Enterprises are presented for the month of February 2009.

Feb. 1 Issued check No. 651 to Rentals R Us for February rent; $3,400.
6 Purchased supplies on account from Sophie's Sundries; $200.
11 Received a bill for advertising from The Daily Bugle; $150.
15 Purchased equipment from Office Suppliers on account; $2,150.
21 Issued check No. 652 to Sophie's Sundries for supplies; $95.
24 Received a bill from Public Gas and Oil for gas bill; $400.
28 Issued check No. 653 to Office Suppliers on account; $1,000.

Required:
Prepare a purchases journal and a cash payments journal for these transactions. The purchases journal should contain the following headings: Date; Account Credited; Ref.; Accounts Payable Cr.; General Supplies Dr.; Other Accounts Dr.; Ref.; and Amount. The cash payments journal should contain the following headings: Date; Check No.; Account Debited; Ref.; Other Accounts Dr.; Accounts Payable Dr.; and Cash Cr. Assume no postings have been made to any subsidiary or general ledger accounts.

E5-24 Recording Transactions in the General Journal **LO3**

Various purchase-related transactions for GenaFlynn, Inc., are presented for the month of December 2009.

Dec. 2 Returned supplies to Suppliers Incorporated on account; $30.
9 Received a credit from The Daily Journal for an advertising billing error; $40.
16 Purchased a delivery truck by issuing a note payable to Dodgge, Inc.; $40,000.
19 Received a check from The Supply Hut for amount overpaid on account; $15.

Required:
Prepare a general journal for these transactions. Assume no postings have been made to any subsidiary or general ledger accounts. If a transaction would not be recorded in the general journal, indicate which special journal it should be recorded in (if any).

E5-25 Recording Transactions in the General Journal **LO3**

Purchase-related transactions for Cryogelf Limited are presented for the month of January 2009.

Jan. 6 Purchased office equipment by issuing a $10,000 note payable to Equipers, Inc.
12 Returned office supplies to Total Office on account; $50.
22 Received a credit from Delivery Enterprises for error on delivery bill; $25.
31 Received a check from the National Inquiry for an amount that Cryogelf overpaid on account; $20.

Required:
Prepare a general journal for these transactions. Assume no postings have been made to any subsidiary or general ledger accounts. If a transaction would not be recorded in the general journal, indicate which special journal it should be recorded in (if any).

E5-26 Posting from the General Journal to Control Account and Subsidiary Ledger **LO3**

Purchase-related transactions for Katanga Company are presented for the month of July 2009.

General Journal — Page 1

Date	Account Titles	Ref.	Debit	Credit
Jul. 8	Accounts Payable—All Country Insurance		400	
	Insurance Expense			400
16	Furniture and Fixtures		6,000	
	Notes Payable			6,000
29	Accounts Payable—Store Suppliers, Inc.		12	
	Store Supplies			12

Required:
Post the transactions shown in Katanga Company's general journal to the subsidiary ledger accounts, as well as the affected general ledger accounts for the month of July. Use appropriate references, dates, and frequency of posting rules described in the chapter. June 30 balances: All Country Insurance—$1,000 and Store Suppliers, Inc.—$140. Use the following general ledger accounts and balances:

Account No.	Account Tittle	June 30 Balance	Account No.	Account Tittle	June 30 Balance
115	Store Supplies	$ 450	250	Notes Payable	$2,400
160	Furniture and Fixtures	4,000	650	Insurance Expense	2,100
210	Accounts Payable	1,140			

LO2, 3

E5-27 Correcting Errors in Accounts Payable Subsidiary Ledger

After all end-of-period postings were made, the accounts payable subsidiary ledger and the Accounts Payable control account for Kramar Enterprises did not agree. After investigating the problem, it was determined that the control account balance of $178,230 was correct. Use the accounts payable subsidiary ledger that follows to perform each of the requirements.

Required:

1. As the new accounts payable clerk for Kramar Enterprises, you have been asked to find the errors made by the previous clerk and identify any corrections that should be made. Write a brief memo to Mary Cliff, the head bookkeeper, listing the errors that were made.
2. After listing the corrections necessary, prove that the accounts payable subsidiary ledger agrees with the Accounts Payable control account by preparing a schedule of accounts payable.

ACCOUNTS PAYABLE SUBSIDIARY LEDGER

Dean Disposables

Date	Item	Ref.	Debit	Credit	Balance
Jul. 31	Bal.				14,000
Aug. 1		CP8	14,000		28,000
18		P4		65,000	93,000

Office Suppliers

Date	Item	Ref.	Debit	Credit	Balance
Jul. 31	Bal.				30,110
Aug. 10		CP8	30,110		60,220
30		P4		25,000	35,220

Nolan Consulting Services

Date	Item	Ref.	Debit	Credit	Balance
Jul. 31	Bal.				9,555
Aug. 12		CP8	9,555		0
29		P4		35,010	35,010

Reliable Equipment

Date	Item	Ref.	Debit	Credit	Balance
Jul. 31	Bal.				72,220
Aug. 11		P4		41,000	51,220
26		CP8	60,000		111,220

Specialists Inc.

Date	Item	Ref.	Debit	Credit	Balance
Jul. 31	Bal.				6,000
Aug. 11		P4		33,000	39,000
26		CP6	39,000		0

Problems—Set A  Available with McGraw-Hill's Homework Manager

PA5-1 Matching Terminology with Definitions

LO1, 2, 3, 4

Following are the terms and definitions covered in Chapter 5. Match each term with its definition by entering the appropriate letter in the space provided. Use one letter for each blank.

Terms	Definitions
____ 1. Crossfoot	A. A general ledger account that summarizes all transactions occurring in its related subsidiary account.
____ 2. Special journal	B. Used to record services rendered to customers on account.
____ 3. Accounts receivable subsidiary ledger	C. Used to record all correcting, adjusting, closing, and unusual entries that cannot be recorded elsewhere.
____ 4. Manual accounting information system	D. The steps in the accounting cycle are performed with the aid of general ledger software.
____ 5. Revenue journal	E. Used to record all cash collections in a business, regardless of the reason for the collection.
____ 6. Accounting information system	F. Individual transactions with creditors on account are collected and maintained.
____ 7. Control account	G. A collection of all accounts used in a business.
____ 8. General ledger	H. Collect, classify, summarize, and report the financial information about a business to interested parties.
____ 9. Foot	I. Used to record all transactions involving the disbursement of cash from a business.
____ 10. Cash payments journal	J. Used to record similar types of transactions in one convenient place.
____ 11. Computerized accounting system	K. Verifies that the total amounts of the debit columns equal the total amounts of the credit columns in a special journal.
____ 12. Purchases journal	L. Used to record all purchases or expenses that are made on account.
____ 13. Accounts payable subsidiary ledger	M. Individual transactions with customers on account are collected and maintained.
____ 14. General journal	N. The steps in the accounting cycle are performed by hand.
____ 15. Cash receipts journal	O. Adding up the dollar amounts in a column.

LO2, 3

PA5-2 Journalizing Transactions in the Cash Receipts Journal; Posting to Control Account and Subsidiary Ledger

Purple Pirates (owned by George Sparrow) performs magic tricks and other entertainment at children's birthday parties. The following selected accounts are taken from the chart of accounts.

105	Cash	310	George Sparrow, Capital
110	Accounts Receivable	410	Fees Earned
115	Supplies		

On September 30, 2009, the accounts receivable subsidiary ledger had the following balances: G. Bridger $200; T. Mato $1,000; H. Potter $800; and JB Rabitt $600. The following transactions occurred during October:

Oct. 2 Received cash from JB Rabitt as payment in full on his account.
4 Received check from T. Mato for $700 as partial payment on his account.
10 George Sparrow invested an additional $6,000 into the business.
16 Performed party services for a client and received immediate cash payment of $500.
20 Received check from H. Potter as payment in full on his account.
25 Received check from G. Bridger for $100 as partial payment on her account.
30 Received cash refund for supplies returned to supplier for $65 because they were defective. (Hint: Reduce the Supplies account for the cost of the returned supplies.)

Required:

1. Journalize the transactions for October in a four-column cash receipts journal using the following column headings: Date; Account Credited; Ref.; Other Accounts Cr.; Accounts Receivable Cr.; Fees Earned Cr.; and Cash Dr.
2. Set up the Accounts Receivable control account and the individual accounts receivable subsidiary ledger accounts by placing the September 30 balances in them.
3. Post the October transactions to the control account and the subsidiary ledger accounts in the manner described in the chapter.
4. Prepare a schedule that proves that the balances in the control account and the subsidiary ledger accounts are equal.

LO2, 3

PA5-3 Journalizing Transactions in the Cash Payments Journal; Posting to Control Account and Subsidiary Ledger

Sally's Sewing does alterations and creates custom fashions for its customers. The following selected accounts were taken from its chart of accounts.

105	Cash	210	Accounts Payable
115	Sewing Supplies	311	Sally Sartoria, Drawing
145	Prepaid Rent	510	Salaries Expense
160	Furniture & Fixtures		

On January 31, 2009, the accounts payable subsidiary ledger had the following balances: Lacey Gayne $300; Ted Knee $800; Lars Pyn $1,100; and Tammy Seem $2,100. The following transactions occurred during February:

Feb. 3 Paid Ted Knee balance due on account, using check #103.
4 Bought needles, pins, seam rippers, etc. from Tammy Seem for $230, using check #104.
11 Purchased a new sofa for her lobby; $1,800, using check #105.
13 Paid Lars Pyn balance due on account, using check #106.
16 Paid Lacey Gayne balance due on account, using check #107.
17 Sally Sartoria withdrew $2,000 cash for her personal use, using check #108.
20 Paid Tammy Seem $400 as a partial payment on the account, using check #109.
28 Paid monthly salary to her employee—Suzee Seemstress; $1,200, using check #110.
28 Paid four months' rent in advance; $4,000, using check #111.

Required:

1. Journalize the transactions for February in a cash payments journal using the following column headings: Date; Check No.; Account Debited; Ref.; Other Accounts Dr.; Accounts Payable Dr.; and Cash Cr.
2. Set up the Accounts Payable control account and the individual accounts payable subsidiary ledger accounts by placing the January 31 balances in them.
3. Post the February transactions to the control account and the subsidiary ledger accounts in the manner described in the chapter.
4. Prepare a schedule that proves that the balances in the control account and the subsidiary ledger accounts are equal.

PA5-4 Posting Accounts Receivable and Accounts Payable Transactions and Preparing Schedules of Accounts Receivable and Accounts Payable

LO2, 3

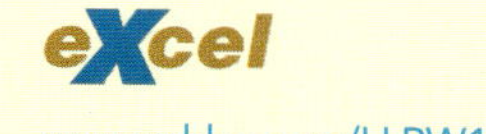

www.mhhe.com/LLPW1e

The Accounts Receivable control account for the Dupree Company as of December 31, 2008, was $10,284, consisting of the following balances: $8,652 from Doe, Inc., and $1,632 from Dosey, Inc. The Accounts Payable control account as of December 31, 2008, was $3,658, consisting of the following balance: $3,658 Redhouse, Inc. Dupree Company's revenue journal, cash receipts journal, purchases journal, and cash payments journal for January 2009 are as follows:

Revenue Journal — Page 2

Date	Invoice No.	Account Debited	Ref.	Accts Receivable Dr. Fees Earned Cr.
Jan. 1	165	Ella Company		4,176
10	166	Doe, Inc.		9,410
14	167	Mand Company		1,400
23	168	Promenade Company		7,823
31	169	Dosey, Inc.		2,011

Cash Receipts Journal — Page 7

Date	Account Credited	Ref.	Other Accounts Cr.	Accounts Receivable Cr.	Fees Earned Cr.	Cash Dr.
Jan. 5	Dosey, Inc.			1,632		1,632
12	Ella Company			4,176		4,176
16	Doe, Inc.			8,652		8,652
25	Mand Company			1,400		1,400
30	Promenade Company			3,000		3,000

Purchases Journal — Page 1

Date	Account Credited	Ref.	Accounts Payable Cr.	Supplies Dr.	Other Accounts Dr.		
					Accounts	Ref.	Amount
Jan. 1	Gonzales Co.		1,140		Advertising Expense		1,140
1	Simms Company		2,388		Rent Expense		2,388
3	Nguyen Inc.		654	654			
8	Tidwell Enterprises		3,858		Furniture & Fixtures		3,858
20	Redhouse Inc.		295	295			

Cash Payments Journal Page 1

Date	Check No.	Account Debited	Ref.	Other Accounts Dr.	Accounts Payable Dr.	Cash Cr.
Jan. 1	101	Prepaid Insurance		6,000		6,000
2	102	Rent Expense		3,450		3,450
18	103	Simms Company			2,388	2,388
20	104	Tidwell Enterprises			3,858	3,858
29	105	Gallagher, Drawing		2,000		2,000
31	106	Nguyen, Inc.			654	654

Required:

1. Set up the Accounts Receivable (No. 110) and Accounts Payable (No. 210) control accounts as well as the corresponding individual subsidiary ledger accounts by placing the December 31 balances in them.
2. Foot and crossfoot the four special journals and post the appropriate information into the subsidiary ledger accounts and control accounts for Accounts Receivable and Accounts Payable in the manner described in the chapter. Do not post to any other general ledger accounts.
3. Prepare schedules of accounts receivable and accounts payable for Dupree Company as of January 31, 2009.

LO2, 3

eXcel

www.mhhe.com/LLPW1e

PA5-5 Journalizing Transactions in the Revenue Journal, Purchases Journal, and General Journal; Posting to Subsidiary Ledgers and Control Accounts

The following selected accounts were taken from the chart of accounts for Lionel Corporation.

110	Accounts Receivable	210	Accounts Payable
115	Office Supplies	410	Fees Earned
160	Furniture & Fixtures	520	Advertising Expense

The following selected transactions occurred in July. All purchases and revenues were on account, unless otherwise indicated.

July 1 Provided services to Talin Jenkins in the amount of $850; invoice #650.
7 Purchased office supplies from Office Emporium; $230.
9 Purchased a new desk for the office from The Furniture Factory; $1,800.
10 Returned office supplies to the Office Emporium that were defective; $30. (Hint: Reduce the Office Supplies account.)
12 Provided services to Franklin Jones in the amount of $390; invoice #651.
17 Received bill from Avian Advertising; $630.
19 Purchased bookcases for $2,420 from The Furniture Factory.
21 Provided services to Ross Butler in the amount of $1,620; invoice #652.
29 Purchased office supplies from Office Emporium; $180.

Required:

1. Journalize the transactions for July in a revenue journal, a purchases journal, and a general journal. Use the following column heading for the purchases journal: Date; Account Credited; Ref.; Accounts Payable Cr.; Office Supplies Dr.; Other Accounts Dr.; Ref. and Amount.
2. Post to the general ledger and subsidiary ledger accounts. (Assume all general ledger accounts and subsidiary ledger accounts have no beginning balances.)
3. Prepare schedules that prove that the balances in the control accounts and the subsidiary ledger accounts are equal.

PA5-6 Journalize Transactions in the Special Journals and General Journal **LO2, 3**

Selected accounts from the chart of accounts of Doyle Company are shown below:

105	Cash	210	Accounts Payable
110	Accounts Receivable	410	Fees Earned
115	Office Supplies	510	Salaries Expense
180	Office Equipment	630	Utilities Expense

The following selected transactions occurred in August. All purchases and revenues were on account, unless otherwise indicated. Doyle Company uses the following journals: revenue journal; purchases journal; cash receipts journal; cash payments journal; and general journal.

Aug. 4 Purchased office supplies on account from Supply Emporium; $150.
6 Purchased office equipment on account from Rose Co.; $1,800.
7 Returned $25 of office supplies purchased on August 4 from Supply Emporium because they were defective. (Hint: Reduce the Office Supplies account.)
12 Fees earned on account from Gorgeous George's; $2,100, invoice #601.
15 Paid salaries to employees $12,300; check #851.
20 Fees earned from cash customers for the week; $1,735.
24 Received $1,000 payment from Gorgeous George's.
28 Paid Supply Emporium the amount owed; check #852.
31 Purchased office supplies from Office Suppliers, Inc. with check #853; $325.
31 Fees earned on account from Little Lola's; $2,600, invoice #602.
31 Received bill for utilities from State Utilities for the month of August; $600.

Required:

1. Record the August transactions in a revenue journal, a purchases journal, a cash receipts journal, a cash payments journal, and a general journal. Use the following headings for the special journals:

   Cash receipts journal: Date; Account Credited; Ref.; Other Accounts Cr.; Accounts Receivable Cr.; Fees Earned Cr.; Cash Dr.

   Purchases journal: Date; Account Credited; Ref.; Accounts Payable Cr.; Office Supplies Dr.; Other Accounts Dr.; Ref.; and Amount.

   Cash payments journal: Date; Check No.; Account Debited; Ref.; Other Accounts Dr.; Accounts Payable Dr.; Cash Cr.
2. Foot and crossfoot all special journals as necessary.
3. Using the methods shown in the chapter, show the posting references that would be made if amounts were posted to the general ledger and subsidiary ledgers (actual posting to the ledger accounts is not required for this problem).

PA5-7 Journalizing Transactions in Revenue and Cash Receipts Journals; Posting; Preparing a Trial Balance; Reconciling Control and Subsidiary Accounts; Preparing a Trial Balance **LO2, 3**

Shown below are the purchases and cash payments journals for Pepperine for its first month of operations, October 2008:

Purchases Journal Page 1

Date	Account Credited	Ref.	Accounts Payable Cr.	Supplies Dr.	Other Accounts Dr.		
					Accounts	Ref.	Amount
Oct. 2	Bitterling, Inc.		2,280		Rent Expense		2,280
2	Aloha Company		1,428		Advertising Expense		1,428
4	Norris Inc.		841	841			
9	Simple Enterprises		1,620		Furniture & Fixtures		1,620
21	Bitterling, Inc.		967	967			
	Totals		7,136	1,808			5,328

www.mhhe.com/LLPW1e

Cash Payments Journal Page 1

Date	Check No.	Account Debited	Ref.	Other Accounts Dr.	Accounts Payable Dr.	Cash Cr.
Oct. 2	810	Prepaid Insurance		3,500		3,500
3	811	Salaries Expense		1,250		1,250
19	812	Aloha Company			1,428	1,428
21	813	Simple Enterprises			1,620	1,620
30	814	Pepperine, Drawing		1,500		1,500
31	815	Norris, Inc.		—	841	841
		Totals		6,250	3,889	10,139

Additionally, the following transactions have not been journalized for October.

Oct. 1 The owner, Sal Pepperine, invests $95,000 in cash.
4 Revenues earned on account, K. Witkowski, $4,895; invoice #460.
5 Cash revenues total $6,100.
7 Revenues earned on account, M. Romero, $2,670; invoice #461.
9 Revenues earned on account, J. DiVincenzo, $1,100; invoice #462.
20 Received payment in full from K. Witkowski.
22 Received payment in full from J. DiVincenzo.
24 Provided services to B. Arredondo for $3,000 on account; invoice #463.
27 Received payment in full from M. Romero.
31 Cash revenues total $5,995.

Required:

1. Open the following accounts in the general ledger:

105	Cash	310	Pepperine, Capital
110	Accounts Receivable	311	Pepperine, Drawing
115	Supplies	410	Fees Earned
140	Prepaid Insurance	510	Salaries Expense
160	Furniture & Fixtures	520	Advertising Expense
210	Accounts Payable	615	Rent Expense

2. Journalize the transactions that have not been journalized by preparing a revenue journal and a cash receipts journal. Use the following headings for the cash receipts journal: Date; Account Credited; Ref.; Other Accounts Cr.; Accounts Receivable Cr.; Fees Earned Cr.; Cash Dr.
3. Foot and crossfoot the revenue and cash receipts journals.
4. Post from *all journals* to the accounts receivable and accounts payable subsidiary ledgers. Complete any other daily and month-end postings that are needed in the order that transactions are presented in the problem.
5. Prepare a trial balance at October 31, 2008.
6. Use the methods described in the chapter to verify that the subsidiary ledgers agree with the control accounts in the general ledger.

LO2, 3

PA5-8 Journalizing in Special Journals; Posting; Preparing a Trial Balance

The post-closing trial balance for Ken Flammer—Attorney at Law is as follows:

Ken Flammer—Attorney at Law Post-Closing Trial Balance December 31, 2008		
	Debit	**Credit**
Cash	16,500	
Accounts Receivable	5,350	
Notes Receivable	6,000	
Office Equipment	32,000	
Accumulated Depreciation—Office Equipment		4,000
Accounts Payable		9,500
K. Flammer, Capital		46,350
Totals	**59,850**	**59,850**

The following detail is contained in the subsidiary ledgers:

- Accounts receivable—B. Baily $1,460; N. Hite $2,320; W. Price $1,570.
- Accounts payable—G. Clump $3,000; P. Dormond $2,800; O. Kadhi $3,700.

The following transactions occurred in January of 2009.

Jan. 1 Paid $14,400 rent for the year; check #500.
1 Received $4,000 as an advance payment for four months of legal representation.
5 Provided services on account to B. Baily; invoice #201 for $1,100.
6 Paid O. Kadhi amount owed in full; check #501.
8 Received partial payment on account of $1,000 from N. Hite.
11 Purchased office supplies from P. Dormond on account $520.
14 Returned office supplies to P. Dormond of $60 because they were defective. (Hint: Reduce the Office Supplies account.)
18 Paid secretary for two weeks' wages; $1,600; check #502.
20 Purchased office equipment with a note payable to G. Clump; $25,000.
21 Paid for advertisements in the local newspaper; check #503 for $220.
25 Provided services on account to W. Price; invoice #202 for $850.
28 Paid P. Dormond $2,800 on account; check #504.
30 Received payment on account of $1,460 from B. Baily.
31 Provided services on account to N. Hite; invoice #203 for $2,300.
31 Recorded cash revenues earned for the month of $6,000.
31 Ken Flammer withdrew $4,000 from the business for personal use; check #505.

Required:

1. Open general ledger accounts and subsidiary ledger accounts for each of the following:

105	Cash	250	Notes Payable
110	Accounts Receivable	260	Unearned Legal Fees
112	Notes Receivable	310	K. Flammer, Capital
115	Office Supplies	311	K. Flammer, Drawing
145	Prepaid Rent	410	Legal Fees Earned
180	Office Equipment	510	Salaries Expense
181	Accumulated Depreciation, Office Equipment	520	Advertising Expense
210	Accounts Payable		

2. Record the January transactions in the revenue journal, cash receipts journal, purchases journal, cash payments journal, and general journal. Use the following headings for the journals:

   Cash receipts journal: Date; Account Credited; Ref.; Other Accounts Cr.; Accounts Receivable Cr.; Fees Earned Cr.; Cash Dr.

   Purchases journal: Date; Account Credited; Ref.; Accounts Payable Cr.; Office Supplies Dr.; Other Accounts Dr.; Ref.; and Amount.

   Cash payments journal: Date; Check No.; Account Debited; Ref.; Other Accounts Dr.; Accounts Payable Dr.; Cash Cr.

3. Post to the general ledger and subsidiary ledger accounts as appropriate.
4. Prepare a trial balance at January 31, 2009.
5. Use the methods described in the chapter to verify that the subsidiary ledgers agree with the control accounts in the general ledger.

Problems—Set B  Available with McGraw-Hill's Homework Manager

LO1, 2, 3, 4

PB5-1 Matching Terminology with Definitions

Following are the terms and definitions covered in Chapter 5. Match each term with its definition by entering the appropriate letter in the space provided. Use one letter for each blank.

Terms

____ 1. General journal
____ 2. Special journal
____ 3. Monthly posting
____ 4. Implementation phase
____ 5. Cash receipts journal
____ 6. Accounting information system
____ 7. Control account
____ 8. Purchases journal
____ 9. Analysis phase
____ 10. Cash payments journal
____ 11. Feedback phase
____ 12. Computerized accounting system
____ 13. Design phase
____ 14. Daily posting
____ 15. Subsidiary ledger

Definitions

A. This may require nothing more than selecting a suitable general ledger software program for a business.
B. Each line represents a separate journal entry consisting of at least one debit to cash and at least one credit to another account.
C. Would be used to record the payment to a creditor on account.
D. Provides the accountant with more time to ensure that all transactions and adjustments have been recorded.
E. Presents the same information as a detailed transaction history, but in a highly summarized form.
F. A critical factor in the ultimate success or failure of an accounting information system.
G. Several columns are needed because a nearly limitless number and variety of accounts could be debited when accounts payable is credited.
H. Used for recording repetitive, frequent transactions.
I. Required for subsidiary ledger accounts because balances must be kept up to date at all times.
J. This must be useful, cost effective, and flexible.
K. Will always be utilized by every business even if special journals are used.
L. Provides detailed history of transactions on account with each individual or business.
M. Control accounts in the general ledger normally only need to be updated when financial statements are prepared.
N. Changes are made to a new information system when problems are discovered.
O. Internal and external user needs are identified.

PB5-2 Journalizing Transactions in the Cash Receipts Journal; Posting to Control Account and Subsidiary Ledger **LO2, 3**

Dave's Dentistry, DDS (owned by David Mastic) provides basic dental care (cleanings, fillings, etc.). The following selected accounts are taken from its chart of accounts.

105	Cash	310	David Mastic, Capital
110	Accounts Receivable	410	Dental Fees Earned
115	Dental Supplies	710	Interest Revenue

On February 28, 2009, the accounts receivable subsidiary ledger had the following balances: R. Cannell $600; Dee Kaye $2,700; Moe Larr $1,400; and Ginger Vytis $3,000. The following transactions occurred during March:

Mar. 4 Received a check from Ginger Vytis as payment in full on her account.
6 Received a check from Moe Larr for $500 as partial payment on his account.
12 David Mastic invested an additional $10,000 into the business.
18 Performed a root canal for Dee Kaye and received immediate cash payment of $2,000.
22 Received check from R. Cannell as payment in full on his account.
27 Received check from Dee Kaye for $1,200 as partial payment on her account.
31 Received a cash refund for dental supplies returned to the supplier for $140 because they were defective. (Hint: Reduce the Dental Supplies account.)

Required:

1. Journalize the transactions for March in a four-column cash receipts journal using the following column headings: Date; Account Credited; Ref.; Other Accounts Cr.; Accounts Receivable Cr.; Dental Fees Earned Cr.; and Cash Dr.
2. Set up the Accounts Receivable control account and the individual accounts receivable subsidiary ledger accounts by placing the February 28 balances in them.
3. Post the March transactions to the control account and the subsidiary ledger accounts in the manner described in the chapter.
4. Prepare a schedule that proves that the balances in the control account and the subsidiary ledger accounts are equal.

PB5-3 Journalizing Transactions in the Cash Payments Journal; Posting to Control Account and Subsidiary Ledger **LO2, 3**

Pete's Packaging packages and ships items worldwide. The following selected accounts were taken from its chart of accounts.

105	Cash	210	Accounts Payable
115	Packaging Supplies	311	Pete Zelin, Drawing
140	Prepaid Insurance	510	Salaries Expense
190	Delivery Truck		

On May 31, the Accounts Payable subsidiary ledger had the following balances: Charlie's Corrugated Boxes $510; Ev'ry Kinda Envelope $950; Packaging Plus $600; Speedy Labels $450. The following transactions occurred during June:

June 4 Paid Speedy Labels the balance due on account, using check #840.
6 Bought mailing tape, black markers, etc. from Ev'ry Kinda Envelope, using check #841; $380.
10 Purchased a new delivery truck $30,000, using check #842.
15 Paid Packaging Plus balance due on account, using check #843.
18 Paid Charlie's Corrugated Boxes balance due on account, using check #844.
19 Pete Zelin withdrew $1,000 cash for his personal use, using check #845.
22 Paid Ev'ry Kinda Envelope $300 as partial payment on the balance due, using check #846.
28 Paid monthly salary to his employee—Yupee Ess, $900, using check #847.
30 Paid annual premium on insurance policy, $10,800, using check #848.

Required:

1. Journalize the transactions for June in a cash payments journal using the following column headings: Date; Check No.; Account Debited; Ref.; Other Accounts Dr.; Accounts Payable Dr.; and Cash Cr.
2. Set up the Accounts Payable control account and the individual accounts payable subsidiary ledger accounts by placing the May 31 balances in them.
3. Post the June transactions to the control account and the subsidiary ledger accounts in the manner described in the chapter.
4. Prepare a schedule that proves that the balances in the control account and the subsidiary ledger accounts are equal.

LO2, 3

PB5-4 Posting Accounts Receivable and Accounts Payable Transactions and Preparing Schedules of Accounts Receivable and Accounts Payable

The Accounts Receivable control account for Grate Plains, Inc., as of April 30, 2009, was $16,500 consisting of the following balances: $5,500 from Pomegranate Company and $11,000 from Star, Inc. The Accounts Payable control account as of April 30, 2009, was $3,000 consisting of the following balances: $2,000 from Fennel Company and $1,000 from Thyme, Inc. The revenue journal, cash receipts journal, purchases journal, and cash payments journal for Grate Plains for May 2009 follow:

Revenue Journal — Page 2

Date	Invoice No.	Account Debited	Ref.	Accts Receivable Dr. Fees Earned Cr.
May 2	451	Mango Company		3,816
12	452	Persimmon, Inc.		8,320
16	453	Papaya Company		2,600
25	454	Pomegranate Company		6,914
30	455	Star, Inc.		3,140

Cash Receipts Journal — Page 7

Date	Account Credited	Ref.	Other Accounts Cr.	Accounts Receivable Cr.	Fees Earned Cr.	Cash Dr.
May 7	Star, Inc.			10,000		10,000
14	Mango Company			3,816		3,816
18	Persimmon, Inc.			6,320		6,320
27	Papaya Company			2,600		2,600
31	Pomegranate Company			5,500		5,500

Purchases Journal — Page 5

Date	Account Credited	Ref.	Accounts Payable Cr.	Supplies Dr.	Other Accounts Dr.		
					Accounts	Ref.	Amount
May 2	Fennel Company		800	800			
9	Parsley Parties		1,900		Rent Expense		1,900
17	Tarragon Ltd.		200	200			
18	Cilantro Sisters, Inc.		6,500		Office Equipment		6,500
24	Basil Company		2,200		Furniture & Fixtures		2,200
28	Cilantro Sisters, Inc.		3,600		Prepaid Insurance		3,600

Cash Payments Journal — Page 9

Date	Check No.	Account Debited	Ref.	Other Accounts Dr.	Accounts Payable Dr.	Cash Cr.
May 1	655	Thyme, Inc.			1,000	1,000
1	656	Fennel Company			2,000	2,000
20	657	Parsley Parties			1,200	1,200
29	658	Cilantro Sisters, Inc.			3,500	3,500
31	659	Tarragon Ltd.			200	200

Required:

1. Set up the Accounts Receivable (No. 110) and Accounts Payable (No. 210) control accounts as well as the corresponding individual subsidiary ledger accounts by placing the April 30 balances in them.
2. Foot and crossfoot the four special journals, post the appropriate information into the subsidiary accounts and control accounts for Accounts Receivable and Accounts Payable in the manner described in the chapter. Do not post to any other general ledger accounts.
3. Prepare schedules of accounts receivable and accounts payable for Grate Plains, Inc., as of May 31, 2009.

PB5-5 Journalizing Transactions in the Revenue Journal, Purchases Journal, and General Journal; Posting to Subsidiary Ledgers and Control Accounts **LO2, 3**

The following selected accounts were taken from the chart of accounts for Cewlio Corporation.

110	Accounts Receivable	210	Accounts Payable
115	Store Supplies	410	Fees Earned
170	Store Equipment	630	Utilities Expense

The following selected transactions occurred in December. All purchases and revenues were on account, unless otherwise indicated.

Dec. 2 Provided services to Judy Crowder in the amount of $1,800; invoice #100.

8 Purchased store supplies from The Store House; $900.

10 Purchased a cash register from Registers R Us; $3,700.

13 Returned store supplies to The Store House that were defective; $100. (Hint: Reduce the Store Supplies account.)

16 Provided services to Gawain Aster in the amount of $925; invoice #101.

18 Received bill from State Gas & Electric; $1,160.

20 Purchased two more cash registers for $7,000 from Registers R Us.

23 Provided services to Scarlet Els in the amount of $640; invoice #102.

30 Purchased store supplies from The Store House; $245.

Required:

1. Journalize the transactions for December in a revenue journal, a purchases journal, and a general journal. Use the following column headings for the purchases journal: Date; Account Credited; Ref.; Accounts Payable Cr.; Store Supplies Dr.; Other Accounts Dr., Ref. and Amount.
2. Post to the general ledger and subsidiary ledger accounts. (Assume all general ledger accounts and subsidiary ledger accounts have zero beginning balances.)
3. Prepare schedules that prove that the balances in the control accounts and the subsidiary ledger accounts are equal.

LO2, 3

PB5-6 Journalizing Transactions in Special Journals and the General Journal

Selected accounts from the chart of accounts of Clover Company are shown below:

105	Cash	210	Accounts Payable
110	Accounts Receivable	410	Fees Earned
115	Office Supplies	510	Salaries Expense
180	Office Equipment	630	Utilities Expense

The following selected transactions occurred in May. All purchases and revenues were on account unless otherwise indicated.

May 3 Purchased office supplies on account from Office Emporium; $225.
7 Purchased office equipment on account from Furniture Liquidators; $3,000.
8 Returned $50 of office supplies purchased on May 3 because they were defective. (Hint: Reduce the Office Supplies account.)
13 Fees earned on account from Peterson Plumbing; $4,000, invoice #630.
16 Paid salaries to employees; $8,500, using check #405.
21 Fees earned from cash customers for the week; $6,200.
25 Received $2,500 payment from Peterson Plumbing.
28 Paid Office Emporium the amount owed using check #406.
29 Purchased office supplies from Office Emporium for cash; $410, using check #407.
31 Fees earned on account from Magna Carta; $4,100, invoice #631.
31 Received bill for utilities from City Utilities for the month of May; $550.

Required:

1. Record the May transactions in a revenue journal, a cash receipts journal, a purchases journal, a cash payments journal, and a general journal. Use the following headings for the special journals:

   Cash receipts journal: Date; Account Credited; Ref.; Other Accounts Cr.; Accounts Receivable Cr.; Fees Earned Cr.; Cash Dr.

   Purchases journal: Date; Account Credited; Ref.; Accounts Payable Cr.; Office Supplies Dr.; Other Accounts Dr.; Ref.; and Amount.

   Cash payments journal: Date; Check No.; Account Debited; Ref.; Other Accounts Dr.; Accounts Payable Dr.; Cash Cr.

2. Foot and crossfoot all special journals.
3. Using the methods shown in the chapter, show the posting references that would be made if amounts were posted to the subsidiary ledgers and general ledger (actual posting to the ledger accounts is not required for this problem).

LO2, 3

PB5-7 Journalizing Transactions in Revenue and Cash Receipts Journals; Posting; Preparing a Trial Balance; Reconciling Control and Subsidiary Accounts; Preparing a Trial Balance

Shown below are the purchases and cash payments journals for Solara Corporation for April 2009, its first month of operations:

Purchases Journal — Page 1

Date	Account Credited	Ref.	Accounts Payable Cr.	Supplies Dr.	Other Accounts Dr.: Accounts	Ref.	Amount
Apr. 1	Gilliland Co.		300	300			
1	Rivera Company		4,000		Advertising Expense		4,000
4	Hawthorne, Inc.		1,310	1,310			
9	Orbon Enterprises		6,146		Furniture & Fixtures		6,146
22	Doan Ltd.		1,244	1,244			
	Totals		13,000	2,854			10,146

Cash Payments Journal Page 1

Date	Check No.	Account Debited	Ref.	Other Accounts Dr.	Accounts Payable Dr.	Cash Cr.
Apr. 1	1001	Prepaid Insurance		2,000		2,000
2	1002	Rent Expense		3,600		3,600
20	1003	Rivera Company			4,000	4,000
23	1004	Orbon Enterprises			6,146	6,146
28	1005	Solara, Drawing		1,200		1,200
30	1006	Hawthorne, Inc.			1,310	1,310
		Totals		6,800	11,456	18,256

Additionally, the following transactions have not been journalized for April.

Apr. 1 The owner, Luz Solara, invests $70,000 in cash.
6 Revenues earned on account, V. Long, $2,220; invoice #261.
7 Cash revenues total $4,300.
9 Revenues earned on account, C. Lara, $3,325; invoice #262.
11 Revenues earned on account, L. Begay, $2,500; invoice #263.
21 Received payment in full from V. Long.
24 Received payment in full from L. Begay.
26 Provided services to S. Lutheran for $4,300 on account; invoice #264.
29 Received payment in full from C. Lara.
30 Cash revenues total $6,294.

Required:

1. Open the following accounts in the general ledger:

105	Cash	310	Solara, Capital
110	Accounts Receivable	311	Solara, Drawing
115	Supplies	410	Fees Earned
140	Prepaid Insurance	520	Advertising Expense
160	Furniture & Fixtures	615	Rent Expense
210	Accounts Payable		

2. Journalize the transactions that have not been journalized in the revenue journal and cash receipts journal. Use the following headings for the cash receipts journal: Date; Account Credited; Ref.; Other Accounts Cr.; Accounts Receivable Cr.; Fees Earned Cr.; Cash Dr.
3. Post to the accounts receivable and accounts payable subsidiary ledgers in the order that transactions are presented in the problem.
4. Post entries to the general ledger.
5. Prepare a trial balance at April 30, 2009.
6. Use the methods described in the chapter to verify that the subsidiary ledgers agree with the control accounts in the general ledger.

PB5-8 Journalizing in Special Journals; Posting; Preparing a Trial Balance **LO2, 3**

The post-closing trial balance for Joe's Accounting Services is as follows:

Joe's Accounting Services
Post-Closing Trial Balance
December 31, 2009

	Debit	Credit
Cash	23,300	
Accounts Receivable	6,500	
Notes Receivable	2,000	
Office Equipment	16,000	
Accumulated Depreciation—Office Equipment		3,200
Accounts Payable		5,000
J. Bency, Capital		39,600
Totals	47,800	47,800

The following detail is contained in the subsidiary ledgers:

- Accounts receivable—N. Bonham $2,150; H. Giahi $1,300; J. Teak $3,050.
- Accounts payable—J. Bright $1,050; S. Cutler $950; J. Storer $3,000.

The following transactions occurred in January of 2010.

Jan.	1	Paid $23,400 rent for the year; check #800.
	1	Received $3,000 as an advance payment for three months of accounting services.
	5	Provided services on account to J. Teak; invoice #501 for $2,350.
	8	Paid J. Storer amount owed in full; check #801.
	8	Received partial payment on account of $2,000 from J. Teak.
	13	Purchased office supplies from S. Cutler on account; $150.
	14	Returned office supplies costing $15 to S. Cutler because they were defective. (Hint: Reduce the Office Supplies account.)
	20	Paid secretary for two weeks' wages; $1,900; check #802.
	22	Purchased office equipment with a Note Payable to J. Romero; $10,000.
	23	Paid for advertisements in the local newspaper; check #803 for $195.
	25	Provided services on account to H. Giahi; invoice #502 for $1,600.
	27	Paid S. Cutler $950 on account; check #804.
	30	Received payment on account of $1,300 from H. Giahi.
	31	Provided services on account to N. Bonham; invoice #503 for $4,400.
	31	Recorded cash revenues earned for the month of $8,500.
	31	Joe Bency withdrew $2,500 from the business for personal use; check #805.

Required:

1. Open general ledger accounts and subsidiary ledger accounts for each of the following:

105	Cash	250	Notes Payable
110	Accounts Receivable	260	Unearned Accounting Fees
112	Notes Receivable	310	J. Bency, Capital
115	Office Supplies	311	J. Bency, Drawing
145	Prepaid Rent	410	Accounting Fees Earned
180	Office Equipment	510	Salaries Expense
181	Accumulated Depreciation, Office Equipment	520	Advertising Expense
210	Accounts Payable		

2. Record the January transactions in the revenue journal, cash receipts journal, purchases journal, cash payments journal, and general journal. Use the following headings for the journals:

   Cash receipts journal: Date; Account Credited; Ref.; Other Accounts Cr.; Accounts Receivable Cr.; Fees Earned Cr.; Cash Dr.

   Purchases journal: Date; Account Credited; Ref.; Accounts Payable Cr.; Office Supplies Dr.; Other Accounts Dr.; Ref.; and Amount.

   Cash payments journal: Date; Check No.; Account Debited; Ref.; Other Accounts Dr.; Accounts Payable Dr.; Cash Cr.

3. Post to the general ledger and subsidiary ledger accounts as appropriate.
4. Prepare a trial balance at January 31, 2010, and determine whether the subsidiary ledgers agree with the control accounts in the general ledger.
5. Use the methods described in the chapter to verify that the subsidiary ledgers agree with the control accounts in the general ledger.

Cases and Projects

CP5-1 Financial Reporting Project: Mini Practice Set

LO1, 2, 3, 4

Young Co. established the following chart of accounts.

105	Cash	211	Salaries Payable	510	Salaries Expense
110	Accounts Receivable	212	Interest Payable	515	Rent Expense
115	Store Supplies	250	Notes Payable	516	Utilities Expense
140	Prepaid Insurance	310	Shawna Young, Capital	518	Store Supplies Expense
170	Store Equipment	311	Shawna Young, Drawing	620	Depreciation Expense
171	Accumulated Depreciation	315	Income Summary	650	Insurance Expense
210	Accounts Payable	410	Fees Earned	810	Interest Expense

Young Co. uses both an accounts receivable and an accounts payable subsidiary ledger. The transactions for Young Co. for the first month of business, March 2009, are presented below.

March	1	The owner, Shawna Young, contributed $25,000 to the business.
	1	Received store supplies and an invoice from Farnswood Co. for $1,300.
	1	Borrowed $10,000 by giving Second State Bank a long-term promissory note.
	1	Paid $1,200 for insurance for one year using check #650.
	1	Paid March rent of $2,900 using check #651.
	2	Purchased store equipment on account for $10,000 from Nelson, Inc.
	5	Earned $3,600 on account from Zachary Makey, Invoice #275.
	5	Returned $200 of damaged supplies received from Farnswood Co. on March 1. (Hint: Reduce the Store Supplies account.)
	6	The owner, Shawna Young, gave store equipment to the business valued at $3,000.
	6	Earned $4,900 on account from John Dilbert, Invoice #276.
	7	Earned $4,300 on account from Edward Solano, Invoice #277.
	11	Sent check #652 to Farnswood Co. in payment of its March 1 invoice.
	12	Purchased store supplies on credit from Corsair Co. $440.
	15	Cash fees earned for the first half of the month were $7,340.
	15	Paid salaries of $7,950 using check #653.
	19	Received payment from Zachary Makey for the March 5 transaction.
	22	Received payment from Edward Solano for the March 7 transaction.
	25	Issued check #654 to Corsair Co. for the March 12 transaction.

26 Earned $6,220 on account from John Dilbert, Invoice #278.
27 Issued check #655 for $2,000 to Nelson, Inc., for partial payment of March 2 transaction.
28 Earned $4,440 on account from Sydney Locke, Invoice #279.
29 Purchased store supplies on credit from Corsair Co., $510.
31 Cash fees earned for the last half of the month were $2,345.
31 Received the utility bill from Texas Utilities for the month of March, $2,400.
31 The owner, Shawna Young, withdrew $2,500 for personal use using check #656.

Required:

1. Record the March transactions in a revenue journal, a cash receipts journal, a purchases journal, a cash payments journal, and a general journal.
2. Complete all necessary daily and end-of-month postings.
3. Prepare an unadjusted trial balance at March 31, 2009.
4. Use the following information to prepare and post adjusting entries, and prepare an adjusted trial balance.
   Adjustment data at March 31, 2009.
   a. Store supplies on hand totaled $185.
   b. Depreciation is $120 on the store equipment.
   c. Interest of $50 is accrued on notes payable at March 31.
   d. Salaries of $2,000 are accrued and unpaid at March 31.
   e. One month insurance has expired.
5. Prepare an Income Statement, an Owner's Equity Statement, and a classified Balance Sheet for March 2009.
   (Note: Young Co. must pay $2,000 on the Notes Payable in the coming year.)
6. Prepare and post closing entries.
7. Prepare a post-closing trial balance.

CP5-2 Implementing a Computerized Accounting Information System: Critical Thinking

Bessie Jacobs is the founder and sole manager of Bessie's Flowers. The business has been operating for nearly 15 years and has developed a loyal customer base consisting of individuals and businesses. Individuals typically purchase flowers on the spur of the moment using cash, whereas most businesses purchase flowers on credit. Bessie has promised to deliver flowers to business customers each week. Bessie's business expenses are modest with her greatest expenses being for flower purchases from several southern states and greenhouses in the Pacific Northwest. Bessie also incurs substantial transportation costs to have her purchases flown in to her shop. Until this year, Bessie has tracked the majority of her business transactions manually. The only computerized application in her business has been the automated cash register. Bessie has come to you for advice on implementing a computerized accounting information system.

Required:

Write a report that advises Bessie about implementing a computerized accounting system. In your report, describe some of the factors she should consider when deciding whether to implement such a system. Also, based on your preliminary understanding of Bessie's business, describe the components that should be included in the system and what information each component would capture.

6 Merchandising Operations

LEARNING OBJECTIVES

After completing this chapter, you should be able to:

Lectured slideshow–LP6-1
www.mhhe.com/LLPW1e

LO1 Distinguish among service, merchandising, and manufacturing operations.

LO2 Explain the use of perpetual and periodic inventory systems and their role in inventory control.

LO3 Analyze merchandise purchases under a perpetual inventory system.

LO4 Analyze merchandise sales under a perpetual inventory system.

LO5 Prepare a merchandiser's multistep income statement.

LO6 Analyze the gross profit percentage.

Focus Company: WAL-MART

"Every Day Low Prices" and Modern Supply-Chain Management Change the World.

www.walmart.com

If you compare your grandparents' first car or TV to the one you own now, you can see how improvements in technology have changed the products you use in daily life. Less obvious are the changes that have taken place in the way we shop for these products. From Bentonville, Arkansas, to Beijing, China, "big-box" stores have changed the world of retailing. Just five of these giants—Wal-Mart, Kmart, Target, Costco, and Sears—account for nearly 60 percent of general merchandise sales in the United States. The leader, Wal-Mart, has done as much as any high-tech company to change American lifestyles over the last 40 years.

Seventeen years after the company was founded, Wal-Mart rang up yearly sales of $1 billion. Fourteen years later, it sold that much in a week. Today, Wal-Mart's sales are approaching $1 billion a day. Wal-Mart's trucks transport goods purchased from hundreds of thousands of suppliers. The store's greeters welcome more than 100 million customers every week in more than 6,100 locations worldwide. To track its huge inventory purchases and sales and ensure that each store is properly stocked and each transaction properly recorded, Wal-Mart needs state-of-the-art accounting systems.

Chapters 1–5 illustrate accounting for the operations of two small companies: Pizza Aroma and a UPS Store. In this chapter, we demonstrate that the same accounting principles apply to much larger companies such as Wal-Mart. The operating activities of Pizza Aroma and a UPS Store also relate to the provision of services rather than to the sale of goods. This chapter focuses on companies such as Wal-Mart that sell merchandise to customers and the way they control and report the unique aspects of their operating activities. You will also learn what to look for in a merchandiser's financial statements.

ORGANIZATION OF THE CHAPTER

OPERATING CYCLES AND INVENTORY SYSTEMS	RECORDING MERCHANDISE PURCHASES	RECORDING MERCHANDISE SALES	PREPARING AND ANALYZING THE INCOME STATEMENT
• Operating Cycles: Service, Merchandising, and Manufacturing Cos. • Inventory Systems: Perpetual and Periodic	• Purchases on Account • Transportation Cost (Freight-In) • Purchase Returns and Allowances • Purchase Discounts • Summary of Purchase-Related Transactions	• Cash Sales • Sales Returns and Allowances • Credit Card Sales • Sales on Account and Sales Discounts • Transportation Cost (Freight-Out) • Summary of Sales-Related Transactions • Comparison of Sales and Purchases Accounting	• Multistep Income Statement for Merchandisers • Gross Profit Percentage • Comparison to Benchmarks

OPERATING CYCLES AND INVENTORY SYSTEMS

Learning Objective 1

Distinguish among service, merchandising, and manufacturing operations.

Operating Cycles

An **operating cycle** is the series of activities that a company undertakes to generate sales and, ultimately, cash**.** Based on their operating cycle, businesses can be classified into three types: (1) service companies, (2) merchandising companies, and (3) manufacturing companies. As in Exhibit 6.1 the operating cycle for **service companies** such as Pizza Aroma and The UPS Store is simple: They use cash to provide services to customers and then collect cash from those customers. The operating cycle for **merchandising companies** has an additional step: These companies use cash to buy inventory, sell the inventory to customers, and then collect cash from customers. Like merchandising companies, **manufacturing companies** such as Ford and Mattel sell physical products, but instead of acquiring ready-to-sell merchandise, they make their own products from raw materials.

This chapter focuses on merchandising companies. In turn, merchandising companies can be classified in two specific subgroups. One group, **retail** merchandising companies, includes companies such as Wal-Mart and American Eagle Outfitters, which sell directly to consumers. Another group, **wholesale** merchandising companies, includes companies such as SYSCO, that sell only to retail businesses for resale to consumers. This chapter applies equally to both retail and wholesale merchandisers.

As the figure in Exhibit 6.1 suggests, the accounting processes that you learned in earlier chapters also apply to merchandising companies. The difference is that merchandising companies must account for the purchase and sale of products. Unlike services, which cannot be stored for future sale, products can be acquired for sale in the future. These stored products, which are called Inventory, present some new accounting issues that you will learn about in this chapter. We begin with a discussion of inventory systems and how they work.

Video 6-1
www.mhhe.com/LLPW1e

Inventory Systems

Learning Objective 2

Explain the use of perpetual and periodic inventory systems and their role in inventory control.

Because inventory management is vital to merchandising operations, companies spend a great deal of time and money tracking their inventory transactions. A strong accounting system plays three roles in this process:

- It provides up-to-date information on inventory quantities and costs so that managers can make informed decisions.
- It provides accurate information for preparing financial statements. Until inventory is sold, it is reported as an asset on the balance sheet. After its sale, it is removed from the

Exhibit 6.1 Operating Cycles for Service, Merchandising, and Manufacturing Companies

Service companies
(Gold's Gym, UPS, Southwest Airlines)

Sell services → Receive cash → Incur operating expenses → Sell services

Merchandising companies
(Wal-Mart, Sears, GAP)

Buy products → Sell products → Receive cash → Incur operating expenses → Buy products

Manufacturing companies
(Ford, Dell, Nike)

Buy raw materials → Make products → Sell products → Receive cash → Incur operating expenses → Buy raw materials

balance sheet and reported on the income statement as an expense, called Cost of Goods Sold.

- It provides information that controls inventory and helps to prevent theft.

To perform these functions, companies can use either of two types of inventory accounting system: perpetual or periodic.

Perpetual Inventory System

A **perpetual inventory system** updates inventory records every time an item is bought, sold, or returned. You may not realize it, but the bar code readers at Wal-Mart's checkouts serve two purposes: (1) they calculate and record the sales revenue for each product you buy and (2) they remove the product and its cost from Wal-Mart's inventory records. Similar scanners

are used in the "employees only" part of the store, where products are unloaded from the trucks or returned to suppliers. As a result of this continuous, or "perpetual," updating, the balances in Wal-Mart's Inventory and Cost of Goods Sold accounts are always up to date.

Periodic Inventory System

A periodic inventory system differs from a perpetual system in several ways, which are described in detail later in this chapter. The main difference is that rather than updating the inventory records immediately after each purchase and sale (as in a perpetual system), a periodic system updates the inventory records only at the end of the period. Most of the time, then, accurate records of the inventory on hand and the inventory that has been sold are unavailable. To determine these amounts, employees must physically count the inventory, which they do at the end of the period, when the store is "closed for inventory." The resulting inventory count is then used to adjust the balances for Inventory and Cost of Goods Sold.

Inventory Control

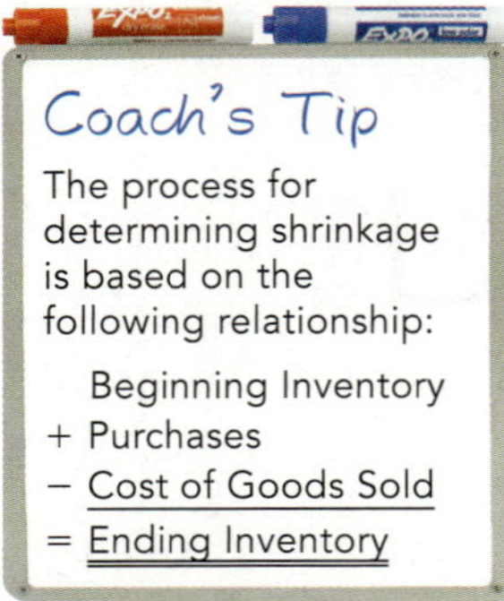

A perpetual inventory system's continuous tracking of transactions allows companies to keep just the right quantity of products on the shelves for just the right amount of time. Doing so saves companies a great deal of money in financing and storage charges. It also benefits consumers, who pay less for the products they buy. When companies use less money or labor to produce a product or service, the productivity of our entire economy goes up. From 1995 to 1999, Wal-Mart's perpetual inventory system accounted for more than 50 percent of U.S. productivity gains in general merchandising.[1] This amazing performance is likely to continue as the company adopts new microchip technologies that transmit data automatically from every inventory item that enters, moves within, and exits its stores.

Another benefit of a perpetual inventory system is that it allows managers to estimate **shrinkage,** the politically correct term for loss of inventory from theft, fraud, and error. How can companies estimate how much of their inventory is missing? They do it by monitoring the transactions that are recorded in their inventory accounts. Here is the procedure:

October 1

October purchases and goods sold

\+

−

1. **Determine how much inventory is on hand at the beginning of the period.**
2. **Monitor every piece of inventory that enters and exits the inventory during the period.**
   a. Add any purchases.
   b. Subtract any goods that are sold.

   If items are tracked in this way, the inventory records should exactly match the quantity of inventory on hand—unless some items have been wrongfully removed.
3. **Count the inventory to determine what is actually there.** If the records say that more inventory is on hand than what was counted, the difference is the amount of shrinkage—that is, the number of items that have been removed from inventory without permission.

Notice that you cannot do this kind of detective work with a periodic inventory system, because it does not provide an up-to-date record of the inventory that should be on hand when you count it. Even if you are using a perpetual inventory system, you still need to count the inventory occasionally (at least once a year) to ensure that the accounting records are accurate and that any shrinkage has been detected.

[1] "Retail: The Wal-Mart Effect," *The McKinsey Quarterly*, no. 1 (2002).

Until recently, perpetual inventory systems were too costly for most merchandisers to implement. Today, however, computerized inventory systems have become so cheap that most merchandisers use a perpetual system. Accordingly, this chapter focuses on the accounting process that perpetual systems use. Because you may still encounter a periodic system, particularly in small companies or large ones that have been slow to switch, Supplement 6A at the end of this chapter discusses the accounting process for periodic systems.

Spotlight On ETHICS

Sources of Inventory Shrinkage

Independent verification of inventory quantities is important. A recent study suggests that more than $37 billion of inventory goes missing from U.S. retailers each year.* Although shoplifting is a major cause of shrinkage (accounting for 33 percent of lost units), an even larger portion (47 percent) results from employee theft. To avoid hiring dishonest employees, companies screen job applicants using employment and criminal background checks. To deter and detect employee theft, they use security tags, closed-circuit TV, and complex computer programs that monitor cash registers.

* Richard Hollinger, "2005 National Retail Security Survey," University of Florida, 2006.

RECORDING MERCHANDISE PURCHASES

Learning Objective 3

Analyze merchandise purchases under a perpetual inventory system.

Purchases on Account

Inventory purchases should be recorded at the point at which ownership is transferred. Most purchase and sales agreements specify one of two possible times:

- When the goods leave the seller's shipping department, known as the FOB (free on board) shipping point.
- When the goods reach the customer at their destination point, known as the FOB destination.

In a perpetual system, all purchases of merchandise inventory are recorded directly into the Inventory account. Because most companies use credit rather than cash to purchase goods, Accounts Payable is usually the other account that is affected. If Wal-Mart purchased $5,000 of DVDs on account, the transaction would be recorded as follows:

Coach's Tip

Inventory includes only merchandise purchased for sale. Other purchases, such as supplies for internal use, are recorded in different accounts.

	Debit	Credit
Inventory (+A)	5,000	
Accounts Payable (+L)		5,000

Assets	=	Liabilities	+	Owners' Equity
Inventory +5,000		Accounts Payable +5,000		

Transportation Cost (Freight-In)

The inventory that Wal-Mart purchases does not magically appear in its stores. It must be shipped from the supplier to Wal-Mart. If the terms are **FOB shipping point,** the purchaser pays for the shipping. If the terms are **FOB destination,** the seller pays for the shipping. When the purchaser pays for the shipping, the additional cost of transporting the goods (called **freight-in**) is added to the Inventory account.

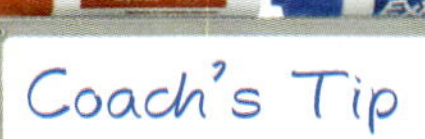

Coach's Tip

When the purchaser incurs the transportation cost (**freight-in**), the amount is added to the purchaser's cost of inventory. When the seller incurs the transportation cost (**freight-out**), it is an operating expense to the seller.

Assume that Wal-Mart pays $300 cash to a trucker who delivers goods to one of its stores. Wal-Mart would account for this transaction as follows:

	Debit	Credit
Inventory (+A)	300	
Cash (−A)		300

Assets		=	Liabilities	+	Owners' Equity
Inventory	+300				
Cash	−300				

In general, a purchaser should include in the Inventory account any costs needed to get the inventory ready for sale. Costs that are incurred after the inventory has been made ready for sale, such as freight-out to deliver goods to customers, should be treated as selling expenses.

Purchase Returns and Allowances

When goods purchased from a supplier arrive in damaged condition or fail to meet specifications, the buyer can (1) return them for a full refund or (2) keep them and ask for a cost reduction, called an allowance. **Purchase returns** and **purchase allowances** are accounted for either by reducing the cost of the inventory and recording a cash refund or by reducing the liability owed to the supplier.

Assume, for example, that Wal-Mart returned merchandise to a supplier and received a $400 reduction in the balance owed. This transaction would be analyzed and recorded as follows:

	Debit	Credit
Accounts Payable (−L)	400	
Inventory (−A)		400

Assets		=	Liabilities		+	Owners' Equity
Inventory	−400		Accounts Payable	−400		

Purchase Discounts

When merchandise is bought on credit, terms such as "2/10, n/30" are sometimes specified. The "2/10" means that if the purchaser pays within 10 days of the date of purchase, a 2 percent **purchase discount** will be deducted from the cost. The "n/30" implies that if payment is not made within the 10-day discount period, the full amount will be due 30 days after the purchase date. If a purchaser fails to pay by the end of that period, interest will be charged. (In the future, the seller may deny credit because of a purchaser's failure to pay on time, and the seller may hire a collection agency to collect the amount owed.) See Exhibit 6.2 for an illustration of a 2/10, n/30 purchase that occurred on November 1.

When offered a purchase discount at the time of purchase, the purchaser accounts for it in two stages. Initially, the purchase is accounted for at **full cost** because it is not clear whether the

Exhibit 6.2 Interpreting Credit Terms

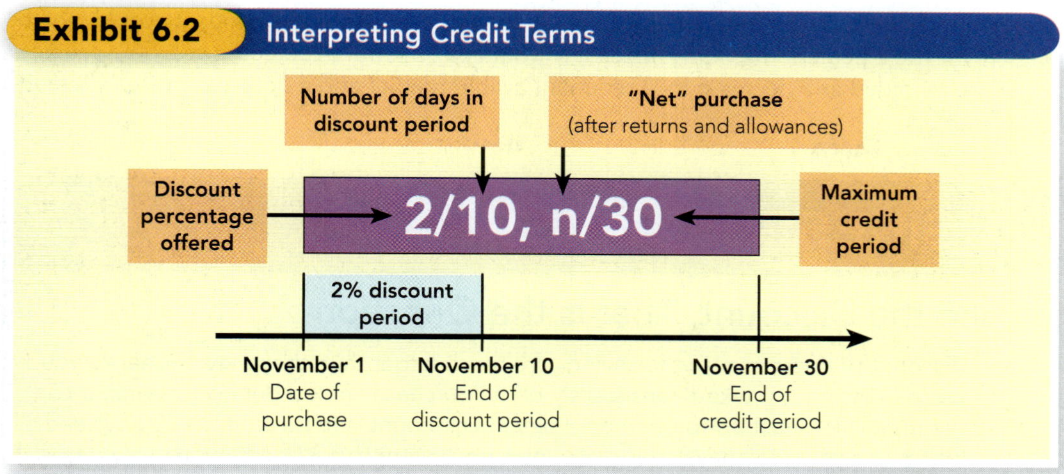

company will take advantage of the discount. Later, by making payment within the discount period, the purchaser reduces the Inventory account by the amount of the discount because it effectively reduces the cost of the inventory.

Assume, for example, that Wal-Mart receives a shipment of LCD televisions bought from Sony. How would a $100,000 purchase with terms of 2/10, n/30 affect Wal-Mart's accounting records? Initially, the purchase would be recorded as follows:

	Debit	Credit
Inventory (+A)	100,000	
Accounts Payable (+L)		100,000

Assets		=	Liabilities		+	Owners' Equity
Inventory	+100,000		Accounts Payable	+100,000		

If Wal-Mart takes advantage of the 2/10, n/30 discount by paying within the 10-day discount period, the discount will effectively reduce the cost of the inventory. The 2 percent discount is calculated using the initial purchase cost (2% × $100,000 = $2,000). Because the discount reduces the inventory cost, the purchaser records it as a reduction of the Inventory account, as follows:

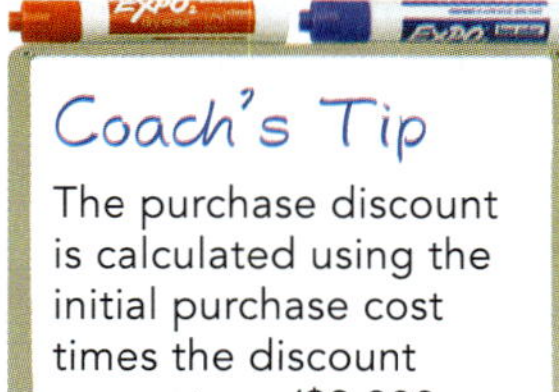

Coach's Tip

The purchase discount is calculated using the initial purchase cost times the discount percentage ($2,000 = 2% × $100,000).

	Debit	Credit
Accounts Payable (−L)	100,000	
Cash (−A) **(98% × 100,000)**		98,000
Inventory (−A) **(2% × 100,000)**		2,000

Assets		=	Liabilities		+	Owners' Equity
Cash	−98,000		Accounts Payable	−100,000		
Inventory	−2,000					

If Wal-Mart paid for the inventory after the 10-day discount period, it would not be eligible for the 2 percent discount. Instead, it would pay the full $100,000 owed. The payment would be recorded as a decrease in Accounts Payable (debit) and a decrease in Cash (credit) of $100,000.[2]

Spotlight On BUSINESS DECISIONS

To Take or Not to Take the Discount, That Is the Question

Purchasers usually pay within the discount period because the savings are much larger than they may appear to you. Although 2 percent might seem a small discount, if taken consistently on all purchases made during the year, it can add up to substantial savings. All the purchaser must do to earn the 2 percent discount is to pay the bill 20 days early (on the 10th day instead of the 30th). Over a year (365 days), this discount is equivalent to a 37 percent annual interest rate.* So even if purchasers must borrow from the bank at a high rate, such as 15 percent, they will still save a great deal by taking the discount.

Summary of Purchase-Related Transactions

You have now seen how several types of purchase-related transactions besides the initial purchase affect the Inventory account on the balance sheet. Before you move on to accounting for merchandise sales, make sure you understand how each of these purchase-related transactions affects Inventory. Cost of Goods Sold is recorded as part of the sales transactions described in the next section. See Exhibit 6.3 for a summary of the effects of the purchase transactions discussed in this section assuming beginning inventory was $75,000.

Exhibit 6.3 Effects of Purchase-Related Transactions on the Inventory Account

Beginning inventory	$ 75,000
Add: Purchases*	105,000
Add: Freight-in	300
Less: Purchase returns and allowances	(400)
Less: Purchase discounts	(2,000)
Cost of goods available for sale	177,900
Less: Cost of goods sold	?
Ending inventory	$?

Recorded as part of the sales transactions described in the next section. (Cost of goods sold and Ending inventory)

*Purchased inventory includes ($105,000 = $5,000 + $100,000).

[2] An alternative approach to accounting for purchase discounts (called the net method) exists, but we leave that topic for discussion in intermediate accounting textbooks.

* To calculate the annual interest rate, first compute the interest rate for the discount period. When taking the 2 percent discount, the customer pays only 98 percent of the gross sales price. For example, on a $100 sale with terms 2/10, n/30, the customer woulds save $2 and pay $98 twenty days early.

The interest rate for the 20-day discount period is computed as follows:

$$\frac{\text{Amount Saved}}{\text{Amount Paid}} = \text{Interest Rate for 20 Days}$$

$$\frac{\$2}{\$98} = 2.04\% \text{ for 20 Days}$$

The annual interest rate is:

$$\text{Interest rate for 20 Days} \times \frac{365 \text{ Days}}{20 \text{ Days}} = \text{Annual Interest Rate}$$

$$2.04\% \times \frac{365 \text{ Days}}{20 \text{ Days}} = 37.23\% \text{ Annual Interest Rate}$$

Spotlight On FINANCIAL REPORTING

Summary of Significant Accounting Policies

Companies must describe how they account for the major items reported on their financial statements in the first note to their financial statements. This note is normally called the Summary of Significant Accounting Policies. Wal-Mart explains the costs included in the cost of sales when the goods are sold as follows:

> ***Cost of Sales***
>
> Cost of sales includes actual product cost, change in inventory, the cost of transportation to the Company's warehouses from suppliers, the cost of transportation from the Company's warehouses to the stores and clubs. . . . Substantially all allowances are accounted for as a reduction of purchases. . . .

This description exactly matches the manner in which we have just accounted for purchased inventory.

SELF-STUDY PRACTICE

How would each of the following independent transactions be recorded in the accounting records?

1. Wal-Mart returns to a supplier damaged boots that cost $1,000. Wal-Mart has not paid for the boots.

	Debit	Credit

Assets	=	Liabilities	+	Owners' Equity

2. Wal-Mart purchases DVD players with an invoice price of $20,000 and payment terms of 2/10, n/30. It then makes the payment within the discount period. Record the purchase and the subsequent payment.

	Debit	Credit

Assets	=	Liabilities	+	Owners' Equity

After you have finished, check your answers with the solutions at the bottom of the next page.

Learning Objective 4

Analyze merchandise sales under a perpetual inventory system.

RECORDING MERCHANDISE SALES

Merchandisers (the sellers) generally record the sale (and the customer records the purchase) at the point at which ownership is transferred to the customer. For a retail merchandiser like Wal-Mart, the transfer occurs when a customer buys and takes possession of the goods at checkout. For a wholesale merchandiser, the transfer of ownership occurs at the time stated in the written sales agreement—either **FOB shipping point** or **FOB destination.**

A perpetual system records two effects when inventory is sold:

1. An increase in Sales Revenue and a corresponding increase in either Cash (for a cash sale) or Accounts Receivable (for a credit sale).
2. A decrease in Inventory and a corresponding increase in Cost of Goods Sold (CGS), an expense account for the cost of inventory sold.

Cash Sales

Assume that Wal-Mart sells a Schwinn mountain bike for $225 cash. The bike's cost to Wal-Mart was $175. Exhibit 6.4 illustrates this transaction.

Notice that Wal-Mart records **the sale of inventory as two transactions.** The first journal entry, which increases Cash and Sales Revenue, is recorded at the selling price ($225). The second part, which increases Cost of Goods Sold and decreases Inventory, is recorded at Wal-Mart's cost ($175). The $50 difference between the selling price and the cost ($225 − 175) is the gross profit. **Gross profit is not recorded directly in an account.** Rather, it is a subtotal that is produced by subtracting the cost of goods sold from the selling price.

Exhibit 6.4 Sale of Merchandise in a Perpetual System

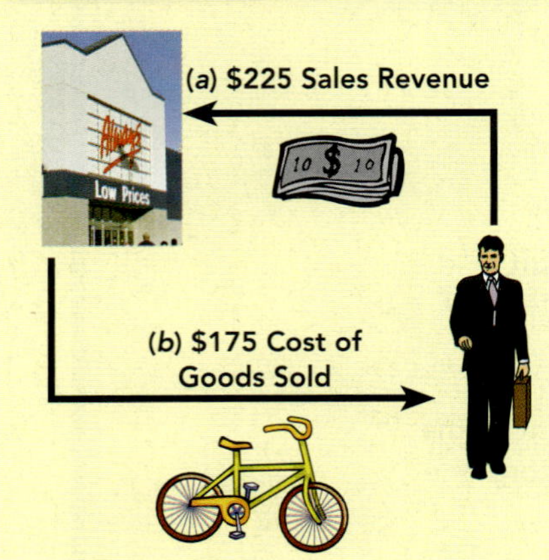

	Debit	Credit
(a) Cash (+A)	225	
Sales Revenue (+R, +OE)		225
(b) Cost of Goods Sold (+E, −OE)	175	
Inventory (−A)		175

Assets		= Liabilities +	Owners' Equity	
(a) Cash	+225		Sales Revenue (+R)	+225
(b) Inventory	−175		Cost of Goods Sold (+E)	−175

Solution to Self-Study Practice

1. Accounts Payable (−L)	1,000	
Inventory (−A)		1,000

Assets	= Liabilities	+ Owners' Equity
Inventory −1,000	Accts. Payable −1,000	

2. Inventory (+A)	20,000	
Accounts Payable (+L)		20,000
Accounts Payable (−L)	20,000	
Inventory (−A) (2% × $20,000)		400
Cash (−A) (98% × $20,000)		19,600

Assets		= Liabilities	+ Owners' Equity
Inventory	+20,000	Accts. Payable +20,000	
Inventory	−400	Accts. Payable −20,000	
Cash	−19,600		

Sales Returns and Allowances

Sales returns and allowances are the same as purchase returns and allowances except that they are recorded from the seller's perspective rather than the purchaser's. Suppose that after Wal-Mart sold the Schwinn mountain bike, the customer returned it to Wal-Mart. Assuming that the bike's condition was still like new, Wal-Mart would refund the purchase price of $225 to the customer.

To account for this transaction, Wal-Mart would make two entries to basically reverse the entries recorded when the bike was sold. We say "basically" because there is one catch: Wal-Mart does not directly reduce its Sales Revenue account. Instead, the company tracks sales returns and allowances in a contra-revenue account that is deducted from total sales revenue.

Just as a contra-asset account such as Accumulated Depreciation reduces the total in an asset account such as Plant and Equipment, a contra-revenue account such as Sales Returns and Allowances reduces the total in a revenue account such as Sales Revenues. **Using a contra-revenue account instead of directly reducing the Sales account allows Wal-Mart to track the value of goods returned,** an indication of whether customers are happy with Wal-Mart's products.[3] Sales returns are recorded as follows:

	Debit	Credit
Sales Returns & Allowances (+xR, −OE)	225	
Cash (−A)		225
Inventory (+A)	175	
Cost of Goods Sold (−E, +OE)		175

Assets		=	Liabilities	+	Owners' Equity	
Cash	−225				Sales Returns & Allowances (+xR)	−225
Inventory	+175				Cost of Goods Sold (−E)	+175

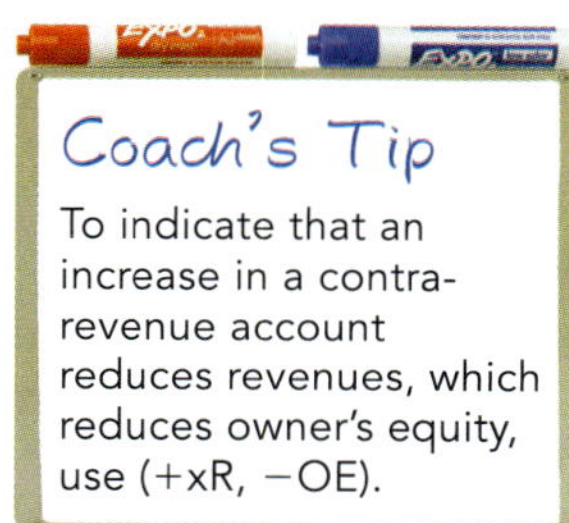

To indicate that an increase in a contra-revenue account reduces revenues, which reduces owner's equity, use (+xR, −OE).

Credit Card Sales

In addition to cash, Wal-Mart accepts credit card payments. Wal-Mart's managers decided to accept credit cards—mainly Visa, Mastercard, and American Express—for a variety of reasons:

1. To increase customer traffic.
2. To avoid the costs of providing credit directly to customers, including credit checks, recordkeeping, and collections.
3. To receive payments faster (credit card receipts can be deposited directly into the seller's bank account).

Credit card companies charge a fee for the service they provide. When Wal-Mart deposits its credit card receipts, it might receive only 99 percent of the sales price. To account for these transactions, the company records the full sales price as sales revenue and then records the 1 percent credit card fee as an expense.

[3] We have assumed that the return occurs in the same period as the sale. When significant returns are likely to occur after the period of sale, the seller records an estimate of those expected returns using methods similar to those described in Chapter 9. We also have assumed the returned bike was as good as new.

Assume, for example, Wal-Mart sold an LCD TV for $500 and received $495 (= 99% × $500) from the credit card company. If the TV cost Wal-Mart $350, the company's accountant would make the following two entries:

	Debit	Credit
Cash (+A) (99% × $500)	495	
Credit Card Fees (+E, −OE) (1% × $500)	5	
Sales Revenue (+R, +OE)		500
Cost of Goods Sold (+E, −OE)	350	
Inventory (−A)		350

Assets		=	Liabilities	+	Owners' Equity	
Cash	+495				Sales Revenue (+R)	+500
					Credit Card Fees (+E)	−5
Inventory	−350				Cost of Goods Sold (+E)	−350

Sales using a retailer-issued credit card (such as Saks) are treated like any sale on account.

Sales on Account and Sales Discounts

You already know that buyers sometimes receive purchase discounts to encourage them to pay promptly for the purchases they make on account. From the seller's point of view, these discounts are called **sales discounts**. As with purchase discounts, sales discounts involve two transactions: (1) the initial sale and (2) the discount given for prompt payment.

Assume Wal-Mart's warehouse store (Sam's Club) sells $1,000 of printer paper on account to a local business with payment terms of 2/10, n/30. The paper cost Sam's Club $670. Wal-Mart records this sale as follows:

	Debit	Credit
Accounts Receivable (+A)	1,000	
Sales Revenue (+R, +OE)		1,000
Cost of Goods Sold (+E, −OE)	670	
Inventory (−A)		670

Assets		=	Liabilities	+	Owners' Equity	
Accounts Receivable	+1,000				Sales Revenue (+R)	+1,000
Inventory	−670				Cost of Goods Sold (+E)	−670

If the customer pays Wal-Mart within the 10-day discount period, it will receive a $20 discount (2% × $1,000). Wal-Mart accounts for the transaction as follows:

Coach's Tip

Sales discounts are calculated after taking into account any sales returns and allowances.

	Debit	Credit
Cash (+A) (98% × $1,000)	980	
Sales Discounts (+xR, −OE) (2% × $1,000)	20	
Accounts Receivable (−A)		1,000

Assets		=	Liabilities	+	Owners' Equity	
Cash	+980				Sales Discounts (+xR)	−20
Accounts Receivable	−1,000					

Exhibit 6.5 Effects of Sales-Related Transactions on Net Sales

Sales revenue	$1,725*
Less: Sales returns and allowances	(225)
Sales discounts	(20)
Net sales (reported on the income statement)	$1,480

* Sales revenue totaled ($1,725 = $225 + $500 + $1,000).

If the customer does not pay by the end of the discount period, Wal-Mart will not allow the customer to take the discount for early payment. Instead, the customer will have to pay the full $1,000. Wal-Mart would record this payment as an increase in Cash (debit) and a decrease in Accounts Receivable (credit). (What if the customer does not pay at all? We will discuss that issue in detail in Chapter 9.)

Before leaving the topic of sales discounts, we should clear up a common misconception. Sales discounts differ from the discount you get as a consumer buying clearance items at a reduced price. The sales discounts discussed in this chapter are given only in business-to-business (B2B) transactions in return for prompt payment. We are sorry to say that as a consumer, you are not likely to be offered this type of discount.

Transportation Cost (Freight-Out)

If Wal-Mart pays to have the printer paper delivered to the business that bought it, its accountant will record the shipping cost (called **freight-out)** as a Delivery Expense. To illustrate, assume Wal-Mart pays UPS $50 cash to deliver the printer paper to the business. Wal-Mart records the cost of transporting the goods to the customer as follows:

	Debit	Credit
Delivery Expense (+E, −OE)	50	
Cash (–A)		50

Assets		=	Liabilities	+	Owners' Equity	
Cash	−50				Delivery Expense (+E)	−50

Summary of Sales-Related Transactions

The sales returns and allowances and sales discounts introduced in this section were recorded using contra-revenue accounts. Exhibit 6.5 summarizes their effects on sales reporting.

Note that **credit card fees** and **freight-out** were recorded as an expense. Normally, both of these transactions would be included in the category **selling, general, and administrative expenses** or **operating expenses.**

Spotlight On FINANCIAL REPORTING

The Makeup of Net Sales

As you have seen, the documentation procedure involving contra-revenue accounts allows managers to monitor and control how sales discounts, returns, and allowances affect the company's revenues. For example, frequent returns of defective products would show up as an increase in the Sales Returns and Allowances account. In response to such an increase, Wal-Mart's managers might decide to discontinue the product or find a new supplier.

Detailed information relating to sales discounts and returns is a key part of a merchandiser's business operations. To avoid revealing these secrets to competitors, most companies report these contra-accounts only on their internal financial statements as in Exhibit 6.5. Externally reported income statements almost never include contra-revenue accounts. Instead, like the one for Wal-Mart, the income statements begin with **Net Sales.**

SELF-STUDY PRACTICE

1. Assume that Wal-Mart's warehouse store (Sam's Club) sells tables on account to a local business for $500 with payment terms of 2/10, n/30. The tables cost Wal-Mart $270. Analyze and record this sale.

Assets	=	Liabilities	+	Owners' Equity

2. The customer pays Wal-Mart for the purchase within the discount period.

Assets	=	Liabilities	+	Owners' Equity

After you have finished, check your answers with the solutions at the bottom of the page.

Comparison of Sales and Purchases Accounting

You may have noticed that when one business sells products to another, the resulting transactions affect the books of both seller and purchaser. An example should clarify these relationships. In the examples just given, Wal-Mart was both the purchaser and the seller of the merchandise. Assume instead that the computer maker HP is the **seller** and Wal-Mart the **purchaser.** Furthermore:

1. HP sold 1,000 notebook computers to Wal-Mart for $500,000 on terms of 3/10, n/30. The computers had an inventory cost to HP of $300,000.

Solution to Self-Study Practice

1. Accounts Receivable (+A)	500	
Sales Revenue (+R, +OE)		500
Cost of Goods Sold (+E, −OE)	270	
Inventory (−A)		270

Assets		=	Liabilities	+	Owners' Equity	
Accts. Rec.	+500				Sales Revenue (+R)	+500
Inventory	−270				Cost of Goods Sold (+E)	−270

2. Cash (+A) (98% × $500)	490	
Sales Discounts (+xR, −OE) (2% × $500)	10	
Accounts Receivable (−A)		500

Assets		=	Liabilities	+	Owners' Equity	
Cash	+490				Sales Discounts (+xR)	−10
Accts. Rec.	−500					

HP (Seller)

Accounts Receivable (+A)	500,000	
Sales Revenue (+R, +OE)		500,000
Cost of Goods Sold (+E, −OE)	300,000	
Inventory (−A)		300,000

Wal-Mart (Purchaser)

Inventory (+A)	500,000	
Accounts Payable (+L)		500,000

2. Wal-Mart returned 200 of those computers, for which the total purchase price was $100,000 (HP's cost was $60,000).

HP (Seller)

Sales Returns and Allowances (+xR, −OE)	100,000	
Accounts Receivable (−A)		100,000
Inventory (+A)	60,000	
Cost of Goods Sold (−E, +OE)		60,000

Wal-Mart (Purchaser)

Accounts Payable (−L)	100,000	
Inventory (−A)		100,000

3. Wal-Mart paid HP for the remaining computers within the discount period.

HP (Seller)

Cash (+A)	388,000	
Sales Discounts (+xR, −OE)	12,000*	
Accounts Receivable (−A)		400,000
*($12,000 = $400,000 × 3%)		

Wal-Mart (Purchaser)

Accounts Payable (−L)	400,000	
Cash (−A)		388,000
Inventory (−A)		12,000

Note that the 3 percent discount is applied to the amount owed after considering the return ($400,000 = $500,000 − $100,000).

As indicated earlier, the terms of sale (**FOB shipping point** or **FOB destination**) determine when the sale and purchase should be recorded. **The same terms indicate which party pays for the shipping.** The purchaser pays for shipping if the terms are FOB shipping point; the seller pays if the terms are FOB destination.

Coach's Tip

Note that **Net Sales** for the seller equals the total cost of the **Inventory** recorded by the purchaser:

$500,000
−100,000
− 12,000
$388,000

HP (Seller)

If HP paid the $1,000 transportation cost on the shipment, it would record the freight–out on its books as a delivery expense:

Delivery Expense (+E, −OE)	1,000	
Cash (−A)		1,000

OR

Wal-Mart (Purchaser)

If Wal-Mart paid the $1,000 transportation cost on the shipment, the freight–in would be recorded on its books as part of inventory:

Inventory (+A)	1,000	
Cash (−A)		1,000

The terms of the sales contract are usually stated in the invoice the seller sends to the buyer. Exhibit 6.6 shows a facsimile of an invoice for the transaction just analyzed with terms 3/10, n/30 and FOB destination (transportation paid by customer).

Exhibit 6.6 Invoice Sent by HP (the seller) to Wal-Mart (the buyer)

Invoice No. 2389

HP

3000 Hanover Street
Palo Alto, CA 94304

Sold to:
Wal-Mart
Bentonville, Arkansas 33302

Date: 07/02/2010	Terms: 3/10, n/30	Freight: Paid by Customer		
Item Number	Description	Quantity	Price	Total
DV6000T	Notebook computer	1,000	$500.00	$500,000
Returns period: 30 days			Total:	$500,000

Learning Objective 5

Prepare a merchandiser's multistep income statement.

PREPARING AND ANALYZING THE INCOME STATEMENT

Multistep Income Statement for Merchandisers

One of the basic facts of merchandising is that to survive, a merchandiser must sell goods for more than their purchase cost. That is the only way companies such as Wal-Mart or Best Buy can generate enough money to cover their operating expenses. To help financial statement users to see how much income merchandising companies earned from product sales, merchandisers often present their income statements in a multistep format.

The multistep format separates revenues and expenses related to core operations from all other items that affect net income. We use the multistep format to prepare the income statement throughout this text. Because the amount of profit earned after deducting the cost of goods sold is a key measure for merchandisers, their multistep income statement also separates the Cost of Goods Sold from other expenses. As Exhibit 6.7 shows, this extra step produces a subtotal called **Gross Profit (Gross Margin)**, or the amount the company earned from selling goods over and above the cost of those goods. If you buy something for $70 and sell it for $100, you will have a gross profit of $30.

Notice that after the gross profit line, the multistep income statement in Exhibit 6.7 presents other items in much the same format as that used by Pizza Aroma in Chapter 4. The category **Selling, General, and Administrative Expenses** (or Operating Expenses) represents a variety of expenses including wages, utilities, advertising, and rent. Those expenses are subtracted from the Gross Profit to yield **Operating Income,** a measure of the company's income from regular operating activities.

Revenues, expenses, gains, and losses from transactions that are not central to ongoing operations (that is, nonoperating items) are added and subtracted next. Typical items in this category include:

1. Interest revenue.
2. Interest expense.
3. Gains on the sale of investments and equipment.
4. Losses on the sale of investments and equipment.

Exhibit 6.7 Sample Multistep Income Statement

Wal-Mart

Wal-Mart Stores, Inc.
Income Statements
Fiscal Years Ended January 31
(amounts in millions)

	2006	2005	2004
Net sales	$ 312,427	$ 285,222	$ 256,329
Cost of goods sold	240,391	219,793	198,747
Gross profit	72,036	65,429	57,582
Selling, general, and administrative expenses	53,506	48,338	42,557
Operating income	18,530	17,091	15,025
Other revenue and expense, net	1,172	986	832
Income before income taxes	17,358	16,105	14,193
Income tax expense	6,127	5,838	5,139
Net income	$ 11,231	$ 10,267	$ 9,054

The first and third of these items increase net income; the second and fourth decrease it. Thus, this line on the statement is called **Other Revenue and Expense, Net.** The term **net** refers to the fact that the amount reported combines amounts that both increase and decrease net income.

Wal-Mart's income statement includes one more subtotal and expense that we did not discuss in Chapter 4. We noted earlier that like many small businesses, Pizza Aroma is organized as a sole proprietorship. In contrast, most large companies are organized as corporations. Because a corporation is a separate legal entity, its owners cannot be held liable for more than their investment in the corporation—a major advantage to investors. Corporations are also taxed separately from their owners, so they normally list the subtotal **Income before Income Taxes** next. Then they subtract the account **Income Tax Expense** to arrive at the "bottom line," **Net Income.** This basic format is used by most merchandising and manufacturing companies.

Coach's Tip

The term **net** included in an account title listed on a financial statement means that positive and negative amounts have been combined.

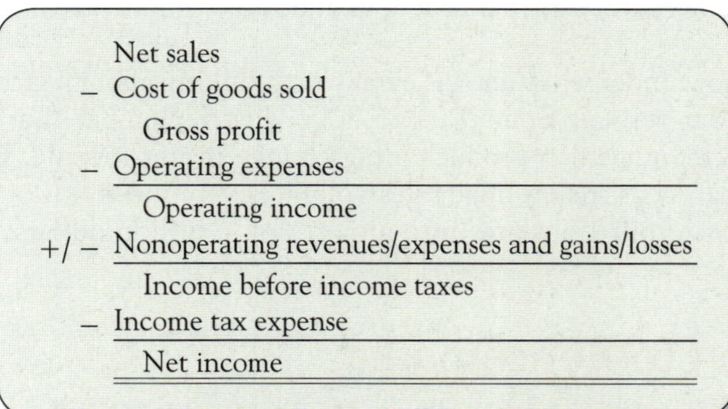

Net sales
– Cost of goods sold
Gross profit
– Operating expenses
Operating income
+/ – Nonoperating revenues/expenses and gains/losses
Income before income taxes
– Income tax expense
Net income

Gross Profit Percentage

Learning Objective 6

Analyze the gross profit percentage.

Let's focus again on the gross profit line on the income statement in Exhibit 6.7. Although the dollar amount of gross profit can be impressive—Wal-Mart really did generate more than $72 billion of gross profit in 2006—by itself, this number is difficult to interpret. According to Exhibit 6.7, Wal-Mart's gross profit increased from 2004 to 2005 to 2006. The problem is that Wal-Mart also increased its sales over those three years, so we do not know whether the increase in gross profit arose because Wal-Mart increased its sales volume or because it generated more profit per sale. To determine the amount of gross profit included in each dollar of sales, analysts typically evaluate the **gross profit percentage.**

Accounting Decision Tools

Name of Measure	Formula	What It Tells You
Gross profit percentage	$\frac{(\text{Net Sales} - \text{CGS})}{\text{Net Sales}} \times 100$	• The percentage of profit earned on each dollar of sales after considering the cost of products sold • A higher ratio means that more profit is available to cover operating and other expenses

The gross profit percentage measures the percentage of profit earned on each dollar of sales. Using the numbers from Wal-Mart's income statement in Exhibit 6.7, Wal-Mart's 2006 gross profit percentage would be computed as follows:

$$\text{Gross Profit Percentage} = \frac{(\text{Net Sales} - \text{CGS})}{\text{Net Sales}} \times 100 = \frac{(\$312{,}427 - \$240{,}391)}{\$312{,}427} \times 100 = 23.1\%$$

This ratio is used (1) to analyze changes in the company's operations over time, (2) to compare one company with another, and (3) to determine whether a company is earning enough revenue on each sale to cover its operating expenses. A higher gross profit percentage means that the company is selling products for a larger markup over their cost.

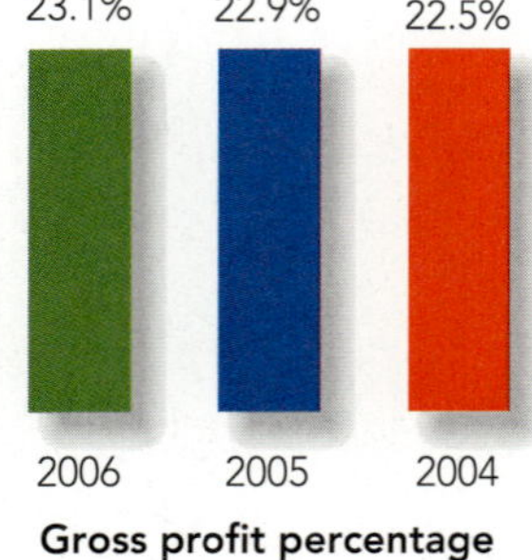

Gross profit percentage

Wal-Mart

As the bar graph in the margin shows, Wal-Mart's gross profit percentage increased ever so slightly from 2004 through 2006. In 2006, each dollar of sales included 23.1 cents of gross profit compared with 22.9 or 22.5 cents of gross profit in the prior two years, respectively. So not only did Wal-Mart sell more in 2006 than in the prior two years but it also generated more profit per sale. How was that possible? To find out, you could read the Management's Discussion and Analysis section of Wal-Mart's annual report. You would find that Wal-Mart was able to reduce inventory shrinkage and markdowns, which yields more profit per dollar of sales.

You might also wonder whether it is even worth talking about a gross profit percentage increase of only 0.6 percent from 2004 to 2006. Just remember that a small change in the gross profit percentage can produce a big change in net income. In Wal-Mart's case, because the company has such a huge sales volume, even one-tenth of a percentage point increase in its gross profit translates into almost half a billion dollars. Yes, that is billion with a **b.**

Comparison to Benchmarks

Be aware that gross profit percentages can vary greatly among different types of companies. Wal-Mart's 23.1 percent is characteristic of its business strategy, which is to sell at "Low Prices, Always." In contrast, Saks' high-end department stores carry fashions with high-end prices, producing a 37.5 percent gross profit percentage. These two companies represent the extremes of merchandising; the typical department store earns a gross profit percentage of 28.1 percent.

Gross profit percentages can vary across industries as well (see Exhibit 6.8). Pharmaceutical companies recently reported an average gross profit percentage of 74.2 percent compared to the 15.2 percent automakers reported. Of course, these cross-industry differences are to be expected. Drug companies need a higher gross profit percentage than carmakers do because their research and development expenses are much higher.

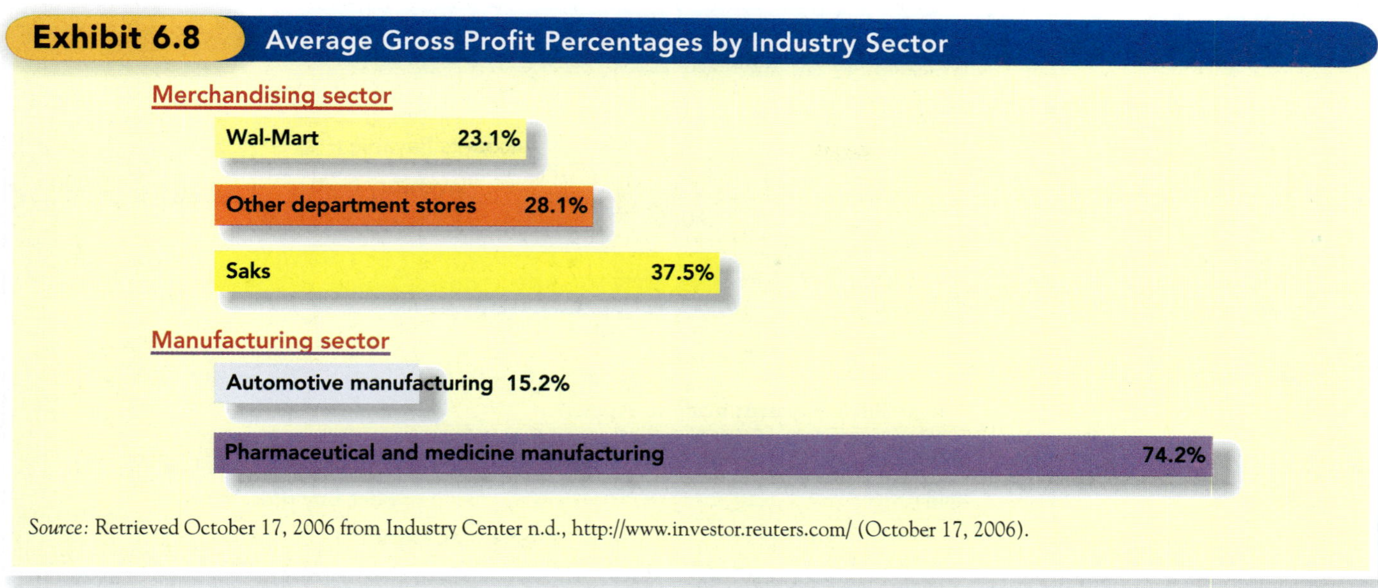

Source: Retrieved October 17, 2006 from Industry Center n.d., http://www.investor.reuters.com/ (October 17, 2006).

Demonstration Case A

Assume that Apple Inc. sold iPods costing $137,200 on account to Best Buy for $405,000 at terms 2/10, n/30. Because some of the merchandise differed from Best Buy's order, the manager returned the merchandise, which had a total purchase price of $5,000 (and a $1,500 cost to Apple). Best Buy satisfied the remaining balance (of $400,000) by paying within the discount period.

Required:

1. Assuming that both companies use a perpetual inventory system, prepare the journal entries that Apple and Best Buy would make to record the following transactions:
   a. Apple's sale to Best Buy.
   b. Best Buy's return of goods to Apple.
   c. Best Buy's payment made to Apple.
2. Compute Apple's Net Sales, assuming that Sales Returns and Allowances and Sales Discounts are treated as contra-revenues.
3. Compute Apple's Gross Profit from this sale.

Suggested Solution

1. **Journal entries:**
   a. **Apple's sale to Best Buy:**

Apple (Seller)

Accounts Receivable (+A)	405,000	
Sales Revenue (+R, +OE)		405,000
Cost of Goods Sold (+E, −OE)	137,200	
Inventory (−A)		137,200

Best Buy (Purchaser)

Inventory (+A)	405,000	
Accounts Payable (+L)		405,000

b. **Best Buy's return of goods to Apple:**

Apple (Seller)

Sales Returns and		
Allowances (+xR, −OE)	5,000	
Accounts Receivable (−A)		5,000
Inventory (+A)	1,500	
Cost of Goods Sold (−E, +OE)		1,500

Best Buy (Purchaser)

Accounts Payable (−L)	5,000	
Inventory (−A)		5,000

c. **Best Buy's payment made to Apple:**

Apple (Seller)

Cash (+A)	392,000	
Sales Discounts (+xR, −OE)	8,000*	
Accounts Receivable (−A)		400,000
*[$8,000 = ($405,000 − $5,000) × 2%]		

Best Buy (Purchaser)

Accounts Payable (−L)	400,000	
Cash (−A)		392,000
Inventory (−A)		8,000

2. **To compute Net Sales, subtract Sales Returns and Allowances and Sales Discounts from Sales Revenue:**

Sales revenue	$405,000
Less: Sales returns and allowances	5,000
Sales discounts [0.02 × ($405,000 − $5,000)]	8,000
Net sales	$392,000

3. **To compute Gross Profit, subtract Cost of Goods Sold from Net Sales:**

Net sales	$392,000
Cost of goods sold ($137,200 − $1,500)	135,700
Gross profit	$256,300

Demonstration Case B

Among membership warehouse stores, Costco Wholesale Corporation is Sam's Club's major competitor. Costco's income statement for the year ended September 3, 2006, included the following revenues and expenses (presented in alphabetical order, in millions of dollars):

Cost of merchandise sold	$ 52,745
Other income and expense, net	+125
Net sales	60,151
Income tax expense	648
Selling, general, and administrative expenses	5,780

Required:

1. Prepare Costco's income statement for the year ended September 3, 2006, using the multistep format presented in this chapter.
2. Compute Costco's gross profit percentage for the year. What does it tell you about the company?

Suggested Solution

1. Multistep income statement:

Costco Wholesale Corporation
Income Statement
Fiscal Year Ended September 3, 2006
(in millions)

Net sales	$ 60,151
Cost of merchandise sold	52,745
Gross profit	7,406
Selling, general, and administrative expenses	5,780
Operating income	1,626
Other income and expense, net	125
Income before income taxes	1,751
Income tax expense	648
Net income	$ 1,103

2. Gross profit percentage:

$$\left(\frac{(\text{Net Sales} - \text{CGS})}{\text{Net Sales}}\right) \times 100$$

$$\frac{(\$60{,}151 - \$52{,}745)}{\$60{,}151} \times 100 = 12.3\%$$

This percentage means that each dollar of sales in 2006 included 12.3 cents of gross profit.

Supplement 6A

Periodic Inventory Records

As you have learned in this chapter, businesses using a periodic inventory system update inventory records only at the end of the accounting period. Unlike a perpetual inventory system, a periodic system does not track the cost of goods sold during the accounting period.

This supplement illustrates some typical journal entries made when using a periodic inventory system. The table that follows contrasts those entries with the entries that would be recorded using a perpetual inventory system. A summary of the effects of the journal entries on the accounting equation follows them. Note that the total effects and the resulting financial statements are identical. Only the timing and nature of the entries differ.

Assume for the purposes of this illustration only that a local cell phone dealer stocks and sells just one item, the MOTORAZR phone and that only the following events occurred in 2010:

Jan. 1	Beginning inventory: 800 units at a unit cost of $50.
Apr. 14	Purchased 1,100 additional units on account at a unit cost of $50.
Nov. 30	Sold 1,300 units on account at a unit sales price of $83.
Dec. 31	Counted 600 units at a unit cost of $50.

Periodic Records

A. Record purchases:
April 14, 2010:

Purchases (+A) (1,100 units at $50)	55,000	
Accounts Payable (+L)		55,000

B. Record sales (but not cost of goods sold):
November 30, 2010:

Accounts Receivable (+A)	107,900	
Sales Revenue (+R, +OE) (1,300 units at $83)		107,900

No cost of goods sold entry

C. Record end-of-period adjustments:

a. Count the number of units on hand.
b. Compute the dollar valuation of the ending inventory.
c. Compute and record the cost of goods sold.

Beginning inventory (last period's ending) (800 units at $50)	$40,000
Add: Net purchases	55,000
Cost of goods available for sale	95,000
Deduct Ending inventory (physical count—600 units at $50)	30,000
Cost of goods sold	$65,000

December 31, 2010:

Transfer beginning inventory and net purchases to cost of goods sold: (act as if all goods were sold)

Cost of Goods Sold (+E, −OE)	95,000	
Inventory (−A) (beginning)		40,000
Purchases (−A)		55,000

Adjust the cost of goods sold by subtracting the amount of ending inventory still on hand (recognize that not all goods were sold):

Inventory (+A) (ending)	30,000	
Cost of Goods Sold (−E, +OE)		30,000

Assets		=	Liabilities		+	Owners' Equity	
Purchases	+55,000		Accounts Payable	+55,000			
Accts. Rec.	+107,900					Sales Revenue (R)	+107,900
Inventory	−40,000					Cost of Goods Sold (E)	−95,000
Purchases	−55,000						
Inventory	+30,000					Cost of Goods Sold (E)	+30,000
Totals	+97,900			+55,000			+42,900

Perpetual Records

A. Record purchases:
April 14, 2010:

Inventory (+A) (1,100 units at $50)	55,000	
Accounts Payable (+L)		55,000

B. Record sales and cost of goods sold:
November 30, 2010:

Accounts Receivable (+A)	107,900	
Sales Revenue (+R, +OE) (1,300 units at $83)		107,900

Cost of Goods Sold (+E, −OE)	65,000	
Inventory (−A) (1,300 units at $50)		65,000

C. Record end-of-period adjustments:

At the end of the accounting period, the balance in the Cost of Goods Sold account is reported on the income statement. Computing the cost of goods sold is not necessary because the **Cost of Goods Sold** account is up to date. Also, the **Inventory** account shows the ending inventory amount reported on the balance sheet. A physical inventory count is still necessary to assess the accuracy of the perpetual records and identify theft and other forms of shrinkage. Any shrinkage would be recorded by reducing the **Inventory** account and increasing an expense account (such as **Inventory Shrinkage** or **Cost of Goods Sold**). This illustration assumes that no shrinkage has been detected.

No entry

Assets		=	Liabilities		+	Owners' Equity	
Inventory	+55,000		Accounts Payable	+55,000			
Accts. Rec.	+107,900					Sales Revenue (R)	+107,900
Inventory	−65,000					Cost of Goods Sold (E)	−65,000
Totals	+97,900			+55,000			+42,900

Supplement 6B

Closing Entries for a Merchandiser

Like service companies, merchandisers must close their temporary accounts. The process is very similar to that followed by a service company. Assume for the purposes of this illustration only that a local cell phone dealer's preclosing trial balance included the following revenues, contra-revenues, and expenses at the end of 2010. The owner, John T. Lyon, organized his business as a sole proprietorship and uses a perpetual inventory system.

	Debit	Credit
Sales Revenue		175,000
Cost of Goods Sold	92,000	
Salaries Expense	28,000	
Rent Expense	24,000	
Shipping Expense (Freight-Out)	2,000	
Interest Income		2,400
Depreciation Expense	3,200	
Sales Returns and Allowances	1,200	
Sales Discounts	600	

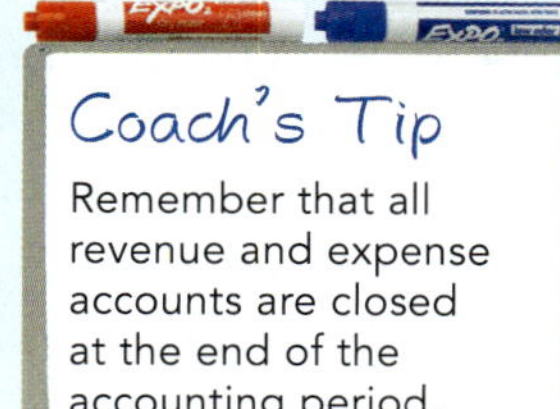

The company would make the following closing entries:

Sales Revenue (−R, −OE)	175,000	
Interest Income (−R, −OE)	2,400	
Income Summary (+OE)		177,400

Income Summary (−OE)	151,000	
Cost of Goods Sold (−E, +OE)		92,000
Salaries Expense (−E, +OE)		28,000
Rent Expense (−E, +OE)		24,000
Shipping Expense (Freight–Out) (−E, +OE)		2,000
Depreciation Expense (−E, +OE)		3,200
Sales Returns and Allowances (−xR, +OE)		1,200
Sales Discounts (−xR, +OE)		600

Income Summary (−OE)	26,400	
John T. Lyon, Capital (+OE)		26,400

Note that the major differences between this merchandising example and the service company examples in Chapter 4 are that the Cost of Goods Sold and the contra-revenue accounts, Sales Returns and Allowances and Sales Discounts, must also be closed to the Income Summary.

Chapter Summary

LO1 Distinguish among service, merchandising, and manufacturing operations. p. 262

- Service companies sell services rather than physical goods; consequently, their income statements show the cost of services rather than the cost of goods sold.
- Merchandise companies sell goods that have been obtained from a supplier. Retail merchandise companies sell directly to consumers. Wholesale merchandise companies sell to retail companies.
- Manufacturing companies sell goods that they have made themselves.

LO2 Explain the use of perpetual and periodic inventory systems and their role in inventory control. p. 262

- A perpetual inventory system updates inventory records every time an item is bought, sold, or returned.
- Rather than update inventory records immediately after each purchase and sale, a periodic system updates inventory records only at the end of the accounting period.

LO3 Analyze merchandise purchases under a perpetual inventory system. p. 265

- The Inventory account should include the purchase price and any costs, such as freight-in, that are needed to prepare the inventory for sale.
- The Inventory account is decreased whenever the purchaser returns goods to the supplier or receives a discount for prompt payment.

LO4 Analyze merchandise sales under a perpetual inventory system. p. 270

- Two entries are made every time inventory is sold: One entry records the sale (and a corresponding debit to Cash or Accounts Receivable) and the other entry records the cost of goods sold (and a corresponding credit to Inventory).
- Sales discounts and sales returns and allowances are reported as contra-revenues, which reduce net sales.
- Credit card discounts and freight-out are recorded as operating expenses.

LO5 Prepare a merchandiser's multistep income statement. p. 276

- One of the key items in a merchandiser's multistep income statement is Gross Profit, which is a subtotal calculated by subtracting the Cost of Goods Sold from Net Sales.
- For both merchandisers and manufacturers, the basic format for the multistep income statement is:

	Net sales
−	Cost of goods sold
	Gross profit
−	Operating expenses
	Operating income
+/−	Nonoperating revenues/expenses and gains/losses
	Income before income taxes
−	Income tax expense
	Net income

LO6 Analyze the gross profit percentage. p. 277

- The gross profit percentage is calculated by dividing the amount of Gross Profit (which is Net Sales minus Cost of Goods Sold) by the Net Sales amount. This measure indicates the amount of gross profit that is included in each dollar of sales.

Financial Analysis Tools

Name of Measure	Formula	What It Tells You
Gross profit percentage	$\frac{(\text{Net Sales} - \text{CGS})}{\text{Net Sales}} \times 100$	• The percentage of profit earned on each dollar of sales after considering the cost of products sold • A higher ratio means that more profit is available to cover operating and other expenses

Key Terms

Cost of Goods Sold (CGS) (p. 270)
FOB Destination (p. 265)
FOB Shipping Point (p. 265)
Gross Profit (or Gross Margin) (p. 276)
Gross Profit Percentage (p. 278)
Manufacturing Company (p. 262)
Merchandising Company (p. 262)
Periodic Inventory System (p. 264)
Perpetual Inventory System (p. 263)
Purchase Discount (p. 266)
Purchase Returns and Allowances (p. 266)
Sales Discount (p. 272)
Sales Returns and Allowances (p. 271)
Service Company (p. 262)

See complete glossary in back of text.

Questions

1. What is the distinction between service and merchandising companies? What is the distinction between merchandising and manufacturing companies? What is the distinction between retail and wholesale merchandising companies?
2. What is the main distinction between perpetual and periodic inventory systems? Which type of system provides better internal control over inventory? Explain why.
3. Why is a physical count of inventory necessary in a periodic inventory system? Why is it still necessary in a perpetual system?
4. Describe how transportation costs to obtain inventory (freight-in) are accounted for by a merchandising company using a perpetual inventory system. Explain the reasoning behind this accounting treatment.
5. What is the distinction between purchase returns and allowances and purchase discounts?
6. What is a purchase discount? Use 1/10, n/30 in your explanation.
7. Describe in words the journal entries that are made in a perpetual inventory system when inventory is sold on credit.
8. What is a credit card fee? How does it affect amounts reported on the income statement?
9. What is a sales discount? Use 1/10, n/30 in your explanation.
10. What is the distinction between sales allowances and sales discounts?
11. Is the amount of sales discount taken recorded (a) at the time the sale is recorded or (b) at the time the collection of the account is recorded?
12. Explain the difference between sales revenue and net sales.
13. Why are contra-revenue accounts used for sales discounts and sales returns and allowances rather than direct deductions from the sales account?
14. What is gross profit? How is the gross profit percentage computed? Illustrate its calculation and interpretation assuming net sales revenue is $100,000 and cost of goods sold is $60,000.

Multiple Choice

1. Mountain Gear, Inc., buys bikes, tents, and climbing supplies from Rugged Rock Corporation for sale to consumers. What type of company is Mountain Gear, Inc.?

   Quiz 6-1
   www.mhhe.com/LLPW1e

   a. Service.
   b. Retail merchandiser.
   c. Wholesale merchandiser.
   d. Manufacturer.

2. Which of the following is false regarding a perpetual inventory system?
   a. Physical counts are never needed since records are maintained on a transaction-by-transaction basis.
   b. The balance in the inventory account is updated with each inventory purchase and sale transaction.
   c. Cost of goods sold is increased as sales are recorded.
   d. The account Purchases is not used as inventory is acquired.

3. Purchase discounts with terms 2/10, n/30 mean:
   a. 10 percent discount for payment within 30 days.
   b. 2 percent discount for payment within 10 days or the full amount (less returns) is due within 30 days.
   c. Two-tenths of a percent discount for payment within 30 days.
   d. None of the above.

4. Which of the following describes how payments to suppliers made within the purchase discount period are recorded in a perpetual inventory system (using the method shown in the chapter)?
   a. Reduce Cash, reduce Accounts Payable.
   b. Reduce Cash, reduce Accounts Payable, reduce Inventory.
   c. Reduce Cash, reduce Accounts Payable, increase Purchase Discounts.
   d. Reduce Cash, reduce Accounts Payable, decrease Purchase Discounts.

5. What is the best description of a credit card fee?
   a. The discount offered by a seller to a consumer for using a national credit card such as VISA.
   b. The fee charged by a seller to a consumer for the right to use a credit card, calculated as a percentage of total revenue for the sale.
   c. The discount offered by a seller to a customer for early payment of an account receivable.
   d. The percentage fee charged by a credit card company to a seller.

6. Sales discounts with terms 2/10, n/30 mean:
   a. 10 percent discount for payment within 30 days.
   b. 2 percent discount for payment within 10 days or the full amount (less returns) is due within 30 days.
   c. Two-tenths of a percent discount for payment within 30 days.
   d. None of the above.

7. Which of the following describes proper accounting for the costs of transporting purchased goods from the seller to the purchaser (freight-in) that is paid for by the purchaser?
   a. The amount is included in the cost of inventory by the purchaser.
   b. The amount is recorded as an other operating expense by the purchaser.

c. The amount is recorded as part of cost of goods sold by the seller.
d. None of the above.

8. Which of the following is not a component of net sales?
   a. Sales returns and allowances.
   b. Sales discounts.
   c. Cost of goods sold.
   d. Sales revenue.

9. A $1,000 sale is made on May 1 with terms 2/10, n/30. Items with a $100 selling price are returned on May 3. What amount, if received on May 9, will be considered payment in full?
   a. $700
   b. $800
   c. $882
   d. $880

10. Earlier this year, your company negotiated larger purchase discounts when paying for its merchandise inventory, which it has consistently taken throughout the year. What effect will this factor have on the company's gross profit percentage this year, in comparison to last year's percentage?
    a. The ratio will not change.
    b. The ratio will increase.
    c. The ratio will decrease.
    d. Either *b* or *c*.

Solutions to Multiple-Choice Questions				
1. b	2. a	3. b	4. b	5. d
6. b	7. a	8. c	9. c	10. b

Mini Exercises  **Available with McGraw-Hill's Homework Manager**

LO1

M6-1 Distinguishing Among Operating Cycles

Identify the type of business as service (S), retail merchandiser (RM), wholesale merchandiser (WM), or manufacturer (M) for each of the following.

1. The company reports no inventory on its balance sheet.
2. The company's customers have been slow in paying their accounts because their own customers have been slow in paying.
3. Approximately one-third of the company's inventory requires further work before it will be ready for sale.

LO2
Nordstrom, Inc.

M6-2 Choosing between a Perpetual and a Periodic Inventory System

Nordstrom, Inc., started in business in 1901. It only took 100 years, but eventually the company changed from a periodic inventory system to a perpetual inventory system (in 2002). Write a brief report describing how this change is likely to improve the company's inventory control.

LO2

M6-3 Calculating Shrinkage in a Perpetual Inventory System

Corey's Campus Store has $50,000 of inventory on hand at the beginning of the month. During the month, the company buys $8,000 of merchandise and sells merchandise that had cost $30,000. At the end of the month, $25,000 of inventory is on hand. How much "shrinkage" occurred during the month?

LO3

M6-4 Preparing Journal Entries for Purchases, Purchase Discounts, and Purchase Returns Using a Perpetual System

Assume Anderson's General Store bought, on credit, a truckload of merchandise from American Wholesaling costing $23,000. The company was charged $650 in transportation cost by National Trucking, immediately returned goods to American Wholesaling costing $1,200, and then took advantage of a 2/10, n/30 purchase discount. Prepare journal entries to record the inventory transactions, assuming Anderson's uses a perpetual inventory system.

LO3

M6-5 Determining Inventory Cost in a Perpetual System

Using the information in M6-4, how much should Anderson's report as the cost of inventory?

LO4

M6-6 Preparing Journal Entries for Credit Card Sales

Credit card sales were $8,000 (credit card fee 3 percent). The goods sold had cost the company $3,500. Prepare journal entries to record these transactions.

LO2, 3, 4, 5

M6-7 Preparing Journal Entries for Purchases and Sales Using a Perpetual Inventory System

Inventory at the beginning of the year cost $13,400. During the year, the company purchased (on account) inventory costing $54,000. Inventory that had cost $60,000 was sold on account for $75,000. At the end of the year, inventory was counted and its cost was determined to be $7,400. (*a*) Prepare journal entries to record these transactions, assuming a perpetual inventory system is used. (*b*) What was the gross profit? (*c*) Was there any shrinkage?

M6-8 Recording Journal Entries for Sales and Sales Discounts **LO4**

Merchandise costing $1,500 is sold for $2,000 on terms 2/10, n/30. The company uses a perpetual inventory system. Prepare the journal entries needed at the time of sale and collection, assuming that the buyer pays within the discount period.

M6-9 Reporting Net Sales and Gross Profit with Sales Discounts **LO4, 5**

Using the information in M6-8, what amount will be reported on the income statement as net sales and as gross profit?

M6-10 Journal Entries to Record Sales Discounts **LO4**

Inventory that cost $500 is sold for $700, with terms of 2/10, n/30. Give the journal entries to record (*a*) the sale of merchandise and (*b*) collection of the accounts receivable assuming that it occurs during the discount period. (Use the method shown in the chapter for recording sales discounts.)

M6-11 Preparing a Multistep Income Statement **LO5**

Sellall Department Stores reported the following amounts in its adjusted trial balance prepared as of its December 31, 2010, fiscal year-end: Administrative Expenses, $2,400; Cost of Goods Sold, $22,728; Income Tax Expense, $3,000; Interest Expense, $1,600; Interest Revenue, $200; Operating Expenses, $2,600; Sales Revenue, $42,000; Sales Discounts, $2,200; Sales Returns and Allowances, $1,920; and Delivery (freight-out) Expense, $300. Prepare a multistep income statement for distribution to external financial statement users.

M6-12 Computing and Interpreting the Gross Profit Percentage **LO6**

Using the information in M6-11, calculate the gross profit percentage for 2010. Evaluate the company's performance using Exhibit 6.8 as a benchmark.

M6-13 Computing and Interpreting the Gross Profit Percentage **LO6**

Ziehart Pharmaceuticals reported net sales of $178,000 and cost of goods sold of $58,000. Candy Electronics Corp. reported net sales of $36,000 and cost of goods sold of $26,200. Calculate the gross profit percentage for both companies. From these calculations, can you determine which company is more successful? Explain.

M6-14 Evaluating the Effect of Discounts and Returns on Gross Profit **LO4, 5, 6**

One of the few companies to report the extent of sales discounts and returns is sunglass maker Oakley, Inc. In the Management's Discussion and Analysis section of its 2005 annual report, Oakley reports the following information about its sales discounts and returns.

	Year ended December 31, (in thousands)		
	2005	2004	2003
Gross sales	$693,342	$621,652	$567,077
Discounts and returns	(45,211)	(36,184)	(39,043)
Net sales	648,131	585,468	528,034
Cost of goods sold	277,230	262,483	245,578
Gross profit	370,901	322,985	282,456

Required:

1. For each year, calculate the percentage of sales discounts and returns by dividing discounts and returns by gross sales and multiplying by 100. Based on these percentages, explain whether sales discounts and returns have a greater impact in 2005 or 2004.
2. For each year, calculate the gross profit percentage using the formula shown in this chapter (i.e., using net sales).

Exercises 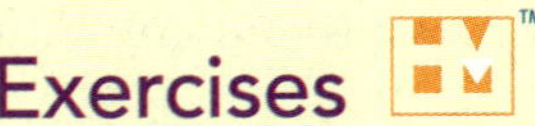 Available with McGraw-Hill's Homework Manager

LO2

E6-1 Inferring Shrinkage Using a Perpetual Inventory System

Calculate the amount of shrinkage for each of the following independent cases:

Cases	Beginning Inventory	Purchases	Cost of Goods Sold	Ending Inventory (as counted)	Shrinkage
A	$100	$700	$300	$420	$?
B	200	800	850	150	?
C	150	500	200	440	?
D	260	600	650	200	?

LO2
JCPenney

E6-2 Inferring Shrinkage Using a Perpetual Inventory System

JCPenney Company, Inc., is a major retailer with department stores in all 50 states. The main part of the company's business consists of providing merchandise and services to consumers through department stores. In 2006 JCPenney reported cost of goods sold of $11,405 million, ending inventory for the current year of $3,234 million, and ending inventory for the previous year (2005) of $3,167 million.

Required:

If you knew that the cost of inventory purchases was $11,474 million, could you estimate the cost of shrinkage during the year? If so, prepare the estimate and, if not, explain why.

LO3

E6-3 Recording the Cost of Purchases for a Merchandiser

Apparel.com purchased 80 new shirts and recorded a total cost of $3,015 determined as follows:

Invoice cost	$2,600
Transportation cost (freight-in)	165
Estimated cost of shipping to customers	250
	$3,015

Required:

Calculate the correct inventory cost.

LO3

E6-4 Recording Journal Entries for Purchases and Purchase Discounts Using a Perpetual Inventory System

During the months of January and February, Axe Corporation purchased goods from three suppliers. The sequence of events was as follows:

Jan.	6	Purchased goods for $1,200 from Green with terms 2/10, n/30.
	6	Purchased goods from Munoz for $900 with terms 2/10, n/30.
	14	Paid Green in full.
Feb.	2	Paid Munoz in full.
	28	Purchased goods for $350 from Reynolds with terms 2/10, n/45.

Required:

Assume Axe uses a perpetual inventory system. The company had no inventory on hand at the beginning of January, and no sales were made during January and February. Prepare journal entries to record the transactions.

LO3

E6-5 Reporting Purchases and Purchase Discounts Using a Perpetual Inventory System

Using the information in E6-4, calculate the cost of inventory as of February 28.

E6-6 Recording Journal Entries for Purchases, Purchase Discounts, and Purchase Returns Using a Perpetual Inventory System **LO3**

During the month of June, Ace Incorporated purchased goods from two suppliers. The sequence of events was as follows:

June 3 Purchased goods for $3,200 from Diamond Ltd. with terms 2/10, n/30.
5 Returned goods costing $1,100 to Diamond Ltd. for full credit.
6 Purchased goods from Club Corp. for $1,000 with terms 2/10, n/30.
11 Paid the balance owed to Diamond.
22 Paid Club Corp. in full.

Required:

Assume Ace uses a perpetual inventory system and that the company had no inventory on hand at the beginning of the month. Prepare journal entries to record the transactions.

E6-7 Reporting Purchases, Purchase Discounts, and Purchase Returns Using a Perpetual Inventory System **LO3**

Using the information in E6-6, calculate the cost of inventory as of June 30.

E6-8 Recording Journal Entries for Net Sales with Credit Sales and Sales Discounts **LO4**

During the months of January and February, Solitare Corporation sold goods to three customers. The sequence of events was as follows:

Jan. 6 Sold goods for $100 to Wizard Inc. with terms 2/10, n/30. The goods cost Solitare $70.
6 Sold goods to SpyderCorp for $80 with terms 2/10, n/30. The goods cost Solitare $60.
14 Collected cash due from Wizard Inc.
Feb. 2 Collected cash due from SpyderCorp.
28 Sold goods for $50 to Bridges with terms 2/10, n/45. The goods cost Solitare $30.

Required:

Assume Solitare uses a perpetual inventory system and that sales discounts are reported as a contra-revenue. Prepare journal entries to record the transactions.

E6-9 Reporting Net Sales with Credit Sales and Sales Discounts **LO4**

Using the information in E6-8, compute net sales for the two months ended February 28.

E6-10 Recording Journal Entries for Net Sales with Credit Sales and Sales Discounts **LO4**

The following transactions were selected from the records of Evergreen Company:

July 12 Sold merchandise to Wally Butler, who paid for the $1,000 purchase with cash. The goods cost Evergreen Company $600.
15 Sold merchandise to Claudio's Chair Company at a selling price of $5,000 on terms 3/10, n/30. The goods cost Evergreen Company $3,500.
20 Sold merchandise to Otto's Ottomans at a selling price of $3,000 on terms 3/10, n/30. The goods cost Evergreen Company $1,900.
23 Collected payment from Claudio's Chair Company from the July 15 sale.
Aug. 25 Collected payment from Otto's Ottomans from the July 20 sale.

Required:

Assume Evergreen Company uses a perpetual inventory system and that sales discounts are reported as a contra-revenue. Prepare journal entries to record the transactions.

E6-11 Reporting Net Sales with Credit Sales and Sales Discounts **LO4**

Using the information in E6-10, compute net sales for the two months ended August 31.

E6-12 Recording Journal Entries for Net Sales with Credit Card Sales, Credit Sales, Sales Discounts, and Sales Returns **LO4**

The following transactions were selected from among those completed by Bear's Retail Store in 2010:

Nov. 20 Sold two items of merchandise to Cheryl Jahn, who charged the $400 sales price on her Visa credit card. Visa charges Bear's a 2 percent credit card fee. The goods cost Bear's $300.

25 Sold 20 items of merchandise to Vasko Athletics at a selling price of $4,000 (total); terms 3/10, n/30. The goods cost Bear's $2,500.

28 Sold 10 identical items of merchandise to Nancy's Gym at a selling price of $6,000 (total); terms 3/10, n/30. The goods cost Bear's $4,000.

29 Nancy's Gym returned one of the items purchased on the 28th. The item was in perfect condition, and credit was given to the customer.

Dec. 6 Nancy's Gym paid the account balance in full.

30 Vasko Athletics paid in full the invoice of November 25, 2010.

Required:

Assume Bear's Retail Store uses a perpetual inventory system and that sales returns and sales discounts are reported as contra-revenues. Prepare journal entries to record the transactions.

LO4

E6-13 Reporting Net Sales with Credit Card Sales, Credit Sales, Sales Discounts, and Sales Returns

Using the information in E6-12, compute net sales for the two months ended December 31, 2010.

LO4, 5

E6-14 Determining the Effects of Credit Sales, Sales Discounts, and Sales Returns and Allowances on Income Statement Categories

Rockland Shoe Company records sales returns and allowances and sales discounts as contra-revenues. Complete the following table for Rockland, indicating the amount and direction of effect (+ for increase, − for decrease, and NE for no effect) of each transaction on each item listed below.

July 12 Rockland sold merchandise to Kristina Zee at its factory store. Kristina paid for the $300 purchase in cash. The goods cost Rockland $160.

July 15 Sold merchandise to Shoe Express at a selling price of $5,000, with terms 3/10, n/30. Rockland's cost was $3,000.

July 20 Collected cash due from Shoe Express.

July 21 Sold merchandise to Fleet Foot Co. at a selling price of $2,000, with terms 2/10, n/30. Rockland's cost was $1,200.

July 23 Fleet Foot Co. returned $1,000 of shoes, and promised to pay for the remaining goods in August. The returned shoes were in perfect condition and had cost Rockland $600.

Transaction	July 12	July 15	July 20	July 21	July 23
Sales Revenue					
Sales Returns and Allowances					
Sales Discounts					
Net Sales					
Cost of Goods Sold					
Gross Profit					

LO3, 4

E6-15 Recording Sales and Purchases with Discounts

Cycle Wholesaling sells merchandise on credit terms of 2/10, n/30. A sale for $800 (cost of goods sold of $500) was made to Sarah's Cycles on February 1, 2010. On March 4, 2010, Cycle Wholesaling purchased bicycles from a supplier on credit, invoiced at $8,000 with terms 1/15, n/30. Assume Cycle Wholesaling uses a perpetual inventory system.

Required:

Sales Transactions:

1. Give the journal entry Cycle Wholesaling would make to record the sale to Sarah's Cycles.
2. Give the journal entry to record the collection of the account, assuming it was collected in full on February 9, 2010.
3. Give the journal entry, assuming instead that the account was collected in full on March 2, 2010.

Purchase Transactions:

4. Give the journal entry to record the purchase on credit.
5. Give the journal entry to record the payment of Cycle Wholesaling's account, assuming it was paid in full on March 12, 2010.
6. Give the journal entry, assuming instead that the account was paid in full on March 28, 2010.

E6-16 Analyzing Sales and Purchases with Discounts and the Gross Profit Percentage — LO3, 4, 6

Refer to the information in E6-15.

Required:

1. Calculate the gross profit percentage for the sale to Sarah's Cycles, assuming the account was collected in full on February 9, 2010.
2. At what cost will the bicycles purchased on March 4 be reported, assuming they are paid for on March 12, 2010?

E6-17 Inferring Missing Amounts Based on Income Statement Relationships — LO5

Supply the missing dollar amounts for the 2010 income statement of Williamson Company for each of the following independent cases:

	Case A	Case B	Case C
Sales revenue	$ 8,000	$ 6,000	$?
Sales returns and allowances	150	?	275
Net sales revenue	?	?	5,920
Cost of goods sold	5,750	4,050	5,400
Gross profit	?	1,450	?

E6-18 Inferring Missing Amounts Based on Income Statement Relationships — LO5

Supply the missing dollar amounts for the 2010 income statement of Lewis Retailers for each of the following independent cases:

Cases	Sales Revenue	Beginning Inventory	Purchases	Cost of Goods Sold	Cost of Ending Inventory	Gross Profit
A	$ 650	$100	$700	$300	?	$?
B	900	200	800	?	150	?
C	?	150	?	200	300	400
D	800	?	600	650	250	?
E	1,000	50	900	?	?	500

E6-19 Analyzing Gross Profit Percentage on the Basis of a Multistep Income Statement — LO5, 6

The following summarized data were provided by the records of Mystery Incorporated for the year ended December 31, 2010:

Sales of merchandise for cash	$240,000
Sales of merchandise on credit	42,000
Cost of goods sold	165,000
Selling expense	40,200
Administrative expense	19,000
Sales returns and allowances	7,000
Income tax expense	17,600

Required:

1. Based on these data, prepare a multistep income statement (showing gross sales, net sales, gross profit, and all other appropriate subtotals).
2. What was the amount of gross profit? What was the gross profit percentage? Explain what these two amounts mean.
3. Evaluate the 2010 results in light of the 38 percent gross profit percentage in 2009.

LO5, 6
Wolverine World Wide

E6-20 Analyzing Gross Profit Percentage on the Basis of an Income Statement

Wolverine World Wide prides itself as being the "world's leading marketer of U.S. branded non-athletic footwear." The following data (in thousands) were taken from its annual report for the year ended 2005:

Sales of merchandise	$1,060,999
Income taxes	36,780
Cash dividends paid	14,814
Selling and administrative expense	291,891
Cost of products sold	655,800
Interest expense	3,647
Other revenues	1,736

Required:

1. Based on these data, prepare a multistep income statement.
2. How much was the gross profit? What was the gross profit percentage (rounded to the nearest tenth of a percent)? Explain what these two amounts mean.
3. Evaluate the 2005 results in light of the 37.7 percent gross profit percentage in 2004.
4. Compare Wolverine's gross profit percentage to Wal-Mart's average gross profit percentage of 23.1 percent. From this information, can you determine which company is more successful? Why or why not?

LO5, 6
Circuit City

E6-21 Comparing Multistep Income Statements

Abbreviated income statements for Circuit City and Best Buy are shown below (in millions) for the year ended February 28, 2006.

	Best Buy	Circuit City
Net sales	$ 30,848	$ 11,598
Cost of goods sold	23,122	8,767
Gross profit	7,726	2,831
Operating expenses	6,082	2,611
Income from operations	1,644	220
Other income and expenses	77	19
Income before income taxes	1,721	239
Income tax expense	581	88
Net income	$ 1,140	$ 151

Required:

1. Which company generated more net income and gross profit?
2. Which company generated a higher gross profit percentage? Show calculations.
3. Interpret your findings from 1 and 2.

E6-22 (Supplement A) Recording Purchases and Sales Using Perpetual and Periodic Inventory Systems

Kangaroo Jim Company reported beginning inventory of 100 units at a per unit cost of $25. It had the following purchase and sales transactions during 2010:

Jan. 14	Sold 25 units at a unit sales price of $45 on account.
Apr. 9	Purchased 15 additional units at a per unit cost of $25 on account.
Sep. 2	Sold 50 units at a unit sales price of $50 on account.
Dec. 31	Counted inventory and determined 40 units were still on hand.

Required:

Record each transaction, assuming that Kangaroo Jim Company uses (*a*) a perpetual inventory system and (*b*) a periodic inventory system.

E6-23 (Supplement B) Closing Entries for a Merchandiser

Koala Joe's preclosing trial balance included the following amounts (among others):

	Debit	Credit
Sales revenue		75,000
Cost of goods sold	42,000	
Sales returns and allowances	1,500	
Sales discounts	500	

Prepare any entries necessary to close these accounts to the Income Summary account.

Problems—Set A  Available with McGraw-Hill's Homework Manager

PA6-1 Journalizing Sales and Purchase Transactions between Wholesale and Retail Merchandisers with Sales/Purchase Allowances and Sales/Purchase Discounts Using Perpetual Inventory Systems LO3, 4

The transactions listed below are typical of those involving New Books and Readers' Corner. New Books is a wholesale merchandiser and Readers' Corner is a retail merchandiser. Assume the following transactions between the two companies occurred in the order listed during the year ended August 31, 2010. Assume all sales of merchandise from New Books to Readers' Corner are made with terms 2/10, n/30, and that the two companies use perpetual inventory systems.

Transactions during the year ended August 31, 2010 are as follows:

a. New Books sold merchandise to Readers' Corner at a selling price of $550,000. The merchandise had cost New Books $415,000.

b. Two days later, Readers' Corner complained to New Books that some of the merchandise differed from what Readers' Corner had ordered. New Books agreed to give an allowance of $10,000 to Readers' Corner.

c. Just three days later, Readers' Corner paid New Books, which settled all amounts owed.

Required:

1. Prepare the journal entries that New Books would record, and show any computations.
2. Prepare the journal entries that Readers' Corner would record, and show any computations.

PA6-2 Reporting Sales and Purchase Transactions between Wholesale and Retail Merchandisers, with Sales/Purchase Allowances and Sales/Purchase Discounts Using Perpetual Inventory Systems LO3, 4, 5

Use the information presented in PA6-1 to complete the following requirements.

Required:

1. For each of the events *a* through *c*, indicate the amount and direction of the effect (+ for increase, − for decrease, and NE for no effect) on New Books in terms of the following items.

Sales Revenues	Sales Returns and Allowances	Sales Discounts	Net Sales	Cost of Goods Sold	Gross Profit

2. Which of the above items are likely to be reported on New Books' external financial statements?
3. Indicate the effect (direction and amount) of each transaction on the balance in Readers' Corner's inventory account.

LO3, 4, 5, 6

www.mhhe.com/LLPW1e

PA6-3 Recording Sales and Purchases with Discounts, Returns, and Credit Card Fees and Computing the Gross Profit Percentage

Hair World Inc. is a wholesaler of hair supplies. Hair World uses a perpetual inventory system. The following transactions (summarized) have been selected from 2010:

a.	Sold merchandise for cash (cost of merchandise $18,600).	$31,200
b.	Received merchandise returned by customers as unsatisfactory, for cash refund (original cost of merchandise $360).	600
c.	Sold merchandise to customers who charged the sales on their credit cards (cost of merchandise $12,000). The credit card fee is 3 percent.	20,000
d.	Purchased merchandise from Cari's Comb Company with terms 3/10, n/30.	1,000
e.	Purchased merchandise from other suppliers with terms 3/10, n/30.	24,000
f.	Purchased equipment for use in the store; paid cash.	400
g.	Purchased office supplies for future use in the store; paid cash.	140
h.	Freight on merchandise purchased; paid cash.	100
i.	Paid Cari's Comb Company after the discount period.	1,000
j.	Paid other suppliers (see part *e*) within the 3 percent discount period.	23,280

Required:

1. Prepare journal entries for transactions *a–j*.
2. Assume that Hair World had inventory on hand at the beginning of the period at a cost of $100,000. At what amount should inventory be reported at the end of the period?
3. Compute gross profit and the gross profit percentage for sales this period.

LO4, 5, 6

www.mhhe.com/LLPW1e

PA6-4 Preparing a Multistep Income Statement with Sales Discounts and Sales Returns and Allowances and Computing the Gross Profit Percentage

Big Tommy Corporation is a local grocery store organized seven years ago as a corporation. The store is in an excellent location, and sales have increased each year. At the end of 2010, the bookkeeper prepared the following statement (assume that all amounts are correct, but note the incorrect terminology and format):

BIG TOMMY CORPORATION
Profit and Loss
December 31, 2010

	Debit	Credit
Sales		$420,000
Cost of goods sold	$279,000	
Sales returns and allowances	10,000	
Sales discounts	6,000	
Selling expense	58,000	
Administrative expense	16,000	
General expenses	1,000	
Income tax expense	15,000	
Net profit	35,000	
Totals	$420,000	$420,000

Required:

1. Compute net sales. Treat sales discounts and sales returns and allowances as contra-revenues.
2. Prepare a multistep income statement, beginning with the amount for net sales.
3. Compute the gross profit percentage and explain its meaning.

PA6-5 (Supplement A) Journalizing Sales and Purchase Transactions between Wholesale and Retail Merchandisers Using Periodic Inventory Systems

Use the information presented in PA6-1 and transaction *a* (only) to complete the following requirements, except assume that both companies use periodic inventory systems.

www.mhhe.com/LLPW1e

Required:

1. Prepare the journal entries that New Books would record for transaction *a* only.
2. Prepare the journal entries that Readers' Corner would record for transaction *a* only.
3. Assume that, during the year, Readers' Corner sold merchandise on credit for $250,000. Prepare the journal entries that Readers' Corner would record.
4. Assume that, at the end of the year, Readers' Corner counted the inventory it had purchased from New Books and determined that its cost was $135,000. There was no beginning inventory. Prepare any adjusting entries that Readers' Corner would record, and show any computations.

PA6-6 (Supplement B) Closing Entries for a Merchandiser

R. Gupta Chemical's preclosing trial balance included the following amounts (among others):

	Debit	Credit
Sales Revenue		615,000
Interest Expense	12,500	
Sales Returns and Allowances	53,200	
Sales Discounts	14,600	
Cost of Goods Sold	376,000	
Selling Expense	23,000	
Rental Expense	27,000	
Shipping Expense (Freight-out)	5,200	
Depreciation Expense	18,000	

Required:

Prepare the entries necessary to close these accounts.

Problems—Set B  Available with McGraw-Hill's Homework Manager

PB6-1 Journalizing Sales and Purchase Transactions between Wholesale and Retail Merchandisers with Sales/Purchase Allowances and Sales/Purchase Discounts Using Perpetual Inventory Systems LO3, 4

The transactions listed below are typical of those involving Southern Sporting Goods and Sports R Us. Southern Sporting Goods is a wholesale merchandiser and Sports R Us is a retail merchandiser. Assume the following transactions between the two companies occurred in the order listed during the year ended December 31, 2010. Assume all sales of merchandise from Southern Sporting Goods to Sports R Us are made with terms 2/10, n/30, and that the two companies use perpetual inventory systems.

Transactions during 2010:

a. Southern Sporting Goods sold merchandise to Sports R Us at a selling price of $125,000. The merchandise had cost Southern Sporting Goods $94,000.

b. Two days later, Sports R Us complained to Southern Sporting Goods that some of the merchandise differed from what Sports R Us had ordered. Southern Sporting Goods agreed to give an allowance of $3,000 to Sports R Us.

c. Just three days later Sports R Us paid Southern Sporting Goods, which settled all amounts owed.

Required:

1. Prepare the journal entries that Southern Sporting Goods would record, and show any computations.
2. Prepare the journal entries that Sports R Us would record, and show any computations.

LO3, 4, 5

PB6-2 Reporting Sales and Purchase Transactions between Wholesale and Retail Merchandisers with Sales/Purchase Allowances and Sales/Purchase Discounts Using Perpetual Inventory Systems

Use the information presented in PB 6-1 to complete the following requirements.

Required:

1. For each of the events *a* through *c*, indicate the amount and direction of the effect (+ for increase, − for decrease, and NE for no effect) on Southern Sporting Goods in terms of the following items.

Sales Revenues	Sales Returns and Allowances	Sales Discounts	Net Sales	Cost of Goods Sold	Gross Profit

2. Which of the above items is likely to be reported on Southern Sporting Goods' external financial statements.
3. Indicate the effect (direction and amount) of each transaction on the balance in Sports R Us's inventory account.

LO3, 4, 5, 6

PB6-3 Recording Sales and Purchases with Discounts, Returns, and Credit Card Fees and Computing the Gross Profit Percentage

Larry's Hardware, Incorporated, is a locally owned and operated hardware store. Larry's Hardware uses a perpetual inventory system. The following transactions (summarized) have been selected from 2010:

a.	Sold merchandise for cash (cost of merchandise $285,000).	$400,000
b.	Received merchandise returned by customers as unsatisfactory, for cash refund (original cost of merchandise $1,900).	3,000
c.	Sold merchandise to customers who charged the sales on their credit cards (cost of merchandise $60,000). The credit card fee is 2 percent.	100,000
d.	Purchased merchandise from Do It Yourself Company with terms 3/10, n/30.	27,000
e.	Purchased merchandise from other suppliers with terms 3/10, n/30.	237,000
f.	Purchased equipment for use in store; paid cash.	5,000
g.	Purchased office supplies for future use in the store; paid cash.	400
h.	Freight on merchandise purchased; paid cash.	350
i.	Paid Do It Yourself Company after the discount period.	27,000
j.	Paid other suppliers (see transaction *e*) within the discount period.	229,890

Required:

1. Prepare journal entries for transactions *a–j*.
2. Assume that Larry's Hardware had inventory on hand at the beginning of the period at a cost of $350,000. At what amount should inventory be reported at the end of the period?
3. Compute gross profit and the gross profit percentage for sales this period.

LO4, 5, 6

PB6-4 Preparing a Multistep Income Statement with Sales Discounts and Sales Returns and Allowances, and Computing the Gross Profit Percentage

Emily's Greenhouse Corporation is a local greenhouse organized 10 years ago as a corporation. The greenhouse is in an excellent location, and sales have increased each year. At the end of 2010, the bookkeeper prepared the following statement (assume that all amounts are correct, but note the incorrect terminology and format):

EMILY'S GREENHOUSE CORPORATION Profit and Loss December 31, 2010		
	Debit	Credit
Sales		$504,000
Cost of goods sold	$311,000	
Sales returns and allowances	11,000	
Sales discounts	8,000	
Selling expense	61,000	
Administrative expense	13,000	
General expenses	3,000	
Income tax expense	18,000	
Net profit	79,000	
Totals	$504,000	$504,000

Required:

1. Compute net sales. Treat sales discounts and sales returns and allowances as contra-revenues.
2. Prepare a multistep income statement, beginning with the amount for net sales.
3. Compute the gross profit percentage and explain its meaning.

PB6-5 (Supplement A) Journalizing Sales and Purchase Transactions between Wholesale and Retail Merchandisers Using Periodic Inventory Systems

Use the information presented in PB6-1 and transaction *a* (only) to complete the following requirements, except assume that both companies use periodic inventory systems.

Required:

1. Prepare the journal entries that Southern Sporting Goods would record for transaction *a* only.
2. Prepare the journal entries that Sports R Us would record for transaction *a* only.
3. Assume that, during the year, Sports R Us sold merchandise on credit for $97,000. Prepare the journal entries that Sports R Us would record.
4. Assume that, at the end of the year, Sports R Us counted the inventory it had purchased from Southern Sporting Goods and determined that its cost was $43,000. There was no beginning inventory. Prepare any adjusting entries that Sports R Us would record, and show any computations.

PB6-6 (Supplement B) Closing Entries for a Merchandiser

Paul Ethan's Skateboard Shop's preclosing trial balance included the following amounts (among others):

	Debit	Credit
Sales Revenue		65,000
Other Income		12,500
Wage Expense	13,000	
Rental Expense	5,000	
Shipping Expense (Freight-out)	500	
Sales Discounts	1,600	
Sales Returns and Allowances	5,200	
Cost of Goods Sold	31,000	
Interest Expense	800	

Required:

Prepare the entries necessary to close these accounts.

Cases and Projects

LO2, 5, 6

CP6-1 Finding Financial Information

Refer to the financial statements of The Home Depot in Appendix A at the end of this book, or download the annual report from the *Cases* section of the text's Web site at www.mhhe.com/LLPW1e.

Required:

1. What amount of Net Sales does the company report during the current year?
2. Assuming that Cost of Sales is the same thing as Cost of Goods Sold, compute the company's gross profit percentage for the most recent two years. Has it risen or fallen? Explain the meaning of the change.
3. Assume that The Home Depot experienced no shrinkage in the most current year. Using the balance sheet and income statement, estimate the amount of purchases in the most recent year. (Hint: Use the cost of goods sold equation to solve for purchases.)

LO4, 5, 6

Lowe's

CP6-2 Comparing Financial Information

Refer to the financial statements of The Home Depot in Appendix A and Lowe's in Appendix B at the end of this book, or download the annual reports from the *Cases* section of the text's Web site at www.mhhe.com/LLPW1e.

1. Does Lowe's report higher or lower Net Sales than The Home Depot during the current year?
2. Assuming that Cost of Sales is the same thing as Cost of Goods Sold, compute Lowe's gross profit percentage for the most recent two years. Is it greater or less than The Home Depot's?
3. Assume that Lowe's and The Home Depot experienced no shrinkage in the most recent year. Using the balance sheet and income statement, estimate the amount of purchases in the most recent year. How much greater (or less) were Lowe's purchases than The Home Depot's for the most recent year? (Hint: Use the cost of goods sold equation to solve for purchases.)

LO1, 6

CP6-3 Examining an Annual Report: Internet-Based Team Research

As a team, select an industry to analyze. Using your Web browser, each team member should acquire the annual report or 10-K for one publicly traded company in the industry, with each member selecting a different company. (See CP1-3 in Chapter 1 for a description of possible resources for these tasks.)

Required:

1. On an individual basis, each team member should write a short report that incorporates the following:
   a. Describe the company's business in sufficient detail to be able to classify it as a service, merchandising, or manufacturing company. What products or services does the company provide?
   b. Calculate the gross profit percentage at the end of the current and prior year, and explain any change between the two years.
2. Then, as a team, write a short report comparing and contrasting your companies using these attributes. Discuss any patterns across the companies that you as a team observe. Provide potential explanations for any differences discovered.

LO5, 6

CP6-4 Making Ethical Decisions: A Mini Case

Assume you work as an accountant in the merchandising division of a large public company that makes and sells athletic clothing. To encourage the merchandising division to earn as much profit on each individual sale as possible, the division manager's pay is based, in part, on the division's gross profit percentage. To encourage control over the division's operating expenses, the manager's pay also is based on the division's net income.

You are currently preparing the division's financial statements. The division had a good year, with sales of $100,000, cost of goods sold of $50,000, sales returns and allowances of $6,000, sales discounts of $4,000, and other selling expenses of $30,000. (Assume the division does not report income taxes.) The division manager stresses that "it would be in your personal interest" to classify sales returns and allowances, and sales discounts as selling expenses rather than as contra-revenues on the division's income statement. He justifies this "friendly advice" by saying that he is not asking you to fake the numbers—he just believes that those items are more accurately reported as expenses. Plus, he claims, being a division of a larger company, you do not have to follow GAAP.

Required:

1. Prepare an income statement for the division using the classifications advised by the manager. Using this income statement, calculate the division's gross profit percentage.
2. Prepare an income statement for the division using the classifications shown in this chapter. Using this income statement, calculate the division's gross profit percentage.
3. What reason (other than reporting "more accurately") do you think is motivating the manager's advice to you?
4. Do you agree with the manager's statement that he "is not asking you to fake the numbers"?
5. Do you agree with the manager's statement about not having to follow GAAP?
6. How should you respond to the division manager's "friendly advice"?

CP6-5 Preparing Multistep Income Statements and Calculating Gross Profit Percentage LO5, 6

Assume that you have been hired by Big Sky Corporation as a summer intern. The company is in the process of preparing their annual financial statements. To help in the process, you are asked to prepare an income statement for internal reporting purposes and an income statement for external reporting purposes. Your boss has also requested that you determine the company's gross profit percentage based on the statements that you are to prepare. The following adjusted trial balance was created from the general ledger accounts on May 31, 2010.

Account Titles	Debit	Credit
Cash	$ 57,000	
Accounts receivable	67,000	
Inventory	103,000	
Property and equipment	252,000	
Accumulated depreciation		$ 103,000
Liabilities		75,000
Owners' equity, June 1, 2009		265,900
Sales revenue		369,000
Sales returns and allowances	9,500	
Sales discounts	14,000	
Cost of goods sold	248,000	
Selling expense	19,000	
Administrative expense	23,000	
General expenses	5,000	
Income tax expense	15,400	
Totals	$ 812,900	$ 812,900

Your boss wants you to create the spreadsheet in a way that automatically recalculates net sales and any other related amounts whenever changes are made to the contra-revenue accounts. To do this, you know that you will have to use formulas throughout the worksheets and even import or link cells from one worksheet to another. Once again, your friend Owen is willing to help.

From: Owen@yahoo.com
To: Helpme@hotmail.com
Cc:
Subject: Excel Help

Sounds like you are going to get some great experience this summer. Okay, to import a number from another spreadsheet, you first click on the cell where you want the number to appear. For example, if you want to enter the Net Sales balance in the external income statement, click on the cell in the external income statement where the net sales number is supposed to appear. Enter the equals sign (=) and then click on the tab that takes you to the worksheet containing the internal income statement. In that worksheet, click on the cell that contains the amount you want to import into the external income statement and then press enter. This will create a link from the internal income statement cell to the external income statement cell. Here is a screen shot showing the formula that will appear after you import the number.

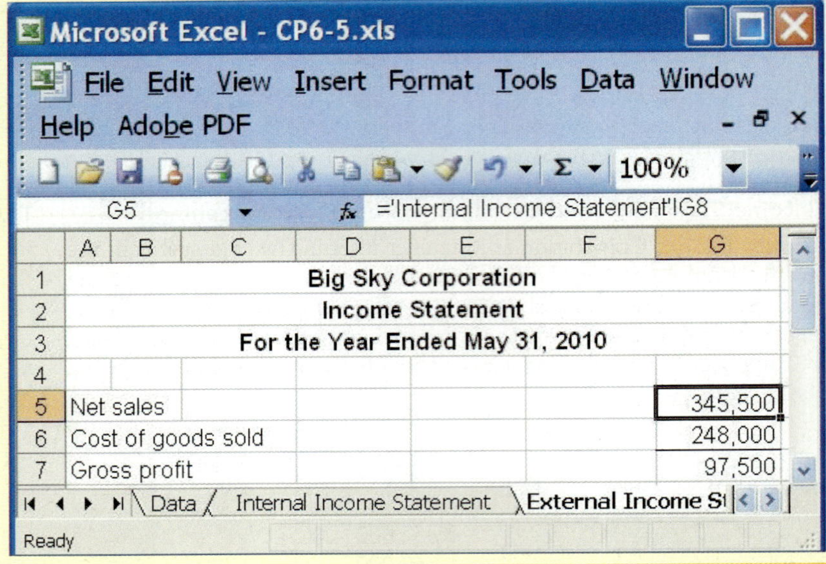

Do not forget to save the file using a name that indicates who you are.

Required:

Enter the trial balance information into a spreadsheet and complete the following:

1. Prepare a multistep income statement that would be used for internal reporting purposes. Classify sales returns and allowances and sales discounts as contra-revenue accounts.
2. Prepare a multistep income statement that would be used for external reporting purposes, beginning with the amount for net sales.
3. Compute the gross profit percentage.

7 Inventories

LEARNING OBJECTIVES

After completing this chapter, you should be able to:

Lectured slideshow–LP7-1
www.mhhe.com/LLPW1e

LO1 Explain how to report inventory and cost of goods sold.

LO2 Explain the cost of goods sold equation.

LO3 Compute inventory costs using four inventory costing methods.

LO4 Report inventory at the lower of cost or market.

LO5 Determine the effects of inventory errors on the income statement and balance sheet.

LO6 Compute and interpret the inventory turnover ratio.

AMERICAN EAGLE OUTFITTERS
ae.com

Focus Company: AMERICAN EAGLE OUTFITTERS

"Relentless Customer Focus Leads to Record Profitability"

www.ae.com

Whether you are shopping for gasoline, groceries, or a new flat-screen TV, prices always seem to be changing. The political situation in oil-producing nations can cause a stunning increase in prices at the pump. A late freeze in Florida can hike the price of orange juice. Increasing competition can dramatically lower the cost of that new TV.

Companies face similar price changes when they purchase or produce the goods they sell. Increases in demand can cause the cost of inventory to increase over time; technological innovation can cause it to decrease. Either way, inventory is likely to include some items that were acquired at a lower unit cost and others that were acquired at a higher unit cost.

Suppose American Eagle Outfitters, the clothing retailer, purchases three batches of its AE Springweight Track Jackets at a cost of $40 per jacket for the first batch, $50 per jacket for the second batch, and $60 per jacket for the third. How would you account for this inventory? Fortunately, there are specific rules to follow in determining the cost of inventory on hand and the cost of inventory sold. The tricky part is that these rules allow accountants to use several different methods, each of which leads to a different number. This flexibility allows managers to choose the method that best fits their business environment. But it also means that you must know which method managers are using and how it works. That is our focus in this chapter.

ORGANIZATION OF THE CHAPTER

REPORTING INVENTORY AND COST OF GOODS SOLD	CHOOSING AMONG INVENTORY COSTING METHODS	REPORTING INVENTORY AT THE LOWER OF COST OR MARKET	IDENTIFYING THE EFFECTS OF INVENTORY ERRORS	EVALUATING INVENTORY MANAGEMENT
• Balance Sheet and Income Statement Reporting • Cost of Goods Sold Equation	• Cost Flow Methods under a Perpetual Inventory System • First-In, First-Out (FIFO) • Last-In, First-Out (LIFO) • Weighted Average Cost • Financial Statement Effects of Inventory Costing Methods		• Income Statement Effects • Balance Sheet Effects	• Inventory Turnover Analysis • Comparison to Benchmarks

REPORTING INVENTORY AND COST OF GOODS SOLD

The generic term **inventory** includes both goods that are held for sale in the normal course of business and goods that are used to produce other goods. Merchandisers such as American Eagle Outfitters hold merchandise inventory, which they usually acquire in finished condition, ready for sale without further processing. Manufacturers often hold three types of inventory, each of which represents a different stage in the manufacturing process. For purposes of this chapter, we focus on merchandise inventory, but be aware that the concepts discussed in this chapter apply to both merchandise and manufacturing inventories.

Learning Objective 1

Explain how to report inventory and cost of goods sold.

Balance Sheet and Income Statement Reporting

Because inventory will be used or converted into cash within one year, it is reported on the balance sheet as a current asset. Goods placed in inventory are initially recorded at cost, which is the amount paid to acquire the asset and prepare it for sale. See Exhibit 7.1 for the way American Eagle's partial balance sheet reports inventory.

AMERICAN EAGLE OUTFITTERS
ae.com

Exhibit 7.1 Reporting Inventory on the Balance Sheet (Partial)

American Eagle Outfitters, Inc.
Consolidated Balance Sheets
At January 31, 2007 and 2006

(in millions)	2007	2006
Assets		
Current assets		
Cash and cash equivalents	$ 60	$131
Short-term investments	767	621
Merchandise inventory	264	211
Accounts and note receivable	26	29
Prepaid expenses and other	34	30

Exhibit 7.2 Reporting Cost of Goods Sold on the Income Statement (Partial)

American Eagle Outfitters, Inc.
Consolidated Income Statements
For the Years Ended January 31, 2007, 2006, and 2005

(in millions)	2007	2006	2005
Net sales	$2,794	$2,322	$1,890
Cost of goods sold	1,454	1,244	1,009
Gross profit	1,340	1,078	881

AMERICAN EAGLE OUTFITTERS
ae.com

When a company sells goods, it removes their cost from the Inventory account and reports the cost on the income statement as the expense Cost of Goods Sold. See Exhibit 7.2 for how American Eagle reports the Cost of Goods Sold (CGS) on its partial income statement. Notice that it follows directly after net sales. The difference between these two line items is a subtotal called gross profit.

COST OF GOODS SOLD EQUATION

Learning Objective 2
Explain the cost of goods sold equation.

Although the cost of inventory and the cost of goods sold are reported on different financial statements, they are related. A company starts each accounting period with a stock of inventory called **beginning inventory (BI).** During the accounting period, new **purchases (P)** are added to the beginning inventory. As in Exhibit 7.3, the sum of these two amounts (BI + P) becomes the cost of goods available for sale during the period.

Some of the goods available for sale will be sold during the period; some will not. The portion that is sold is reported as the cost of goods sold on the income statement. The portion that remains unsold at the end of the period is reported as the **ending inventory (EI)** on the balance sheet. The ending inventory for one accounting period then becomes the beginning

Exhibit 7.3 Relationship between Inventory and Cost of Goods Sold

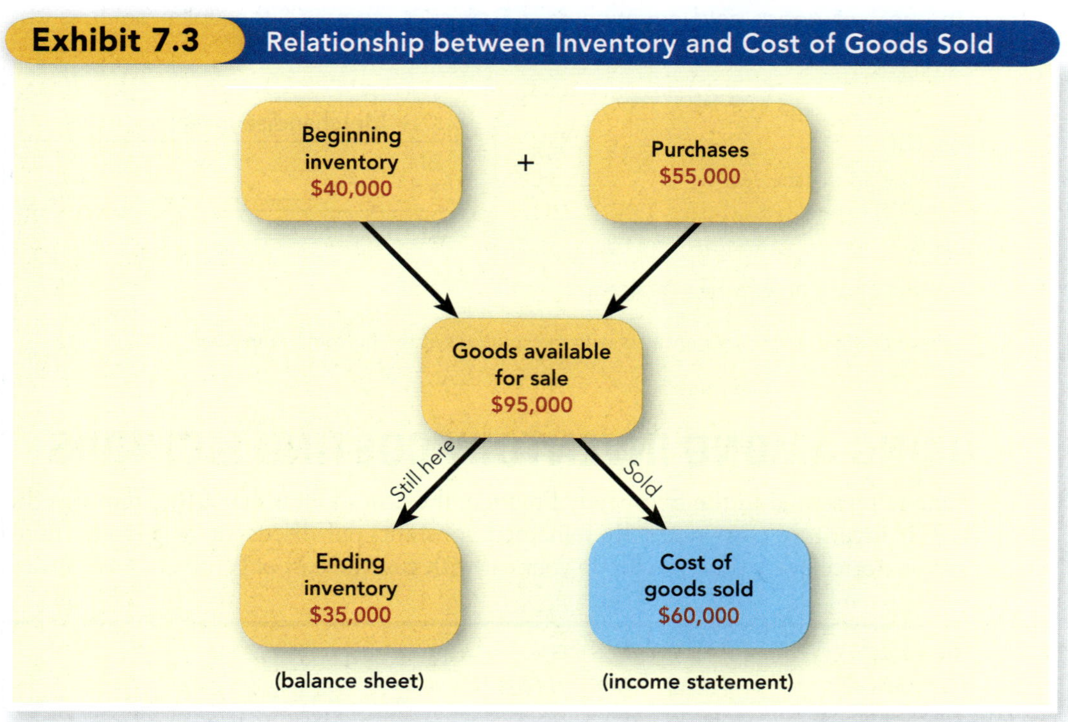

inventory for the next period. The **cost of goods sold (CGS) equation** summarizes the relationships between these inventory amounts:

$$BI + P - CGS = EI$$

To illustrate the CGS equation, assume that, as in Exhibit 7.3, American Eagle Outfitters began the period with $40,000 of Springweight Track Jackets in beginning inventory. During the period, the company purchased more of these jackets for $55,000. The cost of goods sold for the period is $60,000. At the end of the period, $35,000 of jackets was left in inventory. These amounts can be represented in the cost of goods sold equation or by the inventory T-account:

Cost of Goods Sold Calculation

Beginning inventory	$40,000
+ Purchases of merchandise during the period	+ 55,000
Goods available for sale	95,000
− Cost of goods sold	− 60,000
Ending inventory	35,000

+ Merchandise Inventory (A) −			
Beginning Inventory	40,000		
Purchases of Inventory	55,000	60,000	Cost of Goods Sold
Ending Inventory	35,000		

If one of these values is unknown, you can use either the cost of goods sold equation or the inventory T-account to solve for the missing value. See for yourself in the following Self-Study Practice.

SELF-STUDY PRACTICE

Assume the following facts for the AE Eyelet Ts product line for the year 2008:

Beginning inventory (BI) held 500 units at a unit cost of $10.

Purchases (P) of inventory equaled 1,200 units at a unit cost of $10.

Sales equaled 1,100 units at a sales price of $12 (and a unit cost of $10).

Using the cost of goods sold equation or a T-account, compute the dollar amount of Eyelet Ts in inventory at the end of the period.

Beginning inventory (BI)	$ 5,000
+ Purchases of merchandise during the year	____
− Cost of goods sold (CGS)	____
= Ending inventory (EI)	$____

+ Merchandise Inventory (A) −			
BI	____		
P	____	____	CGS
EI	____		

After you have finished, check your answers with the solutions at the bottom of the page.

CHOOSING AMONG INVENTORY COSTING METHODS

In the example presented in the Self-Study Practice, the cost of all units of the item was the same—$10. If inventory costs normally remained constant, our discussion would end here. But just as you notice every time you fill up your car with gas, the cost of goods does not always

Solution to Self-Study Practice

BI = 500 × $10 = $5,000	BI + P − CGS = EI
P = 1,200 × $10 = $12,000	5,000 + 12,000 − 11,000 = EI
CGS = 1,100 × $10 = $11,000	6,000 = EI

stay the same. In recent years, the costs of many items have risen moderately. In other cases, such as LCD TVs, costs have dropped dramatically.

When the costs of inventory change over time, it is not obvious how to determine the cost of goods sold (and the cost of remaining inventory). To see why, think about the following simple example for a new company:

Learning Objective 3

Compute inventory costs using four inventory costing methods.

May 3	Purchased 1 unit of Product A for **$70.**
May 5	Purchased 1 unit of Product A for **$75.**
May 6	Purchased 1 unit of Product A for **$95.**
May 8	Sold 2 units of Product A for $125 each.

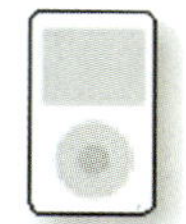

Video 7-1
www.mhhe.com/LLPW1e

The sale on May 8 of two units for $125 each would generate sales revenue of $250 ($125 × 2), but what amount would be considered the cost of goods sold? Because the cost of Product A increased, the answer depends on which goods are assumed to have been sold.

Four generally accepted inventory costing methods are available for determining the cost of goods sold and the cost of goods remaining in ending inventory. Any one of these four methods is acceptable under GAAP in the United States. The specific identification method individually identifies and records the cost of each item sold as part of cost of goods sold. This method requires accountants to keep track of the purchase cost of each item. In the example just given, if the items sold were identified as the ones that cost $70 and $95, the total cost of those items ($70 + 95 = $165) would be reported as the cost of goods sold. The cost of the remaining item ($75) would be reported as inventory on the balance sheet at the end of the period. The specific identification method is used primarily to account for individually expensive and unique items. Toll Brothers, the country's leading builder of luxury homes, reports the costs of home construction using the specific identification method.

Because each unit in a product line is identical, American Eagle Outfitters does not use the specific identification method. Like most companies, American Eagle uses one of the three cost flow methods to account for inventory items. These three other inventory costing methods are **not based on the physical flow** of goods on and off the shelves. Instead, these methods are based on **assumptions** that accountants make about the flow of inventory costs. These three cost flow assumptions are applied to our simple three-unit example in Exhibit 7.4.

Coach's Tip

Remember that generally accepted accounting principles do **not** require a company to use a cost flow assumption that mirrors the physical flow of goods.

1. First-in, first-out (FIFO) assumes that the inventory costs flow out in the order the goods are received. As in Exhibit 7.4, the earliest items received, the $70 and $75 units received on May 3 and 5, become the $145 cost of goods sold on the income statement and the remaining $95 unit received on May 6 becomes ending inventory on the balance sheet.
2. Last-in, first-out (LIFO) assumes that the inventory costs flow out in the opposite of the order the goods are received. As in Exhibit 7.4, the latest items received, the $95 and $75 units received on May 6 and 5, become the $170 cost of goods sold on the income statement, and the remaining $70 unit received on May 3 becomes ending inventory on the balance sheet.
3. Weighted average uses the weighted average of the costs of goods available for sale for both the cost of each item sold and those remaining in inventory. As in Exhibit 7.4, the average of the costs [($70 + 75 + 95) ÷ 3 = $80] is assigned to the two items sold totaling $160 cost of goods sold and the one item totaling $80 ending inventory.

As Exhibit 7.4 illustrates, the choice of cost flow assumption can have a major effect on gross profit on the income statement and inventory on the balance sheet. By one estimate, the combined effect of this decision on the profits of large U.S. corporations exceeds $60 billion a year.[1] Now that you have seen how cost flow assumptions work and why they make a difference in a company's reported results, you are ready for a more complex example.

[1] "Big Oil's Accounting Methods Fuel Criticism," *The Wall Street Journal*, August 8, 2006, C1.

Exhibit 7.4 FIFO, LIFO, and Weighted Average Cost Flow Assumptions

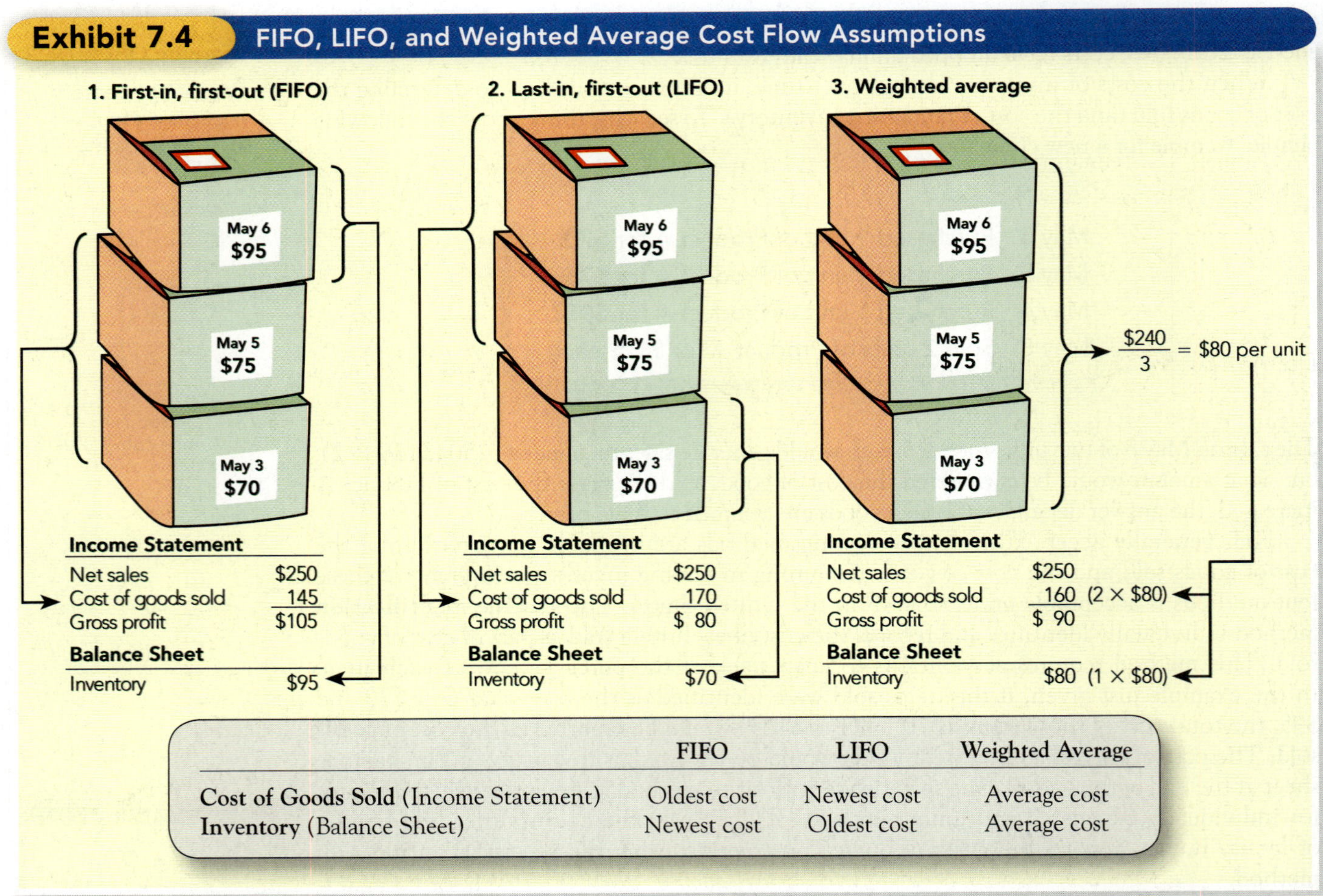

The following sections apply the three cost flow assumptions using a perpetual inventory system. Supplement 7A applies the cost flow assumptions using a periodic inventory system. Your instructor may assign either one or both of these sections.

Cost Flow Methods under a Perpetual Inventory System

In this section, we will apply the cost flow methods using what is called a **perpetual inventory system that records all inventory purchases, sales, and cost of goods sold in sequence as they occur.** Assume American Eagle engaged in the following transactions for its AE Alpine Bomber Jacket product line during the month of January and that all sales were for $150 per unit.

Date	Description	Units	Unit Cost	Total Cost	Balance in Units
Jan 1	Beginning inventory	20	$ 70	$1,400	20
12	Purchase	60	80	4,800	80
17	Sale	50			30
19	Purchase	20	100	2,000	50
26	Sale	32			18
				$8,200	

First-In, First-Out (FIFO)

The **first-in, first-out method (FIFO)** assumes that the oldest goods (the first ones into inventory) are the first ones sold (the first ones out of inventory). So you **use the costs of the**

oldest goods as of the date of sale to calculate the cost of goods sold. The **costs of the newer goods become the costs of the ending inventory.** As in Exhibit 7.5,

- The cost of the 50 units sold on January 17 include the 20 units costing $70 from beginning inventory and 30 of the $80 units from the January 12 purchase (the oldest units). The remaining 30 of the $80 units (the newest units) become ending inventory.
- The 32 items sold on January 26 include the 30 remaining $80 units and 2 of the $100 units (the oldest units). The remaining 18 of the $100 units (the newest units) become ending inventory.

Coach's Tip

FIFO allocates the oldest unit costs to the cost of goods sold and the newest unit costs to the ending inventory.

Last-In, First-Out (LIFO)

The **last-in, first-out method (LIFO)** assumes that the newest goods (the last ones into inventory) are the first ones sold (the first ones out of inventory). So you **use the costs of the newest goods as of the date of sale to calculate the cost of goods sold.** The **costs of the older goods become the costs of the ending inventory.** As in Exhibit 7.6,

- The cost of the 50 units sold on January 17 include 50 of the $80 units from the most recent January 12 purchase (the newest units). The remaining 10 of the $80 units and the 20 units costing $70 from beginning inventory (the oldest units) become ending inventory.

Coach's Tip

LIFO allocates the newest unit costs to the cost of goods sold and the oldest unit costs to the ending inventory.

Exhibit 7.5 FIFO Computations—Perpetual Inventory

FIFO Perpetual Calculations		PURCHASES			COST OF GOODS SOLD			INVENTORY BALANCE		
Date	Description	Units	Unit Cost	Total Cost	Units	Unit Cost	Total Cost	Units	Unit Cost	Total Cost
Jan 1	Beginning inventory							20	$ 70	$1,400
12	Purchase	60	$ 80	$4,800				60	80	4,800
17	Sale				20	$ 70	$1,400			
					30	80	2,400	30	80	2,400
19	Purchase	20	100	2,000				20	100	2,000
26	Sale				30	80	2,400			
					2	100	200	18	100	1,800
	Total	80		$6,800	82		$6,400	18		$1,800

Exhibit 7.6 LIFO Computations—Perpetual Inventory

LIFO Perpetual Calculations		PURCHASES			COST OF GOODS SOLD			INVENTORY BALANCE		
Date	Description	Units	Unit Cost	Total Cost	Units	Unit Cost	Total Cost	Units	Unit Cost	Total Cost
Jan 1	Beginning inventory							20	$ 70	$1,400
12	Purchase	60	$ 80	$4,800				60	80	4,800
17	Sale				50	$ 80	$4,000	20	$ 70	1,400
								10	80	800
19	Purchase	20	100	2,000				20	100	2,000
26	Sale				20	100	2,000			
					10	80	800			
					2	70	140	18	70	1,260
	Total	80		$6,800	82		$6,940	18		$1,260

- The cost of the 32 items sold on January 26 include the 20 most recently purchased $100 units from the January 19 purchase, the remaining 10 of the $80 units, and 2 of the $70 units (the newest units). The remaining 18 of the $70 units from beginning inventory (the oldest units) become ending inventory.

Coach's Tip

In calculating the weighted average cost, be sure to **weight** the costs by the number of units purchased at each cost. Do not just average the unit costs (e.g., $70, $80, $100) without considering the number of units purchased at each cost.

Weighted Average Cost

In the **weighted average cost method,** you calculate the **weighted average cost per unit of the goods available for sale as of the date of sale.** You add the total cost of beginning inventory and purchases before the date of sale to get the total cost of goods available for sale. As in Exhibit 7.7, you then divide this amount by the number of units available for sale to compute the weighted average cost and assign that cost to all units sold and in ending inventory.

- For the January 17 sale, the cost of goods available for sale is computed by adding the $1,400 cost of the beginning inventory and the $4,800 cost of the January 12 purchase and dividing by the 80 total units available ($6,200 ÷ 80 = $77.50). This $77.50 average cost per unit is then assigned to the 50 units sold ($77.50 × 50 = $3,875) and the 30 units that remain in ending inventory ($77.50 × 30 = $2,325).
- For the January 26 sale, the cost of goods available for sale is computed by adding the $2,325 cost of the units remaining after the January 17 sale and the $2,000 cost of the January 19 purchase and dividing by the 50 total units available ($4,325 ÷ 50 = $86.50). This $86.50 average cost per unit is then assigned to the 32 units sold ($86.50 × 32 = $2,768) and the 18 units that remain in ending inventory ($86.50 × 18 = $1,557).

Financial Statement Effects of Inventory Costing Methods

Exhibit 7.8 illustrates the journal entries that would have been made under each method for the purchases and sales transactions assuming that all sales were for $150 cash per unit. Note that the purchases and sales revenue entries are identical across the methods. **For the cost of goods sold entries, the accounts affected are the same, but the amounts are different.**

Exhibit 7.9 summarizes the financial statement effects of the FIFO, LIFO, and weighted average cost methods. Remember that these methods differ only in the way they split the cost of goods available for sale between the cost of goods sold and the ending inventory. Because a cost that goes into ending inventory cannot also go into the cost of goods sold, the method that assigns the highest cost to ending inventory will assign the lowest cost to the cost of goods sold and vice versa.

Exhibit 7.7 Weighted Average Computations—Perpetual Inventory

Weighted Average Perpetual Calculations		PURCHASES			COST OF GOODS SOLD			INVENTORY BALANCE			
Date	Description	Units	Unit Cost	Total Cost	Units	Unit Cost	Total Cost	Units	Unit Cost	Total Cost	
Jan 1	Beginning inventory							20	$70.00	$1,400	$6,200÷80=$77.50 per unit
12	Purchase	60	$ 80	$4,800				60	80.00	4,800	
17	Sale				50	$77.50	$3,875	30	77.50	2,325	$4,325÷50=$86.50 per unit
19	Purchase	20	100	2,000				20	100.00	2,000	
26	Sale				32	86.50	2,768	18	86.50	1,557	
	Total	80		$6,800	82		$6,643	18		$1,557	

Exhibit 7.8 Journal Entries—Perpetual Inventory

		FIFO		LIFO		WEIGHTED AVERAGE	
		Debit	Credit	Debit	Credit	Debit	Credit
Jan 12	Inventory (+A)	4,800		4,800		4,800	
	Accounts Payable (+L)		4,800		4,800		4,800
Jan 17	Cash (+A) (50 × $150)	7,500		7,500		7,500	
	Sales Revenue (+R, +OE)		7,500		7,500		7,500
	Cost of Goods Sold (+E, −OE)	3,800		4,000		3,875	
	Inventory (−A)		3,800		4,000		3,875
Jan 19	Inventory (+A)	2,000		2,000		2,000	
	Accounts Payable (+L)		2,000		2,000		2,000
Jan 26	Cash (+A) (32 × $150)	4,800		4,800		4,800	
	Sales Revenue (+R, +OE)		4,800		4,800		4,800
	Cost of Goods Sold (+E, −OE)	2,600		2,940		2,768	
	Inventory (−A)		2,600		2,940		2,768

Exhibit 7.9 Financial Statement Effects of Inventory Costing Methods

	FIFO	LIFO	Weighted Average
Effect on the Income Statement			
Sales	$12,300	$12,300	$12,300
Cost of goods sold	6,400	6,940	6,643
Gross profit	5,900	5,360	5,657
Effect on the Balance Sheet			
Inventory	$1,800	$1,260	$1,557

Depending on whether costs are rising or falling, different methods have different effects on the financial statements. **When costs are rising,** as they are in our example, FIFO produces a higher inventory value (making the balance sheet **appear** to be stronger) and a lower cost of goods sold (resulting in a higher gross profit, which makes the company **look** more profitable). **When costs are falling,** these effects are reversed; FIFO produces a lower ending inventory value and a higher cost of goods sold—a double whammy. These are not "real" economic effects, however, because the same number of units is sold or held in ending inventory under either method. The following table summarizes the effects:

Effects of Increasing Costs on the Financial Statements

	FIFO	LIFO
Inventory on balance sheet	Higher	Lower
Cost of goods sold on income statement	Lower	Higher

Effects of Decreasing Costs on the Financial Statements

	FIFO	LIFO
Inventory on balance sheet	Lower	Higher
Cost of goods sold on income statement	Higher	Lower

Spotlight On BUSINESS DECISIONS

Choosing Inventory Costing Methods

Given the effects of different inventory costing methods, you might wonder why a company would ever choose a method that produces a lower inventory value and a higher cost of goods sold. American Eagle, like Wal-Mart and the rest of the companies discussed in this text, is a corporation, and corporations must pay income taxes. Faced with increasing costs per unit as in our example, a company that uses FIFO will incur a higher income tax expense. That tax effect is a real economic cost in the sense that the higher income tax will reduce the company's cash. So most companies that face a rising per unit inventory cost choose LIFO. Companies choosing LIFO for their tax returns must also use LIFO on their financial statements.*

Increasing cost companies using LIFO: Harley-Davidson, Ford, General Motors, Exxon.

*In other cases such as choosing depreciation methods, companies may use one method on their tax return and a different method on their financial statements.

A common question that people ask is whether managers are free to choose LIFO one period, FIFO the next, and then LIFO again, depending on whether unit costs are rising or falling at the time. Because doing so would make it difficult to compare financial results across periods, accounting rules require that costing methods be applied consistently. A change in inventory costing method is allowed only if it will improve the accuracy with which a company's financial results and financial position are reported, and that does not happen often. Companies can use different inventory costing methods for different product lines, however, as long as they do so consistently over time.

Spotlight On ETHICS

Just Who Are You Working For?

Given a choice between FIFO and LIFO, most stockholders would want managers to use the method that results in the lowest income taxes. Managers, on the other hand, might prefer the method that produces the highest net income, particularly if they receive a bonus based on reported profits. Clearly, a manager who selected an accounting method that is less than optimal for the company solely to increase his or her own pay would be engaging in questionable ethical behavior.

SELF-STUDY PRACTICE

Assume that a firm had the following inventory purchases and sales during January. Compute the cost of goods sold and the ending inventory using the LIFO method.

Beginning inventory	20 units at $6 each
Purchase January 5	30 units at $8 each
Sale January 8	36 units
Purchase January 28	16 units at $9 each

After you have finished, check your answers with the solutions at the bottom of the next page.

Learning Objective 4

Report inventory at the lower of cost or market.

REPORTING INVENTORY AT THE LOWER OF COST OR MARKET

For two reasons, the value of inventory can sometimes fall below its recorded cost: (1) It can be easily replaced by identical goods at a lower cost or (2) it has become outdated or damaged. The first case typically involves high-tech goods such as cell phones. As companies become more efficient at making these cutting-edge products, they become cheaper to make. The second case commonly occurs with fad items or seasonal goods such as American Eagle's winter coats, which tend to drop in value at the end of the season.

In either instance, when the value of inventory falls below its recorded cost, GAAP requires that the amount that was originally recorded for inventory be written down to its lower market value. This rule is known as reporting inventories at the **lower of cost or market (LCM)**. It is based on the **conservatism** concept, which ensures that inventory assets are not reported at more than they are worth.

Let's look at how the inventory write-down is determined and recorded. Assume that American Eagle's ending inventory includes two items whose replacement costs have recently changed: leather coats and fleece hoodies.[2] The replacement costs of these items can be used as estimates of market value and compared to the original recorded cost per unit. You then take the lower of those two amounts (the lower of cost or market) and multiply it by the number of units on hand. The result is the amount at which the inventory should be reported after all adjustments have been made:

Item	Quantity	Cost per Item	Replacement Cost (Market) per Item	LCM per Item	Total Lower of Cost or Market
Leather coats	1,000	$165	$150	$150	1,000 × $150 = $150,000
Fleece hoodies	400	20	25	20	400 × $ 20 = 8,000

Because the market value of the 1,000 leather coats ($150) is **lower** than the recorded cost ($165), the recorded amount for ending inventory should be written down by $15 per unit ($165 – $150). If American Eagle has 1,000 units in inventory, the total write-down should be $15,000 ($15 × 1,000). The effect of this write-down on the accounting equation and the journal entry to record it would be:

	Debit	Credit
Cost of Goods Sold (+E, –OE)	15,000	
Inventory (–A)		15,000

Assets	=	Liabilities	+	Owners' Equity
Inventory –15,000				Cost of Goods Sold (+E) –15,000

Solution to Self-Study Practice

LIFO Perpetual Calculations		PURCHASES			COST OF GOODS SOLD			INVENTORY BALANCE		
Date	Description	Units	Unit Cost	Total Cost	Units	Unit Cost	Total Cost	Units	Unit Cost	Total Cost
Jan 1	Beginning inventory							20	$6	$120
5	Purchase	30	8	$240				30	8	240
8	Sale				30	$8	$240			
					6	6	36	14	6	84
28	Purchase	16	9	144				16	9	144
	Total	46		$384	36		$276	30		$228

Cost of goods sold is $276; ending inventory is $228.

[2] We apply lower of cost or market on an item basis. It also may be applied on a category or total inventory basis.

Because the market value of the fleece hoodies ($25) is higher than the original cost ($20), no write-down is necessary. The fleece hoodies should remain on the books at their original cost of $20 per unit ($8,000 in total). Their value should not be increased based on the higher replacement cost because GAAP requires that they be reported at the **lower** of cost or market.

Spotlight On FINANCIAL REPORTING

Using Lower of Cost or Market in Practice

AMERICAN EAGLE OUTFITTERS
ae.com

American Eagle explains the use of the LCM rule in Note 2 to its financial statements.

American Eagle Outfitters, Inc.
Notes to the Consolidated Financial Statements

. . . .

2. Summary of Significant Accounting Policies
Merchandise Inventory
Merchandise inventory is valued at the lower of average cost or market. . . .

Learning Objective 5

Determine the effects of inventory errors on the income statement and balance sheet.

IDENTIFYING THE EFFECTS OF INVENTORY ERRORS

Errors in inventory valuations can significantly affect both the balance sheet and the income statement. As the cost of goods sold equation indicates, there is a direct relationship between ending inventory and the cost of goods sold: Items that are not in the ending inventory are assumed to have been sold. Thus, any errors in ending inventory affect both the balance sheet (current assets) and the income statement (cost of goods sold, gross profit, and net income). Furthermore, the effects of inventory errors impact more than one year because the ending inventory for one year becomes the beginning inventory for the next.

Income Statement Effects

To determine the effects of inventory errors on the financial statements in both the current and following years, you use the cost of goods sold equation. Assume, for example, that ending inventory was overstated by $10,000 due to an error that was not discovered until the following year. This error would have the following effects in the current year:

	Current Year
Beginning inventory	Accurate
+ Purchases of merchandise during the year	Accurate
Goods available for sale	Accurate
− Ending inventory (balance sheet)	Overstated $10,000
= Cost of goods sold (income statement)	Understated $10,000

Because the cost of goods sold was understated in the current year, gross profit and net income would be overstated by $10,000 in the same year (ignoring taxes).

The current year's ending inventory becomes next year's beginning inventory. So, the $10,000 overstatement of ending inventory in the current year would have the following effects next year (assuming that ending inventory is calculated correctly that year):

Next Year	
Beginning inventory	**Overstated $10,000**
+ Purchases of merchandise during the year	**Accurate**
Goods available for sale	**Overstated $10,000**
− Ending inventory (balance sheet)	**Accurate**
= Cost of goods sold (income statement)	**Overstated $10,000**

Because the cost of goods sold, which is an expense, is overstated in the next year, gross profit and net income are understated by $10,000 in the same year.

Exhibit 7.10 shows the effects of these errors on net income in each of the two years (ignoring income taxes). Notice that the cost of goods sold is understated in the first year and overstated in the second year. Over the two years, these errors would offset each other. However, inventory errors will "self-correct" in this way only if the ending inventory is calculated accurately at the end of the following year and adjusted to the correct amount.

Balance Sheet Effects

Errors in ending inventory affect two balance sheet accounts. First, the amount used as ending inventory in the cost of goods sold equation becomes the value of the current asset inventory shown on the balance sheet. Second, the cost of goods sold affects the value of owners' equity when it is closed to that account.

Exhibit 7.11 shows both of these effects. Note that they will offset each other over the two years only if the value of the ending inventory is calculated accurately at the end of the second year and adjusted to the correct amount.

Exhibit 7.10 Two-Year Effects of an Inventory Error on the Income Statement

	CURRENT YEAR				NEXT YEAR			
	With an Error		Without an Error		With an Error		Without an Error	
Sales		$120,000		$120,000		$110,000		$110,000
Beginning inventory	$ 50,000		$ 50,000		**$ 45,000**		**$ 35,000**	
Purchases	75,000		75,000		70,000		70,000	
Cost of goods available for sale	125,000		125,000		115,000		105,000	
Ending inventory	**45,000**		**35,000**		20,000		20,000	
Cost of goods sold		80,000		90,000		95,000		85,000
Gross profit		40,000		30,000		15,000		25,000
Operating expenses		10,000		10,000		10,000		10,000
Net income		$ 30,000		$ 20,000		$ 5,000		$ 15,000

Net income overstated by $10,000 → Cancels out ← Net income understated by $10,000

Exhibit 7.11 Two-Year Effects of an Inventory Error on the Balance Sheet

Year	Ending Inventory Error	Assets	Owners' Equity
Current year	Overstated $10,000	Overstated $10,000	Overstated $10,000
Next year	Accurate	Accurate	Accurate

EVALUATING INVENTORY MANAGEMENT

Inventory Turnover Analysis

Learning Objective 6
Compute and interpret the inventory turnover ratio.

If a company's inventory balance increases from $100,000 in one period to $130,000 in the next, is that good news or bad news? If the increase occurs because management is building up stock in anticipation of higher sales, it could be good news. But if it results from an accumulation of old inventory items that nobody wants, it is probably bad news. Those who work inside the company can easily determine whether the change is good or bad news by talking with the sales managers. But if you are looking at the company's financial statements from the outside, how can you tell?

The method most analysts use to evaluate such changes is called **inventory turnover** analysis. Exhibit 7.12 illustrates the idea behind inventory turnover analysis. As a company buys goods, its inventory balance goes up; as it sells goods, its inventory balance goes down. This process of buying and selling, which is called **inventory turnover,** is repeated over and over during each accounting period for each line of products.

Analysts can assess how many times, on average, inventory has been bought and sold during the period by calculating the inventory turnover ratio. A higher ratio indicates that inventory moves more quickly from purchase to sale, reducing storage and obsolescence costs. Because less money is tied up in inventory, the excess can be invested to earn interest or reduce borrowing, which reduces interest expense. More efficient purchasing and production techniques as well as high product demand will boost this ratio. A sudden decline in the inventory turnover ratio may signal an unexpected drop in demand for the company's products or poor inventory management.

Rather than evaluate the **number of times** inventory turns over during the year, some analysts prefer to think in terms of the **length of time** (in days) required to sell inventory. Converting the inventory turnover ratio to the number of days needed to sell the inventory is easy. You simply divide 365 days by the inventory turnover ratio to get the **days to sell.** This measure does not tell analysts anything different about a company's ability to buy and sell inventory; it is just a little easier to interpret than the inventory turnover ratio. In terms of Exhibit 7.12, the inventory turnover ratio indicates the number of loops in a given period; days to sell indicates the average number of days between loops.

Inventory turnover analysis can be applied to merchandisers as well as manufacturers. For manufacturers, inventory turnover refers to the production and delivery of inventory to customers. For merchandisers, it refers to the buying and selling of goods to customers.

Exhibit 7.12 Inventory Turnover Analysis

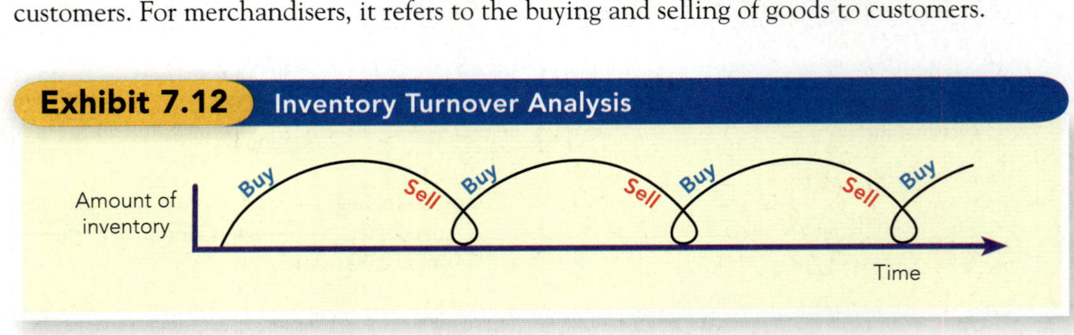

Financial Analysis Tools

Name of Measure	Formula	What It Tells You
Inventory Turnover Ratio	$\frac{\text{Cost of Goods Sold}}{\text{Average Inventory}}$	• The number of times inventory turns over during the period • A higher ratio means faster turnover
Days to Sell	$\frac{365}{\text{Inventory Turnover Ratio}}$	• The average number of days from purchase to sale • A higher number means a longer time to sell

American Eagle's turnover ratio and days to sell would be computed as follows:

$$\text{Inventory Turnover Ratio} = \frac{\text{Cost of Goods Sold}}{\text{Average Inventory}} = \frac{\$1{,}454}{\$(264 + 211)/2} = 6.1 \text{ times}$$

$$\text{Days to Sell} = \frac{365}{\text{Inventory Turnover Ratio}} = \frac{365 \text{ days}}{6.1 \text{ times}} = 59.8 \text{ days}$$

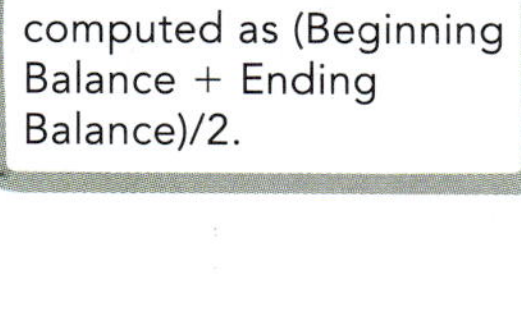

Coach's Tip

The average inventory balance outstanding over the entire year is used in the bottom of the receivables turnover ratio. It is computed as (Beginning Balance + Ending Balance)/2.

Comparison to Benchmarks

Inventory turnover ratios and the number of days to sell can be helpful in comparing different companies' inventory management practices. You should use them cautiously, however, because these measures can vary significantly from one industry to another. As in Exhibit 7.13, Ruby Tuesday had a turnover ratio of 30.0 in 2006, meaning that it took about 12 days to sell its entire food inventory (including the contents of its freezers). Harley-Davidson took more time to produce and sell its motorcycles—as its inventory turnover ratio of 14.0 indicates, about 26 days. American Eagle's inventory turned over only 6.1 times during the year, or just once every 59.8 days.

Given this wide range in ratios among industries and companies, it is usually more useful to compare a company's inventory turnover with its own results in prior periods or to similar (competitor) companies. For practice in computing these measures and comparing them to a competitor, try the following Self-Study Practice, which asks you to calculate the inventory turnover ratio and days to sell.

SELF-STUDY PRACTICE

a. Urban Outfitters reported cost of goods sold of $773 and beginning and ending inventories of $140 and $154 (all in millions) for 2006. Calculate its inventory turnover and days to sell in 2006.

b. Compare its inventory turnover and days to sell to that of American Eagle. How would you interpret the difference?

2006 Inventory Turnover	2006 Days to Sell
$\frac{___}{(___ + ___)/2}$ = ___ = times	$\frac{365 \text{ days}}{___ \text{ times}}$ = ___ days

times

When you have finished, check your answers with the solutions at the bottom of the page.

Solution to Self-Study Practice

a. $\frac{773}{(140 + 154)/2} = 5.3$ times

$365 \div 5.3 = 68.9$ days

b. Urban Outfitters' inventory turnover was lower and days to sell was higher, indicating less efficient inventory management.

Exhibit 7.13 Inventory Turnover Analysis for Three Different Companies

Company	2006 Inventory Turnover	2006 Days to Sell
American Eagle	6.1	59.8 days
Harley-Davidson	14.0	26.1 days
RubyTuesday	30.0	12.2 days

Spotlight On FINANCIAL REPORTING

Impact of Inventory Costing Methods

As you saw in Exhibit 7.4, different cost flow assumptions often yield different amounts for inventory and cost of goods sold. Accounting rules require that any company that chooses to use LIFO must report in the notes to the financial statements what the inventory balance would have been had it used FIFO instead. Deere & Company, the manufacturer of John Deere farm, lawn, and construction equipment, disclosed this information as follows.

Deere & Company

Notes to the Consolidated Financial Statements

Note 13—Inventories

Most inventories owned by Deere & Company and its United States equipment subsidiaries are valued at cost, on the "last-in, first-out" (LIFO) basis. If all inventories had been valued on a FIFO basis, estimated inventories at October 31 in millions of dollars would have been as follows:

	2006	2005
Total FIFO value	$ 3,097	$ 3,267
Adjustment to LIFO basis	1,140	1,132
Inventories	$ 1,957	$ 2,135

Deere & Company

Notice that the cost of inventory under the FIFO assumption ($3,097 in 2006) was more than 1.5 times higher than the cost of inventory under the LIFO assumption ($1,957 in 2006). The lesson here is that in analyzing a company's inventory or cost of goods sold, you should compare that company's results only to its own results in prior periods or to those of another company that uses the same cost flow assumption.

Demonstration Case

Ebert Electronics distributes consumer electronics. One product has been selected for use in this case. Assume the completion of the following summarized transactions during the month of March 2008 in the order given. All transactions involved cash.

	Units	Unit Cost
Beginning inventory (March 1)	11	$200
New inventory purchases (March 15)	5	208
Sales (March 19) (selling price, $420)	12	—
New inventory purchases (March 21)	9	220

Required:

1. Compute the following amounts using the FIFO, LIFO, and weighted average cost methods applied on a perpetual basis:

	ENDING INVENTORY		COST OF GOODS SOLD	
	Units	**Dollars**	**Units**	**Dollars**
FIFO				
LIFO				
Weighted average				

2. Assuming the company's inventory costs are expected to follow the trend for this particular product and Ebert Electronics wants to minimize its income taxes, which inventory costing method would you recommend that the company use to account for inventory? Explain your answer.
3. If Ebert's ending inventory were overstated by $100 at the end of March 2008, how would this affect its cost of goods sold for the month of March 2008?

Suggested Solution

1.

	ENDING INVENTORY		COST OF GOODS SOLD	
	Units	**Dollars**	**Units**	**Dollars**
FIFO	13	$2,812	12	$2,408
LIFO	13	2,780	12	2,440
Weighted average	13	2,790	12	2,430

FIFO Perpetual Calculations		PURCHASES			COST OF GOODS SOLD			INVENTORY BALANCE		
Date	**Description**	**Units**	**Unit Cost**	**Total Cost**	**Units**	**Unit Cost**	**Total Cost**	**Units**	**Unit Cost**	**Total Cost**
Mar 1	Beginning inventory							11	$200	$2,200
15	Purchase	5	$208	$1,040				5	208	1,040
19	Sale				11	$200	$2,200			
					1	208	208	4	208	832
21	Purchase	9	220	1,980				9	220	1,980
	Total	14		$3,020	12		$2,408	13		$2,812

LIFO Perpetual Calculations		PURCHASES			COST OF GOODS SOLD			INVENTORY BALANCE		
Date	**Description**	**Units**	**Unit Cost**	**Total Cost**	**Units**	**Unit Cost**	**Total Cost**	**Units**	**Unit Cost**	**Total Cost**
Mar 1	Beginning inventory							11	$200	$2,200
15	Purchase	5	$208	$1,040				5	208	1,040
19	Sale				5	$208	$1,040			
					7	200	1,400	4	200	800
21	Purchase	9	220	1,980				9	220	1,980
	Total	14		$3,020	12		$2,440	13		$2,780

Weighted Average Perpetual Calculations		PURCHASES			COST OF GOODS SOLD			INVENTORY BALANCE			
Date	Description	Units	Unit Cost	Total Cost	Units	Unit Cost	Total Cost	Units	Unit Cost	Total Cost	
Mar 1	Beginning inventory							11	$200.00	$2,200	
15	Purchase	5	$208	$1,040				5	208.00	1,040	$3,240 ÷ 16 = $202.50 per unit
19	Sale				12	$202.50	$2,430	4	202.50	810	$2,790
21	Purchase	9	220	1,980				9	220.00	1,980	
	Total	14		$3,020	12		$2,430	13		$2,790	

2. LIFO should be selected. Because costs are rising, LIFO produces a higher cost of goods sold, a lower income before income taxes, and lower income taxes.
3. If ending inventory were overstated by $100 at the end of March 2008, cost of goods sold would be understated by the same amount.

Supplement 7A
Cost Flow Methods under a Periodic Inventory System

In this section, we apply the cost flow methods using what is called a **periodic inventory system that makes the computations as if all purchases made during the period take place before any sales or cost of goods sold are recorded.** Assume that American Eagle engaged in the following transactions for its AE Alpine Bomber Jacket product line during the month of January and that all sales were for $150 per unit.

Date	Description	Units	Unit Cost	Total Cost
Jan 1	Beginning inventory	20	$70	$1,400
12	Purchase	60	80	4,800
19	Purchase	20	100	2,000
	Sales during the month	(82)		
				$8,200

Remember that a periodic inventory system records merchandise purchases as they occur but updates the inventory account and records cost of goods sold only at the end of the period. Ending inventory is determined by taking a physical count, and cost of goods sold is computed using the cost of goods sold equation in the following form:

$$BI + P - EI = CGS$$

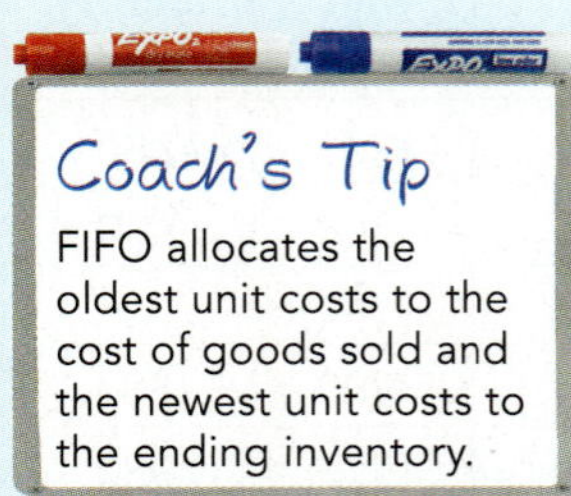

First-In, First-Out Method (FIFO)

The first-in, first-out method (FIFO) assumes that the oldest goods (the first ones into the inventory) are the first ones sold (the first ones out of the inventory). So you use the costs of the **oldest goods to calculate the cost of goods sold** (the 20 units at $70 plus the 60 units at $80 plus 2 units at $100 = $6,400). The **costs of the newer goods become the costs of the ending inventory** (the 18 units at $100 = $1,800).

Cost of Goods Sold and Ending Inventory Calculation (FIFO)

Beginning inventory	(20 units at $70 each)	$1,400
+ Purchases	(60 units at $80 each)	4,800
	(20 units at $100 each)	2,000
Goods available for sale		8,200
− Ending inventory (18 × $100)		1,800
Cost of goods sold (20 × $70) + (60 × $80) + (2 × $100)		$6,400

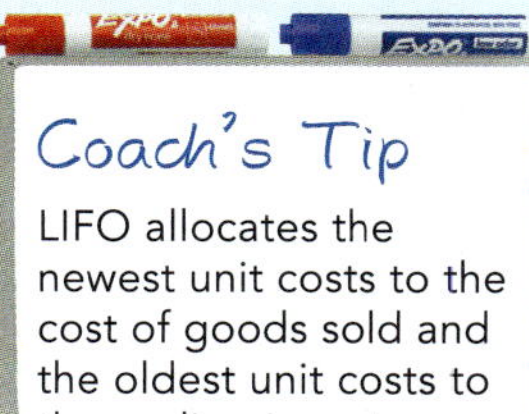

Last-In, First-Out Method (LIFO)

The last-in, first-out method (LIFO) assumes that the **newest** goods (the **last** ones into the inventory) are the first ones sold (the first ones out of the inventory). So you use the **costs of the newest goods to calculate the cost of goods sold** (20 units at $100 plus 60 units at $80 plus 2 units at $70). The **costs of the older costs become the costs of the ending inventory** (18 units at $70).

Cost of Goods Sold and Ending Inventory Calculation (LIFO)

Beginning inventory	(20 units at $70 each)	$1,400
+ Purchases	(60 units at $80 each)	4,800
	(20 units at $100 each)	2,000
Goods available for sale		8,200
− Ending inventory (18 × $70)		1,260
Cost of goods sold (20 × $100) + (60 × $80) + (2 × $70)		$6,940

Coach's Tip

In calculating the weighted average cost, be sure to **weight** the costs by the number of units purchased at each cost. Do not just average the unit costs ($100, $80, $70) without considering the number of units purchased at each cost.

Weighted Average Cost Method

The **weighted average cost method** calculates the weighted average cost per unit of the goods available for sale. The first step is to calculate the total cost of the goods available for sale. You multiply the number of units purchased at each cost by the cost per unit and then add to get the total cost:

Beginning inventory	(20 units at $70 each)	$1,400
+ Purchases	(60 units at $80 each)	4,800
	(20 units at $100 each)	2,000
Goods available for sale	(100 units)	$8,200

Then you calculate the weighted average cost per unit using the following formula:

$$\text{Weighted Average Cost} = \frac{\text{Cost of Goods Available for Sale}}{\text{Number of Units Available for Sale}} = \frac{\$8{,}200}{100 \text{ Units}} = \$82 \text{ per unit}$$

Cost of goods sold and ending inventory are both calculated using the same weighted average cost per unit, $82.

Cost of Goods Sold and Ending Inventory Calculation (Average Cost)

Beginning inventory	(20 units at $70 each)	$1,400
+ Purchases	(60 units at $80 each)	4,800
	(20 units at $100 each)	2,000
Goods available for sale		$8,200
− Ending inventory	(18 units at $82 average cost each)	1,476
Cost of goods sold	(82 units at $82 average cost each)	$6,724

Financial Statement Effects of Inventory Costing Methods

Exhibit 7A.1 summarizes the financial statement effects of the FIFO, LIFO, and weighted average cost methods. Remember that these methods differ only in the way they split the cost of goods available for sale between the cost of goods sold and the ending inventory. Because a cost that goes into ending inventory cannot also go into the cost of goods sold, the method that assigns the highest cost to ending inventory assigns the lowest cost to the cost of goods sold and vice versa.

Depending on whether costs are rising or falling, different methods have different effects on the financial statements. **When costs are rising,** as they are in our example, FIFO produces a higher inventory value (making the balance sheet **appear** to be stronger) and a lower cost of goods sold (resulting in a higher gross profit, which makes the company **look** more profitable). **When costs are falling,** these effects are reversed; FIFO produces a lower ending inventory value and a higher cost of goods sold—a double whammy. These are not "real" economic effects, however, because the same number of units is sold or held in ending inventory under either method. The following table summarizes the effects:

Effects of Increasing Costs on the Financial Statements

	FIFO	LIFO
Inventory on balance sheet	Higher	Lower
Cost of goods sold on income statement	Lower	Higher

Effects of Decreasing Costs on the Financial Statements

	FIFO	LIFO
Inventory on balance sheet	Lower	Higher
Cost of goods sold on income statement	Higher	Lower

Exhibit 7A.1 Financial Statement Effects of Inventory Costing Methods

	FIFO	LIFO	Weighted Average
Effect on the Income Statement			
Sales	$12,300	$12,300	$12,300
Cost of goods sold	6,400	6,940	6,724
Gross profit	5,900	5,360	5,576
Effect on the Balance Sheet			
Inventory	$1,800	$1,260	$1,476

Supplement 7B

Estimating Inventory

Gross Profit Method

When perpetual records and a physical inventory count are unavailable, the cost of goods sold and ending inventory may be estimated using one of two methods. The first, the **gross profit method,** relies on an estimate of the gross profit percentage (discussed in Chapter 6):

$$\text{Gross Profit Percentage} = \frac{(\text{Net Sales} - \text{CGS})}{\text{Net Sales}} \times 100$$

To illustrate, assume the company's accounting records indicate the following:

Beginning inventory	$14,000
Purchases	48,000
Net sales	75,000
Estimated gross profit percentage	40%

The gross profit method involves two steps:

1. Compute the cost of goods sold using the following formula:

   (100% − Gross Profit Percentage) × Net Sales = Cost of Goods Sold
   (100% − 40%) × $75,000 = $45,000

2. Compute the ending inventory using the cost of goods sold equation:

Beginning inventory	$14,000
+ Purchases of merchandise during the year	48,000
Goods available for sale	62,000
− Estimated cost of goods sold	45,000
Estimated ending inventory	$17,000

Retail Inventory Method

When a retailer maintains a record of the retail price of its entire inventory, the **retail inventory method** may be used. This method relies on an estimate of the ratio of cost to the retail price. To illustrate, assume the company's accounting records indicate the following:

	Cost	Retail
Beginning inventory	$24,000	$ 40,000
Purchases	48,000	80,000
Goods available for sale	$72,000	$120,000
Sales		$100,000

The retail method involves three steps:

1. Compute the ratio of cost to retail using the following formula:

$$\text{Ratio of Cost to Retail} = \frac{\text{Goods Available for Sale at Cost}}{\text{Goods Available for Sale at Retail}} = \frac{\$72{,}000}{\$120{,}000} = 0.6$$

2. Compute the ending inventory at retail:

Goods available for sale	$120,000
Sales	100,000
Ending inventory at retail	$ 20,000

3. Compute the ending inventory at estimated cost:

   Ending Inventory at Retail × Ratio of Cost to Retail = Ending Inventory at Cost
   $20,000 × 0.6 = $12,000

Chapter Summary

LO1 Explain how to report inventory and cost of goods sold. p. 304

- Goods held in inventory are recorded initially at cost, which is the amount given up to acquire the assets and prepare them for sale.
- When the goods are sold, their cost is removed from the inventory account and reported on the income statement as an expense called Cost of Goods Sold.

LO2 Explain the cost of goods sold equation. p. 305

Beginning inventory
\+ Purchases of merchandise made during the year
= Goods available for sale
− Ending inventory
= Cost of goods sold

LO3 Compute inventory costs using four inventory costing methods. p. 307

- Any of four generally accepted methods can be used to allocate the cost of inventory available for sale between goods that have been sold and goods that remain on hand at the end of the accounting period.
- The specific identification method assigns costs to ending inventory and the cost of goods sold by identifying and tracking specific inventory items.
- The FIFO method assigns the costs of the goods first in to the cost of goods sold and the costs of the goods last in (the most recent) to the ending inventory.
- The LIFO method assigns the costs of the goods last in to the cost of goods sold and the costs of the goods first in (the oldest) to the ending inventory.
- The weighted average cost method assigns the weighted average cost per unit of inventory to both the cost of goods sold and the ending inventory.

LO4 Report inventory at the lower of cost or market. p. 312

- The LCM rule ensures that inventory assets are not reported at more than they are worth.

LO5 Determine the effects of inventory errors on the income statement and balance sheet. p. 320

- An overstatement of ending inventory results in an understatement of the cost of goods sold in the current year and an overstatement of the cost of goods sold in the following year.
- An understatement of ending inventory has the opposite effects.

LO6 Compute and interpret the inventory turnover ratio. p. 316

- The inventory turnover ratio is calculated by dividing the cost of goods sold by average inventory. It indicates how many times average inventory was acquired and sold during the period and reflects the efficiency of inventory management.
- Days to sell is computed by dividing 365 by the inventory turnover ratio. It indicates the average number of days from purchase to sale.

Financial Analysis Tools

Name of Measure	Formula	What It Tells You
Inventory Turnover Ratio	Cost of Goods Sold / Average Inventory	• The number of times inventory turns over during the period • A higher ratio means faster turnover ☺
Days to Sell	365 / Inventory Turnover Ratio	• The average number of days from purchase to sale • A higher number means a longer time to sell ☹

Key Terms

Cost of Goods Sold (CGS) Equation (p. 306)
First-In, First-Out (FIFO) (p. 307)
Goods Available for Sale (p. 305)
Last-In, First-Out (LIFO) (p. 307)
Lower of Cost or Market (LCM) (p. 313)
Specific Identification (p. 307)
Weighted Average (p. 307)

See complete glossary in back of text.

Questions

1. Define goods available for sale. How does it differ from cost of goods sold?
2. Define beginning inventory and ending inventory.
3. The chapter discussed four inventory costing methods. List the four methods and briefly explain each.
4. Where possible, the inventory costing method should mimic actual product flows. Do you agree? Explain.
5. Contrast the effects of LIFO versus FIFO on ending inventory when (a) costs are rising and (b) costs are falling.
6. Contrast the income statement effect of LIFO versus FIFO (on cost of goods sold and gross profit) when (a) costs are rising and (b) costs are falling.
7. Explain briefly the application of the LCM rule to ending inventory. Describe its effect on the balance sheet and income statement when market is lower than cost.
8. Explain why an error in ending inventory in one period affects the following period.
9. How is the inventory turnover ratio computed?
10. (Supplement A) Distinguish perpetual inventory systems from periodic inventory systems by describing when and how cost of goods sold is calculated.

Multiple Choice

Quiz 7-1
www.mhhe.com/LLPW1e

1. How many of the following statements is/are true regarding cost of goods sold?
   - Cost of goods sold represents the cost that a company incurred to purchase or produce inventory in the current period.
   - Cost of goods sold is an expense on the income statement.
   - Cost of goods sold is affected by the inventory method selected by a company (FIFO, LIFO, etc.).

   a. None.
   b. One.
   c. Two.
   d. Three.
2. The inventory costing method selected by a company can affect
   a. The balance sheet.
   b. The income statement.
   c. Neither statement.
   d. Both statements.
3. An overstatement of ending inventory will affect reported net income in which periods?
   a. The period of the overstatement.
   b. The subsequent period.
   c. The period of the overstatement and the subsequent period.
   d. None of the above.
4. In each period, the cost of goods available for sale is allocated between
   a. Assets and liabilities.
   b. Assets and expenses.
   c. Assets and revenues.
   d. Expenses and liabilities.
5. A New York bridal dress retailer purchased three units of the same dress as follows: January 4: $170, January 12: $180, January 18: $190. It sold one dress on January 21 and one on January 29. What was cost of goods sold during the month of January using FIFO, LIFO, and weighted average costing methods?
   a. FIFO: $370, LIFO: $350, weighted average: $360.
   b. FIFO: $170, LIFO: $190, weighted average: $180.
   c. FIFO: $350, LIFO: $370, weighted average: $360.
   d. None of the above.
6. If costs are rising, which of the following will be true?
   a. The cost of goods sold will be higher if LIFO is used rather than weighted average.
   b. The cost of ending inventory will be higher if FIFO is used rather than LIFO.
   c. The gross profit will be higher if FIFO is used rather than LIFO.
   d. All of the above are true.
7. Which inventory method provides a better matching of current costs with sales revenue on the income statement but also results in older values being reported for inventory on the balance sheet?
   a. FIFO.
   b. Weighted average.
   c. LIFO.
   d. Specific identification.
8. Assume ending inventory included the following items, and the lower of cost or market rule for inventory was applied. What amount would be reported as ending inventory?

		Units	Cost	Market
i.	Item A	20	$35	$25
ii.	Item B	50	$40	$42

   a. $2,600.
   b. $2,700.
   c. $2,500.
   d. None of the above.

9. An increasing inventory turnover ratio
   a. Indicates a longer time span between ordering and receiving inventory.
   b. Indicates a shorter time span between ordering and receiving inventory.
   c. Indicates a shorter time span between the purchase and sale of inventory.
   d. Indicates a longer time span between the purchase and sale of inventory.

10. Which of the following is true regarding companies that report their inventories on a LIFO basis?
   a. They will always have a higher income tax expense.
   b. They will always have a higher inventory balance.
   c. Both of the above.
   d. None of the above.

Solutions to Multiple-Choice Questions									
1. c	2. d	3. c	4. b	5. c	6. d	7. c	8. c	9. c	10. d

Mini Exercises

Available with McGraw-Hill's Homework Manager

LO2 Dillard's

M7-1 Inferring Purchases Using the Cost of Goods Sold Equation

Dillard's, Inc., operates 330 department stores located in 29 states primarily in the Southwest, Southeast, and Midwest. In its annual report for the year ended January 28, 2006, the company reported cost of goods sold of $5,014 million, ending inventory for the current year of $1,803 million, and ending inventory for the previous year of $1,733 million. Is it possible to develop a reasonable estimate of the merchandise purchases for the year? If so, prepare the estimate. If not, explain why.

LO3

M7-2 Matching Financial Statement Effects to Inventory Costing Methods

Complete the following table by indicating which inventory costing method (FIFO or LIFO) would lead to the effects noted in the rows for each of the circumstances described in the columns.

	1. Rising Costs	2. Declining Costs
a. Lowest net income		
b. Lowest ending inventory		

LO3

M7-3 Matching Inventory Costing Method Choices to Company Circumstances

Indicate whether a company interested in minimizing its income taxes should choose the FIFO or LIFO inventory costing method under each of the following circumstances.

a. Declining costs ________

b. Rising costs ________

LO3

M7-4 Calculating Cost of Goods Sold and Ending Inventory under FIFO, LIFO, and Weighted Average (Perpetual Inventory)

Given the following information, calculate sales, cost of goods sold, and gross profit, under (a) FIFO, (b) LIFO, and (c) weighted average. Assume a perpetual inventory system is used.

		Units	Unit Cost	Unit Selling Price
July 1	Beginning inventory	100	$10	
July 13	Purchase	500	13	
July 25	Sold	(200)		$15
July 31	Ending inventory	400		

M7-5 Calculating Cost of Ending Inventory and Cost of Goods Sold under FIFO, LIFO, and Weighted Average (Perpetual Inventory) LO3

Scrappers Supplies uses a perpetual inventory system. At the end of January, its inventory records showed the following:

Transactions	Units	Unit Cost
Beginning inventory, January 1, 2008	200	$30
Transactions:		
a. Purchase, January 15	300	32
b. Sale, January 19 ($46 each)	(350)	
c. Purchase, January 24	250	36

Required:

1. Calculate the cost of the 350 units sold under the *(a)* FIFO, *(b)* LIFO, and *(c)* weighted average cost methods.
2. Calculate the cost of ending inventory using the (*a*) FIFO, (*b*) LIFO, and (*c*) weighted average cost methods.

M7-6 Calculating Cost of Ending Inventory and Cost of Goods Sold under FIFO, LIFO, and Weighted Average (Perpetual Inventory) LO3

Assume Oahu Kiki's uses a perpetual inventory system that shows the following for the month of January. (Round weighted average cost per unit to the nearest cent.)

	Date	Units	Unit Cost	Total Cost
Beginning Inventory	January 1	120	$ 8	$ 960
Purchase	January 15	380	9	3,420
Sale	January 19	240		
Purchase	January 24	200	11	2,200
Total				$6,580

Required:

1. Calculate the cost of the 240 units sold under the *(a)* FIFO, *(b)* LIFO, and *(c)* weighted average cost methods.
2. Calculate the cost of ending inventory using the (*a*) FIFO, (*b*) LIFO, and (*c*) weighted average cost methods.

M7-7 Reporting Inventory under Lower of Cost or Market LO4

The Jewel Fool had the following inventory items on hand at the end of the year.

	Quantity	Cost per Item	Replacement Cost per Item
Necklaces	50	$75	$70
Bracelets	25	60	50

Determine the lower of cost or market per unit and the total amount that should be reported on the balance sheet for each item of inventory.

LO5

M7-8 Determining the Financial Statement Effects of Inventory Errors

Assume the 2007 ending inventory of Shea's Shrimp Shack was understated by $10,000. Explain how this error would affect the amounts reported for cost of goods sold and gross profit for 2007 and 2008.

LO5

M7-9 Determining the Financial Statement Effects of Inventory Errors

Repeat M7-8, except assume the 2007 ending inventory was overstated by $100,000.

LO6
Dillard's
Macy's

M7-10 Calculating the Inventory Turnover Ratio and Days to Sell

Using the data in M7-1, calculate to one decimal place the inventory turnover ratio and days to sell for Dillard's. In a recent year, Macy's reported an inventory turnover ratio of 2.6. Which company's inventory turnover is faster?

M7-11 (Supplement A) Calculating Cost of Goods Sold and Ending Inventory under FIFO, LIFO, and Weighted Average (Periodic Inventory)

Complete the requirements in M7-5 assuming a periodic inventory system is used under FIFO, LIFO, and weighted average cost.

M7-12 (Supplement A) Calculating Cost of Goods Sold and Ending Inventory under FIFO, LIFO, and Weighted Average (Periodic Inventory)

Complete the requirements in M7-6, except assume that the company uses a periodic inventory system.

M7-13 (Supplement B) Estimating Inventory Using the Gross Profit Method

Net sales were $150,000 and the estimated gross profit percentage was 40 percent. Estimate cost of goods sold using the gross profit method.

M7-14 (Supplement B) Estimating Inventory Using the Retail Inventory Method

Net sales were $200,000 and goods available for sale were $250,000 at retail and $150,000 at cost. Compute ending inventory at cost.

Exercises

Available with McGraw-Hill's Homework Manager

LO2

E7-1 Inferring Missing Amounts Based on Income Statement Relationships

Supply the missing dollar amounts for the 2008 income statement of Lewis Retailers for each of the following independent cases:

Case	Sales Revenue	Beginning Inventory	Purchases	Total Available	Ending Inventory	Cost of Goods Sold	Gross Profit	Operating Expenses	Income from Operations
A	$800	$100	$700	$?	$500	$?	$?	$200	$?
B	900	200	700	?	?	?	?	150	0
C	?	150	?	?	250	200	400	100	?
D	800	?	600	?	250	?	?	250	100

LO2
The Gap

E7-2 Inferring Merchandise Purchases

The Gap, Inc., is a specialty retailer that operates stores selling clothes under the trade names Gap, Forth and Towne, Banana Republic, and Old Navy. Assume you are employed as a stock analyst and your boss has just completed a review of the Gap annual report for the year ended January 28, 2006. She provided you with her notes, but they are missing some information that you need. Her notes show that the ending inventory for Gap in the current year was $1,696,000,000 and in the previous year was $1,814,000,000. Net sales for the current year were $16,023,000,000. Gross profit was $5,869,000,000 and net income was $1,113,000,000. For your analysis, you determine that you need to know the amount of purchases and cost of goods sold for the year.

Required:

Do you need to ask your boss for her copy of the annual report, or can you develop the information from her notes? Explain and show calculations.

E7-3 Calculating Cost of Goods Sold and Ending Inventory under FIFO, LIFO, and Weighted Average (Perpetual Inventory) LO3

Given the following information, calculate the cost of ending inventory and cost of goods sold, assuming a perpetual inventory system is used in combination with *(a)* FIFO, *(b)* LIFO, and *(c)* weighted average cost. (Round weighted average cost per unit to the nearest tenth of a cent; three decimal places.)

		Units	Unit Cost
July 1	Beginning Inventory	2,000	$ 20.60
July 5	Sold	1,000	
July 13	Purchased	6,000	22.00
July 17	Sold	3,000	
July 25	Purchased	8,000	25.10
July 27	Sold	5,000	

E7-4 Calculating Cost of Goods Sold and Ending Inventory under FIFO, LIFO, and Weighted Average (Perpetual Inventory) LO3

In its first month of operations, Literacy for the Illiterate opened a new bookstore and bought merchandise in the following order: (1) 300 units at $7 on January 1, (2) 450 units at $8 on January 8, and (3) 750 units at $9 on January 29. Assuming the company sold 350 units on January 12 and 550 units on January 30, calculate the cost of goods sold and ending inventory on January 31 under the *(a)* FIFO, *(b)* LIFO, and *(c)* weighted average cost flow assumptions. Assume a perpetual inventory system is used. (Round weighted average cost per unit to the nearest tenth of a cent; three decimal places.)

E7-5 Evaluating the Effects of Three Inventory Methods on Income from Operations, Income Taxes, and Net Income (Perpetual Inventory) LO3

Courtney Company uses a perpetual inventory system. Data for 2009: beginning merchandise inventory (December 31, 2008), 1,000 units at $35; purchases include 2,000 units at $38 on March 22 and 3,000 units at $40 on July 1; operating expenses (excluding income taxes), $71,000; sales for the year include 1,500 units sold on April 14 and 3,500 sold on September 30; sales price per unit, $70; and income tax expense is 30 percent of income from operations.

Required:

1. Compute cost of goods sold under the FIFO, LIFO, and weighted average costing methods using a format similar to Exhibits 7.5, 7.6, and 7.7. (Round weighted average cost per unit to the nearest tenth of a cent; three decimal places.) Then prepare income statements for each method using a format similar to the following:

	INVENTORY COSTING METHOD		
	FIFO	LIFO	Weighted Average
Income Statement			
Sales revenue	$	$	$
Cost of goods sold			
Gross profit			
Operating expenses			
Income from operations			
Income tax expense			
Net income			

2. Between FIFO and LIFO, which method is preferable in terms of (*a*) maximizing operating income or (*b*) minimizing income taxes? Explain.
3. What would be your answer to requirement 2 if costs were falling? Explain.

LO3

E7-6 Evaluating the Effects of Three Inventory Methods on Income from Operations, Income Taxes, and Net Income (Perpetual Inventory)

Following is partial information for the cost of goods sold calculation and income statement of Timber Company under three different inventory costing methods, assuming the use of a perpetual inventory system:

Transactions
Beginning inventory (330 units @ $34) on Jan. 1
Purchases:
  Jan. 10—175 units purchased at $36
  Jan. 25—300 units purchased at $37
Sales:
  Jan. 12 — 200 units sold at $50 per unit
  Jan. 28 — 95 units sold at $50 per unit
Operating expences: $1,600

Required:

1. Compute cost of goods sold under the FIFO, LIFO, and weighted average inventory costing methods. (Round weighted average cost per unit to the nearest tenth of a cent; three decimal places.)
2. Prepare an income statement (up to income before income taxes) that compares each method.
3. Rank the three methods in order of highest income before income taxes.
4. Calculate income tax expense under each of the three methods, assuming income tax expense equal to 30 percent of income before income taxes.
5. Rank the three methods in order of lowest income taxes.

LO3

E7-7 Choosing LIFO versus FIFO When Costs Are Rising and Falling

Use the following information to complete this exercise: sales, 550 units for $12,500; beginning inventory on January 1 of 300 units; purchases of 100 units on February 18, and 300 units on September 14; sales of 300 units on June 5, and 250 units on October 22; and operating expenses of $4,000. Begin by setting up the following table and then complete the requirements that follow.

	COSTS RISING		COSTS FALLING	
	SITUATION A	SITUATION B	SITUATION C	SITUATION D
	FIFO	LIFO	FIFO	LIFO
Sales revenue	$12,500	$12,500	$12,500	$12,500
Cost of goods sold	_____	_____	_____	_____
Gross profit				
Operating expenses	4,000	4,000	4,000	4,000
Income before income taxes				
Income tax expense (30%)	_____	_____	_____	_____
Net income	=====	=====	=====	=====

Required:

1. First use the included information to calculate the cost of goods sold in Situations A through D, and then complete the table for each situation. In Situations A and B (costs rising), assume the following: beginning inventory, 300 units at $12 = $3,600; February and September purchases

were made at $13. In Situations C and D (costs falling), assume the opposite; that is, beginning inventory, 300 units at $13 = $3,900; subsequent purchases were made at $12. Use perpetual inventory procedures.

2. Describe the relative effects on income from operations as demonstrated by requirement 1 when costs are rising and when costs are falling.
3. Describe the relative effects on income taxes for each situation.
4. Would you recommend FIFO or LIFO? Explain.

E7-8 Reporting Inventory at Lower of Cost or Market LO4

Peterson Furniture Designs is preparing the annual financial statements dated December 31, 2009. Ending inventory information about the five major items stocked for regular sale follows:

	ENDING INVENTORY, 2007				
Item	Quantity on Hand	Unit Cost When Acquired (FIFO)	Replacement Cost (Market) at Year-End	LCM per Item	Total LCM
Alligator armoires	50	$15	$12	______	______
Bear bureaus	75	40	40	______	______
Cougar beds	10	50	52	______	______
Dingo cribs	30	30	30	______	______
Elephant dressers	400	10	6	______	______
Total					______

Required:

Complete the final two columns of the table and then compute the amount that should be reported for the 2009 ending inventory using the LCM rule applied to each item.

E7-9 Reporting Inventory at Lower of Cost or Market LO4

Sandals Company was formed on January 1, 2008, and is preparing the annual financial statements dated December 31, 2008. Ending inventory information about the four major items stocked for regular sale follows:

	ENDING INVENTORY, 2008		
Product Line	Quantity on Hand	Unit Cost When Acquired (FIFO)	Replacement Cost (Market) at Year-End
Air flow	20	$12	$ 14
Blister buster	75	40	38
Coolonite	35	55	50
Dudesly	10	30	35

Required:

1. Compute the amount that should be reported for the 2008 ending inventory using the LCM rule applied to each item.
2. How will the write-down of inventory to lower of cost or market affect the cost of goods sold reported for the year ended December 31, 2008?

E7-10 Preparing the Journal Entry to Record Lower of Cost or Market (LCM) Adjustments LO 4

RadioShack Corporation (RadioShack) sells consumer electronic goods and services through its 4,972 stores and 777 kiosks. In its annual report filed with the SEC for a recent year, the company reported that it wrote down inventory by approximately $62,000,000 because its cost exceeded its market value. Show the journal entry that the company would have made to record this adjustment as well as the effects on the accounting equation.

LO5

E7-11 Analyzing and Interpreting the Impact of an Inventory Error

Dallas Corporation prepared the following two income statements:

	First Quarter 2009		Second Quarter 2009	
Sales revenue		$15,000		$18,000
Cost of goods sold				
Beginning inventory	$ 3,000		$ 4,000	
Purchases	7,000		12,000	
Goods available for sale	10,000		16,000	
Ending inventory	4,000		9,000	
Cost of goods sold		6,000		7,000
Gross profit		9,000		11,000
Operating expenses		5,000		6,000
Operating income		$ 4,000		$ 5,000

During the third quarter, the company's internal auditors discovered that the ending inventory for the first quarter should have been $4,400. The ending inventory for the second quarter was correct.

Required:

1. What effect would the error have on the total operating income for the two quarters combined? Explain.
2. What effect would the error have on the operating income for each of the two quarters? Explain.
3. Prepare corrected income statements for each quarter.

LO5

E7-12 Analyzing and Interpreting the Impact of an Inventory Error

Houston Corporation prepared the same two income statements presented in E7-11. During the third quarter, the company's internal auditors discovered that the ending inventory for the first quarter should have been $3,600. The ending inventory for the second quarter was correct.

Required:

1. What effect would the error have on the total operating income for the two quarters combined? Explain.
2. What effect would the error have on the operating income for each of the two quarters? Explain.
3. Prepare corrected income statements for each quarter.

LO6
Polaris Industries

E7-13 Analyzing and Interpreting the Inventory Turnover Ratio

Polaris Industries Inc. is the biggest snowmobile manufacturer in the world. It reported the following amounts in its recent financial statements (in millions):

	Current Year	Prior Year
Net sales revenue	$1,870	$1,773
Cost of sales	1,452	1,349
Average inventory	188	179

Required:

1. Calculate to one decimal place the inventory turnover ratio and average days to sell inventory for the current and prior years.

2. Comment on any trends, and compare the effectiveness of inventory managers at Polaris to inventory managers at its main competitor, Arctic Cat, where inventory turns over 7.5 times per year (48.7 days to sell). Both companies use the same inventory costing method (FIFO).

E7-14 (Supplement A) Calculating Cost of Ending Inventory and Cost of Goods Sold under Periodic FIFO, LIFO and Weighted-Average

Refer to the information in E7-3. Assume the company uses a periodic inventory system. Calculate the cost of goods sold and the cost of ending inventory using the FIFO, LIFO, and weighted average cost methods (Round weighted average cost per unit to the nearest tenth of a cent; three decimal places.)

E7-15 (Supplement A) Calculating Cost of Ending Inventory and Cost of Goods Sold under Periodic FIFO, LIFO, and Weighted Average

Refer to the information in E7-4. Assume the company uses a periodic inventory system. Calculate the cost of ending inventory and the cost of goods sold using the FIFO, LIFO, and weighted average cost methods. (Round weighted average cost per unit to the nearest tenth of a cent; three decimal places.)

E7-16 (Supplement B) Estimating Inventory Using the Gross Profit Method

Hartman Co.'s accounting records contained the following information related to the month of November:

Beginning inventory	$16,000
Purchases	52,000
Net sales	75,000
Estimated gross profit percentage	30%

Estimate cost of goods sold for the month and ending inventory at month-end using the gross profit method.

E7-17 (Supplement B) Estimating Inventory Using the Retail Inventory Method

Ralph's Clothing's accounting records indicated the following at the end of the quarter:

	Cost	Retail
Beginning inventory	$26,000	$ 41,600
Purchases	48,000	76,800
Goods available for sale	74,000	118,400
Sales		100,400

Compute ending inventory at cost using the retail method.

Problems—Set A

Available with McGraw-Hill's Homework Manager

PA7-1 Analyzing the Effects of Four Alternative Inventory Methods in a Perpetual Inventory System LO3

Gladstone Company uses a perpetual inventory system. At the end of the annual accounting period, December 31, 2007, the accounting records for the most popular item in inventory showed the following:

Transactions	Units	Unit Cost
Beginning inventory, January 1, 2007	1,800	$5.00
Transactions during 2007:		
Purchase, January 30	2,500	6.20
Sale, March 14 ($10 each)	(1,450)	
Purchase, May 1	1,200	8.00
Sale, August 31 ($10 each)	(1,900)	

Required:

1. Compute the ending inventory and cost of goods sold at December 31, 2007, under each of the following inventory costing methods:
   a. First-in, first-out.
   b. Last-in, first-out.
   c. Weighted average cost. (Round weighted average cost per unit to the nearest tenth of a cent; three decimal places.)
   d. Specific identification, assuming that the March 14, 2007, sale was comprised of 580 units from the beginning inventory and 870 units from the purchase of January 30, 2007. Assume that the sale of August 31, 2007, was comprised of 1,220 units from beginning inventory, and 680 units from the purchase of May 1, 2007.
2. Of the four methods, which will result in the highest gross profit? Which will result in the lowest income taxes?

LO3 

www.mhhe.com/LLPW1e

PA7-2 Analyzing and Interpreting the Financial Statement Effects of FIFO, LIFO, and Weighted Average (Perpetual Inventory)

Orion Iron Corp. uses a perpetual inventory system. At the end of the annual accounting period, December 31, 2009, the accounting records provided the following information:

Transactions	Units	Unit Cost
Inventory, December 31, 2008	2,000	$ 8.00
For the year 2009:		
Purchase, April 11	10,000	10.40
Sale, May 1 (sold for $40 per unit)	2,000	
Purchase, June 1	8,000	12.25
Sale, July 3 (sold for $40 per unit)	6,000	
Operating expenses (excluding income tax expense), $195,000		

Required:

1. Compute the cost of goods sold under (*a*) FIFO, (*b*) LIFO, and (*c*) weighted average. (Round weighted average cost per unit to the nearest tenth of a cent; three decimal places.)
2. Prepare an income statement that shows 2009 amounts for the FIFO method in one column, the LIFO method in another column, and the weighted average method in a final column. Include the following line items in the income statement: sales revenue, cost of goods sold, gross profit, operating expenses, and income from operations.
3. Compare the income from operations and the ending inventory amounts that would be reported under the three methods. Explain the similarities and differences.
4. Which inventory costing method may be preferred by Orion Iron Corp. for income tax purposes? Explain.

LO4

www.mhhe.com/LLPW1e

PA7-3 Evaluating the Income Statement and Income Tax Effects of Lower of Cost or Market

Springer Anderson Gymnastics prepared its annual financial statements dated December 31, 2009. The company used the FIFO inventory costing method, but it failed to apply LCM to the ending inventory. The preliminary 2009 income statement follows:

Sales revenue		$140,000
Cost of goods sold		
Beginning inventory	$ 15,000	
Purchases	91,000	
Goods available for sale	106,000	
Ending inventory (FIFO cost)	22,000	
Cost of goods sold		84,000
Gross profit		56,000
Operating expenses		31,000
Income before income taxes		25,000
Income tax expense (30%)		7,500
Net income		$ 17,500

Assume you have been asked to restate the 2009 financial statements to incorporate LCM. You have developed the following data relating to the 2009 ending inventory:

		ACQUISITION COST		CURRENT REPLACEMENT UNIT COST
Item	Quantity	Per Unit	Total	Market
A	1,500	$3	$ 4,500	$4
B	750	4	3,000	2
C	3,500	2	7,000	1
D	1,500	5	7,500	3
			$22,000	

Required:

1. Restate the income statement to reflect LCM valuation of the 2009 ending inventory. Apply LCM on an item-by-item basis and show computations.
2. Compare and explain the LCM effect on each amount that was changed in requirement 1.
3. What is the conceptual basis for applying LCM to merchandise inventories?

PA7-4 Analyzing and Interpreting the Effects of Inventory Errors

LO5

www.mhhe.com/LLPW1e

The income statement for Sherwood Company summarized for a four-year period shows the following:

	2005	2006	2007	2008
Sales revenue	$2,000,000	$2,400,000	$2,500,000	$3,000,000
Cost of goods sold	1,400,000	1,660,000	1,770,000	2,100,000
Gross profit	$ 600,000	$ 740,000	$ 730,000	$ 900,000

An audit revealed that in determining these amounts, the ending inventory for 2006 was overstated by $20,000. The inventory balance on December 31, 2007, was accurately stated.

Required:

1. Restate the income statements to reflect the correct amounts after fixing the inventory error.
2. Compute the gross profit percentage for each year (*a*) before the correction and (*b*) after the correction. Do the results lend confidence to your corrected amounts? Explain.

PA7-5 Calculating and Interpreting the Inventory Turnover Ratio and Days to Sell

LO6

Harman International
Boston Acoustics

Harman International Industries is a world leading producer of loudspeakers and other electronics products, which are sold under brand names like JBL, Infinity, and Harman/Kardon. The company reported the following amounts in its financial statements (in millions):

	Current Year	Previous Year
Net sales revenue	$3,248	$3,031
Cost of sales	2,095	1,999
Beginning inventory	312	292
Ending inventory	345	312

Required:

1. Determine the inventory turnover ratio and average days to sell inventory for the current and previous years.
2. Comment on any changes in these measures, and compare the effectiveness of inventory managers at Harmon to inventory managers at Boston Acoustics, where inventory turns over 3.7 times per year (99 days to sell). Both companies use the same inventory costing method (FIFO).

PA7-6 (Supplement A) Analyzing the Effects of the LIFO Inventory Method in a Periodic Inventory System

Using the information in PA7-1, calculate the cost of goods sold and ending inventory under (*a*) FIFO, (*b*) LIFO, and (*c*) weighted average in combination with a periodic inventory system. (Round the weighted average cost to the nearest tenth of a cent; three decimal places.). Which method will result in the highest gross profit? Which method will result in the lowest taxes?

PA7-7 (Supplement B) Estimating Inventory Using the Gross Profit Method

Bunky's Business Solutions uses the gross profit method to estimate cost of goods sold and ending inventory for its quarterly financial statements. Last year, net sales were $750,000 and cost of goods sold were $540,000. The accounting records for the current quarter contained the following information:

Beginning inventory	$ 40,000
Purchases	112,000
Net sales	181,000

Required:

1. Compute the gross profit percentage for last year.
2. Estimate cost of goods sold for the quarter and ending inventory at quarter-end using the gross profit method.

PA7-8 (Supplement B) Estimating Inventory Using the Retail Inventory Method

Fleming Enterprises' accounting records indicated the following at the end of the quarter:

	Cost	Retail
Beginning inventory	$ 84,000	$112,000
Purchases	318,000	424,000
Goods available for sale	$402,000	$536,000
Sales		$468,000

Required:

1. Compute ending inventory at cost using the retail method.
2. Compute cost of goods sold using the answer to requirement 1.

Problems—Set B

Available with McGraw-Hill's Homework Manager

LO3

PB7-1 Analyzing the Effects of Four Alternative Inventory Methods in a Perpetual Inventory System

Mojo Industries uses a perpetual inventory system. At the end of the accounting period, January 31, 2009, the inventory records showed the following for an item that sold at $9 per unit:

Transactions	Unit Cost	Units	Total Cost
Inventory, January 1, 2009	$2.50	250	$625
Sale, January 10		(200)	
Purchase, January 12	3.00	300	900
Sale, January 17		(150)	
Purchase, January 26	4.00	80	320

Required:

1. Compute the ending inventory and cost of goods sold at January 31, 2009, under each of the following inventory costing methods:
   a. First-in, first-out.
   b. Last-in, first-out.

c. Weighted average cost (Round weighted average unit cost to the nearest tenth of a cent; three decimal places.)

d. Specific identification, assuming that the January 10 sale was from the beginning inventory and the January 17 sale was from the January 12 purchase.

2. Of the four methods, which will result in the highest gross profit? Which will result in the lowest income taxes?

PB7-2 Analyzing and Interpreting the Financial Statement Effects of FIFO, LIFO, and Weighted Average (Perpetual Inventory) LO3

Scoresby Inc. uses a perpetual inventory system. At the end of the annual accounting period, December 31, 2008, the accounting records provided the following information:

Transactions	Units	Unit Cost
Inventory, December 31, 2007	3,000	$7.90
For the year 2008:		
Purchase, March 5	8,000	9.00
Sale, April 15 (sold for $29 per unit)	4,000	
Purchase, September 19	5,000	11.82
Sale, October 31 (sold for $31 per unit)	8,000	
Operating expenses (excluding income tax expense), $240,000		

Required:

1. Compute the cost of goods sold under (*a*) FIFO, (*b*) LIFO, and (*c*) weighted average. (Round weighted average cost per unit to the nearest tenth of a cent; three decimal places.)
2. Prepare an income statement that shows 2008 amounts for the FIFO method in one column, the LIFO method in another column, and the weighted average method in a final column. Include the following line items in the income statement: sales revenue, cost of goods sold, gross profit, operating expenses, and income from operations.
3. Compare the income from operations and the ending inventory amounts that would be reported under the two methods. Explain the similarities and differences.
4. Which inventory costing method may be preferred by Scoresby for income tax purposes? Explain.

PB7-3 Evaluating the Income Statement and Income Tax Effects of Lower of Cost or Market LO4

Mondetta Clothing prepared its annual financial statements dated December 31, 2008. The company used the FIFO inventory costing method, but it failed to apply LCM to the ending inventory. The preliminary 2008 income statement follows:

Sales revenue		$420,000
Cost of goods sold		
Beginning inventory	$ 45,000	
Purchases	273,000	
Goods available for sale	318,000	
Ending inventory (FIFO cost)	66,000	
Cost of goods sold		252,000
Gross profit		168,000
Operating expenses		93,000
Income before income taxes		75,000
Income tax expense (30%)		22,500
Net income		$ 52,500

Assume you have been asked to restate the 2008 financial statements to incorporate LCM. You have developed the following data relating to the 2008 ending inventory:

		ACQUISITION COST		CURRENT REPLACEMENT UNIT COST
Item	Quantity	Per Unit	Total	Market
A	3,000	$4.50	$13,500	$6.00
B	1,500	6.00	9,000	3.00
C	7,000	3.00	21,000	6.00
D	3,000	7.50	22,500	4.50
			$66,000	

Required:

1. Restate the income statement to reflect LCM valuation of the 2008 ending inventory. Apply LCM on an item-by-item basis and show computations.
2. Compare and explain the LCM effect on each amount that was changed in requirement 1.
3. What is the conceptual basis for applying LCM to merchandise inventories?

LO5

PB7-4 Analyzing and Interpreting the Effects of Inventory Errors

"Oops, I Did It Again" was the song being sung by the accountants at Spears & Cantrell when they announced inventory had been overstated by $30 (million) at the end of the second quarter. The error was not discovered and corrected in the company's periodic inventory system until after the end of the third quarter. The following table shows the amounts (in millions) that were originally reported by the company.

	Q1	Q2	Q3
Sales revenue	$3,000	$3,600	$3,750
Cost of goods sold	2,100	2,490	2,655
Gross profit	$ 900	$1,110	$1,095

Required:

1. Restate the income statements to reflect the correct amounts, after fixing the inventory error.
2. Compute the gross profit percentage for each quarter (*a*) before the correction and (*b*) after the correction. Do the results lend confidence to your corrected amounts? Explain.

LO6

amazon.com

Borders

PB7-5 Calculating and Interpreting the Inventory Turnover Ratio and Days to Sell

Amazon.com reported the following amounts in its financial statements (in millions):

	Current Year	Prior Year
Net sales revenue	$8,490	$6,921
Cost of sales	6,451	5,319
Beginning inventory	480	294
Ending inventory	566	480

Required:

1. Determine the inventory turnover ratio and average days to sell inventory for the current and prior years.
2. Comment on any changes in these measures and compare the inventory turnover at Amazon.com to inventory turnover at Borders, where inventory turned over 2.2 times during the current year

(166 days to sell). Based on your own experience, what is the key difference between Amazon.com and Borders that leads one company's results to be the picture of efficiency and the other to seem like a library?

PB7-6 (Supplement A) Analyzing the Effects of Three Inventory Methods in a Periodic Inventory System

Using the information in PB7-1, calculate the cost of goods sold and ending inventory under (*a*) FIFO, (*b*) LIFO, and (*c*) weighted average in combination with a periodic inventory system. (Round the weighted-average cost to the nearest tenth of a cent; three decimal places.) Which method will result in the highest gross profit? Which method will result in the lowest taxes?

PB7-7 (Supplement B) Estimating Inventory Using the Gross Profit Method

Greeley & Morgan, LLP uses the gross profit method to estimate cost of goods sold and ending inventory for its quarterly financial statements. Last year, net sales were $328,125 and cost of goods sold were $210,000. Its accounting records for the current quarter contained the following information:

Beginning inventory	$ 9,000
Purchases	52,000
Net sales	85,000

Required:

1. Compute the gross profit percentage for last year.
2. Estimate cost of goods sold for the quarter and ending inventory at quarter-end using the gross profit method.

PB7-8 (Supplement B) Estimating Inventory Using the Retail Inventory Method

Indieser, Inc.'s accounting records indicated the following at the end of the quarter:

	Cost	Retail
Beginning inventory	$252,000	$ 315,000
Purchases	676,000	845,000
Goods available for sale	928,000	1,160,000
Sales		980,000

Required:

1. Compute ending inventory at cost using the retail method.
2. Compute cost of goods sold using the answer to requirement 1.

Cases and Projects

CP7-1 Finding Financial Information LO1, 2, 6

Refer to the financial statements of The Home Depot in Appendix A at the end of this book, or download the annual report from the *Cases* section of the text's Web site at www.mhhe.com/LLPW1e.

1. How much inventory does the company hold at the end of the most recent year? Does this represent an increase or decrease in comparison to the prior year?
2. What method(s) does the company use to determine the cost of its inventory? Describe where you found this information.
3. Compute to one decimal place the company's inventory turnover ratio and days to sell for the most recent year.

CP7-2 Comparing Financial Information LO1, 2, 6

Lowe's

Refer to the financial statements of The Home Depot in Appendix A and Lowe's in Appendix B at the end of this book, or download the annual reports from the *Cases* section of the text's Web site at www.mhhe.com/LLPW1e.

1. Does Lowe's hold more or less inventory than The Home Depot at the end of the most recent year?
2. What method does Lowe's use to determine the cost of its inventory? Comment on how this affects comparisons you might make between Lowe's and The Home Depot's inventory turnover ratios.
3. Compute to one decimal place Lowe's inventory turnover ratio and days to sell for the most recent year and compare to The Home Depot's. What does this analysis suggest to you?

LO1, 2, 3, 4, 5, 6

CP7-3 Examining an Annual Report: Internet-Based Team Research

As a team, select an industry to analyze. Using your Web browser, each team member should acquire the annual report or 10-K for one publicly traded company in the industry, with each member selecting a different company. (See CP1-3 in Chapter 1 for a description of possible resources for these tasks.)

Required:

1. On an individual basis, each team member should write a short report that incorporates the following:
   a. Describe the types of inventory held by the company. Does the company indicate its inventory management goals anywhere in its annual report?
   b. Describe the inventory costing method that it used. Why do you think the company chose this method rather than the other acceptable methods? Do you think its inventory costs are rising or falling?
   c. Calculate the inventory turnover ratio for the current and prior year, and explain any change between the two years. (To obtain the beginning inventory number for the prior year, you will need the prior year's annual report.)
   d. Search the 10-K for information about the company's approach for applying the LCM rule to inventory. Did the company report the amount of inventory written down during the year?
2. Then, as a team, write a short report comparing and contrasting your companies using these attributes. Discuss any patterns across the companies that you as a team observe. Provide potential explanations for any differences discovered.

LO3

CP7-4 Making Ethical Decisions: A Mini Case

David Exler is the CEO of AquaGear Enterprises, a seven-year-old manufacturer of boats. After many long months of debate with the company's board of directors, David obtained the board's approval to expand into water ski sales. David firmly believed that AquaGear could generate significant profits in this market, despite recent increases in the cost of skis. A board meeting will be held later this month for David to present the financial results for the first quarter of ski sales. As AquaGear's corporate controller, you reported to David that the results were not great. Although sales were better than expected at $165,000 (3,000 units at $55 per unit), the cost of goods sold was $147,500. This left a gross profit of $17,500. David knew this amount would not please the board. Desperate to save the ski division, David asks you to "take another look at the cost calculations to see if there's any way to reduce the cost of goods sold. I know you accountants have different methods for figuring things out, so maybe you can do your magic now when I need it most." You dig out your summary of inventory purchases for the quarter to recheck your calculations, using the LIFO method that has always been used for the company's inventory of boats.

	Date	Units	Unit Cost	Total Cost
Beginning inventory of water skis	January 1	0	—	—
Purchases	January 15	1,500	$ 30	$ 45,000
Purchases	February 18	2,000	45	90,000
Purchases	February 27	2,500	50	125,000

Required:

1. Calculate cost of goods sold using the LIFO method. (Assume all sales took place in March.) Does this confirm the statement you made to David about the gross profit earned on water ski sales in the first quarter?
2. Without doing any calculations, is it likely that any alternative inventory costing method will produce a lower cost of goods sold?
3. Calculate cost of goods sold using the FIFO method. Would use of this method solve David's current dilemma?
4. Is it acceptable within GAAP to report the water skis using one inventory costing method and the boats using a different method?
5. Do you see any problems with using the FIFO numbers for purposes of David's meeting with the board?

LO4
Perfumania

CP7-5 Calculating and Recording the Effects of Lower of Cost or Market (LCM) on Ending Inventory

Assume you recently obtained a job in the Miami head office of Perfumania, the largest specialty retailer of discounted fragrances in the United States. Your job is to estimate the amount of write-down required to value inventory at the lower of cost or market. The cost of inventory is calculated using the weighted average cost method and, at approximately $70 million, it represents the company's largest and most important asset. Assume the corporate controller asked you to prepare a spreadsheet that can be used to determine the amount of LCM write-down for the current year. The controller provides the following hypothetical numbers for you to use in the spreadsheet.

Product Line	Quantity on Hand	Weighted Average Unit Cost	Replacement Cost (Market) at Year-End
Alfred Sung Shi	80	$ 22	$ 20
Animale	75	15	16
Azzaro	50	10	10
Mambo	30	16	17
OP Juice	400	8	7

You realize that you will need to multiply the quantity of each item by the lower of cost or market per unit, but you cannot figure out how to get the spreadsheet to choose the lower number. You e-mailed your friend Billy for help, and here is his reply.

From: Billy@yahoo.com
To: Helpme@hotmail.com
Cc:
Subject: Excel Help

You can do this several different ways, but the easiest is to use the MIN command. Set up your spreadsheet similar to the table you sent me, and then add two new columns. In the first new column, enter the command "=MIN(costcell, marketcell)" where costcell is the cell containing the cost per unit and marketcell is the cell containing the market value per unit. Next, in the second new column, multiply the quantity by the LCM per unit. Here is a screenshot of what this will probably look like in your spreadsheet.

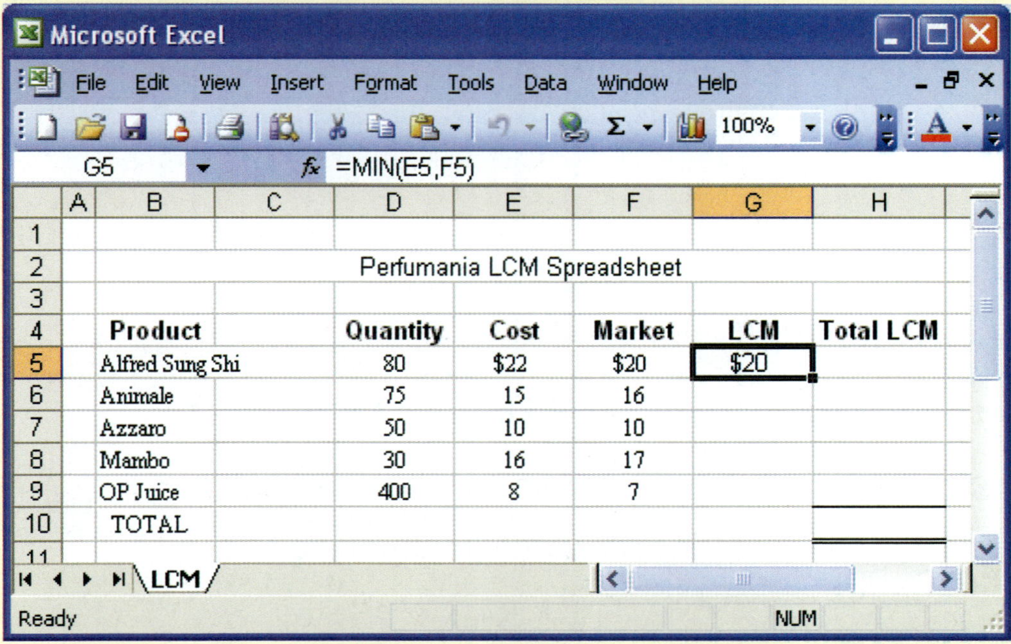

Be sure to enter a formula to sum down the Total LCM column for all the products so that this grand total can be subtracted from the cost presently recorded in the inventory accounting records to determine the write-down.

Required:

1. Prepare a spreadsheet that calculates total LCM for inventory, applied on an item-by-item basis.
2. Prepare a journal entry to record the write-down needed for the five products in this problem.

8 Internal Control and Cash

LEARNING OBJECTIVES

After completing this chapter, you should be able to:

Lectured slideshow–LP8-1
www.mhhe.com/LLPW1e

LO1 Define internal control and explain why it is needed.

LO2 Explain the common principles and limitations of internal control.

LO3 Apply internal control principles to cash receipts and payments.

LO4 Describe the operation of voucher and petty cash systems.

LO5 Prepare a bank reconciliation.

LO6 Describe the reporting of cash and cash equivalents.

Focus Company: THE HOME DEPOT

"You Can Do It. We Can Help."

ir.homedepot.com

The Home Depot's business code of conduct and ethics states that the company's success depends on doing the right thing each and every day for the benefit of employees, customers, vendors, suppliers, and the communities the company serves. A clerk who was working at a Home Depot store in New York recently took these words to heart and provided a phone tip that led to the discovery of "the largest, most remarkable, most extraordinary theft" from a school system in U.S. history. The clerk had become suspicious of a customer who used a school district's Home Depot credit card to buy construction materials for delivery far outside the school district. The clerk's tip prompted an audit and later a criminal investigation, which ultimately revealed an embezzlement of more than $11 million. It turned out that the customer, who was the son of the school's assistant superintendent, had given 74 unauthorized cards to friends and family to use for personal purchases. Other misdeeds and attempted cover-ups involving the school's superintendent, assistant superintendent, auditor, and others resulted in jail terms of up to 12 years and fines ranging from $780,000 to $4.3 million. According to a report issued by the State of New York, the embezzlement was possible because the school district's "internal control weaknesses created an environment that was conducive to fraud and abuse."[1]

You are not likely to find these kinds of internal control problems at The Home Depot. As you will see in this chapter, The Home Depot takes internal control seriously. In fact, the company recently ranked among the top 10 companies in the United States for internal control and other governance practices.[2]

---

[1] "Roslyn Union Free School District: Anatomy of a Scandal," n.d., http://www.osc.state.ny.us/localgov/audits/2005/schools/roslyn2.pdf, February 25, 2007.

[2] "Corporate Governance Quotient: Benchmarking Your Governance Against Your Peers," n.d., http://www.isscorporateservices.com/ratings/cgqtop10.html, February 25, 2007.

ORGANIZATION OF THE CHAPTER

INTERNAL CONTROL	INTERNAL CONTROL OF CASH	FINANCIAL REPORTING OF CASH
• Definition and Purpose • Sarbanes-Oxley Act of 2002 • Common Control Principles • Control Limitations	• Cash Receipts • Cash Payments • Bank Procedures and Reconciliation	• Cash and Cash Equivalents

INTERNAL CONTROL

Definition and Purpose

Learning Objective 1
Define internal control and explain why it is needed.

All businesses have one thing in common: To be successful, they must control their operations. They must hire the right people, pay them the right amount of wages, order and receive the right products, pay suppliers the right amounts at the right times, set the right prices, collect and deposit the right amount of cash, and so on.

To achieve this state of control, each company establishes and follows specific procedures and policies that describe how the business is to be run. These procedures and policies are internal controls. In your personal life, internal controls include basic precautions, such as locking your car door and checking the accuracy of your bank statement. In business, **internal control** is defined as the methods an organization uses to protect against the theft of assets, enhance the reliability of accounting information, promote efficient and effective operations, and ensure compliance with applicable laws, regulations, and codes of ethical conduct.

The ideas behind internal control, which have been around for more than 5,000 years,[3] apply to all government, not-for-profit, and business organizations, both large and small. In simple terms, internal controls are needed to help ensure that people will act in ways that benefit the organization. When internal controls operate effectively, they can improve efficiency and minimize waste, unintentional errors, and fraud. In fact, one group of researchers found companies that emphasized internal control and an ethical culture grew their revenues four times faster and increased their stock prices 12 times as much as companies without those practices.[4] It is little wonder, then, that The Home Depot owes much of its success to the internal controls in place at its 1,500 store locations, which ensure that the 1.3 billion transactions processed by the company each year are completed with consistency, efficiency, accuracy, and honesty.

Sarbanes-Oxley Act of 2002

Although internal control is essential to businesses of all sizes, it has become one of the most important issues facing public companies today. The first decade of this century brought several high-profile accounting scandals involving Enron, WorldCom, and a number of other publicly owned companies. To restore investor confidence and improve the quality of financial reporting in the United States, the U.S. Congress passed the **Sarbanes-Oxley (SOX) Act of 2002**. This new act has led public companies to strengthen their internal controls and to better inform financial statement users of their effectiveness in producing accurate financial statements and preventing fraud. In this section, we explain some of the key features of SOX as summarized in Exhibit 8.1.[5]

[3] See T. A. Lee, "The Historical Development of Internal Control from the Earliest Times to the End of the Seventeenth Century," *Journal of Accounting Research*, Spring 1971, pp. 150–57.

[4] J. P. Kotter and J. L. Heskett, 1992, *Corporate Culture and Performance* (New York: Maxwell MacMillan International).

[5] The triangle in Exhibit 8.1 corresponds to what fraud investigators call the "fraud triangle," meaning the convergence of (1) the opportunity, (2) the incentive, and (3) the unscrupulous character that enables individuals to commit, rationalize, and conceal fraud.

Exhibit 8.1 Significant Changes Introduced by the Sarbanes-Oxley Act of 2002

Reduce opportunities for error and fraud
- Internal control report from management
- Stronger oversight by directors
- Internal control audit by external auditors

Encourage good character
- Anonymous tip lines
- Whistle-blower protection
- Code of ethics

Counteract incentives for fraud
- Stiffer fines and prison terms

Reduce Opportunities for Error and Fraud

A primary goal of SOX is improved internal controls, particularly in relation to financial reporting. SOX aims to achieve this goal in three ways:

1. **Internal control report from management.** Every year managers must review their company's internal controls and issue a report that indicates whether controls over financial reporting were effective. This new requirement means that most marketing managers, for example, now have some accounting responsibilities, such as determining whether their staff members submit accurate sales and expense reports.
2. **Stronger oversight by directors.** Each company must establish an independent audit committee to oversee the company's financial matters. One of the main roles of this committee is to hire external auditors and ensure that they perform their work effectively as described in the following paragraph.
3. **Internal control audit by external auditors.** The company's external auditors must test the effectiveness of the company's internal controls and issue a report that gives an opinion about the effectiveness of the company's internal controls over financial reporting. As was the case before SOX, external auditors must also examine the company's financial statements and report whether they were prepared using GAAP.

Counteract Incentives for Committing Fraud

Under SOX, those who intentionally misstate a company's financial results face much stiffer penalties than before. They must repay any money obtained via fraud and can be assessed additional fines of up to $5 million. Executives cannot avoid these penalties by declaring personal bankruptcy, which explains why a former sales director at Computer Associates will be giving 15 percent of every paycheck he earns for the rest of his life to a fraud restitution fund. SOX also increased the maximum jail sentence for fraudulent financial reporting to 20 years, which can add up because federal sentencing guidelines allow judges to declare consecutive jail terms for each violation.

Encourage Good Character in Employees

Admittedly, it is difficult for a law to make people act appropriately, but SOX introduces new rules that should help employees of good character to confront those of questionable character. For example, audit committees are now required to create tip lines that allow employees to secretly submit concerns they may have about suspicious accounting or auditing practices. SOX gives these "whistle-blowers" legal protection from retaliation by those charged with fraud. That is, if you tattle on your boss for submitting a fraudulent expense claim, you cannot be fired for doing so. Finally, to reinforce good character, public companies must adopt a code of ethics for senior financial officers.

SELF-STUDY PRACTICE

Identify whether each of the following actions is most likely to increase (+) or decrease (–) the risk of error or fraud arising from opportunities (O), incentives (I), or an individual's character (C).

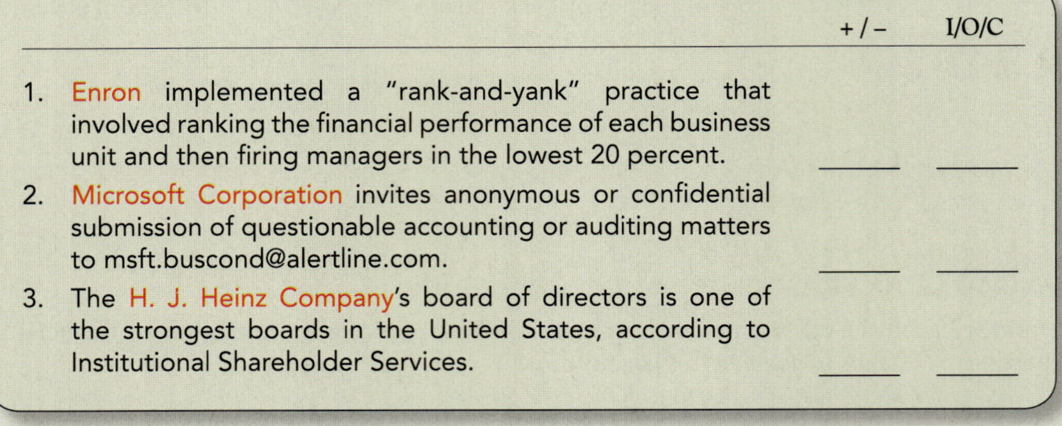

	+/–	I/O/C
1. Enron implemented a "rank-and-yank" practice that involved ranking the financial performance of each business unit and then firing managers in the lowest 20 percent.	_____	_____
2. Microsoft Corporation invites anonymous or confidential submission of questionable accounting or auditing matters to msft.buscond@alertline.com.	_____	_____
3. The H. J. Heinz Company's board of directors is one of the strongest boards in the United States, according to Institutional Shareholder Services.	_____	_____

After you have finished, check your answers with the solution at the bottom of this page.

Learning Objective 2

Explain the common principles and limitations of internal control.

Common Control Principles

From the perspective of a company's chief executive officer (CEO), chief financial officer (CFO), and board of directors, internal control is a broad concept that includes more than accounting. It includes setting strategic objectives, identifying risks the company faces, hiring good employees, instilling ethical principles in them, motivating them to achieve the company's objectives, and providing the resources and information they need to fulfill those objectives. Rather than overwhelm you with the list of 20 control principles that senior executives must think about,[6] we focus on just five basic principles that you are likely to see in your own work. We want you to understand why certain types of control exist so that when you encounter them during your career, you will appreciate them and ensure that others respect them.

All good systems of internal control are based on these five common principles, which are summarized in Exhibit 8.2. These principles are typically applied to all aspects of a company's business activities, including human resource management, finance, marketing, and general business operations. Our focus here, however, is on their relationship to accounting, as follows.

1. **Establish responsibility.** Whenever possible, assign each task to only one employee. Doing so will allow you to determine who caused any errors or thefts that may have occurred. Thus, The Home Depot assigns a separate cash register drawer to each employee at the beginning of a shift. If two cashiers were to use the same drawer, determining which cashier caused the drawer to be short of cash would not be possible. With just one person responsible for adding and removing money from the drawer, however, no doubt exists about who is responsible for a cash shortage.
2. **Segregate duties.** Segregation of duties involves assigning responsibilities so that one employee cannot make a mistake or commit a dishonest act without someone else discovering it. This principle is the reason that cashiers at The Home Depot need a manager's approval for price changes at the checkout counter. Without this control, cashiers could lower the price for a friend or relative. Segregation of duties is most effective when a company assigns the responsibilities for related activities to two or more people and assigns recordkeeping responsibilities to people who do not handle the assets

[6] These 20 principles are outlined in "Internal Control for Financial Reporting—Guidance for Smaller Public Companies," published June 2006 at www.coso.org by The Committee of Sponsoring Organizations (COSO).

Solution to Self-Study Practice

1. + / I (increased pressure to report stronger financial results)
2. – / C (less likelihood that unethical behavior will go unreported)
3. – / O (strong oversight by directors)

Exhibit 8.2 Five Common Principles of Internal Control

Principle	Explanation	Example
1. Establish responsibility.	Assign each task to only one employee.	Each Home Depot cashier uses a different cash drawer.
2. Segregate duties.	Do not make one employee responsible for all parts of a transaction.	Home Depot cashiers, who ring up cash sales, do not also approve price changes.
3. Restrict access.	Do not provide access to assets or information unless it is needed to fulfill assigned responsibilities.	Home Depot secures valuable assets such as cash and access to its computer systems.
4. Document procedures.	Prepare documents to show activities that have occurred.	Home Depot pays suppliers using prenumbered checks.
5. Independently verify.	Check others' work.	Home Depot compares the cash balances in its records to the cash balances reported by its bank and accounts for any differences.

for which they are accounting. A single employee should not initiate, approve, record, and access the items involved in the same transaction.

3. **Restrict access.** Some controls involve rather obvious steps such as physically locking up valuable assets and electronically securing access to other assets and information. The Home Depot restricts access to check-signing equipment, requires a password to open cash registers, and protects computer systems with firewalls. The company provides access to important assets and valuable information on an as-needed basis. If employees do not need assets or information to fulfill their assigned responsibilities, they are denied access.
4. **Document procedures.** Digital and paper documents are such common features of business that you may not realize they represent an internal control. By documenting each business activity, a company creates a record of whether goods were shipped, customers were billed, cash was received, and so on. Without these documents, a company would not know what transactions have been or need to be entered into the accounting system. To enhance this control, most companies assign sequential numbers to their documents and then check at the end of every accounting period to make sure that each document number corresponds to one and only one accounting entry. The Home Depot's computer system automatically assigns sequential numbers to cash sales so that the accounting staff can ensure that every sale has been recorded.
5. **Independently verify.** A business can perform independent verification in various ways. The most obvious is to hire someone (an internal auditor) to check that the work done by others within the company is appropriate and is supported by documentation. Independent verification can also be made part of a person's job. For example, before The Home Depot issues a check to pay for a truckload of lumber, a clerk first verifies that the bill relates to goods that were actually received and that it has been calculated correctly. A third form of independent verification involves comparing the company's accounting information to

Spotlight On CONTROLS

Is That a Control, Too?

The five principles covered in this section do not represent all possible forms of internal control. Many other policies and procedures exist, some of which you might not recognize as contributing to internal control. For example, most businesses establish a mandatory vacation policy for employees who handle cash because it is difficult for them to cover prior thefts while they are away from the business. Another simple control is an anonymous hotline that allows anyone to tip off independent auditors about suspected fraud. The Association of Certified Fraud Examiners claims that more than 45 percent of workplace fraud cases are identified in this way. A final example of a control that can limit losses from theft is **bonding** employees, which involves obtaining an insurance policy that partially reimburses the organization for losses caused by employee fraud.

information kept by an independent third party, such as a bank. For example, the company may compare internal cash records to a statement of account issued by the bank. The next section of this chapter demonstrates this procedure, called a bank reconciliation.

Control Limitations

Internal controls can never completely prevent and detect errors and fraud for two reasons. First, an organization will implement internal controls only to the extent that their benefits exceed their costs. The Home Depot could nearly eliminate shoplifting by body searching every customer who leaves the store, but such an irritating policy would soon drive customers away. The cost of the lost sales would far exceed the benefits of reduced shoplifting. Second, internal controls can fail as a result of human error or fraud. People do make simple mistakes in performing control procedures, especially if they are tired, careless, or confused. Finally, criminally minded employees have been known to **override** (disarm) internal controls or **collude** (work together) to get around them.

SELF-STUDY PRACTICE

Identity the internal control principles suggested in the following diagram. Some principles may appear more than once.

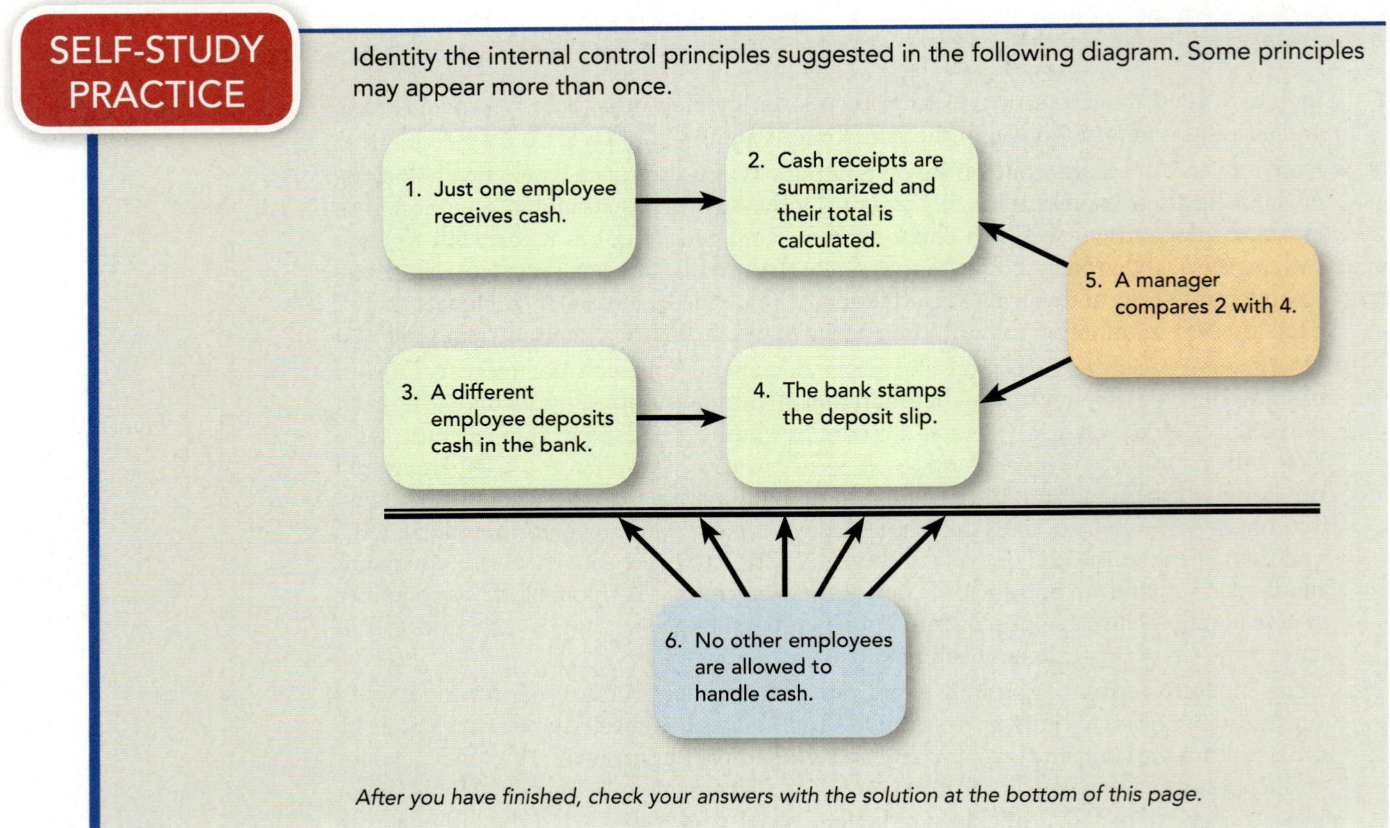

After you have finished, check your answers with the solution at the bottom of this page.

INTERNAL CONTROL OF CASH

Learning Objective 3
Apply internal control principles to cash receipts and payments.

Internal control of cash is important to any organization for two main reasons. First, because the volume of transactions affecting cash is enormous, any errors that are made in handling cash can quickly add up. By our estimates, The Home Depot received about $78 billion from customers in 2007 and paid $72 billion for inventory, wages, and other operating expenses. Second, because cash is valuable, portable, and difficult to specifically identify, thieves often target it. The Association of Certified Fraud Examiners reports that 93 percent of all known

Solution to Self-Study Practice

1. Establish responsibility.
2. Document procedures.
3. Segregate duties.
4. Document procedures.
5. Independently verify.
6. Restrict access.

asset thefts involve cash. The following discussion describes common applications of internal control principles to cash receipts and cash payments.

Cash Receipts

Businesses can receive cash in two different ways. They can receive it **in person** at the time of a sale, or they can receive it **from a remote source** as payment on an account. Most businesses, including The Home Depot, receive cash either physically, in the form of dollars, coins, and checks payable to the business, or through electronic transactions involving credit cards, debit cards, and electronic funds transfers. Generally speaking, The Home Depot applies similar controls to cash received in both these forms, so in the following discussion, we do not distinguish between them. Regardless of the way or form in which a business receives cash, **the primary internal control goal for cash receipts is to ensure that the business receives the appropriate amount of cash and safely deposits it in the bank.**

Cash Received in Person

To properly segregate duties involving cash receipts, specific responsibilities are usually assigned to three different employees. First, a cashier is responsible for collecting cash and issuing a receipt at the point of sale. Second, a supervisor is responsible for taking custody of the cash at the end of each cashier's shift and depositing it in the bank. Third, members of the accounting staff are responsible for ensuring that the receipts from cash sales are properly recorded in the accounting system. If this segregation of duties did not exist, employees could steal the cash and cover up the theft by changing the accounting records. Segregating the duties ensures that those who handle the cash (the cashiers and supervisor) do not have access to those who record it (the accounting staff). Exhibit 8.3 illustrates the steps involved in carrying out these duties, which we explain in the context of The Home Depot's internal control procedures.

As Exhibit 8.3 shows, the control process begins at the cash register. The register performs three important functions: (1) it restricts access to cash, (2) it documents the amount charged for each item sold, and (3) it summarizes the total cash sales. By restricting access, the cash register

Exhibit 8.3 Processing Cash Received in Person

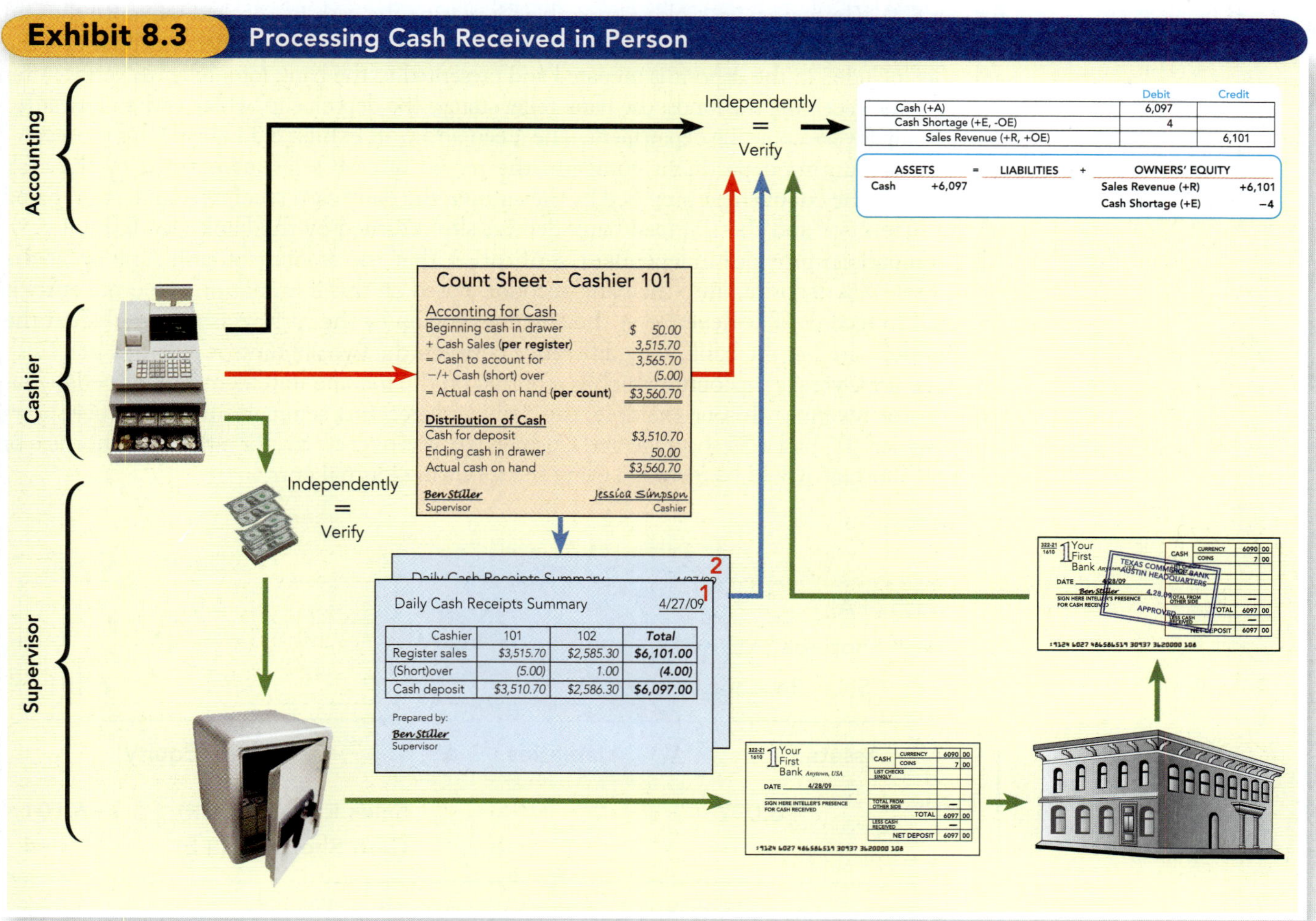

Exhibit 8.4 Sample Cash Count Sheet and Daily Cash Receipts Summary

Count Sheet – Cashier 101

Accounting for Cash	
Beginning cash in drawer	$ 50.00
+ Cash Sales **(per register)**	3,515.70
= Cash to account for	3,565.70
−/+ Cash (short) over	(5.00)
= Actual cash on hand **(per count)**	$3,560.70

Distribution of Cash	
Cash for deposit	$3,510.70
Ending cash in drawer	50.00
Actual cash on hand	$3,560.70

Ben Stiller Supervisor | *Jessica Simpson* Cashier

2

Daily Cash Receipts Summary 4/27/09

Cashier	101	102	**Total**
Register sales	$3,515.70	$2,585.30	**$6,101.00**
(Short) over	(5.00)	1.00	**(4.00)**
Cash deposit	$3,510.70	$2,586.30	**$6,097.00**

Prepared by:
Ben Stiller
Supervisor

reduces the risk of cash being lost or stolen. In documenting each item sold (both on screen and on a paper receipt), the cash register reduces errors by allowing customers to dispute overcharges should they occur. By summarizing the total cash sales, the cash register provides an independent record of the amount of cash the cashier should have collected and passed on for deposit at the bank. This record is securely forwarded to the accounting department (see the **black arrow** in Exhibit 8.3). The cashier also uses it to complete a cash count sheet (see the red arrow in Exhibit 8.3).

Each cashier prepares a **cash count sheet**, shown in detail in Exhibit 8.4, at the end of each shift to determine the amount of cash available for deposit at the bank. The cash count sheet documents the amount of cash the cashier received and determines any cash short or over that occurred during the shift. The supervisor independently verifies and signs each cashier's count sheet (as in Exhibit 8.3). The supervisor then uses each cashier's cash count sheet to prepare a daily cash receipts summary and sends one copy to the accounting department (see the blue arrow in Exhibit 8.3). The supervisor is also responsible for placing the cash in a locked safe until the end of the day at which time it is taken to the bank for deposit. At that time, a deposit slip listing the amounts included in the deposit is prepared and presented to the bank for a teller to verify. After verifying and receiving the funds, the bank teller stamps the deposit slip, which is then forwarded to the company's accounting department. The green arrows in Exhibit 8.3 indicate this process.

The accounting department compares the record of cash sales maintained by the cash register with the count sheet prepared by the cashier, the daily cash receipts summary prepared by the supervisor and the stamped bank deposit slip returned by the bank (see Exhibit 8.3). This comparison provides independent verification that the amount of cash rung up at the time of sale was deposited into the bank account. Based on this information, a journal entry is prepared to record Sales Revenue at the amount rung up by the cash register and Cash at the amount deposited in the bank. Any difference between the two amounts is recorded in a Cash Shortage (or Overage) account, which is reported on the income statement as a miscellaneous expense (or revenue). In our example, the daily cash receipts summary in Exhibit 8.4 shows that Cashier 101 had a $5 shortage and Cashier 102 was over by $1, for a net cash shortage of $4. This shortage would be recorded using the following journal entry.

Account Titles	Debit	Credit
Cash (+A)	6,097	
Cash Shortage (+E, −OE)	4	
Sales Revenue (+R, +OE)		6,101

Assets		=	Liabilities	+	Owners' Equity	
Cash	+6,097				Sales Revenue (+R)	+6,101
					Cash Shortage (+E)	−4

Cash Received from a Remote Source

Cash Received by Mail. Businesses receive checks in the mail when customers pay on account. The Home Depot, for example, allows approved businesses to buy on account and pay their account balances using checks or money orders mailed to The Home Depot's credit division in Nevada. Because this cash is not received in the form of currency and coins, the Nevada office does not have a cashier enter these amounts into a cash register. Instead, the clerk who opens the mail performs this function. In fact, to visualize the following description, you need only glance back at Exhibit 8.3 and replace the cash register with a mail clerk.

Like a cash register, the mail clerk lists all amounts received on the cash receipt list, which also includes the customers' names and the purpose of each payment. The customer typically explains the purpose of the payment using a **remittance advice**, which is a tear-off portion of the monthly bill that the customer includes with the payment. Ideally, someone supervises the clerk who opens the mail to ensure that he or she takes no cash receipts for personal use. As evidence of this supervision, both the mail clerk and the supervisor sign the completed cash receipts list. To ensure that no one diverts the checks for personal use, the clerk stamps each check "For Deposit Only," which instructs the bank to deposit the check in the company's account rather than exchange it for cash.

Coach's Tip

Because payments must be credited to each customer's account, it is important that the cash receipt list include the customer's name and payment purpose.

After these steps have been completed, the cash received is separated from the record of cash received, and each follows a separate route similar to the routes shown in Exhibit 8.3 (page 349). Checks and money orders are given to the person who prepares the bank deposit whereas the cash receipts list and remittance advices are sent to the accounting department. The accounting department then independently verifies that all cash received by mail was deposited in the bank by ensuring that the total on the cash receipts list equals the stamped deposit slip received from the bank. The accounting department then uses the cash receipts list to record the journal entries that debit Cash and credit Accounts Receivable from each customer.

Cash Received Electronically. Businesses also receive payments from customers via **electronic funds transfer (EFT)**. An EFT occurs when a customer electronically transfers funds from its bank account to the company's bank account. The Home Depot encourages customers to use EFTs because they speed The Home Depot's collections. The company may not receive mailed payments for five to seven days, but it receives EFTs immediately. And because these payments are deposited directly into the company's bank account without ever passing through the hands of a Home Depot employee, EFTs eliminate the need for some internal controls. To process an EFT, The Home Depot's accounting department merely records journal entries to debit Cash and credit each customer's account receivable. The Home Depot receives EFT notices from its bank every afternoon and records them in customers' accounts the same day.

Cash Payments

For a business, cash payments usually occur in three situations: (1) writing a check to a supplier for goods or services purchased on account, (2) paying employees via EFT, and (3) reimbursing cash paid by employees for minor business expenses. Regardless of the situation, **the primary goal of internal controls for cash payments is to ensure that the business pays only for properly authorized transactions.** These payments should be made efficiently to minimize the cost to the organization and take advantage of discounts when possible. Internal control is generally more effective and efficient when payments are made using prenumbered checks or EFTs rather than cash.

Cash Paid by Check for Purchases on Account

Learning Objective 4

Describe the operation of voucher and petty cash systems.

Most businesses purchase goods and services on account and pay for them later by check. Purchases and payments cause increases and decreases in Accounts Payable, so they are closely controlled for financial reporting reasons. Control over purchases and payments is also important to avoid inefficiency and fraud. Because companies incur substantial internal costs to process each transaction with a supplier, controls that promote efficiency can significantly improve a company's profits. Companies can also avoid or reduce losses due to fraud by having strong internal controls. A 2006 report by the Association of Certified Fraud Examiners estimated that fraudulent purchases and payments cost small businesses—defined as those with fewer than 100 employees—an average of $150,000 per year.

Most companies rely on a voucher system to control these transactions. A **voucher system** is a process for approving and documenting all purchases and payments made on account. The **voucher** includes the documents prepared at each step in the system. See Exhibit 8.5 for the typical steps involved in obtaining goods or services from a supplier and the documentation prepared at each step. Exhibit 8.5 also gives some examples of the related cash controls. **Study this exhibit in detail,** noticing how at each step employee responsibilities are limited to specific tasks that occur only after obtaining and documenting proper authorization in the prior step. The purchasing, receiving, and bill payment duties are segregated to ensure that the company obtains and pays only for the goods or services that have been properly authorized.

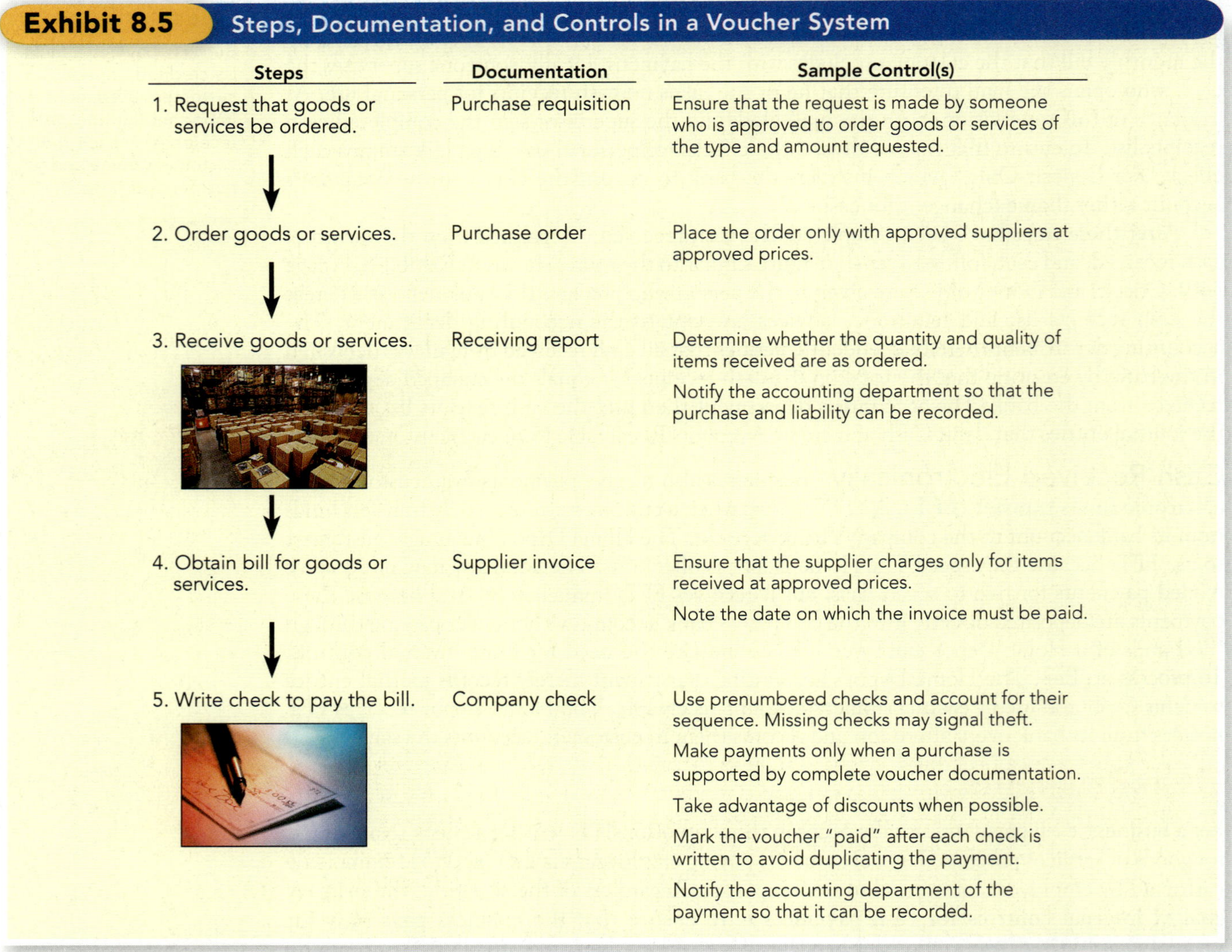

Exhibit 8.5 Steps, Documentation, and Controls in a Voucher System

Steps	Documentation	Sample Control(s)
1. Request that goods or services be ordered.	Purchase requisition	Ensure that the request is made by someone who is approved to order goods or services of the type and amount requested.
2. Order goods or services.	Purchase order	Place the order only with approved suppliers at approved prices.
3. Receive goods or services.	Receiving report	Determine whether the quantity and quality of items received are as ordered. Notify the accounting department so that the purchase and liability can be recorded.
4. Obtain bill for goods or services.	Supplier invoice	Ensure that the supplier charges only for items received at approved prices. Note the date on which the invoice must be paid.
5. Write check to pay the bill.	Company check	Use prenumbered checks and account for their sequence. Missing checks may signal theft. Make payments only when a purchase is supported by complete voucher documentation. Take advantage of discounts when possible. Mark the voucher "paid" after each check is written to avoid duplicating the payment. Notify the accounting department of the payment so that it can be recorded.

Cash Paid to Employees via Electronic Funds Transfer

Most companies pay cash to their employees through EFTs, which are known by employees as **direct deposits.** The company initiates the EFT when it instructs its bank to transfer the net pay due each employee directly from the company's bank account to each employee's checking account. This system is convenient and efficient for the employer because it eliminates the tasks of physically writing and distributing the checks and for the employee who has access to the funds without having to deposit a check. One risk, however, is that the bank might accidentally overpay or underpay an employee by transfering the wrong amount of money out of the company's bank account.

To avoid this risk, many companies use an imprest system for paying employees. An **imprest system** restricts the total amount paid to others by limiting the amount of money available to be transferred. Using an imprest payroll system, the company instructs the bank to transfer the total net pay of all employees for the pay period out of the company's general bank account and into a special payroll account established for that purpose. Then the bank transfers the individual amounts from the payroll account to the employees' checking accounts. If the transfers occur without error, the special payroll account equals zero after all employees have been paid. If the account is overdrawn or a balance remains, the company knows that an error has occurred.

Cash Paid to Reimburse Employees (Petty Cash)

To avoid the time and cost of writing checks for business expenses that are small in amount, most organizations use a petty cash fund. A **petty cash fund** is a system used to reimburse employees for expenditures they have made on behalf of the organization. Like the imprest payroll account described in the last section, a petty cash fund acts as a control by establishing a limited amount of cash to use for specific types of expenses. The main difference between the two is that rather than transfer funds from a general bank account to another special account at the bank, the company removes cash from its general bank account to hold at its premises in a locked cash box. An employee with the title petty cash custodian is responsible for operating the petty cash fund as follows.

1. **Put money into the fund.** The company establishes the fund by writing a check to the petty cash custodian. The amount of the check equals the total estimated payments to be made from the fund over a fairly short period, such as a month or quarter. The custodian cashes the check and places the funds in the locked cash box. At this time, the petty cash still belongs to the company, so it represents an asset that must be recorded in the accounting system. The following journal entry is recorded to establish a $100 petty cash fund.

Account Titles	Debit	Credit
Petty Cash (+A)	100	
Cash (−A)		100

Assets		=	Liabilities	+	Owners' Equity
Petty Cash	+100				
Cash	−100				

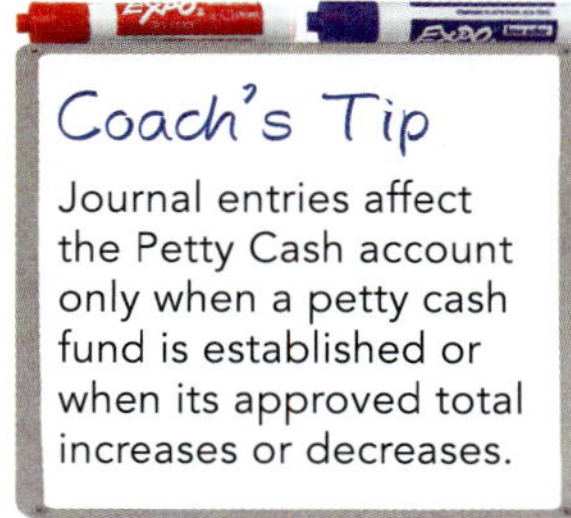

2. **Pay money out of the fund.** The custodian determines when to make payments out of the cash box following policies established by the company's managers. Usually, these policies limit the size and nature of payments to items such as postage, taxi fares, and low-cost supplies. Petty cash policies require that payments be documented using a petty cash receipt signed by both the custodian and the payee as in the following example. The custodian attaches any related documents, such as a bill of sale or an invoice, to the petty cash receipt and places it in the cash box. Documents such as these act as controls to ensure that petty cash payments are made only for approved purchases.

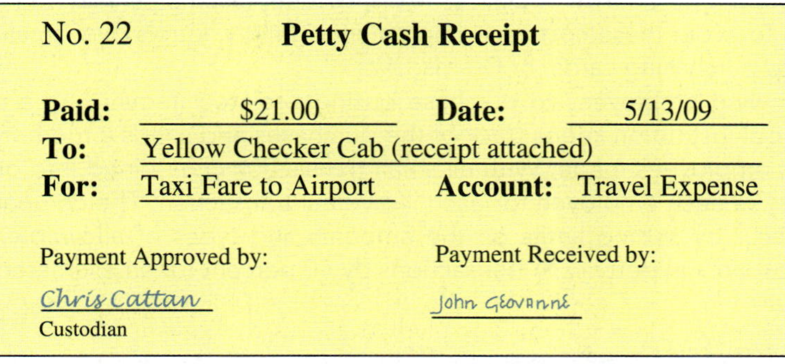
No. 22 **Petty Cash Receipt**

Paid: $21.00 **Date:** 5/13/09
To: Yellow Checker Cab (receipt attached)
For: Taxi Fare to Airport **Account:** Travel Expense

Payment Approved by: Chris Cattan, Custodian
Payment Received by: John Giovanni

Because these receipts involve such small amounts, **payments out of petty cash are not recorded in the accounting system until the fund is replenished.** To ensure that the fund is operating appropriately, however, most companies require that an internal auditor or manager conduct surprise audits of the fund. At any point, the sum of the petty cash receipts and the funds in the cash box should equal the fund's total when it was established.

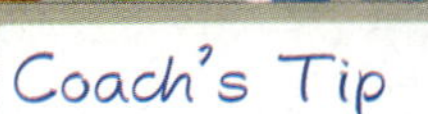

Coach's Tip

If the total of cash and receipts in the cash box is less (or more) than the fund total, the fund is referred to as being **short** (or **over**). Shortages (overages) are recorded in an account called **Cash Short (Over)** and reported on the income statement as miscellaneous expense (or revenue).

3. **Replenish the fund.** When the amount of cash in the cash box runs low, the petty cash custodian asks that the fund be replenished. To support this request, the petty cash custodian presents a summary of payments and all supporting petty cash receipts to the accounting department. After reviewing these items, the accounting department marks the receipts "paid" and issues a check to the custodian for the total amount spent. The amount of the check is recorded as a reduction in Cash (with a credit), and the various items that were paid are recorded in their corresponding accounts (with debits). For example, if the custodian requested a check for $67 to replenish the fund after payments were made for supplies ($40), travel ($21), and a dozen Krispy Kreme donuts awarded to the employee of the month ($6), the following journal entry would be recorded.

Account Titles	Debit	Credit
Supplies (+A)	40	
Travel Expense (+E, −OE)	21	
Office Expense (+E, −OE)	6	
Cash (−A)		67

Assets		=	Liabilities	+	Owners' Equity	
Cash	−67				Travel Expense (+E)	−21
Supplies	+40				Office Expense (+E)	−6

Because petty cash transactions are recorded only when the fund is replenished, some companies have a policy of replenishing all petty cash funds at the end of each accounting period so that the expenses are recorded in the appropriate period. Other companies do not observe this policy on the grounds that unrecorded petty cash transactions are "immaterial" (too small to affect the decisions of financial statement users).

Spotlight On CONTROLS

Pcards: Efficient Control of Small-Dollar Transactions

Until recently, the administrative costs of processing small-dollar purchases often exceeded the cost of the items themselves. For example, a consultant to the City Council of Dallas, Texas, recently estimated that each petty cash transaction costs the city $60 to process. To avoid these costs and implement tighter controls over small-dollar purchases, many organizations have turned to purchasing cards, or Pcards.

Pcards work like a credit card by allowing employees to purchase business-related items using a plastic card issued by a financial institution. The financial institution keeps track of the purchases and sends a monthly bill to the company for all purchases the company's employees made. With all small transactions combined into one monthly bill, the company avoids having to reimburse each employee for each individual transaction. The company can also tighten controls before the purchases occur by setting limits on the amounts and types of allowable purchases. Pcards have helped the City of Dallas to cut annual petty cash transactions by 40 percent for an estimated savings of $1.1 million.*

* www.dallascityhall.com/council_briefings/briefings0806/20060802_P-Card.pdf, n.d., June 20, 2007.

SELF-STUDY PRACTICE

The following transactions occurred during the month. Indicate whether a voucher system (V) or a petty cash system (PC) would be used for each transaction. Then show the journal entry and accounting equation effects when the petty cash fund is replenished after only these transactions.

_______ 1. A $3,000 check is written for inventory purchased from a manufacturer.
_______ 2. A $30 cash payment is made to FedEx for delivery of goods to a customer.
_______ 3. A $300 check is written for supplies purchased from Office Depot.
_______ 4. A $60 cash payment is made to Pizza Hut for an employee luncheon.

After you have finished, check your answers with the solution at the bottom of this page.

Bank Procedures and Reconciliation

Learning Objective 5
Prepare a bank reconciliation.

Banks provide important services to individuals and businesses. They accept deposits, process payments to others, and provide statements that account for these and other transactions. Their services help businesses to control cash in several ways:

1. **Safeguarding.** Because banks provide a secure place to deposit cash, businesses need to keep only a limited amount of cash on hand, which reduces the risk that it will be stolen or misplaced.
2. **Improving efficiency and effectiveness.** By processing payments made by check or EFT, banks facilitate business transactions.
3. **Independently verifying.** Company accountants can use the statement of account prepared by the bank to double-check the accuracy of the cash records. By comparing these two sets of records and investigating any differences, they can verify that the company's records are accurate or identify necessary adjustments.

The process of comparing two sets of records is **reconciling.** Thus, the internal accounting report that compares the company's cash records with the bank's is a bank reconciliation. A bank reconciliation is a key internal control because it provides independent verification of all cash transactions that the bank has processed for the company. This document is prepared monthly, ideally by a company employee whose duties are segregated from recording and handling cash. To prepare a bank reconciliation, you must first understand the items on the bank's statement of account.

Bank Statement

Large businesses such as The Home Depot can have many bank accounts. For each account a business opens, the bank generates a monthly statement of account that it either mails to the business or makes available online. The format varies from bank to bank, but the statement in Exhibit 8.6 is typical. This statement, prepared by Texas Commerce Bank for one of the accounts opened by Habitat Design (HD), provides an overall summary of the activity in the account (labeled ① in Exhibit 8.6). The summary is followed by a list of specific transactions posted to the account (labeled ② through ④) and a running balance in the account (labeled ⑤). In the following section, we explain the transactions that caused changes in the account's balance.

Solution to Self-Study Practice

1. V 2. PC 3. V 4. PC

Account Titles	Debit	Credit
Delivery Expense (+E, −OE)	30	
Office Expense (+E, −OE)	60	
Cash (−A)		90

Assets		=	Liabilities	+	Owners' Equity	
Cash	−90				Delivery Expense (+E)	−30
					Office Expense (+E)	−60

Exhibit 8.6 Sample Bank Statement

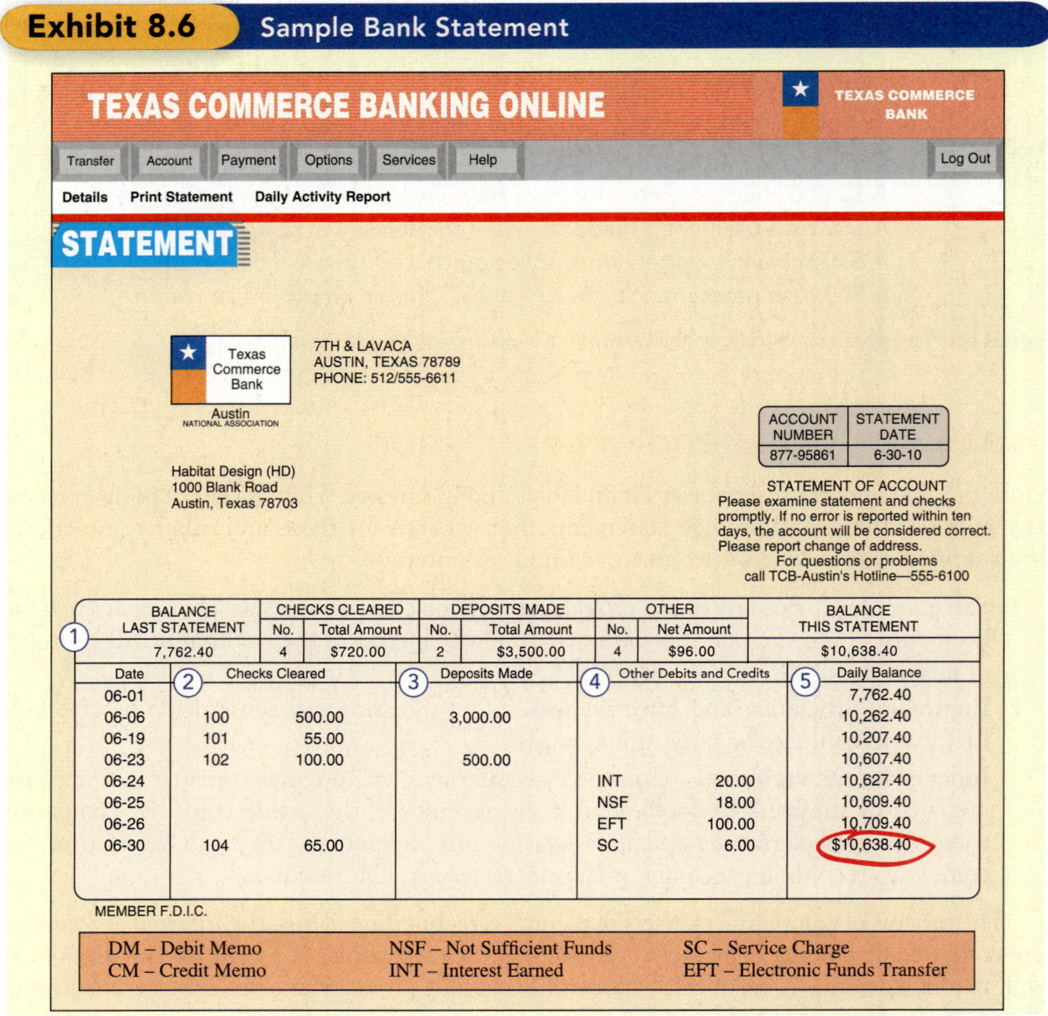

TEXAS COMMERCE BANKING ONLINE

TEXAS COMMERCE BANK

Transfer | Account | Payment | Options | Services | Help | Log Out

Details | Print Statement | Daily Activity Report

STATEMENT

Texas Commerce Bank
Austin
NATIONAL ASSOCIATION

7TH & LAVACA
AUSTIN, TEXAS 78789
PHONE: 512/555-6611

ACCOUNT NUMBER	STATEMENT DATE
877-95861	6-30-10

Habitat Design (HD)
1000 Blank Road
Austin, Texas 78703

STATEMENT OF ACCOUNT
Please examine statement and checks promptly. If no error is reported within ten days, the account will be considered correct. Please report change of address.
For questions or problems call TCB-Austin's Hotline—555-6100

① BALANCE LAST STATEMENT	CHECKS CLEARED No.	CHECKS CLEARED Total Amount	DEPOSITS MADE No.	DEPOSITS MADE Total Amount	OTHER No.	OTHER Net Amount	BALANCE THIS STATEMENT
7,762.40	4	$720.00	2	$3,500.00	4	$96.00	$10,638.40

Date	② Checks Cleared		③ Deposits Made	④ Other Debits and Credits		⑤ Daily Balance
06-01						7,762.40
06-06	100	500.00	3,000.00			10,262.40
06-19	101	55.00				10,207.40
06-23	102	100.00	500.00			10,607.40
06-24				INT	20.00	10,627.40
06-25				NSF	18.00	10,609.40
06-26				EFT	100.00	10,709.40
06-30	104	65.00		SC	6.00	$10,638.40

MEMBER F.D.I.C.

DM – Debit Memo
CM – Credit Memo
NSF – Not Sufficient Funds
INT – Interest Earned
SC – Service Charge
EFT – Electronic Funds Transfer

Coach's Tip

Bank statements often refer to checks as **debits** and deposits as **credits.** This apparent flipping of debit and credit rules occurs because the bank reports from its perspective, not yours. To the bank, your account is a liability that decreases when you take money out (debit the liability) and increases when you deposit money (credit the liability).

Checks Cleared. You may not have thought much about what happens after a check is written. The payee to whom the check is written usually presents the check to a financial institution for deposit or cash. That financial institution contacts the check writer's bank, which in turn withdraws the amount of the check from the check writer's account and reports it as a deduction on the bank statement. The check is then said to have **cleared the bank.**

Checks are listed on the bank statement in the order in which they clear the bank. Look closely at column ② in Exhibit 8.6 and you will see that four checks cleared the bank in June. Because HD's checks are used in their prenumbered order, the bank statement provides a hint that check 103 did not clear the bank this month. (This fact will be important later when we prepare the bank reconciliation.)

Deposits Made. Deposits are listed on the bank statement in the order in which the bank processes them. If you make a deposit after the bank closes (using an ATM or a night deposit chute), it will not appear on the bank statement until the bank processes it the following business day. Knowing this detail will help you to prepare the bank reconciliation.

Other Debits and Credits. The balance in a bank account can change for a variety of reasons other than checks and deposits. For example, the account balance increases when the account earns interest and when funds are transferred into the account electronically. The account balance decreases when the bank charges a service fee or transfers funds out of the account electronically.

To understand how these items are reported on a bank statement, it is important to realize that **the bank statement is presented from the bank's point of view.** The amounts in a company's bank account are liabilities to the bank because they will eventually be used by or returned to the company. As with all liabilities, increases are reported as credits on the bank statement. Amounts that are removed from a bank account reduce the bank's liability, so they are reported as debits on the bank statement. Banks typically explain the reasons for these increases (credits) and decreases (debits) with symbols or in a short memo, appropriately called a credit or debit memo.

Need for Reconciliation

A bank reconciliation involves comparing the company's records to the bank's statement of account to determine whether they agree. The company's records can differ from the bank's records for two basic reasons: (1) the company has recorded some items that the bank does not know about at the time it prepares the statement of account or (2) the bank has recorded some items that the company does not know about until the bank statement arrives. Exhibit 8.7 lists specific causes of these differences, which we discuss below.

1. **Bank errors.** Bank errors happen in real life, just as they do in Monopoly. If you discover a bank error, you should ask the bank to correct its records, but you should not change yours.
2. **Time lags.** Time lags are common. A time lag occurs, for example, when you make a deposit after the bank's normal business hours. *You* know you made the deposit, but your bank does not know until it processes the deposit the next day. Time lags involving deposits are called **deposits in transit**. Another common time lag is an **outstanding check**. This lag occurs when you write and mail a check to a company, but your bank does not find out about it until that company deposits the check in its own bank, which then notifies your bank. As you will see later, although deposits in transit and outstanding checks may be a significant part of a bank reconciliation, they do not require any further action on your part.
3. **Interest deposited.** You may know that your bank pays interest, but you probably do not know exactly how much interest you will receive because it varies depending on the average balance in your account. When you read your bank statement, you will see how much interest to add to your records.
4. **Electronic funds transfer (EFT).** It does not happen every day, but occasionally funds may be transferred into or out of your account without your knowing about it. If you discover these electronic transfers on your bank statement, you will need to adjust your records.
5. **Service charges.** These are the amounts the bank charges for processing your transactions. Rather than send you a bill and wait for you to pay it, the bank just takes the amount directly out of your account. You will need to reduce the Cash balance in your accounting records for these charges.
6. **NSF checks.** Checks that were deposited in the bank but were later rejected ("bounced") because of insufficient funds in the check writer's account are referred to as **NSF (not sufficient funds) checks**. Because the bank increased the account when the check was deposited, it decreases the account when it discovers that the deposit was not valid. You will need to reduce your Cash balance by the amount of these bounced checks (and any additional bank charges), and you will have to try to collect these amounts from the check writer.
7. **Your errors.** You may have made mistakes or forgotten to record some amounts in your checkbook. If so, you will need to adjust your records for these items.

Exhibit 8.7 Reconciling Differences between the Bank Statement and Company Records

Your Bank May Not Know About	You May Not Know About
1. Errors made by the bank	3. Interest the bank has put into your account
2. Time lags	4. EFTs
a. Deposits that you made recently	5. Service charges taken out of your account
b. Checks that you wrote recently	6. Customer checks you deposited but that bounced
	7. Errors you made

Bank Reconciliation

The ending cash balance shown on the bank statement does not usually agree with the ending cash balance in the company's Cash account. For example, HD's Cash account at the end of June might contain the information shown in this T-account.

		+ Cash (A)	–	
June 1	balance	7,762.40		
June 6	deposit	3,000.00	500.00	Check 100 written June 4
June 23	deposit	500.00	55.00	Check 101 written June 17
June 30	deposit	1,800.00	100.00	Check 102 written June 20
			145.00	Check 103 written June 24
			56.00	Check 104 written June 30
			815.00	Check 105 written June 30
Ending balance		11,391.40		

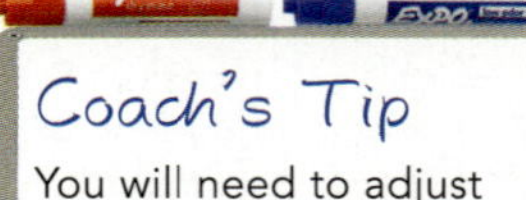

Coach's Tip

You will need to adjust your cash records for items that appear only on the right-hand side of Exhibit 8.8.

Notice that HD's ending cash balance of $11,391.40 differs from the $10,638.40 ending cash balance shown on the bank statement in Exhibit 8.6 (page 356). To determine the appropriate cash balance, these balances must be reconciled.

Exhibit 8.8 presents the bank reconciliation prepared by HD for the month of June. The completed reconciliation shows that the up-to-date cash balance is $11,478.40—an amount that differs from both the bank statement and HD's accounting records. This balance is the amount that HD will report as Cash on its balance sheet after adjusting its records (we discuss the adjusting entries later).

To prepare the bank reconciliation in Exhibit 8.8, HD compared the entries in the Cash account to the bank statement in Exhibit 8.6 with the following goals:

1. **Identify the deposits in transit.** A comparison of HD's recorded deposits with those listed on the bank statement revealed that the bank statement did not list a deposit of $1,800 made on June 30. More than likely, the bank did not process this deposit until July 1. HD did not need to change its records for this item because it was already in HD's books on June 30. Instead, HD entered the amount on the bank reconciliation as an addition to update the bank's records.
2. **Identify the outstanding checks.** A comparison of HD's record of written checks with the checks listed on the bank statement revealed that Checks 103 and 105 were still outstanding at the end of June (that is, they had not cleared the bank). They were entered on the reconciliation as a deduction from the bank account because the bank will reduce the account balance when the checks eventually clear the bank. (HD had already deducted Checks 103 and 105 from its cash records.)
3. **Record other transactions reported on the bank statement.**
   a. **Interest received** from the bank, $20—this amount was entered on the bank reconciliation as an addition to the company's balance because it was included in the bank balance but had not yet been recorded in the company's books.

Exhibit 8.8 Sample Bank Reconciliation

Updates to Bank Statement			Updates to Company's Books		
Ending cash balance per bank statement		$10,638.40	Ending cash balance per books		$11,391.40
Additions			Additions		
(1) Deposit in transit		1,800.00	(3a) Interest received from the bank	$ 20.00	
		12,438.40	(3b) EFT received from customer	100.00	120.00
					11,511.40
Deductions			Deductions		
(2) Outstanding checks:					
103	$145.00		(3c) NSF check of R. Smith	18.00	
105	815.00	960.00	(3d) Bank service charges	6.00	
			(4) Error in recording check no. 104	9.00	33.00
Up-to-date ending cash balance		$11,478.40	Up-to-date ending cash balance		$11,478.40

b. **Electronic funds transfer** received from customer, $100—this amount was entered on the bank reconciliation as an addition to the company's balance because it was included in the bank balance but had not yet been recorded in the company's books.
c. **NSF check** rejected, $18—this amount was entered on the bank reconciliation as a deduction from the company's balance because it was deducted from the bank balance but had not yet been deducted from the company's records.
d. **Service charges,** $6—this amount was entered on the bank reconciliation as a deduction from the company's balance because it had been deducted from the bank balance but had not yet been removed from the company's Cash account.

4. **Determine the impact of errors.** After performing the three steps just listed, HD's accountant found that the reconciliation was still out of balance by $9. In checking the journal entries made during the month, the accountant found that Check 104 had been recorded as $56 when in fact it had been written for $65 (in payment of an account payable). As Exhibit 8.6 (page 356) shows, the bank correctly processed this check on June 30 for $65. To correct the company's error, HD's accountant deducted $9 (= $65 – $56) from the company's side of the bank reconciliation.

Coach's Tip

This example involves the company's error in recording the amount of the check. In other cases, the bank errs if it processes the check at the wrong amount. In all instances, the amount written on the check is the correct amount at which the transaction should be recorded.

Now that we know that the up-to-date ending balance in the Cash account should be $11,478.40, we need to prepare journal entries that will bring the Cash account to that balance. The entries on the Bank Statement side of the bank reconciliation (the deposit in transit and the two outstanding checks) do not require entries because they will work out automatically when the bank processes them next month. **Only the items on the Company's Books side of the bank reconciliation need to be recorded in the company's records** using the following journal entries:

	Account Titles and Explanations	Debit	Credit
(3*a*)	Cash (+A)	20	
	Interest Revenue (+R, +OE)		20
	(To record interest received from the bank.)		
(3*b*)	Cash (+A)	100	
	Accounts Receivable (−A)		100
	(To record EFT received from customer.)		
(3*c*)	Accounts Receivable (+A)	18	
	Cash (−A)		18
	(To record NSF check rejected by bank and still owed by customer.)		
(3*d*)	Office Expense (+E, −OE)	6	
	Cash (−A)		6
	(To record service charges deducted by bank.)		
(3*e*)	Accounts Payable (−L)	9	
	Cash (−A)		9
	(To correct company error on a check paid to a creditor.)		

Coach's Tip

Notice that the changes in Cash correspond to amounts on the right-hand side of the bank reconciliation in Exhibit 8.8.

Assets		=	Liabilities		+	Owners' Equity	
Cash	+87*		Accounts Payable	−9		Interest Revenue (+R)	+20
Accounts Receivable	−82‡					Office Expense (+E)	− 6

*20 + 100 − 18 − 6 − 9 = 87
‡− 100 + 18 = −82

SELF-STUDY PRACTICE

Indicate which of the following items discovered during preparation of a bank reconciliation for Nordstrom will need to be recorded in the Cash account on the company's books.

1. Outstanding checks.
2. Deposits in transit.
3. Bank service charges.
4. NSF checks that were deposited.

After you have finished, check your answers with the solution at the bottom of this page.

Spotlight On CONTROLS

Granny Does Time

Grandmothers seem so trustworthy. In one well-known case, however, a granny stole nearly half a million dollars from the small company where she worked as a bookkeeper. It was easy to do. Because the owner knew very little about accounting, he gave her responsibility for all of the company's accounting and never independently verified her work. Granny realized that this lack of internal control gave her unlimited opportunity, so she wrote checks to herself and recorded them as inventory purchases. Then, when she did the bank reconciliation, she destroyed the checks to cover her tracks. Granny kept this fraud going for eight years until she confessed after becoming overwhelmed by guilt.

Learning Objective 6

Describe the reporting of cash and cash equivalents.

FINANCIAL REPORTING OF CASH

Cash and Cash Equivalents

For the purposes of external financial statement reporting, cash includes **cash** deposited with banks, petty cash, and cash equivalents. **Cash equivalents** are short-term, highly liquid investments obtained within three months of maturity. They are combined with cash and reported as current assets because they are readily convertible to known amounts of cash and are so near to maturity that there is little risk that their value will change. In your personal life, cash equivalents could include checks you have received but not yet deposited into your bank account as well as certificates of deposit (CDs) you purchased within three months of maturity.

The Home Depot held $445 million of Cash and Cash Equivalents at the end of January 2008, only a portion of which was held as cash. In fact, the first note to the financial statements explained that the company held various cash equivalents including money market funds and financial instruments issued by investment-grade companies and the U.S. government.

Solution to Self-Study Practice

1 and 2 represent time lags between the bank's and company's records. Nordstrom does not need to record them because the company recorded them when it wrote the checks and made the deposits.

3. Bank service charges are deducted from the company's bank account, so Nordstrom must reduce Cash and record an expense.

4. When checks are deposited, Nordstrom records them on the books as increases in the Cash account. When the bank later rejects a check as NSF, Nordstrom must decrease Cash and increase the related account receivable.

Demonstration Case A

In June, a local Amtrak office established a petty cash fund with Terrell Noman as its custodian. Terrell received and cashed a company check of $175 to establish the fund. During that month, Terrell paid cash from the fund for supplies ($30), delivery charges ($80), and other minor office expenses ($40). On July 10, he received a company check for $150 to replenish the fund.

Required:

1. Prepare the journal entry required in June.
2. Prepare the journal entry required in July.
3. Explain why it may be appropriate or inappropriate to wait until July to record the payments from the petty cash fund.

Suggested Solution

1.

	Debit	Credit
Petty Cash (+A)	175	
Cash (−A)		175

Assets		=	Liabilities	+	Owners' Equity	
Petty Cash	+175					
Cash	−175					

2.

	Debit	Credit
Supplies (+A)	30	
Delivery Expense (+E, −OE)	80	
Office Expense (+E, −OE)	40	
Cash (−A)		150

Assets		=	Liabilities	+	Owners' Equity	
Cash	−150				Delivery Expense (+E)	−80
Supplies	+ 30				Office Expense (+E)	−40

3. Waiting until July to record payments from the fund may be inappropriate because the expenses occurred in June, and the matching principle suggests that they should therefore be recorded in June—not in July, when the fund is replenished. However, waiting until July may be appropriate because the unrecorded amounts are immaterial—that is, too small to influence the decisions of those who use Amtrak's records.

Demonstration Case B

Kat Bardash, a student at a small state college, has just received her first checking account statement for the month ended September 30. This is her first chance to attempt a bank reconciliation. The bank's statement of account shows the following information:

Bank balance, September 1	$1,150
Deposits during September	650
Checks cleared during September	900
Bank service charge	25
Interest earned	5
Bank balance, September 30	880

Kat is surprised that her bank has not yet reported the $50 deposit that she made on September 29 and pleased that her $200 rent check has not yet cleared her account. Her September 30 checkbook balance is $750.

Required:

1. Complete Kat's bank reconciliation. What adjustments, if any, does she need to make in her checkbook?
2. Why is it important for individuals and businesses to prepare a bank reconciliation each month?

Suggested Solution

1. **Kat's bank reconciliation:**

Updates to Bank Statement		Updates to Kat's Books	
September 30 cash balance	$880	September 30 cash balance	$750
Additions		Additions	
Deposit in transit	50	Interest earned	5
Deductions		Deductions	
Outstanding check	(200)	Bank service charge	(25)
Up-to-date cash balance	$730	Up-to-date cash balance	$730

Kat should increase her checkbook balance by $5 for the interest earned and reduce her checkbook balance by $25 for the service charges.

2. Bank statements, whether personal or business, should be reconciled each month to ensure that the depositor's books reflect a correct balance. Failure to reconcile a bank statement increases the chance that an error will not be discovered and may result in writing NSF checks. Businesses reconcile their bank statements for an additional reason: They report the up-to-date balance calculated during reconciliation on the balance sheet.

Chapter Summary

LO1 Define internal control and explain why it is needed. p. 344

- Internal control encompasses the methods an organization uses to protect against the theft of assets, to enhance the reliability of accounting information, to promote efficient and effective operations, and to ensure compliance with applicable laws and regulations.
- Internal controls are needed to ensure that people will behave in ways that benefit the organization. When internal controls operate effectively, they can improve an organization's efficiency and minimize waste, unintentional errors, and fraud.

LO2 Explain the common principles and limitations of internal control. p. 346

- The concept of internal control is broad. Most employees of a company will encounter five basic internal control principles: (1) establish responsibility for each task, (2) segregate duties so that one employee cannot initiate, approve, record, and handle a single transaction, (3) restrict access to assets and information to those employees who have been assigned responsibility for them, (4) document all procedures, and (5) independently verify work that has been done using information from others inside and outside the business.
- Internal controls are limited because they (1) are implemented only to the extent that their benefits exceed their costs and (2) may fail to operate effectively as a result of error and fraud.

LO3 Apply internal control principles to cash receipts and payments. p. 348

- When applied to cash receipts, internal control principles require that (1) cashiers be held individually responsible for the cash they receive, (2) different individuals be assigned to receive, maintain custody of, and record cash, (3) cash be stored in a locked safe until it has been securely deposited in a bank, (4) cash register receipts, cash count sheets, daily cash summary reports, and bank deposit slips be prepared to document the cash received and deposited, and (5) cash register receipts be matched to cash counts and deposits to independently verify that all cash was received and deposited.
- When applied to cash payments, internal control principles require that (1) only certain individuals or departments initiate purchase requests, (2) different individuals be assigned to order, receive, and pay for purchases, (3) access to checks and

valuable property be restricted, (4) purchase requisitions, purchase orders, receiving reports, and prenumbered checks be used to document the work done, and (5) each step in the payment process occur only after the preceding step has been independently verified using the documents listed in (4).

LO4 Describe the operation of voucher and petty cash systems. p. 351

- A voucher system is used to record most purchases of goods and services. The voucher includes documentation for each step in requesting, ordering, receiving, and paying for goods or services from a supplier. These documents are used for independent verification, which helps to ensure that each step proceeds only after an authorized individual or department has completed the previous steps.
- A petty cash system is used to reimburse employees for relatively small business-related expenditures. The petty cash custodian is involved in establishing, making payments from, and replenishing the fund.

LO5 Prepare a bank reconciliation. p. 355

- Preparing a bank reconciliation involves identifying items in two categories: (1) those that have been recorded in the company's books but not in the bank's statement of account and (2) those that have been reported in the bank's statement of account but not in the company's books. Items in the second category provide the data needed to adjust the cash account to the balance reported on the balance sheet.

LO6 Describe the reporting of cash and cash equivalents. p. 360

- Cash (including petty cash and reconciled bank account balances) and cash equivalents are reported as a current asset on the balance sheet. Cash equivalents are short-term, highly liquid investments acquired within three months of maturity.

Key Terms

Bank Reconciliation (p. 355)
Bonding (p. 347)
Cash (p. 360)
Cash Count Sheet (p. 350)
Cash Equivalents (p. 360)
Collude (p. 348)
Deposits in Transit (p. 357)
Electronic Funds Transfer (EFT) (p. 351)
Imprest System (p. 352)
Internal Control (p. 344)
NSF (Not Sufficient Funds) Checks (p. 357)
Outstanding Check (p. 357)
Override (p. 348)
Petty Cash Fund (p. 353)
Remittance Advice (p. 351)
Sarbanes-Oxley (SOX) Act of 2002 (p. 344)
Segregation of Duties (p. 346)
Voucher (p. 352)
Voucher System (p. 352)

See complete glossary in back of text.

Questions

1. What are internal controls and why are they needed?
2. What aspect(s) of the Sarbanes-Oxley Act of 2002 might counteract the incentive to commit fraud?
3. What aspect(s) of the Sarbanes-Oxley Act of 2002 might reduce opportunities for fraud?
4. What aspect(s) of the Sarbanes-Oxley Act of 2002 might allow the good character of employees to prevail?
5. From the perspective of a CEO or CFO, what does internal control mean?
6. What are five common internal control principles?
7. Why is it a good idea to assign each task to only one employee?
8. Why should responsibilities for certain duties, like cash handling and cash recording, be separated? What specific responsibilities should be separated?
9. What are some of the methods for restricting access?
10. In what ways does documentation act as a control?
11. In what ways can independent verification occur?
12. In what way does a mandatory vacation policy act as a control?
13. What are the three limitations of internal control?
14. What is the primary internal control goal for cash receipts?
15. What internal control functions are performed by a cash register? How are these functions performed when cash is received by mail?
16. How is cash received in person independently verified?
17. What is the primary internal control goal for cash payments?
18. In what ways is a petty cash system similar to and different from an imprest payroll system?
19. Describe three ways in which banking services help businesses control cash.
20. What are the purposes of a bank reconciliation? What balances are reconciled?
21. Define *cash* and indicate the types of items that should be reported as cash. Define *cash equivalents* and give two examples of a cash equivalent.

Multiple Choice

1. Which of the following was required of publicly traded companies prior to the laws arising from SOX?
   a. Internal control report from management.
   b. Internal control audit by external auditors.
   c. Financial statement audit by external auditors.
   d. Tip lines for anonymously submitting concerns about accounting or auditing practices.

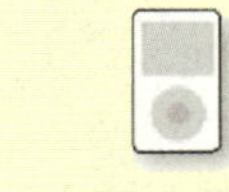

Quiz 8-1
www.mhhe.com/LLPW1e

2. Which of the following does not enhance internal control?
   a. Assigning different duties to different employees.
   b. Ensuring adequate documentation is maintained.
   c. Allowing access only when required to complete assigned duties.
   d. None of the above—all enhance internal control.
3. Which of the following internal control principles is best exemplified by hiring internal auditors?
   a. Segregate duties.
   b. Establish responsibility.
   c. Restrict access.
   d. Independently verify.
4. Which of the following internal control principles underlies the requirement that all customers be given a sales receipt?
   a. Segregate duties.
   b. Establish responsibility.
   c. Restrict access.
   d. Document procedures.
5. At most movie theaters, one employee collects cash and issues a receipt, and another employee collects the tear-away portion of that receipt. Which of the following internal control principles does this description best illustrate?
   a. Segregate duties.
   b. Establish responsibility.
   c. Restrict access.
   d. Document procedures.
6. Which of the following documents is least likely to be included in a voucher?
   a. Purchase order.
   b. Invoice.
   c. Purchase requisition.
   d. Remittance advice.
7. Which of the following explains why almost all businesses use banking services?
   a. Banking services allow the business to keep only a minimal amount of cash on hand.
   b. Banking services make it easier for the business to transact with other businesses.
   c. Banking services enable the business to independently verify the accuracy of its cash records.
   d. All of the above.
8. Upon review of your company's bank statement, you discover that you recently deposited a check from a customer that was rejected by your bank as NSF. Which of the following describes the actions to be taken when preparing your company's bank reconciliation?

Balance per Bank	Balance per Books
a. Decrease	No change
b. Increase	Decrease
c. No change	Decrease
d. Decrease	Increase

9. Upon review of the most recent bank statement, you discover that a check made out to your supplier for $86 was recorded in your Cash and Accounts Payable accounts as $68. Which of the following describes the actions to be taken when preparing your bank reconciliation?

Balance per Bank	Balance per Books
a. Decrease	No change
b. Increase	No change
c. No change	Decrease
d. Decrease	Increase

10. Assume a business has $2,000 cash in its checking account on August 1. On August 2, the business writes a check to establish a $100 petty cash fund. Later in the month, cash payments totaling $20 are made out of the fund and checks totaling $350 are written (including a check to replenish the petty cash fund). If all checks except for one in the amount of $10 clear the bank in August, what amount would the business report as Cash and Cash Equivalents at the end of August? Assume there are no other items affecting cash and cash equivalents.
    a. $1,650.
    b. $1,630.
    c. $1,550.
    d. $1,530.

Solutions to Multiple-Choice Questions

1. c	2. d	3. d	4. d	5. a	6. d
7. d	8. c	9. c	10. a		

Mini Exercises  Available with McGraw-Hill's Homework Manager

M8-1 Classifying Sarbanes-Oxley (SOX) Objectives and Requirements LO1

Match each of the following SOX requirements to the corresponding objective by entering the appropriate letter in the space provided.

____ 1. Establish a tip line for employees to report questionable acts.
____ 2. Increase maximum fines to $5 million.
____ 3. Require management to report on effectiveness of internal controls.
____ 4. Legislate whistle-blower protections.
____ 5. Require external auditors' report on internal control effectiveness.

A. Counteract incentives for fraud.
B. Reduce opportunities for error and fraud.
C. Encourage good character.

M8-2 Identifying Internal Control Procedures and Principles LO2

Fox Erasing has a system of internal control with the following procedures. Match the procedure to the corresponding internal control principle.

Procedure	Internal Control Principle
____ 1. The treasurer signs checks.	A. Establish responsibility.
____ 2. The treasurer is not allowed to make bank deposits.	B. Segregate duties.
____ 3. The company's checks are prenumbered.	C. Restrict access.
____ 4. Unused checks are stored in the vault.	D. Document procedures.
____ 5. A bank reconciliation is prepared each month.	E. Independently verify.

M8-3 Identifying Internal Control Principles Applied by a Merchandiser LO2, 4

Identify the internal control principle represented by each point in the following diagram.

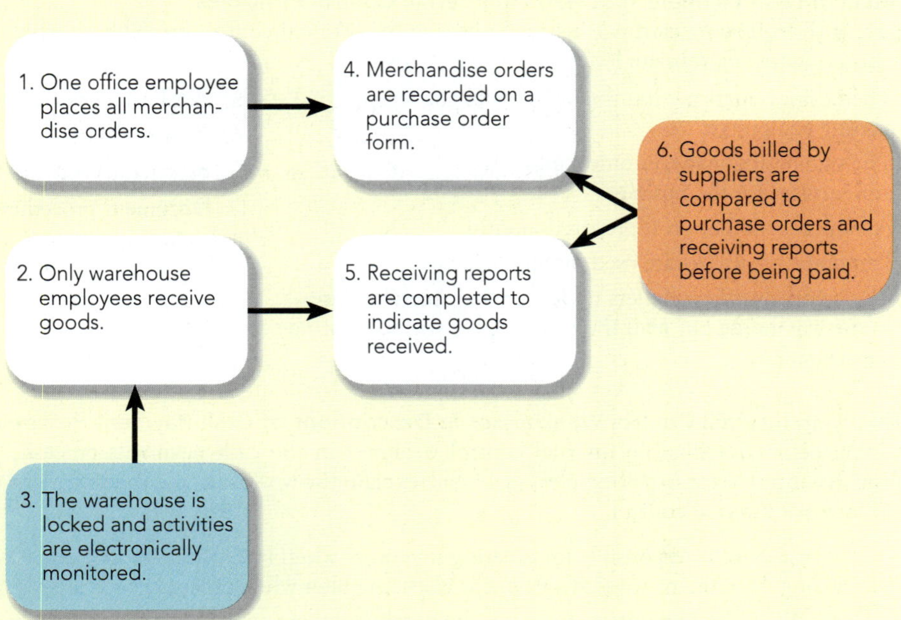

LO3

M8-4 Matching Cash Receipt Processes to Internal Control Principles

Match each of the following cash receipt activities to the internal control principle to which it best relates, by entering the appropriate letter in the space provided.

____ 1. A list of checks received in the mail is prepared.
____ 2. Total cash receipts are compared to the amount on the bank deposit slip.
____ 3. A password is required to open the cash register.
____ 4. Price changes at the checkout require a manager's approval.
____ 5. Each cashier is assigned a separate cash drawer.

A. Establish responsibility.
B. Segregate duties.
C. Restrict access.
D. Document procedures.
E. Independently verify.

LO3

M8-5 Identifying Internal Control Weaknesses in Descriptions of Cash Receipts Process

Each situation below describes an internal control weakness in the cash receipts process. Identify which of the five internal control principles is violated, explain the weakness, and then suggest a change that would improve internal control.

1) Cashiers prepare a cash count summary, attach tapes from the cash register showing total receipts, and then prepare a bank deposit slip, which they take to the bank for deposit. After the deposit is made, all documents are forwarded to the accounting department for review and recording.
2) Each cash register is password protected but, for convenience, the password is written on a note stuck to the side of the cash register.
3) The receptionist opens the mail each morning, sorts it into piles, and then gives checks received from customers to the mail clerk for delivery to the accounting department, where a cash receipts list is prepared.
4) The accounting department receives cash register totals each day and promptly files them by cash register number. The accounting department also receives cash count sheets from cashiers each day and files them by employee number. The accounting department receives stamped bank deposit slips the morning after the bank deposit is made, prepares the journal entry, and files the deposit slips by date.
5) To avoid boredom, the employee who works the cash register at the movie theater trades off with either the employee who collects the tickets or an employee who works at the concessions stand.
6) To enhance efficiency, cashiers are assigned the responsibility of authorizing price changes at the cash register.

LO3

M8-6 Matching Cash Payment Processes to Internal Control Principles

Match each of the following cash payment activities to the internal control principle to which it best relates by entering the appropriate letter in the space provided.

____ 1. The business manager has the only key to the check signing equipment.
____ 2. The purchasing manager orders all goods and services for the business.
____ 3. A bank reconciliation is prepared monthly.
____ 4. Prenumbered checks are used for all payments.
____ 5. The company asks suppliers to deliver their merchandise to the warehouse but mail their invoices to the accounting department.

A. Establish responsibility.
B. Segregate duties.
C. Restrict access.
D. Document procedures.
E. Independently verify.

LO3, 4

M8-7 Identifying Internal Control Weaknesses in Descriptions of Cash Payment Processes

Each situation below describes an internal control weakness in the cash payments process. Identify which of the five internal control principles is violated, explain the weakness, and then suggest a change that would improve internal control.

1) The warehouse clerk is responsible for ordering inventory when levels become low, and advising the accounting department to issue a payment to the supplier when ordered goods are received.
2) For each purchase, the accountant compares the purchase order (prepared by the purchasing manager) to the receiving report (prepared by warehouse employees), and then attaches these documents to the corresponding supplier invoice and files them by supplier name. The accountant then prepares a check, which the owner merrily signs and sends to the mail clerk for mailing.

3) The petty cash custodian prepared a template for petty cash receipts using Microsoft Word and e-mailed a copy of it to employees in his department for them to use when submitting their reimbursement claims.
4) The check-signing machine is stored with a supply of blank checks in the lunch room closet.
5) Purchase orders can be approved by the purchasing manager, accountant, or warehouse supervisor, depending on who is least busy.
6) The petty cash custodian assists the assistant controller by preparing the monthly bank reconciliation.

M8-8 Recognizing Voucher and Petty Cash Systems **LO4**

The following transactions occurred during the month. Indicate whether a voucher (V) or petty cash (PC) system would be used to process each transaction.

____ 1. A $10 cash payment is made to Starbucks to purchase coffee for a business client.
____ 2. A $40 cash payment is made for supplies purchased from Office Depot.
____ 3. A $30 cash payment is made to UPS to deliver goods to a customer.
____ 4. A $300 check is written for supplies purchased on account from Office Max.

M8-9 Accounting for Petty Cash Transactions **LO4**

Refer to M8-8. Prepare the journal entry that would be recorded to replenish the petty cash fund.

M8-10 Accounting for Petty Cash Transactions **LO4**

On September 30, Hector's petty cash fund of $100 is replenished. At the time, the cash box contained $18 cash and receipts for taxi fares ($40), delivery charges ($12), and office supplies ($30). Prepare the journal entry to record the replenishment of the fund.

M8-11 Organizing Items on the Bank Reconciliation **LO5**

Indicate whether the following items would be added (+) to or subtracted (−) from the company's books or the bank statement side of a bank reconciliation.

Reconciling Item	Bank Statement	Company's Books
1. Outstanding checks of $12,000		
2. Bank service charge of $15		
3. Deposit in transit of $2,300		
4. Interest earned of $5		

M8-12 Preparing Journal Entries after a Bank Reconciliation **LO5**

Using the information in M8-11, prepare any journal entries needed to adjust the company's books.

M8-13 Preparing a Bank Reconciliation **LO5**

Prepare a bank reconciliation for Trigger Company, using the following information at June 30, 2009.

Balance per bank	$10,000
Balance per company	9,030
Bank service charges	80
Bank interest earned	50
Deposit in transit	3,000
Outstanding checks	4,000

M8-14 Preparing Journal Entries after a Bank Reconciliation **LO5**

Refer to M8-13. Prepare any journal entries needed to adjust the company's books.

M8-15 Reporting Cash and Cash Equivalents **LO6**

Indicate (Yes or No) whether each of the following would be properly included as Cash and Cash Equivalents.

____ 1. $10,000 of government Treasury bills purchased 10 days prior to their maturity.
____ 2. $5,000 of stock in Zoogle—a private company that operates a lost pet search business.
____ 3. $20,000 of cash owed by customers on sales made within 20 days of year-end.
____ 4. $1,000 of cash in the petty cash custodian's locked cash box.

Exercises

Available with McGraw-Hill's Homework Manager

LO1, 2

E8-1 Identifying Internal Control Principles

At most movie theaters, one employee sells tickets and another employee collects them. One night when you are at the movies, your friend comments that this is a waste of the theater's money.

Required:

1. Identify the control principle to which this situation relates.
2. Explain to your friend what could happen if the same person did both jobs.

LO2

E8-2 Identifying Internal Control Principles

Your student club recently volunteered to go door-to-door collecting cash donations on behalf of a local charity. The charity's accountant went berserk when you said you wrote receipts only for donors who asked for one.

Required:

Identify the control principle that you violated, and explain why the accountant reacted so strongly. What controls might be appropriate to use in the future?

LO3

E8-3 Identifying Internal Control Principles in Cash Receipt Processes

Locker Rentals Corp. (LRC) operates locker rental services at several locations throughout the city including the airport, bus depot, shopping malls, and athletics facilities. Unlike some of the old mechanical lockers that charge a fixed amount per use, LRC's lockers operate electronically and are able to charge based on hours of use. The locker system transmits a daily message to LRC's office indicating the number of hours that lockers have been used, which the office manager uses to determine when cash should be picked up at each location. LRC's cash receipts system is described below.

a. Two employees ("cash collection clerks") are responsible for collecting cash from the lockers. Based on instructions from the office manager, one clerk collects cash from specific locations on the west side of the city and the other collects from specific locations on the east side.

b. When each cash collection clerk returns the cash, a supervisor counts the cash and prepares a cash count sheet.

c. The supervisor summarizes the cash count sheets in a prenumbered daily cash summary and files the prenumbered cash count sheets by date.

d. The supervisor places the cash in a locked cash box until it is taken to the bank for deposit.

e. The supervisor, not the cash collection clerks, takes the cash to the bank for deposit.

f. The supervisor prepares a duplicate deposit slip, which the bank stamps after the deposit is made, to indicate the date and amount of the deposit.

g. The supervisor sends the stamped bank deposit slip and daily cash summary to the accountant, who compares them before preparing a journal entry debiting Cash and crediting Locker Rental Revenue.

Required:

1. For each statement a–g, identify the internal control principle being applied.
2. Prepare a diagram similar to Exhibit 8.3 showing the flow of information and materials. In what two ways does LRC's system differ from Exhibit 8.3?
3. After several months, LRC's supervisor is arrested for stealing nearly $10,000 from the company. Identify the internal control weakness that allowed this theft to occur.
4. After the theft, LRC hired an external auditor to evaluate the company's cash receipts system. One of the auditor's recommendations was for LRC's accountant to verify that the cash collection clerks were returning all the cash received at each locker location. Explain how the accountant could use the electronic information transmitted by each locker location to verify that the cash collection clerks were not stealing from the company.

LO3, 4

E8-4 Identifying Internal Control Principles in Cash Payment Processes

Home Repair Corp. (HRC) operates a building maintenance and repair business. The business has three office employees—a sales manager, a materials/crew manager, and an accountant. HRC's cash payments system is described below.

a. After a contract is signed with a customer, the sales manager prepares a prenumbered purchase requisition form that indicates the materials needed for the work at the repair site.

b. Based on the purchase requisition form, the materials/crew manager prepares and sends a prenumbered purchase order to suppliers of materials, advising them of the specific materials needed and the repair site to which they should be delivered.

c. The materials/crew manager is the only employee authorized to order goods.

d. Upon receiving a supplier's invoice, the accountant compares it to terms indicated on the purchase order, noting in particular the prices charged and quantity ordered.

e. If these documents are in agreement, the accountant prepares a prenumbered check, stamps the invoice "paid," and prepares a journal entry to record the payment. The journal entry explanation references the sequential number on the purchase order.

f. HRC's owner prepares a monthly bank reconciliation and reviews checks returned with the bank statement to ensure they have been issued to valid suppliers.

Required:

1. For each statement a–f, identify the internal control principle being applied.
2. Using the above description, prepare a list of steps and documentation similar to Exhibit 8.5. Which document in Exhibit 8.5 is excluded from the above description?
3. After several months, HRC's materials/crew manager is arrested for having $20,000 of materials delivered to his home, but charged to the company. Identify the internal control weakness that allowed this theft to occur.

E8-5 Recording Petty Cash Transactions LO4

Mountain Air Company established a $200 petty cash fund on January 1. From January 2 through 15, payments were made from the fund, as listed below. On January 17, the fund was replenished with a check for $172.

a. January 3—Paid cash to courier for deliveries to customers—$43.

b. January 8—Paid cash to restaurant for catering lunch—$83.

c. January 10—Paid cash for postage—$14.

d. January 15—Paid cash for office supplies—$32.

Required:

1. Prepare the journal entry, if any, required on January 1.
2. Prepare the journal entries, if any, required on January 2 through 15.
3. Prepare the journal entries, if any, required on January 17.

E8-6 Recording Petty Cash Transactions LO4

Sunshine Health established a $100 petty cash fund on January 1. From January 2 through 10, payments were made from the fund, as listed below. On January 12, the fund had only $10 remaining; a check was written to replenish the fund.

a. January 2—Paid cash to courier for deliveries to customers—$23.

b. January 7—Paid cash for taxi fares—$50.

c. January 10—Paid cash for postage—$13.

Required:

1. Prepare the journal entry, if any, required on January 1.
2. Prepare the journal entries, if any, required on January 2 through 10.
3. Prepare the journal entries, if any, required on January 12.

(**Tip:** The Coach's Tip on page 354 explains how to account for cash shortages when a fund is replenished.)

E8-7 Preparing a Bank Reconciliation and Journal Entries and Reporting Cash LO5, 6

Hills Company's June 30, 2009, bank statement and the June ledger account for cash are summarized here:

BANK STATEMENT

	Checks	Deposits	Other	Balance
Balance, June 1, 2009				$ 7,200
Deposits during June		$18,000		25,200
Checks cleared during June	$19,100			6,100
Bank service charges			$30	6,070
Balance, June 30, 2009				6,070

+ Cash (A) −					
June 1	Balance	6,800			
June	Deposits	19,000	June	Checks written	19,400
June 30	Balance	6,400			

Required:

1. Prepare a bank reconciliation. A comparison of the checks written with the checks that have cleared the bank shows outstanding checks of $700. Some of the checks that cleared in June had been written prior to June. No deposits in transit were noted in May, but a deposit is in transit at the end of June.
2. Give any journal entries that should be made as a result of the bank reconciliation.
3. What is the balance in the Cash account after the reconciliation entries?
4. In addition to the balance in its bank account, Hills Company also has $300 of Petty Cash, which is recorded in a separate account. What is the total amount of Cash and Cash Equivalents that should be reported on the balance sheet at June 30?

LO5, 6

E8-8 Preparing a Bank Reconciliation and Journal Entries and Reporting Cash

The September 30, 2009, bank statement for Cadieux Company and the September ledger account for cash are summarized here:

BANK STATEMENT

	Checks		Deposits	Other	Balance
Balance, September 1, 2009					$ 2,000
September 7				NSF $100	1,900
September 11			$3,000		4,900
September 12	#101	$ 800			4,100
September 17	#102	1,700			2,400
September 26	#103	2,300			100
September 29				EFT 150	250
September 30				Service 20	230

+ Cash (A) −					
Sept 1	Balance	2,000			
Sept 10		3,000	800	Sept 10	101
Sept 30		2,500	1,700	Sept 15	102
			2,300	Sept 22	103
			50	Sept 28	104
Sept 30	Balance	2,650			

No outstanding checks and no deposits in transit were noted in August. However, there were deposits in transit and checks outstanding at the end of September. The NSF check and electronic funds transfer (EFT) involved transactions with Cadieux Company's customers.

Required:

1. Prepare a bank reconciliation.
2. Give any journal entries that should be made as a result of the bank reconciliation.
3. What should the balance in the Cash account be after recording the journal entries in requirement 2?
4. If the company also has $400 in a Petty Cash account, what total amount of Cash and Cash Equivalents should the company report on the September 30 balance sheet?

Problems—Set A

Available with McGraw-Hill's Homework Manager

PA8-1 Evaluating Internal Control Strengths and Weaknesses in Cash Receipts and Disbursements

LO2, 3, 4

The following procedures are used by Richardson Light Works.

a. When customers pay cash for lighting products, it is placed in a cash register and a receipt is issued to the customer.

b. At the end of each day, the cash is counted by the cashier and a cash count sheet is prepared.

c. The manager checks the accuracy of the cash count sheet before taking it to the bank for deposit.

d. The journal entry to record cash sales is prepared using the cash count sheet.

e. Disbursements from the petty cash fund are made for postage, office supplies, and small loans to fellow employees.

f. Checks are written to suppliers immediately after supplier invoices are received.

g. Receiving reports are prepared to indicate the quantity and condition of goods received from suppliers based on inspections made by warehouse personnel.

Required:

1. Indicate whether each procedure represents a strength or weakness. Explain your reasons.
2. For each weakness, describe a change in procedures that would address the weakness.

PA8-2 Controlling and Accounting for Petty Cash Disbursements

LO3, 4

Superior Cabinets maintains a petty cash fund for minor business expenditures. The petty cash custodian, Mo Smith, describes the events that occurred during the last two months:

a. I established the fund by cashing a Superior Cabinets' check for $300 made payable to me.

b. Liz Clay provided a receipt for $50 for various office supplies. I paid $50 cash to her.

c. James Flyer provided a $70 taxi receipt, so I paid $70 cash to him.

d. Ricky Ricota claimed to have photocopied brochures for Superior Cabinets at The UPS Store for $97, but had misplaced the receipt. I took him at his word and paid $97 cash to him.

e. On the last day of the month, I prepared a summary of expenditures and requested the fund be replenished. I received and cashed a Superior Cabinets' check for $217, placing the cash into the locked cash box.

f. James Flyer provided receipts for taxi costs ($65) and airport Internet connection fees ($10), so I paid $75 cash to him.

g. Woo Riun provided a $147 receipt from a local delivery company for an expedited delivery to a customer. I paid her $147 cash.

h. Ricky Ricota claimed to have purchased $20 of envelopes, which were used to mail brochures to potential customers, but again he had misplaced the receipt. He did provide a receipt for $15 of postage, so I paid him $35 cash.

i. On the last day of the month, I prepared a summary of expenditures and discovered that the petty cash fund was $2 short. After requesting that the fund be replenished, I received and cashed a Superior Cabinets' check for $259, placing the cash into the locked cash box.

j. After suggesting that the petty cash fund be increased, I received and cashed a Superior Cabinets' check for $100 cash, which I placed in the locked cash box.

Required:

1. Prepare journal entries where required.
2. From the description of events, identify one control strength and one control weakness.

PA8-3 Preparing a Bank Reconciliation and Journal Entries and Reporting Cash

LO5, 6

Martin Company's bank reconciliation at the end of April 2009 showed a reconciled cash balance of $18,800. No deposits were in transit at the end of April, but a deposit was in transit at the end of May. The bookkeeper at Martin Company has asked you to prepare a bank reconciliation as of May 31, 2009. The May 31, 2009, bank statement and the May T-account for Cash showed the following (summarized):

BANK STATEMENT

	Checks	Deposits	Other	Balance
Balance, May 1, 2009				$18,800
May 2		$ 8,000		26,800
May 5	#301 $11,000			15,800
May 7	#302 6,000			9,800
May 8		10,000		19,800
May 14	#303 500			19,300
May 17			Interest $120	19,420
May 22			NSF 280	19,140
May 27	#304 4,600			14,540
May 31			Service charge 60	14,480
Balance, May 31, 2009				14,480

+ Cash (A) −

May 1 Balance	18,800		
May 1	8,000	11,000	301 May 2
May 7	10,000	6,000	302 May 4
May 29	4,000	500	303 May 11
		4,600	304 May 23
		1,300	305 May 29
May 31 Balance	17,400		

Required:

1. Prepare a bank reconciliation for May.
2. Prepare any journal entries required as a result of the bank reconciliation. Why are they necessary?
3. After the reconciliation journal entries are posted, what balance will be reflected in the Cash account in the ledger?
4. If the company also has $50 of petty cash and $10,000 in government T-bills, which are recorded in different accounts, what total amount of Cash and Cash Equivalents should be reported on the balance sheet at the end of May?

LO5, 6

PA8-4 Identifying Outstanding Checks and Deposits in Transit and Preparing a Bank Reconciliation and Journal Entries

The December 2009 bank statement and Cash T-account for Stewart Company follow:

BANK STATEMENT

Date	Checks	Deposits	Other		Balance
Dec. 1					$48,000
2	$500				47,500
4	7,000				40,500
6	120				40,380
11	550	$28,000			67,830
13	1,900				65,930
17	12,000				53,930
23	60	36,000			89,870
26	900				88,970
28	2,200				86,770
30	17,000	19,000	NSF*	$300	88,470
31	1,650		Interest earned	50	86,870
31			Service charge	150	86,720

* NSF check from J. Left, a customer.

+ Cash (A) –			
Dec. 1 Balance	48,000	Checks written during December:	
Deposits			
Dec. 11	28,000	500	60
23	36,000	7,000	900
30	19,000	120	150
31	13,000	550	17,000
		1,900	3,500
		12,000	1,650
		2,200	
Dec. 31 Balance	96,470		

There were no deposits in transit or outstanding checks at November 30.

Required:

1. Identify and list the deposits in transit at the end of December.
2. Identify and list the outstanding checks at the end of December.
3. Prepare a bank reconciliation for December.
4. Give any journal entries that the company should make as a result of the bank reconciliation. Why are they necessary?
5. After the reconciliation journal entries are posted, what balance will be reflected in the Cash account in the ledger?
6. The company also has $300 of petty cash, $1,000 of government T-bills, and a $20,000 investment in a small privately owned company, each of which is recorded in a different account. What total amount of Cash and Cash Equivalents should be reported on the December 31, 2009, balance sheet?

PA8-5 Preparing a Bank Reconciliation and Journal Entries Including Petty Cash Transactions **LO4, 5, 6**
The August 2009 bank statement for Martha Company and the Cash T-account for August 2009 follow:

BANK STATEMENT

Date	Checks	Deposits	Other	Balance
Aug. 1				$17,470
2	$300			17,170
3		$12,000		29,170
4	400			28,770
5	250			28,520
9	890			27,630
10	310			27,320
15		4,000		31,320
21	400			30,920
24	21,000			9,920
25		7,000		16,920
30	800			16,120
30			Interest earned $20	16,140
31			Service charge 10	16,130

+ Cash (A) −			
Aug. 1 Balance	17,470	Checks written	
Deposits			
Aug. 2	12,000	300	Aug. 1
12	4,000	400	2
24	7,000	250	3
31	5,000	310	4
		890	5
		290	15
		550	17
		800	18
		400	19
		21,000	23
Aug. 31 Balance	20,280		

No deposits were in transit and no checks were outstanding at the end of July.

Required:

1. Identify and list the deposits in transit at the end of August.
2. Identify and list the outstanding checks at the end of August.
3. Prepare a bank reconciliation for August.
4. Give any journal entries that the company should make as a result of the bank reconciliation. Why are they necessary?
5. After the reconciliation journal entries are posted, what balance will be reflected in the Cash account in the ledger?
6. The company also has a petty cash fund of $300, which was established several months ago. The fund was replenished on August 31, 2009, with a payment of $125 to cover office supplies ($50), taxi fares ($60), and postage costs ($15) paid out of the fund. Give any journal entries the company should make when the fund is replenished.
7. If the company also has $5,000 of government T-bills recorded in a different account, what total amount of Cash and Cash Equivalents should be reported on the August 31, 2009, balance sheet?

Problems—Set B  Available with McGraw-Hill's Homework Manager

LO2, 3, 4

PB8-1 Evaluating Internal Control Strengths and Weaknesses in Cash Receipts and Disbursements

The following procedures are used by The Taco Shop.

a. Customers pay cash for all food orders. Cash is placed in a cash register and a receipt is issued upon request by the customer.
b. At the end of each day, the cashier counts the cash, prepares a cash count sheet, and has the manager review and sign the cash count sheet.
c. At three times during the day, excess cash is removed from the cash register and placed in a vault until it is taken for night deposit at the local bank.
d. Orders for drink cups, straws, condiments, and other supplies are written on prenumbered purchase order forms and are approved by the manager before being sent to an authorized supplier.
e. When supplies are received, they are stacked just inside the back door to the kitchen, which is left unlocked because part-time employees frequently arrive and leave at various times during the day.
f. Rather than maintain a formal petty cash system, reimbursement for minor business expenses are paid using cash in the cash register. Employees show a receipt to the cashier on duty, who then files the receipt in a cardboard box under the counter.

Required:

1. Indicate whether each procedure represents a strength or weakness. Explain your reasons.
2. For each weakness, describe a change in procedures that would address the weakness.

PB8-2 Controlling and Accounting for Petty Cash Disbursements **LO3, 4**

Harristown Hockey Club (HHC) maintains a petty cash fund for minor club expenditures. The petty cash custodian, Wayne Crosby, describes the events that occurred during the last two months:

a. I established the fund by cashing a check from HHC for $250 made payable to me.
b. Tom Canuck provided a $70 receipt for repairs to the club's computer, so I paid $70 cash to him.
c. Kim Harra provided a receipt for $50 for various supplies she had used to decorate the arena last month. I paid $50 cash to her.
d. Trainer Jim bought a bag of pucks that the club intends to use for the next few years. He gave me the receipt and I paid him $80.
e. On the last day of the month, I prepared a summary of expenditures and requested the fund be replenished. I received and cashed a check from HHC for $200, placing the cash into a locked cash box.
f. Wendy Wignes provided receipts for chips and sodas purchased for the club's entertainment event. I paid $125 cash to her.
g. Destiny Hook provided a phone bill showing she had paid $30 for calls made to contact referees for the annual tournament. I paid her $30 cash.
h. Gutty McTavish submitted a receipt for $35 for a haircut he received. I did not pay him.
i. I could not make it to the bank in time to take out money for the weekend, so I borrowed $50 from the petty cash box and will repay it next month.
j. On the last day of the month, I prepared a summary of expenditures and discovered that the petty cash fund was $10 short. After requesting that the fund be replenished, I received and cashed a check from HHC for $215, placing the cash into the locked cash box.

Required:

1. Prepare journal entries where required.
2. From the description of events, identify one control strength and one control weakness.

PB8-3 Preparing a Bank Reconciliation and Journal Entries and Reporting Cash **LO5, 6**

The April 30, 2010, bank statement for KMaxx Company and the April ledger account for Cash are summarized here:

BANK STATEMENT

	Checks		Deposits	Other		Balance
Balance, April 1, 2010						$6,000
April 5	#101	$700				5,300
April 9			$2,500			7,800
April 12	#102	200				7,600
April 19	#103	500				7,100
April 22	#104	1,000				6,100
April 27				EFT	$200	5,900
April 30				Service charge	25	5,875

+ Cash (A) −

Apr 1 Balance	6,000		
Apr 8	2,500	700	Apr 2 101
Apr 28	500	200	Apr 10 102
		500	Apr 15 103
		1,100	Apr 20 104
		300	Apr 29 105
Apr 30 Balance	6,200		

No outstanding checks and no deposits in transit were noted in March. However, there are deposits in transit and checks outstanding at the end of April. The electronic funds transfer (EFT) involved an automatic monthly payment to one of KMaxx's creditors. Check 104 was written for $1,100.

Required:

1. Prepare a bank reconciliation for April.
2. Give any journal entries that should be made as a result of the bank reconciliation.
3. What should the balance in the Cash account be after recording the journal entries in requirement 2?
4. If the company also has $500 of petty cash and $10,000 worth of 60-day government treasury bills (T-bills) purchased last month, what total amount of Cash and Cash Equivalents should the company report on the April 30 balance sheet?

LO5, 6

PB8-4 Preparing a Bank Reconciliation and Journal Entries and Reporting Cash

The bookkeeper at Tony Company has asked you to prepare a bank reconciliation as of February 29, 2010. The February 29, 2010, bank statement and the February T-account for Cash showed the following (summarized):

BANK STATEMENT

	Checks		Deposits	Other		Balance
Balance, February 1, 2010						$49,400
February 2	101	$15,000				34,400
February 4			$ 7,000			41,400
February 5				NSF	$320	41,080
February 9	102	11,000				30,080
February 12	103	7,500				22,580
February 14			9,500			32,080
February 19	104	9,000				23,080
February 23			14,150			37,230
February 26	105	6,700				30,530
February 28				Interest	150	30,680
February 29				Service charge	40	30,640

+	Cash (A)	–	
Feb 1 Balance	49,400		
Feb 2	7,000	15,000	Feb 1 101
Feb 13	9,500	11,000	Feb 7 102
Feb 21	14,150	7,500	Feb 11 103
Feb 28	7,800	9,000	Feb 17 104
		6,700	Feb 25 105
		1,200	Feb 29 106
Feb 29 Balance	37,450		

Tony Company's bank reconciliation at the end of January 2010 showed no outstanding checks. No deposits were in transit at the end of January, but a deposit was in transit at the end of February.

Required:

1. Prepare a bank reconciliation for February.
2. Prepare any journal entries required as a result of the bank reconciliation. Why are they necessary?
3. After the reconciliation journal entries are posted, what balance will be reflected in the Cash account in the ledger?
4. The company also has $400 of petty cash, $2,000 of government T-bills, and a $20,000 investment in a small privately owned company, each of which is recorded in a different account. What total amount of Cash and Cash Equivalents should be reported on the February 29, 2010, balance sheet?

PB8-5 Identifying Outstanding Checks and Deposits in Transit and Preparing a Bank Reconciliation and Journal Entries Including Petty Cash **LO4, 5, 6**

The September 2010 bank statement for Terrick Company and the Cash T-account for September 2010 follow:

BANK STATEMENT

Date	Checks	Deposits	Other		Balance
Sept. 1					$ 75,900
2	$620				75,280
4	2,000				73,280
6	1,500				71,780
11	300	14,000			85,480
13	650				84,830
17	10,000				74,830
23	90	27,000			101,740
26	700				101,040
28	8,000				93,040
29	730	17,000	NSF*	$500	108,810
30	400		Interest earned	60	108,470
30			Service charge	40	108,430

* NSF check from B. Frank, a customer.

+ Cash (A) −

		Checks written during September	
Sept. 1 Balance	75,900		
Deposits		620	8,000
Sept. 11	14,000	2,000	730
23	27,000	1,500	400
29	17,000	300	500
30	21,000	650	6,000
		10,000	90
		700	
Sept. 30 Balance	123,410		

There were no deposits in transit or outstanding checks at August 31.

Required:

1. Identify and list the deposits in transit at the end of September.
2. Identify and list the outstanding checks at the end of September.
3. Prepare a bank reconciliation for September.
4. Give any journal entries that the company should make as a result of the bank reconciliation. Why are they necessary?
5. After the reconciliation journal entries are posted, what balance will be reflected in the Cash account in the ledger?
6. The company also has a petty cash fund of $300, which was established several months ago. The fund was replenished on September 30, 2010, with a payment of $175 to cover office supplies ($60), selling expenses ($90), and courier fees ($25) paid out of the fund. Give any journal entries the company should make when the fund is replenished.
7. The company also acquired 60-day government treasury bills (T-bills) last month, now valued at $4,000. What total amount of Cash and Cash Equivalents should be reported on the September 30, 2010, balance sheet?

Cases and Projects

LO6

CP8-1 Finding Financial Information

Refer to the financial statements of The Home Depot in Appendix A at the end of this book, or download the annual report from the Cases and Projects section of the text's Web site at www.mhhe.com/ LLPW1e. How much cash (including cash equivalents) does the company report at February 3, 2008? According to the company's management and external auditors, were internal controls over financial reporting effective at that time?

LO6
Lowe's

CP8-2 Comparing Financial Information

Refer to the financial statements of The Home Depot in Appendix A and Lowe's in Appendix B at the end of this book, or download the annual reports from the Cases section of the text's Web site at www.mhhe.com/ LLPW1e. Does Lowe's report more or less cash (including cash equivalents) than The Home Depot in February 2008? According to the company's management and external auditors, were internal controls over financial reporting effective at that time?

LO1, 6

CP8-3 Examining an Annual Report: Internet-Based Team Research

As a team, select an industry to analyze. Using your Web browser, each team member should access the annual report or 10-K for one publicly traded company in the industry, with each member selecting a different company. (See CP1–3 in Chapter 1 for a description of possible resources for these tasks.)

Required:

1. On an individual basis, each team member should write a short report that incorporates the following:
   a. Read management's report on internal control effectiveness. Did any material weaknesses or deficiencies exist during the year? Did the external auditors agree with management's assessment?
   b. How much did the company report in total Cash and Cash Equivalents? Does the company present sufficient information to determine the proportion of Cash versus Cash Equivalents?
2. Then, as a team, write a short report comparing and contrasting your companies using these attributes. Discuss any patterns across the companies that you as a team observe. Provide potential explanations for any differences discovered.

LO2
Famous Footwear

CP8-4 Making Ethical Decisions: A Real-Life Example

When some people think about inventory theft, they imagine a shoplifter running out of a store with goods stuffed inside a jacket or bag. But that's not what the managers at the Famous Footwear store on Chicago's Madison Street thought. No, they suspected their own employees were the main cause of their unusually high shrinkage. One scam involved dishonest cashiers who would let their friends take a pair of Skechers without paying for them. To make it look like the shoes had been bought, cashiers would ring up a sale, but instead of charging $50 for shoes, they would charge only $2 for a bottle of shoe polish. When the company's managers saw a drop in gross profit, they decided to put the accounting system to work. In just two years, the company cut its Madison Street inventory losses in half. Here's how a newspaper described the store's improvements:

Retailers Crack Down on Employee Theft
SouthCoast Today, September 10, 2000, Chicago
By Calmetta Coleman, *Wall Street Journal* Staff Writer

. . . Famous Footwear installed a chainwide register-monitoring system to sniff out suspicious transactions, such as unusually large numbers of refunds or voids, or repeated sales of cheap goods.

. . . [B]efore an employee can issue a cash refund, a second worker must be present to see the customer and inspect the merchandise.

. . . [T]he chain has set up a toll-free hotline for employees to use to report suspicions about co-workers.

These improvements in inventory control came as welcome news for investors and creditors of Brown Shoe Company, the company that owns Famous Footwear. Although these improvements helped the Chicago store, Brown Shoe has been forced to shut down operations in other cities.

Brown Shoe Company

Required:

1. Explain how the register-monitoring system would allow Famous Footwear to cut down on employee theft.
2. What is the name of the control that is addressed by Famous Footwear's new cash refund procedure?
3. Think of and describe at least four different parties that are harmed by the type of inventory theft described in this case.

CP8-5 Making Ethical Decisions: A Mini Case

LO1, 6

You are an assistant in the accounting department of Hasher Electronics, a small electronics retailer. Hasher has a loan that requires the company to maintain a minimum cash balance of $125,000, as reported on its year-end balance sheet. Although Hasher has struggled in recent years, as of yesterday it looked as though Hasher would be able to meet this requirement. The cash balance in Hasher's general ledger was $130,000 and the company's credit manager was expecting to receive a $30,000 electronic funds transfer that day on account from your biggest customer. Your department supervisor had been worried about meeting the loan requirement, so she had delayed making payments to Hasher's suppliers for several days. But in anticipation of receiving the EFT, she decided yesterday to issue checks to suppliers totaling $15,000.

It is now the last day of the fiscal year and your supervisor approaches you with a problem. Your big customer had backed out at the last minute, indicating it had "some financial issues to sort out" before it can transfer money to Hasher. The supervisor says the only way Hasher can meet its loan requirement is to put the $15,000 back into the Cash account and pretend as if the supplier checks were not issued until after year-end. You questioned whether this would be ethical. Her reply was, "Well, we don't really have a choice. Either we do this, or we violate the terms of the loan agreement and possibly be forced to repay the loan immediately. That could put us out of business. Think of all the people who would lose their jobs! Just make a journal entry today to increase Cash and Accounts Payable. Then tomorrow we can reduce Cash and Accounts Payable—probably before many of our suppliers even get the checks we have written to them."

Required:

1. Who might suffer in the short term if you go along with your supervisor's request? What might happen in the future if you go along with her request this time? If you do not go along, who might suffer in the short term and what could be the long-term consequences?
2. You want to be loyal to your supervisor but honest to others who rely on your work. As an accounting assistant, which of these concerns should be most important? Why?
3. What alternative courses of action can you take? Which of these is "best" given the circumstances?

CP8-6 Analyzing Internal Control Weaknesses: Critical Thinking

LO1, 2, 3

Snake Creek Company has one trusted employee who, as the owner said, "handles all of the bookkeeping and paperwork for the company." This employee is responsible for counting, verifying, and recording cash receipts and payments, making the weekly bank deposit, preparing checks for major expenditures (signed by the owner), making small expenditures from the cash register for daily expenses, and collecting accounts receivable. The owners asked the local bank for a $20,000 loan. The bank asked that an audit be performed covering the year just ended. The independent auditor (a local CPA), in a private conference with the owner, presented some evidence of the following activities of the trusted employee during the past year:

a. Cash sales sometimes were not entered in the cash register, and the trusted employee pocketed approximately $50 per month.
b. Cash taken from the cash register (and pocketed by the trusted employee) was replaced with expense memos with fictitious signatures (approximately $12 per day).

Required:

1. What was the approximate amount stolen during the past year?
2. What would be your recommendations to the owner?

9 Receivables

LEARNING OBJECTIVES

After completing this chapter, you should be able to:

Lectured slideshow–LP9-1
www.mhhe.com/LLPW1e

LO1 Identify the different types of receivables.

LO2 Account for and report the effects of uncollectible accounts.

LO3 Use two different methods to estimate uncollectible accounts.

LO4 Compute and report interest on notes receivable.

LO5 Compute and interpret the receivables turnover ratio.

Focus Company: SKECHERS

"Global Leader in the Lifestyle Footwear Industry"

www.skechers.com

One of the most challenging parts of your academic and professional career will be managing events that you cannot completely control. Think, for example, about a group project that you must complete this term. You may believe that in theory the project should take only six days from start to finish. You know from experience, however, that someone in your group is likely to be late in completing the assigned work or may fail to complete it at all. The problem is that you do not know who it will be or how long the delay will take; these matters are largely beyond your control. To allow for the possibility that someone may be late, you might set a shorter period (say, four days) to complete the work. Establishing a two-day margin of safety will give you a realistic basis for planning and successfully completing the project.

This situation is similar to one faced by many companies, including Skechers, a shoe manufacturer that sells to retailers such as Foot Locker. Skechers' managers know from experience that some of their customers will not pay their bills. The problem is that at the time the sales are made, they cannot identify those customers. In this chapter, you will learn a method of accounting for such uncertainties—one that is similar to the approach you took with your group project. This method allows Skechers to report in a timely manner how much money the company is likely to collect from customers. In doing so, the company provides financial statement users a realistic basis for decision making.

Also in this chapter, you will learn about accounting for receivables, which arise either from selling to customers or from lending to others. As of December 31, 2006, receivables accounted for more than 25 percent of Skechers' total assets. If the company is to be successful, then, it must manage those assets effectively. You will see exactly how companies such as Skechers extend credit to others. Then you will confront the interesting accounting issues that arise when businesses decide to do so.

ORGANIZATION OF THE CHAPTER

TYPES OF RECEIVABLES	ACCOUNTS RECEIVABLE	NOTES RECEIVABLE AND INTEREST REVENUE	EVALUATING RECEIVABLES MANAGEMENT
	• Accounting for Bad Debts: The Allowance Method • Recording Estimated Bad Debt Expense • Methods for Estimating Bad Debts • Other Issues	• Calculating Interest • Recording Notes Receivable and Interest Revenue	• Receivables Turnover Analysis • Comparison to Benchmarks

TYPES OF RECEIVABLES

Learning Objective 1

Identify the different types of receivables.

Receivables may be classified in three common ways. First, they may be classified as either an account receivable or a note receivable. A credit sale on an open account creates an account receivable. For example, an account receivable is created when Skechers sells shoes on open account to Fontana Shoes in Ithaca, New York, or a large chain such as Foot Locker.

A note receivable is a promise made in writing (that is, a formal document) to pay (1) a specified amount of money called the **principal** at a definite future date known as the **maturity date** and (2) a specified amount of **interest** on one or more future dates. The interest is the amount that is charged for use of the principal. Legally, notes receivable are viewed as stronger claims than accounts receivable. Because a new note must be created for every transaction, however, notes receivable are used less frequently than accounts receivable, typically only for expensive items such as vehicles or for transactions with borrowers who do not have an established credit history.

Second, receivables may be classified as trade or nontrade receivables (see Exhibit 9.1). A **trade receivable** is created in the normal course of business when a sale of merchandise or services is made on credit. A **nontrade receivable** arises from transactions other than the normal sale of merchandise or services. If Skechers were to lend money to an employee to finance a home at a new job location, for example, the loan would be classified as a nontrade receivable.

Third, on a classified balance sheet, receivables are classified as either **current** or **noncurrent** (that is, short term or long term), depending on when the company expects to collect cash. Like many companies, Skechers reports Trade Accounts Receivable (from customers) as well as Other Receivables and classifies both as current assets because they are expected to be paid within one year (see Exhibit 9.1).

Skechers, Inc.

Exhibit 9.1 Classification of Accounts Receivable on the Balance Sheet

Skechers U.S.A., Inc.
Partial Consolidated Balance Sheets (in thousands)

	December 31, 2006	December 31, 2005
ASSETS		
Current assets		
Cash and cash equivalents	$220,485	$197,007
Trade accounts receivable, less allowances of $10,558 in 2006 and $7,196 in 2005	177,740	134,600
Other receivables	8,035	6,888
Total receivables	185,775	141,488
Inventories	200,877	136,171
Prepaid expenses and other current assets	15,321	11,628
Deferred tax assets	9,490	5,755
Total current assets	631,948	492,049

ACCOUNTS RECEIVABLE

Accounting for Bad Debts: The Allowance Method

Learning Objective 2

Account for and report the effects of uncollectible accounts.

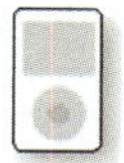

Video 9-1
www.mhhe.com/LLPW1e

You already know from earlier chapters that **accounts receivable** arise from the sale of goods or services on credit. What you may not know is that some accounts receivable are never collected. In fact, a recent study estimated the cost of bad debts to be as high as 5 percent of the net incomes of all U.S. corporations.[1] Like that "friend" of yours who says he will pay you later but for one reason or another never gets around to it, some customers just do not pay their bills.

For billing and collection purposes, Skechers keeps a separate accounts receivable account (called a **subsidiary account**) for each of the retail stores that carries its footwear and apparel. On the balance sheet, the amount for Accounts Receivable represents the total of these individual customer accounts. When Skechers extends credit to these commercial customers, managers know that some of these customers will not pay their debts. If a customer does not pay the bill on time, Skechers first rebills the customer and then attempts to contact the customer to determine the reason for nonpayment. If these measures do not work, Skechers turns the account over to a collection agency.

Managers may not learn which customers will not pay until the **next** accounting period, however. At the end of the period of sale, then, they normally do not know which accounts receivable represent bad debts. To solve this problem and to satisfy both the **matching** principle and the **conservatism** principle, they use the allowance method to measure bad debt expense. The allowance method is based on estimates of the expected amount of bad debts relative to a period's sales. The two major steps in employing the allowance method are:

1. Make an end-of-period adjusting entry to record the **estimated** bad debt expense in the period in which the sale took place.
2. Write off (remove) specific customer balances during the period when they are determined to be uncollectible.

Recording Estimated Bad Debt Expense

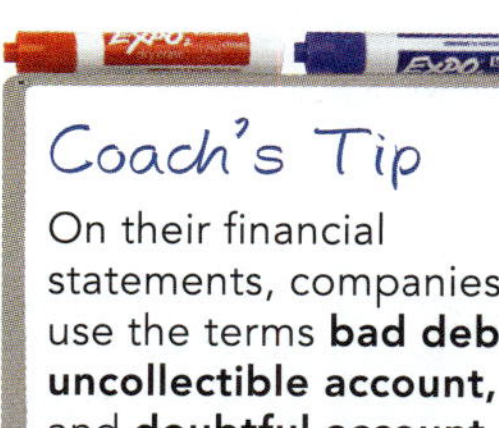

Coach's Tip

On their financial statements, companies use the terms **bad debt, uncollectible account,** and **doubtful account** interchangeably.

Bad debt expense (also called **uncollectible accounts expense**) is the expense associated with estimated uncollectible accounts receivable. **At the end of the accounting period,** accountants will make an **adjusting journal entry** to record the bad debt estimate. For the year ended December 31, 2006, for example, if Skechers estimated bad debt expense to be $4,591 (expressed in thousands of dollars), accountants would make the following adjusting entry to record the expense:

	Debit	Credit
Bad Debt Expense (+E, −OE)	4,591	
Allowance for Doubtful Accounts (+xA, −A)		4,591

Assets		=	Liabilities	+	Owners' Equity	
Allowance for Doubtful Accounts (+xA)	−4,591				Bad Debt Expense (+E)	−4,591

On the income statement, Bad Debt Expense is included under operating expenses. It decreases net income and owners' equity.

Why not credit Accounts Receivable in the adjusting entry? The answer is that at this point, there is no way to know which customers' accounts receivable are involved, and thus which subsidiary ledger accounts to reduce. The credit is made instead to the contra-asset account Allowance for Doubtful Accounts. (**Allowance for Bad Debts** and **Allowance for Uncollectible Accounts** are other common names for this account.) As with other contra-assets, the balance in Allowance for Doubtful Accounts is always subtracted from the balance of the asset Accounts Receivable. Thus, the entry decreases the net book value of Accounts Receivable and total assets. But because the estimated uncollectible portion is not taken

[1] PriceWaterhouse Coopers National Economic Consulting, *Value of Third-Party Debt Collection to the U.S. Economy: Survey and Analysis* (June 27, 2006).

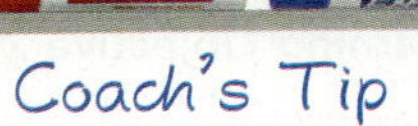

Coach's Tip

Accounts Receivable, net of allowance ("Trade accounts receivable, less allowances" in Exhibit 9.1) is not a separate account. It is a subtotal that is computed by subtracting the contra-asset account Allowance for Doubtful Accounts from the asset account Accounts Receivable.

directly out of Accounts Receivable, Skechers can still track the customers who owe money—even those who are believed to be unlikely to pay.

Of course, like all contra-asset accounts, the Allowance for Doubtful Accounts is a permanent account, so its balance carries forward from one accounting period to the next. The balance of Bad Debt Expense, which is a temporary account, is reduced to zero at the end of each accounting period. Consequently, the balance in the Allowance for Doubtful Accounts equals the balance in Bad Debt Expense only during the first year the Allowance for Doubtful Accounts is established.

Removing (Writing Off) Specific Customer Balances

Throughout the year, whenever it becomes clear that a particular customer will not pay, Skechers removes the customer's account from the accounts receivable records. After removing the receivable, Skechers no longer needs to make an allowance for it, so the company removes the corresponding amount from the Allowance for Doubtful Accounts. Removing the uncollectible account and its corresponding allowance is called a **write off**. In the 2006 annual report, if Skechers stated that it had written off customer accounts totaling $1,229 (in thousands), the effects of these write-offs and the journal entry to record them were as follows:

	Debit	Credit
Allowance for Doubtful Accounts (−xA, +A)	1,229	
Accounts Receivable (−A)		1,229

Assets		=	Liabilities	+	Owners' Equity
Allowance for Doubtful Accounts (−xA)	+1,229				
Accounts Receivable	−1,229				

Note that **a write-off does not affect the income statement accounts.** The estimated bad debt expense related to these uncollectible accounts was recorded with an adjusting entry in the period when the sale was recorded. Therefore, no additional expense is incurred when the account is finally written off. Notice too that the decrease in Accounts Receivable offsets the decrease in Allowance for Doubtful Accounts so that the write-off does not affect the Net Accounts Receivable subtotal on the balance sheet.

Summary of the Allowance Method

Here is a quick summary of the two main steps in the allowance method:

Step	Timing	Journal Entry	Financial Statement Effects: Balance Sheet		Financial Statement Effects: Income Statement	
1. Record adjustment for estimated bad debts	End of the period in which sales are made	Bad Debt Expense (+E, −OE) Allowance for Doubtful Accounts (+xA, −A)	Accounts receivable	*No effect*	Revenues	*No effect*
			Less: Allowance	⇧	Expenses	
			Net accounts receivable	⇩	Bad debt expense	⇧
					Net income	⇩
2. Identify and write off actual bad debts	As accounts are determined uncollectible	Allowance for Doubtful Accounts (−xA, +A) Accounts Receivable (−A)	Accounts receivable	⇩	Revenues	*No effect*
			Less: Allowance	⇩	Expenses	
			Net accounts receivable	*No effect*	Bad debt expense	*No effect*
					Net income	*No effect*

The effects of these two steps on Skechers' 2006 balance sheet can be summarized in terms of the following changes in the related T-accounts:

Accounts Receivable (A)	
Unadj. Bal. 189,527	
	1,229 Write-offs
End. Bal 188,298	

Allow. for Doubtful Accts (xA)	
	7,196 Beg. Bal.
Write-offs 1,229	4,591 Estimate
	10,558 End. Bal.

Ending Balances December 31, 2006

Accounts Receivable	$188,298
−Allowance for Doubtful Accounts	10,558
Accounts Receivable (Net)	177,740

Spotlight On CONTROLS

Segregating Collections and Write-Offs

One way to control accounts receivable is to ensure that the same person does not both receive collections from customers and write off account balances. This segregation of duties helps to prevent errors and fraud. Without adequate segregation between these duties, a single dishonest employee could divert customer payments to his or her own bank account and then cover up the theft by writing off the customer's balance.

SELF-STUDY PRACTICE

Indicate the effect (+ / − / No Effect) of each of the following on net income and total assets.

	Net Income	Total Assets
1. Polaris Industries recorded an increase in estimated bad debts on December 31, 2008.		
2. Kellogg's wrote off 12 customer account balances during 2008.		

After you have finished, check your answers with the solution at the bottom of the page.

Methods for Estimating Bad Debts

Learning Objective 3
Use two different methods to estimate uncollectible accounts.

In the examples given so far, we simply stated the estimated amount of uncollectibles to record. In the real world, companies must estimate the amount that they record in the end-of-period adjusting entry for bad debt expense. Such estimates may be based on either (1) a percentage of total credit sales for the period or (2) an "aging" of accounts receivable. Both methods are acceptable under GAAP and are used widely. The percentage of credit sales method is simpler to apply, but the aging method is generally more accurate. Some companies use the simpler method on a weekly or monthly basis and the more accurate method on a monthly or quarterly basis to check the accuracy of earlier estimates. In our example, both methods produce exactly the same estimate—a result that rarely occurs in the real world.

Solution to Self-Study Practice

	Net Income	Total Assets
1.	−	−
2.	NE	NE*

*The decrease in Accounts Receivable is offset by the decrease in Allowance for Doubtful Accounts.

Percentage of Credit Sales Method

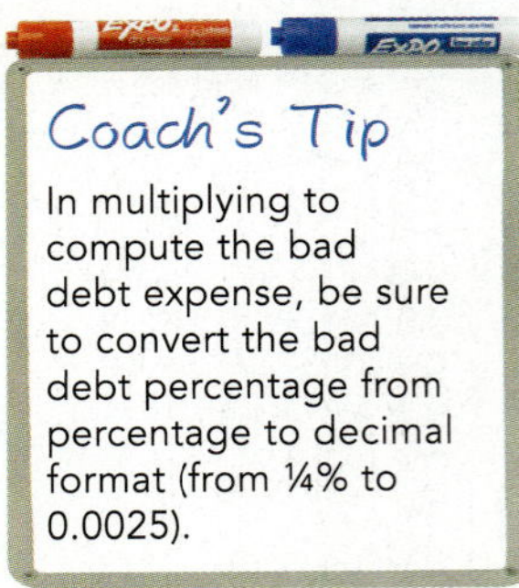

The allowance method of accounting for bad debts requires estimating and recording bad debts in the same period as the sale to which they relate. The **percentage of credit sales method** estimates bad debt expense by multiplying the historical percentage of bad debt losses by the current year's credit sales. Assume, for example, that Skechers has experienced bad debt losses of ¼ of 1 percent of credit sales in past years. If credit sales in the current year total $1,836,400, Skechers could estimate the current year's bad debt expense as:

Credit sales this year	$1,836,400
× Bad debt loss rate (0.25%)	× 0.0025
Bad debt expense this year	$ 4,591

This estimate would be recorded using the following journal entry, which you first saw on page 383:

	Debit	Credit
Bad Debt Expense (+E, −OE)	4,591	
Allowance for Doubtful Accounts (+xA, −A)		4,591

Accounts Receivable Methods

While the percentage of sales method computes the estimated Bad Debt Expense for the period, accounts receivable methods compute the estimated ending balance in the Allowance for Doubtful Accounts. To find the ending balance, managers must first determine the percentage of the total accounts receivable that is likely to be uncollectible. This method is often called the **percentage of accounts receivable method**.

A related, more commonly used and accurate approach for estimating uncollectible amounts is called the **aging of accounts receivable method**. This method gets its name because it is based on the "age" of each amount in accounts receivable. The older and more overdue an account receivable becomes, the less likely it is to be collectible. For example, a receivable that was due in 30 days but has not been paid after 45 days is more likely to be collected than a similar receivable that remains unpaid after 120 days. Based on prior experience, a company can estimate what portion of receivables of a specific age will not be paid.

The aging of accounts receivable method includes three steps as summarized in Exhibit 9.2:

1. **Prepare an aged listing of accounts receivable** with totals for each age category. Most accounting software will produce this report automatically.
2. **Estimate bad debt loss percentages for each category.** The percentage each company uses varies according to its circumstances. Generally, the longer an amount remains unpaid, the less likely it is to be collected. Therefore, a higher percentage is applied to amounts uncollected after 120 days than to those uncollected after 30 days.
3. **Compute the total estimate by multiplying the totals in Step 1 by the percentages in Step 2 and then summing across all categories.** The total across all aging categories ($1,000 + $2,121 + $5,317 + $2,120 = $10,558) equals the balance to which the Allowance for Doubtful Accounts will need to be adjusted at the end of the period.

The amount computed in Step 3 is the desired balance in the Allowance for Doubtful Accounts, not the amount of the adjustment. To compute the amount of the adjustment, you must subtract the existing, unadjusted balance from the desired adjusted balance computed in Step 3. Skechers had a beginning balance in the Allowance for Doubtful Accounts of $7,196 and had written off $1,229 in bad debts during the period, so its unadjusted credit balance would be $5,967 ($7,196 − $1,229). The desired credit balance computed in Exhibit 9.2 was $10,558, so an adjustment of $4,591 (= $10,558 − $5,967) needs to be recorded as a credit to the account. A corresponding amount is debited to Bad Debt Expense.

Exhibit 9.2 Estimating Uncollectible Amounts with an Aging of Accounts Receivable

		NUMBER OF DAYS UNPAID				
Customer	**Total**	**0–30**	**31–60**	**61–90**	**Over 90**	
Adam's Sports Stores	$ 648	$ 405	$ 198	$ 45	—	←Step 1—Age
Backyard Shoe Company	2,345	—	—	—	$2,345	
Other customers	185,305	91,388	52,822	37,935	3,160	
Total receivables	$188,298	$ 91,793	$53,020	$37,980	$5,505	
× Estimated bad debt percentages		1%	4%	14%	40%	←Step 2—Estimate
= **Estimated uncollectible**	$ 10,558	$ 918	$ 2,121	$ 5,317	$2,202	←Step 3—Compute

Desired balance	$ 10,558	Credit
−Unadjusted **credit** balance ($7,196 − $1,229)	5,967	Credit
Required adjustment	$ 4,591	Credit

Beginning balance	$7,196	
−Write-offs	1,229	
Unadjusted balance	$5,967	Credit (Debit if negative)

	Debit	Credit
Bad Debt Expense (+E, −OE)	4,591	
Allowance for Doubtful Accounts (+xA, −A)		4,591

Although the Allowance for Doubtful Accounts normally has a credit balance, it may have a **debit balance** before it is adjusted for uncollectible accounts. This situation occurs when a company has recorded write-offs that exceed previous estimates of uncollectible accounts. If so, you can still calculate the amount of the adjustment needed to reach the desired balance under the aging of accounts receivable method. The only difference is that to reach the desired balance, you need to record an amount equal to the desired balance **plus** the existing debit balance. For example, if the unadjusted balance was a debit of $1,000, the amount of the entry is computed as follows:

Desired balance	$ 10,558	Credit
+Unadjusted **debit** balance	1,000	Debit
Required adjustment	**$11,558**	**Credit**

Comparison of Methods

Students often fail to recognize that the approach to estimating bad debt expense using the percentage of credit sales method is different from that for the aging method. The difference in the approaches is illustrated in the following two T-accounts:

Allowance for Doubtful Accts (xA)			
		7,196	Beg. Bal.
Write-offs	1,229	**4,591**	**Estimate**
		10,558	End. Bal.

Percent of credit sales estimate

Allowance for Doubtful Accts (xA)			
		7,196	Beg. Bal.
Write-offs	1,229	4,591	Estimate
		10,558	**End. Bal.**

Desired balance from aging

- **Percentage of credit sales.** Directly compute the amount to be recorded as **Bad Debt Expense** on the **income statement** for the period in the adjusting journal entry.
- **Aging.** Compute the **desired ending balance** you would like to have in the **Allowance for Doubtful Accounts** on the **balance sheet** after you make the necessary adjusting entry. The difference between the current balance in the account and the desired balance is recorded as the adjusting entry for Bad Debt Expense for the period.

In either case, the balance sheet presentation for 2006 would show Accounts Receivable less Allowance for Doubtful Accounts of $177,740 ($188,298 – $10,558).

SELF-STUDY PRACTICE

In a previous year, Mad Catz reported a beginning balance in the Allowance for Doubtful Accounts of $5,971. It also recorded write-offs of bad accounts amounting to $3,979 (all numbers are expressed in thousands of dollars).

1. Assume that Mad Catz used the percentage of sales method and had estimated its bad debt loss rate to be 2 percent. Its credit sales for the year were $216,850. Compute Bad Debt Expense for the period and the ending balance in the Allowance for Doubtful Accounts.
2. Assume instead that Mad Catz used the aging method. The aging of accounts receivable produced a desired balance of $6,329. Compute Bad Debt Expense for the period and the ending balance in the Allowance for Doubtful Accounts. Use either the following equation or T-account to solve for the missing value.

Desired balance		Credit
–Unadjusted **credit** balance	______	Credit
Required adjustment		Credit

– Allowance for Doubtful Accts (xA) +	
	5,971 Beg. Bal.
	____

After you have finished, check your answers with the solution at the bottom of the next page.

Spotlight On FINANCIAL REPORTING

Bad Debt Policies

Skechers, Inc.

Companies must take action both to minimize the costs of bad debts and to accurately estimate those debts. Skechers described its policies regarding bad debts in its annual report, as follows:

> We provide a reserve against our receivables for estimated losses that may result from our customers' inability to pay. To minimize the likelihood of uncollectibility, customers' credit-worthiness is reviewed periodically based on external credit reporting services and our experience with the account, and it is adjusted accordingly. Should a customer's account become past due, we generally place a hold on the account and discontinue further shipments to that customer, minimizing further risk of loss. We determine the amount of the reserve by analyzing known uncollectible accounts, aged receivables, economic conditions in the customers' country or industry, historical losses and our customers' credit-worthiness. Amounts later determined and specifically identified to be uncollectible are charged or written off against this reserve.

Other Issues

Revising Estimates

Unless managers can see into the future, bad debt estimates always differ from the amounts that are later written off. Rather than go back and revise the initial estimates, companies are required to revise their bad debt estimates for the current period. That is, they correct overestimates in prior periods by lowering estimates in the current period; they correct underestimates in prior periods by raising estimates in the current period.

Account Recoveries

In the same way that someone you have written off as a friend might do something to win you back, a customer might pay an account balance that has been written off. The collection of a previously written off account, called a **recovery,** is accounted for in two parts. First, you put the receivable back on the books by reversing the write-off. Second, you record the collection of the account. To illustrate, let's assume that Skechers collects $50 on an account previously written off. The recovery would be recorded with the following journal entries:

		Debit	Credit
1.	Accounts Receivable (+A)	50	
	Allowance for Doubtful Accounts (+xA, −A)		50
2.	Cash (+A)	50	
	Accounts Receivable (−A)		50

} Reverse the write-off

} Record the collection

Look closely at these journal entries and you will see that Accounts Receivable is first debited and then credited for $50. Although it is tempting to cancel out these two amounts, doing so would create an inaccurate credit history for the customer. After all is said and done, the customer's balance was removed because it was collected, not written off, and the accounting records should reflect that fact.

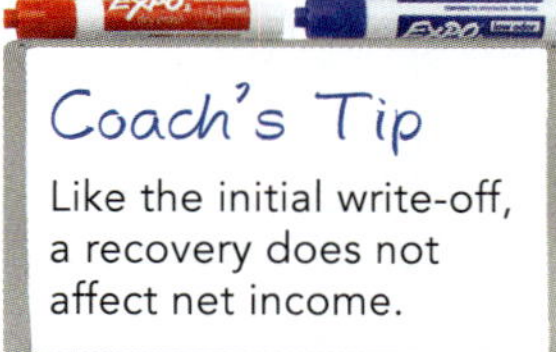
Coach's Tip
Like the initial write-off, a recovery does not affect net income.

Direct Write-Off Method

You should be aware that some small companies do not use the allowance method. Instead, they use an alternative approach called the **direct write-off method**. Using this single-step approach, these companies record bad debt expense only when they write off specific accounts. Although this alternative method is easier to use, it violates both the conservatism and matching principles. Thus, it is not considered a generally accepted accounting method. However, the Internal Revenue Service (IRS) accepts the use of this method for tax purposes, so we demonstrate it in Supplement 9A at the end of this chapter.

Spotlight On BUSINESS DECISIONS

Deciding Whether to Grant Credit

Given the costs of granting credit (recordkeeping, collections, bad debts), why do so many companies grant credit? As in most business decisions, the expected benefits of granting credit outweigh the costs. Consider the following example:

Nutware Productions Inc. generated sales of $30,000 and gross profit of $10,000 last year. The company estimates that it would have generated sales of $60,000 and gross profit of $20,000 by extending credit but would have incurred additional costs totaling $11,000 for recordkeeping, collections, and bad debts. Should the company have extended credit?

Benefits (extra gross profit) ($20,000 − $10,000)	$10,000
Costs (additional recordkeeping, collections & bad debts)	11,000
Gain (Loss) from granting credit	$ (1,000)

In this example, the costs outweigh the benefits, so Nutware was better off by forgoing the additional sales that the company would have generated by granting credit. If the benefits had exceeded the costs, granting credit would have been the right decision.

Solution to Self-Study Practice

1.

Credit sales this year	$216,850
× Bad debt loss rate (2%)	× 0.02
Bad debt expense this year	$ 4,337

Allowance for Doubtful Accts

		5,971	Beg. Bal
Write-offs	3,979	4,337	Estimate
		6,329	End. Bal.

2.

Desired balance	6,329	Credit
−Unadjusted **credit** balance*	1,992	Credit
Required adjustment	4,337	Credit

*Beginning − Write-offs = Unadjusted Balance
$5,971 − $3,979 = $1,992

Allowance for Doubtful Accts

		5,971	Beg. Bal
Write-offs	3,979	4,337	Estimate
		6,329	End. Bal.

Beginning + Bad Debt Estimate − Write-offs = Ending
$5,971 + X − $3,979 = $6,329; X = $4,337

NOTES RECEIVABLE AND INTEREST REVENUE

Learning Objective 4

Compute and report interest on notes receivable.

The accounting issues for notes receivable are similar to those for accounts receivable with one exception. Unlike accounts receivable, which do not normally incur interest until they become overdue, notes receivable start incurring interest the day they are created. Let's look at how to calculate the interest.

Calculating Interest

To calculate interest, you need to consider three variables: (1) the **principal,** which is simply the amount of the note receivable, (2) the **interest rate** charged on the note, and (3) the **time** period covered in the interest calculation. Because **interest rates are always stated as an annual percentage even if the note is for less than a year,** the time period is the portion of a year for which the interest is calculated. Ask yourself how many months out of 12 or how many days out of 365 the interest period covers. Then use the following interest formula to calculate the interest:

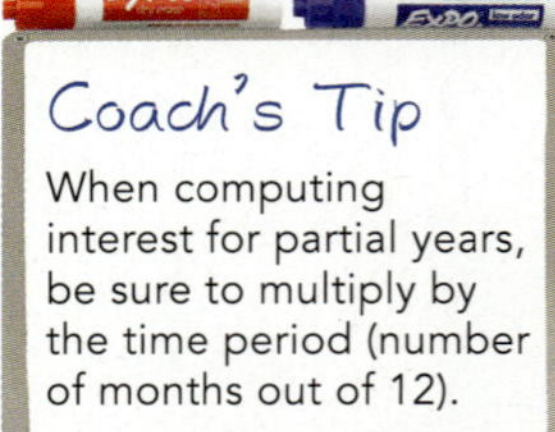

Interest (I) = Principal (P) × Interest Rate (R) × Time (T)

Many financial institutions use the number of days out of 365 to compute interest. In doing homework assignments, assume that the time is measured in terms of number of months out of 12. See Exhibit 9.3 for the computation of interest for three different notes, 6, 8, and 10 percent.

Recording Notes Receivable and Interest Revenue

The four key events that occur with any note are (1) establishing the note, (2) accruing interest earned but not received, (3) recording interest payments received, and (4) recording principal payments received. Assume that on November 1, 2009, Skechers lent $100,000 to an inventor by creating a note that required the inventor to pay Skechers 6 percent interest and the $100,000 principal on October 31, 2010. Skechers prepared year-end financial statements as of December 31, 2009, but made no other adjustments for interest during the year.

Establishing a Note Receivable

The $100,000 loan that created the note receivable has the following accounting equation effects, which Skechers would record using the following journal entry:

	Debit	Credit
Note Receivable (+A)	100,000	
Cash (−A)		100,000

Assets		=	Liabilities	+	Owners' Equity
Note Receivable	+100,000				
Cash	−100,000				

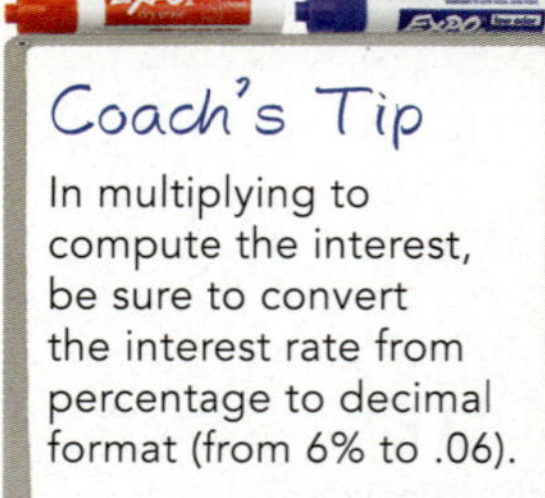

Exhibit 9.3 Sample Interest Computations

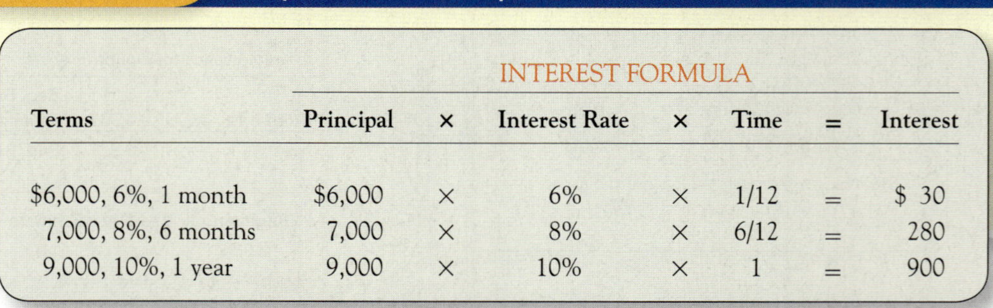

Terms	Principal	×	Interest Rate	×	Time	=	Interest
$6,000, 6%, 1 month	$6,000	×	6%	×	1/12	=	$ 30
7,000, 8%, 6 months	7,000	×	8%	×	6/12	=	280
9,000, 10%, 1 year	9,000	×	10%	×	1	=	900

(INTEREST FORMULA spans Principal through Time columns.)

Exhibit 9.4 Use of a Timeline to Keep Track of Interest Periods

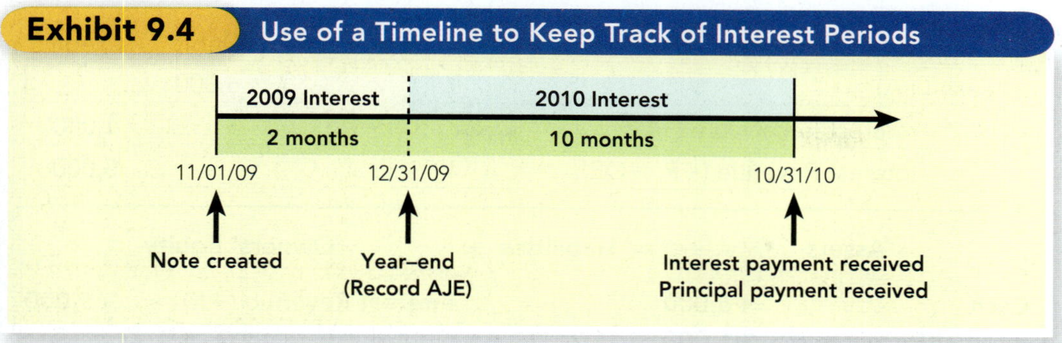

Accruing Interest Earned

Although a note receivable earns interest each day, interest payments might be made only once or twice a year. Thus, a company with a note receivable needs to accrue interest revenue and interest receivable at the end of each accounting period (unless it happens to receive an interest payment on the last day of the period).

The timeline in Exhibit 9.4 shows how Skechers should account for the interest revenue earned from the note over its one-year term. Note that between the date of the note's creation (November 1, 2009) and the year-end (December 31, 2009), Skechers earned two months of interest revenue (the yellow portion of the time line) because the note was outstanding for all of November and December 2009. As you learned in Chapter 4, when a company has earned interest in the current period but has not yet recorded the interest, the company must make an adjusting entry at the end of the current period to accrue the interest earned. The amount of interest to record for the two months of 2009 is computed as follows:

Interest (I)	=	Principal (P)	×	Interest Rate (I)	×	Time (T)
$1,000	=	$100,000	×	6%	×	2/12

The effect of this adjustment, along with the adjusting journal entry to record the $1,000 of interest revenue receivable on December 31, 2009, is as follows.

	Debit	Credit
Interest Receivable (+A)	1,000	
Interest Revenue (+R, +OE)		1,000

Assets		=	Liabilities	+	Owners' Equity	
Interest Receivable	+1,000				Interest Revenue (+R)	+1,000

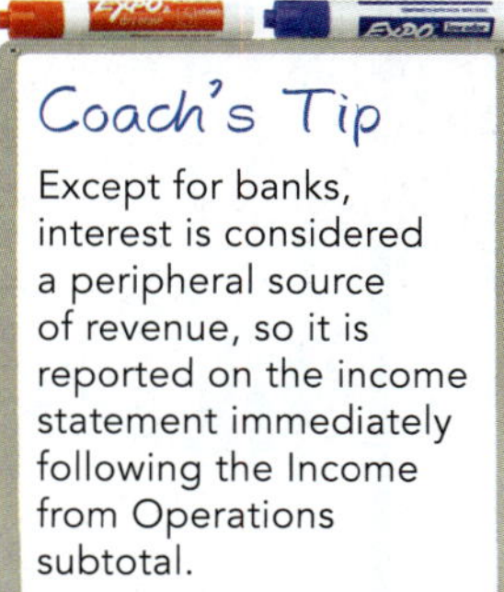

Coach's Tip

Except for banks, interest is considered a peripheral source of revenue, so it is reported on the income statement immediately following the Income from Operations subtotal.

Recording Interest Received

The timeline in Exhibit 9.4 indicates that on October 31, 2010, Skechers received a cash interest payment of $6,000 (= $100,000 × 6% × 12/12). This interest payment included the $1,000 accrued as interest receivable on December 31, 2009, plus the $5,000 earned during the 10-month period from January 1 to October 31, 2010, which had yet to be recorded. When Skechers received this interest, the company's accountant recorded the receipt of $6,000 in cash. Of that amount, $1,000 reduced the Interest Receivable, and the remaining of $5,000 was recorded as Interest Revenue for 2010.

	Debit	Credit
Cash (+A)	6,000	
Interest Receivable (–A)		1,000
Interest Revenue (+R, +OE)		5,000

Assets		=	Liabilities	+	Owners' Equity	
Cash	+6,000				Interest Revenue (+R)	+5,000
Interest Receivable	−1,000					

Recording Principal Received

A company accounts for the collection of a note receivable just as it does the collection of an account receivable. Assuming that Skechers received the $100,000 principal that was due on October 31, 2010, the journal entry would be:

	Debit	Credit
Cash (+A)	100,000	
Note Receivable (–A)		100,000

Assets		=	Liabilities	+	Owners' Equity
Cash	+100,000				
Note Receivable	−100,000				

Accounting for Uncollectible Notes

Just as a customer might fail to pay an accounts receivable balance, some companies might fail to pay the principal (and interest) owed on a note receivable. When a note receivable's collectibility is in doubt, the company should record an allowance for doubtful accounts against the note receivable, just as it records an allowance for doubtful accounts against accounts receivable.

SELF-STUDY PRACTICE

Assume that Mad Catz lent $12,000 to an employee on October 1, 2008, by creating a note that required that the employee pay the principal and 8 percent interest on September 30, 2009. Assume that the company makes adjusting entries only at year-end on December 31.

1. Record the creation of the note.
2. Record any necessary end-of-period adjusting entry to be made at the end of 2008.
3. Record the receipt of interest and principal on September 30, 2009.

After you have finished, check your answers with the solution at the bottom of the page.

Solution to Self-Study Practice

1.	Note Receivable (+A)	12,000	
	Cash (−A)		12,000
2.	Interest Receivable (+A) ($12,000 × 8% × 3/12)	240	
	Interest Revenue (+R, +OE)		240
3.	Cash (+A) ($12,000 × 8% × 12/12)	960	
	Interest Receivable (−A) ($12,000 × 8% × 3/12)		240
	Interest Revenue (+R, +OE) ($12,000 × 8% × 9/12)		720
	Cash (+A)	12,000	
	Note Receivable (−A)		12,000

Spotlight On ETHICS

Resetting the Clock

Earlier in this chapter you saw that as customer balances grow older, the Allowance for Doubtful Accounts should be increased. Because increases in the Allowance for Doubtful Accounts require increases in Bad Debt Expense, the result of an increase in the age of customer accounts should be a decrease in net income.

Managers at MCI knew about these accounting effects. To avoid reducing net income, they "reset the clock" on the amounts customers owed. They did so by making loans to customers, who then used the money to pay off their account balances. By replacing old accounts receivable with new notes receivable, managers avoided recording approximately $70 million in bad debts. Their scheme did not last for long, though. After the fraud was revealed, the managers involved spent several years in prison and are now working to pay off more than $10 million in fines.

EVALUATING RECEIVABLES MANAGEMENT

Receivables Turnover Analysis

Learning Objective 5

Compute and interpret the receivables turnover ratio.

Managers, directors, investors, and creditors can evaluate the effectiveness of a company's credit-granting and collection activities by performing a receivables turnover analysis. The idea behind the analysis is simple. When a company sells goods or services on credit, the receivables balance goes up; when the company collects from customers, the receivables balance goes down. This process of selling and collecting, called **receivables turnover,** is repeated over and over during each accounting period for each customer as in the following diagram.

Receivables Turnover Analysis

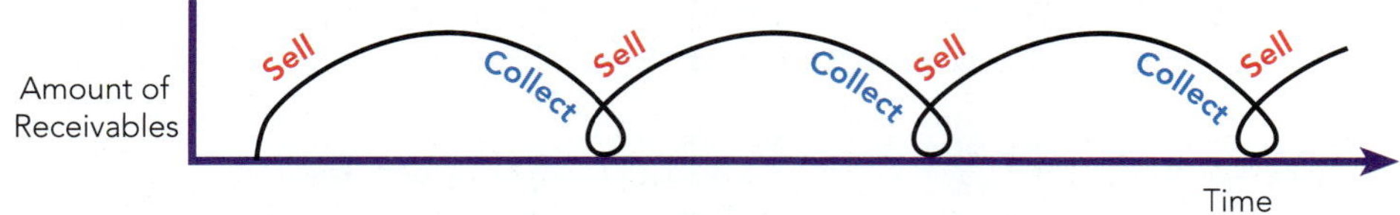

The receivables turnover ratio indicates how many times, on average, this process of selling and collecting is repeated during the period. The higher the ratio, the faster the collection of receivables. A low turnover ratio can be a warning sign, suggesting that the company is allowing too long a time for customers to pay. As you learned earlier in this chapter, the longer an account goes without being collected, the higher is the risk that it will never be collected. Analysts watch for changes in the receivables turnover ratio because a sudden decline may mean that a company is recording sales of merchandise that customers are likely to return later. It also may mean that the company is allowing customers more time to pay their accounts to entice them to buy as much as possible—a practice known as **channel stuffing.**

Coach's Tip

Days to collect is also called days sales outstanding.

Rather than evaluate the **number** of times that accounts receivable turn over during the year, some people find it easier to think in terms of the **length** of time (in days) needed to collect accounts receivable (called **days to collect**). Converting the year's receivables turnover ratio into the average days to collect is easy. Simply divide 365 by the receivables turnover ratio. This alternative measure does not tell analysts anything more about the company's ability to collect receivables than the receivables turnover ratio does.

Financial Analysis Tools

Name of Measure	Formula	What It Tells You
Receivables Turnover Ratio	$\frac{\text{Net Sales Revenue}}{\text{Average Net Receivables}}$	• Number of times receivables turn over during the period • A higher ratio means faster turnover
Days to Collect	$\frac{365}{\text{Receivables Turnover Ratio}}$	• Average number of days from sale on account to collection • A higher number means a longer time to collect

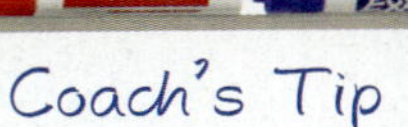

Coach's Tip

The average receivables balance outstanding over the entire year is used in the bottom of the receivables turnover ratio. It is computed as (Beginning Balance + Ending Balance)/2.

Skechers' receivables turnover ratio and days to collect would be computed as follows:

$$\text{Receivables Turnover Ratio} = \frac{\text{Net Sales Revenue}}{\text{Average Net Receivables}} = \frac{\$1{,}205}{(\$177.7 + \$134.6)/2} = 7.7 \text{ times}$$

$$\text{Days to Collect} = \frac{365}{\text{Receivables Turnover Ratio}} = \frac{365 \text{ days}}{7.7 \text{ times}} = 47.4 \text{ days}$$

Comparison to Benchmarks

To Stated Credit Terms

By calculating the days to collect, you can compare a company's collection performance to its stated collections policy. You might recall from Chapter 6 that when companies sell on account, they specify the length of the credit period (as well as any discounts for prompt payment). By comparing the number of days to collect to the length of the credit period, you can gain a sense of whether customers are complying with the stated policy. Managers inside a company watch this measure closely, and so do investors and creditors on the outside. Why? If customers appear to be disregarding the stated credit period, they may be dissatisfied with the product or service they bought.

Spotlight On FINANCIAL REPORTING

Comparing Days to Collect with Stated Credit Terms Kellogg

Kellogg is one of the rare companies that provides information about its normal credit policies in its annual report. In the notes to the financial statements, Kellogg indicates that the stated policy is to require payment from customers 11 to 16 days after making a sale. The company's collection period of 18 to 19 days suggests that customers are generally willing to comply.

> In the United States, the Company generally has required payment for goods sold eleven or sixteen days subsequent to the date of invoice as 2%,10 / net 11 or 1%,15 / net 16, and days sales outstanding (DSO) averages 18–19 days.

To Other Companies or Prior Periods

Receivables turnover ratios and number of days to collect often vary across industries. Compare the ratios for Skechers, Boeing (an airplane manufacturer), and Deere & Co. (a farm implements company) in Exhibit 9.5. As the exhibit shows, Skechers turned its receivables over 7.7 times, or once every 47 days. Boeing had a turnover ratio of 11.7, which translates to a jet-fast collection period of about 31 days. Deere & Co. trailed behind with a ratio of 6.5, or about 56 days to collect.

Given the wide range in ratios among industries, a company's receivables turnover should be compared only to those of other companies in the same industry or to the company's own ratio from prior periods. For practice at computing these ratios and comparing them to those from prior periods, try the following Self-Study Practice, which asks you to calculate Skechers' receivables turnover ratio and days to collect in 2005.

SELF-STUDY PRACTICE

Skechers reported net accounts receivable of $134.6 on December 31, 2005, and $120.4 on December 31, 2004. Credit sales were $1,006 during 2005. (All numbers are in millions.) Use this information to calculate Skechers' receivables turnover and days to collect in 2005.

2005 Receivables Turnover	2005 Days to Collect
$\dfrac{______}{(_____ + _____)/2}$ = _____ times	$\dfrac{365 \text{ days}}{_____ \text{ times}}$ = _____ days

When you have finished, check your answers with the solutions at the bottom of the next page.

Exhibit 9.5 Receivables Turnover in Three Different Industries

Company	Relevant Information (in millions)	2006	2005	2006 Accounts Receivable Turnover Calculation	2006 Days to Collect Calculation
Skechers, Inc.	Net sales	$1,205	$1,006	$\frac{\$1,205}{(\$177.7 + \$134.6)/2} = 7.7$ times	$\frac{365 \text{ days}}{7.7 \text{ times}} = 47.4$ days
	Net accounts receivable	$177.7	$134.6		
		2006	2005		
Boeing	Net sales	$61,530	$54,845	$\frac{\$61,530}{(\$5,285 + \$5,246)/2} = 11.7$ times	$\frac{365 \text{ days}}{11.7 \text{ times}} = 31.2$ days
	Net accounts receivable	$ 5,285	$ 5,246		
		2006	2005		
Deere & Co.	Net sales	$19,884	$19,401	$\frac{\$19,884}{(\$3,038 + \$3,118)/2} = 6.5$ times	$\frac{365 \text{ days}}{6.5 \text{ times}} = 56.2$ days
	Net accounts receivable	$ 3,038	$ 3,118		

Spotlight On BUSINESS DECISIONS

Factoring Receivables

To generate the cash needed to pay for a company's business activities, managers must ensure that the company collects receivables on a timely basis. You might wonder what managers can do to speed up sluggish collections. One approach is to sell outstanding accounts receivable to another company, called a **factor.** In this factoring arrangement, your company receives cash for the receivables it sells to the factor (minus a factoring fee), and the factor receives the right to collect the outstanding amounts your customers owe. In the same way that you can get cash immediately for any check you bring to a local Checks Cashed store, factoring is a fast and easy way for your company to get cash for receivables. This service does come at a cost, however. The factoring fee can amount to as much as 3 percent of the receivables sold.

Demonstration Case A

Shooby Dooby Shoes (SDS) sold $950,000 in merchandise on credit during 2009. During the same year, SDS determined that a $500 account balance owed by a deceased customer (R. Cutler) was uncollectible.

Required:

1. Prepare the journal entry to record the write-off of R. Cutler's account receivable.
2. Assume that SDS uses the aging of accounts receivable method and has collected the information presented in the aging schedule that follows. As of December 31, 2009, the Allowance for

Solution to Self-Study Practice

$$\frac{1,006}{\$(134.6 + 120.4)/2} = 7.9 \text{ times} \quad 365 \div 7.9 = 46.2 \text{ days}$$

Doubtful Accounts had an unadjusted credit balance of $3,000. Compute the desired balance for uncollectible accounts and prepare a journal entry to record the bad debt expense.

		NUMBER OF DAYS UNPAID			
	Total	0–30	31–60	61–90	>90
Total receivables	$171,000	$50,000	$80,000	$40,000	$1,000
× Estimated bad debt %		× 1%	× 5%	× 15%	× 50%
= Estimated uncollectible					

3. Assume SDS reported net accounts receivable of $160,000 on December 31, 2009, and $167,586 on December 31, 2008. Calculate the receivables turnover ratio for 2009.
4. If the receivables turnover ratio was 6.4 in 2008, what was the number of days to collect in 2008? Given your calculations in requirement 3, were SDS collections in 2009 faster or slower than collections in 2008?
5. Assume that SDS uses the percentage of credit sales method (rather than the aging of accounts receivable method) for estimating bad debt expense. If SDS estimates that 1 percent of credit sales will become bad debts, prepare the journal entry to record those effects.

Suggested Solution

1.

Allowance for Doubtful Accounts (−xA, +A)	500	
Accounts Receivable (−A)		500

2. Using the aging of accounts receivable method, you first determine the desired balance in the Allowance for Doubtful Accounts ($11,000) and then subtract its unadjusted balance ($3,000) to determine the amount of the adjustment ($8,000 = $11,000 − 3,000).

		NUMBER OF DAYS UNPAID			
	Total	0–30	31–60	61–90	>90
Total receivable	$171,000	$50,000	$80,000	$40,000	$1,000
× Estimated bad debt %		× 1%	× 5%	× 15%	× 50%
= Estimated uncollectible	$11,000	$500	$4,000	$6,000	$500

Bad Debt Expense (+E, −OE)	8,000	
Allowance for Doubtful Accounts (+xA, −A)		8,000

3. The receivables turnover ratio is calculated as Net Sales ÷ Average Accounts Receivable. The average accounts receivable in 2009 was $163,793 (= ($160,000 + $167,586)/2), so the receivables turnover ratio for 2009 was 5.8 (= $950,000 ÷ $163,793).
4. Days to collect is calculated as 365 ÷ Receivables Turnover Ratio. The 6.4 turnover in 2008 equates to (365 ÷ 6.4 =) 57 days (and the 5.8 turnover in 2009 equates to 63 days). Collections were slower in 2009 than in 2008.
5. In the percentage of credit sales method, you multiply historical bad debt losses (1%) by this period's credit sales ($950,000) to directly estimate the amount of bad debt expense to record ($9,500 = 1% × $950,000).

Bad Debt Expense (+E, −OE) (0.01 × $950,000)	9,500	
Allowance for Doubtful Accounts (+xA, −A)		9,500

Demonstration Case B

On March 1 of a recent year, Rocky Mountain Chocolate Factory, Inc. (RMCF) reported that the company had issued $120,000 of notes receivable at an annual interest rate of 10 percent. As a public company, RMCF prepares financial statements every quarter: on May 31, August 31, November 30, and February 28. Assume the notes were created on March 1, 2009, when RMCF lent money to another company and RMCF receives interest payments semiannually on July 31 and January 31.

Required:

1. Calculate the amount of interest that RMCF earned each month after issuing the notes on March 1.
2. Calculate the amount of the interest payments that RMCF will receive on July 31, 2009, and January 31, 2010.
3. Prepare a timeline showing the amount of interest earned and received during each period.
4. Prepare journal entries to record the note's issuance, the interest earned, and the interest payments received on each given date.

Suggested Solution

1. Interest earned = Principal × Interest Rate × Time
   = $120,000 × 10% × 1/12 = $1,000 per month.

2. The period from March 1 to July 31 is five months. The period from August 1 to January 31 is six months.

   Interest Payment = Principal × Interest Rate × Time
   = $120,000 × 10% × 5/12 = $5,000 on July 31

   Interest Payment = Principal × Interest Rate × Time
   = $120,000 × 10% × 6/12 = $6,000 on January 31

3. Timeline

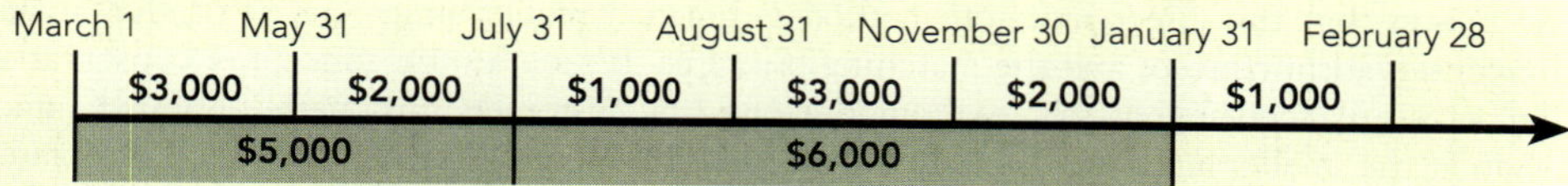

4. Journal Entries

March 1, 2009 (Notes Issued)

Notes Receivable (+A)	120,000	
Cash (−A)		120,000

May 31, 2009 (Interest Accrued)

Interest Receivable (+A)	3,000	
Interest Revenue (+R, +OE)		3,000

July 31, 2009 (Interest Payment Received)

Cash (+A)	5,000	
Interest Receivable (−A)		3,000
Interest Revenue (+R, +OE)		2,000

August 31, 2009 (Interest Accrued)

Interest Receivable (+A)	1,000	
Interest Revenue (+R, +OE)		1,000

November 30, 2009 (Interest Accrued)

Interest Receivable (+A)	3,000	
Interest Revenue (+R, +OE)		3,000

January 31, 2010 (Interest Payment Received)

Cash (+A)	6,000	
Interest Receivable (−A)		4,000
Interest Revenue (+R, +OE)		2,000

February 28, 2010 (Interest Accrued)

Interest Receivable (+A)	1,000	
Interest Revenue (+R, +OE)		1,000

Supplement 9A

Direct Write-Off Method

As noted earlier in this chapter, **the direct write-off method** is an alternative method of accounting for uncollectible accounts. This alternative approach does not estimate bad debts or use an allowance for doubtful accounts. Instead, you report sales when they occur and bad debt expense when you discover it. Again, although this method is acceptable for use on federal income tax returns, it is not acceptable for the preparation of financial statements under generally accepted accounting principles (GAAP).

The reason that the direct write-off method is not acceptable under GAAP is that it ignores both the conservatism concept and the matching principle. It violates the concept of conservatism by reporting accounts receivable at the total amount owed by customers (an overly optimistic amount) rather than at the smaller amount estimated to be collectible (a more realistic amount). It violates the matching principle by recording bad debt expense in the period when customer accounts are determined to be bad rather than in the period when the credit sales are actually made. The failure to match bad debt expense to sales distorts net income both in the period of the sale and in later periods when bad debts are discovered.

The direct write-off method makes no journal entries until the discovery of a bad debt. The journal entry used to record bad debt expense when a $1,000 customer account is determined to be uncollectible would be:

	Debit	Credit
Bad Debt Expense (+E, −OE)	1,000	
Accounts Receivable (−A)		1,000

Assets		=	Liabilities	+	Owners' Equity	
Accounts Receivable	−1,000				Bad Debt Expense (+E)	−1,000

Chapter Summary

LO1 Identify the different types of receivables. p. 382

- A credit sale on open account creates an account receivable. A note receivable is a promise in writing (a formal document) to pay (1) a specified amount of money, called the principal, on a definite future date known as the maturity date and (2) a specified amount of interest on one or more future dates.

- A sale of merchandise or services on credit in the normal course of business creates a trade receivable. A nontrade receivable arises from transactions other than the normal sale of merchandise or services.
- Receivables are classified as either current or noncurrent (short term or long term), depending on when cash is expected to be collected.

LO2 Account for and report the effects of uncollectible accounts. p. 383

- Under generally accepted accounting principles, companies must use the allowance method to account for uncollectibles. This method involves two steps:
    1. Estimate and record uncollectibles with an end-of-period adjusting entry that increases Bad Debt Expense (debit) and increases the Allowance for Doubtful Accounts (credit).
    2. Identify and write off specific customer balances in the period when they are determined to be uncollectible by decreasing the specific customer Account Receivable (credit) and decreasing the Allowance for Doubtful Accounts (debit).
- The adjusting entry (in 1) reduces net income as well as net accounts receivable. The write-off (in 2) affects neither.

LO3 Use two different methods to estimate uncollectible accounts. p. 385

- The percentage of credit sales method estimates bad debt expense by multiplying the historical percentage of bad debt losses by the current year's credit sales.

	Credit sales this year
×	Bad debt loss rate
	Bad debt expense this year

- The aging of accounts receivable method estimates bad debts based on the "age" of each amount in accounts receivable. The older and more overdue accounts receivable become, the less likely they are to be collected. Therefore, for each age category, we multiply an estimated bad debt loss percentage by the amount of the accounts receivable in that category. The total amount is the desired ending balance in the Allowance for Doubtful Accounts.

LO4 Compute and report interest on notes receivable. p. 390

- Calculate interest on a note receivable by multiplying the principal, the interest rate, and the time period (the number of months out of 12). As time passes and interest is earned on the note, accountants record an adjusting entry to accrue the interest revenue receivable on the note.

LO5 Compute and interpret the receivables turnover ratio. p. 393

- The receivables turnover ratio measures the effectiveness of credit-granting and collection activities. It reflects how many times, on average, a company recorded and collected trade receivables during the period.
- Analysts and creditors watch this ratio because a sudden decline may mean that a company is extending payment deadlines in an attempt to prop up lagging sales. Or it may mean that the company is recording sales of merchandise that customers are likely to return later.

Financial Analysis Tools

Name of Measure	Formula	What It Tells You
Receivables Turnover Ratio	$\dfrac{\text{Net Sales Revenue}}{\text{Average Net Receivables}}$	• The number of times receivables turn over during the period • A higher ratio means faster turnover ☺
Days to Collect	$\dfrac{365}{\text{Receivables Turnover Ratio}}$	• Average number of days from sale on account to collection • A higher number means a longer time to collect ☹

Key Terms

Account Receivable (p. 382)

Aging of Accounts Receivable Method (p. 386)

Allowance for Doubtful Accounts (p. 383)

Allowance Method (p. 383)

Bad Debt Expense (p. 383)

Direct Write-Off Method (p. 389)

Interest Formula (p. 390)

Note Receivable (p. 382)

Percentage of Accounts Receivable Method (p. 386)

Percentage of Credit Sales Method (p. 386)

Write-Off (p. 384)

See complete glossary in back of text.

Questions

1. What determines whether receivables are current or noncurrent assets?
2. Which basic accounting principles does the allowance method of accounting for bad debts satisfy?
3. Using the allowance method, is bad debt expense recognized in the period in which (*a*) sales related to the uncollectible account were made or (*b*) the seller learns that the customer is unable to pay?
4. What is the effect of the write-off of uncollectible accounts (using the allowance method) on (*a*) net income and (*b*) net accounts receivable?
5. What is the primary difference between accounts receivable and notes receivable?
6. What are the three components of the interest formula? Explain how this formula adjusts for interest periods that are less than a full year.
7. Are interest revenues most appropriately recognized in the period in which (*a*) a note receivable has remained unpaid or (*b*) the company receives a cash payment for the interest?
8. Does an increase in the receivables turnover ratio generally indicate faster or slower collection of receivables? Explain.
9. What two approaches can managers take to speed up sluggish collections of receivables? List one advantage and one disadvantage for each approach.
10. (Supplement) Describe how (and when) the direct write-off method accounts for uncollectible accounts. What are the disadvantages of this method?

Multiple Choice

Quiz 9-1
www.mhhe.com/LLPW1e

1. When a company using the allowance method writes off a specific customer's account receivable from the accounting system, how many of the following are true?
   - Total owners' equity remains the same.
   - Total assets remain the same.
   - Total expenses remain the same.

   a. None. c. Two.
   b. One. d. Three.
2. When using the allowance method, as bad debt expense is recorded,
   a. Total assets remain the same and owners' equity remains the same.
   b. Total assets decrease and owners' equity decreases.
   c. Total assets increase and owners' equity decreases.
   d. Total liabilities increase and owners' equity decreases.
3. You have determined that Carefree Company estimates bad debt expense using the aging of accounts receivable method. Generally, its estimate of uncollectible receivables resulting from the aging analysis equals:
   a. Bad debt expense for the current period.
   b. The ending balance in the Allowance for Doubtful Accounts for the period.
   c. The change in the Allowance for Doubtful Accounts for the period.
   d. None of the above.
4. Which of the following best describes the proper presentation of Accounts Receivable in the financial statements?
   a. Gross Accounts Receivable plus the Allowance for Doubtful Accounts in the asset section of the balance sheet.
   b. Gross Accounts Receivable in the asset section of the balance sheet and the Allowance for Doubtful Accounts in the expense section of the income statement.
   c. Gross Accounts Receivable less Bad Debt Expense in the asset section of the balance sheet.
   d. Gross Accounts Receivable less the Allowance for Doubtful Accounts in the asset section of the balance sheet.
5. If the Allowance for Doubtful Accounts had a beginning balance of $10,000, included write-offs of $5,000 (with no recoveries) during the period, and had a desired ending balance based on aging of $20,000, what was the amount of bad debt expense?
   a. $5,000.
   b. $10,000.
   c. $15,000.
   d. $20,000.
6. When an account receivable that has been written off is "recovered"
   a. Total assets increase. c. Owners' equity increases.
   b. Total assets decrease. d. None of the above.
7. If a 10 percent note receivable for $10,000 is created on January 1, 2006, and it has a maturity date of December 31, 2010,
   a. No interest revenue will be recorded in 2006.
   b. The note receivable will be classified as a current asset.
   c. Interest revenue of $1,000 will be recorded in 2006.
   d. None of the above.

8. If a 12 percent note receivable for $20,000 is created on December 1, 2009, and interest and principal are due on November 30, 2010, what amount of interest revenue would be reported for the year ended December 31, 2009?
   a. $2,400.
   b. $200.
   c. $2,200.
   d. None of the above.

9. If the receivables turnover ratio decreased during the year,
   a. The days to collect also decreased.
   b. Receivables collections slowed down.
   c. Sales revenues increased at a faster rate than receivables increased.
   d. None of the above.

10. In a recent year, Coca-Cola Company had a receivables turnover ratio of 10.2. Which of the following would cause the ratio to decrease?
    a. Write off additional customer accounts receivable.
    b. Increase the percentages used to estimate bad debts.
    c. Lengthen credit terms from 30 to 60 days.
    d. None of the above.

Solutions to Multiple-Choice Questions

1. d 2. b 3. b 4. d 5. c 6. d 7. c
8. b 9. b 10. c

Mini Exercises  Available with McGraw-Hill's Homework Manager

M9-1 Recording Write-Offs and Bad Debt Expense Using the Allowance Method LO2

Prepare journal entries for each transaction listed.

a. During the period, customer balances in the amount of $17,000 are written off.
b. At the end of the period, bad debt expense is estimated to be $14,000.

M9-2 Determining Financial Statement Effects of Write-Offs and Bad Debt Expense Using the Allowance Method LO2

Using the following categories, indicate the effects of the following transactions. Use + for increase and − for decrease and indicate the accounts affected and the amounts.

a. During the period, customer balances in the amount of $8,000 are written off.
b. At the end of the period, bad debt expense is estimated to be $10,000.

Assets	=	Liabilities	+	Owners' Equity

M9-3 Reporting Accounts Receivable and Recording Write-Offs Using the Allowance Method LO2

At the end of 2008, Extreme Fitness has adjusted balances of $800,000 in Accounts Receivable and $55,000 in the Allowance for Doubtful Accounts. On January 2, 2009, the company learns that certain customer accounts are not collectible, so management authorizes a write-off of these accounts totaling $5,000.

a. Show how the company would have reported its receivable accounts on December 31, 2008. As of that date, what amount did Extreme Fitness expect to collect?
b. Prepare the journal entry to write off the accounts on January 2, 2009.
c. Assuming no other transactions occurred between December 31, 2008, and January 3, 2009, show how Extreme Fitness would have reported its receivable accounts on January 3, 2009. As of that date, what amount did Extreme Fitness expect to collect? Has this changed from December 31, 2008? Explain why or why not.

M9-4 Recording Recoveries Using the Allowance Method LO2

Let's go a bit further with the example from M9-3. Assume that on February 2, 2009, Extreme Fitness received a payment of $500 from one of the customers whose balance had been written off. Prepare the journal entries to record this transaction.

M9-5 Estimating Bad Debts Using the Percentage of Credit Sales Method LO3

Assume Simple Co. had credit sales of $250,000 and cost of goods sold of $150,000 for the period. Simple uses the percentage of credit sales method and estimates that ½ percent of credit sales would result in uncollectible accounts. The balance in the Allowance for Doubtful Accounts before the end-of-period adjustment is made is $250. What amount of bad debt expense would the company record as an end-of-period adjustment?

LO3

M9-6 Estimating Bad Debts Using the Aging Method

Assume that Simple Co. had credit sales of $250,000 and cost of goods sold of $150,000 for the period. Simple uses the aging method and estimates that the appropriate ending balance in the Allowance for Doubtful Accounts is $1,500. The balance in the Allowance for Doubtful Accounts before the end-of-period adjustment is made is $250. What amount of bad debt expense would the company record as an end-of-period adjustment?

LO4

M9-7 Using the Interest Formula to Compute Interest

Complete the following table by computing the missing amounts (?) for the following independent cases.

Principal Amount on Note Receivable	Annual Interest Rate	Time Period	Interest Earned
a. $ 100,000	10%	6 months	?
b. ?	10%	12 months	$ 4,000
c. $ 50,000	?	9 months	$ 3,000

LO4

M9-8 Recording Note Receivable Transactions

Scotia Corporation hired a new corporate controller and agreed to provide her with a $20,000 relocation loan on a six-month, 7 percent note. Prepare journal entries to record the following transactions for Scotia Corporation. Rather than using letters to refer to each transaction, use the date of the transaction.

a. The company loans the money on January 1, 2008.

b. The new employee pays Scotia the full principal and interest on its maturity date.

LO4

M9-9 Recording Note Receivable Transactions

RecRoom Equipment Company received an $8,000, six-month, 6 percent note to settle an $8,000 unpaid balance owed by a customer. Prepare journal entries to record the following transactions for RecRoom. Rather than using letters to reference each transaction, use the date of the transaction.

a. The note is accepted by RecRoom on November 1, 2008, causing the company to increase its notes receivable and decrease its accounts receivable.

b. RecRoom adjusts its records for interest earned to December 31, 2008.

c. RecRoom receives the principal and interest on the note's maturity date.

LO5

M9-10 Determining the Effects of Credit Policy Changes on Receivables Turnover Ratio and Days to Collect

Indicate the most likely effect of the following changes in credit policy on the receivables turnover ratio and days to collect (+ for increase, − for decrease, and NE for no effect).

a. Granted credit with shorter payment deadlines.

b. Increased effectiveness of collection methods.

c. Granted credit to less creditworthy customers.

LO5

M9-11 Evaluating the Effect of Factoring on the Receivables Turnover Ratio and Computing the Cost of Factoring

After noting that its receivables turnover ratio had declined, Imperative Company decided to sell $500,000 of receivables to a factoring company. The factor charges a factoring fee of 3 percent of the receivables sold. All else equal, how will this affect Imperative's receivables turnover ratio in the future? How much cash does Imperative receive on the sale? Calculate the factoring fee and describe how it is reported by Imperative Company.

LO2

CATERPILLAR®

M9-12 Preparing Financial Statements

Caterpillar, Inc., reported the following accounts and amounts (in millions) in its December 31, 2005, year-end financial statements. Prepare the current assets section of a classified balance sheet. Assume that the Allowance for Doubtful Accounts relates to Accounts Receivable rather than Notes Receivable.

Accounts Payable	$3,471	Long-Term Debt	$19,545
Accounts Receivable	7,828	Long-Term Notes Receivable	10,301
Allowance for Doubtful Accounts	302	Notes Receivable—Current	6,442
Cash and Cash Equivalents	1,108	Other Current Assets	2,490
Inventories	5,224	Other Current Liabilities	9,952
Loans Payable—Current	5,569	Other Noncurrent Assets	5,990
		Property, Plant, and Equipment, net	7,888

M9-13 (Supplement) Recording Write-Offs and Reporting Accounts Receivable Using the Direct Write-off Method

Complete all requirements of M9-3, except assume that Extreme Fitness uses the direct write-off method. Note that this means Extreme does not have an Allowance for Doubtful Accounts balance.

Exercises

Available with McGraw-Hill's Homework Manager

E9-1 Recording Bad Debt Expense Estimates and Write-Offs LO2

During 2008, Blackhorse Productions, Inc., estimated bad debt losses of $9,750.

Required:

Prepare journal entries for each transaction.

a. On October 31, 2008, an account receivable for $1,000 from March 2008 was determined to be uncollectible and was written off.

b. The appropriate bad debt expense adjustment was recorded for the year 2008.

E9-2 Determining Financial Statement Effects of Bad Debt Expense Estimates and Write-Offs LO2

Using the following categories, indicate the effects of the transactions in E9-1. Use + for increase and − for decrease and indicate the accounts affected and the amounts.

Assets	=	Liabilities	+	Owners' Equity

E9-3 Recording and Determining the Effects of Write-Offs, Recoveries, and Bad Debt Expense Estimates on the Balance Sheet and Income Statement (Percentage of Sales Method) LO2, 3

Academic Dishonesty Investigations Ltd. operates a plagiarism detection service for universities and community colleges. While most of its customers reliably pay amounts owed, the company has historically experienced a 2 percent rate of bad debts on credit sales. The company estimates bad debts with the percentage of credit sales method.

Required:

1. Prepare journal entries for each transaction below.
   a. On March 31, 2008, 10 customers were billed for detection services totaling $25,000.
   b. On October 31, 2008, a customer balance for $1,500 from a prior year was determined to be uncollectible and was written off.
   c. On December 15, 2008, a customer paid an old balance of $900, which had been written off in a prior year.
   d. On December 31, 2008, the appropriate bad debt expense adjustment was recorded for the year 2008.
2. Complete the following table, indicating the amount and effect (+ for increase, − for decrease, and NE for no effect) of each transaction.

Transaction	Net Receivables	Net Sales	Income from Operations
a.			
b.			
c.			
d.			

LO2, 3

E9-4 Recording, Reporting, and Evaluating a Bad Debt Estimate (Percentage of Credit Sales Method)

During the year ended December 31, 2007, Kelly's Camera Shop had sales revenue of $170,000, of which $85,000 was on credit. At the start of 2007, Accounts Receivable showed a $10,000 debit balance, and the Allowance for Doubtful Accounts showed an $800 credit balance. Collections of accounts receivable during 2007 amounted to $68,000.

Data during 2007 follows:

a. On December 10, 2007, a customer balance of $1,500 from a prior year was determined to be uncollectible, so it was written off.

b. On December 31, 2007, a decision was made to continue the accounting policy of basing estimated bad debt losses on 2 percent of credit sales for the year.

Required:

1. Give the required journal entries for the two events in December 2007.
2. Show how the amounts related to Accounts Receivable and Bad Debt Expense would be reported on the income statement and balance sheet for 2007.
3. On the basis of the data available, does the 2 percent rate appear to be reasonable? Explain.

LO2, 3

E9-5 Recording Write-Offs, Recoveries, and Bad Debt Expense Estimates (Aging Method)

Prior to recording the following, Elite Electronics, Incorporated had a credit balance of $2,000 in its allowance for doubtful accounts.

Required:

Prepare journal entries for each transaction.

a. On August 31, 2008, a customer balance for $300 from a prior year sale was determined to be uncollectible and was written off.

b. On December 15, 2008, the customer balance for $300 written off on August 31, 2008, was collected in full.

c. Based on an aging of accounts receivable, the company determined that the December 31 balance in the Allowance for Doubtful Accounts should be $5,600. On December 31, 2008, the appropriate bad debt adjustment was recorded.

LO2, 3

E9-6 Determining Financial Statement Effects of Write-Offs, Recoveries, and Bad Debt Expense Estimates (Aging Method)

Using the following categories, indicate the effects of the transactions in E9-5.

Use + for increase and − for decrease and indicate the accounts affected and the amounts.

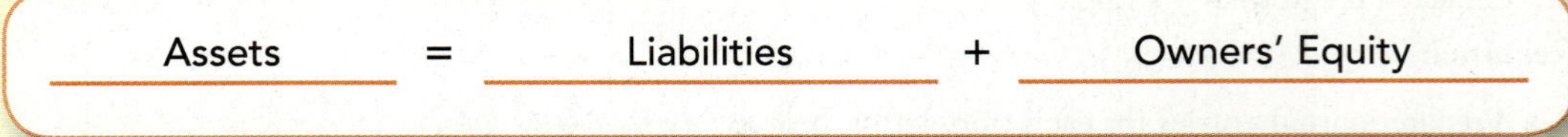

LO2, 3

E9-7 Computing Bad Debt Expense Using Aging of Accounts Receivable Method

Young and Old Corporation (YOC) uses two aging categories to estimate uncollectible accounts. Accounts less than 60 days outstanding are considered young and have a 5 percent uncollectible rate. Accounts more than 60 days outstanding are considered old and have a 35 percent uncollectible rate.

Required:

1. If YOC has $10,000 of young accounts and $40,000 of old accounts, how much should be reported in the Allowance for Doubtful Accounts?
2. If YOC's Allowance for Doubtful Accounts currently has an unadjusted credit balance of $4,000, how much should be credited to the account?

3. If YOC's Allowance for Doubtful Accounts has an unadjusted debit balance of $500, how much should be credited to the account?
4. Explain how YOC's Allowance for Doubtful Accounts could have a debit balance.

E9-8 Computing Bad Debt Expense Using Aging of Accounts Receivable Method LO2, 3

Brown Cow Dairy uses the aging approach to estimate bad debt expense. The balance of each account receivable is aged on the basis of three time periods as follows: (1) 1–30 days old, $12,000, (2) 31–90 days old, $5,000, and (3) more than 90 days old, $3,000. Experience has shown that for each age group, the average loss rate on the amount of the receivable due to uncollectibility is (1) 3 percent, (2) 15 percent, and (3) 30 percent, respectively. At December 31, 2008 (end of the current year), the Allowance for Doubtful Accounts balance was $800 (credit) before the end-of-period adjusting entry is made.

Required:

1. Prepare an aging schedule to estimate an appropriate year-end balance for the Allowance for Doubtful Accounts.
2. What amount should be recorded as Bad Debt Expense for the current year?
3. If the unadjusted balance in the Allowance for Doubtful Accounts was a $600 debit balance, what would be the amount of Bad Debt Expense in 2008?

E9-9 Recording and Reporting Allowance for Doubtful Accounts Using Aging of Accounts Receivable Method LO2, 3

InnovativeTech, Inc. uses the aging approach to estimate bad debt expense. The balance of each account receivable is aged on the basis of three time periods as follows: (1) 1–30 days old, $75,000, (2) 31–90 days old, $10,000, and (3) more than 90 days old, $4,000. Experience has shown that for each age group, the average loss rate on the amount of the receivable due to uncollectibility is (1) 1 percent, (2) 15 percent, and (3) 40 percent, respectively. At December 31, 2009 (end of the current year), the Allowance for Doubtful Accounts balance was $100 (credit) before the end-of-period adjusting entry is made.

Required:

1. Prepare an aging schedule to estimate an appropriate year-end balance for the Allowance for Doubtful Accounts.
2. Prepare the appropriate bad debt expense adjusting entry for the year 2009.
3. Show how the various accounts related to accounts receivable should be shown on the December 31, 2009, balance sheet.

E9-10 Comprehensive Recording and Reporting of Credit Sales and Bad Debts Using Aging LO2, 3

Walgreens

Okay Optical, Inc. (OOI) began operations in January 2008 selling inexpensive sunglasses to large retailers like Walgreens and other smaller stores. Assume the following transactions occurred during its first six months of operations.

January	4	Sold merchandise to Walgreens for $20,000; the cost of these goods to OOI was $12,000.
February	2	Received payment in full from Walgreens.
March	9	Sold merchandise to Tony's Pharmacy on account for $3,000; the cost of these goods to OOI was $1,400.
April	22	Sold merchandise to Travis Pharmaco on account for $8,000. The cost to OOI was $4,400.
May	30	Sold merchandise to Anjuli Stores on account for $2,000; the cost to OOI was $1,200.
June	15	Received $6,500 on account from Travis Pharmaco.

Required:

1. Complete the following aged listing of customer accounts as of June 30, 2008.

Customer	Total Balance	June (1 month)	May (2 months)	April (3 months)	March (>3 months)
Anjuli Stores	$2,000				
Tony's Pharmacy	3,000				
Travis Pharmaco					
Walgreens					

2. Estimate the Allowance for Doubtful Accounts required at June 30, 2008, assuming the following uncollectible rates: one month, 1 percent; two months, 5 percent; three months, 20 percent; more than three months, 40 percent.
3. Show how OOI would report its accounts receivable on its June 30 balance sheet. What amounts would be reported on an income statement prepared for the six-month period ended June 30, 2008?
4. Bonus Question: In July 2008, OOI collected the balance due from Tony's Pharmacy but discovered that the balance due from Travis Pharmaco needed to be written off. Using this information, determine how accurate OOI was in estimating the Allowance for Doubtful Accounts needed for each of these two customers and in total.

LO4

E9-11 Recording Note Receivable Transactions, Including Accrual Adjustment for Interest

The following transactions took place for Smart Solutions Ltd.

2007	July 1	Loaned $70,000 to an employee of the company and received back a one-year, 10 percent note.
	Dec. 31	Accrued interest on the note.
2008	July 1	Received interest and principal on the note. (No interest has been accrued since December 31.)

Required:

Prepare the journal entries that Smart Solutions Ltd. would record for the above transactions.

LO4

E9-12 Recording Note Receivable Transactions, Including Accrual Adjustment for Interest

The following transactions took place for Parker's Grocery.

2008	Jan. 1	Loaned $50,000 to a cashier of the company and received back a one-year, 7 percent note.
	June 30	Accrued interest on the note.
	Dec. 31	Received interest and principal on the note. (No interest has been accrued since June 30.)

Required:

Prepare the journal entries that Parker's Grocery would record for the above transactions.

LO4

E9-13 Recording Note Receivable Transactions, Including Accrual Adjustment for Interest

To attract retailers to its shopping center, the Marketplace Mall will lend money to tenants under formal contracts, provided that they use it to renovate their store space. On November 1, 2008, the company loaned $100,000 to a new tenant on a one-year note with a stated annual interest rate of 6 percent. Interest is to be received by Marketplace Mall on April 30, 2009, and at maturity on October 31, 2009.

Required:

Prepare journal entries that Marketplace Mall would record related to this note on the following dates: (*a*) November 1, 2008; (*b*) December 31, 2008 (Marketplace Mall's fiscal year-end); (*c*) April 30, 2009; and (*d*) October 31, 2009.

LO2, 5
Microsoft

E9-14 Using Financial Statement Disclosures to Infer Write-Offs and Bad Debt Expense and to Calculate the Receivables Turnover Ratio

Microsoft develops, produces, and markets a wide range of computer software including the Windows operating system. Microsoft reported the following information about net sales revenue and accounts receivable (in millions).

	June 30, Current Year	June 30, Prior Year
Accounts receivable, net of allowances of $142 and $171	$ 9,316	$ 7,180
Net revenues	44,282	39,788

According to its Form 10-K, Microsoft recorded bad debt expense of $40 and did not recover any previously written off accounts during the current year.

Required:

1. What amount of accounts receivable was written off during the current year? (Hint: Construct the T-account for the Allowance for Doubtful Accounts and solve for the missing number.)
2. What was Microsoft's receivables turnover ratio for the current year?

E9-15 Using Financial Statement Disclosures to Infer Bad Debt Expense LO2 Sears

The annual report for Sears Holding Corporation contained the following information (in millions):

	Prior Year	Current Year
Accounts receivable	$686	$846
Allowance for doubtful accounts	(40)	(35)
Accounts receivable, net	$646	$811

A footnote to the financial statements disclosed that accounts receivable write-offs amounted to $92 during the current year. Assume Sears did not record any recoveries.

Required:

Determine the bad debt expense for the current year based on the above facts. (Hint: Construct the T-account for the Allowance for Doubtful Accounts and solve for the missing number.)

E9-16 Determining the Effects of Uncollectible Accounts on the Receivables Turnover Ratio LO2, 5

Complete the following table indicating the direction of the effect (+ for increase, − for decrease, and NE for no effect) of each transaction during 2009:

Transaction	Net Credit Sales	Average Net Accounts Receivable	Receivables Turnover Ratio
a. Writing off of $92,000,000 in uncollectible accounts.			
b. Recording bad debt expense.			

E9-17 Analyzing and Interpreting Receivables Turnover Ratio and Days to Collect LO5 FedEx

A recent annual report for FedEx Corporation contained the following data (in millions):

	MAY 31,	
	Current Year	Prior Year
Accounts receivable	$3,660	$3,422
Less: Allowance for doubtful accounts	144	125
Net accounts receivable	$3,516	$3,297
Net sales (assume all on credit)	$32,294	

Required:

1. Determine the accounts receivable turnover ratio and days to collect for the current year.
2. Explain the meaning of each number.

LO2, 5

E9-18 Determining the Effects of Bad Debts on Receivables Turnover Ratio

During 2008, Jesse Enterprises Corporation recorded credit sales of $650,000. Based on prior experience, the company estimates a 1 percent bad debt rate on credit sales. At the beginning of the year, the balance in Net Trade Accounts Receivable was $50,000. At the end of the year, but *before* the bad debt expense adjustment was recorded and before any bad debts had been written off, the balance in Net Trade Accounts Receivable was $55,500.

Required:

1. Assume that on December 31, 2008, the appropriate bad debt expense adjustment was recorded for the year 2008, and accounts receivable totaling $6,000 for the year were determined to be uncollectible and written off. What was the receivables turnover ratio for 2008?
2. Assume instead that on December 31, 2008, the appropriate bad debt expense adjustment was recorded for the year 2008, and $7,000 of accounts receivable was determined to be uncollectible and written off. What was the receivables turnover ratio for 2008?
3. Explain why the answers to requirements 1 and 2 differ or do not differ.

E9-19 (Supplement) Recording Write-Offs and Reporting Accounts Receivable Using the Direct Write-Off Method

Trevorson Electronics is a small company privately owned by Jon Trevorson, an electrician who installs wiring in new homes. Because the company's financial statements are prepared only for tax purposes, Jon uses the direct write-off method. During 2007, its first year of operations, Trevorson Electronics sold $30,000 of services on account. The company collected $26,000 of these receivables during the year, and Jon believed that the remaining $4,000 was fully collectible. In 2008, Jon discovered that none of the $4,000 would be collected, so he wrote off the entire amount. To make matters worse, Jon sold only $5,000 of services during the year.

Required:

1. Prepare journal entries to record the transactions in 2007 and 2008.
2. Using only the information provided (ignore other operating expenses), prepare comparative income statements for 2007 and 2008. Was 2007 really as profitable as indicated by its income statement? Was 2008 quite as bad as indicated by its income statement? What should Jon do if he wants better information for assessing his company's ability to generate profit?

Problems—Set A

Available with McGraw-Hill's Homework Manager

LO2, 3
Kraft Foods

PA9-1 Recording Accounts Receivable Transactions Using the Allowance Method

Kraft Foods Inc. is the second-largest food and beverage company in the world. Assume the company recently reported the following amounts in its unadjusted trial balance as of December 31, 2007 (all amounts in millions):

	Debits	Credits
Accounts Receivable	$3,900	
Allowance for Doubtful Accounts		$ 110
Sales		32,010

Required:

1. Assume Kraft uses the aging of accounts receivable method and estimates that $233 of accounts receivable will be uncollectible. Prepare the adjusting journal entry required at December 31, 2007, for recording bad debt expense.
2. Repeat requirement 1, except this time assume the unadjusted balance in Kraft's Allowance for Doubtful Accounts at December 31, 2007, was a debit balance of $20.
3. If one of Kraft's main customers declared bankruptcy in 2008, what journal entry would be used to write off its $15 balance?

4. Assume Kraft uses ½ of 1 percent of sales to estimate its bad debt expense for the year. If you also assume that no bad debt expense has been recorded for 2007, what adjusting journal entry would be required at December 31, 2007, for bad debt expense?

PA9-2 Interpreting Disclosure of Allowance for Doubtful Accounts

LO2
Stride Rite

Stride Rite, Corp., designs, develops, and markets performance-oriented athletic footwear, athletic apparel, and casual leather footwear. It recently disclosed the following information concerning the Allowance for Doubtful Accounts.

VALUATION AND QUALIFYING ACCOUNTS (DOLLARS IN THOUSANDS)

Allowance for Doubtful Accounts	Balance at Beginning of Year	Additions Charged to Bad Debt Expense	Deductions from Allowance	Balance at End of Year
	$1,547	$1,400	$1,638	$1,309

Required:

1. Record summary journal entries for the year related to (*a*) estimating bad debt expense and (*b*) writing off specific balances.
2. Create a T-account for the Allowance for Doubtful Accounts and enter into it the amounts from the above schedule. Then write the T-account in equation format to prove that the above items account for the changes in the account.
3. If Stride Rite had written off an additional $200 of accounts receivable during the year, how would net receivables have been affected? How would net income have been affected? Explain why.

PA9-3 Recording Notes Receivable Transactions

LO4

www.mhhe.com/LLPW1e

C&S Marketing (CSM) recently hired a new marketing director, Jeff Otos, for its downtown Minneapolis office. As part of the arrangement, CSM agreed on February 28, 2007, to advance Jeff $50,000 on a one-year, 8 percent note, with interest to be paid at maturity on February 28, 2008. CSM prepares financial statements on June 30 and December 31.

Required:

1. Prepare the journal entry that CSM will make to record the establishment of the note.
2. Prepare the journal entries that CSM will make to accrue interest on June 30 and December 31.
3. Prepare the journal entry that CSM will make to record the interest and principal payments on February 28, 2008.

PA9-4 Recording and Reporting Accounts Receivable and Notes Receivable Transactions

LO2, 4

www.mhhe.com/LLPW1e

Merle Adventures, Inc., is a distributor of kayaks, kayaking equipment, and kayaking accessories. The company ships mainly to retail stores in the northeastern United States. Most of its sales are made on account, but some particularly large orders are sold in exchange for notes receivable. Merle Adventures reported the following balances in its December 31, 2008, unadjusted trial balance:

	Debit	Credit
Accounts Receivable	$2,700,000	
Allowance for Doubtful Accounts		$ 11,000
Bad Debt Expense	0	
Interest Receivable	0	
Interest Revenue		0
Notes Receivable	20,000	

Notes Receivable consists of principal owed by a customer on a two-year, 6 percent note accepted on November 1, 2008. The note requires the customer to make annual interest payments on October 31, 2009 and 2010. Merle Adventures has no concerns about the collectibility of this note. Merle Adventures estimates that $25,000 of its accounts receivable will be uncollectible.

Required:

1. Prepare the December 31, 2008, adjusting journal entries related to Accounts Receivable and Notes Receivable.
2. Show how the adjusted balances for the above balance sheet accounts will be reported on Merle Adventures' classified balance sheet as of December 31, 2008.

LO2, 5
Coca-Cola
PepsiCo

PA9-5 Analyzing Allowance for Doubtful Accounts, Receivables Turnover Ratio, and Days to Collect

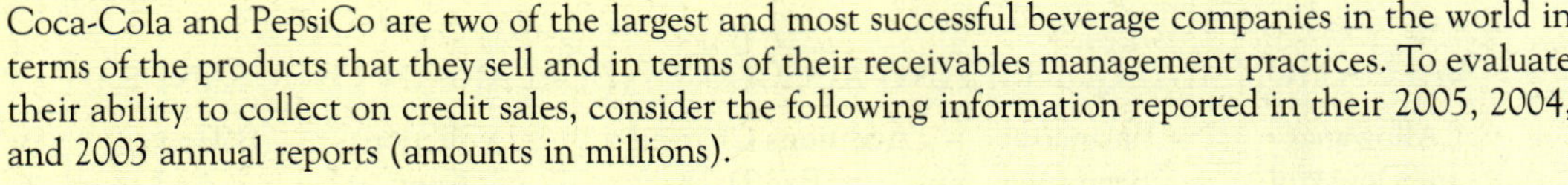
Coca-Cola and PepsiCo are two of the largest and most successful beverage companies in the world in terms of the products that they sell and in terms of their receivables management practices. To evaluate their ability to collect on credit sales, consider the following information reported in their 2005, 2004, and 2003 annual reports (amounts in millions).

www.mhhe.com/LLPW1e

	COCA-COLA			PEPSICO		
Fiscal Year Ended	2005	2004	2003	2005	2004	2003
Net sales	$23,104	$21,742	$20,857	$32,562	$29,261	$26,971
Accounts receivable	$ 2,353	$ 2,313	$ 2,152	$ 3,261	$ 2,999	$ 2,830
Allowance for doubtful accounts	72	69	61	105	116	121
Accounts receivable, net of allowance	$ 2,281	$ 2,244	$ 2,091	$ 3,156	$ 2,883	$ 2,709

Required:

Calculate the receivables turnover ratios and days to collect for Coca-Cola and PepsiCo for 2005 and 2004. (Round to one decimal place.) Which of the companies is quicker to convert its receivables into cash?

Problems—Set B

Available with McGraw-Hill's Homework Manager

LO2, 3

PB9-1 Recording Accounts Receivable Transactions Using the Allowance Method

Intel Corporation is a well-known supplier of computer chips, boards, systems, and software building blocks. Assume the company recently reported the following amounts in its unadjusted trial balance as of December 31, 2008 (all amounts in millions):

	Debits	Credits
Accounts Receivable	$3,300	
Allowance for Doubtful Accounts		$ 65
Sales		32,404

Required:

1. Assume Intel uses the aging of accounts receivable method and estimates that $200 of accounts receivable will be uncollectible. Prepare the adjusting journal entry required at December 31, 2008, for recording bad debt expense.
2. Repeat requirement 1, except this time assume the unadjusted balance in Intel's Allowance for Doubtful Accounts at December 31, 2008, was a debit balance of $20.
3. If one of Intel's main customers declared bankruptcy in 2009, what journal entry would be used to write off its $15 balance?
4. Assume Intel uses ¼ of 1 percent of sales to estimate its bad debt expense for the year. If you also assume that no bad debt expense has been recorded for 2008, what adjusting journal entry would be required at December 31, 2008, for bad debt expense?

LO2

PB9-2 Interpreting Disclosure of Allowance for Doubtful Accounts

Xerox Corporation is the company that made the photocopier popular, although it now describes itself as a technology and services enterprise that helps businesses deploy document management strategies and improve productivity. It recently disclosed the following information concerning the Allowance for Doubtful Accounts.

VALUATION AND QUALIFYING ACCOUNTS (DOLLARS IN MILLIONS)

Allowance for Doubtful Accounts	Balance at Beginning of Year	Additions Charged to Bad Debt Expense	Deductions from Allowance	Balance at End of Year
	$459	$72	$166	$365

Required:

1. Record summary journal entries for the year related to (*a*) estimating bad debt expense and (*b*) writing off specific balances.
2. Create a T-account for the Allowance for Doubtful Accounts and enter into it the amounts from the above schedule. Then, write the T-account in equation format to prove that the above items account for the changes in the account.
3. If Xerox had written off an additional $20 of accounts receivable during the year, how would net accounts receivable have been affected? How would net income have been affected? Explain why.

PB9-3 Recording Notes Receivable Transactions

LO4

Stinson Company recently agreed to loan an employee $100,000 for the purchase of a new house. The loan was established on May 31, 2007, and is a one-year, 6 percent note, with interest payments required on November 30, 2007, and May 31, 2008. Stinson Co. issues quarterly financial statements on March 31, June 30, September 30, and December 31.

Required:

1. Prepare the journal entry that Stinson Co. will make to record the establishment of the note.
2. Prepare the journal entries that Stinson Co. will make to record the interest accruals at each quarter-end and interest payments at each payment date.
2. Prepare the journal entry that Stinson Co. will make to record the principal payment at the maturity date.

PB9-4 Recording and Reporting Accounts Receivable and Notes Receivable Transactions

LO2, 4

Tractors-R-Us is a supplier of garden tractors. Most of its sales are made on account, but some particularly large orders are sold in exchange for notes receivable. Tractors-R-Us reported the following balances in its December 31, 2007, unadjusted trial balance:

	Debit	Credit
Accounts Receivable	$1,650,000	
Allowance for Doubtful Accounts		$ 16,000
Bad Debt Expense	0	
Interest Receivable	0	
Interest Revenue		0
Notes Receivable	115,000	

Notes receivable consists of principal owed by a customer on a two-year, 5 percent note accepted on July 1, 2007. The note requires the customer to make annual interest payments on June 30, 2008 and 2009. Tractors-R-Us has no concerns about the collectibility of this note. Tractors-R-Us does estimate, however, that $25,000 of its accounts receivable will be uncollectible.

Required:

1. Prepare the December 31, 2007, adjusting journal entries related to accounts receivable and notes receivable.
2. Show how the adjusted balances for the above balance sheet accounts will be reported on Tractors-R-Us's classified balance sheet as of December 31, 2007.

LO2, 5
Wal-Mart
Target

PB9-5 Analyzing Allowance for Doubtful Accounts, Receivables Turnover Ratio, and Days to Collect

Wal-Mart and Target are two of the largest and most successful retail chains in the world. To evaluate their ability to collect on credit sales, consider the following information reported in their 2005 and 2004 annual reports (amounts in millions).

	WAL-MART			TARGET		
Fiscal Year Ended	2005	2004	2003	2005	2004	2003
Net sales	$312,427	$285,222	$256,329	$52,620	$46,839	$42,025
Gross accounts receivable	$ 2,662	$ 1,715	$ 1,254	$ 6,117	$ 5,456	$ 4,973
Allowance for doubtful accounts	186	129	90	451	387	352
Accounts receivable, net of allowance	$ 2,476	$ 1,586	$ 1,164	$ 5,666	$ 5,069	$ 4,621

Required:

Calculate the receivables turnover ratios and days to collect for Wal-Mart and Target for 2005 and 2004. (Round to one decimal place.) Which of the companies is quicker to convert its receivables into cash?

Cases and Projects

LO2, 5

CP9-1 Finding Financial Information

Refer to the financial statements of The Home Depot in Appendix A at the end of this book, or download the annual report from the *Cases* section of the text's Web site at www.mhhe.com/LLPW1e.

1. Does the company report an Allowance for Doubtful Accounts on the balance sheet or in the notes? Explain why it does or does not. (*Hint:* The company refers to its Allowance for Doubtful Accounts as a "Valuation Reserve" related to Accounts Receivable.)
2. Compute the company's receivables turnover ratio and days to collect for the most recent year.

LO2, 5
Lowe's

CP9-2 Comparing Financial Information

Refer to the financial statements of Lowe's in Appendix B at the end of this book, or download the annual report from the *Cases* section of the text's Web site at www.mhhe.com/LLPW1e.

1. Does the company report Accounts Receivable or an Allowance for Doubtful Accounts in its financial statements? Explain why it does or does not.
2. Based on your observations for requirement 1, describe the usefulness of the receivables turnover ratio and days to collect analyses for companies that are involved in home improvement retail sales.

LO1, 2, 5

CP9-3 Internet-Based Team Research: Examining an Annual Report

As a team, select an industry to analyze. Using your Web browser, each team member should acquire the annual report or 10-K for one publicly traded company in the industry, with each member selecting a different company. (See CP1-3 in Chapter 1 for a description of possible resources for these tasks.)

Required:

1. On an individual basis, each team member should write a short report that incorporates the following:
   a. Calculate the receivables turnover ratio for the current and prior years, and explain any change between the two years. (To obtain the beginning accounts receivable number for the prior year, you will need the prior year's annual report.)
   b. Look in the 10-K for the Schedule II analysis of "Valuation and Qualifying Accounts," which provides additional disclosures concerning the allowance for doubtful accounts. From this schedule, determine the level of bad debt expense, as a percentage of sales, for the current and prior years.
2. Then, as a team, write a short report comparing and contrasting your companies using these attributes. Discuss any patterns across the companies that you as a team observe. Provide potential explanations for any differences discovered.

CP9-4 Ethical Decision Making: A Mini-Case LO2, 3, 5

Having just graduated with a business degree, you are excited to begin working as a junior accountant at Clear Optics, Inc. The company supplies lenses, frames, and sunglasses to opticians and retailers throughout the country. Clear Optics is currently in the process of finalizing its third quarter (Q3) operating results. All Q3 adjusting entries have been made, except for bad debt expense. The preliminary income statement for Q3 is shown below, along with reported results for Q2 and Q1.

Clear Optics, Inc.
Quarterly Income Statements
(amounts in thousands of U.S. dollars)

	Q3 (preliminary)	Q2 (as reported)	Q1 (as reported)
Net sales	$ 135,800	$ 135,460	$ 130,100
Cost of goods sold	58,400	58,250	55,990
Gross profit	77,400	77,210	74,110
Selling, general, and administrative expenses	56,560	53,975	53,690
Bad debt expense	—	6,050	4,200
Income before income taxes	20,840	17,185	16,220
Income tax expense	5,620	5,155	5,020
Net income	$ 15,220	$ 12,030	$ 11,200

The corporate controller has asked you to examine the Allowance for Doubtful Accounts and use the aged listing of accounts receivable to determine the adjustment needed to record estimated bad debts for the quarter. The controller states, "Although our customers are somewhat slower in paying this quarter, we can't afford to increase the Allowance for Doubtful Accounts. If anything, we need to decrease it—an adjusted balance of about $8,000 is what I'd like to see. Play around with our estimated bad debt loss rates until you get it to work."

You were somewhat confused by what the controller had told you, but you chalked it up to your lack of experience and decided to analyze the Allowance for Doubtful Accounts. You summarized the transactions recorded in the Allowance for Doubtful Accounts using the T-account below:

Allowance for Doubtful Accounts (xA)

		7,900	**January 1 bal. fwd.**
Q1 Write-offs	4,110	4,200	Q1 Bad debts estimate
		7,990	**March 31 adjusted**
Q2 Write-offs	4,120	6,050	Q2 Bad debts estimate
		9,920	**June 30 adjusted**
Q3 Write-offs	4,030	—	
		5,890	**September 30 unadjusted**

Required:

1. What bad debts estimate for Q3 will produce the $8,000 balance that the controller would like to see?
2. Prepare the adjusting journal entry that would be required to record this estimate.
3. If the entry in requirement 2 is made, what does it do to the Q3 income and the trend in earnings? (Assume that income tax expense does not change.)
4. Reconsider the statement the controller made to you. Is his suggestion a logical way to use the aging method to estimate bad debts?
5. What would be the Q3 net income if the bad debt expense estimate was the average of bad debt expense in Q2 and Q1? What would this do to the trend in net income across the three quarters? (Assume that income tax expense does not change.)
6. Is there any evidence of unethical behavior in this case? Explain your answer.

LO3 CP9-5 Using an Aging Schedule to Estimate Bad Debts and Improve Collections from Customers

Assume you were recently hired by Caffe D'Amore, the company that formulated the world's first flavored instant cappuccino and now manufactures several lines of flavored cappuccino mixes. The company recently has experienced tremendous growth in its sales to retailers, given that there are an estimated 8 million weekly drinkers of iced cappuccino nationwide. Given its tremendous sales growth, Caffe D'Amore's receivables also have grown. Your job is to evaluate and improve collections of the company's receivables.

By analyzing collections of accounts receivable over the past five years, you were able to estimate bad debt loss rates for balances of varying ages. To estimate this year's uncollectible accounts, you jotted down the historical loss rates on the last page of a recent aged listing of outstanding customer balances (see below).

		NUMBER OF DAYS UNPAID				
Customer	Total	1–30	31–60	61–90	91–120	Over 120
Subtotal from previous page	$280,000	$150,000	$60,000	$40,000	$20,000	$10,000
Jumpy Jim's Coffee	1,000					1,000
Pasadena Coffee Company	24,500	14,500	8,000	2,000		
Phillips Blender House	17,000	12,000	4,000		1,000	
Pugsly's Trading Post	26,600	19,600	7,000			
Q-Coffee	12,400	8,400	3,000	1,000		
Special Sips	10,000	6,000	4,000			
Uneasy Isaac's	3,500	500				3,000
Total accounts receivable	375,000	211,000	86,000	43,000	21,000	14,000
Bad debt loss rates		1%	5%	10%	15%	30%

Required:

1. With a spreadsheet, use the above information to calculate the total estimated uncollectible accounts.
2. Prepare the year-end adjusting journal entry to adjust the Allowance for Doubtful Accounts to the balance you calculated above. Assume the allowance account has an unadjusted credit balance of $8,000.
3. Of the customer account balances shown above on the last page of the aged listing, which should be your highest priority for contacting and pursuing collection?
4. Assume Jumpy Jim's Coffee account is determined to be uncollectible. Prepare the journal entry to write off the entire account balance.

10 Long-Lived Tangible and Intangible Assets

LEARNING OBJECTIVES

After completing this chapter, you should be able to:

Lectured slideshow–LP10-1
www.mhhe.com/LLPW1e

LO1 Define, classify, and explain the nature of long-lived assets.

LO2 Apply the cost principle to the acquisition of long-lived assets.

LO3 Apply various depreciation methods as economic benefits are used up over time.

LO4 Explain the effect of asset impairment on the financial statements.

LO5 Account for the disposal of long-lived tangible assets that are discarded or sold.

LO6 Account for the acquisition, use, and disposal of long-lived intangible assets.

LO7 Interpret the fixed asset turnover ratio.

LO8 Describe the factors to consider when comparing long-lived assets across companies.

Focus Company: CEDAR FAIR

Owner of the "Best Amusement Park in the World"

www.cedarfair.com

Most people agonize over how much money to spend on a house or which car to buy. After all, they will own these expensive items for many years to come. The same concerns exist when companies acquire long-lived assets. One of the major challenges business managers face is determining the right amount to invest in long-lived assets.

The task is especially challenging for companies such as Disney, Six Flags, and Cedar Fair, which operate amusement parks. Unlike merchandising companies, an amusement park cannot build up an inventory of unused seats to be sold sometime in the future. If managers build more rides than needed to satisfy park-goers, some rides will run with empty seats. Although the company will still incur all the costs of running the rides, it will generate only a fraction of the potential revenue. On the other hand, amusement parks can also run into trouble if they have too few rides to satisfy patrons. Who wants to stand in line for an hour or more? Because most people want to ride the newest, most exciting rides they can find, amusement park managers are always having to decide whether to buy new rides.

In this chapter, by studying specific long-lived asset decisions at Cedar Fair, you will see the significant effect that long-lived assets can have on a company's financial statements. Although manufacturing companies, retailers, and even airlines must deal with the same issues as Cedar Fair, the impact on this amusement park company is particularly significant because it relies almost exclusively on long-lived assets. As of December 31, 2007, in fact, Cedar Fair's rides, hotels, and other long-lived assets accounted for more than 97 percent of its total assets.

ORGANIZATION OF THE CHAPTER

DEFINITION AND CLASSIFICATION	TANGIBLE ASSETS: ACQUISITION, USE, IMPAIRMENT, AND DISPOSAL	INTANGIBLE ASSETS: TYPES, ACQUISITION, USE, AND DISPOSAL	EVALUATION OF LONG-LIVED ASSET USE
• Tangible Assets • Intangible Assets	• Acquisition of Tangible Assets • Use of Tangible Assets • Impairment of Tangible Assets • Disposal and Exchange of Tangible Assets	• Types of Intangible Assets • Acquisition, Use, and Disposal of Intangible Assets	• Turnover Analysis • Impact of Differences in Depreciation

DEFINITION AND CLASSIFICATION

Learning Objective 1

Define, classify, and explain the nature of long-lived assets.

Long-lived assets are business assets acquired for use over one or more years. These assets are not intended for resale. Instead, they are considered "productive" assets in the sense that they enable the business to produce the goods or services that the business then sells to customers. Examples include the ovens in which Pizza Aroma bakes pizza, the stores where Wal-Mart sells merchandise, and the legal rights that restrict use of The UPS Store logo to companies authorized by UPS. So when you hear the term "long-lived assets," think more broadly than just rusty old equipment. This class of assets includes two major types: tangible and intangible.[1]

Tangible Assets

Tangible assets are long-lived assets with physical substance—that is, you can see, touch, or kick them. The most prominent examples of tangible assets are land, buildings, factories, machinery, vehicles, office equipment, and furniture and fixtures. On the balance sheet, these assets are often grouped in the single line item Property, Plant, and Equipment. Because many long-lived tangible assets are fixed in place, these assets are also known as fixed assets. Cedar Fair's tangible assets include roller coasters, hotels, and nearly 5,000 acres of land in the western, midwestern, and northeastern United States.

Intangible Assets

Long-lived intangible assets have special rights but no physical substance. The existence of most intangible assets is indicated only by legal documents that describe their rights. Compared to the tangible assets that you see in daily life, such as store buildings and cash registers, intangible assets are probably less familiar to you. For this reason, we describe the various types of intangible assets in detail later in this chapter. For now, you can think of this category as including brand names, trademarks, and licensing rights such as the ones that allow Cedar Fair to use PEANUTS characters throughout its amusement parks.

See Exhibit 10.1 for the way Cedar Fair reported long-lived assets on its 2007 balance sheet. Looking at this exhibit, you can see how important tangible and intangible assets are to Cedar Fair. Of the $2.4 billion in assets Cedar Fair owned that year, long-lived assets comprised more than $2.3 billion ($1,933,562 + $422,358 = $2,355,920, in thousands).

In the next section, you will see how to account for tangible long-lived assets. The section that follows that one covers intangible assets.

[1] A third type of long-lived asset, one that includes assets that are depleted over time, such as oil wells or gold mines, is common in natural resource industries. Supplement 10A explains how to account for natural resource assets.

Exhibit 10.1 Cedar Fair's Assets

Cedar Fair L.P.

	(in thousands)	
December 31,	**2007**	**2006**
Assets		
Current assets		
Cash	$ 5,501	$ 30,203
Receivables	16,516	21,796
Inventories	26,884	26,377
Prepaids	13,847	26,132
Total current assets	62,748	104,508
Property and equipment		
Land	344,688	325,617
Land improvements	317,811	315,406
Buildings	582,654	580,588
Rides and equipment	1,270,852	1,237,790
Construction in progress	33,997	25,288
	2,550,002	2,484,689
Less: Accumulated depreciation	(616,440)	(498,980)
	1,933,562	1,985,709
Intangible assets	422,358	420,704
Total assets	$2,418,668	$2,510,921

TANGIBLE ASSETS: ACQUISITION, USE, IMPAIRMENT, AND DISPOSAL

Learning Objective 2

Apply the cost principle to the acquisition of long-lived assets.

Most companies own a variety of tangible assets. Earlier chapters introduced you to the most common examples: land, buildings, equipment, and automobiles. Other, less common examples include land improvements and construction in progress—both of which Cedar Fair reported on its balance sheet in Exhibit 10.1. Land improvements differ from land in that they deteriorate over time, whereas land is assumed to last forever. Land improvements include the sidewalks, pavement, landscaping, and trees that are added to improve the usefulness of land. Construction in progress includes the costs of constructing new buildings and equipment. When construction is finished, these costs are moved from this account into the building or equipment account to which they relate.

Acquisition of Tangible Assets

The general rule for accounting for tangible assets under the cost principle is that **all reasonable and necessary costs to acquire and prepare an asset for use should be recorded as a cost of the asset.** Accountants say costs have been capitalized when they are recorded as assets (rather than as expenses).

Deciding whether a cost is a reasonable and necessary cost of acquiring or preparing tangible assets for use can involve a great deal of judgment. Because capitalizing costs has a significant impact on both the balance sheet (it increases assets) and the income statement (it decreases expenses), some dishonest accountants and managers have exploited the judgment involved by capitalizing costs that should have been expensed. A well-known example of this tactic is described in the following Spotlight on Ethics feature. As you read the feature and the next couple of pages, focus on distinguishing between what types of costs should be capitalized and what types should be expensed.

Spotlight On ETHICS

The Biggest and Simplest Accounting Fraud

In the early 2000s, executives at WorldCom (now owned by Verizon) committed an $11 billion accounting fraud in part by capitalizing costs that should have been expensed. Their decision caused WorldCom to report huge increases in assets (rather than expenses) in the periods when the costs were incurred. The result was a balance sheet that appeared stronger (more total assets) and an income statement that appeared more profitable (lower expenses) than would have been the case had the costs been expensed. Learn more about this fraud in Case CP10-4 at the end of this chapter.

The illustration that follows shows the types of cost that should be capitalized when a tangible asset is acquired. All are necessary for acquiring and preparing tangible assets for use. Notice that they are not limited to the amounts paid to purchase or construct the assets. For example, the Land account at Cedar Fair would include legal fees for title searches, fees for land surveys, and commissions paid to brokers when purchasing the land on Ohio's Sandusky Bay shown in the photograph on the left. Take a moment right now to read the lists of costs that should be capitalized when buildings (middle) and equipment (right) are acquired.

Land

Purchase cost
Legal fees
Survey fees
Broker's commissions

Equipment

Purchase/Construction cost
Sales taxes
Transportation costs
Installation costs

Buildings

Purchase/Construction cost
Legal fees
Appraisal fees
Architect fees

If a company buys land, a building, or a piece of used equipment and incurs demolition, renovation, or repair costs before it can be used, the company would capitalize the additional costs as a cost of the land, building, or equipment. These costs are capitalized because they are needed to prepare the asset for use. Cedar Fair spent $10 million in 2006 to relocate its X-Flight roller coaster from Cleveland to Cincinnati. The full cost of the move was capitalized to its Rides and Equipment account.

In some cases, land, buildings, and equipment are purchased together. On June 30, 2006, Cedar Fair bought five amusement parks from Paramount Parks for $1.24 billion. When this type of "basket purchase" occurs, the total cost is split among the assets in proportion to the market value of the assets as a whole. For example, if Cedar Fair were to pay $10 million for a hotel and the land surrounding it, based on an appraisal that estimates that the land contributes 40 percent of the property's value and the building contributes 60 percent, Cedar Fair would record 40 percent of the total cost as land ($4 million) and the other 60 percent as buildings ($6 million). Splitting the total purchase price among individual assets is necessary because the cost of different asset types may be depreciated over different periods. Land is not depreciated, so any costs assigned to Land will remain in that account until Cedar Fair sells the land.

To illustrate how the costs of tangible assets are recorded, consider the Top Thrill Dragster ride, which Cedar Fair purchased in 2002 from Intamin, a Swiss roller-coaster manufacturer.

When it was purchased, the Top Thrill Dragster was the biggest, fastest roller coaster in the world. Some of its specs are shown in the accompanying graphic.

Assume the list price for the roller coaster (including sales tax) was $26 million but that Cedar Fair received a $1 million discount. In other words, the roller coaster's net purchase price to Cedar Fair was $25 million. Assume too that Cedar Fair paid $125,000 to have the roller coaster delivered and another $625,000 to have it assembled and prepared for use. Cedar Fair would calculate the costs to be capitalized for this asset as follows:

Invoice price	$26,000,000
Less: Discount	1,000,000
Net cash invoice price	25,000,000
Add: Transportation costs paid by Cedar Fair	125,000
Installation costs paid by Cedar Fair	625,000
Total cost of the roller coaster	$25,750,000

The total $25,750,000 cost would be the amount Cedar Fair recorded in the Rides and Equipment account regardless of how the company paid for or financed the roller coaster. As you will see next, the method of payment or financing affects only whether the purchase reduces cash, increases liabilities, or both.

Cash Purchase

Assuming that Cedar Fair paid cash for the roller coaster and related transportation and installation costs, the company would record the transaction as follows:

	Debit	Credit
Rides and Equipment (+A)	25,750,000	
Cash (−A)		25,750,000

Assets		=	Liabilities	+	Owners' Equity
Cash	−25,750,000				
Rides and Equipment	+25,750,000				

You may find it hard to believe that Cedar Fair would pay cash for assets that cost more than $25 million, but that is not unusual. Companies often pay with cash generated from operations or with cash that has been borrowed. In addition, the seller may extend credit to the buyer, a situation we examine next.

Credit Purchase

If we assume Cedar Fair signed a note payable for the new roller coaster and paid cash for the transportation and installation costs, the journal entry to record the purchase would be:

	Debit	Credit
Rides and Equipment (+A)	25,750,000	
Cash (−A)		750,000
Note Payable (+L)		25,000,000

Assets		=	Liabilities		+	Owners' Equity
Cash	−750,000		Note Payable	+25,000,000		
Rides and Equipment	+25,750,000					

SELF-STUDY PRACTICE

In a recent year, the New Bakery Company of Ohio opened a new baking plant that can make 3 million hamburger buns a day. The equipment cost $21,000,000. Assume New Bakery financed the purchase cost using a note payable and paid in cash $800,000 of sales taxes, $70,000 of transportation costs, and $50,000 of installation costs before the equipment could be used.

1. What amount should be recorded as the total acquisition cost of the equipment?

   ____

2. Complete the following journal entry to record the acquisition.

	Debit	Credit

After you have finished, check your answers with the solution at the bottom of the page.

Before we leave this section, we should mention that not all fixed asset costs are capitalized. The cost of some fixed assets, such as staplers and hole punches, is such a small amount that it is not worth the trouble of recording and tracking as a fixed asset. Outback Steakhouse, for example, reports in the notes to its financial statements that the company expenses all expenditures of less than $1,000 when incurred. Such policies are acceptable because immaterial (relatively small) amounts will not affect users' analysis of the financial statements. **Other costs that are expensed when incurred include insurance for fixed assets, interest on loans obtained to purchase fixed assets, and—as discussed in the next section—ordinary repairs and maintenance.**

Solution to Self-Study Practice

1. $21,000,000 + $800,000 + $70,000 + $50,000 = $21,920,000

2.

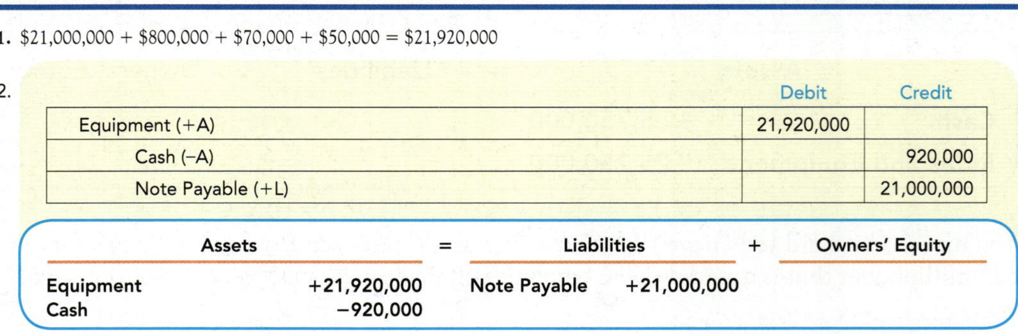

	Debit	Credit
Equipment (+A)	21,920,000	
Cash (−A)		920,000
Note Payable (+L)		21,000,000

Assets		=	Liabilities		+	Owners' Equity
Equipment	+21,920,000		Note Payable	+21,000,000		
Cash	−920,000					

Use of Tangible Assets

Maintenance Costs Incurred during Use

Most tangible assets require substantial expenditures over the course of their lives to maintain or enhance their operation. Maintenance is extremely important in the roller-coaster industry where safety is vital. Despite the tremendous stress created by the frequent use and ultra-fast speeds of the rides, surprisingly few accidents occur at amusement parks. According to some estimates, the odds of a serious injury occurring at an amusement park are 1 in 23 million. In fact, you are 38 times more likely to get hit by lightning than you are to be injured at an amusement park.[2] The companies that run the parks have achieved this high level of safety by spending a lot of money on two types of maintenance: (1) ordinary repairs and maintenance and (2) extraordinary repairs and maintenance.

Ordinary Repairs and Maintenance. **Ordinary repairs and maintenance** are expenditures for the routine maintenance and upkeep of long-lived assets. Like an oil change for your car, these are recurring, relatively small expenditures that do not directly lengthen an asset's useful life. Because they are made to maintain the asset's productive capacity for a short time, they are recorded as expenses in the current period. Because expenses are matched to revenues, ordinary repairs and maintenance costs are sometimes called **revenue expenditures**.

In Cedar Fair's case, ordinary repairs and maintenance would include greasing the tracks on the Steel Venom roller coaster at Valleyfair in Minnesota. It would also include replacing the lights on the eight-story Ferris wheel at Michigan's Adventure and tightening the seams on a water slide at Knott's Soak City in California.

Extraordinary Repairs, Replacements, and Additions. In contrast to ordinary repairs and maintenance, **extraordinary repairs** occur infrequently, involve large expenditures, and increase an asset's economic usefulness through enhanced efficiency, capacity, or lifespan. Examples include additions, major overhauls, complete reconditioning, and major replacements and improvements, such as the complete replacement of the passenger train on a roller coaster. Because these costs increase the usefulness of tangible assets beyond their original condition, they are added to the appropriate long-lived asset accounts. And because doing so means capitalizing these costs, extraordinary repairs, replacements, and additions are sometimes called **capital expenditures**.

[2] "Newtonian Nightmare Rack-and-Pinion Inversions and Pneumatic Accelerators: This Is Fun?" *Forbes*, July 23, 2001, p. 112.

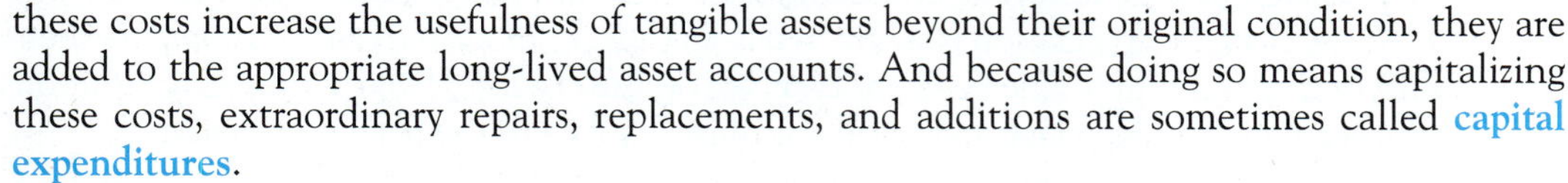

Accounting for Ordinary and Extraordinary Repairs

Companies are required to describe the policies they use to account for any significant expenditures on property, plant, and equipment. In the notes to the financial statements, Cedar Fair clearly indicates that accounting for ordinary repairs differs from that for expenditures on improvements and upgrades (extraordinary repairs).

Cedar Fair
Notes to the Financial Statements
Key Accounting Policies

Expenditures made to maintain assets in their original operating condition are expensed as incurred, and improvements and upgrades are capitalized.

SELF-STUDY PRACTICE

As you know from living in a house, apartment, or dormitory, buildings require continuous maintenance and repair. Indicate whether each of the following expenditures should be expensed in the current period or capitalized as part of the cost of the building.

Expense or Capitalize?

1. Replacing electrical wiring and plumbing throughout the building.
2. Repairing the hinge on the front door of the building.
3. Cleaning the building's air conditioning filters once every year.
4. Making major structural improvements to a clubhouse.

After you have finished, check your answers with the solution at the bottom of the page.

Depreciation Expense

In addition to repairs and maintenance expense, a company reports depreciation expense every period that a tangible asset is used. This expense does not involve new payments for use of the asset. Instead, depreciation is the allocation of existing costs that have already been recorded as a long-lived tangible asset. The idea is that the cost of a long-lived tangible asset is essentially a prepaid cost representing future benefits. Because these benefits are used up when the asset is used, **following the matching principle, a portion of the asset's cost is removed from the balance sheet and reported on the income statement as an expense in the period when the asset is used to generate revenue.** Cedar Fair earns revenues when the rides are open to customers, so depreciation expense is recorded at that time to show the allocated cost of the tangible assets used to generate revenues.

Depreciation is recorded in two accounts. First, the income statement account Depreciation Expense reports the amount of depreciation for the current period. Second, the balance sheet reports a contra-asset account, Accumulated Depreciation, which includes the current period depreciation as well as the depreciation accumulated from all prior periods since the asset was first used. Accumulated Depreciation is subtracted from the cost of related assets to compute their book values, or carrying values. The book (or carrying) value of a long-lived asset is its acquisition cost less the accumulated depreciation from the acquisition date to the balance sheet date.

To see how Cedar Fair reported these items on the balance sheet, take a quick look at Exhibit 10.1 on page 419. You should see that at the end of 2007, Cedar Fair's total cost of property and equipment (in thousands) was $2,550,002. Accumulated depreciation was $616,440 and the book (or carrying) value was $1,933,562 ($2,550,002 – $616,440). In Cedar Fair's 2007 income statement (not shown), depreciation expense of $55,765 was included. Although some companies report depreciation expense as a separate operating expense, many (including Cedar Fair) combine it with other operating expenses for external reporting purposes.

To calculate depreciation expense, you need three amounts:

1. **Asset cost.** The asset cost includes all of the asset's capitalized costs—for example, the purchase cost, sales tax, legal fees, and other costs needed to acquire and prepare the asset for use.
2. **Residual value.** Residual (or salvage or scrap) value is an estimate of the amount the company will receive when it disposes of the asset. Cedar Fair will recover some of the cost of its roller coasters when it disposes of them either by selling them "as is" to local amusement companies or by dismantling them and selling the parts to other roller coaster or scrap metal companies.
3. **Useful life.** Useful life is an estimate of the asset's useful economic life to the company (rather than its economic life to all potential users). It may be expressed in terms of years or units of asset capacity, such as the number of units it can produce or the number

Solution to Self-Study Practice

1. Capitalize—extends life.
2. Expense.
3. Expense.
4. Capitalize—extends life.

of miles it will travel. **Land is the only tangible asset that is assumed to have an unlimited (indefinite) useful life. Thus, land is not depreciated.**

The basic idea behind depreciation is to match the dollar amount of the asset that will be used up (the asset cost minus the residual value) to the periods in which the asset will be used to generate revenue (the useful life). Residual value is considered when calculating depreciation because we want to leave a little of the asset's cost in the accounts after we have finished depreciating it. We do so because when we dispose of the asset, we are likely to get back some of the money we initially paid for it. So the amount to be depreciated over the asset's useful life is the difference between its cost and its residual value, an amount called the **depreciable cost**. A company should record depreciation each year of an asset's useful life until the total accumulated depreciation equals the depreciable cost. After that, the company should report no additional depreciation even if the company continues to use the asset.

Water structures and facilities such as the Hoover Dam are depreciated over periods extending to 100 years.

Source: U.S. Department of the Interior, Bureau of Reclamation, 2005 annual report.

If every company used the same techniques to calculate depreciation, we would stop right here. Because companies own different assets and use them differently, however, accountants have not been able to agree on a single best method of depreciation. As a result, managers are allowed to choose from several different methods based on how well they match the cost of using the assets to the revenues those assets generate over time. These alternative depreciation methods produce different numbers for depreciation. To interpret such differences, you need to understand how the methods work.

Depreciation Methods

Learning Objective 3
Apply various depreciation methods as economic benefits are used up over time.

In this section, we discuss three common depreciation methods:

- Straight line.
- Units of production.
- Declining balance.

Because these methods assume different patterns of depreciation over an asset's useful life, they use different methods to calculate depreciation. Regardless of the method, however, the calculated amount of depreciation should be recorded with the same journal entry you learned in Chapter 4. For example, the journal entry to record $20,000 of depreciation for a given period would be:

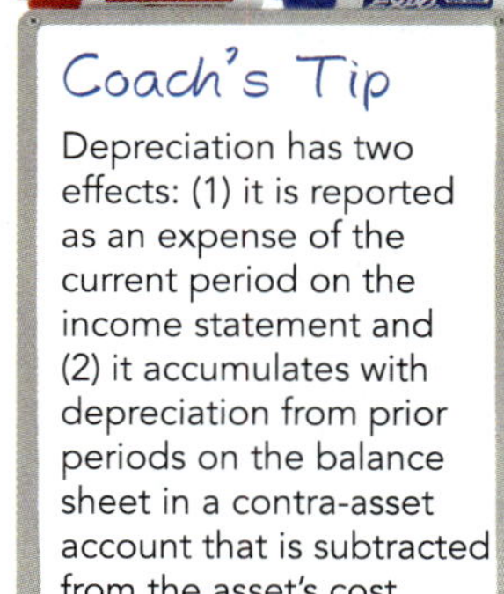

Coach's Tip

Depreciation has two effects: (1) it is reported as an expense of the current period on the income statement and (2) it accumulates with depreciation from prior periods on the balance sheet in a contra-asset account that is subtracted from the asset's cost.

	Debit	Credit
Depreciation Expense (+E, −OE)	20,000	
Accumulated Depreciation (+xA, −A)		20,000

Assets		=	Liabilities	+	Owners' Equity	
Accumulated Depreciation (+xA)	−20,000				Depreciation Expense (+E)	−20,000

To demonstrate how each depreciation method works, we assume that Cedar Fair acquired a new go-cart ride on January 1, 2009. See Exhibit 10.2 for the relevant information.

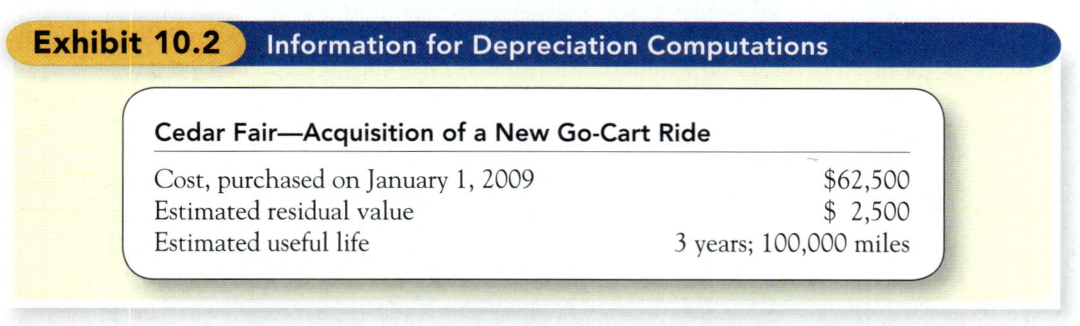

Exhibit 10.2 Information for Depreciation Computations

Cedar Fair—Acquisition of a New Go-Cart Ride

Cost, purchased on January 1, 2009	$62,500
Estimated residual value	$ 2,500
Estimated useful life	3 years; 100,000 miles

Straight-Line Method. The straight-line depreciation method reports an equal amount of depreciation in each period of the asset's estimated useful life. The straight-line formula for estimating annual depreciation expense is:

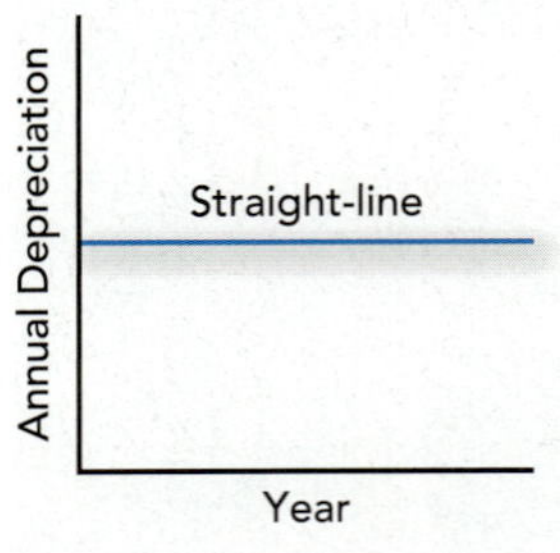

Straight-Line Formula

$$\text{(Cost} - \text{Residual Value)} \times \frac{1}{\text{Useful Life}} = \text{Depreciation Expense}$$

In the straight-line formula, Cost − Residual Value is the total amount to be depreciated (the depreciable cost). The depreciation rate is 1/Useful Life. Using the information in Exhibit 10.2, the depreciation expense for Cedar Fair's new ride is $20,000 per year, calculated in the following depreciation schedule:

Straight-line
(Cost − Residual Value) × (1/Useful Life)

		Income Statement	Balance Sheet		
Year	Yearly Computation	Depreciation Expense	Cost	Accumulated Depreciation	Book Value
At acquisition			$62,500	$ 0	$62,500
2009	($62,500 − $2,500) × (1/3)	$20,000	62,500	20,000	42,500
2010	($62,500 − $2,500) × (1/3)	20,000	62,500	40,000	22,500
2011	($62,500 − $2,500) × (1/3)	20,000	62,500	60,000	2,500
	Total	$60,000			

Take a moment to study the straight-line depreciation schedule. Notice that as the name straight line suggests,

1. Depreciation expense is a constant amount each year.
2. Accumulated depreciation increases by an equal amount each year.
3. Book value decreases by the same equal amount each year.

Notice too that at the end of the asset's life, accumulated depreciation ($60,000) equals the asset's depreciable cost ($62,500 − $2,500), and book value ($2,500) equals residual value.

As you will see with other depreciation methods, the amount of depreciation depends on estimates of an asset's useful life and residual value at the end of that life. A question people often ask is: **How do accountants estimate useful lives and residual values?** While some of this information can be obtained from the asset's supplier or from other sources such as reseller databases or insurance companies, the simple answer is that professional judgment is required. Because useful lives and residual values are difficult to estimate with precision, accountants are encouraged to update their calculations regularly (see Supplement 10B at the end of this chapter).

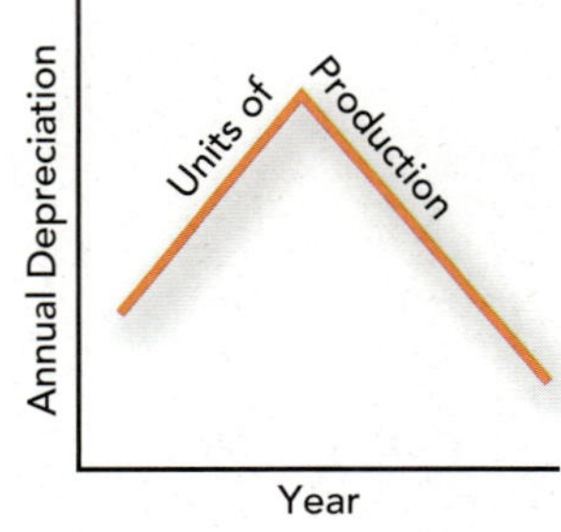

Units-of-Production Method. Whereas the straight-line method bases depreciation on the amount of time that has passed, the units-of-production depreciation method bases it on the amount of asset production. An asset's production is defined in terms of miles, products, or machine-hours. The units-of-production formula for estimating depreciation expense is:

Units-of-Production Formula

$$\text{(Cost} - \text{Residual Value)} \times \frac{\text{Actual Production this Period}}{\text{Estimated Total Production}} = \text{Depreciation Expense}$$

If the go-cart in Exhibit 10.2 was driven 30,000 miles in 2009, 50,000 miles in 2010, and 20,000 miles in 2011, the units-of-production method would calculate depreciation in each year of the asset's life as follows:

Units-of-production
(Cost – Residual Value) × (Actual/Estimated Total Production)

		Income Statement	Balance Sheet		
Year	Yearly Computation	Depreciation Expense	Cost	Accumulated Depreciation	Book Value
At acquisition			$62,500	$ 0	$62,500
2009	($62,500 – $2,500) × (30,000/100,000 miles)	$18,000	62,500	18,000	44,500
2010	($62,500 – $2,500) × (50,000/100,000 miles)	30,000	62,500	48,000	14,500
2011	($62,500 – $2,500) × (20,000/100,000 miles)	12,000	62,500	60,000	2,500
	Total	$60,000			

Notice that **under the units-of-production method, the depreciation expense, accumulated depreciation, and book value vary from period to period, depending on the number of units produced.**

Declining-Balance Method. Under the declining-balance depreciation method, depreciation expense is higher in the early years of an asset's life and lower in the later years. That is why this method is sometimes called an accelerated depreciation method. Although accelerated methods are used infrequently for financial reporting purposes in the United States, they are used commonly in financial reporting in other countries, such as Japan and Canada, as well as in tax reporting in the United States (a point we discuss in greater detail later).

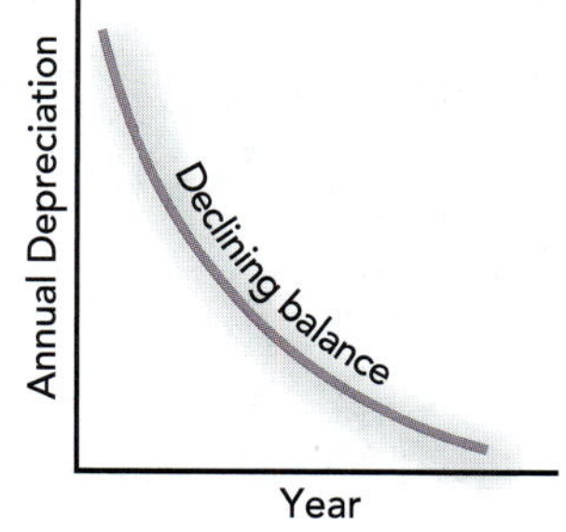

The declining-balance method applies a depreciation rate to the book value of the asset at the beginning of each accounting period. Notice that the following formula uses book value (Cost – Accumulated Depreciation) rather than depreciable cost (Cost – Residual Value). This slight difference in the formula produces declining amounts of depreciation as the asset ages. Because the 2/Useful Life rate used in the formula is double the straight-line rate, this particular version of the declining-balance method is called the double-declining-balance depreciation method.

Double-Declining-Balance Formula

$$\text{(Cost} - \text{Accumulated Depreciation)} \times \frac{2}{\text{Useful Life}} = \text{Depreciation Expense}$$

This formula uses the accumulated depreciation balance at the beginning of each year. In the first year of an asset's life, the beginning balance in Accumulated Depreciation is zero. However, with each passing year as additional depreciation is recorded, the Accumulated Depreciation balance increases, causing the amount of double-declining depreciation expense to decline over time.

Because **residual value is not included in the formula for the declining-balance method of computing depreciation expense,** you must take extra care to ensure that an asset's book value is not depreciated beyond its residual value. If the calculated amount of depreciation for the year would reduce the book value below the asset's residual value, you must record a lower amount of depreciation so that the book value will equal the residual value. The following depreciation schedule illustrates this point.

Coach's Tip

Remember that the declining-balance formula does not include an asset's residual value, so you must consider it separately.

		Income Statement	Balance Sheet		
Double-declining-balance (Cost − Residual Value) × (2/Useful Life)					
Year	**Yearly Computation**	**Depreciation Expense**	**Cost**	**Accumulated Depreciation**	**Book Value**
At acquisition			$62,500	$ 0	$62,500
2009	($62,500 − $0) × (2/3)	$41,667	62,500	41,667	20,833
2010	($62,500 − $41,667) × (2/3)	13,889	62,500	55,556	6,944
2011	($62,500 − $55,556) × (2/3)	~~4,629~~	62,500	~~60,185~~	~~2,315~~
		4,444	62,500	60,000	2,500
	Total	$60,000			

Notice that the calculated depreciation expense for 2011 ($4,629) has not been recorded because it would cause the asset's book value to fall below its residual value. Instead, in the final year of the asset's life, just enough depreciation ($4,444) is recorded to make the book value of the asset equal its residual value of $2,500.

Summary of Depreciation Methods. See Exhibit 10.3 for a summary of the depreciation expense that would be reported in each year of our example under the three alternative depreciation methods. Notice that **the amount of depreciation expense recorded in each year of an asset's life depends on the method that is used. That means that the amount of net income that is reported can vary, depending on the depreciation method used.** At the end of an asset's life, after it has been fully depreciated, the total amount of depreciation will equal the asset's depreciable cost regardless of the depreciation method used.

Exhibit 10.3 Differences in Depreciation Expense by Method

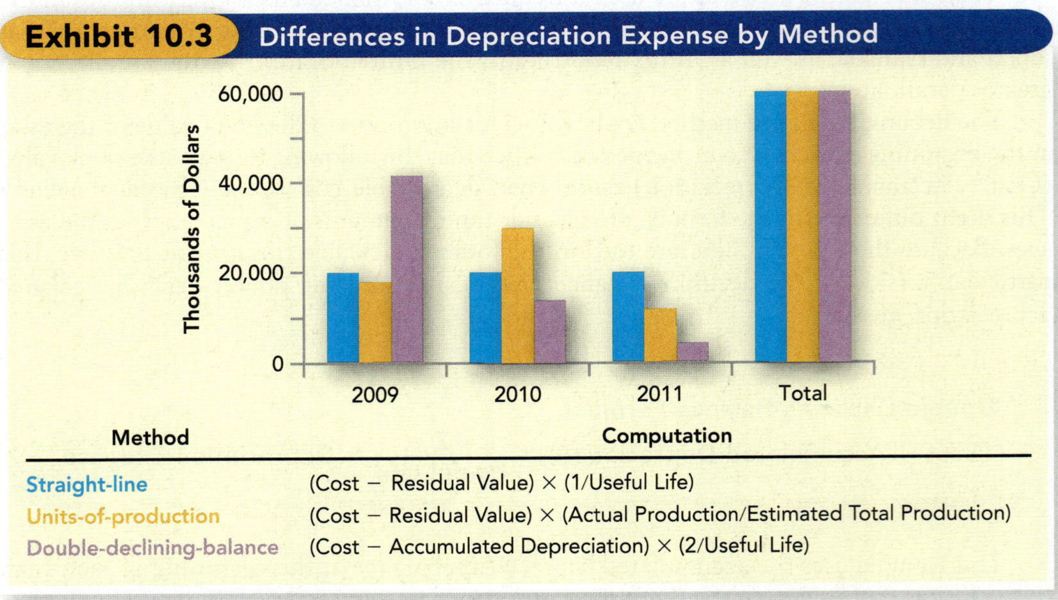

Method	Computation
Straight-line	(Cost − Residual Value) × (1/Useful Life)
Units-of-production	(Cost − Residual Value) × (Actual Production/Estimated Total Production)
Double-declining-balance	(Cost − Accumulated Depreciation) × (2/Useful Life)

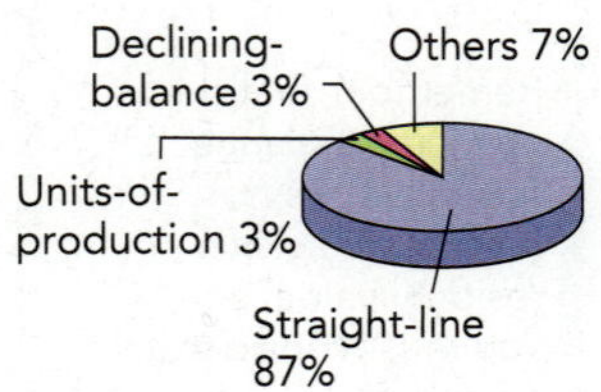

Managers may use any rational and systematic depreciation method provided that the company describes it in the notes to the financial statements. Because tangible assets are not identical, different depreciation methods can be used for different classes of assets provided they are used consistently over time so that financial statement users can compare results across periods. The methods that companies use most frequently are shown in the margin. The straight-line method is the preferred choice because it is the easiest to use and understand, and it does a good job of matching depreciation expense to revenues when assets are used evenly over their useful lives. The units-of-production method is the typical choice when asset use fluctuates significantly from period to period. Declining-balance methods apply best to assets that are most productive when they are new but quickly lose their usefulness as they get older.

SELF-STUDY PRACTICE

Assume that Cedar Fair has acquired new equipment at a cost of $24,000. The equipment has an estimated useful life of six years, an estimated operating life of 5,000 hours, and an estimated residual value of $3,000. Determine the depreciation expense for the second year under each of the following methods:

1. Straight-line method.

   ($24,000 − $_____) × (_____/6) = $_______

2. Units-of-production method (assume that the equipment ran for 800 hours in Year 2).

   ($_____ − $_____) × (_____/5,000) = $_______

3. Double-declining-balance method.

   Year 1: ($24,000 − $_____) × (_____/_____) = $_______

   Year 2: ($24,000 − $_____) × (_____/_____) = $_______

After you have finished, check your answers with the solution at the bottom of the page.

Partial-Year Depreciation Calculations. Purchases of long-lived assets seldom occur on the first or last day of the accounting period. Consequently, the need arises to calculate depreciation for periods shorter than a year. **Under the straight-line and declining-balance methods, the annual depreciation is multiplied by the fraction of the year for which depreciation is being calculated.**

For purposes of these calculations, accountants typically assume that assets were purchased at the beginning of the month nearest to the actual purchase date. For example, if Cedar Fair purchased the go-cart ride on October 7, 2009, it would have owned the asset for about three months during the year ended December 31, 2009. Thus, the depreciation for the ride in 2009 would be calculated by multiplying the annual straight-line depreciation of $20,000 by 3 ÷ 12, representing the 3 months of 12 that Cedar Fair owned it. Similarly, if an asset is disposed of during the year, the annual depreciation is multiplied by the fraction of the year during which the asset was owned. **These partial-year modifications are not required in the units-of-production method because that method is based on actual production for the period.** If the accounting period is shorter than a year, the level of actual production already reflects that shorter period.

Tax Depreciation. Before we leave the topic of depreciation, we should note that if a business is operated as a corporation, it may use one method of depreciation for reporting to owners and a second method for determining the income taxes that a corporation must pay. Keeping two sets of accounting records is both ethical and legal because the objective of GAAP differs from that of the Internal Revenue Code.

Financial Reporting (GAAP)	Tax Reporting (Internal Revenue Code)
The objective of financial reporting is to provide economic information about a business that is useful in projecting future cash flows of the business.	The objective of the Internal Revenue Code is to raise sufficient revenues to pay for the expenditures of the federal government and to encourage certain social and economic behaviors.

One of the behaviors the government wants to encourage is economic renewal and growth. Thus, the IRS allows companies to deduct larger amounts of tax depreciation than GAAP

Solution to Self-Study Practice

1. ($24,000 − $3,000) × (1/6) = $3,500
2. ($24,000 − $3,000) × (800/5,000) = $3,360
3. Year 1: ($24,000 − $0) × (2/6) = $8,000

   Year 2: ($24,000 − $8,000) × (2/6) = $5,333

allows.[3] The larger tax deduction reduces the company's income taxes significantly in the years immediately following the purchase of a long-lived asset.

Although the IRS allows super-sized deductions in the early years of an asset's life, it does not allow a company to depreciate more than an asset's depreciable cost over its life. So the tax savings that companies enjoy in the early years of an asset's life will eventually be returned to the government in later years of that asset's life. The amount of tax that is put off (deferred) as a result of taking large tax deductions for depreciation is reported as a long-term liability, Deferred Income Taxes. Although the deferral delays the payment of taxes only temporarily, it can be worth the effort of keeping two sets of records. The following companies report that they deferred significant tax obligations in recent years by choosing different depreciation methods for tax and financial reporting purposes.

Company	Deferred Tax Liabilities	Percentage due to Applying Different Depreciation Methods
AT&T Corp.	$27,406 million	77%
Southwest Airlines	2,104 million	87
Revlon, Inc.	27 million	99

This table shows that like most individuals, companies follow an economic rule called the **least and the latest rule.** All taxpayers want to pay the least tax that is legally permitted, at the latest possible date. If you had the choice of paying $1,000 to the federal government at the end of this year or at the end of next year, you would choose the end of next year. Doing so would allow you to invest the money for an extra year and earn a significant return on your investment.

Impairment of Tangible Assets

Learning Objective 4

Explain the effect of asset impairment on the financial statements.

As a result of recording depreciation, an asset's book value declines as it ages. However, because **depreciation is not intended to report an asset at its current value,** an asset's book value could exceed its current value, particularly if the asset becomes impaired. **Impairment** occurs when events or changed circumstances cause the estimated future cash flows from a long-lived asset to fall below its book value. If an asset's estimated future cash flows are less than its book value, the book value should be written down to what the asset is worth (called fair value) with the amount of the write-down reported as an impairment loss. Impairment losses are typically included with Other Expenses and Losses, which is reported below the Operating Income line near the bottom of the income statement.

Coach's Tip

Under current U.S. accounting rules, if long-lived tangible assets increase in value, the accounting records are not adjusted to write up their value.

Cedar Fair recorded a write-down in 2002 after a rare engineering phenomenon called "vortex shedding" reportedly caused a steel support tower in a VertiGo slingshot ride to snap during the off-season. Even though only one ride was affected, Cedar Fair dismantled and removed both its VertiGo rides.[4] To see how this bizarre event would be accounted for, assume that the book value of Cedar Fair's VertiGo rides was $8 million. If the fair value of the rides was estimated to be $4.8 million—an amount that represents what other amusement park companies and scrap dealers might be expected to pay for the rides' parts—then the impairment loss would be calculated as $8 million minus $4.8 million. The resulting $3.2 million impairment loss would be recorded using the following journal entry:

	Debit	Credit
Loss Due to Impairment of Assets (+E, −OE)	3,200,000	
Rides and Equipment (−A)		3,200,000

Assets		=	Liabilities	+	Owners' Equity	
Rides and Equipment	−3,200,000				Loss Due to Impairment (+E)	−3,200,000

[3] Most corporations use the IRS-approved Modified Accelerated Cost Recovery System (MACRS) to calculate depreciation expense on their tax returns. MACRS is similar to the declining-balance method and is applied over relatively short asset lives set by the IRS to yield high tax deductions for depreciation expense in the early years.

[4] "Insurer Refuses Damage Payment to Sandusky, Ohio-Based Amusement Park Company," Knight Ridder/Tribune Business News, February 11, 2003.

Exhibit 10.4 Financial Statement Note Describing Impairment

Impairment of Long-Lived Assets During the first quarter . . . , we removed certain fixed assets from service at our parks, and recorded a provision of $3.2 million for the estimated portion of the net book value of these assets that may not be recoverable.

When Cedar Fair reported this loss on the income statement, it caused a huge reduction in net income. Because the loss was so large and unusual in nature, it was reported as the separate line item Nonrecurring Loss. Cedar Fair also described the impairment loss and asset write-down in the notes to its financial statements (see Exhibit 10.4).

Disposal and Exchange of Tangible Assets

Learning Objective 5

Account for the disposal of long-lived tangible assets that are discarded or sold.

In some cases, a business may voluntarily decide not to hold a long-term asset for its entire life. For example, your local gym might decide to replace its treadmills with elliptical trainers. Or, if a company discontinues a product, it may sell the equipment that was used to make the product. To get rid of used assets, companies do just what you do: They discard them in a junkyard, sell them on eBay, or exchange them as a trade-in on a new asset.

Regardless of how a depreciable asset is disposed of, two accounting adjustments are required:

1. **Update the Depreciation Expense and Accumulated Depreciation accounts.** If a long-lived asset is disposed of during the year, it should be depreciated to the date of disposal using the partial-year calculations discussed on page 429.
2. **Record the disposal.** All disposals of long-lived assets require that you account for (1) the book value of the items given up, (2) the market value of the items received, and (3) any difference between the two amounts, which reflects a gain or loss on the disposal. Because the disposal of a long-lived asset is not a core part of a company's operations, any gains or losses on the disposal should be reported as Nonoperating Gains and Losses below the Operating Income line on the income statement (see Exhibit 6.7 on page 277, for example).[5] The specific journal entries to record disposals of long-lived assets depend on whether the asset is discarded, sold, or exchanged as a trade-in. In this section, we illustrate the entries for assets that are discarded or sold. Supplement 10C at the end of this chapter discusses exchanges of assets.

Discarding Assets

Long-lived assets are discarded when they are no longer useful to the company. For example, in May 2005, Cedar Fair discarded its White Water Landing ride, which was acquired in 1982 for $3,400,000. If we assume that this asset was fully depreciated—meaning that the accumulated depreciation equaled the asset's cost—then Cedar Fair would record the following journal entry.

	Debit	Credit
Accumulated Depreciation—Rides (−xA, +A)	3,400,000	
Rides and Equipment (−A)		3,400,000

Assets		=	Liabilities	+	Owners' Equity
Rides and Equipment	−3,400,000				
Accumulated Depreciation (−xA)	+3,400,000				

[5] One exception to reporting gains or losses on the income statement involves asset exchanges that lack commercial substance. This exception is discussed in intermediate accounting.

Notice that **both the cost of the asset and any related accumulated depreciation are removed from the accounting records.** Because the book value of the ride was zero and Cedar Fair received nothing when it discarded the asset, the company recorded no gain or loss.

Selling Assets

To illustrate how companies account for assets that are disposed of through a sale, assume that Cedar Fair sold its Demon Drop ride on December 31, 2008. The ride cost Cedar Fair $2,500,000, and on December 31, 2008, had accumulated depreciation of $2,200,000. In other words, at the time of sale, it had a net book value of $300,000 ($2,500,000 − $2,200,000). If Cedar Fair had sold the ride for more than $300,000, Cedar Fair would record a gain. If the ride were sold for less than $300,000, Cedar Fair would record a loss. Both cases are shown here.

Gain on Sale. If Cedar Fair sold the Demon Drop ride for $350,000 cash, the company would receive an asset (cash) with a value ($350,000) more than the ride's book value ($300,000). In other words, Cedar Fair would receive a gain of $50,000. The required journal entry would be:

	Debit	Credit
Cash (+A)	350,000	
Accumulated Depreciation—Rides (−xA, +A)	2,200,000	
Rides and Equipment (−A)		2,500,000
Gain on Sale of Rides and Equipment (+R, +OE)		50,000

Assets		= Liabilities +	Owners' Equity	
Cash	+ 350,000		Gain on Sale of Rides and Equipment (+R)	+ 50,000
Rides and Equipment	−2,500,000			
Accumulated Depreciation—Rides (−xA)	+2,200,000			

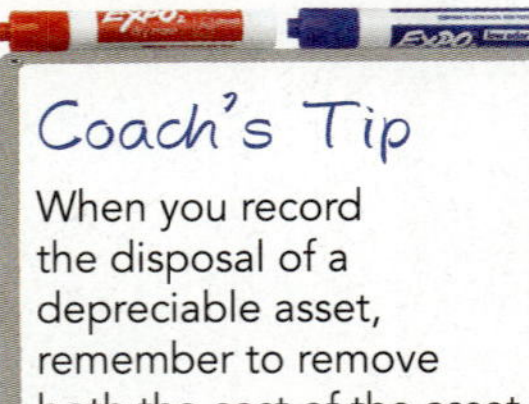

Coach's Tip

When you record the disposal of a depreciable asset, remember to remove both the cost of the asset and its accumulated depreciation.

Loss on Sale. If the Demon Drop ride were sold for $200,000 cash, Cedar Fair would receive an asset (cash) with a value ($200,000) that is less than the ride's book value ($300,000). A $100,000 loss would result. The required journal entry would be:

	Debit	Credit
Cash (+A)	200,000	
Loss on Sale of Rides and Equipment (+E, −OE)	100,000	
Accumulated Depreciation—Rides (−xA, +A)	2,200,000	
Rides and Equipment (−A)		2,500,000

Assets		= Liabilities +	Owners' Equity	
Cash	+ 200,000		Loss on Sale of Rides and Equipment (+E)	−100,000
Rides and Equipment	−2,500,000			
Accumulated Depreciation—Rides (−xA)	+2,200,000			

SELF-STUDY PRACTICE

Assume Cedar Fair sold a hotel on March 31, 2009. The hotel, which had an original cost of $21 million, had been depreciated using the straight-line method with an estimated residual value of $1 million and an estimated useful life of 20 years. Depreciation recorded on December 31, 2008, brought the Accumulated Depreciation balance to $16 million. No depreciation has been recorded since then.

1. What is the hotel's annual amount of straight-line depreciation? What amount of depreciation should be recorded for the hotel on March 31, 2009? To what balance would this adjustment bring the Accumulated Depreciation account?
2. What would be the journal entry if Cedar Fair sold the hotel for $3 million cash?
3. What would be the journal entry if Cedar Fair sold the hotel for $5 million cash?

After you have finished, check your answers with the solution at the bottom of the page.

INTANGIBLE ASSETS: TYPES, ACQUISITION, USE, AND DISPOSAL

Learning Objective 6

Account for the acquisition, use, and disposal of long-lived intangible assets.

Intangible assets are long-lived assets that lack physical substance. Their existence is usually indicated by legal documents of the types described in the following section.

Types of Intangible Assets

Trademarks

A **trademark** is a special name, image, or slogan identified with a product or company, such as the name Kleenex or the image of McDonald's golden arches. The symbol ® signifies a trademark that has been registered with the U.S. Patent and Trademark Office. The symbol™ indicates an unregistered trademark. Both types of trademark are considered intangible assets.

Solution to Self-Study Practice

1. Annual depreciation: (Cost − Residual Value) × (1/Life) = ($21 − $1) × (1/20) = $1 million per year.
   January 1–March 31 = 3 months out of 12; $1 million × (3/12) = $250,000.
   Accumulated Depreciation on March 31 = $16,000,000 + $250,000 = $16,250,000.
2.

		Debit	Credit
March 31	Cash (+A)	3,000,000	
	Loss on Sale of Assets (+E, −OE)	1,750,000	
	Accumulated Depreciation (−xA, +A)	16,250,000	
	Buildings (−A)		21,000,000

Assets		=	Liabilities	+	Owners' Equity	
Cash	+ 3,000,000					
Buildings	−21,000,000				Loss on Sale of Assets (+E)	−1,750,000
Acc. Depn. (−xA)	+16,250,000					

3.

		Debit	Credit
March 31	Cash (+A)	5,000,000	
	Accumulated Depreciation (−xA, +A)	16,250,000	
	Buildings (−A)		21,000,000
	Gain on Sale of Assets (+R, +OE)		250,000

Assets		=	Liabilities	+	Owners' Equity	
Cash	+ 5,000,000					
Buildings	−21,000,000				Gain on Sale of Assets (+R)	+250,000
Acc. Depn. (−xA)	+16,250,000					

Copyrights

A **copyright** gives the owner the exclusive right to publish, use, and sell a literary, musical, artistic, or dramatic work for a period not exceeding 70 years after the author's death. The book you are reading is copyrighted. It is illegal, therefore, for an instructor to copy several chapters from this book and hand them out in class without first obtaining permission from the copyright owner.

Patents

A **patent** is an exclusive right granted by the federal government for a period of 20 years, typically to whoever invents a new product or discovers a new process. The patent declares the owner to be the only person who can use, manufacture, or sell the patented item. This protection is intended to encourage people to be inventive because it prevents others from simply copying an innovation until after the inventor has had time to profit from the new product or process. One of the first roller-coaster patents was granted in 1884 for what was then called a "gravity pleasure road."

Licensing Rights

Licensing rights are limited permissions to use something according to specific terms and conditions. Your university or college has likely obtained the licensing right to make certain computer programs available for use on your campus network. A licensing right also allows Cedar Fair to showcase the PEANUTS character Snoopy at its parks.

Franchises

A **franchise** is a contractual right to sell certain products or services, use certain trademarks, or perform certain activities in a specific geographical region. For example, a business can buy franchise rights that allow it to use the Krispy Kreme name, store format, recipes, and ingredients by paying an up-front fee ranging from $20,000 to $50,000 per store plus ongoing fees of 4.5 to 6.0 percent of store sales.[6]

Goodwill

Goodwill tops the charts as the most frequently reported intangible asset. This asset can encompass a favorable location, an established customer base, a great reputation, and successful business operations. Although many companies have probably built up their own goodwill, GAAP does not allow it to be reported as an intangible asset on the balance sheet unless it has been purchased from another company. To understand the reasons for this rule, keep reading; we explain them in the next section.

Acquisition, Use, and Disposal of Intangible Assets

Acquisition of Intangible Assets

The costs of intangible assets are recorded as assets only if they have been purchased. If an intangible asset was developed internally, its costs are reported as **research and development** expenses. The primary reason that the cost of internally developed intangibles is reported as an expense rather than an asset is that it is easy for managers to claim they developed a valuable (but invisible) intangible asset. To believe the claim, you need to see some evidence that the asset is actually worth what they say it is worth. That evidence is created only when someone gives up hard-earned cash to buy the asset. At that time, the purchaser records the intangible asset at its acquisition cost. This general rule applies to trademarks, copyrights, patents, licensing rights, franchises, and goodwill.

Goodwill is a particularly interesting type of intangible asset because it represents the value paid for another business's unidentifiable assets. You might wonder how anyone can put a value on something that cannot be identified, but it is possible. When one company buys another business, the purchase price is often more than the value of all of the business's **net assets**. Why would a company pay more for a business as a whole than it would for

[6] Krispy Kreme 2007 Form 10-K annual report.

the individual assets? The answer is to obtain the business's goodwill. You could easily buy equipment to produce and sell generic chocolate sandwich cookies, but that strategy probably would not be as successful as acquiring the goodwill associated with Oreos. That is part of the reason that Kraft Foods paid $40 billion more than the value of Nabisco's net assets: to acquire the goodwill associated with Nabisco's Oreo and Ritz snacks.

For accounting purposes, goodwill is defined as the difference between the purchase price of a company as a whole and the fair value of its net assets:

Purchase price
− Fair value of identifiable assets, net of liabilities
= Goodwill to be reported

Both parties to the sale estimate an acceptable amount for the goodwill of the business and add it to the appraised value of the business's net assets. Then they negotiate the sales price of the business. Based on the cost principle, the resulting goodwill is recorded as an intangible asset (but only when it has been purchased at a measurable cost).

Use of Intangible Assets

The rules of accounting for intangible assets after they have been purchased depend on whether the intangible asset has a limited or an unlimited life.

Limited Life. The cost of intangible assets with a limited life (such as copyrights, patents, licensing rights, and franchises) is spread over each period of useful life in a process called **amortization**, which is similar to straight-line depreciation. Most companies do not estimate a residual value for their intangible assets because unlike tangible assets that can be sold as scrap, most intangibles have no value at the end of their useful lives. Amortization is reported as an expense on the income statement each period. It is also subtracted directly from the applicable intangible asset accounts on the balance sheet.[7]

To illustrate, assume that Cedar Fair purchased a patent for an uphill water coaster for $800,000. The company intends to use it for 20 years. Each year, the company would record $40,000 in patent amortization expense ($800,000 ÷ 20 years). The journal entry to record this amortization follows.

	Debit	Credit
Amortization Expense (+E, −OE)	40,000	
Patents (−A)		40,000

Assets		=	Liabilities	+	Owners' Equity	
Patents	−40,000				Amortization Expense (+E)	−40,000

Unlimited Life. Intangibles with unlimited (or indefinite) lives, such as goodwill and trademarks, are not amortized. However, they are tested for possible impairment, just like other long-lived assets. If an intangible asset is impaired, its book value is written down (decreased) to its fair value.

Disposal of Intangible Assets

As with disposals of long-lived tangible assets, disposals of intangible assets result in gains (or losses) if the amounts received on disposal are more than (or less than) their book values.

Exhibit 10.5 summarizes and compares the accounting rules for long-lived tangible and intangible assets.

[7] As in the procedure for recording accumulated depreciation, a company may use an Accumulated Amortization account. In practice, however, most companies reduce the intangible asset account directly.

Exhibit 10.5 Accounting Rules for Long-Lived Tangible and Intangible Assets

Stage	Subject	Tangible Assets	Intangible Assets
Acquire	***Purchased asset***	Capitalize all related costs	Capitalize all related costs
Use	***Repairs and maintenance***		
	Ordinary	Expense related costs	Not applicable
	Extraordinary	Capitalize related costs	Not applicable
	Depreciation/amortization		
	Limited life	One of several methods: • Straight line • Units of production • Declining balance	Straight-line method
	Unlimited life	Do not depreciate (e.g., land)	Do not amortize (e.g., goodwill)
	Impairment test	Write down if necessary	Write down if necessary
Dispose	***Report gain (loss) when . . .***	Receive more (less) on disposal than book value	Receive more (less) on disposal than book value

Learning Objective 7

Interpret the fixed asset turnover ratio.

EVALUATION OF LONG-LIVED ASSET USE

Turnover Analysis

A primary goal of financial analysts is to evaluate how well management uses long-lived tangible assets to generate revenues. The fixed asset turnover ratio provides a good measure of this aspect of managerial performance. It is calculated as shown in the table that follows. The denominator uses the value of **average** net fixed assets over the same period as the revenues in the numerator. You can calculate the average net fixed assets by summing the beginning and ending balances in fixed assets (net of accumulated depreciation) and dividing by 2.

Accounting Decision Tools

Name of Measure	Formula	What It Tells You
Fixed Asset Turnover Ratio	$\frac{\text{Net Sales Revenue}}{\text{Average Net Fixed Assets}}$	• Indicates dollars of sales generated for each dollar invested in fixed assets (long-lived tangible assets) • A higher ratio implies greater efficiency

The fixed asset turnover ratio measures the sales dollars generated by each dollar invested in (tangible) fixed assets. Just as the number of miles per gallon provides a measure of a car's fuel efficiency, the fixed asset turnover ratio provides a measure of fixed asset operating efficiency. Generally speaking, a high or increasing turnover ratio relative to the industry average suggests better than average use of fixed assets in the sense that each dollar of fixed assets is generating higher than average sales.

Be aware that fixed asset turnover ratios can vary across industries because capital intensity—the need for tangible assets—also varies widely. A company such as Yahoo!, for example, needs fewer fixed assets than most companies to generate revenues. So Yahoo! is likely to have a high turnover ratio compared to companies such as Cedar Fair and Six Flags, which must invest considerable money in fixed assets to attract customers. Exhibit 10.6 shows the fixed asset turnover ratios for the three companies in 2007. Practice computing this ratio and comparing it to prior periods by trying the Self-Study Practice that follows Exhibit 10.6.

Exhibit 10.6 Summary of Fixed Asset Turnover Ratio Analyses

Company		Relevant Information (in millions) 2007	2006	2007 Fixed Asset Turnover Calculation
Cedar Fair L.P.	Sales	\$ 987.0	\$ 831.4	$\frac{\$987.0}{(\$1{,}933.6 + \$1{,}985.7) \div 2} = 0.50$
	Net fixed assets	\$1,933.6	\$1,985.7	
Six Flags	Sales	\$ 972.8	\$ 945.7	$\frac{\$972.8}{(\$1{,}641.1 + \$1{,}661.6) \div 2} = 0.59$
	Net fixed assets	\$1,641.1	\$1,661.6	
Yahoo!	Sales	\$6,969.3	\$6,425.7	$\frac{\$6{,}969.3}{(\$1{,}101.4 + \$1{,}331.6) \div 2} = 5.73$
	Net fixed assets	\$1,101.4	\$1,331.6	

SELF-STUDY PRACTICE

Cedar Fair reported net fixed assets of \$967.3 (million) on December 31, 2005.

1. Use this information and that in Exhibit 10.6 to calculate Cedar Fair's fixed asset turnover ratio in 2006.

2006 Fixed Asset Turnover

$$\frac{____}{(___ + ___) \div 2} = ____$$

2. Did Cedar Fair's fixed asset turnover improve or decline in 2007 compared to 2006?

When you have finished, check your answers with the solution at the bottom of the page.

Impact of Differences in Depreciation

Learning Objective 8

Describe the factors to consider when comparing long-lived assets across companies.

Just as differences in the nature of business operations affect financial analyses and the conclusions you draw from them, so too do differences in depreciation. Depreciation varies from one company to the next as a result of differences in depreciation methods, estimated useful lives, and estimated residual values. In this section, we present a simple example to show how different depreciation methods can affect financial analysis throughout the life of a long-lived asset. Do not be fooled by the simplicity of the example. Differences in depreciation can have a significant impact in the real world.

Assume that Cedar Fair and Six Flags each acquired a new roller coaster at the beginning of the year for \$15.5 million. The two companies estimate that the roller coasters will have residual values of \$1.5 million at the end of their seven-year useful lives. Assume too that

Solution to Self-Study Practice

1. $\frac{\$831.4}{(\$1{,}985.7 + \$967.3) \div 2} = 0.56$

2. Cedar Fair's fixed asset turnover declined from 0.56 in 2006 to 0.50 in 2007.

Exhibit 10.7 Straight-Line versus Double-Declining-Balance Depreciation Schedules

Cedar Fair (Straight line)				Six Flags (Double-declining balance)		
Depreciation Expense	Accumulated Depreciation	Book Value	Year	Depreciation Expense	Accumulated Depreciation	Book Value
$2,000,000	$ 2,000,000	$13,500,000	1	$4,429,000	$ 4,429,000	$11,071,000
2,000,000	4,000,000	11,500,000	2	3,163,000	7,592,000	7,908,000
2,000,000	6,000,000	9,500,000	3	2,259,000	9,851,000	5,649,000
2,000,000	8,000,000	7,500,000	4	1,614,000	11,465,000	4,035,000
2,000,000	10,000,000	5,500,000	5	1,153,000	12,618,000	2,882,000
2,000,000	12,000,000	3,500,000	6	823,000	13,441,000	2,059,000
2,000,000	14,000,000	1,500,000	7	559,000	14,000,000	1,500,000

Coach's Tip

For tips and practice involving the calculations in Exhibit 10.7, try CP10-7 at the end of this chapter.

everything about the roller coasters is identical. However, Cedar Fair uses the straight-line depreciation method and Six Flags uses the double-declining-balance method. Exhibit 10.7 shows the yearly depreciation reported by the two companies. Notice that early in the asset's life, before year 4, the straight-line depreciation expense reported by Cedar Fair is less than the declining-balance depreciation expense reported by Six Flags. Thus, even if the two companies attract exactly the same number of customers and earn exactly the same total revenues, their reported net incomes will differ each year simply because they use two different (but equally acceptable) methods of depreciation. This example shows why a user of financial statements needs to understand the accounting methods companies use.

These differences in depreciation affect more than just depreciation expense, however. Taking this example one step further, assume that the two companies sell the roller coasters at the end of year 4 for $6,000,000. Because the disposal occurs on the last day of the year, the companies will record a full year of depreciation prior to the disposal. Thus, at the time of disposal, Cedar Fair's roller coaster will have a book value of $7,500,000, but Six Flags' roller coaster will have a book value of $4,035,000 (see the highlighted line in Exhibit 10.7). To account for the disposal at the end of year 4, the companies record what they received, remove what they gave up (the book value of the asset), and recognize a gain or loss for the difference between what was received and what was given up. Exhibit 10.8 shows the calculations for the two companies.

Based on the information in Exhibit 10.8, which company appears to be better managed? Someone who does not understand accounting is likely to say that Six Flags is better managed because it reported a gain on disposal whereas Cedar Fair reported a loss. You know that cannot be right, however, because both companies experienced exactly the same events. They bought the same asset at the same cost ($15.5 million) and sold it for the same amount of money ($6 million). The only difference between them is that Cedar Fair reported less depreciation over the years leading up to the disposal, so its roller coaster had a larger book value at the time of disposal. Six Flags reported more depreciation, so its roller coaster had a smaller book

Exhibit 10.8 Calculation of Gain/Loss on Disposal, Straight-Line versus Double-Declining-Balance Depreciation

	Cedar Fair	Six Flags
Selling price	$ 6,000,000	$ 6,000,000
Book value (see Exhibit 10.7)	(7,500,000)	(4,035,000)
Gain (loss) on disposal	$(1,500,000)	$ 1,965,000

value at the time of disposal. As a financial statement user, you should realize that any gain or loss on disposal that is reported on the income statement tells you as much about the method used to depreciate the asset as about management's apparent ability to successfully negotiate the sale of long-lived assets.

Although the previous example concerned different depreciation methods, the same effects can occur for two companies that use the same depreciation method but different estimated useful lives or residual values. Useful lives can vary for several reasons including differences in (1) the type of equipment each company used, (2) the frequency of repairs and maintenance, (3) the frequency and duration of use, and (4) the degree of conservatism in management's estimates. How large can these differences be? Even within the same industry, sizable differences can occur. The notes to the financial statements of various companies in the airline industry, for example, reveal the following differences in the estimated useful lives of airplanes and other flight equipment:

Company	Estimated Life (in years)
US Airways	Up to 30
Southwest Airlines	Up to 25
Alaska Airlines	Up to 20
Singapore Airlines	Up to 15

Some analysts try to sidestep such differences in depreciation calculations by focusing on financial measures that exclude the effects of depreciation. One popular measure is called **EBITDA** (pronounced something like *'e bit, duh*), which stands for "earnings before interest, taxes, depreciation, and amortization." Analysts calculate EBITDA by starting with net income and then adding back depreciation and amortization expense (as well as nonoperating expenses such as interest and taxes). The idea is that this measure allows analysts to conduct financial analyses without having to deal with possible differences in depreciation and amortization.

Demonstration Case

Diversified Industries (DI) began operations as a home construction company but recently expanded into heavy construction, ready-mix concrete, sand and gravel, construction supplies, and earth-moving services. The company completed the following transactions during 2009. Amounts have been simplified.

July 1 Management decided to buy a 10-year-old building for $175,000 and, for $130,000, the land on which it was built. DI paid $100,000 in cash and signed a note payable for the rest.

July 3 DI paid $38,000 in cash for renovations to the building prior to its use.

Oct. 10 DI paid $1,200 cash for ordinary repairs on the building.

Dec. 31 DI considered the following information to determine year-end adjustments:

(*a*) The building will be depreciated on a straight-line basis over an estimated useful life of 30 years. Its estimated residual value is $33,000.

(*b*) DI purchased another company several years ago at $100,000 more than the fair values of the net assets acquired. The goodwill has an unlimited life.

(*c*) At the beginning of the year, DI owned equipment with a cost of $650,000 and accumulated depreciation of $150,000. The equipment is being depreciated using the double-declining-balance method with a useful life of 20 years and no residual value.

(*d*) At year-end, DI tested its long-lived assets for possible impairment of their value. Included in its equipment was a piece of old excavation equipment with a cost of $156,000 and a book value of $120,000 after the adjustment made in (*c*). Due to its small size and lack of safety features, the old equipment has limited use. Its future cash flows and fair value are expected to be $35,000. Goodwill was found not to be impaired.

December 31, 2009, is the end of the annual accounting period.

Required:

1. Prepare the journal entries to record each event that occurred during the year and the adjusting journal entries required on December 31. After each entry, show the effects on the accounting equation and explain any supporting decisions or calculations.
2. Show the December 31, 2009, balance sheet classification and amount for each of the following items:
   Fixed assets—land, building, and equipment.
   Intangible asset—goodwill.
3. Assuming that the company had sales of $1,000,000 for the year and a book value of $500,000 for fixed assets at the beginning of the year, compute the fixed asset turnover ratio. Explain its meaning.

Suggested Solution

1. **Journal entries for events during the year:**

July 1, 2009

	Debit	Credit
Land (+A)	130,000	
Building (+A)	175,000	
Cash (−A)		100,000
Note Payable (+L)		205,000

Assets		=	Liabilities		+	Owners' Equity
Cash	−100,000		Note Payable	+205,000		
Land	+130,000					
Building	+175,000					

July 3, 2009

	Debit	Credit
Building (+A)	38,000	
Cash (–A)		38,000

Assets		=	Liabilities	+	Owners' Equity
Cash	−38,000				
Building	+38,000				

The $38,000 expenditure is capitalized because it is necessary to prepare the asset for use.

October 10, 2009

	Debit	Credit
Repairs Expense (+E, −OE)	1,200	
Cash (−A)		1,200

Assets		=	Liabilities	+	Owners' Equity	
Cash	−1,200				Repairs Expense (+E)	−1,200

This is an ordinary repair that should be expensed.

December 31, 2009 (adjusting journal entries)

(*a*) **See page 441 for the calculation of this adjusting journal entry.**

	Debit	Credit
Depreciation Expense (+E, −OE)	3,000	
Accumulated Depreciation (+xA, −A)		3,000

Assets		=	Liabilities	+	Owners' Equity	
Accumulated Depreciation (+xA)	−3,000				Depreciation Expense (+E)	−3,000

Cost of Building		Straight-Line Depreciation
Initial payment	$175,000	($213,000 cost − $33,000 residual value) ×
Renovations prior to use	38,000	(1/30) years = $6,000 annual depreciation
Acquisition cost	$213,000	$6,000 × (6/12) = $3,000

(*b*) No adjusting journal entry is required because goodwill is assumed to have an unlimited (or indefinite) life. Goodwill is tested for impairment annually, but as described in the case, it was found not to be impaired.

(*c*) **Double-declining-balance depreciation**
($650,000 cost − $150,000 accumulated depreciation) × (2/20) years = $50,000 annual depreciation

	Debit	Credit
Depreciation Expense (+E, −OE)	50,000	
Accumulated Depreciation (+xA, −A)		50,000

Assets		=	Liabilities	+	Owners' Equity	
Accumulated Depreciation (+xA)	−50,000				Depreciation Expense (+E)	−50,000

(*d*) **Asset impairment test**
The book value of the old equipment ($120,000) exceeds its expected future cash flows ($35,000). The asset has become impaired, so it should be written down to its fair value.

Impairment loss	
Book value	$120,000
Less: Fair value	− 35,000
Loss due to impairment	$ 85,000

	Debit	Credit
Loss Due to Asset Impairment (+E, −OE)	85,000	
Equipment (−A)		85,000

Assets		=	Liabilities	+	Owners' Equity	
Equipment	−85,000				Loss Due to Asset Impairment (+E)	−85,000

2. **Partial balance sheet, December 31, 2009:**

Assets		
Fixed assets		
Land		$130,000
Building	$213,000	
Less: Accumulated depreciation	3,000	210,000
Equipment ($650,000 − $85,000)	565,000	
Less: Accumulated depreciation ($150,000 + $50,000)	200,000	365,000
Total fixed assets		705,000
Intangible asset		
Goodwill		100,000

3. **Fixed asset turnover ratio:**

$$\frac{\text{Net Sales Revenue}}{(\text{Beginning Net Fixed Asset Balance} + \text{Ending Net Fixed Asset Balance}) \div 2} = \frac{\$1{,}000{,}000}{(\$500{,}000 + \$705{,}000) \div 2} = 1.66$$

This construction company is capital intensive. The fixed asset turnover ratio measures management's efficiency at using the company's investment in property, plant, and equipment to generate sales. On average, approximately $1.66 of sales were generated for each dollar of fixed assets.

Supplement 10A

Natural Resources

Industries such as oil and gas, mining, and timber harvesting rely on a third category of long-lived assets called **natural resources.** These natural resources, whether in the form of oil wells, mineral deposits, or timber tracts, provide the raw materials for products sold by companies such as ExxonMobil and International Paper.

When a company first acquires or develops a natural resource, the cost is recorded in conformity with the **cost principle.** As the natural resource is used up, this cost must be split among the periods in which revenues are earned in conformity with the **matching principle.** The term **depletion** describes this process of allocating a natural resource's cost over the period of its extraction or harvesting. Depletion is often computed using the units-of-production method.

With one important exception, depletion is similar to the concepts of depreciation and amortization discussed in connection with tangible and intangible assets. When a natural resource such as timberland is depleted, the company obtains **inventory.** For example, a timber company obtains an inventory of logs. Because depletion of the natural resource is necessary to obtain the inventory, the depletion that is computed during a period is **added** to the cost of the inventory, not expensed in the period. For example, if a timber tract costing $530,000 is depleted over its estimated cutting life based on a cutting rate of approximately 20 percent per year, it would be depleted by $106,000 each year. The yearly depletion would be recorded with the following journal entry.

	Debit	Credit
Timber Inventory (+A)	106,000	
Timber Tract (−A)		106,000

Assets		=	Liabilities	+	Owners' Equity
Timber Inventory	**+106,000**				
Timber Tract	**−106,000**				

Supplement 10B

Changes in Depreciation

Depreciation is based on two estimates, useful life and residual value, that are made at the time a depreciable asset is acquired. As time goes by, one or both of these estimates may need to be revised. In addition, extraordinary repairs and additions may be added to the original acquisition cost at some time during the asset's use. When it is clear that either estimate should be revised significantly or that the asset's cost has changed, the undepreciated asset balance (less any residual value estimated at that date) should be assigned to the remaining years of estimated life using a new amount of depreciation.

To compute the new depreciation expense, you substitute the book value for the original acquisition cost, the new residual value for the original residual value, and the estimated remaining life for the original useful life. The revised formula to use with the straight-line method is:

Original

$$(\text{Cost} - \text{Residual Value}) \times \frac{1}{\text{Useful Life}} = \text{Depreciation Expense}$$

Revised

$$(\text{Book Value} - \text{New Residual Value}) \times \frac{1}{\text{Remaining Life}} = \text{Depreciation Expense}$$

Assume Cedar Fair purchased the largest, fastest roller coaster in the world for $60,000,000. The equipment had an estimated useful life of 20 years and an estimated residual value of $3,000,000. Shortly after the start of year 5, Cedar Fair changed the estimated total life to 25 years and lowered the estimated residual value to $2,400,000. At the end of year 5, the computation of the new amount of depreciation expense would be as follows:

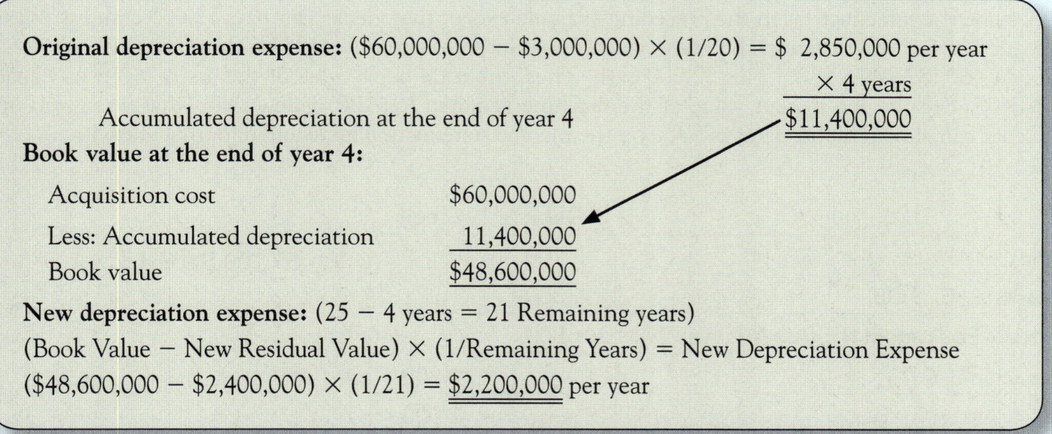

Original depreciation expense: ($60,000,000 − $3,000,000) × (1/20) = $ 2,850,000 per year

× 4 years

Accumulated depreciation at the end of year 4 $11,400,000

Book value at the end of year 4:

Acquisition cost	$60,000,000
Less: Accumulated depreciation	11,400,000
Book value	$48,600,000

New depreciation expense: (25 − 4 years = 21 Remaining years)

(Book Value − New Residual Value) × (1/Remaining Years) = New Depreciation Expense

($48,600,000 − $2,400,000) × (1/21) = $2,200,000 per year

Companies may also change their depreciation method (for example, from declining balance to straight line). Such a change requires significantly more disclosure as described in intermediate accounting textbooks. GAAP requires changes in accounting estimates and depreciation methods to be made only when a new estimate or accounting method better measures the periodic income of the business.

Supplement 10C

Exchanging Assets

In the same way that you may trade in an old car when buying a new one, companies can trade in their used fixed assets when acquiring new ones. Until recently, accounting rules required that these asset exchanges be recorded one way for losses and a different way for gains. Fortunately, that distinction no longer exists for most commercial asset exchanges.

Accounting for an asset exchange is similar to accounting for an asset sale. There are only two small differences: (1) rather than receive cash, you give up cash and (2) rather than simply dispose of the old asset, you also receive a new asset. If the new asset you receive has a market value that is more than the total book value of the cash and old asset that you gave up, you should report a gain on the income statement. You report a loss if the market value of the new asset is less than the total book value of the cash and old asset given up.

Assume, for example, that Cedar Fair trades in a cotton candy machine costing $2,200 with accumulated depreciation of $800 for a new machine worth $3,100. In the first case that follows (a gain), Cedar Fair also pays $1,000 cash as part of the deal.

Gain on Commercial Asset Exchange

The assets given up by Cedar Fair include the cotton candy machine with a book value of $1,400 ($2,200 – $800) and $1,000 cash. Thus, the total book value of the assets given up equals $2,400. Because the market value of the machine acquired ($3,100) is higher than what was given up, Cedar Fair should report a $700 gain on the income statement. The required journal entry is:

	Debit	Credit	
Equipment (new machine) (+A)	3,100		$3,100 Received
Accumulated Depreciation—Equipment (−xA, +A)	800		$2,400 Given up ($2,200 − $800 + $1,000)
Equipment (old machine) (−A)		2,200	
Cash (−A)		1,000	
Gain on Exchange of Assets (+R, +OE)		700	

Assets		=	Liabilities	+	Owners' Equity	
Cash	−1,000				Gain on Exchange of Assets (+R)	+700
Equipment (+3,100 − 2,200)	+ 900					
Accumulated Depreciation—Equipment (−xA)	+ 800					

Loss on Commercial Asset Exchange

Assume the same facts as in the preceding example except that Cedar Fair pays $2,000 cash instead of $1,000. Given these terms, the assets given up include the cotton candy machine with a book value of $1,400 ($2,200 – $800) plus $2,000 cash. Thus, the total book value of the assets given up equals $3,400. Because the market value of the machine acquired ($3,100) is less than what was given up, Cedar Fair should report a loss of $300 on the income statement. The required journal entry is:

	Debit	Credit	
Equipment (new machine) (+A)	3,100		$3,100 Received
Loss on Exchange of Assets (+E, −OE)	300		
Accumulated Depreciation—Equipment (−xA, +A)	800		$3,400 Given up ($2,200 − $800 + $2,000)
Equipment (old machine) (−A)		2,200	
Cash (−A)		2,000	

Assets		=	Liabilities	+	Owners' Equity	
Cash	−2,000				Loss on Exchange of Assets (+E)	−300
Equipment (+3,100 − 2,200)	+ 900					
Accumulated Depreciation—Equipment (−xA)	+ 800					

Chapter Summary

LO1 Define, classify, and explain the nature of long-lived assets. p. 418

- Long-lived assets are those that a business retains for long periods for use in the course of normal operations rather than for sale. They may be divided into tangible assets (land, buildings, and equipment) and intangible assets (including goodwill, patents, and franchises).

LO2 Apply the cost principle to the acquisition of long-lived assets. p. 419

- The acquisition cost of property, plant, and equipment is the cash-equivalent purchase price plus all reasonable and necessary expenditures made to acquire and prepare the asset for its intended use.

- Expenditures made after the asset is in use are expensed if they recur frequently, involve relatively small amounts, and do not directly lengthen the asset's useful life. These expenditures are considered ordinary repairs and maintenance expense.
- Expenditures made after the asset is in use are capitalized as a cost of the asset if they provide benefits for one or more accounting periods beyond the current period. This category includes extraordinary repairs, replacements, and additions.

LO3 Apply various depreciation methods as economic benefits are used up over time. p. 425

- In conformity with the matching principle, the cost of long-lived tangible assets (less any estimated residual value) is allocated to depreciation expense over each period benefited by the assets.
- Depreciation is reported as an expense on the income statement and is accumulated on the balance sheet in the contra-asset account Accumulated Depreciation, which is subtracted from the cost of the long-lived tangible assets to which it relates.
- Common depreciation methods include straight line (a constant amount over time), units of production (a variable amount over time), and double declining balance (a decreasing amount over time).

LO4 Explain the effect of asset impairment on the financial statements. p. 430

- When events or changes in circumstances reduce the estimated future cash flows of a long-lived asset below book value, the book value should be written down and the amount of the write-down reported as an impairment loss.

LO5 Account for the disposal of long-lived tangible assets that are discarded or sold. p. 431

- Disposals occur when assets are discarded or sold; they involve the following adjustments:
  - Record additional depreciation arising since the last depreciation adjustment.
  - Remove the cost of the old asset and its related accumulated depreciation.
  - Recognize the cash proceeds (if any).
  - Recognize a gain (or loss) equal to the amount by which the cash received is more (less) than the asset's book value (cost less accumulated depreciation).

LO6 Account for the acquisition, use, and disposal of long-lived intangible assets. p. 433

- Intangible assets are recorded at cost but only when they are purchased. The costs of most internally developed intangible assets are expensed when they are incurred as research and development costs.
- Intangibles are reported at book value on the balance sheet.
- Amortization is calculated for intangibles with limited useful lives using the straight-line method.
- Intangibles with unlimited useful lives, including goodwill, are not amortized but are reviewed for impairment.

LO7 Interpret the fixed asset turnover ratio. p. 436

- The fixed asset turnover ratio measures management's efficiency in using the company's investments in property, plant, and equipment to generate sales. Higher turnover ratios imply greater efficiency.

LO8 Describe the factors to consider when comparing long-lived assets across companies. p. 437

- Companies in different industries require different levels of investment in long-lived assets. Beyond that, you should consider whether differences exist in depreciation methods, estimated useful lives, and estimated residual values. Such differences can affect the book value of long-lived assets as well as the ratios that are calculated using those book values and any gains or losses reported at the time of an asset's disposal.

Financial Analysis Tools

Name of Measure	Formula	What It Tells You
Fixed Asset Turnover Ratio	$\frac{\text{Net Sales Revenue}}{\text{Average Net Fixed Assets}}$	• Indicates dollars of sales generated for each dollar invested in fixed assets (long-lived tangible assets) • A higher ratio implies greater efficiency

Key Terms

Amortization (p. 435)
Book (or Carrying) Value (p. 424)
Capital Expenditure (p. 423)
Capitalize (p. 419)
Construction in Progress (p. 419)
Copyright (p. 434)
Declining-Balance Depreciation Method (p. 427)
Depreciable Cost (p. 425)
Depreciation (p. 424)
Double-Declining-Balance Depreciation Method (p. 427)
EBITDA (p. 439)
Extraordinary Repairs (p. 423)
Fixed Assets (p. 418)

Franchise (p. 434)
Goodwill (p. 434)
Impairment (p. 430)
Intangible Assets (p. 418)
Land Improvements (p. 419)
Licensing Right (p. 434)
Long-Lived Assets (p. 418)
Net Assets (p. 434)
Ordinary Repairs and Maintenance (p. 423)
Patent (p. 434)
Research and Development (p. 434)
Residual (or Salvage or Scrap) Value (p. 424)
Revenue Expenditure (p. 423)
Straight-Line Depreciation Method (p. 426)
Tangible Assets (p. 418)
Trademark (p. 433)
Units-of-Production Depreciation Method (p. 426)
Useful Life (p. 424)

See complete glossary in back of text.

Questions

1. Define long-lived assets. Identify and describe each of the two common categories of long-lived asset.
2. Under the cost principle, what amounts should be recorded as a cost of a long-lived asset?
3. What is the term for recording costs as assets rather than as expenses? Describe how the decision to record costs as assets rather than expenses affects the balance sheet and income statement.
4. Distinguish between ordinary repairs and extraordinary repairs. How do you account for each?
5. Describe the relationship between the matching principle and accounting for long-lived assets.
6. Why are different depreciation methods allowed?
7. In computing depreciation, three values must be known or estimated. Identify and describe each.
8. What type of depreciation expense pattern is used under each of the following methods, and when is its use appropriate?
   a. The straight-line method.
   b. The units-of-production method.
   c. The double-declining-balance method.
9. What is an *asset impairment?* How do you account for it?
10. What is book value? When equipment is sold for more than book value, how is the transaction recorded? How is it recorded when the selling price is less than book value?
11. Distinguish between depreciation and amortization.
12. Define *goodwill*. When is it appropriate to record goodwill as an intangible asset?
13. How is the fixed asset turnover ratio computed? Explain its meaning.
14. (Supplement 10A) How does depletion affect the balance sheet and income statement? Why is depletion accounted for in a manner that differs from depreciation and amortization?
15. (Supplement 10B) Over what period should an addition to an existing long-lived asset be depreciated? Explain.
16. (Supplement 10C) In what two ways does the disposal of an asset through exchange differ from disposal through discarding or selling the asset?

Multiple Choice

Quiz 10-1
www.mhhe.com/LLPW1e

1. Which of the following should be capitalized when a piece of production equipment is acquired for a factory?
   a. Sales taxes.
   b. Transportation costs.
   c. Installation costs.
   d. All of the above.
2. When recording depreciation, which of the following statements is true?
   a. Total assets increase and owners' equity increases.
   b. Total assets decrease and total liabilities increase.
   c. Total assets decrease and owners' equity increases.
   d. None of the above is true.
3. Under what depreciation method(s) is an asset's book value used to calculate depreciation each year?
   a. Straight-line method.
   b. Units-of-production method.
   c. Declining-balance method.
   d. All of the above.
4. Which of the following decisions will result in a higher net income in the year fixed assets are acquired?
   a. Using MACRS depreciation rates prescribed by the IRS rather than straight-line depreciation.
   b. Using long estimated useful lives.
   c. Using lower estimated residual values.
   d. Using the double-declining-balance method rather than the straight-line method.
5. Barber, Inc., followed the practice of depreciating its building on a straight-line basis. Barber purchased a building on January 1, 2010, that had an estimated useful life of 20 years and a residual value of $20,000. The company's depreciation expense for 2010 was $20,000 on the building. What was the original cost of the building?
   a. $360,000.
   b. $380,000.
   c. $400,000.
   d. $420,000.

6. Under which depreciation method is partial-year depreciation not calculated by multiplying the annual depreciation by the fraction of the year for which the asset has been used?
   a. Straight line.
   b. Units of production.
   c. Declining balance.
   d. None of the above—partial-year depreciation always is calculated by multiplying the annual depreciation by the fraction of the year for which the asset has been used.
7. ACME, Inc., uses straight-line depreciation for all of its depreciable assets. ACME sold a used piece of machinery on December 31, 2010, that it had purchased on January 1, 2009, for $10,000. The asset had a five-year life, zero residual value, and Accumulated Depreciation as of December 31, 2009, of $2,000. If the sales price of the used machine was $7,500, the resulting gain or loss on disposal was which of the following amounts?
   a. Loss of $3,500.
   b. Gain of $3,500.
   c. Loss of $1,500.
   d. Gain of $1,500.
8. What assets should be amortized using the straight-line method?
   a. Land.
   b. Intangible assets with limited useful lives.
   c. Intangible assets with unlimited (or indefinite) lives.
   d. All of the above.
9. How many of the following statements regarding goodwill are true?
   - Goodwill is not reported unless purchased in an exchange.
   - Goodwill must be reviewed annually for possible impairment.
   - Impairment of goodwill results in a decrease in net income.

   a. None. c. Two.
   b. One. d. Three.
10. The Simon Company and the Allen Company each bought a new delivery truck on January 1, 2009. Both companies paid exactly the same cost, $30,000, for their respective vehicles. As of December 31, 2010, the book value of Simon's truck was less than the Allen Company's book value for the same vehicle. Which of the following are acceptable explanations for the difference in book value?
   a. Both companies elected straight-line depreciation, but the Simon Company used a longer estimated life.
   b. The Simon Company estimated a lower residual value, but both estimated the same useful life and both elected straight-line depreciation.
   c. Because GAAP specifies rigid guidelines regarding the calculation of depreciation, this situation is not possible.
   d. None of the above explains the difference in book value.

Solutions to Multiple-Choice Questions

1. d 2. d 3. c 4. b 5. d 6. b 7. d 8. b 9. d 10. b

Mini Exercises  Available with McGraw-Hill's Homework Manager

M10-1 Classifying Long-Lived Assets and Related Cost Allocation Concepts

LO1, 3, 6

For each of the following long-lived assets, indicate its nature and related cost allocation concept. Use the abbreviations shown on the right:

Asset	Nature	Cost Allocation	Nature
1. Operating license	______	______	L Land
2. Property	______	______	B Building
3. New engine for old machine	______	______	E Equipment
4. Delivery vans	______	______	I Intangible
5. Production plant	______	______	
6. Warehouse	______	______	**Cost Allocation**
7. Copyright	______	______	D Depreciation
8. Trademark	______	______	A Amortization
9. Computers	______	______	NO No cost allocation

M10-2 Deciding Whether to Capitalize or Expense

LO2, 6

American Golf Corporation

American Golf Corporation operates over 170 golf courses throughout the country. For each of the following items, enter the correct letter to show whether the cost should be capitalized (C) or expensed (E).

Transactions

____ 1. Purchased a golf course in Orange County, California.

____ 2. Paid a landscaping company to clear 100 acres of land on which to build a new course.

____ 3. Paid a landscaping company to apply fertilizer to the fairways on its Coyote Hills Golf Course.

____ 4. Hired a building maintenance company to build a 2,000 square-foot addition on a clubhouse.

____ 5. Hired a building maintenance company to replace the locks on a clubhouse and equipment shed.

____ 6. Paid an advertising company to create a campaign to build goodwill.

LO2, 6

M10-3 Deciding Whether to Capitalize an Expense

For each of the following items, enter the correct letter to the left to show whether the expenditure should be capitalized (C) or expensed (E).

Transactions

____ 1. Paid $600 for ordinary repairs.

____ 2. Paid $16,000 for extraordinary repairs.

____ 3. Paid cash, $200,000, for addition to old building.

____ 4. Paid for routine maintenance, $250, on credit.

____ 5. Purchased a machine, $70,000; gave long-term note.

____ 6. Purchased a patent, $45,300 cash.

____ 7. Paid $20,000 for monthly salaries.

LO3

M10-4 Computing Book Value (Straight-Line Depreciation)

Calculate the book value of a two-year-old machine that cost $200,000, has an estimated residual value of $40,000, and has an estimated useful life of four years. The company uses straight-line depreciation.

LO3

M10-5 Computing Book Value (Units-of-Production Depreciation)

Calculate the book value of a two-year-old machine that cost $200,000, has an estimated residual value of $40,000, and has an estimated useful life of 20,000 machine hours. The company uses units-of-production depreciation and ran the machine 3,000 hours in year 1 and 8,000 hours in year 2.

LO3

M10-6 Computing Book Value (Double-Declining-Balance Depreciation)

Calculate the book value of a two-year-old machine that cost $200,000, has an estimated residual value of $40,000, and has an estimated useful life of four years. The company uses double-declining-balance depreciation. Round to the nearest dollar.

LO3

M10-7 Computing and Recording Partial-Year Straight-Line Depreciation

Calculate the amount of straight-line depreciation to report during the year ended December 31, 2009, for a machine that was purchased at a cost of $33,000 on September 1, 2009. The machine has an estimated residual value of $3,000, and has an estimated useful life of five years. Round to the nearest dollar. Prepare the journal entry to record the depreciation.

LO3

M10-8 Computing and Recording Partial-Year Double-Declining-Balance Depreciation

Calculate the amount of double-declining-balance depreciation to report during the year ended December 31, 2009, for a machine that was purchased at a cost of $33,000 on September 1, 2009. The machine has an estimated residual value of $3,000, and has an estimated useful life of five years. Round to the nearest dollar. Prepare the journal entry to record the depreciation.

LO4

M10-9 Identifying Asset Impairment

For each of the following impaired assets, indicate the amount of impairment loss to report.

	Book Value	Fair Value	Amount of Loss
a. Machine	$ 17,000	$ 9,000	
b. Copyright	41,000	39,000	
c. Factory building	60,000	30,000	
d. Building	250,000	210,000	

M10-10 Recording the Disposal of a Long-Lived Asset through Sale LO5

Prepare journal entries to record these transactions: (*a*) Morrell Corporation disposed of computer equipment at the end of its useful life. The computer equipment had cost $4,800 and its Accumulated Depreciation balance was $4,800. No residual value was received. (*b*) Assume the same information as (*a*) except that Accumulated Depreciation, updated to the date of disposal, was $3,600.

M10-11 Reporting and Recording the Disposal of a Long-Lived Asset through Sale (Straight-Line Depreciation) LO5

As part of a major renovation at the beginning of the year, Hauser Pharmaceuticals, Inc., sold shelving units (store fixtures) that were 10 years old for $1,000 cash. The shelves originally cost $6,400 and had been depreciated on a straight-line basis over an estimated useful life of 10 years with an estimated residual value of $400. Assuming that depreciation has already been recorded to the date of sale, prepare the journal entry to record the sale of the shelving units and show the effects of the disposal on the accounting equation.

M10-12 Capitalizing versus Expensing Intangible Asset Costs LO6

Most highly visible companies spend significant amounts of money to protect their intellectual property, ensuring that no one uses this property without direct permission. For example, to include logos throughout this book, we had to obtain written permission from each company—a process that stretched over nearly a year and often resulted in requests being denied. Discuss whether companies should capitalize or expense the money paid to employees who evaluate requests for use of their logos and who search for instances where the companies' intellectual property has been used without permission. Draw an analogy to similar costs incurred for employees responsible for the use and upkeep of tangible assets.

M10-13 Computing Goodwill and Patents LO6

Taste-T Company has been in business for 30 years and has developed a large group of loyal restaurant customers. Down Home Foods made an offer to buy Taste-T Company for $6,000,000. The market value of Taste-T's recorded assets, net of liabilities, on the date of the offer is $5,600,000. Taste-T also holds a patent for a fluting machine that the company invented (the patent with a market value of $200,000 was never recorded by Taste-T because it was developed internally). How much has Down Home Foods included for intangibles in its offer of $6,000,000? Assuming Taste-T accepts this offer, which company will report goodwill on its balance sheet?

M10-14 Computing and Evaluating the Fixed Asset Turnover Ratio LO7

The following information was reported by Amuse Yourself Parks (AYP) for 2009:

Net fixed assets (beginning of year)	$8,450,000
Net fixed assets (end of year)	8,250,000
Net sales for the year	4,175,000
Net income for the year	1,700,000

Compute the company's fixed asset turnover ratio for the year. What can you say about AYP's fixed asset turnover ratio when compared to Cedar Fair's 2007 ratio in Exhibit 10.6?

M10-15 (Supplement 10A) Recording Depletion for a Natural Resource

Saskatchewan Forestry Company purchased a timber tract for $600,000, and estimates that it will be depleted evenly over its 10-year useful life with no residual value. Show the journal entry that would be recorded if 10 percent of the total timber is cut and placed into inventory during the current year.

M10-16 (Supplement 10B) Computing Revised Depreciation after Change in Cost and Estimated Life

Thornton Industries purchased a machine for $45,000 and is depreciating it with the straight-line method over a life of 10 years, using a residual value of $3,000. At the beginning of the sixth year, an extraordinary repair was made costing $5,000, the estimated useful life was extended to 13 years, and no change was made to the estimated residual value. Calculate depreciation expense for year 6, rounded to the nearest dollar.

M10-17 (Supplement 10C) Recording the Exchange of Assets

Crosstown Motors acquired a new piece of hydraulic equipment worth $60,000, by paying $50,000 cash and trading in its old equipment. The old equipment had a cost of $40,000 and accumulated depreciation of $35,000. Calculate the amount of the gain or loss that arises from this transaction and prepare the journal entry to record the exchange of assets.

M10-18 (Supplement 10C) Recording the Exchange of Assets

Assume the same facts as M10-17, except that the old equipment has accumulated depreciation of $24,000 at the time of the transaction. Calculate the amount of the gain or loss that arises from the transaction and prepare the journal entry to record the exchange of assets.

Exercises

Available with McGraw-Hill's Homework Manager

LO1
Hasbro, Inc.

E10-1 Preparing a Classified Balance Sheet

The following is a list of account titles and amounts (in millions) reported at December 31, 2006, by Hasbro, Inc., a leading manufacturer of games, toys, and interactive entertainment software for children and families:

Buildings and Improvements	$186	Goodwill	$470
Prepaids and Other Current Assets	243	Machinery and Equipment	368
Allowance for Doubtful Accounts	28	Accumulated Depreciation	379
Other Noncurrent Assets	195	Inventories	203
Cash and Cash Equivalents	715	Other Intangibles, Net	532
Accounts Receivable	584	Land and Improvements	7

Required:

Prepare the asset section of a classified balance sheet for Hasbro, Inc.

LO2, 3

E10-2 Computing and Recording a Basket Purchase and Straight-Line Depreciation

Bridge City Consulting bought a building and the land on which it is located for $182,000 cash. The land is estimated to represent 70 percent of the purchase price. The company also paid renovation costs on the building of $22,000.

Required:

1. Explain how to account for the renovation costs.
2. Give the journal entry to record all expenditures. Assume that all transactions were for cash and they occurred at the start of the year.
3. Compute straight-line depreciation on the building at the end of one year, assuming an estimated 12-year useful life and a $4,600 estimated residual value.
4. What should be the book value of the land and building at the end of year 2?

LO2, 3

E10-3 Recording Asset Acquisition Costs and Straight-Line Depreciation

Conover Company ordered equipment on January 1, 2009, at a purchase price of $30,000. On date of delivery, January 2, 2009, the company paid $8,000 for the equipment and signed a note payable for the balance. On January 3, 2009, it paid $250 for freight on the equipment. On January 5, Conover paid $1,500 cash for installation costs relating to the equipment. On December 31, 2009 (the end of the accounting period), Conover recorded depreciation on the equipment using the straight-line method with an estimated useful life of 10 years and an estimated residual value of $2,750.

Required:

1. Record journal entries, if any, that would be required on January 1, 2, 3, and 5.
2. Compute the acquisition cost of the equipment.
3. Compute the depreciation expense to be reported for 2009, and show the journal entry to record it.
4. What should be the book value of the equipment at the end of 2010?

E10-4 Recording Straight-Line Depreciation and Repairs LO2, 3

Wiater Company operates a small manufacturing facility. At the beginning of 2010, an asset account for the company showed the following balances:

Manufacturing equipment	$160,000
Accumulated depreciation through 2009	110,000

During 2010, the following cash expenditures were made for repairs and maintenance:

Routine maintenance and repairs on the equipment	$ 1,850
Major overhaul of the equipment that improved efficiency	21,000

The equipment is being depreciated on a straight-line basis over an estimated life of 15 years with a $10,000 estimated residual value. The annual accounting period ends on December 31.

Required:

1. Give the adjusting journal entry that would have been made at the end of 2009 for depreciation on the manufacturing equipment.
2. Give the journal entries to record the two expenditures for repairs and maintenance during 2010.

E10-5 Determining Financial Statement Effects of Straight-Line Depreciation and Repairs LO2, 3

Refer to E10-4.

Required:

Indicate the effects (accounts, amounts, and + or −) of the following items on the accounting equation, using the headings shown below.

1. The adjustment for depreciation made at the end of 2009.
2. The two expenditures for repairs and maintenance during 2010.

Item	Assets	=	Liabilities	+	Owners' Equity

E10-6 Computing Depreciation under Alternative Methods LO3

PlasticWorks Corporation bought a machine at the beginning of the year at a cost of $12,000. The estimated useful life was five years, and the residual value was $2,000. Assume that the estimated productive life of the machine is 10,000 units. Expected annual production was 3,000 units in year 1; 3,000 units in year 2; 2,000 units in year 3; 1,000 units in year 4; and 1,000 units in year 5.

Required:

1. Complete a depreciation schedule for each of the alternative methods using a format similar to the one that follows.
   a. Straight line.
   b. Units of production.
   c. Double-declining balance.

		INCOME STATEMENT	BALANCE SHEET		
Year	Computation	Depreciation Expense	Cost	Accumulated Depreciation	Book Value
At acquisition					
1					

2. Which method will result in the highest net income in year 2? Does this higher net income mean the machine was used more efficiently under this depreciation method?

LO3
Sonic Corp.

E10-7 Computing Depreciation under Alternative Methods

Sonic Corp. purchased and installed electronic payment equipment at its drive-in restaurants in San Marcos, Texas, at a cost of $27,000. The equipment has an estimated residual value of $1,500. The equipment is expected to process 255,000 payments over its three-year useful life. Per year, expected payment transactions are 61,200 in year 1; 140,250 in year 2; and 53,550 in year 3.

Required:

Complete a depreciation schedule for each of the alternative methods using a format similar to the one that follows.

1. Straight line.
2. Units of production.
3. Double declining balance.

		INCOME STATEMENT	BALANCE SHEET		
Year	Computation	Depreciation Expense	Cost	Accumulated Depreciation	Book Value
At acquisition					
1					

LO3

E10-8 Computing Partial-Year Depreciation under Alternative Methods

A vehicle was purchased on July 1, 2009, at a cost of $50,000. The vehicle had an estimated useful life of five years and a residual value of $5,000. The company's fiscal year ends on December 31. The vehicle was expected to be driven 30,000 miles in 2009, 40,000 miles in 2010, and 10,000 miles in each of years 2011, 2012, and 2013.

Required:

Compute depreciation for 2009 and 2010, under the following methods.

1. Straight line.
2. Units of production.
3. Double declining balance.

LO3

E10-9 Recording Partial-Year Depreciation under Alternative Methods

Refer to E10-8.

Required:

Prepare journal entries for 2009 and 2010, for each of the alternative methods.

1. Straight line.
2. Units of production.
3. Double declining balance.

LO3
FedEx Corporation

E10-10 Interpreting Management's Choice of Different Depreciation Methods for Tax and Financial Reporting

The annual report for FedEx Corporation includes the following information:

> For financial reporting purposes, we record depreciation and amortization of property and equipment on a straight-line basis over the asset's service life. For income tax purposes, depreciation is generally computed using accelerated methods.

Required:

Explain why FedEx uses different methods of depreciation for financial reporting and tax purposes.

E10-11 Inferring Asset Age from Straight-Line Depreciation LO3

On January 1, 2009, the records of Tuff Turf Corporation (TTC) showed the following regarding production equipment:

Equipment (estimated residual value, $4,000)	$14,000
Accumulated depreciation (straight line, one year)	2,000

Required:
Based on the data given, compute the estimated useful life of the equipment.

E10-12 Exploring Financial Statement Effects of Asset Impairment LO4

Refer to E10-11.

Required:
If TTC's management estimated that the equipment had future cash flows and a fair value of only $6,800 at December 31, 2009, how would this affect TTC's balance sheet and income statement? Explain.

E10-13 Demonstrating the Effect of Book Value on Reporting an Asset Disposal through Sale LO5 FedEx

FedEx is the world's leading express-distribution company. In addition to the world's largest fleet of all-cargo aircraft, the company has more than 46,400 ground vehicles that pick up and deliver packages. Assume that FedEx sold a delivery truck for $16,000. FedEx had originally purchased the truck for $28,000 and had recorded depreciation for three years.

Required:

1. Give the journal entry for the disposal of the truck, assuming that
   a. The accumulated depreciation was $12,000.
   b. The accumulated depreciation was $10,000.
   c. The accumulated depreciation was $15,000.
2. Based on the three preceding situations, explain how the amount of depreciation recorded up to the time of disposal affects the amount of gain or loss on disposal.

E10-14 Demonstrating the Effect of Book Value on Recording an Asset Disposal through Sale LO5

Refer to E10–13.

Required:

1. Calculate the amount of gain or loss on disposal, assuming that
   a. The accumulated depreciation was $12,000.
   b. The accumulated depreciation was $10,000.
   c. The accumulated depreciation was $15,000.
2. Based on the three preceding situations, explain how the amount of depreciation recorded up to the time of disposal affects the amount of gain or loss on disposal.

E10-15 Computing and Reporting the Acquisition and Amortization of Three Different Intangible Assets LO 6

Kreiser Company had three intangible assets at the end of 2009 (end of the accounting year):

a. A patent purchased from J. Miller on January 1, 2009, for a cash cost of $5,640. Miller had registered the patent with the U.S. Patent Office five years ago.
b. A trademark was registered with the federal government for $10,000. Management estimated that the trademark could be worth as much as $200,000 because it has an indefinite life.
c. Computer licensing rights were purchased on January 1, 2008, for $60,000. The rights are expected to have a four-year useful life to the company.

Required:

1. Compute the acquisition cost of each intangible asset.
2. Compute the amortization of each intangible asset for the year ended December 31, 2009.
3. Show how these assets and any related expenses should be reported on the balance sheet and income statement for 2009.

LO4, 6

Nutek, Inc.

E10-16 Recording the Purchase, Amortization, and Impairment of a Patent

Nutek, Inc., holds a patent for the Full Service handi-plate, which the company described in its annual report as "a patented plastic buffet plate that allows the user to hold both a plate and cup in one hand" and that "has a multitude of uses including social gatherings such as backyard barbecues, buffets, picnics, tailgate and parties of any kind." (No, we are not making this up.) Nutek also purchased a patent for $1,000,000 for "a specialty line of patented switch plate covers and outlet plate covers specifically designed to light up automatically when the power fails." Assume the switch plate patent was purchased January 1, 2009, and it is being amortized over a period of 10 years. Assume Nutek does not use an Accumulated Amortization account but instead charges amortization directly against the intangible asset account.

Required:

1. Describe the effects of the purchase and amortization of the switch plate patent on the 2009 balance sheet and income statement.
2. Give the journal entries to record the purchase and amortization of the switch plate patent in 2009.
3. After many months of unsuccessful attempts to manufacture the switch plate covers, Nutek determined the patent was significantly impaired and its book value on January 1, 2010, was written off. Show the journal entry and the accounting effects of recording the asset impairment.

LO7

Apple Inc.

E10-17 Computing and Interpreting the Fixed Asset Turnover Ratio from a Financial Analyst's Perspective

The following data were included in a recent Apple Inc. annual report (in millions):

	2007	2006	2005	2004	2003	2002	2001
Net sales	$24,006	$19,315	$13,931	$8,279	$6,207	$5,742	$5,363
Net property, plant, and equipment	1,832	1,281	817	707	669	669	564

Required:

1. Compute Apple's fixed asset turnover ratio for 2002, 2004, and 2006 (the even years). Round your answers to one decimal place.
2. If you were a financial analyst, what would you say about the results of your analyses?

LO3, 7

E10-18 Computing Depreciation and Book Value for Two Years Using Alternative Depreciation Methods and Interpreting the Impact on the Fixed Asset Turnover Ratio

Torge Company bought a machine for $65,000 cash. The estimated useful life was five years, and the estimated residual value was $5,000. Assume that the estimated useful life in productive units is 150,000. Units actually produced were 40,000 in year 1 and 45,000 in year 2.

Required:

1. Determine the appropriate amounts to complete the following schedule. Show computations.

	DEPRECIATION EXPENSE FOR		BOOK VALUE AT THE END OF	
Method of Depreciation	Year 1	Year 2	Year 1	Year 2
Straight line				
Units of production				
Double-declining balance				

2. Which method would result in the lowest net income for year 1? For year 2?
3. Which method would result in the lowest fixed asset turnover ratio for year 1? Why?

E10-19 Accounting for Operating Activities (Including Depreciation) and Preparing Financial Statements (Comprehensive Exercise) LO2, 3

Grid Iron Prep Inc. (GIPI) is a sole proprietorship created in January 2009 to provide personal training for athletes aspiring to play college football. The following transactions occurred during the year ended December 31, 2009.

(*a*) Gerry Ingalls contributed $90,000 cash to start his sole proprietorship.
(*b*) GIPI purchased a gymnasium building and gym equipment at the beginning of the year for $50,000, 80 percent of which related to the gymnasium and 20 percent to the equipment.
(*c*) GIPI paid $250 cash to have the gym equipment refurbished before it could be used.
(*d*) GIPI collected $36,000 cash in training fees during the year, of which $2,000 was for customer deposits to be earned in 2010.
(*e*) GIPI paid $23,000 of wages and $7,000 in utilities.
(*f*) GIPI provided $3,000 in training during the final month of the year and expected collection in 2010.
(*g*) GIPI will depreciate the gymnasium building using the double-declining-balance method over 20 years. Gym equipment will be depreciated using the straight-line method, with an estimated residual value of $2,250 at the end of its four-year useful life.
(*h*) GIPI received a bill for $350 of advertising done during December. The bill has not been paid or recorded.
(*i*) GIPI will record an estimated 5 percent of its accounts receivable as not collectible.

Required:

1. Prepare journal entries to record the transactions and adjustments listed in *a* through *i*.
2. Prepare GIPI's 2009 income statement, statement of owners' equity, and classified balance sheet.

E10-20 (Supplement 10A) Calculating and Reporting Depletion

Louisiana Oil Company (LOC) paid $3,000,000 for an oil reserve estimated to hold 50,000 barrels of oil. Oil production is expected to be 10,000 barrels in year 1, 30,000 barrels in year 2, and 10,000 barrels in year 3. LOC expects to begin selling barrels from its oil inventory in year 2.

Required:

Assuming these estimates are accurate, describe the amounts, financial statements, and classifications that would be used for the oil reserves and oil inventory at the end of year 1.

E10-21 (Supplement 10B) Recording a Change in Estimate

Refer to E10-4.

Required:

Give the adjusting entry that should be made at the end of 2010 for depreciation of the manufacturing equipment, assuming no change in the original estimated total life or residual value. Show computations.

E10-22 (Supplement 10C) Comparing Exchange of Assets under Two Depreciation Methods

Scrimshaw Industries acquired a new dump truck worth $120,000 on December 31, 2010, by paying $70,000 cash and trading in its used dump truck, which had been purchased three years ago at a cost of $100,000. The old truck had an estimated useful life of five years and a residual value of $20,000.

Required:

1. Calculate the amount of depreciation recorded on the old dump truck on December 31, 2008, 2009, and 2010, assuming (a) straight-line depreciation and (b) double-declining-balance depreciation.
2. Give the journal entry to record the exchange of assets on December 31, 2010, assuming depreciation has already been recorded in 2010 using (a) straight-line and (b) double-declining-balance methods.
3. Does the amount recorded as the cost of the new dump truck differ for situations (a) and (b)? Does the amount recorded as a gain or loss on disposal of the old dump truck differ for situations (a) and (b)? What is responsible for producing any differences between (a) and (b)?

Problems—Set A

Available with McGraw-Hill's Homework Manager

LO1, 2, 3, 4, 5, 6

PA10-1 Recording Transactions and Adjustments for Tangible and Intangible Assets

The following transactions and adjusting entries were completed by a paper-packaging company called Gravure Graphics International. The company uses straight-line depreciation for trucks and other vehicles, double-declining-balance depreciation for buildings, and straight-line amortization for patents.

January 2, 2009	Paid $95,000 cash to purchase storage shed components.
January 3, 2009	Paid $5,000 cash to have the storage shed erected. The storage shed has an estimated life of 10 years, and a residual value of $10,000.
April 1, 2009	Paid $38,000 cash to purchase a pickup truck for use in the business. The truck has an estimated useful life of five years, and a residual value of $8,000.
May 13, 2009	Paid $250 cash for repairs to the pickup truck.
July 1, 2009	Paid $20,000 cash to purchase patent rights on a new paper bag manufacturing process. The patent is estimated to have a remaining useful life of five years.
December 31, 2009	Recorded depreciation and amortization on the pickup truck, storage shed, and patent.
June 30, 2010	Sold the pickup truck for $33,000 cash. (Record the depreciation on the truck prior to recording its disposal.)
December 31, 2010	Recorded depreciation on the storage shed. Determined that the patent was impaired and wrote off its remaining book value (i.e., wrote down the book value to zero).

Required:

Give the journal entries required on each of the above dates.

LO2, 3

PA10-2 Computing Acquisition Cost and Recording Depreciation under Three Alternative Methods

At the beginning of the year, Chemical Control Corporation bought three used machines from Radial Compression Incorporated. The machines immediately were overhauled, installed, and started operating. Because the machines were different, each was recorded separately in the accounts.

	Machine A	Machine B	Machine C
Cost of the asset	$10,000	$31,500	$22,000
Installation costs	1,600	2,100	800
Renovation costs prior to use	600	1,400	1,600
Repairs after production began	500	400	700

By the end of the first year, each machine had been operating 7,000 hours.

Required:

1. Compute the cost of each machine. Explain the rationale for capitalizing or expensing the various costs.
2. Give the journal entry to record depreciation expense at the end of year 1, assuming the following:

	ESTIMATES		
Machine	Life	Residual Value	Depreciation Method
A	4 years	$1,000	Straight line
B	33,000 hours	2,000	Units of production
C	5 years	1,400	Double-declining balance

PA10-3 Recording and Interpreting the Disposal of Long-Lived Assets Sold and Discarded **LO5**

During 2009, Ly Company disposed of two different assets. On January 1, 2009, prior to their disposal, the accounts reflected the following:

Asset	Original Cost	Residual Value	Estimated Life	Accumulated Depreciation (straight line)
Machine A	$24,000	$2,000	5 years	$17,600 (4 years)
Machine B	59,200	3,200	14 years	48,000 (12 years)

The machines were disposed of in the following ways:

a. Machine A: Sold on January 1, 2009, for $7,000 cash.

b. Machine B: On January 1, 2009, this machine suffered irreparable damage from an accident and was removed immediately by a salvage company at no cost.

Required:

1. Give the journal entries related to the disposal of each machine at the beginning of 2009.
2. Explain the accounting rationale for the way that you recorded each disposal.

PA10-4 Determining Financial Statement Effects of Activities Related to Intangible Assets **LO6**

Norton Pharmaceuticals entered into the following transactions that potentially affect intangible assets:

(*a*) On January 1, 2009, the company spent $18,600 cash to buy a patent that expires in 15 years.

(*b*) During 2009, the company spent $25,480 working on a new drug that will be submitted for FDA testing in 2010.

(*c*) Norton Pharmaceuticals purchased the assets of another business in 2009 for a cash lump-sum payment of $650,000. Included in the purchase price was "Goodwill, $75,000."

Required:

1. Give the journal entry for each of these transactions.
2. For each of the intangible assets, compute amortization for the year ended December 31, 2009.

PA10-5 (Supplement 10B) Analyzing and Recording Entries Related to a Change in Estimated Life and Residual Value

Reader's Digest

Reader's Digest is a global publisher of magazines, books, and music and video collections, and is one of the world's leading direct-mail marketers. Many direct-mail marketers use high-speed Didde press equipment to print their advertisements. These presses can cost more than $1 million. Assume that Reader's Digest owns a Didde press acquired at an original cost of $600,000. It is being depreciated on a straight-line basis over a 20-year estimated useful life and has a $75,000 estimated residual value. At the end of 2009, the press had been depreciated for a full eight years. In January 2010, a decision was made, on the basis of improved maintenance procedures, that a total estimated useful life of 25 years and a residual value of $109,500 would be more realistic. The accounting period ends December 31.

Required:

1. Compute (*a*) the amount of depreciation expense recorded in 2009, and (*b*) the book value of the printing press at the end of 2009.
2. Compute the amount of depreciation that should be recorded in 2010. Show computations.
3. Give the adjusting entry for depreciation at December 31, 2010.

Problems—Set B

PB10-1 Recording Transactions and Adjustments for Tangible and Intangible Assets **LO1, 2, 3, 4, 5, 6**

The following transactions and adjusting entries were completed by a local delivery company called Super Swift. The company uses straight-line depreciation for delivery vehicles, double-declining-balance depreciation for buildings, and straight-line amortization for franchise rights.

January 2, 2010	Paid $75,000 cash to purchase a small warehouse building near the airport. The building has an estimated life of 20 years, and a residual value of $15,000.

July 1, 2010	Paid $40,000 cash to purchase a delivery van. The van has an estimated useful life of five years, and a residual value of $8,000.
October 2, 2010	Paid $400 cash to paint a small office in the warehouse building.
October 13, 2010	Paid $150 cash to get the oil changed in the delivery van.
December 1, 2010	Paid $60,000 cash to UPS to begin operating Super Swift business as a franchise using the name The UPS Store. This franchise right expires in five years.
December 31, 2010	Recorded depreciation and amortization on the delivery van, warehouse building, and franchise right.
June 30, 2011	Sold the warehouse building for $64,000 cash. (Record the depreciation on the building prior to recording its disposal.)
December 31, 2011	Recorded depreciation on the delivery van and amortization on the franchise right. Determined that the franchise right was not impaired in value.

Required:

Give the journal entries required on each of the above dates.

LO2, 3

PB10-2 Computing Acquisition Cost and Recording Depreciation under Three Alternative Methods

At the beginning of the year, Oakmont Company bought three used machines from American Manufacturing, Inc. The machines immediately were overhauled, installed, and started operating. Because the machines were different, each was recorded separately in the accounts.

	Machine A	Machine B	Machine C
Amount paid for asset	$19,600	$10,100	$9,800
Installation costs	300	500	200
Renovation costs prior to use	100	300	600
Repairs after production began	220	900	480

By the end of the first year, each machine had been operating 4,000 hours.

Required:

1. Compute the cost of each machine. Explain the rationale for capitalizing or expensing the various costs.
2. Give the journal entry to record depreciation expense at the end of year 1, assuming the following:

	ESTIMATES		
Machine	Life	Residual Value	Depreciation Method
A	7 years	$1,100	Straight line
B	40,000 hours	900	Units of production
C	4 years	2,000	Double-declining balance

LO5

PB10-3 Recording and Interpreting the Disposal of Long-Lived Assets Sold and Discarded

During 2009, Rayon Corporation disposed of two different assets. On January 1, 2009, prior to their disposal, the accounts reflected the following:

Asset	Original Cost	Residual Value	Estimated Life	Accumulated Depreciation (straight line)
Machine A	$60,000	$11,000	7 years	$28,000 (4 years)
Machine B	14,200	1,925	5 years	7,365 (3 years)

The machines were disposed of in the following ways:

a. Machine A: Sold on January 2, 2009, for $33,500 cash.

b. Machine B: On January 2, 2009, this machine suffered irreparable damage from an accident and was removed immediately by a salvage company at no cost.

Required:

1. Give the journal entries related to the disposal of each machine at the beginning of 2009.
2. Explain the accounting rationale for the way that you recorded each disposal.

PB10-4 Determining Financial Statement Effects of Activities Related to Intangible Assets **LO6**

Pandey Company entered into the following transactions that potentially affect intangible assets:

(*a*) Soon after Pandey Company started business, in January 2008, it purchased the assets of another business for a cash lump-sum payment of $400,000. Included in the purchase price was "Goodwill, $60,000." The account balance has not changed in two years.

(*b*) The company purchased a patent at a cash cost of $54,600 on January 1, 2009. The patent has an estimated useful life of 13 years.

(*c*) In 2009, Pandey hired a director of brand development to create a marketable identity for the company's products. The director devoted the entire year to this work, at a cost to the company of $125,000.

Required:

1. Give the journal entries required in 2009.
2. For each of the intangible assets, compute amortization for the year ended December 31, 2009.

PB10-5 (Supplement 10C) Analyzing and Recording Entries Related to an Exchange of Assets

The following transactions and adjusting entries were completed by a glass-cutting company. The company uses straight-line depreciation.

June 30, 2009	Paid $10,000 cash to purchase waterjet cutting equipment. The equipment has an estimated life of three years and residual value of $1,300.
July 1, 2009	Paid $300 cash to have the waterjet cutter installed in the production facility.
December 31, 2009	Recorded depreciation on the waterjet cutting equipment.
April 1, 2010	Paid $10,000 cash and traded in the waterjet cutting equipment to acquire a $19,000 plasmacutter, which will allow the company to cut at higher levels of precision. (Record the depreciation on the old equipment prior to recording its exchange.) The new plasmacutter has an estimated useful life of four years, and a residual value of $1,000.
December 31, 2010	Recorded depreciation on the plasmacutter.

Required:

1. Compute the amount of depreciation expense recorded (*a*) in 2009, and (*b*) for the three months up to April 1, 2010
2. Indicate the (a) cost of the new equipment acquired April 1, 2010, and (b) depreciation on the new equipment for the nine months from April 1 through December 31, 2010. Show computations.
3. Give the journal entries required on each of the above dates.

Cases and Projects

CP10-1 Finding Financial Information **LO2, 3, 6, 7**

Refer to the financial statements of The Home Depot in Appendix A at the end of this book, or download the annual report from the Cases and Projects section of the text's Web site at www.mhhe.com/ LLPW1e.

Required:

1. What method of depreciation does the company use?
2. What is the amount of Accumulated Depreciation at February 3, 2008? What percentage is this of the total cost of property and equipment?

3. For depreciation purposes, what is the range of estimated useful lives for the buildings?
4. What amount of depreciation and amortization expense was reported for the current year? What percentage of net sales is it?
5. What is the fixed asset turnover ratio for the current year?
6. For each of the preceding questions, where did you locate the information?

LO2, 3, 6, 7

CP10-2 Comparing Financial Information

Lowe's

Refer to the financial statements of The Home Depot in Appendix A and Lowe's Companies in Appendix B at the end of this book, or download the annual reports from the Cases section of the text's Web site at www.mhhe.com/ LLPW1e.

Required:

1. What method of depreciation does the company use?
2. What is the amount of Accumulated Depreciation at February 1, 2008? What percentage is this of the total cost of property and equipment? Is this a larger (or smaller) percentage of the total cost of property and equipment than for The Home Depot (in CP10-1)? What does it suggest to you about the length of time the assets have been depreciated?
3. Lowe's estimated useful life of buildings differs from that estimated by The Home Depot. How will this affect the fixed asset turnover ratios of the two companies?
4. What amount of depreciation expense was reported on the income statement for the current year? What percentage of net sales is it? Compare this percentage to that of The Home Depot and describe what this implies about the two companies' operations.
5. What is the fixed asset turnover ratio for the current year? Compare this ratio to that of The Home Depot and describe what it implies about the operations of the two companies.

LO1, 3, 6, 7

CP10-3 Examining an Annual Report: Internet-Based Team Research

As a team, select an industry to analyze. Using your Web browser, each team member should acquire the annual report or 10-K for one publicly traded company in the industry, with each member selecting a different company. (See CP1-3 in Chapter 1 for a description of possible resources for these tasks.)

Required:

1. On an individual basis, each team member should write a short report that incorporates the following:
   a. Describe the depreciation methods used.
   b. Compute the percentage of fixed asset cost that has been depreciated. What does this imply about the length of time the assets have been depreciated?
   c. Compute the fixed asset turnover ratios for the current and prior years. What does this tell you about the efficiency of the company's asset use?
   d. Describe the kinds of intangible assets, if any, that the company reports on the balance sheet.
2. Then, as a team, write a short report comparing and contrasting your companies using these attributes. Discuss any patterns across the companies that you as a team observe. Provide potential explanations for any differences discovered.

LO2, 7

CP10-4 Making Ethical Decisions : A Real-Life Example

Assume you work as a staff member in a large accounting department for a multinational public company. Your job requires you to review documents relating to the company's equipment purchases. Upon verifying that purchases are properly approved, you prepare journal entries to record the equipment purchases in the accounting system. Typically, you handle equipment purchases costing $100,000 or less.

This morning, you were contacted by the executive assistant to the Chief Financial Officer (CFO). She says that the CFO has asked to see you immediately in his office. Although your boss's boss has attended a few meetings where the CFO was present, you have never met the CFO during your three years with the company. Needless to say, you are anxious about the meeting.

Upon entering the CFO's office, you are warmly greeted with a smile and friendly handshake. The CFO compliments you on the great work that you have been doing for the company. You soon feel a little more comfortable, particularly when the CFO mentions that he has a special project for you. He states that he and the CEO have negotiated significant new arrangements with the company's equipment suppliers, which require the company to make advance payments for equipment to be purchased in the future. The CFO says that, for various reasons that he did not want to discuss, he will be processing the payments through the operating division of the company rather than the equipment accounting group. Given that the payments will be made through the operating division, they will initially be classified as operating expenses of the company. He indicates clearly that these advance payments for property and equipment should "obviously" be recorded as assets, so he will be contacting you at the end of every quarter to make an adjusting journal entry to capitalize the amounts inappropriately classified as operating expenses. He advises you that a new account, called Prepaid Equipment, has been established for this purpose. He quickly wraps up the meeting by telling you that it is important that you not talk about the special project with anyone. You assume he does not want others to become jealous of your new important responsibility.

A few weeks later, at the end of the first quarter, you receive a voice mail from the CFO stating, "The adjustment that we discussed is $771,000,000 for this quarter." Before deleting the message, you replay it to make sure you heard it right. Your company generates over $8 billion in revenues and incurs $6 billion in operating expenses every quarter, but you have never made a journal entry for that much money. So, just to be sure there is not a mistake, you send an e-mail to the CFO confirming the amount. He phones you back immediately to abruptly inform you, "There is no mistake. That is the number." Feeling embarrassed that you may have annoyed the CFO, you quietly make the adjusting journal entry.

For each of the remaining three quarters in that year and for the first quarter in the following year, you continue to make these end-of-quarter adjustments. The "magic number" as the CFO liked to call it was $560,000,000 for Q2, $742,745,000 for Q3, $941,000,000 for Q4, and $818,204,000 for Q1 of the following year. During this time, you have had several meetings and lunches with the CFO where he provides you the magic number, sometimes supported with nothing more than a Post-it note with the number written on it. He frequently compliments you on your good work and promises that you will soon be in line for a big promotion.

Despite the CFO's compliments and promises, you are growing increasingly uncomfortable with the journal entries that you have been making. Typically, whenever an ordinary equipment purchase involves an advance payment, the purchase is completed a few weeks later. At that time, the amount of the advance is removed from an Equipment Deposit account and transferred to the appropriate equipment account. This has not been the case with the CFO's special project. Instead, the Prepaid Equipment account has continued to grow, now standing at over $3.8 billion. There has been no discussion about how or when this balance will be reduced, and no depreciation has been recorded for it.

Just as you begin to reflect on the effect the adjustments have had on your company's fixed assets, operating expenses, and operating income, you receive a call from the vice president for internal audit. She needs to talk with you this afternoon about "a peculiar trend in the company's fixed asset turnover ratio and some suspicious journal entries that you have been making."

Required:

1. Complete the following table to determine what the company's accounting records would have looked like had you not made the journal entries as part of the CFO's special project. Comment on how the decision to capitalize amounts, which were initially recorded as operating expenses, has affected the level of operating income in each quarter.

	Q1 Year 1 (March 31)		Q2 Year 1 (June 30)		Q3 Year 1 (September 30)		Q4 Year 1 (December 31)		Q1 Year 2 (March 31)	
(amounts in millions of U.S. dollars)	With the Entries	Without the Entries	With the Entries	Without the Entries	With the Entries	Without the Entries	With the Entries	Without the Entries	With the Entries	Without the Entries
Property and equipment, net	$38,614	$	$35,982	$	$38,151	$	$38,809	$	$39,155	$
Sales revenues	8,825	8,825	8,910	8,910	8,966	8,966	8,478	8,478	8,120	8,120
Operating expenses	7,628		8,526		7,786		7,725		7,277	
Operating income	1,197		384		1,180		753		843	

2. Using the numbers that include the special journal entries that you recorded, compute the fixed asset turnover ratio for the periods ended Q2 through Q4 of year 1 and Q1 of year 2. What does the trend in this ratio suggest to you? Is this consistent with the changes in operating income reported by the company?
3. Before your meeting with the vice president for internal audit, you think about the above computations and the variety of peculiar circumstances surrounding the "special project" for the CFO. What in particular might have raised your suspicion about the real nature of your work?
4. Your meeting with internal audit was short and unpleasant. The vice president indicated that she had discussed her findings with the CFO before meeting with you. The CFO claimed that he too had noticed the peculiar trend in the fixed assets turnover ratio, but that he had not had a chance to investigate it further. He urged internal audit to get to the bottom of things, suggesting that perhaps someone might be making unapproved journal entries. Internal audit had identified you as the source of the journal entries and had been unable to find any documents that approved or substantiated the entries. She ended the meeting by advising you to find a good lawyer. Given your current circumstances, describe how you would have acted earlier had you been able to foresee where it might lead you.
5. In the real case on which this one is based, the internal auditors agonized over the question of whether they had actually uncovered a fraud or whether they were jumping to the wrong conclusion. *The Wall Street Journal* mentioned this on October 30, 2002, by stating, "it was clear . . . that their findings would be devastating for the company. They worried about whether their revelations would result in layoffs. Plus, they feared that they would somehow end up being blamed for the mess." Beyond the personal consequences mentioned in this quote, describe other potential ways in which the findings of the internal auditors would likely be devastating for the publicly traded company and those associated with it.

Epilogue:

World Com
Verizon

This case is based on a fraud committed at WorldCom (now owned by Verizon). The case draws its numbers, the nature of the unsupported journal entries, and the CFO's role in carrying out the fraud from a report issued by WorldCom's bankruptcy examiner. Year 1 in this case was actually 2001 and year 2 was 2002. This case excludes other fraudulent activities that contributed to WorldCom's $11 billion fraud. The 63-year-old CEO was sentenced to 25 years in prison for planning and executing the biggest fraud in the history of American business. The CFO, who cooperated in the investigation of the CEO, was sentenced to five years in prison.

LO3

CP10-5 Making Ethical Decisions: A Mini Case

Assume you are one of three members of the accounting staff working for a small, private company. At the beginning of this year, the company expanded into a new industry by acquiring equipment that will be used to make several new lines of products. The owner and general manager of the company has indicated that, as one of the conditions for providing financing for the new equipment, the company's bank will receive a copy of the company's annual financial statements. Another condition of the loan is that the company's total assets cannot fall below $250,000. Violation of this condition gives the bank the option to demand immediate repayment of the loan. Before making the adjustment for this year's depreciation, the company's total assets are reported at $255,000. The owner has asked you to take a look at the facts regarding the new equipment and "work with the numbers to make sure everything stays onside with the bank."

A depreciation method has yet not been adopted for the new equipment. Equipment used in other parts of the company is depreciated using the double-declining-balance method. The cost of the new equipment was $35,000 and the manager estimates it will be worth "at least $7,000" at the end of its four-year useful life. Because the products made with the new equipment are only beginning to catch on with consumers, the company used the equipment to produce just 4,000 units this year. It is expected that, over all four years of its useful life, the new equipment will make a total of 28,000 units.

Required:

1. Calculate the depreciation that would be reported this year under each of the three methods shown in this chapter. Which of the methods would meet the owner's objective?
2. Evaluate whether it is ethical to recommend that the company use the method identified in requirement 1. What two parties are most directly affected by this recommendation? How would each party be benefited or harmed by the recommendation? Does the recommendation violate any laws or applicable rules? Are there any other factors that you would consider before making a recommendation?

CP10-6 Thinking Critically: Analyzing the Effects of Depreciation Policies on Income

LO3, 5, 8

As an aspiring financial analyst, you have applied to a major Wall Street firm for a summer job. To screen potential applicants, the firm provides them a short case study and asks them to evaluate the financial success of two hypothetical companies that started operations on January 1, 2008. Both companies operate in the same industry, use very similar assets, and have very similar customer bases. Among the additional information provided about the companies are the following comparative income statements.

	FAST CORPORATION		SLOW CORPORATION	
	2009	2008	2009	2008
Net sales	$60,000	$60,000	$60,000	$60,000
Cost of goods sold	20,000	20,000	20,000	20,000
Gross profit	40,000	40,000	40,000	40,000
Selling, general, and administrative expenses	19,000	19,000	19,000	19,000
Depreciation expense	3,555	10,667	5,000	5,000
Operating income	17,445	10,333	16,000	16,000
Other gains (losses)	2,222	—	(2,000)	—
Income before income taxes	$19,667	$10,333	$14,000	$16,000

Required:

Prepare an analysis of the two companies with the goal of determining which company is better managed. If you could request two additional pieces of information from these companies' financial statements, describe specifically what they would be and explain how they would help you to make a decision.

CP10-7 Preparing Depreciation Schedules for Straight-Line and Double-Declining-Balance Methods

LO3

To make some extra money, you have started preparing templates of business forms and schedules for others to download from the Internet (for a small fee). After relevant information is entered into each template, it automatically performs calculations using formulas you have entered into the template. For the depreciation template, you decide to produce two worksheets—one that calculates depreciation and book value under the straight-line method and another that calculates these amounts using the double-declining-balance method. The templates perform straightforward calculations of depreciation and book value, when given the cost of an asset, its estimated useful life, and its estimated residual value. These particular templates will not handle disposals or changes in estimates—you plan to create a deluxe version for those functions. To illustrate that your templates actually work, you enter the information used to produce the depreciation schedules shown in Exhibit 10.7, with Cedar Fair and Six Flags as examples.

Although you are confident you can use appropriate formulas in the spreadsheet to create a template for the straight-line method, you are a little uncertain about how to make the double-declining-balance method work. You e-mail your friend Sally for advice. Here is what she said:

From: Sally@yahoo.com
To: Helpme@hotmail.com
Cc:
Subject: Excel Help

I wish I had thought of charging money for showing how to do ordinary accounting activities. You would have made me rich by now. ☺ Here is how to set up your worksheets. Begin by creating an "input values" section. This section will allow someone to enter the asset cost, residual value, and estimated life in an area removed from the actual depreciation schedule. You do not want someone accidentally entering amounts over formulas that you have entered into the schedule.

The cells from the input values section will be referenced by other cells in the depreciation schedule. You will want to enter formulas in the cells for the first year row, and then copy and paste them to rows for the other years. When doing this, you will need to use what is called an "absolute reference," which means that the cell reference does not change when one row is copied and pasted to a different row. Unlike an ordinary cell reference that has a format of A1, an absolute reference has the format of A1, which prevents the spreadsheet from changing either the column (A) or row (1) when copying the cell to other cells. You may find this useful when preparing both the straight-line and double-declining-balance schedules.

To create the depreciation schedules, use five columns labeled: (1) year, (2) beginning of year accumulated depreciation, (3) depreciation, (4) end-of-year accumulated depreciation, and (5) end-of-year book value.

The double-declining-balance template will be the trickiest to create because you need to be concerned that the book value is not depreciated below the residual value in the last year of the asset's life. To force the template to automatically watch for this, you will need to use the IF function. Here's a screenshot of a template I created, using the IF function to properly calculate depreciation for all years of the asset's life. Notice the formula bar at the top.

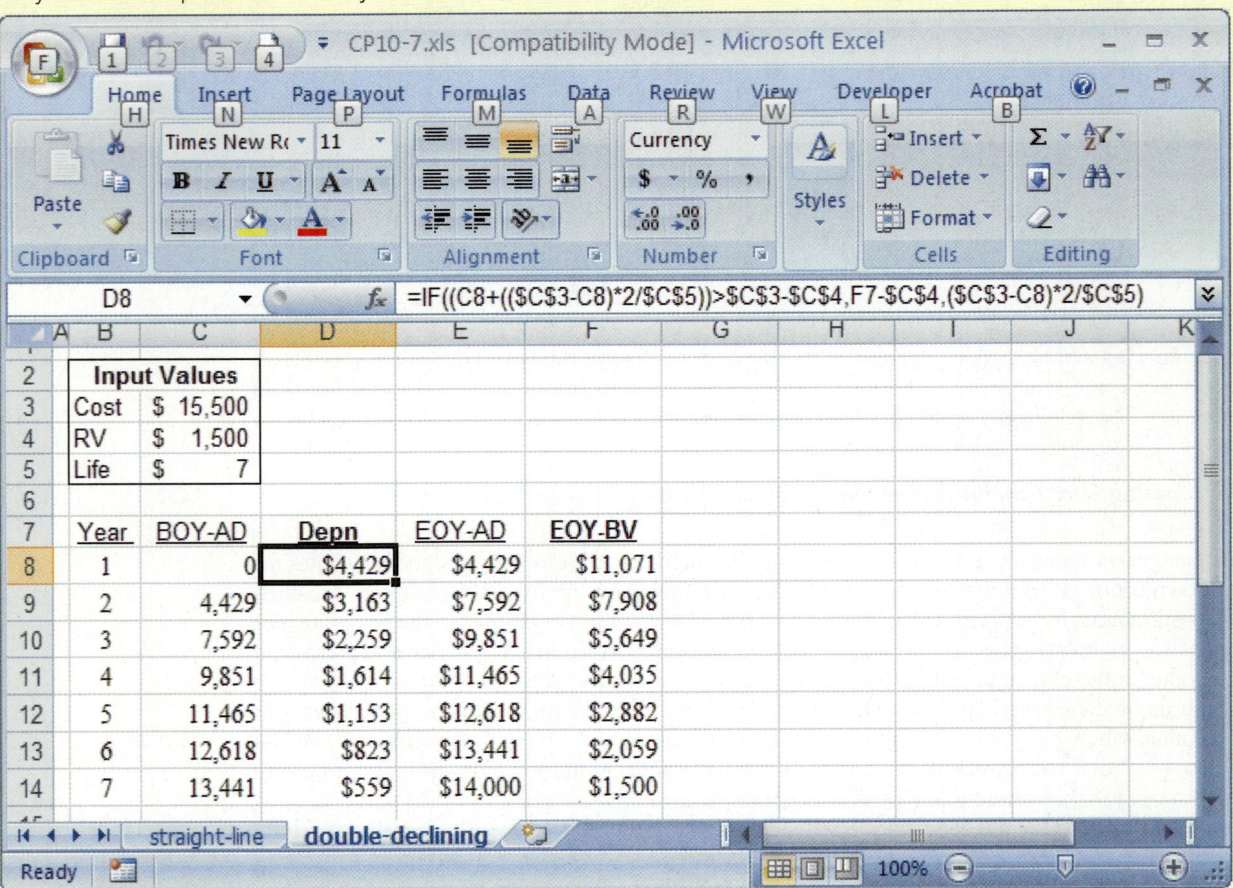

Required:

Create the spreadsheet templates to calculate depreciation and book value using the straight-line and double-declining-balance methods. Demonstrate that the template works by reproducing the schedules in Exhibit 10.7.

Tip: To switch between displaying cell formulas and their values, press CTRL and ~ (tilde) at the same time.

11 Current Liabilities and Payroll

LEARNING OBJECTIVES

After completing this chapter, you should be able to:

LO1 Explain how to report the major types of liabilities.

LO2 Calculate and interpret the current ratio.

LO3 Demonstrate how to account for notes payable and the current portion of long-term debt.

LO4 Demonstrate how to account for sales taxes and unearned revenues.

LO5 Demonstrate how to account for warranties and other contingent liabilities.

LO6 Calculate and record payroll including employer payroll taxes.

Lectured slideshow–LP11-1
www.mhhe.com/LLPW1e

Focus Company: GENERAL MILLS, INC.

Maker of Pillsbury, Green Giant, Cheerios, and More

www.generalmills.com

If you are like most people, you probably owe money to someone. Maybe you used your credit card to buy some new shoes or you took out a student loan to pay your tuition. Whatever the reason, you should make sure you can pay those liabilities when they become due. Americans spend about $14 billion each year just for late fees on their overdue credit card balances. When you consider the interest that is charged on an overdue balance, you can see why the failure to pay liabilities on time is a leading cause of personal bankruptcy. For businesses, too, paying liabilities is a big issue.

General Mills knows the importance of paying its liabilities on time. The cereal and grocery maker buys on account from thousands of suppliers, so the company cannot afford to slip up in paying its liabilities. General Mills also employs more than 28,000 workers to whom at one time or another General Mills will owe salaries and wages. Needless to say, those employees expect General Mills to pay their salaries and wages on time. In this chapter, you will learn how the Big G (Wall Street's nickname for General Mills) accounts for payroll and other short-term liabilities. Later, in Chapter 14, you will learn how the company accounts for long-term liabilities.

ORGANIZATION OF THE CHAPTER

REPORTING LIABILITIES	ACCOUNTING FOR CURRENT LIABILITIES	PAYROLL ACCOUNTING
• Measuring Liabilities • Classifying Liabilities • Calculating and Interpreting the Current Ratio	• Accounts Payable • Notes Payable • Current Portion of Long-Term Debt • Other Current Liabilities	• Calculating the Payroll • Recording the Payroll • Applying Internal Control Principles

REPORTING LIABILITIES

Learning Objective 1

Explain how to report the major types of liabilities.

Businesses record liabilities when they become obligated to pay cash or to provide services in the future. These obligations arise in several ways: from acquiring goods or services on credit with a promise to pay in the future, from borrowing cash with a promise to repay in the future, or from receiving cash before providing future services. In each of these cases, the business records a liability on the date it becomes obligated to pay cash or provide future services. Later, when the cash has been paid or the services have been provided, the business reduces the liability.

Two questions arise when recording liabilities:

1. At what amount should they be measured?
2. Should they be classified as current or long term?

Video 11-1
www.mhhe.com/LLPW1e

Measuring Liabilities

A business must record a liability whenever a transaction or event obligates the company to give up assets or provide services in the future. The dollar amount that is reported for a liability depends on three considerations:

1. **The initial amount of the liability.** Initially, the business records a liability at its cash equivalent, which is the amount of cash a creditor would accept to settle the liability immediately after the transaction or event.
2. **Additional amounts owed to the creditor.** The business increases liabilities whenever additional obligations arise, by purchasing goods and services or incurring interest charges over time.
3. **Payments or services provided to the creditor.** The business reduces liabilities whenever the company makes a payment or provides services to the creditor.

Notice that a liability is first recorded at a cash-equivalent amount, which excludes interest charges. This practice makes sense; if you borrowed $10 from a friend and paid it back a split-second later, you would not need to pay interest. Because interest arises only with the passage of time, it is recorded as a liability only after time has passed.

Classifying Liabilities

Most businesses have liabilities that are to be settled on various dates. General Mills, for example, reports not only accounts payable that must be paid within 30 to 60 days but also loans that are not due to be repaid until the year 2078. To help financial statement users evaluate whether a business will be able to pay its liabilities as they come due, liabilities on the balance sheet are usually classified as either current or long term. Current liabilities are short-term obligations that will be paid with current assets within the business's current operating cycle or one year after the balance sheet date, whichever is longer. Because most companies have an operating cycle that is shorter than one year, the definition of current liabilities can be simplified as liabilities due within one year.

Refer to Exhibit 11.1 for an excerpt from the 2007 balance sheet for General Mills. You can see that the company owed more than $11.7 billion. That may sound like a lot to owe,

Exhibit 11.1 General Mills' Liabilities

LIABILITIES		
(in millions)	2007	2006
Current liabilities		
Accounts payable	$ 778	$ 673
Notes payable	1,254	1,503
Current portion of long-term debt	1,734	2,131
Other current liabilities	2,079	1,831
Total current liabilities	5,845	6,138
Long-term debt	3,218	2,415
Other liabilities	2,663	2,614
Total liabilities	11,726	11,167

but only half of it ($5.8 billion) was payable in the coming year. And General Mills had many current assets to use in satisfying its current liabilities as we will see shortly.

Calculating and Interpreting the Current Ratio

Learning Objective 2
Calculate and interpret the current ratio.

The **current ratio** is a financial measure used to evaluate **liquidity**, which is a concept representing a company's ability to pay the amounts it currently owes. The current ratio indicates whether a business has enough current assets to pay its current liabilities. Generally speaking, a high current ratio suggests good liquidity. An old rule of thumb was that companies should have a current ratio of between 1.0 and 2.0. Today, however, many successful companies use financial management techniques that minimize their current assets. As a result, those companies have current ratios that are less than 1.0.

Financial Analysis Tools		
Name of Measure	Formula	What It Tells You
Current Ratio	$\frac{\text{Current Assets}}{\text{Current Liabilities}}$	• Whether current assets are sufficient to pay current liabilities • A higher ratio means better ability to pay

At the time General Mills owed $5.8 billion in current liabilities (see Exhibit 11.1), the company owned $3.1 billion in current assets. Therefore, its current ratio was calculated as:

$$\text{Current Ratio} = \frac{\text{Current Assets}}{\text{Current Liabilities}} = \frac{\$3.1\text{ billion}}{\$5.8\text{ billion}} = 0.53$$

A current ratio of 0.53 indicates that a company's current assets are only 53 percent as large as its current liabilities. For many companies, a ratio of less than 1.0 (100 percent) would be a significant concern. However, it is not as much of a concern to General Mills because, as the notes to the company's financial statements explain, operating activities generate nearly $5 million in cash each day. In addition, General Mills has arranged a **line of credit**—basically a preapproved bank loan—that the company can use at any time as needed. This arrangement gives General Mills the freedom to invest its cash in assets that generate more income than the interest that is typically paid on cash sitting in a checking account. If General Mills ever has too little cash to pay its current liabilities, the company can borrow more immediately via the line of credit.

ACCOUNTING FOR CURRENT LIABILITIES

Accounts Payable

Most companies purchase goods and services on credit from other companies. Typically, these transactions involve three stages: (1) order the goods or services, (2) receive the goods or services, and (3) pay for the goods or services. Accountants record liabilities at the stage that "obligates the company to give up assets or services." When do you think Big G becomes obligated to pay for the grain it buys for making Wheaties and Cheerios?

If a grain order were never filled, General Mills would not be expected to pay for it. So the point at which the liability is created and recorded is the receipt of goods or services, not the order. Like Big G, most companies call this liability Accounts Payable. According to Exhibit 11.1, General Mills owed $778 million in Accounts Payable at the end of 2007. The great advantage of using accounts payable to buy goods and services is that suppliers do not charge interest on the unpaid balances unless they are overdue.

Video 11-2
www.mhhe.com/LLPW1e

Notes Payable

Learning Objective 3

Demonstrate how to account for notes payable and the current portion of long-term debt.

The next liability reported by General Mills in Exhibit 11.1 is Notes Payable. This liability represents the amount the company owes to others as a result of issuing promissory notes. A **promissory note** is a written document outlining the terms and conditions according to which one company will repay another. In this section, we illustrate an **interest-bearing** note, which requires payment of the borrowed amount (the principal) plus interest calculated using the interest rate stated in the note. In Chapter 14, we illustrate a different type of promissory note, called a discounted note, which does not explicitly state an interest rate.

Chapter 9 showed how a company records Notes Receivable to account for promissory notes created when the company lends money. This section presents the other side of the transaction—the Notes Payable that are created when a company borrows money by issuing promissory notes. Assume that on November 1, 2009, General Mills negotiated an agreement to borrow $100,000 cash on a one-year note. The note specified that General Mills would pay 6 percent interest one year later on October 31, 2010. The principal was also to be repaid on the maturity date (October 31, 2010). See Exhibit 11.2 for a summary of these events assuming that General Mills adjusts its accounting records on December 31, 2009.

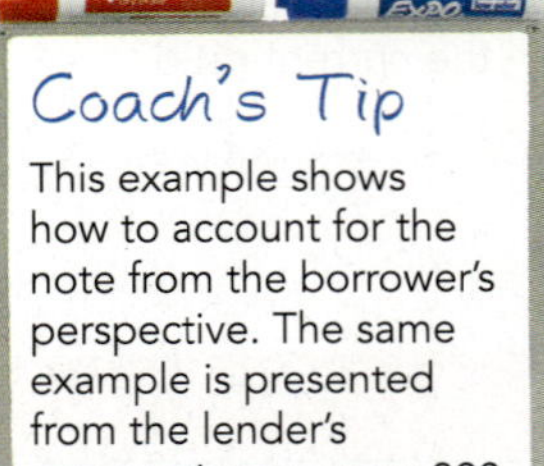

Coach's Tip

This example shows how to account for the note from the borrower's perspective. The same example is presented from the lender's perspective on page 390.

The arrows in Exhibit 11.2 point to three aspects of the note to be accounted for. First, General Mills will need to increase Cash when the company creates the note. Next, **under the matching principle, General Mills will need to adjust its records to account for the interest incurred each accounting period.** In reality, General Mills would make this kind of adjustment every month or quarter, but for simplicity, we have assumed it occurs only once (on December 31, 2009). Finally, the company will decrease Cash when interest and principal are paid. The following discussion addresses these three elements that exist for any promissory note.

1. **The note is issued and cash is received.** When General Mills receives $100,000 cash on November 1, 2009, it becomes obligated to repay that amount. This transaction would be recorded as follows:

	Debit	Credit
Cash (+A)	100,000	
Notes Payable (+L)		100,000

Assets		=	Liabilities		+	Owners' Equity
Cash	+100,000		Notes Payable	+100,000		

2. **Interest is owed at the end of the accounting period.** Interest is like rent for the privilege of using someone else's money. Although interest becomes payable with each day that passes, it is not paid nearly that often. Typically, interest is paid monthly or in some cases once or twice a year. Rather than record the unpaid interest on a daily basis,

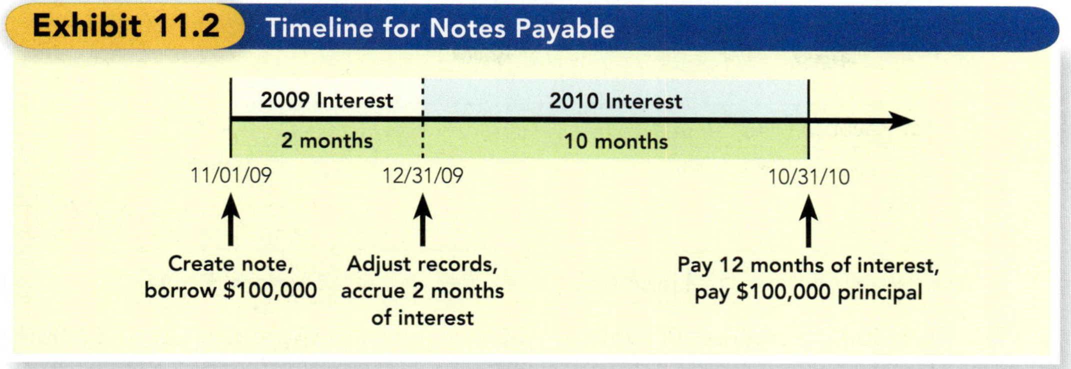

most companies record it at the end of the accounting period. For interest-bearing notes, the interest obligations are recorded in the current liability account Interest Payable.

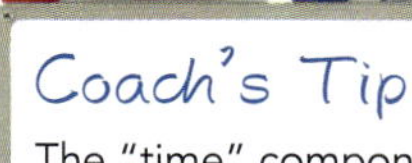

Coach's Tip

The "time" component refers to the portion of a year for which interest is calculated, not the portion of the note's entire life. A 2-month interest calculation on a 3-year note has a time component of 2/12, not 2/36.

When General Mills adjusts its records on December 31, 2009, it records the amount of interest incurred but not paid during the period. This period is represented by the light yellow shading in Exhibit 11.2. As you may recall from Chapter 9, interest is calculated using the following formula:

$$\text{Interest} = \text{Principal} \times \text{Interest Rate} \times \text{Time}$$

As of December 31, the General Mills note has existed for two months, but no interest has been paid, so the unpaid interest is $1,000 (= $100,000 × 6% × 2/12). Notice in this calculation that the principal is the amount owed at the beginning of the interest period, which is equal to the amount of the liability recorded in the Notes Payable account on November 1. The interest rate is the 6 percent annual rate stated on the note, and the time component is the fraction of the year for which the interest is being calculated (2 months out of 12).

The adjusting entry to accrue interest from November 1 to December 31 is as follows.

	Debit	Credit
Interest Expense (+E, −OE)	1,000	
Interest Payable (+L)		1,000

Assets	=	Liabilities		+	Owners' Equity	
		Interest Payable	+1,000		Interest Expense (+E)	−1,000

3. **Payments are made to the lender.** General Mills will pay both the principal and the interest on the October 31, 2010, maturity date. Although the company is likely to pay both amounts with a single check, it is instructive to consider these payments separately. We begin with the interest payment. This payment covers the full year from the time the note was signed until the time it matures on October 31. The total interest payment is $6,000 (= $100,000 × 6% × 12/12). As the following timeline shows, this interest payment includes 2 months of interest recorded as an expense and a liability in 2009 ($1,000) plus 10 months of interest expense related to the period from January 1 to October 31, 2010 ($5,000 = $100,000 × 6% × 10/12).

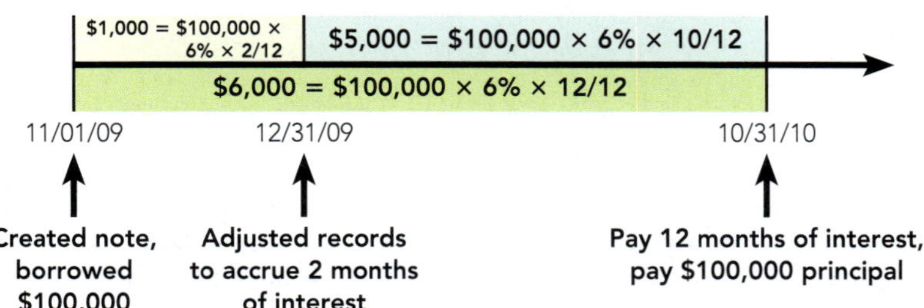

The $6,000 interest payment is recorded as follows:

	Debit	Credit
Interest Payable (−L)	1,000	
Interest Expense (+E, −OE)	5,000	
Cash (−A)		6,000

Assets		=	Liabilities		+	Owners' Equity	
Cash	−6,000		Interest Payable	−1,000		Interest Expense (+E)	−5,000

The principal payment of $100,000 made on October 31, 2010, is recorded as:

	Debit	Credit
Notes Payable (−L)	100,000	
Cash (−A)		100,000

Assets		=	Liabilities		+	Owners' Equity
Cash	−100,000		Notes Payable	−100,000		

Assume Starbucks issues a $12,000 note on December 1 with interest due annually at a rate of 5 percent. Record (1) this transaction and (2) the December 31 interest adjustment.

1.

	Debit	Credit

Assets	=	Liabilities	+	Owners' Equity

2.

	Debit	Credit

Assets	=	Liabilities	+	Owners' Equity

After you have finished, check your answers with the solution at the bottom of the next page.

Current Portion of Long-Term Debt

Remember when you were in the ninth grade and it seemed as if it would be forever before you would graduate from high school? At that time, graduation was something that would happen in the long term. Later, when you became a senior, graduation became a current event—one that was less than a year away. A similar progression occurs with long-term debt.

If a company borrows money with the promise to repay it in two years, the loan is classified as a long-term debt. The company reports only the accrued interest on the loan as a current liability on that year's balance sheet. After a year has passed, however, the loan becomes a current liability (just as your graduation became a current event when you reached your senior year). When that happens, the borrower must report the loan in the Current Liabilities section of the balance sheet. Rather than create a different account, accountants simply remove the amount of principal to be repaid in the upcoming year from the total long-term debt and report it as a current liability, Current Portion of Long-Term Debt.

The third line item in the Current Liabilities section of the General Mills balance sheet (see Exhibit 11.1, page 469) provides an example. Notice that in 2007, General Mills reported a current liability for the $1.7 billion of long-term debt that was expected to be paid in 2008. Similarly, in 2006, current liabilities included $2.1 billion of long-term debt expected to be paid in 2007. This reclassification of long-term debt to a current liability is needed so that the balance sheet will accurately report the dollar amount of liabilities that Big G will pay in the upcoming year.

SELF-STUDY PRACTICE

Assume that on December 31, 2009, Blockbuster borrowed $10,000, a portion of which was to be repaid each year on November 30. Specifically, Blockbuster will make the following principal payments: $1,000 in 2010, $2,000 in 2011, $3,000 in 2012, and $4,000 in 2013. Show how this loan will be reported on the balance sheets on December 31, 2010 and 2009, assuming that the principal payments will be made when required.

	AS OF DECEMBER 31	
	2010	2009
Current liabilities:		
Current portion of long-term debt	$	$
Long-term debt		
Total liabilities	$ 9,000	$ 10,000

After you have finished, check your answers with the solutions at the bottom of the next page.

Other Current Liabilities

Learning Objective 4

Demonstrate how to account for sales taxes and unearned revenues.

Because of the nature of General Mills' business, the company does not report certain current liabilities that are common to other companies. In this section, we examine a few of those liabilities.

Solution to Self-Study Practice

1.

	Debit	Credit
Cash (+A)	12,000	
Notes Payable (+L)		12,000

Assets		=	Liabilities		+	Owners' Equity
Cash	+12,000		Notes Payable	+12,000		

2. $12,000 × 5% × 1/12 = $50

	Debit	Credit
Interest Expense (+E, −OE)	50	
Interest Payable (+L)		50

Assets	=	Liabilities		+	Owners' Equity	
		Interest Payable	+50		Interest Expense (+E)	−50

Sales Tax Payable

Retail companies are required to charge a sales tax in all but five states (Alaska, Delaware, Montana, New Hampshire, and Oregon). Retailers collect sales tax from consumers at the time of sale and forward it to the state government. They report the taxes they collect as a current liability until they forward them to the government. Sales tax is not an expense to the retailer because it is simply collected and passed on to the government. So if Best Buy sold a television for $1,000 cash plus 5 percent sales tax, Best Buy would earn $1,000 in sales revenue and recognize a $50 liability (= 5% × $1,000) for the sales tax collected. The sale would be recorded as follows.

	Debit	Credit
Cash (+A)	1,050	
Sales Tax Payable (+L) ($1,000 × 0.05)		50
Sales Revenue (+R, +OE)		1,000

Assets		=	Liabilities		+	Owners' Equity	
Cash	+1,050		Sales Tax Payable	+50		Sales Revenue (+R)	+1,000

When Best Buy pays the sales tax to the state government, its accountants will reduce Sales Tax Payable (with a debit) and reduce Cash (with a credit).

Unearned Revenue

In Chapter 4, you learned that some companies receive cash before they provide goods or services to customers. IAC, the owner of Ticketmaster and Match.com, provides a great example of this type of liability. Consider what happens when IAC receives cash for subscription services to Match.com. Because IAC receives cash before providing the subscription services, accountants initially record a liability in the account Unearned Revenue. As the subscription services are provided, IAC reduces the liability and reports the subscription fees earned as revenue.

Assume, for example, that on October 1, IAC received cash for a three-month subscription paid in advance at a rate of $10 per month ($30 in total). IAC records this transaction in two steps:

1. **Receive cash and create a liability** (on October 1):

	Debit	Credit
Cash (+A)	30	
Unearned Revenue (+L)		30

Assets		=	Liabilities		+	Owners' Equity
Cash	+30		Unearned Revenue	+30		

Solution to Self-Study Practice

	AS OF DECEMBER 31	
	2010	2009
Current liabilities		
Current portion of long-term debt	$2,000	$ 1,000
Long-term debt	7,000	9,000
Total liabilities	$9,000	$10,000

2. Fulfill part of the liability and earn revenue (on October 31):

	Debit	Credit
Unearned Revenue (−L)	10	
Subscription Revenue (+R, +OE)		10

Assets	=	Liabilities		+	Owners' Equity	
		Unearned Revenue	−10		Subscription Revenue (+R)	+10

As each month passes, IAC would make another adjustment like the one in Step 2 to show that it has continued to fulfill its obligation and to earn subscription revenue. Do not let the small amounts in this example fool you; unearned revenues can be huge. For IAC, they total more than $199 million.

Warranties Payable

Learning Objective 5

Demonstrate how to account for warranties and other contingent liabilities.

Most companies that sell physical items, such as watches and computers, provide a warranty that obligates the company to repair defective products for a limited time. Because the warranty applies to each product that is sold, it is considered a cost of making the sale. **According to the matching principle, warranty costs should be reported as an expense when the sale is recorded.**

Because the company does not pay these costs at the time of the sale, the company records a liability. Like other liabilities discussed in this chapter, the liability for warranty costs requires the company to give up resources in the future. Unlike other current liabilities, however, the precise amount to be given up is not known. Instead, it must be estimated based on the company's history of product repairs and any recent changes in product quality.

To understand how to estimate and record warranty costs, consider the following example. In the second quarter of 2007, Gateway sold 1 million computers. Managers estimated that warranty repairs on the computers would cost $16 million. To come up with the $16 million figure, they estimated both the percentage of computers they expected would require warranty repairs and the average cost of the repairs. Assuming that 10 percent of the computers were expected to require warranty repairs at an average cost of $160 per unit, the managers calculated total estimated warranty repair costs as follows.

Total unit sales in this period	1,000,000
Percent requiring warranty repair	× 10%
Units requiring warranty repair	100,000
Average warranty repair cost	× $160
Estimated cost of warranty repairs	$16,000,000

Based on this estimate, Gateway could record an estimated warranty repair cost each time it sold a computer, but that would be inefficient. Instead, accountants make an adjusting entry to record estimated warranty repair costs at the end of each accounting period. Warranty Expense is reported as a selling expense on the income statement. If the warranty repairs are likely to occur within a year, Warranty Liability is classified as a current liability on the balance sheet.

	Debit	Credit
Warranty Expense (+E, −OE)	16,000,000	
Warranty Liability (+L)		16,000,000

Assets	=	Liabilities		+	Owners' Equity	
		Warranty Liability	+16,000,000		Warranty Expense (+E)	−16,000,000

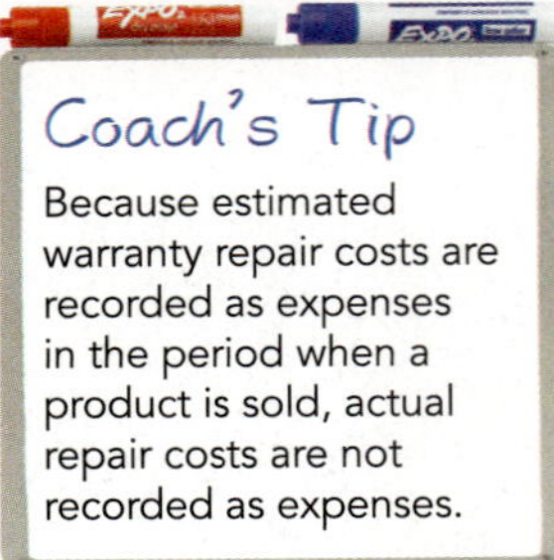

Later, when Gateway actually repairs a computer under warranty, the repair costs will be recorded as a reduction in the Warranty Liability account. For example, if Gateway used $300 of parts to repair a computer under warranty, the accountant makes the following journal entry.

	Debit	Credit
Warranty Liability (−L)	300	
Computer Parts (−A)		300

Assets		=	Liabilities		+	Owners' Equity
Computer Parts	−300		Warranty Liability	−300		

Other repair costs are handled in a similar way. For example, most manufacturers outsource much of their repair work. If Gateway paid a company $2,000 to repair 20 computers under warranty, the accountant makes the following journal entry.

	Debit	Credit
Warranty Liability (−L)	2,000	
Cash (−A)		2,000

Assets		=	Liabilities		+	Owners' Equity
Cash	−2,000		Warranty Liability	−2,000		

At the end of the accounting period, Gateway would evaluate whether the balance in the Warranty Liability account is adequate to cover the work likely to be done in future periods. If the balance is judged to be too low, managers will increase it; if the balance is too high, they will decrease it.

Other Contingent Liabilities

A warranty is one example of a special type of liability called contingent liabilities. **Contingent liabilities** are potential liabilities that arise as a result of past transactions or events, but their ultimate resolution depends (is contingent) on a future event. Gateway's Warranty Liability arises from the warranty promised when the company sells computers, but the exact amount of the liability depends on the extent of repairs that may be required in the future. As is often the case, the challenge for accountants is to anticipate what is likely to happen in the future so that it can be reported now if appropriate.

Many other types of contingent liability exist. The most common is a lawsuit against the company. Unlike warranties, for which future costs can usually be estimated, the cost of a lawsuit is difficult to predict. Some suits will be defended successfully; others may result in huge fines or penalties. Given such uncertainties, accounting rules require the company to evaluate whether it is likely to be found liable and, if so, whether the amount of the liability is estimable. As Exhibit 11.3 indicates, if a contingent liability is possible but not probable or its amount cannot be estimated, a liability should not be recorded. Instead, the potential liability should be described in a note to the financial statements.

Exhibit 11.3 Accounting for Contingent Liabilities

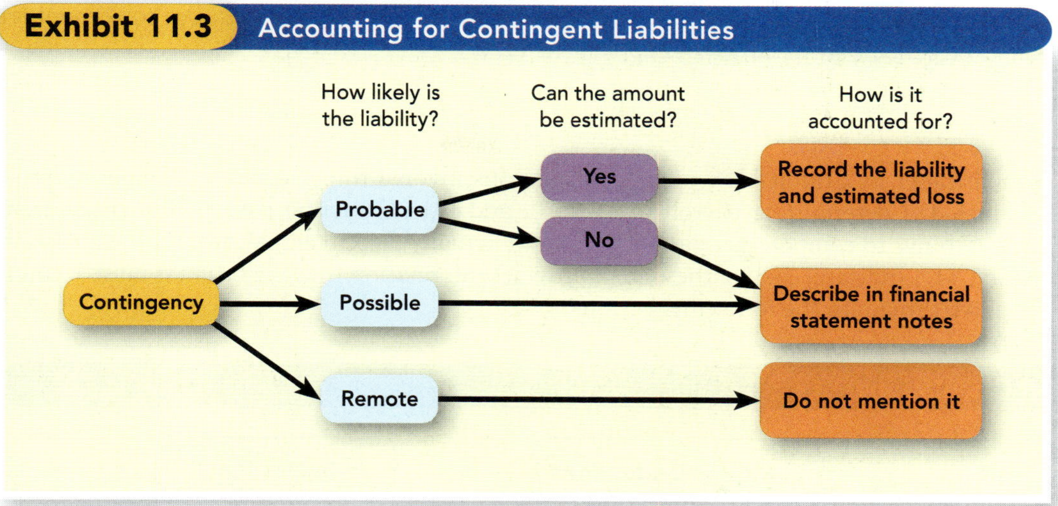

Spotlight On FINANCIAL REPORTING

Disclosure of Contingent Liabilities

Gateway

To forewarn financial statement users of potential liabilities related to existing lawsuits, computer maker Gateway provided the following disclosure in its 2006 annual report:

> Gateway is a party to various lawsuits, claims, including assertions of patent infringements, investigations and administrative proceedings that arise in connection with its business, including ***Lucent Technologies, Inc. v. Gateway, Inc.*** . . . asserting that Gateway infringes seven patents owned by Lucent Technologies, Inc. . . . Gateway reserves for a legal liability when it is both probable that a liability has been incurred and the amount of the loss can be reasonably estimated. At least quarterly Gateway reviews and adjusts these reserves to reflect the impacts of negotiations, settlements, rulings, advice of legal counsel and other information and events pertaining to a particular case. The ultimate outcome of such matters cannot presently be determined or estimated.

PAYROLL ACCOUNTING

Learning Objective 6

Calculate and record payroll including employer payroll taxes.

Payroll refers to the processes followed to pay employees for their work. For large companies, payroll can be a huge and difficult undertaking. At one time, General Mills was managing eight different payroll systems at 47 different production plants. Even small companies can find payroll challenging because all employers are required by law to maintain certain payroll records and to calculate payroll in particular ways. And of course, employees expect this task to be done on time without error.

Payroll costs can be significant in terms of their impact on both current liabilities and operating expenses. At the end of 2007, for example, General Mills owed more than $1.3 billion to employees (included in Other current liabilities in Exhibit 11.1), and payroll expenses for the year totaled many times that amount. Typical payroll costs include salaries, wages, bonuses, employer payroll taxes, and employee benefits. Salaries are fixed amounts that are paid monthly, typically to managerial, sales, and administrative personnel. Wages are based on a rate per hour or per unit of production and are typically paid to clerks, factory workers, and part-time employees. Bonuses are extra amounts paid to employees for outstanding performance. It is not unusual for executive-level employees to receive more in bonuses than in salary as was the case in 2007, when General Mills' chief executive officer received $2.5 million in bonuses and $1.3 million in salary. Employer payroll taxes also add significant costs, as we show later in detail. Finally, employee benefits include amounts employers paid on behalf of employees for health insurance, retirement pensions, and vacation, illness, and family leaves. The methods used to account for employee benefits are discussed in Supplement 11A.

Calculating the Payroll

As illustrated in Exhibit 11.4, payroll calculations involve three steps: (1) computing gross earnings, (2) determining payroll deductions, and (3) subtracting payroll deductions from gross earnings to compute net pay—the amount actually paid to employees. As the arrows in Exhibit 11.4 indicate, each of these steps provides information that the business must account for, as we explain in the following sections.

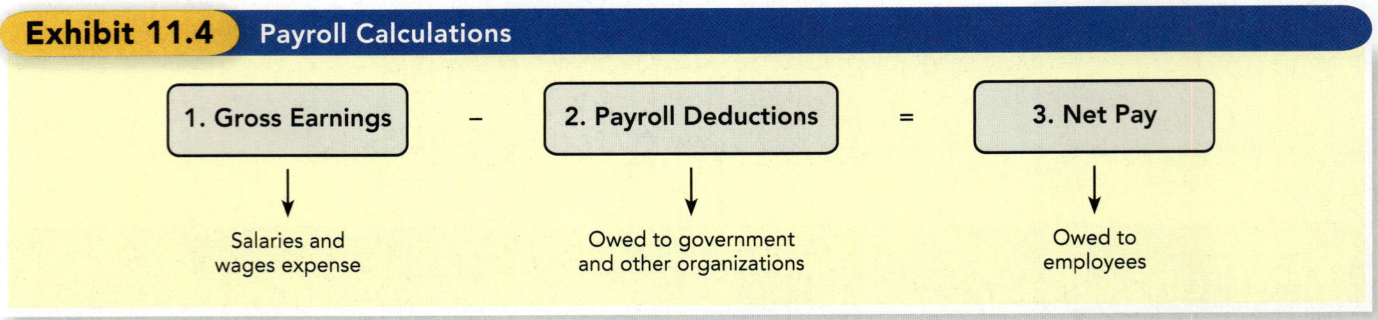

Gross Earnings

Gross earnings represents the amount employees earn as compensation for the work they do. From the employer's point of view, this is an expense called Salaries and Wages Expense. Employers and employees determine salaries and wage rates by agreement. An employee who agrees to a yearly salary of $60,000 would be entitled to $5,000 of gross earnings for each month of work (= $60,000 ÷ 12). An employee who agrees to an hourly wage rate of $10 would be entitled to gross earnings of $400 for 40 hours of work (= 40 × $10).

Most employers are required by law to pay an overtime premium to hourly employees who work more than 8 hours per day or 40 hours per week. Overtime pay is typically calculated as "time and a half," which means 1½ times the regular pay rate. Some employers pay an even higher overtime premium ("double time") to employees who work on weekends or holidays. Assume Nigel Lithgow earns a regular pay rate of $10 per hour for the first 40 hours per week and time and a half for anything over 40 hours. If Nigel works 54 hours during the first week of the year, his gross earnings will be $610, calculated as follows:

	Pay Rate	×	Hours	=	Gross Earnings
Regular	$10		40		$ 400
Overtime	($10 × 1½)		14		210
Total			54		$ 610

Payroll Deductions

Payroll deductions are amounts a company subtracts from each employee's gross earnings. The employer does not keep these deductions but rather pays ("remits") them to another organization or government agency on behalf of employees. Some deductions are required by law; others are made on a voluntary basis as a service to employees. Deductions required by law, such as those for income taxes and FICA taxes (commonly referred to as Social Security taxes), are calculated according to specific rules. Voluntary deductions are amounts for charitable donations, retirement savings, union dues, medical and dental plans, life insurance, parking fees, and so on.

From the employer's perspective, payroll deductions create liabilities, not expenses. They are not expenses because they do not directly increase the employer's salary and wage costs. Instead, they simply redirect part of the salary and wage payments to a government agency or other organization rather than to employees.

Coach's Tip

Always think from the company's perspective, not your own personal perspective. Although payroll deductions seem to be expenses to you on a personal basis, they create liabilities, not expenses, for the employer.

Income Taxes. At a minimum, federal income tax must be deducted ("withheld") from each employee's pay. In addition, deductions may be required for state, county, and city income taxes depending on where employees live. These additional income taxes are often specified as a percentage of federal income tax. To avoid complicating our examples, we assume no state, county, or city income taxes.

The Internal Revenue Service (IRS) explains the methods employers can use to determine the federal income tax deduction for each employee. The simplest method is to look up the amount of the deduction in the tax bracket tables the IRS provides. These tables take into account the employee's gross earnings for a given pay period (as calculated by the employer), as well as "allowances" for other personal factors, such as marital status and number of children and dependents (as each employee indicates on a W-4 Form). Exhibit 11.5 is an excerpt from a tax bracket table. According to this table, the employer should deduct $58 income tax from Nigel Lithgow's pay assuming that he earned $610 during the week, that he is single, and he claimed two allowances.

FICA Taxes. To support Medicare and Social Security, the Federal Insurance Contributions Act requires employees to pay FICA taxes to the government through employee payroll deductions. In 2008, employers were required to deduct 1.45 percent from each employee's earnings for Medicare and 6.2 percent (on earnings of up to $102,000) for Social Security. To simplify calculations, we will assume a total FICA rate of 8 percent. At that rate, Nigel's $610 of gross earnings requires a deduction of $48.80 for FICA taxes (= $610 × 0.08).

Voluntary Deductions. Each employee should approve in writing the amount to be withheld from his or her earnings for voluntary deductions. Just like income tax and FICA tax deductions, the company records voluntary deductions as a liability until the business pays them to the designated charity, savings plan, union, or other organization.

Net Pay

As Exhibit 11.4 showed, net pay is calculated by subtracting payroll deductions from gross earnings. Nigel Lithgow's net pay is calculated as follows, assuming a voluntary deduction of $10 for a United Way contribution.

Gross earnings		$ 610.00
Payroll deductions:		
Federal income tax	$ 58.00	
FICA taxes	48.80	
United Way	10.00	116.80
Net pay		**$ 493.20**

Exhibit 11.5 Table for Determining Income Tax Deductions

SINGLE Persons—**WEEKLY** Payroll Period

If the wages are–		And the number of withholding allowances claimed is–										
At least	But less than	0	1	2	3	4	5	6	7	8	9	10
		The amount of income tax to be withheld is–										
$600	$610	$76	$66	$56	$47	$37	$27	$17	$10	$3	$0	$0
610	620	77	68	58	48	38	28	19	11	4	0	0
620	630	79	69	59	50	40	30	20	12	5	0	0
630	640	80	71	61	51	41	31	22	13	6	0	0
640	650	82	72	62	53	43	33	23	14	7	1	0

Mia Miller worked 42 hours this week. Her regular wage rate is $14 per hour, and the overtime rate is 1½ times the regular pay rate. Her employer pays Mia weekly. She is single, claims three allowances, pays no state, county, or city income tax, and has requested a voluntary deduction of $5 per week for a charity. Using the tax bracket table in Exhibit 11.5 and assuming total FICA taxes of 8 percent, calculate Mia's gross earnings, payroll deductions, and net pay.

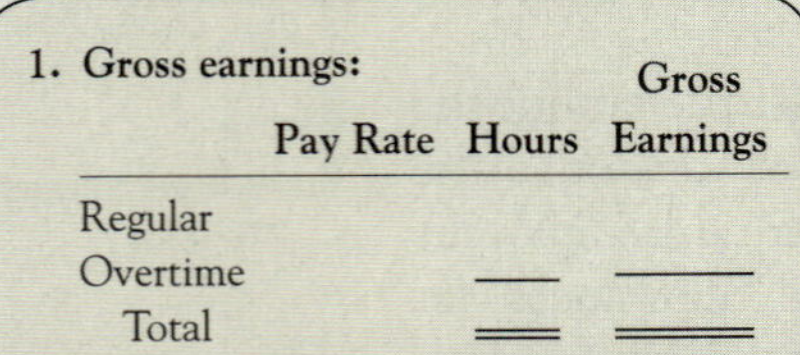

1. Gross earnings:

	Pay Rate	Hours	Gross Earnings
Regular			
Overtime		____	______
Total		====	======

2. Payroll deductions:

Federal income tax	
FICA taxes	
Charitable contribution	______
Total	======

3. Net pay:

Gross earnings	
Payroll deductions	______
Net pay	======

After you have finished, check your answers with the solution at the bottom of the next page.

Recording the Payroll

The system for recording payroll transactions is designed to achieve two objectives: (1) to comply with state and federal laws requiring a cumulative record of each employee's gross earnings, deductions, and net pay and (2) to summarize those amounts to enable the business to record journal entries.

Employee Earnings Records

Payroll computations for each employee are captured each pay period in an employee earnings record. See Exhibit 11.6 for excerpts from Nigel Lithgow's employee earnings record for the year ended December 31, 2009. The calculations for Nigel's first pay period are highlighted in red.

The employee earnings record is used in three ways. First, it is used to determine whether the employee has reached the maximum earnings that are subject to the full FICA tax rate. The Cumulative column in Exhibit 11.6 shows that at no point during the year did Nigel's total earnings exceed the $102,000 FICA limit, so the full FICA rate is applied to all his earnings.

Exhibit 11.6 Employee Earnings Record

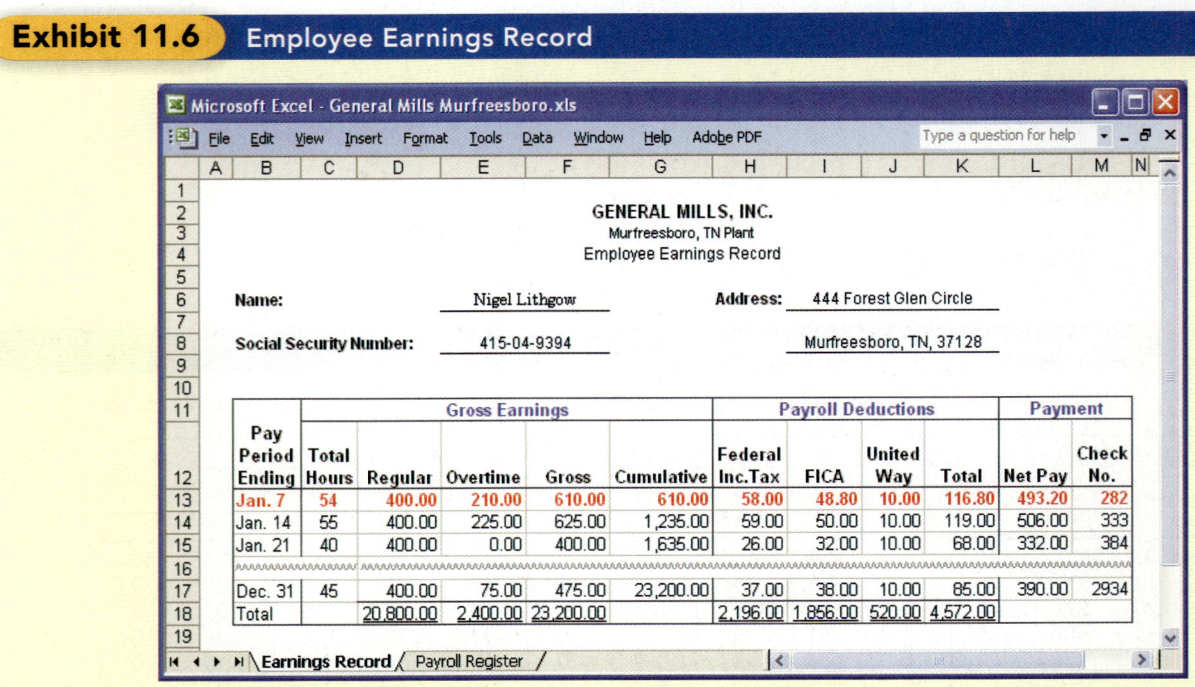

Microsoft Excel - General Mills Murfreesboro.xls

GENERAL MILLS, INC.
Murfreesboro, TN Plant
Employee Earnings Record

Name: Nigel Lithgow **Address:** 444 Forest Glen Circle

Social Security Number: 415-04-9394 Murfreesboro, TN, 37128

		Gross Earnings				Payroll Deductions				Payment	
Pay Period Ending	Total Hours	Regular	Overtime	Gross	Cumulative	Federal Inc.Tax	FICA	United Way	Total	Net Pay	Check No.
Jan. 7	54	400.00	210.00	610.00	610.00	58.00	48.80	10.00	116.80	493.20	282
Jan. 14	55	400.00	225.00	625.00	1,235.00	59.00	50.00	10.00	119.00	506.00	333
Jan. 21	40	400.00	0.00	400.00	1,635.00	26.00	32.00	10.00	68.00	332.00	384
Dec. 31	45	400.00	75.00	475.00	23,200.00	37.00	38.00	10.00	85.00	390.00	2934
Total		20,800.00	2,400.00	23,200.00		2,196.00	1,856.00	520.00	4,572.00		

Earnings Record / Payroll Register

The second function of the employee earnings record is to accumulate information for employees' use in tracking their gross pay, payroll deductions, and net pay. This information is typically conveyed by a statement of earnings, which is either attached to each paycheck or distributed separately. Exhibit 11.7 provides an example. Because this example is for the first pay period of the year, the year-to-date numbers equal the amounts for the current period.

Exhibit 11.7 Paycheck with Detachable Statement of Earnings

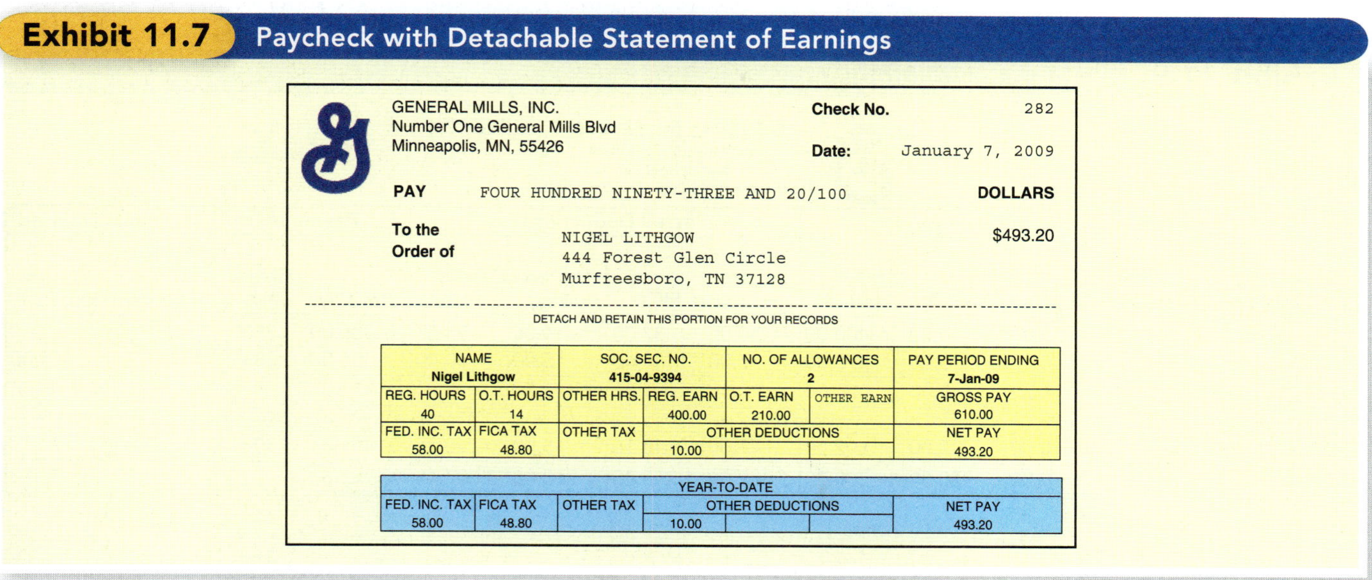

GENERAL MILLS, INC.
Number One General Mills Blvd
Minneapolis, MN, 55426

Check No. 282

Date: January 7, 2009

PAY FOUR HUNDRED NINETY-THREE AND 20/100 DOLLARS

To the Order of NIGEL LITHGOW
444 Forest Glen Circle
Murfreesboro, TN 37128

$493.20

DETACH AND RETAIN THIS PORTION FOR YOUR RECORDS

NAME		SOC. SEC. NO.		NO. OF ALLOWANCES		PAY PERIOD ENDING
Nigel Lithgow		415-04-9394		2		7-Jan-09
REG. HOURS	O.T. HOURS	OTHER HRS.	REG. EARN	O.T. EARN	OTHER EARN	GROSS PAY
40	14		400.00	210.00		610.00
FED. INC. TAX	FICA TAX	OTHER TAX	OTHER DEDUCTIONS			NET PAY
58.00	48.80		10.00			493.20

YEAR-TO-DATE						
FED. INC. TAX	FICA TAX	OTHER TAX	OTHER DEDUCTIONS			NET PAY
58.00	48.80		10.00			493.20

The third function of the employee earnings record is to provide information for preparing quarterly and annual reports for tax, insurance, and other purposes. For example, by January 31 of the following year, employers must prepare for each employee a year-end Wage and Tax Statement (Form W-2) similar to the one in Exhibit 11.8. The employer provides a copy of Form W-2 to each employee for use in preparing personal income taxes. The employer submits another copy to the Social Security Administration, which relays the income information to the IRS.

Exhibit 11.8 Sample Wage and Tax Statement (Form W-2)

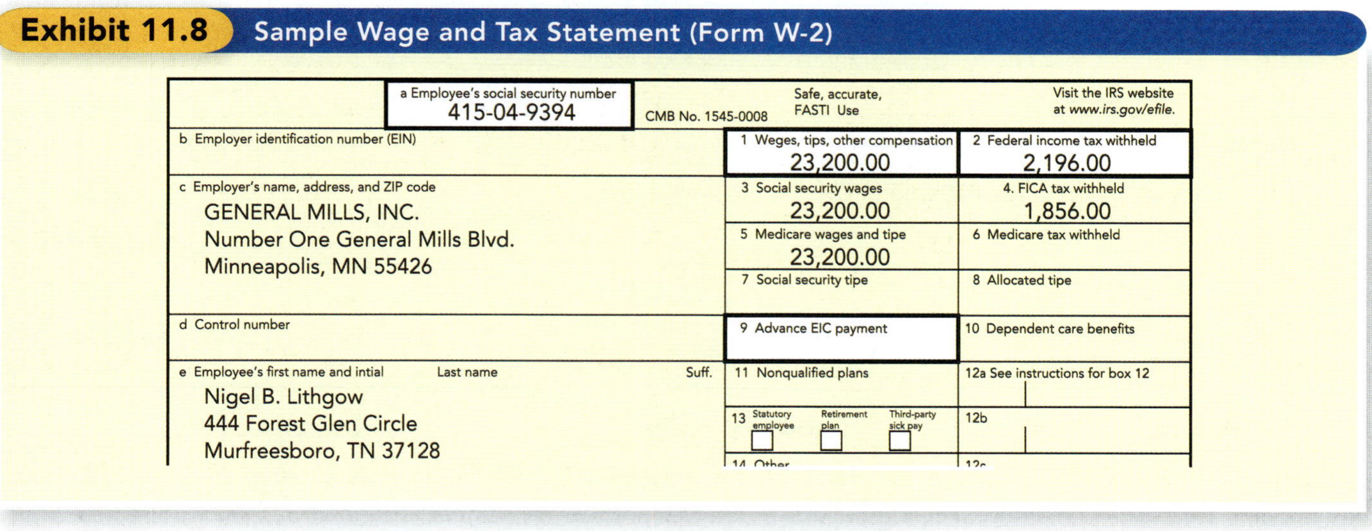

a Employee's social security number 415-04-9394 | CMB No. 1545-0008 | Safe, accurate, FASTI Use | Visit the IRS website at *www.irs.gov/efile.*

b Employer identification number (EIN)	1 Weges, tips, other compensation 23,200.00	2 Federal income tax withheld 2,196.00
c Employer's name, address, and ZIP code GENERAL MILLS, INC. Number One General Mills Blvd. Minneapolis, MN 55426	3 Social security wages 23,200.00	4. FICA tax withheld 1,856.00
	5 Medicare wages and tipe 23,200.00	6 Medicare tax withheld
	7 Social security tipe	8 Allocated tipe
d Control number	9 Advance EIC payment	10 Dependent care benefits
e Employee's first name and intial Last name Suff. Nigel B. Lithgow 444 Forest Glen Circle Murfreesboro, TN 37128	11 Nonqualified plans	12a See instructions for box 12
	13 Statutory employee ☐ Retirement plan ☐ Third-party sick pay ☐	12b
	14 Other	12c

Solution to Self-Study Practice

1. Gross earnings:

	Pay Rate	Hours	Gross Earnings
Regular	$14	40	$ 560
Overtime	($14 × 1½)	2	42
Total		42	$ 602

2. Payroll deductions

Federal income tax	$ 47.00
FICA taxes ($602 × 0.08)	48.16
Charitable contribution	5.00
Total	$100.16

3. Net pay:

Gross earnings	$602.00
Payroll deductions	100.16
Net pay	$501.84

Payroll Register

In addition to computing and reporting payroll information for each employee, the employer's payroll system must summarize the information across all employees so that total payroll costs and liabilities can be recorded in the accounting system. Typically, a payroll register like the one shown in Exhibit 11.9 serves this purpose.

Exhibit 11.9 Sample Payroll Register

GENERAL MILLS, INC.
Murfreesboro, TN Plant
Payroll Register
For the Week Ending January 7, 2009

	Gross Earnings				Payroll Deductions				Payment		Accounts Debited	
Employee	Total Hours	Regular	Overtime	Gross	Federal Inc. Tax	FICA	United Way	Total	Net Pay	Check No.	Office Salaries Expense	Wages Expense
Arent, Jason	40	400.00	0.00	400.00	59.00	32.00	4.00	95.00	305.00	280	400.00	
Caldwell, Nancy	45	400.00	75.00	475.00	37.00	38.00	5.00	80.00	395.00	281		475.00
Lithgow, Nigel	54	400.00	210.00	610.00	58.00	48.80	10.00	116.80	493.20	282		610.00
Zvinakis, Kris	42	560.00	42.00	602.00	47.00	48.16	15.00	110.16	491.84	308	602.00	
Total		14,780.00	950.00	15,730.00	1,489.00	1,258.40	260.00	3,007.40	12,722.60		2,359.50	13,370.50

Reading the payroll register in Exhibit 11.9 from left to right, we see the company incurred $15,730 of gross salaries and wages during the first week of January. From this, payroll deductions were withheld for income tax ($1,489), FICA ($1,258.40), and United Way ($260), leaving net pay of $12,722.60. Of the gross pay, $2,359.50 was for office salaries and $13,370.50 was for wages. General Mills would make the following journal entry to record this payroll information for the pay period ended January 7, 2009.

	Debit	Credit
Office Salaries Expense (+E, −OE)	2,359.50	
Wages Expense (+E, −OE)	13,370.50	
Federal Income Tax Payable (+L)		1,489.00
FICA Taxes Payable (+L)		1,258.40
United Way Payable (+L)		260.00
Cash (−A)		12,722.60

Assets		=	Liabilities		+	Owners' Equity	
Cash	−12,722.60		Federal Inc. Tax Payable	+1,489.00		Office Salaries Expense (+E)	− 2,359.50
			FICA Taxes Payable	+1,258.40		Wages Expense (+E)	−13,370.50
			United Way Payable	+ 260.00			

Note that the third-to-last column in the payroll register shows that employees were paid on January 7 using checks numbered 280–308. Had those checks not been prepared until later in the month, the company would have recorded the expenses and liabilities shown in the journal entry just given, but the credit for $12,722.60 would have been recorded to Salaries and Wages Payable (+L) instead of to Cash (−A).

Employer Payroll Taxes

Salaries and wages are not the only payroll expenses that businesses incur. Like their employees, employers are required to pay FICA taxes. In addition, employers are required to pay unemployment taxes at both the federal and state levels. Employer FICA and unemployment taxes, known generally as **employer payroll taxes**, are calculated and recorded using the methods that follow.

FICA Taxes. Employers are required to match each employee's FICA contribution. In other words, the company's required FICA tax contribution is equal to the total of all employees' contributions. The payroll register shown in Exhibit 11.9 indicates that **employee** FICA contributions totaled $1,258.40. This total implies that the **employer's** FICA contribution for the period was an additional $1,258.40. Until it has been paid, this liability is recorded in the same FICA Taxes Payable account as the amount that is withheld from employees.

Unemployment Taxes. Employers are charged unemployment taxes through the Federal Unemployment Tax Act (FUTA) and state unemployment tax acts (SUTA). This legislation provides limited financial support to employees who lose their jobs through no fault of their own. Typically, federal tax calculations give employers credit for unemployment taxes paid at the state level, so we begin by calculating the state unemployment tax.

An employer calculates the amount of the state unemployment tax by multiplying a tax rate by a specified amount of wages paid to employees during the calendar year. Because the rate and specified amount of wages vary by state, industry, and number of company employees receiving unemployment benefits in prior years, it is difficult to cover all possibilities here.[1] We illustrate the calculation of the tax by assuming a basic rate of 5.4 percent, which is applied to just the first $7,000 of wages. (Unless you are instructed otherwise, use this same assumption in all homework exercises and assignments.) The payroll register in Exhibit 11.9 shows that as of January 7, no employee had earned more than $7,000, so the 5.4 percent tax rate applies to all employees in this pay period. Thus, state unemployment taxes for the week ended January 7 are calculated by multiplying the 5.4 percent rate by the total wages of $15,730.00, yielding $849.42 (= $15,730.00 × 0.054) in state unemployment tax.

The FUTA specifies a federal tax rate of 6.2 percent on taxable wages up to the first $7,000 for each employee. However, if the employer has a good payment history, the tax rate can be reduced by unemployment taxes paid at the state level. The maximum credit for state taxes is 5.4 percent of taxable wages. Assuming that General Mills receives this credit, its federal tax rate would be lowered to 0.8 percent (= 6.2 − 5.4) of taxable wages. Applying this rate to the taxable wages for the week ended January 7 (shown in Exhibit 11.9 as $15,730.00), we find that General Mills owes $125.84 (= 0.008 × $15,730.00) in federal unemployment taxes.

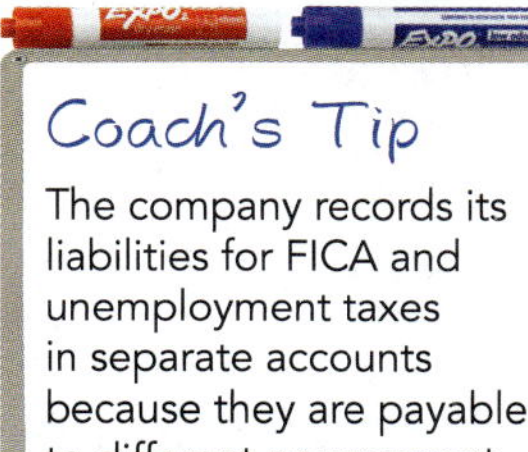

Coach's Tip

The company records its liabilities for FICA and unemployment taxes in separate accounts because they are payable to different government agencies.

These three employer payroll taxes represent additional costs the employer incurs beyond the costs of salaries and wages. The business therefore reports these costs as an expense on the income statement. Until they have been paid, these three taxes are recorded as current liabilities using separate accounts as shown in the following journal entry:

	Debit	Credit
Payroll Tax Expense (+E, −OE)	2,233.66	
FICA Taxes Payable (+L)		1,258.40
State Unemployment Taxes Payable (+L)		849.42
Federal Unemployment Taxes Payable (+L)		125.84

Assets	=	Liabilities		+	Owners' Equity	
		FICA Taxes Payable	+1,258.40		Payroll Tax Expense (+E)	−2,233.66
		State Unemployment Taxes Payable	+849.42			
		Federal Unemployment Taxes Payable	+125.84			

[1] Tax rates and specific wage limitations by state are available from the Department of Labor Employment and Training Administration Web site at www.doleta.gov.

SELF-STUDY PRACTICE

The payroll register for the two weeks ended October 31, 2008, indicates the following:

Gross salaries	$14,000	United Way contributions	$400
Federal income tax deductions	1,093	State unemployment taxes	756
FICA tax deductions	1,120	Federal unemployment taxes	112

Assuming that employees received their net pay on October 31 but no other payments were made for payroll, prepare journal entries to record (1) salaries and wages and (2) employer payroll taxes. Also show the accounting equation effects.

After you have finished, check your answers with the solution at the bottom of the page.

Applying Internal Control Principles

Employers apply to payroll the same internal control principles used for cash receipts and payments. These controls focus on **establishing responsibilities** for: tracking the work done by each employee, approving pay rates, calculating deductions, and distributing net pay. These **duties are segregated** so that an employee cannot both authorize and pay oneself. **Restricted access** to timecards, pay rate files, and check-signing equipment limits the risk of unauthorized activities. Payroll staff members **document procedures** performed using internal records, such as the payroll register, as well as external reports, such as Form W-2. **Independent verification** by each employee helps prevent underpayments, and the imprest payroll system discussed in Chapter 8 (page 352) helps prevent overpayments.

Spotlight On CONTROLS

Biometric Time Tracking: A Replacement for Timecards

Biometric time tracking is quickly replacing time clocks as the internal control method used to track employee work hours. Palm scanners, fingerprint scanners, voice recognition systems, and retinal scanners are all examples of biometric time-tracking devices that record when an employee enters and exits the workplace. Biometric systems can eliminate administrative time spent with timecard records calculating the number of hours worked. They can also reduce theft caused by employees punching in for tardy or absent co-workers and eliminate human error from timecard processing. Studies by the American Payroll Association indicate that such inefficiencies and problems can cost organizations up to 8 percent of their annual gross payroll.

Solution to Self-Study Practice

	Debit	Credit
1. Salaries Expense (+E, −OE)	14,000	
Federal Income Tax Payable (+L)		1,093
FICA Taxes Payable (+L)		1,120
United Way Payable (+L)		400
Cash (−A)		11,387

	Debit	Credit
2. Payroll Tax Expense (+E, −OE)	1,988	
FICA Taxes Payable (+L)		1,120
State Unemployment Taxes Payable (+L)		756
Federal Unemployment Taxes Payable (+L)		112

Assets		=	Liabilities		+	Owners' Equity	
1. Cash	−11,387		Federal Income Tax Payable	+1,093		Salaries Expense (+E)	−14,000
			FICA Taxes Payable	+1,120			
			United Way Payable	+ 400			
2.			FICA Taxes Payable	+1,120		Payroll Tax Expense (+E)	− 1,988
			State Unemployment Taxes Payable	+ 756			
			Federal Unemployment Taxes Payable	+ 112			

Demonstration Case A

Notes Payable, the Current Ratio, and Warranty Liabilities

CATERPILLAR®

On June 30, 2006, Caterpillar Inc. reported $24.3 billion in current assets and $21.1 billion in current liabilities. On August 3, 2006, Caterpillar received $500 million from an issue of promissory notes that will mature in 2016. The notes pay interest on February 15 at an annual rate of 6.05 percent. Caterpillar's fiscal year ends on December 31.

Required:

1. Explain which sections of Caterpillar's classified balance sheet the new promissory notes affect.
2. Give the journal entry on August 3, 2006, to record the issue of notes payable.
3. Give the journal entry on December 31, 2006, to record interest expense, assuming that none had been accrued prior to that date. Calculate interest assuming the notes had been outstanding for five full months.
4. Give the journal entry on February 15, 2007, to record the first interest payment. Calculate the interest payment using a period of 6.5 months.
5. Compute Caterpillar's current ratio on June 30, 2006.
6. Assume that as of December 31, 2006, Caterpillar had not yet used the cash obtained from the issue of notes on August 3, 2006. What is the effect, if any, of the note issue on the company's current ratio at the end of the fiscal year?
7. On January 1, 2007, Caterpillar had accrued product warranty liabilities totaling $953 million. From January 1 to September 30, 2007, the company paid $677 million under existing warranty agreements and accrued $754 million for additional warranties arising from sales made in 2007. Give the journal entries to record the total payment and accrual made during 2007. What is the balance in warranty liability at September 30, 2007?

Suggested Solution

1. Issuing of the notes increases Caterpillar's cash (a current asset) and notes payable (a long-term liability) by $500 million.
2. August 3, 2006 (issue date):

	Debit	Credit
Cash (+A)	500,000,000	
Notes Payable (+L)		500,000,000

3. December 31, 2006 (accrual of interest expense for five months):

	Debit	Credit
Interest Expense (+E, −OE) ($500,000,000 × 6.05% × 5/12)	12,604,167	
Interest Payable (+L)		12,604,167

4. February 15, 2007 (first interest payment date):

	Debit	Credit
Interest Expense (+E, −OE) ($500,000,000 × 6.05% × 1.5/12)	3,781,250	
Interest Payable (−L)	12,604,167	
Cash (−A) ($500,000,000 × 6.05% × 6.5/12)		16,385,417

5. June 30 current ratio:

$$\frac{\text{Current Assets}}{\text{Current Liabilities}} = \frac{\$24{,}300{,}000{,}000}{\$21{,}100{,}000{,}000} = 1.15$$

6. December current ratio:

$$\frac{\text{Current Assets}}{\text{Current Liabilities}} = \frac{(\$24{,}300{,}000{,}000 + \$500{,}000{,}000)}{(\$21{,}100{,}000{,}000 + \$12{,}604{,}167)} = 1.17$$

Issuing the notes increases the current ratio because cash from the notes increased current assets by $500 million, but the only increase in current liabilities was a relatively small amount of interest payable. The $500 million in notes payable increased long-term liabilities.

7. Warranty Payments

	Debit	Credit
Warranty Liabilities (−L)	677,000,000	
Cash (−A)		677,000,000

Warranty Accrual

	Debit	Credit
Warranty Expense (+E, −OE)	754,000,000	
Warranty Liabilities (+L)		754,000,000

Warranty Liabilities (Jan. 1) − Payments (Jan.–Sept) + Additional Accrual (Jan.–Sept.) = Warranty Liabilities (Sept. 30) = $953 − $677 + $754 = $1,030 (million)

Demonstration Case B

Unearned Revenue

Online Games, Inc., reported that it received $120,000 in annual subscription payments during the year ended December 31, 2009. The company will earn these subscription payments equally throughout each month of 2010.

Required:

1. Explain how Online Games should report the 2009 subscription payments on the balance sheet and income statement on (a) December 31, 2009, and (b) January 31, 2010.
2. Give the journal entries for (a) the receipt of annual subscription payments in December 2009 and (b) any required adjustments for the subscription payments on January 31, 2010.

Suggested Solution

1. (a) On December 31, 2009, the $120,000 of advanced subscription payments would be reported on the balance sheet as the current liability Unearned Revenue. No amounts related to 2009 subscription payments would be reported on the 2009 income statement.

   (b) On January 31, 2010, one month of subscription services would be earned, so the Unearned Revenue account on the balance sheet would be reduced by $10,000 (= $120,000 × 1/12), and the Subscription Revenue account on the income statement would be increased by $10,000.

2. (a) December 2009 (receipt of 2009 subscription payments)

	Debit	Credit
Cash (+A)	120,000	
Unearned Revenue (+L)		120,000

Assets		=	Liabilities		+	Owners' Equity
Cash	+120,000		Unearned Revenue	+120,000		

(b) January 31, 2010 (earned one month of 2010 subscriptions)

	Debit	Credit
Unearned Revenue (−L)	10,000	
Subscription Revenue (+R, +OE)		10,000

Assets	=	Liabilities		+	Owners' Equity	
		Unearned Revenue	−1,000		Subscription Revenue (+R)	+1,000

Demonstration Case C

Payroll

Bexco Industries reported the following information in its accounting records on December 31, 2009 related to the December 26 to December 31 payroll.

Gross salaries earned by employees	$3,600
Income taxes withheld from employees	550
FICA taxes withheld from employees	210
Net payment to employees	2,840
State unemployment taxes	194
Federal unemployment taxes	29

Bexco paid employees $2,840 on December 31, 2009 but did not remit the withholdings. Bexco has not recorded employer payroll taxes for the period from December 26 to December 31.

Required:

1. Compute the total payroll costs related to the period from December 26 to December 31, 2009.
2. Give the journal entry on December 31, 2009, to record payroll related to the period from December 26 to December 31, 2009. Separate the journal entry for the employer's payroll expenses from the entry for salaries and wages expense, and show the effects of each on the accounting equation.

Suggested Solution

1. **Computation of total payroll costs**

Salaries and wages		$3,600
Employer payroll taxes		
FICA taxes (matching contribution)	$210	
State unemployment taxes	194	
Federal unemployment taxes	29	433
Total payroll costs		$4,033

2. **Employee-related payroll costs**

	Debit	Credit
Salaries and Wages Expense (+E, −OE)	3,600	
Federal Income Tax Payable (+L)		550
FICA Taxes Payable (+L)		210
Cash (−A)		2,840

Assets		=	Liabilities		+	Owners' Equity	
Cash	−2,840		Federal Income Tax Payable	+550		Salaries and Wages Expense (+E)	−3,600
			FICA Taxes Payable	+210			

Employer-related payroll costs

	Debit	Credit
Payroll Tax Expense (+E, −OE)	433	
FICA Taxes Payable (+L)		210
State Unemployment Taxes Payable (+L)		194
Federal Unemployment Taxes Payable (+L)		29

Assets	=	Liabilities		+	Owners' Equity	
		FICA Taxes Payable	+210		Payroll Tax Expense (+E)	−433
		State Unemployment Taxes Payable	+194			
		Federal Unemployment Taxes Payable	+29			

Supplement 11A
Employee Benefits

Employees earn salaries and wages as direct compensation for their work. They may also receive additional benefits, such as paid leaves and post-retirement benefits. The general principle of accounting for employee benefits is based on the **matching principle.** That is, the employer should record an expense for employee benefits when the employees have earned benefits, not when the employer pays them.

Paid Leaves

Most businesses give employees the opportunity to take paid leaves from work for short periods. General Mills, for example, provides illness, childbirth, adoption, and military leaves to many employees. One of the most common paid leaves is vacation pay, which allows an employee to leave work for a period (several days or weeks) and still be paid.

Why does this topic require special discussion apart from ordinary salaries and wages? Unlike salaries and wages, which are earned and paid within a short time, such as a week or month, vacation pay is often earned over a longer period (a year). In fact, depending on its terms, vacation pay may accumulate and be paid out a long time after it has been earned. Some employers allow vacation pay to accumulate from one year to the next, resulting in a huge payment when the employee leaves the company.

To ensure that vacation pay is properly recorded in the period in which the employee earns it, the company should record a liability (and expense) for the estimated cost of paid vacations that employees will take. For example, if the estimated vacation time earned but not taken by employees in the current pay period is $1,000, it should be recorded as follows:

	Debit	Credit
Vacation Benefits Expense (+E, −OE)	1,000	
Vacation Benefits Payable (+L)		1,000

Assets	=	Liabilities		+	Owners' Equity	
		Vacation Benefits Payable	+1,000		Vacation Benefits Expense (+E)	−1,000

Later, when employees use the vacation time, the liability Vacation Benefits Payable should be reduced (with a debit).

Post-Employment Benefits

Post-employment benefits are benefits that employees receive after they retire as part of the total compensation they earned while working for the company. As the **matching principle** requires, the cost of post-employment benefits is recorded as an expense in the period when the employees work for the company. Because these costs are paid after employees leave the company, the employer must record a liability as the costs are incurred.

Several benefits may be provided after retirement including pensions and medical and life insurance. In this section, we focus on pensions, which operate differently depending on whether they involve defined benefits or defined contributions. In a **defined benefit** pension, the employer promises to pay specified amounts (benefits) to employees after they retire. It is up to the employer to ensure that sufficient funds are invested in the pension plan to cover the promised benefits. In a **defined contribution** pension, the employer is responsible only for making specified contributions to the plan, not for the amounts that are ultimately paid out as pensions. Instead, the amount paid out depends on how much the pension investments earn. On balance, defined benefit plans involve more uncertainty for the employer and much more complex accounting than defined contribution plans. We illustrate accounting for only defined contribution plans because these plans are the most common type of pension plans you will encounter.

The most popular type of defined contribution plan is a 401(k), which gets its name from the section of the Internal Revenue Code that explains how it works. The basic idea is that employees contribute amounts into the plan, and the employer makes matching contributions. The money in the plan is then invested, and any income it generates is accumulated in the plan without being taxed. Employees are not taxed until later when they near retirement and can withdraw amounts from the plan. This deferral of tax and the matching employer contribution are what make this plan so popular.

The matching contribution is the only part of the plan that the employer records in the accounting records. If the employer is required to make a matching contribution of $10,000, the following journal entry should be recorded:

	Debit	Credit
Pension Expense (+E, −OE)	10,000	
Pension Liability (+L)		10,000

Assets	=	Liabilities		+	Owners' Equity	
		Pension Liability	+10,000		Pension Expense (+E)	−10,000

When the employer pays the matching contribution to the pension plan, the Pension Liability should be reduced (with a debit) and Cash should be reduced (with a credit).

Chapter Summary

LO1 Explain how to report the major types of liabilities. p. 468

- Liabilities represent probable future sacrifices of economic benefits that arise from past transactions.
- Liabilities are classified as current if they are due to be paid with current assets within the current operating cycle or within one year of the balance sheet date, whichever is longer. All other liabilities are considered long term.

LO2 Calculate and interpret the current ratio. p. 469

- The current ratio is calculated by dividing current assets by current liabilities. A higher ratio suggests greater liquidity, a concept that represents the company's ability to pay current liabilities using current assets.

LO3 Demonstrate how to account for notes payable and the current portion of long-term debt. p. 470

- Notes payable are initially reported at their cash-equivalent value, which is the amount of cash received when the notes are signed. Interest expense is recorded as time passes; if it is not paid, the liability Interest Payable should be recorded.
- If any principal is owed on long-term debt in the upcoming year (or operating cycle), that amount should be classified as a current liability called Current Portion of Long-term Debt.

LO4 Demonstrate how to account for sales taxes and unearned revenues. p. 473

- Most states require retailers to charge sales tax on the selling price of products. Until they pay the tax, retailers should record sales tax as a current liability.
- Unearned revenues represent cash a business receives before it is earned. Because unearned revenues require the business to provide future services (or return the cash), unearned revenues are reported as current liabilities.

LO5 Demonstrate how to account for warranties and other contingent liabilities. p. 475

- Warranties are promises companies make to provide future repair services on any product sold during the current period. A warranty is considered a contingent liability because the cost of a future repair will not be known until a future event (the repair) occurs. Accounting rules require that estimable costs be recorded as a liability (Warranty Payable) and an expense in the period of sale. Actual repair costs then reduce the Warranty Payable account.
- Similarly, other contingent liabilities that are probable and estimable are recorded in the period when they arise. Contingent liabilities that are possible but not probable or are not estimable are disclosed in the notes to the financial statements.

LO6 Calculate and record payroll including employer payroll taxes. p. 477

- Calculating the payroll involves calculating gross earnings (based on the amount of work done by employees), payroll deductions (as required by law or requested voluntarily by employees), and net pay, which is the amount paid to employees.
- In addition to the cost of salaries and wages, employers incur additional payroll expenses related to FICA taxes and state and federal unemployment taxes.

Financial Analysis Tools

Name of Measure	Formula	What It Tells You
Current Ratio	$\frac{\text{Current Assets}}{\text{Current Liabilities}}$	• Whether current assets are sufficient to pay current liabilities • A higher ratio means better ability to pay

Key Terms

Cash Equivalent (p. 468)
Contingent Liabilities (p. 476)
Current Liabilities (p. 468)
Current Ratio (p. 469)
Employee Earnings Record (p. 480)
Employer Payroll Taxes (p. 483)
Gross Earnings (p. 478)
Line of Credit (p. 469)
Liquidity (p. 469)
Payroll (p. 477)
Payroll Deductions (p. 478)
Payroll Register (p. 482)
Promissory Note (p. 470)
Salaries (p. 477)
Wages (p. 477)

See complete glossary in back of text.

Questions

1. Define *liability*. What is the difference between a current liability and a long-term liability?
2. What three factors influence the dollar amount reported for liabilities?
3. What is the current ratio? How is it related to the classification of liabilities?
4. What is a line of credit? Does a line of credit affect the amount of cash that a company needs to have available to pay current liabilities?
5. Why is the "time" factor included in the formula to compute interest?

6. If a company has a long-term loan that has only two years remaining until it matures, how is it reported on the balance sheet (*a*) this year and (*b*) next year?
7. Why are sales taxes considered liabilities?
8. Why is unearned revenue considered a liability?
9. Why are warranty repair costs estimated and recorded in the period of sale rather than simply recorded when they are provided for customers?
10. How is the liability for warranties similar to and different from liabilities for sales taxes and accounts payable?
11. What is a contingent liability? How is a contingent liability reported?
12. Why are payroll deductions considered current liabilities?
13. Why do you think the federal government requires employers to deduct income taxes from employees' pay? How does this benefit the government? How might it benefit employees?
14. If a company maintains employee earnings records for each employee, is there additional value in maintaining a payroll register?
15. (Supplement 11A) If a company records and pays salaries each month, why is it necessary to estimate and record paid vacations too?
16. (Supplement 11A) Why should employees participate in a 401 (k) plan? Is this a defined contribution or defined benefit plan?

Multiple Choice

Quiz 11-1
www.mhhe.com/LLPW1e

1. Which of the following does not create a current liability?
   a. Cash is received from customers but not yet earned.
   b. Sales taxes are collected but not remitted.
   c. Amounts are withheld from employee wages but not yet remitted.
   d. None of the above—all create current liabilities.

2. Which of the following statements about the current ratio is true?
   a. The current ratio is always more than or equal to 1.0.
   b. The current ratio decreases when a company fulfills its obligation for unearned revenues.
   c. The higher the current ratio, the greater the risk the business will not be able to pay current liabilities.
   d. None of the above—all are false.

3. Assume that Warnaco Group Inc., the makers of Calvin Klein underwear, borrowed $100,000 from the bank to be repaid over the next five years with principal payments beginning next month. Which of the following best describes the presentation of this debt in the balance sheet as of today (the date of borrowing)?
   a. $100,000 in the Long-Term Liability section.
   b. $100,000 plus the interest to be paid over the five-year period in the Long-Term Liability section.
   c. A portion of the $100,000 in the Current Liability section and the remainder of the principal in the Long-Term Liability section.
   d. A portion of the $100,000 plus interest in the Current Liability Section and the remainder of the principal plus interest in the Long-Term Liability section.

4. Assume Speedo International received $400,000 for promissory notes that it issued on November 1. The notes pay interest on April 30 and October 31 at the annual rate of 6 percent. Which of the following journal entries must Speedo make at December 31?

		Debit	Credit
a.	Interest Expense	4,000	
	Interest Payable		4,000
b.	Interest Expense	4,000	
	Cash		4,000
c.	Interest Expense	4,000	
	Interest Payable	8,000	
	Cash		12,000
d.	Interest Expense	8,000	
	Interest Payable	4,000	
	Cash		12,000

5. As of February 28, 2007, American Greetings Corporation had 9,400 full-time and 19,500 part-time employees. Assume that in the last pay period of the year, the company paid $8,000,000 to employees after deducting $2,000,000 for employee income taxes, $612,000 for FICA taxes, and $700,000 of voluntary deductions. The company had made no payments to the government or other organizations relating to these payroll deductions. Which of the following statements is true regarding this pay period?
   a. FICA taxes payable is $612,000.
   b. FICA taxes payable is $1,224,000.
   c. Salaries and wages expense is $4,688,000.
   d. None of the above is true.

6. Which of the following is true when a retailer sells a computer for $1,000 cash and collects a 5 percent sales tax?
   a. Sales Revenue is $1,000.
   b. Sales Taxes Payable is $50.
   c. Cash collected totals $1,050.
   d. All of the above are true.

7. Which of the following accounts is debited when a company pays cash to have its products repaired under warranty?
   a. Warranty Expense.
   b. Cash.
   c. Warranty Liability.
   d. Repairs and Maintenance Expense.

8. Big Hitter Corp. is facing a class-action lawsuit in the upcoming year. It is possible, but not probable, that the company will have to pay a settlement of approximately $2,000,000. How would this fact be reported, if at all, in the financial statements to be issued at the end of the current month?
   a. Report $2,000,000 as a current liability.
   b. Report $2,000,000 as a long-term liability.
   c. Report the potential liability in the notes to the financial statements.
   d. Reporting is not required in this case.

9. Lucinda Perez worked 50 hours this week. She earns $10 for the first 40 hours and $15 for any overtime work. She had $75 in payroll deductions. What is her gross earnings?
   a. $550. c. $475.
   b. $665. d. $590.

10. The payroll records for Coolo Ice Cream Company showed gross employee earnings of $10,000 as well as payroll deductions of $1,200 for income tax, $800 for FICA taxes, and $500 for voluntary deductions. If the company owes $80 in federal unemployment taxes and $540 for state unemployment taxes, what is the total cost for payroll?
    a. $8,120. c. $10,620.
    b. $8,920. d. $11,420.

Solutions to Multiple-Choice Questions

1. d 2. d 3. c 4. a 5. b 6. d 7. c
8. c 9. a 10. d

Mini Exercises  Available with McGraw-Hill's Homework Manager

LO1 **M11-1 Reporting Liabilities in a Classified Balance Sheet**

Prepare the liabilities sections of a classified balance sheet for Electronic Games Inc. using the following balances reported at March 31, 2009: Unearned Revenue of $23,000; Accrued Salaries and Employee benefits of $35,670; Accounts Payable of $180,330; Short-Term Notes Payable of $50,000; Long-Term Debt of $100,000 (including current portion of long-term debt equal to $20,000); and Sales Taxes and Other Current Liabilities of $1,000.

LO2 **M11-2 Computing and Interpreting the Current Ratio**

Refer to M11-1. Compute the Electronic Games current ratio to two decimal places assuming current assets totaled $487,500 at March 31, 2009. Knowing the current ratio was 1.15 on March 31, 2008, would you say the company's liquidity improved or deteriorated in 2009?

LO2 **M11-3 Computing and Interpreting the Current Ratio**

The balance sheet for Shaver Corporation reported the following: total assets, $250,000; noncurrent assets, $150,000; current liabilities, $40,000; total owners' equity, $90,000; net income, $3,320; interest expense, $4,400; and income before income taxes, $5,280. Compute Shaver's current ratio. Based on this ratio alone, does it appear Shaver will be able to meet its obligations to pay current liabilities as they become due?

LO2 **M11-4 Analyzing the Impact of Transactions on the Current Ratio**

BSO, Inc., has a current ratio of 2.0 (= $1,000,000 ÷ $500,000). For each of the following transactions, determine whether the current ratio will increase, decrease, or remain the same.

(*a*) Purchased $20,000 of new inventory on credit.
(*b*) Paid accounts payable in the amount of $50,000.
(*c*) Recorded accrued salaries in the amount of $100,000.
(*d*) Borrowed $250,000 from a local bank to be repaid in 90 days.

LO3 **M11-5 Reporting Current and Noncurrent Portions of Long-Term Debt**

Assume that on December 1, 2008, your company borrowed $14,000, a portion of which is to be repaid each year on November 30. Specifically, your company will make the following principal payments: 2009, $2,000; 2010, $3,000; 2011, $4,000; and 2012, $5,000. Show how this loan will be reported in the December 31, 2009 and 2008, balance sheets, assuming that principal payments will be made when required.

M11-6 Recording a Note Payable LO3

Greener Pastures Corporation borrowed $1,000,000 on November 1, 2008. The note carried a 6 percent interest rate with the principal and interest payable on June 1, 2009. Prepare the journal entries and show the accounting equation effects for (*a*) the note issued on November 1, (*b*) the interest accrual on December 31, and (*c*) the interest and principal payments on June 1, 2009.

M11-7 Reporting Interest and Long-Term Debt, Including Current Portion LO3

Barton Chocolates used a promissory note to borrow $1,000,000 on July 1, 2009, at an annual interest rate of 6 percent. The note is to be repaid in yearly installments of $200,000, plus accrued interest, on June 30 of every year until the note is paid in full (on June 30, 2014). Show how the results of this transaction would be reported in a classified balance sheet prepared as of December 31, 2009.

M11-8 Recording Sales and State Sales Tax on Services LO4

Ahlers Clocks sells and repairs wall clocks, mantles, and grandfather clocks and is located in the Empire Mall in Sioux Falls, South Dakota. Assume that a grandfather clock was repaired for $50 cash plus 4 percent sales tax. Prepare the journal entry and show the accounting equation effects related to this transaction.

M11-9 Recording Sales, State Sales Tax, and Cost of Goods Sold LO4

Assume Ahlers Clock sold a grandfather clock for $5,000 cash plus 4 percent sales tax. Prepare the journal entry and show the accounting equation effects related to this transaction. As part of this transaction, include the cost of goods sold using a perpetual inventory system and assuming the clock cost Ahlers $3,000.

M11-10 Recording Unearned Revenues LO4

A local theater company sells 1,500 season ticket packages at a price of $250 per package. The first show in the five-show season starts this week. Prepare the journal entries and show the related accounting equation effects arising from (*a*) the sale of the season tickets before the first show and (*b*) the revenue earned after the first show.

M11-11 Accounting for Warranty Liabilities LO5

Hugo Watch Company, based in Livingston, Montana, sold $10,000 of watches in January under a six-month warranty. The cost of warranty repairs is estimated to be 5 percent of the sales price. In February and March, customers returned watches for repair under warranty. Hugo paid $480 for a repair company to perform this work. Prepare the journal entries and show the related accounting equation effects related to (*a*) the estimated liability for warranty costs and (*b*) the payment for watch repairs. Does the warranty cost estimate appear accurate? If not, what should Hugo Watch do?

M11-12 Reporting a Contingent Liability LO5

Buzz Coffee Shops is famous for its large servings of hot coffee. After a famous case involving McDonald's, the lawyer for Buzz warned management (during 2007) that it could be sued if someone were to spill hot coffee and be burned. "With the temperature of your coffee, I can guarantee it's just a matter of time before you're sued for $1,000,000." Unfortunately, in 2008, the prediction came true when a customer filed suit. The case went to trial in 2009, and the jury awarded the customer $400,000 in damages, which the company immediately appealed. The company's lawyers believed the lawsuit would be overturned on appeal. During 2010, the customer and the company settled their dispute for $150,000. What is the proper reporting of this liability each year?

M11-13 Calculating Gross Earnings LO6

Dan Carotene earns a regular pay rate of $20 per hour for the first 40 hours per week and time and a half for anything over 40 hours. If Dan works 50 hours during the first week of the year, what is his gross earnings for the week?

M11-14 Calculating Net Pay LO6

Lightning Electronics is a mid-size manufacturer of lithium batteries. The company's payroll records for the November 1–14 pay period show that employees earned wages totaling $100,000 but that federal income taxes totaling $14,000 and FICA taxes totaling $5,250 were withheld from this amount. There were no voluntary deductions. The net pay was directly deposited into the employees' bank accounts. What was the amount of net pay? If the company incurs $90 for federal unemployment taxes and $608 for state unemployment taxes, what is the total payroll cost (including employer payroll taxes) for this period?

M11-15 Recording Net Pay LO6

Refer to M11-14. Prepare the journal entry or entries that Lightning Electronics would use to record the payroll. Include both employee and employer taxes.

  Exercises **Available with McGraw-Hill's Homework Manager**

LO2
Kraft Foods Inc.

E11-1 Calculating and Interpreting the Current Ratio

According to its Web site, Kraft Foods Inc. sells enough Kool-Aid mix to make 1,000 gallons of the drink every minute during the summer and over 560 million gallons each year. At December 31, 2006, the company reported the following amounts (in millions) in its financial statements:

	2005	2006
Total current assets	$ 8,153	$ 8,254
Total current liabilities	8,724	10,473

Required:

1. Compute the current ratio (to two decimal places) for 2005 and 2006.
2. Did Kraft appear to have increased or decreased its ability to pay current liabilities as they become due?

LO2, 3

E11-2 Determining the Impact of Current Liability Transactions Including Analysis of the Current Ratio

Bryant Company sells a wide range of inventories that are initially purchased on accounts payable. Occasionally, a short-term note payable is used to obtain cash for current use. The following transactions were selected from those occurring during 2009:

(*a*) On January 10, 2009, purchased merchandise on credit for $18,000. The company uses a perpetual inventory system.

(*b*) On March 1, 2009, borrowed $40,000 cash from City Bank and gave a $40,000 interest-bearing note payable due in six months plus interest stated an annual rate of 8 percent payable at maturity.

Required:

1. Show the journal entry and accounting equation effects on January 10 and March 1.
2. Describe the impact of each transaction on the current ratio. (Assume Bryant Company's current assets have always been more than its current liabilities.)
3. What amount of cash is paid on the maturity date of the note?

LO3
Target Corporation

E11-3 Journalizing Transactions Involving Notes Payable

Many businesses borrow money during periods of increased business activity to finance inventory and accounts receivable. Target Corporation is one of America's largest general merchandise retailers. Each Christmas, Target builds up its inventory to meet the needs of Christmas shoppers. A large portion of Christmas sales are on credit. As a result, Target often collects cash from the sales several months after Christmas. Assume that on November 1, 2009, Target borrowed $6 million cash from Metropolitan Bank and signed a promissory note that matures in six months. The interest rate was 7.5 percent payable at maturity. The accounting period ends December 31.

Required:

1. Give the journal entry to record the note on November 1, 2009.
2. Give any adjusting entry required on December 31, 2009.
3. Give the journal entry to record payment of the note and interest on the maturity date, April 30, 2010, assuming that interest has not been recorded since December 31, 2009.
4. If Target needs extra cash during every Christmas season, should management borrow money on a long-term basis to avoid the necessity of negotiating a new short-term loan each year? Why or why not?

LO3

E11-4 Journalizing Transactions Involving Notes Payable

Assume that on November 1, 2009, Tops Bakery negotiated an agreement to borrow $200,000 cash on a one-year note. The note specified that Tops would pay 6 percent interest one year later, on October 31, 2010. The principal was also to be repaid on the maturity date (October 31, 2010).

Required:

1. Depict these events on a timeline similar to the one in Exhibit 11.2. How many months of interest are included in the payment on October 31, 2010? How many of these months relate to 2009 versus 2010?
2. Give the journal entry to record the note on November 1, 2009.

3. Give any adjusting entry required on December 31, 2009.
4. Give the journal entry to record payment of the note and interest on the maturity date, October 31, 2010, assuming that interest has not been recorded since December 31, 2009.

E11-5 Journalizing and Reporting Transactions Involving Sales Taxes **LO2, 4**

The Ferrer School (TFS) provides services to customers and collects a 5 percent state sales tax. The business entered into the following transactions.

a. During January 2009, TFS sold $12,000 worth of services to customers and collected $12,600 cash.

b. On February 1, 2009, TFS made a sales tax remittance for sales taxes collected during January 2009.

Required:

1. Give the journal entries to record these events.
2. Describe the impact of these events on the current ratio assuming current assets were $200,000 and current liabilities were $100,000 on January 1, 2009.

E11-6 Determining and Recording the Financial Statement Effects of Unearned Subscription Revenue **LO4** Reader's Digest

Reader's Digest Association is a publisher of magazines, books, and music collections. The following note is from its June 30 annual report:

> **Revenues**
>
> Sales of our magazine subscriptions, less estimated collections, are deferred (as unearned revenue) and recognized as revenues proportionately over the subscription period.

Assume that Reader's Digest collected $394 million in 2008 for magazines that will be delivered in future years. During the 2009 fiscal year, the company delivered $190 million worth of magazines on those subscriptions.

Required:

1. Using the information given above, prepare the journal entries that would be recorded in each year.
2. Using your answers to requirement 1, compute the amount of subscription services that Reader's Digest received in 2008 but must still provide in 2010 and beyond.

E11-7 Journalizing Transactions Involving Warranties **LO5**

During 2008, Bull Manufacturing Inc. (BMI) sold 30,000 lawnmowers with a two-year warranty. The company's production manager estimated that 5 percent of the lawnmowers would require warranty repairs at an average cost of $100 per unit. BMI outsources the warranty work to repair companies and incurred $100,000 in repair costs during 2008, all of which were paid in cash.

Required:

1. What is the total estimated cost of warranty repairs for sales made during 2008?
2. Give the journal entries to record these events.
3. If BMI's estimate is accurate, what total repair cost is yet to be incurred for the lawnmowers sold in 2008?

E11-8 Journalizing Transactions Involving Warranties **LO5**

Paloma Group sells tankless water heaters that come with a 10-year warranty against defects. Assume that during the years ended December 31, 2008 and 2009, the company sold 50,000 and 60,000 units. At the time of sale, the company's engineers estimated that only 1 percent would be returned for repair under warranty. Paloma intends to perform all of its own repair work at an estimated cost of $100 per repair. During 2008, Paloma used parts and supplies costing $5,000 for warranty repairs. In 2009, parts and supplies costing $11,000 were used. (Ignore the associated labor cost.)

Required:

1. What is the total estimated cost of warranty repairs for sales made during 2008? 2009?
2. What was the actual cost of warranty repairs in 2008? 2009?
3. Give the journal entries to record the 2008 and 2009 transactions involving warranties.
4. Does it appear that Paloma's initial estimate of total repair costs was accurate? Explain.

LO6

E11-9 Recording Payroll Costs with Discussion

McLoyd Company completed the salary and wage payroll for March 2009. The payroll provided the following details:

Salaries and wages earned	$230,000	Withholdings for United Way	$ 6,000
Federal income taxes withheld	50,200	Federal unemployment tax	1,840
FICA taxes withheld	16,445	State unemployment tax	12,880

Required:

1. Considering employer payroll taxes, calculate the total labor cost for the company.
2. Prepare the journal entry to record the payroll for March including employee deductions (but excluding employer payroll taxes).
3. Prepare the journal entry to record the employer's payroll taxes.

LO6

E11-10 Calculating and Recording Net Pay

Assume that Nora Jones worked 46 hours this week. Her regular wage rate is $13 per hour, and the overtime rate is 1½ times the regular pay rate. She is single, paid weekly, claims three allowances, pays federal but no state, county, or city income tax, and requested voluntary deductions of $8 each week for WWF (a charitable organization).

Required:

1. Using the tax bracket table in Exhibit 11.5 and assuming total FICA taxes equal to 8 percent, calculate (a) gross earnings, (b) payroll deductions, and (c) net pay. If necessary, round to the nearest penny.
2. Prepare the journal entry to record this payroll assuming Nora is paid by check but the payroll deductions have not been remitted. (Ignore employer payroll taxes.)

LO6

E11-11 Recording Net Pay and Payroll Taxes

The payroll register for the two weeks ended October 31, 2008, indicates the following:

Gross salaries	$140,000	United Way contributions	$3,000
Federal income tax deductions	10,093	State unemployment taxes	7,560
FICA tax deductions	11,120	Federal unemployment taxes	1,120

Required:

1. Calculate net pay.
2. Assuming that employees were paid their net pay on October 31 but no other payments were made for payroll, prepare journal entries to record (a) salaries and wages and (b) employer payroll taxes.

LO6

E11-12 Calculating and Recording Payroll Taxes

The payroll register for Great Southern Hospitality Corp. is shown below. No employees have earned more than $7,000 to date.

GREAT SOUTHERN HOSPITALITY CORP.
Payroll Register
For the Week Ending January 7, 2009

	Gross Earnings				Payroll Deductions				Payment		Accounts Debited	
Employee	Total Hours	Regular	Overtime	Gross	Federal Inc. Tax	FICA	United Way	Total	Net Pay	Check No.	Office Salaries Expense	Wages Expense
Ashworth, Jay	40	400.00	0.00	400.00	59.00	32.00	4.00	95.00	305.00	280	400.00	
Cabot, Noreen	45	400.00	75.00	475.00	37.00	38.00	5.00	80.00	395.00	281		475.00
...												
Zuvin, Katy	42	560.00	42.00	602.00	47.00	48.16	15.00	110.16	491.84	308	602.00	
Total		13,302.00	698.00	14,000.00	1,340.00	1,120.00	290.00	2,750.00	11,250.00		2,100.00	11,900.00

Required:

1. Calculate state unemployment taxes, assuming a 5.4 percent rate. If necessary, round to the nearest cent.
2. Calculate federal unemployment taxes assuming a 6.2 percent rate and a full credit for state unemployment taxes. If necessary, round to the nearest cent.
3. Using information in the payroll register and your answers to requirements 1 and 2, prepare journal entries that would be used to record (a) salaries and wages and (b) employer payroll taxes.

E11-13 Recording Payroll Costs with and without Withholdings **LO6**

Assume an employee of Rocco Rock Company earns $1,000 of gross wages during the current pay period and is required to remit to the government $100 for income tax and $50 for FICA. Consider the following two procedures for paying the employee. (Ignore unemployment taxes.)

Procedure 1 (withholdings)	Procedure 2 (no withholdings)
Rocco Rock Company pays the employee net wages of $850 and will remit income taxes and FICA on behalf of the employee.	Rocco Rock Company pays the employee gross wages of $1,000 and the employee is responsible for remitting income taxes and FICA.

Required:

1. Ignoring employer payroll taxes, under each procedure calculate (a) the total labor cost for the company and (b) the amount by which the employee's cash will increase after satisfying all responsibilities to the government.
2. Explain why procedure 1 (withholdings) is the approach preferred by the government.
3. Considering that employers are responsible for matching the employee's FICA contributions, explain why employers might also prefer procedure 1 over procedure 2.
4. Prepare the journal entries required by the employer under procedure 1 assuming the employee is paid in cash but the withholdings and matching employer FICA contribution have not been paid.

E11-14 (Supplement) Employee Benefits

Heara Whisper Electronics (HWE) is a maker of assistive hearing devices. To attract employees, the company offers three-week paid vacations, which can be used up each year or accumulated over successive years and then paid out in cash. The company also has a defined contribution pension plan to which the company will make contributions that match 100 percent of the contributions made by employees. During 2009, Victor Ree accumulated $1,500 of vacation time, and he contributed $1,000 to the pension plan. The company expects to make cash payments in 2010 totaling $2,500 related to these transactions.

Required:

1. In what year should HWE record these items? Explain.
2. Prepare journal entries that HWE should make to record the effect of these transactions on the company.

Problems—Set A  **Available with McGraw-Hill's Homework Manager**

PA11-1 Journalizing Transactions, Evaluating Current Ratio Effects, and Reporting Liabilities **LO1, 2, 3, 4**

Jack Hammer Company completed the following transactions during 2009. The annual accounting period ends December 31, 2009.

Apr. 30	Received $550,000 from Commerce Bank after signing a 2-year, 6 percent interest-bearing note payable.
June 6	Purchased merchandise on account at a cost of $75,000.
July 15	Paid for the June 6 purchase.

Aug. 31 Signed contract to provide security service to a small apartment complex and collected six months' fees in advance amounting to $12,000. (Use the account Unearned Service Revenue.)

Required:

1. Prepare journal entries for each of the transactions and for adjustments required at year-end.
2. For each transaction, state whether the current ratio is increased, decreased, or remains the same. (Assume Jack Hammer's current assets have always been higher than its current liabilities.)
3. Show how all of the liabilities arising from these transactions are reported on the classified balance sheet at December 31, 2009.

LO1, 2, 3, 5

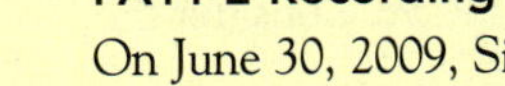

www.mhhe.com/LLPW1e

PA11-2 Recording Notes Payable, Warranties, and Evaluating Impact on Current Ratio

On June 30, 2009, Sideways Movers had $243,000 in current assets and $211,000 in current liabilities. On August 1, 2009, Sideways received $50,000 from an issue of promissory notes that will mature in 2012. The notes pay interest on February 1 at an annual rate of 6 percent. Sideways' fiscal year ends on December 31.

Required:

1. Explain which sections of Sideways' classified balance sheet are affected by the new promissory notes.
2. Give the journal entry on August 1, 2009, to record the issue of notes payable.
3. Give the journal entry on December 31, 2009, to record interest expense assuming that none had been recorded prior to that date.
4. Give the journal entry on February 1, 2010, to record the first interest payment.
5. Compute Sideways' current ratio on June 30, 2009.
6. Assume that as of December 31, 2009, Sideways had not yet used the cash obtained from the issue of notes on August 1, 2009. What is the effect, if any, of the note issue on the company's current ratio at the end of the fiscal year?
7. On January 1, 2010, Sideways had accrued product warranty liabilities totaling $9,530. From January 1 to December 31, 2010, the company paid $6,770 under existing warranty agreements and accrued $7,540 for additional warranties arising from sales made in 2010. Give the journal entries to record the total payment and accrual made during 2010. What is the balance in Warranty Liability at December 31, 2010?

LO1, 4, 6

www.mhhe.com/LLPW1e

PA11-3 Recording and Reporting Unearned Revenue and Payroll

On December 1, 2009, Lakeview Company collected rent of $3,600 for office space rented to another business. The rent collected was for two months from December 1, 2009, to January 31, 2010. Lakeview also reported the following information in its accounting records on December 31, 2009, for the December 22 to December 31 payroll.

Gross salaries earned by employees	7,200
Federal income tax withheld from employees	1,100
FICA taxes withheld from employees	420
State unemployment taxes	388
Federal unemployment taxes	58

Employees were paid $5,680 on December 31, 2009, but the withholdings have not yet been remitted. No employer payroll taxes have been recorded for the period from December 22 to December 31.

Required:

1. Give the journal entries to record (a) the collection of rent on December 1, 2009, and (b) the adjustment for rent on December 31, 2009.
2. Compute the total payroll costs related to the period from December 22 to December 31, 2009.
3. Give the journal entry on December 31, 2009, to record payroll related to the period from December 22 to December 31, 2009. Separate the journal entry for the employer's payroll expenses from the entry for salaries and wages expense.
4. Show how any liabilities related to these transactions should be reported on the company's balance sheet at December 31, 2009.

LO5

Macromedia, Inc.

PA11-4 Determining Financial Statement Reporting of Contingent Liabilities

Macromedia, Inc., is the original maker of shockwave and flash technologies. Its 2002 annual report indicated that a lawsuit had been filed in 2000 against the company and five of its former officers for securities fraud in connection with allegedly making false or misleading statements about its financial results. The lawsuit was settled on January 9, 2002, as described in the following note:

> **Legal**
>
> The settlement amount was $48.0 million, of which approximately $19.5 million was paid by insurance. As a result, the Company recorded a $28.5 million charge as a component of other income (expense) in its consolidated statements of operations during fiscal year 2002.

Required:

Explain why Macromedia did not record a contingent liability in 2000 when the lawsuit was filed.

PA11-5 Journalizing Transactions, Evaluating Current Ratio Effects, and Reporting Liabilities (Comprehensive Problem) **LO2, 3, 4, 5, 6**

www.mhhe.com/LLPW1e

Jinx Hair Salon in Iowa City completed the following transactions.

(*a*) Provided hair styling services and received $9,450, which included $450 in sales taxes.

(*b*) Received $200 for gift cards to be redeemed for future services.

(*c*) Prepared to expand the salon by borrowing $40,000, which was placed in the company's bank account. Signed a 9-month promissory note on February 1, with interest payable at maturity on October 31, 2009, calculated using a 5 percent annual interest rate.

(*d*) Provided hair styling services, which were paid for using gift cards. The total charge of $105 included $5 of sales taxes.

(*e*) Received a letter alleging that a Jinx stylist had ruined a customer's wedding by providing inferior hair care services. The customer was seeking $100,000 to compensate for her anguish. Jinx's lawyer believes the pending lawsuit is without merit.

(*f*) Paid stylists net wages of $5,500. Withheld but did not yet remit $725 for federal income tax, $315 for FICA taxes, and $20 for United Way contributions. Employer payroll costs for FICA, state unemployment taxes ($297), and federal unemployment taxes ($44) have not yet been remitted.

(*g*) Paid interest on the note on October 31, 2009.

(*h*) Paid principal on the note on October 31, 2009.

Required:

1. Prepare journal entries for each of the transactions and for adjustments required at year-end.
2. Indicate the independent effect of each transaction on the current ratio (increase, decrease, no change). When determining the effects, assume Jinx's current ratio at the beginning of the period was 1.1 (= $176,000 ÷ $160,000).

Problems—Set B

Available with McGraw-Hill's Homework Manager

PB11-1 Journalizing Transactions, Evaluating Current Ratio Effects, and Reporting Liabilities **LO1, 2, 3, 4**

Tiger Company completed the following transactions during 2009. The annual accounting period ends December 31, 2009.

Jan. 3 Purchased merchandise on account at a cost of $24,000. (Assume a perpetual inventory system.)

27 Paid for the January 3 purchase.

Apr. 1 Received $80,000 from Atlantic Bank after signing a 12-month, 5 percent interest-bearing note payable.

Aug. 1 Rented out a small office in a building owned by Tiger Company and collected eight months' rent in advance amounting to $8,000. (Use the account Unearned Rent Revenue.)

Required:

1. Prepare journal entries for each of the transactions and for adjustments required at year-end.
2. For each transaction, state whether the current ratio is increased, decreased, or remains the same. (Assume Tiger Company's current assets have always been higher than its current liabilities.)
3. Show how all of the liabilities arising from these transactions are reported on the balance sheet at December 31, 2009.

LO1, 2, 3, 5

PB11-2 Recording Notes Payable, Warranties, and Evaluating Impact on Current Ratio

On January 31, 2009, Dry Ice Inc. (DII) had $486,000 in current assets and $405,000 in current liabilities. On February 1, 2009, DII received $100,000 from an issue of promissory notes that will mature in 2011. The notes pay interest on January 31 at an annual rate of 6 percent. DII's fiscal year ends on December 31.

Required:

1. Explain which sections of DII's classified balance sheet are affected by the new promissory notes.
2. Give the journal entry on February 1, 2009, to record the issue of notes payable.
3. Compute DII's current ratio on January 31, 2009. What would be the effect, if any, of the February 1 note issuance on the company's current ratio?
4. Give the journal entry on December 31, 2009, to record interest expense assuming that none had been recorded prior to that date.
5. Give the journal entry on January 31, 2010, to record the first interest payment.
6. On January 1, 2010, DII had accrued product warranty liabilities totaling $10,000. From January 1 to December 31, 2010, the company paid $9,000 under existing warranty agreements and accrued $12,000 for additional warranties arising from sales made in 2010. Give the journal entries to record the total payment and accrual made during 2010. What is the balance in Warranty Liability at December 31, 2011?

LO1, 4, 6

PB11-3 Recording and Reporting Unearned Revenue and Payroll

On December 1, 2009, Sandler Company collected rent of $3,600, for office space rented to another business. The rent collected was for three months from December 1, 2009, to February 28, 2010. Sandler also reported the following information in its accounting records on December 31, 2009, for the December 17 to December 31 payroll.

Gross salaries earned by employees	18,000
Federal income tax withheld from employees	2,750
FICA taxes withheld from employees	1,050
State unemployment taxes	970
Federal unemployment taxes	145

Employees were paid $14,200 on December 31, 2009, but the withholdings have not yet been remitted. No employer payroll taxes have been recorded for the period from December 17 to December 31.

Required:

1. Give the journal entries to record (a) the collection of rent on December 1, 2009, and (b) the adjustment for rent on December 31, 2009.
2. Compute the total payroll costs related to the period from December 17 to December 31, 2009.
3. Give the journal entry on December 31, 2009, to record payroll related to the period from December 17 to December 31, 2009. Separate the journal entry for the employer's payroll expenses from the entry for salaries and wages expense.
4. Show how any liabilities related to these transactions should be reported on the company's balance sheet at December 31, 2009.

LO5
Brunswick Corporation

PB11-4 Determining Financial Statement Reporting of Contingent Liabilities

Brunswick Corporation is a multinational company that manufactures and sells marine and recreational products. A prior annual report contained the following information:

> **Litigation**
>
> A jury awarded $44.4 million in damages in a suit brought by Independent Boat Builders, Inc., a buying group of boat manufacturers and its 22 members. Under the antitrust laws, the damage award has been tripled, and the plaintiffs will be entitled to their attorney's fees and interest. The Company has filed an appeal contending the verdict was erroneous as a matter of law, both as to liability and damages.

Required:

What are the alternative ways in which Brunswick could account for the loss related to this litigation?

PB11-5 Journalizing Transactions, Evaluating Current Ratio Effects, and Reporting Liabilities (Comprehensive Problem) **LO2, 3, 4, 5, 6**

The Rosa Shell Tennis Center completed the following transactions in August 2009.

(*a*) On August 1, sold 12-month memberships and received $128,400, which included $8,400 in sales taxes required on taxable services.

(*b*) On August 1, purchased a new ball machine for $10,000, which was financed by signing a nine-month promissory note with interest payable at maturity on April 30, 2010, calculated using a 6 percent annual interest rate.

(*c*) Received a letter indicating that the center was being sued by a member for failing to display signs about wet court surfaces. The member was seeking $20,000 to cover medical expenses and mental hardship arising from a sprained ankle. The tennis center's lawyer believes the pending lawsuit is without merit.

(*d*) Paid net wages of $11,000 to staff in the pro shop. Withheld but did not yet remit $1,450 for federal income tax, $630 for FICA taxes, and $40 for Salvation Army contributions. Employer payroll costs for FICA, state unemployment taxes ($594), and federal unemployment taxes ($88) have not yet been remitted.

(*e*) Made month-end adjustments for membership revenues earned and interest expense incurred.

Required:

1. Prepare journal entries for each of the transactions and month-end adjustments.
2. Indicate the independent effect of each transaction or event on the current ratio (increase, decrease, no change). When determining the effects, assume the tennis center's current ratio at the beginning of the period was 1.5 (= $150,000 ÷ $100,000).

Cases and Projects

CP11-1 Finding Financial Information **LO2**

Refer to the financial statements of The Home Depot in Appendix A at the end of this book, or download the annual report from the Cases and Projects section of the text's Web site at www.mhhe.com/LLPW1e.

Required:

Calculate, to two decimal places, the company's current ratio at February 3, 2008. Does this ratio cause you any concern about the company's ability to pay its current liabilities?

CP11-2 Comparing Financial Information **LO2, 5**

Lowe's

Refer to the financial statements of The Home Depot in Appendix A and Lowe's Companies in Appendix B at the end of this book, or download the annual reports from the Cases section of the text's Web site at www.mhhe.com/LLPW1e.

Required:

1. Calculate, to two decimal places, the company's current ratio at February 1, 2008. Does this ratio cause you any concern about the company's ability to pay its current liabilities? Based on your analyses of the current ratio, does Lowe's or The Home Depot appear to be better able to pay its current liabilities?
2. According to Note 1 of the financial statements, what caused reductions and increases in the company's liability for extended warranty claims? Is this liability reported as a current or noncurrent liability?

CP11-3 Examining an Annual Report: Internet-Based Team Research **LO1, 2, 5**

As a team, select an industry to analyze. Using your Web browser, each team member should acquire the annual report or 10-K for one publicly traded company in the industry with each member selecting a different company. (See CP1-3 in Chapter 1 for a description of possible resources for these tasks.)

Required:

1. On an individual basis, each team member should write a short report that incorporates the following:

    a. What are the most significant types of current liabilities owed by the company?

    b. Read the company's financial statement note regarding contingencies. Does the company have any potentially significant liabilities that have not yet been recorded?

    c. Compute and analyze the current ratio.

2. Then, as a team, write a short report comparing and contrasting your companies using these attributes. Discuss any patterns across the companies that you as a team observe. Provide potential explanations for any differences discovered.

LO2

CP11-4 Making Ethical Decisions: A Real-Life Example

A few months ago, you were approached by a charming, young entrepreneur named Barry who had dreams of creating the world's largest carpet cleaning company. He said his business had really taken off, which he backed up with financial statements that showed sales growth from $1,240,524 to $4,845,347 and gross profit growth from $663,830 to $2,794,568 in just one short year. To finance this rapid growth, he had borrowed more than $780,000 using short-term promissory notes, but now he needed new investors. Excerpts from the balance sheets are presented in the following table.

	Year 1	Year 2
ASSETS		
Current assets		
Cash	$ 30,321	$ 87,014
Accounts receivable	0	693,773
Other	76,775	947,186
Total current assets	107,096	1,727,973
LIABILITIES		
Current liabilities		
Notes payable	$ 0	$ 780,507
Taxes payable	0	28,027
Other	2,930	959,901
Total current liabilities	2,930	1,768,435

Required:

1. Calculate, to two decimal places, the current ratios at the end of year 1 and year 2.
2. Does the size of the current ratio in year 2 cause you any concern? Does the change in the ratio cause you concern? Is the change consistent with a company that has reportedly quadrupled its sales and gross profits in just one year? What questions would you ask before investing in his business?

ZZZZ Best

Note: This case is based on the financial statements of ZZZZ Best in 1985 and 1986 as reported in an article by Joseph T. Wells ("Irrational Ratios," *Journal of Accountancy*, August 2001, retrieved on January 17, 2008 from http://www.aicpa.org/PUBS/jofa/aug2001/wells.htm). The founder of ZZZZ Best was convicted of defrauding investors in many different ways, including overstating current assets by accruing accounts receivable for fictitious sales on account.

LO1, 2

CP11-5 Making Ethical Decisions: A Mini Case

Upon reviewing your company's accounting records, you discovered that several customer accounts have credit balances instead of debit balances. Your investigation revealed that these customers had paid their balances but later were dissatisfied with the services your company had provided. Your company's sales staff agreed to fully refund amounts charged to the customers. Being a little short on cash, your company's accounting department decided to apply the refund against future purchases made by these customers, rather than issue a check for the refund. At the end of the year, your company reported total current liabilities of $9,500 and total current assets of $19,000. Included in Accounts Receivable were credit balances totaling $1,000.

Required:

1. Calculate the current ratio using the totals reported by your company.
2. If dissatisfied customers do not make future purchases from your company, they could legitimately ask to be paid the credit balances owed to them. In light of this possibility, the credit balances should be reclassified from Accounts Receivable to Accounts Payable. Recalculate the current ratio after taking into account this reclassification.

3. Your company's accountant has argued that the dollar amount of credit balances is so small that their reclassification is unnecessary. Do you agree? What if your company's bank has the right to a higher interest rate if your company's current ratio falls below 2.0?

CP11-6 Evaluating Effects on Current Ratio: Critical Thinking

LO2

Assume you work as an assistant to the chief financial officer (CFO) of Fashions First, Inc. The CFO reminds you that the fiscal year-end is only two weeks away and that he is looking to you to ensure the company complies with its loan covenant to maintain a current ratio of 1.25 or higher. A review of the general ledger indicates that current assets total $690,000 and current liabilities are $570,000. Your company has an excess of cash ($300,000) and an equally large balance in Accounts Payable ($270,000), although none of the accounts payable are due until next month.

Required:

1. Determine whether the company is currently in compliance with its loan covenant.
2. Assuming the level of current assets and current liabilities remains unchanged until the last day of the fiscal year, evaluate whether Fashions First should pay down $90,000 of its accounts payable on the last day of the year before the accounts payable become due.

12 Partnerships

LEARNING OBJECTIVES

After completing this chapter, you should be able to:

LO1 Compare the partnership form of business with other forms.

LO2 Demonstrate how to account for partnerships.

LO3 Demonstrate the proper treatment for changes of ownership in a partnership.

LO4 Demonstrate the proper treatment for the liquidation of a partnership.

LO5 Calculate and interpret the partner return on equity ratio.

Lectured presentations–12-1
www.mhhe.com/LLPW1e

Focus Company: BLOOM 'N FLOWERS

Fabulously Fresh Flowers.

Perhaps the single most important decision the owners of a new business face is determining the appropriate form of the business. At one time, owners could choose from only three basic forms of business: corporation, general partnership, and sole proprietorship. These forms of business are still used today, but numerous others are now available. As a result, choosing the proper business form has become an increasingly complex decision requiring future owners to wade through mountains of information. Enlisting the services of a CPA or knowledgeable attorney in making this decision is highly advisable.

In this chapter, we investigate the advantages and disadvantages of two forms of business, the general partnership and a newer form called the limited liability company (LLC). We do so by following the story of Hal Flowers and Dawn Bloom, two friends who decided to start a business together.

Hal Flowers and Dawn Bloom both sold flowers to individuals and businesses in their respective neighborhoods. They wished to expand their customer base by moving their business into a large mall located in the center of the city. Because neither had the resources or the time to run a business this large by themselves, they decided to combine their resources and form a new business—Bloom 'N Flowers. The new business would serve more customers and carry a larger inventory of fresh cut flowers than was previously possible when operating separately as sole proprietors.

Hal and Dawn knew that their most important decision would be the form of business they chose for their enterprise. After doing a bit of research, they narrowed the choice to three possibilities: the general partnership, the limited liability company, and the S-corporation.

ORGANIZATION OF THE CHAPTER

PARTNERSHIPS COMPARED TO SIMILAR ORGANIZATIONS	ACCOUNTING FOR PARTNERSHIPS	CHANGES OF OWNERSHIP IN A PARTNERSHIP	LIQUIDATION OF A PARTNERSHIP	RATIO ANALYSIS
• Characteristics of Partnerships • Similar Forms of Business	• Formation: Recording Cash and Noncash Contributions • Division of Income (or Loss): Four Methods • Preparation of Financial Statements	• Admission of a Partner • Withdrawal of a Partner • Death of a Partner	• No Capital Deficiency • Capital Deficiency	• Partner Return on Equity

Learning Objective 1

Compare the partnership form of business with other forms.

PARTNERSHIPS COMPARED TO SIMILAR ORGANIZATIONS

Because Hal and Dawn had little or no knowledge of the options available to them, they did some quick research. The two learned that each form of business has specific characteristics.

Characteristics of Partnerships

The Uniform Partnership Act defines partnership as "the association of two or more persons to carry on as co-owners of a business for profit, whether or not the persons intend to form a partnership." Because partnerships are so easy to form—no formal contract is required—this form of business has the greatest potential for disputes and lawsuits. **To prevent misunderstandings among partners, having a formal partnership agreement, preferably drafted by a lawyer, is advisable.**

Hal and Dawn decided to evaluate the partnership by listing its advantages and disadvantages. Later, they would weigh them against the advantages and disadvantages of other forms of business before deciding on the appropriate form for their own business.

Advantages of the Partnership

- **Pass-through taxation.** Profits from the business flow directly through to the partners' personal tax returns rather than being taxed first at the partnership level.
- **Ease of formation.** Partnerships are relatively easy and inexpensive to establish. In fact, some partnerships may be formed inadvertently through a handshake or a simple "OK."
- **Simplified recordkeeping.** No annual meetings are required and there are few recordkeeping requirements.
- **Favorable taxation.** Most small business partnerships receive favorable tax treatment and often do not have to pay the minimum taxes required of other business forms.
- **Increased ability to raise funds.** Generally, the more people involved in a business, the greater their collective ability to raise funds.

Disadvantages of the Partnership

- **Unlimited liability.** Business partners (both individually and as a group) are liable for all legal and financial obligations of the partnership.
- **Co-ownership of property.** Profits must be shared with the other partners.
- **Limited life.** A partnership ends when a partner dies or withdraws from the business.
- **Mutual agency.** Individual partners bear responsibility for the actions of all other partners.
- **Partner disagreements.** Poorly organized partnerships and those formed orally are susceptible to disputes among owners.

Clearly, a partnership has both significant benefits and serious drawbacks. The unlimited personal liability that each general partner bears for the legal and financial obligations of the business is especially important. Hal and Dawn realized that if they chose to form a partnership, they would need to develop a formal partnership agreement. Exhibit 12.1 lists the most important concerns to address in a partnership agreement.

Exhibit 12.1 Essential Elements of a Partnership Agreement

- Type of business
- Amount of equity invested by each partner
- Method for sharing profits and losses
- Partners' pay/compensation
- Distribution of assets on dissolution
- Provisions for changes to or dissolution of the partnership
- Provisions for settlement of disputes
- Settlement on death or incapacitation of partners
- Restrictions on partners' authority and expenditures
- Length of partnership's life

Similar Forms of Business

After the two friends gained a good understanding of the advantages and disadvantages of partnerships, they were ready to consider the other forms of business that interested them. They decided to look at one of the newest forms of business, the limited liability company.

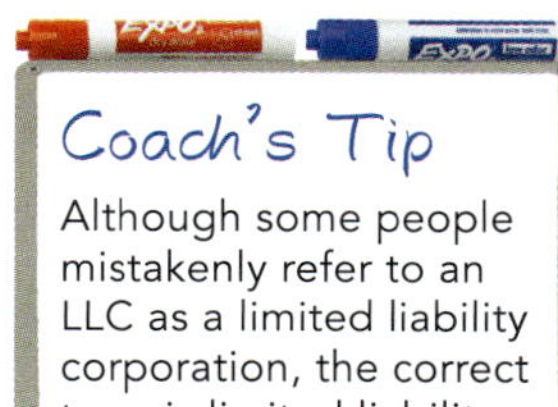

Limited Liability Companies

The limited liability company (LLC) is a relatively new form of business organization created by state legislatures. Because this form of business is primarily state controlled, the laws regarding its formation, fees, and so on vary from state to state.

The LLC combines the most attractive features of a corporation with the best features of the partnership, creating a kind of hybrid business form. As the name suggests, it offers protection to members (owners of the LLC) against personal liability for company debts and other obligations. However, its formation is more complex and formal than that of a general partnership. The primary characteristics of the LLC follow.

Advantages of the Limited Liability Company

- **Limited liability.** If the LLC is properly structured and managed, each member's personal assets will be protected from lawsuits and judgments against the business. Thus, each member's liability is limited to the assets he or she has invested in the company. This statement is true even for owners who participate in the LLC's management.
- **Ease of formation.** An LLC is easier to form than a corporation. Rules regarding the formation of an LLC differ from state to state, but setting one up typically requires only one or two documents. First, every state requires the LLC to file its articles of organization and pay any required fees. The articles of organization set out important details such as the business name, purpose, and operating structure. Because of its importance, this document should be drawn up by a lawyer. A few states require a second document, an operating agreement. It helps to define the LLC's ownership, member responsibilities, and profit sharing. Much like a partnership agreement, it can be invaluable in the event of disagreements among members and is strongly recommended even if the state does not require it.
- **Simplified recordkeeping.** LLCs are not required to hold an annual meeting, keep formal minutes, record resolutions, or observe many other formalities required of corporations. However, they do require more paperwork than partnerships.
- **Favorable taxation.** If an LLC has only one member, the IRS automatically treats it as a sole proprietorship. Similarly, an LLC with multiple members is taxed by default as a partnership. Normal business expenses may be deducted from an LLC's profits before profits are allocated to members for tax purposes. Members report their share of the LLC's profits and losses on their personal tax returns. This arrangement, referred to as pass-through taxation, allows the business to avoid the double taxation to which

corporations are subject. (Double taxation occurs when a corporation pays taxes on its corporate profits and then the individual owners pay taxes on any corporate profits distributed to them in the form of dividends. That is, the same profits are taxed twice, once at the corporate level and again at the personal level.)

- **Flexibility of operations.** An LLC allows members to allocate profits and losses as they see fit, to have great flexibility regarding the number of members, to elect to be managed as a partnership or as a corporation, and to admit new members or modify its membership and investment structure with ease.

Disadvantages of the Limited Liability Company

- **Limited corporate characteristics.** LLCs must not have more than two of the four favorable characteristics that define corporations, or they risk being taxed as a corporation. These characteristics are (1) owners' liability limited to business assets, (2) continuity of life, (3) centralization of (nonowner) management, and (4) free transferability of ownership interests.
- **Limited life.** LLCs dissolve with the death, incapacitation, bankruptcy, retirement, resignation, or expulsion of any member.
- **Lack of legal precedents.** Predicting how an LLC will be treated in the courts may be difficult. To date, relatively few legal cases have involved LLCs. However, as time goes on and LLCs become increasingly common, this disadvantage will become less significant.

Because of its long list of advantages and relatively few disadvantages, the LLC form has become a favorite choice among businesses that meet the following criteria:

- The business has one to three members.
- All members are active participants in a small local business.
- The business has no plans for significant growth.
- The business has no foreseeable need to raise significant amounts of capital.

S-Corporations

An S-corporation is a corporation with 1 to 100 shareholders that passes income (or loss) to shareholders, who are taxed at the individual shareholder level. This is a significant difference from a regular corporation, which is subject to double taxation. S-corporations enjoy many of the benefits of partnerships and LLCs, but the state requirements for forming a corporation, electing to be taxed as an S-corporation, and completing annual filings are complex and time consuming. Because of these complexities and required formalities, Dawn and Hal quickly discarded this form of business as a viable option. To compare the features of the two remaining forms of business, they set up the table in Exhibit 12.2.

Exhibit 12.2 Characteristics of Partnerships and LLCs

Characteristic	Partnership	Limited Liability Company
Ease of formation and recordkeeping	Less difficult	More difficult
Setup costs	Medium to high	High
Limited liability	No, unless limited partnership	Yes
Annual meetings	Recommended, not required	Recommended, not required
Limited life	Yes*	Yes
Corporate tax treatment permitted	No	Yes
Partnership tax treatment permitted	Yes, automatic	Yes, when there are two or more members
Annual state filings and fees	Almost never	Yes
Uniform state laws governing entity	Very little variation in laws	Moderate variation in laws

* Partnerships can appear to achieve unlimited lives if new partners are admitted as old partners exit, but technically these changes cause the dissolution of the existing partnership.

After careful consideration, the two friends decided to form a general partnership. Although the features of an LLC sounded great, they did not think they could limit themselves to only two of the four characteristics of a corporation, and they did not want to invest a lot of time and money in forming their business.

SELF-STUDY PRACTICE

Indicate whether each of the following is a true (T) or false (F) statement regarding partnerships and other forms of business.

1. The partnership agreement is a required document; you will be unable to register your partnership without a properly documented partnership agreement. ________
2. A limited liability company must not have more than three of the four characteristics that define corporations, or it risks being taxed as a corporation. ________
3. One disadvantage of both partnerships and LLCs is pass-through taxation. ________
4. Because of its long list of disadvantages and relatively few advantages, the LLC is rarely the business form of choice for new businesses. ________
5. One disadvantage of the LLC is that it is subject to double taxation. ________

After you have finished, check your answers with the solution at the bottom of the page.

ACCOUNTING FOR PARTNERSHIPS

Learning Objective 2

Demonstrate how to account for partnerships.

Because a partnership is a pass-through entity, each partner reports his or her share of the partnership's income (or loss) as an individual. In this respect, the accounting treatment is very much like that of a sole proprietorship. The only real difference is that the partners must determine how to divide the partnership's income (or loss) among themselves. To keep track of this information, accounting for a partnership requires:

1. A capital account for each partner.
2. A drawing account for each partner.
3. The allocation of the partnership's income (or loss) to each partner according to the terms of the partnership agreement.

As we noted earlier, any new partnership is strongly encouraged to create a formal partnership agreement. Hal and Dawn took this recommendation seriously and asked a lawyer to draw up their partnership agreement. While they were discussing the agreement, the attorney spoke with them about some other matters including how to account for the formation of their partnership, how to allocate the partnership's income (or loss), and how to prepare the partnership's financial statements.

Formation: Recording Cash and Noncash Contributions

When a partnership is formed, the partners can invest any combination of assets and/or liabilities in it. Because both Hal and Dawn had sole proprietorships before forming their partnership, each contributed assets from the "proprietorships" as well as cash. Hal's entire investment in the partnership consisted of cash and accounts receivable; Dawn's included cash and equipment. The partnership did not take on liabilities from the sole proprietorships.

When a partner invests cash in a partnership, that partner's capital account is credited for the amount invested. Other investments are recorded at the fair market value of the assets on the date of transfer to the partnership. Each partner must agree to these assigned values. With

Solution to Self-Study Practice

1. F—although partnerships may be fraught with disagreements among partners, having a partnership agreement is not required for forming a partnership.
2. F—a limited liability company must not have more than two of the four characteristics that define corporations.
3. F—pass-through taxation is a major advantage of the LLC and partnership forms of business.
4. F—the LLC is often the business form of choice for new businesses because of its long list of advantages and relatively few disadvantages.
5. F—the LLC form of business allows members to avoid double taxation.

Exhibit 12.3 Valuation of Contributed Assets

	BOOK VALUE		MARKET VALUE	
	Hal Flowers	Dawn Bloom	Hal Flowers	Dawn Bloom
Cash	$10,000	$ 9,000	$10,000	$ 9,000
Accounts receivable	3,800		3,800	
Allowance for doubtful accounts			(800)	
Store equipment		10,000		8,000
Accumulated depreciation		(1,000)		
	$13,800	$18,000	$13,000	$17,000

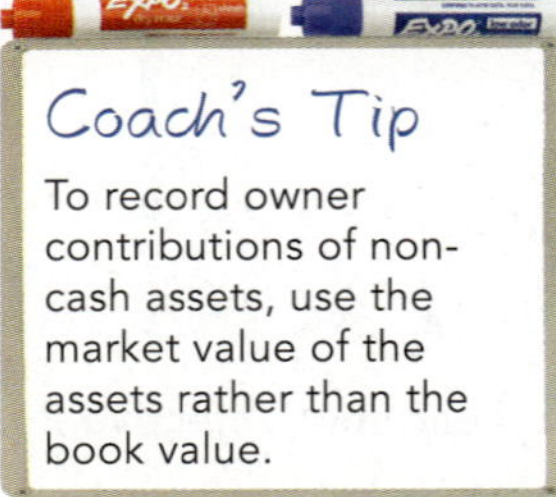

Coach's Tip

To record owner contributions of non-cash assets, use the market value of the assets rather than the book value.

the attorney's help, Hal and Dawn determined and agreed to the market values shown in the two right-hand columns of Exhibit 12.3. Although the table provides both the book values and market values of the contributed assets, **only the market values are used to record the investments.**

Note that the accounts receivable were brought into the partnership at net realizable value (the net amount of cash the partnership expects to collect) by establishing an allowance for doubtful accounts. This account is needed because no one knows which particular customer accounts will not be collected, but experience shows that some portion of the receivables would not be collected. Consequently, the estimated uncollectible portion was deducted from Hal's investment. Finally, note that Dawn's contribution of store equipment did not include the accumulated depreciation from her old business. Instead, its fair market value was used in recording her contribution to the partnership. In essence, the equipment contribution was treated as if the partnership purchased used equipment.

The following journal entries were made to record Hal and Dawn's investments. Once the partners' investments were recorded, the assets were treated just as any other business asset. The receivables were collected, and any uncollectible accounts were written off. At the end of the accounting period, the allowance account was re-evaluated and adjusted accordingly. The equipment was depreciated over its useful life using the method chosen by the partnership.

	Debit	Credit
Cash (+A) ($10,000 + $9,000)	19,000	
Accounts Receivable (+A)	3,800	
Store Equipment (+A)	8,000	
Allowance for Doubtful Accounts (+xA, −A)		800
Hal Flowers, Capital (+OE)		13,000
Dawn Bloom, Capital (+OE)		17,000

Assets		=	Liabilities	+	Owners' Equity	
Cash ($10,000 + $9,000)	+19,000				Hal Flowers, Capital	+13,000
Accounts Receivable	+3,800				Dawn Bloom, Capital	+17,000
Allowance for Doubtful Accounts (+xA)	−800					
Store Equipment	+8,000					

Division of Income (or Loss): Four Methods

A partnership's income (or loss) is divided according to the partnership agreement. Unfortunately, partners do not always draw up an agreement before forming their business. In such situations, the assumption is that the partners intend to share all profits and losses equally regardless of any oral agreements they may have made. To be legally enforceable, profit and loss allocations must be made in writing. When Hal and Dawn met with their attorney, he told them partners can use one of four methods to allocate income or loss among themselves.

1. **The fixed-ratio method** is often used when partners' initial financial contributions are the same or relatively close. This method bases income and loss allocations primarily on the amount of time each partner expects to devote to the business on a regular basis. For example, if partners expect to work equally, they may agree to split profits and losses equally. In this case, the fixed ratio can be stated in three ways: as a percentage (50 percent to 50 percent), as a proportion (1:1), or as a fraction (½ to ½).
2. **The interest on partners' capital balances method** may appeal to partners who wish to earn a specific return on their investments. This method sets a stated rate of interest partners will receive on their capital account balances; any remaining amounts are allocated on a fixed-ratio basis. This method is especially useful to partners who have invested large sums of cash in the partnership but have very little involvement in the business's day-to-day operations. Essentially, their entire return from the partnership hinges on the balances in their capital accounts.
3. **The salaries to partners method** appeals to partners who spend a great deal of time running the business on a daily basis and the partnership is their primary source of personal income. This method requires that the partners' salaries be distributed first; any remaining income (or loss) is allocated on a fixed-ratio basis.
4. **The salaries to partners and interest on partners' capital balances method** is the most complicated method. It is appropriate when the partners' needs, financial contributions, and time contributions are so diverse that some combination of each of the previous methods is necessary. With this method, the partners receive salaries and earn interest on their capital account balances. Any remaining amounts are allocated to them on a fixed-ratio basis.

Hal and Dawn asked the attorney to show them examples of each of these four allocation methods. The attorney was happy to oblige. **The following examples assume that Hal and Dawn's partnership earned a profit of $10,000 for the year and that Hal withdrew $2,600 from the partnership and Dawn withdrew $1,400.**

Fixed-Ratio Method

Assume that Hal and Dawn decided to share the $10,000 profit according to the fixed proportions of 8:2 (that is, $8 for Hal to every $2 for Dawn). These proportions are based on the relative time and effort each partner planned to contribute to the partnership. When you use proportions as the allocation basis, each partner's individual portion is divided by the total of the partners' numbers (8 + 2 = 10).

Hal's portion of the profit [$10,000 × (8 ÷ 10)]	$ 8,000
Dawn's portion of the profit [$10,000 × (2 ÷ 10)]	2,000
Total profit allocated	$10,000

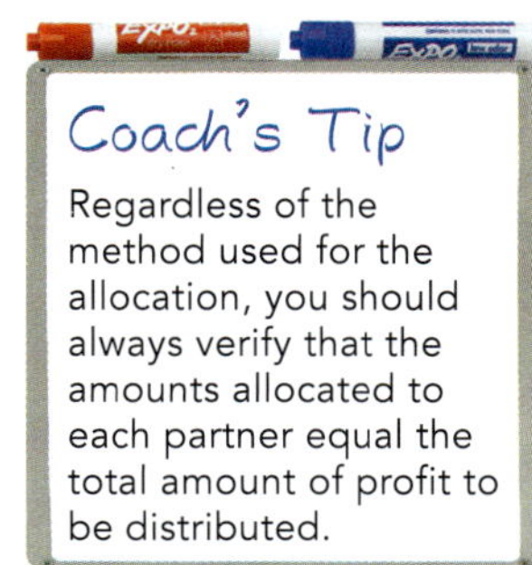

Regardless of the allocation method used, the partners' capital accounts do not reflect the allocated amounts until the closing entries for the period have been made. The closing process for a partnership is nearly identical to that shown for a sole proprietorship in Chapter 4 on page 164. In this chapter, we assume that all revenues and expenses have been closed and that the net profit (or loss) of the business is now in the Income Summary account. In our example, the partnership had a $10,000 profit, so the Income Summary account needs to be debited and each individual partner's capital account credited for the amount of profit allocated to him or her. The entry to allocate the partnership profits to each partner under the fixed-ratio method follows.

	Debit	Credit
Income Summary (−OE)	10,000	
Hal Flowers, Capital (+OE)		8,000
Dawn Bloom, Capital (+OE)		2,000

Assets	=	Liabilities	+	Owners' Equity	
				Income Summary	−10,000
				Hal Flowers, Capital	+8,000
				Dawn Bloom, Capital	+2,000

Next the partners' drawing accounts must be closed. The balance in each partner's drawing account is credited with corresponding debits to the capital accounts. Because this entry remains the same regardless of the allocation method used, it is presented only once. However, recognize that this entry would be made for each of the allocation methods presented. The entry to close the partners' drawing accounts would be:

Coach's Tip

Do not confuse the allocation of income with the partners' withdrawals. The allocation represents how much profit each partner has **earned** from the business. The withdrawal represents how much of the partners' income has actually been taken out of the business (usually as cash).

	Debit	Credit
Hal Flowers, Capital (−OE)	2,600	
Dawn Bloom, Capital (−OE)	1,400	
Hal Flowers, Drawing (+OE)		2,600
Dawn Bloom, Drawing (+OE)		1,400

Assets	=	Liabilities	+	Owners' Equity	
				Hal Flowers, Capital	−2,600
				Dawn Bloom, Capital	−1,400
				Hal Flowers, Drawing	+2,600
				Dawn Bloom, Drawing	+1,400

Interest on Partners' Capital Balances Method

To illustrate this method, we will use Hal and Dawn's original capital contributions, $13,000 and $17,000, respectively. We also assume both Hal and Dawn wanted to earn 12 percent on their beginning capital balances. Under the interest on partners' capital balances method, **the interest must first be allocated to the partners.** Then, the remaining profit is allocated according to a fixed ratio. For this example, we will use a fixed ratio of 80 percent to Hal and 20 percent to Dawn. See Exhibit 12.4 for the way this method allocates the profit.

Exhibit 12.4 Allocation of Income with Interest on Partners' Capital Balances

	Hal Flowers	Dawn Bloom	Total Allocated	Remainder to Allocate
Net income to allocate				$10,000
Interest				
Hal: $13,000 × 12%	$1,560		$ 1,560	(1,560)
Dawn: $17,000 × 12%		$2,040	2,040	(2,040)
Remainder (allocate on a fixed ratio)				6,400
Hal: $6,400 × 80%	5,120		5,120	(5,120)
Dawn: $6,400 × 20%		1,280	1,280	(1,280)
Total	$6,680	$3,320	$10,000	$ 0

When the partners' contributions of time and/or money differ significantly, this method or one of the remaining ones may be used to ensure that income allocation is based fairly on the individual partners' contributions of time and/or assets. The following entry records each partner's share of the partnership's income using the interest on partners' capital balances method.

	Debit	Credit
Income Summary (−OE)	10,000	
Hal Flowers, Capital (+OE)		6,680
Dawn Bloom, Capital (+OE)		3,320

Assets	=	Liabilities	+	Owners' Equity	
				Income Summary	**−10,000**
				Hal Flowers, Capital	**+6,680**
				Dawn Bloom, Capital	**+3,320**

SELF-STUDY PRACTICE

Jack Clumsy and Jill Mimic began the Hill Partnership on January 1, 2009. On December 31, 2009, the partnership has $18,000 of profit to allocate. Determine the amount of profit to be allocated to each partner under each of the following independent situations.

1. Fixed ratio of 3:6 to Jack and Jill, respectively.
2. Interest on capital balances of 12 percent with the remainder on a ratio of 3:6. Assume capital balances of $2,000 for Jack and $8,000 for Jill.

After you have finished, check your answers with the solution at the bottom of the page.

Salaries to Partners Method

The salaries to partners method allocates income first to cover the partners' salaries and then the remainder of the income according to a fixed ratio. Assume Hal and Dawn agreed to the following salaries and fixed ratios:

	Salaries	Fixed Ratio
Hal Flowers	$6,000	80%
Dawn Bloom	2,000	20

See Exhibit 12.5 for the allocation of the partnership's net income of $10,000.

Solution to Self-Study Practice

1. Jack receives $6,000 (=$18,000 × 3/9), and Jill receives $12,000 (=$18,000 × 6/9).
2. Jack and Jill receive the following:

	Jack		Jill		Total Allocated	Remainder to Allocate
Net income to allocate						$ 18,000
Interest	$2,000 × 12% =	$ 240	$8,000 × 12% =	$ 960	$ 1,200	(1,200)
						16,800
Remainder (allocate on a fixed ratio)	$16,800 × 3/9 =	5,600	$16,800 × 6/9 =	11,200	16,800	(16,800)
Total allocation		$ 5,840		$ 12,160	$18,000	$ 0

Exhibit 12.5 Allocation of Income with Salaries to Partners

	Hal Flowers	Dawn Bloom	Total Allocated	Remainder to Allocate
Net income to allocate				$10,000
Salary allocations	$6,000	$2,000	$8,000	(8,000)
Remainder (allocate on a fixed ratio)				2,000
Hal: $2,000 × 80%	1,600		1,600	(1,600)
Dawn: $2,000 × 20%		400	400	(400)
Total	$7,600	$2,400	$10,000	$ 0

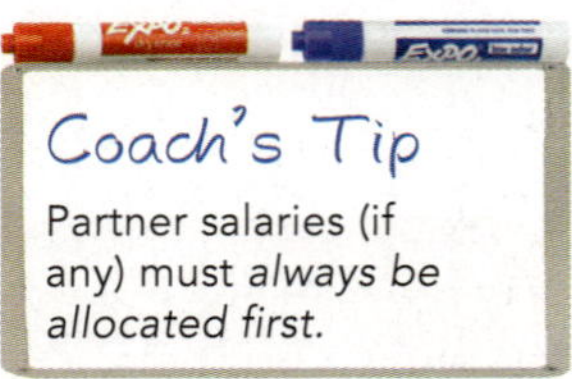

Coach's Tip

Partner salaries (if any) must *always* be allocated first.

Whenever salaries are allocated to the partners, they must be taken out of the partnership's income before any other allocations can be made. Once again, always verify that the total of the amounts allocated to each partner equals the total partnership income (or loss). The following journal entry would be used to allocate income under this method.

	Debit	Credit
Income Summary (−OE)	10,000	
Hal Flowers, Capital (+OE)		7,600
Dawn Bloom, Capital (+OE)		2,400

Assets	=	Liabilities	+	Owners' Equity	
				Income Summary	−10,000
				Hal Flowers, Capital	+7,600
				Dawn Bloom, Capital	+2,400

Salaries to Partners and Interest on Partners' Capital Balances Method

The salaries to partners and interest on partners' capital balances method allocates income first to the partners' salaries and second to the interest on the partners' capital accounts. Any remaining income is allocated according to a fixed ratio. Assume the following salaries, interest rate, and fixed ratios:

	Salaries	Interest	Fixed Ratio
Hal Flowers	$6,000	12%	80%
Dawn Bloom	2,000	12	20

See Exhibit 12.6 for the allocation of the partnership's $10,000 net income under this method. Study it carefully; it is tricky. Needless to say, this example illustrates why a proof of the allocation is so important. Sometimes allocating profit (or loss) according to the partnership agreement creates a situation in which the partnership's income is insufficient to give each partner the salaries and interest required in the partnership agreement. Nevertheless, **these amounts must be allocated** even if doing so results in the allocation of a negative amount. Any negative amount is allocated using the fixed ratio.

Exhibit 12.6 Allocation of Income under the Salaries to Partners and Interest on Partners' Capital Balances Method

	Hal Flowers	Dawn Bloom	Total Allocated	Remainder to Allocate
Net income to allocate				$10,000
Salary allocations	$6,000	$2,000	$ 8,000	(8,000)
Remaining after salary allocations				2,000
Interest				
Hal: $13,000 × 12%	$1,560		1,560	(1,560)
Dawn: $17,000 × 12%		$2,040	2,040	(2,040)
Remainder (overallocated)				(1,600)
Hal: ($1,600) × 80%	(1,280)		(1,280)	1,280
Dawn: ($1,600) × 20%		(320)	(320)	320
Total	$6,280	$3,720	$10,000	$ 0

The entry to record the allocation of income under this method would be:

	Debit	Credit
Income Summary (−OE)	10,000	
Hal Flowers, Capital (+OE)		6,280
Dawn Bloom, Capital (+OE)		3,720

Assets	=	Liabilities	+	Owners' Equity	
				Income Summary	−10,000
				Hal Flowers, Capital	+6,280
				Dawn Bloom, Capital	+3,720

Coach's Tip

A fixed ratio is used to allocate the remainder amount for every allocation method. So, it is important to select a fixed ratio for each partner even when the fixed ratio method is not used for allocating profit.

SELF-STUDY PRACTICE

Jack and Jill began the Hill Partnership on January 1, 2009. On December 31, 2009, the partnership has $18,000 profit to allocate. Determine the amount of profit to be allocated to each partner under the salaries to partners and interest on capital balances method using the following.

	Salaries	Interest	Capital	Fixed Ratio
Jack	$ 7,800	12%	$2,000	3
Jill	13,500	12	8,000	6

After you have finished, check your answers with the solution at the bottom of the page.

Solution to Self-Study Practice

	Jack		Jill		Total Allocated	Remainder to Allocate
Net income to allocate						$18,000
Salary		$ 7,800		$13,500	$21,300	(21,300)
Interest	$2,000 × 12% =	240	$8,000 × 12% =	960	1,200	(1,200)
						(4,500)
Remainder (overallocated)	($4,500) × 3/9 =	(1,500)	($4,500) × 6/9 =	(3,000)	(4,500)	4,500
Total/proof		$ 6,540		$11,460	$18,000	$ 0

After listening intently to their attorney's advice and carefully considering their options for allocating the partnership's income, Hal and Dawn asked the attorney to allocate all income (or loss) using the salaries to partners method (method 3). They chose this method because Hal agreed to take on more managerial responsibilities than Dawn, and this method rewards him for his commitment of additional time.

Preparation of Financial Statements

The financial statements of a partnership are very similar to those of a sole proprietorship. There are only three differences: (1) net income is allocated among the partners, (2) the balance sheet shows a capital account for each partner, and (3) the partners' capital statement replaces the owner's equity statement.

Net income on the partnership's income statement is calculated and reported in exactly the same way as for a sole proprietorship. The allocation of this net income to each partner's capital account is reported on the **partners' capital statement**. This statement begins with each partner's beginning capital account balance, which is increased by the portion of income allocated to each partner and reduced by withdrawals made by each partner. An illustration of this statement is shown in Exhibit 12.7, given the following assumptions.

	Capital Contributions	Net Income (allocated)	Partner Drawings
Hal Flowers	$13,000	$7,600	$2,600
Dawn Bloom	17,000	2,400	1,400

Exhibit 12.7 Partners' Capital Statement

Bloom 'N Flowers
Partners' Capital Statement
December 31, 2008

	Hal Flowers	Dawn Bloom	Total
Capital, January 1, 2008	$ 0	$ 0	$ 0
Add: Partner capital contributions	13,000	17,000	30,000
Net income	7,600	2,400	10,000
	20,600	19,400	40,000
Less: Partner drawings	2,600	1,400	4,000
Capital, December 31, 2008	$18,000	$18,000	$36,000

After the partners' capital statement is complete, the balance sheet can be prepared. See Exhibit 12.8 for the owners' equity section of the balance sheet for Bloom 'N Flowers partnership. Notice that the capital account balances in Exhibits 12.7 and 12.8 are equal.

Exhibit 12.8 Partial Balance Sheet

Bloom 'N Flowers
Balance Sheet (partial)
December 31, 2008

Total liabilities [for illustration purposes only]		$ 8,000
Owners' equity		
Hal Flowers, capital	$18,000	
Dawn Bloom, capital	18,000	
Total owners' equity		36,000
Total liabilities and owners' equity		$44,000

CHANGES OF OWNERSHIP IN A PARTNERSHIP

Learning Objective 3
Demonstrate the proper treatment for changes of ownership in a partnership.

Hal and Dawn later toyed with the idea of admitting another partner to their business. Hal had a friend, Bud Green, who specialized in marketing—a field with which Hal and Dawn have little experience. The two partners knew that marketing would be critical to the success of their business, however.

Admission of a Partner

The lawyer was pleased that Hal and Dawn had brought up the idea of admitting a new partner **before** actually going through with it. Although adding a new partner has little economic impact on a partnership, it does have a major legal effect called partnership dissolution. Specifically, adding a partner causes the dissolution of the existing partnership (consisting of the old partners) and the creation of a new partnership (consisting of the new partners).

Of course, additional capital and drawing accounts would need to be created for the new partner. Then the existing partners would need to decide how to complete the admission of the new partner. Legally, a new partner cannot be admitted into a partnership unless all existing partners agree to it. Assuming all current partners have agreed to admit a new partner, the new partner can be admitted in two ways: through a purchase made among partners or by the investment of additional assets.

Purchase among Partners

A purchase among partners transfers a portion of one or more existing partners' capital account balances to the new partner's capital account. This transaction is a **personal** transaction involving **only** those individuals involved in the purchase. The only impact on the partnership is that a journal entry is required to transfer amounts from the existing partners' capital accounts to the new partner's capital account.

Assume that on January 1, 2009, Bud was admitted to the partnership with a $33^1/_3$ percent ownership. Bud agreed to pay each partner $8,000 in exchange for 1/3 of each partner's capital account balance ($18,000 × 1/3 = $6,000). The following journal entry was made to record Bud's admission to the partnership, based on the capital balances on the balance sheet as of December 31, 2008 (see Exhibit 12.8).

	Debit	Credit
Hal Flowers, Capital (−OE)	6,000	
Dawn Bloom, Capital (−OE)	6,000	
Bud Green, Capital (+OE)		12,000

Assets	=	Liabilities	+	Owners' Equity	
				Hal Flowers, Capital	−6,000
				Dawn Bloom, Capital	−6,000
				Bud Green, Capital	+12,000

Hal and Dawn's attorney explained some important features of the purchase among partners method of admitting a new partner. First, the amount of money that each partner accepts in return for his or her capital is strictly a private matter between the new partner and the individuals who have agreed to give up a portion of their capital. Theoretically, neither Hal nor Dawn need to be aware of the amount the other receives for his or her share of the capital.

Furthermore, because the partnership is not involved in the transaction, the entry to record the transaction would be the same whether Bud paid each partner $100 or $100,000. The fact that Bud paid a total of $16,000 for a $12,000 capital account balance affects the partners' personal income tax returns but it does not affect the partnership's accounting records.

As the following T-accounts show, the **total** capital in the partnership would be the same **after** Bud's admission to the partnership as **before** he was admitted (that is, $36,000). After his admission, each **individual** partner's capital is $12,000 or exactly one-third of the total ($36,000 × 1/3). The three friends become equal partners, each of whom would own $33^1/_3$ percent of the partnership.

Hal Flowers, Capital	
	Bal. 18,000
Jan.1 6,000	
	12,000

Dawn Bloom, Capital	
	Bal. 18,000
Jan.1 6,000	
	12,000

Bud Green, Capital	
	Bal. 0
	Jan. 1 12,000
	12,000

Investment of Additional Assets

The other way to admit a new partner is for the incoming partner to invest new assets into the partnership. Unlike the purchase among partners method, the investment method alters the partnership's assets.

Assume that Bud was admitted to Hal and Dawn's partnership as a new partner. Hal and Dawn's original capital balances did not change. They were still $18,000 each, or $36,000 in total. Bud invested $18,000 of additional cash in the partnership.

Under the investment of additional assets method, Bud's contribution affected only the partnership's net assets (cash) and Bud's capital account. The existing partners' capital accounts were unaffected. The journal entry made to record the admission of the new partner follows.

	Debit	Credit
Cash (+A)	18,000	
Bud Green, Capital (+OE)		18,000

Assets		=	Liabilities	+	Owners' Equity	
Cash	+18,000				Bud Green, Capital	+18,000

After Bud's investment, the partners' capital accounts had the following balances:

Hal Flowers, Capital	
	Bal. 18,000

Dawn Bloom, Capital	
	Bal. 18,000

Bud Green, Capital	
	Bal. 0
	Jan. 1 18,000
	18,000

Bud's ownership of one-third of the partnership would not necessarily entitle him to one-third of the profits. Once again, the partnership agreement would dictate how to allocate profits (or losses) to the partners. The original partners may or may not have agreed to give him an equal share of the profits. If no written agreement exists, the profits would be allocated equally among all the partners whether or not that was their intention.

The example we have just presented assumed that the new partner's contribution **exactly equaled** his or her share of the partnership's total equity. Sometimes, however, the new partner contributes **more** or **less** than that amount. Let's see how these variations in the new partner's contribution affect the existing partners.

Bonus to the Existing Partners. In some situations, the existing partners require an extra contribution from the new partner in return for admission to the partnership. This situation is common when the fair market value of the partnership's assets is higher than the asset book value. When paying more than the book value of the assets he or she is acquiring, the new partner is effectively giving the existing partners a bonus.

Instead of contributing $18,000 to the partnership, let's assume that Bud contributed $24,000 in exchange for one-third of the partnership capital. The steps to determine the appropriate journal entry follow.

1. **Calculate the total capital in the partnership after the new partner's contribution.**

Total partnership capital before contribution	$36,000
New partner's contribution	24,000
Partnership capital after contribution	$60,000

2. **Calculate the amount of the new partner's capital account.** Multiply the result from Step 1 by the portion of the partnership that the new partner is purchasing.

Result from Step 1	$60,000
New partner's ownership portion	× 1/3
New partner's capital account balance	$20,000

3. **Calculate the total bonus to the existing partners.**
   The total bonus to the existing partners is the difference between the amount contributed by the new partner and the amount of capital the new partner received.

Amount contributed by new partner	$24,000
Amount of capital given to the new partner	(20,000)
Total bonus to the existing partners	$ 4,000

4. **Allocate the bonus to the existing partners using their fixed ratios.** The existing partners' fixed ratios (after salaries) were 80 percent to Hal and 20 percent to Dawn. Therefore, the bonus allocation was as follows:

Hal's portion of the bonus ($4,000 × 80%)	$ 3,200
Dawn's portion of the bonus ($4,000 × 20%)	800
Total bonus allocated	$ 4,000

The following journal entry would be made to record the transaction.

	Debit	Credit
Cash (+A)	24,000	
Bud Green, Capital (+OE)		20,000
Hal Flowers, Capital (+OE)		3,200
Dawn Bloom, Capital (+OE)		800

Assets		=	Liabilities	+	Owners' Equity	
Cash	+24,000				Bud Green, Capital	+20,000
					Hal Flowers, Capital	+3,200
					Dawn Bloom, Capital	+800

Bonus to the New Partner. Sometimes the opposite situation occurs: The new partner may receive a capital account balance that exceeds the amount he or she invests in the partnership. This situation results in a bonus to the new partner. It can arise when the partnership desperately needs cash or the new partner has knowledge or skills that the original partners are eager to obtain. For example, Hal and Dawn may have needed Bud's marketing expertise so much that they were willing to give him a capital account that was **more** than his cash contribution.

To illustrate this situation, we assume that Bud contributed $9,000 (instead of $24,000) to the partnership in exchange for a one-third ownership interest. The steps required to determine the resulting journal entry are:

1. **Calculate the total capital in the partnership after the new partner's contribution.**

Total partnership capital before contribution	$36,000
New partner's contribution	9,000
Partnership capital after contribution	$45,000

2. **Calculate the amount of the new partner's capital account.** Multiply the result from Step 1 by the portion of the partnership that the new partner is purchasing.

Result from Step 1	$45,000
New partner's ownership portion	× 1/3
New partner's capital account balance	$15,000

3. **Calculate the total bonus to the new partner.** The total bonus to the new partner is the difference between the amount of capital the new partner received and the amount the new partner contributed.

Amount of capital given to the new partner	$15,000
Amount contributed by the new partner	(9,000)
Total bonus given by the existing partners	$ 6,000

4. **Allocate the bonus to the new partner using the fixed ratios.** The existing partners' fixed ratios (after their salaries) were 80 percent to Hal and 20 percent to Dawn. Therefore, the bonus given by the existing partners was allocated as follows:

Hal's portion of the bonus ($6,000 × 80%)	$4,800
Dawn's portion of the bonus ($6,000 × 20%)	1,200
Total bonus allocated	$6,000

In this case, the $6,000 bonus to the new partner was accomplished by removing a portion of the existing partners' capital balances. The entry that would be made to record the transaction is:

	Debit	Credit
Cash (+A)	9,000	
Hal Flowers, Capital (–OE)	4,800	
Dawn Bloom, Capital (–OE)	1,200	
Bud Green, Capital (+OE)		15,000

Assets		=	Liabilities	+	Owners' Equity	
Cash	+9,000				Hal Flowers, Capital	−4,800
					Dawn Bloom, Capital	−1,200
					Bud Green, Capital	+15,000

After Hal and Dawn's attorney had explained the ins and outs of admitting a new partner, the two friends decided to admit Bud in return for an $18,000 cash investment to the partnership. Following Bud's admission, each partner had a capital balance of $18,000, and each owned one-third of the partnership. The new partnership agreement specified that Hal, Dawn, and Bud would share the profits and losses according to a fixed ratio of 40 percent to 40 percent to 20 percent, respectively.

SELF-STUDY PRACTICE

Billie, Mandie, and Grimm agree to allow Crustie into their partnership and to give him a 25 percent ownership interest in the partnership on January 1, 2009. Prior to Crustie's entry, the following information was available.

	Capital	Fixed Ratio
Billie	$20,000	10%
Mandie	50,000	60
Grimm	30,000	30

1. Assume Crustie pays the partnership $30,000 for 25 percent of the partnership capital. Calculate the bonus to the new partner and the amounts that will be debited to the capital account for each of the existing partners.
2. Assume Crustie pays the partnership $40,000 for 25 percent of the partnership capital. Calculate the bonus to the existing partners and the amount that will be credited to Crustie's capital account.

After you have finished, check your answers with the solution at the bottom of the next page.

Withdrawal of a Partner

After his admission, Bud joined Hal and Dawn in all meetings with their attorney because he was a full partner. During one visit, Dawn asked the attorney to explain what would happen if one of the partners withdrew from the partnership. The attorney replied that as with the addition of a new partner, the withdrawal of a partner causes the immediate dissolution of the partnership. After dissolution, the remaining partners may carry on the business, but the partnership is legally new and different.

A partner can withdraw from a partnership in two ways: (1) voluntarily through the sale of his or her interest in the partnership to the remaining partner(s) or (2) involuntarily for one of several reasons. Death, insanity, mandatory retirement, and removal by the remaining partners (an unusual occurrence) can cause a partner's involuntary withdrawal from the partnership.

A properly prepared partnership agreement should cover the procedures, terms, and conditions for a partner's withdrawal. Similar to the admission of a new partner, certain options are available to the partners when a partner withdraws. Specifically, the remaining partners can purchase the exiting partner's capital account in one of two ways: They can pay the exiting partner with their own personal assets or with the partnership's assets. As we discuss in the following sections, the first option involves the partnership only insofar as a journal entry must be made to record the transfer of capital from the exiting partner to the remaining partner(s). The second option, in which the partnership uses its own assets to buy out the exiting partner, is more complicated.

Purchase among Partners

When partners use their own personal assets to pay the exiting partner, the partnership does nothing more than make a journal entry to transfer the balance in the exiting partner's capital account to the remaining partners' capital accounts. The dollar amount of the purchase and all other particulars are treated as personal transactions among the partners; the partnership itself is not involved.

Assume, for example, that on January 1, 2011 (after the partnership had been operating for several years), Dawn Bloom voluntarily withdrew from the partnership. At that time, each partner had a capital account balance of $30,000 (or a total of $90,000 for the partnership). Hal and Bud each agreed to purchase half of Dawn's interest in the partnership for $20,000. The entry made to record Dawn's withdrawal in this example follows:

	Debit	Credit
Dawn Bloom, Capital (−OE)	30,000	
Hal Flowers, Capital (+OE)		15,000
Bud Green, Capital (+OE)		15,000

Assets	=	Liabilities	+	Owners' Equity	
				Dawn Bloom, Capital	−30,000
				Hal Flowers, Capital	+15,000
				Bud Green, Capital	+15,000

In this case, the amount Dawn accepted for her capital account balance was strictly a private matter between her and the other partners. Theoretically, as in the admission of a new partner, each of the remaining partners may have been unaware of the amount the other paid

Solution to Self-Study Practice

1.

Step 1	Capital before contribution ($20,000 + $50,000 + $30,000)	$100,000
	Crustie's contribution	30,000
	New partnership capital	$130,000
2	New partner's capital account balance ($130,000 × 25%)	$ 32,500
3	Bonus to new partner ($32,500 − $30,000)	$ 2,500
4	Allocate bonus of new partner to existing partners	
	Billie: $2,500 × 10% = $250	
	Mandie: $2,500 × 60% = $1,500	
	Grimm: $2,500 × 30% = $750	

2.

Step 1	Capital before contribution ($20,000 + $50,000 + $30,000)	$100,000
	Crustie's contribution	40,000
	New partnership capital	$140,000
2	New partner's capital account balance ($140,000 × 25%)	$ 35,000
3	Bonus to existing partners ($40,000 − $35,000)	$ 5,000
4	Allocate bonus to existing partners	
	Billie: $5,000 × 10% = $500	
	Mandie: $5,000 × 60% = $3,000	
	Grimm: $5,000 × 30% = $1,500	

for his half of Dawn's capital account balance. The financial impact of the transaction, if any, is handled by the partners on their individual income tax returns, not by the partnership.

As the following T-accounts show, the **total** capital in the partnership was the same **before and after** Dawn's withdrawal from the partnership ($90,000). After the withdrawal, each **remaining** partner's capital was worth $45,000—exactly half the total ($90,000 × ½). The two remaining partners each own 50 percent of the partnership's net assets.

Hal Flowers, Capital	
	Bal. 30,000
	Jan. 1 15,000
	45,000

Dawn Bloom, Capital	
	Bal. 30,000
Jan. 1 30,000	
	0

Bud Green, Capital	
	Bal. 30,000
	Jan. 1 15,000
	45,000

Although each remaining partner owns one-half the partnership's net assets, that does not necessarily mean that each is entitled to half the partnership's profits. The allocation of the partnership's profit (or loss) is determined by the partnership agreement. The agreement may or may not state that profits will be split 50–50 after a partner exits. If no written agreement exists, the profits would be allocated equally among the partners whether or not that was their intention.

Withdrawal of Assets

The other means of a partner's withdrawal is to use the partnership's assets (usually cash) to purchase the exiting partner's capital account. Unlike the purchase among partners method, this method has an obvious impact on the partnership.

We assume, as before, that when Dawn withdrew from the partnership, all three partners had a capital account balance of $30,000. In this case, however, Dawn received $30,000 in cash from the partnership in return for her voluntary withdrawal. Under this method, only the partnership's net assets (cash) and Dawn's capital account were affected by her exit. The remaining partners' capital accounts were unaffected. The entry that would be made to record Dawn's withdrawal from the partnership follows.

	Debit	Credit
Dawn Bloom, Capital (−OE)	30,000	
Cash (−A)		30,000

Assets		=	Liabilities	+	Owners' Equity	
Cash	−30,000				Dawn Bloom, Capital	−30,000

After the $30,000 payment to Dawn, the remaining partners' capital accounts had the following balances:

Hal Flowers, Capital	
	Bal. 30,000

Dawn Bloom, Capital	
	Bal. 30,000
Jan. 1 30,000	
	0

Bud Green, Capital	
	Bal. 30,000

As before, the remaining partners then owned 50 percent of the partnership's net assets except that those net assets have decreased by $30,000. Before Dawn's withdrawal, the partnership's net assets (Assets − Liabilities = Owners' Equity) were $90,000 (= $30,000 + $30,000 + $30,000). After her withdrawal, its net assets were $60,000 (= $30,000 + $30,000).

In this case, we assumed that the partnership paid Dawn the exact amount of her capital account—that is, one-third of the partnership's total capital. In some cases, however, the partnership may pay the exiting partner **more or less** than his or her capital account balance. In the following sections, we consider both possibilities.

Bonus to the Remaining Partners. Sometimes the cash payment to the exiting partner is less than that partner's capital balance. A reduced payment is possible for several reasons. The fair market value of the partnership's assets may be less than their book value, or the exiting partner may wish to leave the partnership as quickly as possible, no matter what payment is offered. Whatever the reason, the remaining partners effectively receive a bonus from the withdrawing partner.

Assume that instead of receiving $30,000 for her interest in the partnership, Dawn received only $24,000. The steps to follow in determining the journal entry to record the transaction are:

1. **Calculate the total bonus to the remaining partners.** The total bonus to the remaining partners is the difference between the amount in the exiting partner's capital account and the amount the exiting partner receives at withdrawal from the partnership.

Amount in exiting partner's capital account	$30,000
Amount of cash paid to the exiting partner	24,000
Total bonus to the remaining partners	$ 6,000

2. **Allocate the bonus to the remaining partners using their fixed ratios.** Referring to the partnership agreement that was drawn up after Bud's admission to the partnership, the fixed ratios for Hal, Dawn, and Bud were 40 percent, 40 percent, and 20 percent, respectively. With Dawn's withdrawal, the allocation was based on the remaining percentages, 40 percent and 20 percent.

   Because the remaining percentages total 60 percent (= 40 percent + 20 percent), allocations were made on that basis. Therefore, the bonus was allocated as follows:

Hal's portion of the bonus [$6,000 × 40/60]	$4,000
Bud's portion of the bonus [$6,000 × 20/60]	2,000
Total bonus allocated	$6,000

The entry to record this transaction would be:

	Debit	Credit
Dawn Bloom, Capital (−OE)	30,000	
Cash (−A)		24,000
Hal Flowers, Capital (+OE)		4,000
Bud Green, Capital (+OE)		2,000

Assets		=	Liabilities	+	Owners' Equity	
Cash	−24,000				Dawn Bloom, Capital	−30,000
					Hal Flowers, Capital	+ 4,000
					Bud Green, Capital	+ 2,000

Bonus to the Exiting Partner. Now let's examine the reverse situation. In this case, the partnership paid the exiting partner **more** than her capital account balance such that she received a bonus. This situation may occur for several reasons. The other partners may have been eager to see Dawn leave, the fair market value of the partnership's assets may have been higher than their book value, or the partnership may have enjoyed exceptional earnings and/or generated goodwill within the partnership.

To illustrate, assume that the partnership paid Dawn $33,000 (instead of $24,000) in exchange for her interest in the partnership. The procedure to account for this transaction is as follows:

1. **Calculate the bonus to the exiting partner.** The bonus to Dawn is the difference between the amount of cash she receives from the partnership and the balance in her capital account at the time of her withdrawal.

Amount of cash paid to the exiting partner	$33,000
Capital account balance of exiting partner	30,000
Total bonus to the exiting partner	$ 3,000

2. **Allocate the exiting partner's bonus to the remaining partners using their fixed ratios.** The remaining partner's fixed income ratios are the same as those shown in the last example. Therefore, the bonus would have been allocated as follows:

Hal's portion of the bonus [$3,000 × (40/60)]	$2,000
Bud's portion of the bonus [$3,000 × (20/60)]	1,000
Total bonus allocated	$3,000

The $3,000 bonus to the exiting partner came out of the remaining partners' capital accounts. The assumption is that the remaining partners are willing to give up some of their own capital account balances to obtain the exiting partner's withdrawal. The following entry would have been made to record this transaction.

	Debit	Credit
Dawn Bloom, Capital (−OE)	30,000	
Hal Flowers, Capital (−OE)	2,000	
Bud Green, Capital (−OE)	1,000	
Cash (−A)		33,000

Assets		=	Liabilities	+	Owners' Equity	
Cash	−33,000				Dawn Bloom, Capital	−30,000
					Hal Flowers, Capital	−2,000
					Bud Green, Capital	−1,000

Death of a Partner

Although the death of a partner is not something most partners want to consider, the sobering fact is that no one knows when a partner's death might occur. When a partner dies, the existing partnership is dissolved. Because the partner's equity in the partnership will pass to his or her estate after death, the partnership agreement should include provisions for a settlement with the estate.

To determine the balance in the deceased partner's equity account on the date of death, the partnership is required to (1) calculate the partnership's net income up to the date of death, (2) close the books, and (3) prepare financial statements. If the partnership agreement requires it, the partnership's net assets may be restated at their fair market value, and an audit of the accounting records may be required.

In some cases, the remaining partners personally purchase the deceased partner's interest in the partnership. In other cases, the partnership's assets may be used to finance the buyout. Because a profitable and successful partnership can be worth hundreds of thousands, if not millions, of dollars, many partnerships purchase life insurance policies on all general partners to cover the potential cost of a buyout.

SELF-STUDY PRACTICE

Klock voluntarily withdraws from the 4K partnership on January 1, 2009. Prior to Klock's withdrawal, the following information is available.

	Capital	Fixed Ratio
Kharge	$15,000	10%
Klock	20,000	20
Knot	25,000	30
Katt	60,000	40

1. Assume the partnership pays Klock $18,000 for the balance in her capital account. Calculate the bonus allocated to each of the remaining partners.
2. Assume the partnership pays Klock $23,000 for the balance in her capital account. Calculate the bonus to her and the amount that will be debited to the capital accounts of each of the remaining partners.

After you have finished, check your answers with the solution at the bottom of the page.

LIQUIDATION OF A PARTNERSHIP

Learning Objective 4

Demonstrate the proper treatment for the liquidation of a partnership.

Although Hal, Dawn, and Bud's partnership had been successful for many years (Dawn never actually withdrew from the partnership), the three friends became weary of the time required and the stress involved in running a business. Increasingly, they talked of dissolving their partnership. As a result, they decided to meet with their attorney again to discuss the possibility of a dissolution—the process that ultimately ends in the liquidation and distribution of partnership assets.

A **partnership liquidation** may be caused by the death of a partner, the imminent bankruptcy of the partnership, or by mutual agreement among all partners. The attorney informed the three friends that when a partnership is liquidated, the assets are sold (for cash), any outstanding debts and liabilities are paid, and the remaining cash, if any, is distributed to the partners. Before the process begins, however, the accounting cycle should be completed. That is, adjustments should be made, financial statements prepared, and closing entries recorded and posted. At that point, only the permanent accounts reported on the balance sheet should contain balances.

Solution to Self-Study Practice

1.

Amount of Klock's capital account	$20,000
Cash paid to Klock	18,000
Bonus to remaining partners	$ 2,000

Kharge: $2,000 × [10/(10 + 30 + 40)] = $250

Knot: $2,000 × [30/(10 + 30 + 40)] = $750

Katt: $2,000 × [40/(10 + 30 + 40)] = $1,000

2.

Amount paid to Klock	$23,000
Capital balance of Klock	20,000
Bonus to Klock	$ 3,000

Kharge: $3,000 × [10/(10 + 30 + 40)] = $375

Knot: $3,000 × [30/(10 + 30 + 40)] = $1,125

Katt: $3,000 × [40/(10 + 30 + 40)] = $1,500

The four steps in the liquidation process follow.

1. **Sell.** All assets (except cash) must be sold for cash and the resulting gain or loss recognized.
2. **Allocate.** After all assets have been liquidated (that is, converted to cash), the gain or loss calculated in Step 1 must be allocated among the partners according to their fixed ratios.
3. **Pay.** The partnership's cash is then used to pay all of the partnership's liabilities.
4. **Distribute.** Any remaining cash can then be distributed to the partners according to their fixed ratios.

The attorney advised the partners that

- **These four steps must be performed in order.** Executing them in any other order could result in serious financial consequences to the partners.
- A journal entry must be recorded for each and every step in the liquidation process.
- All liabilities, debts, and/or other obligations **must** be paid before the partners receive anything.

After the business has been operating for several years, partners' capital account balances will differ from one another for several reasons. The partners may have received different percentages of the profit (or loss), or their drawings may have varied. Over the years, these additions and/or withdrawals may have greatly impacted their capital accounts. Two possibilities exist with regard to the partners' capital accounts: (1) no capital deficiency—that is, every partner has a credit balance in his or her capital account and (2) a capital deficiency—that is, one or more partners have a debit balance (deficit) in his or her capital account. These different situations dramatically affect the partnership liquidation process, as we show in the following examples.

Assume that after many years of successful operations, Hal, Dawn, and Bud decided to liquidate their partnership. Exhibit 12.9 shows the partnership's account balances just before liquidation. In the following sections, we investigate how the existence or nonexistence of a capital deficiency affects the liquidation of a partnership.

No Capital Deficiency

After deciding to liquidate the partnership, Hal, Dawn, and Bud followed their lawyer's instructions to the letter. They completed the four steps in the liquidation process in order, as follows.

1. **Sell the partnership's assets (except cash).** The partners accepted an offer from Plantland, Inc., to purchase the partnership's assets (except cash) for \$240,000. The book value of these assets at the time of the transaction is \$229,000 (=\$94,000 − \$8,000 + \$85,000 + \$105,000 − \$47,000).

Exhibit 12.9 Partnership Account Balances before Liquidation

Assets		Liabilities and Owners' Equity	
Cash	\$ 51,000	Accounts payable	\$ 79,000
Accounts receivable	94,000	Notes payable	118,000
Allowance for doubtful accounts	(8,000)		
Inventory	85,000	Hal Flowers, capital	47,000
Store equipment	105,000	Dawn Bloom, capital	31,000
Accumulated depreciation	(47,000)	Bud Green, capital	5,000
	\$280,000		\$280,000

The entry to record the resulting $11,000 gain on the sale of the assets ($240,000 − $229,000) was:

	Debit	Credit
Cash (+A)	240,000	
Allowance for Doubtful Accounts (−xA, +A)	8,000	
Accumulated Depreciation (−xA, +A)	47,000	
Accounts Receivable (−A)		94,000
Inventory (−A)		85,000
Store Equipment (−A)		105,000
Gain on Liquidation (+OE)		11,000

Assets		=	Liabilities	+	Owners' Equity	
Cash	+240,000				Gain on Liquidation	+11,000
Allowance for Doubtful Accounts (−xA)	+8,000					
Accumulated Depreciation (−xA)	+47,000					
Accounts Receivable	−94,000					
Inventory	−85,000					
Store Equipment	−105,000					

2. **Allocate any gain or loss from the sale of the assets to the partners.** The partners allocated the $11,000 gain from Step 1 according to the partners' fixed ratios: 40 percent to Hal, 40 percent to Dawn, and 20 percent to Bud.

Hal's portion of the gain ($11,000 × 40%)	$ 4,400
Dawn's portion of the gain ($11,000 × 40%)	4,400
Bud's portion of the gain ($11,000 × 20%)	2,200
Total gain allocated	$11,000

The entry to record the allocation of the gain was:

	Debit	Credit
Gain on Liquidation (−OE)	11,000	
Hal Flowers, Capital (+OE)		4,400
Dawn Bloom, Capital (+OE)		4,400
Bud Green, Capital (+OE)		2,200

Assets	=	Liabilities	+	Owners' Equity	
				Hal Flowers, Capital	+ 4,400
				Dawn Bloom, Capital	+ 4,400
				Bud Green, Capital	+ 2,200
				Gain on Liquidation	−11,000

After posting the entry to allocate the gain, the partners' capital accounts appeared as follows.

Hal Flowers, Capital		Dawn Bloom, Capital		Bud Green, Capital	
	Bal. 47,000		Bal. 31,000		Bal. 5,000
	(2) 4,400		(2) 4,400		(2) 2,200
	51,400		35,400		7,200

3. **Pay all outstanding liabilities.** After the sale of assets, the partnership had $291,000 in cash ($51,000 + $240,000). This cash was used to pay the outstanding liabilities. The following entry was made to record the payment.

	Debit	Credit
Accounts Payable (−L)	79,000	
Notes Payable (−L)	118,000	
Cash (−A)		197,000

Assets		=	Liabilities		+	Owners' Equity
Cash	−197,000		Accounts Payable	−79,000		
			Notes Payable	−118,000		

4. **Distribute the remaining cash to the partners.** After paying all outstanding debts, the partnership had $94,000 cash remaining to distribute to the partners ($51,000 + $240,000 − $197,000). Because the partners completed each of the steps in the liquidation process properly and in sequence, the total balance in their capital accounts exactly equaled the amount of cash available for distribution ($51,400 + $35,400 + $7,200 = $94,000). The distribution of cash to the partners is shown in the following journal entry. After posting the entry, the balances in the capital accounts equaled zero, cash was zero, and the liquidation was complete.

	Debit	Credit
Hal Flowers, Capital (−OE)	51,400	
Dawn Bloom, Capital (−OE)	35,400	
Bud Green, Capital (−OE)	7,200	
Cash (−A)		94,000

Assets		=	Liabilities	+	Owners' Equity	
Cash	−94,000				Hal Flowers, Capital	−51,400
					Dawn Bloom, Capital	−35,400
					Bud Green, Capital	−7,200

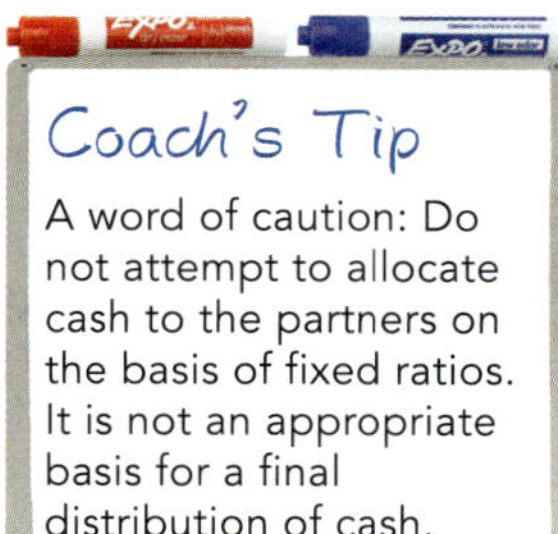
Coach's Tip

A word of caution: Do not attempt to allocate cash to the partners on the basis of fixed ratios. It is not an appropriate basis for a final distribution of cash.

Capital Deficiency

The liquidation process is not always smooth. Sometimes one or more partners do not have a large enough balance in their capital accounts to cover all transactions the liquidation requires. This situation can occur when the partnership has suffered numerous losses over its life. It can also occur when one or more partners have made disproportionately large withdrawals or when the partnership incurs large losses in the liquidation process. The procedure for dealing with this situation is as follows.

1. **Sell the partnership's assets (except cash).** Assume that Hal, Dawn, and Bud could not find a buyer for the business's assets and were forced to auction them off for far less than their fair market value. In total, the partnership collected $150,000 for assets (except cash) whose book value was $229,000 (= $94,000 − $8,000 + $85,000 + $105,000 − $47,000). Because the partnership received only $150,000 for assets recorded on the books for $229,000, it incurred a loss on liquidation of $79,000 ($229,000 − $150,000). The following entry was made to record the loss and the sale of the assets.

	Debit	Credit
Cash (+A)	150,000	
Allowance for Doubtful Accounts (−xA, +A)	8,000	
Accumulated Depreciation (−xA, +A)	47,000	
Loss on Liquidation (−OE)	79,000	
Accounts Receivable (−A)		94,000
Inventory (−A)		85,000
Store Equipment (−A)		105,000

Assets		=	Liabilities	+	Owners' Equity	
Cash	+150,000				Loss on Liquidation	−79,000
Allowance for Doubtful Accounts (−xA)	+8,000					
Accumulated Depreciation (−xA)	+47,000					
Accounts Receivable	−94,000					
Inventory	−85,000					
Store Equipment	−105,000					

2. **Allocate any gain or loss from the sale of assets to the partners.** The loss was allocated according to the partners' fixed income ratios: 40 percent to Hal, 40 percent to Dawn, and 20 percent to Bud.

Hal's portion of the loss ($79,000 × 40%)	$ 31,600
Dawn's portion of the loss ($79,000 × 40%)	31,600
Bud's portion of the loss ($79,000 × 20%)	15,800
Total loss allocated	$ 79,000

This entry was made to record allocation of the loss.

	Debit	Credit
Hal Flowers, Capital (–OE)	31,600	
Dawn Bloom, Capital (–OE)	31,600	
Bud Green, Capital (–OE)	15,800	
Loss on Liquidation (+OE)		79,000

Assets	=	Liabilities	+	Owners' Equity	
				Hal Flowers, Capital	−31,600
				Dawn Bloom, Capital	−31,600
				Bud Green, Capital	−15,800
				Loss on Liquidation	+79,000

3. **Pay the partnership's outstanding liabilities.** After selling the assets, the partnership had cash of $201,000 (= $51,000 + $150,000). This cash was used to pay the outstanding liabilities. The following entry was made to record the payment.

	Debit	Credit
Accounts Payable (−L)	79,000	
Notes Payable (−L)	118,000	
Cash (−A)		197,000

Assets		=	Liabilities		+	Owners' Equity
Cash	−197,000		Accounts Payable	−79,000		
			Notes Payable	−118,000		

4. **Distribute the remaining cash to the partners.** After paying all outstanding debts, the partnership had $4,000 cash (= $51,000 + $150,000 − $197,000) remaining to distribute to the partners. Normally, the partners receive the balances in their capital accounts after the first three transactions have been posted. However, as the debit balances in the following capital accounts show, both Bud and Dawn had a **capital deficiency**. Dawn owed the partnership $600, and Bud owed $10,800.

Hal Flowers, Capital		Dawn Bloom, Capital		Bud Green, Capital	
	Bal. 47,000		Bal. 31,000		Bal. 5,000
(2) 31,600		(2) 31,600		(2) 15,800	
	15,400	600		10,800	

The three friends realize that this was exactly the type of situation that a limited liability company (LLC) is formed to avoid. In a general partnership, each partner bears unlimited liability for the partnership's debts. So legally, Hal had an enforceable claim against both Dawn and Bud for the deficient funds. Hal could even have accessed their personal assets in an attempt to collect the deficiencies. Alternatively, Hal could have collected **the combined deficiency of both partners' capital accounts from just one of the two partners.** Often one partner has a great deal of personal wealth and another has very little. If Hal wanted, he could try to collect the entire amount from the wealthy partner. This ability to collect from any or all partners is called **joint** (all partners) **and several** (any partner) **liability.**

A capital deficiency can be resolved during the liquidation of a partnership in two ways: (1) the partner pays the deficiency and (2) the partner fails to pay the deficiency.

Deficiency Paid by Partner

Assume that Dawn decided to pay her $600 capital deficiency. The following entry was made to record the payment.

	Debit	Credit
Cash (+A)	600	
Dawn Bloom, Capital (+OE)		600

Assets		=	Liabilities	+	Owners' Equity	
Cash	+600				Dawn Bloom, Capital	+600

As the following T-accounts show, after the entry was posted, Dawn's capital account had a zero balance. She received no cash when the final distribution was made, but she owed nothing more. The partnership's Cash account then had increased to $4,600 (= $4,000 + $600).

Hal Flowers, Capital		Dawn Bloom, Capital		Bud Green, Capital	
	Bal. 47,000		Bal. 31,000		Bal. 5,000
(2) 31,600		(2) 31,600	(4a) 600	(2) 15,800	
	15,400		0	10,800	

Deficiency Not Paid by Partner

Suppose that Bud could not pay his $10,800 capital deficiency. When a partner cannot pay the deficit in a capital account, the partners who have credit balances in their capital accounts must absorb the deficit. Normally, the partnership's fixed ratio would be used to allocate the deficit, but because Hal was the only partner with a credit balance, he had to absorb the entire deficit. The following entry was made to record the absorption of the deficit by the remaining partner.

	Debit	Credit
Hal Flowers, Capital (–OE)	10,800	
Bud Green, Capital (+OE)		10,800

Assets	=	Liabilities	+	Owners' Equity	
				Hal Flowers, Capital	−10,800
				Bud Green, Capital	+10,800

With the deficit resolved, the partners' capital accounts had the following balances after the entry was posted.

Hal Flowers, Capital

Debit		Credit	
		Bal.	47,000
(2)	31,600		
(4b)	10,800		
			4,600

Dawn Bloom, Capital

Debit		Credit	
		Bal.	31,000
(2)	31,600	(4a)	600
			0

Bud Green, Capital

Debit		Credit	
		Bal.	5,000
(2)	15,800	(4b)	10,800
			0

The partnership had $4,600 cash, including the $600 that Dawn paid to resolve her deficit. Note that Hal's capital account **also** had a $4,600 balance. The final distribution to Hal could then be made. The final entry in the partnership liquidation was:

	Debit	Credit
Hal Flowers, Capital (–OE)	4,600	
Cash (–A)		4,600

Assets		=	Liabilities	+	Owners' Equity	
Cash	−4,600				Hal Flowers, Capital	−4,600

Even then, neither Bud nor Dawn was completely free of obligation to Hal. Hal had the right to collect the remaining $10,800 that he was owed from **either or both of them.** So even though Dawn may have thought she was in the clear because she paid her deficit, she still had unlimited liability.

SELF-STUDY PRACTICE

At the time of liquidation, AB Partners reported $2,000 in cash, $5,000 in other assets, $4,000 in liabilities, $2,600 in Ali Augo's capital account, and $400 in Bradyn Bad's capital account. For the following two independent cases, determine (a) the amount of cash available after the assets are sold and liabilities paid, and (b) the total balances in the partners' capital accounts after any gain (or loss) is allocated 50-50 between partners.

1. The assets (other than cash) are sold for $7,500.
2. The assets (other than cash) are sold for $3,000.

After you have finished, check your answers with the solution at the bottom of the next page.

RATIO ANALYSIS

Partner Return on Equity

Learning Objective 5
Calculate and interpret the partner return on equity ratio.

In our scenario, the partners certainly received their money's worth from their attorney, who gave them one last bit of information free of charge. He offered to provide the three partners a financial analysis tool called the **partner return on equity.**

Of the numerous financial measures used to analyze a business's performance, the partner return on equity is of particular interest to partnerships. An informative measure of profitability and managerial performance in a partnership, partner return on equity is calculated and interpreted as follows:

Financial Analysis Tools

Name of Measure	Formula	What It Tells You
Partner Return on Equity Ratio	$\frac{\text{Net Income}}{\text{Average Partner Equity}}$	• Measures a company's efficiency at generating profits from every dollar of equity invested (or retained) in the partnership. • A higher ratio indicates a greater efficiency.

Take Hal, Dawn, and Bud's partnership, for example:

	Total	Hal Flowers	Dawn Bloom	Bud Green
Balance 1/1/2009	$54,000	$18,000	$18,000	$18,000
Net income	15,000	6,000	6,000	3,000
Drawings	(12,000)	(2,000)	(3,000)	(7,000)
Balance 12/31/2009	$57,000	$22,000	$21,000	$ 14,000
Partner Return on Equity:				
Net Income / Average Partner Equity	$15,000 / (($54,000 + $57,000)/2)	$6,000 / (($18,000 + $22,000)/2)	$6,000 / (($18,000 + $21,000)/2)	$3,000 / (($18,000 + $14,000)/2)
=	**0.270 or 27.0%**	**0.300 or 30.0%**	**0.308 or 30.8%**	**0.188 or 18.8%**

Notice that the partnership's return on equity (in the Total column) is vastly different from the individual return on equity (ROE) calculated for each partner. Bud's ROE, in particular, appears relatively low when compared to the others. This should not be a surprise, though, because Bud receives a smaller income allocation than the other partners.

Solution to Self-Study Practice

1. (a) Cash = $2,000 + $7,500 − $4,000 = $5,500
   (b) Gain = $7,500 − $5,000 = $2,500 ($1,250 to Ali, $1,250 to Bradyn)
   A. Augo, Capital = $2,600 + $1,250 = $3,850
   B. Bad, Capital = $ 400 + $1,250 = 1,650
   Total $5,500

2. (a) Cash = $2,000 + $3,000 − $4,000 = $1,000
   (b) Gain (loss) = $3,000 − $5,000 = ($2,000) ($1,000 to Ali, $1,000 to Bradyn)
   A. Augo, Capital = $2,600 − $1,000 = $1,600
   B. Bad, Capital = $ 400 − $1,000 = (600)
   Total $1,000

In practice, very few businesses have a consistent return on equity of more than 30 percent. Moreover, maintaining ROE in a partnership at the same level over time is nearly impossible. That is because income is closed to the partners' equity accounts. Assuming the partners leave most of their earnings in the partnership to encourage its growth, the business's capital keeps increasing. To keep the partner ROE ratio high, then, income must also increase continually.

Another thing to watch for in relation to ROE is debt because a partnership can increase its ROE by relying more on debt. Assume, for example, that our partnership's beginning capital balance of $54,000 was made up entirely of partner contributions. Had the partnership instead borrowed $30,000 and required that much less in partner contributions, beginning capital would have been $24,000 rather than $54,000. In that situation, the ROE would have been a staggering 58.8%—[= $15,000/($24,000 + 27,000)/2]. But would you really want to take on all that debt just to achieve a high ROE? For this reason, the ROE should not be the only financial measure used to evaluate a business.

SELF-STUDY PRACTICE

Indicate whether each of the following is a true (T) or false (F) statement regarding partner return on equity.

1. Partner return on equity calculation is: Average Partner Equity ÷ Partner Net Income. ____________
2. Each individual partner's ROE can vary substantially from the ROE of the partnership as a whole. ____________
3. The ROE for most partnerships consistently exceeds 30 percent.____________
4. Assume a partner begins the year with $20,000 in partner equity and ends the year with $35,000. Her allocated net income for the year is $34,000. In this case, her ROE is 123.6 percent. ____________
5. Replacing capital with debt can increase the ROE. ____________

After you have finished, check your answers with the solution at the bottom of the page.

Demonstration Case A

Division of Partnership Income

Alwin and Teddy Ernest formed a partnership to provide accounting services. Assume that their partnership net income was $600,000, and other relevant information (immediately prior to allocating partnership net income) follows.

Partner	Capital Account Balances	Salaries	Interest	Fixed Ratio
Alwin Ernest	$200,000	$100,000	6%	1/3
Teddy Ernest	$300,000	$140,000	6%	2/3

Solution to Self-Study Practice

1. F—ROE is calculated as Partner Net Income ÷ Average Partner Equity.
2. T—Each partner's capital balance and allocated net income may be greater or less than others in the partnership.
3. F—It is rare for a partnership to consistently maintain an ROE in excess of 30 percent.
4. T—$34,000 / [($20,000 + $35,000) / 2] = 123.6%.
5. T—This reduces the bottom number in the ROE formula.

Required:

Allocate net income to each partner under the following four independent assumptions:

1. Fixed ratio.
2. Interest on partners' capital balances.
3. Salaries to partners.
4. Salaries to partners and interest on partners' capital balances.

Suggested Solution

1. Alwin Ernest: $600,000 × 1/3 = $200,000
   Teddy Ernest: $600,000 × 2/3 = $400,000

2.

	Alwin	Teddy	Total Allocated	Remainder to Allocate
Net income to allocate				$600,000
Interest:				
Alwin Ernest: $200,000 × 6%	$ 12,000		$ 12,000	(12,000)
Teddy Ernest: $300,000 × 6%		$ 18,000	18,000	(18,000)
Remainder (allocate on a fixed ratio):				570,000
Alwin Ernest: $570,000 × 1/3	190,000		190,000	(190,000)
Teddy Ernest: $570,000 × 2/3		380,000	380,000	(380,000)
Total	$202,000	$398,000	$600,000	$ 0

3.

	Alwin	Teddy	Total Allocated	Remainder to Allocate
Net income to allocate				$600,000
Salaries	$100,000	$140,000	$240,000	(240,000)
Remainder (allocate on a fixed ratio):				360,000
Alwin Ernest: $360,000 × 1/3	120,000		120,000	(120,000)
Teddy Ernest: $360,000 × 2/3		240,000	240,000	(240,000)
Total	$220,000	$380,000	$600,000	$ 0

4.

	Alwin	Teddy	Total Allocated	Remainder to Allocate
Net income to allocate				$600,000
Salaries	$100,000	$140,000	$240,000	(240,000)
Remainder				360,000
Interest:				
Alwin Ernest: $200,000 × 6%	12,000		12,000	(12,000)
Teddy Ernest: $300,000 × 6%		18,000	18,000	(18,000)
Remainder (allocate on a fixed ratio):				330,000
Alwin Ernest: $330,000 × 1/3	110,000		110,000	(110,000)
Teddy Ernest: $330,000 × 2/3		220,000	220,000	(220,000)
Total	$222,000	$378,000	$600,000	$ 0

Demonstration Case B

Admission and Withdrawal of Partners

In the year following Case A, Ernest & Ernest admits two new partners. Fred Whiney is admitted as an equal partner by purchasing half of Teddy's partnership interest. At the time, Teddy's capital account balance was $400,000 and Alwin's was $200,000. At the end of the year, Arthur Yong is admitted as an equal partner by investing $280,000 cash in the partnership and receiving a 25% partnership interest. At the time of Arthur's admission, the accounting records and partnership agreement contain the following information.

Partner	Capital Account Balances	Fixed Ratio
Alwin Ernest	$220,000	1/3
Teddy Ernest	250,000	1/3
Fred Whiney	250,000	1/3
Total	$720,000	

In the following year, Teddy Ernest retires and the partnership pays him $190,000 for his partnership interest. At the time, his capital account balance was $250,000.

Required:

Prepare the journal entry to record:

1. Admission of Fred Whiney.
2. Admission of Arthur Yong.
3. Withdrawal of Teddy Ernest.

Suggested Solution

1. Because Fred Whiney is admitted by a purchase among partners, the journal entry must only reallocate the existing balances in capital accounts. The total in the capital accounts was $600,000 ($400,000 + $200,000). Equal partnership implies 1/3 of this amount for each partner, or $200,000 (= $600,000 × 1/3). Alwin's capital account balance already equals $200,000, so a portion of only Teddy's account is reallocated.

Teddy Ernest, Capital (−OE)	200,000	
Fred Whiney, Capital (+OE)		200,000

2. Arthur Yong is admitted by an investment of additional assets ($280,000 cash). The journal entry must record this additional investment, and account for any bonus to the new partner or to the existing partners.

Step 1 Calculate the total partnership capital after Arthur's investment.

Total partnership capital before contribution	$ 720,000
Arthur Yong's contribution	280,000
Partnership capital after contribution	$1,000,000

Step 2 Calculate the amount of Arthur's capital account.

Total partnership capital after contribution	$1,000,000
Arthur's ownership portion	× 25%
Arthur's capital account balance	$ 250,000

Step 3 Calculate the total bonus to existing partners.

Amount contributed by Arthur	$280,000
Amount of capital given to Arthur	(250,000)
Total bonus to existing partners	$ 30,000

Step 4 Allocate the bonus to existing partners.

Alwin's portion ($30,000 × 1/3)	$10,000
Teddy's portion ($30,000 × 1/3)	10,000
Fred's portion ($30,000 × 1/3)	10,000
Total bonus to existing partners	$30,000

Cash (+A)	280,000	
Alwin Ernest, Capital (+OE)		10,000
Teddy Ernest, Capital (+OE)		10,000
Fred Whiney, Capital (+OE)		10,000
Arthur Yong, Capital (+OE)		250,000

3. Upon his retirement, Teddy Ernest withdraws $190,000 of partnership assets (cash). The journal entry must record this asset distribution, and account for any bonus to the exiting partner or to the remaining partners.

Step 1 Calculate the total bonus to the remaining partners.

Amount in Teddy Ernest's capital account	$ 250,000
Amount of cash paid to Teddy Ernest	(190,000)
Total bonus to remaining partners	$ 60,000

Step 2 Allocate the bonus to remaining partners.

Alwin Ernest's portion ($60,000 × 1/3)	$20,000
Fred Whiney's portion ($60,000 × 1/3)	20,000
Arthur Yong's portion ($60,000 × 1/3)	20,000
Total bonus to existing partners	$60,000

Teddy Ernest, Capital (–OE)	250,000	
Alwin Ernest, Capital (+OE)		20,000
Fred Whiney, Capital (+OE)		20,000
Arthur Yong, Capital (+OE)		20,000
Cash (–A)		190,000

Demonstration Case C

Liquidation of Partnership

After many years of success, the partnership of Ernest, Whiney, & Yong is dissolved and liquidated. The partnership sold its assets (other than cash) to a competitor for $1,710,000, then paid its liabilities in full, and distributed the remaining cash to its three partners. The partnership reported the following book values at the time of liquidation.

Assets		Liabilities and Owners' Equity	
Cash	$ 50,000	Accounts payable	$ 80,000
Supplies	10,000	Alwin Ernest, Capital	450,000
Equipment	1,800,000	Fred Whiney, Capital	490,000
Accumulated depreciation	(400,000)	Arthur Yong, Capital	440,000
	$1,460,000		$1,460,000

Required:

Prepare journal entries for the partnership to record the:

1. Sale of assets.
2. Allocation of gain on sale. (Assume partners' fixed ratios remain at 1/3 each.)
3. Payment of liabilities.
4. Final cash distribution to partners.

Suggested Solution

1. **Sale of assets.** The partnership received $1,710,000 for assets with a total book value of $1,410,000, resulting in a gain on liquidation equal to $300,000 ($1,710,000 − $1,410,000). (The book value of assets sold includes supplies and equipment less accumulated depreciation, calculated as $10,000 + $1,800,000 − $400,000 = $1,410,000.) The journal entry to record the cash received, assets sold, and gain follows.

Account	Debit	Credit
Cash (+A)	1,710,000	
Accumulated Depreciation (−xA, +A)	400,000	
Supplies (−A)		10,000
Equipment (−A)		1,800,000
Gain on Liquidation (+OE)		300,000

2. **Allocation of gain.** With a 1/3 fixed ratio for each partner, the $300,000 gain is allocated as $100,000 per partner (= $300,000 × 1/3).

Account	Debit	Credit
Gain on Liquidation (−OE)	300,000	
Alwin Ernest, Capital (+OE)		100,000
Fred Whiney, Capital (+OE)		100,000
Arthur Yong, Capital (+OE)		100,000

3. **Payment of liabilities.** The journal entry to record payment for $80,000 of accounts payable follows.

Account	Debit	Credit
Accounts Payable (−L)	80,000	
Cash (−A)		80,000

4. **Final cash distribution to partners.** The new balance in Cash, after receiving $1,710,000 (in step 1) and paying $80,000 (in step 3) is $1,680,000 (= $50,000 + $1,710,000 − $80,000). The new balances in the capital accounts (after step 2) include Alwin $550,000 (= $450,000 + $100,000), Fred $590,000 (= $490,000 + $100,000), and Arthur $540,000 (= $440,000 + $100,000), for a total of $1,680,000 (= $550,000 + $590,000 + $540,000). The journal entry to record the final cash distribution and liquidation of capital account balances follows.

Alwin Ernest, Capital (−OE)	550,000	
Fred Whiney, Capital (−OE)	590,000	
Arthur Yong, Capital (−OE)	540,000	
Cash (−A)		1,680,000

Demonstration Case D

Partner Return on Equity

Refer to Demonstration Case A. Assume partnership income is allocated using the fixed ratio method, and the partners did not make withdrawals or contributions during the year.

Required:
Calculate and interpret the return on equity (ROE) for the partnership as a whole and for each individual partner.

Suggested Solution

Remember to calculate the average balance in the Capital accounts using the beginning balances (provided in Case A) and the ending balances (after taking into account the allocated partnership income determined in Case A).

ROE formula: $$\frac{\text{Net income}}{[\text{Beginning capital} + \text{Ending capital}]/2}$$

Partnership: $$\frac{\$600{,}000}{[\$500{,}000 + (\$500{,}000 + \$600{,}000)]/2} = 0.750 \text{ or } 75.0\%$$

Alwin: $$\frac{\$200{,}000}{[\$200{,}000 + (\$200{,}000 + \$200{,}000)]/2} = 0.667 \text{ or } 66.7\%$$

Teddy: $$\frac{\$400{,}000}{[\$300{,}000 + (\$300{,}000 + \$400{,}000)]/2} = 0.800 \text{ or } 80.0\%$$

Because minimal amounts of cash and other assets are needed to start an accounting firm, the amount invested in the partnership is small relative to the amount of income generated. The very high ROEs are consistent with this. The ROE for Teddy is greater than for Alwin because Teddy receives twice as much partnership income as Alwin (2/3 versus 1/3), but Teddy did not contribute twice the amount of capital ($300,000 versus $200,000).

Chapter Summary

LO1 Compare the partnership form of business with other forms. p. 506

- A partnership is the association of two or more persons to carry on as co-owners of a business for profit, whether or not the persons intend to form a partnership.
- Advantages of partnerships include pass-through taxation, ease of formation, simplified recordkeeping, favorable taxation, and increased ability to raise funds.
- Disadvantages of partnerships include unlimited liability, co-ownership of property, limited life, mutual agency, and partner disagreements.

- The fees and procedures for forming a limited liability company (LLC) vary among states.
- Advantages of the LLC include limited liability, ease of formation, simplified recordkeeping, favorable taxation, and flexibility of operations.
- Disadvantages of LLCs include limited life, lack of legal precedents, limited corporate characteristics—no more than two of the following four corporate characteristics: (1) owners' liability limited to business assets, (2) continuity of life, (3) centralization of management, and (4) free transferability of assets.
- An S-Corporation is a corporation with 1 to 100 shareholders that enjoys pass-through taxation of profits. The formation requirements, annual filings, and required elections are complex and time consuming.

LO2 Demonstrate how to account for partnerships p. 509

- Partnership accounting requires a capital account for each partner, a drawing account for each partner, and an allocation of the partnership's income (or loss) to each partner based on the partnership agreement.
- Partner cash contributions are recorded at the amount of the cash contributed; noncash assets are recorded at the asset's market value. The contributing partner's capital account is credited for the net assets contributed.
- Partnership income (or loss) is allocated to the partners using one of four methods: (1) fixed-ratio method, (2) interest on partners' capital balances method, (3) salaries to partners method, or (4) salaries to partners and interest on partners' capital balances method.
- Closing entries must be made to transfer the allocated amounts of income (or loss) to each partner's capital account.
- The procedures for preparing financial statements is the same as for a proprietorship except a partnership (1) allocates net income among the partners, (2) shows a capital account on the balance sheet for each partner, and (3) replaces the owner's equity statement with the partners' capital statement.

LO3 Demonstrate the proper treatment for changes of ownership in a partnership. p. 517

- The admission of a new partner legally requires that all existing partners agree to it and causes the dissolution of the existing partnership and the creation of a new partnership.
- A new partner can be admitted in two ways: (1) a purchase among partners or (2) the investment of additional assets by the new partner. A purchase among partners is a personal transaction between individuals resulting in a journal entry made to transfer amounts from the original partners' capital accounts to the new partner's capital account. The investment of additional assets can result in a bonus to the new partner (or a bonus to existing partners) if the additional investment is less (or more) than the value of the partnership interest received.
- The withdrawal of a partner can also be accomplished in two ways: (1) a purchase among partners or (2) the withdrawal of assets. A purchase among partners is a personal transaction between individuals resulting in a journal entry made to transfer amounts from the exiting partner's capital account to the remaining partners' capital accounts. The withdrawal of assets can result in a bonus to the exiting partner (or the remaining partners) if the withdrawal is greater (or less) than the balance in the exiting partner's capital account.

LO4 Demonstrate the proper treatment for the liquidation of a partnership. p. 526

- The liquidation of a partnership may result from the death of a partner, the partnership's imminent bankruptcy, or mutual agreement among all partners.
- The four steps in the liquidation process that must be performed in sequence are (1) selling all assets (except cash) for cash and recognizing the resulting gain or loss, (2) allocating this gain or loss among the partners according to their fixed ratios, (3) using the cash in the partnership to pay off all partnership liabilities, (4) distributing any remaining cash according to the partners' fixed income ratios.
- The balance in the partners' capital accounts just before liquidation may have either no capital deficiency or a capital deficiency.
- If, after posting any gain or loss on the sale of the partnership assets, no capital deficiency exists in any of the partners' capital accounts, the outstanding debts of the partnership are paid. With the remaining cash, each partner receives a distribution equal to the balance in his or her capital account.
- If, after posting any gain or loss on the sale of the partnership assets, a capital deficiency exists in any of the partners' capital accounts, two possibilities exist: (1) that partner pays the deficiency or (2) that partner fails to pay the deficiency. When the partner pays the deficiency, the partnership has sufficient cash to pay the capital account balances of other partners. When the partner is unable to pay the capital deficiency, the partners who have credit balances in their capital accounts must absorb the deficit; the allocation of the deficit is based on the partners' fixed ratio.

LO5 Calculate and interpret the partner return on equity ratio. p. 533

- The partner return on equity ratio measures the profitability and managerial performance for each individual partner in a partnership.

Financial Analysis Tools

Name of Measure	Formula	What It Tells You
Partner Return on Equity Ratio	$\frac{\text{Net Income}}{\text{Average Partner Equity}}$	• Measures a company's efficiency at generating profits from every dollar of equity invested (or retained) in the partnership. • A higher ratio indicates a greater efficiency.

Key Terms

Articles of Organization (p. 507)
Capital Deficiency (p. 531)
Limited Liability Company (LLC) (p. 507)
Operating Agreement (p. 507)
Partner Return on Equity (p. 533)
Partners' Capital Statement (p. 516)
Partnership (p. 506)
Partnership Agreement. (p. 506)
Partnership Dissolution (p. 517)
Partnership Liquidation (p. 526)
Pass-Through Taxation (p. 507)
S-Corporation (p. 508)

See complete glossary in back of text.

Questions

1. What is a partnership?
2. List at least two advantages and at least two disadvantages of a partnership.
3. Define unlimited liability and limited liability. Which would you prefer if you were starting a new business? Explain.
4. What is mutual agency? Is it considered an advantage or disadvantage of a partnership? Why?
5. What are the essential elements of a partnership agreement? Is this a required document? Why or why not?
6. Define limited liability company (LLC). Why is this new form of business so popular?
7. List the two documents often required to form a limited liability company (LLC). Which is always a requirement and which is often simply a recommended document?
8. What is double taxation? Which form of business is subject to double taxation?
9. List the four characteristics of a corporation used to evaluate a limited liability company (LLC). What is the maximum number of these characteristics that a limited liability company can possess without risking its status as an LLC? Explain.
10. List the three things necessary for partnership accounting.
11. What amount is used to record partner investments into the partnership?
12. List three ways that the fixed ratio for dividing partnership profits and losses can be expressed.
13. When a new partner is admitted using the purchase among partners method, who is (are) the other party(ies) to the transaction?
14. When a new partner is admitted using the investment of additional assets method and the existing partners' capital accounts are debited, do the existing partners or the new partner receive a bonus?
15. When a partner withdraws, why might the partnership give a bonus to the withdrawing partner?
16. A dissolution is the same as a liquidation. Do you agree with this statement? Why or why not?
17. What are the four steps in the liquidation process?
18. If a capital deficiency exists upon the liquidation of a partnership, what are two possible resolutions to the situation?
19. What is one thing that can cause partner ROE to increase?

Multiple Choice

1. Which of the following is not a disadvantage of the partnership form of business?
   a. Mutual agency.
   b. Pass-through taxation.
   c. Unlimited liability.
   d. Limited life.

Quiz 12-1
www.mhhe.com/LLPW1e

2. Which of the following is a disadvantage of the limited liability company form of business?
   a. Ease of formation.
   b. Limited liability.
   c. Simplified recordkeeping.
   d. Limited corporate characteristics.

3. The limited liability company (LLC) has become a favorite entity choice of businesses meeting all of the following criteria except:
   a. The business has plans for significant growth.
   b. All members are active participants in a small local business.
   c. The business will have one to three members.
   d. All of the above.

4. To accurately keep track of income and/or loss for individual partners, which of the following is not required for partnership accounting?
   a. Provisions for the addition or withdrawal of a partner.
   b. A drawings account for each partner.
   c. A capital account for each partner.
   d. An allocation of the partnership income/loss to each partner, according to the terms of the partnership agreement.

5. Which of the following is not a true statement regarding partnership formation?
   a. The partner's capital account is credited for the amount of assets invested.
   b. Partners can invest any combination of assets and/or liabilities into the partnership.
   c. Partnership investments are recorded at the book value of the assets on the date they are transferred into the partnership.
   d. Partnerships may be formed through a handshake.

6. A partnership has four partners who share income/loss on an 8:4:3:1 ratio according to the partnership agreement. Assuming the partnership has net income of $20,000, how much will be allocated to each partner, respectively?
   a. $8,000, $4,000, $3,000, and $1,000.
   b. $10,000, $5,000, $3,750, and $1,250.
   c. $12,000, $4,000, $3,000, and $1,000.
   d. None of the above is the correct allocation of net income.

7. Joe is admitted into a partnership with Jack and Jill. Joe invests $25,000 into the partnership in exchange for a $22,000 capital account balance. This transaction is referred to as:
   a. A purchase among partners with a bonus to the new partner.
   b. A purchase among partners with a bonus to the original partners.
   c. An investment of assets into the partnership with a bonus to the new partner.
   d. An investment of assets into the partnership with a bonus to the original partners.

8. Stan withdraws from the partnership of Stan, Lee, and Brick and the partnership pays him $54,000. Assuming the balance in his capital account at that time is $50,000, which of the following is true?
   a. There is no bonus because this transaction is personal between the withdrawing partner and each individual remaining partner.
   b. A bonus of $4,000 is allocated to Stan, Lee, and Brick.
   c. A bonus of $4,000 is allocated to Lee and Brick.
   d. A bonus of $4,000 goes to Stan.

9. Which of the following is not a true statement regarding a partnership liquidation?
   a. All liabilities, debts, and/or other obligations of the partnership must be paid before the partners receive anything.
   b. The steps in the liquidation process can be performed in any sequence.
   c. Liquidation may result from the death of a partner, partnership bankruptcy, or agreement among the partners.
   d. A journal entry must be recorded for each step in the liquidation process.

10. What is the partner return on equity for Greg assuming his average partnership equity is $62,800 and his allocated net income from the partnership is $24,000?
    a. 76.4 percent.
    b. 38.2 percent.
    c. 261.7 percent.
    d. Cannot be calculated without ending capital.

Multiple-Choice Solutions						
1. b	2. d	3. a	4. a	5. c	6. b	7. d
8. d	9. b	10. b				

Mini Exercises

Available with McGraw-Hill's Homework Manager

LO1, 2

M12-1 Journalizing Partnership Formation

Prepare the journal entry that would be made for the formation of the DL Partnership given the following information: Doe invests $10,000 cash and equipment with a book value of $7,000 (cost $9,000). Lee invests $12,000 cash and inventory with a cost of $6,000 to the partnership. Fair market values of the equipment and inventory are $6,500 and $4,500, respectively.

LO2

M12-2 Dividing and Journalizing Income with Fixed Ratio

Tram and Quyen share income and loss based on a fixed ratio of 5/8 and 3/8, respectively. Net income for the current year is $24,000. Determine the amount of net income allocated to each partner and prepare the corresponding journal entry to record the allocation.

M12-3 Dividing of Income with Salaries, Interest, and Fixed Ratio
LO2

Blaine Partnership earned $20,000 this year. The partnership agreement states that income should be allocated to Romine and Roach using the salaries to partners and interest on capital balances method. Calculate the amount of Blaine's net income that will be allocated to each partner, assuming the following for each partner.

	Romine	Roach
Salary	$ 8,000	$ 4,000
Interest	10%	10%
Fixed ratio	60%	40%
Capital account balance	$15,000	$22,000

M12-4 Dividing Income When Allocation Exceeds Net Income
LO2

Use the same facts as in M12-3 except that Blaine Partnership earned $14,000 this year. Calculate the amount of Blaine's net income that will be allocated to each partner.

M12-5 Journalizing the Division of Income (Various Situations)
LO2

Perform the following tasks:

1. Prepare the journal entry to record the division of income made in M12-3.
2. Prepare the journal entry to record the division of income made in M12-4.

M12-6 Preparing Partners' Capital Statement
LO2

A. Jel and O. Tin are partners in the Jel N Tin Partnership. Using the following information, prepare a partners' capital statement on December 31, 2009.

	Capital 1/1/09	Capital Contributions	Net Income (allocated)	Partner Drawings
A. Jel	$39,000	$8,000	$14,900	$16,400
O. Tin	27,000	6,000	11,200	7,700

M12-7 Journalizing Admission of Partner as a Purchase among Partners
LO3

Dot and Dash are equal partners in the DD partnership. They agree to admit Dee into the partnership. It is agreed that Dee will pay Dot and Dash $40,000 each in exchange for one-third of each partner's current capital balance. Currently, Dot and Dash each has a capital balance of $90,000. Prepare the journal entry to admit Dee as a partner.

M12-8 Admitting a Partner by Investment with Bonus to the Existing Partners
LO3

Calculate the bonus to each of the existing partners with the admission of a new partner in the following situation: Juniper, Pine, and Fir are equal partners in a partnership. They agree to admit Pinion into the partnership. Pinion invests $35,000 in the partnership in exchange for a 25 percent partnership interest. The partnership agreement stipulates that bonuses be allocated on the basis of the fixed ratios prior to the admission of a new partner. The following information is available prior to the admission of Pinion.

	Juniper	Pine	Fir
Capital balances	$25,000	$35,000	$40,000
Fixed ratio	30%	30%	40%

M12-9 Admitting a Partner by Investment with Bonus to the New Partner
LO3

Calculate the bonus to each of the existing partners with the admission of a new partner in the following situation: Juniper, Pine, and Fir are equal partners in a partnership. They agree to admit Pinion into the partnership. Pinion invests $20,000 into the partnership in exchange for a 25 percent partnership interest. The partnership agreement stipulates that bonuses be allocated on the basis of the fixed ratios prior to the admission of a new partner. The following information is available prior to the admission of Pinion.

	Juniper	Pine	Fir
Capital balances	$25,000	$35,000	$40,000
Fixed ratio	30%	30%	40%

LO3

M12-10 Journalizing the Admission of a Partner (Various Situations)

Perform the following tasks:

1. Prepare the journal entry to record the admission of the partner as calculated in M12-8.
2. Prepare the journal entry to record the admission of the partner as calculated in M12-9.

LO3

M12-11 Calculating Bonus to Remaining Partners upon Withdrawal of Partner (Payment from Partnership)

Calculate the bonus allocated to each remaining partner upon the withdrawal of a partner in the following situation: Ima, Owda, and Hier are equal partners in a partnership. Owda decides to withdraw from the partnership and is very eager to leave. The partnership agrees to pay Owda $76,000 for her partnership interest. The partnership agreement requires that bonuses be allocated on the basis of the partners' fixed ratios prior to the withdrawal. The following information is available prior to Owda's withdrawal:

	Ima	Owda	Hier
Capital balances	$96,000	$84,000	$108,000
Fixed ratio	25%	20%	55%

LO3

M12-12 Calculating Bonus to Exiting Partner upon Withdrawal of Partner (Payment from Partnership)

Assume the same facts as in M12-11 except that the partnership agrees to pay Owda $90,400 for her partnership interest. Calculate the bonus allocated to each remaining partner.

LO3

M12-13 Journalizing the Withdrawal of a Partner (Various Situations)

Perform the following tasks:

1. Prepare the journal entry to record the withdrawal of the partner as calculated in M12-11.
2. Prepare the journal entry to record the withdrawal of the partner as calculated in M12-12.

LO4

M12-14 Liquidating Partnership with No Capital Deficiency

For the liquidation of DDT partnership, calculate the final distribution to each partner. The partnership's net assets have been sold, and the gain/loss has been recorded. Assume the following information:

Assets		Liabilities and Owners' Equity	
Cash	$ 57,000	Notes payable	$ 40,000
		Doun, capital	9,000
		Da, capital	6,000
		Toobes, capital	2,000
	$ 57,000		$ 57,000

LO4

M12-15 Liquidating Partnership with Capital Deficiency

For the liquidation of DDT partnership, calculate the final distribution to each partner. The partnership's net assets have been sold, and the gain/loss has been recorded. Assume the following information and that Toobes does not pay the deficiency.

Assets		Liabilities and Owners' Equity	
Cash	$ 57,000	Notes payable	$ 40,000
		Doun, capital (fixed ratio: 20%)	12,000
		Da, capital (fixed ratio: 30%)	9,000
		Toobes, capital (fixed ratio: 50%)	(4,000)
	$ 57,000		$ 57,000

M12-16 Journalizing the Liquidation of a Partnership (Various Situations) LO4

Perform the following tasks:

1. Prepare the journal entry to record the final payments to the partners of DDT partnership assuming the liquidation scenario in M12-14.
2. Prepare the journal entries to record the allocation of deficit and the final payments to the partners of DDT partnership assuming the liquidation scenario in M12-15.

M12-17 Calculating Partnership Return on Equity LO5

Using the information in the following table, calculate the ROE for each partner.

	Capital 1/1/09	Capital Contributions	Net Income	Partner Drawings	Capital 12/31/09
A. Jel	$39,000	$8,000	$14,900	$16,400	$45,500
O. Tin	27,000	6,000	11,200	7,700	36,500

Exercises  Available with McGraw-Hill's Homework Manager

E12-1 Identifying Advantages and Disadvantages of a Partnership LO1

The following are characteristics of a partnership. Determine whether each characteristic is an advantage (A) or a disadvantage (B).

Partnership Characteristic	Advantage or Disadvantage
___ 1. Limited life.	A. Advantage
___ 2. Co-ownership of property.	B. Disadvantage
___ 3. Mutual agency.	
___ 4. Ability to raise funds.	
___ 5. Partner disagreements.	
___ 6. Ease of formation.	
___ 7. Simplified recordkeeping.	
___ 8. Pass-through taxation.	

E12-2 Identifying Advantages and Disadvantages of a Limited Liability Company (LLC) LO1

Following are characteristics of a limited liability company. Determine whether each characteristic is an advantage (A) or a disadvantage (B).

Limited Liability Company Characteristic	Advantage or Disadvantage
___ 1. Limited liability.	A. Advantage
___ 2. Limited life.	B. Disadvantage
___ 3. Ease of formation.	
___ 4. Limited corporate characteristics.	
___ 5. Flexible profit and loss allocations.	
___ 6. Limited legal precedents.	

E12-3 Journalizing Partnership Formation—Cash and Noncash Contributions LO2

Georgy Cloon and Alfred Nunley form a partnership. The book and fair market values of the contributed assets follow:

	BOOK VALUE		FAIR MARKET VALUE	
	G. Cloon	A. Nunley	G. Cloon	A. Nunley
Cash	$11,000	$20,000	$11,000	$20,000
Accounts receivable		36,000		34,000
Allowance for doubtful accounts		(2,000)		(3,000)
Furniture and fixtures	54,000		42,000	
Accumulated depreciation	(5,000)			
	$60,000	$54,000	$53,000	$51,000

Required:
Based on the information presented, prepare the journal entry to record the contributions made by each partner to the partnership.

LO2

E12-4 Journalizing Division of Income—Various Allocations

Crane, Del, and Egbert are partners in the CDE partnership. Partnership net income for the current year is $70,000. Other relevant information appears in the following table.

	Capital Balance	Salary	Interest	Fixed Ratio
Crane	$65,000	$20,000	9%	5/8
Del	82,000	25,000	9	2/8
Egbert	53,000	18,000	9	1/8

Required:
Determine the allocation of net income to each partner under each of the following three independent assumptions:

1. Fixed-ratio method.
2. Interest on partners' capital balances and any remaining amounts on a fixed ratio.
3. Salaries to partners, interest on partners' capital balances, and any remaining on a fixed ratio.

LO2

E12-5 Dividing Income and Preparing Partners' Capital Statement

L. Len, S. Squigg, and S. Shirl are partners in the Shirl Len Squigg partnership. Partnership net income for the current year is $23,652. Other relevant information appears in the following table.

	Capital 1/1/08	Capital Contributions	Fixed Ratio	Partner Drawings
L. Len	$4,000	$2,500	1/6	$4,650
S. Squigg	5,000	1,500	2/6	5,200
S. Shirl	6,000	3,500	3/6	5,000

Required:

1. Allocate the net income to the partners using the fixed ratio method.
2. Prepare the partners' capital statement at December 31, 2008.

LO3

E12-6 Journalizing Admission of a Partner—Investment with Bonus to Existing Partners

Click and Clack are partners in the CC partnership. They agree to admit Cluck into the partnership. Cluck invests $45,000 into the partnership in exchange for a one-third interest in the partnership. Assume any bonuses will be allocated on the basis of the fixed ratios prior to the admission of the new partner.

Additional information prior to the admission of Cluck:

	Click	Clack
Capital account balance	$48,000	$21,000
Fixed ratio	70%	30%

Required:

1. Determine the capital account balance for each partner after the new partner is admitted.
2. Prepare the journal entry to admit the new partner.

E12-7 Journalizing Admission of a Partner—Investment with Bonus to New Partner LO3

Assume the same facts as in E12-6 except that Cluck invests $31,950.

Required:

1. Determine the capital account balance for each partner after the new partner is admitted.
2. Prepare the journal entry to admit the new partner.

E12-8 Journalizing Withdrawal of Partner—Payment from Partnership with Bonus to Remaining Partners LO3

Wallice, Gromett, Victer, and Warerabbit are partners in the Gromwell partnership. Warerabbit decides to withdraw from the partnership. Additional information available prior to the withdrawal follows:

	Wallice	Gromett	Victer	Warerabbit
Capital balances	$105,000	$122,000	$136,000	140,000
Fixed ratio	21%	28%	35%	14%

Required:

According to the partnership agreement, any bonuses resulting from a partner's withdrawal from the partnership should be allocated on the basis of fixed ratios prior to the withdrawal. Assuming the partnership pays Warerabbit $124,280 for his partnership interest,

1. Calculate the amount of the bonus allocated to each of the remaining partners.
2. Prepare the journal entry to record Warerabbit's withdrawal.
3. Determine the capital account balance for each remaining partner after the withdrawal.

E12-9 Journalizing Withdrawal of Partner—Payment from Partnership with Bonus to Exiting Partner LO3

Assume the facts in E12-8.

Required:

According to the partnership agreement, any bonuses resulting from a partner's withdrawal from the partnership should be allocated on the basis of fixed ratios prior to the withdrawal. Assume the partnership pays Warerabbit $146,000 for his partnership interest.

1. Calculate the amount of the bonus allocated to each of the remaining partners.
2. Prepare the journal entry to record Warerabbit's withdrawal.
3. Determine the capital account balance for each remaining partner after the withdrawal.

E12-10 Journalizing Admission and Withdrawal of a Partner—Among Partners LO3

Frey, Dones, and Bance are partners in the FDB partnership. Additional information available prior to the admission or withdrawal of any partners follows:

	Frey	Dones	Bance
Capital balances	$10,000	$20,000	$30,000
Fixed ratio	16%	39%	45%

Required:
Each of the following is an independent transaction.

1. Prepare the journal entry to admit a new partner given the following assumptions: Amos is admitted to the partnership with a 25 percent partnership interest and agrees to pay each partner $7,000 in exchange for receiving 25 percent of the capital account balances of Frey, Dones, and Bance.
2. Prepare the journal entry for the withdrawal of Frey assuming the following: Using the original information (i.e., assuming Amos was not admitted to the partnership), Frey decides to withdraw from the partnership. Dones and Bance agree to purchase one-half of Frey's capital account balance for $4,000 each.

LO4

E12-11 Liquidating a Partnership—No Capital Deficiency

The partnership of Law Dee Daw liquidates, and the account balances before liquidation follow.

Assets		Liabilities and Owners' Equity	
Cash	$ 6,000	Accounts payable	$19,000
Other partnership assets (net)	44,000	Notes payable	8,000
		L. Law, capital (3/5 fixed ratio)	4,000
		D. Dee capital (1/5 fixed ratio)	7,000
		D. Daw, capital (1/5 fixed ratio)	12,000
	$50,000		$50,000

Assume the assets of Law Dee Daw partnership (except cash) are sold for $40,000.

Required:
Determine the amount of cash to be distributed to the partners upon liquidation.

LO4

E12-12 Liquidating a Partnership—Capital Deficiency (payment by partner)

Refer to E12-11.

Assume the same facts except that the assets of Law Dee Daw partnership (except cash) are sold for $28,000.

Required:
Determine the amount of cash to be distributed to the remaining partners upon liquidation. Assume any capital deficiencies are paid to the partnership.

LO4

E12-13 Liquidating a Partnership—Capital Deficiency (nonpayment by partner)

Refer to E12-11.
Assume the same facts except that the assets of Law Dee Daw partnership (except cash) are sold for $28,000.

Required:
Determine the amount of cash to be distributed to the remaining partners upon liquidation. Assume any capital deficiencies are not paid but rather are absorbed by other partners.

LO5

E12-14 Calculating Partnership Return on Equity

Assume the following information for the partnership of Domee and Gleegal.

	Capital 1/1/08	Capital Contributions	Net Income	Partner Drawings
Domee	$28,000	$ 5,000	$16,500	$10,500
Gleegal	32,000	7,000	9,400	12,000
Total	$60,000	$12,000	$25,900	$22,500

Required:

1. Calculate the ending capital balance for each partner.
2. Calculate the return on equity (ROE) for each partner.
3. Explain the primary cause of any differences in the partners' ROE.

Problems—Set A  Available with McGraw-Hill's Homework Manager

PA12-1 Identifying Characteristics of Partnerships and Limited Liability Companies (LLCs) LO1

Following are various characteristics of partnerships and LLCs discussed in the chapter. For each characteristic, indicate the form(s) of business, partnership (A) or limited liability company (B), the characteristic describes. Some characteristics may describe more than one form of business.

Characteristic	Form of Business
___ 1. Ability to raise funds	A. Partnership
___ 2. Ease of formation	B. Limited Liability Company (LLC)
___ 3. Favorable tax treatment	
___ 4. Few legal precedents	
___ 5. Flexible profit/loss allocations	
___ 6. Limited corporate characteristics	
___ 7. Limited liabilities	
___ 8. Limited life	
___ 9. Pass-through taxation	
___ 10. Simplified recordedkeeping	
___ 11. Unlimited liability	

PA12-2 Forming a Partnership—Cash and Noncash Contributions, Making Journal Entries, and Creating Owners' Equity Section of the Balance Sheet LO2

M. Arsee, P. Ann, and G. Tsosi form the MAT partnership on January 8, 2009. The book and fair market values of the contributed assets follow.

	BOOK VALUE			FAIR MARKET VALUE		
	M. Arsee	P. Ann	G. Tsosi	M. Arsee	P. Ann	G. Tsosi
Cash	$ 9,000	$ 6,000	$17,000	$ 9,000	$ 6,000	$17,000
Accounts receivable			19,000			18,000
Allowance for doubtful accounts			(900)			(1,000)
Inventory	26,000			25,000		
Furniture and fixtures		45,000			35,000	
Accumulated depreciation		(8,000)				
Notes payable		(7,000)			(7,000)	
Net assets contributed	$35,000	$36,000	$35,100	$34,000	$34,000	$34,000

Required:

1. Based on the information presented, prepare the journal entry to record the contributions each partner made to the partnership.
2. Prepare the Liabilities and Owners' Equity section of the partnership balance sheet immediately following the partner contributions on January 8, 2009.

PA12-3 Dividing Income—All Four Methods LO2

www.mhhe.com/LLPW1e

Mills and Cross are partners in the MC partnership. Partnership net income for the current year is $52,200. Other relevant information follows.

	Capital Balances	Salaries	Interest	Fixed Ratio
Mills	$18,000	$21,000	7%	3/4
Cross	32,000	30,000	7	1/4

Required:
Determine the allocation of net income to each of the partners under each of the following four independent assumptions:

1. Fixed ratio.
2. Interest on partners' capital balances and any remaining amounts on a fixed ratio.
3. Salaries to partners and any remaining amounts on a fixed ratio.
4. Salaries to partners, interest on partners' capital balances, and any remaining amounts on a fixed ratio.

LO2

PA12-4 Dividing Income, Journalizing, and Preparing Partners' Capital Statement

A. Batt, B. Robbin, and F. Catt are partners in the Batt R Catt partnership. Partnership net income for 2009 is $46,000. Other relevant information follows:

	Capital 1/1/09	Capital Contributions	Fixed Ratio	Partner Drawings
A. Batt	$ 7,000	$4,400	25%	$4,000
B. Robbin	12,000	3,300	30	7,000
F. Catt	15,000	2,200	45	6,000

Required:

1. Allocate the net income to the partners based on fixed ratios.
2. Prepare the partners' capital statement at December 31, 2009.

LO3

www.mhhe.com/LLPW1e

PA12-5 Admitting a Partner—Journalizing Purchase and Investment Situations

Dick and Jane are partners in the DJ partnership. They agree to admit Spot into the partnership. According to the partnership agreement, any bonuses will be allocated on the basis of the fixed ratio prior to the admission of the new partner. Additional information available prior to Spot's admission follows.

	Dick	Jane
Capital account balance	$61,000	$57,000
Fixed ratio	58%	42%

Required:
Prepare journal entries to record the admission of Spot, under each of the following independent assumptions.

1. Spot pays Dick and Jane $19,000 each. In exchange he receives 30 percent of each partner's capital account balance.
2. Spot invests $25,000 into the partnership in exchange for a 25 percent interest in the partnership.
3. Spot invests $62,000 into the partnership in exchange for a 30 percent interest in the partnership.

LO2

PA12-6 Journalizing Partner Withdrawals

Carrtman, Kennie, and Kile are partners in the Southe Parke partnership. Kennie's death required his withdrawal from the partnership. According to the partnership agreement, any bonuses will be allocated on the basis of fixed ratios prior to the withdrawal. Additional information available prior to the withdrawal follows.

	Carrtman	Kennie	Kile
Capital account balance	$54,000	$64,000	$42,000
Fixed ratio	42%	30%	28%

Required:
Prepare journal entries to record the withdrawal of Kennie, under each of the following independent assumptions.

1. Carrtman and Kile agree to purchase ½ of Kennie's capital account balance for $40,000 each.
2. The partnership pays Kennie's estate $80,000 for his partnership interest.
3. The partnership pays Kennie's estate $59,000 for his partnership interest.

PA12-7 Liquidating a Partnership with No Capital Deficiency and Making Journal Entries LO4

www.mhhe.com/LLPW1e

Assume when the partnership of Shasta, Sheba, Sheeva liquidates, account balances before liquidation are as follows.

Assets		Liabilities and Owners' Equity	
Cash	$ 4,000	Accounts payable	$ 3,000
Inventory	8,000	Notes payable	8,000
Furniture and fixtures	16,000	Shasta, capital (35% fixed ratio)	2,000
Accumulated depreciation	(4,000)	Sheba capital (13% fixed ratio)	5,000
		Sheeva, capital (52% fixed ratio)	6,000
	$24,000		$24,000

Required:
Assume the Shasta, Sheba, and Sheeva partnership sold its assets (except cash) for $18,000. Record the following entries:

1. Sale of the partnership assets (except cash).
2. Allocation of gain or loss to each of the partners.
3. Payment of outstanding partnership liabilities.
4. Distribution of remaining cash to partners.

PA12-8 Liquidating a Partnership with Capital Deficiency (payment and nonpayment by partner) and Making Journal Entries LO4

Assume the same facts as in PA12-7.

Required:
Assume the Shasta, Sheba, and Sheeva partnership sold its assets (except cash) for $12,000. Record the following entries:

1. Sale of the partnership assets (except cash).
2. Allocation of gain or loss to each of the partners.
3. Payment of outstanding liabilities of partnership.
4. Distribution of remaining cash to partners assuming Shasta pays the deficiency.
5. Distribution of remaining cash to partners assuming Shasta does not pay the deficiency.

PA12-9 Calculating Partner Return on Equity (ROE) LO5

Gren, Bare, and Rett are partners in the GBR partnership. Information related to the partners follows.

	Total	Gren	Bare	Rett
Balance 1/1/2008	$71,000	$20,000	$30,000	$21,000
Contributions	20,000	10,000	5,000	5,000
Net Income	33,000	11,000	11,000	11,000
Drawings	(30,000)	(2,000)	(20,000)	(8,000)
Balance 12/31/2008	$94,000	$39,000	$26,000	$29,000

Required:

1. Calculate the partnership ROE.
2. Calculate the ROE for each partner.
3. Which partner has the best ROE? Why?

Problems—Set B

Available with McGraw-Hill's Homework Manager

PB12-1 Matching Terminology with Definitions

LO1 Following are the terms and definitions covered in Chapter 12. Match each term with its definition by entering the appropriate letter in the space provided. Use one letter for each blank.

Terms	Definitions
___ 1. Mutual agency	A. Lack of sufficient capital in a partner's capital account to absorb losses resulting from the liquidation of a partnership.
___ 2. Partners' capital statement	B. Document recommended when an LLC is formed to address potential problem areas in the LLC.
___ 3. Capital deficiency	C. Association of two or more persons to carry on as co-owners of a business for profit.
___ 4. Partnership agreement	D. Allows profits from a business to flow directly to the owners avoiding taxation at the business level.
___ 5. S-corporation	E. Document recommended when a partnership is formed to address potential problem areas in the partnership.
___ 6. Partner return on equity	F. Business form that offers its members limited liability protection and pass-through taxation.
___ 7. Partnership dissolution	G. Process of selling assets of the partnership, paying liabilities and distributing remaining cash to the partners.
___ 8. Articles of organization	H. Sufficient capital in a partner's capital account to absorb losses resulting from the liquidation of a partnership.
___ 9. Partnership	I. Shows all changes to capital for each partner in a partnership and replaces the owner's equity statement.
___ 10. Operating agreement	J. Occurs when a partner voluntarily or involuntarily leaves a partnership.
___ 11. Partnership liquidation	K. Corporation that allows profits to pass to the owners' personal income tax returns and provides owners limited liability.
___ 12. Pass-through taxation	L. Partnership characteristic that holds each partner accountable for the actions of all partners in the partnership.
___ 13. Limited liability company	M. Document required in states to form an LLC; provides important information about its operations and structure.
___ 14. No capital deficiency	N. Measures a company's efficiency in generating profits from every dollar of equity invested or retained by partners.

LO2

PB12-2 Forming a Partnership—Cash and Noncash Contributions, Making Journal Entries, and Creating Owners' Equity Section of the Balance Sheet

R. Tex, T. Ark, and L. Ana form the TexArkAna partnership on November 16, 2009. The book and fair market values of the contributed assets follow.

	BOOK VALUE			FAIR MARKET VALUE		
	R. Tex	T. Ark	L. Ana	R. Tex	T. Ark	L. Ana
Cash	$ 13,500	$ 9,000	$25,500	$13,500	$ 9,000	$25,500
Accounts receivable			28,500			27,000
Allowance for doubtful accounts			(1,350)			(1,500)
Inventory	39,000			37,500		
Furniture and fixtures		67,500			52,500	
Accumulated depreciation		(12,000)				
Notes payable		(10,500)			(10,500)	
Net assets contributed	$ 52,500	$54,000	$52,650	$51,000	$51,000	$51,000

Required:

1. Based on the information presented, prepare the journal entry to record the contributions each partner made to the partnership.
2. Prepare the Liabilities and Owners' Equity section of the partnership balance sheet immediately following the partner contributions on November 16, 2009.

PB12-3 Dividing Income—All Four Methods LO2

Toffee and Bonnie are partners in the Toffnie partnership. Partnership net income for the current year is $81,000. Other relevant information follows.

	Capital Balances	Salaries	Interest	Fixed Ratio
Toffee	$27,000	$31,500	10%	1/3
Bonnie	48,000	45,000	10	2/3

Required:
Determine the allocation of net income to each of the partners under each of the following four independent assumptions:

1. Fixed Ratio.
2. Interest on partners' capital balances and any remaining amounts on a fixed ratio.
3. Salaries to partners and any remaining amounts on a fixed ratio.
4. Salaries to partners, interest on partners' capital balances and any remaining amounts on a fixed ratio.

PB12-4 Dividing Income, Journalizing, and Preparing Partners' Capital Statement LO2

C. Crow, R. Beare, and K. Marin are partners in the CRM partnership. Partnership net income for 2009 is $59,000. Other relevant information follows.

	Capital 1/1/09	Capital Contributions	Fixed Ratio	Partner Drawings
C. Crow	$10,500	$6,000	32%	$ 8,000
R. Beare	18,000	4,500	17	7,000
K. Marin	22,500	3,000	51	10,000

Required:

1. Allocate the net income to the partners based on the fixed ratio.
2. Prepare the partners' capital statement at December 31, 2009.

LO3

PB12-5 Admitting a Partner—Journalizing Purchase and Investment Situations

Dott and Latta are partners in the DL partnership. They agree to admit Caspar into the partnership. Assume any bonuses will be allocated on the basis of the fixed ratio prior to the admission of the new partner. Additional information available prior to Caspar's admission follows.

	Dott	Latta
Capital account balance	$ 91,500	$ 85,500
Fixed ratio	60%	40%

Required:
Prepare journal entries to record the admission of Caspar, under each of the following independent assumptions.

1. Caspar pays Dott and Latta $28,500 each. In exchange he receives 25% of each partner's capital account balance.
2. Caspar invests $40,000 into the partnership in exchange for a 20% interest in the partnership.
3. Caspar invests $90,000 into the partnership in exchange for a 30% interest in the partnership.

LO3

PB12-6 Journalizing Partner Withdrawals

Pinkey, Brainne, and Snobal are partners in the Take Over partnership. Snobal decides to withdraw from the partnership. According to the partnership agreement, any bonuses will be allocated on the basis of fixed ratios prior to the withdrawal. Additional information available prior to the withdrawal follows.

	Pinkey	Brainne	Snobal
Capital account balance	$40,500	$48,000	$31,500
Fixed ratio	35%	45%	20%

Required:
Prepare journal entries to record the withdrawal of Snobal, under each of the following independent assumptions.

1. Pinkey and Brainne agree to purchase 50 percent of Snobal's capital account balance for $17,000 each.
2. The partnership pays Snobal $29,500 for his partnership interest.
3. The partnership pays Snobal $35,100 for his partnership interest.

LO4

PB12-7 Liquidating a Partnership with No Capital Deficiency and Making Journal Entries

Assume when the partnership of Flour, Rice, and Salt liquidates, account balances before liquidation are as follows.

Assets		Liabilities and Owners' Equity	
Cash	$ 16,000	Accounts payable	$ 12,000
Inventory	32,000	Notes payable	48,000
Furniture and fixtures	64,000	Flour, capital (30% fixed ratio)	5,000
Accumulated depreciation	(12,000)	Rice, capital (15% fixed ratio)	15,000
		Salt, capital (55% fixed ratio)	20,000
	$100,000		$100,000

Required:
Assume the Flour, Rice, and Salt partnership sold its assets (except cash) for $80,000. Record the following entries:

1. Sale of the partnership assets (except cash).
2. Allocation of gain or loss to each of the partners.
3. Payment of outstanding partnership liabilities.
4. Distribution of remaining cash to partners.

PB12-8 Liquidating a Partnership with Capital Deficiency (Payment and Nonpayment by Partner) and Making Journal Entries LO4

Assume the same facts as in PB12-7, except that the fixed ratios for Flour, Rice, and Salt are 25%, 30%, and 45%, respectively.

Required:

Assume the assets of Flour, Rice, and Salt partnership sold all assets (except cash) for $60,000. Record the following entries:

1. Sale of the partnership assets (except cash).
2. Allocation of gain or loss to each of the partners.
3. Payment of outstanding liabilities of partnership
4. Distribution of remaining cash to partners assuming Flour pays the deficiency.
5. Distribution of the remaining cash to partners assuming Flour does not pay the deficiency.

PB12-9 Calculating Partner Return on Equity (ROE) LO5

Preppen, Somme, and Allison are partners in the PSA partnership. Information related to the partners follows.

	Total	Preppen	Somme	Allison
Balance 1/1/2008	$40,000	$5,000	$10,000	$25,000
Contributions	6,000	2,000	2,000	2,000
Net income	25,000	8,000	10,000	7,000
Drawings	(18,000)	(6,000)	(9,000)	(3,000)
Balance 12/31/2008	$53,000	$9,000	$13,000	$31,000

Required:

1. Calculate the partnership ROE.
2. Calculate the ROE for each partner.
3. Which partner has the best ROE? Why?

Cases and Projects

CP12-1 Making Key Partnership Decisions LO1, 2

Harrison and Daniel are two brothers who have been developing video games for several years as a hobby. Their games have proven to be very popular, so they recently decided to turn their hobby into a business venture. Harrison—the older and more responsible brother—has accumulated $30,000 to contribute to the business to get it started. Daniel, on the other hand, has relatively little capital to contribute ($3,000), but he has tremendous creativity and energy. After the business is established, Harrison is likely to work 20 hours per week developing games for the business and Daniel will work 40 hours per week. The brothers get along well, and do not anticipate any problems working together, however their oldest brother Tiger claims that eventually relationships change so they should plan for that possibility. Tiger claims that someday he might even be interested in joining them in running the business, or helping their kids to take over the business. Harrison and Daniel do not want to invest a lot of time or energy establishing the new business, so they have come to you for advice.

Required:

1. Should Harrison and Daniel form a partnership or limited liability company? List the differences between these two forms of business and then make a recommendation based on the facts you know about Harrison and Daniel.
2. Assume Harrison and Daniel decide to form a partnership. Explain the elements they should include in the partnership agreement. Provide specific advice for the division of profits and losses, taking into account the different contributions of capital and time that they plan to make.

CP12-2 Resolving Inequitable Partnership Contributions LO2

Last year, Mick and Sayesha entered into a partnership to establish and run a local music promotions business called MuSick Promos (MSP). Both partners contributed $2,000 to the business to get MSP off the ground. They had verbally agreed to contribute their own special talents to MSP in approximately equal proportions. Mick was in his final year as a marketing major at a local university and Sayesha was a struggling musician who had many contacts in the local music scene. For that first year, Sayesha worked about 20 hours a week finding bands to represent and promoting to clubs and other venues in the city. Mick spent an equal amount of time building relationships with local clubs that would hire bands to play at weekend events. Both Mick and Sayesha succeeded in their efforts. Mick had found about 15 clubs that regularly hired the artists promoted by MSP, and Sayesha had signed an equal number of bands to represent.

As MSP entered its second year of operations, Mick and Sayesha started having problems. Sayesha complained that now that Mick had graduated and taken a full-time sales job with a newspaper company, he spent only a few hours a week on MSP business, yet she still spent about 15 hours a week drumming up bands to represent. Mick responded by explaining that his hard work during the first year had led to long-lasting relationships with the clubs, so he had little to do except occasionally keep in touch with the clubs' managers. In contrast, the bands signed by Sayesha frequently broke up or moved to other cities as their popularity fell or grew. Mick tried to further justify his situation by saying that his new job allowed him to leave his share of MSP's profits in the business. In contrast, he complained, Sayesha had withdrawn most of her share to pay her rent and other living costs. Mick said this imbalance in capital account balances caused differences in the partners' return on equity ratios, which were unfair to him.

Required:

1. Evaluate the validity of each argument expressed by Mick and Sayesha. Are these arguments reasonable and equally valid? With whom would you side if you were asked to reconcile their situation?
2. Could the conflict have been avoided? How? Can something be done now to improve the partners' future relations?

LO5 CP12-3 Making Ethical Decisions: A Mini-Case

Frank was recently hired as an accountant for the TMM Partnership. When the partnership published its quarterly figures, Frank noticed the return on equity figures seemed odd. After asking a few co-workers, he found that the figures were artificially and intentionally inflated each quarter. This type of reporting seemed to be a recurring event that co-workers questioned but accepted because they resulted in higher bonuses and "nobody" was hurt by it. The published results became a water cooler topic that Frank's co-workers were laughing about all the way to the bank. Frank saw the funding that the partnership was receiving based on the figures and realized that it was providing him and his co-workers with a great deal of job security. Frank thought, Who is it hurting anyway? Why should I put all of these benefits in jeopardy by saying something? With this reasoning, Frank decided to do nothing.

Required:

1. Describe the ethical dilemma that Frank faces.
2. Who benefits and who is harmed by reporting inflated ROE figures?
3. Do you think Frank handled the situation correctly? Would you have handled it differently?

LO1 CP12-4 Forming a Partnership or Limited Liability Company

Assume you are considering forming a general partnership or a limited liability company (LLC) in your state. Search the Internet for the required documents and forms needed to establish such business forms in your state. A good starting place for this search is the Web site smallbusiness.findlaw.com.

Required:

1. Prepare a checklist of key steps to follow when starting a partnership.
2. Locate and provide copies of any forms that must be filed to form a limited liability company (LLC).

13 Accounting for Corporations

LEARNING OBJECTIVES

After completing this chapter, you should be able to:

Lectured presentations–13-1
www.mhhe.com/LLPW1e

LO1 Describe the characteristics of corporations.

LO2 Demonstrate how to account for transactions involving common stock, preferred stock, and treasury stock.

LO3 Demonstrate how to account for cash dividends, stock dividends, and stock splits.

LO4 Analyze the earnings per share (EPS) and price/earnings (P/E) ratios.

Focus Company: SONIC CORP.

America's Drive-In

www.sonicdrivein.com

News about shares of stock is everywhere. You can read it in the *Wall Street Journal,* listen to it on MSNBC, or search for it at Yahoo!Finance. Behind this fascination with stock is a dream many people share: taking a small amount of money and turning it into a fortune.

That is what Sonic Corp.—America's largest drive-in restaurant chain—has managed to do. When Sonic first started operations as a hamburger and root beer stand about 35 years ago, the company was selling 100 shares of stock to store owners for $100. As the company grew larger and more profitable, the value of its stock increased. By 1995, Sonic was selling 100 shares to investors for $2,125. Since then, those shares have split five times, causing 100 shares to multiply into 760 shares. Sonic is now buying back its stock at over $19 a share. That is more than $14,400 for the 100 shares bought in 1995, or an increase of nearly 700 percent in little more than a decade!

In this chapter, you will see how companies such as Sonic Corp. account for various stock transactions, including stock issues, stock splits, and stock dividends. Soon you'll understand many of the stock terms used in the financial news.

ORGANIZATION OF THE CHAPTER

CHARACTERISTICS OF THE CORPORATE FORM	ACCOUNTING FOR STOCK TRANSACTIONS	ACCOUNTING FOR DIVIDENDS AND SPLITS	FINANCIAL RATIO ANALYSIS
• Ownership • Laws and Taxes • Formation • Financing	• Common and Preferred Stock • Treasury Stock • Financial Statement Reporting	• Cash Dividends on Common Stock • Cash Dividends on Preferred Stock • Stock Dividends • Stock Splits • Statement of Retained Earnings	• Earnings per Share (EPS) • Price/Earnings (P/E) Ratio

CHARACTERISTICS OF THE CORPORATE FORM

Learning Objective 1

Describe the characteristics of corporations.

Video 13-1
www.mhhe.com/LLPW1e

If you were to write down the names of 50 familiar businesses, probably all of them would be corporations. According to Bizstats.com, corporations account for 85 percent of the total sales reported by U.S. businesses. Furthermore, many people own shares in corporations, either directly or indirectly, through a mutual fund or pension program. You probably recall from Chapter 1 that the act of creating a corporation is costly. Why, then, is the corporate form so popular?

Ownership

The secret to the popularity of the corporate form is that investors both large and small can easily participate in a corporation's ownership. This widespread participation gives corporations one critical advantage over sole proprietorships and partnerships: They can raise large amounts of money. Several factors encourage investors to participate in corporate ownership:

1. **Shares of stock can be purchased in small amounts.** According to Yahoo!Finance, on January 21, 2008, you could have become one of Sonic Corp.'s owners by buying a single share of the company's stock for just $19. Owners of corporations are called stockholders or shareholders.
2. **Ownership interests are transferable.** Shares of a company's stock can be bought and sold, allowing new investors to become owners and existing owners to leave the business. If a corporation is a public company, any member of the public can buy or sell the company's shares through a stock market, such as the New York Stock Exchange. Sonic is a public company, but not all corporations are public companies. Chick-fil-A and Cargill, for example, are private companies whose shares are bought and sold privately.
3. **Stockholders are not liable for the corporation's debts.** Creditors have no legal claim on stockholders' personal assets as they do on the personal assets of those who own sole proprietorships and partnerships. So, if you owned stock in the old Montgomery Ward department store, which went bankrupt and was liquidated in 2000, you could lose only what you paid to buy the stock. You would not be liable for the hundreds of millions of dollars of debt that the company could not pay back.

Laws and Taxes

The law recognizes a corporation as a separate legal entity. It may own assets, incur liabilities, expand and contract in size, sue others and be sued, and enter into contracts independently of its owners. Because a corporation exists separate and apart from its owners, it does not die when its owners die. Thomas Edison died in 1931, but the company he founded—General Electric—continues in existence today.

As a separate legal entity, a corporation is obligated to pay taxes on the net income it generates. This obligation is reported on the balance sheet as the current liability Income Taxes

Payable. Because income taxes are a necessary cost of being a corporation, they are reported as an expense on the income statement.

Formation

To protect everyone's rights, the law tightly regulates the creation and oversight of corporations. Owners create corporations by submitting an application to a state government (not the federal government). Because laws vary from state to state, you might decide to create a corporation in a state that differs from the one(s) where it operates. Although Sonic has its headquarters in Oklahoma City, it was actually incorporated in Delaware. More than half of the largest corporations in the United States are incorporated in Delaware because it has some of the most favorable laws for establishing corporations. If the application is approved, the state issues a charter, which specifies the corporation's name and address, the nature of its business, and the type and number of shares that the corporation can issue.

The type and number of shares can vary greatly from one corporation to the next. In its most basic form, a corporation must have one type of share, appropriately called common stock. Owners of common stock usually enjoy the following benefits:

- **Voting rights.** For each share you own, you get one vote on major issues, such as which accounting firm will audit the company's books and who will serve on the board of directors. As Exhibit 13.1 illustrates, the board of directors appoints the corporation's executive officers and governs top management.
- **Dividends.** Dividends can be declared as a way of distributing the corporation's profits to its stockholders.
- **Residual claim.** If a corporation ceases to operate, stockholders share in any remaining assets after the company has paid all of its debts.
- **Preemptive rights.** Existing stockholders may be given the first chance to buy newly issued stock before it is offered to others.

In addition to common stock, corporations can issue preferred stock to a select group of investors. This special form of stock differs from common stock, typically in the following ways:

1. **Preferred stock generally does not include voting rights.** As a result, preferred stock does not appeal to investors who want some control over a company's operations. However, it does appeal to existing common stockholders because the company can sell preferred stock to raise funds without reducing common stockholders' voting control.

Exhibit 13.1 Typical Organizational Structure of a Corporation

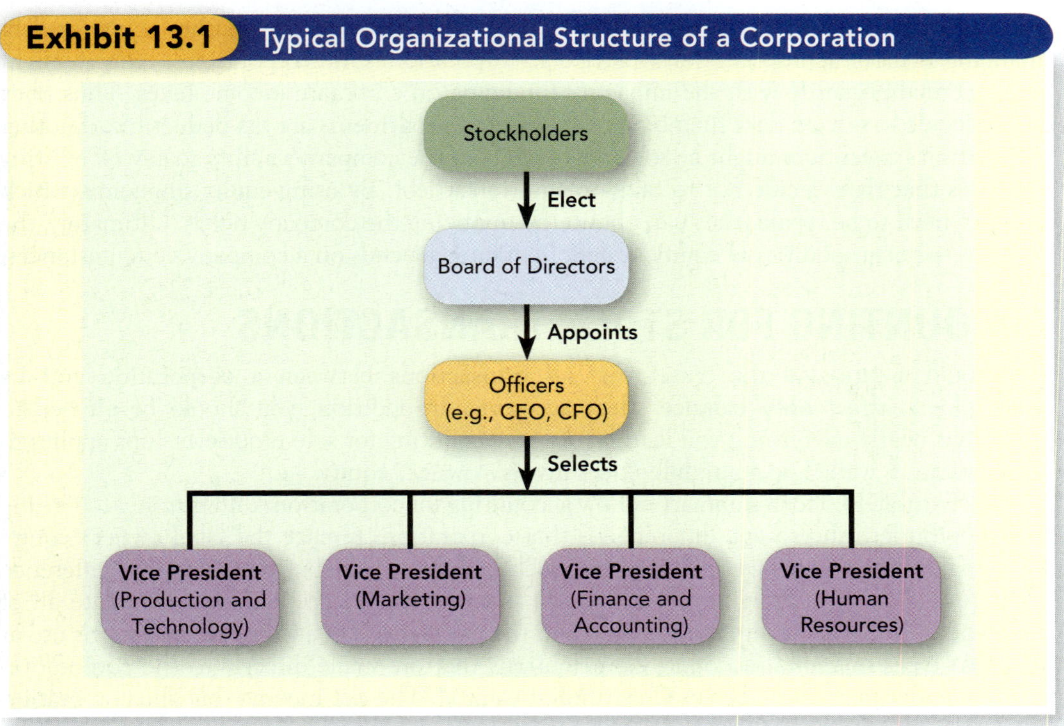

2. **Dividends on preferred stock, if any, are paid at a fixed rate,** specified as either a dollar amount or a percentage per share. For example, if dividends are declared on "6 percent preferred stock," the dividend will equal 6 percent of the stock's par value. A fixed dividend can be attractive to certain investors, such as retirees or company founders, who seek a stable income from their investments.
3. **Preferred stock carries priority over common stock.** Preferred stockholders have higher priority than common stockholders if a corporation distributes assets to its owners through dividends or at liquidation. That is, any dividends the corporation declares must be paid to preferred stockholders before they can be paid to common stockholders. Also, if the corporation goes out of business, its assets will be sold and used to pay creditors and then preferred stockholders. Common stockholders are paid last from whatever assets remain after paying preferred stockholders.

Financing

Whenever a corporation needs a large amount of long-term financing, its executives must decide whether to obtain it by issuing new stock to investors (equity financing) or by borrowing money from lenders (debt financing). Both these forms of financing have certain advantages as listed in Exhibit 13.2.

Exhibit 13.2 Advantages of Equity versus Debt Financing

Advantages of Equity Financing	Advantages of Debt Financing
1. Equity does not have to be repaid. Debt must be repaid or refinanced.	1. Interest on debt is tax deductible. Dividends on stock are not tax deductible.
2. Dividends are optional. Interest must be paid on debt.	2. Debt does not change stockholder control. In contrast, a stock issue gives new stockholders the right to vote and share in the earnings, diluting existing stockholders' control.

These relative advantages play a significant role in determining whether equity or debt financing is more appropriate for a particular corporation. One corporation's officers might be concerned primarily with the impact of financing on corporate income taxes. Thus, they might decide to rely on debt financing because interest payments are tax deductible. Another corporation's executives might be so concerned about the company's ability to pay off existing liabilities that they decide not to take on additional debt. By using equity financing, which does not need to be repaid, they can obtain the financing the company needs. Ultimately, the decision to pursue additional equity or debt financing depends on a company's circumstances.

ACCOUNTING FOR STOCK TRANSACTIONS

Learning Objective 2
Demonstrate how to account for transactions involving common stock, preferred stock, and treasury stock.

We should mention at the outset that **all transactions between a corporation and its stockholders affect only balance sheet accounts.** In addition, you should be pleased to know that nearly everything you learned about accounting for sole proprietorships applies to corporations as well. The main differences involve owner's equity.

See Exhibit 13.3 for a summary of how accounting for corporations differs from accounting for sole proprietorships. One difference is that corporations replace the label owner's equity with **stockholders' equity** to indicate that stockholders own the business. Another difference is that unlike sole proprietorships, which use just one capital account to accumulate all of the owner's investments and withdrawals and the company's net income, corporations use at least two types of capital account. Contributions that are made directly to the corporation by stockholders are referred to as **Contributed Capital**. The net income that the corporation generates each year through profitable operations is accumulated in a separate account,

Exhibit 13.3 Accounting Differences for Sole Proprietorships and Corporations

Sole Proprietorships						
Owner's Equity						
Joe Smith, Capital	=	Contributions	+	Net Income	−	Withdrawals
Corporations						
Stockholders' Equity						
Contributed Capital	=	Contributions				
Retained Earnings	=			Net Income	−	Dividends

Retained Earnings. Unlike a sole proprietor, who may take money out of the business in the form of withdrawals, stockholders must rely on dividends. Dividends are subtracted from Retained Earnings as shown in Exhibit 13.3.

In the following section, we look more closely at transactions that affect Contributed Capital. Those transactions include issues of common stock and preferred stock and the repurchase of shares in the form of treasury stock.

Common and Preferred Stock

Stock Authorization

The corporate charter authorizes and defines the specific rights and characteristics of a corporation's stock. This authorization does not directly affect the accounting records, but it does establish certain characteristics that will later affect how to account for the stock.

One characteristic of importance is the stock's par value. Oddly enough, par value has little meaning today. It was originally introduced to prevent stockholders from removing their contributed capital after discovering that the business was going bankrupt. Today, stronger laws and regulations prevent that from happening, so the concept of par value is no longer critical to this aspect of the business.

Many states still require corporations to specify a par value for their stock. Typically, they set par value at a minimal amount, such as $0.01 per share, as Sonic did with its common stock. Other states have dropped the requirement to specify a par value and instead allow corporations to issue no-par value stock. No-par value stock is just like stock with par value except that it does not have a specified legal value per share. Although par value is a legal concept that is not related in any way to the share's market value, it does affect how to account for stock as you will see in the next section.

Stock Issues

Par Value Common Stock Issued for Cash. The sale of stock from the corporation to an investor is called a stock issue. In most cases, these sales are cash transactions. To see how to account for an issue of par value stock, assume that during the next fiscal year, Sonic receives cash for 100,000 shares of its $0.01 par value common stock issued when the market price is $30 per share. This stock issue would be accounted for as follows:

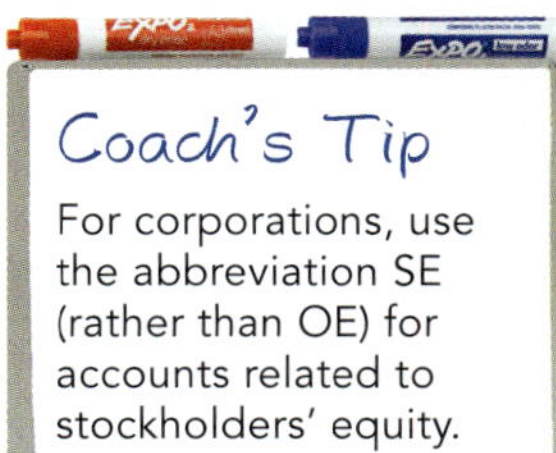

Coach's Tip
For corporations, use the abbreviation SE (rather than OE) for accounts related to stockholders' equity.

	Debit	Credit
Cash (+A) (100,000 × $30)	3,000,000	
Common Stock (+SE) (100,000 × $0.01)		1,000
Additional Paid-In Capital (+SE) ($3,000,000 − $1,000)		2,999,000

Assets		=	Liabilities	+	Stockholders' Equity	
Cash	+3,000,000				Common Stock	+1,000
					Additional Paid-In Capital	+2,999,000

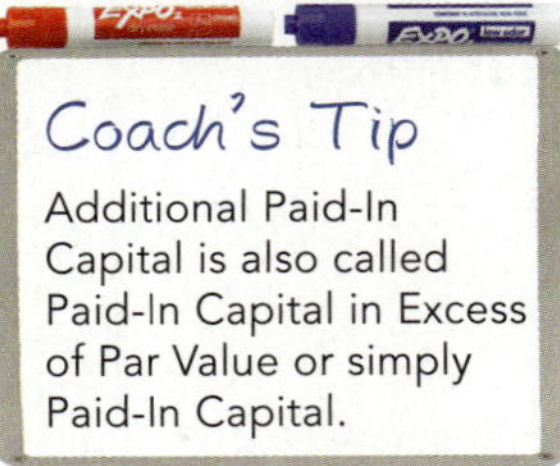

Additional Paid-In Capital is also called Paid-In Capital in Excess of Par Value or simply Paid-In Capital.

Notice that the account Common Stock is used to indicate the type of stock issued. The increase in the Common Stock account is the number of shares sold times the par value per share (100,000 × \$0.01). Any amount received in excess of the par value is recorded in a separate account appropriately named Additional Paid-In Capital. These two accounts are reported in the Stockholders' Equity section of the balance sheet; together, they represent Contributed Capital.

No-Par Value Common Stock Issued for Cash. If the corporate charter does not specify a par value for the stock, the total cash received from the sale of stock is entered in the Common Stock account. For example, if 100,000 shares of no-par common stock were issued for \$30 per share, the journal entry would be:

	Debit	Credit
Cash (+A) (100,000 × \$30)	3,000,000	
Common Stock (+SE) (100,000 × \$30)		3,000,000

Assets		=	Liabilities	+	Stockholders' Equity	
Cash	+3,000,000				Common Stock	+3,000,000

Common Stock Issued for Noncash Assets. In some cases, a corporation might receive items other than cash in exchange for its shares. This situation occurs most often when someone starts a private company and contributes land, buildings, or equipment to the corporation.

Noncash transactions such as this are accounted for using the value of the items contributed to or given up by the corporation, whichever is easier to determine. Typically, the value of a private company's stock is difficult to determine because it is bought and sold infrequently. So usually the transaction is recorded using the value of the items contributed to the corporation. For example, if equipment valued at \$50,000 were contributed to a private company in exchange for 10,000 common shares with a par value of \$0.01 per share, the transaction would be recorded as:

	Debit	Credit
Equipment (+A)	50,000	
Common Stock (+SE) (10,000 × \$0.01)		100
Additional Paid-In Capital (+SE) (\$50,000 − \$100)		49,900

Assets		=	Liabilities	+	Stockholders' Equity	
Equipment	+50,000				Common Stock	+100
					Additional Paid-In Capital	+49,900

Preferred Stock. Just like common stock, preferred stock may be designated par value or no-par value and may be issued for cash or noncash assets. If preferred stock specifies a par value, any contributions in excess of par value are recorded as "Additional Paid-In Capital (APIC)—Preferred" to distinguish it from Additional Paid-In Capital related to common stock. In all other respects, **preferred stock issues are accounted for in the same way as common stock issues.** To illustrate, if Sonic issued 10,000 shares of \$0.01 par value preferred stock for \$40 per share, the company records the following journal entry:

	Debit	Credit
Cash (+A) (10,000 × $40)	400,000	
Preferred Stock (+SE) (10,000 × $0.01)		100
Additional Paid-In Capital— Preferred (+SE) ($400,000 − $100)		399,900

Assets		=	Liabilities	+	Stockholders' Equity	
Cash	+400,000				Preferred Stock	+100
					APIC—Preferred	+399,900

Stock Sold between Investors. When a company issues stock to an investor, the transaction is between the issuing corporation and the investor so it is recorded by the corporation. After the initial sale, investors can sell shares to other investors without directly affecting the corporation or its accounting records.

Assume, for example, that investor Aaron Cadieux sold 1,000 shares of Sonic stock to Tara Rink. Aaron received cash for the shares he sold, and Tara received shares for the cash she paid, but Sonic did not receive or pay anything. Following the separate entity assumption (see Chapter 1), Sonic would not record a journal entry on its books because the transaction involved only the stock's owners, not the corporation itself. (Think of an auto dealer who records the sale of a car to a customer but does nothing when the customer later sells the car to someone else.)

Stock Used to Compensate Employees. To encourage employees to work hard, many corporations offer a combination of base pay, cash bonuses, and stock options. Stock options allow employees to buy company stock at a predetermined price during a specified period. The idea is that if employees work hard to meet the company's goals, the stock price is likely to increase. If it increases before the options expire, employees can exercise their right to buy stock at the lower price and then sell it at the higher market price for an immediate profit. If the stock price declines, employees have not lost anything. Accounting rules require that when granting stock options, a company must report an expense for the estimated cost associated with stock options. The procedures for doing so are complex, so they are discussed in intermediate accounting courses.

Spotlight On ETHICS

Stock Options Motivate, but at Whose Expense?

Some critics claim that stock options, which are intended to give senior executives of a company the same goals as stockholders, are often granted at the expense of existing stockholders. When senior executives exercise their stock options to buy new stock, existing stockholders lose voting power because their percentage of ownership in the company is diluted. Furthermore, critics contend that stock options encourage senior executives to overstate financial results in an attempt to increase the company's stock price so they can reap huge personal gains.

Treasury Stock

Although corporations are never obligated to buy back their own stock, some companies find it desirable to do so. A corporation may repurchase its own stock (1) to signal to investors that the company believes its stock is worth purchasing, (2) to obtain shares that can be reissued as payment for purchases of other companies, or (3) to obtain shares to reissue to employees as part of stock option plans. When a corporation buys its own stock back from stockholders, the stock is called **treasury stock**. While the corporation holds these shares, they do not offer voting, dividend, or other stockholder rights.

Acquisition of Treasury Stock

Most companies record the purchase of treasury stock based on the cost of the shares that are purchased. This approach is called the cost method. If a company bought 50,000 shares of its common stock at a market price of $25 per share, the total cost of $1,250,000 (= 50,000 shares × $25) would be recorded as follows:

	Debit	Credit
Treasury Stock (+xSE, −SE)	1,250,000	
Cash (−A)		1,250,000

Assets		=	Liabilities	+	Stockholders' Equity	
Cash	−1,250,000				Treasury Stock (+xSE)	−1,250,000

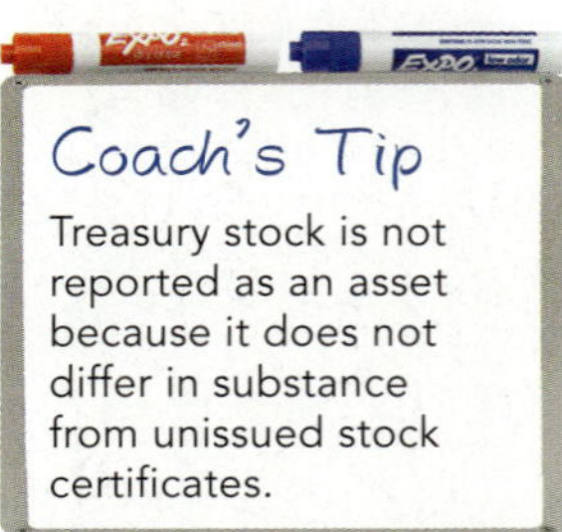

Coach's Tip

Treasury stock is not reported as an asset because it does not differ in substance from unissued stock certificates.

Treasury stock is recorded in a contra stockholders' equity account, which we indicate using the abbreviation xSE. Treasury Stock is subtracted from total stockholders' equity on the balance sheet as shown in the example in Exhibit 13.4.

Reissue of Treasury Stock

When a corporation reissues shares of treasury stock, the company receives cash. The amount of cash received may be more or less than the amount the company initially paid to acquire it, depending on the market price for the stock. The accounting effects depend on whether treasury stock is reissued above or below its initial cost.

Reissue above Cost. To illustrate this case, we extend the example in which the treasury stock was acquired at a cost of $25 per share. If the company resold 5,000 shares of the

Exhibit 13.4 Excerpt from Sonic Corp.'s Balance Sheet — SONIC DRIVE-IN

Sonic Corp.
Partial Balance Sheet
November 30, 2006
(dollars in thousands)

STOCKHOLDERS' EQUITY	
Contributed Capital	
Common Stock, Par Value $0.01 per share	
Authorized: 245,000,000 Shares	
Issued: 115,183,800 Shares	$ 1,152
Additional Paid-In Capital	178,115
Preferred Stock, Par Value $0.01 per share; none outstanding	—
Retained Earnings	491,980
Other	(4,035)
	667,212
Treasury Stock, at cost 47,171,602 Common Shares	(666,584)
Total Stockholders' Equity	$ 628

treasury stock for $27 per share, the required journal entry is:

	Debit	Credit
Cash (+A) (5,000 × $27)	135,000	
Treasury Stock (−xSE, +SE) (5,000 × $25)		125,000
Additional Paid-In Capital—Treasury (+SE) [5,000 × ($27 − $25)]		10,000

Assets		=	Liabilities	+	Stockholders' Equity	
Cash	+135,000				Treasury Stock (−xSE)	+125,000
					APIC—Treasury	+10,000

Reissue below Cost. Assume the company resold 5,000 shares of treasury stock for $24 per share. Again, the company initially paid $25 per share to repurchase the stock. In this case, the required journal entry is:

	Debit	Credit
Cash (+A) (5,000 × $24)	120,000	
Additional Paid-In Capital—Treasury (−SE) [5,000 × ($25 − $24)]	5,000	
Treasury Stock (−xSE, +SE) (5,000 × $25)		125,000

Assets		=	Liabilities	+	Stockholders' Equity	
Cash	+120,000				Treasury Stock (−xSE)	+125,000
					APIC—Treasury	−5,000

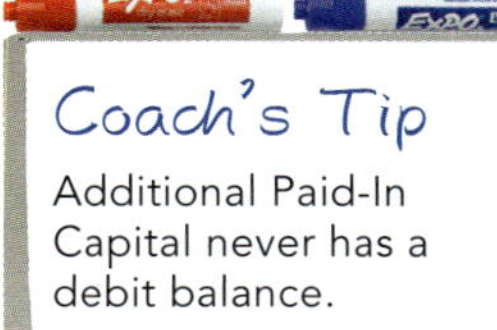

If a company fully depletes its balance in Additional Paid-In Capital—Treasury, any excess should be debited to Retained Earnings.

Financial Statement Reporting

In addition to reporting the dollar amounts for common stock, preferred stock, and treasury stock, corporations must disclose the number of shares related to those amounts. Most companies report this information on the balance sheet, as in Exhibit 13.4. Note in the exhibit that the **authorized** number of shares was 245 million common shares, but only 115,183,800 common shares had actually been **issued**. Unless the company buys them back, these shares will be owned forever by one investor or another. As you can see in the next-to-last line of Exhibit 13.4, Sonic held 47,171,602 shares of treasury stock that had been repurchased from the previously issued common shares.

Shares that have been issued but the corporation has not bought back are called **outstanding shares**. Based on Exhibit 13.4, you should be able to compute the number of Sonic shares still outstanding. As Exhibit 13.5 shows, of the 115,183,800 common shares issued, 47,171,602

Exhibit 13.5 Authorized, Issued, Outstanding, and Treasury Stock

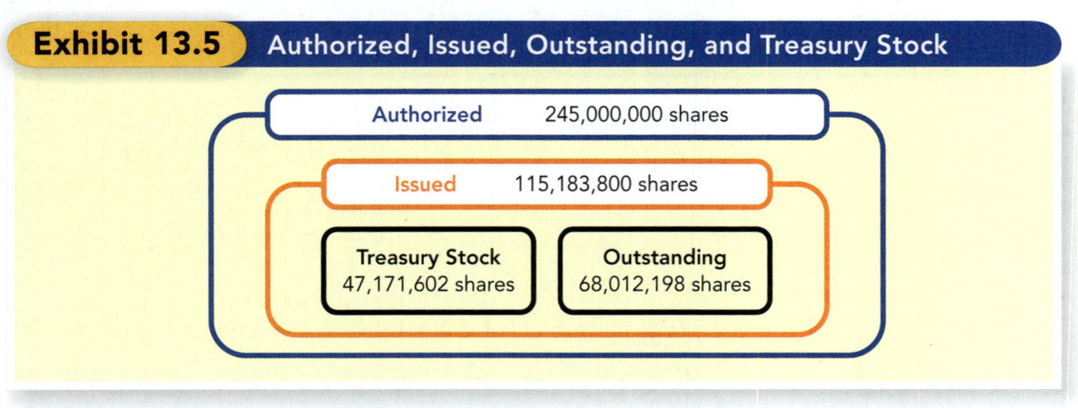

were repurchased, which means that 68,012,198 (= 115,183,800 − 47,171,602) were still outstanding. This number is important to financial analysts who need to express certain dollar amounts on a per share basis. Earnings per share (EPS)—a key financial ratio discussed later in this chapter—is expressed in terms of the number of outstanding shares.

SELF-STUDY PRACTICE

1. Assume that Aéropostale, Inc. issued 1,000 shares of its common stock, par value $0.01, for $21,900. Show the journal entry to record this transaction.

	Debit	Credit

2. Assume that Aéropostale, Inc. repurchased 500 of its common shares when the stock was selling for $20 per share. Show the journal entry to record this transaction at cost.

	Debit	Credit

3. Assume that Aéropostale, Inc. reissued 100 shares of its treasury stock at a market value of $25 per share. Show the journal entry to record this transaction.

	Debit	Credit

After you have finished, check your answers with the solution at the bottom of the page.

Learning Objective 3

Demonstrate how to account for cash dividends, stock dividends, and stock splits.

ACCOUNTING FOR DIVIDENDS AND SPLITS

Cash Dividends on Common Stock

Investors buy common stock because they expect a return on their investment. That return can come in two forms: dividends and increases in the stock price. Some investors prefer to buy stocks that pay little or no dividends (called "growth stocks") because companies that reinvest most of their earnings tend to increase their future earnings potential as well as their

Solution to Self-Study Practice

1.

	Debit	Credit
Cash (+A)	21,900	
Common Stock (+SE) (1,000 × $0.01)		10
Additional Paid-In Capital (+SE)		21,890

2.

	Debit	Credit
Treasury Stock (+xSE, −SE)	10,000	
Cash (−A) ($20 × 500)		10,000

3.

	Debit	Credit
Cash (+A) ($25 × 100)	2,500	
Treasury Stock (−xSE, +SE)		2,000
Additional Paid-In Capital—Treasury (+SE)		500

$2,000 = 100 shares × $20
$ 500 = 100 shares × ($25 − $20)

stock prices. Dell Corporation, for example, has never paid a dividend, yet if you had bought 100 shares in Dell when they were first issued on June 22, 1988, for $850, your investment would have been worth about $200,000 when this chapter was written. Other investors, such as retired people who need a steady income, prefer to receive their return in the form of dividends. These people often seek stocks that pay dividends consistently (called "income stocks"), such as Coca-Cola, which has paid cash dividends each year since 1893.

Video 13-2
www.mhhe.com/LLPW1e

A corporation does not have a legal obligation to pay dividends. The board of directors makes the decision each time a dividend is to be paid. Whenever the board of directors formally declares a dividend, a liability is created.

Dividend Dates

If Sonic were to declare a dividend, its press release would contain three important dates. In the following announcement, note the declaration date (May 20), the date of record (June 14), and the date of payment (July 1).

SONIC DRIVE-IN

Sonic Corp. Announces Cash Dividend

Oklahoma City, Okla., May 20, 2008—Sonic Corp. (Nasdaq: SONC) announced today that the Company's Board of Directors declared a cash dividend of $.02 per common share, payable on or about July 1, 2008 to stockholders of record as of June 14, 2008.

Declaration Date. The declaration date (in this case, May 20) is the date on which the board of directors officially approves the dividend. As soon as the board makes the declaration, the company records an increase in its liabilities and a corresponding decrease in Retained Earnings. **Dividends are distributions of a company's accumulated prior earnings,** so they are reported as a reduction in Retained Earnings on the balance sheet. **Dividends are not reported on the income statement because they are not expenses.**

With over 68 million common shares outstanding, the $0.02 dividend per share would equal $1,360,244 (= $0.02 × 68,012,198). The journal entry to record them is:

	Debit	Credit
Retained Earnings (−SE)	1,360,244	
Dividends Payable (+L)		1,360,244

Assets	=	Liabilities		+	Stockholders' Equity	
		Dividends Payable	+1,360,244		Retained Earnings	−1,360,244

Date of Record. The next date, the record date (here, June 14), is the date on which the corporation prepares the list of current stockholders based on its records. The dividend is payable only to those names listed on the record date. Sonic makes no journal entry on this date.

Date of Payment. The third date, the payment date (July 1 in this example), is the date on which Sonic disburses cash to pay the dividend liability. When the dividend is paid and the liability is satisfied on July 1, the journal entry is:

	Debit	Credit
Dividends Payable (−L)	1,360,244	
Cash (−A)		1,360,244

Assets		=	Liabilities		+	Stockholders' Equity
Cash	−1,360,244		Dividends Payable	−1,360,244		

Exhibit 13.6 Dividend Timeline: Declaration Date, Date of Record, and Date of Payment

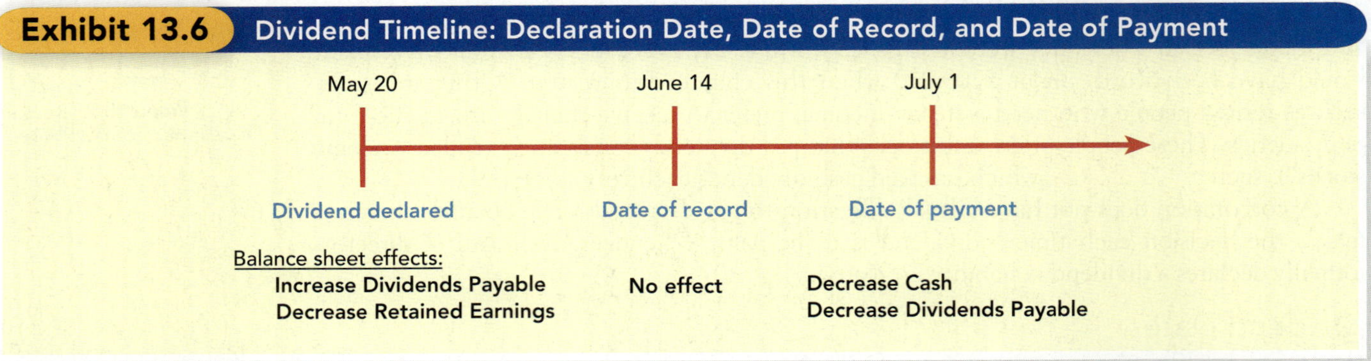

The timeline in Exhibit 13.6 summarizes these three dates and the corresponding balance sheet effects.

Dividend Requirements

Notice in Exhibit 13.6 that the declaration of a cash dividend decreases Retained Earnings. Notice too that payment of the cash dividend later reduces the Cash account by the same amount. These two observations explain the **two fundamental requirements for payment of a cash dividend:** sufficient retained earnings and sufficient cash.

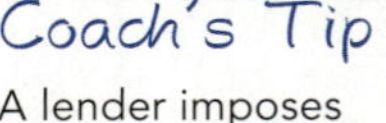

Coach's Tip

A lender imposes dividend restrictions because it does not want to lend money to a corporation and then have the corporation give it to stockholders via dividends rather than use it to grow the business.

Sufficient Retained Earnings. The corporation must have accumulated a sufficient amount of retained earnings to cover the amount of the dividend. State laws often restrict cash dividends to the balance in the Retained Earnings account. The company may be further restricted by clauses in loan agreements that require an even larger minimum balance in Retained Earnings. If the company were to violate such a clause, a lender could demand immediate repayment of outstanding loans. Because such a restriction can severely limit a company's ability to pay dividends, accounting rules require that companies disclose it in their notes to the financial statements.

Sufficient Cash. The corporation must have sufficient cash to pay the dividend. The company can use cash for a variety of purposes other than just paying dividends. Sonic may use cash to install new debit machines at its drive-ins or to pay down some of its debt. So in addition to considering the balance in Retained Earnings, corporations must ensure that they have sufficient cash available to pay any dividends that are declared.

SELF-STUDY PRACTICE

Answer the following questions concerning dividends:

1. On which dividend date is a liability created?
2. A cash outflow occurs on which dividend date?
3. What are the two fundamental requirements for paying a cash dividend?

After you have finished, check your answers with the solution at the bottom of the page.

Cash Dividends on Preferred Stock

Because purchasers of preferred stock give up the voting rights available to owners of common stock, preferred stock offers them dividend preferences in return. The two most common dividend preferences are called current and cumulative preferences.

Current Dividend Preference

A **current dividend preference** requires preferred dividends to be paid before paying any dividends to holders of common stock. This preference is a feature of all preferred stock. After

Solution to Self-Study Practice

1. Declaration date.
2. Date of payment.
3. Dividends can be paid only if both sufficient retained earnings and sufficient cash are available.

the current dividend preference has been met, and if no other preference exists, dividends may be paid to the common stockholders.

When a company declares dividends, the current preferred dividend preference must be met first; then any remaining declared dividends go to common stockholders. Consider the following example:

Checker Company

Preferred stock outstanding, 6%, par $20; 2,000 shares
Common stock outstanding, par $10; 5,000 shares

Assume the preferred stock carries only a current dividend preference and Checker declared dividends totaling $8,000 and $10,000 in 2009 and 2010, respectively. In each year, a portion of the total dividends would go first to the preferred stockholders; the remaining amount would go to the common stockholders, as follows.

Year	Total Dividends Declared	Dividends on 6% Preferred Stock*	Dividends on Common Stock†
2009	$ 8,000	$2,400	$5,600
2010	10,000	2,400	7,600

* Dividends on Preferred Stock = 2,000 Shares × $20 Par Value × 6% Dividend = $2,400
† Dividends on Common Stock = Total Dividends Declared − Dividends on Preferred Stock

If Checker Company did not declare dividends in 2009, preferred stockholders would have been entitled to dividends of $2,400 in 2010 only. The current dividend preference does not carry over to later years unless the preferred stock is designated as cumulative, as we discuss next.

Cumulative Dividend Preference

A **cumulative dividend preference** states that if a company does not pay all or part of the current dividend in full, the cumulative unpaid amount, known as **dividends in arrears**, must be paid in the future before any other dividends may be paid. To illustrate, assume Checker Company has the same amount of stock outstanding as in the previous example but dividends have been in arrears for two years. In this case, when Checker declares dividends in 2009, preferred stockholders first receive $4,800 for the dividends in arrears (2 years × $2,400) and then they receive $2,400 for the current year (2009). Any remaining dividend goes to common stockholders:

		DIVIDENDS ON 6% PREFERRED STOCK		
Year	Total Dividends Declared	In Arrears*	Current†	Dividends on Common Stock‡
2009	$ 8,000	$4,800	$2,400	$ 800
2010	10,000	—	2,400	7,600

* Dividends in Arrears Preference = 2,000 Shares × $20 Par Value × 6% Dividend × 2 Years = $4,800
† Current Dividend Preference = 2,000 Shares × $20 Par Value × 6% Dividend = $2,400
‡ Dividends on Common Stock = Total Dividends Declared − Total Dividends on Preferred Stock

Notice that after the dividends in arrears have been satisfied (in 2009), the dividend preference reverts back to just a current dividend preference (in 2010).

Spotlight On FINANCIAL REPORTING

Dividends in Arrears

American Skiing

Because dividends do not represent a liability until the board of directors declares them, dividends in arrears are not reported on the balance sheet. Instead, they are disclosed in the notes to the financial statements. The following note from American Skiing, a company that operates ski, snowboard, and golf resorts throughout the United States, is typical:

> Cumulative dividends in arrears totaled approximately $23.7 million and $109.3 million for the Series C-1 Preferred Stock and Series C-2 Preferred Stock, respectively.

Stock Dividends

The term dividend, when used alone with no adjectives, implies a cash dividend. However, some dividends are not paid in cash but in additional shares of stock. These dividends, called **stock dividends**, are distributed to a corporation's stockholders on a pro rata basis at no cost to the stockholder. The phrase "pro rata basis" means that each stockholder receives additional shares based on the percentage of shares held. A stockholder who owns 10 percent of the outstanding shares would receive 10 percent of any additional shares issued as a stock dividend.

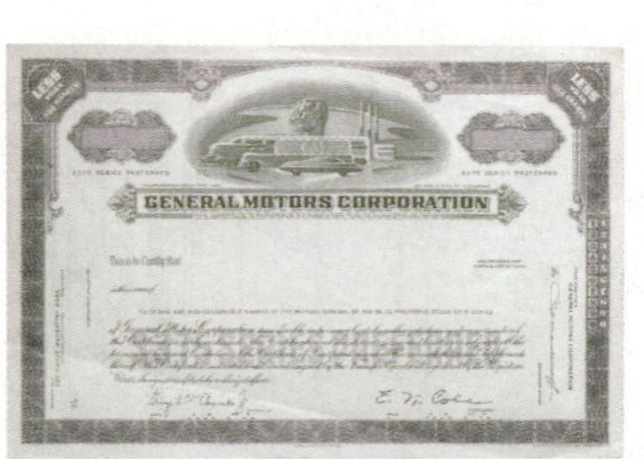

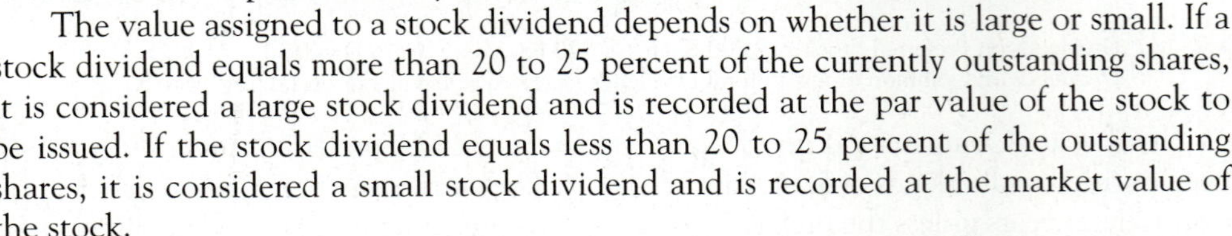

The value assigned to a stock dividend depends on whether it is large or small. If a stock dividend equals more than 20 to 25 percent of the currently outstanding shares, it is considered a large stock dividend and is recorded at the par value of the stock to be issued. If the stock dividend equals less than 20 to 25 percent of the outstanding shares, it is considered a small stock dividend and is recorded at the market value of the stock.

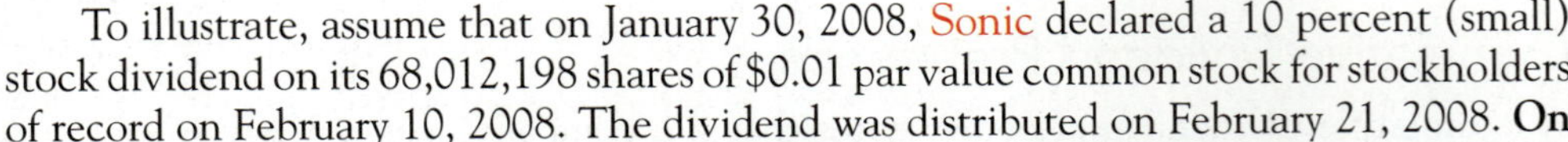

To illustrate, assume that on January 30, 2008, Sonic declared a 10 percent (small) stock dividend on its 68,012,198 shares of $0.01 par value common stock for stockholders of record on February 10, 2008. The dividend was distributed on February 21, 2008. **On the declaration date** (January 30), Sonic would record this small stock dividend at the shares' market value. Assuming that the stock price is $30 per share, the value of the dividend would be $204,036,594 (=$30 per share × 68,012,198 shares × 10% dividend). The par value of the stock to be issued would be $68,012 (=$0.01 per share × 68,012,198 shares × 10% dividend).

Until the stock is actually distributed, this amount would be recorded in the stockholders' equity account Common Stock Dividend Distributable. The difference between the total market value and the par value of the stock to be issued ($204,036,594 – $68,012 = $203,968,582) would be recorded as Additional Paid-In Capital, as follows:

	Debit	Credit
Retained Earnings (−SE)	204,036,594	
Common Stock Dividend Distributable (+SE)		68,012
Additional Paid-In Capital (+SE)		203,968,582

Assets	=	Liabilities	+	Stockholders' Equity	
				Retained Earnings	−204,036,594
				Common Stock Dividend Distributable	+68,012
				Additional Paid-In Capital	+203,968,582

Along with Common Stock, Additional Paid-In Capital, and Retained Earnings, Common Stock Dividend Distributable is reported in the Stockholders' Equity section of the balance sheet. It is not reported as a liability because assets will not be used to pay the dividend. Notice in the accounting equation effects shown that the stock dividend does not change total stockholders' equity. It changes only the balances in some of the accounts that make up stockholders' equity.

On the date of record (February 10), no journal entry would be made. **On the date of distribution** (February 21), the following journal entry would be made:

	Debit	Credit
Common Stock Dividend Distributable (−SE)	68,012	
Common Stock (+SE)		68,012

Assets	=	Liabilities	+	Stockholders' Equity	
				Common Stock	+68,012
				Common Stock Dividend Distributable	−68,012

Large stock dividends (greater than 20 to 25 percent of the outstanding shares) are accounted for in the same way as small stock dividends, except that they are recorded at the stock's par value rather than its market value. Consequently, the Additional Paid-In Capital account is not affected when a large stock dividend is declared.

Stock Splits

Stock splits are not dividends. They are similar to a stock dividend, but they are quite different in terms of how they occur and how they affect the stockholders' equity accounts. With a stock split, the corporation increases the total number of authorized shares by a specified amount, such as 2 for 1. In this example, the corporation calls in each share and issues two new shares in its place. At the same time, the par value of each share decreases, so the total par value of the shares remains unchanged. For example, if a company with 1 million shares outstanding of $0.01 par value stock executes a 2-for-1 stock split, it decreases the par value of its stock from $0.01 to $0.005 and doubles the number of shares outstanding. (Think of taking a four-piece pizza and cutting each piece into two halves.)

Because the decrease in par value per share offsets the increase in the number of shares, the company's financial position does not change, and **no journal entry is needed when stock is split.** Similarly, the market price of each share will decrease to offset the increase in the number of shares, so investors are no wealthier after the split than they were before.

	Before a 2-for-1 Stock Split	After a 2-for-1 Stock Split
Number of shares outstanding	1,000,000	2,000,000
Par value per share	$ 0.01	$ 0.005
Total par value outstanding	$ 10,000	$ 10,000

If you are like most new financial managers, you are probably wondering how a company's board of directors chooses between a 2-for-1 stock split and a "large" 100 percent stock dividend when both have the same effect—that of doubling the number of shares outstanding

Exhibit 13.7 Comparison of a 2-for 1 Stock Split, a 100 percent Stock Dividend, and a Cash Dividend

	BEFORE	AFTER		
Stockholders' Equity		2-for-1 Stock Split	100% Stock Dividend	$10,000 Cash Dividend
Contributed capital				
Number of common shares outstanding	1,000,000	2,000,000	2,000,000	1,000,000
Par value per common share	$ 0.01	$ 0.005	$ 0.01	$ 0.01
Common stock, at par	$ 10,000	$ 10,000	$ 20,000	$ 10,000
Additional paid-in capital	30,000	30,000	30,000	30,000
Retained earnings	650,000	650,000	640,000	640,000
Total stockholders' equity	$ 690,000	$ 690,000	$ 690,000	$ 680,000

and reducing the per share market price. The answer, it seems, is closely related to the method of accounting for stock dividends and splits. A stock dividend causes a reduction in Retained Earnings, whereas a stock split does not (see Exhibit 13.7).

By itself, this accounting difference might not mean much. Remember, though, that to declare a cash dividend, a company must maintain an adequate balance in Retained Earnings. If you are managing a company that you expect will struggle financially in the future, you will prefer a 2-for-1 stock split rather than a 100 percent stock dividend because the stock split does not reduce Retained Earnings, so it does not reduce your ability to declare cash dividends in the future. On the other hand, if you expect your company to be financially successful in the near future, you will not care that a stock dividend reduces Retained Earnings because future earnings will rebuild that account to allow cash dividends to be declared. In fact, you will probably **want** to declare a stock dividend to show how confident you are of your company's financial outlook. This reasoning suggests that **a company's board of directors may declare a stock dividend rather than a stock split to signal to financial statement users that the company expects to be sufficiently profitable to replenish the reduction in Retained Earnings caused by the stock dividend.**

SELF-STUDY PRACTICE

To reduce the market price of its stock, which was $50 per share, Vandalay Industries declared a 10 percent (small) stock dividend on its 1,000,000 outstanding shares of common stock (par value $10).

1. Prepare the journal entry that Vandalay would use to record this transaction.
2. What journal entry would be required if the transaction instead involved a 2-for-1 split? Theoretically, what would be the new stock price after the split?

After you have finished, check your answers with the solution at the bottom of the page.

Statement of Retained Earnings

Retained Earnings represents the total earnings retained in the company after distributing dividends to stockholders. You have already seen that whenever the corporation declares a cash dividend or stock dividend, the balance in Retained Earnings decreases. Its balance increases each year the company reports net income, as you will see next.

Solution to Self-Study Practice

1.

Retained Earnings (−SE)	5,000,000	
Common Stock Dividend Distributable (+SE)		1,000,000
Additional Paid-in Capital (+SE)		4,000,000

($5,000,000 = 1,000,000 × 10% × $50; $1,000,000 = 1,000,000 × 10% × $10)

2. No journal entry is required in the case of a stock split. Theoretically, the new price would be one-half of what it was before the split ($50 × ½ = $25).

Assume, for example, Sonic determined it had $78 million of net income after closing revenues and expenses to the Income Summary account. Sonic records the following journal entry to transfer that amount to Retained Earnings:

	Debit	Credit
Income Summary (−SE)	78,000,000	
Retained Earnings (+SE)		78,000,000

Assets	=	Liabilities	+	Stockholders' Equity	
				Income Summary	−78,000,000
				Retained Earnings	+78,000,000

To report the causes of increases and decreases in Retained Earnings, a Statement of Retained Earnings is prepared each accounting period.[1] (This report replaces the Statement of Owner's Equity that is prepared for sole proprietorships.) Exhibit 13.8 shows an example of this statement for Sonic, assuming a net income of $78 million, cash dividends on common stock of $1,360,244, stock dividends on common stock of $204,036,594, no cash dividends or stock dividends on preferred stock, and a beginning balance in Retained Earnings of $476 million.

Exhibit 13.8 Statement of Retained Earnings — SONIC DRIVE-IN

Sonic Corp.
Statement of Retained Earnings
For the Year Ended August 31, 2010
(in thousands of dollars)

Retained Earnings, August 31, 2009	$476,000
Net Income	78,000
Cash Dividends on Common Stock	(1,360)
Stock Dividends on Common Stock	(204,037)
Retained Earnings, August 31, 2010	$348,603

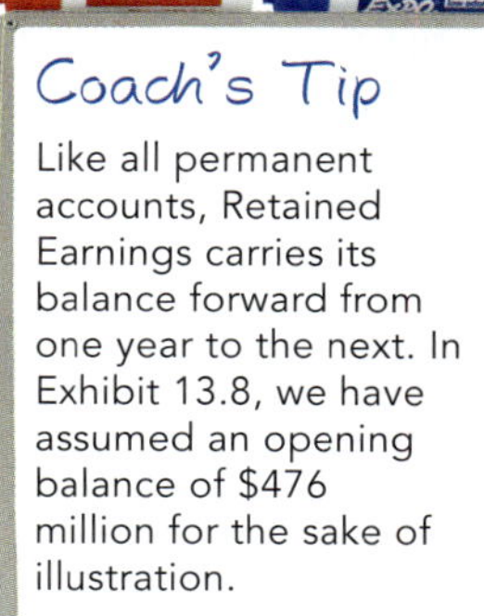

Coach's Tip

Like all permanent accounts, Retained Earnings carries its balance forward from one year to the next. In Exhibit 13.8, we have assumed an opening balance of $476 million for the sake of illustration.

FINANCIAL RATIO ANALYSIS

You have seen how, on the inside, a corporation accounts for stockholders' equity transactions. Now it is time to consider two ratios that outsiders use to evaluate how well a company has used its capital to generate returns for the company and its stockholders.

Financial Analysis Tools

Name of Measure	Formula	What It Tells You
Earnings per share (EPS)	$\frac{\text{Net Income} - \text{Preferred Dividends}}{\text{Average Number of Common Shares Outstanding}}$	• The amount of income generated for each share of common stock owned by stockholders • The higher the number, the greater the profitability
Price/Earnings (P/E) ratio	$\frac{\text{Current Stock Price (per share)}}{\text{Earnings per Share (annual)}}$	• How many times more than the current year's earnings investors are willing to pay for a company's stock • The higher the number, the more investors anticipate an improvement in the company's future results

[1] A more comprehensive Statement of Stockholders' Equity may be presented instead of the Statement of Retained Earnings. A Statement of Stockholders' Equity shows the causes of increases and decreases in each stockholders' equity account, not just Retained Earnings. Preparing this statement is beyond the scope of this course.

Learning Objective 4

Analyze the earnings per share (EPS) and price/earnings (P/E) ratios.

Earnings Per Share (EPS)

The most famous of all financial ratios, earnings per share (EPS), reports how much profit is earned for each share of common stock outstanding. The calculation of EPS can involve many details and intricacies that are appropriately discussed in detail in intermediate accounting courses. In its basic form, EPS is computed by dividing net income by the average number of common shares outstanding. (If the company has declared dividends on preferred stock, they are first subtracted from net income.) Most companies report EPS on the income statement immediately below Net Income or in the notes to the financial statements.

You may be wondering why earnings per share is such a popular measure when dividends and stock prices ultimately determine the return to stockholders. The reason is that current earnings can predict future dividends and stock prices. If a company generates increased earnings in the current year, it will be able to pay higher dividends in future years. In other words, current EPS influences expectations about future dividends, which investors factor into the current stock price. That explains why Sonic Corp.'s stock price increased nearly 4 percent on January 4, 2008, immediately after the company announced that its EPS for the quarter was higher than in the preceding year.

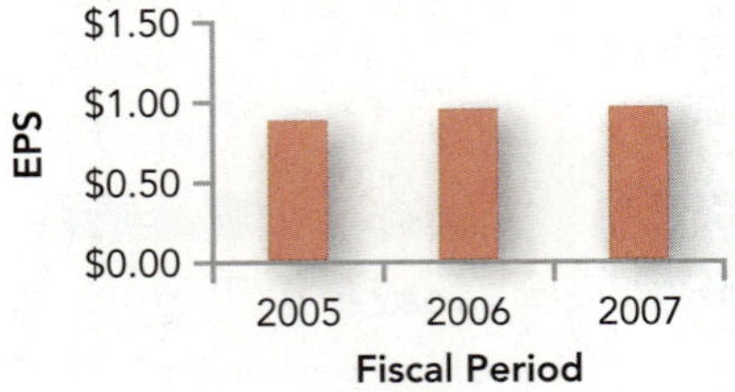

Another reason that EPS is such a popular measure is that it allows investors to make quick comparisons over time. Net income stated in dollars is more difficult to interpret. For example, in fiscal year 2007, Sonic earned a net income of $64 million compared to $78 million in the preceding year. It is hard to know whether that decrease was bad for stockholders because the decrease in Sonic's net income may have been accompanied by a decrease in the number of shares outstanding. By converting earnings to a per share basis, we adjust for the effect of any repurchased stock which gives a clearer picture of what decreased earnings might mean for each investor. As you can see from the accompanying graph, the decrease in net income in 2007 actually translated into higher EPS, from $0.91 to $0.94 per share, because fewer shares were outstanding.

Exhibit 13.9 shows how to calculate EPS for Sonic and a much larger fast food competitor, McDonald's Corporation. We should caution you to resist the temptation of comparing different companies' EPS ratios. The number of shares outstanding for one company can differ dramatically from the number of shares outstanding for a different company simply because

Exhibit 13.9 Earnings per Share (EPS) and Price/Earnings (P/E) Ratios

Company	Relevant Information (in millions)			2007 EPS	2007 P/E
Sonic America's Drive-In		2007	2006		
	Net income	$64.2	$78.7		
	Preferred dividends	0.0	0.0	$\frac{\$64.2-0}{68.3}$	$\frac{\$24.59}{\$0.94}$
	Average number of shares	68.3	86.5	=$0.94	=26.2
	Stock price	$24.59	$22.65		
McDonald's		2007	2006		
	Net income	$2,395.1	$3,544.2		
	Preferred dividends	0.0	0.0	$\frac{\$2,395.1-0}{1,188.3}$	$\frac{\$56.00}{\$2.02}$
	Average number of shares	1,188.3	1,234.0	=$2.02	=27.7
	Stock price	$56.00	$46.00		

one chooses to issue or repurchase more shares than the other. Also, as you have seen in earlier chapters, net income can be affected by more than just operating performance. Accounting differences in assigning inventory costs (Chapter 7), estimating bad debts (Chapter 9) and contingent liabilities (Chapter 11), and depreciating long-lived assets (Chapter 10) can reduce its comparability between companies. So while the EPS ratio is a useful measure for evaluating one company's performance over time, it is not appropriate for cross-company comparisons.

Price/Earnings (P/E) Ratio

The EPS ratio is useful for evaluating a company's ability to generate profits for stockholders, but it does not help investors determine a reasonable price for a company's stock. Advanced finance courses teach sophisticated techniques for valuing a company, but you will likely find it helpful to start with a much simpler tool. The price/earnings (P/E) ratio is the most basic way of determining the value investors place on a company's common stock. This ratio measures how many times more than the current year's earnings investors are willing to pay for a company's stock. The more they value the company, the more they will pay for its stock relative to the earnings the company generated. The P/E ratio is calculated by dividing a company's stock price by its earnings per share for the year (see Exhibit 13.9).

Generally, a relatively high P/E ratio means that investors expect the company to increase its profits in the future and they have factored those future earnings into the current stock price. A relatively low P/E ratio typically means that investors do not expect strong performance in the future. Because P/E ratios can vary significantly across industries, they are most meaningful when used to compare a company's performance over time or to compare competitors in the same industry. In 2007, Sonic's P/E ratio of 26.2 was similar to both McDonald's P/E ratio (27.7) and the overall industry average (24.6 according to Yahoo!Finance), suggesting that investors anticipated that Sonic would be at least as successful as other fast food restaurants.

SELF-STUDY PRACTICE

1. Use the information in Exhibit 13.9 to calculate Sonic's earnings per share (EPS) and price/earnings (P/E) ratio for 2006.

2006 EPS	2006 P/E
____ / ____	____ / ____

2. Did Sonic's EPS improve or decline from 2006 (calculated in part 1) to 2007 (shown in Exhibit 13.9)? Does Sonic's 2006 P/E ratio suggest that investors anticipated the changes that occurred in 2007? As a point of reference, the average P/E ratio for the industry was 19.5 in 2006.

After you have finished, check your answers with the solution at the bottom of the page.

Demonstration Case A

Stock Issue, Repurchase, and Financial Statement Reporting

This case focuses on selected transactions from the first year of operations of Zoogle Corporation, a lost-pet search business that became a public company on January 1, 2009. Zoogle's charter authorized it to issue the following:

Common stock, $0.10 par value; 20,000 shares.

Preferred stock, 5 percent cumulative, $100 par value; 5,000 shares.

Solution to Self-Study Practice

1. EPS: $78.7 / 86.5 = $0.91
   P/E: $22.65 / $0.91 = 24.9

2. Sonic's EPS improved, increasing from $0.91 in 2006 to $0.94 in 2007. Investors appeared to anticipate the improved performance because they were willing to pay 24.9 times earnings to buy a share of Sonic in 2006 when they were willing to pay only 19.5 times earnings for other companies in the industry.

The following transactions, selected from 2009, were completed on the dates indicated:

(*a*) Jan. 1 Issued a total of 8,000 shares of $0.10 par value common stock for cash at $50 per share.

(*b*) Feb. 1 Sold 2,000 shares of preferred stock at $100 per share; cash collected in full.

(*c*) July 1 Purchased 400 shares of common stock that had been issued earlier. Zoogle paid the stockholders $54 per share for the stock and currently holds the shares in treasury.

(*d*) Aug. 1 Sold 30 shares of the common treasury stock at $56 per share.

(*e*) Dec. 31 The board decided not to declare any dividends for the current year.

Required:

1. Give the appropriate journal entries; show your calculations for each transaction.
2. Prepare the Stockholders' Equity section of the balance sheet for Zoogle Corporation on December 31, 2009. Assume that the Retained Earnings account on that date totaled $31,000.

Suggested Solution

1. Journal entries:

			Debit	Credit
(*a*)	Jan. 1, 2009	Cash (+A) ($50 × 8,000 shares)	400,000	
		Common Stock (+SE) ($0.10 × 8,000 shares)		800
		Additional Paid-In Capital—Common (+SE)		399,200
(*b*)	Feb. 1, 2009	Cash (+A) ($100 × 2,000 shares)	200,000	
		Preferred Stock (+SE) ($100 par × 2,000 shares)		200,000
(*c*)	July 1, 2009	Treasury Stock (+xSE, −SE)	21,600	
		Cash (−A) (400 shares × $54)		21,600
(*d*)	Aug. 1, 2009	Cash (+A) (30 × $56)	1,680	
		Treasury Stock (−xSE, +SE) (30 shares × $54)		1,620
		Additional Paid-In Capital—Treasury (+SE) ($1,680 − $1,620)		60
(*e*)	Dec. 31, 2009	No journal entry is required. Dividends in arrears from the current year (2,000 shares × $100 × 5% = $10,000) would be reported in the notes to Zoogle's financial statements.		

2. Stockholders' equity section of the balance sheet:

Zoogle Corporation
Partial Balance Sheet
At December 31, 2009

Stockholders' Equity	
Contributed capital	
Common stock ($0.10 par value; authorized 20,000 shares, issued 8,000 shares of which 370 shares are held as treasury stock)	$ 800
Additional paid-in capital, common stock	399,200
Additional paid-in capital, treasury stock	60
Preferred stock, 5% cumulative (par value $100; 5,000 authorized shares, 2,000 issued and outstanding shares)	200,000
Total contributed capital	$600,060
Retained earnings	31,000
Treasury stock, at cost, 370 common shares	(19,980)
Total stockholders' equity	$611,080

Demonstration Case B

Dividends, Stock Split, and Retained Earnings

This case extends Demonstration Case A by focusing on dividends and other stock transactions that occurred during Zoogle Corporation's second year. The following transactions selected from 2010 were completed on the dates indicated:

(*a*) Nov. 1 The board declared a cash dividend on the preferred stock for the current year as well as payment of the prior year's dividends in arrears, payable on November 22 to stockholders of record as of November 15.

(*b*) Dec. 1 The board declared a 10 percent stock dividend on the outstanding common stock, distributable on December 18 to shareholders of record as of December 16. The stock price was $60 per share.

(*c*) Dec. 21 Zoogle Corporation completed a 2-for-1 stock split on its common stock.

(*d*) Dec. 31 The $50,000 balance in the Income Summary account was closed to Retained Earnings.

Required:

1. Give the appropriate journal entries; show your calculations for each transaction.
2. Prepare a Statement of Retained Earnings for the year ended December 31, 2010.

Suggested Solution

1.

			Debit	Credit
(*a*)	Nov. 1, 2010	Retained Earnings (−SE)	20,000	
		Dividends Payable (+L)		20,000
		(2,000 preferred shares × $100 par × 5% dividend rate × 2 years)		
	Nov. 15, 2010	No journal entry is required on the date of record.		
	Nov. 22, 2010	Dividends Payable (−L)	20,000	
		Cash (−A)		20,000
(*b*)	Dec. 1, 2010	Retained Earnings (−SE)	45,780	
		Common Stock Dividend Distributable (+SE)		76
		Additional Paid-In Capital (+SE)		45,704
		$45,780 = (8,000 common shares issued − 370 in treasury) × 10% × $60		
		$76 = (8,000 common shares issued − 370 in treasury) × 10% × $0.10		
		$45,704 = $45,780 − $76		
	Dec. 16, 2010	No journal entry is required on the date of record.		
	Dec. 18, 2010	Common Stock Dividend Distributable (−SE)	8	
		Common Stock (+SE)		8
(*c*)	Dec. 21, 2010	No journal entry is required to record a stock split.		
(*d*)	Dec. 31, 2010	Income Summary (−SE)	50,000	
		Retained Earnings (+SE)		50,000

2.

Zoogle Corporation
Statement of Retained Earnings
For the Year Ended December 31, 2010

Retained earnings, December 31, 2009	$31,000
Net income	50,000
Cash dividends on preferred stock	(20,000)
Stock dividends on common stock	(45,780)
Retained earnings, December 31, 2010	$15,220

Chapter Summary

LO1 Describe the characteristics of corporations. p. 560

- The law recognizes corporations as separate legal entities. Owners invest in a corporation and receive capital stock that can be bought from and sold to other investors.
- Common stock provides a number of rights, including the rights to vote, to receive dividends, to share in the corporation's residual assets at liquidation, and to preempt others from purchasing newly issued stock.
- Preferred stock gives investors certain advantages, including current dividend preferences and preference in asset distributions if the corporation is liquidated. If preferred stock carries cumulative dividend rights, any part of a current dividend that is not paid (dividends in arrears) must be paid in full before any additional dividends can be paid.

LO2 Demonstrate how to account for transactions involving common stock, preferred stock, and treasury stock. p. 562

- All transactions involving common stock, preferred stock, and treasury stock affect only the balance sheet. Corporations do not report income from gains or losses on transactions involving their own stock.
- If a stock specifies a par value, any amounts received in excess of par value are recorded in the stockholders' equity account Additional Paid-In Capital.
- If the corporation repurchases a stock, it is called treasury stock. The cost method records treasury stock at the cost to reacquire it in a contra-account that is subtracted from the Stockholders' Equity section on the balance sheet. If treasury stock is reissued, the treasury stock account is decreased by the cost of the treasury stock, and any excess amount received on reissue is recorded as Additional Paid-In Capital—Treasury.

LO3 Demonstrate how to account for cash dividends, stock dividends, and stock splits. p. 568

- Cash dividends reduce stockholders' equity (Retained Earnings) and create a liability (Dividends Payable) when the board of directors declares them. The liability is reduced when the dividends are paid.
- Stock dividends are pro rata distributions of a company's stock to existing owners. If the stock dividend is a small proportion of the outstanding stock, the transaction is accounted for by reducing Retained Earnings by the market value of the distributed stock, increasing Common Stock by the par value of the distributed stock, and increasing Additional Paid-In Capital for the excess of market value over par value. If the stock dividend is large (more than 20 to 25 percent), it is recorded at the par value of the stock.
- A stock split also involves the distribution of additional shares to owners, but no additional amount is transferred to Common Stock. Instead, the per share par value of the stock is reduced.

LO4 Analyze the earnings per share (EPS) and price/earnings (P/E) ratios. p. 576

- The earnings per share (EPS) ratio is calculated by dividing net income (less any dividends on preferred stock) by the average number of shares of common stock outstanding during the year. This ratio is helpful in comparing a corporation's earnings over time. It does not allow reliable comparisons across companies because it does not adjust for likely differences in the number of outstanding shares in each company and in the accounting methods used by each company.
- The price-earnings (P/E) ratio relates the corporation's current stock price to its most recent annual earnings per share. It indicates the value that investors place on the company's stock.

Financial Analysis Tools

Name of Measure	Formula	What It Tells You
Earnings per share (EPS)	$\frac{\text{Net Income} - \text{Preferred Dividends}}{\text{Average Number of Common Shares Outstanding}}$	• The amount of income generated for each share of common stock owned by stockholders • The higher the number, the greater the profitability
Price/Earnings (P/E) ratio	$\frac{\text{Current Stock Price (per share)}}{\text{Earnings per Share (annual)}}$	• How many times more than the current year's earnings investors are willing to pay for a company's stock • The higher the number, the more investors anticipate an improvement in the company's future results

Key Terms

Authorized Shares (p. 567)
Common Stock (p. 561)
Contributed Capital (p. 562)
Cumulative Dividend Preference (p. 571)
Current Dividend Preference (p. 570)
Declaration Date (p. 569)
Dividends in Arrears (p. 571)
Issued Shares (p. 567)
No-Par Value Stock (p. 563)

Outstanding Shares (p. 567)
Par Value (p. 563)
Payment Date (p. 569)
Preferred Stock (p. 561)
Private Companies (p. 560)
Public Companies (p. 560)
Record Date (p. 569)
Retained Earnings (p. 563)
Stock Dividend (p. 572)
Stockholders (p. 560)
Stockholders' Equity (p. 562)
Stock Split (p. 573)
Treasury Stock (p. 565)

See complete glossary in the back of text.

Questions

1. Identify the primary advantages of the corporate form of business.
2. What four benefits do owners of common stock usually enjoy?
3. What are the differences between common stock and preferred stock?
4. What are the usual characteristics of preferred stock?
5. What are the relative advantages of equity versus debt financing?
6. In what ways does owner's equity differ for proprietorships and for corporations?
7. Explain each of the following terms: (*a*) authorized common stock, (*b*) issued common stock, and (*c*) outstanding common stock.
8. What is the distinction between par value and no-par value capital stock?
9. What is treasury stock? Why do corporations acquire treasury stock?
10. How is treasury stock reported on the balance sheet? How do the financial statements report the "gain or loss" on treasury stock reissued above or below cost?
11. What three dates are significant for dividends? What changes are made to the financial statement accounts on each of these three dates?
12. What are the two basic requirements to support the declaration of a cash dividend? What are the effects of a cash dividend on assets and stockholders' equity?
13. What is unique about cumulative preferred stock?
14. What is a stock dividend? How does a stock dividend differ from a cash dividend?
15. Why might a corporation's board declare a stock dividend rather than a stock split?
16. Why is the EPS number so popular? What are its limitations?
17. How do stock repurchases affect the EPS ratio?
18. Generally speaking, what does a high P/E ratio suggest?

Multiple Choice

Quiz 13-1
www.mhhe.com/LLPW1e

1. Which feature is not applicable to common stock ownership?
   a. Right to receive dividends before preferred stock shareholders.
   b. Right to vote on appointment of external auditor.
   c. Right to receive residual assets of the company should it cease operations.
   d. None of the above (all are applicable to common stock ownership).
2. Which statement regarding treasury stock is false?
   a. Treasury stock is considered to be issued but not outstanding.
   b. Treasury stock has no voting, dividend, or liquidation rights.
   c. Treasury stock reduces total stockholders' equity on the balance sheet.
   d. None of the above.
3. Which of the following statements about stock dividends is true?
   a. Stock dividends are reported on the income statement.
   b. Stock dividends increase total stockholders' equity.
   c. Stock dividends decrease total stockholders' equity.
   d. None of the above.
4. Which of the following is ordered from the largest number of shares to the smallest number of shares?
   a. Shares authorized, shares issued, shares outstanding.
   b. Shares issued, shares outstanding, shares authorized.
   c. Shares outstanding, shares issued, shares authorized.
   d. Shares in treasury, shares outstanding, shares issued.
5. Which of the following statements about the relative advantages of equity and debt financing is false?
   a. An advantage of equity financing is that it does not have to be repaid.
   b. An advantage of equity financing is that dividends are optional.
   c. An advantage of equity financing is that new stockholders get to vote and share in the earnings of the company.
   d. An advantage of debt financing is that interest is tax deductible.
6. A journal entry is not recorded on what date?
   a. Date of declaration.
   b. Date of record.
   c. Date of payment.
   d. None of the above. (A journal entry is recorded on all of the above dates.)
7. Which of the following transactions will increase the return on equity?
   a. Declare and issue a stock dividend.
   b. Split the stock 2-for-1.
   c. Repurchase the company's stock.
   d. None of the above.

8. Which statement regarding dividends is false?
   a. Dividends represent a sharing of corporate profits with owners.
   b. Both stock and cash dividends reduce retained earnings.
   c. Cash dividends paid to stockholders reduce net income.
   d. None of the above.
9. When treasury stock is purchased with cash, what is the impact on the balance sheet equation?
   a. No change—the reduction of the asset Cash is offset with the addition of the asset Treasury Stock.
   b. Assets decrease and Stockholders' Equity increases.
   c. Assets increase and Stockholders' Equity decreases.
   d. Assets decrease and Stockholders' Equity decreases.
10. In what situation does an investor's personal wealth increase immediately?
   a. When receiving a cash dividend.
   b. When receiving a stock dividend.
   c. When a stock split is announced.
   d. In all of the above situations.

Solutions to Multiple-Choice Questions

1. a 2. d 3. d 4. a 5. c 6. b 7. c 8. c 9. d 10. a

Mini Exercises

Available with McGraw-Hill's Homework Manager

LO1

M13-1 Favoring Equity versus Debt Financing

Indicate whether each of the following favors the use of equity (E) or debt (D) financing.

____ 1. Interest is tax deductible.
____ 2. Dividends are optional.
____ 3. Debt must be repaid.
____ 4. Additional stock issuances dilute existing stockholders' control.

LO1

M13-2 Evaluating Stockholders' Rights

Name four rights of common stockholders. Which of these seems most important? Why?

LO2

M13-3 Computing the Number of Unissued Shares

The balance sheet for Crutcher Corporation reported 147,000 shares outstanding, 300,000 shares authorized, and 10,000 shares in treasury stock. Compute the maximum number of new shares that Crutcher could issue.

LO2

M13-4 Recording the Sale of Common Stock

To expand operations, Aragon Consulting issued 100,000 shares of previously unissued common stock with a par value of $1. The selling price for the stock was $75 per share. Record the journal entry for this sale of stock. Would your answer be different if the par value were $2 per share? If so, record the sale of stock with a par value of $2.

LO2

M13-5 Recording the Sale of Common Stock

Refer to M13-4. Assume the issued stock has no par value. Record the journal entry for the sale of no-par value stock at $75. Do the effects on total assets, total liabilities, and total stockholders' equity differ from those in M13-4?

LO2
Sonic Corporation

M13-6 Comparing Common Stock and Preferred Stock

Your parents have just retired and have asked you for some financial advice. They have decided to invest $100,000 in a company very similar to Sonic Corp. The company has issued both common and preferred stock. Which type of stock would you recommend? What factors would you consider in giving them advice?

LO2

M13-7 Determining the Effects of Treasury Stock Transactions

Trans Union Corporation sold 5,000 shares for $50 per share in 2007, and it sold 10,000 shares for $37 per share in 2008. In 2009, the company purchased 2,000 shares of its own stock for $45 per share. Determine the impact (increase, decrease, or no change) of each of these transactions on the following classifications:

1. Total assets.
2. Total liabilities.
3. Total stockholders' equity.
4. Net income.

M13-8 Comparing Stockholder's Equity to Owner's Equity LO2

On January 1, Daniel Harrison contributed $20,000 to start his business. At the end of that year, the business had generated $30,000 in sales revenues, incurred $18,000 in operating expenses, and distributed $5,000 for Daniel to use to pay some personal expenses. Prepare the section of the balance sheet showing (*a*) his stockholder's equity, assuming this is a corporation with no-par value stock or (*b*) his owner's equity, assuming this is a sole proprietorship.

M13-9 Determining the Amount of a Dividend LO3

Netpass Company has 300,000 shares of common stock authorized, 270,000 shares issued, and 50,000 shares of treasury stock. The company's board of directors declares a dividend of 50 cents per share on common stock. What is the total amount of the dividend that will be paid?

M13-10 Recording Dividends LO3

On April 15, 2009, the board of directors for Auction.com declared a cash dividend of 40 cents per share payable to stockholders of record on May 20. The dividends will be paid on June 14. The company has 500,000 shares of stock outstanding. Prepare any necessary journal entries for each date.

M13-11 Determining the Impact of a Stock Dividend LO3

Sturdy Stone Tools, Inc., announced a 100 percent stock dividend. Determine the impact (increase, decrease, no change) of this dividend on the following:

1. Total assets.
2. Total liabilities.
3. Common stock.
4. Total stockholders' equity.
5. Market value per share of common stock.

M13-12 Determining the Impact of a Stock Split LO3

Complete the requirements of M13-11 assuming that the company announced a 2-for-1 stock split.

M13-13 Recording a Small Stock Dividend LO3

Shriver Food Systems, Inc., declared a 10 percent stock dividend on May 1. The company has 800,000 shares authorized and 200,000 shares outstanding. The par value of the stock is $1 per share and the market value is $100 per share. The dividend was issued on May 21. Prepare the journal entries to record the declaration and issuance of this stock dividend.

M13-14 Recording a Large Stock Dividend LO3

Refer to M13-13. Assume the company declared and issued a 50 percent stock dividend on the dates indicated. Prepare the journal entries to record the declaration and issuance.

M13-15 Determining the Amount of a Preferred Dividend LO3

Colliers, Inc., has 100,000 shares of cumulative preferred stock outstanding. The preferred stock pays dividends in the amount of $2 per share but because of cash flow problems, the company did not pay any dividends last year. The board of directors plans to pay dividends in the amount of $1 million this year. What amount will go to preferred stockholders? How much will be available for common stock dividends?

M13-16 Calculating and Interpreting Earnings per Share (EPS) LO4

Academy Driving School reported the following amount in its financial statements:

	2010	2009
Number of common shares	11,500	11,500
Net income	$23,000	$18,000
Cash dividends paid on common stock	$ 3,000	$ 3,000

Calculate 2010 EPS. Another driving school in the same city reported a higher net income ($45,000) in 2010, yet its EPS ratio was lower than that for the Academy Driving School. Explain how this apparent inconsistency could occur.

LO4

M13-17 Determining the Impact of Transactions on Earnings per Share (EPS)
Identify and explain the direction of effect (+ for increase, − for decrease, or NE for no effect) of each of the following transactions on EPS.

a. Purchased 50 shares into treasury.
b. Declared and paid a cash dividend.
c. Declared and issued a stock dividend.
d. Sold inventory at an amount more than cost.
e. Sold and issued 6,000 shares of common stock for cash.

LO4

M13-18 Inferring Financial Information Using the P/E Ratio
In 2008, Rec Room Sports reported earnings per share of $8.50 when its stock was selling for $212.50. In 2009, its earnings increased by 20 percent. If all other relationships remain constant, what is the price of the stock in 2009? Explain.

Exercises  Available with McGraw-Hill's Homework Manager

LO2
Big Dog Holdings

E13-1 Computing Shares Outstanding
Big Dog Holdings reported that, as of September 30, 2007, 30 million shares of common stock had been authorized. As of that date, 11,182,808 shares had been issued and 1,710,598 shares were held as treasury stock.

Required:
Determine the number of shares outstanding on September 30, 2007.

LO2, 3

E13-2 Reporting Stockholders' Equity and Determining Dividend Policy
Incentive Corporation was organized as a corporation in 2008 to operate a financial consulting business. The charter authorized the following capital stock: common stock, par value $4 per share, 12,000 shares. During the first year, the following selected transactions were completed:

a. Sold and issued 6,000 shares of common stock for cash at $20 per share.
b. Sold and issued 2,000 shares of common stock for cash at $23 per share.

Required:

1. Give the journal entry required for each of these transactions.
2. At year-end, the Income Summary account reflected a profit of $10,000. Give the journal entry to close this account to Retained Earnings.
3. Prepare the Stockholders' Equity section as it should be reported on the 2008 year-end balance sheet.
4. Incentive Corporation has $30,000 cash in the company's bank account. What is the maximum amount of cash dividends the company can declare at this time? Explain.

LO2

E13-3 Reporting the Stockholders' Equity Section of the Balance Sheet
North Wind Aviation received its corporate charter during January 2009. The charter authorized the following capital stock:

Common stock: par $7, authorized 50,000 shares.
Preferred stock: 8 percent, par $10, authorized 20,000 shares.

During 2009, the following transactions occurred in the order given:

a. Issued a total of 40,000 shares of the common stock to the company's founders for $11 per share.
b. Sold 5,000 shares of the preferred stock at $18 per share.
c. Sold 3,000 shares of the common stock at $14 per share and 1,000 shares of the preferred stock at $28.
d. Net income for the first year was $48,000, and no dividends were declared.

Required:
Prepare the Stockholders' Equity section of the balance sheet at December 31, 2009.

LO2, 3

E13-4 Reporting the Stockholders' Equity Section of the Balance Sheet
Shelby Corporation was organized in January 2010 by 10 stockholders to operate an air conditioning sales and service business. The charter issued by the state authorized the following capital stock:

Common stock, $1 par value, 200,000 shares.
Preferred stock, 6 percent, $8 par value, 50,000 shares.

During January and February 2010, the following stock transactions were completed:

a. Collected $40,000 cash from each of the 10 organizers and issued 2,000 shares of common stock to each of them.

b. Sold 15,000 shares of preferred stock at $25 per share; collected the cash and immediately issued the stock.

Net income for 2010 was $40,000; cash dividends declared and paid at year-end were $10,000.

Required:
Prepare the Stockholders' Equity section of the balance sheet at December 31, 2010.

E13-5 Determining the Effects of the Issuance of Common and Preferred Stock LO2

Inside Incorporated was issued a charter on January 15, 2009, that authorized the following capital stock:

Common stock, $6 par, 100,000 shares, one vote per share.
Preferred stock, 7 percent, par value $10 per share, 5,000 shares, nonvoting.

During 2009, the following selected transactions were completed in the order given:

a. Sold and issued 20,000 shares of the $6 par common stock at $18 cash per share.

b. Sold and issued 3,000 shares of preferred stock at $22 cash per share.

c. At the end of 2009, the Income Summary account included net income of $38,000.

Required:

1. Prepare journal entries to record transactions *a* and *b*, and to close Income Summary to Retained Earnings in *c*.
2. Prepare the Stockholders' Equity section of the balance sheet at December 31, 2009.
3. Assume that you are a common stockholder. If Inside Incorporated needed additional capital, would you prefer to have it issue additional common stock or additional preferred stock? Explain.

E13-6 Recording and Reporting Stockholders' Equity Transactions LO2

AvA School of Learning obtained a charter at the start of 2009 that authorized 50,000 shares of no-par common stock and 20,000 shares of preferred stock, par value $10, 5% noncumulative dividend. During 2009, the following selected transactions occurred:

a. Collected $40 cash per share from four individuals and issued 5,000 shares of common stock to each.

b. Sold and issued 6,000 shares of common stock to an outside investor at $40 cash per share.

c. Sold and issued 8,000 shares of preferred stock at $15 cash per share.

Required:

1. Give the journal entries indicated for each of these transactions.
2. Prepare the Stockholders' Equity section of the balance sheet at December 31, 2009. At the end of 2009, the accounts reflected net income of $36,000.

E13-7 Finding Amounts Missing from the Stockholders' Equity Section LO2

The Stockholders' Equity section on the December 31, 2009, balance sheet of Chemfast Corporation follows:

Stockholders' Equity	
Contributed capital	
Preferred stock (par $20; authorized 10,000 shares, ? issued, of which 500 shares are held as treasury stock)	$104,000
Additional paid-in capital, preferred	14,300
Common stock (no par; authorized 20,000 shares, issued and outstanding 8,000 shares)	600,000
Retained earnings	30,000
Cost of 500 shares of preferred treasury stock	9,500

Required:

Complete the following statements and show your computations.

1. The number of shares of preferred stock issued was ______.
2. The number of shares of preferred stock outstanding was ______.
3. The average sales price of the preferred stock when issued was $______ per share.
4. The average issue price of the common stock was $______.
5. The treasury stock transaction increased (decreased) stockholders' equity by ______.
6. How much did the treasury stock cost per share? $______.
7. Total stockholders' equity is $______.

LO2

E13-8 Recording Treasury Stock Transactions and Analyzing Their Impact

During 2009, the following selected transactions affecting stockholders' equity occurred for Corner Corporation:

a. Feb. 1 Purchased 400 shares of the company's own common stock at $22 cash per share.
b. Jul. 15 Sold 100 of the shares purchased on February 1, 2009, for $24 cash per share.
c. Sept. 1 Sold 60 more of the shares purchased on February 1, 2009, for $20 cash per share.

Required:

1. Give journal entries for each of the transactions.
2. What impact does the purchase of treasury stock have on dividends paid?
3. What impact does the sale of treasury stock for an amount higher than the purchase price have on net income?

LO2, 3

E13-9 Comparing Owners' Equity Sections for a Sole Proprietorship and Corporation

Assume for each of the following independent cases that the annual accounting period ends on December 31, 2009, and that the Income Summary held a credit balance of $20,000.

Case A: Assume that the company is a *sole proprietorship* owned by Proprietor A. Prior to the closing entries, the capital account reflected a credit balance of $50,000 and the drawings account a balance of $8,000.

Case B: Assume that the company is a *corporation*. Prior to the closing entries, the stockholders' equity accounts showed the following: Common Stock, par $10, 30,000 shares authorized, 15,000 shares issued and outstanding; Additional Paid-In Capital, $5,000; Retained Earnings, $65,000. No dividends were declared.

Required:

1. Give all the closing entries required at December 31, 2009, for each case.
2. Show the body of (a) a statement of owner's equity and (b) a statement of retained earnings for the year ended December 31, 2009.
3. Show how the Equity section of the balance sheet would appear at December 31, 2009, for each case.

LO2, 3

E13-10 Recording Stockholders' Equity Transactions

The annual report for Malibu Beachwear reported the following transactions affecting stockholders' equity:

a. Purchased $35,000 in treasury stock.
b. Declared cash dividends in the amount of $25,420.
c. Paid cash dividends in the amount of $25,420.
d. Declared 10 percent common stock dividend, which would require issuing 20,000 additional $1 par value shares with a market price of $15 per share.
e. Issued the stock dividend in transaction d.

Required:

1. Prepare journal entries to record each of these transactions.
2. Indicate the effect (increase, decrease, or no effect) of each of these transactions on total assets, liabilities, and stockholders' equity.

E13-11 Computing Dividends on Common and Preferred Stock and Analyzing Differences LO3

The records of Hoffman Company reflected the following balances in the stockholders' equity accounts at December 31, 2009:

Common stock, par $12 per share, 40,000 shares outstanding.

Preferred stock, 8 percent, par $10 per share, 6,000 shares outstanding.

Retained earnings, $220,000.

On January 1, 2010, the board of directors was considering the distribution of a $62,000 cash dividend. No dividends were paid during 2008 and 2009.

Required:

1. Determine the total and per share amounts that would be paid to the common stockholders and to the preferred stockholders under two independent assumptions:
   a. The preferred stock is noncumulative.
   b. The preferred stock is cumulative.
2. Briefly explain why the dividends per share of common stock were less for the second assumption.
3. What factors would cause a more favorable dividend for the common stockholders?

E13-12 Recording the Payment of Dividends and Preparing a Statement of Retained Earnings LO3

The 2009 annual report for Sneers Corporation disclosed that the company declared and paid preferred dividends in the amount of $119.9 million in 2009. It also declared and paid dividends on common stock in the amount of $2 per share. During 2009, Sneers had 1,000,000,000 shares of common authorized; 387,570,300 shares had been issued; and 41,670,300 shares were in treasury stock. The balance in Retained Earnings was $1,554 million on December 31, 2008 and net income was $858 million for 2009.

Required:

1. Prepare journal entries to record the declaration of dividends on (a) preferred stock and (b) common stock.
2. Prepare journal entries to record the payment of dividends on (a) preferred stock and (b) common stock.
3. Prepare a journal entry to close 2009 net income into Retained Earnings from Income Summary.
4. Using the information given above, prepare a statement of retained earnings for the year ended December 31, 2009.

E13-13 Analyzing Stock Dividends LO3

On December 31, 2008, the Stockholders' Equity section of the balance sheet of R & B Corporation reflected the following:

Common stock (par $10; authorized 60,000 shares, outstanding 25,000 shares)	$250,000
Additional paid-in capital	12,000
Retained earnings	75,000

On February 1, 2009, the board of directors declared a 12 percent stock dividend to be issued April 30, 2009. The market value of the stock on February 1, 2009, was $18 per share.

Required:

1. For comparative purposes, prepare the Stockholders' Equity section of the balance sheet both (a) immediately before the stock dividend and (b) immediately after the stock dividend. Consider using side-by-side columns for the amounts in parts (a) and (b).
2. Explain the effects of this stock dividend on the assets, liabilities, and stockholders' equity.
3. How would your answers to requirements 1 and 2 change if the stock dividend were 100 percent?

E13-14 Recording Dividends LO3

BLACK&DECKER

Black & Decker is a leading global manufacturer and marketer of power tools, hardware, and home improvement products. A press release on October 17, 2007, contained the following announcement:

> ... its Board of Directors declared a quarterly cash dividend of $0.42 per share on the Corporation's outstanding common stock payable December 28, 2007, to stockholders of record at the close of business on December 14, 2007.

At the time of the press release, Black & Decker had 150,000,000 shares authorized and 62,536,000 outstanding. The par value for the company's stock is $.50 per share.

Required:
Prepare journal entries as appropriate for each of the three dates mentioned above.

LO3

E13-15 Comparing Stock Dividends and Splits

On July 1, 2009, Jones Corporation had the following capital structure:

Common stock, $1 par, 200,000 authorized shares, 150,000 issued and outstanding	$150,000
Additional paid-in capital	88,000
Retained earnings	172,000
Treasury stock	None

Required:
Complete the following table based on three independent cases involving stock transactions:

Case 1: The board of directors declared and issued a 10 percent stock dividend when the stock was selling at $8 per share.

Case 2: The board of directors declared and issued a 100 percent stock dividend when the stock was selling at $8 per share.

Case 3: The board of directors voted a 2-for-1 stock split. The market price prior to the split was $8 per share.

		CASE 1	CASE 2	CASE 3
Items	Before Stock Transactions	After 10% Stock Dividend	After 100% Stock Dividend	After Stock Split
Number of shares outstanding				
Par per share	$ 1	$	$	$
Common stock account	$	$	$	$
Additional paid-in capital	88,000			
Retained earnings	172,000			
Total stockholders' equity	$	$	$	$

LO2, 3

E13-16 Analyzing Dividends in Arrears

Mission Critical Software, Inc., was a leading provider of systems management software for Windows NT network and Internet infrastructure. Like many start-up companies, Mission Critical struggled with cash flows as it developed new business opportunities. A student found a financial statement for Mission Critical that stated that the increase in dividends in arrears on preferred stock this year was $264,000.

The student who read the note suggested that the Mission Critical preferred stock would be a good investment because of the large amount of dividend income that would be earned when the company started paying dividends again: "As the owner of the stock, I'll get dividends for the period I hold the stock plus some previous periods when I didn't even own the stock." Do you agree? Explain.

LO3

E13-17 Determining the Impact of Cash and Stock Dividends

Superior Corporation has the following capital stock outstanding on January 1, 2009:

Common stock, par $8, outstanding shares, 30,000.

Preferred stock, 6 percent, par $15, outstanding shares, 8,000.

On October 1, 2009, the board of directors declared dividends that would be paid, or issued, to stockholders of record on December 1, 2009:

Common stock: 10 percent common stock dividend, to be issued on December 20, 2009.

Preferred stock: Cash dividend, 6 percent, payable December 20, 2009.

On October 1, 2009, the market prices were preferred stock, $40, and common stock, $32. On December 20, 2009, the dividends were paid, or issued.

Required:
At each date indicated above, present journal entries for the dividends on (a) preferred stock and (b) common stock.

E13-18 Determining the Financial Statement Effects of Cash and Stock Dividends LO3

Lynn Company has outstanding 60,000 shares of $10 par value common stock and 25,000 shares of $20 par value preferred stock (8 percent). On December 1, 2009, the board of directors voted an 8 percent cash dividend on the preferred stock and a 10 percent stock dividend on the common stock. At the date of declaration, the common stock was selling at $35 and the preferred at $20 per share. The dividends are to be paid, or issued, on February 15, 2010. The annual accounting period ends December 31.

Required:
Explain the comparative effects of the two dividends on the assets, liabilities, and stockholders' equity (*a*) through December 31, 2009, (*b*) on February 15, 2010, and (*c*) overall from December 1, 2009, through February 15, 2010. A schedule using the following structure might be helpful:

	COMPARATIVE EFFECTS EXPLAINED	
Item	Cash Dividend on Preferred	Stock Dividend on Common
(*a*) Through December 31, 2009:		
Effect on assets		
Effect on liabilities		
Effect on stockholders' equity		

E13-19 Preparing a Statement of Retained Earnings and Partial Balance Sheet and Evaluating Dividend Policy LO2, 3, 4

The following account balances were selected from the records of Blake Corporation at December 31, 2009, after all adjusting entries were completed. The company had not issued or repurchased any additional shares this year.

Common stock (par $15; authorized 100,000 shares, issued 35,000 shares, of which 1,000 shares are held as treasury stock)	$525,000
Additional paid-in capital	180,000
Dividends on common stock declared and paid in 2009	28,000
Retained earnings, January 1, 2009	76,000
Treasury stock at cost (1,000 shares)	20,000
Net income for the year.	48,000

Required:

1. Prepare the statement of retained earnings for the year ended December 31, 2009, and the Stockholders' Equity section of the balance sheet at December 31, 2009.
2. Determine the number of shares of stock that received dividends.
3. Compute the EPS ratio for the year ended December 31, 2009. Is it better or worse than the $1.32 earnings per share in 2008?

E13-20 Analyzing Stock Repurchases and Stock Dividends LO3, 4 Winnebago

Winnebago is a familiar name on vehicles traveling U.S. highways. The company manufactures and sells large motor homes for vacation travel. These motor homes can be quickly recognized because of the company's "flying W" trademark. An April 12, 2006, press release contained the following information:

> Winnebago Industries, Inc., (NYSE: WGO) announced that in a meeting held today, the Company's Board of Directors announced a new $60 million stock repurchase authorization. Winnebago Industries has repurchased approximately 24.4 million shares of common stock for approximately $356.8 million since December 31, 1997.

Required:

1. Explain the impact of a $60 million stock repurchase on the financial statements.
2. Why do you think the board decided to repurchase the stock?
3. Assuming that Winnebago continues its current level of annual dividend payments, what impact will this purchase have on Winnebago's future dividends per share?
4. On January 14, 2004, the company's board of directors declared a 100 percent stock dividend that was distributed on March 5, 2004. Why would Winnebago choose a stock dividend rather than a 2-for-1 stock split?
5. What impact would this stock dividend have had on Winnebago's financial statements? What impact would it have had on the EPS ratio?

Problems—Set A  Available with McGraw-Hill's Homework Manager

LO2

PA13-1 Recording Journal Entries and Preparing a Partial Balance Sheet after Stock Issue, Purchase, and Reissue Transactions

Worldwide Company obtained a charter from the state in January 2009, which authorized 200,000 shares of common stock, $10 par value. During the first year, the company earned $38,200, and the following selected transactions occurred in the order given:

a. Sold 60,000 shares of the common stock at $12 per share.

b. Purchased 2,000 shares at $15 cash per share from one of the 30 stockholders who needed cash and wanted to sell the stock back to the company.

c. Resold 1,000 of the shares of the treasury stock purchased in transaction *b* two months later to another individual at $18 cash per share.

Required:

1. Prepare journal entries to record each transaction.
2. Prepare the Stockholders' Equity section of the balance sheet at December 31, 2009. Because this is the first year of operations, Retained Earnings has a zero balance at the beginning of the year.

LO3
Macy's

PA13-2 Recording Dividends

Prior to changing its corporate name to Macy's, Inc., on June 1, 2007, Federated Department Stores issued a press release with the following information:

> CINCINNATI—May 19, 2006—The Board of Directors of Federated Department Stores, Inc. (NYSE:FD) today approved a split of the company's common stock on a two-for-one basis. Additional shares issued as a result of the stock dividend will be distributed after close of trading on June 9, 2006, to shareholders of record on May 26, 2006. At the company's Annual Meeting this morning, Federated shareholders approved an increase in the number of authorized shares of Federated common stock from 500 million to 1 billion. With the stock split, Federated's quarterly dividend will be 12.75 cents per outstanding common share, payable July 3, 2006, to Federated shareholders of record at the close of business on June 16, 2006.

Required:

1. Although the press release refers to a stock split, the transaction actually involved a 100 percent stock dividend, to be recorded at par value. Prepare any journal entries that Federated Department Stores should have made as the result of the stock dividend and the cash dividend. Assume that, at the time of the stock dividend, the company had 175 million shares outstanding, the par value was $0.01 per share, and the market value was $73 per share.
2. What two requirements would the board of directors have considered before making the dividend decision?

PA13-3 Finding Missing Amounts LO2, 3, 4

At December 31, 2009, the records of Nortech Corporation provided the following selected and incomplete data:

Authorized shares of common stock, 200,000.

Balance in common stock account $1,250,000 (par $10; no changes during 2009).

Common stock issued in prior year at a price of $17 per share.

Shares held as treasury stock, 3,000 shares, cost $20 per share (no changes during 2009).

Net income for 2009, $118,000.

Dividends declared and paid during 2009, $73,200.

Retained earnings balance, January 1, 2009, $155,000.

Required:

1. Complete the following:
   Shares authorized _______.
   Shares issued _______.
   Shares outstanding _______.
2. The balance in the Additional Paid-In Capital account would be $ _______.
3. Earnings per share is $ _______.
4. Dividends paid per share of common stock is $ _______.
5. Treasury stock should be reported in the Stockholders' Equity section of the balance sheet in the amount of $ _______.
6. Assume that the board of directors approved a 2-for-1 stock split. After the stock split, the par value per share will be $_____ and the number of outstanding shares will be ______. (The treasury stock was acquired after the split was issued.)
7. Disregard the stock split (assumed above). Assume instead a 100 percent stock dividend was declared and issued after the treasury stock was acquired, when the market price of the common stock was $21. Give any journal entry that should be made.

PA13-4 Recording Journal Entries and Preparing a Partial Balance Sheet after Common Stock Issue, Purchase, Reissue, and Cash Dividends LO2, 3

www.mhhe.com/LLPW1e

American Laser, Inc. reported the following stockholders' equity account balances on January 1, 2009.

Common stock, 10,000 shares of $1 par	$ 10,000
Retained earnings	120,000
Additional paid-in capital—common	90,000
Treasury stock	0

The company entered into the following transactions during 2009.

Jan. 15	Issued 5,000 shares of $1 par common stock for $50,000 cash.
Feb. 15	Purchased 3,000 shares of $1 par common stock into treasury for $33,000 cash.
Mar. 15	Reissued 2,000 shares of treasury stock for $24,000 cash.
Aug. 15	Reissued 600 shares of treasury stock for $4,600 cash.
Sept. 15	Declared (but did not pay) a $1 cash dividend on each outstanding share of common stock.

Required:

1. Prepare journal entries to record each transaction.
2. Prepare the Stockholders' Equity section of the balance sheet at December 31, 2009. At the end of 2009, the accounts reflected net income of $20,000. The company was authorized to issue 200,000 shares.

LO2, 3

www.mhhe.com/LLPW1e

PA13-5 Comparing Stock and Cash Dividends

Water Tower Company had the following stock outstanding and retained earnings at December 31, 2009:

Common stock (par $8; outstanding, 30,000 shares)	$240,000
Preferred stock, 7% (par $10; outstanding, 6,000 shares)	60,000
Retained earnings	280,000

The board of directors is considering the distribution of a cash dividend to the common and preferred stockholders. No dividends were declared during 2007 or 2008. Three independent cases are assumed:

Case A: The preferred stock is noncumulative; the total amount of dividends is $30,000.

Case B: The preferred stock is cumulative; the total amount of dividends is $12,600.

Case C: Same as Case B, except the amount is $66,000.

Required:

1. Compute the amount of dividends, in total and per share (rounded to the nearest penny), that would be payable to each class of stockholders for each case. Show computations.
2. Assume that a 100 percent common stock dividend was issued when the market value per share was $24. Complete the following schedule.

	AMOUNT OF DOLLAR INCREASE (DECREASE)	
Item	Cash Dividend, Case C	Stock Dividend
Assets	$	$
Liabilities		
Stockholders' equity		

LO4

Aaron Rents, Inc.
Rent-A-Center, Inc.

www.mhhe.com/LLPW1e

PA13-6 Computing and Interpreting Earnings per Share (EPS) and Price/Earnings (P/E) Ratios

Aaron Rents, Inc., and Rent-A-Center, Inc., are two publicly traded rental companies. They reported the following in their 2006 financial statements (in thousands, except per share amounts):

	AARON RENTS, INC.		RENT-A-CENTER, INC.	
	2005	2006	2005	2006
Average number of common shares	49,994	52,423	72,977	69,657
Average number of preferred shares	0	0	0	0
Net income	$ 57,993	$ 78,635	$ 135,738	$ 103,092
Stock price when annual results reported	23.10	27.60	20.80	28.50

Required:

1. Compute the 2006 EPS for each company (rounded to the nearest penny). In 2005, Aaron Rents reported EPS of $1.16, whereas Rent-A-Center reported EPS of $1.86. Which company appears to have improved its performance in 2006?
2. Compute the 2006 P/E ratio for each company. Do investors appear to value one company more than the other? Explain.

Problems—Set B  Available with McGraw-Hill's Homework Manager

PB13-1 Recording Journal Entries and Preparing a Partial Balance Sheet after Stock Issue and Purchase Transactions

LO2

Global Marine obtained a charter from the state in January 2009, which authorized 1,000,000 shares of common stock, $5 par value. During the first year of operations, the company earned $429,000, and the following selected transactions occurred in the order given:

a. Sold 700,000 shares of the common stock at $54 per share. Collected the cash and issued the stock.

b. Purchased 25,000 shares at $50 cash per share to use as stock incentives for senior management.

Required:

1. Prepare journal entries to record each transaction.
2. Prepare the Stockholders' Equity section of the balance sheet at December 31, 2009.

PB13-2 Recording Dividends

LO3

National Beverage Corp.

National Beverage Corp. produces soft drinks, bottled waters, and juices sold under the brand names Shasta, Faygo, and Everfresh. A press release contained the following information:

> March 5—National Beverage Corp. today announced that its Board of Directors has declared a special "one-time" cash dividend of $1.00 per share on approximately 36.6 million outstanding shares. The dividend will be paid on or before April 30 to shareholders of record at the close of business on March 26.

Required:

1. Prepare any journal entries that National Beverage Corp. should make to record the cash dividend.
2. On March 5, National Beverage Corp. also declared a 100 percent stock dividend, which was distributed on March 22. Prepare any journal entries that National Beverage Corp. should have made to record this stock dividend. Assume that the company had 18.3 million shares outstanding on March 5, the par value is $0.01 per share, and the market value is $10 per share.
3. What two requirements would the board of directors have considered before making the dividend decisions?

PB13-3 Finding Missing Amounts

LO2, 3, 4

At December 31, 2009, the records of Kozmetsky Corporation provided the following selected and incomplete data:

Common stock (par $1; no changes during 2009).
Shares authorized, 5,000,000.
Shares issued, __?__; issue price $80 per share.
Shares held as treasury stock, 100,000 shares, cost $60 per share (no changes during 2009).
Net income for 2009, $4,800,000.
Common Stock account, $1,500,000.
Dividends declared and paid during 2009, $2 per share.
Retained Earnings balance, January 1, 2009, $82,900,000.

Required:

1. Complete the following:
   Shares issued _______.
   Shares outstanding_______.
2. The balance in the Additional Paid-In Capital account would be $_______.
3. Earnings per share is $_______.
4. Total dividends paid on common stock during 2009 is $_______.
5. Treasury stock should be reported in the Stockholders' Equity section of the balance sheet in the amount of $_______.

6. Assume that the board of directors voted a 2-for-1 stock split. After the stock split, the par value per share will be $______, and the number of outstanding shares will be______. The treasury stock was acquired after the split was issued.
7. Disregard the stock split (assumed above). Assume instead a 100 percent stock dividend was declared and issued after the treasury stock was acquired, when the market price of the common stock was $21. Explain how stockholders' equity will change.

LO2, 3

PB13-4 Recording Journal Entries and Preparing a Partial Balance Sheet after Common Stock Issue, Purchase, Reissue, and Cash Dividends

Waste Control, Inc. reported the following stockholders' equity account balances on January 1, 2009.

Common stock, 20,000 shares of $1 par	$ 20,000
Retained earnings	110,000
Additional paid-in capital—common	180,000
Treasury stock	0

The company entered into the following transactions during 2009.

Jan. 12	Issued 5,000 shares of $1 par common stock for $50,000 cash.
Feb. 3	Purchased 3,000 shares of $1 par common stock into treasury for $27,000 cash.
Mar. 4	Reissued 2,000 shares of treasury stock for $20,000 cash.
Aug. 5	Reissued 600 shares of treasury stock for $5,400 cash.
Sept. 15	Declared (but did not pay) a $2 cash dividend on each outstanding share of common stock.

Required:

1. Prepare journal entries to record each transaction.
2. Prepare the Stockholders' Equity section of the balance sheet at December 31, 2009. At the end of 2009, the accounts reflected net income of $50,000. The company was authorized to issue 500,000 shares.

LO2, 3

PB13-5 Comparing Stock and Cash Dividends

Ritz Company had the following stock outstanding and Retained Earnings at December 31, 2009:

Common stock (par $1; outstanding, 500,000 shares)	$500,000
Preferred stock, 8% (par $10; outstanding, 21,000 shares)	210,000
Retained earnings	900,000

The board of directors is considering the distribution of a cash dividend to the common and preferred stockholders. No dividends were declared during 2007 or 2008. Three independent cases are assumed:

Case A: The preferred stock is noncumulative; the total amount of dividends is $30,000.

Case B: The preferred stock is cumulative; the total amount of dividends is $30,000.

Case C: Same as Case B, except the amount is $75,000.

Required:

1. Compute the amount of dividends, in total and per share (rounded to the nearest penny), payable to each class of stockholders for each case. Show computations.
2. Assume that the company issued a 100 percent stock dividend on the outstanding common shares when the market value per share was $50. Complete the following schedule.

	AMOUNT OF DOLLAR INCREASE (DECREASE)	
Item	Cash Dividend, Case C	Stock Dividend
Assets	$	$
Liabilities		
Stockholders' equity		

PB13-6 Computing and Interpreting Earnings per Share (EPS) and Price/Earnings (P/E) Ratios LO4

Two magazine companies reported the following in their 2008 financial statements:

	BUSINESSWORLD		FUN AND GAMES	
	2007	2008	2007	2008
Average number of common shares	20,000	22,000	40,000	45,000
Net income	$65,000	$76,000	$84,000	$180,000
Preferred dividends	10,000	10,000	0	0
Stock price when annual results reported	54.60	51.00	32.55	59.60

Required:

1. Compute the 2008 EPS for each company. In 2007, BusinessWorld reported EPS of $2.75, whereas Fun and Games reported EPS of $2.10. Which company appears to have improved its performance in 2008?
2. Compute the 2008 P/E ratio for each company. Do investors appear to value one company more than the other? Explain.

Cases and Projects

CP13-1 Finding Financial Information LO2, 3, 4

Refer to the financial statements of The Home Depot in Appendix A at the end of this book, or download the annual report from the Cases and Projects section of the text's Web site at www.mhhe.com/LLPW1e.

Required:

1. As of February 3, 2008, how many shares of common stock were authorized? How many shares were issued? How many shares were held in treasury? What does this suggest to you about the number of shares outstanding?
2. According to the Retained Earnings column in the Statement of Stockholders' Equity, how much did the company declare in dividends during the year ended February 3, 2008?
3. According to the income statement, how has The Home Depot's net earnings changed over the past three years? Has the company's basic earnings per share changed over the past three years? How do you explain these seemingly inconsistent patterns?

CP13-2 Comparing Financial Information LO2, 3, 4

Lowe's

Refer to the financial statements of The Home Depot in Appendix A and Lowe's in Appendix B at the end of this book, or download the annual reports from the Cases and Projects section of the text's Web site at www.mhhe.com/LLPW1e.

Required:

1. Did Lowe's have more or fewer authorized shares of common stock than The Home Depot at the beginning of February 2008?
2. From the Retained Earnings column in the statement of stockholders' equity, what total amount of cash dividends did Lowe's declare during the year ended February 1, 2008? Compared to The Home Depot, is Lowe's policy on dividends better, worse, or just different?
3. How have Lowe's net earnings changed over the past three years? How has the company's basic earnings per share changed over the past three years? According to financial statement note 11, were the changes in EPS caused only by changes in Lowe's net earnings?

CP13-3 Examining an Annual Report: Internet-Based Team Research LO3, 4

As a team, select an industry to analyze. Using your Web browser, each team member should acquire the annual report or 10-K for one publicly traded company in the industry, with each member selecting a different company. (See CP1-3 in Chapter 1 for a description of possible resources for these tasks.)

Required:

1. On an individual basis, each team member should write a short report that incorporates the following:
   a. Has the company declared cash or stock dividends during the past three years?
   b. What is the trend in the company's EPS over the past three years?
   c. Compute and analyze the P/E ratio over the past two years.
2. Then, as a team, write a short report comparing and contrasting your companies using these attributes. Discuss any patterns across the companies that you as a team observe. Provide potential explanations for any differences discovered.

LO2

CP13-4 Making Ethical Decisions: A Real-Life Example

Activision, Inc.

Activision became a public company with an initial public offering of stock on June 9, 1983, at $12 per share. In June 2002, Activision issued 7.5 million additional shares to the public at approximately $33 per share. In October 2002, when its stock was trading at about $22 per share, Activision executives announced that the company would spend up to $150 million to buy back stock from investors. On January 8, 2003, *The Wall Street Journal* reported that several analysts were criticizing Activision's executives because the company had sold the shares to the public at a high price ($33) and then were offering to buy them back at the going market price, which was considerably lower than the issue price in 2002.

Required:

1. Do you think it was inappropriate for Activision to offer to buy back the stock at a lower price in October 2002?
2. Would your answer to requirement 1 be different if Activision had not issued additional stock in June 2002?
3. *The Wall Street Journal* article also reported that Activision executives had purchased over 530,000 shares of company stock in December 2002 at the then-current price of $13.32 per share. If you were an investor, how would you feel about executives buying stock in their own company?
4. Would your answer to requirement 3 be different if you also learned that the executives had sold nearly 2.5 million shares of Activision stock earlier that year, when the price was at least $26.08 per share?

LO3

CP13-5 Making Ethical Decisions: A Mini Case

You are the president of a very successful Internet company that has had a remarkably profitable year. You have determined that the company has more than $10 million in cash generated by operating activities not needed in the business. You are thinking about paying it out to stockholders as a special dividend. You discuss the idea with your vice president, who reacts angrily to your suggestion:

> Our stock price has gone up by 200 percent in the last year alone. What more do we have to do for the owners? The people who really earned that money are the employees who have been working 12 hours a day, six or seven days a week to make the company successful. Most of them didn't even take vacations last year. I say we have to pay out bonuses and nothing extra for the stockholders.

As president, you know that you are hired by the board of directors, which is elected by the stockholders.

Required:

What is your responsibility to both groups? To which group would you give the $10 million? Why?

LO3

CP13-6 Thinking Critically Making a Decision as an Investor

You have retired after a long and successful career as a business executive and now spend a good portion of your time managing your retirement portfolio. You are considering two basic investment alternatives. You can invest in (1) conservative stocks that pay substantial dividends (typically 5 percent of the stock price every year) or (2) growth-oriented technology stocks that pay no dividends.

Required:

Analyze each of these alternatives and select one. Justify your selection.

CP13-7 Charting Stock Price Movement around Important Announcement Dates — LO3

Using a Web search engine like Google, find either an earnings or dividend announcement for two different companies. Using a source such as bigcharts.com, determine the closing stock price for each company for each day during the five business days before and after the announcement. Using a separate worksheet for each company, prepare a line chart of its stock price movement.

Required:

Examine the charts for each company. Does the stock price appear to change as a consequence of their announcements? Explain why or why not.

14 Long-Term Liabilities

LEARNING OBJECTIVES

After completing this chapter, you should be able to:

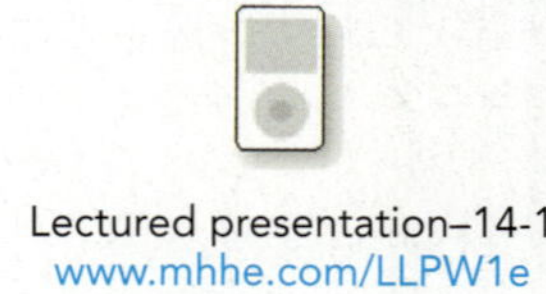

Lectured presentation–14-1
www.mhhe.com/LLPW1e

LO1 Explain how to measure long-term liabilities.

LO2 Demonstrate how to account for discounted notes payable.

LO3 Demonstrate how to account for bonds payable.

LO4 Explain how to account for lease liabilities.

LO5 Calculate and interpret the debt-to-assets and times interest earned ratios.

Focus Company: GENERAL MILLS, INC.

Maker of Pillsbury, Green Giant, Cheerios, and More

www.generalmills.com

After turning in their report, they eagerly await their grade. They are expecting an A and would be devastated if they got a B. A group of high-achieving students waiting for their project grade? They could be, but these hopeful characters are actually the Jolly Green Giant, Lucky the Leprechaun, Poppin' Fresh, and their corporate bosses at General Mills.

That's right, this magically delicious company and all its brands receive a letter grade just as you do. The grading process is a bit different from yours because credit-rating agencies such as Standard & Poor's, Fitch, and Moody's assign their grades based on the company's ability to pay its liabilities on time. And instead of ranging from A to F, their grade can range from AAA to D. The AAA rating is given only to companies in rock-solid financial condition, and the D goes to those likely to pay less than half of what they owe. In general, any grade above a BB is considered a good to high-quality credit rating, which is what General Mills typically earns.

In this chapter, you will learn about the accounting procedures and financial ratios used to report and interpret long-term liabilities and how they influence a company's credit rating. Although we focus on business reporting and analysis, this chapter can also help you understand information that is used to assess your personal credit rating.

ORGANIZATION OF THE CHAPTER

LONG-TERM LIABILITIES	ACCOUNTING FOR LONG-TERM LIABILITIES	ANALYZING LONG-TERM LIABILITIES
• Making Financing Decisions • Measuring Liabilities	• Discounted Notes • Bonds Payable • Lease Liabilities	• Debt-to-Assets Ratio • Times Interest Earned Ratio

Learning Objective 1

Explain how to measure long-term liabilities.

LONG-TERM LIABILITIES

Making Financing Decisions

Businesses of all forms, including sole proprietorships, partnerships, and corporations, usually require long-term financing at some time during their lives. This financing may be used to purchase new equipment, expand buildings, or acquire other businesses. Long-term financing generally involves borrowing money from lenders (debt) or obtaining money from owners (equity). Chapter 13 introduced the relative advantages of these two sources of financing when evaluated by corporations. See Exhibit 14.1 for similar ideas that apply to other organizational forms.

After a decision is made to rely on long-term debt financing, further decisions must be made about the type of debt to use. **Long-term debt** includes any liabilities that will require repayment over more than one year or if longer, the company's operating cycle. These long-term liabilities, which we explain in the following sections of this chapter, include notes payable, bonds payable, and lease liabilities. Although important differences for these types of debt exist, all liabilities are reported in the financial statements using the same principles, which we discuss next.

Measuring Liabilities

In Chapter 11, we noted that all liabilities are first recorded at their **cash-equivalent amount**—that is, the amount of cash that would be accepted in full settlement of the liability at the moment it is created. This amount excludes interest. Interest arises and is recorded as an expense as time passes.

In many instances, the cash-equivalent amount is readily apparent. For example, bank loans or interest-bearing notes (discussed in Chapter 11) refer specifically to separate principal and interest components. In these situations, the principal clearly represents the cash-equivalent amount. To illustrate, consider a $100,000 interest-bearing note that requires principal and

Exhibit 14.1 Reasons to Use Debt or Equity Financing

Reasons to Use Debt Financing	Reasons to Use Equity Financing
1. Owners may not have sufficient resources to contribute to the business. 2. Interest paid on business loans is tax deductible, but withdrawals paid to owners are not tax deductible. 3. Debt does not usually change an owner's control, but admitting new owners does.	1. A business must repay (or refinance) debt when it matures. Equity contributions by owners do not mature or require repayment. 2. Interest on debt must be repaid regardless of the financial condition of the business. Owners may forgo withdrawals to help the business survive its financial difficulties.

Exhibit 14.2 Recording Principal and Interest on an Interest-Bearing Note

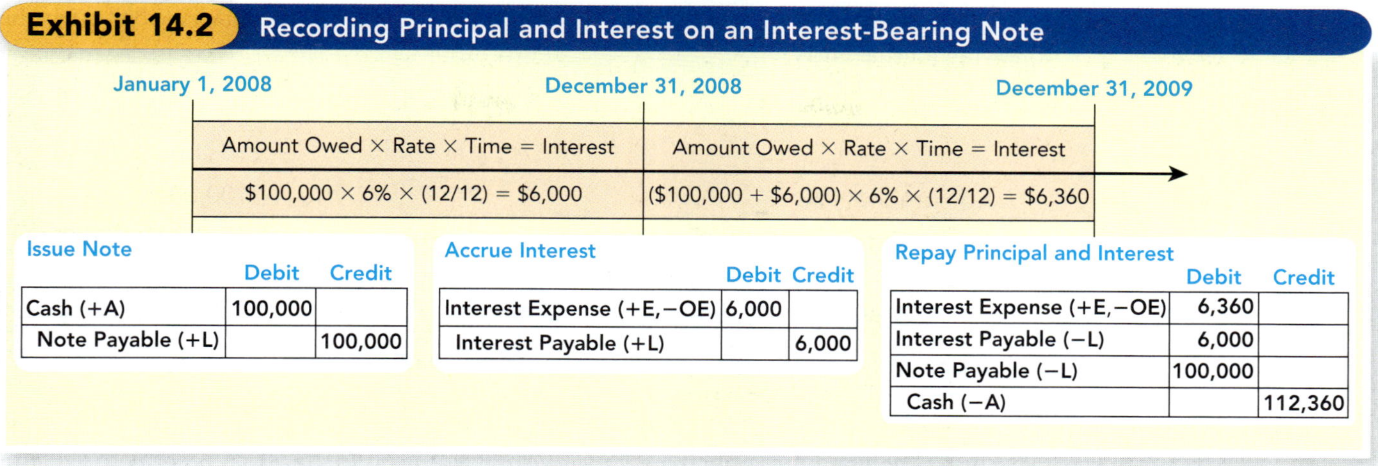

Issue Note

	Debit	Credit
Cash (+A)	100,000	
Note Payable (+L)		100,000

Accrue Interest

	Debit	Credit
Interest Expense (+E, −OE)	6,000	
Interest Payable (+L)		6,000

Repay Principal and Interest

	Debit	Credit
Interest Expense (+E, −OE)	6,360	
Interest Payable (−L)	6,000	
Note Payable (−L)	100,000	
Cash (−A)		112,360

interest payments in two years with interest calculated at the rate of 6 percent of the unpaid balance each year. In this example, the principal is $100,000 and the total interest over the two years is $12,360. See Exhibit 14.2 for a review of how to calculate and record the principal and interest on the note. This long-term note is accounted for the same way as the short-term note payable you encountered in Chapter 11 except the long-term note is outstanding for two years rather than one.

The liabilities discussed in the remainder of this chapter apply these same principles, but they do not explicitly separate the principal and interest components. The separate components do exist, but they must be calculated before they can be recorded as principal or interest. A *discounted note payable*, for example, typically describes only the dollar amounts to be paid, such as requiring a payment of $112,360 in two years. Of this payment, part represents the principal and part is assumed to be built-in interest covering the two-year period. The accountant must determine what part is principal and what part is interest so that the cash-equivalent amount (the amount of the principal) can be initially recorded as a Note Payable. As time passes, interest is calculated and recorded, as you will see in the next section.

The procedures used for recording discounted notes are also used to record bonds and lease liabilities, as you will see in later sections. So take your time when learning about discounted notes, and you will find the other topics easier to learn.

The method that accountants use to determine the principal or cash-equivalent amount is called discounting or present value analysis. In effect, discounting allows accountants to remove the built-in interest component, leaving a **present value** that represents the note's principal (cash-equivalent) component on the date the liability was created. Supplement 14A explains the steps used in discounting various long-term liabilities.

ACCOUNTING FOR LONG-TERM LIABILITIES

Discounted Notes

Learning Objective 2

Demonstrate how to account for discounted notes payable.

Discounted notes are accounted for in the same way as interest-bearing notes with two exceptions. First, the accountant must discount the payments to be made on the note to determine the principal (cash-equivalent) amount to record in Notes Payable. Second, interest on a discounted note is accrued in the Notes Payable account. (Interest on interest-bearing notes is accrued in the Interest Payable account.)

Video 14-1
www.mhhe.com/LLPW1e

Assume that on January 1, 2008, General Mills buys a new piece of equipment. Rather than pay cash, General Mills offers a note that promises to pay $112,360 on December 31, 2009. General Mills typically borrows at a 6 percent interest rate. Because this note does not explicitly state an interest rate, it must be discounted to remove the 6 percent interest that is presumed to be built into the $112,360 payment. By discounting the $112,360 payment using the steps explained in Supplement 14A (see page 616), we can determine that the note's present value on January 1, 2008, is $100,000. That amount is the principal, or cash-equivalent, amount of the note. The liability is recorded as a Note Payable using the following journal entry:

	Debit	Credit
Equipment (+A)	100,000	
Note Payable (+L)		100,000

Assets		=	Liabilities		+	Owners' Equity
Equipment	+100,000		Note Payable	+100,000		

Under the matching principle, General Mills **will need to adjust its records to account for the interest incurred each accounting period.** In reality, General Mills would make such an adjustment every month or quarter, but for the sake of simplicity, we assume that it occurs only once each year on December 31. Interest for the year ended December 31, 2008, is calculated by multiplying the amount of the liability by the interest rate for the full 12 months of the year ($100,000 × 6% × 12/12 = $6,000). This amount is an expense in 2008, and because it has not yet been paid, it also increases liabilities, as recorded in the following journal entry:

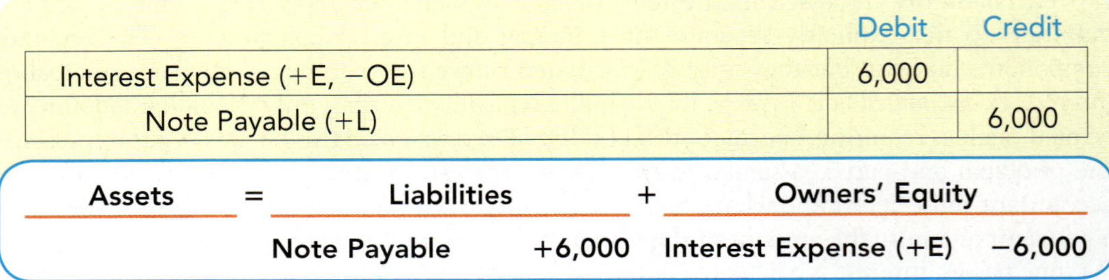

	Debit	Credit
Interest Expense (+E, −OE)	6,000	
Note Payable (+L)		6,000

Assets	=	Liabilities		+	Owners' Equity	
		Note Payable	+6,000		Interest Expense (+E)	−6,000

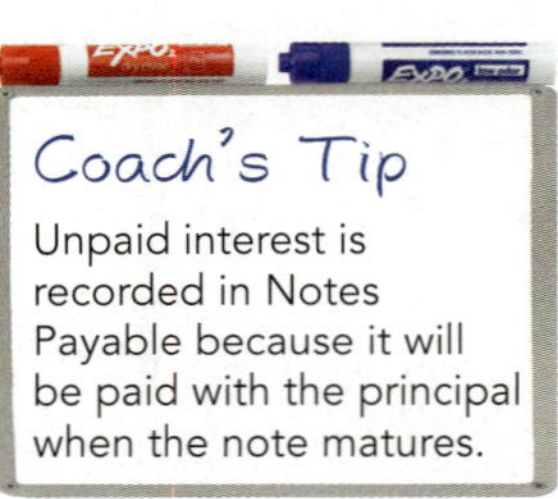

Coach's Tip

Unpaid interest is recorded in Notes Payable because it will be paid with the principal when the note matures.

After this journal entry has been recorded, the balance in the Note Payable account increases from $100,000 to $106,000. We use this new balance in calculating the interest for the following year ($106,000 × 6% × 12/12 = $6,360). This amount is matched to the period in which it was incurred by recording the following journal entry on December 31, 2009, when General Mills makes the required payment of $112,360:

	Debit	Credit
Interest Expense (+E, −OE)	6,360	
Note Payable (−L)	106,000	
Cash (−A)		112,360

Assets		=	Liabilities		+	Owners' Equity	
Cash	−112,360		Note Payable	−106,000		Interest Expense (+E)	−6,360

Refer to Exhibit 14.3 for a summary of these calculations and journal entries. If you compare Exhibit 14.3 to Exhibit 14.2 (page 601), you will see that recording the liability and interest on discounted notes is similar to recording them on interest-bearing notes.

Before moving to bonds payable, try the following Self-Study Practice to make sure you understand how to account for discounted notes.

Exhibit 14.3 Recording Principal and Interest on a Discounted Note

January 1, 2008	December 31, 2008	December 31, 2009
Amount Owed × Rate × Time = Interest	Amount Owed × Rate × Time = Interest	
$100,000 × 6% × (12/12) = $6,000	($100,000 + $6,000) × 6% × (12/12) = $6,360	

Issue Note

	Debit	Credit
Equipment	100,000	
Note Payable		100,000

Accrue Interest

	Debit	Credit
Interest Expense	6,000	
Note Payable		6,000

Repay Principal and Interest

	Debit	Credit
Interest Expense	6,360	
Note Payable	106,000	
Cash		112,360

SELF-STUDY PRACTICE

Starbucks

Assume that Starbucks issued a discounted note on January 1, 2008, to acquire new equipment. The note requires a payment of $55,125 on December 31, 2009. Using an annual interest rate of 5 percent to discount the payment, you determine that the note's present value on January 1, 2008, was $50,000. Record the journal entries and accounting equation effects for (1) the equipment purchase, (2) the interest adjustment on December 31, 2008, and (3) the $55,125 payment on December 31, 2009.

1.

	Debit	Credit

Assets	=	Liabilities	+	Owners' Equity

2.

	Debit	Credit

Assets	=	Liabilities	+	Owners' Equity

3.

	Debit	Credit

Assets	=	Liabilities	+	Owners' Equity

After you have finished, check your answers with the solution at the bottom of the next page.

Bonds Payable

Learning Objective 3

Demonstrate how to account for bonds payable.

Video 14-2
www.mhhe.com/LLPW1e

Occasionally, governments and very large companies such as General Mills need to borrow more money than any single lender can provide. In 2007, for example, General Mills needed to borrow $700 million. Because issuing a promissory note for such a large amount of money was impractical, the company instead issued bonds. A sample bond certificate is shown here.

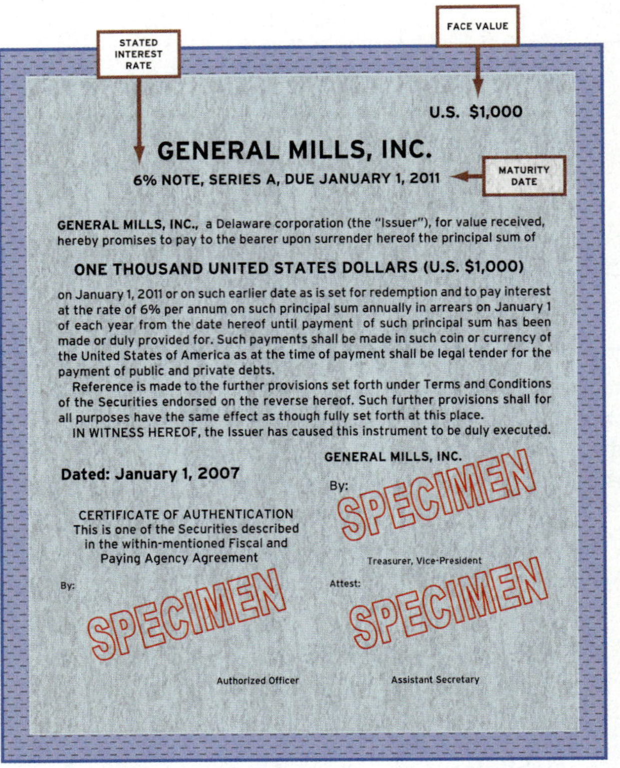

U.S. $1,000

GENERAL MILLS, INC.

6% NOTE, SERIES A, DUE JANUARY 1, 2011

GENERAL MILLS, INC., a Delaware corporation (the "Issuer"), for value received, hereby promises to pay to the bearer upon surrender hereof the principal sum of

ONE THOUSAND UNITED STATES DOLLARS (U.S. $1,000)

on January 1, 2011 or on such earlier date as is set for redemption and to pay interest at the rate of 6% per annum on such principal sum annually in arrears on January 1 of each year from the date hereof until payment of such principal sum has been made or duly provided for. Such payments shall be made in such coin or currency of the United States of America as at the time of payment shall be legal tender for the payment of public and private debts.

Reference is made to the further provisions set forth under Terms and Conditions of the Securities endorsed on the reverse hereof. Such further provisions shall for all purposes have the same effect as though fully set forth at this place.

IN WITNESS HEREOF, the Issuer has caused this instrument to be duly executed.

Dated: January 1, 2007

GENERAL MILLS, INC.

By: SPECIMEN

Treasurer, Vice-President

CERTIFICATE OF AUTHENTICATION
This is one of the Securities described in the within-mentioned Fiscal and Paying Agency Agreement

By: SPECIMEN

Authorized Officer

Attest: SPECIMEN

Assistant Secretary

Bonds are financial instruments that outline the future payments a company promises to make in exchange for receiving a sum of money now. From the company's perspective, the bond is a long-term liability. From the bondholder's perspective, the bond is an investment. After a company issues the bonds, they can be traded on established exchanges such as the New York Bond Exchange. The ability to sell a bond on the bond exchange is attractive to bondholders because it provides them liquidity, or the ability to receive cash for the bond whenever they wish to sell it. In return for this liquidity, bondholders will accept a lower interest rate, which benefits the company by lowering the cost of long-term borrowing.

As you can see from the sample bond certificate shown here, three key elements of a bond are (1) the **maturity date**, (2) the amount payable on the maturity date (often called the **face value**), and (3) the **stated interest rate**. In most cases, the face value of each bond is $1,000.

Coach's Tip

An alternative term for stated interest rate is coupon rate.

Solution to Self-Study Practice

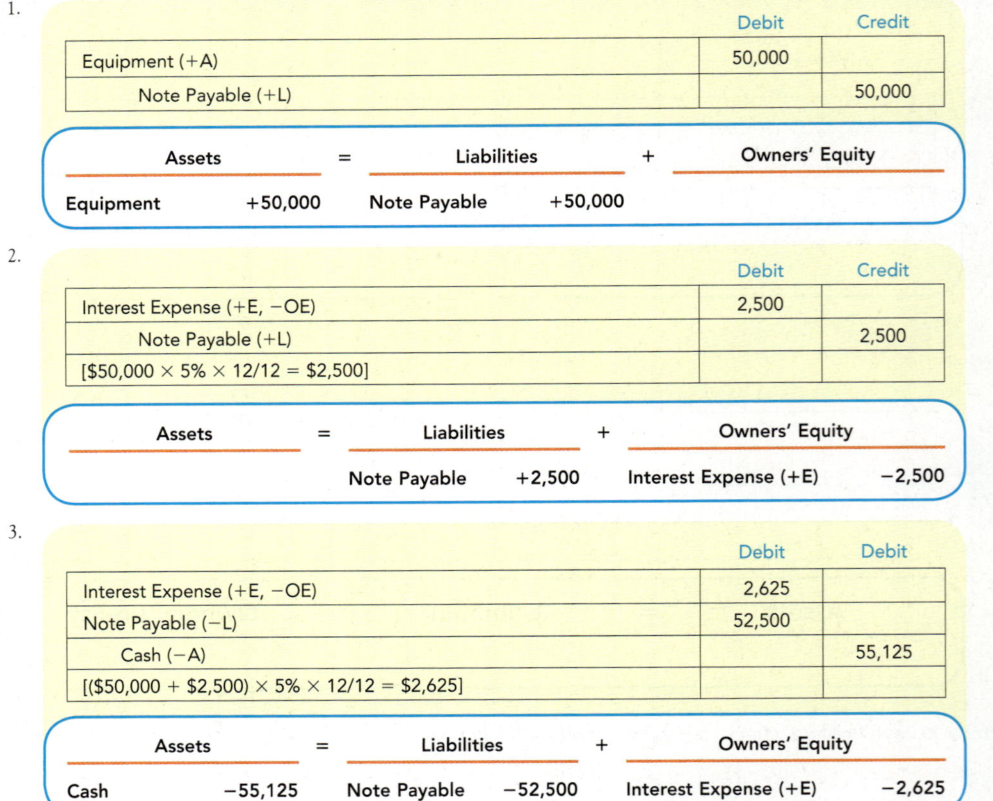

1.

	Debit	Credit
Equipment (+A)	50,000	
Note Payable (+L)		50,000

Assets		=	Liabilities		+	Owners' Equity	
Equipment	+50,000		Note Payable	+50,000			

2.

	Debit	Credit
Interest Expense (+E, −OE)	2,500	
Note Payable (+L)		2,500
[$50,000 × 5% × 12/12 = $2,500]		

Assets		=	Liabilities		+	Owners' Equity	
			Note Payable	+2,500		Interest Expense (+E)	−2,500

3.

	Debit	Debit
Interest Expense (+E, −OE)	2,625	
Note Payable (−L)	52,500	
Cash (−A)		55,125
[($50,000 + $2,500) × 5% × 12/12 = $2,625]		

Assets		=	Liabilities		+	Owners' Equity	
Cash	−55,125		Note Payable	−52,500		Interest Expense (+E)	−2,625

The stated interest rate is always expressed as an annual rate although some bonds require interest payments every six months (that is, semiannually). Each interest payment is computed by multiplying the face value times the stated interest rate (times the fraction of the year if payments are made semiannually). As you will see later, for good economic reasons, bonds may be sold at amounts above or below their face value. A bond's selling price does not affect the amount of each interest payment, however. For example, a 6 percent bond with a face value of $1,000 will always pay interest of $60 cash each year (= $1,000 × 6% × 12/12).

Spotlight On FINANCIAL REPORTING

The financial press reports bond prices each day based on transactions that occurred on the bond exchange. The following is typical of the information you will find:

Company Bond	Close	Yield	Volume	Change
Safeway 5.5 2013	97.2	6.80	58	−1/4
General Mills 6.0 2011	101.4	5.77	250	+3/8
Harrah's 7.0 2020	104.1	6.90	580	−7/8

GENERAL MILLS

This listing reports that the General Mills bond has a stated interest rate of 6.0 percent and will mature in the year 2011. The bond's price is quoted as a percentage of face value; in this case, 101.4 percent of face value, or $1,014 ($1,000 × 1.014). At this price, the bond payments represent a cash yield of 5.77 percent. On the date reported, 250 bonds were sold, and the price increased 3/8 of a point from the closing price on the day before (a point is 1 percent).

Daily changes in bond prices arise from transactions among bondholders, which do not directly involve the company. Consequently, they do not affect the company's financial statements. The company accounts for its bonds using the historical face value and historical interest rates that existed when the bonds were first sold to the public.

Bond Pricing

Neither the company nor its financial advisers determine the price at which bonds sell. Instead, the market determines the price by discounting the cash payments that the company promises to make on the bond. Supplement 14A at the end of this chapter shows the calculations for the $1,000, 6 percent General Mills bond (see page 616). Although it is useful to know how to do these calculations, they are not a necessary step in accounting for a bond issue. Instead, what we really need to know is the amount of cash received from the market when the bonds were first sold. This cash-equivalent amount is the value at which the liability for the bonds is recorded.

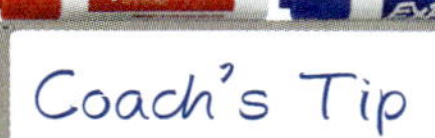

Coach's Tip

Bond prices are typically quoted as a percentage of face value (although the percentage symbol is often omitted).

Because the market determines the price at which bonds sell, the company may receive an amount of cash that is equal to the face value, above the face value, or below the face value. A bond issued for more than its face value is said to have been issued at a **premium**, which is the excess of the bond's issue price over its face value. A bond issued for less than its face value is said to have been issued at a **discount**, which is the amount by which the issue price falls short of the bond's face value. The following sections show how to account for bonds issued at face value, at a premium, and at a discount.

Bonds Issued at Face Value. If General Mills receives $100,000 cash in exchange for issuing 100 bonds at their $1,000 face value, the company's accountants will record the following journal entry:

	Debit	Credit
Cash (+A)	100,000	
Bonds Payable (+L)		100,000

Assets		=	Liabilities		+	Owners' Equity
Cash	+100,000		Bonds Payable	+100,000		

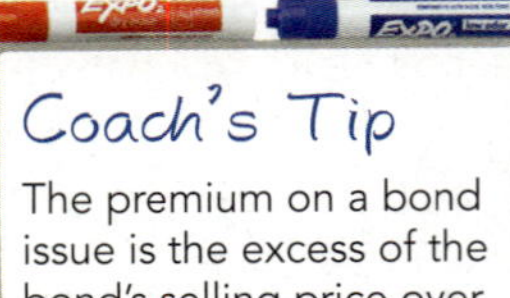

Coach's Tip

The premium on a bond issue is the excess of the bond's selling price over its face value.

Bonds Issued at a Premium. If General Mills receives $107,260 for bonds with a total face value of $100,000, the cash-equivalent amount is $107,260, which represents the total liability on that date. The company's accountants will distinguish the $100,000 face value from the $7,260 premium by recording them in separate liability accounts as in the following journal entry:

	Debit	Credit
Cash (+A)	107,260	
Bonds Payable (+L)		100,000
Premium on Bonds Payable (+L)		7,260

Assets		=	Liabilities		+	Owners' Equity
Cash	+107,260		Bonds Payable	+100,000		
			Premium on Bonds Payable	+7,260		

Why would bondholders be willing to pay a premium? For the same reason that you might pay a premium to acquire tickets to a great concert or a big game. If a bond offers something attractive, such as a high interest rate, bondholders may be willing to pay a premium to acquire it.

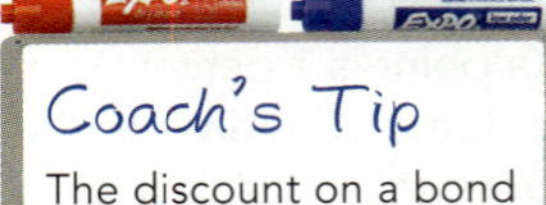

Coach's Tip

The discount on a bond issue is the amount by which the bond issue price falls short of its face value.

Bonds Issued at a Discount. If General Mills receives $93,376 for bonds with a total face value of $100,000, the cash-equivalent amount is $93,376, which represents the liability on that date. The discount of $6,624 (= $100,000 − $93,376) offsets the face value, so accountants will record it in a contra-account. A contra-account to a liability is recorded as a debit as in the following journal entry:

	Debit	Credit
Cash (+A)	93,376	
Discount on Bonds Payable (+xL, −L)	6,624	
Bonds Payable (+L)		100,000

Assets		=	Liabilities		+	Owners' Equity
Cash	+93,376		Bonds Payable	+100,000		
			Discount on Bonds Payable (+xL)	−6,624		

Why would companies such as General Mills be willing to discount a bond? The answer is that they must if they want to sell it. If a bond promises to pay interest at a stated rate of 6 percent when other financial instruments offer 8 percent, no one will be willing to buy the bond unless the company discounts it. The discount reduces the initial price of the bond without changing the interest payments and the face value to be paid at maturity. In effect, a discount increases the return that bondholders earn on their initial investment.

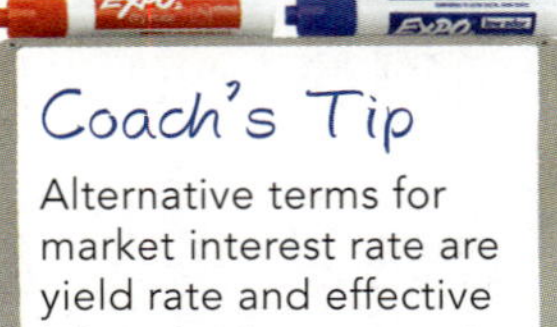

Coach's Tip

Alternative terms for market interest rate are yield rate and effective interest rate.

To illustrate, suppose you could buy a $1,000 bond that pays a stated interest rate of 6 percent and matures in one year. After one year, you would receive the stated interest of $60 ($1,000 × 6% × 12/12) plus the face value of $1,000. If you had paid $1,000 for the bond, you would receive 1.06 times as much as your initial investment [($60 + $1,000) ÷ $1,000]—a return of 6 percent. If instead the bond price were discounted $19, so that you paid only $981 for it, you would receive 1.08 times as much your initial investment [($60 + $1,000) ÷ $981 = 1.08]—a return of 8 percent. This percentage represents both the bondholder's rate of return and the company's cost of borrowing. It is commonly referred to as the **market interest rate**.

Exhibit 14.4 Balance Sheet Reporting of Bond Liabilities

Bonds issued at a premium

Bonds payable	$100,000
Premium on bonds payable	7,260
Unpaid bond liability	107,260

Bonds issued at face value

Bonds payable	$100,000

Bonds issued at a discount

Bonds payable	$100,000
Discount on bonds payable	(6,624)
Unpaid bond liability	93,376

Reporting Bond Liabilities. The total face value of a bond plus any related premium or minus any related discount is reported in the liabilities section of the balance sheet as in Exhibit 14.4 for our three examples. The amount of the unpaid bond liability, after taking into account any premium or discount, is referred to as the bond's **carrying value**.

To determine whether a bond will be issued at a premium, at face value, or at a discount, you need consider only the relationship between the stated interest rate on the bond (what the bond pays in cash) and the market interest rate (the return that bondholders require). Exhibit 14.5 illustrates this relationship.

Exhibit 14.5 Relationships between Interest Rates and Bond Pricing

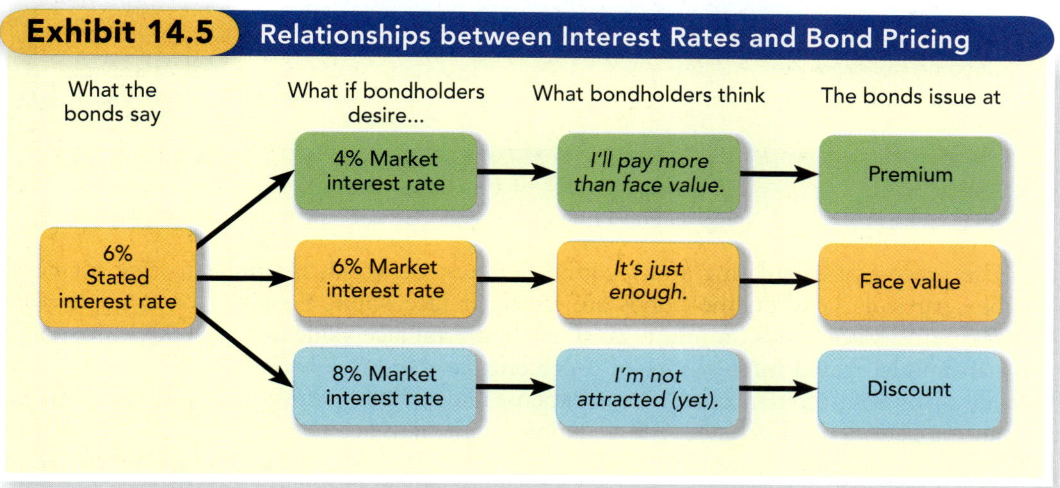

Before you continue, try the following Self-Study Practice to make sure you understand how bonds are priced.

SELF-STUDY PRACTICE

For each of the following independent situations, indicate whether the bonds were issued at a premium, at a discount, or at face value.

1. Stated interest rate = 7% and market interest rate = 7%. ________
2. Stated interest rate = 5% and market interest rate = 6%. ________
3. Bond issue price = $10,100 and bond face value = $10,000. ________

After you have finished, check your answers with the solution at the bottom of the page.

Interest Expense

As time passes, a bond liability creates interest expense, which is matched to each period in which the liability is outstanding. Because interest expense arises from a financing decision (not an operating decision), it is reported below the Income from Operations line on the company's income statement as in Exhibit 14.6.

Solution to Self-Study Practice

1. Face value.
2. Discount—the market requires a better rate of return than the interest stated on the bond.
3. Premium—the market is willing to pay more than face value to obtain the bond's higher interest rate.

Exhibit 14.6 Reporting Interest Expense on the Income Statement

General Mills, Inc.
Income Statement
For the Quarter Ended August 26, 2007
(in millions)

Net sales	$3,072.0
Cost of sales	1,915.8
Selling, general, and administrative expenses	631.6
Other operating expenses	14.5
	2,561.9
Income from operations	510.1
Interest expense	**113.3**
Other expenses (revenues)	(22.4)
Income before income taxes	419.2
Income tax expense	130.3
Net income	$ 288.9

The process of calculating and recording interest on bonds is similar to that for notes payable, particularly when the bonds are issued at face value. Assume, for example, that General Mills issues bonds on July 1, 2009, at their total face value of $100,000. If the bonds carry an annual stated interest rate of 6 percent payable in cash on June 30 of each year, General Mills will need to accrue both an expense and a liability for interest at the end of each accounting period. On December 31, assuming no previous accrual of interest, General Mills would record interest of $3,000 (= $100,000 × 6% × 6/12) with the following entry:

	Debit	Credit
Interest Expense (+E, −OE)	3,000	
Interest Payable (+L)		3,000

Assets	=	Liabilities		+	Owners' Equity	
		Interest Payable	+3,000		Interest Expense (+E)	−3,000

General Mills reports Interest Payable as a current liability because the company will pay this amount within the coming year. When it is paid, Interest Payable will be debited and Cash will be credited.

In comparison to this procedure for reporting interest expense on bonds issued at face value, the procedures for reporting interest expense on bonds issued at a premium or a discount are slightly more complicated. The complication arises because the premium or discount represents an adjustment to the interest rate stated on the bond. A premium reduces the company's cost of borrowing, so it reduces Interest Expense over the life of the bond. A discount increases the company's cost of borrowing, so it increases Interest Expense over the life of the bond. The process of recording these adjustments to interest expense is called amortization. Two methods may be used to amortize premiums and discounts, the effective-interest method (explained in Supplement 14B) and the straight-line method (explained in Supplement 14C).

Bond Retirement

Most bonds are retired (paid off) at maturity. If interest has been fully paid at the time of maturity, the only remaining account to settle will be Bonds Payable. Assuming the General

Mills bonds in our example were retired with a payment equal to their $100,000 face value, the following journal entry would be recorded:

	Debit	Credit
Bonds Payable (−L)	100,000	
Cash (−A)		100,000

Assets		=	Liabilities		+	Owners' Equity
Cash	−100,000		Bonds Payable	−100,000		

Rather than wait until the maturity date to retire the bonds, however, the company may retire them early. Companies with a lot of cash often retire their bonds early to reduce future interest expense and increase net income. Even companies that do not have extra cash may decide to retire their bonds early if interest rates have fallen since issuing the original bonds. In this case, the companies would issue new bonds at the lower interest rate and use the money they receive from the new bonds to retire the old ones before maturity. Again, this decision reduces future interest expense, which increases future earnings.

The early retirement of bonds has three financial effects. The company (1) pays cash, (2) eliminates the bond liability, and (3) reports either a gain or a loss. A gain arises if the cash paid to retire the bonds is less than the carrying value of the bond liability. A loss is incurred if the company pays more than the carrying value at the time of retirement.

To illustrate these effects, assume that in 2000, General Mills issued $100,000 of bonds at face value. Nine years later, in 2009, the company retired the bonds early. At the time, the bond price was 103, so General Mills made a payment of $103,000 (= $100,000 × 103%) to retire the bonds. The following journal entry recorded the retirement:

	Debit	Credit
Bonds Payable (−L)	100,000	
Loss on Bond Retirement (+E, −OE)	3,000	
Cash (−A)		103,000

Assets		=	Liabilities		+	Owners' Equity	
Cash	−103,000		Bonds Payable	−100,000		Loss on Bond Retirement (+E)	−3,000

Notice two features of this example. First, because the bond retirement is a financing decision, the loss would be reported after the Income from Operations line on the income statement. In Exhibit 14.6, this loss would be included in Other Expenses; a gain would be included in Other Revenues. Second, this retirement does not involve the removal of a bond discount or bond premium account because the bonds were issued at face value. If the bonds had been issued below or above face value, any premium or discount balance that existed at the time of retirement would need to be removed as well.

Types of Bonds

When you first start learning about bonds, it may seem the number of new terms that describe the bonds are limitless. These terms can generally be grouped into two categories: (1) those that describe the type of organization that issued the bonds and (2) those that describe specific features of the bond. In the first category are bonds issued by the U.S. Treasury Department ("treasuries"); municipal organizations such as states, cities, counties, and towns ("munis"); and corporations ("corporates"). In the second category are bonds that are backed by collateral ("secured") or not ("debentures"), that the issuing corporation can call in and exchange for cash ("callable") or convert into shares of its stock ("convertible"), and that mature in a series of installments ("serial bonds") or include no periodic interest payments ("zero-coupon bonds" and "strips"). The basic procedures shown in the previous sections for recording bond liabilities and interest expense apply equally to these various types of bonds.

Be sure you understand the basics of bond accounting by trying the following Self-Study Practice before you move to the next section.

SELF-STUDY PRACTICE

In January 2008, Target Corporation issued bonds with a face value of $2,250,000, a stated interest rate of 7.0 percent, and a maturity date of January 15, 2038. The bonds issued at a price of 99.318. Based on this issue price, (1) indicate whether the market interest rate was higher or lower than the stated interest rate at the time of issue and (2) prepare the journal entry to record the bond issue.

After you have finished, check your answers with the solution at the bottom of the page.

Learning Objective 4

Explain how to account for lease liabilities.

Lease Liabilities

A lease is a rental agreement between the owner of property (the lessor) and the renter of that property (the lessee). Depending on the terms of the rental agreement, a lease may be accounted for as an operating lease or a capital lease.

Operating Leases

An **operating lease** allows a company to use property temporarily while the lessor continues to own it. An apartment lease and a daily or weekly car rental from Hertz or Avis are examples of operating leases.

When a company obtains the use of property through an operating lease, accountants record the payments made or owed to the lessor as an operating expense. For example, in 2007, General Mills rented warehouse space at a total cost of $46 million. Assuming that the company paid $40 million in cash and owed $6 million at the end of the year, accountants would record the following journal entry (in millions):

	Debit	Credit
Rent Expense (+E, −OE)	46	
Rent Payable (+L)		6
Cash (−A)		40

Assets		=	Liabilities		+	Owners' Equity	
Cash	−40		Rent Payable	+6		Rent Expense (+E)	−46

Capital Leases

A **capital lease** allows a lessee to use rented property in exchange for payments to the lessor, but unlike an operating lease, it transfers virtually all risks and rewards of owning the property to the lessee. In effect, the lessee purchases the property from the lessor through a series of payments made over the term of the lease. To account for this arrangement, the lessee records the property and the lease liability at the cash-equivalent amount. The cash-equivalent amount is calculated by discounting the payments the lessee will make over the term of the lease. Supplement 14A explains the procedure for discounting the payments (see page 616).

Solution to Self-Study Practice

1. The bonds are issued at a discount (99.318 percent of face value), which implies that the stated interest rate was not as attractive as other interest rates available in the market. That is, the market interest rate was higher than the stated interest rate.
2. Issue price = $2,250,000 × .99318 = $2,234,655.

	Debit	Credit
Cash (+A)	2,234,655	
Discount on Bonds Payable (+xL, −L)	15,345	
Bonds Payable (+L)		2,250,000

General Mills obtains some of its equipment through capital leases. To illustrate the accounting, assume that the company has promised to make payments over a five-year period that equate to the cash-equivalent (discounted) amount of $42,124. When the equipment is obtained, General Mills would record the following journal entry:

	Debit	Credit
Equipment (+A)	42,124	
Lease Liability (+L)		42,124

Assets		=	Liabilities		+	Owners' Equity
Equipment	+42,124		Lease Liability	+42,124		

In the periods that follow, General Mills would record Depreciation Expense on the equipment and Interest Expense on the lease liability.

ANALYZING LONG-TERM LIABILITIES

Learning Objective 5

Calculate and interpret the debt-to-assets and times interest earned ratios.

In evaluating a company's ability to pay its liabilities, a good place to start is with the reports credit-rating agencies issue. These agencies do not report on all companies, however, particularly the smaller ones. Even if they did, their reports might not address your specific concerns. So, you need to know how to analyze a set of financial statements in the same way that a credit rater would.

Essentially, you want to assess what proportion of a company's assets are financed by liabilities and whether or not the company is likely to generate the resources needed to pay the interest on those liabilities. Two financial ratios are commonly used to make these assessments: the debt-to-assets ratio and the times interest earned ratio.

Financial Analysis Tools

Name of Measure	Formula	What It Tells You
Debt-to-assets ratio	$\frac{\text{Total Liabilities}}{\text{Total Assets}}$	• The proportion of assets financed by liabilities • The higher the number the greater the financing risk
Times interest earned ratio	$\frac{\text{(Net Income + Interest Expense + Income Tax Expense)}}{\text{Interest Expense}}$	• Whether sufficient resources are generated to cover interest costs • The higher the number the better the coverage

Debt-to-Assets Ratio

The debt-to-assets ratio compares total liabilities to total assets. Usually calculated to three decimal places, it can be expressed as a percentage by multiplying it by 100. This ratio indicates the proportion of total assets that are financed by debt. It is important to know how much debt is used to finance assets because debt must be repaid whether or not a company is doing well. If a company finances its assets mainly by debt rather than equity, then the debt-to-assets ratio will be high, suggesting that the company's financing strategy is risky. Ultimately, a company can be forced into bankruptcy if it takes on more debt than it could ever repay.

Refer to Exhibit 14.7 for an illustration of how debt plays a major role in financing General Mills' assets: 64.5 percent of the company's assets were financed by debt at the end of 2007. That percentage is not nearly as large, however, as the one for rival Kellogg's, whose debt-to-assets ratio was more than 80 percent. Although these ratios are typical of the food processing industry, they are high compared to other industries. Companies in the video game industry, for example, have much lower debt-to-assets ratios (Activision's is 13.7 percent).

Exhibit 14.7 Debt-to-Assets Ratios in the Food Processing Industry

Company	Relevant Information (in millions)			2007 Debt-to-Assets Ratio
GENERAL MILLS		2007	2006	
	Total liabilities	\$11,726	\$11,167	\$11,726 / \$18,184 = 0.645 or 64.5%
	Total assets	18,184	18,075	
Kellogg's		2007	2006	
	Total liabilities	\$ 8,645	\$ 8,291	\$ 8,645 / \$10,714 = 0.807 or 80.7%
	Total assets	10,714	10,575	

Spotlight on ETHICS

Doctoring the Debt-to-Assets Ratio

The debt-to-assets ratio can be a useful measure of the extent to which a company relies on debt to finance its assets. Analysts should be aware, however, that seemingly normal transactions that occur just before the end of an accounting period can influence this ratio. For example, the ratio can be reduced by repaying a loan just prior to the financial statement date. Although this transaction decreases total liabilities and total assets by the same amount, it has a greater impact on liabilities than on assets, thus reducing the ratio. If a company's debt-to-assets ratio is 10 to 15 (67 percent) before repayment of a \$5 loan, it will be 5 to 10 (50 percent) after repayment.

Times Interest Earned Ratio

One way to judge a company's ability to pay interest is to ask whether it has generated enough income to cover its interest expense. The measure that most analysts use for this purpose is the **times interest earned ratio**.

The financial analysis tools box (on page 611) showed the formula for the times interest earned ratio. It is reproduced after the following paragraph. Notice that in this ratio, interest and income tax expenses are added back into net income. The reason for this is simple: Analysts want to know whether a company generates enough income to cover its interest expense **before the costs of financing and taxes.** In general, a high times interest earned ratio is viewed more favorably than a low one. A high ratio indicates an extra margin of protection should the company's profitability decline in the future.

Using the information in the income statement in Exhibit 14.6 on page 608, we can compute the times interest earned ratio for General Mills as follows.

$$\frac{\text{Net Income} + \text{Interest Expense} + \text{Income Tax Expense}}{\text{Interest Expense}} = \frac{\$288.9 + \$113.3 + \$130.3}{\$113.3} = 4.70$$

This ratio means that General Mills generates \$4.70 of income (before the costs of financing and taxes) for each dollar of interest expense. No doubt this ratio is part of the reason that General Mills has earned a favorable credit rating of BBB or higher.

Every now and then you will see a times interest earned ratio that is less than 1.0 or even negative. **When the times interest earned ratio is less than 1.0, a company is not generating enough income to cover its interest expense.** Most companies with a negative times interest earned ratio survive only a couple of years before declaring bankruptcy.

Before you conclude your reading of this chapter, try the following Self-Study Practice to make sure you understand how to analyze long-term liabilities.

SELF-STUDY PRACTICE

1. Use the information in Exhibit 14.7 to calculate the 2006 debt-to-assets ratios for General Mills and Kellogg's. Show the ratios as whole numbers calculated to three decimal places and as percentages.
2. Compare the ratios calculated in part (1) to the ratios in Exhibit 14.7. Did the two companies' financing risk increase or decrease in 2007 relative to 2006?

After you have finished, check your answers with the solutions at the bottom of the page.

Demonstration Case A

Discounted Notes

On January 1, 2008, Central University (CU) bought new gymnastics equipment. Rather than pay cash, CU gave a note that promised payment of $20,000 on January 1, 2011. CU typically borrows at a 4 percent interest rate. Using a 4 percent interest rate to discount the $20,000 payment, CU determined that the present value of this liability on January 1, 2008, was $17,780.

Required:

1. Give the journal entry required to record the equipment purchase on January 1, 2008.
2. Calculate the interest expense on the note in 2008. If this amount is added to the note amount on December 31, 2008, what will be the new balance in Note Payable on December 31, 2008? Continue these calculations for 2009 and 2010. What will be the balance in Notes Payable immediately prior to payment of the note on January 1, 2011? Round all calculations to the nearest dollar.
3. Assuming CU adjusts its accounting records once each year on December 31, give the journal entries required to accrue interest on the note on December 31, 2008, 2009, and 2010.

Suggested Solution

1.

	Debit	Credit
Equipment (+A)	17,780	
Note Payable (+L)		17,780

Assets		=	Liabilities		+	Owners' Equity
Equipment	+17,780		Note Payable	+17,780		

2.

	Note Payable, January 1	Interest Expense	Note Payable, December 31
2008	$17,780	$17,780 × 4% × 12/12 = $711	$17,780 + $711 = $18,491
2009	18,491	18,491 × 4% × 12/12 = 740	18,491 + 740 = 19,231
2010	19,231	19,231 × 4% × 12/12 = 769	19,231 + 769 = 20,000

Solution to Self-Study Practice

1. General Mills = $11,167 / $18,075 = 0.618 or 61.8%.
   Kellogg's = $8,291 / $10,575 = 0.784 or 78.4%.
2. Both companies increased their reliance on debt in 2007, suggesting an increase in the risk that they would be unable to repay their borrowings.

3. December 31, 2008:

	Debit	Credit
Interest Expense (+E, −OE)	711	
Note Payable (+L)		711

Assets	=	Liabilities		+	Owners' Equity	
		Note Payable	+711		Interest Expense (+E)	−711

December 31, 2009:

	Debit	Credit
Interest Expense (+E, −OE)	740	
Note Payable (+L)		740

Assets	=	Liabilities		+	Owners' Equity	
		Note Payable	+740		Interest Expense (+E)	−740

December 31, 2010:

	Debit	Credit
Interest Expense (+E, −OE)	769	
Note Payable (+L)		769

Assets	=	Liabilities		+	Owners' Equity	
		Note Payable	+769		Interest Expense (+E)	−769

Demonstration Case B

Bonds

On February 1, 2006, Black & Decker Corporation issued 300,000 bonds at 5.75 percent, each with a face value of $1,000 and a maturity date of January 31, 2016. The bonds were issued at 99.6. Of the cash received from the issue, $154.6 million was used to retire some 7 percent bonds. Assume the 7 percent bonds had been previously issued at a face value of $155 million.

Required:

1. How much cash did Black & Decker Corporation receive from the sale of the bonds payable? Show your computations.
2. What was the amount of the premium or discount on the bonds payable?
3. Give the journal entry for recording the issue of the 5.75 percent bonds on February 1, 2006.
4. Show how the bonds would be reported on the balance sheet on February 1, 2006.
5. Give the journal entry to record the retirement of the 7 percent bonds.

Suggested Solution

1. Sale price of the bonds: 300,000 bonds × $1,000 face value × 99.6% = $298,800,000, or $298.8 million.
2. Discount on the bonds payable: $300 million − $298.8 million = $1.2 million.

3. February 1, 2006 (in millions):

	Debit	Credit
Cash (+A)	298.8	
Discount on Bonds Payable (+xL, −L)	1.2	
Bonds Payable (+L)		300.0

Assets		=	Liabilities		+	Owners' Equity
Cash	+298.8		Bonds Payable	+300.0		
			Discount on Bonds Payable (+xL)	−1.2		

4. Balance sheet reporting (long-term liabilities) (in millions):

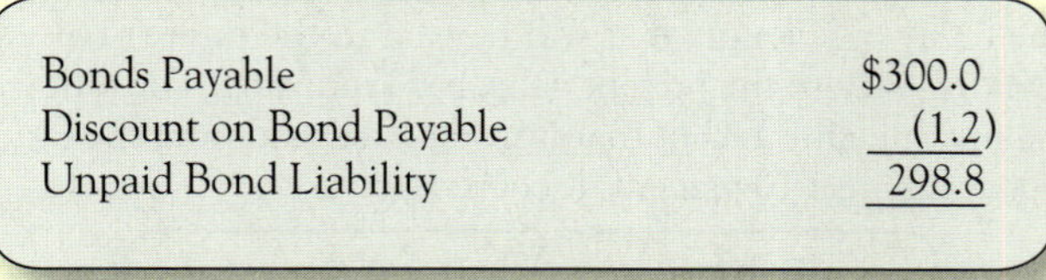

Bonds Payable	$300.0
Discount on Bond Payable	(1.2)
Unpaid Bond Liability	298.8

5. (in millions)

Face value	$ 155.0
Paid to retire	(154.6)
Gain	$ 0.4

	Debit	Credit
Bonds Payable (−L)	155.0	
Gain on Bond Retirement (+R, +OE)		0.4
Cash (−A)		154.6

Assets		=	Liabilities		+	Owners' Equity	
Cash	−154.6		Bonds Payable	−155.0		Gain on Bond Retirement (+R)	+0.4

Demonstration Case C

Leases

AMR Corporation provides air transportation to customers through its American Airlines and American Eagle business units. As of December 31, 2006, AMR operated 1,003 aircraft, 231 of which were obtained through operating leases and 90 through capital leases. For the year ended December 31, 2006, AMR incurred $606 million in aircraft rental expense. At the end of the year, the company owed $927 million for aircraft obtained via capital leases. The aircraft were capitalized as a noncurrent asset at a total cost of $1,744 million.

AMR

Required:

1. Does the aircraft rental expense relate to operating leases or capital leases?
2. Describe the two adjustments that would be made each year with respect to the aircraft and obligations related to capital leases.

Suggested Solution

1. The aircraft rental expense relates to operating leases. (When payments are made for capital leases, they are reported as interest expense and reductions in the principal owed on the lease liability.)
2. An adjustment would be recorded each accounting period for (a) depreciation on the aircraft obtained through capital leases and (b) interest on the lease liability. (Rent on the operating leases would be accrued as well.)

Supplement 14A

Discounting Future Payments

This supplement is based on the simple notion that you can invest cash today to earn interest over time, resulting in a larger amount in the future. The future value of your investment is larger than its present value because interest is added to the original investment, in a process called compounding. The following timeline shows how $1,000 invested today at a 10 percent interest rate becomes $1,100 one year from now ($1,000 × 1.10 = $1,100):

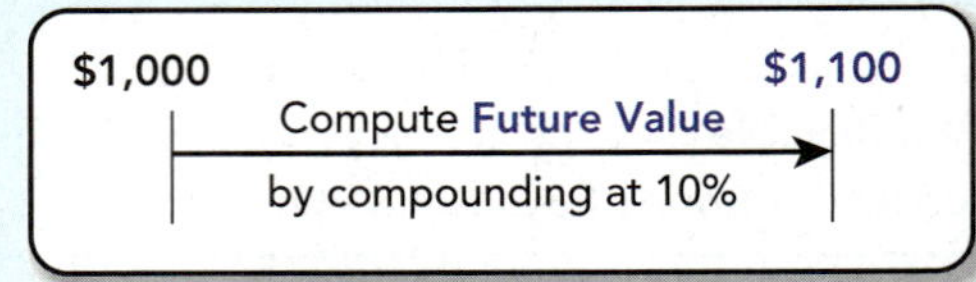

In finance, many problems involve determining the future value that can be generated from some present value. In accounting, however, our focus is just the opposite: We want to know the present (cash-equivalent) value today of amounts that will be paid in the future. This process of starting with the future value and working back to the present value is **discounting**. The following timeline shows the same situation as in the first timeline except that it works backward from the future value of $1,100 to a present value of $1,000, assuming a 10 percent discount rate:

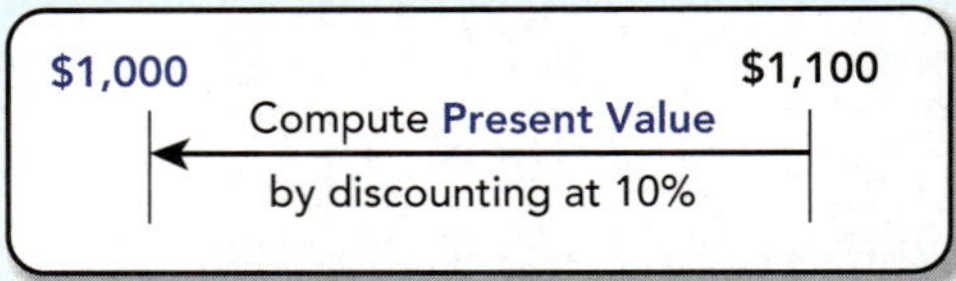

Two different discounting situations arise in business. The first involves discounting a **single amount** paid only once. This situation is illustrated in our timeline. To calculate the present value of a single amount, you divide the future payment by the rate at which interest accumulates in each period. Because our example involves only one period, the calculation is straightforward: $1,100 ÷ 1.10 = $1,000.

As the number of periods increases, this method becomes tiresome. An alternative approach is to use present value tables. Table 14A-1 shows the present value of $1 at various combinations of interest rates

Table 14A-1 Present Value of $1

Periods	2%	3%	3.75%	4%	4.25%	5%	6%	7%	8%
1	0.9804	0.9709	0.9639	0.9615	0.9592	0.9524	0.9434	0.9346	0.9259
2	0.9612	0.9426	0.9290	0.9246	0.9201	0.9070	0.8900	0.8734	0.8573
3	0.9423	0.9151	0.8954	0.8890	0.8826	0.8638	0.8396	0.8163	0.7938
4	0.9238	0.8885	0.8631	0.8548	0.8466	0.8227	0.7921	0.7629	0.7350
5	0.9057	0.8626	0.8319	0.8219	0.8121	0.7835	0.7473	0.7130	0.6806
6	0.8880	0.8375	0.8018	0.7903	0.7790	0.7462	0.7050	0.6663	0.6302
7	0.8706	0.8131	0.7728	0.7599	0.7473	0.7107	0.6651	0.6227	0.5835
8	0.8535	0.7894	0.7449	0.7307	0.7168	0.6768	0.6274	0.5820	0.5403
9	0.8368	0.7664	0.7180	0.7026	0.6876	0.6446	0.5919	0.5439	0.5002
10	0.8203	0.7441	0.6920	0.6756	0.6595	0.6139	0.5584	0.5083	0.4632
20	0.6730	0.5537	0.4789	0.4564	0.4350	0.3769	0.3118	0.2584	0.2145

Periods	9%	10%	11%	12%	13%	14%	15%	20%	25%
1	0.9174	0.9091	0.9009	0.8929	0.8850	0.8772	0.8696	0.8333	0.8000
2	0.8417	0.8264	0.8116	0.7972	0.7831	0.7695	0.7561	0.6944	0.6400
3	0.7722	0.7513	0.7312	0.7118	0.6931	0.6750	0.6575	0.5787	0.5120
4	0.7084	0.6830	0.6587	0.6355	0.6133	0.5921	0.5718	0.4823	0.4096
5	0.6499	0.6209	0.5935	0.5674	0.5428	0.5194	0.4972	0.4019	0.3277
6	0.5963	0.5645	0.5346	0.5066	0.4803	0.4556	0.4323	0.3349	0.2621
7	0.5470	0.5132	0.4817	0.4523	0.4251	0.3996	0.3759	0.2791	0.2097
8	0.5019	0.4665	0.4339	0.4039	0.3762	0.3506	0.3269	0.2326	0.1678
9	0.4604	0.4241	0.3909	0.3606	0.3329	0.3075	0.2843	0.1938	0.1342
10	0.4224	0.3855	0.3522	0.3220	0.2946	0.2697	0.2472	0.1615	0.1074
20	0.1784	0.1486	0.1240	0.1037	0.0868	0.0728	0.0611	0.0261	0.0115

and time periods. To solve the problem in our example, we would look for the value at the intersection of 10 percent and one period, which is 0.9091. This value implies that $1 paid one year from now equals $0.9091 today. To apply it to a $1,100 payment in one year, we would simply multiply it by $1,100 to obtain a present value of $1,000 (rounded).

The second type of discounting situation that arises in business involves a series of equal amounts, called an **annuity**. The following timeline illustrates an annuity:

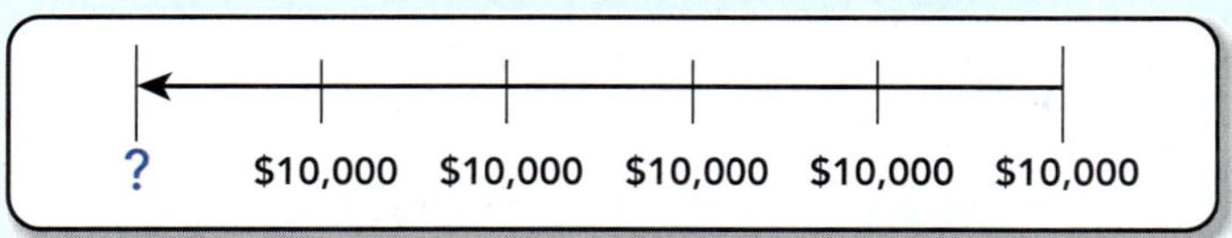

Although we could treat each payment in this annuity as a single amount to be discounted separately (and then totaled), such an approach would be cumbersome. To save time, we can use Table 14A-2, which shows the present value of a $1 annuity received at the end of several periods given various combinations of interest rates and periods. Assuming an interest rate of 6 percent for five years, we simply multiply the discounting factor in the table, 4.2124, by the annuity amount of $10,000 to obtain a present value of $42,124.

The following sections show how to apply these discounting techniques to discounted notes, bonds payable, and capital leases.

Discounted Notes

Assume that General Mills has just signed a note that requires a $112,360 payment in two years. The note does not state an interest rate, but General Mills typically incurs a 6 percent annual rate.

Table 14A-2 Present Value of Annuity of $1

Periods*	2%	3%	3.75%	4%	4.25%	5%	6%	7%	8%
1	0.9804	0.9709	0.9639	0.9615	0.9592	0.9524	0.9434	0.9346	0.9259
2	1.9416	1.9135	1.8929	1.8861	1.8794	1.8594	1.8334	1.8080	1.7833
3	2.8839	2.8286	2.7883	2.7751	2.7620	2.7232	2.6730	2.6243	2.5771
4	3.8077	3.7171	3.6514	3.6299	3.6086	3.5460	3.4651	3.3872	3.3121
5	4.7135	4.5797	4.4833	4.4518	4.4207	4.3295	4.2124	4.1002	3.9927
6	5.6014	5.4172	5.2851	5.2421	5.1997	5.0757	4.9173	4.7665	4.6229
7	6.4720	6.2303	6.0579	6.0021	5.9470	5.7864	5.5824	5.3893	5.2064
8	7.3255	7.0197	6.8028	6.7327	6.6638	6.4632	6.2098	5.9713	5.7466
9	8.1622	7.7861	7.5208	7.4353	7.3513	7.1078	6.8017	6.5152	6.2469
10	8.9826	8.5302	8.2128	8.1109	8.0109	7.7217	7.3601	7.0236	6.7101
20	16.3514	14.8775	13.8962	13.5903	13.2944	12.4622	11.4699	10.5940	9.8181

Periods*	9%	10%	11%	12%	13%	14%	15%	20%	25%
1	0.9174	0.9091	0.9009	0.8929	0.8550	0.8772	0.8696	0.8333	0.8000
2	1.7591	1.7355	1.7125	1.6901	1.6681	1.6467	1.6257	1.5278	1.4400
3	2.5313	2.4869	2.4437	2.4018	2.3612	2.3216	2.2832	2.1065	1.9520
4	3.2397	3.1699	3.1024	3.0373	2.9745	2.9137	2.8550	2.5887	2.3616
5	3.8897	3.7908	3.6959	3.6048	3.5172	3.4331	3.3522	2.9906	2.6893
6	4.4859	4.3553	4.2305	4.1114	3.9975	3.8887	3.7845	3.3255	2.9514
7	5.0330	4.8684	4.7122	4.5638	4.4226	4.2883	4.1604	3.6046	3.1611
8	5.5348	5.3349	5.1461	4.9676	4.7988	4.6389	4.4873	3.8372	3.3289
9	5.9952	5.7590	5.5370	5.3282	4.1317	4.9464	4.7716	4.0310	3.4631
10	6.4177	6.1446	5.8892	5.6502	5.4262	5.2161	5.0188	4.1925	3.5705
20	9.1285	8.5136	7.9633	7.4694	7.0248	6.6231	6.2593	4.8696	3.9539

*There is one payment each period.

We use that rate to discount the future payment of $112,360 to today's present value as in the following timeline:

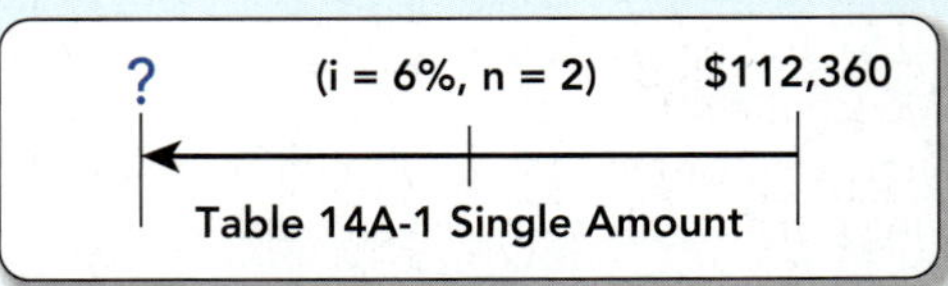

Table 14A-1 shows that at an interest rate of 6 percent over two periods, the discounting factor we should use is 0.8900. So, we can compute the present value of the note as follows:

0.8900 × $112,360 = $100,000 Present Value

Bonds Payable

A bond represents a promise to pay a specified **face value** at maturity plus a **stated interest rate** each period until maturity. The following timeline illustrates these payments using the example in which General Mills issued 100 bonds, each with a face value of $1,000, to be repaid at maturity in four years. The stated interest rate of 6 percent is to be paid annually, which means a total annual interest payment of $6,000 (100 bonds × $1,000 × 6%). The two question marks on the timeline indicate that the $100,000 face value (a single amount) should be discounted separately from the $6,000 interest payments (an annuity). The total of the two present values will equal the value that the bond market places on these bonds.

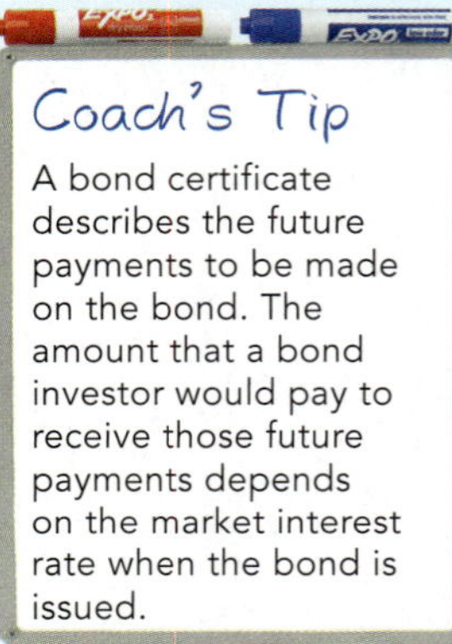

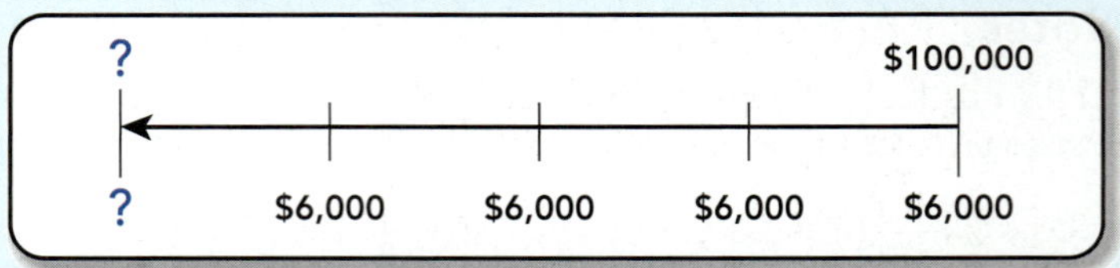

The value the market places on bond payments depends on three factors: (1) the amount of the payments for face value and interest, (2) the period covered by each payment, and (3) the market interest rate when the bond is issued. The following examples show how differences in the market interest rate affect the computations.

Bonds Issued at Face Value.

Exhibit 14.5 (on page 607) shows that bonds will be issued at their face value if their stated interest rate (what the bond pays) equals the market interest rate (what the market demands). To illustrate, assume that the market interest rate is 6 percent, which equals the 6 percent stated interest rate used to compute the interest payments shown in the timeline. Table 14A-1 shows that the discounting factor for a single amount at 6 percent for four periods is 0.7921; Table 14A-2 shows that the discounting factor for an annuity at 6 percent for four periods 3.4651. We can multiply these factors by the future payments to get the present values:

Present value of $100,000 face value ($100,000 × 0.7921)	$ 79,210
Present value of $6,000 annuity ($6,000 × 3.4651)	20,790
Total present value of bond	$100,000

We should mention that, because the discounting factors are rounded to four decimal places, small rounding errors can arise. For example, if you calculate $6,000 × 3.4651 in the previous example, you will find it equals $20,790.60. We have rounded this down so that the total present value equals $100,000.

Bonds Issued above Face Value (at a Premium).

Bonds will be issued at a premium if their stated interest rate is higher than the market interest rate. Assume, for example, that the stated interest rate is 6 percent, but the market interest rate is only 4 percent. The discounting factor for a single amount at 4 percent for four periods is 0.8548 (see Table 14A-1); the discounting factor for an annuity at the same 4 percent interest rate for the same number of periods is 3.6299 (see Table 14A-2). If we multiply these factors by the future payments, we get the present values:

Present value of $100,000 face value ($100,000 × 0.8548)	$ 85,480
Present value of $6,000 annuity ($6,000 × 3.6299)	21,780
Total present value of bond	$107,260

Bonds Issued below Face Value (at a Discount).

Bonds will be issued at a discount if their stated interest rate is lower than the market interest rate. Assume, for example, that the stated interest rate is 6 percent, but the market interest rate is 8 percent. The discounting factor for a single amount at 8 percent for four periods is 0.7350 (see Table 14A-1); the discounting factor for an annuity at the same 8 percent rate for the same number of periods is 3.3121 (see Table 14A-2). If we multiply these factors by the future payments, we get the present values:

Present value of $100,000 face value ($100,000 × 0.7350)	$73,503
Present value of $6,000 annuity ($6,000 × 3.3121)	19,873
Total present value of bond	$93,376

Again, we need to mention that because the present value factors are rounded to four decimal places, small rounding differences may arise. In the preceding calculation, for example, we have shown $73,503, which is the actual present value unaffected by rounding, rather than the amount obtained by multiplying $100,000 by the rounded factor of 0.7350.

Capital Leases

A capital lease is a rental agreement that typically requires the lessee to make a series of equal payments over the term of the lease. Those payments represent an annuity. To compute the present (cash-equivalent) value of the annuity when a company enters into the lease, we can simply multiply the payment by the appropriate annuity factor in Table 14A-2.

To illustrate, assume General Mills has agreed to rent a piece of equipment for five years in return for five annual payments of $10,000 at an implied interest rate of 6 percent. The discounting factor for an annuity at 6 percent over five periods is 4.2124 (see Table 14A-2). We can use this factor to calculate the present (cash-equivalent) value of the five payments when a company enters into the agreement as follows:

$10,000 × 4.2124 = $42,124 present value

Interest Rates and Interest Periods

The preceding illustrations assumed annual interest periods. Although interest *rates* are always quoted on an annual basis, interest *periods* may cover less than a year. For example, semiannual interest implies two interest periods each year; quarterly interest implies four periods per year. When interest periods are less than a year, both the number of periods and the interest rate must be restated to be consistent with the length of the interest period.

To illustrate, 12 percent interest compounded annually for five years implies an interest rate of 12 percent and five periods. If interest is compounded quarterly, however, the interest period is one-quarter of a year (four periods per year), and the quarterly interest rate is one-quarter of the annual rate (3 percent per quarter). Therefore, 12 percent interest compounded quarterly for five years implies an interest rate of 3 percent per period over 20 interest periods (5 years × 4 periods per year).

Supplement 14B

Effective-Interest Method of Amortization

When a bond is issued at a premium or a discount, the amount of the bond premium or discount must be matched to the periods in which the bond is outstanding. This process, called bond amortization, may be accomplished using the effective-interest method, which ensures that interest expense represents the company's actual cost of borrowing. To calculate the interest expense for each interest period, accountants multiply the unpaid bond liability by the market interest rate that existed when the bonds were issued. Then they record the difference between the interest expense and the amount of interest paid (or accrued) that period as a reduction in the bond premium or discount as in the following examples.

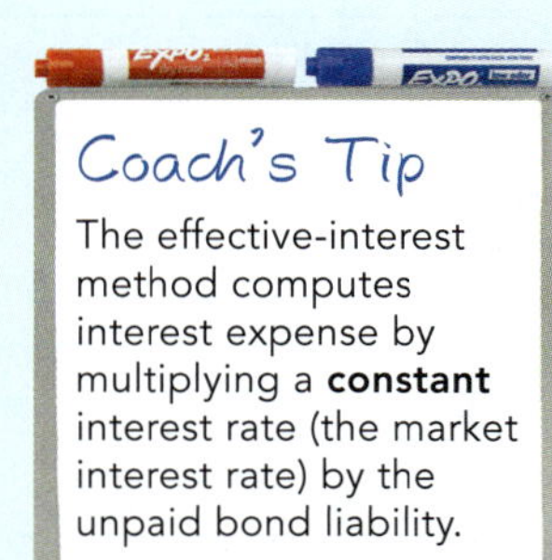

Bond Premiums

A premium arises when the bond issuer receives more cash than the issuer repays at maturity. In effect, the premium reduces the company's cost of borrowing, so that in each accounting period, interest expense is lower than the actual interest payment. The excess of the interest payment over the interest expense is recorded as a reduction in the Premium on Bonds Payable liability account.

In our earlier example, General Mills received $107,260 for bonds with a total face value of $100,000. The company received a premium because the stated interest rate on the bonds (6 percent) was higher than the market interest rate at the time the bonds were issued (4 percent). The stated interest rate determines the interest payment that is made each period ($100,000 × 6% × 12/12 = $6,000). Interest expense, however, is based on the market interest rate, as follows:

Interest Expense = Unpaid Bond Liability × Market Interest Rate × n/12

Unpaid Bond Liability = Bonds Payable + Premium on Bonds Payable

n = Number of Months in Each Interest Period

For the first year ended December 31, 2007, interest expense for these bonds would be $4,290 ($107,260 × 4% × 12/12). The interest payment is $6,000 ($100,000 × 6% × 12/12). You can think of the difference between the $6,000 payment and the $4,290 interest expense ($6,000 − $4,290 = $1,710) as a partial repayment of the Premium on Bonds Payable. These effects would be recorded on December 31, 2007, in the following journal entry:

	Debit	Credit
Interest Expense (+E, −OE)	4,290	
Premium on Bonds Payable (−L)	1,710	
Cash (−A)		6,000

Assets		=	Liabilities		+	Owners' Equity	
Cash	−6,000		Premium on Bonds Payable	−1,710		Interest Expense (+E)	−4,290

Coach's Tip

The beginning balance on January 1, 2008, is the same as the ending balance on December 31, 2007.

Now that the journal entry has reduced the Premium on Bonds Payable, the unpaid bond liability in 2008 is smaller than it was in 2007 ($107,260 − $1,710 = $105,550). Thus, the calculation of Interest Expense in 2008 reflects this change, by multiplying the unpaid bond liability on January 1, 2008, by the market rate of interest for the full year ($105,550 × 4% × 12/12 = $4,222). Again, think of the difference between the $6,000 payment in 2008 and the $4,222 interest expense as another partial repayment of the Premium on Bonds Payable ($6,000 − $4,222 = $1,778). These effects would be recorded with the following journal entry:

	Debit	Credit
Interest Expense (+E, −OE)	4,222	
Premium on Bonds Payable (−L)	1,778	
Cash (−A)		6,000

Assets		=	Liabilities		+	Owners' Equity	
Cash	−6,000		Premium on Bonds Payable	−1,778		Interest Expense (+E)	−4,222

In each remaining year, General Mills will pay $6,000 as promised on the bond certificate. As you have just seen, a portion of that payment will represent Interest Expense and a portion reduces the original Premium on Bonds Payable. The following bond amortization schedule summarizes these effects:

BOND PREMIUM AMORTIZATION SCHEDULE: EFFECTIVE-INTEREST METHOD

	CHANGES DURING THE PERIOD			ENDING BOND LIABILITY BALANCES		
Period Ended	(A) Interest Expense	(B) Interest Payable	(C) (= B − A) Amortization of Premium	(D) Bonds Payable	(E) Premium on Bonds Payable	(F) (= D + E) Unpaid Bond Liability
01/01/07	—	—	—	$100,000	$7,260	$107,260
12/31/07	$4,290	$6,000	$1,710	100,000	5,550	105,550
12/31/08	4,222	6,000	1,778	100,000	3,772	103,772
12/31/09	4,151	6,000	1,849	100,000	1,923	101,923
12/31/10	4,077	6,000	1,923	100,000	0	100,000

Bond Discounts

A discount arises when the bond issuer receives less cash than the issuer must repay at maturity. In effect, the discount increases the company's cost of borrowing so that in each accounting period, interest expense is higher than the company's interest payment. The excess amount represents an increase in the unpaid bond liability, which will be paid at maturity. To report this effect, accountants record a decrease in the contra-liability account Discount on Bonds Payable. Decreasing this contra-liability increases the carrying value of the bond liability.

In our earlier example, General Mills received \$93,376 for bonds with a total face value of \$100,000. The company gave buyers a discount because the stated interest rate on the bonds (6 percent) was less than the market interest rate at the time the bonds were issued (8 percent). The stated interest rate determines the interest payment that must be made each period (\$100,000 × 6% × 12/12 = \$6,000). The interest expense is based on the market interest rate, as follows:

Interest Expense = Unpaid Bond Liability × Market Interest Rate × n/12

Unpaid Bond Liability = Bonds Payable − Discount on Bonds Payable

n = Number of Months in Each Interest Period

For the first year ended December 31, 2007, interest expense on these bonds would be \$7,470 (\$93,376 × 8% × 12/12). The interest payment is \$6,000 (\$100,000 × 6% × 12/12). The difference between the interest expense and the payment (\$7,470 − \$6,000 = \$1,470) represents the amortization of the bond discount in 2007. These effects would be recorded on December 31, 2007, in the following journal entry:

	Debit	Credit
Interest Expense (+E, −OE)	7,470	
Discount on Bonds Payable (−xL, +L)		1,470
Cash (−A)		6,000

Assets	=	Liabilities	+	Owners' Equity
Cash −6,000		Discount on Bonds Payable (−xL) +1,470		Interest Expense (+E) −7,470

Because the 2007 interest expense was not paid in full, the unpaid bond liability at the beginning of 2008 will be more than it was in the last year (\$93,376 + \$1,470 = \$94,846). Interest expense for the following year will reflect this change in the unpaid bond liability. Interest expense in 2008 would be calculated by multiplying the unpaid bond liability on January 1, 2008, by the market rate of interest for the full year (\$94,846 × 8% × 12/12 = \$7,588). Again, the difference between the \$7,588 interest expense and the \$6,000 interest paid in 2008 represents amortization of the bond discount in 2008 (\$7,588 − \$6,000 = \$1,588). These effects would be recorded with the following journal entry:

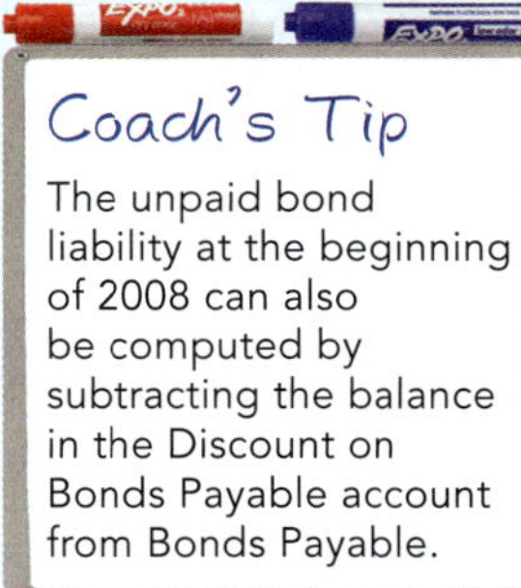

	Debit	Credit
Interest Expense (+E, −OE)	7,588	
Discount on Bonds Payable (−xL, +L)		1,588
Cash (−A)		6,000

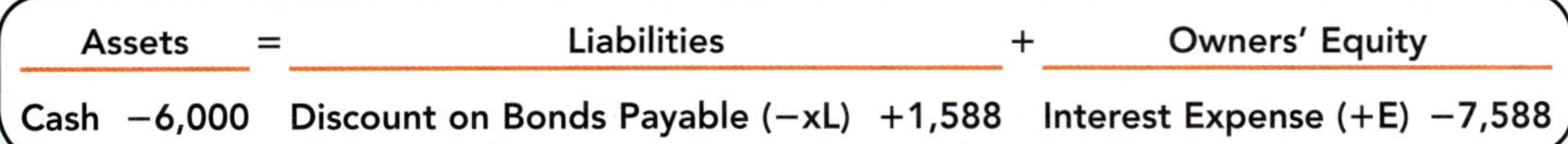

Assets	=	Liabilities	+	Owners' Equity
Cash −6,000		Discount on Bonds Payable (−xL) +1,588		Interest Expense (+E) −7,588

In each remaining year, General Mills will pay \$6,000 interest, as promised on the bond certificate. As we have seen, however, this payment will be less than the interest expense, so the unpaid bond liability will continue to increase (through decreases in the contra-liability account Discount on Bonds Payable). These effects are summarized in the following bond amortization schedule:

BOND DISCOUNT AMORTIZATION SCHEDULE: EFFECTIVE-INTEREST METHOD						
	CHANGES DURING THE PERIOD			ENDING BOND LIABILITY BALANCES		
Period Ended	(A) Interest Expense	(B) Interest Payable	(C) (= A − B) Amortization of Discount	(D) Bonds Payable	(E) Discount on Bonds Payable	(F) (= D − E) Unpaid Bond Liability
01/01/07	—	—	—	$100,000	$6,624	$ 93,376
12/31/07	$7,470	$6,000	$1,470	100,000	5,154	94,846
12/31/08	7,588	6,000	1,588	100,000	3,566	96,434
12/31/09	7,715	6,000	1,715	100,000	1,851	98,149
12/31/10	7,851	6,000	1,851	100,000	0	100,000

Coach's Tip

The straight-line method amortizes a bond premium or discount by adjusting Interest Expense each period by a **constant** dollar amount.

Supplement 14C

Straight-Line Method of Amortization

The aim of the straight-line method of amortization is to **match** any bond premium or discount to the periods in which the bond liability remains unpaid. Rather than adjust the rate used to calculate the interest expense, the straight-line method allocates the total premium or discount evenly over each year. Because this method results in an equal amount of interest expense each period, it is easy to apply. However, constant interest expense does not reflect reality because the bond liability changes each period. Consequently, the straight-line method may be used only when it does not materially differ from the effective-interest method of amortization (presented in Supplement 14B).

Bond Premiums

A premium arises when the bond issuer receives more cash than the issuer repays at maturity. In effect, a premium reduces the company's cost of borrowing, so amortization of the premium causes interest expense to be lower than the interest payment each period. The difference is recorded as a reduction in the Premium on Bonds Payable liability account.

In our earlier example, General Mills received $107,260 for four-year bonds with a total face value of $100,000, implying a premium of $7,260. Using the straight-line method, amortization of the premium in each of the four years that the bonds remain unpaid would be $1,815 (= $7,260 ÷ 4). This amount would be subtracted from the interest to be paid ($6,000) to arrive at the amount of interest expense ($4,185). The effects would be recorded in the following journal entry:

	Debit	Credit
Interest Expense (+E, −OE)	4,185	
Premium on Bonds Payable (−L)	1,185	
Cash (−A)		6,000

Assets		=	Liabilities		+	Owners' Equity	
Cash	−6,000		Premium on Bonds Payable	−1,815		Interest Expense (+E)	−4,185

This journal entry would be recorded each year on December 31 until the bonds mature. The following bond amortization schedule summarizes the effects:

BOND PREMIUM AMORTIZATION SCHEDULE: STRAIGHT-LINE METHOD						
	CHANGES DURING THE PERIOD			ENDING BOND LIABILITY BALANCES		
Period Ended	(A) Interest Payable	(B) Amortization of Premium	(C) (= A − B) Interest Expense	(D) Bonds Payable	(E) Premium on Bonds Payable	(F) (= D + E) Unpaid Bond Liability
01/01/07	—	—	—	$100,000	$7,260	$107,260
12/31/07	$6,000	$1,815	$4,185	100,000	5,445	105,445
12/31/08	6,000	1,815	4,185	100,000	3,630	103,630
12/31/09	6,000	1,815	4,185	100,000	1,815	101,815
12/31/10	6,000	1,815	4,185	100,000	0	100,000

Bond Discounts

A discount arises when the bond issuer receives less cash than the issuer repays at maturity. In effect, a discount increases the company's cost of borrowing, so amortization of the discount causes interest expense to be higher than the interest payment each period. To report this effect, accountants record a decrease in Discount on Bonds Payable and an increase in Interest Expense.

In our earlier example, General Mills received $93,376 for four-year bonds with a total face value of $100,000, implying a discount of $6,624. Using the straight-line method, amortization of the discount in each of the four years that the bonds remain unpaid would be $1,656 (= $6,624 ÷ 4). This amount would be added to the interest to be paid ($6,000) to calculate the amount of Interest Expense ($7,656). The effects would be recorded in the following journal entry:

	Debit	Credit
Interest Expense (+E, −OE)	7,656	
Discount on Bonds Payable (−xL, +L)		1,656
Cash (−A)		6,000

Assets	=	Liabilities	+	Owners' Equity
Cash −6,000		Discount on Bonds Payable (−xL) +1,656		Interest Expense (+E) −7,656

This journal entry would be recorded each year on December 31 until the bonds mature. The effects are summarized in the following bond amortization schedule:

BOND DISCOUNT AMORTIZATION SCHEDULE: STRAIGHT-LINE METHOD						
	CHANGES DURING THE PERIOD			ENDING BOND LIABILITY BALANCES		
Period Ended	(A) Interest Payable	(B) Amortization of Discount	(C) (= A + B) Interest Expense	(D) Bonds Payable	(E) Discount on Bonds Payable	(F) (= D − E) Unpaid Bond Liability
01/01/07	—	—	—	$100,000	$6,624	$ 93,376
12/31/07	$6,000	$1,656	$7,656	100,000	4,968	95,032
12/31/08	6,000	1,656	7,656	100,000	3,312	96,688
12/31/09	6,000	1,656	7,656	100,000	1,656	98,344
12/31/10	6,000	1,656	7,656	100,000	0	100,000

Chapter Summary

LO1 Explain how to measure long-term liabilities. p. 600

- Long-term liabilities are first recorded at their cash-equivalent amount, which is the amount of cash that would be accepted as full settlement of the liability at the moment it is created.

- The cash-equivalent amount is calculated using the discounting techniques explained in Supplement 14A. It excludes interest that arises (and is later recorded) with the passage of time.

LO2 Demonstrate how to account for discounted notes payable. p. 601

- Discounted notes are recorded at their cash-equivalent amount, which is computed using the discounting techniques explained in Supplement 14A.
- As time passes, interest on a discounted note is accrued in the Note Payable account.

LO3 Demonstrate how to account for bonds payable. p. 604

- The account Bonds Payable reports the face value of the bonds, which must be paid at maturity.
- If a company receives more cash when a bond is issued than the amount it promises to repay at maturity (perhaps because the bond pays an attractive rate of interest), the excess is recorded as a liability Premium on Bonds Payable.
- If the company receives less cash when a bond is issued than the amount it promises to repay at maturity (perhaps because the bond pays an unattractive rate of interest), the difference is recorded as a Discount on Bonds Payable, a contra-liability account that is deducted from Bonds Payable.
- Interest expense is the cost of borrowing; it equals the periodic interest payments plus (or minus) the amount of the bond discount (or premium) amortized in the current interest period.
- When a bond is retired, three financial effects are recorded: (1) a reduction in Cash for the amount paid, (2) the elimination of any balances in the bond liability account(s), and (3) a gain (or loss) if the amount paid is less (or more) than the carrying value of the bond liability accounts.

LO4 Explain how to account for lease liabilities. p. 610

- An operating lease allows a company (the lessee) to temporarily use property belonging to another company (the lessor) in exchange for payments that the lessee records as Rent Expense.
- A capital lease allows a lessee to use rented property in exchange for paying the lessor, but unlike an operating lease, it transfers virtually all risks and rewards of owning the property to the lessee. To account for a capital lease, the lessee records the property as an asset and a long-term lease liability equal to the cash-equivalent amount of the future lease payments.

LO5 Calculate and interpret the debt-to-assets and times interest earned ratios. p. 611

- The debt-to-assets ratio measures the extent to which a company's total assets have been financed by liabilities.
- The times interest earned ratio measures a company's ability to meet its interest obligations using resources generated by profit-making activities.

Financial Analysis Tools

Name of Measure	Formula	What It Tells You
Debt-to-assets ratio	$\frac{\text{Total Liabilities}}{\text{Total Assets}}$	• The proportion of assets financed by liabilities • The higher the number the greater the financing risk
Times interest earned ratio	$\frac{\text{(Net Income + Interest Expense + Income Tax Expense)}}{\text{Interest Expense}}$	• Whether sufficient resources are generated to cover interest costs • The higher the number the greater the coverage

Key Terms

Bonds (p. 604)
Cash-Equivalent Amount (p. 600)
Capital Lease (p. 610)
Carrying Value (p. 607)
Debt-to-Assets Ratio (p. 611)
Discount (p. 605)
Discounting (p. 601)
Face Value (p. 604)
Long-term Debt (p. 600)
Market Interest Rate (p. 606)
Maturity Date (p. 604)
Operating Lease (p. 610)
Premium (p. 605)
Stated Interest Rate (p. 604)
Times Interest Earned Ratio (p. 612)

See complete glossary in back of text.

Questions

1. Why might a business finance using debt rather than equity? Why might a different business rely on equity rather than debt?
2. What term describes the amount at which liabilities are first recorded? Does this include interest? Why or why not?
3. How does a discounted note payable differ from an interest-bearing note payable, a topic introduced in Chapter 11? In what two ways does the accounting for these notes differ?
4. What accounting principle requires that interest expense be recorded each period even when interest has not been paid?
5. What are the three key elements of a bond, and which is/are indicated on the face of a bond certificate?
6. How are bond prices typically quoted? If an issuer sells 900 bonds, each with a face value of $1,000, at an issue price of 99.8, how much cash is received by the issuer? Describe how this would be reported by the issuer in the financial statements on the date of issue.
7. What are the reasons that some bonds are issued at a discount and others are issued at a premium?
8. Assuming simple annual compounding, how much should you pay for a one-year bond with a stated interest rate of 5 percent and a face value of $1,000 if you want to earn a return of 5 percent? What is the maximum you would be willing to pay if you want to earn a return of 8 percent? What is the maximum you would be willing to pay if you require a return of 4 percent?
9. What is the difference between the stated interest rate and the market interest rate on a bond?
10. Will the stated interest rate be higher than the market interest rate or will the market interest rate be higher than the stated interest rate when a bond is issued at (*a*) face value, (*b*) a discount, and (*c*) a premium?
11. In the context of bonds payable, to what does the term "carrying value" refer? In this same context, to what does the term "amortization" refer?
12. What three financial effects arise when a bond is retired early?
13. What two categories can be used to characterize seemingly limitless types of bonds?
14. What aspect of a lease agreement distinguishes a capital lease from an operating lease? In what ways does the accounting for capital leases differ from the accounting for operating leases?
15. If a company's debt-to-assets ratio increases, is it more or less likely to be able to pay the amounts it owes? If a company's times interest earned ratio decreases, has it become a better or worse credit risk?
16. (Supplement 14A) How does the purpose of compounding differ from the purpose of discounting? Which procedure (compounding or discounting) is more likely to be used in accounting?
17. (Supplement 14A) If you are asked to compute the present value of an amount compounded quarterly using an annual rate of 8 percent for five years, what combination of interest rates and interest periods should you use?
18. (Supplement 14B) How is interest expense calculated using the effective-interest method of amortization for a bond issued at (*a*) a discount and (*b*) a premium?
19. (Supplement 14C) How is interest expense calculated using the straight-line method of amortization for a bond issued at (*a*) a discount and (*b*) a premium?

Multiple Choice

Quiz 14-1
www.mhhe.com/LLPW1e

1. Which of the following best describes a reason for using debt rather than equity financing?
   a. Owners may not have sufficient resources available to contribute to the business.
   b. Debt must be repaid (or refinanced) when it matures.
   c. Owners may forgo withdrawals to help the business survive its financial difficulties.
   d. None of the above.
2. A company purchases a piece of equipment and pays for it by signing a discounted note payable that requires a single payment of $134,776 in three years. How does the company account for this transaction?
   a. The payment of $134,776 is reported as a noncurrent liability on the date of purchase.
   b. Nothing is reported until the payment of $134,776 is made.
   c. The accountant computes the present value of $134,776 and records that amount as a noncurrent liability on the date of purchase.
   d. The accountant computes the future value of $134,776 and records that amount as a noncurrent liability on the date of purchase.
3. A three-year discounted note payable, which requires a payment of $595,508 at maturity on December 31, 2010, had an adjusted balance of $530,000 at December 31, 2008. Assuming 6 percent annual interest, which of the following adjusting journal entries should be recorded on December 31, 2009?

	Account	Debit	Credit
a.	Interest Expense	31,800	
	Interest Payable		31,800
b.	Interest Expense	31,800	
	Cash		31,800
c.	Interest Expense	31,800	
	Note Payable		31,800
d.	Interest Expense	65,508	
	Note Payable	530,000	
	Cash		595,508

4. A corporate bond issued at 102 is currently trading at 97. Which of the following is true?
   a. The corporation reports a bond discount on the balance sheet.
   b. The corporation reports a bond premium on the income statement.
   c. The stated interest rate was less than the market interest rate on the date of issue.
   d. None of the above.
5. Which of the following does not impact the calculation of the cash interest payments to be made to bondholders?
   a. Face value of the bond.
   b. Stated interest rate.
   c. Market interest rate.
   d. Length of time between payments.
6. Which of the following is false when a bond is issued at a premium?
   a. The bond is issued at an amount above its face value.
   b. Interest expense will exceed the cash interest payments.
   c. The market interest rate is lower than the stated interest rate.
   d. The issue price will be quoted at a number more than 100.
7. Which of the following terms describes bonds that are issued without security?
   a. Zero coupon.
   b. Debentures.
   c. Serial.
   d. Callable.
8. To determine whether a bond will be issued at a premium, discount, or at face value, one must know which of the following pairs of information?
   a. The face value and the stated interest rate on the date the bonds were issued.
   b. The face value and the market interest rate on the date the bonds were issued.
   c. The stated interest rate and the market interest rate on the date the bonds were issued.
   d. You cannot tell without having more information.
9. For the year ended December 31, 2006, Land O' Lakes, Inc., reported income from operations of $124,195, net income of $88,666, interest expense of $58,360, and income tax expense of $7,806. What was this dairy company's times interest earned ratio for the year?
   a. 0.65
   b. 1.51
   c. 2.13
   d. 2.65
10. Which of the following expenses is recorded on an operating lease?
   a. Depreciation Expense.
   b. Interest Expense.
   c. Rent Expense.
   d. All of the above.

Solutions to Multiple-Choice Questions

1. a 2. c 3. c 4. d 5. c 6. b 7. b 8. c 9. d 10. c

Mini Exercises  Available with McGraw-Hill's Homework Manager

LO2

M14-1 Recording Discounted Note Issue and Interest Accruals

On January 1, 2008, Steelmet Furniture purchased new welding equipment by issuing a note that promises to pay $27,783 on December 31, 2010. Assuming a 5 percent annual interest rate, the cash-equivalent amount on January 1, 2008, is $24,000. Prepare journal entries needed on (a) January 1, 2008, (b) December 31, 2008, and (c) December 31, 2009.

LO2

M14-2 Recording Discounted Note Issue and Interest Accruals

On January 1, 2009, Shaw Cable purchased new computer switching equipment by issuing a note that promises to pay $115,762.50 on December 31, 2011. Assuming a 5 percent annual interest rate, the cash-equivalent amount on January 1, 2009, is $100,000. Prepare journal entries needed on (a) January 1, 2009, (b) December 31, 2009, and (c) December 31, 2010.

LO2

M14-3 Recording Discounted Note Issue, Interest, and Maturity Repayment

On January 1, 2008, Touchstone Developments purchased a new excavator by issuing a note that promises to pay $22,898 on December 31, 2009. Assuming a 7 percent annual interest rate, the cash-equivalent amount on January 1, 2008, is $20,000. Prepare journal entries needed on (a) January 1, 2008, (b) December 31, 2008, and (c) December 31, 2009.

LO2

M14-4 Recording Discounted Note Issue, Interest, and Maturity Repayment

On January 1, 2009, ACME Corporation purchased new aviation equipment by issuing a note that promises to pay $110,250 on December 31, 2010. Assuming a 5 percent annual interest rate, the cash-equivalent amount on January 1, 2009, is $100,000. Prepare journal entries needed on (a) January 1, 2009, (b) December 31, 2009, and (c) December 31, 2010.

LO3
Ford Motor Company

M14-5 Determining Bond Discount or Premium from Quoted Price

On October 1, 2006, biz.yahoo.com quoted a bond price of 101.5 for Ford Motor Company's 9.875 percent bonds maturing on August 10, 2011. Were the bonds selling at a discount or premium? Does this mean the market interest rate for comparable bonds was higher or lower than 9.875 percent?

M14-6 Computing and Reporting a Bond Liability at an Issuance Price of 98 LO3

E-Tech Initiatives Limited plans to issue $500,000, 10-year, 4 percent bonds. Interest is payable annually on December 31. All of the bonds will be issued on January 1, 2009. Show how the bonds would be reported on the January 2, 2009, balance sheet if they are issued at 98.

M14-7 Computing and Reporting a Bond Liability at an Issuance Price of 103 LO3

Repeat M14-6 assuming the bonds are issued at 103.

M14-8 Recording Bonds Issued at Face Value LO3

Schlitterbahn Waterslide Company issued 25,000, 10-year, 6 percent, $100 bonds on January 1, 2009, at face value. Interest is payable each December 31. Show the journal entries and accounting equation effects for (*a*) the bond issue on January 1, 2009, and (*b*) the interest payment on December 31, 2009.

M14-9 Recording Bonds Issued at Face Value LO3

Shark's Pool Company issued 2,000, 10-year, 6 percent, $1,000 bonds on July 1, 2009, at face value. Interest is payable each June 30. Show the journal entries and accounting equation effects for (*a*) the issuance of these bonds on July 1, 2009, and (*b*) accrual of interest on December 31, 2009.

M14-10 Determining Financial Statement Effects of an Early Retirement of Debt LO3

If the market price of a bond increased after it was issued and the company decided to retire its debt early, would you expect the company to report a gain or loss on debt retirement? Describe the financial statement effects of a debt retirement under these circumstances.

M14-11 Recording Early Retirement of Bonds LO3

Refer to M14-9. Prepare journal entries that would be recorded if the bonds were retired early by repurchasing them at a price of (a) 99 or (b) 100.5. Explain why an early bond retirement is likely to result in a gain or loss.

M14-12 Recording Operating and Capital Leases LO4

Prepare the journal entries that Hamilton Property should make on June 30, 2008, to record the following transactions, in which Hamilton is the lessee.

a. Made a lease payment of $8,000 on June 30, 2008, for equipment rented in June under an operating lease agreement.
b. Leased a new building, which requires 10 annual payments of $50,000. Assuming an annual interest rate of 6 percent, the cash-equivalent amount on June 30, 2008, is $368,005.

M14-13 Computing the Debt-to-Assets Ratio and the Times Interest Earned Ratio LO5

The balance sheet for Food Maker Corporation (FMC) reported the following: total assets, $250,000; noncurrent assets, $150,000; current liabilities, $40,000; total stockholders' equity, $90,000; net income, $3,320; interest expense, $4,400; and income before income taxes, $5,280. Compute FMC's debt-to-assets ratio and times interest earned ratio. Based on these calculations and the ratios reported in Exhibit 14.7, does it appear FMC will be able to meet its obligations to pay liabilities and interest obligations as they become payable?

M14-14 Analyzing the Impact of Transactions on the Debt-to-Assets Ratio LO5

BSO, Inc., has total liabilities of $500,000 and total assets of $1,000,000, resulting in a debt-to-assets ratio of 0.50 (or 50 percent). For each of the following independent events, determine whether the debt-to-assets ratio will increase, decrease, or remain the same.

a. Purchased $20,000 of new inventory on credit.
b. Paid accounts payable in the amount of $50,000.
c. Recorded accrued salaries in the amount of $10,000.
d. Borrowed $250,000 from a local bank on an interest-bearing note to be repaid in 90 days.

M14-15 (Supplement 14A) Calculating Present Values

Refer to M14-1. Show how Steelmet's accountants determined that the cash-equivalent amount on January 1, 2008, was $24,000.

M14-16 (Supplement 14A) Calculating Present Values

Refer to M14-2. Show how Shaw's accountants determined that the cash-equivalent amount on January 1, 2009, was $100,000.

M14-17 (Supplement 14A) Calculating Present Values

Refer to M14-3. Show how Touchstone's accountants determined that the cash-equivalent amount on January 1, 2008, was $20,000.

M14-18 (Supplement 14A) Calculating Present Values

Refer to M14-4. Show how ACME's accountants determined that the cash-equivalent amount on January 1, 2009, was $100,000.

M14-19 (Supplement 14A) Calculating Present Values

Refer to M14-12. Show how Hamilton's accountants determined that the cash-equivalent amount on June 30, 2008, was $368,005.

M14-20 (Supplement 14B) Recording Bond Issuance and Interest Payment (Effective-Interest Amortization)

Clem Company issued $800,000, 10-year, 5 percent bonds on January 1, 2009. The bonds sold for $741,000. Interest is payable annually on January 1. Using effective-interest amortization, prepare journal entries to record (*a*) the bond issuance on January 1, 2009, and (*b*) the payment of interest on January 1, 2010. The market interest rate on the bonds is 6 percent.

M14-21 (Supplement 14C) Recording Bond Issuance and Interest Payment (Straight-Line Amortization)

Simko Company issued $600,000, 10-year, 5 percent bonds on January 1, 2009. The bonds were issued for $580,000. Interest is payable annually on January 1. Using straight-line amortization, prepare journal entries to record (*a*) the bond issuance on January 1, 2009, and (*b*) the payment of interest on January 1, 2010.

Exercises  Available with McGraw-Hill's Homework Manager

LO1

E14-1 Choosing between Debt and Equity Financing

Novelty Productions is operated as a sole proprietorship by its founder, Tina Wilkins. Tina is an inventor who recently created a new product that is growing in popularity. Tina needs to expand the business but has already contributed all personal resources to the business. Tina estimates that $100,000 is needed to purchase new equipment, and is confident that this investment will return about $25,000 cash each year for the next five years. Given the secret nature of the business, Tina is reluctant to admit partners. She rarely withdraws funds from the sole proprietorship.

Required:

How should Tina finance the expansion of her business? Provide reasons supporting your recommendation.

LO1

E14-2 Accounting for an Interest-Bearing Note Issue, Interest, and Maturity

Right Foot Shoes issued a two-year, $50,000 interest-bearing note on January 1, 2008, in exchange for new equipment. Interest accrues at 6 percent annually but is not paid until maturity.

Required:

Record the journal entries and accounting equation effects for each of the following.

1. The equipment purchase on January 1, 2008.
2. The interest adjustment on December 31, 2008.
3. The payment on December 31, 2009.

LO2

E14-3 Accounting for a Discounted Note Issue, Interest, and Maturity

Left Foot Shoes issued a discounted note on January 1, 2008, in exchange for new equipment. The note requires a payment of $56,180 on December 31, 2009. Using an annual interest rate of 6 percent to discount the payment, you determine that the note's present value on January 1, 2008, was $50,000.

Required:

Record the journal entries and accounting equation effects for each of the following.

1. The equipment purchase on January 1, 2008.
2. The interest adjustment on December 31, 2008.
3. The $56,180 payment on December 31, 2009.

LO2

E14-4 Accounting for a Discounted Note Issue, Interest, and Maturity

Deep Powder Corporation issued a discounted note on January 1, 2008, in exchange for new snow-making equipment. The note requires a $121,551 payment on December 31, 2011. Using an annual interest rate of 5 percent to discount the payment, you determine that the note's present value on January 1, 2008, was $100,000.

Required:
Record the journal entries for each of the following. (Round interest calculations to the nearest dollar.)

1. The equipment purchase on January 1, 2008.
2. The interest adjustments on December 31, 2008, 2009, and 2010.
3. The $121,551 payment on December 31, 2011.

E14-5 Accounting for Bonds Issued at Face Value with Interest Accrual and Early Retirement LO3
On October 1, 2009, Garden Equipment Corporation issued 2,000 bonds at face value. The bond certificates indicate a face value of $1,000, a stated interest rate of 7 percent paid annually on September 30, and a September 30, 2020 maturity date.

Required:

1. Give the journal entry to record the bond issue on October 1, 2009.
2. Give the adjusting entry required on December 31, 2009.
3. Assume Garden Equipment retires the bond early on October 1, 2012, at a price of 103. Give the journal entry to record this early retirement.

E14-6 Accounting for Bonds Issued at Face Value with Interest Accrual and Maturity Repayment LO3
On January 1, 2009, Arena Enterprises issued 300 bonds at face value. The bond certificates indicate a face value of $1,000, a stated interest rate of 6 percent paid annually on December 31, and a December 31, 2010, maturity date.

Required:

1. Give the journal entry to record the bond issue on January 1, 2009.
2. Give the journal entry required on December 31, 2009.
3. Give the journal entry to record the payment on December 31, 2010.

E14-7 Determining Bond Price and Preparing Journal Entries to Record Bond Issue and Interest Payment LO3
On January 1, 2008, Applied Technologies Corporation (ATC) issued 600 bonds, each with a face value of $1,000 and a maturity date of December 31, 2017. The bonds have a stated interest rate of 10 percent. When the bonds were issued, the market interest rate was 10 percent. The bonds pay interest once per year on December 31.

Required:

1. Determine the price at which the bonds were issued and the amount of cash that ATC received.
2. Prepare the journal entry to record the bond issue.
3. Prepare the journal entry to record the interest payment on December 31, 2008.

E14-8 Preparing Journal Entries to Record Issuance of a Bond at Face Value, Payment of Interest, and Early Retirement LO3
On January 1, 2009, Innovative Solutions, Inc., issued 200 bonds at face value ($1,000 each). The bonds have a stated interest rate of 6 percent, mature in 10 years, and pay interest annually on December 31.

Required:

1. Prepare the journal entry to record the bond issue.
2. Prepare the journal entry to record the interest payment on December 31, 2009.
3. Assume the bond was retired immediately after the first interest payment on January 1, 2010, at a quoted price of 102. Prepare the journal entry to record the early retirement of the bond.

E14-9 Describing the Effects of a Premium Bond Issue and Interest Payment on the Financial Statements, Debt-to-Assets Ratio, and Times Interest Earned Ratio LO3, 5
Grocery Corporation received $300,328 for $250,000, 11 percent bonds issued on January 1, 2008, at a market interest rate of 8 percent. The bonds stated that interest would be paid each December 31 and that they mature on December 31, 2017.

Required:

1. Describe how the bond issue affects the balance sheet and income statement, specifically identifying the account names and direction of effects (ignore amounts). Also, describe its impact on the debt-to-assets ratio and times interest earned ratio.
2. Without doing calculations, describe which balance sheet and income statement accounts are affected by the recording of interest on December 31, 2008.

LO3

E14-10 Computing Price for One-Year Bond

Speedy Housing issued 200 bonds, each with a face value of $1,000 and stated interest rate of 5 percent to be paid out exactly one year after the issue date.

Required:

Determine your return on the 200 bonds if you purchased them all on the issue date for

1. $200,000.
2. $201,924.
3. $198,114.

LO4

E14-11 Recording Lease Transactions

On June 1, 2009, National Equipment Rental leased equipment to the Glendale Community Club and Craig Legal Services. Glendale signed a lease indicating the club would rent portable tables for the month of June 2009 at a cost of $1,000 to be paid in July 2009. Craig Legal Services signed a lease indicating that the business would rent computer equipment for the three-year period ended May 31, 2012. Craig is required to pay $10,000 at the end of each year; these payments equate to a present value of $26,730 on June 1, 2009.

Required:

1. Prepare the journal entry that Glendale Community Club should record on June 30, 2009.
2. Prepare the journal entry that Craig Legal Services should record on June 1, 2009.

LO5
Kraft

E14-12 Calculating and Interpreting the Debt-to-Assets Ratio and Times Interest Earned Ratio

According to its Web site, Kraft Foods Inc. sells enough Kool-Aid mix to make 1,000 gallons of the drink every minute during the summer and more than 560 million gallons each year. At December 31, 2007, the company reported the following amounts (in millions) in its financial statements:

	2007	2006
Total assets	$ 67,993	$ 55,574
Total liabilities	40,698	27,019
Interest expense	698	579
Income tax expense	1,137	951
Net income	2,590	3,060

Required:

1. Compute the debt-to-assets ratio (to three decimal places) and times interest earned ratio (to two decimal places) for 2007 and 2006.
2. Does the trend in these ratios suggest Kraft has relied more or less on debt financing? Is Kraft's financial position more or less risky than that for the companies in Exhibit 14.7?

LO5
TJX Companies Inc.

E14-13 Reporting Long-term Liabilities on a Classified Balance Sheet

TJX Companies, Inc., owns discount clothing stores operating in the United States under the store names Marshall's and TJ Maxx. For its year ended January 27, 2007, TJX Companies reported the following liabilities (all amounts in thousands). Prepare the Liabilities section of its classified balance sheet.

Accounts payable	$1,372,352	Bond debentures payable	$200,000
Accrued liabilities	1,008,774	Discount on bond debentures payable	183
Other long-term liabilities	604,572	Zero-coupon bonds payable	517,497
Lease liability, long-term	22,382	Discount on zero-coupon bonds payable	126,485
Lease liability, short-term	1,854	Other long-term borrowings	194,816

E14-14 (Supplement 14A) Calculating Present Values

Refer to E14-3. Show how, Left Foot Shoes determined that the cash-equivalent amount on January 1, 2008, was $50,000.

E14-15 (Supplement 14A) Calculating Present Values

Refer to E14-4. Show how Deep Powder's accountants determined that the cash-equivalent amount on January 1, 2008, was $100,000.

E14-16 (Supplement 14A) Calculating Present Values
Refer to E14-9. Show how investors determined the price of Grocery Corporation's bonds on January 1, 2008 to be $300,328.

E14-17 (Supplement 14A) Calculating Present Values
Refer to E14-11. Show how Craig Legal Services determined the cash-equivalent amount of $26,730 on June 1, 2009. What interest rate does this imply?

E14-18 (Supplement 14B) Recording the Effects of a Premium Bond Issue and First Interest Payment (Effective-Interest Amortization)
Refer to the information in E14-9 and assume Grocery Corporation uses the effective-interest method to amortize the bond premium.

Required:

1. Prepare the journal entry to record the bond issue.
2. Prepare the journal entries to record the December 31 interest payments in 2008 and 2009.

E14-19 (Supplement 14C) Recording the Effects of a Premium Bond Issue and First Interest Payment (Straight-Line Amortization)
Refer to the information in E14-9 and assume Grocery Corporation uses the straight-line method to amortize the bond premium.

Required:

1. Prepare the journal entry to record the bond issue.
2. Prepare the journal entries to record the December 31 interest payments in 2008 and 2009.

E14-20 (Supplement 14B) Recording the Effects of a Discount Bond Issue and First Interest Payment and Preparing a Discount Amortization Schedule (Effective-Interest Amortization)
On January 1, 2009, when the market interest rate was 9 percent, Seton Corporation sold a $200,000, 8 percent bond issue for $187,163. The bonds were dated January 1, 2009, pay interest each December 31, and mature December 31, 2018. Seton amortizes the bond discount using the effective-interest method.

Required:

1. Prepare the journal entry to record the bond issue.
2. Prepare the journal entry to record the interest payment on December 31, 2009.
3. Prepare a bond discount amortization schedule for these bonds using the format shown in Supplement 14B.

E14-21 (Supplement 14C) Recording the Effects of a Discount Bond Issue and First Interest Payment and Preparing a Discount Amortization Schedule (Straight-Line Amortization)
Refer to the information in E14-20 but assume Seton Corporation uses the straight-line method to amortize the bond discount.

Required:

1. Prepare the journal entry to record the bond issuance.
2. Prepare the journal entry to record the interest payment on December 31, 2009.
3. Prepare a bond discount amortization schedule for these bonds, using the format shown in Supplement 14C.

Problems—Set A

Available with McGraw-Hill's Homework Manager

PA14-1 Comparing and Recording a Discounted Note Payable and Capital Lease Liability **LO2, 4 ,5**
Rockwell Industries is evaluating whether to purchase a piece of equipment or rent it. The company is a little short on cash, so a purchase would require Rockwell to finance the equipment's cost by signing a promissory note that requires a single payment of $100,000 three years after the purchase date. The present value of this payment is $83,960. If Rockwell were to rent the equipment, the company would pay $31,410.40 at the end of each of the following three years. This rental agreement would transfer to Rockwell virtually all risks and rewards of owning the equipment. The present value of these payments is $83,960. Rockwell's bank requires that the company's debt-to-assets ratio not exceed 0.50. Prior to acquiring the equipment, Rockwell has liabilities totaling $490,000 and assets totaling $1,000,000.

Required:

1. Prepare the journal entry to record the purchase of the equipment by issuing a promissory note.
2. Prepare the journal entry to record acquisition of the equipment through a capital lease.
3. Describe any significant differences in your answers to requirements 1 and 2.
4. Calculate the debt-to-assets ratio before and after the equipment acquisition. What are the possible consequences of acquiring the equipment through purchase or capital lease? How would you advise Rockwell to proceed?

LO3

PA14-2 Comparing Bonds Issued at Face Value, Discount, and Premium

Sikes Corporation, whose annual accounting period ends on December 31, issued the following bonds:

Date of bonds: January 1, 2008.
Maturity amount and date: $200,000 due in 10 years (December 31, 2017).
Interest: 10 percent per year payable each December 31.
Date issued: January 1, 2008.

Required:

1. Provide the following amounts to be reported on the January 1, 2008, financial statements immediately after the bonds are issued:

	Case A (issued at 100)	Case B (issued at 96)	Case C (issued at 102)
a. Bonds payable	$	$	$
b. Unamortized premium or discount			
c. Unpaid bond liability			

2. Assume that a retired person has written to you (an investment adviser) asking, "Why should I buy a bond at a premium when I can find one at a discount? Is it not the case that paying a premium is like paying list price for a car instead of negotiating a discount?" Write a brief message in response to the question.

PA14-3 (Supplement 14A) Comparing and Recording a Discounted Note Payable and Capital Lease Liability with Present Value Computations

Refer to PA14-1. Assume Rockwell Industries can acquire a comparable piece of equipment by signing a promissory note that requires a single payment of $80,000 three years after the purchase date or rent it by paying $25,128.32 at the end of each of the following three years. Rockwell typically borrows at a 6 percent annual interest rate.

Required:

1. Calculate the present value of the promissory note, and prepare the journal entry to record the purchase of the equipment.
2. Calculate the present value of the lease payments, and prepare the journal entry to record acquisition of the equipment through a capital lease.
3. Describe any significant differences in your answers to requirements 1 and 2.
4. Calculate the debt-to-assets ratio before and after the equipment acquisition. What are the possible consequences of acquiring the equipment through purchase or capital lease? How would you advise Rockwell to proceed?

www.mhhe.com/LLPW1e

PA14-4 (Supplement 14B) Recording Bond Issue, Interest Payments (Effective-Interest Amortization), and Early Retirement

Southwest Corporation issued bonds with the following details:

Face value: $600,000.
Interest: 9 percent per year paid each December 31.
Terms: Bonds issued January 1, 2009, maturing on December 31, 2013.

The annual accounting period ends December 31. The bonds were issued at 104 on January 1, 2009, implying an 8 percent market interest rate. Assume the company uses effective-interest amortization.

Required:

1. Compute the bond issue price (show computations).
2. Give the journal entry to record the bond issue.
3. Give the journal entries to record the interest payments on December 31, 2009 and 2010.

4. How much interest expense would be reported on the income statements for 2009 and 2010? Show how the liability related to the bonds should be reported on the balance sheets at December 31, 2009 and 2010.
5. Assume the bonds are retired on January 1, 2011, at a price of 101. Give the journal entry to record the bond retirement.

PA14-5 (Supplement 14C) Recording Bond Issue, Interest Payments (Straight-Line Amortization), and Early Retirement

www.mhhe.com/LLPW1e

Complete the requirements of PA14-4, assuming Southwest Corporation uses straight-line amortization.

PA14-6 (Supplement 14B) Interpreting and Completing an Amortization Schedule (Effective-Interest Amortization)

Hondor Corporation issued bonds and received cash for the issue price. The bonds were dated and issued on January 1, 2008. The stated interest rate was payable at the end of each year. The bonds mature at the end of four years. The following schedule has been completed (amounts in thousands):

Date	Cash Paid	Interest Expense	Amortization	Unpaid Bond Liability
January 1, 2008	—	—	—	$6,101
End of year 2008	$450	$427	$23	6,078
End of year 2009	450	426	24	6,054
End of year 2010	450	?	?	?
End of year 2011	450	?	28	6,000

Required:

1. What was the total face value to be paid at maturity?
2. How much cash was received at date of issuance (sale) of the bonds?
3. Was there a premium or a discount? If so, which was it and how much was it?
4. How much cash will be paid for interest each period and in total for the full life of the bond issue?
5. What is the stated interest rate?
6. What is the market interest rate?
7. Complete the amortization schedule by replacing the four ?s with appropriate amounts.
8. What amount should be reported on the income statement each year?
9. Show how the bonds should be reported on the balance sheet at the end of 2008 and 2009.

PA14-7 (Supplement 14C) Interpreting and Completing an Amortization Schedule (Straight-Line Amortization)

The Peg Corporation (TPC) issued bonds and received cash in full for the issue price. The bonds were dated and issued on January 1, 2009. The stated interest rate was payable at the end of each year. The bonds mature at the end of four years. The following schedule has been prepared (amounts in thousands):

Date	Cash Paid	Interest Expense	Amortization	Unpaid Bond Liability
January 1, 2009	—	—	—	$6,101
End of year 2009	$450	$425	$25	?
End of year 2010	450	?	25	6,051
End of year 2011	450	?	25	6,026
End of year 2012	450	424	26	6,000

Required:

1. What was the total face value to be paid at maturity?
2. How much cash was received at date of issuance (sale) of the bonds?
3. Was there a premium or a discount? If so, which was it and how much was it?
4. How much cash will be paid for interest each period and in total for the full life of the bond issue?
5. What is the stated interest rate?
6. Complete the amortization schedule by replacing the three ?s with appropriate amounts.
7. What amount should be reported on the income statement each year?
8. Show how the bonds should be reported on the balance sheet at the end of 2009 and 2010.

PA14-8 (Supplements 14A and 14B) Computing Bond Issue Price with Present Values, and Recording Bond Issue, Interest Payments (Effective-Interest Amortization), and Early Bond Retirement

www.mhhe.com/LLPW1e

On January 1, 2008, Surreal Manufacturing issued 600 bonds, each with a face value of $1,000, a stated interest rate of 3 percent paid annually on December 31, and a maturity date of December 31, 2010. On the issue date, the market interest rate was 4 percent. Surreal uses the effective-interest method of amortization.

Required:

1. Compute the bond issue price (show computations).
2. Prepare a bond amortization schedule similar to that shown in Supplement 14B.
3. Give the journal entry to record the bond issue.
4. Give the journal entries to record the interest payments on December 31, 2008 and 2009.
5. Give the journal entry to record the interest and face value payment on December 31, 2010.
6. Assume, instead, that the bonds are retired on January 1, 2010, at a price of 101. Give the journal entry to record the bond retirement.

PA14-9 (Supplements 14A and 14C) Computing Bonds Issue Price with Present Values, and Recording Bond Issue, Interest Payments (Straight-Line Amortization), and Early Bond Retirement

On January 1, 2008, Loop Raceway issued 600 bonds, each with a face value of $1,000, a stated interest rate of 5 percent paid annually on December 31, and a maturity date of December 31, 2010. On the issue date, the market interest rate was 6 percent. Loop uses the straight-line method of amortization.

Required:

1. Compute the bond issue price (show computations).
2. Prepare a bond amortization schedule similar to that shown in Supplement 14C.
3. Give the journal entry to record the bond issue.
4. Give the journal entries to record the interest payments on December 31, 2008 and 2009.
5. Give the journal entry to record the interest and face value payment on December 31, 2010.
6. Assume, instead, that the bonds are retired on January 1, 2010, at a price of 98. Give the journal entry to record the bond retirement.

Problems—Set B

Available with McGraw-Hill's Homework Manager

LO2, 4, 5

PB14-1 Comparing and Recording a Discounted Note Payable and Capital Lease Liability

Bridge Construction Company is evaluating whether to purchase a piece of equipment or rent it. The company is short on cash, so a purchase would require Bridge to finance the equipment's cost by signing a promissory note that requires a single payment of $200,000 three years after the purchase date. The present value of this payment is $167,920. If Bridge were to rent the equipment, the company would pay $62,820.80 at the end of each of the following three years. This rental agreement would transfer to Bridge virtually all risks and rewards of owning the equipment. The present value of these payments is $167,920. Bridge's bank requires that the company's debt-to-assets ratio not exceed 0.50. Prior to acquiring the equipment, Bridge has liabilities totaling $980,000 and assets totaling $2,000,000.

Required:

1. Prepare the journal entry to record the purchase of the equipment by issuing a promissory note.
2. Prepare the journal entry to record acquisition of the equipment through a capital lease.
3. Describe any significant differences in your answers to requirements 1 and 2.
4. Calculate the debt-to-assets ratio before and after the equipment acquisition. What are the possible consequences of acquiring the equipment through purchase or capital lease? How would you advise Bridge to proceed?

LO3

PB14-2 Comparing Bonds Issued at Par, Discount, and Premium

Net Work Corporation, whose annual accounting period ends on December 31, issued the following bonds:

Date of bonds: January 1, 2009.

Maturity amount and date: $200,000 due in 10 years (December 31, 2018).

Interest: 10 percent per year payable each December 31.

Date issued: January 1, 2009.

Required:

1. Provide the following amounts to be reported on the January 1, 2009, financial statements immediately after the bonds were issued:

	Case A (issued at 100)	Case B (issued at 97)	Case C (issued at 101)
a. Bonds payable	$	$	$
b. Unamortized premium or discount			
c. Unpaid bond liability			

2. Assume that a retired person has written to you (an investment adviser) asking, "Why did you encourage me to buy a bond at a premium when my friend bought a different one at a discount? Have I paid too much for the bond I bought?" Write a brief message in response to the question.

PB14-3 (Supplement 14A) Comparing and Recording a Discounted Note Payable and Capital Lease Liability with Present Value Computations

Refer to PB14-1. Assume that Bridge Construction Company can acquire a comparable piece of equipment by signing a promissory note that requires a single payment of $160,000 three years after the purchase date, or rent it by paying $50,256.64 at the end of each of the following three years. Bridge typically borrows at a 6% annual interest rate.

Required:

1. Calculate the present value of the promissory note, and prepare the journal entry to record the purchase of the equipment.
2. Calculate the present value of the lease payments, and prepare the journal entry to record acquisition of the equipment through a capital lease.
3. Describe any significant differences in your answers to requirements 1 and 2.
4. Calculate the debt-to-assets ratio before and after the equipment acquisition. What are the possible consequences of acquiring the equipment through purchase or capital lease? How would you advise Bridge to proceed?

PB14-4 (Supplement 14B) Recording Bond Issue, Interest Payments (Effective-Interest Amortization), and Early Retirement

WestCoast Airlines Corporation issued bonds with the following details:

Face value: $500,000.

Interest: 7 percent per year paid each December 31.

Terms: Bonds issued January 1, 2009, maturing on December 31, 2014.

The annual accounting period ends December 31. The bonds were issued at 95.38 on January 1, 2009, implying an 8 percent market interest rate. Assume the company uses effective-interest amortization.

Required:

1. Compute the bond issue price (show computations).
2. Give the journal entry to record the bond issue.
3. Give the journal entries to record the interest payments on December 31, 2009 and 2010.
4. How much interest expense would be reported on the income statements for 2009 and 2010? Show how the liability related to the bonds should be reported on the balance sheets at December 31, 2009 and 2010.
5. Assume the bonds are retired on January 1, 2011, at a price of 101. Give the journal entry to record the bond retirement.

PB14-5 (Supplement 14C) Recording Bond Issue, Interest Payments (Straight-Line Amortization), and Early Retirement

Complete the requirements of PA14-4, assuming WestCoast Airlines Corporation uses straight-line amortization.

PB14-6 (Supplement 14B) Interpreting and Completing an Amortization Schedule (Effective-Interest Amortization)

Amhert Corporation issued bonds and received cash for the issue price. The bonds were dated and issued on January 1, 2008. The stated interest rate was payable at the end of each year. The bonds mature at the end of four years. The following schedule has been completed (amounts in thousands):

Date	Cash Paid	Interest Expense	Amortization	Unpaid Bond Liability
January 1, 2008	—	—	—	$11,800
End of year 2008	$900	$944	$44	11,844
End of year 2009	900	?	48	11,892
End of year 2010	900	?	?	?
End of year 2011	900	957	57	12,000

Required:

1. What was the total face value to be paid at maturity?
2. How much cash was received at date of issuance (sale) of the bonds?
3. Was there a premium or a discount? If so, which was it and how much was it?
4. How much cash will be paid for interest each period and in total for the full life of the bond issue?
5. What is the stated interest rate?
6. What is the market interest rate?
7. Complete the amortization schedule by replacing the four ?s with appropriate amounts.
8. What amount should be reported on the income statement each year?
9. Show how the bonds should be reported on the balance sheet at the end of 2008 and 2009.

PB14-7 (Supplement 14C) Interpreting and Completing an Amortization Schedule (Straight-Line Amortization)

Toon Corporation (TC) issued bonds and received cash in full for the issue price. The bonds were dated and issued on January 1, 2009. The stated interest rate was payable at the end of each year. The bonds mature at the end of four years. The following schedule has been prepared (amounts in thousands):

Date	Cash Paid	Interest Expense	Amortization	Unpaid Bond Liability
January 1, 2009	—	—	—	$11,800
End of year 2009	$900	$950	$50	?
End of year 2010	900	?	50	11,900
End of year 2011	900	?	50	11,950
End of year 2012	900	950	50	12,000

Required:

1. What was the total face value to be paid at maturity?
2. How much cash was received at date of issuance (sale) of the bonds?
3. Was there a premium or a discount? If so, which was it and how much was it?
4. How much cash will be paid for interest each period and in total for the full life of the bond issue?
5. What is the stated interest rate?
6. Complete the amortization schedule by replacing the three ?s with appropriate amounts.
7. What amount should be reported on the income statement each year?
8. Show how the bonds should be reported on the balance sheet at the end of 2009 and 2010.

PB14-8 (Supplements 14A and 14B) Computing Bond Issue Price with Present Values, and Recording Bond Issue, Interest Payments (Effective-Interest Amortization), and Early Bond Retirement

On January 1, 2008, Methodical Manufacturing issued 100 bonds, each with a face value of $1,000, a stated interest rate of 5 percent paid annually on December 31, and a maturity date of December 31, 2010. On the issue date, the market interest rate was 4.25 percent. Methodical uses the effective-interest method of amortization.

Required:

1. Compute the bond issue price (show computations).
2. Prepare a bond amortization schedule similar to that shown in Supplement 14B.
3. Give the journal entry to record the bond issue.
4. Give the journal entries to record the interest payments on December 31, 2008 and 2009.
5. Give the journal entry to record the interest and face value payment on December 31, 2010.
6. Assume the bonds are retired on January 1, 2010, at a price of 101. Give the journal entries to record the bond retirement.

PB14-9 (Supplements 14A and 14C) Computing Bond Issue Price with Present Values, and Recording Bond Issue, Interest Payments (Straight-Line Amortization), and Early Bond Retirement
Refer to PB14-8. Assume Methodical uses the straight-line method of amortization.

Required:

1. Compute the bond issue price (show computations).
2. Prepare a bond amortization schedule similar to that shown in Supplement 14C.
3. Give the journal entry to record the bond issue.
4. Give the journal entries to record the interest payments on December 31, 2008 and 2009.
5. Give the journal entry to record the interest and face value payment on December 31, 2010.
6. Assume the bonds are retired on January 1, 2010, at a price of 102. Give the journal entry to record the bond retirement.

Cases and Projects

CP14-1 Finding Financial Information

LO5

Refer to the financial statements of The Home Depot in Appendix A at the end of this book, or download the annual report from the Cases and Projects section of the text's Web site at www.mhhe.com/LLPW1e.

Required:

1. Calculate, to two decimal places, the company's debt-to-assets ratio using amounts reported in its financial statements for the years ended February 3, 2008, and January 28, 2007. What do the changes in this ratio suggest about the company's ability to pay its liabilities?
2. Calculate, to two decimal places, the company's times interest earned ratio for the year ended February 3, 2008. Does this ratio cause you any concern about the company's ability to meet future interest obligations as they become due?

CP14-2 Comparing Financial Information

LO5

Lowe's

Refer to the financial statements of The Home Depot in Appendix A and Lowe's in Appendix B at the end of this book, or download the annual reports from the Cases and Projects section of the text's Web site at www.mhhe.com/LLPW1e.

Required:

1. Calculate, to two decimal places, the companies' debt-to-assets ratios using amounts reported in the financial statements for the years ending in early 2008 and 2007. What do the changes in this ratio suggest about the companies' ability to pay their liabilities? Does it appear that Lowe's or The Home Depot has a greater financing risk?
2. Calculate, to two decimal places, the companies' times interest earned ratios for the year ended in February 2008. Does it appear that Lowe's or The Home Depot will be better able to meet future interest obligations as they become payable?

CP14-3 Examining an Annual Report: Internet-Based Team Research

LO1, 5

As a team, select an industry to analyze. Using your Web browser, each team member should acquire the annual report or 10-K for one publicly traded company in the industry, with each member selecting a different company. (See CP1-3 in Chapter 1 for a description of possible resources for these tasks.)

Required:

1. On an individual basis, each team member should read the company's financial statement note regarding long-term debt and then write a short report that incorporates the following:
   a. What are the types of long-term debt owed by the company?
   b. Does the company have any significant amounts coming due in the next five years?
   c. Compute and analyze the debt-to-assets ratios and times interest earned ratios for the two most recent years.
2. Then, as a team, write a short report comparing and contrasting your companies using these attributes. Discuss any patterns across the companies that you as a team observe. Provide potential explanations for any differences discovered.

LO3

CP14-4 Making Ethical Decisions: A Real-Life Example

Many retired people invest a significant portion of their money in bonds of corporations because of their relatively low level of risk. During the 1980s, significant inflation caused some interest rates to rise to as high as 15 percent. Retired people who bought bonds that paid only 6 percent continued to earn at the lower rate. During the 1990s, inflation subsided and interest rates declined. Many corporations took advantage of the callability feature of these bonds and retired the bonds early. Many of these early retirements of high interest rate bonds were replaced with low interest rate bonds.

Required:

In your judgment, is it ethical for corporations to continue paying low interest rates when rates increase but to call bonds when rates decrease? Why or why not?

LO3

CP14-5 Making Ethical Decisions: A Mini Case

Assume you are a portfolio manager for a large insurance company. The majority of the money you manage is from retired school teachers who depend on the income you earn on their investments. You have invested a significant amount of money in the bonds of a large corporation and have just read a news release from the company's president explaining that it is unable to meet its current interest obligations because of deteriorating business operations related to increased international competition. The president has a recovery plan that will take at least two years. During that time, the company will not be able to pay interest on the bonds and, she admits, if the plan does not work, bondholders will probably lose more than half of their money. As a creditor, you can force the company into immediate bankruptcy and probably get back at least 90 percent of the bondholders' money. You also know that your decision will cause at least 10,000 people to lose their jobs if the company ceases operations.

Required:

Given only these two options, what should you do? Consider who would be helped or harmed by the two options.

LO1, 5

CP14-6 Thinking Critically: Evaluating Effects on Debt-to-Assets Ratio

Assume you work as an assistant to the chief financial officer (CFO) of Little Chip Company. The CFO reminds you that the fiscal year end is only one month away and that he is looking to you to ensure the company adheres to its loan covenant to maintain a debt-to-assets ratio of 0.50 or lower. A review of the general ledger indicates that assets total $1,690,000 and total liabilities are $820,000. Your company will soon need additional warehouse space that could be obtained by issuing a long-term, interest-bearing promissory note for $200,000 and using that money to purchase a nearby building. Alternatively, the building owner is willing to rent the space on either a long-term or month-to-month basis.

Required:

1. Determine whether the company is currently in compliance with its loan covenant. Show calculations (to three decimal places) in support of your answer.
2. Evaluate whether Little Chip should purchase the building before year-end. Show calculations in support of your answer.
3. Evaluate whether Little Chip should enter into a lease agreement before year-end. Explain your answer.

CP14-7 (Supplement 14B) Preparing a Bond Amortization Schedule (Effective-Interest Amortization)

Assume the authors of a popular accounting principles text have hired you to create spreadsheets that will calculate bond discount amortization schedules like those shown in Supplements 14B and 14C.

You e-mail your friend Sally for some guidance. Much to your disappointment, you receive an auto-reply message from Sally indicating that she's gone skiing in New Zealand. After a bit of panicking, you realize you can refer to Sally's previous e-mail messages for spreadsheet advice that will help you complete this task. From her advice for Chapter 10, you decide to create a data input section for the stated interest rate, market interest rate, face value, issue price, and years to maturity. The spreadsheet file also will have a separate amortization schedule worksheet that contains only formulas, references to the cells in the data input section, and references to other cells in the amortization schedule. All amounts will be rounded to the nearest dollar (using the Round function in Excel), which means the discount amortization in the final year might be off a few dollars (unless you use the If function in Excel to eliminate any remaining discount in the final year of the bond's life, in the same way that Sally showed in Chapter 10 for declining-balance depreciation).

Required:

Prepare a worksheet that reproduces the effective-interest bond discount amortization schedule shown in Supplement 14B (page 622). Provide a printout showing both the amortization schedule and the formulas underlying it. (Formulas can be revealed in Excel by entering Ctrl ~).

CP14-8 (Supplement 14C) Preparing a Bond Amortization Schedule (Straight-Line Amortization)

Refer to the information in CP14-7 and prepare a worksheet that reproduces the straight-line bond discount amortization schedule shown in Supplement 14C (page 623). Provide a printout showing both the amortization schedule and the formulas underlying it. (Formulas can be revealed in Excel by entering Ctrl ~).

15 Accounting for Investments

LEARNING OBJECTIVES

After studying this chapter, you should be able to:

Lectured presentations–15-1
www.mhhe.com/LLPW1e

LO1 Explain why companies invest in debt and stock securities.

LO2 Identify investment types and the related accounting methods.

LO3 Analyze and report bond investments held to maturity.

LO4 Analyze and report passive investments in securities using the market value method.

LO5 Analyze and report investments involving significant influence using the equity method.

LO6 Explain the reporting of investments in controlling interests.

LO7 Analyze and interpret the return on assets ratio.

Focus Company: THE WASHINGTON POST COMPANY

Investment Strategies

www.washpostco.com

Have you ever wondered how big companies become big? The answer, for many companies, is by investing in other companies. One such business is The Washington Post Company, best known for publishing the most important newspaper in our nation's capital. However, The Washington Post Company does much more than that. It owns television stations, *Newsweek* magazine, Cable One (a TV cable company), and a variety of community newspapers.

Many users of this text have already been Washington Post customers without knowing it. The company also owns Kaplan, Inc., the king of admissions test preparation services that will even help you prepare for the certified public accountant or chartered financial analyst exams. The Washington Post Company also recognizes that new technologies bring increased efficiency to its operations while expanding business opportunities. For example, it publishes electronic versions of *The Washington Post* and *Newsweek* and shares news resources with NBC News and MSNBC.

The company has achieved its diversity in part by investing in the stock of other companies. For example, it spent $350 million over the last three years to purchase other companies including the online magazine *Slate* and a variety of private education companies around the world. It jointly owns (with another publisher) the company that produces the European, Middle Eastern, and African editions of *Newsweek*. It also jointly owns one of the major providers of the paper on which *The Washington Post* is printed. In addition, the company's investment portfolio consists of more than $350 million worth of stock of other companies.

In this chapter, you will see how to account for four different types of investments. To understand these investments and the reasons why they are accounted for in certain ways, you first need to answer the following question: Why do companies invest in other companies?

ORGANIZATION OF THE CHAPTER

AN OVERVIEW	ACCOUNTING FOR PASSIVE INVESTMENTS	ACCOUNTING FOR INFLUENTIAL INVESTMENTS	EVALUATING TOTAL INVESTED CAPITAL

• Reasons Companies Invest
• Identifying Investment Types and Accounting Methods
  • Passive Investments in Debt and Equity Securities
  • Investments in Stock for Significant Influence
  • Investments in Stock for Control
	• Debt Investments Held to Maturity: Amortized Cost Method
	• Securities Available for Sale: Market Value Method
	• Comparison of Available-for-Sale and Trading Securities
		• Investments for Significant Influence: Equity Method
		• Investments with Controlling Interests: Consolidated Statements
			• Return on Assets (ROA)
			• Comparison to Benchmarks

Learning Objective 1

Explain why companies invest in debt and stock securities.

AN OVERVIEW

Reasons Companies Invest

Many factors motivate managers to invest in securities. Some do so **because the very nature of their business requires it.** For example, pension funds, insurance companies, and mutual funds receive large sums of cash from their clients. To generate earnings—an important source of revenue in these companies—they invest the cash in the securities of other companies. Investments are significant assets to these companies. State Farm Mutual Automobile Insurance Company, for example, holds more than $90 billion in securities that generate more than $3 billion in income each year.

Other managers invest in securities **to even out seasonal fluctuations in cash.** A manager whose company has extra cash at the end of a busy season may want to earn a return on the idle funds until they are needed for other purposes, such as repaying loans, purchasing property and equipment, or paying dividends. Excess cash can be invested in the stocks and bonds of other companies, either long or short term. Managers may also invest excess cash to provide a cushion against future downturns in the economy or unanticipated emergencies. Such investments in securities are referred to as **passive investments** because the investors are not interested in influencing or controlling the companies that issued the securities. The Washington Post Company's 2006 balance sheet in Exhibit 15.1 reflects both short-term and long-term Investments in Marketable Securities accounts—passive investments.

Sometimes managers want to expand their company's presence in a related industry or market. They do so by investing in another company **with the purpose of influencing, but not controlling, the company's policies and activities.** Washington Post's balance sheet reports these types of investments as Investments in Affiliates in Exhibit 15.1—investments for significant influence.

Finally, managers may want **to control another company,** either by purchasing it directly or by becoming the majority shareholder. In this case, the two companies combine their financial reports into **consolidated** financial statements, as Washington Post has done (see the title to its "consolidated" balance sheet). In the notes to the annual report, we find that Washington Post's recent acquisitions include PMBR, a bar exam test preparation company, and *Slate* magazine. As you saw in Chapter 10, when one company purchases another for more than the fair value of its assets and liabilities, the company records the difference as Goodwill (see Exhibit 15.1).

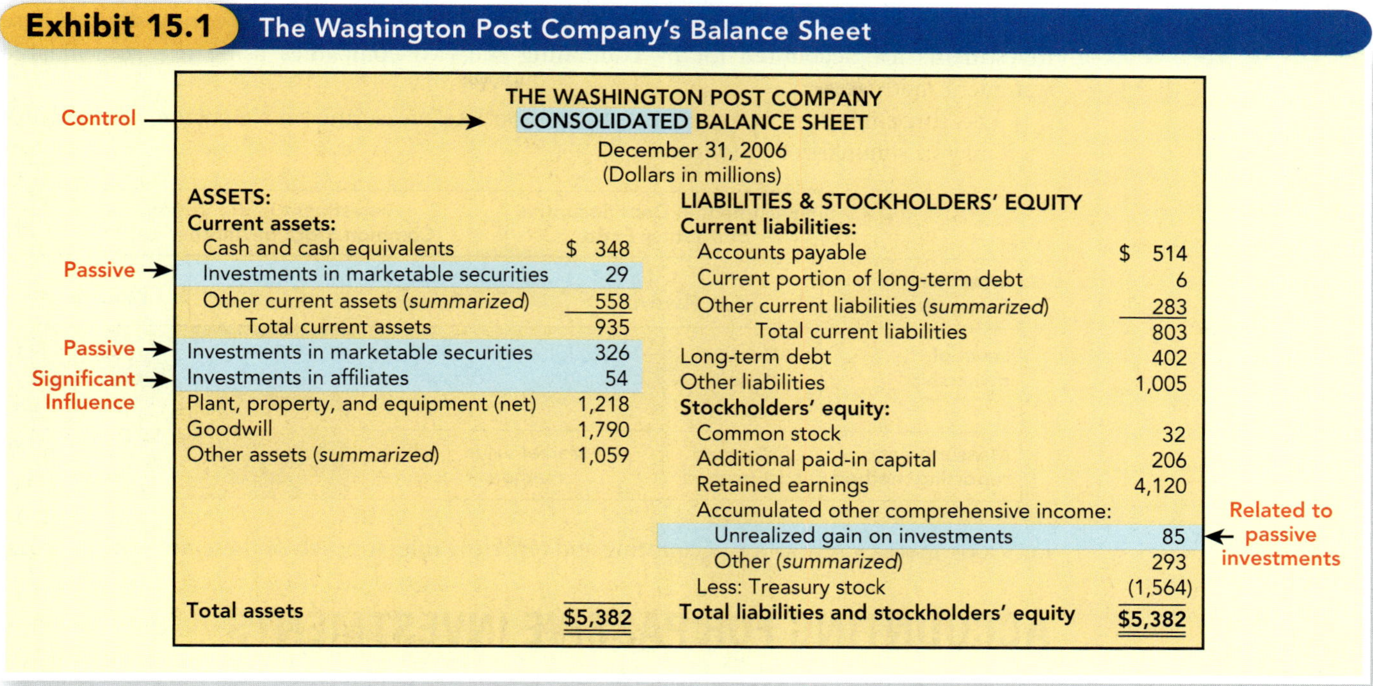

Exhibit 15.1 The Washington Post Company's Balance Sheet

THE WASHINGTON POST COMPANY
CONSOLIDATED BALANCE SHEET
December 31, 2006
(Dollars in millions)

	ASSETS:		LIABILITIES & STOCKHOLDERS' EQUITY		
	Current assets:		**Current liabilities:**		
	Cash and cash equivalents	$ 348	Accounts payable	$ 514	
Passive →	Investments in marketable securities	29	Current portion of long-term debt	6	
	Other current assets (*summarized*)	558	Other current liabilities (*summarized*)	283	
	Total current assets	935	Total current liabilities	803	
Passive →	Investments in marketable securities	326	Long-term debt	402	
Significant Influence →	Investments in affiliates	54	Other liabilities	1,005	
	Plant, property, and equipment (net)	1,218	**Stockholders' equity:**		
	Goodwill	1,790	Common stock	32	
	Other assets (*summarized*)	1,059	Additional paid-in capital	206	
			Retained earnings	4,120	
			Accumulated other comprehensive income:		
			Unrealized gain on investments	85	← Related to passive investments
			Other (*summarized*)	293	
			Less: Treasury stock	(1,564)	
	Total assets	$5,382	**Total liabilities and stockholders' equity**	$5,382	

Identifying Investment Types and Accounting Methods

The accounting methods used to record investments are directly related to the purpose of the investment.

Learning Objective 2

Identify investment types and the related accounting methods.

Passive Investments in Debt and Equity Securities

Investors make **passive investments** to earn a high rate of return on funds that may be needed in the future for either short- or long-term purposes. This category includes investments in both debt securities (bonds and notes) and equity securities (stock):

- **Investments in equity securities** are presumed to be passive if the investing company owns less than 20 percent of the other company's outstanding voting shares or any amount of nonvoting shares. The market value method is used to measure and report these investments.
- **Investments in debt securities** are always considered to be passive. If they are meant to be sold before maturity, they are treated as equity securities and reported using the market value method (also called fair market value method). If the company intends and has the ability to hold them until the maturity date, however, the company measures and reports them at amortized cost.

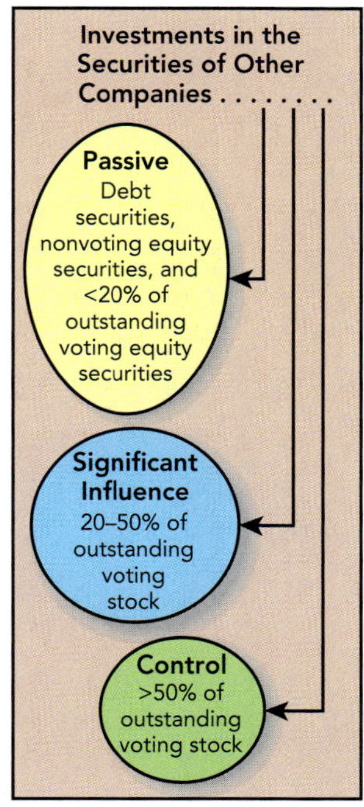

Investments in Stock for Significant Influence

Active investments are those in which a company owns enough stock in another business to influence or control that business. An investor or company that owns enough shares of voting stock of another company to have an important impact on its operating and financing policies is said to have **significant influence.** Significant influence is presumed to exist if the investing company owns from 20 to 50 percent of the outstanding voting shares. However, other factors may also indicate significant influence, including membership on the board of directors of the other company, participation in its policy-making processes, evidence of material transactions between the two companies, an interchange of managerial personnel, and technological dependency. The equity method is used to measure and report this type of investment.

Investments in Stock for Control

Control is the ability to determine the operating and financial policies of another company through ownership of its voting stock. For all practical purposes, control is presumed when the investing company owns more than 50 percent of the outstanding voting stock. These investments are accounted for by combining the two companies using the consolidated statement method.

The three investment types and the appropriate measuring and reporting methods for each may be summarized as follows:

	Investment in Debt Securities of Another Entity		Investment in the Voting Common Stock of Another Entity		
Investment Category	Passive		Passive	Significant Influence	Control
Level of ownership	Held to maturity	Not held to maturity	<20% of outstanding shares	20–50% of outstanding shares	>50% of outstanding shares
Measuring and reporting method	Amortized cost method	Market value method		Equity method	Consolidation method

Let's look more closely at the accounting and reporting rules for each of these investment types.

ACCOUNTING FOR PASSIVE INVESTMENTS

Debt Investments Held to Maturity: Amortized Cost Method

Learning Objective 3

Analyze and report bond investments held to maturity.

When management plans to hold a bond investment until the maturity date (when the principal is due), it is reported in the account appropriately named **Investments Held to Maturity**. Bonds should be classified as investments held to maturity if management has both the intent and the ability to hold them until the maturity date. These bonds are reported at amortized cost—that is, at cost adjusted for the amortization of any bond discount or premium. We illustrate how to account for these investments from their purchase date through the maturity date.

Bond Purchases

On the date of purchase, a bond may be acquired at the maturity amount (at par), for less than the maturity amount (at a discount), or for more than the maturity amount (at a premium).[1] Following the cost principle, the bond's total cost, including all acquisition costs such as transfer fees and brokers' commissions, is debited to the Investments Held to Maturity account.

To illustrate, assume that on October 1, 2010, The Washington Post Company paid the par value of $100 million[2] for 8 percent bonds due to mature on October 1, 2015. The 8 percent interest is paid each September 30. Management plans and has the ability to hold the bonds for five years until their maturity date. The journal entry to record the purchase of the bonds on October 1, 2010, is:

(In millions)	Debit	Credit
Investments Held to Maturity (+A)	100	
Cash (−A)		100

Assets		=	Liabilities	+ Owners' Equity
Investments Held to Maturity	+100			
Cash	−100			

[1] The price of the bond is determined based on the present value techniques discussed in Chapter 14. Many analysts refer to a bond price as a percentage of par. For example, *The Wall Street Journal* might report that an ExxonMobil bond with a par value of $1,000 is selling at 82.97. This statement means that the bond costs $829.70 (82.97 percent of $1,000).

[2] When bond investors accept an interest rate that is the same as the rate stated on the bonds, the bonds will sell at par (that is, at 100 percent of face value).

Interest Earned

In this illustration, the company purchased the bonds at par, or face value. Because there is no premium or discount to amortize, the book value remains constant over the life of the investment. In such situations, the revenue earned on the investment each period is measured as the amount of interest collected in cash or accrued at year-end. The following journal entry records the accrual of $2 million in interest on December 31 [$100 million face value × 0.08 (or 8%) × 3/12 of a year (since the October 1 purchase)]:

(In millions)	Debit	Credit
Interest Receivable (+A)	2	
Interest Revenue (+R, +OE)		2

Assets		=	Liabilities	+	Owners' Equity	
Interest Receivable	+2				Interest Revenue (+R)	+2

On September 30, 2011, when the investor receives a full year of interest ($2 million each quarter × 4 quarters = $8 million), the following journal entry is made:

(In millions)	Debit	Credit
Cash (+A)	8	
Interest Receivable (−A)		2
Interest Revenue (+R, +OE)		6

Assets		=	Liabilities	+	Owners' Equity	
Cash	+8				Interest Revenue (+R)	+6
Interest Receivable	−2					

The same entry is made for succeeding interest payments. On the income statement, Interest Revenue is reported in the Other Items section.

Principal at Maturity

When the bonds mature on October 1, 2015, the journal entry to record receipt of the $100 million principal payment is:

(In millions)	Debit	Credit
Cash (+A)	100	
Investments Held to Maturity (−A)		100

Assets		=	Liabilities	+	Owners' Equity
Cash	+100				
Investments Held to Maturity	−100				

Note the following:

- If the bond investment is sold before maturity, any difference between the market value (the proceeds from the sale) and the net book value (the unamortized cost) is reported in the income statement as a gain or loss on the sale.
- If management intends to sell the bonds before (or is unable to hold them until) the maturity date, they should be treated in the same way as stock investments classified as securities available for sale, which we discuss in the next section.

SELF-STUDY PRACTICE

On February 1, 2011, Rodriguez Company had $200,000 in excess cash. The company invested it in a three-year bond, purchased at par, which pays 12 percent interest each year on January 31. Rodriguez expects and is able to hold the bond to maturity. Answer the following questions.

1. What type of investment is this, and how should Rodriguez account for it?
2. Record the journal entry on the purchase date, February 1, 2011.

	Debit	Credit

3. Record the journal entry on December 31, 2011, the company's year-end.

	Debit	Credit

4. Record the journal entry on the first interest payment date, January 31, 2012.

	Debit	Credit

5. Record the journal entry on the maturity date, February 1, 2014.

	Debit	Credit

After you have finished, check your answers with the solution at the bottom of the next page.

Learning Objective 4

Analyze and report passive investments in securities using the market value method.

Securities Available for Sale: Market Value Method

When the investing company owns less than 20 percent of the outstanding voting stock in another company or any level of nonvoting stock, its investment in equity securities is considered passive. Among the assets and liabilities shown on the balance sheet, only passive investments in marketable securities (that is, stock and debt that is not held to maturity) are reported using the **market value method**.

Classifying Passive Investments

Depending on management's intent, passive investments may be classified as either trading securities or securities available for sale:

Trading Securities. **Trading securities** are traded actively with the objective of generating short-term profits on changes in the securities' price. This approach is similar to the one taken by many mutual funds whose portfolio managers actively buy and sell securities. On the balance sheet, **Trading Securities** are classified as current assets.

Securities Available for Sale. Most companies do not actively trade the securities of other companies. Instead they invest in them to earn a return on funds they may need in the near future for operating purposes. These investments are called **Securities Available for Sale**.

On the balance sheet, they are classified as either current or noncurrent assets, depending on whether management intends to sell them within the next year.

Because securities available for sale are the most common type of passive investment, we focus on this category in the next section by analyzing Washington Post's investing activities.

Recording and Reporting Securities Available for Sale

Washington Post's Investments in Marketable Securities accounts are reported for the year 2006 at $29 million for the current asset and $326 million for the noncurrent asset (see Exhibit 15.1). The notes to Washington Post's annual report contain the following information concerning this investment portfolio:

WASHINGTON POST

2006 Annual Report

NOTES TO CONSOLIDATED FINANCIAL STATEMENTS

A. SUMMARY OF SIGNIFICANT ACCOUNTING POLICIES

Investments in Marketable Equity Securities. The Company's investments in marketable equity securities are classified as **available-for-sale** and therefore are recorded at fair market value in the Consolidated Balance Sheets, with the change in fair market value during the period excluded from earnings and recorded net of tax as a separate component of comprehensive income. Marketable equity securities the Company expects to hold long term are classified as non-current assets. If the fair market value of a marketable equity security declines below its cost basis, and the decline is considered other than temporary, the Company will record a write-down, which is included in earnings [*emphasis added*].

Here is how the market value method is applied:

- Washington Post invests in equity securities, acquiring a passive interest in the stock of other companies. These assets are reported on the balance sheet (Exhibit 15.1) as both current and noncurrent assets. The note to the annual report indicates both groups are accounted for as securities available for sale. Like most companies, Washington Post does not invest in trading securities.
- When the company purchases securities available for sale, accountants record them at cost in the account Securities Available for Sale (part of Investments in Marketable Securities on Washington Post's balance sheet).

Solution to Self-Study Practice

1. Because Rodriguez intends to hold the bond until maturity, it is a passive investment called Investments Held to Maturity. It should be accounted for using the amortized cost method.

2.

	Debit	Credit
Investments Held to Maturity (+A)	200,000	
Cash (−A)		200,000

3.

	Debit	Credit
Interest Receivable (+A)	22,000	
Interest Revenue (+R, +OE)		22,000
[$200,000 × 0.12 × 11/12]		

4.

	Debit	Credit
Cash (+A)	24,000	
Interest Receivable (−A)		22,000
Interest Revenue (+R, +OE)		2,000

5.

	Debit	Credit
Cash (+A)	200,000	
Investments Held to Maturity (−A)		200,000

A realized gain or loss occurs when a company actually **sells** its investments. Gains or losses from simply **holding** the available-for-sale investments are not realized because no sale has occurred.

- In reporting the market value of the investments on the balance sheet at year-end, accountants record an adjusting entry for any temporary change up or down in the stock's market value since it was acquired. These changes are called **unrealized holding gains or losses.** Accountants use a special account, a valuation allowance, to show the change in the market value above or below acquisition cost. If the investments' market value has increased since they were purchased, the valuation allowance is added to the cost of the securities in the Securities Available for Sale account. If their market value has decreased, the valuation allowance is subtracted from the cost of the investments.
- Because a journal entry must affect at least two accounts, the other half of the adjusting entry is made to another account, reported in the Stockholders' Equity section of the balance sheet under Accumulated Other Comprehensive Income. Note in Exhibit 15.1 that Washington Post reported unrealized gains of $85 million in Stockholders' Equity. Because the amount reported for the long-term asset Investments in Marketable Securities was $326 million, the **cost** of the securities available for sale must have been $241 million with a valuation allowance of $85 million for unrealized gains ($326 million reported – $85 million unrealized gain = $241 million cost).

This process may sound complicated. To illustrate the market value method, let's assume that Washington Post had no passive investments at the end of 2009. In the following example, we apply the market value method, the accounting policy used by Washington Post, to a sample securities purchase.

Purchase of Stock. Assume that on January 2, 2010, Washington Post purchased 1,000,000 shares of Internet Financial News[3] (IFN) common stock for $60 per share, paying $60,000,000. On that date, 10,000,000 shares were outstanding, so Washington Post owned 10 percent of IFN (1,000,000 ÷ 10,000,000). This investment would be treated as a passive investment that is recorded initially (on January 2, 2010) at cost:

(In millions)	Debit	Credit
Securities Available for Sale (+A)	60	
Cash (−A)		60

Assets		=	Liabilities	+	Owners' Equity
Securities Available for Sale	+60				
Cash	−60				

See Exhibit 15.2 on page 651 for this entry and those that follow posted to T-accounts.

Dividends Earned. Investments in equity securities earn a return from two sources: (1) price increases and (2) dividend income. Price increases (or decreases) are analyzed both at year-end and when a security is sold. On the income statement, dividends earned are reported as Investment Income (or Dividend Revenue) and included in the computation of net income for the period. Let's assume that on December 15, 2010, Washington Post received a $1 per share cash dividend from IFN totaling $1,000,000 ($1 × 1,000,000 shares). The entry to record the receipt is:

(In millions)	Debit	Credit
Cash (+A)	1	
Investment Income (+R, +OE)		1

Assets		=	Liabilities	+	Owners' Equity	
Cash	+1				Investment Income (+R)	+1

This entry is the same for both trading securities and available-for-sale securities.

[3] Internet Financial News is a fictitious company.

Year-End Valuation. At the end of the accounting period, Washington Post reports passive investments on the balance sheet **at their market value.** Assume that IFN had a $58 per share market value at the end of the year. That is, the investment lost value ($60 − $58 = $2 per share). Because the shares were not sold, however, the loss is a holding loss, not a realized loss.

Reporting securities available for sale at market value requires adjusting the account to market value at the end of each period using the valuation account **Market Value Allowance.** The offset to the Market Value Allowance is the **Unrealized Gain (or Loss) on Investments** account. If the Market Value Allowance account has a **debit balance,** it is **added** to the Securities Available for Sale account. If it has a **credit balance,** it is **subtracted.** The Unrealized Gain (or Loss) on Investments account is then reported in the Stockholders' Equity section of the balance sheet under Accumulated Other Comprehensive Income. Thus, the balance sheet remains in balance.

Coach's Tip

Because there were no passive investments at the end of the prior year, the beginning balance in the Market Value Allowance account is $0.

The following chart shows the computation of any unrealized gain or loss in the securities available for sale portfolio. The amounts are given in millions of dollars:

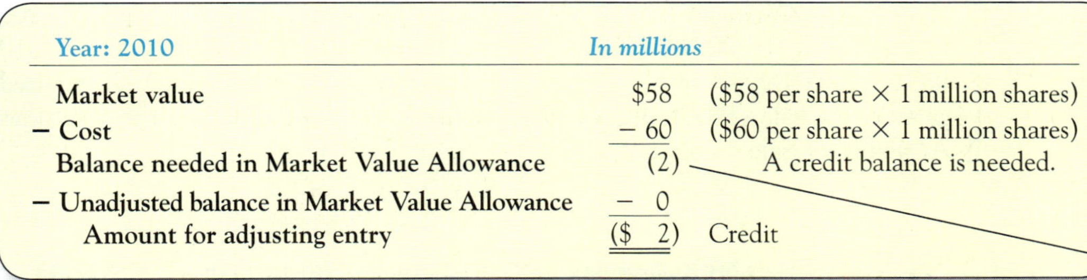

Year: 2010	In millions	
Market value	$58	($58 per share × 1 million shares)
− Cost	− 60	($60 per share × 1 million shares)
Balance needed in Market Value Allowance	(2)	A credit balance is needed.
− Unadjusted balance in Market Value Allowance	− 0	
Amount for adjusting entry	($ 2)	Credit

Market Value Allowance

	0 12/31/09
	2 AJE
	2 12/31/10

The adjusting entry on December 31, 2010, would be recorded as follows:

(In millions)	Debit	Credit
Unrealized Gain (Loss) on Investments (−OE)	2	
Market Value Allowance (−A)		2

Assets		=	Liabilities	+	Owners' Equity	
Market Value Allowance	−2				Unrealized Gain (Loss) on Investments	−2

On the 2010 balance sheet under Investments in Marketable Securities, Washington Post reports securities available for sale of $58,000,000 ($60,000,000 cost − the $2,000,000 credit balance in the valuation allowance). The company also reports, under Accumulated Other Comprehensive Income (Stockholders' Equity), Unrealized Loss on Investments of $2,000,000 for securities available for sale. Because these investments are expected to be held into the future, the company does not report the unrealized holding loss as part of net income. (Recall that only when a security is sold are any realized gains or losses included in net income.) The only item that would be reported on the income statement for 2010 is investment income of $1,000,000 (from dividends earned), classified under Other Items.

On the Balance Sheet:	*(in millions)*
Assets	
Investments in Marketable Securities	$ 60
Market Value Allowance	(2)
Net investment	$ 58
Stockholders' Equity	
Other Comprehensive Income:	
Unrealized Loss on Investments	$(2)

Now let's assume that Washington Post held the IFN securities through the year 2011. At the end of 2011, the stock had a market value of $61 per share. The adjustment for 2011 is computed as follows:

Year: 2011	In millions	
Market value	$ 61	($61 per share × 1 million shares)
− Cost	− 60	($60 per share × 1 million shares)
Balance needed in Market Value Allowance	1	
− Unadjusted balance in Market Value Allowance	− (2)	
Amount for adjusting entry	$ 3	Debit

Market Value Allowance

	0 12/31/09
	2 AJE
	2 12/31/10
AJE 3	
12/31/11 1	

The adjusting entry on December 31, 2011, is:

(in millions)	Debit	Credit
Market Value Allowance (+A)	3	
Unrealized Gain (Loss) on Investments (+OE)		3

Assets		=	Liabilities	+	Owners' Equity	
Market Value Allowance	+3				Unrealized Gain (Loss) on Investments	+3

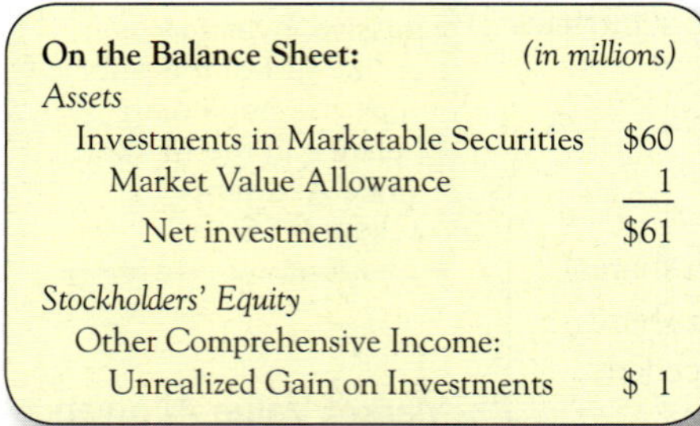

On the Balance Sheet:	*(in millions)*
Assets	
Investments in Marketable Securities	$60
Market Value Allowance	1
Net investment	$61
Stockholders' Equity	
Other Comprehensive Income:	
Unrealized Gain on Investments	$ 1

Sale of Stock. Let's assume that on March 17, 2012, Washington Post sold all of its investment in IFN for $64 per share. The company receives $64,000,000 in cash ($64 × 1,000,000 shares) for stock purchased at $60,000,000 in 2010 ($60 × 1,000,000 shares). On that date, accountants record a $4,000,000 **realized gain** on the sale ($64 million − $60 million) and then eliminate the Securities Available for Sale account.

(in millions)	Debit	Credit
Cash (+A)	64	
Securities Available for Sale (−A)		60
Gain on Sale of Investments (+R, +OE)		4

Assets		=	Liabilities	+	Owners' Equity	
Cash	+64				Gain on Sale of Investments (+R)	+4
Securities Available for Sale	−60					

You may be wondering what a company does with the Market Value Allowance and the Unrealized Gain (Loss) on Investments accounts when investments are sold. The answer is that they adjust the account balances to $0 at the end of the year, similar to the process in the preceding example. Because Washington Post has no investment in IFN at December 31, 2012, it would eliminate the $1 balance in each account.

(in millions)	Debit	Credit
Unrealized Gain (Loss) on Investments (−OE)	1	
Market Value Allowance (−A)		1

Assets		=	Liabilities	+	Owners' Equity	
Market Value Allowance	−1				Unrealized Gain (Loss) on Investments	−1

You now can review the T-accounts for all of the transactions from 2010 to 2012 in Exhibit 15.2.

Comparison of Available-for-Sale and Trading Securities

The impact of unrealized holding gains or losses on the financial statements depends on whether an investment is a trading security or a security available for sale.

Available-for-Sale Securities

As you learned in the last section, the balance in the Unrealized Gain (Loss) on Investments account is reported as a separate component of stockholders' equity under **Accumulated Other**

Exhibit 15.2 T-Accounts for the Illustrated Transactions

Balance Sheet Accounts (in millions)

Securities Available for Sale (at cost) (A)

Debit		Credit	
12/31/09	0		
1/2/10 Purchase	60		
12/31/10	60		
12/31/11	60	60	Sale 3/17/12
12/31/12	0		

Market Value Allowance (A)

Debit		Credit	
		0	12/31/09
		2	AJE 12/31/10
		2	12/31/10
12/31/11 AJE	3		
12/31/11	1		
		1	AJE 12/31/12
		0	12/31/12

Unrealized Gain (Loss) on Investments (OE)

Debit		Credit	
12/31/09	0		
12/31/10 AJE	2		
12/31/10	2		
		3	AJE 12/31/11
		1	12/31/11
12/31/12 AJE	1		
12/31/12	0		

Income Statement Accounts (in millions)

Investment Income (R)

Debit	Credit	
	1	Earned 12/15/10
	1	12/31/10

Gain on Sale of Investments (R)

Debit	Credit	
	4	Sale 3/17/12
	4	12/31/12

Comprehensive Income. It is not reported on the income statement because it does not affect net income.

However, at the time of sale, the difference between the proceeds from the sale and the original cost of the investment is recorded as a gain or loss on the sale of investments. It is reported on the income statement because the gain has been realized. At the end of the year, the Unrealized Gain (Loss) on Investments account and the Market Value Allowance account are adjusted.

Trading Securities

For trading securities, the amount of the adjustment to record a holding gain or loss is included **in each period's income statement** (that is, it is treated as realized). Holding gains increase net income, and holding losses decrease net income. The amount that is recorded as Unrealized Gain (Loss) on Trading Securities is also closed to Retained Earnings at the end of the period as are other temporary accounts on the income statement. When a trading security is sold, the affected accounts are Cash, Trading Securities, and Market Value Allowance plus any additional Gain (Loss) on Sale of Investments.

EFFECT ON INCOME STATEMENT (in millions)

	Trading Securities	Securities Available for Sale
2010 Investment income	$1	$1
2010 Unrealized loss	(2)	—
2011 Unrealized gain	3	—
2012 Gain on sale	3	4
Total income	$5	$5

See Exhibit 15.3 for a comparison of the treatment of trading securities and securities available for sale using Washington Post's transactions from 2010 to 2012. **Note that the total investment income reported for the three years is the same for both trading securities and securities available for sale ($5 million). Only the allocation across periods differs.**

Spotlight On FINANCIAL REPORTING

Equity Securities and Earnings Management

Most managers prefer to treat passive investments as investments available for sale. This treatment generally reduces variations in reported earnings by avoiding recognition of unrealized holding gains and losses that result from quarter-to-quarter changes in stock prices. It also allows managers to smooth out fluctuations in earnings by selling securities with unrealized gains when earnings decline and securities with unrealized losses when earnings increase. Analysts can see through this strategy, however, by examining the required note on investments in the financial statements.

Exhibit 15.3 Comparison of Accounting for Trading and Available-for-Sale Securities

Part A: Journal Entries	Trading Securities (in millions)			Securities Available for Sale (in millions)		
2010						
• Purchase (for $60 million cash)	Trading Securities (+A)	60		Securities Available for Sale (+A)	60	
	Cash (−A)		60	Cash (−A)		60
• Receipt of dividends ($1 million cash)	Cash (+A)	1		Cash (+A)	1	
	Investment Income (+R, +OE)		1	Investment Income (+R, +OE)		1
• Year-end adjustment to market (market = $58 million)	Unrealized Loss on Trading Securities (+E, −OE)	2		Unrealized Gain (Loss) on Investments (−OE)	2	
	Market Value Allowance (−A)		2	Market Value Allowance (−A)		2
2011						
• Year-end adjustment to market (market = $61 million)	Market Value Allowance (+A)	3		Market Value Allowance (+A)	3	
	Unrealized Gain on Trading Securities (+R, + OE)		3	Unrealized Gain (Loss) on Investments (+OE)		3
2012						
• Sale (for $64 million)	Cash (+A)	64		Cash (+A)	64	
	Trading Securities (−A)		60	Securities Available for Sale (−A)		60
	Market Value Allowance (−A)		1	Gain on Sale of Investments (+R, + OE)		4
	Gain on Sale of Investments (+R, +OE)		3			
• Year-end adjustment to market (market = $0 because investments have been sold)	None			Unrealized Gain (Loss) on Investments (−OE)	1	
				Market Value Allowance (−A)		1

Part B: Financial Statements	Trading Securities				Securities Available for Sale			
Balance Sheet	*Assets*	*2012*	*2011*	*2010*	*Assets*	*2012*	*2011*	*2010*
	Investment in marketable securities	—	$60	$60	Investment in marketable securities	—	$60	$60
	Market value allowance	—	1	(2)	Market value allowance	—	1	(2)
	Net investment in trading securities	—	$61	$58	Net investments available for sale	—	$61	$58
					Stockholders' Equity			
					Unrealized gain (loss) on investments	—	$ 1	$(2)
Income Statement		*2012*	*2011*	*2010*		*2012*	*2011*	*2010*
	Investment income	—	—	$ 1	Investment income	—	—	$1
	Unrealized gain (loss) on trading securities.	—	$3	$(2)	Gain on sale of investments	$4	—	—
	Gain on sale of investments	$3	—	—				

SELF-STUDY PRACTICE

Let's reconstruct the investment activities Washington Post undertook in a recent year, with a few transactions assumed. Use the following T-accounts to infer the amounts. Then prepare journal entries and answer questions. The dollars are stated in millions.

Balance Sheet Accounts

Securities Available for Sale

1/1	361		
Purchase	43	?	Sale
12/31	355		

Market Value Allowance

1/1	58	
AJE	?	
12/31	85	

(In Accumulated Other Comprehensive Income)

Unrealized Gain (Loss) on Investments

	58	1/1
	?	AJE
	85	12/31

Income Statement Accounts

Investment Income

	?	Earned
	73	12/31

Gain on Sale of Investments

	34	Sale
	34	12/31

1. Purchased securities available for sale for cash as a noncurrent asset. Prepare the journal entry.
2. Received cash dividends on the investments. Prepare the journal entry.
3. Sold securities available for sale at a gain. Prepare the journal entry.
4. At year-end, the securities available for sale portfolio had a market value of \$440. Prepare the adjusting entry.
5. What would be reported for investments on the balance sheet on December 31? On the income statement for the year? Indicate classifications, account titles, and amounts.
6. How would year-end reporting change if the investments were categorized as trading securities instead of securities available for sale? Assume the market value allowance for the trading securities sold was \$20.

After you have finished, check your answers with the solution at the bottom of the page.

Solution to Self-Study Practice

1.	Securities Available for Sale (+A)	43	
	Cash (−A)		43
2.	Cash (+A)	73	
	Investment Income (+R, +OE)		73
3.	Cash (+A)	83	
	Gain on Sale of Investments (+R +OE)		34
	Securities Available for Sale (−A)		49
	(Beg. bal. \$361 + purchase \$43 − end. bal. \$355 = \$49 cost of securities sold)		
4.	Market Value Allowance (+A)	27	
	Unrealized Gain (Loss) on Investments (+OE)		27

	In Millions
Market value	\$440
− Cost	− 355
Balance needed in Market Value Allowance	85
− Unadjusted balance in Market Value Allowance	− 58
Amount for adjusting entry	\$ 27

5.

Balance Sheet		**Income Statement**	
Assets (noncurrent)		*Other Items*	
Investments in Marketable Securities	\$440	Gain on Sale of Investments	\$ 34
Stockholders' Equity		Investment Income	73
Accumulated Other Comprehensive Income:			
Unrealized Gain (Loss) on Investments	85		

6.

Balance Sheet		**Income Statement**	
Assets (Current)		*Other Items*	
Investments in Marketable Securities	\$440	Gain on Sale of Investments	\$ 14
		Investment Income	73

When trading securities were sold, the journal entry was:

Cash (+A)	83		
Investments in Marketable Securities (−A)		49	
Market Value Allowance (−A)		20	Assumed
Gain on Sale of Investments (+R, +OE)		14	

Spotlight On FINANCIAL REPORTING

Passive Investments and the Fair Value Option

Both U.S. GAAP and international financial reporting standards (IFRS) allow the option to account for bonds held to maturity and securities available for sale at **fair value.** Fair value is the price the seller would receive if the assets were sold. The election is made when each security is purchased. If a company decides to account for a held-to-maturity or available-for-sale security at fair value, it is transferred to the trading securities portfolio and is accounted for in the same manner as other trading securities.

ACCOUNTING FOR INFLUENTIAL INVESTMENTS

Investments for Significant Influence: Equity Method

Learning Objective 5

Analyze and report investments involving significant influence using the equity method.

For a variety of reasons, an investor may want to exert significant influence (by owning 20 to 50 percent of a company's outstanding voting stock) without becoming the controlling shareholder (by acquiring over 50 percent of the voting stock). For example:

- A retailer may want to influence a manufacturer to ensure obtaining certain products designed to its specifications.
- A manufacturer may want to influence a computer consulting firm to incorporate the firm's cutting-edge technology in its manufacturing processes.
- A manufacturer may recognize that a parts supplier lacks experienced management and could prosper with additional managerial support.

When an investor can exert **significant influence** over an **investee** (the company it partially owns), accountants must use the **equity method** to value the investment. As you have seen, when Washington Post invests in securities as a passive investor, the company reports those investments on the balance sheet as Investments in Marketable Securities. However, when Washington Post owns 20 to 50 percent of the outstanding voting stock, the company is presumed to be taking a more active role as an investor. On the balance sheet, Washington Post reports these long-term **investments for significant influence** as Investments in Affiliates (see Exhibit 15.1). Washington Post reported one primary investment in an affiliated company in its 2006 annual report. It sold another affiliated company during 2006:

WASHINGTON POST
2006 Annual Report

NOTES TO FINANCIAL STATEMENTS

A. SUMMARY OF SIGNIFICANT ACCOUNTING POLICIES

Investments in Affiliates. The Company uses the equity method of accounting for its investments in and earnings or losses of associated companies that it does not control, but over which it does exert significant influence. . . .

C. INVESTMENTS

. . .

Investments in Affiliates. The Company's investments in affiliates at December 31, 2006 and January 1, 2006 include the following (in millions):

	2006	**2005**
Bowater Mersey Paper Company	$49	$55
BrassRing	—	11
Other	5	1
	$54	$67

At the end of 2006, the Company's investments in affiliates consisted of a 49% interest in the common stock of Bowater Mersey Paper Company Limited, which owns and operates a newsprint mill in Nova Scotia, and other investments.

. . . On November 13, 2006, the Company sold its 49% interest in BrassRing and recorded a $43.2 million pre-tax gain that is included in "Other income (expense), net" in the Consolidated Statements of Income.

Recording Investments under the Equity Method

With a passive investment (less than 20 percent stock ownership), an investor usually cannot influence the investee's operating and financing activities—for example, by compelling the investee to pay dividends. So, the investor reports any dividends received from the investee as dividend revenue.

Under the equity method, however, the investor's 20 to 50 percent ownership in a company presumes significant influence over the investee's operating and financing policies. Often the investee's board of directors may include a representative of the investor who influences the investee's board to declare dividends among other decisions. Because of this influence, the investment is accounted for as if the two companies were one. That is, the net income the investee earned increases the investee's net assets (assets − liabilities). Likewise, the investor should report a portion of the investee's net income as its income and an increase in the investment account. Dividends paid by the investee decrease the investee's net assets. Similarly, the receipt of dividends by the investor is treated as a reduction of the investment account, not revenue. A summary follows:

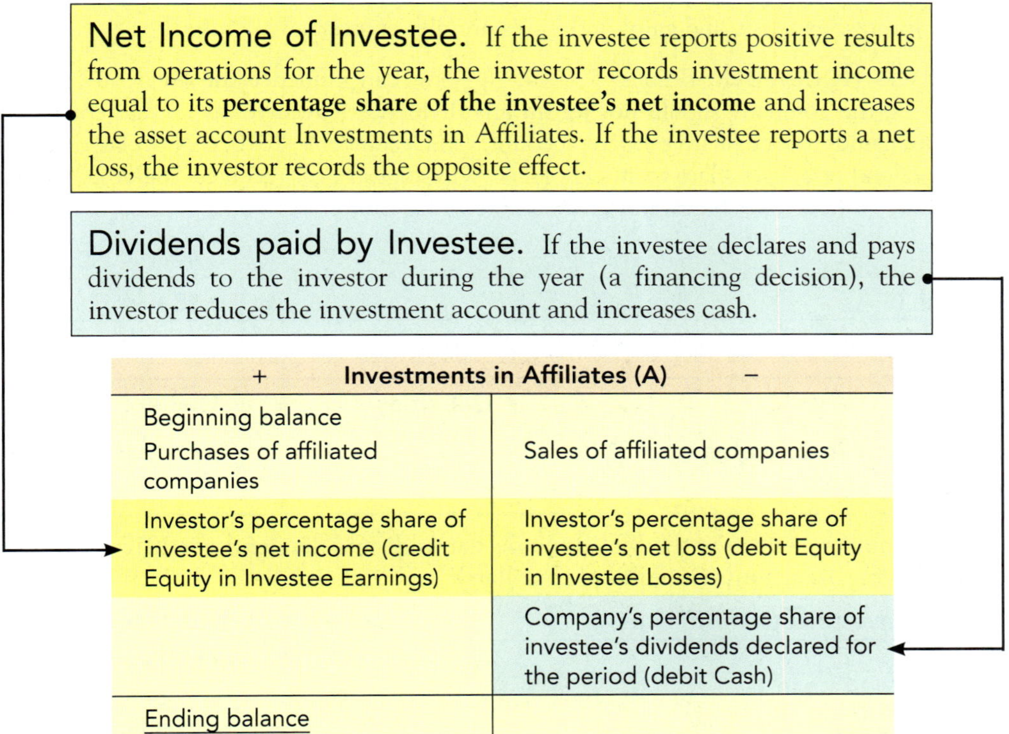

Purchase of Stock. For simplicity, let's assume that at the end of 2009, Washington Post had no long-term investments in companies over which it exerted significant influence. On January 2, 2010, Washington Post purchased 4 million shares of the outstanding voting stock of IFN for $240,000,000 cash. Because IFN had 10 million shares of common stock outstanding, Washington Post acquired a 40 percent interest (4 million ÷ 10 million shares) and was presumed to have significant influence over the investee. Therefore, Washington Post must use the equity method to account for the investment. The purchase of the asset would be recorded on January 2, 2010, at cost in Investments in Affiliates.

(in millions)	Debit	Credit
Investments in Affiliates (+A)	240	
Cash (−A)		240

Assets		=	Liabilities	+	Owners' Equity
Investments in Affiliates	+240				
Cash	−240				

Investee Earnings. Because the investor can influence the investee's income-earning process, the investor bases its investment income on the investee's earnings rather than on the dividends paid. In 2010, IFN reported net income of $50,000,000. Washington Post's percentage share of that income, $20,000,000 (40% × $50,000,000), would be recorded on December 31, 2010, as follows:

(in millions)	Debit	Credit
Investments in Affiliates (+A)	20	
Equity in Investee Earnings (+R, +OE)		20

Assets		=	Liabilities	+	Owners' Equity	
Investments in Affiliates	**+20**				**Equity in Investee Earnings (+R)**	**+20**

If reporting a net loss, the investor records its share of the loss by decreasing the investment account and recording the loss under Equity in Investee Losses. Equity in Investee Earnings (or Losses) is reported in the Other Items section of the income statement along with interest revenue, interest expense, and gains and losses on sales of assets.

Dividends Received. Because Washington Post can influence the dividend policies of its investees, the company should **not** record any dividends it receives as investment income. Instead, dividends reduce its investment account. On December 1, 2010, IFN declared and paid a cash dividend of $2 per share to stockholders. Washington Post received $8,000,000 in cash ($2 per share × 4,000,000 shares) from IFN, and recorded this on December 1, 2010, as follows:

(in millions)	Debit	Credit
Cash (+A)	8	
Investments in Affiliates (−A)		8

Assets		=	Liabilities	+	Owners' Equity
Investments in Affiliates	**−8**				
Cash	**+8**				

The cumulative effects of the IFN purchase, earnings, and dividends for 2010 are reflected in the following T-accounts (in millions of dollars):

Investments in Affiliates			
1/1/10	0		
Purchases	240		
Share of investee net earnings	20	8	Share of investee dividends
12/31/10	252		

Equity in Investee Earnings			
		0	1/1/10
		20	Share of investee net earnings
		20	12/31/10

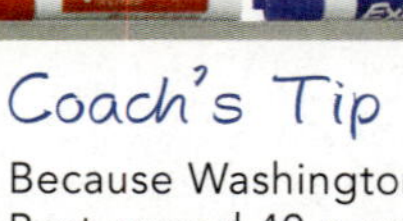

Coach's Tip

Because Washington Post owned 40 percent of IFN prior to the sale (4 million of the 10 million shares outstanding), it will then own 30 percent (3 million of 10 million shares) after the sale. Thus, **it must still apply the equity method.**

Sale of Stock. Companies record any sale of stock in affiliated companies in the same way as sales of other assets. Investment in Affiliates is reduced by the percentage of stock sold, Cash is debited, and the difference is recorded as either a Gain (or Loss) on Sale of Investments.

Let's assume that on January 2, 2011, Washington Post decided to sell 1,000,000 of the 4,000,000 shares of stock it owned in IFN for $70 million. That represents 25 percent of Washington Post's Investment in Affiliates. One-fourth of the balance in the account is equal to $63 million ($252 million × ¼), so the entry in January 2011 is:

(in millions)	Debit	Credit
Cash (+A)	70	
Investments in Affiliates (−A)		63
Gain on Sale of Investments (+R, +OE)		7

Assets		=	Liabilities	+	Owners' Equity	
Cash	**+70**				**Gain on Sale of Investments (+R)**	**+7**
Investments in Affiliates	**−63**					

Reporting Investments under the Equity Method

On the balance sheet, Investments in Affiliates is reported as a long-term asset. However, as the year-end entries show, the investment account does not reflect either cost or market value. Instead, the following occurs:

- The investment account increases with the cost of the purchased shares and the proportional share of the investee's income.
- The investment account decreases with the dividends received from the investee, the proportional share of any investee losses, and any sale of shares in the investee.

At the end of the accounting period, accountants **do not adjust the investment account to reflect changes in the market value** of the securities. When the securities are sold, accountants record the difference between the cash received and the book value of the investment as a Gain (Loss) on Sale of Investments and report the amount on the income statement in the Other Items section.

Spotlight On ETHICS

Improper Influence

A key assumption in accounting is that all transactions occur at "arm's length." That is, each party to the transaction is acting in his or her own self-interest. But when one company exerts significant influence over another (that is, when it owns 20 to 50 percent of the voting common stock), it is unreasonable to assume that transactions between the two companies are made at arm's length.

Consider what might happen if an investor company could affect the investee's dividend policy. If the investor reported dividends paid by the investee as dividend income, the investor could manipulate its own income by influencing the other company's dividend policy. In a bad year, the investor might request large dividend payments to bolster its income. In a good year, it might try to cut dividend payments to build up the investee's retained earnings, which would support large dividends in the future.

The equity method prevents this type of manipulation. Instead of recognizing dividends as income, this method bases income from the investment on a percentage of the affiliated company's reported net income.

SELF-STUDY PRACTICE

Let's reconstruct some actions Washington Post undertook recently regarding its investments in affiliated companies with a few transactions assumed. Prepare the following journal entries and answer the following questions. Use the T-accounts that follow to infer the amounts. The dollars are given in millions.

Investments in Affiliates			
1/1	67		
Purchases	3	15	Sales of investments
Share of investee earnings	?	2	Share of investee dividends
12/31	54		

Equity in Investee Earnings			
		0	1/1
		1	Share of investee earnings
		1	12/31

1. Purchased additional investments in affiliated companies for cash. Prepare the journal entry.
2. Sold a portion of investments in affiliated companies for $58 cash. Prepare the journal entry.
3. Received cash dividends on the investments. Prepare the journal entry.
4. At year-end, the affiliated companies reported a total of $5 in net income, and investments in affiliates had a market value of $42. Prepare the adjusting entry. What percentage of the investee's stock is owned by the Washington Post?
5. What would be reported on the year-end balance sheet regarding the investments in affiliates? What would be reported on the income statement for the year?

After you have finished, check your answers with the solution at the bottom of the next page.

Spotlight On FINANCIAL REPORTING

Selecting Accounting Methods

Managers can choose freely between LIFO and FIFO for measuring inventory or between accelerated depreciation and straight-line depreciation for measuring the use of long-lived assets. In the case of minority investments (50 percent or less), however, they may **not** choose between the market value and equity methods. Investments in less than 20 percent of a company's outstanding stock are usually accounted for using the market value method. Investments of 20 to 50 percent are accounted for using the equity method.

However, managers may be able to structure acquisitions in a way that permits them to use the accounting methods they prefer. For example, a company that wants to use the market value method could purchase only 19.9 percent of the outstanding stock of another company and achieve essentially the same investment goals as it would with a 20 percent investment. Why might managers want to avoid using the equity method? Most managers prefer to minimize variations in reported earnings. If a company were planning to buy stock in a firm that reported large earnings in some years and large losses in others, it might want to use the market value method to avoid reporting its share of the investee's earnings and losses.

In short, analysts who compare companies must understand management's reporting choices and the way in which differences between the market value and equity methods can affect a company's earnings.

Investments with Controlling Interests: Consolidated Statements

Learning Objective 6

Explain the reporting of investments in controlling interests.

Why Control Other Companies?

Before we discuss financial reporting of investments that involve ownership of more than 50 percent of another company's outstanding voting stock, we should consider the reasons for acquiring this level of ownership. Following are some of these reasons:

1. **Vertical integration.** In this type of acquisition, one company acquires another company that operates on a different level in the distribution channel. For example, Washington Post owns a newsprint company that provides raw materials.
2. **Horizontal growth.** Horizontal acquisitions involve companies that operate on the same level of the distribution channel. For example, Washington Post has expanded internationally by creating or acquiring newspaper companies in major international markets.

Solution to Self-Study Practice

1.	Investments in Affiliates (+A)	3	
	Cash (−A)		3
2.	Cash (+A)	58	
	Investments in Affiliates (−A)		15
	Gain on Sale of Investments (+R, +OE)		43
3.	Cash (+A)	2	
	Investments in Affiliates (−A)		2
4.	Investments in Affiliates (+A)	1	
	Equity in Investee Earnings (+R, +OE)		1
	Washington Post owns 20 percent of affiliates' stock (20% × \$5 net income = \$1 equity in investee earnings).		

Under the equity method, there is no entry at year-end to adjust the Investments in Affiliates account to market value.

5.

Balance Sheet		Income Statement	
Assets (under noncurrent assets)		*Other Items*	
Investments in Affiliates	\$54	Equity in Investee Earnings	\$ 1
		Gain on Sale of Investments	43

3. **Synergy.** Two companies operating together may be more profitable than two companies operating separately. Washington Post has created or purchased a number of broadcast and Internet services. Merging these companies and sharing news content may create more profits than operating separate entities could.

Understanding why one company has acquired control over other companies is a key factor in understanding that company's business strategy.

What Are Consolidated Statements?

Any corporate acquisition involves two companies. A **merger** occurs when one company purchases all assets and liabilities of another company and the **acquired company goes out of existence.** When the acquired company remains in business, the company that gains control over it by acquiring all or a majority of the voting stock is the **parent company.** The **subsidiary company** is the company that the parent acquired.[4] Following is a list of three corporations and some of the well-known companies they own:

The Gap, Inc.	YUM! Brands, Inc.	The Walt Disney Company
Gap	Pizza Hut	ABC Television Network
Old Navy	KFC	ESPN
Banana Republic	Taco Bell	Disneyland
Forth & Towne	Long John Silver's	Pixar Animation Studios
	A&W All-American Restaurants	Touchstone Pictures

Coach's Tip

Because a single set of financial statements covers both the parent company and its subsidiaries, external users such as stockholders and banks (and you) will not be able to obtain financial statements for individual subsidiaries.

When one company acquires another, the results of their operations must be reported together in consolidated statements. **Consolidated financial statements combine the operations of two or more companies into a single set of statements,** usually identified by the word consolidated in the statement titles. For example, the title of the statement in Exhibit 15.1 is *Consolidated* Balance Sheet. Consolidated statements may be thought of as adding together the financial statements for two or more companies so that they appear to be a single company. Thus, the cash accounts for the companies are summed, along with the inventory accounts, the land accounts, and all other accounts. Combining all financial information into one set of consolidated statements gives users better information on the size and scope of operations in companies controlled by the parent corporation.

The notes to Washington Post's 2006 annual report provide the following information:

WASHINGTON POST
2006 Annual Report

NOTES TO FINANCIAL STATEMENTS

A. SUMMARY OF SIGNIFICANT ACCOUNTING POLICIES

Principles of Consolidation. The accompanying financial statements include the accounts of the Company and its subsidiaries; significant intercompany transactions have been eliminated.

As the note indicates, when consolidated statements are prepared, intercompany items such as loans from the parent company to the subsidiaries must be eliminated. Remember that consolidated statements imply that a single company exists when in fact there are two or more separate legal entities. Intercompany items do not exist in a single corporation. For example, a debt Washington Post (the parent) owes to its newsprint subsidiary is not reported

[4] The discussion assumes acquisition of 100 percent of another company. Any acquisition of 51 to 99 percent of another company creates a minority interest that is discussed in advanced accounting courses.

on a consolidated statement because a company cannot owe money to itself. Accounting for business acquisitions and preparing consolidated financial statements are discussed in detail in advanced accounting courses.

EVALUATING TOTAL INVESTED CAPITAL

Learning Objective 7
Analyze and interpret the return on assets ratio.

Return on Assets (ROA)

Investments are assets that are used to generate profits for their owners. To assess how well management has used the company's assets to earn income, analysts and managers compute the **return on assets (ROA)** ratio.

Accounting Decision Tools

Name of Measure	Formula	What It Tells You
Return on assets (ROA)	$\frac{\text{Net Income*}}{\text{Average Total Assets}^{\dagger}} \times 100$	• The percentage of income earned on each dollar invested in assets • The higher the ratio, the more effectively managers are using total assets

* In more complicated analyses, interest expense (net of tax) and minority interest are added back to net income because the measure assesses return on assets independent of their source.

† Average Total Assets = (Beginning Total Assets + Ending Total Assets) ÷ 2

The ROA ratio measures how much the firm earned for each dollar invested in assets. It is the broadest measure of profitability and managerial effectiveness independent of financial strategy. Using the information from Washington Post's 2006 10-K report (with dollars given in thousands), the company's ROA is computed as follows:

$$\text{Return on Assets} = \frac{\text{Net Income}}{\text{Average Total Assets}} \times 100 = \frac{\$324{,}469}{(\$5{,}381{,}372 + \$4{,}584{,}773) \div 2} \times 100 = 6.5\%$$

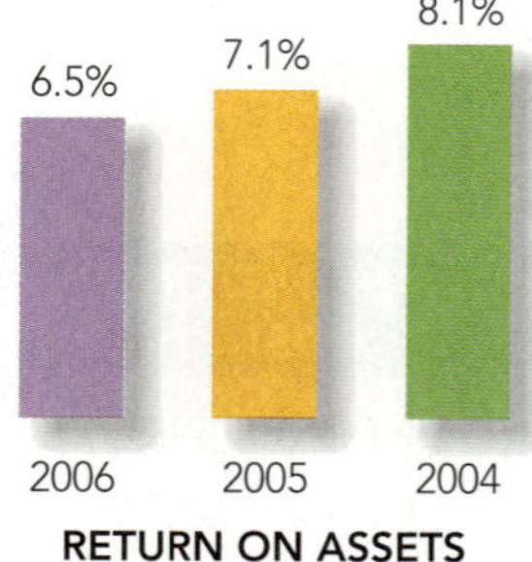

RETURN ON ASSETS

The Washington Post

The return on assets ratio is helpful both in analyzing management's effectiveness in using assets to generate profits and in comparing one company or division to another. Companies often compute this measure on a division-by-division basis and then use it to evaluate divisional managers' performance. A higher ROA means that the managers are doing a better job at selecting new investments in assets, all other things held equal.

As you can see from the graph in the margin, Washington Post's ROA for 2006 was below its ROA for the preceding two years. In 2006, Washington Post generated 6.5 cents of income for every dollar of assets; in 2005 and 2004, the company generated 7.1 cents and 8.1 cents of income, respectively, for every dollar of assets. ROA allows investors to compare management's investment performance against alternative investment options. Firms with higher ROAs are doing a better job of selecting new investments, all other things equal.

Comparison to Benchmarks

Comparing a company's ROA ratio to those of competing companies provides additional information on management's effectiveness. As noted in Exhibit 15.4, in 2006, the Gannett Co., Inc., and the Tribune Company reported ROAs of 7.3 percent and 4.7 percent, respectively. By comparison, Washington Post's 2006 ROA of 6.5 percent was in the middle.

Be aware that ROAs can vary greatly from one industry to the next. As noted in Exhibit 15.4, footwear companies recently reported an average return on assets ratio of 16.4 percent compared to 1.0 percent for banks and 13.6 percent for nonalcoholic beverage companies.

Exhibit 15.4 Average Return on Assets Ratio by Industry

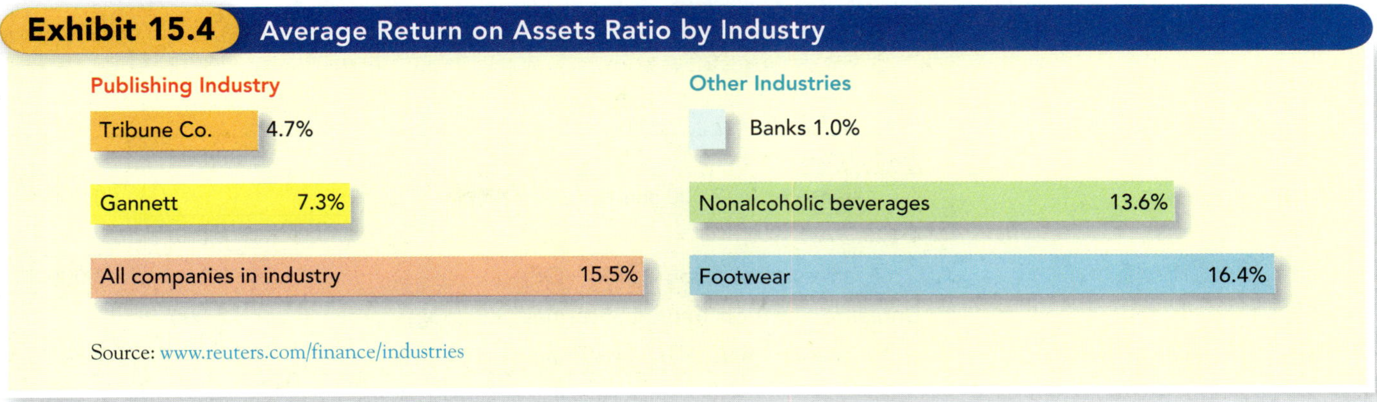

Source: www.reuters.com/finance/industries

Spotlight On BUSINESS DECISIONS

The Big Get Bigger

We began this chapter by asking how big companies become big and suggesting that acquisitions of stock in other companies is a common strategy. As this chapter was being written, Dow Jones, another major player in the publishing industry, was acquired by News Corporation, a diversified entertainment company headquartered in Australia with worldwide operations in film (e.g., 20th Century Fox), television and cable network programming (e.g., Fox network), magazines (e.g., *TV Guide*), newspapers (e.g., *New York Post*), and other segments. News Corporation has more than $62 billion in total assets, and its annual revenues exceed $28 billion. With the $5 billion Dow Jones acquisition, News Corporation will grow by 8 percent. On December 13, 2007, Dow Jones issued the following press release:

> **NEW YORK** — Dow Jones & Company, Inc. (NYSE: DJ) announced today that its stockholders voted at a special meeting to approve the previously announced merger agreement with News Corporation. The stockholder vote satisfies the final condition for the completion of the transaction. The merger is expected to close and become effective at approximately the close of business on Dec. 13, 2007.

2007 Press Release

Demonstration Case A

(Try to resolve the following requirements before proceeding to the suggested solution that follows.) Howell Equipment Corporation sells and services a major line of farm equipment. Both sales and service operations have been profitable. The following transactions affected the company during 2009:

a. Jan. 1 Purchased 2,000 shares of common stock in Dear Company at $40 per share. Purchase represented 1 percent of the shares outstanding. Management intends to trade these shares actively.

b. Dec. 28 Received $4,000 cash dividend on Dear Company stock.

c. Dec. 31 Determined that the current market price of Dear stock was $39.

Required:

1. Prepare the journal entry for each of these transactions.
2. What accounts and amounts will be reported on the balance sheet at the end of 2009 and on the income statement for 2009?

Suggested Solution for Case A

1.

a.	Trading Securities (+A)	80,000	
	Cash (−A) (2,000 shares × $40)		80,000
b.	Cash (+A)	4,000	
	Investment Income (+R, +OE)		4,000
c.	Unrealized Loss on Trading Securities (+E −OE)	2,000	
	Market Value Allowance (−A)		2,000

Year: 2009

Market value	$78,000	($39 per share × 2,000 shares)
− Cost	−80,000	($40 per share × 2,000 shares)
Balance needed in Market Value Allowance	(2,000)	A credit balance
− Unadjusted balance in Market Value Allowance	− 0	
Amount for adjusting entry	$ (2,000)	An unrealized loss to income

2. On the balance sheet — On the income statement

Current Assets		*Other Items*	
Investment in Marketable Securities ($80,000 cost − $2,000 allowance)	$78,000	Investment Income	$4,000
		Unrealized Loss on Trading Securities	(2,000)

Demonstration Case B

Assume the same facts as in Case A except that the shares were purchased as securities available for sale rather than as trading securities.

Required:

1. Prepare the journal entry for each of these transactions.
2. What accounts and amounts will be reported on the balance sheet at the end of 2009 and on the income statement for 2009?

Suggested Solution for Case B

1.

a.	Securities Available for Sale (+A)	80,000	
	Cash (−A) (2,000 shares × $40)		80,000
b.	Cash (+A)	4,000	
	Investment Income (+R, +OE)		4,000
c.	Unrealized Gain (Loss) on Investments (−OE)	2,000	
	Market Value Allowance (−A)		2,000

Year: 2009

Market value	$78,000	($39 per share × 2,000 shares)
− Cost	− 80,000	($40 per share × 2,000 shares)
Balance needed in Market Value Allowance	(2,000)	A credit balance
− Unadjusted balance in Market Value Allowance −	0	
Amount for adjusting entry	$ (2,000)	An unrealized loss to owners' equity

2. On the balance sheet | On the income statement

Current or noncurrent assets		*Other items*	
Investments in marketable securities ($80,000 cost − $2,000 allowance)	$78,000	Investment income	$4,000
Owners' equity			
Accumulated other comprehensive income:			
Unrealized loss on investments	(2,000)		

Demonstration Case C

On January 1, 2010, Connaught Company purchased 40 percent of the outstanding voting shares of London Company on the open market for $85,000 cash. London declared $10,000 in cash dividends on December 1, 2010, and reported net income of $60,000 for the year on December 31, 2010.

Required:

1. Prepare the journal entries for 2010.
2. What accounts and amounts were reported on Connaught's balance sheet at the end of 2010 and on Connaught's income statement for 2010?

Suggested Solution for Case C

1.

Jan. 1	Investments in Affiliates (+A)	85,000	
	Cash (−A)		85,000
Dec. 1	Cash (+A) (40% × $10,000)	4,000	
	Investments in Affiliates (−A)		4,000
Dec. 31	Investments in Affiliates (+A) (40% × $60,000)	24,000	
	Equity in Investee Earnings (+R, +OE)		24,000

2. On the balance sheet | On the income statement

Noncurrent assets		*Other items*	
Investments in affiliates	$105,000	Equity in investee earnings	$24,000
$ 85,000 cost			
− 4,000 dividends			
+ 24,000 percentage of investee's net income			
$105,000 balance in Investments account			

Chapter Summary

LO1 Explain why companies invest in debt and stock securities. p. 642

- Businesses that receive large amounts of cash invest in the debt and stock securities of other companies to generate earnings.
- Companies with seasonal businesses that have extra cash on hand at the end of the busy season may invest in the stocks and bonds of other companies to earn a return on idle funds.
- Companies with a growth strategy may acquire the stock of other companies to significantly influence their financial and operating policies or to actually control their activities

LO2 Identify investment types and the related accounting methods. p. 643

- **Passive investments in debt and equity securities**
    - Debt securities that are accounted for and reported as
        - Held-to-maturity investments, accounted for under the cost method or
        - Investments not intended to be held to maturity, accounted for under the market value method.
    - Equity securities (stock) amounting to less than 20 percent of the outstanding voting stock of another company, accounted for and reported under the market value method.
- **Investments in stock for significant influence**
    - Investments that amount to 20 to 50 percent of the outstanding voting stock of another company are presumed to result in significant influence over the other company. These investments are accounted for and reported under the equity method.
- **Investments in stock for control**
    - Investments that amount to more than 50 percent of the outstanding voting stock of another company result in control over that company. These investments are combined with the parent company in consolidated financial statements.

LO3 Analyze and report bond investments held to maturity. p. 644

- **Debt investments held to maturity: Amortized cost**
    - When management intends to hold a bond investment until it matures, the bond is recorded at **cost** when acquired and at amortized cost on the balance sheet. Any interest earned during the period is reported on the income statement.

LO4 Analyze and report passive investments in securities using the market value method. p. 646

- **Securities available for sale: Market value method**
    - Depending on management's intent, passive investments may be classified as either
        - Trading securities (those that are actively traded to maximize their return) or
        - Securities available for sale (those that earn a return but are not as actively traded). Most companies classify investments as available for sale.
    - Debt securities that are not intended to be held to maturity and passive stock investments are recorded at cost and adjusted to market value at year-end. A valuation allowance is increased or decreased to arrive at the market value. The resulting unrealized holding gain or loss is recorded
        - For trading securities, in net income.
        - For securities available for sale, as a component of stockholders' equity in Accumulated Other Comprehensive Income.
    - Any dividends or interest earned are reported in the Other Items section of the income statement along with any gains or losses on sales of passive investments.
- **Comparing available-for-sale and trading securities**
    - Trading securities are always classified as current assets.
    - Accounting for trading securities is almost identical to accounting for securities available for sale. The primary difference is that any unrealized holding gains or losses are reported directly on the income statement.

LO5 Analyze and report investments involving significant influence using the equity method. p. 654

- **Investments for significant influence: Equity method**
    - Under the equity method, the investor records an investment at cost on the acquisition date. Each period after that, the investment's value is increased (or decreased) by the investor's percentage share of the investee's reported net income (or loss) and decreased by the investor's percentage share of the dividends declared by the investee. Each period, the investor recognizes as revenue its share of the net income (or loss) reported by the investee.
    - Equity in the investee's earnings or losses (that is, the investor's percentage share of the investee's net income or loss for the period) is reported in the Other Items section of the income statement along with any gains or losses on the sale of investments.

LO6 Explain the reporting of investments in controlling interests. p. 658

- **Investments with controlling interest: Consolidated statements**
  - A company acquires control of another company by purchasing more than 50 percent of the acquired company's outstanding voting shares. Often acquisitions are made to achieve vertical integration (with a different level in the distribution channel), horizontal growth (on the same level of the distribution channel), or synergy (more efficient operations, which increase profitability).
  - Mergers occur when one company purchases all net assets of another and the acquired company ceases to exist as a separate legal entity. When the acquired company remains in business, the purchaser is the parent company and the acquired company is the subsidiary.
  - The concept of consolidation is based on the view that a parent company and its subsidiaries constitute a single economic entity. Therefore, their separate income statements, balance sheets, and statements of cash flows should be combined each period on an item-by-item basis to form a single set of consolidated financial statements.

LO7 Analyze and interpret the return on assets ratio. p. 660

- **Return on assets (ROA)**
  - The return on assets ratio is computed by dividing net income by average total assets. This ratio measures how much income a company earned with each dollar of assets. It provides information on both a company's profitability and management's effectiveness in using assets. An increasing ratio suggests increased managerial efficiency.

Accounting Decision Tools

Name of Measure	Formula	What It Tells You
Return on assets (ROA)	$\frac{\text{Net Income*}}{\text{Average Total Assets}^{\dagger}} \times 100$	• The percentage of income earned on each dollar invested in assets • The higher the ratio, the more effectively managers are using total assets

* In more complicated analyses, interest expense (net of tax) and minority interest are added back to net income because the measure assesses return on assets independent of their source.

† Average Total Assets = (Beginning Total Assets + Ending Total Assets) ÷ 2

Key Terms

Active Investments (p. 643)
Amortized Cost (p. 644)
Consolidated Financial Statements (p. 659)
Equity Method (p. 654)
Investments Held to Maturity (p. 644)
Investments for Significant Influence (p. 654)
Market Value Method (p. 646)
Merger (p. 659)
Parent Company (p. 659)
Passive Investments (p. 643)
Return on Assets (ROA) (p. 660)
Securities Available for Sale (p. 646)
Subsidiary Company (p. 659)
Trading Securities (p. 646)
Unrealized Holding Gains or Losses (p. 648)

See complete glossary in the back of text.

Questions

1. Explain the difference between a short-term investment and a long-term investment.
2. Why do companies invest in debt and stock securities?
3. What are
   a. Passive investments?
   b. Investments for significant influence?
   c. Investments for control?
4. What are the accounting methods used for passive investments, investments in which the investor can exert significant influence, and investments in which the investor has control over another entity?
5. Explain how to report bonds held to maturity on the balance sheet.
6. What are trading securities? How are they reported on the balance sheet, and how is income determined and reported on the income statement?
7. What are securities available for sale? How are they reported on the balance sheet, and how is income determined and reported on the income statement?
8. Under the market value method, when and how does the investor company measure investment revenue?

9. Under the equity method, why does the investor company measure revenue on a proportionate basis when the investee company reports income rather than when dividends are declared?
10. Under the equity method, dividends received from the investee company are not recorded as revenue. To record dividends as revenue involves double counting. Explain.
11. What is a parent–subsidiary relationship?
12. Explain the basic concept underlying consolidated statements.

Multiple Choice

Quiz 15-1
www.mhhe.com/LLPW1e

1. Company A owns 40 percent of Company B and exercises significant influence over Company B management. Therefore, Company A uses what method of accounting for and reporting its ownership of stock in Company B?
   a. Amortized cost method.
   b. Market-value method.
   c. Equity method.
   d. Consolidation of the financial statements of companies A and B.
2. Company A purchases 10 percent of Company X and intends to hold the stock for at least five years. At the end of the current year, how would Company A report on its December 31 (year-end) balance sheet its investment in Company X?
   a. At original cost in the Current Assets section.
   b. At the December 31 market value in the Current Assets section.
   c. At original cost in the Long-Term Assets section.
   d. At the December 31 market value in the Long-Term Assets section.
3. Dividends received from a stock that is reported as a security available for sale in the Long-Term Assets section of the balance sheet are reported as which of the following?
   a. Increase to cash and a decrease to the Investment in Marketable Securities account.
   b. Increase to cash and an unrealized gain on the balance sheet.
   c. Increase to cash and an increase to revenue.
   d. Increase to cash and an unrealized gain on the income statement.
4. Realized gains and losses are recorded on the income statement for which of the following transactions in Trading Securities and Securities Available for Sale?
   a. When adjusting a trading security to its market value.
   b. When adjusting a security available for sale to its market value.
   c. Only when recording the sale of a trading security.
   d. When recording the sale of either a trading security or an available-for-sale security.
5. When recording dividends received from a stock investment accounted for using the equity method, which of the following statements is true?
   a. Total assets are increased and net income is increased.
   b. Total assets are increased and total owners' equity is increased.
   c. Total assets are decreased and total owners' equity is decreased.
   d. Total assets and total owners' equity do not change.
6. When using the equity method, when is revenue recorded on the books of the investor company?
   a. When the market value of the investee stock increases.
   b. When a dividend is received from the investee.
   c. When the investee company reports net income.
   d. Both (b) and (c).
7. Kelly Company acquired 500 shares of stock of Drucker Company at $60 per share as a long-term investment. This represents 10 percent of the outstanding voting shares of Drucker. During the year, Drucker paid stockholders $2 per share in dividends. At year-end, Drucker reported net income of $40,000. Drucker's stock price at year-end was $63 per share. The amount of investments reported on the balance sheet at year-end and the amount reported on the income statement for the year would be:

	Balance Sheet	Income Statement
a.	$31,500	$1,000
b.	$30,000	$1,000
c.	$33,000	$4,000
d.	$31,500	$4,000

8. Kelly Company acquired 500 shares of stock of Drucker Company at $60 per share as a long-term investment. This represents 40 percent of the outstanding voting shares of Drucker. During the year, Drucker paid stockholders $2 per share in dividends. At year-end, Drucker reported net income of $40,000. Drucker's stock price at year-end was $63 per share. The amount of investments reported on the balance sheet at year-end and the amount reported on the income statement for the year would be:

	Balance Sheet	Income Statement
a.	$31,500	$ 1,000
b.	$45,000	$16,000
c.	$31,000	$ 0
d.	$31,500	$16,000

9. Consolidated financial statements are required in which of the following situations?
   a. Only when a company can exert significant influence over another company.
   b. Only when a company acquires another company for more than it is valued.

c. Only when a parent company can exercise control over its subsidiary.
d. Only when a company acquires another company for passive investment.

10. Which of the following is true regarding the use of the return on assets ratio?
    a. Evaluates the efficiency of a company given the capital contributed by owners.
    b. Evaluates the financing strategy of a company.
    c. Evaluates the profit generated for every dollar of sales.
    d. Evaluates how efficiently a company uses its total assets to earn income.

Solutions to Multiple-Choice Questions

1. c 2. d 3. c 4. d 5. d 6. c 7. a 8. b 9. c 10. d

Mini Exercises  Available with McGraw-Hill's Homework Manager

M15-1 Matching Measurement and Reporting Methods LO2

Match the following. Answers may be used more than once.

Measurement Method

A. Market value method
B. Equity method
C. Consolidation
D. Amortized cost

1. _______ More than 50 percent ownership
2. _______ Bonds held to maturity
3. _______ Less than 20 percent ownership
4. _______ At least 20 but not more than 50 percent ownership
5. _______ Current market value
6. _______ Original cost less any amortization of premium or discount associated with the purchase
7. _______ Original cost plus proportionate part of the income of the investee less proportionate part of the dividends declared by investee

M15-2 Recording a Bond Investment LO3

Wall Company purchased $1,000,000, 8 percent bonds issued by Janice Company on January 1, 2010. The purchase price of the bonds was $1,070,000. Management plans and has the ability to hold bonds until their maturity date. Interest is payable semiannually each June 30 and December 31. Record the purchase of the bonds on January 1, 2010.

M15-3 Recording Trading Securities Transactions LO4

During 2009, Princeton Company acquired some of the 50,000 outstanding shares of the common stock, par $10, of Cox Corporation as trading securities. The accounting period for both companies ends December 31. Give the journal entries for each of the following transactions that occurred during 2009:

July	2	Purchased 8,000 shares of Cox common stock at $28 per share.
Dec.	15	Recorded receipt of Cox Corporation's cash dividends of $2 per share.
	31	Determined the current market price of Cox stock to be $25 per share.

M15-4 Recording Available-for-Sale Securities Transactions LO4

Using the data in M15-3, assume Princeton Company purchased the voting stock of Cox Corporation for the available-for-sale portfolio instead of the trading securities portfolio. Give the journal entries for each of the transactions listed.

M15-5 Determining Financial Statement Effects of Trading Securities Transactions LO4

Using the information in M15-3, indicate in the following table the effects and amounts of each transaction listed. Use + for increase, − for decrease, and NE for no effect.

	BALANCE SHEET			INCOME STATEMENT		
Transaction	Assets	Liabilities	Owners' Equity	Revenues/ Gains	Expenses/ Losses	Net Income
July 2						
Dec. 15						
Dec. 31						

LO4

M15-6 Determining Financial Statement Effects of Available-for-Sale Securities Transactions

Using the information in M15-4, indicate in the following table the effects and amounts of each transaction listed. Use + for increase, − for decrease, and NE for no effect.

	BALANCE SHEET			INCOME STATEMENT		
Transaction	Assets	Liabilities	Owners' Equity	Revenues/ Gains	Expenses/ Losses	Net Income
July 2						
Dec. 15						
Dec. 31						

LO5

M15-7 Recording Equity Method Securities Transactions

On January 1, 2011, Ubuy.com acquired 25 percent (10,000 shares) of the common stock of E-Net Corporation. The accounting period for both companies ends December 31. Give the journal entries for each of the following transactions that occurred during 2011:

July 2 E-Net declared and paid a cash dividend of $3 per share.
Dec. 31 E-Net reported net income of $200,000.

LO5

M15-8 Determining Financial Statement Effects of Equity Method Securities

Using the information in M15-7, indicate in the following table the effects and amounts of each transaction listed. Use + for increase, − for decrease, and NE for no effect.

	BALANCE SHEET			INCOME STATEMENT		
Transaction	Assets	Liabilities	Owners' Equity	Revenues/ Gains	Expenses/ Losses	Net Income
July 2						
Dec. 31						

LO7

M15-9 Computing and Interpreting Return on Assets Ratio

M.A.D. Company reported the following information at the end of each year:

Year	Net Income	Total Assets
2008	$152,000	$ 52,000
2009	195,000	68,000
2010	201,000	134,000
2011	212,000	145,000

Compute return on assets for 2009, 2010, and 2011. What do the results suggest about M.A.D. Company?

Exercises  Available with McGraw-Hill's Homework Manager

LO3
Macy's, Inc.

E15-1 Explaining Investing Decisions and Recording Bonds Held to Maturity

Macy's, Inc. (formerly Federated Department Stores, Inc.) operates more than 880 department and furniture stores under the names of Macy's and Bloomingdales. The company does more than $20 billion in sales each year.

Assume that as part of its cash management strategy, Macy's purchased $10 million in bonds at par for cash on July 1, 2009. The bonds pay 10 percent annual interest each June 30 and December 31 and mature in 10 years. Macy's plans to hold the bonds until maturity.

Required:

1. Record the purchase of the bonds on July 1, 2009.
2. Record the receipt of interest on December 31, 2009.

E15-2 Comparing Market Value and Equity Methods LO4, 5

Company A purchased a certain number of Company B's outstanding voting shares at $19 per share as a long-term investment. Company B had outstanding 20,000 shares of $10 par value stock.

Required:

Complete the following matrix relating to the measurement and reporting by Company A after the acquisition of the shares of Company B stock.

	Market Value Method	Equity Method
1. What is the applicable level of ownership by Company A of Company B to apply the method?	______%	______%
For 2, 3, 6, 7, and 8, assume the following:		
Number of shares acquired of Company B stock	1,000	5,000
Net income reported by Company B in the first year	$50,000	$50,000
Dividends declared by Company B in the first year	$10,000	$10,000
Market price at end of the first year, Company B stock	$ 15	$ 15
2. What is the percentage ownership of Company B by Company A?	______	______
3. At acquisition, the investment account on the books of Company A should be debited at what amount?	______	______
4. When should Company A recognize revenue earned on the stock of Company B? Explanation required.	______	______
5. After the acquisition date, how should Company A change the balance of the investment account net of the allowance with respect to the stock owned in Company B (other than for disposal of the investment)? Explanation required.	______	______
6. What is the net amount of investment reported on the balance sheet of Company A at the end of the first year?	______	______
7. What amount of revenue from the investment in Company B should Company A report at the end of the first year?	______	______
8. What amount of unrealized loss should Company A report at the end of the first year?	______	______

E15-3 Recording Transactions in the Trading Securities Portfolio LO4

On June 30, 2009, MetroMedia, Inc., purchased 10,000 shares of Mitek stock for $20 per share. Management purchased the stock for speculative purposes and recorded the stock in the trading securities portfolio. The following information pertains to the price per share of Mitek stock:

	Price
12/31/2009	$24
12/31/2010	31
12/31/2011	25

MetroMedia sold all of the Mitek stock on February 14, 2012, at a price of $22 per share. Prepare any journal entries that are required by the facts presented in this case.

E15-4 Recording Transactions in the Available-for-Sale Portfolio LO4

Using the data in E15-3, assume MetroMedia's management purchased the Mitek stock for the available-for-sale portfolio instead of the trading securities portfolio. Prepare any journal entries required by the facts presented in the case.

E15-5 Recording Transactions in the Trading Securities Portfolio LO4

On March 10, 2009, General Solutions, Inc., purchased 5,000 shares of MicroTech stock for $50 per share. Management purchased the stock for speculative purposes and recorded it in the trading securities portfolio. The following information pertains to the price per share of MicroTech stock:

	Price
12/31/2009	$55
12/31/2010	40
12/31/2011	42

General Solutions sold all of the MicroTech stock on September 12, 2012, at a price of $39 per share. Prepare any journal entries required by the facts presented in this case.

LO4

E15-6 Recording Transactions in the Available-for-Sale Portfolio

Using the data in E15-5, assume General Solutions' management purchased the MicroTech stock for the available-for-sale portfolio instead of the trading securities portfolio. Prepare any journal entries required by the facts presented in the case.

LO5

E15-7 Recording and Reporting an Equity Method Investment

Felicia Company acquired some of the 60,000 shares of outstanding common stock (no par) of Nueces Corporation during 2010 as a long-term investment. The annual accounting period for both companies ends December 31. The following transactions occurred during 2010:

Jan. 10 Purchased 21,000 shares of Nueces common stock at $12 per share.

Dec. 31
a. Received the 2010 financial statements of Nueces Corporation that reported net income of $90,000.
b. Nueces Corporation declared and paid a cash dividend of $0.60 per share.
c. Determined the market price of Nueces stock to be $11 per share.

Required:

1. What accounting method should the company use? Why?
2. Give the journal entries for each of these transactions. If no entry is required, explain why.
3. Show how the long-term investment and the related revenue should be reported in the 2010 financial statements of the company.

LO6
The Colgate-Palmolive Company

E15-8 Determining the Appropriate Accounting Treatment for an Acquisition

The notes of Colgate-Palmolive's recent financial statements contained the following information:

Note 3

Acquisitions

On May 1, 2006, the Company completed the purchase of 84% of the outstanding shares of Tom's of Maine, Inc., for approximately $100 plus transaction costs. Tom's of Maine gives Colgate the opportunity to enter the fast-growing health and specialty trade channel where Tom's of Maine toothpaste and deodorant are market leaders.

How would Colgate-Palmolive report the acquisition? Explain why.

LO7
Timberland

E15-9 Analyzing and Interpreting the Return on Assets Ratio

The Timberland Company is a leading designer of shoes and clothing. In a recent year, it reported the following (in thousands of dollars):

	Current Year	Prior Year
Revenue	$1,567,619	$1,565,681
Net income	106,432	164,624
Total assets	843,105	788,654
Total stockholders' equity	560,817	528,187

Required:

1. Determine the return on assets ratio for the current year.
2. Explain the meaning of the ratio.
3. The footwear industry ratio is 16.4 percent. What do your results for Timberland suggest about the company?

Problems—Set A  Available with McGraw-Hill's Homework Manager

PA15-1 Determining Financial Statement Effects for Bonds Held to Maturity

LO3

Starbucks Corporation

Starbucks is a rapidly expanding company that provides high-quality coffee products. Assume as part of its expansion strategy, Starbucks plans to open numerous new stores in Mexico in five years. The company has $5 million to support the expansion and has decided to invest the funds in corporate bonds until the money is needed. Assume Starbucks purchased bonds with $5 million face value at par for cash on July 1, 2010. The bonds pay 8 percent interest each June 30 and December 31 and mature in five years. Starbucks plans to hold the bonds until maturity.

Required:

1. What accounts are affected when the bonds are purchased on July 1, 2010?
2. What accounts are affected when interest is received on December 31, 2010?
3. Should Starbucks prepare a journal entry if the market value of the bonds decreased to $4,000,000 on December 31, 2010? Explain.

PA15-2 Recording Passive Investments

LO4

www.mhhe.com/LLPW1e

On March 1, 2009, HiTech Industries purchased 10,000 shares of Integrated Services Company for $20 per share. The following information applies to the stock price of Integrated Services:

	Price
12/31/2009	$17
12/31/2010	24
12/31/2011	31

Required:

1. Prepare journal entries to record the facts in the case assuming HiTech purchased the shares for the trading portfolio.
2. Prepare journal entries to record the facts in the case assuming HiTech purchased the shares for the available-for-sale portfolio.

PA15-3 Reporting Passive Investments

LO4

During January 2010, Nash Glass Company purchased the following shares as a long-term investment:

Stock	Number of Shares Outstanding	Purchase	Cost per Share
Q Corporation Common (no par)	90,000	12,600	$ 5
R Corporation Preferred, nonvoting (par $10)	20,000	12,000	30

Subsequent to acquisition, the following data were available:

	2010	2011
Net income reported at December 31		
Q Corporation	$30,000	$36,000
R Corporation	40,000	48,000
Dividends declared and paid per share during the year		
Q Corporation common stock	$ 0.85	$ 0.90
R Corporation preferred stock	1.00	1.10
Market value per share at December 31		
Q Corporation common stock	$ 4.00	$ 4.00
R Corporation preferred stock	29.00	31.00

Required:

1. What accounting method should the company use for the investment in Q Corporation common stock? In R Corporation preferred stock? Why?
2. Give the journal entries for the company for each year in parallel columns (if none, explain why) for each of the following:
   a. Purchase of the investments.
   b. Income reported by Q and R corporations.

   c. Dividends received from Q and R corporations.
   d. Market value effects at year-end.
3. For each year, show how the following items and their balances should be reported on the financial statements:
   a. Long-term investments.
   b. Owners' equity—unrealized gains and losses.
   c. Revenues.

LO4, 5

eXcel

www.mhhe.com/LLPW1e

PA15-4 Recording Passive Investments and Investments for Significant Influence

On August 4, 2009, Coffman Corporation purchased 1,000 shares of Dittman Company for $45,000. The following information applies to the stock price of Dittman Company:

	Price
12/31/2009	$52
12/31/2010	47
12/31/2011	38

Dittman Company declares and pays cash dividends of $2 per share on June 1 of each year.

Required:

1. Prepare journal entries to record the facts in the case assuming Coffman purchased the shares for the trading portfolio.
2. Prepare journal entries to record the facts in the case assuming Coffman purchased the shares for the available-for-sale portfolio.
3. Prepare journal entries to record the facts in the case assuming Coffman used the equity method to account for the investment. Coffman owns 30 percent of Dittman and Dittman reported $50,000 in income each year.

LO4, 5

PA15-5 Comparing Methods to Account for Various Levels of Ownership of Voting Stock

Company Chi had outstanding 30,000 shares of common stock, par value $10 per share. On January 1, 2009, Company Delta purchased some of these shares as a long-term investment at $25 per share. At the end of 2009, Company Chi reported the following: income, $50,000, and cash dividends declared and paid during the year, $25,500. The market value of Company Chi stock at the end of 2009 was $22 per share.

Required:

1. For each of the following cases (in the tabulation), identify the method of accounting that Company Delta should use. Explain why.
2. Give the journal entries for Company Delta at the dates indicated for each of the two independent cases, assuming that the investments will be held long term. If no entry is required, explain why. Use the following format:

Tabulation of Items	Case A: 3,600 Shares Purchased	Case B: 10,500 Shares Purchased
1. Accounting method?		
2. Journal entries:		
a. To record the acquisition at January 1, 2009.		
b. To recognize the income reported by Company Chi for 2009.		
c. To recognize the dividends declared and paid by Company Chi.		
d. To recognize the market value effect at the end of 2009.		

3. Complete the following schedule to show the separate amounts that should be reported on the 2009 financial statements of Company Delta:

	DOLLAR AMOUNTS	
	Case A	Case B
Balance sheet		
Investments		
Owners' equity		
Income statement		
Investment income		
Equity in investee earnings		

4. Explain why assets, owners' equity, and revenues for the two cases are different.

PA15-6 Comparing the Market Value and Equity Methods

LO4, 5, 6

www.mhhe.com/LLPW1e

Ship Corporation had outstanding 100,000 shares of no-par common stock. On January 10, 2011, Shore Company purchased a block of these shares in the open market at $20 per share for long-term investment purposes. At the end of 2011, Ship reported net income of $300,000 and cash dividends of $.60 per share. At December 31, 2011, Ship's stock was selling at $18 per share. This problem involves two separate cases:

Case A: Purchase of 10,000 shares of Ship common stock.

Case B: Purchase of 40,000 shares of Ship common stock.

Required:

1. For each case, identify the accounting method that Shore Company should use. Explain why.
2. For each case, in parallel columns, give the journal entries for each of the following (if no entry is required, explain why):
   a. Acquisition.
   b. Revenue recognition.
   c. Dividends received.
   d. Market value effects.
3. For each case, show how the following should be reported on the 2011 financial statements:
   a. Long-term investments.
   b. Owners' equity.
   c. Revenues.
4. Explain why the amounts reported for the two cases in requirement 3 differ.
5. Explain whether either of the two cases requires preparing consolidated financial statements? Why?

PA15-7 Comparing Methods for Sales of Securities

LO4, 5

Using the data in PA15-6, assume that Shore Company management sold 10,000 shares of its investment in Ship Corporation stock on January 10, 2012, at $19 per share. This problem involves two separate cases.

Required:

1. For each case, what level of ownership did Shore Company have in Ship Corporation after the sale?
2. For each case, what method should Shore Company use for its investment in Ship Corporation after the sale?
3. For each case, give the journal entry for the sale of the investment and any entry needed on December 31, 2012.

PA15-8 Interpreting the Return on Assets Ratio

LO7

The Cheesecake Factory Incorporated operates more than 120 upscale casual dining restaurants. The following information was reported in the company's 10-K annual report dated January 2, 2007:

(in thousands)	2006	2005	2004	2003
Net income	$ 81,282	$ 87,948	$ 65,366	$ 55,585
Total assets	1,039,731	926,250	758,994	610,116

Required:

1. Compute the return on assets ratio for 2006, 2005, and 2004.
2. What do the results in requirement 1 suggest about The Cheesecake Factory?

Problems—Set B  Available with McGraw-Hill's Homework Manager

LO3
Sonic Corporation

PB15-1 Determining Financial Statement Effects for Bonds Held to Maturity

Sonic Corporation operates and franchises a chain of quick-service drive-in restaurants in most of the United States and in Mexico. Customers drive up to a canopied parking space and order food through an intercom speaker system. A carhop then delivers the food to the customer. Assume Sonic has $10 million in cash to support future expansion and has decided to invest the funds in corporate bonds until the money is needed. Sonic purchases bonds with a face value of $10 million for $10.3 million cash on January 1, 2011. The bonds pay 8 percent interest each June 30 and December 31 and mature in four years. Sonic plans to hold the bonds until maturity.

Required:

1. What accounts were affected when the bonds were purchased on January 1, 2011?
2. What accounts were affected when interest was received on June 30, 2011?
3. Should Sonic prepare a journal entry if the market value of the bonds decreased to $9,700,000 on December 31, 2011? Explain.

LO4

PB15-2 Recording Passive Investments

On September 15, 2010, James Media Corporation purchased 5,000 shares of Community Broadcasting Company for $32 per share. The following information applies to the stock price of Community Broadcasting:

	Price
12/31/2010	$34
12/31/2011	25
12/31/2012	21

Required:

1. Prepare journal entries to record the facts in the case assuming James Media purchased the shares for the trading portfolio.
2. Prepare journal entries to record the facts in the case assuming James Media purchased the shares for the available-for-sale portfolio.

LO4

PB15-3 Reporting Passive Investments

During January 2009, Stevie's Bike Shop purchased the following shares as a long-term investment:

Stock	Number of Shares Outstanding	Purchase	Cost per Share
Chrome Corporation Common (no par)	100,000	15,000	$ 25
Leather Company Preferred, nonvoting (par $10)	30,000	20,000	10

Subsequent to acquisition, the following data were available:

	2009	2010
Net income reported at December 31		
Chrome Corporation	$60,000	$72,000
Leather Company	80,000	96,000
Dividends declared and paid per share during the year		
Chrome Corporation common stock	$ 1.20	$ 1.00
Leather Company preferred stock	2.00	1.20
Market value per share at December 31		
Chrome Corporation common stock	$ 24.00	$ 24.00
Leather Company preferred stock	9.00	11.00

Required:

1. What accounting method should Stevie's Bike Shop use for the investment in Chrome Corporation common stock? In Leather Company preferred stock? Why?
2. Give the journal entries for Stevie's Bike Shop for each year in parallel columns (if none, explain why) for each of the following:
   a. Purchase of the investments.
   b. Income reported by Chrome Corporation and Leather Company.
   c. Dividends received from Chrome Corporation and Leather Company.
   d. Market value effects at year-end.
3. For each year, show how the following amounts should be reported on the financial statements:
   a. Long-term investments.
   b. Owners' equity—unrealized gain/loss.
   c. Revenues.

PB15-4 Recording Passive Investments and Investments for Significant Influence **LO4, 5**

On March 1, 2010, St. Denis Corporation purchased 10,000 shares of Carey Company for $520,000. The following information applies to the stock price of Carey Company:

	Price
12/31/2010	$54
12/31/2011	49
12/31/2012	40

Carey Company declares and pays cash dividends of $1.50 per share on June 1 of each year.

Required:

1. Prepare journal entries to record the facts in the case assuming St. Denis purchased the shares for the trading portfolio.
2. Prepare journal entries to record the facts in the case assuming St. Denis purchased the shares for the available-for-sale portfolio.
3. Prepare journal entries to record the facts in the case assuming St. Denis used the equity method to account for the investment. St. Denis owns 30 percent of Carey and Carey reported $150,000 in income each year.

PB15-5 Comparing Methods to Account for Various Levels of Ownership of Voting Stock **LO4, 5**

Zeta Company had outstanding 100,000 shares of common stock, par-value $5 per share. On January 1, 2010, Beta Company purchased some of these shares as a long-term investment at $15 per share. At the end of 2010, Zeta Company reported the following: income, $100,000, and cash dividends declared and paid during the year, $2,500. The market value of Zeta Company stock at the end of 2010 was $12 per share.

Required:

1. For each of the following cases (in the tabulation), identify the method of accounting that Beta Company should use. Explain why.
2. Give the journal entries for Beta Company at the dates indicated for each of the two independent cases assuming the investments will be held long term. If no entry is required, explain why. Use the following format:

Tabulation of Items	Case A: 4,000 Shares Purchased	Case B: 40,000 Shares Purchased
1. Accounting method?		
2. Journal entries:		
a. To record the acquisition at January 1, 2010.		
b. To recognize the income reported by Zeta Company for 2010.		
c. To recognize the dividends declared and paid by Zeta Company.		
d. To recognize the market value effect at the end of 2010.		

3. Complete the following schedule to show the separate amounts that should be reported on the 2010 financial statements of Beta Company:

	DOLLAR AMOUNTS	
	Case A	Case B
Balance sheet		
Investments		
Owners' equity		
Income statement		
Investment income		
Equity in investee earnings		

4. Explain why assets, owners' equity, and revenues for the two cases are different.

LO4, 5, 6

PB15-6 Comparing the Market Value and Equity Methods

Boston Corporation had outstanding 200,000 shares of common stock. On October 1, 2009, Packer Company purchased a block of these shares in the open market at $15 per share for long-term investment purposes. At the end of 2009, Boston reported net income of $560,000 and cash dividends of $1.20 per share. At December 31, 2009, Boston's stock was selling at $17 per share. This problem involves two separate cases:

Case A: Purchase of 30,000 shares of Boston common stock.
Case B: Purchase of 80,000 shares of Boston common stock.

Required:

1. For each case, identify the accounting method that Packer Company should use. Explain why.
2. For each case, in parallel columns, give the journal entries for each of the following (if no entry is required, explain why).
   a. Acquisition.
   b. Revenue recognition.
   c. Dividends received.
   d. Market value effects.
3. For each case, show how the following should be reported on the 2009 financial statements:
   a. Long-term investments.
   b. Owners' equity.
   c. Revenues.
4. Explain why the amounts reported for the two cases in requirement 3 are different.
5. Explain whether either of the two cases requires preparing consolidated financial statements? Why?

LO4, 5

PB15-7 Comparing Methods for Sales of Securities

Using the data in PB15–6, assume that Packer Company's management sold 20,000 shares of its investment in Boston Corporation stock on January 10, 2010, at $16 per share. This problem involves two separate cases.

Required:

1. For each case, what level of ownership did Packer Company have in Boston Corporation after the sale?
2. For each case, what method should Packer Company use for its investment in Boston Corporation after the sale?
3. For each case, give the journal entry for the sale of the investment and any entry needed on December 31, 2010.

LO7
Marriott International, Inc.

PB15-8 Interpreting the Return on Assets Ratio

Marriott International, Inc., is a global leader in the hospitality industry operating or franchising more than 2,800 lodging units and 2,000 furnished corporate housing units around the world. The following information was reported in the company's 2006 annual report (in millions of dollars):

(in millions)	2006	2005	2004	2003
Net income	$ 608	$ 669	$ 596	$ 502
Total assets	8,588	8,530	8,668	8,117

Required:

1. Compute the return on assets ratio for 2006, 2005, and 2004.
2. What do the results in requirement 1 suggest about Marriott?

Cases and Projects

CP15-1 Finding Financial Information

LO4, 5, 6

Refer to the financial statements of The Home Depot in Appendix A at the end of this book, or download the annual report from the *Cases* section of the text's Web site at www.mhhe.com/LLPW1e.

Required:

1. What was the balance in short-term investments reported by the company on February 3, 2008?
2. How much cash did the company realize from investments that matured or were sold during the year ended February 3, 2008?
3. What companies did The Home Depot acquire in 2007? What was the total purchase price of these acquisitions for the year?

CP15-2 Comparing Financial Information

LO4, 5, 6, 7

Lowe's

Refer to the financial statements of The Home Depot in Appendix A and Lowe's in Appendix B at the end of this book, or download the annual reports from the *Cases* section of the text's Web site at www.mhhe.com/LLPW1e.

Required:

1. What was the balance in short-term investments reported by Lowe's on February 1, 2008? By The Home Depot on February 3, 2008? What types of securities were included in short-term investments for each company?
2. Compute the net profit margin, total asset turnover, and return on assets ratios for both The Home Depot and Lowe's for the current year. Which company provided the higher return on its total investments during the current year?
3. Was the difference in ROA due primarily to profitability or efficiency differences? How did you know?

CP15-3 Examining an Annual Report: Internet-Based Team Research Project

LO2, 3, 4, 5, 6, 7

As a team, select an industry to analyze. Using your Web browser, each team member should acquire the annual report or 10-K for one publicly traded company in the industry with each member selecting a different company.

Required:

1. On an individual basis, each team member should write a short report that answers the following questions:
   a. Determine whether the company prepared consolidated financial statements. How do you know?
   b. Does the company use the equity method for any of its investments?
   c. Does the company hold any investments in securities? If so, what is their market value? Does the company have any unrealized gains or losses?
   d. Identify the company's lines of business. Why does management want to engage in these business activities?
   e. Compute the return on assets ratio for the two most recent years reported. What do the results suggest about your company?
2. Discuss any patterns that you as a team observe. Then, as a team, write a short report comparing and contrasting your companies according to the preceding attributes. Provide potential explanations for any differences discovered.

LO1

CP15-4 Evaluating an Ethical Dilemma: Using Inside Information

Assume you are on the board of directors of a company that has decided to buy 80 percent of the outstanding stock of another company within the next three or four months. The discussions have convinced you that this company is an excellent investment opportunity, so you decide to buy $10,000 worth of the company's stock.

Required:

1. Is there an ethical problem with your decision?
2. Would your answer be different if you planned to invest $500,000?
3. Are there different ethical considerations if you do not buy the stock but recommend that your brother do so?

LO6

CP15-5 Evaluating an Acquisition from the Standpoint of a Financial Analyst

Assume you are a financial analyst for a large investment banking firm. You are responsible for analyzing companies in the retail sales industry. You have just learned that a large West Coast retailer has acquired a large East Coast retail chain for a price more than the net book value of the acquired company. You have reviewed the separate financial statements for the two companies before the announcement of the acquisition.

Required:

Write a brief report explaining what will happen when the financial results of the companies are consolidated as well as the impact on the return on assets ratio.

16 Reporting and Interpreting the Statement of Cash Flows

LEARNING OBJECTIVES

After completing this chapter, you should be able to:

Lectured presentation–16-1
www.mhhe.com/LLPW1e

LO1 Identify cash flows from operating, investing, and financing activities.

LO2 Report cash flows from operating activities using the indirect method.

LO3 Report cash flows from investing activities.

LO4 Report cash flows from financing activities.

LO5 Prepare and evaluate the statement of cash flows.

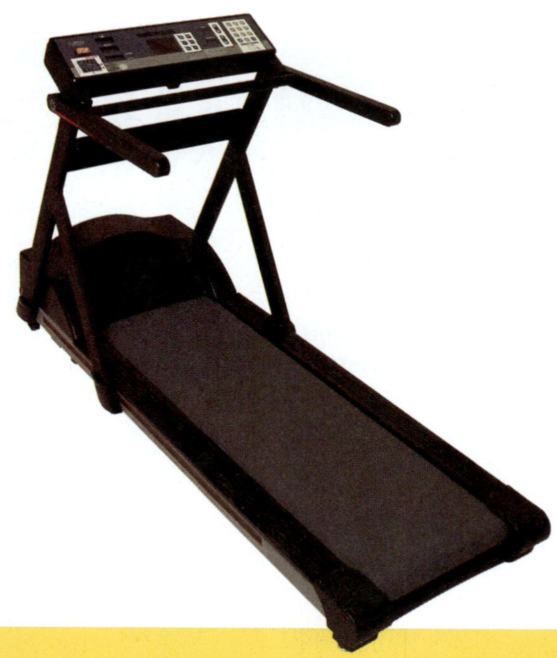

Focus Company: NAUTILUS INC.

"Helping People Achieve a Fit and Healthy Lifestyle Through Proper Exercise, Rest and Nutrition."

www.nautilusinc.com

Have you ever studied your bank statements to see how much money you bring in and pay out during a typical month? You do not have to be a financial genius to know that if you are spending more than you earn, your savings will quickly disappear, and you will need to get a loan or some other source of financing to see you through.

Most businesses face the same issues you do. In 2005, for example, Nautilus Inc.—maker of Stairmaster and Bowflex fitness equipment—reported a net cash outflow from day-to-day operating activities. To ensure the company's long-term survival, managers had to stay on top of this change in the cash situation. Fortunately, the company had saved a great deal of cash in prior years. Managers were also able to negotiate some new loans to keep the business from running out of cash. By 2006, the company was again experiencing a positive net cash inflow from operating activities.

Investors and creditors also monitor a company's cash inflows and outflows to predict whether they are likely to receive dividends and other amounts they are owed. They can find the information they need to make such predictions reported in the statement of cash flows, which is similar to your bank statement in that it reports changes in the company's cash situation. In this chapter, we will investigate how cash flows from operating, investing, and financing activities are classified and reported on the statement of cash flows. We also examine some of the tools investors and creditors use to evaluate the statement of cash flows.

ORGANIZATION OF THE CHAPTER

CLASSIFICATIONS OF THE STATEMENT OF CASH FLOWS	REPORTING CASH FLOWS FROM OPERATING ACTIVITIES—INDIRECT METHOD	REPORTING CASH FLOWS FROM INVESTING ACTIVITIES	REPORTING CASH FLOWS FROM FINANCING ACTIVITIES	PREPARING AND EVALUATING THE STATEMENT OF CASH FLOWS
• The Relationship between Business Activities and Cash Flows • Cash Flows from Operating Activities • Cash Flows from Investing Activities • Cash Flows from Financing Activities • Net Increase (Decrease) in Cash • Relationships to the Balance Sheet and Income Statement	• Depreciation and Gains and Losses on Sale of Long-Term Assets • Changes in Current Assets and Current Liabilities	• Plant and Equipment • Land and Investments	• Long-Term Debt • Contributed Capital • Retained Earnings	• Format for the Statement of Cash Flows • Noncash Investing and Financing Activities • Supplemental Cash Flow Information • Free Cash Flow • Quality of Income Ratio

Learning Objective 1

Identify cash flows from operating, investing, and financing activities.

Video 16-1
www.mhhe.com/LLPW1e

CLASSIFICATIONS OF THE STATEMENT OF CASH FLOWS

To this point, we have analyzed business activities to identify their financial effects on assets, liabilities, owners' equity, revenues, and expenses. We have emphasized that business activities have financial effects even when they do not involve cash. That is why accrual accounting exists. When accurately reported, accrual-based net income is the best measure of whether a company has been profitable during the period.

Despite the importance of net income as a measure of profit, however, companies cannot use net income to pay wages, dividends, or loans. Because those activities require cash, financial statement users need information about the company's cash situation.

The Relationship between Business Activities and Cash Flows

Neither the balance sheet nor the income statement provides all of the needed information about the company's cash situation. Although the balance sheet shows a company's cash balance at a point in time, it does not indicate where the cash came from. Cash might have been generated by the company's day-to-day operations, by the sale of the company's buildings, or by the negotiation of new loans. What financial statement users really need is a report that identifies the activities that produced the amount of cash reported on the balance sheet.

Furthermore, the timing of cash receipts and payments may differ from the items shown on the income statement, which reports revenues when they are earned and expenses when they are incurred. Nautilus, for example, reported a hefty amount of net income in each quarter of 2006, yet its cash flows were negative in two of those four quarters. Such differences between net income and cash flows are the reason that GAAP requires every company to report a statement of cash flows.

The statement of cash flows shows each major type of business activity that caused a company's cash to increase or decrease during the accounting period. For the purposes of this statement, cash is defined to include cash and cash equivalents. As you have seen before, cash equivalents are short-term, highly liquid investments that are both (1) readily convertible to known amounts of cash and (2) so near to maturity that there is little risk their value will change. All of a company's cash inflows and outflows must be classified under operating, investing, or financing activities. Exhibit 16.1 shows the general form of the statement. Note that each category of activities can result in net cash inflows (represented by a positive number)

Exhibit 16.1 Categories in the Statement of Cash Flows

Net cash provided by (used for) operating activities
± Net cash provided by (used for) investing activities
± Net cash provided by (used for) financing activities
Net increase (decrease) in cash and cash equivalents
+ Cash and cash equivalents at beginning of period
Cash and cash equivalents at end of period

or net cash outflows (represented by a negative number in brackets). The sum of the three categories of cash flows explains the change in cash on the balance sheet for the period.

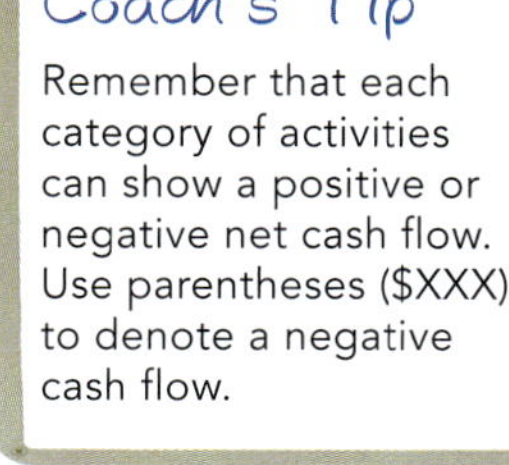

Coach's Tip

Remember that each category of activities can show a positive or negative net cash flow. Use parentheses ($XXX) to denote a negative cash flow.

Cash Flows from Operating Activities

Cash flows from operating activities (or cash flows from operations) are the cash inflows and outflows related directly to the revenues and expenses reported on the income statement. Operating activities involve day-to-day business activities with customers, suppliers, employees, landlords, and others. Typical cash flows from operating activities include:

Inflows	Outflows
Cash provided by	*Cash used for*
Customers	Purchase of goods for resale and services (electricity, etc.)
Dividends and interest on investments	Salaries and wages
	Income taxes
	Interest on liabilities

The difference between these cash inflows and outflows is reported on the statement of cash flows as a subtotal, Net Cash Provided by (Used for) Operating Activities.

The two different methods for presenting the operating activities in the cash flow statement are:

1. The direct method reports the total cash inflow or outflow from each major type of transaction (that is, transactions with customers, suppliers, etc.). The difference between those cash inflows and outflows equals the Net Cash Provided by (Used for) Operating Activities.
2. The indirect method starts with net income from the income statement and adjusts it by removing items that do not involve cash and adding items that do involve cash. Adjusting net income for these items yields the amount of Net Cash Provided by (Used for) Operating Activities.

Net income
± Adjustments
Net cash provided by (used for) operating activities

The point to remember about these two methods is that they are simply different ways to arrive at the same number. **Net cash flows provided by (used for) operating activities is the same under both methods.** Also, the choice between the two methods affects only the operating activities section of the statement of cash flows, not the investing and financing sections.

Each company's management is allowed to choose which method to use. Nearly 99 percent of large U.S. companies, including Nautilus, choose the indirect method.[1] For this reason, we

[1] American Institute of Certified Public Accountants, *Accounting Trends & Techniques* (New York: AICPA, 2006). Some people have speculated that the indirect method is preferred so overwhelmingly because the FASB requires that companies using the direct method also report a reconciliation of net income to cash flow. That reconciliation is identical to the indirect method.

examine the indirect method in detail within this chapter. We present the less commonly used direct method in Supplement 16A at the end of the chapter.

Cash Flows from Investing Activities

Cash flows from investing activities are the cash inflows and outflows related to the purchase and disposal of investments and long-lived assets. Typical cash flows from investing activities include:

Inflows	Outflows
Cash provided by	*Cash used for*
Sale or disposal of property, plant, and equipment	Purchase of property, plant, and equipment
Sale or maturity of investments in securities	Purchase of investments in securities

The difference between these cash inflows and outflows is reported on the statement of cash flows as a subtotal, Net Cash Provided by (Used for) Investing Activities.

Cash Flows from Financing Activities

Cash flows from financing activities include exchanges of cash with stockholders and cash exchanges with lenders (for principal on loans). Common cash flows from financing activities include:

Inflows	Outflows
Cash provided by	*Cash used for*
Borrowing from lenders through formal debt contracts	Repaying principal to lenders
Issuing stock to owners	Repurchasing stock from owners
	Paying dividends to owners

The difference between these cash inflows and outflows is reported on the statement of cash flows as a subtotal, Net Cash Provided by (Used for) Financing Activities.

Net Increase (Decrease) in Cash

Together, **the net cash flows from operating activities, investing activities, and financing activities must equal the net increase (decrease) in cash** for the period. For 2006, Nautilus reported a net decrease in cash of $1,000. That explains the change in cash on the company's balance sheet from the beginning balance of $8,000 to the ending balance of $7,000 (all amounts in $thousands):

Net cash provided by operating activities	$29,000
− Net cash used for investing activities	(11,000)
− Net cash used for financing activities	(19,000)
Net decrease in cash and cash equivalents	(1,000)
+ Cash and cash equivalents at beginning of period	8,000
Cash and cash equivalents at end of period	$ 7,000

In the next section, we examine Nautilus's statement of cash flows in more detail, including the way in which it relates to the balance sheet and income statement. Then we see how each section of the statement describes a set of important decisions made by Nautilus's management, and how financial analysts use those sections to evaluate the company's performance. But first, to make sure you understand how to classify cash flows, complete the following Self-Study Practice.

SELF-STUDY PRACTICE

Brunswick Corporation

Brunswick Corporation produces the Life Fitness line of gym equipment, which competes head to head with Nautilus. A list of some of the company's cash flows follows. Indicate whether each item should be disclosed in the operating activities (O), investing activities (I), or financing activities (F) section of the statement of cash flows.

____ 1. Stock issued to owners for cash

____ 2. Collections from customers

____ 3. Interest paid on debt

____ 4. Purchase of equipment

____ 5. Purchase of investment securities

____ 6. Dividends paid to owners

After you have finished, check your answers with the solution at the bottom of the page.

Spotlight On ETHICS

Cash Is Not Estimated

Critics of accrual-based net income claim that it can be manipulated because it includes many estimated amounts (for bad debts, the market values of inventory, and assets' useful lives, for example). Because cash flows are not estimated, these critics claim the cash flows are not so easily manipulated. Indeed, a cash balance changes only when cash has been received or paid.

One particularly dramatic illustration of the subjectivity of net income compared to cash is the bankruptcy of a department store chain operated by W. T. Grant Company. Through biased estimates, the company reported net income for nine consecutive years and then shocked everyone by declaring bankruptcy and closing. At the time, GAAP did not require a statement of cash flows. Had this been required, it would have shown that the company's operations led to net cash outflows in 7 of the company's last 10 years.

Relationships to the Balance Sheet and Income Statement

One way to classify cash flows into operating, investing, and financing categories is to think about the balance sheet accounts to which the cash flows relate. Although exceptions exist, the general rule is that operating cash flows cause changes in current assets and current liabilities; investing cash flows affect long-lived assets; and financing cash flows affect noncurrent liabilities or owners' equity accounts.[2] See Exhibit 16.2 for the way this general rule relates the three sections of the statement of cash flows to the main sections of the classified balance sheet.

The statement of cash flows is intended to provide a cash-based view of a company's business activities during the accounting period. So, a company cannot prepare this statement directly from the ledger accounts because those amounts are based on accrual accounting. Instead, the company must analyze the numbers recorded under the accrual method and convert them to a cash basis. To prepare a statement of cash flows, you need the following:

1. **Comparative balance sheets**, showing beginning and ending balances for use in calculating the cash flows from all activities (operating, investing, and financing).
2. **A complete income statement** for use primarily in calculating cash flows from operating activities.
3. **Additional details** concerning selected accounts that increase and decrease as a result of investing and/or financing activities.

[2] Intermediate accounting discusses exceptions to this general rule in detail. They include investing activities that affect current assets (for example, short-term investments) and financing activities that affect current liabilities (for example, dividends payable and short-term notes payable).

Solution to Self-Study Practice

1. F
2. O
3. O
4. I
5. I
6. F

Exhibit 16.2 Relationships between Balance Sheet and Cash Flow Categories

Operating Activities Affect	
Current assets	Current liabilities
Investing Activities Affect	**Financing Activities Affect**
Noncurrent assets	Noncurrent liabilities
	Owners' equity

This approach to preparing the cash flow statement focuses on changes in the balance sheet accounts. It relies on a simple rearrangement of the balance sheet equation:

Assets = Liabilities + Owners' Equity

First, assets can be separated into cash and all other assets, which we call noncash assets:

Cash + Noncash Assets = Liabilities + Owners' Equity

If we move the noncash assets to the right side of the equation, we get

Cash = Liabilities + Owners' Equity − Noncash Assets

Given this relationship, the changes (Δ) in cash from the beginning to the end of the period must equal the changes (Δ) in the amounts on the right side of the equation from the beginning to the end of the period:

Δ Cash = Δ Liabilities + Δ Owners' Equity − Δ Noncash Assets

This equation says that **changes in cash must be accompanied by, and can be explained by, changes in liabilities, owners' equity, and noncash assets.** See Exhibit 16.3 for examples of this basic idea using selected cash transactions.

Before beginning to prepare the statement of cash flows, it is helpful to compute the change in each balance sheet account (that is, the ending balance minus the beginning

Exhibit 16.3 Effects of Cash Transactions on Other Balance Sheet Accounts

Category	Transaction	Cash Effect	Other Account Affected
Operating	Collect accounts receivable	+ Cash	− Accounts Receivable (A)
	Pay accounts payable	− Cash	− Accounts Payable (L)
	Prepay rent	− Cash	+ Prepaid Rent (A)
	Pay interest	− Cash	− Retained Earnings (OE)
	Sell goods/services for cash	+ Cash	+ Retained Earnings (OE)
Investing	Purchase equipment for cash	− Cash	+ Equipment (A)
	Sell investment securities for cash	+ Cash	− Investments (A)
Financing	Pay back debt to bank	− Cash	− Bank Loan Payable (L)
	Issue stock for cash	+ Cash	+ Contributed Capital (OE)

balance). The next step is to relate each account to operating (O), investing (I), or financing (F) activities by marking it with the appropriate letter. **Operating activities** typically affect the following accounts:

- ***Current assets*** are used up or converted into cash through the company's regular operating activities. For example, the sale of inventories creates accounts receivable, which are turned into cash when they are collected. When marking an O beside the current assets related to operating activities, you should exclude cash (because the change in cash is what you are trying to explain).
- ***Current liabilities*** such as accounts payable and accrued liabilities arise from the purchase of goods or services that are used in the company's operations. Mark these items with an O.
- ***Accumulated Depreciation*** is a contra-asset account that increases each period by the amount of depreciation expense and decreases when the asset is sold. Because depreciation expense affects net income, this account is related to operating activities.
- ***Retained Earnings*** increases each period by the amount of net income, which is the starting point for the operating activities section. It decreases when dividends are declared and paid (a financing activity). To show that this account relates to both operating and financing activities, mark it with an O and an F.

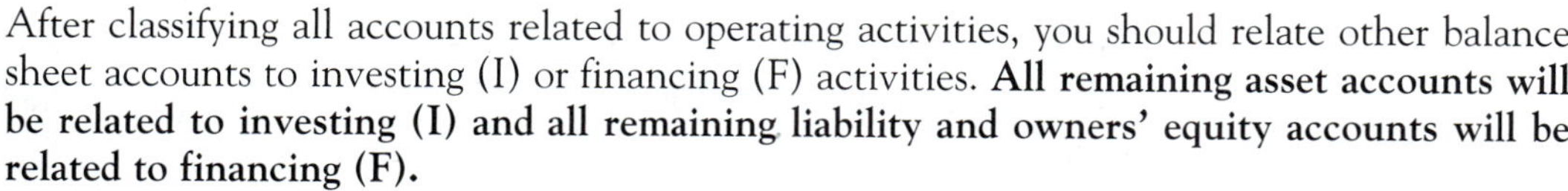

After classifying all accounts related to operating activities, you should relate other balance sheet accounts to investing (I) or financing (F) activities. **All remaining asset accounts will be related to investing (I) and all remaining liability and owners' equity accounts will be related to financing (F).**

In Exhibit 16.4, the left-hand column shows how to classify the balance sheet accounts for Nautilus. The right-hand column shows the changes in the account balances, which we use in the following sections.

REPORTING CASH FLOWS FROM OPERATING ACTIVITIES—INDIRECT METHOD

Learning Objective 2

Report cash flows from operating activities using the indirect method.

As we defined them earlier, operating cash flows are cash inflows and outflows that are directly related to the revenues and expenses reported on the income statement. These cash flows arise from transactions with customers, suppliers, employees, landlords, and others.

The indirect method begins with the creation of a schedule of operating activities in the following format:

Operating Activities
Net income
Add/Subtract to convert to cash basis
+ Depreciation expense
− Gain on sale of long-term assets
+ Loss on sale of long-term assets
+ Decreases in current assets
+ Increases in current liabilities
− Increases in current assets
− Decreases in current liabilities
Net cash flow from operating activities

As the format suggests, the conversion process begins with net income, which is taken from the bottom line of the company's income statement. The schedule for Nautilus is in Exhibit 16.5. Notice that the schedule begins with the $31,000 net income reported on the income statement in Exhibit 16.4.

Exhibit 16.4 Nautilus, Inc.: Comparative Balance Sheet and Current Income Statement — Nautilus

Nautilus, Inc.
Balance Sheet*
(in thousands)

Related Cash Flow Section		December 31, 2006	December 31, 2005	*Change*
	Assets			
	Current assets			
Change in Cash	Cash and cash equivalents	$ 7,000	$ 8,000	**−1,000**
O	Accounts receivable	138,000	117,000	**+21,000**
O	Inventories	76,000	96,000	**−20,000**
O	Prepaid expenses	33,000	24,000	**+9,000**
	Total current assets	254,000	245,000	
I	Plant and equipment	219,000	203,000	**+16,000**
O	Less: Accumulated depreciation	(54,000)	(47,000)	**−7,000**
I	Land	10,000	12,000	**−2,000**
	Total assets	$429,000	$413,000	
	Liabilities and Stockholders' Equity			
	Current liabilities			
O	Accounts payable	$ 64,000	$ 61,000	**+3,000**
O	Accrued liabilities	38,000	37,000	**+1,000**
	Total current liabilities	102,000	98,000	
F	Long-term debt	67,000	63,000	**+4,000**
	Total liabilities	169,000	161,000	
	Stockholders' equity			
F	Contributed capital	5,000	4,000	**+1,000**
O, F	Retained earnings†	255,000	248,000	**+7,000**
	Total stockholders' equity	260,000	252,000	
	Total liabilities and stockholders' equity	$429,000	$413,000	

Nautilus, Inc.
Income Statement*
For the Year Ended December 31, 2006
(in thousands)

Net sales	$680,000
Cost of goods sold	382,000
Gross profit	298,000
Operating expenses	
Selling, general, and administrative expenses	250,000
Depreciation	7,000
Total operating expenses	257,000
Operating income	41,000
Gain on sale of land	3,000
Interest revenue (expense)	(1,000)
Net income before taxes	43,000
Income tax expense	12,000
Net income	$ 31,000

*Certain balances have been adjusted to simplify the presentation.

† This line item includes transactions related to both operating and financing activities.

Exhibit 16.5 Schedule for Conversion of Net Income to Net Cash Flow from Operating Activities

Items	Amount (in thousands)	Explanation
Net income	$31,000	From income statement.
Add (subtract) to convert to cash basis		
Depreciation	+7,000	Add because depreciation expense does not affect cash but was subtracted in computing net income.
Gain on sale of land	−3,000	Subtract because all cash collected from sale of long-lived assets are investing cash flows.
Accounts receivable increase	−21,000	Subtract because cash collected from customers was less than accrual-based revenues.
Inventory decrease	+20,000	Add because purchases were less than cost of goods sold expense.
Prepaid expense increase	−9,000	Subtract because cash prepayments for expenses were more than accrual-based expenses.
Accounts payable increase	+3,000	Add because amounts purchased on account (that is, borrowed from suppliers) were more than cash payments made to suppliers.
Accrued liabilities increase	+1,000	Add because accrual-based expenses were more than cash payments for expenses.
Net cash inflow (outflow)	$29,000	Subtotal for the operating cash flows section.

By starting with net income, it appears we are assuming all revenues resulted in cash inflows and all expenses resulted in cash outflows. Because we know that is not true, however, we must adjust net income for the effects of the items we marked with an O on the balance sheet (see Exhibit 16.4). Those items reflect differences in the timing of accrual-basis net income and cash flows. The process of adjusting net income has two steps.

Depreciation and Gains and Losses on Sale of Long-Term Assets

Step 1 **Adjust net income for depreciation expense and gains and losses on sale of long-term assets.** On the income statement, depreciation is subtracted to determine net income. But depreciation does not affect cash, so we must eliminate its effect by adding it back to net income. In the case of Nautilus, we remove its effect by adding back the $7,000 of depreciation expense that had been subtracted to determine net income: See Exhibit 16.5.[3]

If Nautilus sells plant and equipment or land or investments at a gain or loss, the amount of cash received would be classified as an investing cash inflow. Because all of the cash received is an investing cash flow, an adjustment must also be made in the operating activities section to avoid double counting the gain or loss. **Gains on sales of property, plant, and equipment or investments are subtracted, and losses on such sales are added** to convert net income to cash flow from operating activities. Nautilus sold land at a gain of $3,000 ($5,000 cash received less cost of $2,000) that must be subtracted in Exhibit 16.5.

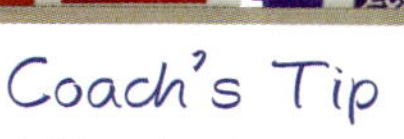

Coach's Tip

Adding back depreciation is not intended to suggest that depreciation creates an increase in cash. Rather, it shows that depreciation does not cause a decrease in cash. This is a subtle but very important point.

Changes in Current Assets and Current Liabilities

Step 2 **Adjust net income for changes in current assets and current liabilities.** Each change in current assets (other than cash) and current liabilities causes a difference between

[3] Amortization expense for intangible assets and depletion expense for natural resources (discussed in Chapter 10) is handled in exactly the same way as depreciation expense.

net income and cash flow from operating activities. In converting net income to cash flow from operating activities, apply the following general rules:

- **Add the change when a current asset decreases or a current liability increases.**
- **Subtract the change when a current asset increases or a current liability decreases.**

Understanding what causes current assets and current liabilities to increase and decrease is the key to understanding the logic behind these additions and subtractions. Take your time reading the following explanations and make sure you understand the reasons for the changes.

Change in Accounts Receivable

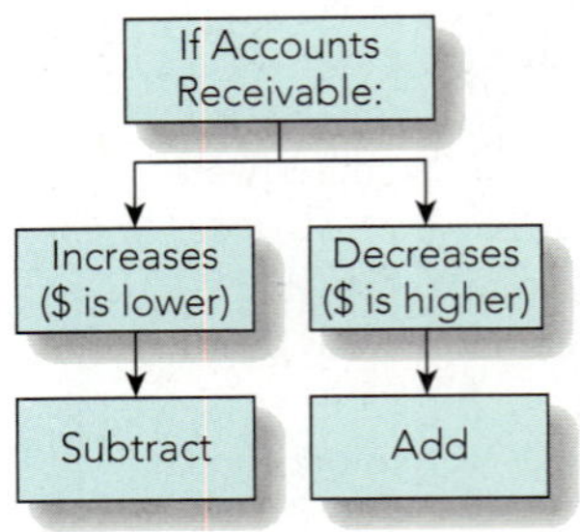

The first operating item (O) listed on the Nautilus balance sheet in Exhibit 16.4 is Accounts Receivable. Remember that the income statement reflects sales revenue, but the cash flow statement must reflect cash collections from customers. As the following T-account for accounts receivable shows, when sales revenues are recorded, Accounts Receivable increases; when cash is collected from customers, the amount in the Accounts Receivable account decreases.

Accounts Receivable (A)		
Beginning balance	117,000	
Sales revenue (on account)	680,000	Cash collected from customers 659,000
Ending balance	138,000	

Change +$21,000

In the case of Nautilus, Accounts Receivable increased, which means that sales revenue was greater than cash collected from customers. To convert from the higher sales amount included in net income to the lower amount of cash collected from customers, we must subtract the difference ($680,000 − $659,000 = $21,000), which is the same as the change in Accounts Receivable.

Ending balance	$138,000
− Beginning balance	117,000
Change	$ 21,000

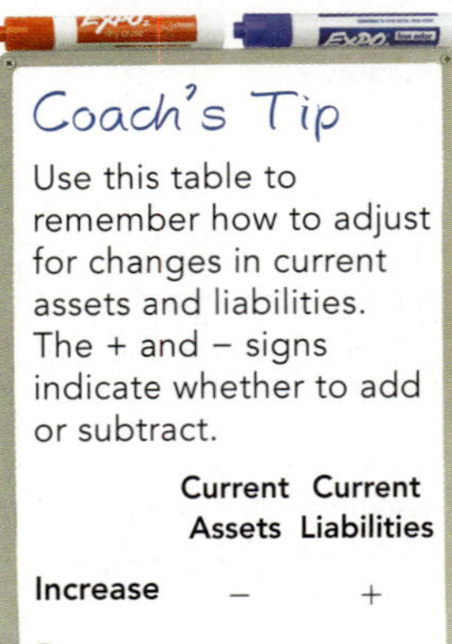

This procedure suggests a shortcut for determining adjustments to net income: Simply adjust for the **changes** in the current asset and current liability accounts that are related to operating activities. The sign of the adjustment fits the general rule just given. In the case of Nautilus, the net increase in Accounts Receivable is subtracted from net income. If Accounts Receivable had decreased, the net decrease would be added to net income.

Accounts Receivable (A)		
Beg. bal.	117,000	
Increase	21,000	
End. bal.	138,000	

Cash Flows from Operating Activities	
Net income	31,000
Accts rec. increase	(21,000)
. . .	. . .
Net cash inflow	

Change in Inventory

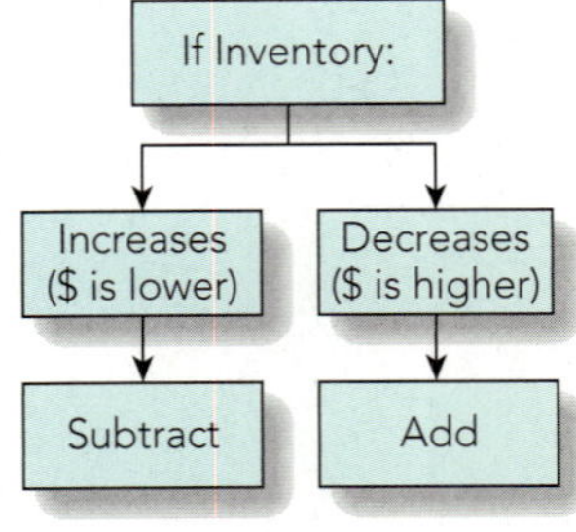

The income statement reports the cost of merchandise sold during the period, but cash flow from operating activities must report cash purchases of inventory. As the following T-accounts show, recording purchases of goods (left) increases the balance in the Inventories account; recording cost of goods sold (right) decreases the balance in the Inventories account:

Inventories (A)	
Beg. bal.	
Purchases	Cost of goods sold
End. bal.	

Inventories (A)			
Beg. bal.	96,000		
		Decrease	20,000
End. bal.	76,000		

The balance sheet in Exhibit 16.4 indicates that Nautilus's inventory decreased by $20,000, which means that purchases were less than the amount of merchandise sold. This decrease (that is, the use of existing inventories) must be added to net income to convert to cash flow from operating activities: See Exhibit 16.5. (An increase in inventories would be subtracted.)

Change in Prepaid Expenses

The income statement reports expenses for the period, but cash flow from operating activities must report cash payments. As the following T-accounts show, cash prepayments increase the balance in Prepaid Expenses; the recording of expenses decreases the balance:

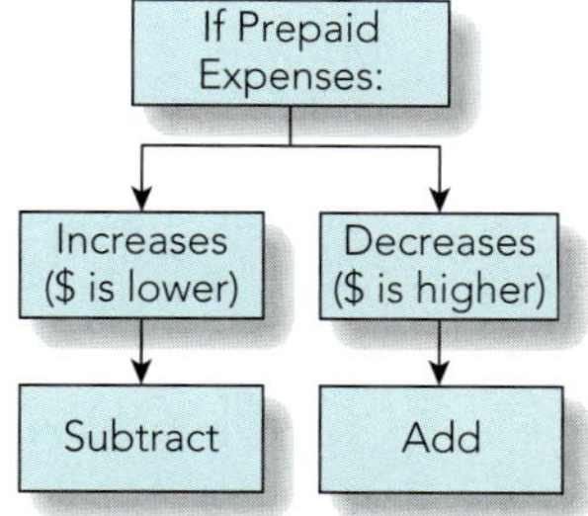

Prepaid Expenses (A)	
Beg. bal.	
Cash prepayments	Used up/expensed
End. bal.	

Prepaid Expenses (A)		
Beg. bal.	24,000	
Increase	9,000	
End. bal.	33,000	

The balance sheet for Nautilus (see Exhibit 16.4) shows a $9,000 increase in Prepaid Expenses, which means that new cash prepayments were more than recorded expenses. This increase (the extra cash prepayments) must be subtracted from net income in Exhibit 16.5. (A decrease in Prepaid Expenses would be added.)

Change in Accounts Payable

Cash flow from operations must reflect cash purchases, but not all purchases are paid for in cash. Purchases made on account increase Accounts Payable; cash paid to suppliers decreases Accounts Payable:

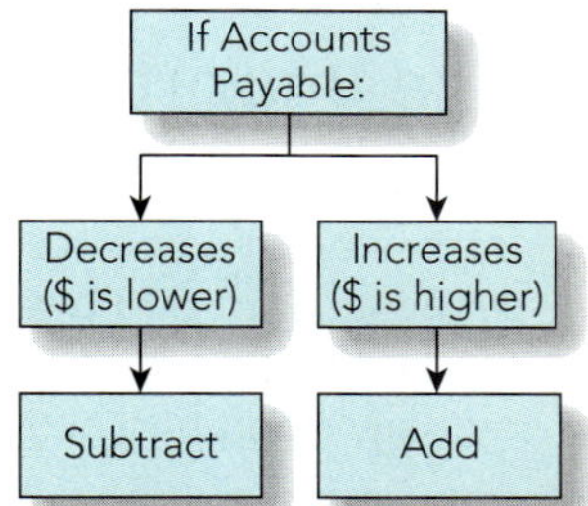

Accounts Payable (L)	
	Beg. bal.
Cash payments	Purchases on account
	End. bal.

Accounts Payable (L)		
	Beg. bal.	61,000
	Increase	3,000
	End. bal.	64,000

For Nautilus, Accounts Payable increased by $3,000 during the period (see Exhibit 16.4). That means cash payments to suppliers were less than purchases made on account. This increase in Accounts Payable must be added to net income in Exhibit 16.5. (A decrease in Accounts Payable would be subtracted.)

Change in Accrued Liabilities

The income statement reports all accrued expenses, but the cash flow statement must report actual payments for those expenses. Recording accrued expenses increases the balance in the Accrued Liabilities account; cash payments for these expenses decrease Accrued Liabilities:

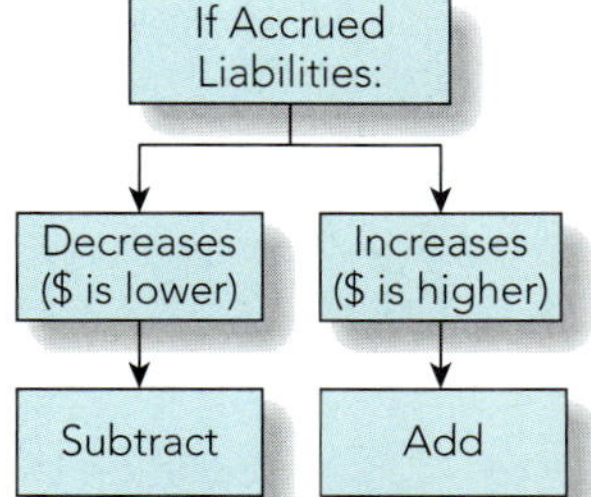

Accounts Liabilities (L)	
	Beg. bal.
Cash payments	Accrued expenses
	End. bal.

Accrued Liabilities (L)		
	Beg. bal.	37,000
	Increase	1,000
	End. bal.	38,000

According to Exhibit 16.4, Nautilus's Accrued Liabilities increased by $1,000, which means that cash payments were less than accrued expenses. This increase in Accrued Liabilities must be added to net income in Exhibit 16.5. (A decrease in Accrued Liabilities would be subtracted.)

Summary

We can summarize the typical additions and subtractions required to reconcile net income with cash flow from operating activities as follows:

Item	ADDITIONS AND SUBTRACTIONS TO RECONCILE NET INCOME TO CASH FLOW FROM OPERATING ACTIVITIES	
	When Item Increases	When Item Decreases
Depreciation and amortization	+	NA
Gain on sale of long-term asset	−	NA
Loss on sale of long-term asset	+	NA
Accounts receivable	−	+
Inventory	−	+
Prepaid expenses	−	+
Accounts payable	+	−
Accrued liabilities	+	−

Notice that to reconcile net income to cash flow from operations, you must:

- **Add the change when a current asset decreases or a current liability increases.**
- **Subtract the change when a current asset increases or a current liability decreases.**

Spotlight On BUSINESS DECISIONS

The Importance of Cash Flow from Operations

In an established business, operating activities are important to investors and creditors. Financial statement users are interested in a company's ability to generate enough cash flows from operations to continue investing in assets and repay its debt on time. Creditors and investors will tolerate poor operating cash flows only so long before they stop lending to or investing in a company. For a company to survive over the long run, then, the amount of cash generated by daily operating activities must exceed the amount of cash spent on them.

SELF-STUDY PRACTICE

Compute cash flow from operating activities assuming the following list includes all amounts related to operating activities.

Net income	$10,000	Inventory decrease	$ 300
Accounts receivable increase	600	Loss on sale of investments	100
Accounts payable decrease	700	Depreciation expense	3,000

After you have finished, check your answers with the solution at the bottom of the page.

Solution to Self-Study Practice

Net income	$10,000
+ Depreciation expense	3,000
+ Loss on sale of investments	100
− Accounts receivable increase	(600)
+ Inventory decrease	300
− Accounts payable decrease	(700)
Cash Flow from Operating Activities	$12,100

REPORTING CASH FLOWS FROM INVESTING ACTIVITIES

Learning Objective 3

Report cash flows from investing activities.

To prepare the second section of the statement of cash flows, we must analyze the accounts related to investments and to property, plant, and equipment.[4] In the operating activities section, we were concerned with only the **net** change in selected accounts. In the investing activities section, however (as well as in the financing activities section), we must identify the causes of **both** increases and decreases in selected accounts. The following activities and their related accounts are the ones you will encounter most often:

Related Balance Sheet Accounts	Investing Activity	Cash Flow Effect
Investments	Purchase of investment securities for cash	Outflow
	Sale (maturity) of investment securities for cash	Inflow
Property, Plant, and Equipment	Purchase of property, plant, and equipment for cash	Outflow
	Sale of property, plant, and equipment for cash	Inflow

In the case of Nautilus, the balance sheet in Exhibit 16.4 shows two investment-related accounts (noted with an I) that changed during the year: Plant and Equipment, and Land. To determine the cause(s) for the changes in these accounts, we need to examine the records for these accounts. Purchases of plant and equipment or land increase the account; sales decrease it.

Plant and Equipment

Assume Nautilus purchased equipment for $16,000 cash. This purchase caused a cash outflow, which we must subtract on the schedule of investing activities in Exhibit 16.6. This purchase explains the change in the Plant and Equipment account.

Plant and Equipment (A)			
Beg. bal.	203,000		
Purchases	16,000	Sales	0
End. bal.	219,000		

Exhibit 16.6 Nautilus, Inc.: Schedule for Net Cash Flow from Investing Activities

Items	Amount (in thousands)	Explanations
Purchases of plant and equipment	$(16,000)	Payment of cash for equipment
Sales of land	5,000	Sale of land for cash
Net cash inflow (outflow)	$(11,000)	Subtotal for the statement of cash flows

[4] Although they are not shown here, cash flows for intangible assets are similar to those for property, plant, and equipment.

If Nautilus had sold any plant and equipment during the period, regardless of the amount of any gain or loss on the sale, the total amount of cash received would have been an investing cash inflow.

Land and Investments

Nautilus sold land for $5,000 in cash. The land's book value on the balance sheet at the time of sale was $2,000. Consequently, a gain of $3,000 ($5,000 − $2,000) occurred on the sale. Regardless of the amount of any gain or loss on the sale, the total amount of cash received from the sale, $5,000, is an investing cash inflow.

Land (A)			
Beg. bal.	12,000		
Purchases	0	Sales	2,000
End. bal.	10,000		

If Nautilus had purchased or sold any investments during the period, they would be treated in the same manner as the land in this example.

SELF-STUDY PRACTICE

Compute cash flow from investing activities assuming the following list includes all amounts related to purchases and sales of plant and equipment, land, and investments.

a. Purchased investments for cash, $10,000.
b. Sold land with a book value of $17,000 for $18,000 cash.
c. Purchased plant and equipment for $25,000 cash.
d. Sold investments with a book value of $15,000 for $12,000 cash.

After you have finished, check your answers with the solution at the bottom of the page.

Learning Objective 4

Report cash flows from financing activities.

REPORTING CASH FLOWS FROM FINANCING ACTIVITIES

The third section of the statement of cash flows includes changes in the liabilities owed to owners (such as dividends payable) and financial institutions (such as bank loans payable, notes payable, and long-term debt) as well as changes in owners' equity. (Because earning interest is considered an operating activity, it is excluded from cash flows from financing.) The following activities and their related accounts are the ones you will encounter most often:

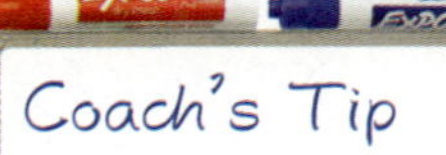

Coach's Tip

Remember that the dividends received from investing in other companies, as well as interest received and interest paid, affect net income. Thus, they are reported as **operating** (not investing or financing) cash flows.

Related Balance Sheet Accounts	Financing Activity	Cash Flow Effect
Notes Payable	Borrowing cash from banks or other financial institutions	Inflow
	Repayment of loan principal	Outflow
Long-Term Debt	Issuance of bonds for cash	Inflow
	Repayment of bond principal	Outflow
Contributed Capital	Issuance of stock for cash	Inflow
	Repurchase of stock with cash	Outflow
Retained Earnings	Payment of cash dividends	Outflow

Solution to Self-Study Practice

Purchased plant and equipment	($25,000)
Purchased investments	(10,000)
Sold land	18,000
Sold investments	12,000
Cash flow from investing activities	($ 5,000)

To compute the cash flows from financing activities, we must review the changes in all debt and owners' equity accounts. Looking at changes in Nautilus's balance sheet (Exhibit 16.4), we find that the Long-Term Debt, Contributed Capital, and Retained Earnings accounts (noted with an F) all changed during the period. In the financing activities section (as in the investing activities section), we must **separately** identify the causes of both increases and decreases in selected accounts. This means that, in addition to the change in the balance sheet account, the accounting records related to the account must be examined.

Long-Term Debt

Suppose the accounting records indicate that the $4,000 increase in Long-Term Debt on the balance sheet resulted from a combination of new borrowing of $6,000 and repayment of $2,000 in **principal** on existing debt. We will include both the inflow and outflow in the schedule of financing activities in Exhibit 16.7.

Long-Term Debt (L)			
		Beg. bal.	63,000
Repayments	2,000	Borrowings	6,000
		End. bal.	67,000

Contributed Capital

The change in the Contributed Capital account resulted from an issue of company stock for $1,000 in cash, which produced a cash inflow. This $1,000 increase in contributed capital should be listed on the schedule of financing activities in Exhibit 16.7.

Contributed Capital (OE)			
		Beg. bal.	4,000
		Issuance of stock	1,000
		End. bal.	5,000

Retained Earnings

Net income increases the amount in the Retained Earnings account; dividends decrease Retained Earnings. We have already included the cash effects related to net income in the operating activities section of the statement of cash flows. The only change in retained earnings that remains to be accounted for is the cash outflow for any dividends paid.

From the income statement in Exhibit 16.4, we know that Nautilus reported net income of $31,000. From the statement of retained earnings (or statement of owners' equity), we know that Nautilus declared dividends of $24,000. The balance sheet does not report any dividends payable, so the full amount of dividends must have been paid in cash. This outflow is included in the schedule of financing activities in Exhibit 16.7. Together, net income

Exhibit 16.7 Nautilus, Inc.: Schedule for Net Cash Flow from Financing Activities

Items	Amount (in thousands)	Explanation
Additional borrowings of long-term debt	$ 6,000	Cash received when new loan obtained
Repayment of principal on existing debt	(2,000)	Cash paid to repay principal on existing debt
Issuance of company stock	1,000	Cash received from issuing stock
Cash dividends paid	(24,000)	Cash paid to stockholders as dividend
Net cash inflow (outflow)	$(19,000)	Subtotal for the statement of cash flows

and dividends account for the $7,000 increase in Retained Earnings as in the following T-account.

Retained Earnings (OE)			
		Beg. bal.	248,000
Dividends	24,000	Net Income	31,000
		End. bal.	255,000

SELF-STUDY PRACTICE

Compute cash flow from financing activities assuming the following list includes all financing activities of the period and some nonfinancing activities

Purchased investments for cash	$10,000	Additional short-term borrowing from bank	$19,000
Dividends paid	25,000	Interest paid	8,000

After you have finished, check your answers with the solution at the bottom of the page.

PREPARING AND EVALUATING THE STATEMENT OF CASH FLOWS

Format for the Statement of Cash Flows

Learning Objective 5

Prepare and evaluate the statement of cash flows.

Now that we have determined the cash flows for the three main types of business activity, we can prepare the statement of cash flows. In Exhibit 16.8, we show the format for the statement of cash flows using the indirect method. The statement of cash flows combines cash flows from operating, investing, and financing activities to produce an overall net increase (or decrease) in cash. This net change is added to the beginning cash balance to arrive at the ending cash balance, which is the same as the cash balance reported on the balance sheet.

Noncash Investing and Financing Activities

Certain transactions are important investing and financing activities but have no cash flow effects. These are called **noncash investing and financing activities.** For example, the purchase of a $100,000 building with a $100,000 mortgage given by the former owner does not cause either an inflow or an outflow of cash. As a result, these noncash activities are not listed in the three main sections of the cash flow statement. However, supplemental disclosure of these transactions is required, in either narrative or schedule form. Nautilus statement of cash flows does not list any noncash investing and financing activities. However, when Northwest Airlines purchases airplanes from AIRBUS or Boeing, the manufacturer provides some of the

Solution to Self-Study Practice

Dividends paid	($25,000)
Additional short-term borrowing from bank	19,000
Cash flow from financing activities	($6,000)

Exhibit 16.8 Format for the Statement of Cash Flows—Indirect Method

Nautilus

Nautilus, Inc.
Statement of Cash Flows*
For the Year Ended December 31, 2006
(in thousands)

Cash Flows from Operating Activities	
Net income	$31,000
Adjustments to reconcile net income to net cash provided by operating activities:	
Depreciation	7,000
Gain on sale of land	(3,000)
Changes in assets and liabilities:	
Accounts receivable	(21,000)
Inventories	20,000
Prepaid expenses	(9,000)
Accounts payable	3,000
Accrued liabilities	1,000
Net cash provided by operating activities	29,000
Cash Flows from Investing Activities	
Purchases of plant and equipment	(16,000)
Sales of land	5,000
Net cash used by investing activities	(11,000)
Cash Flows from Financing Activities	
Additional borrowings of long-term debt	6,000
Repayment of principal on existing debt	(2,000)
Issuance of common stock	1,000
Cash dividends paid	(24,000)
Net cash used by financing activities	(19,000)
Net decrease in cash and cash equivalents	(1,000)
Cash and cash equivalents at beginning of period	8,000
Cash and cash equivalents at end of period	$ 7,000

*Certain amounts have been adjusted to simplify the presentation.

financing for those purchases. These amounts are disclosed as follows at the bottom of its cash flow statement:

Northwest

NORTHWEST AIRLINES CORPORATION

(in millions)	**Year ended December 31,**		
Investing and Financing Activities Not Affecting Cash:	**2007**	**2006**	**2005**
Manufacturer financing of aircraft and other non-cash transactions	$ 502	$ 280	$ 344

Supplemental Cash Flow Information

Companies that use the indirect method of presenting cash flows from operations also must provide two other figures: cash paid for interest and cash paid for income taxes. These are normally listed at the bottom of the statement or in the notes.

Free Cash Flow

In evaluating the statement of cash flows, a good place to start is with the subtotals in each of the three main sections. Cash flow patterns differ from one company to the next, depending on how well established a company is. A healthy, well-established company will show positive cash flows from operations that are large enough to pay for the replacement of current property, plant, and equipment and pay dividends to stockholders.

Any additional cash beyond that required to meet a company's basic needs is called **free cash flow.** Free cash flow can be used (a) to expand the business through additional investing activities, (b) for financing (for example, to pay down debt or pay future dividends), or (c) simply to build the company's cash balance.

Financial Analysis Tools

Name of Measure	Formula	What It Tells You
Free Cash Flow	Net Cash Flow from Operating Activities – Purchases of Property and Equipment – Dividends Paid	• Ability to make additional capital investments without external financing. • Ability to pay down debt or repurchase stock. • Ability to pay future dividends.

Nautilus's free cash flow would be computed as follows:

Free Cash Flow = Net Cash Flow from Operating Activities – Purchases of Property and Equipment – Dividends Paid
= $29,000 – $16,000 – $24,000 = ($11,000)

Quality of Income Ratio

The operating activities section of the statement of cash flows indicates how well a company can generate cash internally through its operations and its management of current assets and current liabilities. Most analysts believe this section is the most important one because in the long run, operations are the only continuing source of cash. Investors will not invest in a company if they do not believe that cash generated from operations will be available to pay dividends or expand the company. Similarly, creditors will not lend money if they believe that cash generated from operations will not be sufficient to repay them.

In evaluating the operating activities section of the statement of cash flows, consider the absolute amount of the cash flow; is it positive or negative? Keep in mind that for a company to be successful, operating cash flows must be positive over the long run. You can also look at the relationship between operating cash flows and net income by using the quality of income ratio. This ratio measures the portion of net income that was generated in cash. All other things held equal, a quality of income ratio near 1.0 indicates a high likelihood that revenues are realized in cash and that expenses are associated with cash outflows.

Financial Analysis Tools

Name of Measure	Formula	What It Tells You
Quality of income ratio	$\frac{\text{Net Cash Flow from Operating Activities}}{\text{Net Income}}$	• Portion of net income generated in cash • Ratio near 1.0 means that operating cash flows and net income are in sync.

Nautilus's quality of income ratio would be computed as follows:

$$\text{Quality of Income Ratio} = \frac{\text{Net Cash Flow from Operating Activities}}{\text{Net Income}} = \frac{\$29{,}000}{\$31{,}000} = 0.94 \text{ times}$$

The quality of income ratio is most useful when it is compared to those of competitors in the same industry or to that of the same company in prior periods. Any major deviations—say, below 0.5 or above 1.5—should be investigated. In some cases, a deviation may be nothing to worry about, but in others it could be the first sign of serious problems.

There are three potential causes of deviations in this ratio. The first is **the corporate life cycle, or growth in sales.** New companies often experience rapid sales growth. When sales are increasing, accounts receivable and inventory normally increase faster than cash flows from sales. This lag in collections often reduces operating cash flows below net income, which in turn reduces the ratio. The problem is not serious provided that the company can get sufficient cash from financing activities to meet its needs until operating activities begin to generate positive cash flows.

A second potential cause of a deviation in the quality of income ratio is a **change in management of operating activities.** If a company's operating assets (such as Accounts Receivable and Inventories) are allowed to grow out of control, its operating cash flows and quality of income ratio will decrease. More efficient management will have the opposite effect. To investigate this potential cause more closely, use the inventory and accounts receivable turnover ratios covered in prior chapters

A third cause of deviation in this ratio is a **change in revenue and expense recognition.** Most cases of fraudulent financial reporting involve aggressive revenue recognition (that is, recording revenues before they are earned) or delayed expense recognition (that is, failing to report expenses). Both tactics cause net income to increase in the current period, suggesting that the company has improved its performance. However, neither of these tactics affects cash flows from operating activities. As a result, if revenue and expense recognition policies are used to artificially boost net income, the quality of income ratio will drop, providing one of the first warning signs that the financial statements might contain errors or fraud.

Demonstration Case A: Indirect Method

For a recent quarter ended March 31, Brunswick Corporation reported net income of $3,800 (all numbers in thousands). On December 31 of the year before, the balance in cash and cash equivalents had been $351,400; by March 31, it was $280,000. The company reported the following additional activities:

a. Received $2,200 from debt borrowings.
b. Accounts receivable increased by $40,300.
c. Paid $31,800 in cash for purchase of property, plant, and equipment.
d. Recorded depreciation of $35,600.
e. Salaries payable increased by $10,210.
f. Other accrued liabilities decreased by $35,000.
g. Prepaid expenses decreased by $14,500.

h. Inventories increased by $20,810.

i. Accounts payable decreased by $10,200.

j. Issued stock to employees for $400 in cash.

Required:
Based on this information, prepare the statement of cash flows using the indirect method. Evaluate the cash flows reported in the statement.

Suggested Solution

Brunswick Corporation
Statement of Cash Flows
For the Quarter Ended March 31
(in thousands)

Cash flows from operating activities	
Net income	$ 3,800
Adjustments	
Depreciation	35,600
Increase in accounts receivable	(40,300)
Increase in inventories	(20,810)
Decrease in prepaid expenses	14,500
Decrease in accounts payable	(10,200)
Increase in salaries payable	10,210
Decrease in other accrued liabilities	(35,000)
Net cash provided by (used for) operating activities	(42,200)
Cash flows from investing activities	
Additions to property, plant, and equipment	(31,800)
Net cash provided by (used for) investing activities	(31,800)
Cash flows from financing activities	
Proceeds from debt borrowings	2,200
Proceeds from issuance of stock to employees	400
Net cash provided by (used for) financing activities	2,600
Increase (decrease) in cash and cash equivalents	(71,400)
Cash and cash equivalents, December 31	351,400
Cash and cash equivalents, March 31	$280,000

Despite reporting a profit this quarter, the company has experienced negative cash flow from operations. The drop was caused primarily by a buildup of accounts receivable and inventories with no corresponding reduction in spending on accounts payable and other accrued liabilities. This negative cash flow from operations could be troublesome because it suggests that the company may be encountering difficulties in selling its products and collecting on past sales. In addition to the drain on cash for operating activities, the company spent more than $30 million for additional property, plant, and equipment. Financing activities had relatively little effect on cash flows during the period, however. The company entered the quarter with a lot of cash (more than $350 million). Despite the shortfall in cash flow, it still has a lot of cash remaining to finance future activities.

Supplement 16A

Reporting Cash Flows from Operating Activities—Direct Method

The direct method summarizes all operating transactions that result in either a debit or a credit to Cash. It is prepared by adjusting each revenue and expense on the income statement from an accrual basis to a cash basis. We demonstrate this process using the revenues and expenses reported in Nautilus's income statement (Exhibit 16.4). See Exhibit 16A.1 for the schedule for converting from an accrual to a cash basis using the direct method. Notice that in this method, we work directly with each revenue and expense listed on the income statement, ignoring any totals or subtotals (such as net income).

Exhibit 16A.1 **Nautilus Inc.: Schedule for Net Cash Flow from Operating Activities—Direct Method**

Cash flows from operating activities	
Cash collected from customers	$ 659,000
Cash payments to suppliers	(359,000)
Cash payments for operating expenses	(258,000)
Cash paid for interest	(1,000)
Cash payments for income taxes	(12,000)
Net cash inflow (outflow)	$ 29,000

Nautilus

Converting Sales Revenues to a Cash Inflow

When a company records sales, its Accounts Receivable increases; when the company collects cash, Accounts Receivable decreases. Thus, if Accounts Receivable increases by $21,000, sales on account must have been $21,000 more than cash collections. To convert sales revenue to cash collected, then, we need to subtract $21,000 from sales revenue. The following diagram shows this process:

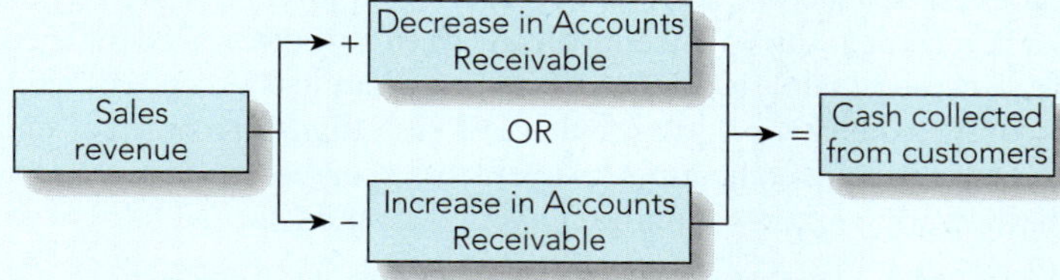

Using information from Nautilus's income statement and balance sheet in Exhibit 16.4, we can compute cash collected from customers as follows:

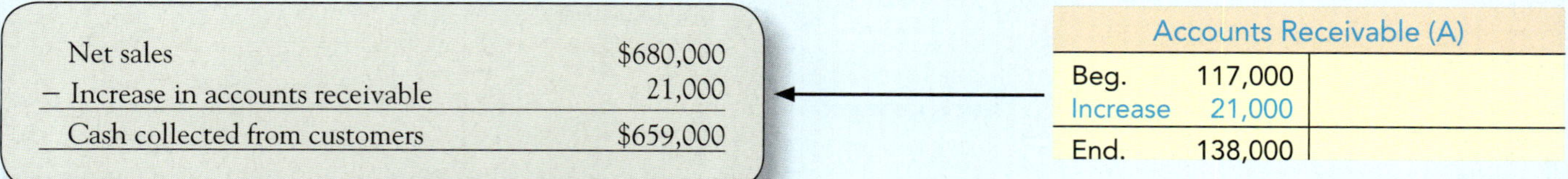

Net sales	$680,000
− Increase in accounts receivable	21,000
Cash collected from customers	$659,000

Accounts Receivable (A)		
Beg.	117,000	
Increase	21,000	
End.	138,000	

Converting Cost of Goods Sold to Cash Paid to Suppliers

Cost of goods sold represents the cost of merchandise sold during the accounting period. It may be more or less than the amount of cash paid to suppliers during the period. In the case of Nautilus, inventory decreased during the year because the company sold more merchandise than it purchased. If the company paid cash to inventory suppliers, it would have paid less cash than the amount of cost of goods sold. So, the decrease in inventory must be subtracted from the cost of goods sold to compute the cash paid to suppliers.

Typically, companies buy their inventory on account from suppliers (as indicated by an accounts payable balance on the balance sheet). Consequently, we need to consider more than just the change in Inventory to convert the cost of goods sold to cash paid to suppliers. We must also consider the credit purchases and payments recorded in Accounts Payable. Credit purchases increase Accounts Payable; cash payments decrease it. The overall increase in Accounts Payable reported by Nautilus in Exhibit 16.4 indicates that cash payments were less than credit purchases, so we must subtract the difference to compute the total cash payments to suppliers. In other words, to fully convert the cost of goods sold to a cash basis, we must consider the changes in both Inventory and Accounts Payable, in the following manner:

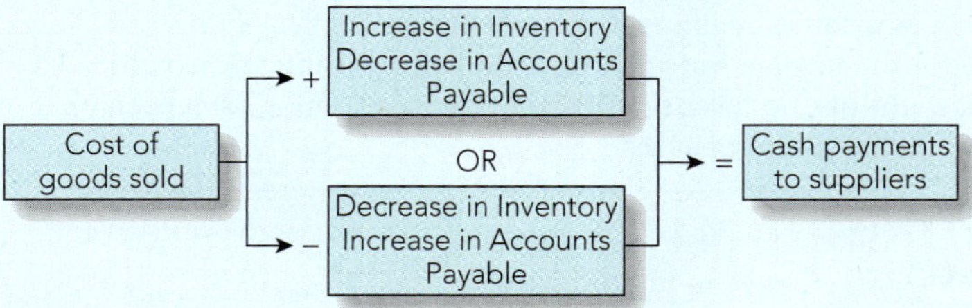

Using information from Exhibit 16.4, we can compute cash paid to suppliers as follows:

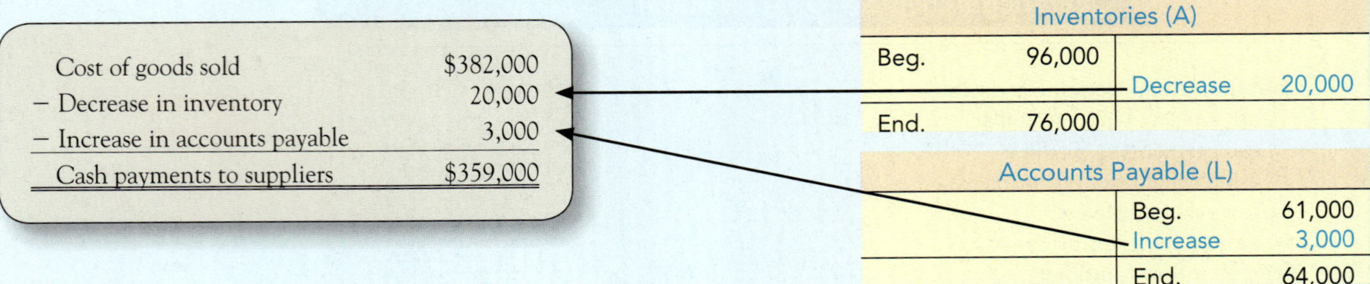

Converting Operating Expenses to a Cash Outflow

The total amount of expense on the income statement may differ from the cash outflow associated with that activity. Some amounts, such as that for prepaid rent, are paid **before** they are recognized as expenses. When prepayments are made, the balance in the asset Prepaid Expenses increases. When expenses are recorded, Prepaid Expenses decreases. When Nautilus's Prepaid Expenses increase by $9,000, we know that the company paid more cash than it recorded in operating expenses. This increase in Prepaid Expenses must be added to net income to determine cash paid for operating expenses.

Some operating expenses, such as accrued wages, are paid **after** they are recorded. In that case, when the expenses are recorded, the balance in the Accrued Liabilities account increases. When the payments are made, Accrued Liabilities decreases. When Nautilus's Accrued Liabilities increase by $1,000, then we know the company paid that much less cash than it recorded as operating expenses. This amount must be subtracted in computing cash paid for expenses.

Generally, other operating expenses can be converted from an accrual basis to a cash basis in the following manner:

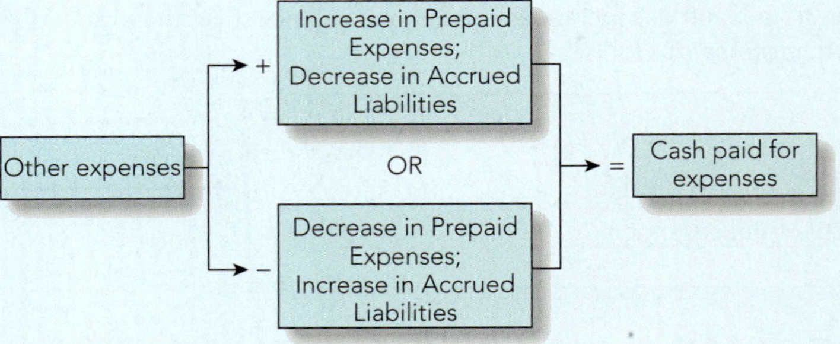

Using income statement information from Exhibit 16.4, we can compute cash paid for expenses as follows:

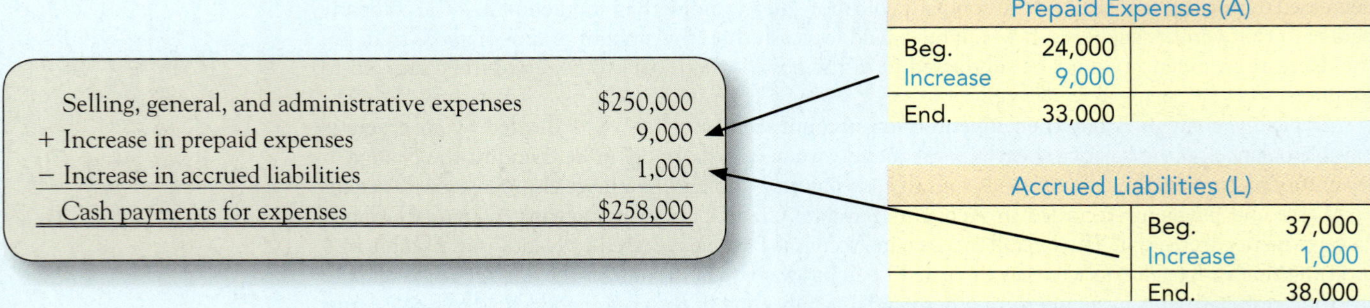

It is easy to convert depreciation expense to a cash basis because depreciation does not involve cash. Thus, the direct method of preparing the statement of cash flows omits noncash expenses such as depreciation (as well as revenues, gains, and losses that do not affect cash).

The next line on the income statement in Exhibit 16.4 is interest expense of $1,000. Because the Interest Payable account has no balance, all interest expense must have been paid in cash. Thus, the interest expense equals the interest paid:

Interest expense	$1,000
No change in interest payable	0
Cash payments for interest	$1,000

The same logic can be applied to income taxes. Nautilus reported income tax expense of $12,000. Because Income Taxes Payable (or any other tax account) on the balance sheet in Exhibit 16.4 has no balance, the income tax paid must equal the income tax expense:

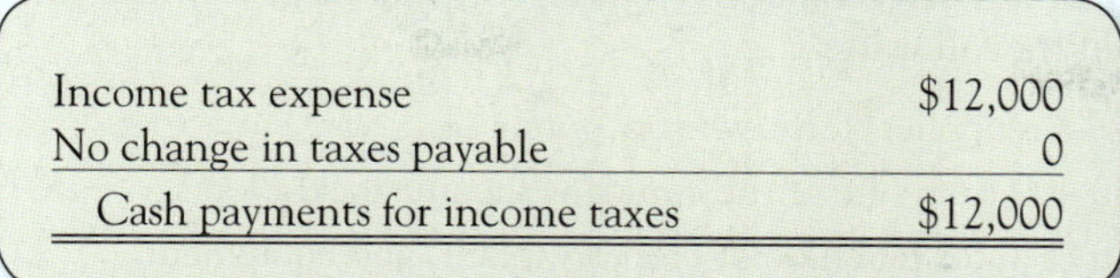

Income tax expense	$12,000
No change in taxes payable	0
Cash payments for income taxes	$12,000

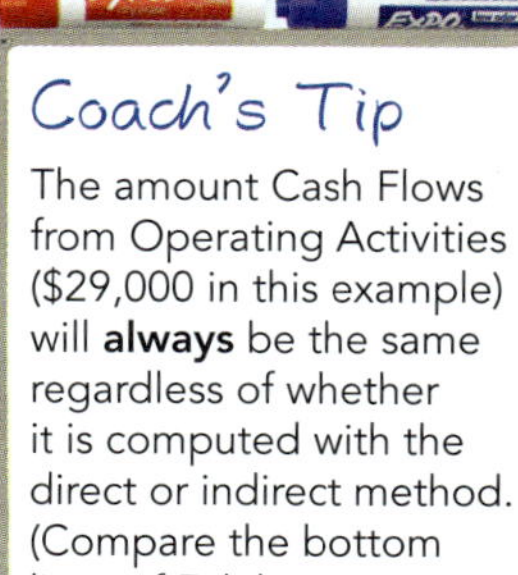

Coach's Tip

The amount Cash Flows from Operating Activities ($29,000 in this example) will **always** be the same regardless of whether it is computed with the direct or indirect method. (Compare the bottom lines of Exhibits 16A.1 and 16.5.)

Now that we have considered all of the line items shown on the income statement in Exhibit 16.4, it is time to gather all operating cash inflows and outflows that we have calculated (See Exhibit 16A.1). If Nautilus were to report its statement of cash flows using the direct method, Exhibit 16A.1 would replace the Cash Flows from Operating Activities section in Exhibit 16.8.

The following chart summarizes the adjustments that must be made to convert income statement items to operating cash flows. Before you move to the next section, review it carefully and then complete the self-study practice that follows to make sure you understand how to compute cash flow from operations (direct method).

Income Statement Account	± Change in Balance Sheet Account(s)	= Operating Cash Flow
Sales Revenue	+Decrease in Accounts Receivable (A)	
	−Increase in Accounts Receivable (A)	= Collections from customers
Cost of Goods Sold	+Increase in Inventory (A)	
	−Decrease in Inventory (A)	
	−Increase in Accounts Payable (L)	
	+Decrease in Accounts Payable (L)	= Payments to suppliers of inventory
Other Expenses	+Increase in Prepaid Expenses (A)	
	−Decrease in Prepaid Expenses (A)	
	−Increase in Accrued Expenses (L)	= Payments to suppliers of services
	+Decrease in Accrued Expenses (L)	(e.g., rent, utilities, wages, interest)
Interest Expense	−Increase in Interest Payable (L)	
	+Decrease in Interest Payable (L)	= Payments of interest
Income Tax Expense	+Increase in Prepaid Income Taxes (Deferred Taxes) (A)	
	−Decrease in Prepaid Income Taxes (Deferred Taxes) (A)	
	−Increase in Income Taxes Payable (Deferred Taxes) (L)	
	+Decrease in Income Taxes Payable (Deferred Taxes) (L)	= Payments of income taxes

SELF-STUDY PRACTICE

Indicate which of the following items taken from a cash flow statement would be added (+), subtracted (−), or not included (0) when calculating cash flow from operations using the direct method.

___1. Payments to suppliers of inventories.
___2. Payment of dividends to stockholders.
___3. Cash collections from customers.
___4. Purchase of plant and equipment for cash.
___5. Payments of interest to lenders.
___6. Payment of taxes to the government.

After you have finished, check your answers with the solution at the bottom of the page.

Solution to Self-Study Practice

1. − 2. 0 3. + 4. 0 5. − 6. −

Demonstration Case B: Direct Method (Supplement A)

During a recent quarter ended March 29, Cybex International reported that cash and cash equivalents had increased from $216 on December 31 to $469 on March 29 (all amounts in thousands). The company also reported the following:

a. Paid $13,229 to suppliers for inventory purchases.
b. Borrowed $2,400 from one of the company's main stockholders.
c. Paid $554 in cash for purchase of property, plant, and equipment.
d. Reported sales on account of $20,608 (accounts receivable were $13,628 at the beginning of the quarter and $12,386 at the end of the quarter).
e. Paid operating expenses totaling $6,188.
f. Made cash payments for interest totaling $1,060.
g. Made payments of $2,625 for principal owed on long-term debt.
h. Paid $284 cash for other financing activities.
i. Paid $57 cash for income taxes.

Required:
Based on this information, prepare the statement of cash flows using the direct method. Evaluate the cash flows reported in the statement.

Suggested Solution

Cybex International
Statement of Cash Flows
For the Quarter Ended March 29
(in thousands)

Operating activities	
Cash collected from customers ($20,608 + $13,628 − $12,386)	$ 21,850
Cash paid to suppliers	(13,229)
Cash paid for operating expenses	(6,188)
Cash paid for interest	(1,060)
Cash paid for income taxes	(57)
Net cash provided by operating activities	1,316
Investing activities	
Additions to property, plant, and equipment	(554)
Net cash used for investing activities	(554)
Financing activities	
Borrowed cash from related party (stockholder)	2,400
Repaid principal owed on long-term debt	(2,625)
Cash paid for other financing activities	(284)
Net cash used for financing activities	(509)
Increase in cash and cash equivalents	253
Cash and cash equivalents, December 31	216
Cash and cash equivalents, March 29	$ 469

Cybex reported a net cash inflow of $1,316 from operating activities during the quarter. This cash inflow was more than enough to pay for the property, plant, and equipment purchased during the quarter. Some of the extra cash from operations (that is, free cash flow) that was not needed to purchase property, plant, and equipment could have been used to pay down debt or increase the company's cash balance. The Financing Activities section suggests that the company did pay down a significant amount of long-term debt ($2,625) in part by borrowing funds from a related party ($2,400). Borrowing from a related party—particularly a major stockholder—is unusual, and would prompt analysts to investigate further. The company's quarterly report explains that lenders had demanded immediate repayment of their loans after the company violated its debt covenants. A major stockholder lent money to the company to make the repayment.

Supplement 16B
Spreadsheet Approach: Indirect Method

As a company's situation becomes more complex, the analytical approach that we used to prepare the statement of cash flows for Nautilus becomes cumbersome and inefficient. In practice, many companies use a spreadsheet to prepare the statement of cash flows. This approach is based on the same logic as our earlier approach. Its primary advantage is its systematic way of keeping track of detailed information. You may find it useful even in simple situations.

Exhibit 16B.1 is a spreadsheet for Nautilus, which we created using the following procedure:

1. Starting from the right side of the spreadsheet, set up four columns to record dollar amounts. The first column should hold the beginning balances for the items reported on the balance sheet. The next two columns should show debit and credit changes in those balances. The final column should show the ending balances in these balance sheet accounts.
2. On the top half of the spreadsheet, on the left side, enter each account name from the balance sheet.
3. On the bottom half of the spreadsheet, on the left side, enter the name of each item to be reported on the statement of cash flows. Do this as you analyze the change in each balance sheet account.

Think of the bottom half of the spreadsheet as a big Cash T-account.

Note that in the top half of the spreadsheet, you analyze changes in the balance sheet accounts in terms of debits and credits. In the bottom half of the spreadsheet, you record the offsetting debits and credits in terms of their impact on cash flows. Each change in the noncash balance sheet accounts explains part of the change in the Cash account.

Let's go through each of the entries in the spreadsheet in Exhibit 16B.1, starting with the first one in the bottom half:

a. Net income of $31,000 is shown as an inflow in the operating activities section. The corresponding credit in the top half of the spreadsheet goes to Retained Earnings (to show that net income increased Retained Earnings).

b. Depreciation expense of $7,000 is added back to net income because this expense does not cause a cash outflow. The corresponding credit explains the increase in the Accumulated Depreciation account during the period.

c. The $21,000 increase in Accounts Receivable means that cash collections from customers were less than sales made on account. Because net income includes the sales made on account, we must subtract that amount to adjust to the actual cash collected. This adjustment appears on the spreadsheet as a credit to Cash and a corresponding debit to Accounts Receivable.

d. This $20,000 entry reconciles purchases of inventory with the cost of goods sold. The amount is added to net income because more inventory was sold than was purchased.

e. This $9,000 entry reconciles the prepayment of expenses with their expiration. The amount is subtracted from net income because cash prepayments were more than the amounts reported as expired expenses.

f. This $3,000 entry reconciles cash paid to suppliers with purchases made on account. The amount is added because more was borrowed (by purchasing on account) than was paid in cash.

g. This $1,000 entry reconciles the accrual of liabilities for operating expenses with payments for those expenses. The amount is added because the cash paid for accrued liabilities was less than the expenses recorded for accrued liabilities. Note that the debit to Cash corresponds to the net credit to Accrued Liabilities.

h. This $16,000 entry records purchases of new equipment for cash.

i. This $5,000 entry records the sale of land for cash.

j. This $2,000 entry records cash repaid for principal on existing debt.

k. This $6,000 entry records cash obtained through additional long-term debt.

l. This $1,000 entry records cash received from an issue of company stock.

m. This $24,000 entry records the payment of dividends in cash.

n. This $1,000 entry shows that the change in cash (on the top part of the spreadsheet) is accounted for by the net cash flows listed on the bottom part of the spreadsheet.

Finally, check to make sure that the debits equal the credits on your spreadsheet. If they do not, you have missed something. If they do, you can then use the bottom part of the spreadsheet to prepare the statement of cash flows in Exhibit 16.8.

Exhibit 16B.1 Spreadsheet to Prepare Statement of Cash Flows, Indirect Method — Nautilus

Nautilus, Inc.
For the Year Ended December 31, 2006
(in thousands)

	Beginning Balances, December 31, 2005	ANALYSIS OF CHANGES Debit		Credit		Ending Balances, December 31, 2006
Items from Balance Sheet						
Cash and cash equivalents (A)	8,000			*(n)*	1,000	7,000
Accounts receivable (A)	117,000	*(c)*	21,000			138,000
Inventories (A)	96,000			*(d)*	20,000	76,000
Prepaid expenses (A)	24,000	*(e)*	9,000			33,000
Plant and Equipment (A)	203,000	*(h)*	16,000			219,000
Accumulated depreciation (xA)	(47,000)			*(b)*	7,000	(54,000)
Land (A)	12,000			*(i)*	2,000	10,000
Accounts payable (L)	(61,000)			*(f)*	3,000	(64,000)
Accrued liabilities (L)	(37,000)			*(g)*	1,000	(38,000)
Long-term debt (L)	(63,000)	*(j)*	2,000	*(k)*	6,000	(67,000)
Contributed capital (OE)	(4,000)			*(l)*	1,000	(5,000)
Retained earnings (OE)	(248,000)	*(m)*	24,000	*(a)*	31,000	(255,000)

	CASH Inflows		Outflows		Subtotals
Statement of Cash Flows					
Cash flows from operating activities					
Net income	*(a)*	31,000			
Adjustments to reconcile net income to cash provided by operating activities					
Depreciation	*(b)*	7,000			
Gain on sale of land			*(i)*	3,000	
Changes in assets and liabilities					
Accounts receivable			*(c)*	21,000	
Inventories	*(d)*	20,000			
Prepaid expenses			*(e)*	9,000	
Accounts payable	*(f)*	3,000			
Accrued liabilities	*(g)*	1,000			
					29,000
Cash flows from investing activities					
Purchases of equipment			*(h)*	16,000	
Sale of land	*(i)*	5,000			
					(11,000)
Cash flows from financing activities					
Repayment of principal on existing debt			*(j)*	2,000	
Additional long-term debt borrowed	*(k)*	6,000			
Stock issuance	*(l)*	1,000			
Cash dividends paid			*(m)*	24,000	
					(19,000)
Net decrease in cash and cash equivalents	*(n)*	1,000			
		147,000		147,000	(1,000)

Chapter Summary

LO1 Identify cash flows from operating, investing, and financing activities. p. 682

- The statement of cash flows has three main sections: cash flows from operating activities, which are related to income earned from normal operations; cash flows from investing activities, which are related to the acquisition and sale of productive assets; and cash flows from financing activities, which are related to external financing of the enterprise.
- The net cash inflow or outflow for the period equals the increase or decrease in cash and cash equivalents on the balance sheet for the period. Cash equivalents are highly liquid investments with original maturities of less than three months.

LO2 Report cash flows from operating activities using the indirect method. p. 687

- The indirect method for reporting cash flows from operating activities converts net income to net cash flow from operating activities.
- The conversion involves additions and subtractions for (1) expenses (such as depreciation expense) and revenues that do not affect cash and gains and losses from sale of long-lived assets and (2) changes in each of the individual current assets (other than cash) and current liabilities that reflect differences in the timing of accrual-based net income and cash flows.

LO3 Report cash flows from investing activities. p. 693

- Investing activities reported on the statement of cash flows include cash payments to acquire property, plant, and equipment, investments, and cash proceeds from their sale.

LO4 Report cash flows from financing activities. p. 694

- Cash inflows from financing activities include cash proceeds from the issue of debt and common stock. Cash outflows include cash repayments of principal on debt, cash paid for the repurchase of the company's stock, and cash dividend payments. (Cash payments associated with interest are a cash flow from operating activities.)

LO5 Prepare and evaluate the statement of cash flows. p. 696

- A healthy company will generate positive cash flows from operations, some of which will be used to pay for purchases of property, plant, and equipment. Any additional cash, called free cash flow, can be used to further expand the business or pay down some of the company's debt, or it can be returned to owners. A company is in trouble if it cannot generate positive cash flows from operations over the long run because creditors will eventually stop lending to the company, and stockholders will stop investing in it.
- Two common measures for assessing operating, investing, and financing cash flows are free cash flow and the quality of income ratio.

Financial Analysis Tools

Name of Measure	Formula	What It Tells You
Free Cash Flow	Net Cash Flow from Operating Activities − Purchases of Property and Equipment − Dividends Paid	• Ability to make additional capital investments without external financing. • Ability to pay down debt or repurchase stock. • Ability to pay future dividends.
Quality of income ratio	$\dfrac{\text{Net Cash Flow from Operating Activities}}{\text{Net Incomes}}$	• Portion of net income generated in cash • Ratio near 1.0 means that operating cash flows and net income are in sync.

Key Terms

Cash Equivalents (p. 682)

Cash Flows from Financing Activities (p. 684)

Cash Flows from Investing Activities (p. 684)

Cash Flows from Operating Activities (Cash Flows from Operations) (p. 683)

Direct Method (p. 683)

Indirect Method (p. 683)

See complete glossary in back of text.

Questions

1. Compare the purposes of the income statement, the balance sheet, and the statement of cash flows.
2. What information does the statement of cash flows report that is not reported on the other required financial statements?
3. What are cash equivalents? How are they reported on the statement of cash flows?
4. What are the major categories of business activities reported on the statement of cash flows? Define each of these activities.
5. What are the typical cash inflows from operating activities? What are the typical cash outflows from operating activities?
6. Describe the types of items used to compute cash flows from operating activities under the two alternative methods of reporting.
7. Under the indirect method, depreciation expense is added to net income to report cash flows from operating activities. Does depreciation cause an inflow of cash?
8. Explain why cash outflows during the period for purchases and salaries are not specifically reported on a statement of cash flows prepared using the indirect method.
9. Explain why a $50,000 increase in inventory during the year must be included in computing cash flows from operating activities under the indirect method.
10. What are the typical cash inflows from investing activities? What are the typical cash outflows from investing activities?
11. What are the typical cash inflows from financing activities? What are the typical cash outflows from financing activities?
12. What are noncash investing and financing activities? Give one example. How are noncash investing and financing activities reported on the statement of cash flows?

Multiple Choice

Quiz 16-1
www.mhhe.com/LLPW1e

1. Where is the change in cash shown in the statement of cash flows?
   a. In the top part, before the operating activities section.
   b. In one of the operating, investing, or financing activities sections.
   c. In the bottom part, following the financing activities section.
   d. None of the above.
2. In what order do the three sections of the statement of cash flows appear when reading from top to bottom?
   a. Financing, investing, operating.
   b. Investing, operating, financing.
   c. Operating, financing, investing.
   d. Operating, investing, financing.
3. Total cash inflow in the operating section of the statement of cash flows should include which of the following?
   a. Cash received from customers at the point of sale.
   b. Cash collections from customer accounts receivable.
   c. Cash received in advance of revenue recognition (unearned revenue).
   d. All of the above.
4. If the balance in Prepaid Expenses increased during the year, what action should be taken on the statement of cash flows when following the indirect method, and why?
   a. The change in the account balance should be subtracted from net income because the net increase in Prepaid Expenses did not impact net income but did reduce the Cash balance.
   b. The change in the account balance should be added to net income because the net increase in Prepaid Expenses did not impact net income but did increase the Cash balance.
   c. The net change in Prepaid Expenses should be subtracted from net income to reverse the income statement effect that had no impact on Cash.
   d. The net change in Prepaid Expenses should be added to net income to reverse the income statement effect that had no impact on Cash.

Coach's Tip
To practice more multiple choice questions, go to www.mhhe.com/LLPW1e.

5. Which of the following would not appear in the investing section of the statement of cash flows?
   a. Purchase of inventory.
   b. Sale of investments.
   c. Purchase of land.
   d. All of the above would appear in the investing section of the statement of cash flows.
6. Which of the following items would not appear in the financing section of the statement of cash flows?
   a. The issuance of the company's own stock.
   b. The repayment of debt.
   c. The payment of dividends.
   d. All of the above would appear in the financing section of the statement of cash flows.
7. Which of the following is not added when computing cash flows from operations using the indirect method?
   a. The net increase in Accounts Payable.
   b. The net decrease in Accounts Receivable.
   c. The net decrease in Inventory.
   d. None of the above.

8. If a company engages in a material transaction that is noncash, which of the following is required?
   a. The company must include an explanatory narrative or schedule accompanying the statement of cash flows.
   b. No disclosure is necessary.
   c. The company must include an explanatory narrative or schedule accompanying the balance sheet.
   d. It must be reported in the investing and financing sections of the statement of cash flows.
9. The **total** change in cash as shown near the bottom of the statement of cash flows for the year should agree with which of the following?
   a. The difference in retained earnings when reviewing the comparative balance sheet.
   b. Net income or net loss as found on the income statement.
   c. The difference in cash when reviewing the comparative balance sheet.
   d. None of the above.
10. Which of the following is a ratio or amount used to assess whether cash flows from operations are sufficiently large to pay for replacing current property, plant, and equipment and to pay dividends to stockholders?
   a. Free cash flow.
   b. Fixed asset turnover ratio.
   c. Cash coverage ratio.
   d. Quality of income ratio.

Solutions to Multiple-Choice Questions

1. c 2. d 3. d 4. a 5. a 6. d 7. d 8. a 9. c 10. a

Mini-Exercises  Available with McGraw-Hill's Homework Manager

M16-1 Identifying Companies from Cash Flow Patterns

LO1, 5

Based on the cash flows shown, classify each of the following cases as a growing start-up company (S), a healthy established company (E), or an established company facing financial difficulties (F).

	Case 1	Case 2	Case 3
Cash provided by (used for) operating activities	$(120,000)	$ 3,000	$ 80,000
Cash provided by (used for) investing activities	10,000	(70,000)	(40,000)
Cash provided by (used for) financing activities	75,000	75,000	(30,000)
Net change in cash	(35,000)	8,000	10,000
Cash position at beginning of year	40,000	2,000	30,000
Cash position at end of year	$ 5,000	$10,000	$ 40,000

M16-2 Matching Items Reported to Cash Flow Statement Categories (Indirect Method)

LO1
Buckle

The Buckle, Inc., operates more than 330 stores in 38 states, selling brand name apparel such as Lucky Jeans and Fossil belts and watches. Some of the items included in its recent statement of cash flows presented using the indirect method are listed here. Indicate whether each item is disclosed in the operating activities (O), investing activities (I), or financing activities (F) section of the statement or (NA) if the item does not appear on the statement.

_______1. Purchase of investments.
_______2. Proceeds from issuance of stock.
_______3. Purchase of property and equipment.
_______4. Depreciation.
_______5. Accouts payable (decrease).
_______6. Inventories (increase).

M16-3 Determining the Effects of Account Changes on Cash Flows from Operating Activities (Indirect Method)

LO2

Indicate whether each item would be added (+) or subtracted (−) in the computation of cash flow from operating activities using the indirect method.

_______1. Depreciation.
_______2. Inventories (decrease).
_______3. Accounts payable (decrease).
_______4. Accounts receivable (increase).
_______5. Accrued liabilities (increase).

LO2

M16-4 Computing Cash Flows from Operating Activities (Indirect Method)

For each of the following independent cases, compute cash flows from operating activities. Assume the following list includes all balance sheet accounts related to operating activities.

	Case A	Case B
Net income	$ 200,000	$ 360,000
Depreciation expense	40,000	80,000
Accounts receivable increase (decrease)	100,000	(20,000)
Inventory increase (decrease)	(50,000)	50,000
Accounts payable increase (decrease)	(110,000)	70,000
Accrued liabilities increase (decrease)	60,000	(80,000)

LO2

M16-5 Computing Cash Flows from Operating Activities (Indirect Method)

For the following two independent cases, show the Cash Flows from Operating Activities section of the 2011 statement of cash flows using the indirect method.

	CASE A		CASE B	
	2011	2010	2011	2010
Sales revenue	$ 10,000	$ 9,000	$ 21,000	$ 18,000
Cost of goods sold	6,000	5,500	12,000	11,000
Gross profit	4,000	3,500	9,000	7,000
Depreciation expense	1,000	1,000	2,000	1,500
Salaries expense	2,500	2,000	5,000	5,000
Net income	500	500	2,000	500
Accounts receivable	300	400	750	600
Inventories	600	500	790	800
Accounts payable	800	700	800	850
Salaries payable	1,000	1,200	200	250

LO3

M16-6 Computing Cash Flows from Investing Activities

Based on the following information, compute cash flows from investing activities.

Cash collections from customers	$800
Purchase of used equipment	850
Depreciation expense	200
Proceeds from sale of investments	300

LO4

M16-7 Computing Cash Flows from Financing Activities

Based on the following information, compute cash flows from financing activities.

Purchase of investments	$ 250
Dividends paid	800
Interest paid	400
Additional short-term borrowing from bank	2,000

LO3, 4, 5

M16-8 Reporting Noncash Investing and Financing Activities

Which of the following transactions would be considered noncash investing and financing activities?

_______1. Additional borrowing from bank.

_______2. Purchase of equipment with investments.

_______3. Dividends paid in cash.

_______4. Purchase of building with promissory note.

LO5

M16-9 Interpreting Cash Flows from Operating, Investing, and Financing Activities

Quantum Dots, Inc., is a nanotechnology company that manufactures "quantum dots," which are tiny pieces of silicon consisting of 100 or more molecules. Quantum dots can be used to illuminate very small objects, enabling scientists to see the blood vessels beneath a mouse's skin ripple with each heartbeat, at the rate of 100 times per second. Evaluate this research intensive company's cash flows assuming the following was reported in its statement of cash flows.

	Current Year	Previous Year
Cash flows from operating activities		
Net cash provided by (used for) operating activities	$ (50,790)	$ (46,730)
Cash flows from investing activities		
Purchases of research equipment	(250,770)	(480,145)
Proceeds from selling all short-term investments	35,000	—
Net cash provided by (used for) investing activities	(215,770)	(480,145)
Cash flows from financing activities		
Additional long-term debt borrowed	100,000	200,000
Proceeds from stock issuance	140,000	200,000
Cash dividends paid	—	(10,000)
Net cash provided by (used for) financing activities	240,000	390,000
Net increase (decrease) in cash	(26,560)	(136,875)
Cash at beginning of period	29,025	165,900
Cash at end of period	$ 2,465	$ 29,025

M16-10 Calculating and Interpreting Free Cash Flow LO5

Capital Corporation reported the following information in its statement of cash flows:

	2010	2011	2012
Net cash flow from operating activities	$35,000	$32,000	$23,000
Dividends paid	2,000	3,000	2,500
Income taxes paid	9,000	8,500	6,500
Purchases of property, plant, and equipment	31,818	22,857	20,325

Calculate the total free cash flow for the period covering 2010–2012 and the free cash flow for each year during the period. What does this analysis tell you about the company's need for using external financing to replace property, plant, and equipment and pay dividends?

M16-11 Calculating and Interpreting the Quality of Income Ratio LO5

Dan's Products, Inc., reported net income of $80,000, depreciation expense of $2,000, and cash flow from operations of $60,000. Compute the quality of income ratio. What does the ratio tell you about the company's accrual of revenues and/or deferral of expenses?

M16-12 (Supplement A) Matching Items Reported to Cash Flow Statement Categories (Direct Method)

Prestige Manufacturing Corporation reports the following items in its 2011 statement of cash flows presented using the direct method. Indicate whether each item is disclosed in the operating activities (O), investing activities (I), or financing activities (F) section of the statement or (NA) if the item does not appear on the statement.

_______ 1. Payment for equipment purchase.
_______ 2. Repayments of bank loan.
_______ 3. Dividends paid.
_______ 4. Proceeds from issuance of stock.
_______ 5. Interest paid.
_______ 6. Receipts from customers.

M16-13 (Supplement A) Computing Cash Flows from Operating Activities (Direct Method)

For each of the following independent cases, compute cash flows from operating activities using the direct method. Assume the following list includes all items relevant to operating activities.

	Case A	Case B
Sales revenue	$ 70,000	$ 55,000
Cost of goods sold	35,000	32,000
Depreciation expense	10,000	2,000
Other operating expenses	5,000	13,000
Net income	20,000	8,000
Accounts receivable increase (decrease)	(1,000)	4,000
Inventory increase (decrease)	2,000	0
Accounts payable increase (decrease)	0	3,000
Accrued liabilities increase (decrease)	1,000	(2,000)

M16-14 (Supplement A) Computing Cash Flows from Operating Activities (Direct Method)
Refer to the two cases presented in M16-5, and show the Cash Flow from Operating Activities section of the 2011 statement of cash flows using the direct method.

Exercises

Available with McGraw-Hill's Homework Manager

LO1, 2
Nike

E16-1 Matching Items Reported to Cash Flow Statement Categories (Indirect Method)
Nike, Inc., is the best-known sports shoe, apparel, and equipment company in the world because of its association with sports stars such as LeBron James. Some of the items included in its recent statement of cash flows presented using the indirect method are listed here.

Indicate whether each item is disclosed in the operating activities (O), investing activities (I), or financing activities (F) section of the statement or (NA) if the item does not appear on the statement.

_______ 1. Additions to long-term debt (new borrowing).
_______ 2. Depreciation.
_______ 3. Additions to property, plant, and equipment (paid in cash).
_______ 4. Increase (decrease) in notes payable. (The amount is owed to financial institutions.)
_______ 5. (Increase) decrease in other current assets.
_______ 6. Cash received from disposal of property, plant, and equipment.
_______ 7. Reductions in long-term debt (repayment).
_______ 8. Issuance of stock (for cash).
_______ 9. (Increase) decrease in inventory.
_______ 10. Net income.

LO1, 2

E16-2 Comparing the Direct and Indirect Methods
To compare statement of cash flows reporting under the direct and indirect methods, enter check marks to indicate which line items are reported on the statement of cash flows with each method.

	Statement of Cash Flows Method	
Cash Flows (and Related Changes)	Direct	Indirect
1. Net income.	_______	_______
2. Receipts from customers.	_______	_______
3. Accounts receivable increase or decrease.	_______	_______
4. Payments to suppliers.	_______	_______
5. Inventory increase or decrease.	_______	_______
6. Accounts payable increase or decrease.	_______	_______
7. Payments to employees.	_______	_______
8. Wages payable, increase or decrease.	_______	_______
9. Depreciation expense.	_______	_______
10. Cash flows from operating activities.	_______	_______
11. Cash flows from investing activities.	_______	_______
12. Cash flows from financing activities.	_______	_______
13. Net increase or decrease in cash during the period.	_______	_______

LO2

E16-3 Reporting Cash Flows from Operating Activities (Indirect Method)
The following information pertains to Guy's Gear Company for 2010:

Sales		$80,000
Expenses		
Cost of goods sold	$50,000	
Depreciation expense	6,000	
Salaries expense	12,000	68,000
Net income		$12,000

Partial Balance Sheet	2010	2009
Accounts receivable	$ 15,000	$ 20,000
Merchandise inventory	18,000	10,000
Salaries payable	2,500	2,000

Required:
Present the operating activities section of the statement of cash flows for Guy's Gear Company using the indirect method.

E16-4 Reporting and Interpreting Cash Flows from Operating Activities from an Analyst's Perspective (Indirect Method) **LO2, 5**
New Vision Company completed its income statement and balance sheet for 2010 and provided the following information:

Service revenue		$66,000
Expenses		
Salaries	$42,000	
Depreciation	7,300	
Utilities	7,000	
Loss on sale of machine	1,700	58,000
Net income		$ 8,000

Partial Balance Sheet	2010	2009
Accounts receivable	$12,000	$24,000
Salaries payable	19,000	10,000
Other accrued liabilities	5,000	9,000
Land	52,000	57,000

Required:
1. Present the operating activities section of the statement of cash flows for New Vision Company using the indirect method.
2. Of the potential causes of differences between cash flow from operations and net income, which are the most important to financial analysts?

E16-5 Reporting and Interpreting Cash Flows from Operating Activities from an Analyst's Perspective (Indirect Method) **LO2, 5**
Sizzler, Inc., operates 700 family restaurants around the world. The company's annual report contained the following information (in thousands):

Operating Activities	
Net loss	$(9,482)
Depreciation	33,305
Increase in receivables	170
Decrease in inventories	643
Increase in prepaid expenses	664
Decrease in accounts payable	2,282
Decrease in accrued liabilities	719
Increase in income taxes payable	1,861
Reduction of long-term debt	12,691
Additions to equipment	29,073

Required:
1. Based on this information, compute cash flow from operating activities using the indirect method.
2. What were the major reasons that Sizzler was able to report a net loss but positive cash flow from operations?
3. Of the potential causes of differences between cash flow from operations and net income, which are the most important to financial analysts?

LO2, 3
AMC Theatres

E16-6 Determining Cash Flows from the Sale of Property (Indirect Method)
The first in the theatre industry to introduce a customer loyalty program (like frequent flyer miles for movie watchers) was AMC Theatres. During the prior year, the company sold property for $5,494,000 cash and recorded a gain on sale of $1,385,000. During the current year, the company sold property for $9,289,000 cash and recorded a gain on sale of $2,590,000.

Required:
For the property sold by AMC each year, show how the disposals would be reported on the comparative statements of cash flows using the following format (which assumes the indirect method). Indicate the sign and amount of the effects.

	Prior Year	Current Year
Cash flows from operating activities		
Gain on sale of property	______	______
Cash flows from investing activities		
Proceeds from disposition of property	______	______

LO2, 3
Gymboree

E16-7 Determining Cash Flows from the Sale of Property (Indirect Method)
The Gymboree Corporation, a specialty retailer, offers apparel, accessories, and play programs for children in the United States and Canada. During the prior year, the company sold property for $18,823,000 cash and recorded a loss on sale of $4,419,000. During the current year, the company sold property for $12,648,000 cash and recorded a loss on sale of $2,964,000.

Required:
For the property sold by Gymboree each year, show how the disposals would be reported on the comparative statements of cash flows, using the following format (which assumes the indirect method). Indicate the sign and amount of the effects.

	Prior Year	Current Year
Cash flows from operating activities		
Loss on sale of property	______	______
Cash flows from investing activities		
Proceeds from disposition of property	______	______

LO2
Colgate-Palmolive

E16-8 Inferring Balance Sheet Changes from the Cash Flow Statement (Indirect Method)
Colgate-Palmolive was founded in 1806. Its statement of cash flows for the first quarter of a recent year reported the following information (in millions):

Operating Activities	
Net income	$ 952.2
Depreciation	243.5
Cash effect of changes in	
Accounts receivable	(122.9)
Inventories	(128.9)
Accounts payable	122.8
Other	303.2
Net cash provided by operations	$1,369.9

Required:
Based on the information reported in the operating activities section of the statement of cash flows for Colgate-Palmolive, determine whether the following accounts increased or decreased during the period: Accounts Receivable, Inventories, and Accounts Payable.

LO2
Apple

E16-9 Inferring Balance Sheet Changes from the Cash Flow Statement (Indirect Method)
The statement of cash flows for Apple for the six-month period ended April 1 of a recent year contained the following information (in millions):

Operating Activities	
Net income	$975
Depreciation	102
Changes in assets and liabilities	
Accounts receivable	34
Inventories	(39)
Other current assets	(892)
Accounts payable	329
Other adjustments	(351)
Net cash provided by operations	$158

Required:
For each of the asset and liability accounts listed in the operating activities section of the statement of cash flows, determine whether the account balances increased or decreased during the period.

E16-10 Analyzing Cash Flows from Operating Activities (Indirect Method) and Calculating and Interpreting the Quality of Income Ratio LO2, 5 PepsiCo

A recent annual report for PepsiCo contained the following information for the period (in millions):

Net income	$4,078
Cash dividends paid	1,642
Depreciation	1,308
Increase in accounts receivable	272
Increase in inventory	132
Increase in prepaid expense	56
Increase in accounts payable	188
Increase in taxes payable	609
Decrease in other liabilities related to operations	791

Required:

1. Compute cash flows from operating activities for PepsiCo using the indirect method.
2. Compute the quality of income ratio to one decimal place.
3. What was the main reason that PepsiCo's quality of income ratio did not equal 1.0?

E16-11 Calculating and Understanding Operating Cash Flows Relating to Inventory Purchases (Indirect Method) LO2

The following information was reported by three companies. When completing the requirements, assume that any and all purchases on account are for inventory.

	Aztec Corporation	Bikes Unlimited	Campus Cycles
Cost of goods sold	$175	$175	$350
Inventory purchases from suppliers made using cash	200	0	200
Inventory purchases from suppliers made on account	0	200	200
Cash payments to suppliers on account	0	160	160
Beginning inventory	100	100	200
Ending inventory	125	125	250
Beginning accounts payable	0	80	80
Ending accounts payable	0	120	120

Required:

1. What amount did each company deduct on the income statement related to inventory?
2. What total amount did each company pay in cash during the period related to inventory?
3. By what amount do your answers in 1 and 2 differ for each company?

4. By what amount did each company's inventory increase (decrease)? By what amount did each company's accounts payable increase (decrease)?
5. Using the indirect method of presentation, what amount(s) must each company add (deduct) from net income to convert from accrual to cash basis?
6. Describe any similarities in your answers to requirements 3 and 5. Are these answers the same? Why or why not?

LO3, 4

E16-12 Reporting Cash Flows from Investing and Financing Activities

Randell Furniture Corporation is a North Carolina–based manufacturer of furniture. In a recent quarter, it reported the following activities:

Net income	$ 4,135
Purchase of property, plant, and equipment	871
Borrowings under line of credit (bank)	1,417
Proceeds from issuance of stock	11
Cash received from customers	29,164
Payments to reduce long-term debt	46
Sale of investments	134
Proceeds from sale of property and equipment	6,594
Dividends paid	277
Interest paid	90

Required:

Based on this information, present the cash flows from investing and financing activities sections of the cash flow statement.

LO3, 4, 5

E16-13 Reporting and Interpreting Cash Flows from Investing and Financing Activities with Discussion of Management Strategy

Gibraltar Steel Corporation is a Buffalo, New York–based manufacturer of steel products. In a recent year, it reported the following activities:

Net income	$ 5,213
Purchase of property, plant, and equipment	10,468
Payments of notes payable (bank)	8,598
Net proceeds of stock issuance	26,061
Depreciation	3,399
Long-term debt reduction	17,832
Proceeds from sale of investments	131
Proceeds from sale of property, plant, and equipment	1,817
Proceeds from long-term debt borrowed	10,242
Decrease in accounts receivable	1,137
Proceeds from notes payable (bank)	3,848

Required:

1. Based on this information, present the cash flows from investing and financing activities sections of the cash flow statement.
2. Referring to your response to requirement 1, comment on what you think Gibraltar's management plan was for the use of the cash generated by the stock issuance.

LO5
Disney

E16-14 Calculating and Interpreting Free Cash Flow

The Disney Company reported the following in its 2007 annual report.

	2007	2006	2005
Net income	$4,687	$3,374	$2,533
Net cash provided by operating activities	5,421	6,058	4,269
Purchase of parks, resorts, and other property	(1,566)	(1,299)	(1,823)
Cash paid for interest	551	617	641
Cash paid for income taxes	2,796	1,857	1,572
Cash paid for dividends	637	519	490

Required:

1. Calculate the total free cash flow for the period covering 2005–2007 and the free cash flow for each year.
2. Interpret the results of your calculation in requirement 1. What do they suggest about the company's need for external financing to acquire property and equipment and pay dividends?

E16-15 Calculating and Interpreting the Quality of Income Ratio

LO5
Disney

Refer to the information about the Disney Company in E16-14.

Required:

1. Calculate to one decimal place the quality of income ratio for each year.
2. Interpret the results of your calculations in requirement 1. Given what you know about the Walt Disney Company from your own personal observations, provide one reason that could explain the sizable difference between net income and net cash provided by operating activities.

E16-16 (Supplement A) Reporting and Interpreting Cash Flows from Operating Activities from an Analyst's Perspective (Direct Method)

Refer to the information for New Vision Company in E16-4.

Required:

1. Present the operating activities section of the statement of cash flows for New Vision Company using the direct method. Assume other accrued liabilities relate to other expenses on the income statement.
2. Of the potential causes of differences between cash flow from operations and net income, which are the most important to financial analysts?

E16-17 (Supplement A) Reporting and Interpreting Cash Flows from Operating Activities from an Analyst's Perspective (Direct Method)

Refer to the information given for E16-5 plus the following summarized income statement for Sizzler, Inc.:

Revenues	$136,500
Cost of sales	45,500
Gross margin	91,000
Salary expense	56,835
Depreciation	33,305
Other expenses	7,781
Net loss before income taxes	(6,921)
Income tax expense	2,561
Net loss	$ (9,482)

Required:

1. Based on this information, compute the cash flow from operating activities using the direct method. Assume prepaid expenses and accrued liabilities relate to other expenses.
2. What were the major reasons that Sizzler was able to report a net loss but positive cash flow from operations?
3. Of the potential causes of differences between cash flow from operations and net income, which are the most important to financial analysts?

E16-18 (Supplement B) Preparing a Statement of Cash Flows, Indirect Method: Complete Spreadsheet

To prepare a statement of cash flows for Golf Champion Store, you examined the company's accounts, noting the following transactions:

a. Purchased equipment, $20,000, and issued a promissory note in full payment.

b. Purchased a long-term investment for cash, $15,000.

c. Paid cash dividend, $12,000.

d. Sold land for $24,000 cash (the land was purchased for $21,000).

e. Issued shares of stock, 500 shares at $12 per share cash.

You also created the following spreadsheet to use when preparing the statement of cash flows.

	Beginning Balances, December 31, 2010	ANALYSIS OF CHANGES Debit	Credit	Ending Balances, December 31, 2011
Income statement items				
Sales			$140,000	
Cost of goods sold		$59,000		
Depreciation		3,000		
Wage expense		28,000		
Income tax expense		9,000		
Interest expense		5,000		
Other expenses		15,800		
Gain on the sale of land			3,000	
Net income		23,200		
Balance sheet items				
Cash	$ 20,500			$ 37,200
Accounts receivable	22,000			22,000
Merchandise inventory	68,000			75,000
Investments	0			15,000
Land	21,000			0
Equipment	114,500			134,500
Total debits	$246,000			$283,700
Accumulated depreciation	$ 32,000			$ 35,000
Accounts payable	17,000			14,000
Wages payable	2,500			1,500
Income taxes payable	3,000			4,500
Notes payable	75,000			95,000
Contributed capital	100,000			106,000
Retained earnings	16,500			27,700
Total credits	$246,000			$283,700
		Inflows	Outflows	
Statement of Cash Flows				
Cash flows from operating activities				
Cash flows from investing activities				
Cash flows from financing activities				
Net increase (decrease) in cash				
Totals				

Required:

Prepare a spreadsheet to prepare the statement of cash flows using the indirect method. Follow the format in Exhibit 16B.1.

Problems—Set A  Available with McGraw-Hill's Homework Manager

PA16-1 Determining Cash Flow Statement Effects of Transactions

LO1

Motif Furniture is an Austin-based furniture company. For each of the following first-quarter transactions, indicate whether operating (O), investing (I), or financing activities (F) are affected and whether the effect is a cash inflow (+) or outflow (−), or (NE) if the transaction has no effect on cash.

_______ 1. Bought used equipment for cash.
_______ 2. Paid cash to purchase new equipment.
_______ 3. Declared and paid cash dividends to stockholders.
_______ 4. Collected payments on account from customers.
_______ 5. Recorded an adjusting entry to record accrued salaries expense.
_______ 6. Recorded and paid interest on debt to creditors.
_______ 7. Repaid principal on loan from bank.
_______ 8. Prepaid rent for the following period.
_______ 9. Made payment to suppliers on account.

PA16-2 Computing Cash Flows from Operating Activities (Indirect Method)

LO2

www.mhhe.com/LLPW1e

The income statement and selected balance sheet information for Direct Products Company for the year ended December 31, 2011, follow.

Income Statement	
Sales revenue	$49,600
Expenses	
Cost of goods sold	21,000
Depreciation expense	2,000
Salaries expense	9,000
Rent expense	4,500
Insurance expense	1,900
Interest expense	1,800
Utilities expense	1,400
Loss on sale of land	1,000
Net income	$ 7,000

Selected Balance Sheet Accounts	2011	2010
Accounts receivable	$560	$580
Merchandise inventory	990	770
Accounts payable	440	460
Salaries payable	100	70
Utilities payable	20	15
Prepaid rent	25	20
Prepaid insurance	25	28

Required:

Prepare the Cash Flows from Operating Activities section of the 2011 statement of cash flows using the indirect method.

PA16-3 Preparing a Statement of Cash Flows (Indirect Method)

LO2, 3, 4, 5

XS Supply Company is developing its annual financial statements at December 31, 2011. The statements are complete except for the statement of cash flows. The completed comparative balance sheets and income statement are summarized:

	2011	2010
Balance sheet at December 31		
Cash	$ 34,000	$ 29,000
Accounts receivable	35,000	28,000
Merchandise inventory	41,000	38,000
Property and equipment	121,000	100,000
Less: Accumulated depreciation	(30,000)	(25,000)
	$201,000	$170,000
Accounts payable	$ 36,000	$ 27,000
Wages payable	1,200	1,400
Note payable, long term	38,000	44,000
Contributed capital	88,600	72,600
Retained earnings	37,200	25,000
	$201,000	$170,000
Income statement for 2011		
Sales	$120,000	
Cost of goods sold	70,000	
Other expenses	37,800	
Net income	$ 12,200	

Additional Data:

a. Bought equipment for cash, $21,000.

b. Paid $6,000 on the long-term note payable.

c. Issued new shares of stock for $16,000 cash.

d. No dividends were declared or paid.

e. Other expenses included depreciation, $5,000; wages, $20,000; taxes, $6,000; other, $6,800.

f. Accounts Payable includes only inventory purchases made on credit. Because there are no liability accounts relating to taxes or other expenses, assume that these expenses were fully paid in cash.

Required:

1. Prepare the statement of cash flows for the year ended December 31, 2011, using the indirect method.
2. Evaluate the statement of cash flows.

LO2, 3, 4, 5

www.mhhe.com/LLPW1e

PA16-4 Preparing and Interpreting a Statement of Cash Flows (Indirect Method)

Heads Up Company was started several years ago by two hockey instructors. The company's comparative balance sheets and income statement with additional information follow.

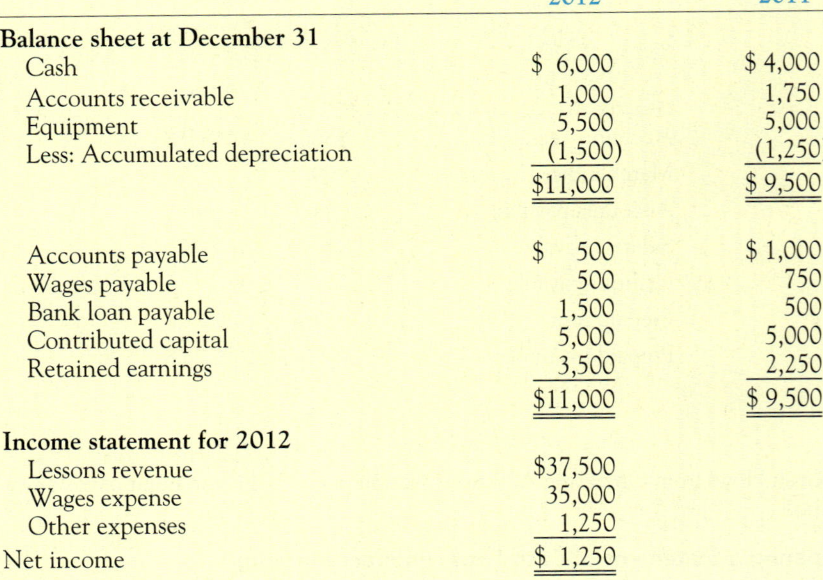

	2012	2011
Balance sheet at December 31		
Cash	$ 6,000	$ 4,000
Accounts receivable	1,000	1,750
Equipment	5,500	5,000
Less: Accumulated depreciation	(1,500)	(1,250)
	$11,000	$ 9,500
Accounts payable	$ 500	$ 1,000
Wages payable	500	750
Bank loan payable	1,500	500
Contributed capital	5,000	5,000
Retained earnings	3,500	2,250
	$11,000	$ 9,500
Income statement for 2012		
Lessons revenue	$37,500	
Wages expense	35,000	
Other expenses	1,250	
Net income	$ 1,250	

Additional Data:

a. Bought new hockey equipment for cash, $500.

b. Borrowed $1,000 cash from the bank during the year.

c. Other expenses included depreciation, $250; rent, $500; taxes, $500.

d. Accounts Payable includes only purchases of services made on credit for operating purposes. Because there are no liability accounts relating to utilities or taxes, assume that these expenses were fully paid in cash.

Required:

1. Prepare the statement of cash flows for the year ended December 31, 2012, using the indirect method.
2. Use the statement of cash flows to evaluate the company's cash flows.

TIP: The demonstration cases provide good examples of information to consider when evaluating cash flows.

PA16-5 (Supplement A) Computing Cash Flows from Operating Activities (Direct Method)

Refer to the information in PA16-2.

Required:

Prepare the cash flows from the operating activities section of the 2011 statement of cash flows using the direct method.

PA16-6 (Supplement A) Preparing and Interpreting a Statement of Cash Flows (Direct Method)

Refer to PA16-4.

Required:

Complete requirements 1 and 2 using the direct method.

Problems—Set B  Available with McGraw-Hill's Homework Manager

PB16-1 Determining Cash Flow Statement Effects of Transactions LO1

Fantatech Inc. designs, develops, and produces high-tech entertainment products, including VirtuaSports, that allow novice players to experience hazardous and difficult real-life sports in virtual reality. The company also produces a 4D theater system that combines 3D visual effects with special effects such as vibrating chairs, simulated drops, and scented air blasts. For each of the following transactions listed in Fantatech's annual report, indicate whether operating (O), investing (I), or financing activities (F) are affected and whether the effect is a cash inflow (+) or outflow (−), or (NE) if the transaction has no effect on cash.

_______1. Received deposits from customers for products to be delivered the following period.

_______2. Principal repayments on loan.

_______3. Paid cash to purchase new equipment.

_______4. Received proceeds from loan.

_______5. Collected payments on account from customers.

_______6. Recorded and paid salaries to employees.

_______7. Paid cash for building construction.

_______8. Recorded and paid interest to debt holders.

PB16-2 Computing Cash Flows from Operating Activities (Indirect Method) LO2

The income statement and selected balance sheet information for Calendars Incorporated for the year ended December 31, 2011, follow.

Income Statement	
Sales revenue	$78,000
Expenses	
Cost of goods sold	36,000
Depreciation expense	16,000
Salaries expense	10,000
Rent expense	2,500
Insurance expense	1,300
Interest expense	1,200
Utilities expense	1,000
Net income	$10,000

Selected Balance Sheet Accounts

	2011	2010
Merchandise inventory	$ 430	$ 490
Accounts receivable	1,800	1,500
Accounts payable	1,200	1,300
Salaries payable	450	300
Utilities payable	100	0
Prepaid rent	50	100
Prepaid insurance	70	90

Required:
Prepare the Cash Flows from Operating Activities section of the 2011 statement of cash flows using the indirect method.

LO2, 3, 4, 5

PB16-3 Preparing a Statement of Cash Flows (Indirect Method)
Audio City, Inc., is developing its annual financial statements at December 31, 2011. The statements are complete except for the statement of cash flows. The completed comparative balance sheets and income statement are summarized:

	2011	2010
Balance sheet at December 31		
Cash	$ 63,000	$ 65,000
Accounts receivable	15,000	20,000
Merchandise inventory	22,000	20,000
Property and equipment	210,000	150,000
Less: Accumulated depreciation	(60,000)	(45,000)
	$250,000	$210,000
Accounts payable	$ 8,000	$ 19,000
Wages payable	2,000	1,000
Note payable, long term	60,000	75,000
Contributed capital	100,000	70,000
Retained earnings	80,000	45,000
	$250,000	$210,000
Income statement for 2011		
Sales	$190,000	
Cost of goods sold	90,000	
Other expenses	60,000	
Net income	$ 40,000	

Additional Data:

a. Bought equipment for cash, $60,000.
b. Paid $15,000 on the long-term note payable.
c. Issued new shares of stock for $30,000 cash.
d. Paid dividends of $5,000 in cash.
e. Other expenses included depreciation, $15,000; wages, $20,000; taxes, $25,000.
f. Accounts Payable includes only inventory purchases made on credit. Because a liability relating to taxes does not exist, assume they were fully paid in cash.

Required:
1. Prepare the statement of cash flows for the year ended December 31, 2011, using the indirect method.
2. Evaluate the statement of cash flows.

PB16-4 Preparing and Interpreting a Statement of Cash Flows (Indirect Method) LO2, 3, 4, 5

Dive In Company was started several years ago by two diving instructors. The company's comparative balance sheets and income statement with additional information follow.

	2012	2011
Balance sheet at December 31		
Cash	$ 3,200	$ 4,000
Accounts receivable	1,000	500
Prepaid expenses	100	50
	$ 4,300	$ 4,550
Wages payable	$ 350	$ 1,100
Contributed capital	1,200	1,000
Retained earnings	2,750	2,450
	$ 4,300	$ 4,550
Income statement for 2012		
Lessons revenue	$33,950	
Wages expense	30,000	
Other expenses	3,650	
Net income	$ 300	

Additional Data:

a. Prepaid expenses relate to rent paid in advance.
b. Other operating expenses were paid in cash.
c. An owner contributed capital by paying $200 cash in exchange for the company's stock.

Required:

1. Prepare the statement of cash flows for the year ended December 31, 2012, using the indirect method.
2. Use the statement of cash flows to evaluate the company's cash flows.

PB16-5 (Supplement A) Computing Cash Flows from Operating Activities (Direct Method)

Refer to the information in PB16-2.

Required:

Prepare the Cash Flows from Operating Activities section of the 2011 statement of cash flows using the direct method.

PB16-6 (Supplement A) Preparing and Interpreting a Statement of Cash Flows (Direct Method)

Refer to PB16-4.

Required:

Complete requirements 1 and 2 using the direct method.

Cases and Projects

CP16-1 Finding Financial Information LO1, 5

Refer to the financial statements of The Home Depot in Appendix A at the end of this book, or download the annual report from the *Cases* section of the text's Web site at www.mhhe.com/LLPW1e.

Required:

1. Which of the two basic reporting approaches for the cash flows from operating activities did The Home Depot use?
2. What amount of tax payments did The Home Depot make during the current year? Where did you find this information?
3. In the most recent year reported, The Home Depot generated $5,727 million from operating activities. Where did The Home Depot spend this money? List the two largest cash outflows.

LO1, 5

CP16-2 Comparing Financial Information

Lowe's

Refer to the financial statements of The Home Depot in Appendix A and Lowe's in Appendix B at the end of this book, or download the annual reports from the *Cases* section of the text's Web site at www.mhhe.com/LLPW1e.

Required:

1. Which of the two basic reporting approaches for the cash flows from operating activities did Lowe's use? Is this the same as what The Home Depot used?
2. What amount of cash did Lowe's receive during fiscal 2007 from issuing long-term debt?
3. In fiscal 2007, Lowe's generated $4,347 million from operating activities. Where did Lowe's spend this money? List the two largest cash outflows reported in the investing or financing activities sections. Do Lowe's uses differ significantly from The Home Depot's?

LO5

CP16-3 Examining an Annual Report: Internet-Based Team Research

As a team, select an industry to analyze. Using your Web browser, each team member should acquire the annual report or 10-K for one publicly traded company in the industry, with each member selecting a different company. (See CP1-3 in Chapter 1 for a description of possible resources for these tasks.)

Required:

1. On an individual basis, each team member should write a short report that incorporates the following:
   a. Has the company generated positive or negative operating cash flows during the past three years?
   b. Has the company been expanding over the period? If so, what appears to have been the source of financing for this expansion (operating cash flow, additional borrowing, issuance of stock)?
   c. Compute and analyze the quality of income ratio in each of the past three years.
2. Then, as a team, write a short report comparing and contrasting your companies using these attributes. Discuss any patterns across the companies that you as a team observe. Provide potential explanations for any differences discovered.

LO1, 2, 5

CP16-4 Making Ethical Decisions: A Mini Case

Assume you serve on the board of a local golf and country club. In preparation for renegotiating the club's bank loans, the president indicates that the club needs to increase its operating cash flows before the end of the current year. With a wink and sly smile, the club's treasurer reassures the president and other board members that he knows a couple of ways to boost the club's operating cash flows. First, he says, the club can sell some of its accounts receivable to a collections company that is willing to pay the club $97,000 up front for the right to collect $100,000 of the overdue accounts. That will immediately boost operating cash flows. Second, he indicates that the club paid about $200,000 last month to relocate the 18th fairway and green closer to the clubhouse. The treasurer indicates that although these costs have been reported as expenses in the club's own monthly financial statements, he feels an argument can be made for reporting them as part of land and land improvements (a long-lived asset) in the year-end financial statements that would be provided to the bank. He explains that, by recording these payments as an addition to a long-lived asset, they will not be shown as a reduction in operating cash flows.

Required:

1. Does the sale of accounts receivable to generate immediate cash harm or mislead anyone? Would you consider it an ethical business activity?
2. If cash is spent on long-lived assets, such as land improvements, how is it typically classified in the statement of cash flows? If cash is spent on expenses, such as costs for regular upkeep of the grounds, how is it typically classified in the statement of cash flows?
3. What facts are relevant to deciding whether the costs of the 18th hole relocation should be reported as an asset or as an expense? Is it appropriate to make this decision based on the impact it could have on operating cash flows?
4. As a member of the board, how would you ensure that an ethical decision is made?

LO2

CP16-5 Thinking Critically: Interpreting Adjustments Reported on the Statement of Cash Flows from a Management Perspective (Indirect Method)

QuickServe, a chain of convenience stores, was experiencing some serious cash flow difficulties because of rapid growth. The company did not generate sufficient cash from operating activities to finance its new stores, and creditors were not willing to lend money because the company had not produced any income for the previous three years. The new controller for QuickServe proposed a reduction in the estimated life of store equipment to increase depreciation expense; thus, "we can improve cash flows from operating activities because depreciation expense is added back on the statement of cash flows." Other executives were not sure that this was a good idea because the increase in depreciation would make it more difficult to have positive earnings: "Without income, the bank will never lend us money."

Required:

What action would you recommend for QuickServe? Why?

CP16-6 Using a Spreadsheet that Calculates Cash Flows from Operating Activities (Indirect Method) LO2

You've recently been hired by B2B Consultants to provide financial advisory services to small business managers. B2B's clients often need advice on how to improve their operating cash flows and, given your accounting background, you are frequently called upon to show them how operating cash flows would change if they were to speed up their sales of inventory and their collections of accounts receivable or delay their payment of accounts payable. Each time you are asked to show the effects of these business decisions on the cash flows from operating activities, you get the uneasy feeling that you might inadvertently miscalculate their effects. To deal with this once and for all, you e-mail your friend Owen and ask him to prepare a template that automatically calculates the net operating cash flows from a simple comparative balance sheet. You received his reply today.

From: Owentheaccountant@yahoo.com
To: Helpme@hotmail.com
Cc:
Subject: Excel Help

Hey, pal. I like your idea of working smarter, not harder. Too bad it involved me doing the thinking. Anyhow, I've created a spreadsheet file that contains four worksheets. The first two tabs (labeled BS and IS) are the input sheets where you would enter the numbers from each client's comparative balance sheet and income statement. Your clients are small, so this template allows for only the usual accounts. Also, I've assumed that depreciation is the only reason for a change in accumulated depreciation. If your clients' business activities differ from these, you'll need to contact me for more complex templates. The third worksheet calculates the operating cash flows using the indirect method, and the fourth does this calculation using the direct method. I'll attach the screenshots of each of the worksheets so you can create your own. To answer "what if" questions, all you'll need to do is change selected amounts in the balance sheet and income statement.

Microsoft Excel

	B	C	D	E
2	Small Business Client			
3	Balance Sheet			
4	As of December 31			
5	ASSETS	Current Year	Prior Year	Change
6	Cash	$ 8,000	$ 12,000	-4,000
7	Accounts receivable	16,900	8,500	+8,400
8	Inventories	37,600	25,900	+11,700
9	Total Current Assets	62,500	46,400	
10	Property, plant, and equipment	105,000	105,000	0
11	Less: accumulated depreciation	(20,000)	(10,000)	-10,000
12	*Total Assets*	$ 147,500	$ 141,400	
13	LIABILITIES			
14	Accounts payable	$ 31,400	$ 30,000	+1,400
15	Income taxes payable	3,000	4,000	-1,000
16	Interest payable	4,000	1,800	+2,200
17	Other accrued liabilities	11,000	14,000	-3,000
18	Total Current Liabilities	49,400	49,800	
19	Long-term debt	40,000	40,000	0
20	Total Liabilities	89,400	89,800	
21	STOCKHOLDERS' EQUITY			
22	Contributed Capital	10,000	10,000	0
23	Retained Earnings	48,100	41,600	+6,500
24	Total Stockholders' Equity	58,100	51,600	
25	*Total Liabilities and Stockholders' Equity*	$ 147,500	$ 141,400	

BS / IS / Indirect / Direct

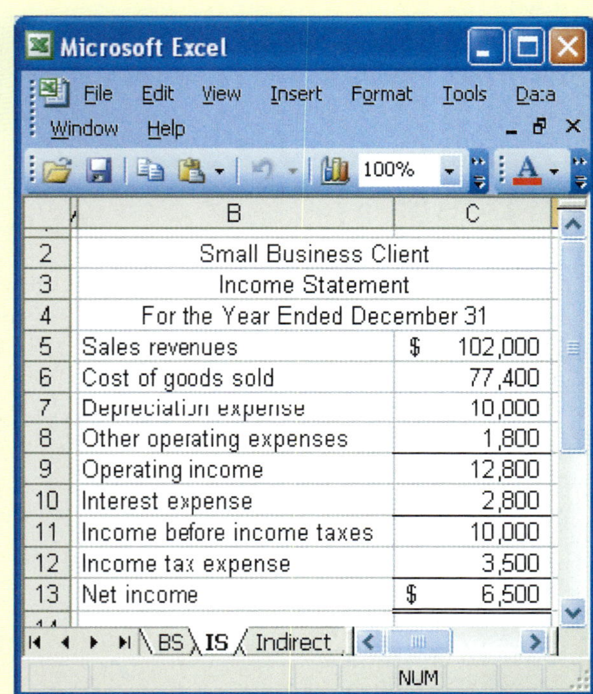

	B	C
2	Small Business Client	
3	Income Statement	
4	For the Year Ended December 31	
5	Sales revenues	$ 102,000
6	Cost of goods sold	77,400
7	Depreciation expense	10,000
8	Other operating expenses	1,800
9	Operating income	12,800
10	Interest expense	2,800
11	Income before income taxes	10,000
12	Income tax expense	3,500
13	Net income	$ 6,500

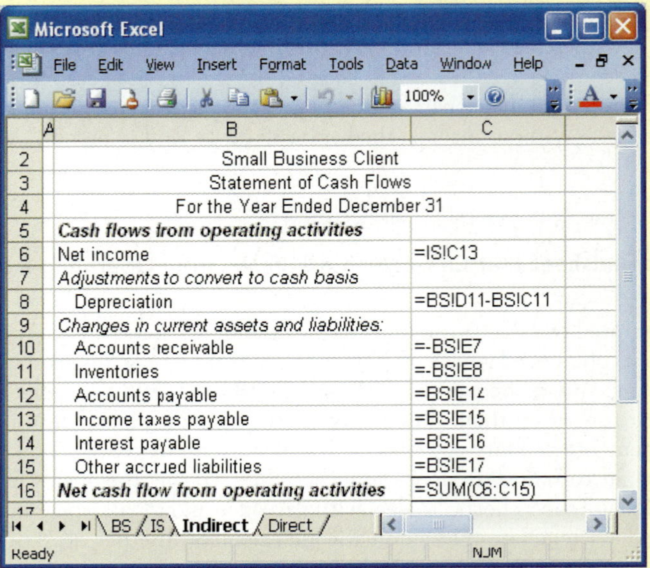

	A	B	C
2		Small Business Client	
3		Statement of Cash Flows	
4		For the Year Ended December 31	
5		***Cash flows from operating activities***	
6		Net income	=IS!C13
7		*Adjustments to convert to cash basis*	
8		Depreciation	=BS!D11-BS!C11
9		*Changes in current assets and liabilities:*	
10		Accounts receivable	=-BS!E7
11		Inventories	=-BS!E8
12		Accounts payable	=BS!E14
13		Income taxes payable	=BS!E15
14		Interest payable	=BS!E16
15		Other accrued liabilities	=BS!E17
16		***Net cash flow from operating activities***	=SUM(C6:C15)

Required:

Copy the information from the worksheets for the balance sheet, income statement, and statement of cash flows (indirect method only) into a spreadsheet file. What was the net cash flow from operating activities?

17 Financial Statement Analysis

LEARNING OBJECTIVES

After completing this chapter, you should be able to:

LO1 Describe how financial statement information is communicated to external users.

Lectured presentations–17-1
www.mhhe.com/LLPW1e

LO2 Use horizontal (trend) analysis to recognize financial changes that unfold over time.

LO3 Use vertical (common size) analysis to understand important relationships within financial statements.

LO4 Calculate and use financial ratios to assess profitability, liquidity, and solvency.

Focus Company: LOWE'S

"Let's Build Something Together"

www.lowes.com

Measuring and evaluating financial performance is like judging gymnastics or figure skating at the Olympics. You have to know three things: (1) the general categories to evaluate for each event, (2) the particular elements to consider within each category, and (3) how to measure performance for each element. On the financial side, analysts follow the same process. They evaluate general categories such as profitability, liquidity, and solvency, which are separated into particular elements such as gross profit margin and net profit margin. For each of these elements, analysts measure performance by computing various percentages and ratios, which themselves are based on information reported in the financial statements.

In this chapter, we focus on Lowe's, the second largest home improvement retailer in the world. Lowe's is a giant with nearly 1,400 stores and 210,000 employees. Yet the company's continued success still requires innovations to increase sales in existing markets and to successfully enter new markets. At the same time, Lowe's must control costs while maintaining a high level of customer service in their stores. Finally, Lowe's management must anticipate the actions of its larger rival, The Home Depot, and deal with changes in overall demand for building products over which it has no control.

How do analysts, investors, and creditors assess Lowe's success in meeting these challenges? This is the purpose of financial statement analysis. Our discussion begins with an explanation of how companies release their financial statement information and where that information can be found. We then explain how to use trend and ratio analysis to understand the financial results of a company's business activities. We conclude the chapter with a review of the key accounting decisions analysts consider when evaluating financial statements.

ORGANIZATION OF THE CHAPTER

RELEASE OF FINANCIAL INFORMATION	HORIZONTAL (TREND) ANALYSIS	VERTICAL (COMMON SIZE) ANALYSIS	FINANCIAL RATIOS
• Preliminary Press Release • Quarterly and Annual Reports • Securities and Exchange Commission (SEC) Filings • Investor Information Web Sites	• Preparing Comparative Balance Sheets and Comparative Income Statements • Revealing Changes through Trend Analyses	• Preparing a Common Size Balance Sheet and Income Statement • Interpreting Common Size Statements	• Profitability Ratios • Liquidity Ratios • Solvency Ratios • Accounting Decisions and Ratio Analysis

RELEASE OF FINANCIAL INFORMATION

Preliminary Press Release

Learning Objective 1

Describe how financial statement information is communicated to external users.

To provide timely information to external users, public companies such as Lowe's announce their annual and quarterly financial results in a press release sent to news agencies three to five weeks after the accounting period ends. The press release typically includes key figures, a discussion of the results of the company's business activities, and a condensed income statement and balance sheet. During the time between the end of the company's year and the date of the press release, accountants are busy making adjusting journal entries and preparing the financial statements, and managers are preparing their analysis and discussion of the results.

Video 17-1
www.mhhe.com/LLPW1e

Today, many companies, including Lowe's, follow up the press release with a conference call that is broadcast over the Internet. This call allows analysts to grill senior executives about the company's financial results. By listening to these calls, investors can learn much about a company's business strategy, its expectations for the future, and the key factors analysts consider when they evaluate a company. (To access this useful source of information, visit a company's Web site or check the archive of conference calls at biz.yahoo.com/cc.)

Quarterly and Annual Reports

Several weeks after the preliminary press release, public companies release their complete financial statements as part of the annual or quarterly report. The annual report has two main sections. The first half usually begins with a friendly letter to investors from the company's CEO followed by glossy photographs of the company's products and glowing commentaries on the company's brilliant future. After developing the right mood with these jazzy marketing tactics, the company then presents the financial section, the meat and potatoes of the report. See Exhibit 17.1 for a list of the typical elements of the financial section and the information they contain. The third column of the exhibit gives the pages in Appendix A (at the end of this book) where you will find an example of each element.

A company's quarterly report looks like a condensed version of its annual report. Following a short letter to stockholders and abbreviated discussion of the financial results, a quarterly report presents a condensed income statement for the quarter, a condensed balance sheet dated at the end of the quarter, and a condensed statement of cash flows. These condensed financial statements typically show less detail than the annual statements, often omitting the statement of retained earnings or stockholders' equity and many notes to the financial statements. Items 4, 7, 8, and 9 in Exhibit 17.1 are typically omitted. Because the quarterly financial statements are not audited, they are labeled unaudited. With these limitations, the quarterly reports are not as informative as the annual reports, but they are released on a timelier basis (every three months rather than every year). So, they also have a major impact on investor and creditor judgments about the company.

Exhibit 17.1 Typical Elements of the Financial Section of an Annual Report

Name of Financial Section	Information Presented
1. Summarized financial data	• Key figures covering a period of 5 or 10 years
2. Management's discussion and analysis (MD&A)	• Honest and detailed analysis of the company's financial condition and operating results—a must-read for any serious financial statement user
3. Management's report on internal control	• Statements that describe management's responsibility for ensuring adequate internal control over financial reporting and report on the effectiveness of those controls during the year
4. Auditor's report	• Auditor's conclusion about whether GAAP was followed (and for public companies, whether internal controls were effective)
5. Comparative financial statements	• Multiyear presentation of the four basic statements
6. Financial statement notes	• Further information about the financial statements, crucial to understanding the financial statement data
7. Recent stock price data	• Brief summary of highs and lows during the year
8. Unaudited quarterly data	• Condensed summary of each quarter's results
9. Directors and officers	• List of the individuals who are overseeing and running the company

Securities and Exchange Commission (SEC) Filings

To ensure that timely information is available to investors, the SEC requires public companies to file certain reports with the SEC electronically. These reports include an annual report on Form 10-K, quarterly reports on Form 10-Q, and current event reports on Form 8-K. Several of these reports include information beyond that reported in the quarterly or annual reports. For example, Lowe's 2006 10-K describes the significant business risks the company faces and outlines the strategies for addressing those risks. The 8-K reports significant business events that occurred between financial statement dates, such as the acquisition of another company or a change in auditor.

These filings are available to the public as soon as the SEC's Electronic Data Gathering and Retrieval Service (EDGAR) receives them. As a result, most users can get all the details of a company's financial results from the SEC filings several weeks before the company's glossy reports reach them in the mail. (To find a company's SEC filings, click on "Search for Company Filings" at www.sec.gov.)

Investor Information Web Sites

Investor information Web sites such as Hoovers.com, TheStreet.com, Fool.com, and Yahoo!Finance offer information about public companies. Some sections of these Web sites provide useful information for evaluating and predicting a company's financial performance. For example, at Yahoo!Finance, you can obtain valuable financial information about Lowe's and its industry sector including financial ratios similar to those you will read about later in this chapter. It is important to note that many Web sites do not show the formulas used to calculate the ratios. That can be a serious drawback because ratios and amounts with similar-sounding names may be calculated differently.

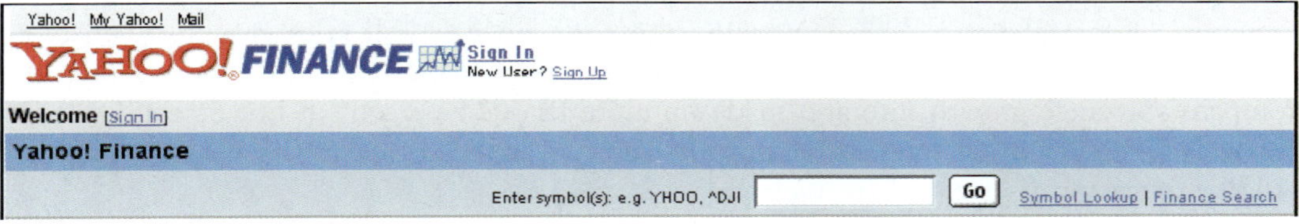

Most good stories have a plot, one the reader comes to understand as it unfolds over time. In the same way, the story of a business and its activities unfolds gradually. To understand and evaluate the results of business activities, then, you need to look at a company over time from many different angles. Only after you have combined the results of all your evaluations into a complete story will you understand whether or not a business is truly successful and why. The first financial analysis tool that we discuss is horizontal or trend analysis.

HORIZONTAL (TREND) ANALYSIS

Learning Objective 2

Use horizontal (trend) analysis to recognize financial changes that unfold over time.

Horizontal (trend) analysis helps financial statement users to recognize financial changes that unfold over time. This approach compares individual financial statement items from year to year with the general goal of identifying significant sustained changes or trends. For example, trend analysis can be used to determine the dollar and percentage changes in the cost of goods sold this year relative to prior years. Because this type of analysis compares the results on each line of the financial statements across several years, trend analysis is also known as horizontal analysis. Because it compares results over a series of periods, it is sometimes called **time-series analysis.**

Preparing Comparative Balance Sheets and Comparative Income Statements

Regardless of the name, trend analyses are usually calculated in terms of year-to-year dollar and percentage changes. A year-to-year percentage change expresses the current year's dollar change as a percentage of the prior year's total by using the following calculation:

$$\text{Year-to-Year Change (\%)} = \frac{\text{Change This Year}}{\text{Prior Year's Total}} \times 100 = \frac{(\text{Current Year's Total} - \text{Prior Year's Total})}{\text{Prior Year's Total}} \times 100$$

To demonstrate how to calculate a trend, we analyze Lowe's financial statements. Summaries of Lowe's balance sheets and income statements from three recent years appear in Exhibits 17.2 and 17.3. Dollar and percentage changes from fiscal year 2005 to 2006[1] are shown to the right of the balance sheet and income statement. The dollar changes were calculated by subtracting the 2005 balances from the 2006 balances. The percentage changes were calculated by dividing those differences by the 2005 balances. For example, according to Exhibit 17.2, Cash decreased by \$59 = (\$364 − \$423) in 2006 relative to 2005 (all numbers in millions). That dollar amount represented a decrease of 13.9% [= (\$59 ÷ \$423) × 100]. To avoid focusing on unimportant changes, use the percentage changes to identify potentially significant changes and then check the dollar change to make sure that it too is significant.

Revealing Changes through Trend Analyses

Data in Exhibits 17.2 and 17.3 indicate that Lowe's grew significantly in 2006 despite a slowdown in the housing market. Exhibit 17.2, for example, shows that total assets increased approximately 12.7 percent in 2006. Similarly, Exhibit 17.3 shows that net sales revenues, gross profit, and net income also rose in 2006 by 8.5, 9.5, and 12.3 percent, respectively.

The major drivers of these changes are explained in the Management's Discussion and Analysis (MD&A) section of the company's 2006 annual report. Lowe's opened 155 new stores in 2006 and was planning to open more than 400 additional stores in the future. Installed sales, which reflect a trend away from do-it-yourself projects and toward do-it-for-me projects, increased by 9 percent in 2006, outpacing the company's overall sales growth. Even more impressive was growth in sales to commercial businesses, which grew at nearly double the company's average growth rate and made up more than 25 percent of Lowe's total sales in 2006. To expand online sales, the company also continued to refine the functionality and product offerings on its corporate Web site.

[1] Like many retail companies, Lowe's fiscal year ends at the end of January.

Exhibit 17.2 Trend (Horizontal) Analysis of Lowe's Summarized Balance Sheets Lowe's

Lowe's
Balance Sheets
(in millions)

			INCREASE (DECREASE)	
Year Ended:	**Fiscal 2006**	**Fiscal 2005**	**Amount**	**Percent**
ASSETS				
Current assets				
Cash	$ 364	$ 423	$ (59)	(13.9)%
Short-term investments	432	453	(21)	(4.6)
Accounts receivable			—	0.0
Inventories	7,144	6,635	509	7.7
Other current assets	374	277	97	35.0
Total current assets	8,314	7,788	526	6.8
Property and equipment, net	18,971	16,354	2,617	16.0
Long-term Investments and other assets	482	497	(15)	(3.0)
Total assets	$27,767	$24,639	$3,128	12.7
LIABILITIES and STOCKHOLDERS' EQUITY				
Current liabilities	$ 6,539	$ 5,832	$ 707	12.1
Long-term liabilities	5,503	4,511	992	22.0
Total liabilities	12,042	10,343	1,699	16.4
Stockholders' equity	15,725	14,296	1,429	10.0
Total liabilities and stockholders' equity	$27,767	$24,639	$3,128	12.7

Exhibit 17.3 Trend (Horizontal) Analysis of Lowe's Summarized Income Statements Lowe's

Lowe's
Income Statements
(in millions)

			INCREASE (DECREASE)	
Year Ended:	**Fiscal 2006**	**Fiscal 2005**	**Amount**	**Percent**
Net sales revenue	$46,927	$43,243	$3,684	8.5%
Cost of revenues	30,729	28,453	2,276	8.0
Gross profit	16,198	14,790	1,408	9.5
Operating and other expenses	11,046	10,136	910	9.0
Interest expense	154	158	(4)	(2.5)
Income tax expense	1,893	1,731	162	9.4
Net income	$ 3,105	$ 2,765	$ 340	12.3
Earnings per share	$ 2.02	$ 1.78	$ 0.24	13.5

In sum, the story told by our trend analysis is that Lowe's grew significantly from 2005 to 2006. While that growth increased sales and gross profit, it also increased operating expenses. Fortunately, the growth in sales more than offset the growth in expenses.

Learning Objective 3

Use vertical (common size) analysis to understand important relationships within financial statements.

VERTICAL (COMMON SIZE) ANALYSIS

A second type of analysis, **vertical (common size) analysis**, focuses on important relationships within financial statements. When a company is growing or shrinking overall, it is difficult to tell from the dollar amounts whether the proportions within each statement category are changing. Common size financial statements provide this information by expressing each financial statement amount as a percentage of another amount on that statement. The usefulness of common size statements is illustrated by the fact that Lowe's presents its balance sheet and income statements in the common size format illustrated in Exhibits 17.4 and 17.5.

Exhibit 17.4 Vertical (Common Size) Analysis of Lowe's Summarized Balance Sheets — Lowe's

Lowe's
Balance Sheets
(in millions)

	FISCAL 2006		FISCAL 2005	
Year Ended	**Amount**	**Percent**	**Amount**	**Percent**
ASSETS				
Current assets				
Cash	$ 364	1.3%	$ 423	1.7%
Short-term investments	432	1.6	453	1.8
Inventories	7,144	25.7	6,635	26.9
Other current assets	374	1.3	277	1.1
Property and equipment, net	18,971	68.3	16,354	66.4
Long-term investments and other assets	482	1.7	497	2.0
Total assets	$27,767	100.0%	$24,639	100.0%
LIABILITIES and STOCKHOLDERS' EQUITY				
Current liabilities	$ 6,539	23.5%	$ 5,832	23.7%
Long-term liabilities	5,503	19.8	4,511	18.3
Stockholders' equity	15,725	56.6	14,296	58.0
Total liabilities and stockholders' equity	$27,767	100.0%	$24,639	100.0%

Exhibit 17.5 Vertical (Common Size) Analysis of Lowe's Summarized Income Statements — Lowe's

Lowe's
Income Statements
(in millions)

	FISCAL 2006		FISCAL 2005	
Year Ended	**Amount**	**Percent**	**Amount**	**Percent**
Net sales revenue	$46,927	100.0%	$43,243	100.0%
Cost of revenues	30,729	65.5	28,453	65.8
Gross profit	16,198	34.5	14,790	34.2
Operating and other expenses	11,046	23.5	10,136	23.4
Interest expense	154	0.3	158	0.4
Income tax expense	1,893	4.0	1,731	4.0
Net income	$ 3,105	6.6%	$ 2,765	6.4%

Preparing a Common Size Balance Sheet and Income Statement

In a common size balance sheet, each asset appears as a percent of total assets, and each liability or stockholders' equity item appears as a percent of total liabilities and stockholders' equity. For example, in Exhibit 17.4, which presents Lowe's common size balance sheets, cash was 1.3% of total assets [= ($364 ÷ $27,767) × 100] at the end of fiscal 2006.

The common size income statement reports each income statement item as a percentage of sales. For example, cost of revenues was equal to 65.5 percent of net sales revenue in 2006 [= ($30,729 ÷ $46,927) × 100]. Exhibit 17.5 presents common size income statements for Lowe's for 2005 and 2006.

Interpreting Common Size Statements

Although Lowe's balance sheet indicates growth during 2006, the common size balance sheet suggests that the increase on the assets side reflected relative increases in property and equipment resulting from the opening of new stores combined with relative declines in most other assets as a percentage of total assets. The decline in inventory reflects both lower costs of certain materials sold by Lowe's and the expected slowdown in the housing market in 2007. These increases in assets were financed more by increases in long-term liabilities than by current liabilities or stockholders' equity as evidenced by the increase in the long-term liabilities percentage.

The common size income statements tell us how Lowe's was able to increase its net income as a percent of sales from 6.4 percent to 6.6 percent. Lowe's accomplished this feat by reducing cost of goods sold as a percent of sales by 0.3 percent, which was partially offset by small increases in operating and other expenses. In its MD&A, Lowe's explains the improvement as resulting from a shift in sales mix to more profitable products and a switch to lower cost foreign-made products. A 0.3 percent decrease in cost of goods sold as a percent of sales may seem to be a small effect at first. But this improvement accounted for $141 million of Lowe's net income for 2006.

These findings from the vertical (common size) analysis are consistent with the results of the horizontal (trend) analysis discussed earlier. Opening 155 new stores involves a significant additional investment in property and equipment and start-up efforts at the new stores tend to add to other operating expenses.

For the year ended January 28, 2007, The Home Depot reported net income of $5.76 billion on sales of $90.8 billion. If the company's cost of sales in fiscal 2006 was $61.1 billion, what percentages would be shown on a common size income statement for gross profit and net income? If sales were $81.5 billion in 2005, what was the year-to-year percentage increase in 2006? Round your answers to one decimal place.

$$\text{Gross Profit Percentage} = \frac{(\$____ - ____)\text{ billion}}{\$90.8\text{ billion}} \times 100$$

$$\text{Net Profit Margin} = \frac{\$5.76\text{ billion}}{\$____} \times 100$$

$$\text{Sales Increase (Percentage)} = \frac{(\$____ - ____)\text{ billion}}{\$____\text{ billion}} \times 100$$

After you have finished, check your answers with the solution at the bottom of the page.

Solution to Self-Study Practice

Gross profit percentage = [($90.8 − $61.1) ÷ 90.8] × 100
= 32.7%
Net profit margin = [$(5.76) ÷ 90.8] × 100 = 6.3%
Sales increase (percentage) = [($90.8 − $81.5) ÷ 81.5] ÷ 100
= 11.4%

FINANCIAL RATIOS

Learning Objective 4

Calculate and use financial ratios to assess profitability, liquidity, and solvency.

Ratio analyses help financial statement users to understand relationships among various items reported in the financial statements. This type of analysis compares the amounts for one or more line items to the amounts for other line items in the same year. Like common size statements, ratio analyses are useful because they consider differences in the size of the amounts being compared, which allows users to evaluate how well a company has performed given the level of its other resources. In fact, some of the most popular ratios, such as net profit margin and debt to assets ratios, are taken directly from the common size statements.

Most analysts classify ratios into three categories:

1. Profitability ratios, which relate to the company's performance in the current period—in particular, the company's ability to generate income.
2. Liquidity ratios, which relate to the company's short-term survival—in particular, the company's ability to use current assets to repay liabilities as they become due.
3. Solvency ratios, which relate to the company's long-run survival—in particular, the company's ability to repay lenders when debt matures and to make the required interest payments prior to the date of maturity.

These three categories emphasize different aspects of a company's performance, which may or may not be important depending on the purpose of the analysis.

In the next section, we demonstrate how to calculate financial trends and ratios. We must emphasize at the start, however, that **no analysis is complete unless it leads to an interpretation that helps financial statement users to understand and evaluate a company's financial results.** Without interpretation, trends and ratios are nothing more than a list of apparently unrelated numbers. See Exhibit 17.6 for a summary of the most commonly used ratios, many of which were introduced in Chapters 4–16, categorized as profitability, liquidity, or solvency ratios.

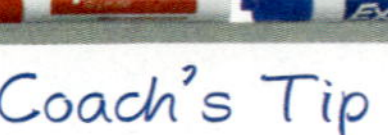

Coach's Tip

Industry averages are reported in the *Annual Statement Studies* published by the Risk Management Association. You can also get industry averages from reuters.com/finance or finance.yahoo.com, which were available free of charge at the time this book was written.

As you have seen in other chapters, benchmarks help to interpret a company's ratios. Benchmarks can include the company's prior year results and those of close competitors, as well as industry averages. In a competitive economy, companies strive to outperform one another, so comparisons with other companies can suggest which are likely to survive and thrive in the long run.

For Lowe's, the industry average encompasses home improvement stores of all sizes and types. The Home Depot, the largest home improvement retailer in the world, is Lowe's closest competitor, with 2,147 stores located in the United States, Canada, China, and Mexico. (Both Lowe's and The Home Depot's annual reports for fiscal 2007 are reproduced in Appendix A and B at the end of this book.) Lowe's is the second largest company in the industry. Its customer-oriented marketing strategy focuses on attracting women. The Home Depot's marketing strategy focuses on contractors and other experienced builders as well as homeowners with a do-it-yourself attitude. In the following sections, we compare Lowe's financial ratios to the prior year and in some cases to those for The Home Depot and the industry as a whole.

Profitability Ratios

The financial analyses in this section focus on the level of profits Lowe's generated during the period. We will compute and interpret ratios (1) through (8) in Exhibit 17.6. The computation shown for each ratio is for 2006 and is based on the statements in Exhibits 17.4 and 17.5. Our first two profitability ratios come right from the common size income statement in Exhibit 17.5.

Net Profit Margin

Net profit margin indicates the percentage of sales revenues that remain in net income after expenses have been deducted. Using the equation in Exhibit 17.6, Lowe's net profit margin in each of the last two years was:

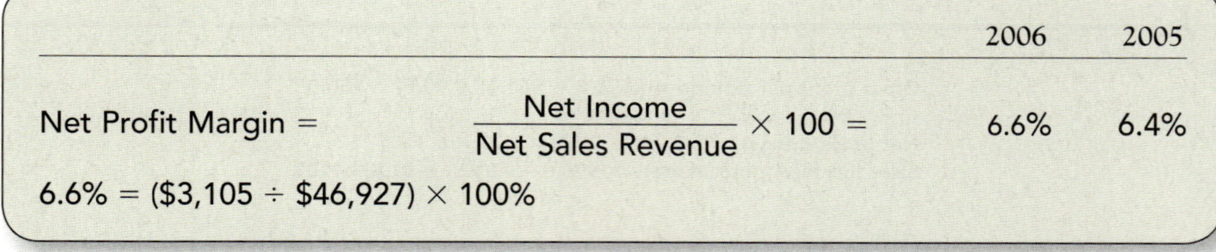

		2006	2005
Net Profit Margin =	$\frac{\text{Net Income}}{\text{Net Sales Revenue}} \times 100 =$	6.6%	6.4%

6.6% = (\$3,105 ÷ \$46,927) × 100%

Exhibit 17.6 Common Ratios Used in Financial Statement Analysis

Profitability Ratios

(1) Net Profit Margin = $\dfrac{\text{Net Income}}{\text{Net Sales Revenue}} \times 100$

(2) Gross Profit Percentage = $\dfrac{\text{Net Sales Revenue} - \text{Cost of Goods Sold}}{\text{Net Sales Revenue}} \times 100$

(3) Asset Turnover = $\dfrac{\text{Net Sales Revenue}}{\text{Average Total Assets}}$

(4) Fixed Asset Turnover = $\dfrac{\text{Net Sales Revenue}}{\text{Average Net Fixed Assets}}$

(5) Return on Assets (ROA) = $\dfrac{\text{Net Income*}}{\text{Average Total Assets}} \times 100$

(6) Return on Equity (ROE) = $\dfrac{\text{Net Income}}{\text{Average Stockholders' Equity}} \times 100$

(7) Earnings per Share (EPS) = $\dfrac{\text{Net Income} - \text{Preferred Dividends}}{\text{Average Number of Common Shares Outstanding}}$

(8) Price/Earnings = $\dfrac{\text{Stock Price}}{\text{EPS}}$

Liquidity Ratios

(9) Receivables Turnover = $\dfrac{\text{Net Sales Revenue}}{\text{Average Net Receivables}}$

Days to Collect = $\dfrac{365}{\text{Receivables Turnover Ratio}}$

(10) Inventory Turnover = $\dfrac{\text{Cost of Goods Sold}}{\text{Average Inventory}}$

Days to Sell = $\dfrac{365}{\text{Inventory Turnover Ratio}}$

(11) Current Ratio = $\dfrac{\text{Current Assets}}{\text{Current Liabilities}}$

(12) Quick Ratio = $\dfrac{\text{Quick Assets}}{\text{Current Liabilities}}$

Solvency Ratios

(13) Debt to Assets = $\dfrac{\text{Total Liabilities}}{\text{Total Assets}}$

(14) Times Interest Earned = $\dfrac{\text{Net Income} + \text{Interest Expense} + \text{Income Tax Expense}}{\text{Interest Expense}}$

(15) Free Cash Flow = Net Cash Flow from Operating Activities − Purchases of Property and Equipment − Dividends Paid

* In more complex ROA analyses, interest expense (net of tax) and minority interest are added back to net income in the numerator because the ratio assesses return on capital independent of source.

The net profit margin of 6.6 percent for 2006 indicates that for each dollar of sales, Lowe's generated 6.6 cents of net income. That is quite good compared to the average home improvement retailer, which according to Yahoo!Finance enjoyed a net profit margin of 5.9 percent that year. The seemingly small increase from 6.4 percent in 2005 to 6.6 percent in 2006 was significant, yielding an additional $94 million in profit on the company's $47 billion in sales.

Gross Profit Percentage

Our earlier analysis indicated that Lowe's gross profits from 2005 to 2006 increased in terms of total dollars, but it did not indicate whether those increases were caused by more total sales or more profit per sale. The gross profit percentage is particularly helpful in this kind of analysis because it indicates how much profit was made, on average, on each dollar of sales after deducting the cost of goods sold. Lowe's gross profit percentage for the last two years was:

	2006	2005
$\text{Gross Profit Percentage} = \dfrac{\text{Net Sales} - \text{Cost of Goods Sold}}{\text{Net Sales}} \times 100 =$	34.5%	34.2%
34.5% = [($46,927 − $30,729) ÷ $46,927] × 100		

This analysis shows that in 2006, after payment of the cost of merchandise sold, 34.5 cents of each sales dollar were left to cover other costs, such as employee wages, advertising, and utilities and to provide profits to the stockholders. The increase in the gross profit percentage from 2005 to 2006 (34.5% − 34.2%) means that Lowe's made 0.3¢ more gross profit on each dollar of sales in 2006 than in 2005. There are two potential explanations for this increase: (1) Lowe's charged higher selling prices without paying a corresponding increase in the cost of merchandise and (2) Lowe's obtained merchandise at a lower unit cost. The MD&A section of Lowe's annual report explains that the increase in gross profit percentage came from a reduction in the cost of merchandise, primarily because of an increase in the proportion of imported goods.

Asset Turnover

The asset turnover ratio indicates the amount of sales revenue generated for each dollar invested in assets. Lowe's ratios for the two years were:

	2006	2005
$\text{Asset Turnover} = \dfrac{\text{Net Sales Revenue}}{\text{Average Total Assets}} =$	1.8	1.9
1.79 = $46,927 ÷ [($27,767 + $24,639) ÷ 2]		

The asset turnover ratio suggests that Lowe's assets did not generate sales as efficiently in 2006 as in the prior year. To understand why, it is helpful to focus on the key assets used to generate sales. For a retailer such as Lowe's, the key asset is store properties, which we can compare to sales using the fixed asset turnover ratio, discussed next.

Fixed Asset Turnover

The fixed asset turnover ratio indicates how much revenue the company generates in sales for each dollar invested in fixed assets, such as store buildings and the property they sit on. Lowe's fixed asset turnover ratios for the two years were:

	2006	2005
$\text{Fixed Asset Turnover} = \dfrac{\text{Net Sales Revenue}}{\text{Average Net Fixed Assets}} =$	2.7	2.9
2.7 = $46,927 ÷ [($18,971 + $16,354) ÷ 2]		

This analysis shows that Lowe's had $2.66 of sales in 2006 for each dollar invested in fixed assets. Although the decline from 2005 was not good, it is understandable because Lowe's added 155 stores during these two years. Those stores will likely need some time to establish a strong customer base and begin generating sales at full capacity. Moreover, as additional stores are opened, they are likely to be located in areas of greater competition. Still, Lowe's fixed asset turnover ratio is low compared to that of its main competitor, The Home Depot, whose fixed asset turnover ratio was 3.53 in 2006. In terms of using fixed assets to generate sales revenue, The Home Depot has a competitive advantage over Lowe's. In other words, Lowe's is operating less efficiently than its major competitor.

Return on Assets (ROA)

The return on assets ratio compares the amount of net income to average total assets. ROA measures how much the firm earned for each dollar of investment. It is the broadest measure of profitability and management effectiveness, independent of financing strategy. ROA allows investors to compare management's investment performance against alternative investment options. Firms with higher ROA are doing a better job of selecting new investments, all other things equal. Company managers often compute the measure on a division-by-division basis and use it to evaluate division managers' relative performance.[2]

	2006	2005
Return on Assets (ROA) = $\frac{\text{Net Income}}{\text{Average Total Assets}} \times 100 =$	11.8%	12.1%

11.8% = ($3,105 ÷ [($27,767 + $24,639) ÷ 2]) × 100

Even though Lowe's net income increased in 2006, its ROA fell slightly because of the increase in assets during the period. Net profit margin and total asset turnover affect return on assets in the following fashion:

$$\text{ROA} = \text{Net Profit Margin} \times \text{Asset Turnover}$$
$$11.8\% = 6.6\% \times 1.79$$

The decline resulted from the decline in total asset turnover discussed earlier, which was partially offset by the increase in net profit margin.

Return on Equity (ROE)

The return on equity ratio compares the amount of net income to average stockholders' equity. ROE reports the net amount earned during the period as a percentage of each dollar contributed by stockholders and retained in the business. Lowe's ROE ratios for the past two years were:

	2006	2005
Return on Equity (ROE) = $\frac{\text{Net Income}}{\text{Average Stockholders' Equity}} \times 100 =$	20.7%	21.4%

20.7% = ($3,105 ÷ [($15,725 + $14,296) ÷ 2]) × 100

Lowe's ROE fell to 20.7 percent because average stockholders' equity increased. Lowe's ROE was close to the industry average of 20.0 percent in 2006, but it lagged behind The Home Depot's, which was 22.2 percent. Lowe's ROE is higher than its ROA because it is earning a higher return on its borrowed funds than it is paying to creditors for interest.

[2] In more complex ROA analyses, interest expense (net of tax) and minority interest are added back to net income in the numerator because the ratio assesses return on capital independent of source.

Earnings Per Share (EPS)

Earnings per share (EPS) indicates the amount of earnings generated for each share of outstanding common stock. It is reported on the income statement. Lowe's reported average shares outstanding of 1,535 and 1,555 in 2006 and 2005, respectively. It has no preferred dividends. Despite the decline in Lowe's ROE, its EPS ratio increased in 2006 because the company repurchased some of its shares (which reduced the number of common shares outstanding). Lowe's EPS for the past two years was:

		2006	2005
Earnings per Share (EPS) =	$\frac{\text{Net Income} - \text{Preferred Dividends}}{\text{Average Number of Common Shares}}$ =	\$2.02	\$1.78

\$2.02 = \$3,105 ÷ 1,535

Price/Earnings (P/E) Ratio

The P/E ratio relates the company's stock price to its EPS, as follows:

		2006	2005
Price/earnings =	$\frac{\text{Stock Price}}{\text{EPS}}$ =	15.3	16.3

15.3 = \$31 ÷ \$2.02

Using the going price for Lowe's stock when its 2006 earnings were announced, its P/E ratio was 15.3, meaning that investors were willing to pay 15.3 times its earnings per share to buy a share of stock. According to Yahoo! Finance, the average P/E ratio for home improvement stores at that time was about 14.8, suggesting that investors were more willing to buy stock in Lowe's than in other home improvement retailers.

Let's pause to summarize what we have learned so far. Despite a slowdown in the housing market, Lowe's increased its profit margin in 2006. Management did so primarily by (1) reducing merchandise costs by importing more merchandise and (2) growing sales by opening new stores, increasing sales to commercial builders, and placing more emphasis on online sales. These increases in gross profit were partly eaten up by operating expenses, which grew at a rate of 9 percent. Despite a decline in ROE during 2006, the company's EPS ratio increased as a result of share repurchases. Asset turnover and fixed asset turnover both declined, meaning that the company was not using its assets to generate sales as efficiently as in the past. Lowe's P/E ratio, which was slightly higher than the industry average, suggests that investors were willing to overlook those declines and were more willing to buy stock in Lowe's than in other home improvement retailers. The bottom line is that Lowe's has fared reasonably well during the housing slump, although the company currently trails its main competitor, The Home Depot, on a number of key ratios.

Liquidity Ratios

The analyses in this section focus on Lowe's ability to survive in the short term by converting its assets to cash to pay current liabilities as they come due. We interpret ratios (9) through (12) from Exhibit 17.6.

Receivables Turnover

Most home improvement retailers have low levels of accounts receivable relative to sales revenue because they collect the majority of their sales immediately in cash. Lowe's sells its small amounts of accounts receivable to a bank. Although the formula for this ratio calls for net **credit** sales in the numerator, companies rarely report their credit sales and cash sales separately. Consequently, financial statement users must use total sales revenue in the numerator, which results in a receivables turnover ratio that is not terribly meaningful for businesses that make few sales on account. This ratio is presented in Exhibit 17.6 simply to remind you of how it is calculated.

Inventory Turnover

The inventory turnover ratio indicates how many times inventory is bought and sold during the year. The ratio "days to sell" converts inventory turnover into the number of days needed to sell each purchase of inventory.

		2006	2005
Inventory Turnover =	$\frac{\text{Cost of Goods Sold}}{\text{Average Inventory}}$ =	4.5	4.5
4.5 = \$30,729 ÷ [(\$7,144 + \$6,635) ÷ 2]			
Days to sell =	$\frac{365}{\text{Inventory Turnover Ratio}}$ =	81.1	81.1
81.1 days = 365 ÷ 4.5			

The inventory turnover ratio is critical to Lowe's because the company wants to offer customers the right product when they need it at a price that beats the competition. Historically, The Home Depot has enjoyed a significant advantage over Lowe's in terms of inventory management. However, in recent years, Lowe's has been able to close the gap. In 2006, The Home Depot had an inventory turnover ratio of 5.04—only slightly better than Lowe's ratio of 4.5.

Turnover ratios vary significantly from one industry to the next. Companies in the food industry (restaurants and grocery stores) have high inventory turnover ratios because their inventory is subject to spoilage. Companies that sell expensive merchandise (automobiles and high-fashion clothes) have much lower ratios because sales of those items are infrequent, but customers want to have a wide selection to choose from when they do buy.

Current Ratio

The current ratio compares current assets to current liabilities, as follows:

		2006	2005
Current Ratio =	$\frac{\text{Current Assets}}{\text{Current Liabilities}}$ =	1.27	1.34
1.27 = \$8,314 ÷ \$6,539			

This ratio measures the company's ability to pay its current liabilities. The slight drop in Lowe's current ratio from 2005 to 2006 probably is not something to be concerned about so long as the decline does not continue. The 2006 current ratio of 1.27 indicates that the company's current assets were 127 percent of its current liabilities. Most analysts would judge that ratio to be very strong, especially considering Lowe's ability to generate cash. In this industry, a current ratio of more than 1.0 is considered to be acceptable.

Quick Ratio

The quick ratio compares the sum of cash, accounts receivable, and short-term investments to current liabilities as follows:

		2006	2005
Quick Ratio =	$\dfrac{\text{Quick Assets}}{\text{Current Liabilities}}$ =	0.12	0.15

0.12 = ($364 + $432) ÷ $6,539

The quick ratio is a more stringent test of short-term liquidity than is the current ratio. The quick ratio compares quick assets, defined as cash and near-cash assets, to current liabilities. Quick assets include cash, short-term investments, and accounts receivable (net of the allowance for doubtful accounts). Inventory is omitted from quick assets because of the uncertainty of the timing of cash flows from its sale. Prepaid expenses are also excluded from quick assets.

Solvency Ratios

The analyses in this section focus on Lowe's ability to survive over the long term—that is, its ability to repay debt when it matures, pay interest until that time, and finance the replacement and/or expansion of long-term assets. We interpret ratios (13) through (15) from Exhibit 17.6.

Debt to Assets

The debt-to-assets ratio indicates the proportion of total assets that creditors finance. Remember that creditors must be paid regardless of how difficult a year the company may have had. The higher this ratio, the riskier is the company's financing strategy. Lowe's ratio for the two years was:

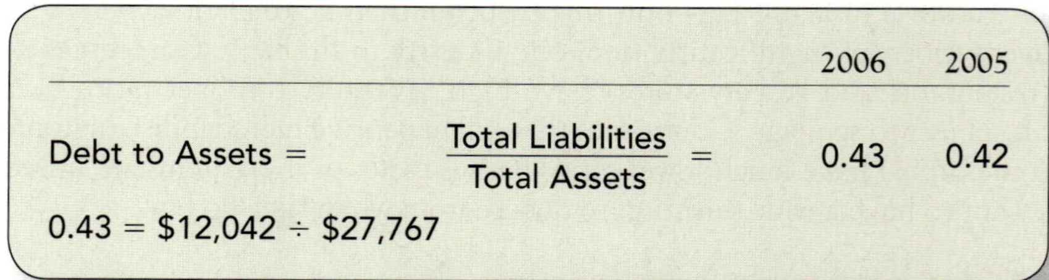

		2006	2005
Debt to Assets =	$\dfrac{\text{Total Liabilities}}{\text{Total Assets}}$ =	0.43	0.42

0.43 = $12,042 ÷ $27,767

Coach's Tip

Instead of the debt-to-assets ratio, analysts might use the **debt-to-equity ratio,** which gives the same basic information as debt to assets. The debt-to-equity ratio is typically calculated as Total Liabilities ÷ Total Stockholders' Equity. As with debt to assets, the higher the debt-to-equity ratio, the more the company relies on debt (rather than equity) financing.

Lowe's ratio of 0.43 in 2006 indicates that creditors contributed 43 percent of the company's financing, implying that stockholders' equity was the company's main source of financing at 57 percent. This ratio did not change significantly from 2005 to 2006. Lowe's currently relies less on debt financing than The Home Depot, which had a debt-to-assets ratio of 52 percent in 2006.

Times Interest Earned

The times interest earned ratio indicates how many times the company's interest expense was covered by its operating results. This ratio is calculated using accrual-based interest expense and net income before interest and income taxes, as follows:

		2006	2005
Times Interest Earned =	$\dfrac{\text{Net Income + Interest Expense + Income Tax Expense}}{\text{Interest Expense}}$ =	33.5	29.5

33.5 = ($3,105 + $154 + $1,893) ÷ $154

Coach's Tip

If a company reports a net loss instead of net income, you should include the loss in the formula as a negative number. A negative ratio indicates that the company's operating results (before the costs of financing and taxes) do not cover its interest costs.

A times interest earned ratio higher than 1.0 indicates that net income (before the costs of financing and taxes have been deducted) is sufficient to cover the company's interest expense. Lowe's ratio of 33.5 indicates that the company is generating more than enough profit to cover its interest expense.

Free Cash Flow

Free cash flow measures a company's ability to make capital investments and pay dividends from its operating cash flows. Lowe's free cash flow for the two years was:

			2006	2005
Free Cash Flow =	Net Cash Flow from Operating Activities −Purchases of Property and Equipment −Dividends Paid	=	$366	$323

$366 = $4,502 − $3,860 − $276

The amounts in the computation come from the cash flow statement, which is not shown in this chapter. The positive free cash flow in the two years (in millions) indicates that Lowe's is a healthy company with enough cash flow from operations to purchase property, plant, and equipment and pay dividends to stockholders.

In sum, these solvency ratios suggest that Lowe's has grown significantly and has financed its growth through both operating cash flows and debt financing. Lowe's reliance on debt financing has remained relatively steady, and the company is in an excellent position to cover the interest expense associated with its debt. Overall, analysts would consider Lowe's to have a low-risk profile, one that bodes well for the company's long-term survival.

SELF-STUDY PRACTICE

Lowe's

1. Show the computations for the following two ratios for Lowe's for 2005. Use the information in Exhibits 17.2 and 17.3 (all numbers are in millions).
   a. Gross profit percentage ratio.
   b. Current ratio.
2. Assume that in 2006, Lowe's recorded a $25 (in millions) expiration of prepaid expenses. Complete the following table by showing its impact (+, −, or no change) on selected measures of profitability, and liquidity.

	Impact of Prepaid Expense Expiration
a. Net profit margin ratio.	
b. Current ratio.	

After you have finished, check your answers with the solution at the bottom of the page.

Solution to Self-Study Practice

1.

$$\frac{\text{Net Sales Revenue} - \text{Cost of Goods Sold}}{\text{Net Sales Revenue}} = \frac{\$43,243 - \$28,453}{\$43,243} \times 100 = 34.2\%$$

$$\frac{\text{Current Assets}}{\text{Current Liabilities}} = \frac{\$7,788}{\$5,832} = 1.34$$

2. The expiration of prepaid expenses would decrease prepaid expenses on the balance sheet and increase expenses on the income statement. The effects on the ratios are:
   a. "–" net income, the numerator of the ratio, decreases when expenses increase, so the ratio decreases
   b. "–" current assets, the numerator of the ratio, decreases when prepaid expenses decreases, so the ratio decreases

Exhibit 17.7 Comparison of Accounting Methods Used by Three Home Improvement Retailers

	Lowe's	The Home Depot	Builder's FirstSource
Inventory	FIFO	FIFO	Weighted Average Cost
Depreciation	Straight line Buildings: 10–40 yrs Equipment: 3–15 yrs	Straight line Buildings: 10–45 yrs Equipment: 3–20 yrs	Straight line Buildings: 20–40 yrs Equipment: 3–10 yrs

Accounting Decisions and Ratio Analysis

In the analyses just presented, we compared Lowe's results with those of The Home Depot. When appropriate, we discussed how differences in the two companies' strategies (for example, relying on debt versus equity financing) and business operations (for example, targeting do-it-yourselfers versus professionals) affected their financial ratios. We should also consider whether differences between the two companies' financial ratios might be caused by differences in their accounting decisions.

Information about a company's accounting decisions is presented in a note to the financial statements. Data in Exhibit 17.7 compare the policies that three home improvement retailers follow in accounting for inventory and depreciation—two line items that can have a noticeable impact on a retailer's results. Take a moment to study the exhibit.

As you can see, the three companies follow similar but not identical policies. Lowe's and The Home Depot use the FIFO method of accounting for ending inventory and the cost of goods sold; Builder's FirstSource uses the weighted average method. Although these two methods result in different numbers, the overall impact on the companies' financial ratios should be minor.

All three companies calculate depreciation using the straight-line method with a similar range of estimated useful lives for buildings and equipment. Because buildings and equipment make up such a large portion of each company's assets, these similarities go a long way toward making their financial results comparable. In conclusion, although the companies' accounting policies have some differences, they are unlikely to have a major impact on our comparisons.

Spotlight On FINANCIAL REPORTING

International Differences in Accounting Standards

Cross-national differences in accounting standards also create differences in the accounting methods different companies use. Many countries, including the members of the European Union, are committed to adopting the international financial reporting standards (IFRS) issued by the International Accounting Standards Board (IASB). Although IFRS are similar to GAAP, several important differences exist. Two of the differences relate to inventory accounting.

Difference	U.S. GAAP	IFRS
Last-in, first-out method for inventory	Permitted	Prohibited
Reversal of inventory write-downs	Prohibited	Required

These differences would make it difficult to compare a U.S. automaker such as Ford that follows U.S. GAAP with a European competitor such as BMW that follows IFRS.

Source: *Deloitte IAS Plus*, February 2007.

Demonstration Case

The following information was taken from The Home Depot's recent annual report.

(in millions of dollars)	Year ended January 28, 2007	
Net sales revenue	$90,837	
Cost of goods sold	61,054	
Net income	5,761	
	January 28, 2007	**January 29, 2006**
Inventory	$12,822	$11,401
Current assets	18,000	15,269
Net property and equipment	26,605	24,901
Total assets	52,263	44,405
Current liabilities	12,931	12,706
Total liabilities	27,233	17,496

Required:

1. Compute the following ratios for The Home Depot for the year ended January 28, 2007.

   Fixed Asset Turnover
   Return on Equity
   Days to Sell
   Current Ratio
   Debt to Assets

2. Interpret the meaning of the ratios you calculated in requirement 1.

Suggested Solution

1. Calculating ratios:

Fixed Asset Turnover
= Net Sales Revenue/Average Net Fixed Assets
= $90,837 ÷ [(26,605 + 24,901) ÷ 2]
= 3.53

Return on Equity
= Net Income/Average Stockholders' Equity
= $5,761 ÷ [(25,030 + 26,909) ÷ 2]
= 0.2218, or 22.2%

Days to Sell
= 365 ÷ Inventory Turnover Ratio
= 365 ÷ (Cost of Goods Sold/Average Inventory)
= 365 ÷ [61,054 ÷ [(12,822 + 11,401) ÷ 2]]
= 72

Current Ratio
= Current Assets/Current Liabilities
= $18,000 ÷ 12,931
= 1.39

Debt to Assets
= Total Liabilities/Total Assets
= $27,233 ÷ 52,263
= 0.52

2. Interpreting ratios

- The fixed asset turnover ratio of 3.53 means that on average, The Home Depot generated $3.53 of sales for each dollar of fixed assets.
- The return on equity of 22.2 percent means that The Home Depot's net income for the year was 22.2 percent of the amount investors contributed to and left in the company.
- The days to sell ratio of 72 means that on average, 72 days elapsed between the time The Home Depot acquired the inventory and the time the company sold it.

- The current ratio of 1.39 means that at year-end, The Home Depot had $1.39 of current assets for each dollar of current liabilities.
- The debt-to-assets ratio of 0.52 means that The Home Depot relied on short-term and long-term debt to finance 52 percent of its assets, implying that stockholders' equity financed 48 percent (=100 − 52) of its total assets.

Supplement 17A

Nonrecurring and Other Special Items

Until 2005, three different types of nonrecurring item were reported in income statements: discontinued operations, extraordinary items, and the cumulative effects of changes in accounting methods. Recently, however, **new accounting standards have nearly eliminated reporting of extraordinary items and the cumulative effects of changes in accounting methods.** In fact, the definition of the term **extraordinary** has become so restricted that few events—not even losses that arose from the terrorist attacks of September 11, 2001—now qualify as extraordinary. The cumulative effects of changes in accounting methods are reported as adjustments to retained earnings rather than as part of the income statement in the period when the change is made. That leaves only one remaining nonrecurring item, discontinued operations.

Discontinued operations result from the abandonment or sale of a major business component. The discontinued operations line on the income statement includes any gain or loss on the disposal of the discontinued operation as well as any operating income generated before its disposal. Because gains or losses from discontinued operations appear below the income tax expense line on the income statement, any additional tax effects related to those gains or losses are included in the reported amounts. Obviously, the sale of a particular business unit can happen only once, so these results are reported separately to inform users that they will not affect the company's future results. Exhibit 17A.1 shows how Newell Rubbermaid reported discontinued operations in 2005 and 2006 when the company divested its Little Tikes division and its Home Décor Europe and European Cookware operations.

In some cases, additional items may appear after the net income (loss) line on the income statement. Those items may be added to or subtracted from net income to arrive at the amount of **comprehensive income.** As you can learn in detail in intermediate financial accounting courses, those items represent gains or losses related to changes in the value of certain balance sheet accounts. While most gains and losses are included in the computation of net income, some (those related to changes in foreign currency exchange rates and the value of certain investments, for example) are excluded from net income and included only in comprehensive income. The main reason for excluding these gains and losses from net income is that the changes in value that created them may well disappear before the gains or losses are

Exhibit 17A.1 Reporting of Nonrecurring Items on the Income Statement — Newell Rubbermaid

Newell Rubbermaid
Condensed Income Statements
December 31,
(in millions)

	2006	2005
Net sales	$6,201.0	$5,717.2
Cost of products sold	4,131.0	3,959.1
Selling, general, and administrative expenses	1,347.0	1,117.7
Impairment charges and restructuring costs	66.4	73.0
Operating income (loss)	656.6	567.4
Interest and other expenses, net	141.7	104.0
Income (loss) before income taxes	514.9	463.4
Income tax expense (benefit)	44.2	57.1
Net income (loss) from continuing operations	470.7	406.3
Gain (loss) on sale of discontinued operations, net of income taxes	(85.7)	(155.0)
Net income (loss)	$ 385.0	$ 251.3

ever realized (when the company sells the related assets or liabilities). For this reason, most analysts will take a moment to consider the size of these special items in relation to net income. If the amount is not large, they will exclude the items in calculating profitability ratios.[3]

Chapter Summary

LO1 Describe how financial statement information is communicated to external users. p. 730

- The issuance of quarterly and annual reports is preceded by press releases containing preliminary results.
- Publicly owned companies file with the Securities and Exchange Commission more detailed information on Forms 10-Q, 10K, and 8-K, which are available first on the Web.

LO2 Use horizontal (trend) analysis to recognize financial changes that unfold over time. p. 732

- Horizontal analysis (also called trend analysis) compares financial statement items to comparable amounts in prior periods with the goal of identifying sustained changes, or trends.
- Trend analysis involves computing the dollar amount by which each account changes from one period to the next and expressing that change as a percentage of the balance for the prior period.

LO3 Use vertical (common size) analysis to understand important relationships within financial statements. p. 734

- Common size financial statements express each line of the income statement (or balance sheet) as a percentage of total sales (or total assets).
- The statements tell the reader whether the proportions within each statement category are changing.

LO4 Calculate and use financial ratios to assess profitability, liquidity, and solvency. p. 736

- Financial ratios are commonly classified with relation to profitability, liquidity, or solvency. Exhibit 17.6 lists common ratios in these three categories and shows how to compute them.
- Profitability ratios focus on measuring the adequacy of a company's income by comparing it to other items reported on the financial statements.
- Liquidity ratios measure a company's ability to meet its current debt obligations.
- Solvency ratios measure a company's ability to meet its long-term debt obligations.
- In comparing trends and ratios over time and across companies, watch for possible differences in accounting policies and nonrecurring events that could affect reported financial results.

Key Terms

Horizontal (Trend) Analysis (p. 732)
Liquidity (p. 736)
Profitability (p. 736)
Solvency (p. 736)
Vertical (Common Size) Analysis (p. 734)

See complete glossary in back of text.

Questions

1. What are the major categories of information in the annual report financial section?
2. What is the general goal of trend analysis?
3. How is a year-to-year percentage change calculated?
4. What is ratio analysis? Why is it useful?
5. What benchmarks are commonly used for interpreting ratios?
6. Into what three categories of performance are most financial ratios classified? To what in particular does each of these categories relate?
7. (Supplement 17A) Name the most commonly reported nonrecurring item, and explain where and how it is reported on the income statement.

Multiple Choice

1. Which of the following ratios is not used to analyze profitability?
   a. Fixed asset turnover ratio.
   b. Gross profit percentage.
   c. Current ratio.
   d. Return on equity.

Quiz 17-1
www.mhhe.com/LLPW1e

2. Which of the following would not directly change the receivables turnover ratio for your company?
   a. Increases in the selling prices of your inventory.
   b. A change in your credit policy.
   c. Increases in the cost you incur to purchase inventory.
   d. None of the above.

[3] Instead of showing the computation of comprehensive income on the face of the income statement, companies are allowed to show it in either a statement of stockholders' equity or a separate statement of comprehensive income. One survey indicates that about 70 percent of companies show the computation in a statement of stockholders' equity. See American Institute of Public Accountants (New York: AICPA, 2006). *Accounting Trends & Techniques*.

3. Which of the following ratios is used to analyze liquidity?
   a. Earnings per share.
   b. Debt to assets.
   c. Current ratio.
   d. Both debt to assets and current ratio.

4. Analysts use ratios to
   a. Compare different companies in the same industry.
   b. Track a company's performance over time.
   c. Compare a company's performance to industry averages.
   d. All of the above.

5. Which of the following incorporates cash flows from operations?
   a. Inventory turnover.
   b. Earnings per share.
   c. Free cash flow.
   d. All of the above.

6. Given the following ratios for four companies, which company is least likely to experience problems paying its current liabilities promptly?

	Current Ratio	Receivables Turnover Ratio
a.	1.2	7.0
b.	1.2	6.0
c.	1.0	6.0
d.	0.5	7.0

7. A decrease in selling and administrative expenses would directly impact what ratio?
   a. Fixed asset turnover ratio.
   b. Times interest earned.
   c. Current ratio.
   d. Gross profit percentage.

8. A bank is least likely to use which of the following ratios when analyzing the likelihood that a borrower will pay interest and principal on its loans?
   a. Free cash flow.
   b. Debt-to-assets ratio.
   c. Times interest earned ratio.
   d. Return on equity ratio.

9. Which of the following accounting concepts do accountants and auditors assess by using financial analyses?
   a. Cost benefit.
   b. Materiality.
   c. Industry practices.
   d. Going-concern assumption.

10. (Supplement 17A) Which of the following items is reported net of related income taxes?
    a. Gain or loss from discontinued operations.
    b. Gain or loss from disposal of property, plant, and equipment.
    c. Interest on long-term debt.
    d. Gain or loss from early extinguishment of debt.

Solutions to Multiple-Choice Questions

1. c 2. c 3. c 4. d 5. c 6. a 7. b
8. d 9. d 10. a

Mini Exercises  Available with McGraw-Hill's Homework Manager

LO2 **M17-1 Calculations and Interpretations of Horizontal (Trend) Analyses**

Lockey Fencing Corporation
Income Statements
For the Years Ended December 31

	2009	2008
Net sales	$100,000	$75,000
Cost of goods sold	58,000	45,000
Gross profit	42,000	30,000
Selling, general, and administrative expenses	9,000	4,500
Interest expense	3,000	3,750
Income before income taxes	30,000	21,750
Income tax expense	9,000	6,525
Net income	$ 21,000	$15,225

What are the two most significant year-to-year changes in terms of dollars and in terms of percentages?

LO3 **M17-2 Calculations and Interpretations of Vertical (Common Size) Analyses**

Using the information in M17-1, prepare common size income statements to determine how the company increased its net income as a percent of revenues in 2009.

M17-3 Computing the Return on Equity Ratio LO4

Given the following data, compute the 2008 return on equity ratio (expressed as a percentage to one decimal place).

	2008	2007
Net income	$ 1,850,000	$ 1,600,000
Stockholders' equity	10,000,000	13,125,000
Total assets	24,000,000	26,000,000
Interest expense	400,000	300,000

M17-4 Analyzing the Inventory Turnover Ratio LO4

A manufacturer reported an inventory turnover ratio of 8.6 during 2009. During 2010, management introduced a new inventory control system that was expected to reduce average inventory levels by 25 percent without affecting sales volume or cost of goods sold. Given these circumstances, would you expect the inventory turnover ratio to increase or decrease during 2010? Explain.

M17-5 Analyzing the Impact of Accounting Alternatives LO4

Nevis Corporation operates in an industry in which costs are falling. The company is considering changing its inventory method from FIFO to LIFO and wants to determine the impact that the change would have on selected accounting ratios in future years. In general, what impact would you expect on the following ratios: net profit margin, fixed asset turnover, and current ratio?

M17-6 Inferring Financial Information Using the P/E Ratio LO4

In 2009, Big W Company reported earnings per share of $2.50 when its stock was selling for $50.00. In 2010, its earnings increased by 10 percent. If all other relationships remain constant, what is the price of the stock? Explain.

M17-7 Identifying Relevant Ratios LO4

Identify the ratio that is relevant to answering each of the following questions.

1. How much net income does the company earn from each dollar of sales?
2. Is the company financed primarily by debt or equity?
3. How many dollars of sales were generated for each dollar invested in fixed assets?
4. How many days, on average, does it take the company to collect on credit sales made to customers?
5. How much net income does the company earn for each dollar owners have invested in it?
6. Does the company have sufficient assets to convert into cash for paying liabilities as they come due in the upcoming year?

M17-8 Interpreting Ratios LO4

Generally speaking, do the following indicate good or bad news?

1. Increase in times interest earned ratio.
2. Decrease in days to sell.
3. Increase in gross profit percentage.
4. Decrease in EPS.
5. Increase in asset turnover ratio.

Exercises

Available with McGraw-Hill's Homework Manager

E17-1 Preparing and Interpreting a Horizontal (Trend) Analysis LO2 Chevron

The average price of a gallon of gas in 2005 jumped $0.43 (24 percent) from $1.81 in 2004 to $2.24 in 2005. Let's see whether these changes are reflected in the income statement of Chevron Corp. for the year ended December 31, 2005 (amounts in millions).

	2005	2004
Total revenues	$198,200	$155,300
Costs of crude oil and products	140,902	104,948
Other operating costs	32,101	29,801
Income before income tax expense	25,197	20,551
Income tax expense	11,098	7,223
Net income	$ 14,099	$ 13,328

Required:

Conduct a horizontal analysis by calculating the year-to-year changes in each line item expressed in dollars and in percentages (rounded to one decimal place). How did the change in gas prices compare to the changes in Chevron Corp.'s total revenues and costs of crude oil and products?

LO3
Chevron

E17-2 Preparing and Interpreting a Vertical (Common Size) Analysis

Use the information for Chevron Corp. in E17-1 to conduct a vertical (common size) analysis of the income statements and then answer the following questions.

Required:

1. Was Chevron able to raise gas prices to offset the increase in its costs of crude oil and products?
2. How did you know?
3. Did other operating costs rise as fast as gas prices? How did you know? Why do you think this is so?

LO4
Chevron

E17-3 Computing and Interpreting Profitability Ratios

Use the information for Chevron Corp. in E17-1 to complete the following requirements.

Required:

1. Compute the gross profit percentage for each year (one decimal place). Assuming the change for 2004 to 2005 is the beginning of a sustained trend, is Chevron likely to earn more or less gross profit from each dollar of sales in 2006?
2. Compute the net profit margin for each year (expressed as a percentage with one decimal place). Given your calculations here and in requirement 1, explain whether Chevron did a better or worse job of controlling expenses other than the costs of crude oil and products in 2005 relative to 2004.
3. Chevron reported average net fixed assets of $54.2 billion in 2005 and $45.1 billion in 2004. Compute the fixed asset turnover ratios for both years (round to two decimal places). Did the company better utilize its investment in fixed assets to generate revenues in 2005 or 2004?
4. Chevron reported average stockholders' equity of $54.0 billion in 2005 and $40.8 billion in 2004. Compute the return on equity ratios for both years (expressed as a percentage with one decimal place). Did the company generate higher returns for stockholders in 2005 or 2004?

LO4
Chevron

E17-4 Computing a Commonly Used Solvency Ratio

Use the information for Chevron Corp. in E17-1 to complete the following requirement.

Required:

Interest expense in the amount of $482 million was included with Other Operating Costs in 2005 ($406 million in 2004). Compute the times interest earned ratios for each year (round to one decimal place). In your opinion, does Chevron generate sufficient net income (before taxes and interest) to cover the cost of debt financing?

LO2

E17-5 Preparing and Interpreting a Horizontal (Trend) Analysis

The average selling price of low-end laptops fell about $200 (25 percent) from $800 in 2008 to $600 in 2009. Let's see whether these changes are reflected in the income statement of Computer Tycoon Inc. for the year ended December 31, 2009.

	2008	2009
Sales revenues	$121,761	$98,913
Cost of goods sold	71,583	59,249
Operating expenses	36,934	36,943
Interest expense	474	565
Income before income tax expense	12,770	2,156
Income tax expense	5,540	1,024
Net income	$ 7,230	$ 1,132

Required:

Conduct a horizontal analysis by calculating the year-to-year changes in each line item expressed in dollars and in percentages (rounded to one decimal place). How did the change in computer prices compare to the changes in Computer Tycoon's sales revenues?

E17-6 Preparing and Interpreting a Vertical (Common Size) Analysis LO3

Use the information in E17-5 to conduct a vertical (common size) analysis of Computer Tycoon's income statements and then answer the following questions.

Required:

1. Was Computer Tycoon able to lower its costs of goods to offset the decrease in selling price? How did you know?
2. What was the main reason Computer Tycoon's net income as a percent of revenues decreased?

E17-7 Computing Profitability Ratios LO4

Use the information in E17-5 for Computer Tycoon to complete the following requirements.

Required:

1. Compute the gross profit percentage for each year (one decimal place). Assuming that the change for 2008 to 2009 is the beginning of a sustained trend, is Computer Tycoon likely to earn higher or lower gross profit from each dollar of sales in 2010?
2. Compute the net profit margin for each year (expressed as a percentage with one decimal place). Given your calculations here and in requirement 1, explain whether Computer Tycoon did a better or worse job of controlling operating expenses in 2009 relative to 2008.
3. Computer Tycoon reported average net fixed assets of $54,200 in 2009 and $45,100 in 2008. Compute the fixed asset turnover ratio for each year (round to two decimal places). Did the company better utilize its investment in fixed assets to generate revenues in 2009 or 2008?
4. Computer Tycoon reported average stockholders' equity of $54,000 in 2009 and $40,800 in 2008. Compute the return on equity ratio for each year (expressed as a percentage with one decimal place). Did the company generate greater returns for stockholders in 2009 or 2008?

E17-8 Computing a Commonly Used Solvency Ratio LO4

Use the information in E17-5 for Computer Tycoon to complete the following requirement.

Required:

Compute the times interest earned ratios for 2009 and 2008. In your opinion, does Computer Tycoon generate sufficient net income (before taxes and interest) to cover the cost of debt financing?

E17-9 Matching Each Ratio with Its Computational Formula LO4

Match each ratio or percentage with its formula by entering the appropriate letter for each numbered item.

	Ratios or Percentages	Formula
___	1. Current ratio	A. Net income ÷ Net sales revenue.
___	2. Net profit margin	B. (Net sales revenue − Cost of goods sold) ÷ Net sales revenue.
___	3. Inventory turnover	C. Current assets ÷ Current liabilities.
___	4. Asset turnover	D. Cost of goods sold ÷ Average inventory.
___	5. Fixed asset turnover	E. Net credit sales revenue ÷ Average net receivables.
___	6. Free cash flow	F. Net income ÷ Average number of common shares outstanding.
___	7. Return on equity	G. Total liabilities ÷ Total assets.
___	8. Times interest earned	H. (Net income + Interest expense + Income tax expense) ÷ Interest expense.
___	9. Debt to assets	I. Net cash flows from operating activities − Purchases of property and equipment − Dividends paid
___	10. Price/earnings	J. Current stock price per share ÷ Earnings per share.
___	11. Receivables turnover	K. Net income ÷ Average total stockholders' equity.
___	12. Earnings per share	L. Net sales revenue ÷ Average total assets
___	13. Gross profit percentage	M. Net sales revenue ÷ Average net fixed assets.

LO4

E17-10 Computing and Interpreting Selected Liquidity Ratios

DuckWing Stores (DWS) reported sales of $600,000 for the year; one-half of sales were on credit. The average gross profit percentage was 40 percent on sales. Account balances follow:

	Beginning	Ending
Accounts receivable (net)	$45,000	$55,000
Inventory	60,000	40,000

Required:

1. Compute the turnover ratios for accounts receivable and inventory (round to one decimal place).
2. Calculate the average days to collect receivables and the average days to sell inventory (round to one decimal place).
3. Explain what each of these ratios and measures means.

LO4

E17-11 Computing and Interpreting Liquidity Ratios

Cintas Corporation is the largest uniform supplier in North America. More than 5 million people wear Cintas clothing each day. Selected information from a recent balance sheet follows. For Year 2, the company reported sales revenue of $2,686,585 and cost of goods sold of $1,567,377 (in thousands).

Cintas	Year 2	Year 1
Balance Sheet (amounts in thousands)		
Cash	$ 32,239	$ 52,182
Accounts receivable, less allowance of $7,737 and $9,229	278,147	225,735
Inventories	228,410	164,906
Prepaid expenses	7,607	7,237
Other current assets	25,420	57,640
Accounts payable	53,909	60,393
Wages payable	25,252	29,004
Income taxes payable	69,545	73,163
Accrued liabilities	127,882	131,705
Long-term debt due within one year	28,251	18,369

Required:

Assuming that 60 percent of sales are on credit, compute the current ratio (two decimal places), inventory turnover ratio (one decimal place), and accounts receivable turnover ratio (one decimal place) for Year 2. Explain what each ratio means.

E17-12 Analyzing the Impact of Selected Transactions on the Current Ratio LO4

In its most recent annual report, Appalachian Beverages reported current assets of $54,000 and a current ratio of 1.80. Assume that the following transactions were completed: (1) purchased merchandise for $6,000 on account and (2) purchased a delivery truck for $10,000, paying $1,000 cash and signing a two-year promissory note for the balance.

Required:

Compute the updated current ratio, rounded to two decimal places, after each transaction.

E17-13 Analyzing the Impact of Selected Transactions on the Current Ratio LO4

In its most recent annual report, Sunrise Enterprises reported current assets of $1,090,000 and current liabilities of $602,000.

Required:

Determine the impact of the following transactions on the current ratio for Sunrise:

1. Sold long-term assets for cash.
2. Accrued severance pay for terminated employees.
3. Wrote down the carrying value of certain inventory items that were deemed to be obsolete.
4. Acquired new inventory by signing an 18-month promissory note (the supplier was not willing to provide normal credit terms).

E17-14 Analyzing the Impact of Selected Transactions on the Current Ratio LO4 Sports Authority

Sports Authority, Inc., is the country's largest private full-line sporting goods retailer. Stores are operated under four brand names: Sports Authority, Gart Sports, Oshman's, and Sportmart. Assume one of the Sports Authority stores reported current assets of $88,000 and its current ratio was 1.75. Assume also the following transactions were completed: (1) paid $6,000 on accounts payable, (2) purchased a delivery truck for $10,000 cash, (3) wrote off a bad account receivable for $2,000 under the allowance method, and (4) paid previously declared dividends in the amount of $25,000 (the dividends were declared in the prior period and paid in the current period).

Required:

Compute the updated current ratio, rounded to two decimal places, after each transaction.

E17-15 Analyzing the Impact of Selected Transactions on the Current Ratio LO4

Current assets totaled $500,000, the current ratio was 2.00, and the company uses the perpetual inventory method. Assume that the following transactions were completed: (1) sold $12,000 in merchandise on short-term credit for $15,000, (2) declared but did not pay dividends of $50,000, (3) paid prepaid rent in the amount of $12,000, (4) paid previously declared dividends in the amount of $50,000, (5) collected an account receivable in the amount of $12,000, and (6) reclassified $40,000 of long-term debt as a current liability.

Required:

Compute the updated current ratio, rounded to two decimal places, after each transaction.

E17-16 Computing the Accounts Receivable and Inventory Turnover Ratios LO4 P&G

Procter & Gamble is a multinational corporation that manufactures and markets many products that are probably in your home or dorm room. In 2006, sales for the company were $68,222 (all amounts in millions). The annual report did not report the amount of credit sales, so we assume all sales were on credit. The average gross profit percentage was 51 percent. Account balances follow:

	Beginning	Ending
Accounts receivable (net)	$5,266	$7,336
Inventory	5,006	6,291

Required:

1. Compute the turnover ratios (rounded to one decimal place) for accounts receivable and inventory.
2. Calculate the average days to collect receivables and the average days to sell inventory.
3. Interpret what these ratios and measures mean.

LO4
Dollar General

E17-17 Inferring Financial Information from Profitability and Liquidity Ratios

Dollar General Corporation operates approximately 8,250 general merchandise stores that feature quality merchandise at low prices to meet the needs of middle-, low-, and fixed-income families in southern, eastern, and midwestern states. For the year ended February 3, 2006, the company reported average inventories of $1,425 (in millions) and an inventory turnover of 4.3. Average total fixed assets were $1,137 (million), and the fixed asset turnover ratio was 7.5.

Required:

1. Calculate Dollar General's gross profit percentage (expressed as a percentage with one decimal place). What does this imply about the amount of gross profit made from each dollar of sales?
2. Is this an improvement from the gross profit percentage of 29.5 percent earned during the year ended January 28, 2005?

TIP: Work backward from the fixed asset turnover and inventory turnover ratios to compute the amounts needed for the gross profit percentage.

LO4

E17-18 Using Financial Information to Identify Mystery Companies

The following selected financial data pertain to four unidentified companies (balance sheet amounts reported in millions):

	COMPANY			
	1	2	3	4
Balance Sheet Data				
Cash	$ 5.1	$ 8.8	$ 6.3	$ 10.4
Accounts receivable	13.1	41.5	13.8	4.9
Inventory	4.6	3.6	65.1	35.8
Property and equipment	53.1	23.0	8.8	35.7
Selected Ratios				
Gross profit percentage	N/A*	N/A	45.2	22.5
Net profit margin ratio (%)	0.3	16.0	3.9	1.5
Current ratio	0.7	2.2	1.9	1.4
Inventory turnover	N/A	N/A	1.4	15.5
Debt to assets	0.7	0.5	0.6	0.7

* N/A = Not applicable.

This financial information pertains to the following companies:

a. Cable TV company.
b. Grocery store.
c. Accounting firm.
d. Retail jewelry store.

Required:
Match each company with its financial information, and explain the basis for your answers.

LO4

E17-19 Analyzing the Impact of Alternative Inventory Methods on Selected Ratios

Company A uses the FIFO method to cost inventory, and Company B uses the LIFO method. The two companies are exactly alike except for the difference in inventory costing methods. Costs of inventory items for both companies have been falling steadily in recent years, and each company has increased its inventory each year. Ignore income tax effects.

Required:
Identify which company will report the higher amount for each of the following ratios. If it is not possible to identify which will report the higher amount, explain why.

1. Current ratio.
2. Debt-to-assets ratio.
3. Earnings per share.

Problems—Set A

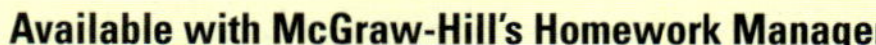

PA17-1 Analyzing Financial Statements Using Horizontal (Trend) and Vertical (Common Size) Analysis

LO2, 3

www.mhhe.com/LLPW1e

The comparative financial statements prepared at December 31, 2009, for Pinnacle Plus showed the following summarized data:

			INCREASE (DECREASE) 2009 OVER 2008	
	2009	2008	Amount	Percentage
Income Statement				
Sales revenue*	$110,000	$ 99,000		
Cost of goods sold	52,000	48,000		
Gross profit	58,000	51,000		
Operating expenses	36,000	33,000		
Interest expense	4,000	4,000		
Income before income taxes	18,000	14,000		
Income tax expense (30%)	5,400	4,200		
Net income	$ 12,600	$ 9,800		
Balance Sheet				
Cash	$ 49,500	$ 18,000		
Accounts receivable (net)	37,000	32,000		
Inventory	25,000	38,000		
Property and equipment (net)	95,000	105,000		
Total assets	$206,500	$193,000		
Accounts payable	$ 42,000	$ 35,000		
Income taxes payable	1,000	500		
Note payable, long term	40,000	40,000		
Total liabilities	83,000	75,500		
Common stock (par $10)	90,000	90,000		
Retained earnings†	33,500	27,500		
Total liabilities and stockholders' equity	$206,500	$193,000		

* One-half of all sales are on credit.

† During 2009, cash dividends amounting to $6,600 were declared and paid.

Required:

1. Complete the Amount and Percentage columns in Pinnacle Plus's comparative financial statements to prepare a horizontal (trend) analysis. Round the percentages to one decimal place. Does anything significant jump out at you from the year-to-year analyses?
2. Prepare common size income statements and balance sheets for the two years. Round the percentages to one decimal place. What significant changes have taken place in the relationship among items in the balance sheet and income statement?

PA17-2 Analyzing Comparative Financial Statements Using Selected Ratios

LO4

Use the data given in PA17-1 for Pinnacle Plus.

Required:

1. Compute the gross profit percentages in 2009 and 2008. Round the percentages to one decimal place. Is the trend going in the right direction?
2. Compute the net profit margin ratios in 2009 and 2008. Round the percentages to one decimal place. Is the trend going in the right direction?
3. Compute the earnings per share for 2009 and 2008. Does the trend look good or bad? Explain.
4. Stockholders' equity totaled $100,000 at the end of 2007. Compute the return on equity (ROE) ratios for 2008 and 2009. Express the ROE as percentages rounded to one decimal place. Is the trend going in the right direction?
5. Net property and equipment totaled $110,000 at the end of 2007. Compute the fixed asset turnover ratios for 2009 and 2008. Round the ratios to two decimal places. Is the trend going in the right direction?
6. Compute the debt-to-assets ratios for 2009 and 2008. Round the ratios to two decimal places. Is debt providing financing for a larger or smaller proportion of the company's asset growth? Explain.
7. Compute the times interest earned ratios for 2009 and 2008. Round the ratios to one decimal place. Do they look good or bad? Explain.
8. After Pinnacle Plus released its 2009 financial statements, the company's stock was trading at $18. After the release of its 2008 financial statements, the company's stock price was $15 per share. Compute the P/E ratios for both years rounded to one decimal place. Does it appear that investors have become more (or less) optimistic about Pinnacle's future success?

LO4
Coca-Cola & Pepsico

PA17-3 Interpreting Profitability, Liquidity, Solvency, and P/E Ratios

Coke and Pepsi are well-known international brands. Coca-Cola sells more than $23 billion worth of beverages each year while annual sales of Pepsi products exceed $32 billion. Compare the two companies as a potential investment based on the following ratios:

Ratio	Coca-Cola	PepsiCo
Gross profit percentage	48.5 %	49.0 %
Net profit margin	2.6 %	4.1 %
Return on equity	66.2 %	23.3 %
EPS	$ 3.40	$ 1.54
Receivables turnover	11.5	9.8
Inventory turnover	15.1	12.8
Current ratio	1.47	1.40
Debt to assets	0.94	0.72
Price/Earnings	16.4	18.7

Required:

1. Which company appears more profitable? Describe the ratio(s) that you used to reach this decision.
2. Which company appears more liquid? Describe the ratio(s) that you used to reach this decision.
3. Which company appears more solvent? Describe the ratio(s) that you used to reach this decision.
4. Are the conclusions from your analyses in requirements 1–3 consistent with the value of the two companies suggested by the P/E ratio of each company? If not, offer one explanation for any apparent inconsistency.

LO4

PA17-4 Using Ratios to Compare Loan Requests from Two Companies

The 2008 financial statements for Royale and Cavalier companies are summarized here:

www.mhhe.com/LLPW1e

	Royale Company	Cavalier Company
Balance Sheet		
Cash	$ 25,000	$ 45,000
Accounts receivable (net)	55,000	5,000
Inventory	110,000	25,000
Property and equipment (net)	550,000	160,000
Other assets	140,000	57,000
Total assets	$880,000	$292,000
Current liabilities	$120,000	$ 15,000
Long-term debt	190,000	55,000
Capital stock (par $20)	480,000	210,000
Additional paid-in capital	50,000	4,000
Retained earnings	40,000	8,000
Total liabilities and stockholders' equity	$880,000	$292,000
Income Statement		
Sales revenue	$800,000	$280,000
Cost of goods sold	(480,000)	(150,000)
Expenses (including interest and income tax)	(240,000)	(95,000)
Net income	$ 80,000	$ 35,000
Selected Data from 2007 Statements		
Accounts receivable, net	$ 47,000	$ 11,000
Long-term debt	190,000	55,000
Property and equipment, net	550,000	160,000
Inventory	95,000	38,000
Total stockholders' equity	570,000	202,000
Other Data		
Per share price at end of 2008	$ 14.00	$ 11.00
Average income tax rate	30%	30%

These two companies are in the same line of business and in the same state but in different cities. One-half of Royale's sales are on credit whereas one-quarter of Cavalier's sales are on credit. Each company has been in operation for about 10 years. Both companies received an unqualified audit opinion on the financial statements, which means the independent auditors found nothing wrong. Royale Company wants to borrow $75,000 cash, and Cavalier Company is asking for $30,000. The loans will be for a two-year period. Both companies estimate bad debts based on an aging analysis, but Cavalier has estimated slightly higher uncollectible rates than Royale.

Required:

1. Complete a schedule that reflects the following ratios for each company: return on equity, gross profit percentage, net profit margin, earnings per share, fixed asset turnover, price earnings, current, receivables turnover, inventory turnover, debt to assets.
2. Assume you work in the loan department of a local bank. You have been asked to analyze the situation and recommend which loan is preferable. Based on the data given, your analysis prepared in requirement 1, and any other information, give your choice and the supporting explanation.

PA17-5 Analyzing an Investment by Comparing Selected Ratios LO4

You have the opportunity to invest $10,000 in one of two companies from a single industry. The only information you have is shown here. The word *high* refers to the top third of the industry; *average* is the middle third; *low* is the bottom third.

Ratio	Company A	Company B
Current	Low	High
Inventory turnover	High	Low
Debt to assets	Low	Average
Times interest earned	High	Average
Price/earnings	High	Average

Required:
Which company would you select? Write a brief explanation for your recommendation.

Problems—Set B  Available with McGraw-Hill's Homework Manager

LO2, 3 **PB17-1 Analyzing Financial Statements Using Ratios and Percentage Changes**
The comparative financial statements prepared at December 31, 2010, for Tiger Audio showed the following summarized data:

			INCREASE (DECREASE) 2010 OVER 2009	
	2010	2009	Amount	Percentage
Income Statement				
Sales revenue*	$222,000	$185,000		
Cost of goods sold	127,650	111,000		
Gross profit	94,350	74,000		
Operating expenses	39,600	33,730		
Interest expense	4,000	3,270		
Income before income taxes	50,750	37,000		
Income tax expense (30%)	15,225	11,100		
Net income	$ 35,525	$ 25,900		
Balance Sheet				
Cash	$ 40,000	$ 38,000		
Accounts receivable (net)	18,500	16,000		
Inventory	25,000	22,000		
Property and equipment (net)	127,000	119,000		
Total assets	$210,500	$195,000		
Accounts payable	$ 27,000	$ 25,000		
Income taxes payable	3,000	2,800		
Note payable, long term	75,500	92,200		
Total liabilities	105,500	120,000		
Capital stock (par $1)	25,000	25,000		
Retained earnings†	80,000	50,000		
Total liabilities and stockholders' equity	$210,500	$195,000		

* One-half of all sales are on credit.
† During 2010, cash dividends amounting to $5,525 were declared and paid.

Required:

1. Complete the Amount and Percentage columns in Tiger Audio's comparative financial statements to prepare a horizontal (trend) analysis. Round the percentages to one decimal place. Does anything significant jump out at you from the year-to-year analyses?
2. Prepare common size income statements and balance sheets for the two years. Round the percentages to one decimal place. What significant changes have taken place in the relationship among items in the balance sheet and income statement?

PB17-2 Analyzing Comparative Financial Statements Using Selected Ratios LO4

Use the data given in PB17-1 for Tiger Audio.

Required:

1. Compute the gross profit percentages in 2010 and 2009. Is the trend going in the right direction?
2. Compute the net profit margin ratios in 2010 and 2009. Is the trend going in the right direction?
3. Compute the earnings per share for 2010 and 2009. Does the trend look good or bad? Explain.
4. Stockholders' equity totaled $65,000 at the end of 2008. Compute the return on equity ratios for 2010 and 2009. Is the trend going in the right direction?
5. Net property and equipment totaled $115,000 at the end of 2008. Compute the fixed asset turnover ratios for 2010 and 2009. Is the trend going in the right direction?
6. Compute the debt-to-assets ratios for 2010 and 2009. Is debt providing financing for a larger or smaller proportion of the company's asset growth? Explain.
7. Compute the times interest earned ratios for 2010 and 2009. Do they look good or bad? Explain.
8. After Tiger released its 2010 financial statements, the company's stock was trading at $17. After the release of its 2009 financial statements, the company's stock price was $12 per share. Compute the P/E ratios for both years rounded to one decimal place. Does it appear that investors have become more (or less) optimistic about Tiger Audio's future success?

PB17-3 Interpreting Profitability, Liquidity, Solvency, and P/E Ratios LO4

Mattel and Hasbro are the two largest makers of games and toys in the world. Mattel sells more than $5 billion of products each year while annual sales of Hasbro products exceed $3 billion. Compare the two companies as a potential investment based on the following ratios:

Hasbro

Ratio	Mattel	Hasbro
Gross profit percentage	48.3 %	58.7 %
Net profit margin	10.3 %	5.7 %
Return on equity	23.6 %	13.6 %
EPS	$ 1.23	$ 0.91
Receivables turnover	7.2	6.4
Inventory turnover	5.5	5.7
Current ratio	1.86	1.89
Debt to assets	0.24	0.33
Price/Earnings	15.2	18.9

Required:

1. Which company appears more profitable? Describe the ratio(s) that you used to reach this decision.
2. Which company appears more liquid? Describe the ratio(s) that you used to reach this decision.
3. Which company appears more solvent? Describe the ratio(s) that you used to reach this decision.
4. Are the conclusions from your analyses in requirements 1–3 consistent with the value of the two companies suggested by the P/E ratio of each company? If not, offer one explanation for any apparent inconsistency.

LO4

PB17-4 Using Ratios to Compare Loan Requests from Two Companies

The 2010 financial statements for Thor and Gunnar Companies are summarized here:

	Thor Company	Gunnar Company
Balance Sheet		
Cash	$ 35,000	$ 54,000
Accounts receivable (net)	77,000	6,000
Inventory	154,000	30,000
Property and equipment (net)	770,000	192,000
Other assets	196,000	68,400
Total assets	$1,232,000	$ 350,400
Current liabilities	$ 168,000	$ 18,000
Long-term debt (12% interest rate)	266,000	66,000
Capital stock (par $20)	672,000	252,000
Additional paid-in capital	70,000	4,800
Retained earnings	56,000	9,600
Total liabilities and stockholders' equity	$1,232,000	$ 350,400
Income Statement		
Sales revenue	$1,120,000	$ 336,000
Cost of goods sold	(672,000)	(180,000)
Expenses (including interest and income tax)	(336,000)	(114,000)
Net income	$ 112,000	$ 42,000
Selected Data from 2009 Statements		
Accounts receivable, net	$ 65,800	$ 13,200
Inventory	133,000	45,600
Property and equipment, net	770,000	192,000
Long-term debt (12% interest rate)	266,000	66,000
Total stockholders' equity	798,000	266,400
Other Data		
Per share price at end of 2010	$ 13.20	$ 19.60
Average income tax rate	30%	30%

These two companies are in the same line of business and in the same state but in different cities. One-half of Thor's sales are on credit, whereas one-quarter of Gunnar's sales are on credit. Each company has been in operation for about 10 years. Both companies received an unqualified audit opinion on the financial statements, which means the independent auditors found nothing wrong. Thor Company wants to borrow $105,000 cash, and Gunnar Company is asking for $36,000. The loans will be for a two-year period.

Required:

1. Complete a schedule that reflects the following ratios for each company: return on equity, gross profit percentage, net profit margin, earnings per share, fixed asset turnover, price earnings, current, receivables turnover, inventory turnover, debt to assets.
2. Assume you work in the loan department of a local bank. You have been asked to analyze the situation and recommend which loan is preferable. Based on the data given, your analysis prepared in requirement 1, and any other information, give your choice and the supporting explanation.

LO4

PB17-5 Analyzing an Investment by Comparing Selected Ratios

You have the opportunity to invest $10,000 in one of two companies from a single industry. The only information you have is shown here. The word *high* refers to the top third of the industry; *average* is the middle third; *low* is the bottom third.

Ratio	Company A	Company B
EPS	High	High
Return on equity	High	Average
Debt to assets	High	Low
Current	Low	Average
Price/Earnings	Low	High

Required:

Which company would you select? Write a brief explanation for your recommendation.

Cases and Projects

CP17-1 Finding Financial Information

LO4

Refer to the financial statements of The Home Depot in Appendix A at the end of this book, or download the annual report from the *Cases* section of the text's Web site at www.mhhe.com/LLPW1e. Compute and interpret the ratios discussed in the chapter for the most recent year presented. Assume that the stock price was $30.44.

CP17-2 Comparing Financial Information

LO4

Lowe's

Refer to the financial statements of Lowe's in Appendix B at the end of this book, or download the annual report from the *Cases* section of the text's Web site at www.mhhe.com/LLPW1e. From the list of ratios that were discussed in this chapter, compute and interpret the ratios that help you compare Lowe's to the results for The Home Depot for the most recent year presented. Assume that Lowe's stock price was $25.55 and The Home Depot's stock price was $30.44.

CP17-3 Examining an Annual Report: Internet-Based Team Research

LO1, 2, 3, 4

As a team, select an industry to analyze. Using your Web browser, each team member should acquire the annual report or 10-K for one publicly traded company in the industry with each member selecting a different company. (See CP1-3 in Chapter 1 for a description of possible resources for these tasks.)

Required:

1. On an individual basis, each team member should write a short report that incorporates trend analysis and as many of the ratios from the chapter as are applicable given the nature of the selected company.
2. Then, as a team, write a short report comparing and contrasting your companies using these attributes. Discuss any patterns across the companies that you as a team observe. Provide potential explanations for any differences discovered.

CP17-4 Making Ethical Decisions: A Real-Life Example

LO4

During its deliberations on the Sarbanes-Oxley Act, the U.S. Senate considered numerous reports evaluating the quality of work done by external auditors. One study by Weiss Ratings, Inc., focused on auditors' ability to predict bankruptcy. The study criticized auditors for failing to identify and report going-concern problems for audit clients that later went bankrupt. Based on a sample of 45 bankrupt companies, the Weiss study concluded that had auditors noted unusual levels for just two of seven typical financial ratios, they would have identified 89 percent of the sample companies that later went bankrupt. A follow-up to the Weiss study found that had the criteria in the Weiss study been applied to a larger sample of nonbankrupt companies, 46.9 percent of nonbankrupt companies would have been predicted to go bankrupt.* In other words, the Weiss criteria would have incorrectly predicted bankruptcy for nearly half of the companies in the follow-up study and would have led the auditors to report that these clients had substantial going-concern problems when, in fact, they did not.

* Michael D. Akers, Meredith A. Maher, and Don E. Giacomino, "Going-Concern Opinions: Broadening the Expectations Gap," *CPA Journal*, October 2003 (n. d.), www.nysscpa.org/cpajournal/2003/1003/features/f103803.htm (November 20, 2006).

Required:

Discuss the negative consequences that arise when auditors fail to predict companies that go bankrupt. Who is harmed by these failures? Discuss the negative consequences that arise when auditors incorrectly predict bankruptcy. Who is harmed by these errors? In your opinion, which of the potential consequences is worse?

LO4

CP17-5 Making Ethical Decisions: A Mini Case

Capital Investments Corporation (CIC) requested a sizable loan from First Federal Bank to acquire a large piece of land for future expansion. CIC reported current assets of $1,900,000 (including $430,000 in cash) and current liabilities of $1,075,000. First Federal denied the loan request for a number of reasons, including the fact that the current ratio was below 2:1. When CIC was informed of the loan denial, the controller of the company immediately paid $420,000 that was owed to several trade creditors. The controller then asked First Federal to reconsider the loan application.

Required:

Based on these abbreviated facts, would you recommend that First Federal approve the loan request? Why? Are the controller's actions ethical?

LO4

CP17-6 Thinking Critically: Analyzing the Impact of Alternative Depreciation Methods on Ratio Analysis

Speedy Company uses the double-declining-balance method to depreciate its property, plant, and equipment. Turtle Company uses the straight-line method. The two companies are exactly alike except for the difference in depreciation methods.

Required:

1. Identify the financial ratios discussed in this chapter that are likely to be affected by the difference in depreciation methods.
2. Which company will report the higher amount for each ratio that you have identified? If you cannot be certain, explain why.

LO4

CP17-7 Using a Spreadsheet to Calculate Financial Statement Ratios

Use the financial statement information from Exhibits 17.2, and 17.3.

Required:

Enter the financial information for each exhibit into two separate worksheets in one spreadsheet file. Create a third worksheet that uses the formulas in Exhibit 17.6 to recalculate ratios (1) through (14) for Lowe's for 2006. (For the EPS ratio, simply import the amount reported on the face of the income statement stock price is $31 per share.)

THE HOME DEPOT, INC. 2007 ANNUAL REPORT*

* This appendix contains excerpts. Go to the text Web site at www.mhhe.com/LLPW1e for the complete report.

DEAR SHAREHOLDERS, ASSOCIATES, CUSTOMERS, SUPPLIERS AND COMMUNITIES:

This past year was one of the most difficult our company has faced. Year-over-year retail sales declined by 2.1 percent, with comp sales down 6.7 percent. Our operating margin declined 186 basis points and our earnings per share from continuing operations were down 11 percent.

We began the year with the objectives of focusing on our retail business, investing in our associates and stores, and improving our customer service. We stayed true to those objectives despite the economic headwinds and invested over $2 billion in five key priorities: **associate engagement, product excitement, product availability, shopping environment and own the pro.** These investments put additional pressure on earnings in a difficult environment, but we are convinced the right long-term strategy starts with the customer experience in our stores. In each priority area, we made significant progress.

ASSOCIATE ENGAGEMENT:

Our founders emphasized the importance of taking care of our associates who take care of our customers. This is as important today as it was twenty years ago. It is an investment we know will strengthen our market leadership position. This past year, we took significant steps to improve the compensation and recognition of our associates and to build on the expertise in our stores. We implemented a new restricted stock bonus program for our assistant store managers. We are the only retailer of our size to award equity grants at that level of management. For us, it is important that our assistant store managers feel and act like owners. We significantly increased participation and payout of our Success Sharing bonuses for hourly associates and rolled out a new Homer Badge merit program to recognize great customer service. I hope as you shop our stores you will notice the associates who are proudly wearing these badges. We hired more than 2,500 Master Trade Specialists in our plumbing and electrical departments. These associates are licensed plumbers and electricians and provide both knowledgeable service to our customers and great training for associates. As a result of these and other efforts, full time voluntary attrition was down almost 20 percent in 2007.

PRODUCT EXCITEMENT:

Our customers expect great value and exciting products in our stores. In 2007, as in the past, we focused on meeting those expectations. We invested significantly in merchandising resets, drove product innovation through our successful launch of the Ryobi Lithium One+ line of power tools and our Eco Options program, and revamped product lines to drive greater value for our customers. We are particularly proud of the leadership we maintained in a number of categories including appliances, outdoor living, live goods, and paint.

PRODUCT AVAILABILITY:

In 2007, we took an important first step in transforming our supply chain. We piloted a new distribution network and technology - Rapid Deployment Centers (RDCs). The pilot was successful, and we will be rolling out RDCs throughout 2008 and 2009. We are confident that our future supply chain will dramatically improve our supply chain efficiency, improve our in stock levels, improve our asset efficiency, and improve our ability to meet increasingly differentiated customer needs.

SHOPPING ENVIRONMENT:

Our store base is getting older, and we have to protect one of our most important assets. We increased store maintenance in 2007, spending 38 percent more than our 2006 maintenance levels and two times our 2005 maintenance levels. We developed a sustainable programmatic approach to maintenance, with specific schedules for polishing floors, remodeling restrooms, and replacing major equipment such as air conditioners and service desks. As shown through our "Voice of the Customer" surveys, our customers appreciate these investments.

OWN THE PRO:

We know that the professional customer is a critically important customer for us. This year we rolled out several programs aimed at better serving our pros. One of these is our pro bid room, which allows us to better manage large customer orders. Our professional customers look to us for the right products in the right quantities to make their jobs easier. We reinforced our job lot quantity program in our stores and revised our delivery service for better utilization. We are also leveraging our customer data to build stronger relationships with this key customer segment.

INTERNATIONAL:

While discussing progress in 2007, I'd like to give special recognition to our international businesses in Mexico, Canada and China. Our stores in Mexico had double digit positive comps for the year. Our stores in Canada posted positive comps. In China, once we launched our Home Depot brand in August 2007, our stores posted positive comps. Our international stores contributed almost 10 percent of sales and 12 percent of operating profit in 2007. These results demonstrate how well our format translates and the sizable opportunity to

VALUES WHEEL

expand to new areas such as Guam, where we opened our first store this year.

As I complete my first year in this role, I want to thank the Board of Directors for their support and dedication. I would especially like to recognize our directors that are retiring this year: John Clendenin, Claudio González, Mitch Hart, and Ken Langone – one of our founders. Their guidance and counsel has been instrumental in the success of our company.

OUR STRATEGY IS SIMPLE:

We have clearly defined The Home Depot as a retail business. The sale of HD Supply in August of 2007 was the critical step in achieving that clarity and focus. We also defined our capital allocation strategy: We will be focused on improving our return on invested capital and will benchmark all uses of excess cash against the value created for shareholders through share repurchases. With that in mind, we used the proceeds from the sale of HD Supply and cash on hand to buy back $10.7 billion of stock. This puts us approximately halfway through our announced $22.5 billion recapitalization plan. Our cash flow will help determine the timing of the remaining steps in the recapitalization plan, as we look to maintain an adjusted debt/EBITDAR ratio of 2.5 times. We are targeting a payout ratio of 30 percent, amongst the highest ratios in retail.

Our strategy: focus on our retail business, invest in our people, improve our stores, bring great products at great value to our customers, drive a high return on invested capital, and return excess cash to our shareholders.

For 2008, we are expecting a year every bit as challenging as 2007. We plan on opening fewer stores than has been our historical practice as we continue to invest and sharpen our focus on existing stores. We will continue to invest in our business along the five priorities set out in 2007. As part of our investment plan, we have aggressive plans to build out our U.S. supply chain, to put more associates on the selling floor through a major "aprons on the floor" initiative, and to take the first step in transforming our information technology infrastructure by converting our Canadian business to an Enterprise Resource Planning platform focused on enhancing our merchandising and customer facing activities. As our market improves and as the benefits of these investments in our business take hold, we look forward over the next four years to returning to a double digit operating margin.

We will also continue to build relationships and strengthen ties with our communities. This has been a hallmark of The Home Depot. One of the best parts of my job is hearing about the extraordinary things our associates do to help each other, help our customers and help our communities every day. We are a values based business, and we do our best to live and celebrate the values represented on the wheel depicted on this page. We recognize the self-reinforcing strength of these values builds great customer service. I hope, as you shop in our stores, you will notice our continuing improvement and the value of the investments we are making.

Frank

Francis S. Blake
Chairman & Chief Executive Officer
April 3, 2008

Item 8. Financial Statements and Supplementary Data.

Management's Responsibility for Financial Statements

The financial statements presented in this Annual Report have been prepared with integrity and objectivity and are the responsibility of the management of The Home Depot, Inc. These financial statements have been prepared in conformity with U.S. generally accepted accounting principles and properly reflect certain estimates and judgments based upon the best available information.

The financial statements of the Company have been audited by KPMG LLP, an independent registered public accounting firm. Their accompanying report is based upon an audit conducted in accordance with the standards of the Public Company Accounting Oversight Board (United States).

The Audit Committee of the Board of Directors, consisting solely of outside directors, meets five times a year with the independent registered public accounting firm, the internal auditors and representatives of management to discuss auditing and financial reporting matters. In addition, a telephonic meeting is held prior to each quarterly earnings release. The Audit Committee retains the independent registered public accounting firm and regularly reviews the internal accounting controls, the activities of the independent registered public accounting firm and internal auditors and the financial condition of the Company. Both the Company's independent registered public accounting firm and the internal auditors have free access to the Audit Committee.

Management's Report on Internal Control over Financial Reporting

Our management is responsible for establishing and maintaining adequate internal control over financial reporting, as such term is defined in Rules 13a-15(f) promulgated under the Securities Exchange Act of 1934, as amended. Under the supervision and with the participation of our management, including our chief executive officer and chief financial officer, we conducted an evaluation of the effectiveness of our internal control over financial reporting as of February 3, 2008 based on the framework in *Internal Control – Integrated Framework* issued by the Committee of Sponsoring Organizations of the Treadway Commission (COSO). Based on our evaluation, our management concluded that our internal control over financial reporting was effective as of February 3, 2008 in providing reasonable assurance regarding the reliability of financial reporting and the preparation of financial statements for external purposes in accordance with generally accepted accounting principles. The effectiveness of our internal control over financial reporting as of February 3, 2008 has been audited by KPMG LLP, an independent registered public accounting firm, as stated in their report which is included on page 32 in this Form 10-K.

/s/ FRANCIS S. BLAKE	**/s/ CAROL B. TOMÉ**
Francis S. Blake **Chairman &** **Chief Executive Officer**	**Carol B. Tomé** **Chief Financial Officer &** **Executive Vice President – Corporate Services**

Report of Independent Registered Public Accounting Firm

The Board of Directors and Stockholders
The Home Depot, Inc.:

We have audited The Home Depot Inc.'s internal control over financial reporting as of February 3, 2008, based on criteria established in *Internal Control – Integrated Framework* issued by the Committee of Sponsoring Organizations of the Treadway Commission (COSO). The Home Depot Inc.'s management is responsible for maintaining effective internal control over financial reporting and for its assessment of the effectiveness of internal control over financial reporting, included in the accompanying Management's Report on Internal Control Over Financial Reporting. Our responsibility is to express an opinion on the Company's internal control over financial reporting based on our audit.

We conducted our audit in accordance with the standards of the Public Company Accounting Oversight Board (United States). Those standards require that we plan and perform the audit to obtain reasonable assurance about whether effective internal control over financial reporting was maintained in all material respects. Our audit included obtaining an understanding of internal control over financial reporting, assessing the risk that a material weakness exists, and testing and evaluating the design and operating effectiveness of internal control based on the assessed risk. Our audit also included performing such other procedures as we considered necessary in the circumstances. We believe that our audit provides a reasonable basis for our opinion.

A company's internal control over financial reporting is a process designed to provide reasonable assurance regarding the reliability of financial reporting and the preparation of financial statements for external purposes in accordance with generally accepted accounting principles. A company's internal control over financial reporting includes those policies and procedures that (1) pertain to the maintenance of records that, in reasonable detail, accurately and fairly reflect the transactions and dispositions of the assets of the company; (2) provide reasonable assurance that transactions are recorded as necessary to permit preparation of financial statements in accordance with generally accepted accounting principles, and that receipts and expenditures of the company are being made only in accordance with authorizations of management and directors of the company; and (3) provide reasonable assurance regarding prevention or timely detection of unauthorized acquisition, use, or disposition of the company's assets that could have a material effect on the financial statements.

Because of its inherent limitations, internal control over financial reporting may not prevent or detect misstatements. Also, projections of any evaluation of effectiveness to future periods are subject to the risk that controls may become inadequate because of changes in conditions, or that the degree of compliance with the policies or procedures may deteriorate.

In our opinion, The Home Depot, Inc. maintained, in all material respects, effective internal control over financial reporting as of February 3, 2008, based on criteria established in *Internal Control – Integrated Framework* issued by the Committee of Sponsoring Organizations of the Treadway Commission.

We also have audited, in accordance with the standards of the Public Company Accounting Oversight Board (United States), the Consolidated Balance Sheets of The Home Depot, Inc. and subsidiaries as of February 3, 2008 and January 28, 2007, and the related Consolidated Statements of Earnings, Stockholders' Equity and Comprehensive Income, and Cash Flows for each of the fiscal years in the three-year period ended February 3, 2008, and our report dated March 28, 2008 expressed an unqualified opinion on those consolidated financial statements.

/s/ KPMG LLP

Atlanta, Georgia
March 28, 2008

Report of Independent Registered Public Accounting Firm

The Board of Directors and Stockholders
The Home Depot, Inc.:

We have audited the accompanying Consolidated Balance Sheets of The Home Depot, Inc. and subsidiaries as of February 3, 2008 and January 28, 2007, and the related Consolidated Statements of Earnings, Stockholders' Equity and Comprehensive Income, and Cash Flows for each of the fiscal years in the three-year period ended February 3, 2008. These Consolidated Financial Statements are the responsibility of the Company's management. Our responsibility is to express an opinion on these Consolidated Financial Statements based on our audits.

We conducted our audits in accordance with the standards of the Public Company Accounting Oversight Board (United States). Those standards require that we plan and perform the audit to obtain reasonable assurance about whether the financial statements are free of material misstatement. An audit includes examining, on a test basis, evidence supporting the amounts and disclosures in the financial statements. An audit also includes assessing the accounting principles used and significant estimates made by management, as well as evaluating the overall financial statement presentation. We believe that our audits provide a reasonable basis for our opinion.

In our opinion, the Consolidated Financial Statements referred to above present fairly, in all material respects, the financial position of The Home Depot, Inc. and subsidiaries as of February 3, 2008 and January 28, 2007, and the results of their operations and their cash flows for each of the fiscal years in the three-year period ended February 3, 2008, in conformity with U.S. generally accepted accounting principles.

As discussed in Note 6 to the consolidated financial statements, effective January 29, 2007, the beginning of the fiscal year ended February 3, 2008, the Company adopted Financial Accounting Standards Board Interpretation No. 48, *Accounting for Uncertainty in Income Taxes* . Also, as discussed in Note 3 to the consolidated financial statements, effective January 30, 2006, the beginning of the fiscal year ended January 28, 2007, the Company adopted Securities and Exchange Commission Staff Accounting Bulletin No. 108, *Considering the Effects of Prior Year Misstatements when Quantifying Misstatements in the Current Year Financial Statements* .

We also have audited, in accordance with the standards of the Public Company Accounting Oversight Board (United States), The Home Depot, Inc.'s internal control over financial reporting as of February 3, 2008, based on criteria established in *Internal Control – Integrated Framework* issued by the Committee of Sponsoring Organizations of the Treadway Commission (COSO), and our report dated March 28, 2008 expressed an unqualified opinion on the effectiveness of the Company's internal control over financial reporting.

/s/ KPMG LLP

Atlanta, Georgia
March 28, 2008

THE HOME DEPOT, INC. AND SUBSIDIARIES

CONSOLIDATED STATEMENTS OF EARNINGS

amounts in millions, except per share data	Fiscal Year Ended (1) February 3, 2008	January 28, 2007	January 29, 2006
NET SALES	**$ 77,349**	$ 79,022	$ 77,019
Cost of Sales	**51,352**	52,476	51,081
GROSS PROFIT	**25,997**	26,546	25,938
Operating Expenses:			
Selling, General and Administrative	**17,053**	16,106	15,480
Depreciation and Amortization	**1,702**	1,574	1,411
Total Operating Expenses	**18,755**	17,680	16,891
OPERATING INCOME	**7,242**	8,866	9,047
Interest (Income) Expense:			
Interest and Investment Income	**(74)**	(27)	(62)
Interest Expense	**696**	391	142
Interest, net	**622**	364	80
EARNINGS FROM CONTINUING OPERATIONS BEFORE PROVISION FOR INCOME TAXES	**6,620**	8,502	8,967
Provision for Income Taxes	**2,410**	3,236	3,326
EARNINGS FROM CONTINUING OPERATIONS	**4,210**	5,266	5,641
EARNINGS FROM DISCONTINUED OPERATIONS, NET OF TAX	**185**	495	197
NET EARNINGS	**$ 4,395**	$ 5,761	$ 5,838
Weighted Average Common Shares	**1,849**	2,054	2,138
BASIC EARNINGS PER SHARE FROM CONTINUING OPERATIONS	**$ 2.28**	$ 2.56	$ 2.64
BASIC EARNINGS PER SHARE FROM DISCONTINUED OPERATIONS	**$ 0.10**	$ 0.24	$ 0.09
BASIC EARNINGS PER SHARE	**$ 2.38**	$ 2.80	$ 2.73
Diluted Weighted Average Common Shares	**1,856**	2,062	2,147
DILUTED EARNINGS PER SHARE FROM CONTINUING OPERATIONS	**$ 2.27**	$ 2.55	$ 2.63
DILUTED EARNINGS PER SHARE FROM DISCONTINUED OPERATIONS	**$ 0.10**	$ 0.24	$ 0.09
DILUTED EARNINGS PER SHARE	**$ 2.37**	$ 2.79	$ 2.72

(1) Fiscal year ended February 3, 2008 includes 53 weeks. Fiscal years ended January 28, 2007 and January 29, 2006 include 52 weeks.

See accompanying Notes to Consolidated Financial Statements.

THE HOME DEPOT, INC. AND SUBSIDIARIES

CONSOLIDATED BALANCE SHEETS

amounts in millions, except share and per share data	February 3, 2008	January 28, 2007
ASSETS		
Current Assets:		
Cash and Cash Equivalents	**$ 445**	$ 600
Short-Term Investments	**12**	14
Receivables, net	**1,259**	3,223
Merchandise Inventories	**11,731**	12,822
Other Current Assets	**1,227**	1,341
Total Current Assets	**14,674**	18,000
Property and Equipment, at cost:		
Land	**8,398**	8,355
Buildings	**16,642**	15,215
Furniture, Fixtures and Equipment	**8,050**	7,799
Leasehold Improvements	**1,390**	1,391
Construction in Progress	**1,435**	1,123
Capital Leases	**497**	475
	36,412	34,358
Less Accumulated Depreciation and Amortization	**8,936**	7,753
Net Property and Equipment	**27,476**	26,605
Notes Receivable	**342**	343
Goodwill	**1,209**	6,314
Other Assets	**623**	1,001
Total Assets	**$ 44,324**	$ 52,263
LIABILITIES AND STOCKHOLDERS' EQUITY		
Current Liabilities:		
Short-Term Debt	**$ 1,747**	$ —
Accounts Payable	**5,732**	7,356
Accrued Salaries and Related Expenses	**1,094**	1,307
Sales Taxes Payable	**445**	475
Deferred Revenue	**1,474**	1,634
Income Taxes Payable	**60**	217
Current Installments of Long-Term Debt	**300**	18
Other Accrued Expenses	**1,854**	1,924
Total Current Liabilities	**12,706**	12,931
Long-Term Debt, excluding current installments	**11,383**	11,643
Other Long-Term Liabilities	**1,833**	1,243
Deferred Income Taxes	**688**	1,416
Total Liabilities	**26,610**	27,233
STOCKHOLDERS' EQUITY		
Common Stock, par value $0.05; authorized: 10 billion shares; issued 1.698 billion shares at February 3, 2008 and 2.421 billion shares at January 28, 2007; outstanding 1.690 billion shares at February 3, 2008 and 1.970 billion shares at January 28, 2007	**85**	121
Paid-In Capital	**5,800**	7,930
Retained Earnings	**11,388**	33,052
Accumulated Other Comprehensive Income	**755**	310
Treasury Stock, at cost, 8 million shares at February 3, 2008 and 451 million shares at January 28, 2007	**(314)**	(16,383)
Total Stockholders' Equity	**17,714**	25,030
Total Liabilities and Stockholders' Equity	**$ 44,324**	$ 52,263

See accompanying Notes to Consolidated Financial Statements.

THE HOME DEPOT, INC. AND SUBSIDIARIES

CONSOLIDATED STATEMENTS OF STOCKHOLDERS' EQUITY AND COMPREHENSIVE INCOME

amounts in millions, except per share data	Common Stock		Paid-In Capital	Retained Earnings	Accumulated Other Comprehensive Income (Loss)	Treasury Stock		Stockholders' Equity	Total Comprehensive Income
	Shares	Amount				Shares	Amount		
BALANCE, JANUARY 30, 2005	**2,385**	**$ 119**	**$ 6,542**	**$ 23,962**	**$ 227**	**(200)**	**$ (6,692)**	**$ 24,158**	
Net Earnings	—	—	—	5,838	—	—	—	5,838	$ 5,838
Shares Issued Under Employee Stock Plans	16	1	409	—	—	—	—	410	
Tax Effect of Sale of Option Shares by Employees	—	—	24	—	—	—	—	24	
Translation Adjustments	—	—	—	—	182	—	—	182	182
Stock Options, Awards and Amortization of Restricted Stock	—	—	174	—	—	—	—	174	
Repurchase of Common Stock	—	—	—	—	—	(77)	(3,020)	(3,020)	
Cash Dividends ($0.40 per share)	—	—	—	(857)	—	—	—	(857)	
Comprehensive Income									$ 6,020
BALANCE, JANUARY 29, 2006	**2,401**	**$ 120**	**$ 7,149**	**$ 28,943**	**$ 409**	**(277)**	**$ (9,712)**	**$ 26,909**	
Cumulative Effect of Adjustment Resulting from the Adoption of SAB 108, net of tax	—	—	201	(257)	—	—	—	(56)	
ADJUSTED BALANCE, JANUARY 29, 2006	**2,401**	**$ 120**	**$ 7,350**	**$ 28,686**	**$ 409**	**(277)**	**$ (9,712)**	**$ 26,853**	
Net Earnings	—	—	—	5,761	—	—	—	5,761	$ 5,761
Shares Issued Under Employee Stock Plans	20	1	351	—	—	—	—	352	
Tax Effect of Sale of Option Shares by Employees	—	—	18	—	—	—	—	18	
Translation Adjustments	—	—	—	—	(77)	—	—	(77)	(77)
Cash Flow Hedges	—	—	—	—	(22)	—	—	(22)	(22)
Stock Options, Awards and Amortization of Restricted Stock	—	—	296	—	—	—	—	296	
Repurchase of Common Stock	—	—	—	—	—	(174)	(6,671)	(6,671)	
Cash Dividends ($0.675 per share)	—	—	—	(1,395)	—	—	—	(1,395)	
Other	—	—	(85)	—	—	—	—	(85)	
Comprehensive Income									$ 5,662
BALANCE, JANUARY 28, 2007	**2,421**	**$ 121**	**$ 7,930**	**$ 33,052**	**$ 310**	**(451)**	**$ (16,383)**	**$ 25,030**	
Cumulative Effect of the Adoption of FIN 48	—	—	—	(111)	—	—	—	(111)	
Net Earnings	—	—	—	4,395	—	—	—	4,395	$ 4,395
Shares Issued Under Employee Stock Plans	12	1	239	—	—	—	—	240	
Tax Effect of Sale of Option Shares by Employees	—	—	4	—	—	—	—	4	
Translation Adjustments	—	—	—	—	455	—	—	455	455
Cash Flow Hedges	—	—	—	—	(10)	—	—	(10)	(10)
Stock Options, Awards and Amortization of Restricted Stock	—	—	206	—	—	—	—	206	
Repurchase of Common Stock	—	—	—	—	—	(292)	(10,815)	(10,815)	
Retirement of Treasury Stock	(735)	(37)	(2,608)	(24,239)	—	735	26,884	—	
Cash Dividends ($0.90 per share)	—	—	—	(1,709)	—	—	—	(1,709)	
Other	—	—	29	—	—	—	—	29	
Comprehensive Income									$ 4,840
BALANCE, FEBRUARY 3, 2008	**1,698**	**$ 85**	**$ 5,800**	**$ 11,388**	**$ 755**	**(8)**	**$ (314)**	**$ 17,714**	

See accompanying Notes to Consolidated Financial Statements.

THE HOME DEPOT, INC. AND SUBSIDIARIES

CONSOLIDATED STATEMENTS OF CASH FLOWS

amounts in millions	Fiscal Year Ended (1) February 3, 2008	January 28, 2007	January 29, 2006
CASH FLOWS FROM OPERATING ACTIVITIES:			
Net Earnings	**$ 4,395**	$ 5,761	$ 5,838
Reconciliation of Net Earnings to Net Cash Provided by Operating Activities:			
Depreciation and Amortization	**1,906**	1,886	1,579
Stock-Based Compensation Expense	**207**	297	175
Changes in Assets and Liabilities, net of the effects of acquisitions and disposition:			
Decrease (Increase) in Receivables, net	**116**	96	(358)
Increase in Merchandise Inventories	**(491)**	(563)	(971)
Decrease (Increase) in Other Current Assets	**109**	(225)	16
(Decrease) Increase in Accounts Payable and Accrued Liabilities	**(465)**	531	148
(Decrease) Increase in Deferred Revenue	**(159)**	(123)	209
(Decrease) Increase in Income Taxes Payable	**—**	(172)	175
(Decrease) Increase in Deferred Income Taxes	**(348)**	46	(609)
Increase (Decrease) in Other Long-Term Liabilities	**186**	(51)	151
Other	**271**	178	267
Net Cash Provided by Operating Activities	**5,727**	7,661	6,620
CASH FLOWS FROM INVESTING ACTIVITIES:			
Capital Expenditures, net of $19, $49 and $51 of non-cash capital expenditures in fiscal 2007, 2006 and 2005, respectively	**(3,558)**	(3,542)	(3,881)
Proceeds from Sale of Business, net	**8,337**	—	—
Payments for Businesses Acquired, net	**(13)**	(4,268)	(2,546)
Proceeds from Sales of Property and Equipment	**318**	138	164
Purchases of Investments	**(11,225)**	(5,409)	(18,230)
Proceeds from Sales and Maturities of Investments	**10,899**	5,434	19,907
Net Cash Provided by (Used in) Investing Activities	**4,758**	(7,647)	(4,586)
CASH FLOWS FROM FINANCING ACTIVITIES:			
Proceeds from (Repayments of) Short-Term Borrowings, net	**1,734**	(900)	900
Proceeds from Long-Term Borrowings, net of discount	**—**	8,935	995
Repayments of Long-Term Debt	**(20)**	(509)	(24)
Repurchases of Common Stock	**(10,815)**	(6,684)	(3,040)
Proceeds from Sale of Common Stock	**276**	381	414
Cash Dividends Paid to Stockholders	**(1,709)**	(1,395)	(857)
Other Financing Activities	**(105)**	(31)	(136)
Net Cash Used in Financing Activities	**(10,639)**	(203)	(1,748)
(Decrease) Increase in Cash and Cash Equivalents	**(154)**	(189)	286
Effect of Exchange Rate Changes on Cash and Cash Equivalents	**(1)**	(4)	1
Cash and Cash Equivalents at Beginning of Year	**600**	793	506
Cash and Cash Equivalents at End of Year	**$ 445**	$ 600	$ 793
SUPPLEMENTAL DISCLOSURE OF CASH PAYMENTS MADE FOR:			
Interest, net of interest capitalized	**$ 672**	$ 270	$ 114
Income Taxes	**$ 2,524**	$ 3,963	$ 3,860

(1) Fiscal year ended February 3, 2008 includes 53 weeks. Fiscal years ended January 28, 2007 and January 29, 2006 include 52 weeks.

See accompanying Notes to Consolidated Financial Statements.

NOTES TO CONSOLIDATED FINANCIAL STATEMENTS

1. SUMMARY OF SIGNIFICANT ACCOUNTING POLICIES

Business, Consolidation and Presentation

The Home Depot, Inc. and its subsidiaries (the "Company") operate The Home Depot stores, which are full-service, warehouse-style stores averaging approximately 105,000 square feet in size. The stores stock approximately 35,000 to 45,000 different kinds of building materials, home improvement supplies and lawn and garden products that are sold to do-it-yourself customers, do-it-for-me customers, home improvement contractors, tradespeople and building maintenance professionals. In addition, the Company operates EXPO Design Center stores ("EXPO"), which offer products and services primarily related to design and renovation projects. At the end of fiscal 2007, the Company was operating 2,234 stores in total, which included 1,950 The Home Depot stores, 34 EXPO stores, five Yardbirds stores and two THD Design Center stores in the United States, including the territories of Puerto Rico, the Virgin Islands and Guam ("U.S."), 165 The Home Depot stores in Canada, 66 The Home Depot stores in Mexico and 12 The Home Depot stores in China.

Information related to the Company's discontinued HD Supply business is discussed in Note 2. The Consolidated Financial Statements include the accounts of the Company and its wholly-owned subsidiaries. All significant intercompany transactions have been eliminated in consolidation.

Fiscal Year

The Company's fiscal year is a 52- or 53-week period ending on the Sunday nearest to January 31. Fiscal year ended February 3, 2008 ("fiscal 2007") includes 53 weeks and fiscal years ended January 28, 2007 ("fiscal 2006") and January 29, 2006 ("fiscal 2005") include 52 weeks.

Use of Estimates

Management of the Company has made a number of estimates and assumptions relating to the reporting of assets and liabilities, the disclosure of contingent assets and liabilities, and reported amounts of revenues and expenses in preparing these financial statements in conformity with generally accepted accounting principles in the U.S. Actual results could differ from these estimates.

Fair Value of Financial Instruments

The carrying amounts of Cash and Cash Equivalents, Receivables, Short-Term Debt and Accounts Payable approximate fair value due to the short-term maturities of these financial instruments. The fair value of the Company's investments is discussed under the caption "Short-Term Investments" in this Note 1. The fair value of the Company's Long-Term Debt is discussed in Note 5.

Cash Equivalents

The Company considers all highly liquid investments purchased with original maturities of three months or less to be cash equivalents. The Company's Cash Equivalents are carried at fair market value and consist primarily of high-grade commercial paper, money market funds and U.S. government agency securities.

Short-Term Investments

Short-Term Investments are recorded at fair value based on current market rates and are classified as available-for-sale.

Accounts Receivable

The Company has an agreement with a third-party service provider who directly extends credit to customers, manages the Company's private label credit card program and owns the related receivables. We evaluated the third-party entities holding the receivables under the program and concluded that they should not be consolidated by the Company in accordance with the provisions of Financial Accounting Standards Board ("FASB") Interpretation No. 46(R), "Consolidation of Variable Interest Entities." The agreement with the third-party service provider expires in 2011, with the Company having the option, but no obligation, to purchase the receivables at the end of the agreement. The deferred interest charges incurred by the Company for its deferred financing programs offered to its customers are included in Cost of Sales. The interchange fees charged to the Company for the customers' use of the cards and the profit sharing with the third-party administrator are included in Selling, General and Administrative expenses ("SG&A").

In addition, certain subsidiaries of the Company extend credit directly to customers in the ordinary course of business. The receivables due from customers were $57 million and $1.8 billion as of February 3, 2008 and January 28, 2007, respectively, a decrease resulting from the sale of HD Supply. The Company's valuation reserve related to accounts receivable was not material to the Consolidated Financial Statements of the Company as of the end of fiscal 2007 or 2006.

Merchandise Inventories

The majority of the Company's Merchandise Inventories are stated at the lower of cost (first-in, first-out) or market, as determined by the retail inventory method. As the inventory retail value is adjusted regularly to reflect market conditions, the inventory valued using the retail method approximates the lower of cost or market. Certain subsidiaries, including retail operations in Mexico and China, and distribution centers record Merchandise Inventories at the lower of cost (first-in, first-out) or market, as determined by the cost method. These Merchandise Inventories represent approximately 11% of the total Merchandise Inventories balance. The Company evaluates the inventory valued using the cost method at the end of each quarter to ensure that it is carried at the lower of cost or market. The valuation allowance for Merchandise Inventories valued under the cost method was not material to the Consolidated Financial Statements of the Company as of the end of fiscal 2007 or 2006.

Independent physical inventory counts or cycle counts are taken on a regular basis in each store and distribution center to ensure that amounts reflected in the accompanying Consolidated Financial Statements for Merchandise Inventories are properly stated. During the period between physical inventory counts in stores, the Company accrues for estimated losses related to shrink on a store-by-store basis based on historical shrink results and current trends in the business. Shrink (or in the case of excess inventory, "swell") is the difference between the recorded amount of inventory and the physical inventory. Shrink may occur due to theft, loss, inaccurate records for the receipt of inventory or deterioration of goods, among other things.

Income Taxes

The Company provides for federal, state and foreign income taxes currently payable, as well as for those deferred due to timing differences between reporting income and expenses for financial statement purposes versus tax purposes. Federal, state and foreign tax benefits are recorded as a reduction of income taxes. Deferred tax assets and liabilities are recognized for the future tax consequences attributable to temporary differences between the financial statement carrying amounts of existing assets and liabilities and their respective tax bases. Deferred tax assets and liabilities are measured using enacted income tax rates expected to apply to taxable income in the years in which those temporary differences are expected to be recovered or settled. The effect of a change in income tax rates is recognized as income or expense in the period that includes the enactment date.

The Company and its eligible subsidiaries file a consolidated U.S. federal income tax return. Non-U.S. subsidiaries and certain U.S. subsidiaries, which are consolidated for financial reporting purposes, are not eligible to be included in the Company's consolidated U.S. federal income tax return. Separate provisions for income taxes have been determined for these entities. The Company intends to reinvest substantially all of the unremitted earnings of its non-U.S. subsidiaries and postpone their remittance indefinitely. Accordingly, no provision for U.S. income taxes for these non-U.S. subsidiaries was recorded in the accompanying Consolidated Statements of Earnings.

Depreciation and Amortization

The Company's Buildings, Furniture, Fixtures and Equipment are recorded at cost and depreciated using the straight-line method over the estimated useful lives of the assets. Leasehold Improvements are amortized using the straight-line method over the original term of the lease or the useful life of the improvement, whichever is shorter. The Company's Property and Equipment is depreciated using the following estimated useful lives:

	Life
Buildings	10-45 years
Furniture, Fixtures and Equipment	3-20 years
Leasehold Improvements	5-45 years

Capitalized Software Costs

The Company capitalizes certain costs related to the acquisition and development of software and amortizes these costs using the straight-line method over the estimated useful life of the software, which is three to six years. These costs are included in Furniture, Fixtures and Equipment in the accompanying Consolidated Balance Sheets. Certain development costs not meeting the criteria for capitalization are expensed as incurred.

Revenues

The Company recognizes revenue, net of estimated returns and sales tax, at the time the customer takes possession of merchandise or receives services. The liability for sales returns is estimated based on historical return levels. When the Company receives payment from customers before the customer has taken possession of the merchandise or the service has been performed, the amount received is recorded as Deferred Revenue in the accompanying Consolidated Balance Sheets until the sale or service is complete. The Company also records Deferred Revenue for the sale of gift cards and recognizes this revenue upon the redemption of gift cards in Net Sales. Gift card breakage income is recognized based upon historical redemption patterns and represents the balance of gift cards for which the Company believes the likelihood of redemption by the customer is remote. During fiscal 2007, 2006 and 2005, the Company recognized $36 million, $33 million and $52 million, respectively, of gift card breakage income. Fiscal 2005 was the first year in which the Company recognized gift card breakage income, and therefore, the amount recognized includes the gift card breakage income related to gift cards sold since the inception of the gift card program. This income is recorded as other income and is included in the accompanying Consolidated Statements of Earnings as a reduction in SG&A.

Services Revenue

Net Sales include services revenue generated through a variety of installation, home maintenance and professional service programs. In these programs, the customer selects and purchases material for a project and the Company provides or arranges professional installation. These programs are offered through the Company's stores. Under certain programs, when the Company provides or arranges the installation of a project and the subcontractor provides material as part of the installation, both the material and labor are included in services revenue. The Company recognizes this revenue when the service for the customer is complete.

All payments received prior to the completion of services are recorded in Deferred Revenue in the accompanying Consolidated Balance Sheets. Services revenue was $3.5 billion, $3.8 billion and $3.5 billion for fiscal 2007, 2006 and 2005, respectively.

Self-Insurance

The Company is self-insured for certain losses related to general liability, product liability, automobile, workers' compensation and medical claims. The expected ultimate cost for claims incurred as of the balance sheet date is not discounted and is recognized as a liability. The expected ultimate cost of claims is estimated based upon analysis of historical data and actuarial estimates.

Prepaid Advertising

Television and radio advertising production costs, along with media placement costs, are expensed when the advertisement first appears. Included in Other Current Assets in the accompanying Consolidated Balance Sheets are $31 million and $44 million, respectively, at the end of fiscal 2007 and 2006 relating to prepayments of production costs for print and broadcast advertising as well as sponsorship promotions.

Vendor Allowances

Vendor allowances primarily consist of volume rebates that are earned as a result of attaining certain purchase levels and advertising co-op allowances for the promotion of vendors' products that are typically based on guaranteed minimum amounts with additional amounts being earned for attaining certain purchase levels. These vendor allowances are accrued as earned, with those allowances received as a result of attaining certain purchase levels accrued over the incentive period based on estimates of purchases.

Volume rebates and certain advertising co-op allowances earned are initially recorded as a reduction in Merchandise Inventories and a subsequent reduction in Cost of Sales when the related product is sold. Certain advertising co-op allowances that are reimbursements of specific, incremental and identifiable costs incurred to promote vendors' products are recorded as an offset against advertising expense. In fiscal 2007, 2006 and 2005, gross advertising expense was $1.2 billion, $1.2 billion and $1.1 billion, respectively, which was recorded in SG&A. Advertising co-op allowances were $120 million, $83 million and $50 million for fiscal 2007, 2006 and 2005, respectively, and were recorded as an offset to advertising expense in SG&A.

Cost of Sales

Cost of Sales includes the actual cost of merchandise sold and services performed, the cost of transportation of merchandise from vendors to the Company's stores, locations or customers, the operating cost of the Company's sourcing and distribution network and the cost of deferred interest programs offered through the Company's private label credit card program.

The cost of handling and shipping merchandise from the Company's stores, locations or distribution centers to the customer is classified as SG&A. The cost of shipping and handling, including internal costs and payments to third parties, classified as SG&A was $571 million, $545 million and $480 million in fiscal 2007, 2006 and 2005, respectively.

Goodwill and Other Intangible Assets

Goodwill represents the excess of purchase price over the fair value of net assets acquired. The Company does not amortize goodwill, but does assess the recoverability of goodwill in the third quarter of each fiscal year by determining whether the fair value of each reporting unit supports its carrying value. The fair values of the Company's identified reporting units were estimated using the expected present value of discounted cash flows.

The Company amortizes the cost of other intangible assets over their estimated useful lives, which range from 1 to 20 years, unless such lives are deemed indefinite. Intangible assets with indefinite lives are tested in the third quarter of each fiscal year for impairment. The Company recorded no impairment charges for goodwill or other intangible assets for fiscal 2007, 2006 or 2005.

Impairment of Long-Lived Assets

The Company evaluates the carrying value of long-lived assets when management makes the decision to relocate or close a store or other location, or when circumstances indicate the carrying amount of an asset may not be recoverable. A store's assets are evaluated for impairment by comparing its undiscounted cash flows with its carrying value. If the carrying value is greater than the undiscounted cash flows, a provision is made to write down the related assets to fair value if the carrying value is greater than the fair value. Impairment losses are recorded as a component of SG&A in the accompanying Consolidated Statements of Earnings. When a location closes, the Company also recognizes in SG&A the net present value of future lease obligations, less estimated sublease income.

In fiscal 2005 the Company recorded $91 million in SG&A related to asset impairment charges and on-going lease obligations associated with closing 20 of its EXPO stores. Additionally, the Company recorded $29 million of expense in Cost of Sales in fiscal 2005 related to inventory markdowns in these stores. The Company also recorded impairments on other closings and relocations in the ordinary course of business, which were not material to the Consolidated Financial Statements of the Company in fiscal 2007, 2006 and 2005.

Stock-Based Compensation

Effective February 3, 2003, the Company adopted the fair value method of recording stock-based compensation expense in accordance with Statement of Financial Accounting Standards ("SFAS") No. 123, "Accounting for Stock-Based Compensation" ("SFAS 123"). The Company selected the prospective method of adoption as described in SFAS No. 148, "Accounting for Stock-Based Compensation – Transition and Disclosure," and accordingly, stock-based compensation expense was recognized for stock options granted, modified or settled and expense related to the Employee Stock Purchase Plan ("ESPP") after the beginning of fiscal 2003. Effective January 30, 2006, the Company adopted the fair value recognition provisions of SFAS No. 123(R), "Share-Based Payment" ("SFAS 123(R)"), using the modified prospective transition method. Under the modified prospective transition method, the Company began expensing unvested options granted prior to fiscal 2003 in addition to continuing to recognize stock-based compensation expense for all share-based payments awarded since the adoption of SFAS 123 in fiscal 2003. During fiscal 2006, the Company recognized additional stock compensation expense of approximately $40 million as a result of the adoption of SFAS 123(R). Results of prior periods have not been restated.

The per share weighted average fair value of stock options granted during fiscal 2007, 2006 and 2005 was $9.45, $11.88 and $12.83, respectively. The fair value of these options was determined at the date of grant using the Black-Scholes option-pricing model with the following assumptions:

	Fiscal Year Ended		
	February 3, 2008	**January 28, 2007**	**January 29, 2006**
Risk-free interest rate	**4.4%**	4.7%	4.3%
Assumed volatility	**25.5%**	28.5%	33.7%
Assumed dividend yield	**2.4%**	1.5%	1.1%
Assumed lives of option	**6 years**	5 years	5 years

The following table illustrates the effect on Net Earnings and Earnings per Share as if the Company had applied the fair value recognition provisions of SFAS 123(R) to all stock-based compensation in each period (amounts in millions, except per share data):

	Fiscal Year Ended		
	February 3, 2008	**January 28, 2007**	**January 29, 2006**
Net Earnings, as reported	**$ 4,395**	$ 5,761	$ 5,838
Add: Stock-based compensation expense included in reported Net Earnings, net of related tax effects	**131**	186	110
Deduct: Total stock-based compensation expense determined under fair value based method for all awards, net of related tax effects	**(131)**	(186)	(197)
Pro forma net earnings	**$ 4,395**	$ 5,761	$ 5,751
Earnings per Share:			
Basic – as reported	**$ 2.38**	$ 2.80	$ 2.73
Basic – pro forma	**$ 2.38**	$ 2.80	$ 2.69
Diluted – as reported	**$ 2.37**	$ 2.79	$ 2.72
Diluted – pro forma	**$ 2.37**	$ 2.79	$ 2.68

Derivatives

The Company uses derivative financial instruments from time to time in the management of its interest rate exposure on long-term debt and its exposure on foreign currency fluctuations. The Company accounts for its derivative financial instruments in accordance with SFAS No. 133, "Accounting for Derivative Instruments and Hedging Activities."

Comprehensive Income

Comprehensive Income includes Net Earnings adjusted for certain revenues, expenses, gains and losses that are excluded from Net Earnings under generally accepted accounting principles in the U.S. Adjustments to Net Earnings and Accumulated Other Comprehensive Income consist primarily of foreign currency translation adjustments.

Foreign Currency Translation

Assets and Liabilities denominated in a foreign currency are translated into U.S. dollars at the current rate of exchange on the last day of the reporting period. Revenues and Expenses are generally translated using average exchange rates for the period and equity transactions are translated using the actual rate on the day of the transaction.

Segment Information

The Company operates within a single operating segment primarily within North America. Net Sales for the Company outside of the U.S. were $7.4 billion, $6.3 billion and $5.2 billion for fiscal 2007, 2006 and 2005, respectively. Long-lived assets outside of the U.S. totaled $3.1 billion and $2.5 billion as of February 3, 2008 and January 28, 2007, respectively.

Reclassifications

Certain amounts in prior fiscal years have been reclassified to conform with the presentation adopted in the current fiscal year.

2. DISPOSITION AND ACQUISITIONS

On August 30, 2007, the Company closed the sale of HD Supply. The Company received $8.3 billion of net proceeds for the sale of HD Supply and recognized a $4 million loss, net of tax, on the sale of the business, subject to the finalization of working capital adjustments. Also in connection with the sale, the Company purchased a 12.5% equity interest in the newly formed HD Supply for $325 million, which is included in Other Assets in the accompanying Consolidated Balance Sheets.

Also in connection with the sale, the Company guaranteed a $1.0 billion senior secured loan ("guaranteed loan") of HD Supply. The fair value of the guarantee, which was determined to be approximately $16 million, is recorded as a liability of the Company and included in Other Long-Term Liabilities. The guaranteed loan has a term of five years and the Company would be responsible for up to $1.0 billion and any unpaid interest in the event of non-payment by HD Supply. The guaranteed loan is collateralized by certain assets of HD Supply.

In accordance with Statement of Financial Accounting Standards No. 144, "Accounting for the Impairment or Disposal of Long-Lived Assets" ("SFAS 144"), the Company reclassified the results of HD Supply as discontinued operations in its Consolidated Statements of Earnings for all periods presented.

The following table presents Net Sales and Earnings of HD Supply through August 30, 2007 which have been reclassified to discontinued operations in the Consolidated Statements of Earnings for fiscal 2007, 2006 and 2005 (amounts in millions):

	Fiscal Year Ended		
	February 3, 2008	**January 28, 2007**	**January 29, 2006**
Net Sales	**$ 7,391**	$ 11,815	$ 4,492
Earnings Before Provision for Income Taxes	**$ 291**	$ 806	$ 315
Provision for Income Taxes	**(102)**	(311)	(118)
Loss on Discontinued Operations, net	**(4)**	—	—
Earnings from Discontinued Operations, net of tax	**$ 185**	$ 495	$ 197

During fiscal 2007, the Company acquired Ohio Water & Waste Supply, Inc. and Geosynthetics, Inc. These acquisitions operated under HD Supply and were included in the disposition. The aggregate purchase price for acquisitions in fiscal 2007, 2006 and 2005 was $25 million, $4.5 billion and $2.6 billion, respectively, including $3.5 billion for Hughes Supply in fiscal 2006. The Company recorded Goodwill related to the HD Supply businesses of $20 million, $2.8 billion and $1.8 billion for fiscal 2007, 2006 and 2005, respectively, and recorded no Goodwill related to its retail businesses for fiscal 2007 compared to $229 million and $111 million for fiscal 2006 and 2005, respectively, in the accompanying Consolidated Balance Sheets.

3. STAFF ACCOUNTING BULLETIN NO. 108

In fiscal 2006, the Company adopted Staff Accounting Bulletin No. 108, "Considering the Effects of Prior Year Misstatements when Quantifying Misstatements in Current Year Financial Statements" ("SAB 108"). SAB 108 addresses the process of quantifying prior year financial statement misstatements and their impact on current year financial statements. The provisions of SAB 108 allowed companies to report the cumulative effect of correcting immaterial prior year misstatements, based on the Company's historical method for evaluating misstatements, by adjusting the opening balance of retained earnings in the financial statements of the year of adoption rather than amending previously filed reports. In accordance with SAB 108, the Company adjusted beginning Retained Earnings for fiscal 2006 in the accompanying Consolidated Financial Statements for the items described below. The Company does not consider these adjustments to have a material impact on the Company's consolidated financial statements in any of the prior years affected.

Historical Stock Option Practices

During fiscal 2006, the Company requested that its Board of Directors review its historical stock option granting practices. A subcommittee of the Audit Committee undertook the review with the assistance of independent outside counsel, and it has completed its review. The principal findings of the 2006 review were as follows:

- All options granted in the period from 2002 through the present had an exercise price based on the market price of the Company's stock on the date the grant was approved by the Board of Directors or an officer acting pursuant to delegated authority. During this period, the stock administration department corrected administrative errors retroactively and without separate approvals. The administrative errors included inadvertent omissions of grantees from lists that were approved previously and miscalculations of the number of options granted to particular employees on approved lists.

- All options granted from December 1, 2000 through the end of 2001 had an exercise price based on the market price of the Company's stock on the date of a meeting of the Board of Directors or some other date selected without the benefit of hindsight. The February 2001 annual grant was not finally allocated to recipients until several weeks after the grant was approved. During this period, the stock administration department also corrected administrative errors retroactively and without separate approvals as in the period 2002 to the present.

- For annual option grants and certain quarterly option grants from 1981 through November 2000, the stated grant date was routinely earlier than the actual date on which the grants were approved by a committee of the Board of Directors. In almost every instance, the stock price on the apparent approval date was higher than the price on the stated grant date. The backdating occurred for grants at all levels of the Company. Management personnel, who have since left the Company, generally followed a practice of reviewing closing prices for a prior period and selecting a date with a low stock price to increase the value of the options to employees on lists of grantees subsequently approved by a committee of the Board of Directors.

- The annual option grants in 1994 through 2000, as well as many quarterly grants during this period, were not finally allocated among the recipients until several weeks after the stated grant date. Because of the absence of records prior to 1994, it is unclear whether allocations also postdated the selected grant dates from 1981 through 1993. Moreover, for many of these annual and quarterly grants from 1981 through December 2000, there is insufficient documentation to determine with certainty when the grants were actually authorized by a committee of the Board of Directors. Finally, the Company's stock administration department also retroactively added employees to lists of approved grantees, or changed the number of options granted to specific employees, without authorization of the Board of Directors or a board committee, to correct administrative errors.

- Numerous option grants to rank-and-file employees were made pursuant to delegations of authority that may not have been effective under Delaware law.

- In numerous instances, and primarily prior to 2003, beneficiaries of grants who were required to report them to the SEC failed to do so in a timely manner or at all.

- The subcommittee concluded that there was no intentional wrongdoing by any current member of the Company's management team or its Board of Directors.

The Company believes that because of these errors, it had unrecorded expense over the affected period (1981 through 2005) of $227 million in the aggregate, including related tax items. In accordance with the provisions of SAB 108, the Company decreased beginning Retained Earnings for fiscal 2006 by $227 million within the accompanying Consolidated Financial Statements.

As previously disclosed, the staff of the SEC began in June 2006 an informal inquiry into the Company's stock option practices, and the U.S. Attorney for the Southern District of New York has also requested information on the subject. The Company is continuing to cooperate with these agencies. While the Company cannot predict the outcome of these matters, it does not believe that they will have a material adverse impact on its consolidated financial condition or results of operations.

The Company does not believe that the effect of the stock option adjustment was material, either quantitatively or qualitatively, in any of the years covered by the review of these items. In reaching that determination, the following quantitative measures were considered (dollars in millions):

Fiscal Year	Net After-tax Effect of Adjustment	Reported Net Earnings	Percent of Reported Net Earnings
2005	$ 11	$ 5,838	0.19%
2004	18	5,001	0.36
2003	18	4,304	0.42
2002	21	3,664	0.57
1981-2001	159	14,531	1.09
Total	$ 227	$ 33,338	0.68%

Vendor Credits

The Company records credits against vendor invoices for various issues related to the receipt of goods. The Company previously identified that it was not recording an allowance for subsequent reversals of these credits based on historical experience. Beginning Retained Earnings for fiscal 2006 was decreased by $30 million in the accompanying Consolidated Financial Statements to reflect the appropriate adjustments to Merchandise Inventories and Accounts Payable, net of tax.

Impact of Adjustments

The impact of each of the items noted above, net of tax, on fiscal 2006 beginning balances are presented below (amounts in millions):

	Cumulative Effect as of January 30, 2006		
	Stock Option Practices	Vendor Credits	Total
Merchandise Inventories	$ —	$ 9	$ 9
Accounts Payable	—	(59)	(59)
Deferred Income Taxes	11	20	31
Other Accrued Expenses	(37)	—	(37)
Paid-In Capital	(201)	—	(201)
Retained Earnings	227	30	257
Total	$ —	$ —	$ —

4. INTANGIBLE ASSETS

The Company's intangible assets at the end of fiscal 2007 and 2006, which are included in Other Assets in the accompanying Consolidated Balance Sheets, consisted of the following (amounts in millions):

	February 3, 2008	January 28, 2007
Customer relationships	$ 11	$ 756
Trademarks and franchises	83	106
Other	29	67
Less accumulated amortization	(23)	(151)
Total	$ 100	$ 778

The decrease in intangible assets from January 28, 2007 to February 3, 2008 was a result of the sale of HD Supply. Amortization expense related to intangible assets in continuing operations was $9 million, $10 million and less than $1 million for fiscal 2007, 2006 and 2005, respectively. Estimated future amortization expense for intangible assets recorded as of February 3, 2008 is $8 million, $8 million, $8 million, $5 million and $4 million for fiscal 2008 through fiscal 2012, respectively.

5. DEBT

The Company has commercial paper programs that allow for borrowings up to $3.25 billion. All of the Company's short-term borrowings in fiscal 2007 and 2006 were under these commercial paper programs. In connection with the commercial paper programs, the Company has a back-up credit facility with a consortium of banks for borrowings up to $3.0 billion. The credit facility, which expires in December 2010, contains various restrictions, none of which is expected to materially impact the Company's liquidity or capital resources.

Short-Term Debt under the commercial paper program was as follows (dollars in millions):

	February 3, 2008	January 28, 2007
Balance outstanding at fiscal year-end	**$ 1,747**	$ —
Maximum amount outstanding at any month-end	**$ 1,747**	$ 1,470
Average daily short-term borrowings	**$ 526**	$ 300
Weighted average interest rate	**5.0%**	5.1%

The Company's Long-Term Debt at the end of fiscal 2007 and 2006 consisted of the following (amounts in millions):

	February 3, 2008	January 28, 2007
3.75% Senior Notes; due September 15, 2009; interest payable semi-annually on March 15 and September 15	$ **998**	$ 997
Floating Rate Senior Notes; due December 16, 2009; interest payable on March 16, June 16, September 16 and December 16	**750**	750
4.625% Senior Notes; due August 15, 2010; interest payable semi-annually on February 15 and August 15	**998**	997
5.20% Senior Notes; due March 1, 2011; interest payable semi-annually on March 1 and September 1	**1,000**	1,000
5.25% Senior Notes; due December 16, 2013; interest payable semi-annually on June 16 and December 16	**1,244**	1,243
5.40% Senior Notes; due March 1, 2016; interest payable semi-annually on March 1 and September 1	**3,017**	2,986
5.875% Senior Notes; due December 16, 2036; interest payable semi-annually on June 16 and December 16	**2,959**	2,958
Capital Lease Obligations; payable in varying installments through January 31, 2055	**415**	419
Other	**302**	311
Total Long-Term Debt	**11,683**	11,661
Less current installments	**300**	18
Long-Term Debt, excluding current installments	$ **11,383**	$ 11,643

At February 3, 2008, the Company had outstanding interest rate swaps, accounted for as fair value hedges, with notional amounts of $2.0 billion that swap fixed rate interest on the Company's $3.0 billion 5.40% Senior Notes for variable rate interest equal to LIBOR plus 60 to 149 basis points that expire on March 1, 2016. At February 3, 2008, the approximate fair value of these agreements was an asset of $29 million, which is the estimated amount the Company would have received to settle similar interest rate swap agreements at current interest rates.

At February 3, 2008, the Company had outstanding an interest rate swap, accounted for as a cash flow hedge, with a notional amount of $750 million that swaps variable rate interest on the Company's $750 million floating rate Senior Notes for fixed rate interest at 4.36% that expires on December 16, 2009. At February 3, 2008, the approximate fair value of this agreement was a liability of $17 million, which is the estimated amount the Company would have paid to settle similar interest rate swap agreements at current interest rates.

In December 2006, the Company issued $750 million of floating rate Senior Notes due December 16, 2009 at par value, $1.25 billion of 5.25% Senior Notes due December 16, 2013 at a discount of $7 million and $3.0 billion of 5.875% Senior Notes due December 16, 2036 at a discount of $42 million, together the "December 2006 Issuance." The net proceeds of the December 2006 Issuance were used to fund, in part, the Company's common stock repurchases, to repay outstanding commercial paper and for general corporate purposes. The $49 million discount and $37 million of issuance costs associated with the December 2006 Issuance are being amortized to interest expense over the term of the related Senior Notes.

Additionally in October 2006, the Company entered into a forward starting interest rate swap agreement with a notional amount of $1.0 billion, accounted for as a cash flow hedge, to hedge interest rate fluctuations in anticipation of the issuance of the 5.875% Senior Notes due December 16, 2036. Upon issuance of the hedged debt in December 2006, the Company settled its forward starting interest rate swap agreements and recorded an $11 million decrease, net of income taxes, to Accumulated Other Comprehensive Income, which will be amortized to interest expense over the life of the related debt.

In March 2006, the Company issued $1.0 billion of 5.20% Senior Notes due March 1, 2011 at a discount of $1 million and $3.0 billion of 5.40% Senior Notes due March 1, 2016 at a discount of $15 million, together the "March 2006 Issuance." The net proceeds of the March 2006 Issuance were used to pay for the acquisition price of Hughes Supply, Inc. and for the repayment of the Company's 5.375% Senior Notes due April 2006 in the aggregate principal amount of $500 million. The $16 million discount and $19 million of issuance costs associated with the March 2006 Issuance are being amortized to interest expense over the term of the related Senior Notes.

Additionally in March 2006, the Company entered into a forward starting interest rate swap agreement with a notional amount of $2.0 billion, accounted for as a cash flow hedge, to hedge interest rate fluctuations in anticipation of the issuance of the 5.40% Senior Notes due March 1, 2016. Upon issuance of the hedged debt, the Company settled its forward starting interest rate swap agreements and recorded a $12 million decrease, net of income taxes, to Accumulated Other Comprehensive Income, which will be amortized to interest expense over the life of the related debt.

In August 2005, the Company issued $1.0 billion of 4.625% Notes due August 15, 2010 ("August 2005 Issuance") at a discount of $5 million. The net proceeds of $995 million were used to pay for a portion of the acquisition price of National Waterworks, Inc. The $5 million discount and $7 million of issuance costs associated with the August 2005 Issuance are being amortized to interest expense over the term of the related Senior Notes.

The Company also had $1.0 billion of 3.75% Senior Notes due September 15, 2009 outstanding as of February 3, 2008, collectively referred to with the December 2006 Issuance, March 2006 Issuance and August 2005 Issuance as "Senior Notes." The Senior Notes may be redeemed by the Company at any time, in whole or in part, at a redemption price plus accrued interest up to the redemption date. The redemption price is equal to the greater of (1) 100% of the principal amount of the Senior Notes to be redeemed, or (2) the sum of the present values of the remaining scheduled payments of principal and interest to maturity. Additionally, if a Change in Control Triggering Event occurs, as defined by the terms of the December 2006 Issuance, holders of the December 2006 Issuance have the right to require the Company to redeem those notes at 101% of the aggregate principal amount of the notes plus accrued interest up to the redemption date.

The Company is generally not limited under the indenture governing the Senior Notes in its ability to incur additional indebtedness or required to maintain financial ratios or specified levels of net worth or liquidity. However, the indenture governing the Senior Notes contains various restrictive covenants, none of which is expected to impact the Company's liquidity or capital resources.

Interest Expense in the accompanying Consolidated Statements of Earnings is net of interest capitalized of $46 million, $47 million and $51 million in fiscal 2007, 2006 and 2005, respectively. Maturities of Long-Term Debt are $300 million for fiscal 2008, $1.8 billion for fiscal 2009, $1.0 billion for fiscal 2010, $1.0 billion for fiscal 2011, $23 million for fiscal 2012 and $7.5 billion thereafter.

As of February 3, 2008, the market value of the Senior Notes was approximately $10.5 billion. The estimated fair value of all other long-term borrowings, excluding capital lease obligations, was approximately $307 million compared to the carrying value of $302 million. These fair values were estimated using a discounted cash flow analysis based on the Company's incremental borrowing rate for similar liabilities.

6. INCOME TAXES

The components of Earnings From Continuing Operations before Provision for Income Taxes for fiscal 2007, 2006 and 2005 were as follows (amounts in millions):

	Fiscal Year Ended		
	February 3, 2008	**January 28, 2007**	**January 29, 2006**
United States	**$ 5,905**	$ 7,915	$ 8,427
Foreign	**715**	587	540
Total	**$ 6,620**	$ 8,502	$ 8,967

The Provision for Income Taxes consisted of the following (amounts in millions):

	Fiscal Year Ended		
	February 3, 2008	**January 28, 2007**	**January 29, 2006**
Current:			
Federal	**$ 2,055**	$ 2,557	$ 3,316
State	**285**	361	493
Foreign	**310**	326	155
	2,650	3,244	3,964
Deferred:			
Federal	**(242)**	(2)	(553)
State	**17**	(1)	(110)
Foreign	**(15)**	(5)	25
	(240)	(8)	(638)
Total	**$ 2,410**	$ 3,236	$ 3,326

The Company's combined federal, state and foreign effective tax rates for fiscal 2007, 2006 and 2005, net of offsets generated by federal, state and foreign tax benefits, were approximately 36.4%, 38.1% and 37.1%, respectively.

The reconciliation of the Provision for Income Taxes at the federal statutory rate of 35% to the actual tax expense for the applicable fiscal years was as follows (amounts in millions):

	Fiscal Year Ended		
	February 3, 2008	January 28, 2007	January 29, 2006
Income taxes at federal statutory rate	**$ 2,317**	$ 2,976	$ 3,138
State income taxes, net of federal income tax benefit	**196**	234	249
Other, net	**(103)**	26	(61)
Total	**$ 2,410**	$ 3,236	$ 3,326

The tax effects of temporary differences that give rise to significant portions of the deferred tax assets and deferred tax liabilities as of February 3, 2008 and January 28, 2007, were as follows (amounts in millions):

	February 3, 2008	January 28, 2007
Current:		
Deferred Tax Assets:		
Accrued self-insurance liabilities	**$ 155**	$ 94
Other accrued liabilities	**601**	603
Current Deferred Tax Assets	**756**	697
Deferred Tax Liabilities:		
Accelerated inventory deduction	**(118)**	(137)
Other	**(113)**	(29)
Current Deferred Tax Liabilities	**(231)**	(166)
Current Deferred Tax Assets, net	**525**	531
Noncurrent:		
Deferred Tax Assets:		
Accrued self-insurance liabilities	**285**	325
State income taxes	**105**	—
Capital loss carryover	**56**	—
Net operating losses	**52**	66
Other	**54**	—
Valuation allowance	**(7)**	—
Noncurrent Deferred Tax Assets	**545**	391
Deferred Tax Liabilities:		
Property and equipment	**(1,133)**	(1,365)
Goodwill and other intangibles	**(69)**	(361)
Other	**(31)**	(74)
Noncurrent Deferred Tax Liabilities	**(1,233)**	(1,800)
Noncurrent Deferred Tax Liabilities, net	**(688)**	(1,409)
Net Deferred Tax Liabilities	**$ (163)**	$ (878)

Current deferred tax assets and current deferred tax liabilities are netted by tax jurisdiction and noncurrent deferred tax assets and noncurrent deferred tax liabilities are netted by tax jurisdiction, and are included in the accompanying Consolidated Balance Sheets as follows (amounts in millions):

	February 3, 2008	January 28, 2007
Other Current Assets	**$ 535**	$ 561
Other Assets	**—**	7
Other Accrued Expenses	**(10)**	(30)
Deferred Income Taxes	**(688)**	(1,416)
Net Deferred Tax Liabilities	**$ (163)**	$ (878)

The Company believes that the realization of the deferred tax assets is more likely than not, based upon the expectation that it will generate the necessary taxable income in future periods and, except for certain net operating losses discussed below, no valuation reserves have been provided. As a result of disposition of HD Supply, $139 million of net deferred tax liabilities were transferred to the purchaser.

At February 3, 2008, the Company had state and foreign net operating loss carryforwards available to reduce future taxable income, expiring at various dates from 2010 to 2027. Management has concluded that it is more likely than not that the tax benefits related to the net operating losses will be realized. However, certain foreign net operating losses are in jurisdictions where the expiration period is too short to be assured of utilization. Therefore, a $7 million valuation allowance has been provided to reduce the deferred tax asset related to net operating losses to an amount that is more likely than not to be realized. Total valuation allowances at February 3, 2008 were $7 million.

As a result of its sale of HD Supply, the Company incurred a tax loss, resulting in a net capital loss carryover of approximately $159 million. The tax loss on sale resulted primarily from the Company's tax basis in excess of its book investment in HD Supply. The net capital loss carryover will expire in 2012. However, the Company has concluded that it is more likely than not that the tax benefits related to the capital loss carryover will be realized based on its ability to generate adequate capital gain income during the carryover period. Therefore, no valuation allowance has been provided.

The Company has not provided for U.S. deferred income taxes on approximately $1.3 billion of undistributed earnings of international subsidiaries because of its intention to indefinitely reinvest these earnings outside the U.S. The determination of the amount of the unrecognized deferred U.S. income tax liability related to the undistributed earnings is not practicable; however, unrecognized foreign income tax credits would be available to reduce a portion of this liability.

The Company's income tax returns are routinely under audit by domestic and foreign tax authorities. These audits generally include questions regarding the timing and amount of depreciation deductions and the allocation of income among various tax jurisdictions. In 2005, the U.S. Internal Revenue Service ("IRS") completed its examination of the Company's U.S. federal income tax returns for fiscal years 2001 and 2002. During 2007, the IRS also completed its examination of the Company's fiscal 2003 and 2004 income tax returns. Certain issues relating to the examinations of fiscal years 2001 through 2004 are under appeal, but only years after fiscal 2004 remain subject to future examination. The Mexican government is currently auditing the Mexican operating subsidiaries' fiscal year 2005 returns, although years after 2001 remain subject to audit. The Canadian governments, including various provinces, are currently auditing income tax returns for the years 2001 through 2005. There are also U.S. state and local audits covering tax years 2001 to 2005. At this time, the Company does not expect the results from any income tax audit to have a material impact on the Company's financial statements.

On January 29, 2007, the Company adopted FASB Interpretation No. 48, "Accounting for Uncertainty in Income Taxes – an Interpretation of FASB Statement No. 109" ("FIN 48"). Among other things, FIN 48 requires application of a "more likely than not" threshold to the recognition and derecognition of tax positions. It further requires that a change in judgment related to prior years' tax positions be recognized in the quarter of such change. The adoption of FIN 48 reduced the Company's Retained Earnings by $111 million. As a result of the implementation, the gross amount of unrecognized tax benefits at January 29, 2007 for continuing operations totaled $667 million. A reconciliation of the beginning and ending amount of gross unrecognized tax benefits for continuing operations is as follows (amounts in millions):

		February 3, 2008
Unrecognized tax benefits balance at January 29, 2007	$	**667**
Additions based on tax positions related to the current year		**66**
Additions for tax positions of prior years		**25**
Reductions for tax positions of prior years		**(115)**
Reductions due to settlements		**(31)**
Reductions due to lapse of statute of limitations		**(4)**
Unrecognized tax benefits balance at February 3, 2008	$	**608**

The gross amount of unrecognized tax benefits as of February 3, 2008 includes $368 million of net unrecognized tax benefits that, if recognized, would affect the annual effective income tax rate.

During fiscal 2007, the Company increased its interest accrual associated with uncertain tax positions by approximately $32 million and paid interest of approximately $8 million. Total accrued interest as of February 3, 2008 is $140 million. There were no penalty accruals during fiscal 2007. Interest and penalties are included in net interest expense and operating expenses, respectively. Our classification of interest and penalties did not change as a result of the adoption of FIN 48.

The Company believes that some individual adjustments under appeal for the completed IRS and Canada audits, as well as other state audits, will be agreed upon within the next twelve months. The IRS issues generally concern the useful life of assets and relevant transfer pricing for intangible assets provided to foreign operations. The Canada issues generally concern the relevant transfer pricing for intangible assets provided from the U.S. State issues generally concern related party expense add-back provisions and forced combination filings. The Company has classified approximately $6 million of the reserve for unrecognized tax benefits as a short-term liability in the accompanying Consolidated Balance Sheets. In addition, there is a reasonable possibility that the Company may resolve the Quebec assessment from prior years, which totaled $65 million at February 3, 2008, within the next twelve months. Final settlement of these audit issues may result in payments that are more or less than these amounts, but the Company does not anticipate the resolution of these matters will result in a material change to its consolidated financial position or results of operations.

7. EMPLOYEE STOCK PLANS

The Home Depot, Inc. 2005 Omnibus Stock Incentive Plan ("2005 Plan") and The Home Depot, Inc. 1997 Omnibus Stock Incentive Plan ("1997 Plan" and collectively with the 2005 Plan, the "Plans") provide that incentive and non-qualified stock options, stock appreciation rights, restricted shares, performance shares, performance units and deferred shares may be issued to selected associates, officers and directors of the Company. Under the 2005 Plan, the maximum number of shares of the Company's common stock authorized for issuance is 255 million shares, with any award other than a stock option reducing the number of shares available for issuance by 2.11 shares. As of February 3, 2008, there were 224 million shares available for future grants under the 2005 Plan. No additional equity awards may be issued from the 1997 Plan after the adoption of the 2005 Plan on May 26, 2005.

Under the Plans, as of February 3, 2008, the Company had granted incentive and non-qualified stock options for 177 million shares, net of cancellations (of which 127 million have been exercised). Under the terms of the Plans, incentive stock options and non-qualified stock options are to be priced at or above the fair market value of the Company's stock on the date of the grant. Typically, incentive stock options and non-qualified stock options vest at the rate of 25% per year commencing on the first anniversary date of the grant and expire on the tenth anniversary date of the grant. The non-qualified stock options also include performance options which vest on the later of the first anniversary date of the grant and the date the closing price of the Company's common stock has been 25% greater than the exercise price of the options for 30 consecutive trading days. The Company recognized $61 million, $148 million and $117 million of stock-based compensation expense in fiscal 2007, 2006 and 2005, respectively, related to stock options.

Under the Plans, as of February 3, 2008, the Company had issued 16 million shares of restricted stock, net of cancellations (the restrictions on 5 million shares have lapsed). Generally, the restrictions on the restricted stock lapse according to one of the following schedules: (1) the restrictions on 100% of the restricted stock lapse at 3, 4 or 5 years, (2) the restrictions on 25% of the restricted stock lapse upon the third and sixth year anniversaries of the date of issuance with the remaining 50% of the restricted stock lapsing upon the associate's attainment of age 62, or (3) the restrictions on 25% of the restricted stock lapse upon the third and sixth year anniversaries of the date of issuance with the remaining 50% of the restricted stock lapsing upon the earlier of the associate's attainment of age 60 or the tenth anniversary date. The restricted stock also includes the Company's performance shares, the payout of which is dependent on the Company's total shareholders return percentile ranking compared to the performance of individual companies included in the S&P 500 index at the end of the three-year performance cycle. Additionally, certain awards may become non-forfeitable upon the attainment of age 60, provided the associate has had five years of continuous service. The fair value of the restricted stock is expensed over the period during which the restrictions lapse. The Company recorded stock-based compensation expense related to restricted stock of $122 million, $95 million and $32 million in fiscal 2007, 2006 and 2005, respectively.

In fiscal 2007, 2006 and 2005, there were 593,000, 417,000 and 461,000 deferred shares, respectively, granted under the Plans. Each deferred share entitles the associate to one share of common stock to be received up to five years after the vesting date of the deferred shares, subject to certain deferral rights of the associate. The Company recorded stock-based compensation expense related to deferred shares of $10 million, $37 million and $10 million in fiscal 2007, 2006 and 2005, respectively.

As of February 3, 2008, there were 2.5 million non-qualified stock options outstanding under non-qualified stock option plans that are not part of the Plans.

The Company maintains two ESPPs (U.S. and non-U.S. plans). The plan for U.S. associates is a tax-qualified plan under Section 423 of the Internal Revenue Code. The non-U.S. plan is not a Section 423 plan. The ESPPs allow associates to purchase up to 152 million shares of common stock, of which 128 million shares have been purchased from inception of the plans. The purchase price of shares under the ESPPs is equal to 85% of the stock's fair market value on the last day of the purchase period. During fiscal 2007, there were 3 million shares purchased under the ESPPs at an average price of $28.25. Under the outstanding ESPPs as of February 3, 2008, employees have contributed $8 million to purchase shares at 85% of the stock's fair market value on the last day (June 30, 2008) of the purchase period. The Company had 24 million shares available for issuance under the ESPPs at February 3, 2008. The Company recognized $14 million, $17 million and $16 million of stock-based compensation in fiscal 2007, 2006 and 2005, respectively, related to the ESPPs.

In total, the Company recorded stock-based compensation expense, including the expense of stock options, ESPPs, restricted stock and deferred stock units, of $207 million, $297 million and $175 million, in fiscal 2007, 2006 and 2005, respectively.

The following table summarizes stock options outstanding at February 3, 2008, January 28, 2007 and January 29, 2006, and changes during the fiscal years ended on these dates (shares in thousands):

	Number of Shares	Weighted Average Exercise Price
Outstanding at January 30, 2005	86,394	$ 36.12
Granted	17,721	37.96
Exercised	(11,457)	28.83
Canceled	(8,626)	38.65
Outstanding at January 29, 2006	84,032	$ 37.24
Granted	257	39.53
Exercised	(10,045)	28.69
Canceled	(8,103)	40.12
Outstanding at January 28, 2007	66,141	$ 38.20
Granted	2,926	37.80
Exercised	(6,859)	28.50
Canceled	(9,843)	40.68
Outstanding at February 3, 2008	52,365	$ 38.98

The total intrinsic value of stock options exercised during fiscal 2007 was $63 million.

As of February 3, 2008, there were approximately 52 million stock options outstanding with a weighted average remaining life of five years and an intrinsic value of $30 million. As of February 3, 2008, there were approximately 42 million options exercisable with a weighted average exercise price of $39.43 and an intrinsic value of $28 million. As of February 3, 2008, there were approximately 51 million shares vested or expected to ultimately vest. As of February 3, 2008, there was $84 million of unamortized stock-based compensation expense related to stock options which is expected to be recognized over a weighted average period of two years.

The following table summarizes restricted stock outstanding at February 3, 2008 (shares in thousands):

	Number of Shares	Weighted Average Grant Date Fair Value
Outstanding at January 29, 2006	5,308	$ 35.76
Granted	7,575	41.37
Restrictions lapsed	(1,202)	38.03
Canceled	(1,551)	39.00
Outstanding at January 28, 2007	10,130	$ 39.20
Granted	7,091	39.10
Restrictions lapsed	(2,662)	39.01
Canceled	(2,844)	39.37
Outstanding at February 3, 2008	11,715	$ 39.14

As of February 3, 2008, there was $267 million of unamortized stock-based compensation expense related to restricted stock which is expected to be recognized over a weighted average period of three years.

8. LEASES

The Company leases certain retail locations, office space, warehouse and distribution space, equipment and vehicles. While most of the leases are operating leases, certain locations and equipment are leased under capital leases. As leases expire, it can be expected that, in the normal course of business, certain leases will be renewed or replaced.

Certain lease agreements include escalating rents over the lease terms. The Company expenses rent on a straight-line basis over the life of the lease which commences on the date the Company has the right to control the property. The cumulative expense recognized on a straight-line basis in excess of the cumulative payments is included in Other Accrued Expenses and Other Long-Term Liabilities in the accompanying Consolidated Balance Sheets.

The Company has a lease agreement under which the Company leases certain assets totaling $282 million. This lease was originally created under a structured financing arrangement and involves two special purpose entities. The Company financed a portion of its new stores opened in fiscal years 1997 through 2003 under this lease agreement. Under this agreement, the lessor purchased the properties, paid for the construction costs and subsequently leased the facilities to the Company. The Company records the rental payments under the terms of the operating lease agreements as SG&A in the accompanying Consolidated Statements of Earnings.

The $282 million lease agreement expires in fiscal 2008 with no renewal option. The lease provides for a substantial residual value guarantee limited to 79% of the initial book value of the assets and includes a purchase option at the original cost of each property. During fiscal 2005, the Company committed to exercise its option to purchase the assets under this lease for $282 million at the end of the lease term in fiscal 2008.

In the first quarter of fiscal 2004, the Company adopted the revised version of FASB Interpretation No. 46(R), "Consolidation of Variable Interest Entities" ("FIN 46"). FIN 46 requires consolidation of a variable interest entity if a company's variable interest absorbs a majority of the entity's expected losses or receives a majority of the entity's expected residual returns, or both. In accordance with FIN 46, the Company was required to consolidate one of the two aforementioned special purpose entities that, before the effective date of FIN 46, met the requirements for non-consolidation. The second special purpose entity that owns the assets leased by the Company totaling $282 million is not owned by or affiliated with the Company, its management or its officers. Pursuant to FIN 46, the Company was not deemed to have a variable interest, and therefore was not required to consolidate this entity.

FIN 46 requires the Company to measure the assets and liabilities at their carrying amounts, which amounts would have been recorded if FIN 46 had been effective at the inception of the transaction. Accordingly, during the first quarter of fiscal 2004, the Company recorded Long-Term Debt of $282 million and Long-Term Notes Receivable of $282 million on the Consolidated Balance Sheets. During fiscal 2007, the liability was reclassified to Current Installments of Long-Term Debt as it is due in fiscal 2008. The Company continues to record the rental payments under the operating lease agreements as SG&A in the Consolidated Statements of Earnings. The adoption of FIN 46 had no economic impact on the Company.

Total rent expense, net of minor sublease income for fiscal 2007, 2006 and 2005 was $824 million, $768 million and $720 million, respectively. Certain store leases also provide for contingent rent payments based on percentages of sales in excess of specified minimums. Contingent rent expense for fiscal 2007, 2006 and 2005 was approximately $6 million, $9 million and $9 million, respectively. Real estate taxes, insurance, maintenance and operating expenses applicable to the leased property are obligations of the Company under the lease agreements.

The approximate future minimum lease payments under capital and all other leases at February 3, 2008 were as follows (in millions):

Fiscal Year	Capital Leases	Operating Leases
2008	$ 79	$ 802
2009	80	716
2010	82	644
2011	82	582
2012	82	523
Thereafter through 2097	882	5,664
	1,287	$ 8,931
Less imputed interest	872	
Net present value of capital lease obligations	415	
Less current installments	15	
Long-term capital lease obligations, excluding current installments	$ 400	

Short-term and long-term obligations for capital leases are included in the accompanying Consolidated Balance Sheets in Current Installments of Long-Term Debt and Long-Term Debt, respectively. The assets under capital leases recorded in Property and Equipment, net of amortization, totaled $327 million and $340 million at February 3, 2008 and January 28, 2007, respectively.

9. EMPLOYEE BENEFIT PLANS

The Company maintains active defined contribution retirement plans for its employees ("the Benefit Plans"). All associates satisfying certain service requirements are eligible to participate in the Benefit Plans. The Company makes cash contributions each payroll period up to specified percentages of associates' contributions as approved by the Board of Directors.

The Company also maintains a restoration plan to provide certain associates deferred compensation that they would have received under the Benefit Plans as a matching contribution if not for the maximum compensation limits under the Internal Revenue Code. The Company funds the restoration plan through contributions made to a grantor trust, which are then used to purchase shares of the Company's common stock in the open market.

The Company's contributions to the Benefit Plans and the restoration plan were $152 million, $135 million and $122 million for fiscal 2007, 2006 and 2005, respectively. At February 3, 2008, the Benefit Plans and the restoration plan held a total of 22 million shares of the Company's common stock in trust for plan participants.

10. BASIC AND DILUTED WEIGHTED AVERAGE COMMON SHARES

The reconciliation of basic to diluted weighted average common shares for fiscal 2007, 2006 and 2005 is as follows (amounts in millions):

	Fiscal Year Ended		
	February 3, 2008	**January 28, 2007**	**January 29, 2006**
Weighted average common shares	**1,849**	2,054	2,138
Effect of potentially dilutive securities:			
Stock Plans	**7**	8	9
Diluted weighted average common shares	**1,856**	2,062	2,147

Stock plans include shares granted under the Company's employee stock plans as described in Note 7 to the Consolidated Financial Statements. Options to purchase 43.4 million, 45.4 million and 55.1 million shares of common stock at February 3, 2008, January 28, 2007 and January 29, 2006, respectively, were excluded from the computation of Diluted Earnings per Share because their effect would have been anti-dilutive.

11. COMMITMENTS AND CONTINGENCIES

At February 3, 2008, the Company was contingently liable for approximately $730 million under outstanding letters of credit and open accounts issued for certain business transactions, including insurance programs, trade contracts and construction contracts. The Company's letters of credit are primarily performance-based and are not based on changes in variable components, a liability or an equity security of the other party.

The Company is a defendant in numerous cases containing class-action allegations in which the plaintiffs are current and former hourly associates who allege that the Company forced them to work "off the clock" or failed to provide work breaks, or otherwise that they were not paid for work performed. The complaints generally seek unspecified monetary damages, injunctive relief or both. Class or collective-action certification has yet to be addressed in most of these cases. The Company cannot reasonably estimate the possible loss or range of loss which may arise from these lawsuits. These matters, if decided adversely to or settled by the Company, individually or in the aggregate, may result in a liability material to the Company's consolidated financial condition or results of operations. The Company is vigorously defending itself against these actions.

12. QUARTERLY FINANCIAL DATA (UNAUDITED)

The following is a summary of the quarterly consolidated results of operations from continuing operations for the fiscal years ended February 3, 2008 and January 28, 2007 (dollars in millions, except per share data):

	Net Sales	Gross Profit	Earnings from Continuing Operations	Basic Earnings per Share from Continuing Operations	Diluted Earnings per Share from Continuing Operations
Fiscal Year Ended February 3, 2008:					
First Quarter	$ 18,545	$ 6,263	$ 947	$ 0.48	$ 0.48
Second Quarter	22,184	7,341	1,521	0.78	0.77
Third Quarter	18,961	6,339	1,071	0.59	0.59
Fourth Quarter	17,659	6,054	671	0.40	0.40
Fiscal Year	$ 77,349	$ 25,997	$ 4,210	$ 2.28	$ 2.27
Fiscal Year Ended January 28, 2007:					
First Quarter	$ 19,378	$ 6,636	$ 1,391	$ 0.66	$ 0.66
Second Quarter	22,592	7,456	1,701	0.82	0.82
Third Quarter	19,648	6,604	1,333	0.65	0.65
	17,404	5,850	841	0.42	0.42
Fiscal Year	$ 79,022	$ 26,546	$ 5,266	$ 2.56	$ 2.55

Note: The quarterly data may not sum to fiscal year totals.

10-Year Summary of Financial and Operating Results
The Home Depot, Inc. and Subsidiaries

amounts in millions, except where noted	10-Year Compound Annual Growth Rate	2007 (1)	2006	2005
STATEMENT OF EARNINGS DATA (2)				
Net sales	12.3%	**$ 77,349**	$ 79,022	$ 77,019
Net sales increase (%)	—	**(2.1)**	2.6	8.3
Earnings before provision for income taxes	13.3	**6,620**	8,502	8,967
Net earnings	13.8	**4,210**	5,266	5,641
Net earnings increase (%)	—	**(20.1)**	(6.6)	14.6
Diluted earnings per share ($)	15.9	**2.27**	2.55	2.63
Diluted earnings per share increase (%)	—	**(11.0)**	(3.0)	18.5
Diluted weighted average number of common shares	(2.1)	**1,856**	2,062	2,147
Gross margin – % of sales	—	**33.6**	33.6	33.7
Total operating expenses – % of sales	—	**24.3**	22.4	21.9
Net interest expense (income) – % of sales	—	**0.8**	0.5	0.1
Earnings before provision for income taxes – % of sales	—	**8.6**	10.8	11.6
Net earnings – % of sales	—	**5.4**	6.7	7.3
BALANCE SHEET DATA AND FINANCIAL RATIOS (3)				
Total assets	14.7%	**$ 44,324**	$ 52,263	$ 44,405
Working capital	(0.2)	**1,968**	5,069	2,563
Merchandise inventories	12.5	**11,731**	12,822	11,401
Net property and equipment	15.5	**27,476**	26,605	24,901
Long-term debt	24.2	**11,383**	11,643	2,672
Stockholders' equity	9.6	**17,714**	25,030	26,909
Book value per share ($)	12.5	**10.48**	12.71	12.67
Long-term debt-to-equity (%)	—	**64.3**	46.5	9.9
Total debt-to-equity (%)	—	**75.8**	46.6	15.2
Current ratio	—	**1.15:1**	1.39:1	1.20:1
Inventory turnover (2)	—	**4.2x**	4.5x	4.7x
Return on invested capital (%) (2)	—	**13.9**	16.8	20.4
STATEMENT OF CASH FLOWS DATA				
Depreciation and amortization	21.0%	**$ 1,906**	$ 1,886	$ 1,579
Capital expenditures	9.3	**3,558**	3,542	3,881
Payments for businesses acquired, net	(14.3)	**13**	4,268	2,546
Cash dividends per share ($)	30.5	**0.900**	0.675	0.400
STORE DATA				
Number of stores	13.6%	**2,234**	2,147	2,042
Square footage at fiscal year-end	13.5	**235**	224	215
Increase in square footage (%)	—	**4.9**	4.2	7.0
Average square footage per store (in thousands)	(0.1)	**105**	105	105
STORE SALES AND OTHER DATA				
Comparable store sales increase (decrease) (%) (4)(5)	—	**(6.7)**	(2.8)	3.1
Weighted average weekly sales per operating store (in thousands)	(2.3)%	**$ 658**	$ 723	$ 763
Weighted average sales per square foot ($)	(2.0)	**332**	358	377
Number of customer transactions	9.3	**1,336**	1,330	1,330
Average ticket ($)	2.8	**57.48**	58.90	57.98
Number of associates at fiscal year-end (3)	10.3	**331,000**	364,400	344,800

(1) Fiscal years 2007 and 2001 include 53 weeks; all other fiscal years reported include 52 weeks.
(2) Fiscal years 2003 through 2007 include Continuing Operations only. The discontinued operations prior to 2003 were not material.
(3) Fiscal year 2007 amounts include Continuing Operations only. Fiscal years 1998-2006 amounts include discontinued operations, except as noted.

	2004	2003	2002	2001 (1)	2000	1999	1998
STATEMENT OF EARNINGS DATA (2)							
Net sales	$ 71,100	$ 63,660	$ 58,247	$ 53,553	$ 45,738	$ 38,434	$ 30,219
Net sales increase (%)	11.7	9.3	8.8	17.1	19.0	27.2	25.1
Earnings before provision for income taxes	7,790	6,762	5,872	4,957	4,217	3,804	2,654
Net earnings	4,922	4,253	3,664	3,044	2,581	2,320	1,614
Net earnings increase (%)	15.7	16.1	20.4	17.9	11.3	43.7	31.9
Diluted earnings per share ($)	2.22	1.86	1.56	1.29	1.10	1.00	0.71
Diluted earnings per share increase (%)	19.4	19.2	20.9	17.3	10.0	40.8	29.1
Diluted weighted average number of common shares	2,216	2,289	2,344	2,353	2,352	2,342	2,320
Gross margin – % of sales	33.4	31.7	31.1	30.2	29.9	29.7	28.5
Total operating expenses – % of sales	22.4	21.1	21.1	20.9	20.7	19.8	19.7
Net interest expense (income) – % of sales	—	—	(0.1)	—	—	—	—
Earnings before provision for income taxes – % of sales	11.0	10.6	10.1	9.3	9.2	9.9	8.8
Net earnings – % of sales	6.9	6.7	6.3	5.7	5.6	6.0	5.3
BALANCE SHEET DATA AND FINANCIAL RATIOS (3)							
Total assets	$ 39,020	$ 34,437	$ 30,011	$ 26,394	$ 21,385	$ 17,081	$ 13,465
Working capital	3,818	3,774	3,882	3,860	3,392	2,734	2,076
Merchandise inventories	10,076	9,076	8,338	6,725	6,556	5,489	4,293
Net property and equipment	22,726	20,063	17,168	15,375	13,068	10,227	8,160
Long-term debt	2,148	856	1,321	1,250	1,545	750	1,566
Stockholders' equity	24,158	22,407	19,802	18,082	15,004	12,341	8,740
Book value per share ($)	11.06	9.93	8.38	7.71	6.46	5.36	3.95
Long-term debt-to-equity (%)	8.9	3.8	6.7	6.9	10.3	6.1	17.9
Total debt-to-equity (%)	8.9	6.1	6.7	6.9	10.3	6.1	17.9
Current ratio	1.37:1	1.40:1	1.48:1	1.59:1	1.77:1	1.75:1	1.73:1
Inventory turnover (2)	4.9x	5.0x	5.3x	5.4x	5.1x	5.4x	5.4x
Return on invested capital (%) (2)	19.9	19.2	18.8	18.3	19.6	22.5	19.3
STATEMENT OF CASH FLOWS DATA							
Depreciation and amortization	$ 1,319	$ 1,076	$ 903	$ 764	$ 601	$ 463	$ 373
Capital expenditures	3,948	3,508	2,749	3,393	3,574	2,618	2,094
Payments for businesses acquired, net	727	215	235	190	26	101	6
Cash dividends per share ($)	0.325	0.26	0.21	0.17	0.16	0.11	0.08
STORE DATA							
Number of stores	1,890	1,707	1,532	1,333	1,134	930	761
Square footage at fiscal year-end	201	183	166	146	123	100	81
Increase in square footage (%)	9.8	10.2	14.1	18.5	22.6	23.5	22.8
Average square footage per store (in thousands)	106	107	108	109	108	108	107
STORE SALES AND OTHER DATA							
Comparable store sales increase (decrease) (%) (4)(5)	5.1	3.7	(0.5)	—	4	10	7
Weighted average weekly sales per operating store (in thousands)	$ 766	$ 763	$ 772	$ 812	$ 864	$ 876	$ 844
Weighted average sales per square foot ($)	375	371	370	394	415	423	410
Number of customer transactions	1,295	1,246	1,161	1,091	937	797	665
Average ticket ($)	54.89	51.15	49.43	48.64	48.65	47.87	45.05
Number of associates at fiscal year-end (3)	323,100	298,800	280,900	256,300	227,300	201,400	156,700

(4) *Includes Net Sales at locations open greater than 12 months, including relocated and remodeled stores. Stores become comparable on the Monday following their 365 th day of operation. Comparable store sales is intended only as supplemental information and is not a substitute for Net Sales or Net Earnings presented in accordance with generally accepted accounting principles.*

(5) *Comparable store sales in fiscal years prior to 2002 were reported to the nearest percent.*

Corporate and Shareholder Information

STORE SUPPORT CENTER
The Home Depot, Inc.
2455 Paces Ferry Road, NW
Atlanta, GA 30339-4024
Telephone: (770) 433-8211

THE HOME DEPOT WEB SITE
www.homedepot.com

TRANSFER AGENT AND REGISTRAR
Computershare Trust Company, N.A.
P.O. Box 43078
Providence, RI 02490-3078
Telephone: (800) 577-0177
Internet address: www.computershare.com/investor

INDEPENDENT REGISTERED PUBLIC ACCOUNTING FIRM
KPMG LLP
Suite 2000
303 Peachtree Street, NE
Atlanta, GA 30308

STOCK EXCHANGE LISTING
New York Stock Exchange
Trading symbol – HD

ANNUAL MEETING
The Annual Meeting of Shareholders will be held at 9 a.m., Eastern Time, May 22, 2008, at Cobb Galleria Centre in Atlanta, Georgia.

NUMBER OF SHAREHOLDERS
As of March 24, 2008, there were approximately 160,000 shareholders of record and approximately 1,400,000 individual shareholders holding stock under nominee security posting listings.

DIVIDENDS DECLARED PER COMMON SHARE

	First Quarter	Second Quarter	Third Quarter	Fourth Quarter
Fiscal 2007	**$0.225**	**$0.225**	**$0.225**	**$0.225**
Fiscal 2006	$0.150	$0.150	$0.225	$0.225

New investors may make an initial investment, and shareholders of record may acquire additional shares of our common stock through our direct stock purchase and dividend reinvestment plan. Subject to certain requirements, initial cash investments, cash dividends and/or additional optional cash purchases may be invested through this plan. To obtain enrollment materials including the prospectus, access The Home Depot web site, or call (877) HD-SHARE or (877) 437-4273. For all other communications regarding these services, contact Computershare.

FINANCIAL AND OTHER COMPANY INFORMATION
Our Annual Report on Form 10-K for the fiscal year ended February 3, 2008 is available on our web site at www.homedepot.com under the Investor Relations section. In addition, financial reports, filing with the Securities and Exchange Commission, news releases and other information are available on The Home Depot web site.

The Home Depot, Inc. has included as exhibits to its Annual Report on Form 10-K for the fiscal year ended February 3, 2008 certifications of The Home Depot's Chief Executive Officer and Chief Financial Officer. The Home Depot's Chief Executive Officer has also submitted to the New York Stock Exchange (NYSE) a certificate certifying that he is not aware of any violations by The Home Depot of the NYSE corporate governance listing standards.

QUARTERLY STOCK PRICE RANGE

	First Quarter	Second Quarter	Third Quarter	Fourth Quarter
Fiscal 2007				
High	**$41.76**	**$40.94**	**$38.31**	**$31.51**
Low	**$36.74**	**$36.75**	**$30.70**	**$24.71**
Fiscal 2006				
High	$43.95	$41.61	$38.24	$41.84
Low	$38.50	$32.85	$33.07	$35.77

Concept and Design: Sagepath (www.sagepath.com)
Photography: Doug Coulter, Craig Bromley, Kim Steele
Printer: Cenveo

APPENDIX B

LOWE'S COMPANIES, INC. 2007 FORM 10-K ANNUAL REPORT*

* This appendix contains excerpts. Go to the text Web site at www.mhhe.com/LLPW1e for the complete report.

Management's Report on Internal Control Over Financial Reporting

Management of Lowe's Companies, Inc. and its subsidiaries is responsible for establishing and maintaining adequate internal control over financial reporting (Internal Control) as defined in Rule 13a-15(f) under the Securities Exchange Act of 1934, as amended. Our Internal Control was designed to provide reasonable assurance to our management and the board of directors regarding the reliability of financial reporting and the preparation and fair presentation of published financial statements.

All internal control systems, no matter how well designed, have inherent limitations, including the possibility of human error and the circumvention or overriding of controls. Therefore, even those systems determined to be effective can provide only reasonable assurance with respect to the reliability of financial reporting and financial statement preparation and presentation. Further, because of changes in conditions, the effectiveness may vary over time.

Our management, with the participation of the Chief Executive Officer and Chief Financial Officer, evaluated the effectiveness of our Internal Control as of February 1, 2008. In evaluating our Internal Control, we used the criteria set forth by the Committee of Sponsoring Organizations of the Treadway Commission (COSO) in *Internal Control—Integrated Framework* . Based on our management's assessment, we have concluded that, as of February 1, 2008, our Internal Control is effective.

Deloitte & Touche LLP, the independent registered public accounting firm that audited the financial statements contained in this report, was engaged to audit our Internal Control . Their report appears on page 27.

Report of Independent Registered Public Accounting Firm

To the Board of Directors and Shareholders of Lowe's Companies, Inc.
Mooresville, North Carolina

We have audited the accompanying consolidated balance sheets of Lowe's Companies, Inc. and subsidiaries (the "Company") as of February 1, 2008 and February 2, 2007, and the related consolidated statements of earnings, shareholders' equity, and cash flows for each of the three fiscal years in the period ended February 1, 2008. These financial statements are the responsibility of the Company's management. Our responsibility is to express an opinion on these financial statements based on our audits.

We conducted our audits in accordance with the standards of the Public Company Accounting Oversight Board (United States). Those standards require that we plan and perform the audit to obtain reasonable assurance about whether the financial statements are free of material misstatement. An audit includes examining, on a test basis, evidence supporting the amounts and disclosures in the financial statements. An audit also includes assessing the accounting principles used and significant estimates made by management, as well as evaluating the overall financial statement presentation. We believe that our audits provide a reasonable basis for our opinion.

In our opinion, such consolidated financial statements present fairly, in all material respects, the financial position of the Company at February 1, 2008 and February 2, 2007, and the results of its operations and its cash flows for each of the three fiscal years in the period ended February 1, 2008, in conformity with accounting principles generally accepted in the United States of America.

We have also audited, in accordance with the standards of the Public Company Accounting Oversight Board (United States), the Company's internal control over financial reporting as of February 1, 2008, based on the criteria established in *Internal Control—Integrated Framework* issued by the Committee of Sponsoring Organizations of the Treadway Commission and our report dated April 1, 2008 expressed an unqualified opinion on the Company's internal control over financial reporting.

/s/ Deloitte & Touche LLP

Charlotte, North Carolina
April 1, 2008

Report of Independent Registered Public Accounting Firm

To the Board of Directors and Shareholders of Lowe's Companies, Inc.
Mooresville, North Carolina

We have audited the internal control over financial reporting of Lowe's Companies, Inc. and subsidiaries (the "Company") as of February 1, 2008 based on criteria established in *Internal Control — Integrated Framework* issued by the Committee of Sponsoring Organizations of the Treadway Commission. The Company's management is responsible for maintaining effective internal control over financial reporting and for its assessment of the effectiveness of internal control over financial reporting, included in the accompanying Management's Report on Internal Control Over Financial Reporting. Our responsibility is to express an opinion on the Company's internal control over financial reporting based on our audit.

We conducted our audit in accordance with the standards of the Public Company Accounting Oversight Board (United States). Those standards require that we plan and perform the audit to obtain reasonable assurance about whether effective internal control over financial reporting was maintained in all material respects. Our audit included obtaining an understanding of internal control over financial reporting, assessing the risk that a material weakness exists, testing and evaluating the design and operating effectiveness of internal control based on the assessed risk, and performing such other procedures as we considered necessary in the circumstances. We believe that our audit provides a reasonable basis for our opinion.

A company's internal control over financial reporting is a process designed by, or under the supervision of, the company's principal executive and principal financial officers, or persons performing similar functions, and effected by the company's board of directors, management, and other personnel to provide reasonable assurance regarding the reliability of financial reporting and the preparation of financial statements for external purposes in accordance with generally accepted accounting principles. A company's internal control over financial reporting includes those policies and procedures that (1) pertain to the maintenance of records that, in reasonable detail, accurately and fairly reflect the transactions and dispositions of the assets of the company; (2) provide reasonable assurance that transactions are recorded as necessary to permit preparation of financial statements in accordance with generally accepted accounting principles, and that receipts and expenditures of the company are being made only in accordance with authorizations of management and directors of the company; and (3) provide reasonable assurance regarding prevention or timely detection of unauthorized acquisition, use, or disposition of the company's assets that could have a material effect on the financial statements.

Because of the inherent limitations of internal control over financial reporting, including the possibility of collusion or improper management override of controls, material misstatements due to error or fraud may not be prevented or detected on a timely basis. Also, projections of any evaluation of the effectiveness of the internal control over financial reporting to future periods are subject to the risk that the controls may become inadequate because of changes in conditions, or that the degree of compliance with the policies or procedures may deteriorate.

In our opinion, the Company maintained, in all material respects, effective internal control over financial reporting as of February 1, 2008, based on the criteria established in *Internal Control — Integrated Framework* issued by the Committee of Sponsoring Organizations of the Treadway Commission.

We have also audited, in accordance with the standards of the Public Company Accounting Oversight Board (United States), the consolidated financial statements as of and for the fiscal year ended February 1, 2008 of the Company and our report dated April 1, 2008 expressed an unqualified opinion on those financial statements.

/s/ Deloitte & Touche LLP

Charlotte, North Carolina
April 1, 2008

Lowe's Companies, Inc.
Consolidated Statements of Earnings

(In millions, except per share and percentage data) Fiscal years ended on	February 1, 2008	% Sales	February 2, 2007	% Sales	February 3, 2006	% Sales
Net sales (Note 1)	**$ 48,283**	**100.00%**	**$ 46,927**	**100.00%**	**$ 43,243**	**100.00%**
Cost of sales (Notes 1 and 14)	31,556	65.36	30,729	65.48	28,453	65.80
Gross margin	**16,727**	**34.64**	**16,198**	**34.52**	**14,790**	**34.20**
Expenses:						
Selling, general and administrative (Notes 1, 8, 9 and 12)	10,515	21.78	9,738	20.75	9,014	20.84
Store opening costs (Note 1)	141	0.29	146	0.31	142	0.33
Depreciation (Notes 1 and 3)	1,366	2.83	1,162	2.48	980	2.27
Interest - net (Note 15)	194	0.40	154	0.33	158	0.37
Total expenses	**12,216**	**25.30**	**11,200**	**23.87**	**10,294**	**23.81**
Pre-tax earnings	**4,511**	**9.34**	**4,998**	**10.65**	**4,496**	**10.39**
Income tax provision (Notes 1 and 10)	1,702	3.52	1,893	4.03	1,731	4.00
Net earnings	**$ 2,809**	**5.82%**	**$ 3,105**	**6.62%**	**$ 2,765**	**6.39%**
Basic earnings per share (Note 11)	**$ 1.90**		**$ 2.02**		**$ 1.78**	
Diluted earnings per share (Note 11)	**$ 1.86**		**$ 1.99**		**$ 1.73**	
Cash dividends per share	**$ 0.29**		**$ 0.18**		**$ 0.11**	

See accompanying notes to the consolidated financial statements.

Lowe's Companies, Inc.
Consolidated Balance Sheets

(In millions, except par value and percentage data)		February 1, 2008	% Total	February 2, 2007	% Total
Assets					
Current assets:					
Cash and cash equivalents (Note 1)		$ 281	0.9%	$ 364	1.3%
Short-term investments (Notes 1 and 2)		249	0.8	432	1.6
Merchandise inventory - net (Note 1)		7,611	24.6	7,144	25.7
Deferred income taxes - net (Notes 1 and 10)		247	0.8	161	0.6
Other current assets (Note 1)		298	1.0	213	0.8
Total current assets		**8,686**	**28.1**	**8,314**	**30.0**
Property, less accumulated depreciation (Notes 1 and 3)		21,361	69.2	18,971	68.3
Long-term investments (Notes 1 and 2)		509	1.7	165	0.6
Other assets (Note 1)		313	1.0	317	1.1
Total assets		**$ 30,869**	**100.0%**	**$ 27,767**	**100.0%**
Liabilities and shareholders' equity					
Current liabilities:					
Short-term borrowings (Note 4)		$ 1,064	3.5%	$ 23	0.1%
Current maturities of long-term debt (Note 5)		40	0.1	88	0.3
Accounts payable (Note 1)		3,713	12.0	3,524	12.7
Accrued salaries and wages		424	1.4	425	1.5
Self-insurance liabilities (Note 1)		671	2.2	650	2.4
Deferred revenue (Note 1)		717	2.3	731	2.6
Other current liabilities (Note 1)		1,122	3.6	1,098	3.9
Total current liabilities		**7,751**	**25.1**	**6,539**	**23.5**
Long-term debt, excluding current maturities (Notes 5, 6 and 12)		5,576	18.1	4,325	15.6
Deferred income taxes - net (Notes 1 and 10)		670	2.2	735	2.7
Other liabilities (Note 1)		774	2.5	443	1.6
Total liabilities		**14,771**	**47.9**	**12,042**	**43.4**
Commitments and contingencies (Note 13)					
Shareholders' equity (Note 7) :					
Preferred stock - $5 par value, none issued		-	-	-	-
Common stock - $.50 par value;					
Shares issued and outstanding					
February 1, 2008	1,458				
February 2, 2007	1,525	729	2.3	762	2.7
Capital in excess of par value		16	0.1	102	0.4
Retained earnings		15,345	49.7	14,860	53.5
Accumulated other comprehensive income (Note 1)		8	-	1	-
Total shareholders' equity		**16,098**	**52.1**	**15,725**	**56.6**
Total liabilities and shareholders' equity		**$ 30,869**	**100.0%**	**$ 27,767**	**100.0%**

See accompanying notes to the consolidated financial statements.

Lowe's Companies, Inc.
Consolidated Statements of
Shareholders' Equity

(In millions)	Common Stock Shares	Common Stock Amount	Capital in Excess of Par Value	Retained Earnings	Accumulated Other Comprehensive Income	Total Shareholders' Equity
Balance January 28, 2005	**1,548**	**$ 774**	**$ 1,127**	**$ 9,597**	**$ -**	**$ 11,498**
Comprehensive income (Note 1):						
Net earnings				2,765		
Foreign currency translation					1	
Total comprehensive income						2,766
Tax effect of non-qualified stock options exercised			59			59
Cash dividends				(171)		(171)
Share-based payment expense (Note 8)			76			76
Repurchase of common stock (Note 7)	(25)	(12)	(762)			(774)
Conversion of debt to common stock (Note 5)	28	14	551			565
Employee stock options exercised and other (Note 8)	15	7	205			212
Employee stock purchase plan (Note 8)	2	1	64			65
Balance February 3, 2006	**1,568**	**$ 784**	**$ 1,320**	**$ 12,191**	**$ 1**	**$ 14,296**
Comprehensive income (Note 1):						
Net earnings				3,105		
Foreign currency translation					(2)	
Net unrealized investment gains (Note 2)					2	
Total comprehensive income						3,105
Tax effect of non-qualified stock options exercised			21			21
Cash dividends				(276)		(276)
Share-based payment expense (Note 8)			59			59
Repurchase of common stock (Note 7)	(57)	(28)	(1,549)	(160)		(1,737)
Conversion of debt to common stock (Note 5)	4	2	80			82
Employee stock options exercised and other (Note 8)	7	3	96			99
Employee stock purchase plan (Note 8)	3	1	75			76
Balance February 2, 2007	**1,525**	**$ 762**	**$ 102**	**$ 14,860**	**$ 1**	**$ 15,725**
Cumulative effect adjustment (Note 10):				(8)		(8)
Comprehensive income (Note 1):						
Net earnings				2,809		
Foreign currency translation					7	
Total comprehensive income						2,816
Tax effect of non-qualified stock options exercised			12			12
Cash dividends				(428)		(428)
Share-based payment expense (Note 8)			99			99
Repurchase of common stock (Note 7)	(76)	(38)	(349)	(1,888)		(2,275)
Conversion of debt to common stock (Note 5)	1	-	13			13
Employee stock options exercised and other (Note 8)	5	3	61			64
Employee stock purchase plan (Note 8)	3	2	78			80
Balance February 1, 2008	**1,458**	**$ 729**	**$ 16**	**$ 15,345**	**$ 8**	**$ 16,098**

See accompanying notes to the consolidated financial statements.

Lowe's Companies, Inc.
Consolidated Statements of Cash Flows

(In millions) Fiscal years ended on	February 1, 2008	February 2, 2007	February 3, 2006
Cash flows from operating activities:			
Net earnings	$ 2,809	$ 3,105	$ 2,765
Adjustments to reconcile earnings to net cash provided by operating activities:			
Depreciation and amortization	1,464	1,237	1,051
Deferred income taxes	2	(6)	(37)
Loss on disposition/writedown of fixed and other assets	51	23	31
Share-based payment expense	99	62	76
Changes in operating assets and liabilities:			
Merchandise inventory - net	(464)	(509)	(785)
Other operating assets	(64)	(135)	(38)
Accounts payable	185	692	137
Other operating liabilities	265	33	642
Net cash provided by operating activities	**4,347**	**4,502**	**3,842**
Cash flows from investing activities:			
Purchases of short-term investments	(920)	(284)	(1,829)
Proceeds from sale/maturity of short-term investments	1,183	572	1,802
Purchases of long-term investments	(1,588)	(558)	(354)
Proceeds from sale/maturity of long-term investments	1,162	415	55
Increase in other long-term assets	(7)	(16)	(30)
Fixed assets acquired	(4,010)	(3,916)	(3,379)
Proceeds from the sale of fixed and other long-term assets	57	72	61
Net cash used in investing activities	**(4,123)**	**(3,715)**	**(3,674)**
Cash flows from financing activities:			
Net increase in short-term borrowings	1,041	23	-
Proceeds from issuance of long-term debt	1,296	989	1,013
Repayment of long-term debt	(96)	(33)	(633)
Proceeds from issuance of common stock under employee stock purchase plan	80	76	65
Proceeds from issuance of common stock from stock options exercised	69	100	225
Cash dividend payments	(428)	(276)	(171)
Repurchase of common stock	(2,275)	(1,737)	(774)
Excess tax benefits of share-based payments	6	12	-
Net cash used in financing activities	**(307)**	**(846)**	**(275)**
Net decrease in cash and cash equivalents	(83)	(59)	(107)
Cash and cash equivalents, beginning of year	364	423	530
Cash and cash equivalents, end of year	**$ 281**	**$ 364**	**$ 423**

See accompanying notes to the consolidated financial statements.

NOTES TO CONSOLIDATED FINANCIAL STATEMENTS
YEARS ENDED FEBRUARY 1, 2008, FEBRUARY 2, 2007 AND FEBRUARY 3, 2006

NOTE 1 - Summary of Significant Accounting Policies:

Lowe's Companies, Inc. and subsidiaries (the Company) is the world's second-largest home improvement retailer and operated 1,534 stores in the United States and Canada at February 1, 2008. Below are those accounting policies considered by the Company to be significant.

Fiscal Year - The Company's fiscal year ends on the Friday nearest the end of January. The fiscal years ended February 1, 2008 and February 2, 2007 contained 52 weeks. The fiscal year ended February 3, 2006 contained 53 weeks. All references herein for the years 2007, 2006 and 2005 represent the fiscal years ended February 1, 2008, February 2, 2007 and February 3, 2006, respectively.

Principles of Consolidation - The consolidated financial statements include the accounts of the Company and its wholly-owned or controlled operating subsidiaries. All material intercompany accounts and transactions have been eliminated.

Use of Estimates - The preparation of the Company's financial statements in accordance with accounting principles generally accepted in the United States of America requires management to make estimates that affect the reported amounts of assets, liabilities, sales and expenses, and related disclosures of contingent assets and liabilities. The Company bases these estimates on historical results and various other assumptions believed to be reasonable, all of which form the basis for making estimates concerning the carrying values of assets and liabilities that are not readily available from other sources. Actual results may differ from these estimates.

Cash and Cash Equivalents - Cash and cash equivalents include cash on hand, demand deposits and short-term investments with original maturities of three months or less when purchased. The majority of payments due from financial institutions for the settlement of credit card and debit card transactions process within two business days and are, therefore, classified as cash and cash equivalents.

Investments - The Company has a cash management program which provides for the investment of cash balances not expected to be used in current operations in financial instruments that have maturities of up to 10 years. Variable-rate demand notes, which have stated maturity dates in excess of 10 years, meet this maturity requirement of the cash management program because the maturity date of these investments is determined based on the interest rate reset date or par value put date for the purpose of applying this criteria.

Investments, exclusive of cash equivalents, with a stated maturity date of one year or less from the balance sheet date or that are expected to be used in current operations, are classified as short-term investments. All other investments are classified as long-term. As of February 1, 2008, investments consisted primarily of money market funds, certificates of deposit, municipal obligations and mutual funds. Restricted balances pledged as collateral for letters of credit for the Company's extended warranty program and for a portion of the Company's casualty insurance and installed sales program liabilities are also classified as investments.

The Company has classified all investment securities as available-for-sale, and they are carried at fair market value. Unrealized gains and losses on such securities are included in accumulated other comprehensive income in shareholders' equity.

Merchandise Inventory - Inventory is stated at the lower of cost or market using the first-in, first-out method of inventory accounting. The cost of inventory also includes certain costs associated with the preparation of inventory for resale and distribution center costs, net of vendor funds.

The Company records an inventory reserve for the loss associated with selling inventories below cost. This reserve is based on management's current knowledge with respect to inventory levels, sales trends and historical experience. Management does not believe the Company's merchandise inventories are subject to significant risk of obsolescence in the near term, and management has the ability to adjust purchasing practices based on anticipated sales trends and general economic conditions. However, changes in consumer purchasing patterns could result in the need for additional reserves. The Company also records an inventory reserve for the estimated shrinkage between physical inventories. This reserve is based primarily on actual shrink results from previous physical inventories. Changes in the estimated shrink reserve may be necessary based on the results of physical inventories. Management believes it has sufficient current and historical knowledge to record reasonable estimates for both of these inventory reserves.

Derivative Financial Instruments - The Company occasionally utilizes derivative financial instruments to manage certain business risks. However, the amounts were not material to the Company's consolidated financial statements in any of the years presented. The Company does not use derivative financial instruments for trading purposes.

Credit Programs - The majority of the Company's accounts receivable arises from sales of goods and services to Commercial Business Customers. In May 2004, the Company entered into an agreement with General Electric Company and its subsidiaries (GE) to sell its then-existing portfolio of commercial business accounts receivable to GE. During the term of the agreement, which ends on December 31, 2016, unless terminated sooner by the parties, GE also purchases at face value new commercial business accounts receivable originated by the Company and services these accounts. The Company accounts for these transfers as sales of accounts receivable. When the Company sells its commercial business accounts receivable, it retains certain interests in those receivables, including the funding of a loss reserve and its obligation related to GE's ongoing servicing of the receivables sold. Any gain or loss on the sale is determined based on the previous carrying amounts of the transferred assets allocated at fair value between the receivables sold and the interests retained. Fair value is based on the present value of expected future cash flows, taking into account the key assumptions of anticipated credit losses, payment rates, late fee rates, GE's servicing costs and the discount rate commensurate with the uncertainty involved. Due to the short-term nature of the receivables sold, changes to the key assumptions would not materially impact the recorded gain or loss on the sales of receivables or the fair value of the retained interests in the receivables.

Total commercial business accounts receivable sold to GE were $1.8 billion in both 2007 and 2006, and $1.7 billion in 2005. During 2007, 2006 and 2005, the Company recognized losses of $34 million, $35 million and $41 million, respectively, on these sales as selling, general and administrative (SG&A) expense, which primarily relates to the fair value of the obligations incurred related to servicing costs that are remitted to GE monthly. At February 1, 2008 and February 2, 2007, the fair value of the retained interests was insignificant and was determined based on the present value of expected future cash flows.

Sales generated through the Company's proprietary credit cards are not reflected in receivables. Under an agreement with GE, credit is extended directly to customers by GE. All credit program-related services are performed and controlled directly by GE. The Company has the option, but no obligation, to purchase the receivables at the end of the agreement in December 2016. Tender costs, including amounts associated with accepting the Company's proprietary credit cards, are recorded in SG&A in the consolidated financial statements.

The total portfolio of receivables held by GE, including both receivables originated by GE from the Company's private label credit cards and commercial business accounts receivable originated by the Company and sold to GE, approximated $6.6 billion at February 1, 2008, and $6.0 billion at February 2, 2007.

Property and Depreciation - Property is recorded at cost. Costs associated with major additions are capitalized and depreciated. Capital assets are expected to yield future benefits and have useful lives which exceed one year. The total cost of a capital asset generally includes all applicable sales taxes, delivery costs, installation costs and other appropriate costs incurred by the Company in the case of self-constructed assets. Upon disposal, the cost of properties and related accumulated depreciation are removed from the accounts, with gains and losses reflected in SG&A expense in the consolidated statements of earnings.

Depreciation is provided over the estimated useful lives of the depreciable assets. Assets are depreciated using the straight-line method. Leasehold improvements are depreciated over the shorter of their estimated useful lives or the term of the related lease, which may include one or more option renewal periods where failure to exercise such options would result in an economic penalty in such amount that renewal appears, at the inception of the lease, to be reasonably assured. During the term of a lease, if a substantial additional investment is made in a leased location, the Company reevaluates its definition of lease term to determine whether the investment, together with any penalties related to non-renewal, would constitute an economic penalty in such amount that renewal appears, at the time of the reevaluation, to be reasonably assured.

Long-Lived Asset Impairment/Exit Activities - The carrying amounts of long-lived assets are reviewed whenever events or changes in circumstances indicate that the carrying amount may not be recoverable.

For long-lived assets held for use, a potential impairment has occurred if projected future undiscounted cash flows expected to result from the use and eventual disposition of the assets are less than the carrying value of the assets. An impairment loss is recognized when the carrying amount of the long-lived asset is not recoverable and exceeds its fair value. The Company estimates fair value based on projected future discounted cash flows.

For long-lived assets to be abandoned, the Company considers the asset to be disposed of when it ceases to be used. Until it ceases to be used, the Company continues to classify the assets as held for use and tests for potential impairment accordingly. If the Company commits to a plan to abandon a long-lived asset before the end of its previously estimated useful life, depreciation estimates are revised.

For long-lived assets held for sale, an impairment charge is recorded if the carrying amount of the asset exceeds its fair value less cost to sell. Fair value is based on a market appraisal or a valuation technique that considers various factors, including local market conditions. A long-lived asset is not depreciated while it is classified as held for sale.

The net carrying value for relocated stores, closed stores and other excess properties that are expected to be sold within the next 12 months are classified as held for sale and included in other current assets in the consolidated balance sheets. Assets held for sale totaled $28 million at February 1, 2008. Assets held for sale at February 2, 2007 were not significant. The net carrying value for relocated stores, closed stores and other excess properties that do not meet the held for sale criteria are included in other assets (non-current) in the consolidated balance sheets and totaled $91 million and $113 million at February 1, 2008 and February 2, 2007, respectively.

When operating leased locations are closed, a liability is recognized for the fair value of future contractual obligations, including property taxes, utilities and common area maintenance, net of estimated sublease income. The liability, which is included in other current liabilities in the consolidated balance sheets, was $11 million and $19 million at February 1, 2008 and February 2, 2007, respectively.

The charge for impairment is included in SG&A expense and totaled $28 million, $5 million and $16 million in 2007, 2006 and 2005, respectively.

Leases - For lease agreements that provide for escalating rent payments or free-rent occupancy periods, the Company recognizes rent expense on a straight-line basis over the non-cancelable lease term and option renewal periods where failure to exercise such options would result in an economic penalty in such amount that renewal appears, at the inception of the lease, to be reasonably assured. The lease term commences on the date that that Company takes possession of or controls the physical use of the property. Deferred rent is included in other long-term liabilities in the consolidated balance sheets.

Assets under capital lease are amortized in accordance with the Company's normal depreciation policy for owned assets or, if shorter, over the non-cancelable lease term and any option renewal period where failure to exercise such option would result in an economic penalty in such amount that renewal appears, at the inception of the lease, to be reasonably assured. The amortization of the assets is included in depreciation expense in the consolidated financial statements. During the term of a lease, if a substantial additional investment is made in a leased location, the Company reevaluates its definition of lease term.

Accounts Payable - In June 2007, the Company entered into a customer-managed services agreement with a third party to provide an accounts payable tracking system which facilitates participating suppliers' ability to finance payment obligations from the Company with designated third-party financial institutions. Participating suppliers may, at their sole discretion, make offers to finance one or more payment obligations of the Company prior to their scheduled due dates at a discounted price to participating financial institutions. The Company's goal in entering into this arrangement is to capture overall supply chain savings, in the form of pricing, payment terms or vendor funding, created by facilitating suppliers' ability to finance payment obligations at more favorable discount rates, while providing them with greater working capital flexibility.

The Company's obligations to its suppliers, including amounts due and scheduled payment dates, are not impacted by suppliers' decisions to finance amounts under this arrangement. However, the Company's right to offset balances due from suppliers against payment obligations is restricted by this arrangement for those payment obligations that have been financed by suppliers. As of February 1, 2008, the Company had placed $77 million of payment obligations on the accounts payable tracking system, and participating suppliers had financed $48 million of those payment obligations to participating financial institutions.

Self-Insurance - The Company is self-insured for certain losses relating to workers' compensation, automobile, property, and general and product liability claims. The Company has stop-loss coverage to limit the exposure arising from these claims. The Company is also self-insured for certain losses relating to extended warranty and medical and dental claims. Self-insurance claims filed and claims incurred but not reported are accrued based upon management's estimates of the discounted ultimate cost for uninsured claims incurred using actuarial assumptions followed in the insurance industry and historical experience. Although management believes it has the ability to reasonably estimate losses related to claims, it is possible that actual results could differ from recorded self-insurance liabilities.

Income Taxes - The Company establishes deferred income tax assets and liabilities for temporary differences between the tax and financial accounting bases of assets and liabilities. The tax effects of such differences are reflected in the balance sheet at the enacted tax rates expected to be in effect when the differences reverse. A valuation allowance is recorded to reduce the carrying amount of deferred tax assets if it is more likely than not that all or a portion of the asset will not be realized. The tax balances and income tax expense recognized by the Company are based on management's interpretation of the tax statutes of multiple jurisdictions.

The Company establishes a reserve for tax positions for which there is uncertainty as to whether or not the position will be ultimately sustained. The Company includes interest related to tax issues as part of net interest in the consolidated financial statements. The Company records any applicable penalties related to tax issues within the income tax provision.

Revenue Recognition - The Company recognizes revenues, net of sales tax, when sales transactions occur and customers take possession of the merchandise. A provision for anticipated merchandise returns is provided through a reduction of sales and cost of sales in the period that the related sales are recorded. Revenues from product installation services are recognized when the installation is completed. Deferred revenues associated with amounts received for which customers have not yet taken possession of merchandise or for which installation has not yet been completed were $332 million and $364 million at February 1, 2008, and February 2, 2007, respectively.

Revenues from stored value cards, which include gift cards and returned merchandise credits, are deferred and recognized when the cards are redeemed. The liability associated with outstanding stored value cards was $385 million and $367 million at February 1, 2008, and February 2, 2007, respectively, and these amounts are included in deferred revenue in the accompanying consolidated balance sheets. The Company recognizes income from unredeemed stored value cards at the point at which redemption becomes remote. The Company's stored value cards have no expiration date or dormancy fees. Therefore, to determine when redemption is remote, the Company analyzes an aging of the unredeemed cards based on the date of last stored value card use.

Extended Warranties - Lowe's sells separately-priced extended warranty contracts under a Lowe's-branded program for which the Company is ultimately self-insured. The Company recognizes revenue from extended warranty sales on a straight-line basis over the respective contract term. Extended warranty contract terms primarily range from one to four years from the date of purchase or the end of the manufacturer's warranty, as applicable. The Company's extended warranty deferred revenue is included in other liabilities (non-current) in the accompanying consolidated balance sheets. Changes deferred revenue for extended warranty contracts are summarized as follows:

(In millions)		2007		2006
Extended warranty deferred revenue, beginning of period	$	315	$	206
Additions to deferred revenue		175		148
Deferred revenue recognized		(83)		(39)
Extended warranty deferred revenue, end of period	$	407	$	315

Incremental direct acquisition costs associated with the sale of extended warranties are also deferred and recognized as expense on a straight-line basis over the respective contract term. Deferred costs associated with extended warranty contracts were $91 million and $81 million at February 1, 2008 and February 2, 2007, respectively. The Company's extended warranty deferred costs are included in other assets (non-current) in the accompanying consolidated balance sheets. All other costs, such as costs of services performed under the contract, general and administrative expenses and advertising expenses are expensed as incurred.

The liability for extended warranty claims incurred is included in self-insurance liabilities in the accompanying consolidated balance sheets. Changes in the liability for extended warranty claims are summarized as follows:

(In millions)		2007		2006
Liability for extended warranty claims, beginning of period	$	10	$	-
Accrual for claims incurred		41		17
Claim payments		(37)		(7)
Liability for extended warranty claims, end of period	$	14	$	10

Cost of Sales and Selling, General and Administrative Expenses - The following lists the primary costs classified in each major expense category:

Cost of Sales

- Total cost of products sold, including:
  - Purchase costs, net of vendor funds;
  - Freight expenses associated with moving merchandise inventories from vendors to retail stores;
  - Costs associated with operating the Company's distribution network, including payroll and benefit costs and occupancy costs;
- Costs of installation services provided;
- Costs associated with delivery of products directly from vendors to customers by third parties;
- Costs associated with inventory shrinkage and obsolescence.

Selling, General and Administrative

- Payroll and benefit costs for retail and corporate employees;
- Occupancy costs of retail and corporate facilities;
- Advertising;
- Costs associated with delivery of products from stores to customers;
- Third-party, in-store service costs;
- Tender costs, including bank charges, costs associated with credit card interchange fees, and amounts associated with accepting the Company's proprietary credit cards;
- Costs associated with self-insured plans, and premium costs for stop-loss coverage and fully insured plans;
- Long-lived asset impairment charges and gains/losses on disposal of assets;
- Other administrative costs, such as supplies, and travel and entertainment.

Vendor Funds - The Company receives funds from vendors in the normal course of business principally as a result of purchase volumes, sales, early payments or promotions of vendors' products. Based on the provisions of the vendor agreements in place, management develops accrual rates by estimating the point at which the Company will have completed its performance under the agreement and the amount agreed upon will be earned. Due to the complexity and diversity of the individual vendor agreements, the Company performs analyses and reviews historical trends throughout the year to ensure the amounts earned are appropriately recorded. As a part of these analyses, the Company validates its accrual rates based on actual purchase trends and applies those rates to actual purchase volumes to determine the amount of funds accrued by the Company and receivable from the vendor. Amounts accrued throughout the year could be impacted if actual purchase volumes differ from projected annual purchase volumes, especially in the case of programs that provide for increased funding when graduated purchase volumes are met.

Vendor funds are treated as a reduction of inventory cost, unless they represent a reimbursement of specific, incremental and identifiable costs incurred by the customer to sell the vendor's product. Substantially all of the vendor funds that the Company receives do not meet the specific, incremental and identifiable criteria. Therefore, the Company treats the majority of these funds as a reduction in the cost of inventory as the amounts are accrued, and recognizes these funds as a reduction of cost of sales when the inventory is sold.

Advertising - Costs associated with advertising are charged to expense as incurred. Advertising expenses were $788 million, $873 million and $812 million in 2007, 2006 and 2005, respectively. Cooperative advertising vendor funds are recorded as a reduction of these expenses with the net amount included in SG&A expense. Cooperative advertising vendor funds were $5 million in 2007 but insignificant in both 2006 and 2005.

Shipping and Handling Costs - The Company includes shipping and handling costs relating to the delivery of products directly from vendors to customers by third parties in cost of sales. Shipping and handling costs, which include salaries and vehicle operations expenses relating to the delivery of products from stores to customers, are classified as SG&A expense. Shipping and handling costs included in SG&A expense were $307 million, $310 million and $312 million in 2007, 2006 and 2005, respectively.

Store Opening Costs - Costs of opening new or relocated retail stores, which include payroll and supply costs incurred prior to store opening and grand opening advertising costs, are charged to operations as incurred.

Comprehensive Income - The Company reports comprehensive income in its consolidated statements of shareholders' equity. Comprehensive income represents changes in shareholders' equity from non-owner sources and is comprised primarily of net earnings plus or minus unrealized gains or losses on available-for-sale securities, as well as foreign currency translation adjustments. Unrealized gains on available-for-sale securities classified in accumulated other comprehensive income on the accompanying consolidated balance sheets were $2 million at both February 1, 2008 and February 2, 2007. Foreign currency translation gains classified in accumulated other comprehensive income on the accompanying consolidated balance sheets were $6 million at February 1, 2008, and foreign currency translation losses were $1 million at February 2, 2007. The reclassification adjustments for gains/losses included in net earnings for 2007, 2006 and 2005 were insignificant.

Recent Accounting Pronouncements – In September 2006, the Financial Accounting Standards Board (FASB) issued Statement of Financial Accounting Standards (SFAS) No. 157, "Fair Value Measurements". SFAS No. 157 provides a single definition of fair value, together with a framework for measuring it, and requires additional disclosure about the use of fair value to measure assets and liabilities. SFAS No. 157 also emphasizes that fair value is a market-based measurement, not an entity-specific measurement, and sets out a fair value hierarchy with the highest priority being quoted prices in active markets. Under SFAS No. 157, fair value measurements are required to be disclosed by level within that hierarchy. SFAS No. 157 is effective for fiscal years beginning after November 15, 2007, and interim periods within those fiscal years. However, FASB Staff Position (FSP) No. FAS 157-2, "Effective Date of FASB Statement No. 157," issued in February 2008, delays the effective date of SFAS No. 157 for all nonfinancial assets and nonfinancial liabilities, except for items that are recognized or disclosed at fair value in the financial statements on a recurring basis, to fiscal years beginning after November 15, 2008, and interim periods within those fiscal years. The Company does not expect the adoption of SFAS No. 157 to have a material impact on its consolidated financial statements.

In February 2007, the FASB issued SFAS No. 159, "The Fair Value Option for Financial Assets and Financial Liabilities." SFAS No. 159 provides entities with an option to measure many financial instruments and certain other items at fair value, including available-for-sale securities previously accounted for under SFAS No. 115, "Accounting for Certain Investments in Debt and Equity Securities." Under SFAS No. 159, unrealized gains and losses on items for which the fair value option has been elected will be reported in earnings at each subsequent reporting period. SFAS No. 159 is effective for fiscal years beginning after November 15, 2007. The Company does not expect the adoption of SFAS No. 159 to have a material impact on its consolidated financial statements.

In June 2007, the Emerging Issues Task Force (EITF) reached a consensus on Issue No. 06-11, "Accounting for Income Tax Benefits of Dividends on Share-Based Payment Awards." EITF 06-11 states that an entity should recognize a realized tax benefit associated with dividends on nonvested equity shares, nonvested equity share units and outstanding equity share options charged to retained earnings as an increase in additional paid in capital. The amount recognized in additional paid in capital should be included in the pool of excess tax benefits available to absorb potential future tax deficiencies on share-based payment awards. EITF 06-11 should be applied prospectively to income tax benefits of dividends on equity-classified share-based payment awards that are declared in fiscal years beginning after December 15, 2007. The Company does not expect the adoption of EITF 06-11 to have a material impact on its consolidated financial statements.

In December 2007, the FASB issued SFAS No. 141(R), "Business Combinations" and SFAS No. 160, "Noncontrolling Interests in Consolidated Financial Statements – an amendment of ARB No. 51". SFAS No. 141(R) and SFAS No. 160 significantly change the accounting for and reporting of business combinations and noncontrolling interests in consolidated financial statements. Under SFAS No. 141(R), more assets and liabilities will be measured at fair value as of the acquisition date instead of the announcement date. Additionally, acquisition costs will be expensed as incurred. Under SFAS No. 160, noncontrolling interests will be classified as a separate component of equity. SFAS No. 141(R) and SFAS No. 160 should be applied prospectively for fiscal years beginning on or after December 15, 2008, with the exception of the presentation and disclosure requirements of SFAS No. 160, which should be applied retrospectively. The Company does not expect the adoption of SFAS No. 141(R) and SFAS No. 160 to have a material impact on its consolidated financial statements.

Segment Information – The Company's operating segments, representing the Company's home improvement retail stores, are aggregated within one reportable segment based on the way the Company manages its business. The Company's home improvement retail stores exhibit similar long-term economic characteristics, sell similar products and services, use similar processes to sell those products and services, and sell their products and services to similar classes of customers. The amount of long-lived assets and net sales outside the U.S. was not significant for any of the periods presented.

Reclassifications - Certain prior period amounts have been reclassified to conform to current classifications.

NOTE 2 - Investments:

The Company's investment securities are classified as available-for-sale. The amortized costs, gross unrealized holding gains and losses, and fair values of the investments at February 1, 2008, and February 2, 2007, were as follows:

	February 1, 2008			
Type (In millions)	Amortized Cost	Gross Unrealized Gains	Gross Unrealized Losses	Fair Value
Municipal obligations	$ 117	$ 1	$ -	$ 118
Money market funds	128	-	-	128
Certificates of deposit	3	-	-	3
Classified as short-term	**248**	**1**	**-**	**249**
Municipal obligations	462	5	-	467
Mutual funds	42	1	(1)	42
Classified as long-term	**504**	**6**	**(1)**	**509**
Total	**$ 752**	**$ 7**	**$ (1)**	**$ 758**

	February 2, 2007			
Type (In millions)	Amortized Cost	Gross Unrealized Gains	Gross Unrealized Losses	Fair Value
Municipal obligations	$ 258	$ -	$ (1)	$ 257
Money market funds	148	-	-	148
Corporate notes	26	-	-	26
Certificates of deposit	1	-	-	1
Classified as short-term	**433**	**-**	**(1)**	**432**
Municipal obligations	127	-	-	127
Mutual funds	35	3	-	38
Classified as long-term	**162**	**3**	**-**	**165**
Total	**$ 595**	**$ 3**	**$ (1)**	**$ 597**

The proceeds from sales of available-for-sale securities were $1.2 billion, $412 million and $192 million for 2007, 2006 and 2005, respectively. Gross realized gains and losses on the sale of available-for-sale securities were not significant for any of the periods presented. The municipal obligations classified as long-term at February 1, 2008, will mature in one to 32 years, based on stated maturity dates.

Short-term and long-term investments include restricted balances pledged as collateral for letters of credit for the Company's extended warranty program and for a portion of the Company's casualty insurance and installed sales program liabilities. Restricted balances included in short-term investments were $167 million at February 1, 2008 and $248 million at February 2, 2007. Restricted balances included in long-term investments were $172 million at February 1, 2008 and $32 million at February 2, 2007.

NOTE 3 - Property and Accumulated Depreciation:

Property is summarized by major class in the following table:

(In millions)	Estimated Depreciable Lives, In Years	February 1, 2008	February 2, 2007
Cost:			
Land	N/A	$ 5,566	$ 4,807
Buildings	7-40	10,036	8,481
Equipment	3-15	8,118	7,036
Leasehold improvements	3-40	3,063	2,484
Construction in progress	N/A	2,053	2,296
Total cost		**28,836**	**25,104**
Accumulated depreciation		(7,475)	(6,133)
Property, less accumulated depreciation		**$ 21,361**	**$ 18,971**

Included in net property are assets under capital lease of $523 million, less accumulated depreciation of $294 million, at February 1, 2008, and $533 million, less accumulated depreciation of $274 million, at February 2, 2007.

NOTE 4 - Short-Term Borrowings and Lines of Credit:

In June 2007, the Company entered into an Amended and Restated Credit Agreement (Amended Facility) to modify the senior credit facility by extending the maturity date to June 2012 and providing for borrowings of up to $1.75 billion. The Amended Facility supports the Company's commercial paper and revolving credit programs. Borrowings made are unsecured and are priced at a fixed rate based upon market conditions at the time of funding, in accordance with the terms of the Amended Facility. The Amended Facility contains certain restrictive covenants, which include maintenance of a debt leverage ratio as defined by the Amended Facility. The Company was in compliance with those covenants at February 1, 2008. Seventeen banking institutions are participating in the Amended Facility. As of February 1, 2008, there was $1.0 billion outstanding under the commercial paper program. The weighted-average interest rate on the outstanding commercial paper was 3.92%. As of February 2, 2007, there was $23 million of short-term borrowings outstanding under the senior credit facility, but no outstanding borrowings under the commercial paper program. The interest rate on the short-term borrowing was 5.41%.

In October 2007, the Company established a Canadian dollar (C$) denominated credit facility in the amount of C$50 million, which provides revolving credit support for the Company's Canadian operations. This uncommitted facility provides the Company with the ability to make unsecured borrowings, which are priced at a fixed rate based upon market conditions at the time of funding in accordance with the terms of the credit facility. As of February 1, 2008, there were no borrowings outstanding under the credit facility.

In January 2008, the Company entered into a C$ denominated credit agreement in the amount of C$200 million for the purpose of funding the build out of retail stores in Canada and for working capital and other general corporate purposes. Borrowings made are unsecured and are priced at a fixed rate based upon market conditions at the time of funding in accordance with the terms of the credit agreement. The credit agreement contains certain restrictive covenants, which include maintenance of a debt leverage ratio as defined by the credit agreement. The Company was in compliance with those covenants at February 1, 2008. Three banking institutions are participating in the credit agreement. As of February 1, 2008, there was C$60 million or the equivalent of $60 million outstanding under the credit facility. The interest rate on the short-term borrowing was 5.75%.

Five banks have extended lines of credit aggregating $789 million for the purpose of issuing documentary letters of credit and standby letters of credit. These lines do not have termination dates and are reviewed periodically. Commitment fees ranging from .225% to .50% per annum are paid on the standby letters of credit amounts outstanding. Outstanding letters of credit totaled $299 million as of February 1, 2008, and $346 million as of February 2, 2007.

NOTE 5 - Long-Term Debt:

(In millions) Debt Category	Interest Rates	Fiscal Year of Final Maturity	February 1, 2008	February 2, 2007
Secured debt: [1]				
Mortgage notes	6.00 to 8.25%	2028	$ 33	$ 30
Unsecured debt:				
Debentures	6.50 to 6.88%	2029	694	693
Notes	8.25%	2010	499	498
Medium-term notes - series A	7.35 to 8.20%	2023	20	27
Medium-term notes - series B [2]	7.11 to 7.61%	2037	217	267
Senior notes	5.00 to 6.65%	2037	3,271	1,980
Convertible notes	0.86 to 2.50%	2021	511	518
Capital leases and other		2030	371	400
Total long-term debt			**5,616**	**4,413**
Less current maturities			40	88
Long-term debt, excluding current maturities			**$ 5,576**	**$ 4,325**

1 *Real properties with an aggregate book value of $47 million were pledged as collateral at February 1, 2008, for secured debt.*

2 *Approximately 46% of these medium-term notes may be put at the option of the holder on the twentieth anniversary of the issue at par value. The medium-term notes were issued in 1997. None of these notes are currently putable.*

Debt maturities, exclusive of unamortized original issue discounts, capital leases and other, for the next five years and thereafter are as follows: 2008, $10 million; 2009, $10 million; 2010, $501 million; 2011, $1 million; 2012, $552 million; thereafter, $4.3 billion.

The Company's debentures, notes, medium-term notes, senior notes and convertible notes contain certain restrictive covenants. The Company was in compliance with all covenants in these agreements at February 1, 2008.

Senior Notes

In September 2007, the Company issued $1.3 billion of unsecured senior notes, comprised of three tranches: $550 million of 5.60% senior notes maturing in September 2012, $250 million of 6.10% senior notes maturing in September 2017 and $500 million of 6.65% senior notes maturing in September 2037. The 5.60%, 6.10% and 6.65% senior notes were issued at discounts of approximately $2.7 million, $1.3 million and $6.3 million, respectively. Interest on the senior notes is payable semiannually in arrears in March and September of each year until maturity, beginning in March 2008. The discount associated with the issuance is included in long-term debt and is being amortized over the respective terms of the senior notes. The net proceeds of approximately $1.3 billion were used for general corporate purposes, including capital expenditures and working capital needs, and for repurchases of shares of the Company's common stock.

In October 2006, the Company issued $1.0 billion of unsecured senior notes, comprised of two tranches: $550 million of 5.40% senior notes maturing in October 2016 and $450 million of 5.80% senior notes maturing in October 2036. The 5.40% senior notes and the 5.80% senior notes were each issued at a discount of approximately $4.4 million. Interest on the senior notes is payable semiannually in arrears in April and October of each year until maturity, beginning in April 2007. The discount associated with the issuance is included in long-term debt and is being amortized over the respective terms of the senior notes. The net proceeds of approximately $991 million were used for general corporate general corporate purposes, including capital expenditures and working capital needs, and for repurchases of common stock.

In October 2005, the Company issued $1.0 billion of unsecured senior notes comprised of two $500 million tranches maturing in October 2015 and October 2035, respectively. The first $500 million tranche of 5.0% senior notes was sold at a discount of $4 million. The second $500 million tranche of 5.5% senior notes was sold at a discount of $8 million. Interest on the senior notes is payable semiannually in arrears in April and October of each year until maturity, beginning in April 2006. The discount associated with the issuance is included in long-term debt and is being amortized over the respective terms of the senior notes. The net proceeds of approximately $988 million were used for the repayment of $600 million in outstanding notes due December 2005, for general corporate purposes, including capital expenditures and working capital needs, and for repurchases of common stock.

The senior notes issued in 2007, 2006 and 2005 may be redeemed by the Company at any time, in whole or in part, at a redemption price plus accrued interest to the date of redemption. The redemption price is equal to the greater of (1) 100% of the principal amount of the senior notes to be redeemed, or (2) the sum of the present values of the remaining scheduled payments of principal and interest thereon, discounted to the date of redemption on a semiannual basis at a specified rate. The indenture under which the 2007 senior notes were issued also contains a provision that allows the holders of the notes to require the Company to repurchase all or any part of their notes if a change in control triggering event occurs. If elected under the change in control provisions, the repurchase of the notes will occur at a purchase price of 101% of the principal amount, plus accrued and unpaid interest, if any, on such notes to the date of purchase. The indenture governing the senior notes does not limit the aggregate principal amount of debt securities that the Company may issue, nor is the Company required to maintain financial ratios or specified levels of net worth or liquidity. However, the indenture contains various restrictive covenants, none of which is expected to impact the Company's liquidity or capital resources.

Upon the issuance of each of the series of senior notes previously described, the Company evaluated the optionality features embedded in the notes and concluded that these features do not require bifurcation from the host contracts and separate accounting as derivative instruments.

Convertible Notes

The Company has $578.7 million aggregate principal, $497.1 million aggregate carrying amount, of senior convertible notes issued in October 2001 at an issue price of $861.03 per note. Cash interest payments on the notes ceased in October 2006. In October 2021 when the notes mature, a holder will receive $1,000 per note, representing a yield to maturity of approximately 1%. Holders of the notes had the right to require the Company to purchase all or a portion of their notes in October 2003 and October 2006, at a price of $861.03 per note plus accrued cash interest, if any, and will have the right in October 2011 to require the Company to purchase all or a portion of their notes at a price of $905.06 per note. The Company may choose to pay the purchase price of the notes in cash or common stock or a combination of cash and common stock. Holders of an insignificant number of notes exercised their right to require the Company to repurchase their notes during 2003 and 2006, all of which were purchased in cash. The Company may redeem for cash all or a portion of the notes at any time, at a price equal to the sum of the issue price plus accrued original issue discount on the redemption date.

Holders of the senior convertible notes may convert their notes into 34.424 shares of the Company's common stock only if: the sale price of the Company's common stock reaches specified thresholds, or the credit rating of the notes is below a specified level, or the notes are called for redemption, or specified corporate transactions representing a change in control have occurred. The conversion ratio of 34.424 shares per note is only adjusted based on normal antidilution provisions designed to protect the value of the conversion option.

The Company's closing share prices reached the specified threshold such that the senior convertible notes became convertible at the option of each holder into shares of common stock during specified quarters of 2006 and 2007. Holders of an insignificant number of senior convertible notes exercised their right to convert their notes into shares of the Company's common stock during 2007 and 2006. The senior convertible notes will not be convertible in the first quarter of 2008 because the Company's closing share prices did not reach the specified threshold during the fourth quarter of 2007.

The Company has $19.7 million aggregate principal, $13.8 million aggregate carrying amount, of convertible notes issued in February 2001 at an issue price of $608.41 per note. Interest will not be paid on the notes prior to maturity in February 2021, at which time the holders will receive $1,000 per note, representing a yield to maturity of 2.5%. Holders of the notes had the right to require the Company to purchase all or a portion of their notes in February 2004, at a price of $655.49 per note, and will have the right in February 2011 to require the Company to purchase all or a portion of their notes at a price of $780.01 per note. The Company may choose to pay the purchase price of the notes in cash or common stock, or a combination of cash and common stock. Holders of an insignificant number of notes exercised their right to require the Company to purchase their notes during 2004, all of which were purchased in cash.

Holders of the convertible notes issued in February 2001 may convert their notes at any time on or before the maturity date, unless the notes have been previously purchased or redeemed, into 32.896 shares of the Company's common stock per note. The conversion ratio of 32.896 shares per note is only adjusted based on normal antidilution provisions designed to protect the value of the conversion option. During 2007, holders of $18 million principal amount, $13 million carrying amount, of the Company's convertible notes issued in February 2001 exercised their right to convert their notes into 0.6 million shares of the Company's common stock at the rate of 32.896 shares per note. During 2006, holders of $118 million principal amount, $80 million carrying amount, of the Company's convertible notes issued in February 2001 exercised their right to convert their notes into 3.9 million shares of the Company's common stock.

Upon the issuance of each of the series of convertible notes previously described, the Company evaluated the optionality features embedded in the notes and concluded that these features do not require bifurcation from the host contracts and separate accounting as derivative instruments.

NOTE 6 - Financial Instruments:

Cash and cash equivalents, accounts receivable, short-term borrowings, accounts payable and accrued liabilities are reflected in the financial statements at cost, which approximates fair value due to their short-term nature. Short- and long-term investments classified as available-for-sale securities, which include restricted balances, are reflected in the financial statements at fair value. Estimated fair values for long-term debt have been determined using available market information. For debt issues that are not quoted on an exchange, interest rates that are currently available to the Company for issuance of debt with similar terms and remaining maturities are used to estimate fair value. However, considerable judgment is required in interpreting market data to develop the estimates of fair value. Accordingly, the estimates presented herein are not necessarily indicative of the amounts that the Company could realize in a current market exchange. The use of different market assumptions and/or estimation methodologies may have a material effect on the estimated fair value amounts. The fair value of the Company's long-term debt, excluding capital leases and other, is as follows:

	February 1, 2008		February 2, 2007	
(In millions)	Carrying Amount	Fair Value	Carrying Amount	Fair Value
Liabilities:				
Long-term debt (excluding capital leases and other)	$ 5,245	$ 5,406	$ 4,013	$ 4,301

NOTE 7 - Shareholders' Equity:

Authorized shares of common stock were 5.6 billion ($.50 par value) at February 1, 2008 and February 2, 2007.

The Company has 5.0 million ($5 par value) authorized shares of preferred stock, none of which have been issued. The Board of Directors may issue the preferred stock (without action by shareholders) in one or more series, having such voting rights, dividend and liquidation preferences, and such conversion and other rights as may be designated by the Board of Directors at the time of issuance.

NOTE 11 - Earnings Per Share:

Basic earnings per share (EPS) excludes dilution and is computed by dividing the applicable net earnings by the weighted-average number of common shares outstanding for the period. Diluted earnings per share is calculated based on the weighted-average shares of common stock as adjusted for the potential dilutive effect of share-based awards and convertible notes as of the balance sheet date. The following table reconciles EPS for 2007, 2006 and 2005:

(In millions, except per share data)	2007	2006	2005
Basic earnings per share:			
Net earnings	**$ 2,809**	**$ 3,105**	**$ 2,765**
Weighted-average shares outstanding	**1,481**	**1,535**	**1,555**
Basic earnings per share	**$ 1.90**	**$ 2.02**	**$ 1.78**
Diluted earnings per share:			
Net earnings	$ 2,809	$ 3,105	$ 2,765
Net earnings adjustment for interest on convertible notes, net of tax	4	4	11
Net earnings, as adjusted	**$ 2,813**	**$ 3,109**	**$ 2,776**
Weighted-average shares outstanding	1,481	1,535	1,555
Dilutive effect of share-based awards	8	9	10
Dilutive effect of convertible notes	21	22	42
Weighted-average shares, as adjusted	**1,510**	**1,566**	**1,607**
Diluted earnings per share	**$ 1.86**	**$ 1.99**	**$ 1.73**

Stock options to purchase 7.8 million, 6.8 million and 5.6 million shares of common stock for 2007, 2006 and 2005, respectively, were excluded from the computation of diluted earnings per share because their effect would have been antidilutive.

NOTE 12 - Leases:

The Company leases store facilities and land for certain store facilities under agreements with original terms generally of 20 years. For lease agreements that provide for escalating rent payments or free-rent occupancy periods, the Company recognizes rent expense on a straight-line basis over the non-cancelable lease term and any option renewal period where failure to exercise such option would result in an economic penalty in such amount that renewal appears, at the inception of the lease, to be reasonably assured. The lease term commences on the date that the Company takes possession of or controls the physical use of the property. The leases generally contain provisions for four to six renewal options of five years each.

Some agreements also provide for contingent rentals based on sales performance in excess of specified minimums. In 2007, 2006 and 2005, contingent rentals were insignificant.

The Company subleases certain properties that are no longer held for use in operations. Sublease income was not significant for any of the periods presented.

Certain equipment is also leased by the Company under agreements ranging from three to five years. These agreements typically contain renewal options providing for a renegotiation of the lease, at the Company's option, based on the fair market value at that time.

The future minimum rental payments required under capital and operating leases having initial or remaining non-cancelable lease terms in excess of one year are summarized as follows:

NOTE 14 – Related Parties:

A brother-in-law of the Company's Executive Vice President of Business Development is a senior officer of a vendor that provides millwork and other building products to the Company. In both 2007 and 2006, the Company purchased products in the amount of $101 million from this vendor, while in 2005 the Company purchased products in the amount of $84 million from this vendor. Amounts payable to this vendor were insignificant at February 1, 2008 and February 2, 2007.

NOTE 15 - Other Information:

Net interest expense is comprised of the following:

(In millions)	2007	2006	2005
Long-term debt	$ 247	$ 183	$ 171
Capitalized leases	32	34	39
Interest income	(45)	(52)	(45)
Interest capitalized	(65)	(32)	(28)
Other	25	21	21
Net interest expense	**$ 194**	**$ 154**	**$ 158**

Supplemental disclosures of cash flow information:

(In millions)	2007	2006	2005
Cash paid for interest, net of amount capitalized	$ 198	$ 179	$ 173
Cash paid for income taxes	$ 1,725	$ 2,031	$ 1,593

Noncash investing and financing activities:			
Noncash fixed asset acquisitions, including assets acquired under capital lease	$ 99	$ 159	$ 175
Conversions of long-term debt to equity	$ 13	$ 82	$ 565

Lowe's Companies, Inc.
Selected Financial Data (Unaudited)

Selected Statement of Earnings Data: (In millions, except per share data)	**2007**	**2006**	**2005***	**2004**	**2003**
Net sales	**$ 48,283**	**$ 46,927**	**$ 43,243**	**$ 36,464**	**$ 30,838**
Gross margin	**16,727**	**16,198**	**14,790**	**12,240**	**9,533**
Earnings from continuing operations	**2,809**	**3,105**	**2,765**	**2,167**	**1,807**
Earnings from discontinued operations, net of tax	-	-	-	-	15
Net earnings	**2,809**	**3,105**	**2,765**	**2,167**	**1,822**
Basic earnings per share - continuing operations	1.90	2.02	1.78	1.39	1.15
Basic earnings per share – discontinued operations	-	-	-	-	0.01
Basic earnings per share	**1.90**	**2.02**	**1.78**	**1.39**	**1.16**
Diluted earnings per share - continuing operations	1.86	1.99	1.73	1.35	1.12
Diluted earnings per share – discontinued operations	-	-	-	-	0.01
Diluted earnings per share	**1.86**	**1.99**	**1.73**	**1.35**	**1.13**
Dividends per share	$ 0.29	$ 0.18	$ 0.11	$ 0.08	$ 0.06

Selected Balance S heet Data:					
Total assets	$ 30,869	$ 27,767	$ 24,639	$ 21,101	$ 18,667
Long-term debt, excluding current maturities	$ 5,576	$ 4,325	$ 3,499	$ 3,060	$ 3,678

Note: The selected financial data has been adjusted to present the 2003 disposal of the Contractor Yards as a discontinued operation for all periods.
* Fiscal year 2005 contained 53 weeks, while all other years contained 52 weeks.

Selected Quarterly Data: (In millions, except per share data)	**First**	**Second**	**Third**	**Fourth**
2007				
Net sales	$ 12,172	$ 14,167	$ 11,565	$ 10,379
Gross margin	4,259	4,883	3,964	3,620
Net earnings	739	1,019	643	408
Basic earnings per share	0.49	0.68	0.44	0.28
Diluted earnings per share	$ 0.48	$ 0.67	$ 0.43	$ 0.28

(In millions, except per share data)	**First**	**Second**	**Third**	**Fourth**
2006				
Net sales	$ 11,921	$ 13,389	$ 11,211	$ 10,406
Gross margin	4,169	4,478	3,865	3,687
Net earnings	841	935	716	613
Basic earnings per share	0.54	0.61	0.47	0.40
Diluted earnings per share	$ 0.53	$ 0.60	$ 0.46	$ 0.40

APPENDIX C

TIME VALUE OF MONEY

TIME VALUE OF MONEY

The **time value of money** is the idea that, quite simply, money received today is worth more than money to be received one year from today (or at any other future date), because it can be used to earn interest. If you invest $1,000 today at 10 percent, you will have $1,100 in one year. So $1,000 in one year is worth $100 less than $1,000 today because you lose the opportunity to earn the $100 in interest.

In some business situations, you will know the dollar amount of a cash flow that occurs in the future and will need to determine its value now. This type of situation is known as a **present value** problem. The opposite situation occurs when you know the dollar amount of a cash flow that occurs today and need to determine its value at some point in the future. These situations are called **future value** problems. The value of money changes over time because money can earn interest. The following table illustrates the basic difference between present value and future value problems:

	Now	Future
Present value	?	$1,000
Future value	$1,000	?

Present and future value problems may involve two types of cash flow: a single payment or an annuity (which is the fancy word for a series of equal cash payments). Thus, you need to learn how to deal with four different situations related to the time value of money:

1. Future value of a single payment
2. Present value of a single payment
3. Future value of an annuity
4. Present value of an annuity

Most inexpensive handheld calculators and any spreadsheet program can perform the detailed arithmetic computations required to solve future value and present value problems. In later courses and in all business situations, you will probably use a calculator or computer to solve these problems. At this stage, we encourage you to solve problems using Tables C.1 through C.4 at the end of this appendix. We believe that using the tables will give you a better understanding of how and why present and future value concepts apply to business problems. The tables give the value of a $1 cash flow (single payment or annuity) for different periods (n) and at different interest rates (i). If a problem involves payments other than $1, it is necessary to multiply the value from the table by the amount of the payment.[1] In the final section of this appendix, we explain how to use Excel to compute present values.

COMPUTING FUTURE AND PRESENT VALUES OF A SINGLE AMOUNT

Future Value of a Single Amount

In future value of a single amount problems, you will be asked to calculate how much money you will have in the future as the result of investing a certain amount in the present. If you were to receive a gift of $10,000, for instance, you might decide to put it in a savings account and use the money as a down payment on a house after you graduate. The future value computation would tell you how much money will be available when you graduate.

To solve a future value problem, you need to know three items:

1. Amount to be invested.
2. Interest rate (i) the amount will earn.
3. Number of periods (n) in which the amount will earn interest.

[1] Present value and future value problems involve cash flows. The basic concepts are the same for cash inflows (receipts) and cash outflows (payments). No fundamental differences exist between present value and future value calculations for cash payments versus cash receipts.

The future value concept is based on compound interest, which simply means that interest is calculated on top of interest. Thus, the amount of interest for each period is calculated using the principal plus any interest not paid out in prior periods. Graphically, the calculation of the future value of $1 for three periods at an interest rate of 10 percent may be represented as follows:

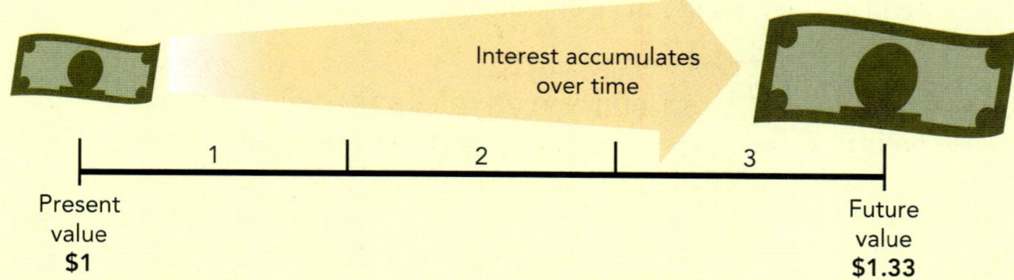

Assume that on January 1, 2009, you deposit $1,000 in a savings account at 10 percent annual interest, compounded annually. At the end of three years, the $1,000 will have increased to $1,331 as follows:

Year	Amount at Start of Year	+	Interest During the Year	=	Amount at End of Year
1	$1,000	+	$1,000 × 10% = $100	=	$1,100
2	1,100	+	1,100 × 10% = 110	=	1,210
3	1,210	+	1,210 × 10% = 121	=	1,331

We can avoid the detailed arithmetic by referring to Table C.1, Future Value of $1, on page C14. For $i = 10\%$, $n = 3$, we find the value 1.3310. We then compute the balance at the end of year 3 as follows:

From Table C.1, Interest rate = 10% $n = 3$

$1,000 × 1.3310 = $1,331

Note that the increase of $331 is due to the time value of money. It is interest revenue to the owner of the savings account and interest expense to the bank.

Present Value of a Single Amount

The present value of a single amount is the worth to you today of receiving that amount some time in the future. For instance, you might be offered an opportunity to invest in a financial instrument that would pay you $1,000 in 3 years. Before you decided whether to invest, you would want to determine the present value of the instrument.

To compute the present value of an amount to be received in the future, we must discount (a procedure that is the opposite of compounding) at i interest rate for n periods. In discounting, the interest is subtracted rather than added, as it is in compounding. Graphically, the present value of $1 due at the end of the third period with an interest rate of 10 percent can be represented as follows:

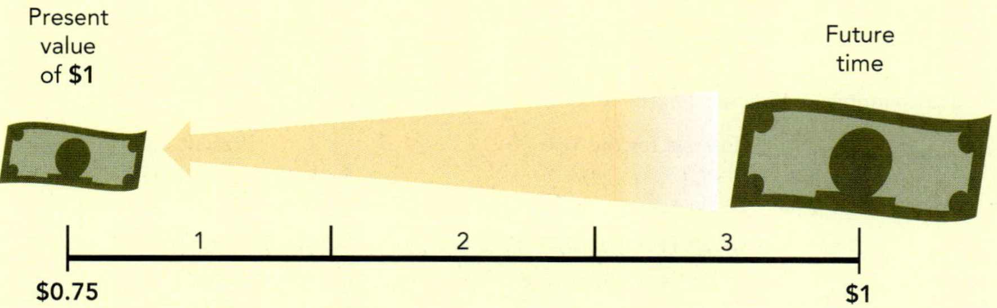

Assume that today is January 1, 2009, and you have the opportunity to receive $1,000 cash on December 31, 2011. At an interest rate of 10 percent per year, how much is the $1,000 payment worth to you on January 1, 2009? You could discount the amount year by year,[2] but it is easier to use Table C.2, Present Value of $1, on pages C14–C15. For $i = 10\%$, $n = 3$, we find that the present value of $1 is 0.7513. The present value of $1,000 to be received at the end of three years can be computed as follows:

From Table C.2,
Interest rate = 10%
$n = 3$

$1,000 × 0.7513 = $751.30

It is important to learn not only how to compute a present value but also to understand what it means. The $751.30 is the amount you would pay now to have the right to receive $1,000 at the end of three years, assuming an interest rate of 10 percent. Conceptually, you should be indifferent between having $751.30 today and receiving $1,000 in three years. If you had $751.30 today but wanted $1,000 in three years, you could simply deposit the money in a savings account that pays 10% interest and it would grow to $1,000 in three years. Alternatively, if you had a contract that promised you $1,000 in three years, you could sell it to an investor for $751.30 in cash today because it would permit the investor to earn the difference in interest.

What if you could only earn 6 percent during the three-year period from January 1, 2009, to December 31, 2011? What would be the present value on January 1, 2009, of receiving $1,000 on December 31, 2011? To answer this we would take the same approach, using Table C.2, except that the interest rate would change to $i = 6\%$. Referring to Table C.2, we see the present value factor for $i = 6\%$, $n = 3$, is 0.8396. Thus, the present value of $1,000 to be received at the end of three years, assuming a 6 percent interest rate, would be computed as $1,000 × 0.8396 = $839.60. Notice that when we assume a 6 percent interest rate the present value is greater than when we assumed a 10 percent interest rate. The reason for this difference is that, to reach $1,000 three years from now, you would need to deposit more money in a savings account now if it earns 6 percent interest than if it earns 10 percent interest.

SELF-STUDY PRACTICE

1. If the interest rate in a present value problem increases from 8 percent to 10 percent, will the present value increase or decrease?
2. What is the present value of $10,000 to be received 10 years from now if the interest rate is 5 percent, compounded annually?
3. If $10,000 is deposited now in a savings account that earns 5 percent interest compounded annually, how much will it be worth 10 years from now?

After you have finished, check your answers with the solution at the bottom of the next page.

COMPUTING FUTURE AND PRESENT VALUES OF AN ANNUITY

Instead of a single payment, many business problems involve multiple cash payments over a number of periods. An **annuity** is a series of consecutive payments characterized by

1. An equal dollar amount each interest period.
2. Interest periods of equal length (year, half a year, quarter, or month).
3. An equal interest rate each interest period.

[2] The detailed discounting is as follows:

Periods	Interest for the Year	Present Value*
1	$1,000 = ($1,000 × 1/1.10) = $90.91	$1,000 − $90.91 = $909.09
2	$909.09 = ($909.09 × 1/1.10) = $82.65	$909.09 − $82.65 = $826.44
3	$826.44 = ($826.44 × 1/1.10) = $75.14†	$826.44 − $75.14 = $751.30

*Verifiable in Table C.2.
†Adjusted for rounding

Examples of annuities include monthly payments on a car or house, yearly contributions to a savings account, and monthly pension benefits.

Future Value of an Annuity

If you are saving money for some purpose, such as a new car or a trip, you might decide to deposit a fixed amount of money in a savings account each month. The future value of an annuity computation will tell you how much money will be in your savings account at some point in the future.

The future value of an annuity includes compound interest on each payment from the date of payment to the end of the term of the annuity. Each new payment accumulates less interest than prior payments, only because the number of periods remaining in which to accumulate interest decreases. The future value of an annuity of $1 for three periods at 10 percent may be represented graphically as

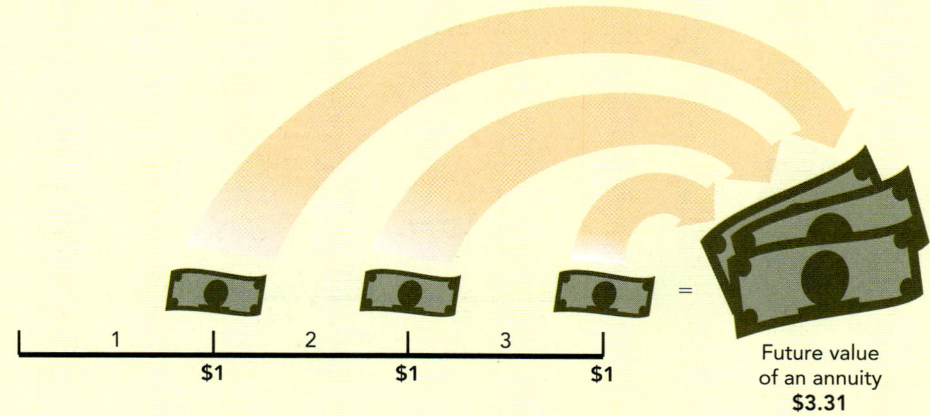

Assume that each year for three years, you deposit $1,000 cash in a savings account at 10 percent interest per year. You make the first $1,000 deposit on December 31, 2009, the second one on December 31, 2010, and the third and last one on December 31, 2011. The first $1,000 deposit earns compound interest for two years (for a total principal and interest of $1,210); the second deposit earns interest for one year (for a total principal and interest of $1,100). The third deposit earns no interest because it was made on the day that the balance is computed. Thus, the total amount in the savings account at the end of three years is $3,310 ($1,210 + $1,100 + $1,000).

To calculate the future value of this annuity, we could compute the interest on each deposit, similar to what is described above. However, a faster way is to refer to Table C.3, Future Value of an Annuity of $1 for $i = 10\%$, $n = 3$ to find the value 3.3100. The future value of your three deposits of $1,000 each can be computed as follows:

From Table C.3, Interest rate = 10%
$n = 3$

$1,000 × 3.3100 = $3,310

The Power of Compounding

Compound interest is a remarkably powerful economic force. In fact, the ability to earn interest on interest is the key to building economic wealth. If you save $1,000 per year for the first 10 years of your career, you will have more money when you retire than you would if you had saved $15,000 per year for the last 10 years of your career. This surprising outcome occurs because the money you save early in your career will earn more interest than the money you save at the end of your career. If you start saving money now, the majority of your wealth will not be the money you saved but the interest your money was able to earn.

Solution to Self-Study Practice

1. The present value will decrease.
2. $10,000 × 0.6139 = $6,139.
3. $10,000 × 1.6289 = $16,289.

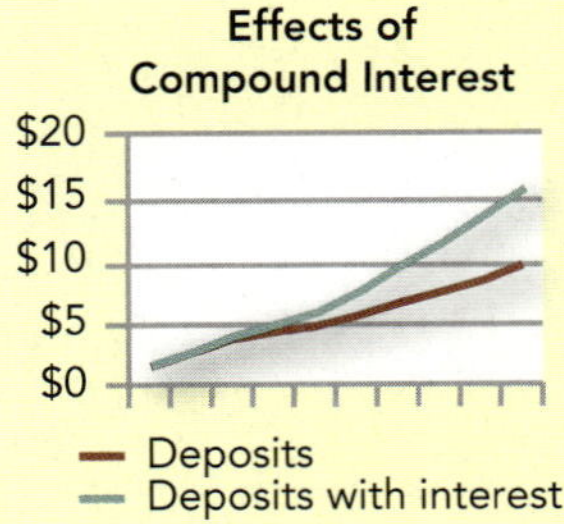

The chart in the margin illustrates the power of compounding over a brief 10-year period. If you deposit $1 each year in an account earning 10 percent interest, at the end of just 10 years, only 63 percent of your balance will be made up of money you have saved. The rest will be interest you have earned. After 20 years, only 35 percent of your balance will be from saved money. The lesson associated with compound interest is that even though saving money is hard, you should start now.

Present Value of an Annuity

The present value of an annuity is the value now of a series of equal amounts to be received (or paid out) for some specified number of periods in the future. It is computed by discounting each of the equal periodic amounts. A good example of this type of problem is a retirement program that offers employees a monthly income after retirement. The present value of an annuity of $1 for three periods at 10 percent may be represented graphically as

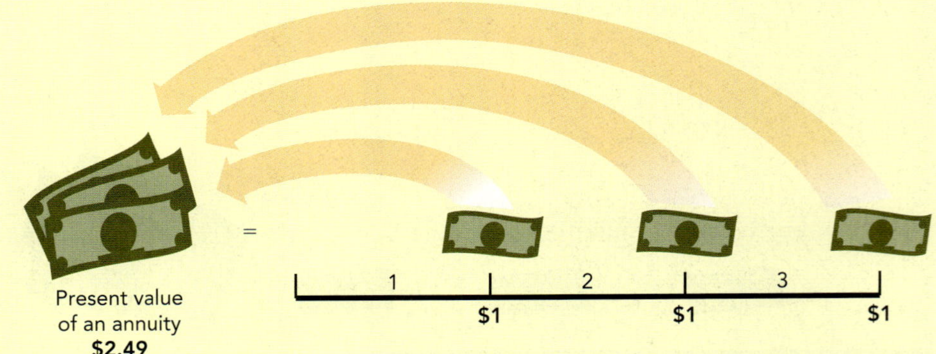

Assume you are to receive $1,000 cash on each December 31, 2009, 2010, and 2011. How much would the sum of these three $1,000 future amounts be worth on January 1, 2009, assuming an interest rate of 10 percent per year? One way to determine this is to use Table C.2 to calculate the present value of each single amount as follows:

			FACTOR FROM TABLE C.2		
Year	Amount		$i = 10\%$		Present Value
1	$1,000	×	0.9091 ($n = 1$)	=	$ 909.10
2	$1,000	×	0.8264 ($n = 2$)	=	826.40
3	$1,000	×	0.7513 ($n = 3$)	=	751.30
			Total present value	=	$2,486.80

Alternatively, we can compute the present value of this annuity more easily by using Table C.4, as follows:

From Table C.4, Interest rate = 10%
$n = 3$

$1,000 × 2.4869 = $2,487 (rounded)

Interest Rates and Interest Periods

The preceding illustrations assumed annual periods for compounding and discounting. Although interest rates are almost always quoted on an annual basis, many compounding periods encountered in business are less than one year. When interest periods are less than a year, the values of n and i must be restated to be consistent with the length of the interest compounding period.

To illustrate, 12 percent interest compounded annually for five years requires the use of $n = 5$ and $i = 12\%$. If compounding is quarterly, however, there will be four interest periods per year (20 interest periods in five years), and the quarterly interest rate is one quarter of the annual rate (3 percent per quarter). Therefore, 12 percent interest compounded quarterly for five years requires use of $n = 20$ and $i = 3\%$.

ACCOUNTING APPLICATIONS OF PRESENT VALUES

Many business transactions require the use of future and present value concepts. In finance classes, you will see how to apply future value concepts. In this section, we apply present value concepts to three common accounting cases.

Case A—Present Value of a Single Amount

On January 1, 2009, General Mills bought some new delivery trucks. The company signed a note and agreed to pay $200,000 on December 31, 2010, an amount representing the cash equivalent price of the trucks plus interest for two years. The market interest rate for this note was 12 percent.

1. How should the accountant record the purchase?

Answer: This case requires the computation of the present value of a single amount. In conformity with the cost principle, the cost of the trucks is their current cash equivalent price, which is the present value of the future payment. The problem can be shown graphically as follows:

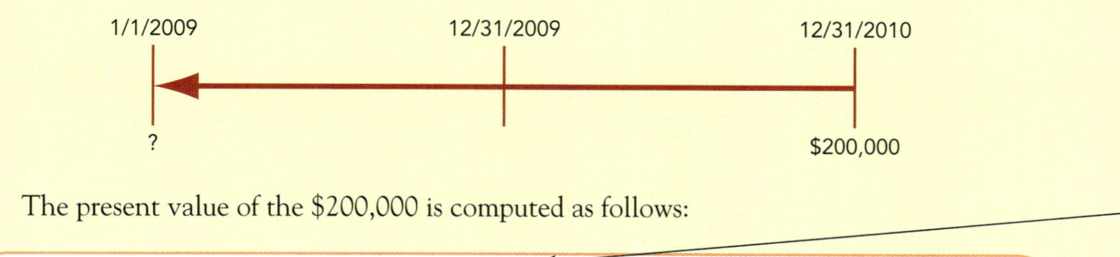

The present value of the $200,000 is computed as follows:

From Table C.2, Interest rate = 12%, n = 2

$200,000 × 0.7972 = $159,440

This transaction would be recorded with the journal entry shown below.

	Debit	Credit
Delivery Trucks (+A)	159,440	
Note Payable (+L)		159,440

Assets		=	Liabilities		+	Owners' Equity
Delivery Trucks	+159,440		Note Payable	+159,440		

2. How should the effects of interest be reported at the end of 2009 and 2010?

Answer: Interest expense would be calculated and recorded as follows:

<u>December 31, 2009</u>

Interest = Principal × Rate × Time
= $159,440 × 12% × 12/12 = $19,132 (rounded)

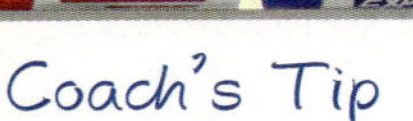

Coach's Tip

The interest is recorded in the Note Payable account because it would be paid as part of the note at maturity.

	Debit	Credit
Interest Expense (+E, −OE)	19,132	
Note Payable (+L)		19,132

Assets	=	Liabilities		+	Owners' Equity	
		Note Payable	+19,132		Interest Expense (+E)	−19,132

December 31, 2010

Interest = Principal × Rate × Time
= ($159,440 + 19,132) × 12% × 12/12 = $21,428 (rounded)

	Debit	Credit
Interest Expense (+E, −OE)	21,428	
Note Payable (+L)		21,428

Assets	=	Liabilities		+	Owners' Equity	
		Note Payable	+21,428		Interest Expense (+E)	−21,428

Note Payable (L)		
	159,440	Jan. 1, 2009
	19,132	Interest 2009
	21,428	Interest 2010
	200,000	Dec. 31, 2010

3. What is the effect of the $200,000 debt payment made on December 31, 2010?

Answer: At this date the amount to be paid is the balance in *Note Payable*, after it has been updated for interest pertaining to 2010, as shown in the T-account in the margin. Notice that, just prior to its repayment, the balance for the note on December 31, 2010 is the same as the maturity amount on the due date.

The debt payment would be recorded with the journal entry shown below.

	Debit	Credit
Note Payable (−L)	200,000	
Cash (−A)		200,000

Assets		=	Liabilities		+	Owners' Equity
Cash	−200,000		Note Payable	−200,000		

Case B—Present Value of an Annuity

On January 1, 2009, General Mills bought new milling equipment. The company elected to finance the purchase with a note payable to be paid off in three years in annual installments of $163,686. Each installment includes principal plus interest on the unpaid balance at 11 percent per year. The annual installments are due on December 31, 2009, 2010, and 2011. This problem can be shown graphically as follows:

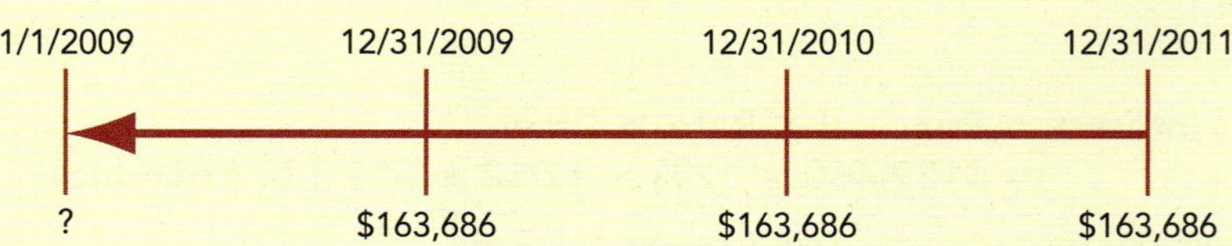

1. What is the amount of the note?

Answer: The note is the present value of each installment payment, $i = 11\%$ and $n = 3$. This is an annuity because the note repayment is made in three equal installments. The amount of the note is computed as follows:

From Table C.4, Interest rate = 11%, n = 3

$163,686 × 2.4437 = $400,000

The acquisition on January 1, 2009, would be accounted for as follows:

	Debit	Credit
Milling Equipment (+A)	400,000	
Note Payable (+L)		400,000

Assets	=	Liabilities	+	Owners' Equity
Milling Equipment +400,000		Note Payable +400,000		

2. How should the payments made at the end of each year be accounted for?

Answer:

December 31, 2009

Each payment includes both interest and principal. The interest part of the first payment is calculated as:

Interest = Principal × Rate × Time
= $400,000 × 11% × 12/12 = $44,000

Now that we know the interest component, the principal portion of the first payment of $163,686 can be calculated ($163,686 − $44,000 = $119,686). Thus, the first payment on December 31, 2009, would be accounted for as:

	Debit	Credit
Interest Expense (+E, −OE)	44,000	
Note Payable (−L) ($163,686 − $44,000)	119,686	
Cash (−A)		163,686

Assets	=	Liabilities	+	Owners' Equity
Cash −163,686		Note Payable −119,686		Interest Expense (+E) −44,000

December 31, 2010

The interest portion of the second and third payments would be calculated in the same way, although notice that the principal balance in the Note Payable account changes after each payment.

Interest = Principal × Rate × Time
= [($400,000 − $119,686) × 11% × 12/12] = $30,835
Principal = Payment − Interest
= $163,686 − $30,835 = $132,851

	Debit	Credit
Interest Expense (+E, −OE)	30,835	
Note Payable (−L)	132,851	
Cash (−A)		163,686

Assets	=	Liabilities	+	Owners' Equity
Cash −163,686		Note Payable −132,851		Interest Expense (+E) −30,835

December 31, 2011

Interest = Principal × Rate × Time
= [($400,000 − $119,686 − $132,851) × 11% × 12/12]
= $16,223 (adjusted to accommodate rounding)

Principal = Payment − Interest
= $163,686 − $16,223 = $147,463

Note Payable (L)		
	400,000	Jan. 1, 2009
Dec. 31, 2009 119,686		
Dec. 31, 2010 132,851		
Dec. 31, 2011 147,463		
	0	Dec. 31, 2011

	Debit	Credit
Interest Expense (+E, −OE)	16,223	
Note Payable (−L)	147,463	
Cash (−A)		163,686

Assets	=	Liabilities	+	Owners' Equity
Cash −163,686		Note Payable −147,463		Interest Expense (+E) −16,223

Case C—Present Value of a Single Amount and an Annuity

On January 1, 2009, General Mills issued 100 four-year, $1,000 bonds. The bonds pay interest annually at a rate of 6 percent of face value. What total amount would investors be willing to pay for the bonds if they require an annual return of: (*a*) 4 percent, (*b*) 6 percent, or (*c*) 8 percent?

Answer: This case requires the computation of the present value of a single amount (the $100,000 face value paid at maturity) plus the present value of an annuity (the annual interest payments of $6,000). The problem can be shown graphically as follows:

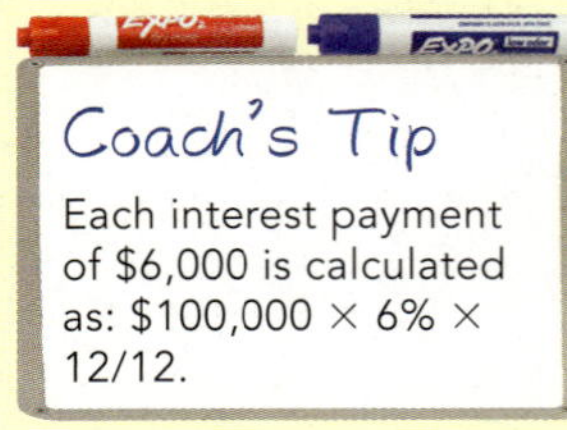

(a) 4 Percent Market Interest Rate

The present value of the $100,000 face value is computed as follows:

From Table C.2, Interest rate = 4% n = 4

$100,000 × 0.8548 = $85,480

The present value of the $6,000 annuity is computed as follows:

From Table C.4,
Interest rate = 4%
n = 4

$6,000 × 3.6299 = $21,780*

*Adjusted to accommodate rounding in the present value factor.

The present value of the total bond payments, computed using the discount rate of 4 percent, is $107,260 (= $85,480 + $21,780).

(b) 6 Percent Market Interest Rate

The present value of the $100,000 face value is computed as follows:

From Table C.2,
Interest rate = 6%
n = 4

$100,000 × 0.7921 = $79,210

The present value of the $6,000 annuity is computed as follows:

From Table C.4,
Interest rate = 6%
n = 4

$6,000 × 3.4651 = $20,790*

* Adjusted to accommodate rounding in the present value factor.

The present value of the total bond payments, computed using the discount rate of 6%, is $100,000 (= $79,210 + $20,790).

(c) 8 Percent Market Interest Rate

The present value of the $100,000 face value is computed as follows:

From Table C.2,
Interest rate = 8%
n = 4

$100,000 × 0.7350 = $73,503*

* Adjusted to accommodate rounding in the present value factor.

The present value of the $6,000 annuity is computed as follows:

From Table C.4,
Interest rate = 8%
n = 4

$6,000 × 3.3121 = $19,873

The present value of the total bond payments, computed using the discount rate of 8%, is $93,376 (= $73,503 + $19,873).
The following table summarizes these calculations:

Coach's Tip

The present values in *a*, *b*, and *c* demonstrate the calculation of the bond issue prices used in Chapter 14.

	MARKET INTEREST RATES		
	4%	6%	8%
Present value of $100,000 face value (principal) paid four years from now	$ 85,480	$ 79,210	$73,503
Present value of $6,000 (interest) paid once a year for four years	21,780	20,790	19,873
Amount to pay	$107,260	$100,000	$93,376

Of course, these calculations are just the starting point for understanding how bond liabilities are determined and reported. You'll need to read Chapter 14 for information about how bond liabilities are accounted for.

PRESENT VALUE COMPUTATIONS USING EXCEL

While the present value tables are useful for educational purposes, most present value problems in business are solved with calculators or Excel spreadsheets. Because of the widespread availability of Excel, we will show you how to solve present value problems using Excel. There are slightly different versions of Excel available, depending on the age of the computer. The illustrations in this text are based on Microsoft Office 2007.

Present Value of a Single Payment

The calculation of a present value amount is based on a fairly simple mathematical formula:

$$PV = \text{Payment}/(1+i)^n$$

In this formula, *payment* is the cash payment made at some point in the future, i is the interest rate each period, and n is the number of periods in the problem. We could use this formula to solve all problems involving the present value of a single payment. It is, of course, easier to use a present value table (like the one at the end of this appendix) which is derived by solving the present value formula for various interest rates and numbers of periods. Unfortunately, a table that included all interest rates and numbers of periods actually encountered in business would be too large to work with. As a result, most accountants and analysts use Excel to compute a present value.

To compute the present value of a single payment in Excel, you enter the present value formula in a cell, using the format required by Excel. You should select a cell and enter the following formula:

$$= \text{Payment}/(1+i)\text{\^{}}n$$

To illustrate, if you want to solve for the present value of a $100,000 payment to be made in five years with an interest rate of 10%, you would enter the following in the function field:

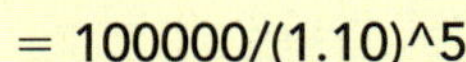

= 100000/(1.10)^5

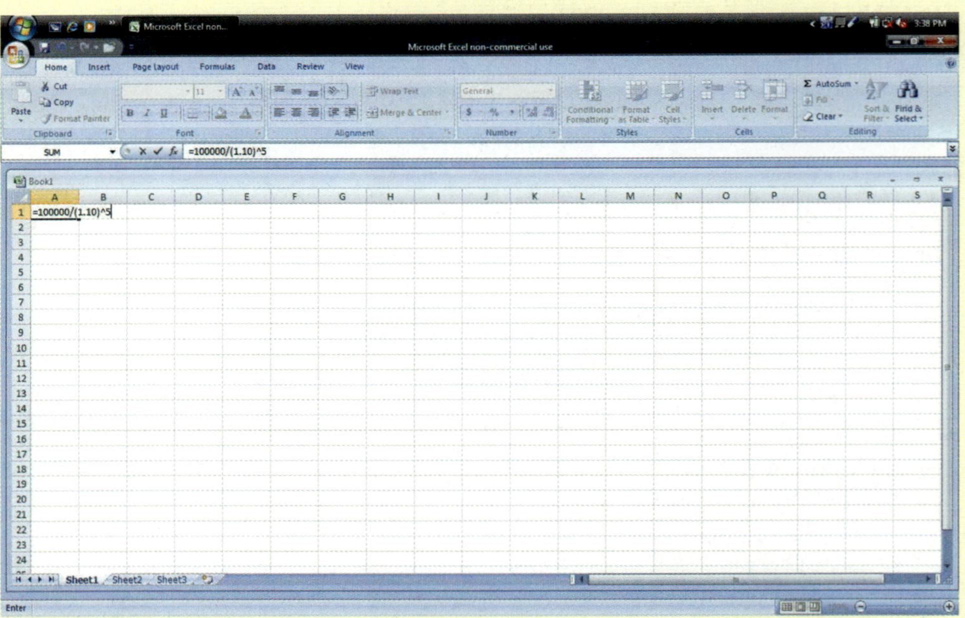

Based on this entry, Excel would compute the present value of $62,092.13. This answer is slightly different from the answer you would have if you used the present value tables at the end of this appendix. The tables are rounded based on four digits. Excel does not round and, therefore, provides a more accurate computation.

Present Value of an Annuity

The formula for computing the present value of an annuity is a little more complicated than the present value of a single payment. As a result, Excel has been programmed to include the formula so that you do not have to enter it yourself.

To compute the present value of an annuity in Excel, select a cell and click on the insert function button (f_x). The following dropdown box will appear:

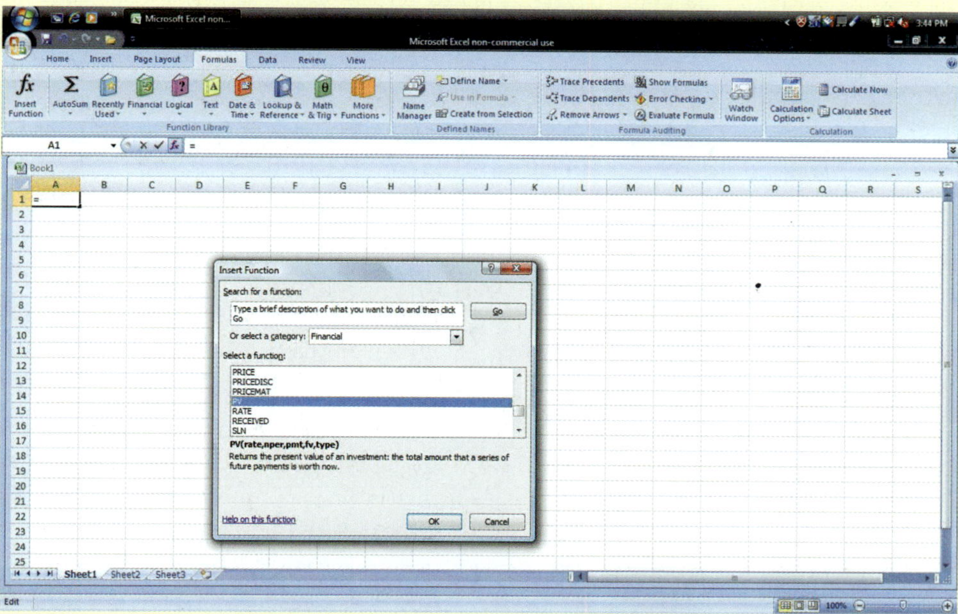

Under the Select Category heading, you should pick "Financial," scroll down under "Select a Function," and click on PV. Then, click on "OK" and a new dropdown box will appear:

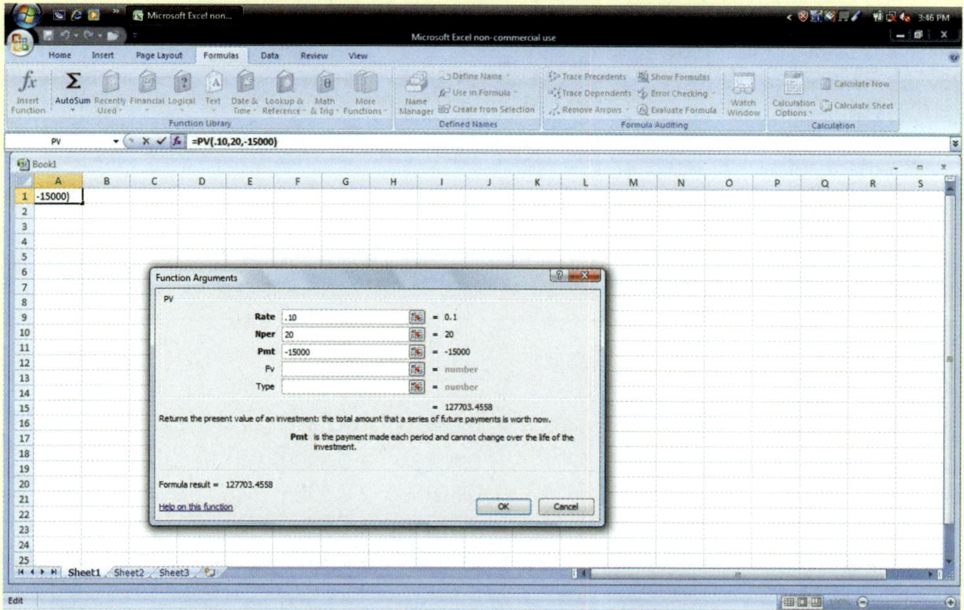

In this box, you should enter the interest rate, 10% in this example, under Rate. Notice that the rate must be entered as a decimal (i.e., 0.10). Enter the number of periods (20) under Nper. Excel has an unusual convention associated with the payment. It must be entered as a negative amount (−15000) under Pmt. Notice also that a comma should not be included in the amount you enter. When you click on OK, Excel will enter the present value in the cell you selected. In this example, the value determined by Excel is $127,703.46.

Table C.1 Future Value of $1

Periods	2%	3%	3.75%	4%	4.25%	5%	6%	7%	8%
0	1.	1.	1.	1.	1.	1.	1.	1.	1.
1	1.02	1.03	1.0375	1.04	1.0425	1.05	1.06	1.07	1.08
2	1.0404	1.0609	1.0764	1.0816	1.0868	1.1025	1.1236	1.1449	1.1664
3	1.0612	1.0927	1.1168	1.1249	1.1330	1.1576	1.1910	1.2250	1.2597
4	1.0824	1.1255	1.1587	1.1699	1.1811	1.2155	1.2625	1.3108	1.3605
5	1.1041	1.1593	1.2021	1.2167	1.2313	1.2763	1.3382	1.4026	1.4693
6	1.1262	1.1941	1.2472	1.2653	1.2837	1.3401	1.4185	1.5007	1.5869
7	1.1487	1.2299	1.2939	1.3159	1.3382	1.4071	1.5036	1.6058	1.7138
8	1.1717	1.2668	1.3425	1.3686	1.3951	1.4775	1.5938	1.7182	1.8509
9	1.1951	1.3048	1.3928	1.4233	1.4544	1.5513	1.6895	1.8385	1.9990
10	1.2190	1.3439	1.4450	1.4802	1.5162	1.6289	1.7908	1.9672	2.1589
20	1.4859	1.8061	2.0882	2.1911	2.2989	2.6533	3.2071	3.8697	4.6610

Periods	9%	10%	11%	12%	13%	14%	15%	20%	25%
0	1.	1.	1.	1.	1.	1.	1.	1.	1.
1	1.09	1.10	1.11	1.12	1.13	1.14	1.15	1.20	1.25
2	1.1881	1.2100	1.2321	1.2544	1.2769	1.2996	1.3225	1.4400	1.5625
3	1.2950	1.3310	1.3676	1.4049	1.4429	1.4815	1.5209	1.7280	1.9531
4	1.4116	1.4641	1.5181	1.5735	1.6305	1.6890	1.7490	2.0736	2.4414
5	1.5386	1.6105	1.6851	1.7623	1.8424	1.9254	2.0114	2.4883	3.0518
6	1.6771	1.7716	1.8704	1.9738	2.0820	2.1950	2.3131	2.9860	3.8147
7	1.8280	1.9487	2.0762	2.2107	2.3526	2.5023	2.6600	3.5832	4.7684
8	1.9926	2.1436	2.3045	2.4760	2.6584	2.8526	3.0590	4.2998	5.9605
9	2.1719	2.3579	2.5580	2.7731	3.0040	3.2519	3.5179	5.1598	7.4506
10	2.3674	2.5937	2.8394	3.1058	3.3946	3.7072	4.0456	6.1917	9.3132
20	5.6044	6.7275	8.0623	9.6463	11.5231	13.7435	16.3665	38.3376	86.7362

Table C.2 Present Value of $1

Periods	2%	3%	3.75%	4%	4.25%	5%	6%	7%	8%
1	0.9804	0.9709	0.9639	0.9615	0.9592	0.9524	0.9434	0.9346	0.9259
2	0.9612	0.9426	0.9290	0.9246	0.9201	0.9070	0.8900	0.8734	0.8573
3	0.9423	0.9151	0.8954	0.8890	0.8826	0.8638	0.8396	0.8163	0.7938
4	0.9238	0.8885	0.8631	0.8548	0.8466	0.8227	0.7921	0.7629	0.7350
5	0.9057	0.8626	0.8319	0.8219	0.8121	0.7835	0.7473	0.7130	0.6806
6	0.8880	0.8375	0.8018	0.7903	0.7790	0.7462	0.7050	0.6663	0.6302
7	0.8706	0.8131	0.7728	0.7599	0.7473	0.7107	0.6651	0.6227	0.5835
8	0.8535	0.7894	0.7449	0.7307	0.7168	0.6768	0.6274	0.5820	0.5403
9	0.8368	0.7664	0.7180	0.7026	0.6876	0.6446	0.5919	0.5439	0.5002
10	0.8203	0.7441	0.6920	0.6756	0.6595	0.6139	0.5584	0.5083	0.4632
20	0.6730	0.5537	0.4789	0.4564	0.4350	0.3769	0.3118	0.2584	0.2145

Table C.2 Present Value of $1 (*continued*)

Periods	9%	10%	11%	12%	13%	14%	15%	20%	25%
1	0.9174	0.9091	0.9009	0.8929	0.8850	0.8772	0.8696	0.8333	0.8000
2	0.8417	0.8264	0.8116	0.7972	0.7831	0.7695	0.7561	0.6944	0.6400
3	0.7722	0.7513	0.7312	0.7118	0.6931	0.6750	0.6575	0.5787	0.5120
4	0.7084	0.6830	0.6587	0.6355	0.6133	0.5921	0.5718	0.4823	0.4096
5	0.6499	0.6209	0.5935	0.5674	0.5428	0.5194	0.4972	0.4019	0.3277
6	0.5963	0.5645	0.5346	0.5066	0.4803	0.4556	0.4323	0.3349	0.2621
7	0.5470	0.5132	0.4817	0.4523	0.4251	0.3996	0.3759	0.2791	0.2097
8	0.5019	0.4665	0.4339	0.4039	0.3762	0.3506	0.3269	0.2326	0.1678
9	0.4604	0.4241	0.3909	0.3606	0.3329	0.3075	0.2843	0.1938	0.1342
10	0.4224	0.3855	0.3522	0.3220	0.2946	0.2697	0.2472	0.1615	0.1074
20	0.1784	0.1486	0.1240	0.1037	0.0868	0.0728	0.0611	0.0261	0.0115

Table C.3 Future Value of Annuity of $1

Periods*	2%	3%	3.75%	4%	4.25%	5%	6%	7%	8%
1	1.	1.	1.	1.	1.	1.	1.	1.	1.
2	2.02	2.03	2.0375	2.04	2.0425	2.05	2.06	2.07	2.08
3	3.0604	3.0909	3.1139	3.1216	3.1293	3.1525	3.1836	3.2149	3.2464
4	4.1216	4.1836	4.2307	4.2465	4.2623	4.3101	4.3746	4.4399	4.5061
5	5.2040	5.3091	5.3893	5.4163	5.4434	5.5256	5.6371	5.7507	5.8666
6	6.3081	6.4684	6.5914	6.6330	6.6748	6.8019	6.9753	7.1533	7.3359
7	7.4343	7.6625	7.8386	7.8983	7.9585	8.1420	8.3938	8.6540	8.9228
8	8.5830	8.8923	9.1326	9.2142	9.2967	9.5491	9.8975	10.2598	10.6366
9	9.7546	10.1591	10.4750	10.5828	10.6918	11.0266	11.4913	11.9780	12.4876
10	10.9497	11.4639	11.8678	12.0061	12.1462	12.5779	13.1808	13.8164	14.4866
20	24.2974	26.8704	29.0174	29.7781	30.5625	33.0660	36.7856	40.9955	45.7620

Periods*	9%	10%	11%	12%	13%	14%	15%	20%	25%
1	1.	1.	1.	1.	1.	1.	1.	1.	1.
2	2.09	2.10	2.11	2.12	2.13	2.14	2.15	2.20	2.25
3	3.2781	3.3100	3.3421	3.3744	3.4069	3.4396	3.4725	3.6400	3.8125
4	4.5731	4.6410	4.7097	4.7793	4.8498	4.9211	4.9934	5.3680	5.7656
5	5.9847	6.1051	6.2278	6.3528	6.4803	6.6101	6.7424	7.4416	8.2070
6	7.5233	7.7156	7.9129	8.1152	8.3227	8.5355	8.7537	9.9299	11.2588
7	9.2004	9.4872	9.7833	10.0890	10.4047	10.7305	11.0668	12.9159	15.0735
8	11.0285	11.4359	11.8594	12.2997	12.7573	13.2328	13.7268	16.4991	19.8419
9	13.0210	13.5975	14.1640	14.7757	15.4157	16.0853	16.7858	20.7989	25.8023
10	15.1929	15.9374	16.7220	17.5487	18.4197	19.3373	20.3037	25.9587	33.2529
20	51.1601	57.2750	64.2028	72.0524	80.9468	91.0249	102.4436	186.6880	342.9447

* *There is one payment each period.*

Table C.4 Present Value of Annuity of $1

Periods*	2%	3%	3.75%	4%	4.25%	5%	6%	7%	8%
1	0.9804	0.9709	0.9639	0.9615	0.9592	0.9524	0.9434	0.9346	0.9259
2	1.9416	1.9135	1.8929	1.8861	1.8794	1.8594	1.8334	1.8080	1.7833
3	2.8839	2.8286	2.7883	2.7751	2.7620	2.7232	2.6730	2.6243	2.5771
4	3.8077	3.7171	3.6514	3.6299	3.6086	3.5460	3.4651	3.3872	3.3121
5	4.7135	4.5797	4.4833	4.4518	4.4207	4.3295	4.2124	4.1002	3.9927
6	5.6014	5.4172	5.2851	5.2421	5.1997	5.0757	4.9173	4.7665	4.6229
7	6.4720	6.2303	6.0579	6.0021	5.9470	5.7864	5.5824	5.3893	5.2064
8	7.3255	7.0197	6.8028	6.7327	6.6638	6.4632	6.2098	5.9713	5.7466
9	8.1622	7.7861	7.5208	7.4353	7.3513	7.1078	6.8017	6.5152	6.2469
10	8.9826	8.5302	8.2128	8.1109	8.0109	7.7217	7.3601	7.0236	6.7101
20	16.3514	14.8775	13.8962	13.5903	13.2944	12.4622	11.4699	10.5940	9.8181
Periods*	**9%**	**10%**	**11%**	**12%**	**13%**	**14%**	**15%**	**20%**	**25%**
1	0.9174	0.9091	0.9009	0.8929	0.8550	0.8772	0.8696	0.8333	0.8000
2	1.7591	1.7355	1.7125	1.6901	1.6681	1.6467	1.6257	1.5278	1.4400
3	2.5313	2.4869	2.4437	2.4018	2.3612	2.3216	2.2832	2.1065	1.9520
4	3.2397	3.1699	3.1024	3.0373	2.9745	2.9137	2.8550	2.5887	2.3616
5	3.8897	3.7908	3.6959	3.6048	3.5172	3.4331	3.3522	2.9906	2.6893
6	4.4859	4.3553	4.2305	4.1114	3.9975	3.8887	3.7845	3.3255	2.9514
7	5.0330	4.8684	4.7122	4.5638	4.4226	4.2883	4.1604	3.6046	3.1611
8	5.5348	5.3349	5.1461	4.9676	4.7988	4.6389	4.4873	3.8372	3.3289
9	5.9952	5.7590	5.5370	5.3282	5.1317	4.9464	4.7716	4.0310	3.4631
10	6.4177	6.1446	5.8892	5.6502	5.4262	5.2161	5.0188	4.1925	3.5705
20	9.1285	8.5136	7.9633	7.4694	7.0248	6.6231	6.2593	4.8696	3.9539

* *There is one payment each period.*

Key Terms

Annuity (p. C4)
Future Value (p. C2)
Present Value (p. C2)
Time Value of Money (p. C2)

See complete glossary in back of text.

Questions

1. Explain the concept of the time value of money.
2. Explain the basic difference between future value and present value.
3. If you deposited $10,000 in a savings account that earns 10 percent, how much would you have at the end of 10 years? Use a convenient format to display your computations.
4. If you hold a valid contract that will pay you $8,000 cash 10 years from now and the going rate of interest is 10 percent, what is its present value? Use a convenient format to display your computations.
5. What is an annuity?
6. Use tables C.1 to C.4 to complete the following schedule:

	TABLE VALUES		
	$i = 5\%, n = 4$	$i = 10\%, n = 7$	$i = 14\%, n = 10$
FV of $1			
PV of $1			
FV of annuity of $1			
PV of annuity of $1			

7. If you deposit $1,000 at the end of each period for 10 interest periods and you earn 8 percent interest, how much would you have at the end of period 10? Use a convenient format to display your computations.

Multiple Choice

1. You are saving up for a Porsche Carrera Cabriolet, which currently sells for nearly half a million dollars. Your plan is to deposit $15,000 at the end of each year for the next 10 years. You expect to earn 5 percent each year. How much will you have saved after 10 years, rounded to the nearest 10 dollars?
   a. $150,000.
   b. $188,670.
   c. $495,990.
   d. None of the above.

2. Which of the following is a characteristic of an annuity?
   a. An equal dollar amount each interest period.
   b. Interest periods of equal length.
   c. An equal interest rate each interest period.
   d. All of the above are characteristics of an annuity.

3. Which of the following is most likely to be an annuity?
   a. Monthly payments on a credit card bill.
   b. Monthly interest earned on a checking account.
   c. Monthly payments on a home mortgage.
   d. Monthly utility bill payments.

4. Assume you bought a state of the art entertainment system, with no payments to be made until two years from now, when you must pay $6,000. If the going rate of interest on most loans is 5 percent, which table in this appendix would you use to calculate the system's equivalent cost if you were to pay for it today?
   a. Table C.1 (Future Value of $1)
   b. Table C.2 (Present Value of $1)
   c. Table C.3 (Future Value of Annuity of $1)
   d. Table C.4 (Present Value of Annuity of $1)

5. Assuming the facts in question 4, what is the system's equivalent cost if you were to pay for it today?
   a. $5,442
   b. $6,615
   c. $11,100
   d. $12,300

6. Assume you bought a car using a loan that requires payments of $3,000 to be made at the end of every year for the next three years. The loan agreement indicates the annual interest rate is 6 percent. Which table in this appendix would you use to calculate the car's equivalent cost if you were to pay for it in full today?
   a. Table C.1 (Future Value of $1)
   b. Table C.2 (Present Value of $1)
   c. Table C.3 (Future Value of Annuity of $1)
   d. Table C.4 (Present Value of Annuity of $1)

7. Assuming the facts in question 6, what is the car's equivalent cost if you were to pay for it today? Round to the nearest hundred dollars.
   a. $2,600
   b. $3,600
   c. $8,000
   d. $9,600

8. Which of the following statements are true?
   a. When the interest rate increases, the present value of a single amount decreases.
   b. When the number of interest periods increase, the present value of a single amount increases.
   c. When the interest rate increases, the present value of an annuity increases.
   d. None of the above are true.

9. Which of the following describes how to calculate a bond's issue price?

	Face Value	Interest Payments
a.	Present value of single amount.	Future value of annuity.
b.	Future value of single amount.	Present value of annuity.
c.	Present value of single amount.	Present value of annuity.
d.	Future value of single amount.	Future value of annuity.

10. If interest is compounded quarterly, rather than yearly, how do you adjust the number of years and annual interest rate when using the present value tables?

	Number of years	Annual interest rate
a.	Divide by 4	Divide by 4
b.	Divide by 4	Multiply by 4
c.	Multiply by 4	Divide by 4
d.	Multiply by 4	Multiply by 4

Solutions to Multiple-Choice Questions

1. b 2. d 3. c 4. b 5. a 6. d 7. c 8. a 9. c 10. c

Mini Exercises

MC-1 Computing the Present Value of a Single Payment

What is the present value of $500,000 to be paid in 10 years, with an interest rate of 8 percent?

MC-2 Computing the Present Value of an Annuity

What is the present value of 10 equal payments of $15,000, with an interest rate of 10 percent?

MC-3 Computing the Present Value of a Complex Contract

As a result of a slowdown in operations, Mercantile Stores is offering to employees who have been terminated a severance package of $100,000 cash; another $100,000 to be paid in one year; and an annuity of $30,000 to be paid each year for 20 years. What is the present value of the package, assuming an interest rate of 8 percent?

MC-4 Computing the Future Value of an Annuity

You plan to retire in 20 years. Calculate whether it is better for you to save $25,000 a year for the last 10 years before retirement or $15,000 for each of the 20 years. Assume you are able to earn 10 percent interest on your investments.

Exercises

EC-1 Computing Growth in a Savings Account: A Single Amount

On January 1, 2009, you deposited $6,000 in a savings account. The account will earn 10 percent annual compound interest, which will be added to the fund balance at the end of each year.

Required (round to the nearest dollar):

1. What will be the balance in the savings account at the end of 10 years?
2. What is the interest for the 10 years?
3. How much interest revenue did the fund earn in 2009? 2010?

EC-2 Computing Deposit Required and Accounting for a Single-Sum Savings Account

On January 1, 2009, Alan King decided to transfer an amount from his checking account into a savings account that later will provide $80,000 to send his son to college (four years from now). The savings account will earn 8 percent, which will be added to the fund each year-end.

Required (show computations and round to the nearest dollar):

1. How much must Alan deposit on January 1, 2009?
2. Give the journal entry that Alan should make on January 1, 2009 to record the transfer.
3. What is the interest for the four years?
4. Give the journal entry that Alan should make on (*a*) December 31, 2009, and (*b*) December 31, 2010.

EC-3 Recording Growth in a Savings Account with Equal Periodic Payments

On each December 31, you plan to transfer $2,000 from your checking account into a savings account. The savings account will earn 9 percent annual interest, which will be added to the savings account balance at each year-end. The first deposit will be made December 31, 2009 (at the end of the period).

Required (show computations and round to the nearest dollar):

1. Give the required journal entry on December 31, 2009.
2. What will be the balance in the savings account at the end of the 10th year (i.e., 10 deposits)?
3. What is the total amount of interest earned on the 10 deposits?
4. How much interest revenue did the fund earn in 2010? 2011?
5. Give all required journal entries at the end of 2010 and 2011.

EC-4 Computing Growth for a Savings Fund with Periodic Deposits

On January 1, 2009, you plan to take a trip around the world upon graduation four years from now. Your grandmother wants to deposit sufficient funds for this trip in a savings account for you. On the basis of a budget, you estimate that the trip currently would cost $15,000. Being the generous and sweet lady she is, your grandmother decided to deposit $3,500 in the fund at the end of each of the next four years, starting on December 31, 2009. The savings account will earn 6 percent annual interest, which will be added to the savings account at each year-end.

Required (show computations and round to the nearest dollar):

1. How much money will you have for the trip at the end of year 4 (i.e., after four deposits)?
2. What is the total amount of interest earned over the four years?
3. How much interest revenue did the fund earn in 2009, 2010, 2011, and 2012?

EC-5 Computing Value of an Asset Based on Present Value

You have the chance to purchase an oil well. Your best estimate is that the oil well's net royalty income will average $25,000 per year for five years. There will be no residual value at that time. Assume that the cash inflow occurs at each year-end and that considering the uncertainty in your estimates, you expect to earn 15 percent per year on the investment.

Required:

What should you be willing to pay for this investment right now?

EC-6 Comparing Options Using Present Value Concepts
After hearing a knock at your front door, you are surprised to see the Prize Patrol from a large, well-known magazine subscription company. It has arrived with the good news that you are the big winner, having won "$20 million." You discover that you have three options: (1) you can receive $1 million per year for the next 20 years, (2) you can have $8 million today, or (3) you can have $2 million today and receive $700,000 for each of the next 20 years. Your financial adviser tells you that it is reasonable to expect to earn 10 percent on investments.

Required:
Which option do you prefer? What factors influence your decision?

Problem—Set A

PAC-1 Comparing Options Using Present Value Concepts
After completing a long and successful career as senior vice president for a large bank, you are preparing for retirement. After visiting the human resources office, you have found that you have several retirement options: (1) you can receive an immediate cash payment of $1 million, (2) you can receive $60,000 per year for life (your remaining life expectancy is 20 years), or (3) you can receive $50,000 per year for 10 years and then $70,000 per year for life (this option is intended to give you some protection against inflation). You have determined that you can earn 8 percent on your investments. Which option do you prefer and why?

Problem—Set B

PBC-1 Comparing Options Using Present Value Concepts
After incurring a serious injury caused by a manufacturing defect, your friend has sued the manufacturer for damages. Your friend received three offers from the manufacturer to settle the lawsuit; (1) receive an immediate cash payment of $100,000, (2) receive $6,000 per year for life (your friend's remaining life expectancy is 20 years), or (3) receive $5,000 per year for 10 years and then $7,000 per year for life (this option is intended to compensate your friend for increased aggravation of the injury over time). Your friend can earn 8 percent interest and has asked you for advice. Which option would you recommend and why?

APPENDIX D

INTERNATIONAL FINANCIAL REPORTING STANDARDS

It has become an old cliché but business really has gone global. Abercrombie is opening stores in Sweden, and Swedish companies like IKEA and H&M are opening stores throughout the United States. Similar trends are occurring in the investing world, where shares of foreign companies like Benetton and British Airways are traded on the New York Stock Exchange (NYSE). Until recently, investors struggled to compare the financial statements of companies like these because different countries used different accounting rules. All this is changing now, with the increasing acceptance of International Financial Reporting Standards (abbreviated IFRS, pronounced "eye-furs").

IFRS are developed by the International Accounting Standards Board (IASB), which is the international counterpart to the Financial Accounting Standards Board (FASB) in the United States. Over 100 different countries including Australia, China, the European Union, South Africa, and New Zealand currently require or permit the use of IFRS, or a local version of IFRS. This number is continuing to grow with IFRS becoming official in the near future in Brazil (2010), Canada (2011), India (2011), and other countries. Although the United States has not yet switched to IFRS, such a change is believed to be coming in the next six years or so. The Securities and Exchange Commission (SEC) has already begun moving in this direction by allowing foreign companies like Benetton and British Airways to issue stock in the United States without having to convert their IFRS-based accounting numbers to U.S. GAAP. The SEC plans to allow some U.S. companies to use IFRS in 2009, and aims to require IFRS starting in 2014. Many foreign-owned private companies in the United States, such as Mack Trucks and Dreyer's Ice Cream, already use IFRS to make it easy to combine their financial statements with their foreign owners' financial statements.

Although IFRS differ from the generally accepted accounting principles currently used in the United States, they do not dramatically alter what you have learned in this course. IFRS use the same system of analyzing, recording, and summarizing the results of business activities that you learned in Chapters 1–4. The most significant differences between IFRS and U.S. GAAP relate to technical issues that are typically taught in intermediate and advanced accounting courses. For the topics discussed in this course, differences between IFRS and U.S. GAAP are limited, which we summarize briefly in the table on the following page.

As we look to the future, it seems clear that U.S. GAAP and IFRS will converge as the FASB and IASB work together to remove differences between the two sets of accounting rules and to develop new rules through joint projects. One of the most exciting of these projects currently being worked on is the development of a new format for organizing items on the financial statements. Although it has not yet been finalized, a current proposal is to separately report the results of operating, investing, and financing activities in each of the financial statements similar to what is currently required for the statement of cash flows. Having learned the differences between typical financing and investing activities (in Chapter 2) and operating activities (in Chapter 3), you will be well-prepared to handle evolutions such as these as they arise during your career.

Chapter Topic	U.S. GAAP	IFRS
7: Inventories	• Allows 4 cost flow methods (p. 307) • LCM rule bases market value on replacement cost (p. 313) • Inventory write-down required but reversal disallowed (p. 314)	• Does not allow LIFO • LCM bases market value on net realizable value (selling price less selling costs) • Both write-down and reversal required
10: Long-Lived Tangible and Intangible Assets	• "Basket purchases" of assets are separated into components (p. 420) • Do not revalue unless impaired (p. 430)	• Individual assets may be separated into significant components • Regular revaluation at fair value permitted
11: Current Liabilities and Payroll	• Contingent liabilities accrued if estimable and probable (p. 477)	• Contingent liabilities accrued if estimable and "more likely than not"
13: Corporations	• Most preferred stock is reported as equity (p. 564)	• Most preferred stock is reported as debt
16: Statement of Cash Flows	• Interest paid, interest received, and dividends received are classified as operating (p. 694) • Dividends paid are classified as financing (p. 694)	• Interest paid can be either operating or financing; interest and dividends received can be either operating or investing • Dividends paid can be either operating or financing

Glossary

A

Account p. 57 Individual record of both increases and decreases in a specific asset, liability, owner's equity, revenue, or expense.

Account Receivable p. 382 Amount owed on open account to a business by a customer.

Accounting p. 6 Information system designed to capture and communicate a business's financial condition and financial performance to decision makers inside and outside the organization.

Accounting Cycle p. 57 Activities during the accounting period: Analyze transactions, record the effects of the transactions in the journal, and post the effects to the ledger. Activities at the end of the accounting period: Take a trial balance, adjust the accounts, prepare financial statements, and close the records.

Accounting Information System (AIS) p. 204 Collects, classifies, summarizes, and reports the financial information about a business to interested parties.

Accounts Payable Subsidiary Ledger p. 206 Used to collect and maintain all individual transactions with creditors that occurred on account.

Accounts Receivable Subsidiary Ledger p. 206 Used to collect and maintain all individual transactions with customers that occurred on account.

Accrual Basis Accounting (accrual accounting) p. 101 Principle that revenues are recorded when earned (i.e., the company performs the service or delivers goods to customers) and expenses are recorded when incurred to generate revenues in the same period.

Accrued Expenses p. 147 Expenses that are incurred but not recorded until the end of the period because cash is paid after the goods or services are used.

Accrued Revenues p. 147 Revenues earned but not recorded until the end of the period because cash is received after the services are performed or goods delivered.

Active Investments p. 643 Investments in stock of another business to influence or control that business; acquisition of 20 percent or more of the voting stock of a company is presumed to be an active investment.

Adjusted Trial Balance p. 160 Listing of all accounts and their balances after adjustments have been posted to the accounts to verify that debits equal credits.

Adjusting Entries p. 147 Entries necessary at the end of the accounting period to measure all revenues when earned and expenses when incurred during that period.

Aging of Accounts Receivable Method p. 386 Method that estimates the uncollectible accounts balance based on the age of each account receivable.

Allowance for Doubtful Accounts p. 383 Contra-asset containing the estimated portion of accounts receivable that will not be paid.

Allowance Method p. 383 Method of accounting that reduces accounts receivable (as well as net income) for an estimate of uncollectible accounts (bad debts).

Amortization p. 435 Name given to allocation of the cost of intangible assets over their limited useful lives.

Amortized Cost p. 644 Cost of bonds adjusted for the amortization of any bond discount or premium.

Articles of Organization p. 507 Document required in all states to form an LLC; provides important information about its operations and structure.

Asset p. 9 Measurable economic resource owned by the business that is likely to provide future benefits.

Authorized Shares p. 567 Shares of stock a corporation can issue as specified in the charter.

B

Bad Debt Expense p. 383 Estimated expense for the period related to customers who will fail to pay.

Balance Sheet p. 51 Financial statement that reports the amount of a business's assets, liabilities, and owner's equity at a specific point in time.

Bank Reconciliation p. 355 Internal accounting report that uses both the bank statement and the cash accounts of a business to determine the appropriate amount of cash in a bank account after considering delays or errors in processing cash transactions.

Bonding p. 347 Obtaining an insurance policy that partially reimburses the organization for losses caused by employee fraud.

Bonds p. 604 Financial instruments that outline future payments a company promises to make in exchange for receiving cash now.

Book (or Carrying) Value p. 424 Acquisition cost of an asset less accumulated depreciation (amount used in prior periods).

C

Capital Deficiency p. 531 Lack of sufficient capital in a partner's capital account to absorb losses resulting from the liquidation of the partnership.

Capital Expenditure p. 423 Amount paid to increase a long-lived asset's economic usefulness through increased efficiency, increased capacity, or longer life; capitalized as a cost of the asset.

Capital Lease p. 610 Similar to an operating lease, except that virtually all risks and rewards of owning the rented property transfer to the company that obtains the use of the property.

Capitalize p. 419 To record a cost as an asset rather than an expense.

Carrying Value p. 607 Amount at which an item is reported ("carried at") on the balance sheet after considering related contra-accounts.

Cash Basis Accounting p. 100 Concept that revenues are recorded when cash is received and expenses are recorded when cash is paid. Cash basis accounting is not a generally accepted accounting principle.

Cash Count Sheet p. 350 Internal document on which a cashier records the amount of cash received from cash register sales and determines any cash shortage or overage.

Cash Equivalent p. 360 Amount of cash that a creditor would accept to settle a liability for a transaction or event immediately after it occurs.

Cash-Equivalent Amount p. 600 Amount of cash that would be accepted as full settlement of a liability the moment the liability is created.

Cash Equivalents p. 468 Short-term, highly liquid investments obtained within three months of maturity.

Cash Equivalents p. 682 Short-term, highly liquid investments that are both (1) readily convertible to known amounts of cash and (2) so near to maturity that there is little risk their value will change.

Cash Flows from Financing Activities p. 684 Cash inflows and outflows related to financing sources external to the company (owners and lenders).

Cash Flows from Investing Activities p. 684 Cash inflows and outflows related to the purchase or sale of investments and long-lived assets.

Cash Flows from Operating Activities (Cash Flows from Operations) p. 683 Cash inflows and outflows related to components of net income.

Cash p. 360 Money or any instrument that banks will accept for deposit and immediate credit to a bank account, such as a check, money order, or bank draft.

Cash Payments Journal p. 217 Used to record all transactions involving the payment of cash from a business.

Cash Receipts Journal p. 212 Used to record all cash receipts/collections in a business regardless of the reason for the receipt.

Certified Public Accountant p. 6 Individual who becomes a licensed accounting professional.

Classified Balance Sheet p. 68 Balance sheet separated into classifications: Current assets are listed separately from noncurrent assets; current liabilities are listed separately from noncurrent liabilities.

Closing the Books p. 164 Process of making all temporary accounts have a zero balance for the start of the next accounting period; the balances in the temporary accounts are transferred to owner's capital to update its balance.

Code of Professional Conduct p. 24 Rules established by the American Institute of Certified Public Accountants to govern the ethical performance of professional services by CPAs.

Collude p. 348 To work with another party to circumvent or avoid internal controls, rendering them ineffective.

Common Stock p. 561 Basic voting stock a corporation issues to stockholders.

Comparable p. 23 Characteristic of financial information stating that information is more useful when it can be compared against information for other companies.

Computerized (Electronic) Accounting Information System p. 204 Performs all steps in the accounting cycle electronically with the aid of general ledger software packages.

Conservatism p. 69 Accounting concept that, when doubt exists about the amount at which assets and liabilities should be reported, the least optimistic measurement should be used.

Consistent p. 23 Characteristic of financial information stating that information is more useful when it can be compared over time.

Consolidated Financial Statements p. 659 Single set of financial statements representing the combination of the operations of two or more companies.

Construction in Progress p. 419 Account used to accumulate construction costs for projects not yet complete.

Contingent Liabilities p. 476 Potential liabilities that arise as a result of past transactions or events and whose resolution depends (is "contingent") on a future event.

Continuity Assumption p. 74 Accounting concept that assumes a business will continue operating long enough to meet its contractual commitments and plan; it will continue to operate into the foreseeable future.

Contra-account p. 152 Account directly related to another but with an opposite balance.

Contributed Capital p. 562 Contributions made directly to a corporation by its owners (stockholders).

Control Account p. 206 Account in the general ledger that summarizes all transactions occurring in its related subsidiary ledger.

Copyright p. 434 Form of protection provided to the original authors of literary, musical, artistic, dramatic, and other works of authorship.

Corporation p. 5 Legal and accounting entity that sells shares of stock to owners.

Cost of Goods Sold (CGS) p. 270 Expense account including the total cost of inventory sold during the period.

Cost of Goods Sold Equation p. 306 BI + P − CGS = EI

Credit p. 58 Special accounting name for the right side of accounts.

Crossfoot p. 213 To verify that the total amounts of the Debit columns equal the total amounts of the Credit columns in a multicolumn special journal.

Cumulative Dividend Preference p. 571 Feature of preferred stock that requires dividends in arrears to be paid before current dividends.

Current Assets p. 68 Resources the business will use or turn into cash within one year.

Current Dividend Preference p. 570 Feature of preferred stock that grants priority to preferred dividends over dividends on common stock.

Current Liabilities p. 68 Short-term obligations that will be paid with current assets or settled by providing goods or services within the current operating cycle of the business or within one year of the balance sheet date, whichever is longer.

Current Ratio p. 469 Ratio measuring the extent to which current assets are sufficient to pay current liabilities; calculated by dividing current assets by current liabilities.

D

Debit p. 58 Special accounting name for the left side of accounts.

Debt-to-Assets Ratio p. 611 Measures the extent of financing risk by indicating the proportion of total assets financed by liabilities.

Declaration Date p. 569 Date on which the board of directors officially approves a dividend.

Declining-Balance Depreciation Method p. 427 Method that assigns more depreciation to early years of an asset's life and less depreciation to later years.

Deposits in Transit p. 357 Reconciling items on a bank reconciliation representing deposits made and recorded by the business but not yet shown on the bank statement.

Depreciable Cost p. 425 Portion of an asset's cost that will be used in generating revenue; calculated as asset cost minus residual value; allocated to depreciation expense throughout the asset's life.

Depreciation p. 152 Allocation of the cost of long-lived tangible assets over their estimated productive lives using a systematic and rational method.

Direct Method p. 683 Method of presenting the Operating Activities section of the cash flow statement to report the components of cash flows from operating activities as gross receipts and gross payments.

Direct Write-Off Method p. 389 Method of accounting that records bad debt expense only when a company writes off specific accounts.

Discount p. 605 Excess of a bond's face value over its issue price.

Discounting p. 601 Process of calculating the cash-equivalent "present value" of future payments by removing the interest component that is built into future payments.

Dividends in Arrears p. 571 Dividend rights from prior years that must be satisfied before dividends of the current year can be paid.

Double-Declining-Balance Depreciation Method p. 427 Type of declining-balance depreciation calculated using double the straight-line depreciation rate.

E

EBITDA p. 439 Abbreviation for "earnings before interest, taxes, depreciation, and amortization," which is a measure of operating performance that some managers and analysts use in place of net income.

Electronic Funds Transfer (EFT) p. 351 Cash transferred into or out of a bank account using electronic means, such as the Internet or wire transfer.

Employee Earnings Record p. 480 Employer's internal record that indicates payroll computations for each employee for a particular pay period.

Employee Payroll Taxes p. 483 Amounts employers are legally required to pay in addition to salaries and wages; typically includes FICA taxes and state and federal unemployment taxes.

Equity Method p. 654 Active investments that are increased (decreased) by the investor's share of the investee's net income or loss (reported as income by the investor) and decreased by the investor's share of the dividends declared by the investee (not reported as income by the investor).

Ethics p. 24 Standards of conduct for judging right from wrong, honest from dishonest, and fair from unfair.

Expenses p. 98 Dollar amount of resources an entity uses to earn revenues during a period.

Extraordinary Repairs p. 423 Expenditures that increase a tangible asset's economic usefulness in the future and are recorded as increases in asset accounts, not as expenses.

F

Face Value p. 604 Amount a bond promises to pay on its maturity date.

Financial Accounting p. 8 Accounting area focused on providing financial information to external users primarily to make investing and lending decisions.

Financial Accounting Standards Board (FASB) p. 23 Entity with the primary responsibility (as designated by the Securities and Exchange Commission) of setting underlying rules of accounting in the United States.

Financing Activities p. 18 Business activities involving borrowing from banks, repaying bank loans, receiving investments from owners, and distributing profits to owners (through withdrawals for proprietors and partnerships and through dividends to stockholders).

First-In, First-Out (FIFO) p. 307 Assumption that the oldest goods (the ones first in) are used first to calculate cost of goods sold.

Fixed Assets p. 418 Alternative name for long-lived tangible assets reflecting assets that are physically fixed in place.

FOB Destination p. 265 Sales term indicating that ownership changes when goods reach the buyer's premises and the seller pays the freight charges.

FOB Shipping Point p. 265 Sales term indicating that ownership changes when goods leave the seller's premises and the buyer pays the freight charges.

Foot p. 213 To add the dollar amounts in a column.

Franchise p. 434 Contractual right to sell certain products or services, use certain trademarks, or perform activities in a certain geographical region.

Fundamental Accounting Equation p. 9 Basic equation stating that assets equal liabilities plus owner's equity.

G

Generally Accepted Accounting Principles (GAAP) p. 23 Accounting measurement and reporting rules to be applied by businesses.

Goods Available for Sale p. 305 Sum of the beginning inventory and purchases of the period.

Goodwill p. 434 Premium a company pays to obtain the favorable reputation associated with another company.

Gross Earnings p. 478 Amounts employees earn as compensation for the work they provide.

Gross Profit (or Gross Margin) p. 276 Amount the company earned from selling goods over and above their cost.

Gross Profit Percentage p. 278 Percentage of profit earned on each dollar of sales after considering the cost of products sold.

H

Historical Cost p. 9 Accounting principle stating that assets are initially measured at the total cost to acquire them.

Horizontal (Trend) Analysis p. 732 Comparison of individual financial statement items from year to year with the general goal of identifying significant sustained changes or trends.

I

Impairment p. 430 Loss that occurs when the cash to be generated by an asset is estimated to be less than the carrying value of that asset.

Imprest System p. 352 System that acts as an internal control to restrict the amount paid to others by limiting the amount of money available to be paid; typically used for payroll and petty cash.

Income Statement p. 14 Financial statement that reports the performance of a business for a period of time.

Income Summary p. 164 Temporary account used only during the closing process; all revenues and expenses are closed to Income Summary and then Income Summary is closed to owner's capital.

Indirect Method p. 683 Method that starts with net income from the income statement and then adjusts it by removing items that do not involve cash but were included in net income and adding items that involved cash but were not yet included in net income.

Intangible Assets p. 418 Long-lived assets that lack physical substance.

Interest Formula p. 390 $I = P \times R \times T$ where I = interest calculated, P = principal, R = annual interest rate, and T = time period covered in the interest calculation (number of months out of 12).

Internal Controls p. 344 Methods an organization uses to protect against theft of assets, to enhance the reliability of accounting information, to promote efficient and effective operations, and to ensure compliance with applicable laws, regulations, and codes of ethical conduct.

Investing Activities p. 18 Business activities involving buying and selling productive resources with long lives.

Investments for Significant Influence p. 654 Investments in 20 percent or more of the voting stock of other companies to obtain significant influence or control over the financing and operating activities of those companies.

Investments Held to Maturity p. 654 Investments in bonds that management intends and has the ability to hold until the maturity date.

J

Journal Entry p. 58 Form used to record the effects of a transaction in the journal. Accounts to be debited are listed first with the amounts indicated in the left column; accounts to be credited are listed below the debited accounts with amounts indicated in the right column.

Journal p. 57 Chronological record of the effects of transactions on accounts.

L

Land Improvements p. 419 Enhancements made to land that are expected to deteriorate over time.

Last-In, First Out (LIFO) p. 307 Assumption that the costs of the newest goods (the last ones in) are used first to calculate cost of goods sold.

Ledger p. 57 Record used to accumulate the effects of transactions on individual accounts.

Liabilities p. 9 Measurable and probable obligations that require the business to pay goods or services to others in the future.

Licensing Right p. 434 Limited permission to use property according to specific terms and conditions set out in a contract.

Limited Liability Company (LLC) p. 507 Business organizational form that offers its members limited liability protection and pass-through taxation.

Line of Credit p. 469 Preapproved loan that allows a business to borrow money (up to a predetermined limit) on an as-needed basis.

Liquidity p. 469 Measure of an organization's ability to pay amounts currently owed.

Liquidity p. 736 Ratio indicating the extent to which a company is able to pay its currently maturing obligations.

Long-Lived Assets p. 418 Resources owned by a business that enable it to produce the goods or services the business sells to customers.

Long-Term Debt p. 600 Liabilities requiring repayment over more than one year or if longer, the company's operating cycle.

Lower of Cost or Market (LCM) p. 313 Process that writes inventory down to market value when the market value of inventory items falls below cost.

M

Managerial Accounting p. 7 Accounting area focused on providing information to assist managers in making business decisions.

Manual Accounting Information System p. 204 Performs all steps in the accounting cycle by hand without the aid of a computerized program.

Manufacturing Company p. 262 Company that sells goods it has made itself.

Market Interest Rate p. 606 Interest rate that the bond market ultimately obtains by purchasing a bond at a premium, a discount, or face value; represents a company's cost of borrowing.

Market Value Method p. 646 Adjust investments in available for sale and trading securities to market value at the end of each reporting period.

Matching Principle p. 103 Principle that costs incurred to generate revenues should be recognized (recorded) in the same period to match the costs with benefits.

Maturity Date p. 604 Date on which a bond's face value is scheduled to be paid to bondholders.

Merchandising Company p. 262 Company that sells goods (merchandise) obtained from a supplier.

Merger p. 659 Event that occurs when one company acquires the assets and liabilities of another company and the acquired company goes out of existence.

Monetary Unit Assumption p. 15 Theoretical concept stating that financial information is reported in the standard monetary denomination of the country in which the business operated.

N

Net Assets p. 434 Shorthand term used to refer to assets minus liabilities.

Net Book Value (also called book value or carrying value) p. 152 Amount reported on the balance sheet (e.g., original cost of equipment minus accumulated depreciation).

Net Income p. 15 Positive difference between revenues earned during a period and the expenses that were incurred to generate the revenues during the period.

Net Loss p. 16 Result when expenses exceed revenues during a period.

Net Profit Margin p. 169 Ratio that measures how effective managers were at generating profit on every dollar of sales.

No-Par Value Stock p. 563 Capital stock that has no par value specified in the corporate charter.

Note Receivable p. 382 Promise made in writing that requires another party to pay the business.

Notes p. 18 Additional information provided to accompany the basic financial statements to assist users in understanding amounts reported on the financial statements or other items that may affect their decisions.

NSF (Not Sufficient Funds) Checks p. 357 Checks written for an amount more than the funds available to cover them.

O

Operating (Cash-to-Cash) Cycle p. 99 Process by which a company acquires and pays for goods and services and then sells goods and services to customers who pay cash to the company.

Operating Activities p. 18 Business activities directly related to earning profits.

Operating Agreement p. 507 Document recommended when an LLC is formed to address potential problem areas.

Operating Lease p. 610 Rental agreement that allows a company to obtain temporary use of property in exchange for future payments to the property's owner.

Ordinary Repairs and Maintenance p. 423 Expenditures for routine operating upkeep of long-lived assets; recorded as expenses.

Outstanding Check p. 357 Reconciling item on a bank reconciliation representing checks written and recorded by the business but that have not yet cleared the bank.

Outstanding Shares p. 567 Issued shares currently held by stockholders, not the corporation itself.

Override p. 348 To disarm or cancel internal controls, rendering them ineffective.

Owner's Equity p. 9 Difference between the assets the business owns and the liabilities the business owes. It represents the owner's stake in the business.

P

Par Value p. 563 Value assigned to each share of capital stock as specified in the charter.

Parent Company p. 659 Company acquiring another for control.

Partner Return on Equity p. 533 Ratio that measures a company's efficiency in generating profits from every dollar of equity invested in and retained by a partnership.

Partner Return on Equity p. 533 Ratio that measures a company's efficiency in generating profits from every dollar of equity invested or retained by partners.

Partner's Capital Statement p. 516 Financial statement that replaces the owner's equity statement and shows all changes to capital for each partner in a partnership.

Partnership p. 506 An unincorporated business owned by two or more individuals.

Partnership Agreement p. 506 Recommended document when a partnership is formed to address potential problem areas.

Partnership Dissolution p. 517 When a partner is added, it causes the dissolution of the existing partnership (consisting of the old partners) and the creation of a new partnership (consisting of the new partners).

Partnership Liquidation p. 526 Process to terminate a partnership that involves selling the partnership assets, paying its liabilities, and distributing cash to partners.

Passive Investments p. 643 Investments in debt and stock instruments for the purpose of earning a return on the funds; acquisition of less than 20 percent of the voting stock of a company is presumed to be a passive investment.

Pass-Through Taxation p. 507 Taxation rule that allows profits from a business to flow directly through to the owners, avoiding taxation at the business level.

Patent p. 434 Right to exclude others from making, using, selling, or importing an invention.

Payment Date p. 569 Date on which a corporation pays a cash dividend to the stockholders of record.

Payroll p. 477 Process followed to pay employees for their work.

Payroll Deductions p. 478 Amounts subtracted from each employee's gross earnings so that they can be remitted to another organization or government agency on behalf of that employee.

Payroll Register p. 482 Internal record that accumulates payroll costs across all employees for a particular pay period; the basis for recording payroll journal entries.

Percentage of Accounts Receivable Method p. 386 Method that estimates the uncollectible accounts balance based on a single percentage of total accounts receivable that are likely to be uncollectible.

Percentage of Credit Sales Method p. 386 Method that estimates bad debt expense by multiplying the historical percentage of bad debt losses by the current year's credit sales.

Periodic Inventory System p. 264 Inventory system that updates the inventory records "periodically," that is, at the end of the accounting period.

Permanent Accounts p. 164 Accounts that retain their balances from period to period (they are not closed); assets, liabilities, and owner's equity accounts are permanent.

Perpetual Inventory System p. 263 Inventory system that updates the inventory records "perpetually," that is, every time inventory is bought, sold, or returned.

Petty Cash Fund p. 353 Fund from which money is taken to reimburse employees for expenditures they have made on behalf of the organization.

Preferred Stock p. 561 Stock that has specified rights over common stock.

Premium p. 605 Excess of a bond's issue price over its face value.

Prepaid Expenses p. 147 Previously recorded assets that must be adjusted for the amount of expense incurred by using the asset during the period to generate revenues.

Private Accounting p. 6 Sector of the accounting profession in which accountants are employed by a single business or nonprofit organization.

Private Companies p. 560 Companies whose stock is bought and sold through private transactions.

Profitability p. 736 Profitability is the extent to which a company generates income.

Promissory Note p. 470 Written document outlining terms and conditions by which one individual or business will pay another.

Public Accounting p. 6 Sector of the accounting profession in which accountants charge fees for services to a variety of organizations.

Public Companies p. 560 Companies whose stock is bought and sold publicly on stock exchanges.

Public Company Accounting Oversight Board (PCAOB) p. 23 Entity that sets rules for auditors in the United States.

Purchase Discount p. 266 Cash discount received for prompt payment of a purchase on account.

Purchase Return and Allowance p. 266 Reduction in the cost of inventory purchases associated with unsatisfactory goods.

Purchases Journal p. 216 Used to record all purchases made or expenses incurred on account.

R

Record Date p. 569 Date on which the corporation prepares the list of current stockholders; dividends are paid only to the stockholder who owns stock on this date.

Relevant p. 23 Characteristic of financial information stating that information that is helpful in making decisions should be reported.

Reliable p. 23 Characteristic of financial information stating that information is most useful when it is unbiased and verifiable.

Remittance Advice p. 351 Form that explains the reasons for a payment, often a tear-away attachment to a supplier's invoice or company check.

Research and Development p. 434 Expenditures that may some day lead to patents, copyrights, or other intangible assets but the uncertainty about their future benefits requires that they be expensed.

Residual (or Salvage or Scrap) Value p. 124 Estimated amount to be recovered at the end of the company's estimated useful life of an asset.

Retained Earnings p. 563 Account used by corporations to accumulate the profits or losses generated each year (minus any dividends declared) since the corporation was first created.

Return on Assets p. 660 Ratio that measures how much the firm earned for each dollar invested in assets.

Revenue Expenditure p. 423 Amounts paid to maintain an asset's original operating capacity; matched to revenues as an expense in the period incurred.

Revenue Journal p. 209 Used to record services rendered to customers on account.

Revenue Principle p. 101 Concept that revenue should be recognized in the period earned (i.e., in which the company has performed a service or delivered goods to customers). Also known as the revenue recognition rule.

Revenues p. 10 Amounts earned when goods or services are delivered to customers.

S

Salaries p. 477 Fixed amounts paid monthly, typically to managerial, sales, and administrative personnel.

Sales Discount p. 272 Discount given to customers for prompt payment of an account receivable.

Sales Returns and Allowances p. 271 Reductions in the amount owed by customers after goods have been found unsatisfactory.

Sarbanes-Oxley (SOX) Act of 2002 p. 344 Act passed by Congress to restore investor confidence in and improve the quality of financial reporting by publicly traded companies in the United States.

S-Corporation p. 508 Corporation that allows profits to pass through to the owners' personal income tax returns and provides owners limited liability.

Securities and Exchange Commission (SEC) p. 23 Governmental agency that supervises the work of the Financial Accounting Standards Board and the Public Company Accounting Oversight Board.

Securities Available for Sale p. 646 Passive investments not actively traded; reported at market value as current and/or noncurrent assets, depending on management's intent; unrealized gains or losses are reported in stockholders' equity on the balance sheet.

Segregation of Duties p. 346 Internal control principle that involves separating employees' duties so that the work of one person can be used to check the work of another person.

Separate Entity Assumption p. 10 Assumption that activities of the business are reported separately from activities of its owners.

Service Company p. 262 Company that sells services rather than physical goods.

Sole Proprietorship p. 4 Business owned by one individual.

Solvency p. 736 Solvency is the ability to survive long enough to repay lenders when debt matures.

Special Journal p. 209 Used to record similar types of transactions in one convenient place.

Specific Identification p. 307 Inventory costing method that individually identifies and records the cost of each item sold.

Stated Interest Rate p. 604 Interest rate stated on the face of a bond certificate, which when multiplied by the face value indicates the dollar amount of interest paid each year.

Statement of Cash Flows p. 18 Financial statement that reports the business's cash inflows (receipts) and outflows (payments) by business activity (operating, investing, and financing) for a period of time.

Statement of Owner's Equity p. 16 Financial statement that reports the changes in owner's equity during the period.

Stock Dividend p. 572 Distribution of additional shares of a corporation's own stock.

Stock Split p. 573 Increase in the total number of authorized and issued shares by a specified ratio; often is accompanied by a corresponding reduction in the per share value, resulting in no change to the stockholders' equity accounts.

Stockholders p. 560 Owners of a corporation who hold stock certificates indicating their share of ownership.

Stockholders' Equity p. 562 Category of the balance sheet that reports stockholders' claims on the resources of the corporation.

Straight-Line Depreciation Method p. 426 Method that allocates the depreciable cost of an asset in equal periodic amounts over its useful life.

Subsidiary Company p. 659 Company acquired by another company gaining control.

Subsidiary Ledger p. 206 Group of accounts that share a common feature.

T

T-account p. 61 Simplification of a page in the ledger, written in the form of a T with debit effects on the left of the T and credit effects on the right.

Tangible Assets p. 418 Long-lived assets that have physical substance.

Temporary Accounts p. 164 Accounts that accumulated data for the current accounting period only (they are closed at the end of the period to owner's capital, a permanent account); revenues, expenses, and owner's drawing accounts are temporary.

Time Period Assumption p. 99 Assumption that, to measure income for a specific period of time, the long life of a company can be reported in shorter time periods.

Times Interest Earned Ratio p. 612 Measures the extent to which a company's income before the costs of financing and taxes are sufficient to cover interest expense.

Trademark p. 433 Special name, image, or slogan identified with a product or company.

Trading Securities p. 646 Investments in stocks and bonds that management actively trades; reported at market value in current assets section of balance sheet; unrealized gains or losses are reported on the income statement.

Transactions p. 68 Business activities that affect the accounting equation.

Treasury Stock p. 565 Issued shares that the corporation has repurchased.

Trial Balance p. 65 List of individual accounts, usually in financial statement order, with their ending balances from the ledger (T-accounts) indicated in the appropriate column (debits on the left and credits on the right). Its purposes are to ensure that debits equal credits, summarize account balances, review and analyze necessary adjustments, and prepare financial statements.

U

Unadjusted Trial Balance p. 112 List of individual accounts, usually in financial statement order, with their ending balances from the ledger (T-accounts) indicated in the appropriate column (debits on the left and credits on the right). The purpose is to check the accounting system to ensure that debits equal credits.

Unearned Revenues p. 147 Previously recorded liabilities, created when cash was received in advance of being earned, that need to be adjusted for the amount of revenue earned during the period.

Units-of-Production Depreciation Method p. 426 Method that allocates the depreciable cost of an asset over its useful life based on the relationship of its periodic output to its total estimated output.

Unrealized Holding Gains or Losses p. 648 Temporary changes in the market value of passive investments.

Useful Life p. 424 Expected service life of an asset to the present owner.

V

Vertical (Common Size) Analysis p. 734 Analytic technique that expresses each line of the income statement (or balance sheet) as a percentage of total sales (or total assets).

Voucher p. 352 The accumulated documentation of each step in a voucher system.

Voucher System p. 352 Process for approving and documenting all purchases and payments made on account.

W

Wages p. 477 Amounts paid based on a rate per hour or per unit of production, typically to clerks, factory workers, and part-time employees.

Weighted Average p. 307 Inventory costing method that uses the weighted average cost of goods available for sale as the unit cost for cost of goods sold and ending inventory.

Write Off p. 384 To remove an uncollectible account and its corresponding allowance from the accounting records.

Credits

CHAPTER 1

Opener (Page 3): © Erica Chadwick/Jupiter Images. The **P&G** logo used by permission of Procter & Gamble. The **Oakley** logo used by permission of Oakley, Inc. The **Tootsie Roll** logo used by permission Tootsie Roll Industries. The **Dave & Buster's** logo used by permission of Dave & Buster's Inc. The **Tech Data** logo used by permission of Tech Data Corporation. The **General Mills** logo is a registered trademark of General Mills and is used with permission. The **Best Buy** logo used by permission of Best Buy Co. Inc. **The Cheesecake Factory** logo used by permission of The Cheesecake Factory Incorporated. **The Home Depot** logo used by permission of The Home Depot.

CHAPTER 2

Opener (Page 49): © Yellow Dog Productions/Taxi/Getty. The **Toro** logo used by permission of The Toro Company. The **3M** logo used by permission of the 3M Company. The **Trump Entertainments Resorts** logo used by permission of Trump Entertainment Resorts, Inc. The **Ethan Allen** logo used by permission of Ethan Allen Interiors. **The Home Depot** logo used by permission of The Home Depot.

CHAPTER 3

Opener (Page 97): © Chris Ware/The Image Works. **Page 101:** © Patricia Libby. **The Home Depot** logo used by permission of The Home Depot.

CHAPTER 4

Opener (Page 145): © Ted Pink/Alamy. The **Papa John's** logo used by permission of Papa John's. The **Dell** logo used by permission of Dell, Inc. **The Home Depot** logo used by permission of The Home Depot. The **Safety-Kleen** logo used by permission of Safety-Kleen Corp.

CHAPTER 5

Opener (Page 203): AP Photo/Douglas C. Pizac. **Page 205 (left):** © Image Source/Corbis; **page 205 (right):** AP Photo/Paul Sakuma.

CHAPTER 6

Opener (Page 261): © Gilles Mingasson/Getty Images. Page **263:** © Steve Cole/Getty Images. **Page 264:** © Alistair Berg / Photodisc/Getty Images. The **Costco** logo used by permission of Costco Wholesale Corporation. **Page 270:** (c) Johnny Crawford/The Image Works. The **Oakley** logo used by permission of Oakley, Inc. The **Best Buy** logo used by permission of Best Buy Co. Inc. **The Home Depot** logo use by permission of The Home Depot.

CHAPTER 7

Opener (Page 303): © James Leynse/Corbis. **Page. 313:** © James Leynse/Corbis. The **American Eagle** Outfitters logo used by permission of American Eagle Outfitters. The **RadioShack** logo used by permission of RadioShack Corporation. The **Harman International** logo used by permission of Harman International Industries. The **amazon.com** logo used by permission of Amazon.com. The **Home Depot** logo used by permission of The Home Depot.

CHAPTER 8

Opener (Page 343): AP Photo/Mark Duncan. **Page 347 (top):** © C Squared Studios/Getty Images; **page 347 (bottom):** © TRBfoto/Getty Images. **Page 349 (cash register):** © Comstock/PunchStock; **page 349 (safe):** © PhotoDisc/Getty Images. Page **352 (top):** © Royalty-Free/Corbis; **page 352 (bottom):** © Jonnie Miles /Getty Images. **The Home Depot** logo used by permission of The Home Depot.

CHAPTER 9

Opener (Page 381): © Aniel Barry/Bloomberg News /Landov. The **Mad Catz** logo used by permission of Mad Catz. The **Boeing** logo used Courtesy of The Boeing Company. The **Rocky Mountain Chocolate Factory** logo used by permission of The Rocky Mountain Chocolate Factory, Inc. The **Caterpillar** logo used by permission of Caterpillar, Inc. The **Walgreens** logo used by permission of Walgreens. The **Intel** logo used by permission of the Intel Corporation. The **Xerox** logo used courtesy of Xerox Corporation. **The Home Depot** logo used by permission of The Home Depot.

CHAPTER 10

Opener (Page 417): © David Sanger Photography /Alamy. **Page. 420 (all); page 423:** Courtesy of Cedar Fair, C.P. **Page 425:** © Royalty-Free/Corbis. The **Cedar Fair** logo used by permission of Cedar Fair, L.P. The **Six Flags** logo used by permission of Six Flags. The **Yahoo!** logo used by permission of Yahoo!. **The Home Depot** logo used by permission of The Home Depot.

CHAPTER 11

Opener (Page 467): AP Photo/Janet Hostetter. The **General Mills** logo is a registered trademark of General Mills and is used with permission. The **Caterpillar** logo used by permission of Caterpillar, Inc. **The Home Depot** logo used by permission of The Home Depot.

CHAPTER 12

Opener (Page 505): © Mel Yates/Cultura/Getty.

CHAPTER 13

Opener (Page 559): © Mike Booth /Alamy. The **Black & Decker** logo used by permission of Black & Decker. **The Home Depot** logo used by permission of The Home Depot.

CHAPTER 14

Opener (Page 599): © Photo by General Mills for Business Wire via Getty Images. The **General Mills** logo is a registered trademark of General Mills and is used with permission. The **Black & Decker** logo used by permission of Black & Decker. **The Home Depot** logo used by permission of The Home Depot.

CHAPTER 15

Opener (Page 641): © AP Photo/Pablo Martinez Monsivais. Page 659: PRNewsFoto/Newsweek. The **Timberland** logo used by permission of the Timberland Company. **The Cheesecake Factory** logo used by permission of The Cheesecake Factory Incorporated. **The Home Depot** logo used by permission of The Home Depot.

CHAPTER 16

Opener (Page 681): © Comstock Images/Alamy. Page 687: © DAG/Getty. The **Gibralter** logo used by permission of Gibralter Steel Corporation. The **Home Depot** logo used by permission of The Home Depot.

CHAPTER 17

Opener (Page 729): Photo/Nell Redmond. The **Cintas** logo used by permission of the Cintas Corporation. The **P&G** logo used by permission of Procter & Gamble. The **Mattel** logo used by permission of Mattel. **The Home Depot** logo used by permission of The Home Depot.

Business Index

Page numbers followed by n indicate footnotes.

A

Aaron Rents, Inc., 592
Abercrombie and Fitch Co., 136, D-1
Activision, Inc., 596, 611
Aeropostale, Inc., 568
AIRBUS, 696
Amazon.com, 338–339
AMC Theatres, 714
American Airlines, 615
American Eagle Outfitters, 113, 262, 615
  balance sheet reporting, 304–305
  business description, 303
  comparison to benchmarks, 317
  cost of goods sold equation, 305–306
  income statement reporting, 304–305
  inventory costing methods, 306–314, 320–322
  inventory turnover analysis, 318
American Express, 271
American Golf Corporation, 447–448
American Red Cross, 6
American Skiing, 572
AMR Corporation, 615
Apple Inc., 169, 279–280, 454, 714–715
Avis, 610

B

Benetton, D-1
Best Buy Co., Inc., 4, 42, 276, 279–280, 292, 474
Big Dog Holdings, 584
Black & Decker Corporation, 614–615
Blockbuster, Inc., 78, 473
Bloom 'n Flowers
  admission of partner, 517–521
  business description, 505
  division of income (loss), 511–516
  financial statements, 516–517
  formation, 509–510
  partner return on equity, 533–534
  partnership accounting, 509–517
  partnership agreement, 506–507
  partnership liquidation, 526–532
  withdrawal of partner, 521–525
Boeing, 394, 395, 696
Borders, 338–339
Boston Acoustics, 335
British Airways, D-1
Brown Shoe Company, 379
Brunswick Corporation, 500, 685, 699–700
Builder's FirstSource, 744

C

Cargill, 560
Caterpillar Inc., 127, 402–403, 485–486
Cedar Fair, L.P.
  business description, 417
  depreciation of assets, 424–433, 437–439, 443
  disposal or exchange of tangible assets, 431–433, 443–444
  fixed asset turnover ratio, 436, 437
  impairment of tangible assets, 430–431
  intangible assets, 418, 419, 435, 436
  tangible assets, 418, 419–433, 436
The Cheesecake Factory Incorporated, 44, 169, 673
Chevron, 750
Chick-fil-A, 560
Cintas Corporation, 752–753
Circuit City, 292
Coach, Inc., 184–185
Coca-Cola Company, 37, 169, 410, 569, 756
The Colgate-Palmolive Company, 670, 714
Computer Associates, 114, 345
Costco Wholesale Corporation, 261, 280–281
Cybex International, 704–705

D

Dave & Buster's Inc., 35–36
Deere & Company, 187, 318, 394, 395
Dell Corporation, 569
Dell Inc., 4, 192, 263
Dillard's, 328
Disney, 417, 659, 716–717
Dollar General Corporation, 754
Domino's, 97, 170
Dow Jones & Company, Inc., 661
Dreyers Ice Cream, D-1

E

Electronic Arts, 39
Elizabeth Arden, 87
Enron, 24, 114, 344
Escalade, Inc., 200–201
Estee Lauder, 91, 92
Ethan Allen Interiors, Inc., 89–90, 99
Exxon, 312
ExxonMobil, 442, 644n

F

Famous Footwear, 378
Federal Express Corporation (FedEx), 35, 49, 52, 196, 407, 452, 453
Federated Department Stores, 590–591
FedEx Kinko's, 196
Fitch, 599
Fontana Shoes, 382
Fool.com, 731
Foot Locker, Inc., 381, 382
Ford Motor Company, 262, 263, 312, 626

G

Gannett Co., Inc., 660, 661
The Gap, Inc., 5, 263, 328–329, 659
Gateway, Inc., 475–477
General Electric, 560
General Mills, Inc., 34, 37
  accounts payable, 470
  amortization methods, 619–623
  bonds payable, 604–610, 619–623
  business description, 467, 599
  contingent liabilities, 476–477
  current portion of long-term debt, 472–473
  current ratio, 469
  debt-to-assets ratio, 611, 612
  discounted notes, 601–603, 613n, 617–618
  income statement, 608
  lease liabilities, 610–611, 619
  liability classification, 468–469
  notes payable, 470–472
  other current liabilities, 473–477
  payroll accounting, 477–484, 488–489
  times interest earned ratio, 612
General Motors Corporation, 312
Gibraltar Industries, 716
Global Crossing, 24
Gold's Gym, 263
Grant (W. T.) Company, 685
Greek Peak, 128
Green Bay Packers, Inc., 14
Gymboree, 714

H

Harley-Davidson, 312, 317, 318
Harman International Industries, 335
Hasbro, Inc., 77, 450, 759
Hertz, 610
Hewlett-Packard Company (HP), 274–276
Hilton Hotels, 4
H&M, D-1
The Home Depot, Inc., 5, 45, 92, 139, 199, 298, 339, 378, 412, 459–460, 501, 595, 637, 677, 724, 736, 739, 741, 744, 761
  annual report, A-1–A-29

The Home Depot, Inc.,—*Cont.*
business description, 343
financial reporting of cash, 360
internal control of cash, 348–360
internal control principles, 344–348
Hoovers.com, 731
H&R Block, 125
Hush Puppies, 127

I

IAC, 474–475
IKEA, D-1
Intamin, 420–421
Intel, 410
International Paper, 442
Internet Financial News (IFN), 648, 649

J

JCPenney Company, Inc., 288

K

Kaplan, Inc., 130, 641
Kellogg's, 394, 611, 612, 613n
Kmart, 261
Kraft Foods Inc., 408–409, 435, 494, 630
Krispy Kreme, 434, 434n

L

The Limited, 136
Linens 'n Things, 4
Lowe's Companies, Inc., 45, 92–93, 139–140, 199, 298, 339, 378, 412, 460, 501, 595, 637, 677, 724, 761
annual report, B-1–B-19
balance sheets, 733, 734
business description, 729
horizontal (trend) analysis, 732–733
income statements, 733, 734
liquidity ratios, 740–742
profitability ratios, 736–740
ratio analysis, 736–744
release of financial information, 730–732
solvency ratios, 742–743
vertical (common size) analysis, 734–735
Lucent Technologies, Inc., 477

M

Mack Trucks, D-1
Macromedia, Inc., 498–499
Macy's, Inc., 4, 328, 590–591, 668
Marriott International, Inc., 676–677
Mastercard, 271
Match.com, 474
Mattel, Inc., 14, 113, 262, 759
McDonald's Corporation, 433, 576–577
Microsoft Corporation, 32, 37, 39, 406–407
MicroStrategy, 24
Montgomery Ward, 560
Moody's, 599
MSNBC, 559, 641

N

Nabisco, 435
National Beverage Corp., 593
Nautilus Inc.
balance sheet, 688, 689
business activities and cash flows of, 682, 684
business description, 681
cash flows from financing activities, 694–696
cash flows from investing activities, 693–694
cash flows from operating activities, 700–705
change in current assets and liabilities, 689–692
income statement, 688, 689
statement of cash flows, 696–699, 705–706
New Bakery Company, 422
Newell Rubbermaid
income statements, 746
nonrecurring and other special items, 746–747
News Corporation, 661
New York Post, 661
Nike, Inc., 81, 263, 712
Nintendo, 39
Nordstrom, Inc., 286
Northwest Airlines, 696, 697
Nutek, Inc., 454

O

Oakley, Inc., 34, 287
OSI Restaurant Partners, Inc., 41
Outback Steakhouse, 422

P

Pacific Sunwear of California, Inc., 196
Papa John's International, Inc., 5, 52n, 97
balance sheet, 69
competitor analysis, 170
Paramount Parks, 420
Peachtree Complete, 6, 205, 221–227
PepsiCo, Inc., 410, 715, 756
Perfumania, 340–341
Pizza Aroma, 262, 418
accounting cycle summary, 70–71
accounting equation and, 10–14, 53
accounting needs of, 6–8
accounting records of, 62–64
accounting tools used by, 49
accrual basis accounting, 101–103
adjusted trial balance, 160–161
adjusting accounts, 145–146, 148–159
analyzing financial information, 145–146, 169–170
balance sheet, 17–18, 51–52, 67–71, 161, 163–164
business activities of, 10–13, 14, 50–56
business description, 3
business type, 4, 5, 6
cash-based measurement, 100–101
chart of accounts, 99
closing the books, 145–146, 164–169
competitor analysis, 69, 170
epilogue, 26
ethical conduct and, 24–25
expense measurement, 102–103, 113
financial reporting by, 8–21
financing transactions, 54
generally accepted accounting principles (GAAP) and, 23
income statement, 14–16, 99, 112–114, 161, 162
investing transactions, 56, 62–63, 64
opening the doors, 97–98
operating activities, 98–110
operating cycle, 99–100
post-closing trial balance, 167–169
professional standards and, 22–23
relationships among financial statements, 19–21, 161–162
revenue measurement, 101–102, 113
statement of cash flows, 18, 19
statement of owner's equity, 16, 161, 162–163
transaction analysis, 53–60, 103–110
trial balance, 64–67
unadjusted trial balance, 112, 148
Pizza Hut, Inc., 69, 97, 170
PMBR, 642
Polaris Industries, 332–333
PricewaterhouseCoopers LLC, 383n
Procter & Gamble, 32, 753

R

RadioShack Corporation, 331–332
Reader's Digest Association, 149, 457, 495
Rent-A-Center, Inc., 592
Reuters, 45
Rite-Aid Corporation, 114
Rocky Mountain Chocolate Factory, Inc., 397–398
Ruby Tuesday, 317, 318

S

Safety-Kleen Corp., 199–200
Saks, 272, 278, 279
Sam's Club, 272, 274, 280–281
Sara Lee Corporation, 184–185
Sears, 261, 263, 407
Security Exchange Company, 93
Sigil Games Online, 132–133
Six Flags, 417, 437–439
Skechers, Inc.
  accounts receivable accounting, 383, 384–389
  bad debt accounting, 383–389
  business description, 381
  notes receivable accounting, 390–393
  receivables turnover, 394, 395
  types of receivables, 382
Sonic Corporation, 452, 582, 674
  balance sheet, 566
  business description, 559
  cash dividends on common stock, 568–570
  earnings per share (EPS), 576
  financial statement reporting, 567–568
  formation of corporation, 561–562
  ownership of, 560
  price/earnings (p/e) ratio, 577
  statement of retained earnings, 575
  stock authorization, 563
  stock sold between investors, 565
Sony Corporation, 39, 267
Sony Online Entertainment, 132–133
Southwest Air Lines, 4, 263
Sports Authority, 753
Standard & Poor's, 599
Starbucks Corporation, 90–91, 192–193, 472, 603, 671
State Farm Mutual Automobile Insurance Company, 642
TheStreet.com, 731
Stride Rite Corp., 409
Sysco, 128, 262

T

Target Corporation, 261, 412, 494
Tech Data Corporation, 37
Texas Commerce Bank, 355, 356
3M Company, 78
Ticketmaster, 474
Timberland Company, 670
TJX Companies Inc., 630
Toll Brothers Inc., 307
Tootsie Roll Industries, 34, 155
The Toro Company, 78
Toys R Us, 99
Tribune Company, 660, 661
Trump Entertainment Resorts, Inc., 79
20th Century Fox, 661

U

United Air Lines, 149
United Parcel Service (UPS), 203, 263, 273
United Way, 4n
UPS Store, 262, 418
  accounts payable subsidiary ledger, 208
  accounts receivable subsidiary ledger, 206–208
  business description, 203
  cash payments journal, 217–218
  cash receipts journal, 212–216, 223–224
  computerized accounting information system of, 223–225
  customer ledgers, 224
  general journal, 218–219
  general ledger accounts, 224–225
  purchases journal, 216–217
  revenue journal, 209–211
  sales journal, 223
Urban Outfitters, Inc., 317, 317n

V

Verizon Communications, Inc., 24, 114, 420, 462
Visa, 271

W

W. T. Grant Company, 685
Walgreen Co., 405
The Wall Street Journal, 644n
Wal-Mart Stores, Inc., 4, 155, 169, 312, 412, 418
  business description, 261
  cash sales, 270
  comparison of sales and purchases accounting, 274–276
  comparison to benchmarks, 278–279
  credit card sales, 271–272
  gross profit percentage, 277–278
  inventory control, 264–265
  multi-step income statement, 276–277
  net sales, 273
  perpetual inventory system, 263–264
  purchase discounts, 266–268
  purchase returns and allowances, 266
  sales discounts, 272–273
  sales on account, 272
  sales returns and allowances, 271
  summary of significant accounting policies, 269
  transportation cost (freight-in), 265–266
The Walt Disney Company, 417, 659, 716–717
The Washington Post Company, 130
  balance sheet, 642, 643
  business description, 641
  comparison to benchmarks, 660–661
  consolidated statements, 642–643, 658–660
  influential investments, 654–660
  notes to financial statements, 642, 654, 659
  passive investments, 642, 643, 644–654
  return on assets (ROA), 660–661
Weiss Ratings, Inc., 761–762
Wolverine World Wide, Inc., 127, 292
WorldCom, 24, 114, 344, 393, 420, 462

X

Xerox Corporation, 24, 410–411

Y

Yahoo!, 437
Yahoo!Finance, 560, 731, 738, 740
Yum! Brands, Inc., 170, 659

Z

ZZZZ Best, 114, 502

Subject Index

Page numbers followed by n indicate footnotes.

A

Accelerated depreciation, 427–428, 429, 438
Account(s)
 balance sheet, 51–52
 defined, 57
 impact of transactions on, 52–62
 income statement, 98–99
Accounting
 accrual basis, 101–103
 assumptions of, 73–74
 careers in, 27–28
 cash basis, 100–101
 defined, 6
 as language of business, 6
 managerial. *See* Managerial accounting
 nature of business transactions, 50–51
 payroll. *See* Payroll accounting
 principles of, 74
 private, 6, 28
 public, 6, 28
 scandals in, 24, 114, 344, 345, 420
 for stock transactions, 562–568
 users of financial information, 6–8
Accounting communication
 ethics and, 24–25
 financial reporting in. *See* Financial reporting
 financial statements in. *See* Financial statement(s)
 managerial reporting in. *See* Managerial accounting
Accounting cycle
 defined, 57
 during-period steps in, 57, 146
 end-of-period steps in, 57, 146, 147, 164–169, 383
 summary of, 70–71
Accounting equation. *See* Fundamental accounting equation
Accounting information system (AIS), 202–228
 cash payments journal, 217–218, 220
 cash receipts journal, 212–216, 220, 223–224
 components of, 206–209
 computerized, 204–205, 222–225
 defined, 204
 developmental phases, 221–222
 general journal, 57, 58–62, 209, 218–219, 220
 manual, 204–205
 overview of, 7
 purchases journal, 216–217, 220
 revenue journal, 209–211, 220
 summary of recording process, 219–220
 theory of, 221–222
 underlying assumptions, 221
Accounting methods, 658
Accounting period, 14
Accounting professionals
 careers, 27–28
 certifications, 6, 8, 347–349, 351
Accounting standards. *See also* Generally accepted accounting principles (GAAP)
 Financial Accounting Standards Board (FASB), 23, 683n, D-1
 International Accounting Standards Board (IASB), 23, 654, 744, D-1–D-2
Accounting worksheets, 175–177
Account recoveries, 388–389
Accounts payable, 53, 470
 operating activities and, 691
Accounts payable subsidiary ledger, 208–209
 control account, 219
 defined, 206
 nature of, 208
Accounts receivable, 383–389
 aging of, 386–388
 bad debts and, 383–389
 on the balance sheet, 382, 383
 cash flows from operating activities and, 687, 690
 defined, 382
 in partnership formation, 510
 receivables turnover, 393–395, 737, 740–741
 schedule of, 207, 214
 uncollectible, 383–385, 388
Accounts receivable general ledger, 214
Accounts receivable subsidiary ledger, 206–208
 control account, 206
 defined, 206
 information contained in, 206, 207
 nature of, 206
Account titles, 12–13
 balance sheet, 51–52
 income statement, 98–99
Accrual basis accounting, 101–103
Accrued expenses, 153–157
 defined, 147
 types of, 153–155
Accrued liabilities
 operating activities and, 691
 payroll taxes, 483
Accrued revenues, 101–102, 147, 155
 defined, 147
 types of, 150, 391
Accumulated amortization, 435n
Accumulated depreciation, 424, 427, 431–432, 435n
 defined, 152
 operating activities and, 687, 689
Accumulated other comprehensive income, 650–651
Acquisition cost, of natural resources, 442
Active investments
 for control, 642, 643–644, 658–660
 defined, 642, 643
 for significant influence, 642, 643, 644, 654–657
Additional Paid-In Capital, 564, 567
Adjusted trial balance, 160–161
Adjusting entries, 145–159
 accrued expenses, 147, 153–157
 accrued revenues, 101–102, 147, 150, 155, 157, 391
 for bad debt expense estimates, 383
 defined, 147
 end of the accounting period, 57, 146, 147–159, 164–169, 383
 ethics and, 158–159
 for expenses, 147, 150–157, 383
 prepaid expenses, 147, 150–153, 155, 157
 purpose of, 146–147
 for revenues, 147, 148–150
 types of, 147
 unearned revenues, 147, 148–150, 155, 157
Aging of accounts receivable, 386–388
Allowance for bad debts, 383–385
Allowance for doubtful accounts, 383–389, 393
Allowance method, 383
American Institute of Certified Public Accountants (AICPA), 24, 683n
American Payroll Association, 484
Amortization
 accumulated, 435n
 of debt investments held to maturity, 644–646
 defined, 435
 effective-interest method of, 619–622
 of long-term liabilities, 619–623
 straight-line method of, 622–623
Amortized cost method
 amortized cost, defined, 644
 for debt investments held to maturity, 644–646
Annual reports
 elements of financial section, 730, 731

Home Depot, Inc., A-1–A-29
Lowe's Companies, Inc., B-1–B-19
release of, 730
SEC filings, 731
Annuity
future value of, C-5–C-6, C-15
present value of, 617, C-6, C-8–C-11, C-12–C-13, C-16
Arm's-length transactions, 657
Articles of organization, 507
Asset(s). *See also specific assets*
adjusting entries, 147
amortization of, 435
on balance sheet, 418, 419
contra-accounts, 384
current, 68, 469
debt to, 611–612, 737, 742
defined, 9
depreciation of. *See* Depreciation
disposal of, 431–433, 435, 436
exchanging, 443–444
in fundamental accounting equation, 19
gains (losses) on sale of, 432, 436, 689
historical cost principle and, 9, 69, 74, 442
impairment of, 430–431, 436
intangible, 418, 433–436
nature of, 9, 73
in T-accounts, 58
tangible, 418, 419–433, 436–437
typical account titles, 13, 51
Asset cost, 424
Asset turnover, 737, 738
Association of Certified Fraud Examiners, 347, 348–349, 351
Auditors, internal control and, 345
Authorized shares, 567

B

Bad debt(s), 383–389
account recoveries, 388–389
accounts receivable methods, 386–387
allowance method, 383–385
direct write-off method, 389
estimating, 385–388
percentage of accounts receivable method, 386
percentage of credit sales method, 386
recording, 383–389
writing off specific uncollectible accounts, 384, 385
Bad debt expense, 383–389
Balance sheet, 17–18. *See also* Current liabilities; Financial statement(s)
account balances on, 57–64
accounts of, 51–52
accounts receivable on, 382, 383
assets on, 418, 419
bonds payable on, 607
chart of accounts, 51–52
classified, 67–68, 161, 163–164
comparative, 685, 688, 732, 733
consolidated, 643
defined, 51
effects of inventory errors on, 315–316
elements of, 17
format of, 161
formula for, 9–10, 58
fundamental accounting equation and, 9–13, 52, 53, 58, 686, 687–692
inventory reporting and, 304–305
limitations of, 68–69
of merchandising companies, 304–305
partnership, 516–517
permanent (real) accounts, 161, 164, 168
preparing, 67–71
purpose of, 17, 21
relationships with other financial statements, 19–21, 161, 685–687, 688
statement of owners' equity, 161
structure of, 21
temporary (nominal) accounts, 161, 164–165, 168
transaction analysis, 52–60
trend (horizontal) analysis of, 732, 733
vertical (common size) analysis of, 734–735
Balance sheet equation. *See* Fundamental accounting equation
Bank(s)
as creditors, 8
debit cards, 58
services provided by, 355
Bank reconciliation
defined, 355
need for, 357
process of, 355, 358–359
sample, 358
Bank service charges, 357, 359
Bank statements, 355–357
bank reconciliation and, 355, 357–359
checks cleared, 356
deposits made, 351, 356
other debits and credits, 356–357
Basket purchases, 420
Beginning inventory (BI), in cost of goods sold, 305–306
Benchmarks, comparison to, 170, 278–279, 317–318, 394–395, 660–661
Biometric time tracking, 484
Board of directors, internal control and, 345, 346
Bonding employees, 347
Bond investments, 644–646
interest earned, 645
principal at maturity, 645
purchases, 644
Bond pricing, 605–607
bonds issued at a discount, 606, 608, 619, 621–622, 623
bonds issued at face value, 604–605, 608, 618
bonds issued at premium, 606, 608, 618, 619–620, 622–623
interest periods in, 619
interest rates and, 607, 619
Bonds payable, 604–610
bond pricing and, 605–607
bond retirement, 608–609
bonds, defined, 604
interest expense, 607–608
present value of, 618–619
reporting bond liabilities, 607
types of bonds, 609–610
Bonuses
to existing partners in partnership dissolution, 519
to exiting partner, 524–525
to new partners in partnership dissolution, 520–521
to remaining partners on withdrawal of partner, 523–524
Book (carrying) value, 152, 424, 607
Book value, net, 152
Borrowing, in fundamental accounting equation, 11
Business entities, types of, 4–5. *See also* Corporations; Partnership(s); Sole proprietorships
Butler, Jeff, 132

C

Calendar year reporting, 14
Callable bonds, 609
Capital deficiency
defined, 531
not paid by partner, 532
paid by partner, 531
in partnership liquidation, 529–532
Capital expenditures, 423
Capital gains. *See also* Capital losses
on commercial asset exchange, 444
on passive investments, 649–654
on sale of assets, 432, 436
on stock held for significant influence, 656–657
Capitalization, of tangible assets, 419–420
Capital leases
described, 610–611, 619
present value of, 619
Capital losses. *See also* Capital gains
on commercial asset exchange, 444
on passive investments, 649–654

Capital losses. *See also* Capital gains—*Cont.*
on sale of assets, 432, 436
on stock held for significant influence, 656–657
Careers in accounting, 27–28
Carrying (book) value, 152, 424, 607
Cash
cash flows. *See* Cash flows
common stock issued for, 563–564
defined, 360
dividends and, 570
excess, investing. *See* Investment(s)
financial reporting of, 360
internal control of, 348–360
net increase (decrease) in, 684
Cash basis accounting, 100–101
Cash contributions, to partnership, 509–510
Cash count sheet, 350
Cash dividends
common stock, 561, 568–570, 574
compared with stock dividends, 574
compared with stock splits, 574
preferred stock, 562, 570–571
Cash-equivalent amount, 468, 600–601
Cash equivalents
defined, 360, 682
financial reporting of, 360
internal control of, 348–360
in liability recording, 468
Cash flows. *See also* Statement of cash flows
from financing activities, 684, 694–696
from investing activities, 18, 684, 693–694
negative, 18
from operating activities, 683–684, 687–692, 699–706
relationship between business activities and, 682–683
Cash payments, 351–354
cash paid by check for purchases on account, 351–352
cash paid to employees via electronic funds transfer, 352–353
cash paid to reimburse employees (petty cash), 353–354
journal for. *See* Cash payments journal
Cash payments journal, 217–218
defined, 217
frequency of posting from, 220
information contained in, 217
postings to general ledger, 218, 220
Cash purchases, of tangible assets, 421–422
Cash receipts, 349–351
cash received from remote source, 351
cash received in person, 349–350
journal for. *See* Cash receipts journal
Cash receipts journal, 212–216
in computerized accounting information systems, 223–224
contents of, 212–213
defined, 212
frequency of posting from, 220
postings to general ledger, 213–215, 220
Cash sales, 270
Cash shortage (overage), 350, 354
Cash-to-cash (operating) cycle, 99–100
Certified financial managers (CFMs), 28
Certified fraud examiners (CFEs), 28
Certified internal auditors (CIAs), 28
Certified management accountants (CMAs), 28
Certified public accountants (CPAs), 6, 28
Channel stuffing, 393
Chartered financial analysts (CFAs), 28
Chart of accounts
balance sheet, 51–52
income statement, 98–99
Checks
cash received by mail, 351
checks cleared, 356
deposits of, 351, 356
NSF (not sufficient funds) checks, 357, 359
outstanding, 357, 358
paychecks, 480–481
Chief executive officer (CEO)
internal control and, 346
Sarbanes-Oxley Act (SOX) of 2002 and, 24, 344–345
Chief financial officer (CFO)
internal control and, 346
Sarbanes-Oxley Act (SOX) of 2002 and, 24, 344–345
Chronological order, of journal entries, 58–60
Classified balance sheet, 67–68, 161, 163–164
Classified income statement, 112–113, 161, 162
Closing the books, 145–146, 164–169, 283
Code of professional conduct, 24
Collateralized (secured) bonds, 609
Collusion, 348
Committee of Sponsoring Organizations (COSO), 346n
Common size (vertical) analysis, 734–735
Common stock
authorization of, 563
cash dividends on, 561, 568–570, 574
characteristics of, 561
defined, 561
earnings per share (EPS), 568, 575, 576–577, 737, 740
financial statement reporting, 567–568, 574–575
price/earnings (P/E) ratio, 575, 576, 577, 737, 740
stock issues, 563–565
Comparable financial information, 23, 73
Comparative balance sheet, 685, 688, 732, 733
Comparative income statement, 732, 733
Compensation. *See also* Bonuses; Employee benefits; Partnership(s); Payroll accounting; Salaries
definitions, 477–478
employee benefits, 477–478, 488–489
salaries expense in, 153
stock options used as, 565
stock used as, 565
Competitor analysis, 69, 170
Complete income statement, 685, 688
Compound entries, 59
Compounding. *See* Future value
Computerized (electronic) accounting information systems, 204–205, 222–225
advantages of, 222–223
comparison with manual accounting information systems, 204
defined, 204
disadvantages of, 223
illustration of, 223–224
Conservatism principle, 69, 70, 74, 383
Consistent financial information, 23, 73
Consolidated financial statements
balance sheet, 643
defined, 642
nature of, 659–660
Construction in progress, 419
Contingent liabilities, 475–477
accounting for, 477
defined, 476
disclosure of, 477
legal, 477
warranties payable, 475–476
Continuity assumption, 74
Contra-accounts, 152–153
contra-asset accounts, 384
contra-liability accounts, 606
stockholders' equity, 566
Contributed capital, 562
cash flows from financing activities and, 694, 695
Control, investing for, 642, 643–644, 658–660
Control account
accounts payable subsidiary ledger, 219

accounts receivable subsidiary ledger, 206
defined, 206
Controlling interests
control, defined, 643
investing for, 642, 643–644, 658–660
Convertible bonds, 609
Copyrights, 434
Corporate bonds, 609
Corporate charter, 563
Corporate governance, 24
Corporate life cycle, 699
Corporations, 558–580
accounting differences between sole proprietorships and, 563
accounting for stock transactions, 562–568
cash dividends, 561, 568–572
characteristics of, 560–562
common stock. *See* Common stock
defined, 5
financial statement reporting, 567–568, 574–575
financing activities, 562. *See also* Financing activities
formation of, 561–562
laws concerning, 476, 560–561
organizational structure, 561
ownership of, 5, 560. *See also* Owners' equity
preferred stock. *See* Preferred stock
S-Corporations, 508–509
stock authorization, 563
stock dividends, 572–573
stock issues, 563–565
stock splits, 573–574
taxes and, 560–561
treasury stock, 565–568, 574–575
Cost effectiveness, of accounting information systems, 221
Cost of goods sold (CGS), 268, 276, 282
converting to cash paid to suppliers, 701–702, 703
defined, 270
equation for, 305–306
relationship between inventory and, 305
reporting in income statement, 305
Cost of goods sold equation, 305–306
Credit(s)
bank account, 356
defined, 58
in T-accounts, 58, 59, 62
Credit balances, 387
Credit card sales, 271–272, 273
Creditors
accounting scandals and, 24, 114
decision to grant credit, 389
as external users of information, 8
recording payments made to, 471–472
relationships among financial statements and, 19–20
types of, 8
Credit purchases, of tangible assets, 422
Credit sales
bad debts, 383–389
decision to grant credit, 389
Credit terms, 266–268, 394
Crossfooting columns, 213
Cumulative dividend preference, 571, 572
Current assets
in current ratio, 469, 737, 741
defined, 68
operating activities and, 687, 689–692
Current dividend preference, 570–571
Current liabilities
accounts payable, 53, 470, 691
current portion of long-term debt, 472–473
deferred revenues, 102, 147, 148–150, 157, 474–475
defined, 68, 468
notes payable, 470–472
operating activities and, 687, 689–692
other contingent liabilities, 476–477
sales tax payable, 474
unearned revenue, 102, 147, 148–150, 157, 474–475
warranties payable, 475–476
Current portion of long-term debt, 472–473
Current ratio, 469, 737, 741
Current receivables, 382
Customer(s)
customer ledgers, in computerized accounting information systems, 224
as external users of information, 8

D

Date of record, 569
Days to collect, 393, 394, 737
Days to sell, 316–317, 737
Death of partner, 525
Debit(s)
bank account, 356
defined, 58
in T-accounts, 58, 59, 62
Debit balances, 105, 387
Debit cards, 58
Debt. *See also* Bad debt(s); Notes payable
current portion of long-term, 472–473
equity versus debt financing, 562, 600
notes receivable, 382, 390–393
Debt securities
amortized cost method of accounting for, 644–646
passive investment in, 643, 644–654
Debt to assets, 611–612, 737, 742
Debt to equity, 742
Declaration date, 569
Declining-balance depreciation method, 427–428, 429, 438
Deductions, payroll, 478–482
Deferred (unearned) revenues, 102
adjusting entries, 147, 148–150, 155, 157
defined, 147, 474
examples of, 157
recording, 474–475
Defined benefit pensions, 489
Defined contribution pensions, 489
Depletion
defined, 442
of natural resources, 442
Deposits, 351, 356
direct deposits, 352–353
in transit, 357, 358
Depreciable cost, 425
Depreciation, 424–433
accelerated, 427–428, 429, 438
accounting for, 436
accumulated, 152, 424, 427, 431–432, 435n
calculating, 424–425, 429
changes in estimates, 443
declining-balance method, 427–428, 429, 438
defined, 152, 424
effects of, 425
on equipment, 152–153
impact of differences in, 437–439
manager choice of method, 429–430
partial-year calculations, 429
sale of long-term assets, 687, 689
straight-line method, 426, 428, 429, 438, 443
summary of methods, 428
in tax reporting, 429–430
units-of-production method, 426–427, 428
Direct deposits, 352–353
Direct method, of reporting cash flows from operating activities, 683, 700–705
Direct write-off method for bad debts, 389
Discarding assets, 431–432, 436
Disclosure. *See* Financial statement(s)
Discontinued operations, 746–747
Discount(s)
bonds issued at, 606, 608, 619, 621–622, 623
deciding to take, 268
defined, 605

Discount(s)—*Cont.*
purchase, 266–268
sales, 272–273
Discounted notes payable, 470
accounting for, 601–603
defined, 601
present value of, 617–618
Discounting. *See also* Present value
defined, 601, 616
Disposal of assets, 431–433, 435, 436
Dividends
cash, 561–562, 568–572, 574
on common stock, 561, 568–570, 574
dividend dates, 569–570
on preferred stock, 562, 570–571
requirements for, 570
on securities purchased, 648, 656
stock, 572–573, 574
Dividends in arrears, 571, 572
Document(s), 52
Documenting procedures, in internal control, 347, 484
Double-declining-balance method of depreciation, 427, 428, 429, 438
Double-entry bookkeeping, 52
Doubtful accounts, allowance for, 383–389, 393
During-period steps, in accounting cycle, 57, 146

E

Earning(s)
defined, 10
on investments for significant influence, 655–656
on investments held to maturity, 645
net, 14
Earnings management, 651
Earnings per share (EPS), 568, 575, 576–577, 737, 740
Ebbers, Bernie, 114
EBITDA (earnings before interest, taxes, depreciation, and amortization), 439
Edison, Thomas, 560
Effective-interest method, of amortization, 619–622
Electronic funds transfer (EFT)
bank reconciliation and, 357, 359
cash paid to employees via, 352–353
cash received electronically, 351
defined, 351
Employee(s). *See also* Compensation
cash paid to, via electronic funds transfer, 352–353
cash paid to reimburse (petty cash), 353–354
income taxes, 481–483
Employee benefits, 477–478, 488–489. *See also* Payroll accounting
Employee compensation. *See* Compensation
Employee earnings records, 480–481
Employee income taxes, 481, 483
Employee payroll taxes, 483
Ending inventory, in cost of goods sold, 305–306
End of the accounting period
adjusting entries, 57, 146, 147–159, 164–169, 383
interest owed at, 470–471
inventory in, 305–306
steps in accounting cycle, 57, 146, 147, 164–169, 383
Equipment. *See also* Property, plant, and equipment
as prepaid expense, 151–153
Equity. *See also* Common stock; Owners' equity; Preferred stock
active investment in, 643–644
debt to, 742
passive investment in, 643, 644, 646–654
Equity financing
debt financing versus, 562, 600
nature of, 562
Equity method
for investments for significant influence, 654–658
managers' choice to use, 658
Errors
bank reconciliation and, 357, 359
internal control and, 345, 348
inventory, effects of, 314–316
reducing opportunities for, 345
in trial balance, 67
Estimates
bad debt expense, 383–389
of expenses at year-end, 147
revising, 388
of useful life, 424–425, 439, 443
Ethics
accounting communication and, 24–25
accounting scandals, 24, 114, 344, 345, 420
adjusting entries and, 158–159
allowance for doubtful accounts, 393
code of professional conduct and, 24
conservatism principle, 70
debt-to-assets ratio and, 612
defined, 24
improper influence, 657
internal control and, 344–360
inventory costing method and, 312
inventory shrinkage, 265
management incentives to violate accounting rules, 114
separate records for tax and financial reporting, 429–430
stock options as compensation, 565
subjectivity of net income, 685
Exchanges
of assets, 443–444
nature of, 52–53
in transaction analysis, 52–53
Expenses
accrued, 147, 153–157
adjusting entries, 147, 150–157
bad debt, 383–389
change in recognition of, 699
credit card fees, 273
defined, 98
estimating at year end, 147
in fundamental accounting equation, 11
interest. *See* Interest expense
measuring, 102–103
operating, 98–99, 102–103, 113, 273
prepaid, 52, 54, 147, 150–153, 155, 157
repair and maintenance, 423, 436
selling, general, and administrative, 273, 276
typical account titles, 13
External decision makers, 7
External events, 50
External investors, 8
External users of information, 8
Extraordinary repairs, 423, 436

F

Face value
bonds issued at, 604–605, 608, 618
of bonds payable, 604–605
defined, 618
Factoring receivables, 395
Fair value, 430
Fair value option, 654
Federal Bureau of Investigation, 6
Federal Income Tax Withheld (FITW), 481
Federal Unemployment Tax Act (FUTA), 483
FICA taxes, 478, 479, 483
Financial accounting
defined, 8
external decision makers and, 7
nature of, 8
Financial Accounting Standards Board (FASB), 23, 683n, D-1
Financial ratios. *See* Ratio analysis
Financial reporting. *See also* Financial statement(s); Generally accepted accounting principles (GAAP)
bad debt policies, 388
basic financial reports, 8–21
bond pricing and, 605–607
of cash, 360
contingent liabilities, 477

disclosure of contingent liabilities, 477
dividends in arrears, 572
equity securities and earnings management, 651
international differences in accounting standards, 654, 744
inventory costing methods in, 318
manager choice of depreciation method, 429–430
net sales, 273, 275
objective of, 73
ordinary and extraordinary repairs, 423, 436
passive investments, 651, 654
selecting accounting methods, 658
separate records for tax reporting and, 429–430
summary of significant accounting policies, 269
unearned revenue, 149

Financial statement(s), 160–164. *See also* Financial reporting; Generally accepted accounting principles (GAAP)
accounts on, 98–99
adjusted trial balance, 160–161
analysis of. *See* Financial statement analysis
business activities causing changes in, 52–56
consolidated, 642, 643, 659–660
elements of, 73
formats of, 161
inventory costing methods and, 310–316, 322
nature of, 8
notes to. *See* Notes to financial statements
overview of, 10–21
partnership, 516–517
relationships among, 19–21, 161–162, 685–687, 688
stock reporting and, 567–568, 574–575
timing of preparation, 14
types of, 10–21. *See also* Balance sheet; Income statement; Statement of cash flows; Statement of owners' equity

Financial statement analysis, 145–146, 728–747. *See also* Ratio analysis
annual reports, 730–731
discontinued operations, 746–747
horizontal (trend) analysis, 732–733
investor information Web sites, 731–732
Management's Discussion and Analysis (MD&A) in, 732–733, 735
nonrecurring items, 746–747
other special items, 746–747
quality of income ratio, 698–699
quarterly reports, 730, 731
release of financial information, 730–732
Securities and Exchange Commission (SEC) filings, 731
T-accounts in, 57–64
vertical (common size) analysis, 734–735

Financing activities
cash flows from, 684, 694–696
defined, 18
equity versus debt, 562, 600
events in, 54
noncash, 696–697
on statement of cash flows, 18

First-in, first-out (FIFO) inventory method
described, 307, 308–309
financial statement effects of, 310–316, 322
managers' choice of, 312, 658
in periodic inventory system, 320–321

Fiscal year reporting, 14

Fixed assets
defined, 418
fixed asset turnover, 436–437, 737, 738–739

Fixed-ratio method, 511–512

Flexibility, of accounting information systems, 221

FOB destination, 265–266, 270, 275

FOB shipping point, 265–266, 270, 275

Footing columns, 213

Footnotes. *See* Notes to financial statements

Form 8-K, 731

Form 10-K, 731

Form 10-Q, 731

Form W-2 (Wage and Tax Statement), 481

Franchises, 434

Fraud. *See also* Ethics
accounting scandals, 24, 114, 344, 345, 420
counteracting incentives for committing, 345
encouraging good character in employees, 345
fraud triangle, 344n, 345
internal control and, 344–348, 360
reducing opportunities for, 345

Free cash flow, 698, 737, 743

Freight-in, 265–266

Freight-out, 265, 273

Full cost, 266–267

Fundamental accounting equation
balancing, 53, 58
changes in cash and, 686, 687–692
components of, 9–10
described, 9–10
impact of common activities on, 10–13
for sole proprietorship, 52

Future value
of an annuity, C-5–C-6, C-15
of a single amount, C-2–C-3, C-14
tables, C-14, C-15

G

GAAP. *See* Generally accepted accounting principles (GAAP)

Gains
on commercial asset exchange, 444
on sale of assets, 432, 436, 689

General journal, 57, 58–62
frequency of posting from, 220
special journals versus, 209
use of, 218–219

General ledger, 57, 58–62, 206
cash payments journal and, 218, 220
cash receipts journal and, 213–215, 220
in computerized accounting information systems, 224–225
purchases journal and, 217
revenue journal and, 210–211
summary of recording process, 219–220

Generally accepted accounting principles (GAAP), 73, 345
defined, 23
depreciation method and, 429–430, 443
fair value option for passive investments, 654
international standards compared with, 23, D-1–D-2
subjectivity of net income, 685

Going-concern assumption, 74

Goods available for sale, 305

Goodwill, 434–435

Governments, as external users of information, 8

Grass, Martin, 114

Gross earnings, in payroll accounting, 478

Gross profit (gross margin), defined, 276

Gross profit method of inventory costing, 323

Gross profit percentage, 277–278, 279, 737, 738

Growth stocks, 568

H

Headd, Brian, 16n

Heskett, J. L., 344n

Historical cost principle, 9, 69, 74, 442

Holding gains, 651
Hollinger, Richard, 265n
Horizontal (trend) analysis, 732–733
Horizontal growth, 658

I

Immediate return, investors and, 20
Impairment
  defined, 430
  of tangible assets, 430–431, 436
Imprest system, 352–353
Improper influence, 657
Income
  division of partnership, 511–516, 534–535
  net, 10, 14, 277
  operating, 276
Income before income taxes, 277
Income (loss) of partnership, 511–516, 534–535
  fixed-ratio method, 511–512
  interest on partners' capital method, 511, 512–513
  salaries to partners and interest on partners' capital balances method, 511, 514–516
  salaries to partners method, 511, 513–514
Income statement, 14–16, 98–110
  accrual basis accounting, 101–103
  chart of accounts, 98–99
  classified, 112–113, 161, 162
  comparative, 732, 733
  complete, 685, 688
  defined, 14
  effects of inventory errors on, 314–315
  elements of, 14–15
  format of, 14–15, 21, 161, 162
  gross profit percentage, 277–278, 279, 737, 738
  inventory reporting and, 304–305
  limitations of, 114
  of merchandising companies, 276–281
  multistep, 276–277
  operating cycle, 99–100
  preparing, 112–114
  purpose of, 14, 21
  relationships with other financial statements, 19–21, 161, 685–687, 688
  structure of, 14–15, 21, 161, 162
  transaction analysis, 103–110
  trend (horizontal) analysis of, 732, 733
  vertical (common size) analysis of, 734–735
  write-offs and, 384
Income stocks, 569
Income summary, 164, 164n
Income taxes. *See also* Tax reporting
  converting to cash outflow, 702–703
  employee, 481–483
  income before, 277
  income taxes payable, 483
  income tax expense, 277
  in payroll accounting, 479
Independent verification, in internal control, 347–348, 484
Indirect method, of reporting cash flows from operating activities, 683, 687–692, 699–700, 705–706
Industry factors
  comparison to benchmarks, 170, 278–279, 317–318, 394–395, 660–661
  competitor analysis, 69, 170
Influential investments
  for control, 642, 643–644, 658–660
  for significant influence, 642, 643, 654–658
Insurance, as prepaid expense, 151
Intangible assets, 433–436
  accounting rules for, 436
  acquisition of, 434–435
  amortization of, 435
  defined, 418
  disposal of, 435
  types of, 433–434
  use of, 435
Interest-bearing notes, 470
Interest expense, 113
  on bonds payable, 607–608
  converting to cash paid to suppliers, 703
  on discounted notes payable, 602–603
Interest formula, 390, 471
Interest on partners' capital method, 511, 512–513
Interest payable, as accrued expense, 154–156
Interest periods
  in bond pricing, 619
  time value of money and, C-6–C-7
Interest rates
  bond pricing and, 607
  on bonds payable, 604–605, 618
  on notes receivable, 390
  quoting, 619
  time value of money and, C-6–C-7
Interest revenue
  accrued, 391
  on bonds, 645
  calculating interest, 390
  deposits to bank account, 357, 358
  on notes receivable, 390–392
Internal control, 342–363
  of cash, 348–360
  common control principles, 346–348, 484
  defined, 344
  documenting procedures, 347, 484
  limitations of, 348
  in payroll accounting, 484
  Sarbanes-Oxley (SOX) Act of 2002 and, 24, 344–345
Internal control of cash, 348–360
  bank procedures and reconciliation, 355–359
  cash payments, 351–354
  cash receipts, 349–351
Internal decision makers, 7. *See also* Manager(s)
  choice of depreciation method, 429–430
  choice of inventory costing method, 312
Internal events, 50–51
Internal Revenue Service (IRS), 6, 389, 429–430, 479
Internal users of information, 7
International Accounting Standards Board (IASB), 23, 744, D-1–D-2
International financial reporting standards (IFRS), 23, 654, 744, D-1–D-2
Inventory, 302–325
  beginning, 305–306
  cash flows from operating activities and, 687, 690–691
  defined, 304
  effects of purchase-related transactions on, 268
  ending, 305–306
  errors, effects of, 314–316
  natural resource as, 442
  relationship between cost of goods sold and, 305
  types of, 304
Inventory control
  periodic inventory system, 264, 281–282, 320–322
  perpetual inventory system, 263–265, 270, 282, 308, 310, 311
Inventory costing methods, 306–316
  cost flow assumptions in, 307–310
  financial statement effects of, 310–316, 322
  first-in, first-out (FIFO) method, 307, 308–316, 320–322, 658
  gross profit method, 323
  impact of, 318
  last-in, first-out (LIFO) method, 307, 308, 309–316, 321, 322, 658
  lower of cost or market, 312–314
  managers' choice of, 312, 658
  under perpetual inventory system, 308, 310
  retail inventory method, 323–324
  specific identification, 307
  weighted average, 307, 308, 310, 321–322

Inventory Cost of Goods Sold, 268, 276, 282
Inventory management, 316–318
  comparison to benchmarks, 317
  inventory turnover analysis, 316–317, 737, 741
Inventory systems
  of merchandisers, 262–265, 270, 281–282
  periodic, 264, 281–282, 320–322
  perpetual, 263–265, 270, 282, 310, 311
  purpose of, 262–263
Inventory turnover analysis, 316–317, 737, 741
Investing activities, 10
  cash flows from, 18, 684, 693–694
  events in, 54, 56
  nature of, 18
  noncash, 696–697
  on statement of cash flows, 18
Investment(s), 640–665. *See also* Investing activities
  of additional assets in partnership, 518–521
  cash and noncash contributions to partnership, 509–510
  cash flows from investing activities and, 18, 684, 693, 694
  consolidated financial statements and, 642, 643, 659–660
  for control, 642, 643–644, 658–660
  passive, 642, 643, 644–654
  return on assets (ROA), 660–661, 737, 739
  for significant influence, 642, 643, 654–658
Investments Held to Maturity, 644–646
Investors. *See also* Stockholders (shareholders)
  corporate ownership and, 560
  as external users of information, 8
  investor information Web sites, 731–732
  relationships among financial statements and, 20
  stock sold between, 565
Issued shares, 567

J

Journal(s), 57
Journal entries. *See also* General journal; Special journals
  adjusting, 147–148
  balance sheet, 53–56
  chronological order and, 58–60
  defined, 58
  income statement, 103–110
  nature of, 58–69
  for partnership formation, 510
  posting transaction effects, 60–62
  in transaction analysis, 58–60, 103–110

K

Kotter, J. P., 344n
Kumar, Sanjay, 114

L

Land, cash flows from investing activities and, 694
Land improvements, 419
Language of business, accounting as, 6
Last-in, first-out (LIFO) inventory method, 308
  defined, 307, 309–310
  financial statement effects of, 310–316, 322
  managers' choice of, 312, 658
  in periodic inventory system, 321
Lease liabilities, 610–611
  capital leases, 610–611, 619
  operating leases, 610
Least-latest rule, 430
Ledger. *See also* General ledger; Subsidiary ledgers
  defined, 57
Lee, T. A., 344n
Legal issues
  for corporations, 476, 560–561
  legal liability, 476
Lenders. *See* Creditors
Liabilities, 466–490
  adjusting entries, 147
  classifying, 468–469
  contingent, 475–477
  contra-accounts, 606
  current. *See* Current liabilities
  defined, 9
  in fundamental accounting equation, 19
  historical cost principle, 69, 74
  long-term. *See* Long-term liabilities
  maturity order of, 68
  measuring, 468, 600–601
  nature of, 9, 73, 468
  payroll, 477–484
  recording, 468, 600–601
  in T-accounts, 58
  typical account titles, 13, 51, 52
Licensing rights, 434
Limited liability companies (LLC), 5n, 507–508
  characteristics of, 507–508
  defined, 507
Limited life, of intangible assets, 435, 436
Line of credit, 469
Liquidation of partnership, 526–532, 538–539
  capital deficiency, 529–532
  causes of, 526
  defined, 526
  no capital deficiency, 527–529
  steps in, 527
Liquidity, 67–68, 469
Liquidity ratios, 736, 737, 740–742
  current ratio, 469, 737, 741
  days to collect, 393, 394, 737
  days to sell, 316–317, 737
  inventory turnover, 316–317, 737, 741
  quick ratio, 737, 742
  receivables turnover, 393–395, 737, 740–741
Long-lived assets, 416–446. *See also* Property, plant, and equipment
  cash flows from operating activities and, 687, 689–692
  classifying, 418
  defined, 418
  depreciation of, 424–433, 437–439, 689
  intangible, 418, 433–436
  sale of, 689
  tangible, 418, 419–433, 436
  turnover analysis, 436–437
Long-term debt
  cash flows from financing activities and, 694, 695
  current portion, 472–473
  defined, 600
Long-term liabilities, 598–624
  amortization of, 619–623
  analyzing, 611–612
  bonds payable, 604–610, 618–623
  debt-to-assets ratio, 611–612, 737, 742
  defined, 473
  discounted notes payable, 601–603, 617–618
  discounting future payments, 616–619
  effective-interest method of amortization, 619–622
  leases, 610–611, 619
  measuring, 600–601, 607
  straight-line method of amortization, 622–623
  times interest earned ratio, 612, 737, 742–743
Long-term return, investors and, 20
Losses
  on commercial asset exchange, 444
  on division of partnership, 511–516, 534–535
  on sale of assets, 432, 436, 689
  on statement of owners' equity, 16n
Lower of cost or market (LCM) inventory valuation, 312–314

M

Mail, cash received by, 351
Maintenance expenses, 423, 436
Management's Discussion and Analysis (MD&A), 732–733, 735
Manager(s). *See also* Ethics
  accounting scandals and, 24, 114, 344, 345, 420
  choice of depreciation method, 429–430
  choice of inventory costing method, 312, 658
  incentives to violate accounting rules, 114
  internal control and, 24, 344–346
  as internal decision makers, 7
  internal users of information and, 7
Managerial accounting
  defined, 7
  internal decision makers and, 7
  nature of, 7
Managerial decision-making process
  irrelevant costs in, 722
  relevant costs in, 722
Manual accounting information systems, 204–205
  comparison with computerized accounting information systems, 204
  defined, 204
Manufacturing companies
  defined, 262
  inventory types, 304
  nature of, 4, 262
  operating cycles of, 262, 263
  types of, 262
Market value
  managers' choice to use, 658
  of passive investments, 646–650, 658
Matching principle, 101–103, 147, 383, 424–425, 442, 470, 488, 489, 602, 622
Maturity date
  bond retirement and, 608–609
  of bonds payable, 604–605, 608–609
  debt investments held to maturity, 644–646
  of notes receivable, 382
Maturity order, of liabilities, 68
McQuaid, Brad, 132
Merchandising companies, 260–284
  balance sheet reporting of inventory, 304–305
  balance sheets of, 304–305
  closing entries, 283
  comparison to benchmarks, 278–279, 317–318
  defined, 262
  gross profit percentage, 277–278, 279, 737, 738
  income statement reporting of inventory, 304–305
  income statements of, 276–281
  inventory systems of, 262–265, 270, 281–282
  multistep income statement, 276–277
  nature of, 4, 262
  operating cycles of, 262, 263
  recording merchandise purchases, 265–269
  recording merchandise sales, 270–276
  sales tax payable, 474
  types of, 5, 262
Mergers
  consolidated financial statements following, 642, 643, 659–660
  defined, 659
Minkow, Barry, 114
Modified Accelerated Cost Recovery System (MACRS), 430n
Monetary unit assumption, 15, 73
Money orders, cash received by mail, 351
Multistep income statement, 276–277
Municipal bonds (munis), 609

N

Natural resources
  accounting for, 418n
  acquisition of, 442
  defined, 442
  depletion of, 442
Negative cash flows, 18
Net assets, 434–435
Net book value, 152, 424
Net earnings, 14
Net income, 277
  conversion to net cash flow from operating activities, 689
  defined, 15
  direct method of reporting cash flows from operating activities, 683, 700–705
  in fundamental accounting equation, 10
  indirect method of reporting cash flows from operating activities, 683, 687–692, 699–700, 705–706
  subjectivity of, 685
Net loss, 16
Net pay, 479
Net profit margin, 169–170, 736–738
Net sales, 273, 275
New York Stock Exchange (NYSE), D-1
Noncash contributions
  common stock issued for, 564
  to corporation, 564
  to partnership, 509–510
Noncash investing and financing activities, 696–697
Noncurrent receivables, 382
Nonoperating gains and losses, 431
Nontrade receivables, 382
No-par value stock, 563, 564
Notes payable, 470–472
  cash flows from financing activities and, 694
  defined, 470
  discounted, 470, 601–603, 617–618
  promissory notes, 470–472
  timeline for, 471
Notes receivable, 390–393
  defined, 382
  interest calculations, 390
  recording, 390–392
  uncollectible, 392
Notes to financial statements, 423
  defined, 18
  depreciation in, 431
  dividends in arrears, 572
  investments in affiliates, 654
  investments in marketable securities, 647
  principles of consolidation, 659–660
NSF (not sufficient funds) checks, 357, 359

O

Operating activities
  accounts affected by, 687
  accrual basis accounting, 101–103, 691
  cash basis accounting, 100–101
  cash flows from, 683–684, 687–692, 699–706
  defined, 18
  direct method of reporting cash flows from, 683, 700–705
  expense measurement, 102–103
  impact of change in, 699
  indirect method of reporting cash flows from, 683, 687–692, 699–700, 705–706
  matching principle, 101–103
  nature of, 18
  quality of income ratio, 698–699
  recognition and measurement of, 98–110
  revenue principle, 101–102
  on statement of cash flows, 18
Operating agreement, 507
Operating (cash-to-cash) cycle, 99–100
  defined, 262
  income statement and, 99–100
  of manufacturers, 262, 263
  of merchandisers, 262, 263
  of service companies, 262, 263
Operating expenses, 98–99, 102–103, 113, 273
  converting to cash outflow, 702–703

Operating income, 276
Operating leases, described, 610
Operating revenues, 98, 113
Ordinary repairs and maintenance, 423, 436
Organizational forms, 4–5. *See also* Corporations; Partnership(s); Sole proprietorships
Organizational structure, corporation, 561
Other revenue and expenses, net, 277
Outstanding checks, 357, 358
Outstanding shares, 567–568
Overriding internal controls, 348
Overtime pay, 478
Owner-managers, incentives to violate accounting rules, 114
Owners' equity. *See also* Statement of owners' equity; Stockholders' equity
  on balance sheet, 17–18
  defined, 9
  in fundamental accounting equation, 19
  interpreting, 16–17
  nature of, 9–10, 73
  typical account titles, 13
Ownership
  corporate, 5, 560
  partnership, 517–525

P

Pacioli, Luca, 23
Paid leaves, 488–489
Parent company
  consolidated financial statements following merger, 642, 643, 659–660
  defined, 659
Partner return on equity, 533–534, 539
Partners' capital statement
  capital deficiency, 529–532
  defined, 516
  no capital deficiency, 527–529
Partnership(s), 504–541
  accounting for, 509–517
  admission of partner, 517–521, 536–537
  characteristics of, 506–507, 508
  death of partner, 525
  defined, 5, 506
  division of income (loss), 511–516, 534–535
  financial statements, 516–517
  formation of, 509–510
  internal users of information and, 7
  liquidation of, 526–532, 538–539
  ownership changes, 517–525
  partner return on equity, 533–534, 539
  similar forms of business, 507–509
  withdrawal of partner, 521–525, 536–537
Partnership agreement, 506
Partnership dissolution
  admission of partner and, 517–521, 536–537
  bonus to existing partners, 519
  bonus to new partner, 520–521
  defined, 517
Par value, 563
  no-par value stock, 563, 564
  par value common stock issued for cash, 563–564
Passive investments
  accounting for, 644–654
  amortized cost method and, 644–646
  debt investments held to maturity, 644–646
  in debt securities, 643, 644–650
  defined, 642, 643
  in equity securities, 643, 644, 646–652
  market value method and, 646–650, 658
  sale of stock, 650
  securities available for sale, 646–654
  trading securities, 646, 651
Pass-through taxation
  for limited liability companies (LLC), 507–508
  for S-Corporations, 508
Patents, 434
Payment date, 569–570
Payroll accounting, 477–484
  biometric tracking versus timecards, 484
  calculating payroll, 478–479
  components of, 477–478
  deductions, 478–482
  definitions, 477–478
  employee benefits, 477–478, 488–489
  internal control principles for, 484
  payroll, defined, 477
  recording payroll, 480–483
Payroll deductions, 478–482
Payroll register, 482
Pcards (purchasing cards), 354
Pension plans, 489
Percentage analysis. *See* Ratio analysis
Percentage of accounts receivable method for bad debts, 386
Percentage of credit sales method for bad debts, 386
Periodic inventory system, 281–282
  compared with perpetual inventory system, 282
  cost flow methods under, 320–322
  defined, 264
Peripheral transactions, 113
Permanent (real) accounts, 161, 164, 168
Perpetual inventory system
  advantages and disadvantages of, 264–265
  compared with periodic inventory system, 282
  cost flow methods under, 308, 310
  defined, 263–264
  journal entries, 311
  merchandise sales in, 270
Petty cash fund, 353–354
Plant and equipment. *See* Property, plant, and equipment
Ponzi, Charles, 93
Ponzi schemes, 93
Post-closing trial balance, 167–169
Post-employment benefits, 489
Pre-closing trial balance entries, 165
Preferred stock
  authorization of, 563
  cash dividends on, 562, 570–571
  characteristics of, 561–562
  cumulative dividend preference, 571, 572
  current dividend preference, 570–571
  defined, 561
  financial statement reporting, 567–568, 574–575
  stock issues, 564
Premium
  bonds issued at, 606, 608, 618, 619–620, 622–623
  defined, 605
Prepaid expenses
  adjusting entries, 147, 150–153, 155, 157
  as assets, 52, 54
  converting to cash outflow, 702
  defined, 147, 150
  operating activities and, 691
  types of, 150–153
Present value
  accounting applications of, 616–619, C-7–C-11
  of an annuity, 617, C-6, C-8–C-11, C-12–C-13, C-16
  of bonds payable, 618–619
  of capital leases, 619
  computations using Excel, C-12–C-13
  defined, 601
  of discounted notes payable, 617–618
  of a single amount, 616–617, C-3–C-4, C-7–C-8, C-10–C-12, C-14–C-15
  tables, 616, 617, C-14–C-16
Press release, preliminary, 730

Price/earnings (P/E) ratio, 575, 576, 577, 737, 740
Principal
  on investments held to maturity, 645
  on notes payable, 603
  on notes receivable, 382, 390, 392
Private accounting
  careers in, 28
  defined, 6
Private companies, 560
Professional standards, 22–23, 24. *See also* Ethics
Profit(s)
  defined, 10
  in fundamental accounting equation, 12
Profitability ratios, 736–740
  asset turnover, 737, 738
  earnings per share (EPS), 568, 575, 576–577, 737, 740
  fixed asset turnover, 436–437, 737, 738–739
  gross profit percentage, 277–278, 279, 737, 738
  net profit margin, 169–170, 736–738
  price/earnings (P/E) ratio, 575, 576, 577, 737, 740
  return on assets (ROA), 660–661, 737, 739
  return on equity (ROE), 533–534, 539, 737, 739
  return on partner equity, 533–534, 539
Profit margin, net, 169–170, 736–738
Promissory notes, 470–472
Property, plant, and equipment, 419–433. *See also* Equipment
  asset impairment, 430–431, 436
  cash flows from investing activities and, 693, 694
  classifying long-lived assets, 418
  depreciation of, 152–153, 424–430, 436
  disposal of, 431–433, 436
  fixed asset turnover, 436–437, 737, 738–739
  maintenance expenses, 423, 436
  as prepaid expense, 151–153
  purchases in fundamental accounting equation, 11
  repairs, 423, 436
Public accounting
  careers in, 28
  defined, 6
Public Accounting Reform and Investor Protection Act (Sarbanes-Oxley Act) of 2002, 24, 344–345
Public companies, 560
Public Company Accounting Oversight Board (PCAOB), 23
Purchases
  cash paid by check for purchases on account, 351–352
  comparison with sales accounting, 274–276
  in cost of goods sold, 305–306
  discounts on, 266–268
  events in, 55
  in fundamental accounting equation, 11–12
  of inventory on account, 265
  of investments for significant influence, 655
  among partners, 517–518
  among partners on withdrawal of partner, 522–523
  recording merchandise, 265–269
  returns and allowances, 266
  of securities available for sale, 648
  summary of purchase-related transactions, 268
  of tangible assets, 419–422
  transportation cost (freight-in), 265–266
Purchases journal, 216–217
  defined, 216
  frequency of posting from, 220
  information contained in, 216–217
  postings to general ledger, 217
Purchasing cards (Pcards), 354

Q

Quality of income ratio, 698–699
Quarterly reports
  release of, 730
  SEC filings, 731
Quick ratio, 737, 742

R

Ratio analysis, 169–175, 736–744
  accounting decisions and, 744
  comparisons to benchmarks, 170, 278–279, 317–318, 394–395, 660–661
  defined, 736
  investor information Web sites and, 731–732
  key ratios, 169
  liquidity ratios, 736, 737, 740–742
  profitability ratios, 736–740
  quality of income ratio, 698–699
  solvency ratios, 736, 737, 742–743
Receivables, 380–399
  accounts receivable, 382, 383–389, 687, 690
  factoring, 395
  nontrade receivables, 382
  notes receivable, 382, 390–393
  receivables turnover analysis, 393–395, 737, 740–741
  trade receivables, 382
Receivables turnover, 393–395, 737, 740–741
Record date, 569
Recovery, 388–389
Relevant financial information, 23, 73
Reliable financial information, 23, 73
Remittance advice, 351
Rent, as prepaid expense, 151
Repair expenses, 423, 436
Replacement, of tangible assets, 423
Research and development expenses, 434
Residual claim on assets
  common stock, 561
  preferred stock, 562
Residual (salvage) value, 424, 427–428, 443
Responsibility, establishing, in internal control, 346, 347, 484
Restricting access, in internal control, 347, 484
Retailers, 5, 262, 474. *See also* Merchandising companies
Retail inventory method, 323–324
Retained earnings. *See also* Statement of retained earnings
  cash flows from financing activities and, 694, 695–696
  defined, 563
  dividends and, 570
  operating activities and, 687
Retirement plans, 489
Return on assets (ROA), 660–661, 737
  comparison to benchmarks, 660–661
  defined, 660, 739
Return on equity (ROE), 533–534, 539, 737, 739
Returns and allowances
  purchase, 266
  sales, 271, 273
Revenue(s)
  accrued, 101–102, 147, 150, 155, 391
  adjusting entries, 147, 148–150
  cash receipts versus, 101–102
  defined, 10, 98
  estimating at year end, 147
  in fundamental accounting equation, 11
  impact of change in, 699
  operating, 98, 113
  typical account titles, 13
  unearned, 147, 148–150, 155, 157, 474–475
Revenue journal, 209–211. *See also* Sales journal
  contents of, 209–210

defined, 209
frequency of posting from, 220
postings to subsidiary ledger and general ledger, 210–211
Revenue principle, 101–102, 147

S

Salaries. *See also* Compensation; Payroll accounting
defined, 477
salaries payable, as accrued expense, 153
salaries to partners and interest on partners' capital balances method, 511, 514–516
salaries to partners method, 511, 513–514
Sales
on account, 272–273
cash, 270
comparison with purchases accounting, 274–276
corporate life cycle and, 699
credit card, 271–272, 273
discounts on, 272–273
growth of, 699
net sales, 273, 275
recording merchandise, 270–276
returns and allowances, 271, 273
revenues from. *See* Sales revenues
of stock held for significant influence, 656–657
summary of sales-related transactions, 273
transportation cost (freight-out), 265, 273
Sales journal, in computerized accounting information systems, 223
Sales revenues
converting to cash inflow, 701, 703
credit sales, 383–389
Sales tax payable, 474
Salvage (residual) value, 424, 427–428, 443
Sarbanes-Oxley (SOX) Act of 2002, 24, 344–345
Scandals, accounting, 24, 114, 344, 345, 420
Schedule of accounts receivable, 207, 214
S-Corporations, 508–509
characteristics of, 508–509
defined, 508
SEC. *See* U.S. Securities and Exchange Commission (SEC)
Secured bonds, 609
Securities and Exchange Commission (SEC), 23
Electronic Data Gathering and Retrieval Service (EDGAR), 731
filings with, 731
Securities available for sale, 646–650
accounting for, 647–654
defined, 646–647
nature of, 650–651
trading securities versus, 650–652
Segregation of duties, 346–347
in internal control, 349, 484
Selling, general, and administrative expenses, 273, 276
Selling assets, 432
Separate entity assumption, 10, 73, 560–561
Service companies
nature of, 4, 262
operating cycles of, 262, 263
Shareholders, 8
Shareholders' equity. *See* Owners' equity; Stockholders' equity
Shoplifting, 265
Shrinkage, 282
defined, 264
sources of, 265
Significant influence
equity method and, 654–658
investing for, 642, 643, 644, 654–658
Single payment
future value of, C-2–C-3, C-14
present value of, 616–617, C-3–C-4, C-7–C-8, C-10–C-12, C-14–C-15
Sole proprietorships
accounting differences between corporations and, 563
defined, 4
internal users of information and, 7
Solvency ratios, 736, 737, 742–743
debt to assets, 611–612, 737, 742
free cash flow, 698, 737, 743
times interest earned, 611, 612, 737, 742–743
Source documents, 52
Special journals, 209–218
cash payments, 217–218, 220
cash receipts, 212–216, 220, 223–224
frequency of posting from, 220
general journals versus, 209
purchases, 216–217, 220
revenue, 209–211, 220
summary of recording process, 219–220
Specific identification method, 307
Spreadsheet approach, to preparing statement of cash flows, 705–706
Stated credit terms, 394
Stated interest rate
on bonds payable, 604–605, 618
defined, 618
Statement of cash flows, 680–707. *See also* Financial statement(s)
cash flows from financing activities, 684, 694–696
cash flows from investing activities, 18, 684, 693–694
cash flows from operating activities, 683–684, 687–692, 699–706
categories in, 683
classifications of, 682–687
defined, 18
direct method of preparing, 683, 700–705
elements of, 18, 19
format of, 696, 697
free cash flow, 698, 737, 743
indirect method of preparing, 683, 687–692, 699–700, 705–706
net increase (decrease) in cash, 684
noncash financing activities, 696–697
noncash investing activities, 696–697
preparing and evaluating, 696–699
purpose of, 18, 21
quality of income ratio, 698–699
relationship between business activities and cash flows, 682–683
relationships with other financial statements, 19–21, 161, 685–687, 688
spreadsheet approach to preparing, 705–706
structure of, 21
supplemental cash flow information, 698
Statement of earnings. *See* Income statement
Statement of financial position. *See* Balance sheet
Statement of income. *See* Income statement
Statement of operations. *See* Income statement
Statement of owners' equity
elements of, 16
format of, 21, 161, 162–163
nature of, 16
purpose of, 21
relationship among statements, 161
structure of, 21, 161, 162–163
Statement of retained earnings, 574–575
State unemployment tax acts (SUTA), 483
Stock, 5. *See also* Common stock; Preferred stock
accounting for stock transactions, 562–568
financial statement reporting and, 567–568, 574–575
treasury stock, 565–568, 574–575

Stock authorization, 563
Stock dividends, 572–573
  compared with cash dividends, 574
  compared with stock splits, 574
Stock issues
  common stock, 563–565
  preferred stock, 564
Stock options, as compensation, 565
Stock splits, 573–574
Stockholders (shareholders), 8
  accounting for stock transactions, 562–568
  corporate ownership and, 5, 560
Stockholders' equity. *See also* Owners' equity
  contra account, 566
  defined, 562
Straight-line method
  of amortization, 622–623
  of depreciation, 426, 428, 429, 438, 443
Strips, 609
Subjectivity, of net income, 685
Subsidiary accounts, 383
Subsidiary company
  consolidated financial statements following, 659–660
  defined, 659
Subsidiary ledgers
  accounts payable, 206, 208–209, 219
  accounts receivable, 206–208
  advantages of, 208–209
  defined, 206
  general journal entry for, 208
  summary of recording process, 219–220
Summary of significant accounting policies, 269
Suppliers
  cash paid to, 701–702
  as creditors, 8
  as external users of information, 8
Supplies
  as prepaid expenses, 150–151
  purchases in fundamental accounting equation, 11–12
Synergy, 659

T

T-accounts
  in accounting information systems, 206
  closing entries, 165–166
  credits in, 58, 59, 62
  debits in, 58, 59, 62
  defined, 61
  structure of, 57–58
  in transaction analysis, 57–64, 103–110, 156
Tangible assets, 419–433
  accounting rules for, 436
  acquisition of, 419–422
  defined, 418
  depreciation of, 424–433
  disposal of, 431–433, 435, 436
  fixed asset turnover analysis, 436–437, 737, 738–739
  impairment of, 430–431, 436
  use of, 423–430
Tax reporting. *See also* Income taxes
  corporate, 560–561
  depreciation in, 429–430
  employee payroll taxes, 483
  pass-through taxation, 507–508
  sales tax payable, 474
  separate records for financial reporting and, 429–430
Temporary (nominal) accounts, 161, 164–165, 168
Time lags, bank reconciliation and, 357
Time period assumption, 99
Time value of money
  computations using Excel, C-12–C-13
  future value of an annuity, C-5–C-6, C-15
  future value of a single amount, C-2–C-3, C-14
  interest periods and, C-6–C-7
  interest rates and, C-6–C-7
  nature of, C-2
  present value of an annuity, 617, C-6, C-8–C-11, C-12–C-13, C-16
  present value of a single amount, 616–617, C-3–C-4, C-7–C-8, C-10–C-12, C-14–C-15
  tables, 616, 617, C-14–C-16
Times interest earned ratio, 611, 612, 737, 742–743
Trade accounts payable. *See* Accounts payable
Trademarks, 433
Trade receivables, 382
Trading securities
  nature of, 646, 651
  securities available for sale versus, 650–652
Transaction(s)
  defined, 50, 68
  impact on accounts, 52–60
  nature of, 50–51
  reliance on, 68
Transaction analysis
  account balances and, 57–64
  analytical tools for, 58–60
  balance sheet, 52–60
  direction of transaction effects, 58, 59
  dual effects of, 52–53
  illustration of, 62–64, 65
  income statement, 103–110
  journal entries, 58–60, 103–110
  posting transaction effects, 60–62
  principles of, 52–53
  recording transaction effects, 58–60
  steps in, 53, 105
  T-accounts in, 57–64, 103–110, 156
Transportation cost
  freight-in, 265–266
  freight-out, 265, 273
Treasury stock, 565–567
  acquisition of, 566
  defined, 565
  financial statement reporting, 567–568, 574–575
  reissue of, 566–567
Trend (horizontal) analysis, 732–733
Trial balance
  adjusted, 160–161
  defined, 65
  errors in, 67
  post-closing, 167–169
  pre-closing entries, 165
  preparing, 64–67
  unadjusted, 112, 148–150
Turnover
  asset, 737, 738
  fixed asset, 436–437, 737, 738–739
  inventory, 316–317, 737, 741
  receivables, 393–395, 737, 740–741
2/10, n/30, 266–268

U

Unadjusted amounts, 145
Unadjusted trial balance, 112, 148–150
Uncollectible accounts
  estimating, 383–389
  writing off, 384, 385
Uncollectible notes, 392
Unearned (deferred) revenues, 102
  adjusting entries, 147, 148–150, 155, 157
  defined, 147, 474
  examples of, 157
  recording, 474–475
Unemployment taxes, 483
Uniform Partnership Act, 506
U.S. Patent and Trademark Office, 433–434
U.S. Securities and Exchange Commission (SEC), 23
  adjusting entries, 159
  ethical issues, 199–200
  international financial reporting standards and, D-1
U.S. Small Business Administration, 4n
U.S. Treasury bonds (treasuries), 609
Units-of-production depreciation method, 426–427, 428

Unlimited life, of intangible assets, 435, 436
Unrealized gain (loss) on investments, 649–653
Useful life, 424–425, 439, 443
Usefulness, of accounting information systems, 221
Utilities payable, as accrued expense, 153–154

V

Valuation
  inventory. *See* Inventory costing methods
  of passive investments, 649–650
Vertical (common size) analysis, 734–735
Vertical integration, 658
Voluntary deductions, 478, 479
Voting rights
  common stock, 561
  preferred stock, 561
Vouchers, 352
Voucher system, 352

W

Wage and Tax Statement (Form W-2), 481
Wages. *See also* Payroll accounting
  defined, 477
  wages payable, as accrued expense, 153
Warranties payable, 475–476
Weighted average inventory method, 308, 310, 321–322
  defined, 307
Whistleblowers, 345
Wholesalers, 5, 262. *See also* Merchandising companies
Withdrawal of partner, 521–525, 536–537
  purchase among partners, 522–523
  withdrawal of assets, 523–525
Worksheets, accounting, 175–177
Write-offs
  defined, 384
  direct write-off method, 389
  impact on income statement, 384
  segregating, 385

Y

Year-end reporting, 14

Z

Zero-coupon bonds, 609

Expanded Transaction Analysis Model

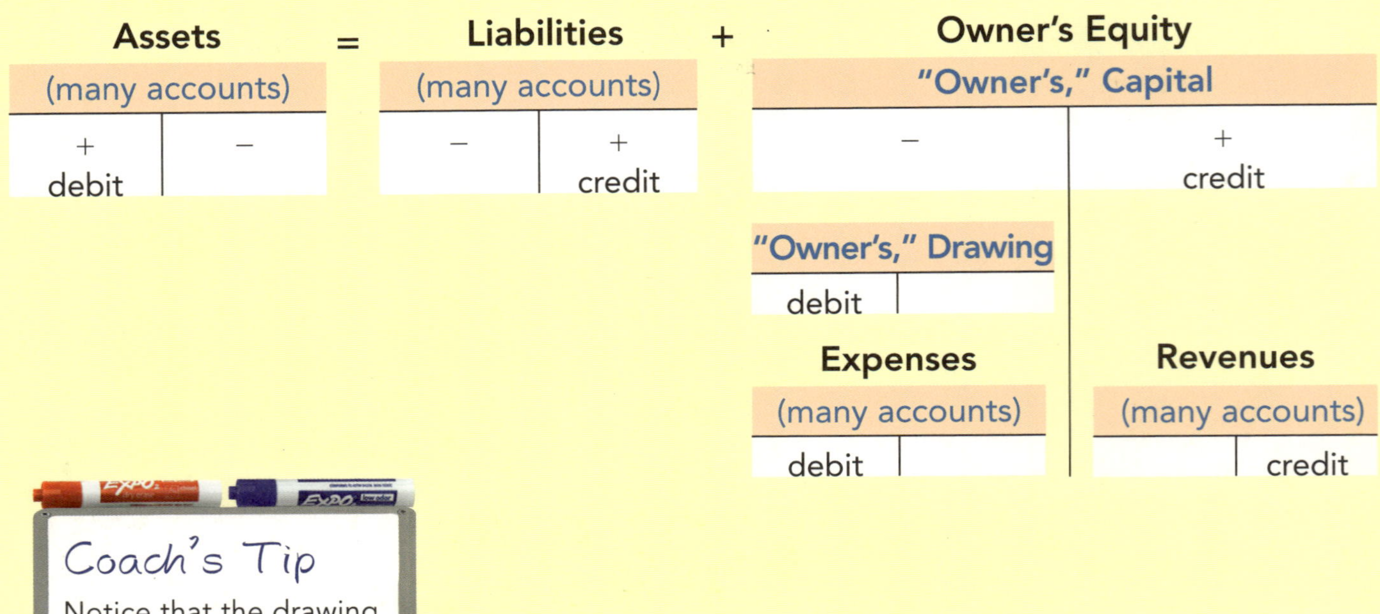

Coach's Tip

Notice that the drawing and expense accounts increase with debits. As these accounts increase, owner's equity decreases.